seventh edition

HUMAN RESOURCE MANAGEMENT

Derek Torrington

Laura Hall

Stephen Taylor

 Prentice Hall
FINANCIAL TIMES

An imprint of **Pearson Education**

Harlow, England • London • New York • Boston • San Francisco • Toronto
Sydney • Tokyo • Singapore • Hong Kong • Seoul • Taipei • New Delhi
Cape Town • Madrid • Mexico City • Amsterdam • Munich • Paris • Milan

Pearson Education Limited
Edinburgh Gate
Harlow
Essex CM20 2JE
England

and Associated Companies throughout the world

Visit us on the World Wide Web at:
www.pearsoned.co.uk

First published in Great Britain under the Prentice Hall Europe imprint in 1987
Second edition published 1991
Third edition published 1995
Fourth edition published 1998
Fifth edition published 2002
Sixth edition published 2005
Seventh edition published 2008

ISBN: 978-0-273-71075-2

British Library Cataloguing-in-Publication Data
A catalogue record for this book is available from the British Library

10 9 8 7 6 5 4 3 2
11 10 09

Typeset in 10/12.5 Sabon MT by 35
Printed and bound by Rotolito Lombarda, S. p. A., Milan, Italy

The publisher's policy is to use paper manufactured from sustainable forests.

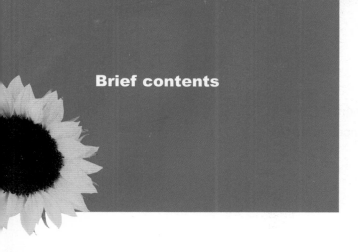

Brief contents

Supporting resources

Visit www.pearsoned.co.uk/torrington to find valuable online resources

Companion Website for students
- Over 250 multiple choice questions to test your understanding
- Extra case studies and exercises
- Extensive links to valuable resources on the web
- An online glossary to explain key terms

For instructors
- Complete, downloadable Instructor's Manual
- Over 1,000 PowerPoint slides that can be downloaded and used for presentations
- Testbank of question material

Also: The Companion Website provides the following features:

- Search tool to help locate specific items of content
- E-mail results and profile tools to send results of quizzes to instructors
- Online help and support to assist with website usage and troubleshooting

For more information please contact your local Pearson Education sales representative or visit www.pearsoned.co.uk/torrington

Pearson Custom publishing

Our Custom publishing programme allows academics to pick and choose content from one or more Pearson Education texts for their course and combine it into a definitive course text.

Here are some common examples of Custom solutions which have helped over 500 courses across Europe:

- Different chapters from across our publishing imprints combined into one book
- Lecturer's own material combined together with textbook chapters or published in a separate booklet
- Third party cases and articles that you are keen for your students to read as part of the course
- Or any combination of the above

The Pearson Education Custom text published for your course is professionally produced and bound- just as you would expect from a normal Pearson Education text. You can even choose your own cover design and add your university logo. Since many of our titles have online resources accompanying them we can even build a Custom website that matches your course text.

Whatever your choice, our dedicated Editorial and Production teams will work with you throughout the process, right until you receive a copy of your Custom text.

Some lecturers teaching *Human Resource Management* have found that the flexibility of Custom publishing has allowed them to include additional material on certain aspects of their course.

To give you an idea of combinations which have proved popular, here is a list of subject areas in which Pearson Education publish one or more key texts that could provide extra chapters to match the emphasis of your course:

- Human Resource Management
- Employment/Industrial Relations
- Human Resource Development
- Human Resource Strategy
- Organisational Behaviour
- Leadership and Change Management
- Management Skills

For more details on any of these books or to browse other material from our entire portfolio, please visit:
www.pearsoned.co.uk

If, once you have had time to review this title, you feel Custom publishing might benefit you and your course, please do get in contact. However minor, or major the change – we can help you out.

You can contact us at: www.pearsoncustom.co.uk
or via your local representative at: www.pearsoned.co.uk/replocator

Contents

Contents

Contents

Contents

Guided tour

NAVIGATION AND SETTING THE SCENE

The book is divided into seven **parts,** each of which opens with a visual guide to the chapters and topics covered.

Learning objectives enable you to focus on what you should have learned by the end of the chapter.

Follow the **Web icon** in the margin of the text to find a range of resources on the website **(www.pearsoned.co.uk/torrington)** which will help you to check your understanding of key topics

AIDING YOUR UNDERSTANDING

Figures and Tables illustrate key concepts and processes, visually reinforcing your learning.

Activity boxes allow you to review and apply your learning at regular intervals throughout the text.

Summary propositions recap and reinforce the key points to take away from the chapter. They also provide a useful revision tool.

Multiple choice questions on the Companion Website give you the chance to check what you have learnt and get instant feedback.

HUMAN RESOURCE MANAGEMENT IN CONTEXT

Windows on practice provides a range of interesting and topical illustrations of HRM in practice.

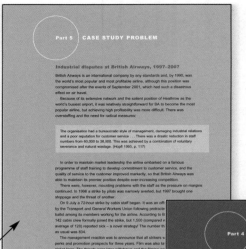

Focus on skills appears at the end of each part, offering clear guidance and a range of exercises to help you develop the skills required of a Human Resource Manager.

Case study problems at the end of each part help consolidate your learning of major themes by applying them to real-life examples.

Annotated weblinks allow you to develop your understanding of relevant organisations.

Preface

This book and its antecedent *Personnel Management* have been through many editions over nearly thirty years, and it has steadily evolved in line with the development of the personnel/HR function and the changing mix of students studying the subject.

We have been very glad to see the number of people buying the book increase year by year and the steady growth of editions in foreign languages, with Russian, Portuguese and Mandarin being the latest versions. It is also gratifying to see that the use of the text is equally strong at all academic levels from specialist masters', through MBA to all undergraduate and professional courses, and that it is also being used by many practitioners.

For this seventh edition we have comprehensively updated and revised the material to encompass legislative changes, emerging issues of professional and academic debate, findings and commentary from our own recent research into contemporary business practices, and other recent data and survey findings. Despite adding much new material we have maintained the same general structure that has been appreciated in the past, taking each of the main functional areas of HRM in turn. We have also been careful to retain all of the material that regularly receives special commendation and requests for permission to copy.

We have moved the chapter on the international dimension into the first part of the book to reflect its increasing importance and have introduced many more international cases and examples, without lessening its main focus on British practice. Parts 3 and 5 have some slight reorganisation and we have brought in two new chapters, one on the future of work and the other on the changing HR function.

We have also increased the level of integration between the book and its companion website www.pearsoned.co.uk/torrington, which has a great deal of supplementary material.

There is a range of assessment material and illustrations, as well as several design features to assist readers further in using and learning from the text; these include:

- Integrated **Window on Practice Boxes** provide a range of illustrative material throughout the text, including examples of real company practice, survey results, anecdotes and quotes, and court cases.

- Integrated **Activity Boxes** encourage readers to review and critically apply their under-standing at regular intervals throughout the text, either by responding to a question or by undertaking a small practical assignment, individually or as part of a group. In recognition that this text is used on both professional and academic courses, most of the exercises reflect the fact that many students will have little or no business experience. Others may appear to exclude students who are not in employment by asking readers to consider an aspect in their own organisation; however, the organisation could be a college or university, the students' union, a political body or sports team.

- **Discussion Topics**: at the end of each chapter there are two or three short questions intended for general discussion in a tutorial or study group.
- **Case Study Problems**: at the end of each Part we have included one short case study with several questions to enable readers to review, link and apply their understanding of the previous chapters to a business scenario.
- **Web Links** are given as appropriate at various points in the text. These are either to the text's companion website, where there is a great deal of further material, or to other websites containing useful information relating to the topics covered.
- **Annotated Readings** for each chapter suggest further relevant readings, with guidance on their value.
- Each Part of the text includes **a brief introduction** to its scope and purpose.
- **Chapter objectives** to open and **Summary propositions** to conclude each chapter set up the readers' expectations and review their understanding progressively.
- There are full **references** at the end of each chapter to aid further exploration of the chapter material, as required.
- Each Part of the book concludes with a **Focus on Skills** dealing with the face-to-face situations that make up a large part of the HR manager's day, followed by a review of the Part of the text which they conclude.
- The **Website**, www.pearsoned.co.uk/torrington, has more material, including further case studies or exercises for each chapter and support for both tutor and student. The HRP exercise is directly referred to in Chapter 3, as this is an integral part of the chapter. This exercise is a case study giving worked examples of how the techniques have been used.

Figure P.1 represents the contents of this book in the six main parts. After the four-chapter introduction in Part 1 come the six parts, which each have the same format: strategic aspects, operational features and a concluding Focus on skills which highlights an interaction that is central to that set of operations. This is the HRM process, a strategic core with operational specialist expertise and a strong focus on dealing with people face to face.

Figure P.1
The
Honeycomb
of HRM

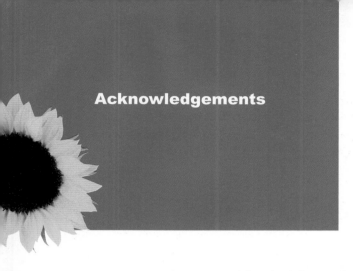

Acknowledgements

We are grateful to the following for permission to reproduce copyright material:

Ralph Windle for his poem 'The Business Consultant' from The Bottom Line: A Book of Business Ballads by Bertie Ramsbottom published by Century Hutchinson (Random House) 1985. (Bertie Ramsbottom is the pen-name of Ralph Windle); Pearson Education Ltd for an extract adapted from *Finding and Keeping the Right People* by Jon Billsberry 1996; Roisin Woolnough for an extract adapted from 'Racism reinforces the glass ceiling' published in *The Guardian* November 2000; IRS Ltd for an extract 'Arriva, dramatic results on diversity' by C. Wolff published in *Equal Opportunities Review* no. 160, January 2007 and News International Syndication Ltd for an extract 'BA is plunging toward disaster' by Harvey Elliott published in *The Times* July 1997. NF 2.2 from Managing Human Assets,Free Press, (Beer, M., Spector, B., Lawrence, P.R., Quinn Mills, D. and Walton, R.E. 1984); NF 2.3 and 2.4 from Strategic Human Resource Management, John Wiley and Sons, (Fombrun, C., Tichy, N.M. and Devanna, M.A. 1984), Reprinted with permission of John Wiley and Sons, Inc; NF 3.1 from Human Resource Strategic Visioning and Strategic Planning in 'The Fall and Rise of Strategic', Harvard Business Review, (Mintzberg, H. 1994); NF 5.2 from 'Strategic Determinants of Managerial Labour Markets', (Sonnenfield et al, J.A. 1992), Reprinted with permission of John Wiley and Sons, Inc; T6.3 based on: Labour Market: Incidence of part-time employment, OECD Factbook 2007, Economic, Environmental and Social Statistics, © OECD 2007; T7.2 from Methods of obtaining a job, Labour Market Trends (2002) in *Labour Market Spotlight*, HMSO, reproduced under the terms of the click-use licence; F12.1 from The Learning Company, McGraw-Hill, (Pedler, M., Burgoyne, J. and Boydell, T. 1991), Reproduced with the kind permission of The McGraw-Hill Publishing Company; F12.2 from Becoming a Learning Organisation, Addison-Wesley, (Swieringa, J. and Wierdsma, A. 1992); T17.1 from Level Three Management Standards in Management Standards Organisation, www.managementstandards.org; T17.2 and 17.3 from The Competant Manager, John Wiley, (Boyatzis, R. 1982), Reprinted with permission of John Wiley and Sons, Inc; T18.1 from 'Planned and Emergent Learning: A Framework and a Method; Executive Development, Vol. 7, (Megginson, D. 1994), Republished with kind permission of Emerald Group Publishing Limited; T20.2 from Categories of Management Styles in Employee Relations in Strategies and Practice in the Management of Industrial Relations: Blackwell, (Purcell, J. and Sisson, K. 1983); F24.1 from Conceptual model of Diversity, Human Resource Management, Vol. 31, Nos 1 and 2, Spring/Summer, (Jackson, B.W., LaFasto, F., Schultz, H.G. and Kelly, D. 1992).

We are grateful to the Financial Times Limited for permission to reprint the following material:

Aviva says job cuts will save £250m annually, © Financial Times, 15 September 2006; When the ideal applicant is too good to be true, © Financial Times, 12 January 2004.

PART 1

INTRODUCTION

The first part of the book has four chapters and a Focus on skills to introduce various dimensions of what human resource management involves. Chapter 1 sets the scene by describing the way in which human resource management works today and then explains how it has evolved to its present form over the hundred years of its existence as a separate function of management. It shows that present-day practice is not only a response to contemporary business demands and social expectations, but also an amalgam of different features which built up throughout the twentieth century and continue in the twenty-first. Later there is a philosophy for human resource management. This is followed by summaries of major debates in the field. Chapter 2 concentrates on strategy in human resource management. We see the way in which HR specialists make their strategic contribution, drawing a distinction between a human resource strategy and strategic human resources.

Chapter 3 is different from the others in having a strong focus on the analytical techniques and processes involved in planning relating to jobs and people. Understanding issues is an essential feature of HR work, but careful, systematic analysis is a vital underpinning for all decision and action. Chapter 4 reviews the international dimension to human resource management. Earlier versions of the book have had this chapter towards the end of the book, but we have moved it nearer the beginning because of its growing significance as a dimension of the work done by almost all HR specialists. The Part 1 Focus on skills begins a series of treatments of the way in which being effective in different face-to-face situations is a fundamental feature of life for all in human resource management.

CHAPTER 1

THE NATURE OF HUMAN RESOURCE MANAGEMENT

THE OBJECTIVES OF THIS CHAPTER ARE TO:

1 Review key current developments in human resource management

2 Explain the different ways in which the term 'human resource management' is used

3 Set out the main objectives of the human resource function

4 Review the historical evolution of the modern HR function

5 Explain the philosophy of HRM that is adopted in this book

6 Introduce some major current debates in the field of HRM

Human resource management (HRM) is the basis of all management activity, but it is not the basis of all business activity. A business may depend fundamentally on having a unique product, like the Dyson vacuum cleaner, or on obtaining the necessary funding, like the London bid to stage the Olympic Games, or on identifying a previously unnoticed market niche, like Saga Services. The basis of management is always the same: getting the people of the business to make things happen in a productive way, so that the business prospers and the people thrive.

HUMAN RESOURCE MANAGEMENT FOR THE TWENTY-FIRST CENTURY

Businesses are diverse. Prisons, restaurants, oil companies, corner shops, fire brigades, churches, hotel chains, hospitals, schools, newspapers, charities, doctors' and dentists' surgeries, professional sports teams, airlines, barristers' chambers and universities are all businesses in the sense that they have overall corporate missions to deliver and these have to be achieved within financial constraints. They all need to have their human resources managed, no matter how much some of the resourceful humans may resent aspects of the management process which limit their individual freedom of action.

Managing resourceful humans requires a constant balancing between meeting the human aspirations of the people and meeting the strategic and financial needs of the business. At times the balance can shift too far in one direction. Through the 1960s and 1970s the human aspirations of senior people in companies and public sector operations tended to produce large staffs, with heavyweight, hierarchical **bureaucracies** and stagnant businesses. One consultancy in the 1970s produced monthly comparative data measuring company success in terms of profitability and the number of employees – the more the better. At the same time the aspirations of employees lower down in the bureaucracy tended to maintain the status quo and a concentration on employee benefits that had scant relevance to business effectiveness. By the end of the twentieth century financial imperatives had generated huge reactions to this in the general direction of '**downsizing**' or reducing the number of people employed to create businesses that were lean, fit and flexible. **Hierarchies** were '**delayered**' to reduce numbers of staff and many functions were '**outsourced**', so as to simplify the operation of the business, concentrating on core expertise at the expense of peripheral activities, which were then bought in as needed from consultants or specialist suppliers. Reducing headcount became a fashionable criterion for success.

By the beginning of the twenty-first century the problems of the scales being tipped so considerably towards rationalisation were beginning to show. Businesses became more than slim; some became anorexic. Cost cutting achieved impressive short-tem results, but it cannot be repeated year after year without impairing the basic viability of the business. Steadily the number of problem cases mounted. In Britain there was great public discussion about problems with the national rail network and the shortage of skilled staff to carry out maintenance and repairs or the lack of trained guards.

WINDOW ON PRACTICE

In February 2003 the Columbia space shuttle disintegrated over Texas during re-entry to the earth's atmosphere. All seven crew died. In August an official inquiry was severe and unequivocal in its condemnation of cost cutting that took no account of safety requirements. NASA staff had been reduced from 32,000 to 19,000 and its budget had been cut by 40 per cent. Much of the responsibility for safety had been subcontracted to Boeing, and NASA's safety culture had become 'reactive, complacent and dominated by unjustified optimism, displaying no interest in understanding a problem and its implications'.

HR managers need to be particularly aware of the risks associated with cost cutting, as they may be the greatest culprits. The British National Health Service has long been criticised for inefficient use of resources, so large numbers of managers and administrators have been recruited to make things more efficient. Many of these new recruits are HR people who may be perceived by health professionals as creating inefficient and costly controls at the expense of employing more health professionals. We are not suggesting that these criticisms are necessarily justified, but there are undoubtedly situations in which the criticisms *are* justified.

There is now a move towards redressing that balance in search for an equilibrium between the needs for financial viability and success in the **marketplace** on the one hand and the need to maximise **human capital** on the other.

BUSINESSES, ORGANISATIONS AND HUMAN RESOURCE MANAGEMENT

Most books on management and the academic study of management use the term 'organisation' as the classifier: organisational behaviour, organisational psychology, organisational sociology and organisation theory are standard terms because they focus on the interaction between the organisation as an entity and its people or with the surrounding society. So far we have used the word 'business'. We will not stick to this throughout the book, but we have used it to underline the fact that HR people are concerned with the management of resourceful humans *not* employed within the organisation as well as those who are. The above criticism of NASA's complacency was because they had lost the sense of ownership and responsibility for a human capital input simply because the people were employed by a different organisation. HR people have to be involved in the effective management of all the people of the business, not only those who are directly employed within the organisation itself. We need to remember that organisation is a process as well as an entity.

ACTIVITY 1.1

We use the word 'organisation' to describe an entity when we are describing the place where we work ('my organisation'), a particular business enterprise ('Shell is an international organisation') or as a general term to describe undertakings ('over 200 organisations were represented at the conference'). Organisation as a process describes how something is done ('the organisation of the conference was very efficient'; 'the project failed due to poor organisation'). Think of examples of HR work which are organisation as a process.

Human resource managers administer the **contract of employment**, which is the legal basis of the employment relationship, but within that framework they also administer a psychological contract for **performance**. To have a viable business the employer obviously requires those who do its work to produce an appropriate and effective performance and the performance may come from employees, but is just as likely to come from non-employees. A business which seeks to be as lean and flexible as it can needs to reduce long-term cost commitments and focus its efforts on the activities which are the basis of its **competitive advantage**. It may be wise to buy in standard business services, as well as expertise, from specialist providers. Performance standards can be unambiguously agreed and monitored (although they rarely are), while the contract can be ended a great deal more easily than is the case with a department full of employees.

We refer to a **contract** for performance because both parties have an interest in performance. The employer needs it from the employee, but an employee also has a psychological need to perform, to do well and to fulfil personal needs that for many can best be met in the employment context. Schoolteachers cannot satisfy their desire to teach without a school to provide premises, equipment and pupils. A research chemist can do little without a well-equipped laboratory and qualified colleagues; very few coach drivers can earn their living unless someone else provides the coach.

DEFINING HUMAN RESOURCE MANAGEMENT

The term 'human resource management' is not easy to define. This is because it is commonly used in two different ways. On the one hand it is used generically to describe the body of management activities covered in books such as this. Used in this way HRM is really no more than a more modern and supposedly imposing name for what has long been labelled 'personnel management'. On the other hand, the term is equally widely used to denote a particular approach to the management of people which is clearly distinct from 'personnel management'. Used in this way 'HRM' signifies more than an updating of the label; it also suggests a distinctive philosophy towards carrying out people-oriented organisational activities: one which is held to serve the modern business more effectively than 'traditional' personnel management. We explore the substance of these two meanings of human resource management in the following paragraphs, referring to the first as 'HRM mark 1' and the second as 'HRM mark 2'.

HRM mark 1: the generic term

The role of the human resource functions is explained by identifying the key **objectives** to be achieved. Four objectives form the foundation of all HR activity.

Staffing objectives

Human resource managers are first concerned with ensuring that the business is appropriately staffed and thus able to draw on the human resources it needs. This involves designing organisation structures, identifying under what type of contract different groups of employees (or subcontractors) will work, before recruiting, selecting and developing the people required to fill the roles: the right people, with the right skills to provide their services when needed. There is a need to compete effectively in the employment market by recruiting and retaining the best, affordable workforce that is available. This involves developing employment packages that are sufficiently attractive to maintain the required employee skills levels and, where necessary, disposing of those judged no longer to have a role to play in the organisation. The tighter a key employment market becomes, the harder it is to find and then to hold on to the people an organisation needs in order to compete effectively. In such circumstances increased attention has to be given to developing competitive pay packages, to the provision of valued training and development opportunities and to ensuring that the experience of working in the organisation is, as far as is possible, rewarding and fulfilling.

Performance objectives

Once the required workforce is in place, human resource managers seek to ensure that people are well motivated and committed so as to maximise their performance in their different roles. Training and development has a role to play, as do reward systems to maximise effort and focus attention on performance targets. In many organisations, particularly where trade unions play a significant role, human resource managers negotiate improved performance with the workforce. The achievement of performance objectives also requires HR specialists to assist in disciplining employees effectively and equitably where individual conduct and/or performance standards are unsatisfactory. Welfare functions can also assist performance by providing constructive assistance to people whose performance has fallen short of their potential because of illness or difficult personal circumstances. Last but not least, there is the range of employee involvement initiatives to raise levels of commitment and to engage employees in developing new ideas. It is increasingly recognised that a key determinant of superior competitive performance is a propensity on the part of an organisation's employees to demonstrate **discretionary effort**. Essentially this means that they choose to go further in the service of their employer than is strictly required in their contracts of employment, working longer hours perhaps, working with greater enthusiasm or taking the initiative to improve systems and relationships. Willingness to engage in such behaviour cannot be forced by managers. But they can help to create an environment in which it is more likely to occur.

Change-management objectives

A third set of core objectives in nearly every business relates to the role played by the HR function in effectively managing change. Frequently change does not come along in readily defined episodes precipitated by some external factor. Instead it is endemic and well-nigh continuous, generated as much by a continual need to innovate as from definable environmental pressures. Change comes in different forms. Sometimes it is merely structural, requiring reorganisation of activities or the introduction of new people into particular roles. At other times cultural change is sought in order to alter attitudes, philosophies or long-present organisational norms. In any of these scenarios the HR function can play a central role. Key activities include the recruitment and/or development of people with the necessary leadership skills to drive the change process, the employment of change agents to encourage acceptance of change and the construction of reward systems which underpin the change process. Timely and effective employee involvement is also crucial because 'people support what they help to create'.

Administration objectives

The fourth type of objective is less directly related to achieving competitive advantage, but is focused on underpinning the achievement of the other forms of objective. In part it is simply carried out in order to facilitate an organisation's smooth running. Hence there is a need to maintain accurate and comprehensive data on individual employees, a record of their achievement in terms of performance, their attendance and training records, their terms and conditions of employment and their personal details. However, there is also a legal aspect to much administrative activity, meaning that it is done because the business is required by law to comply. Of particular significance is the requirement that payment is administered professionally and lawfully, with itemised monthly pay statements being provided for all employees. There is also the need to make arrangements for the deduction of taxation and national insurance, for the payment of pension fund contributions and to be on top of the complexities associated with Statutory Sick Pay and Statutory Maternity Pay, as well as maternity and paternity leave. Additional legal requirements relate to the monitoring of health and safety systems and the issuing of contracts to new employees. Accurate record keeping is central to ensuring compliance with a variety of newer legal obligations such as the National Minimum Wage and the Working Time Regulations. HR professionals often downgrade the significance of effective administration, seeking instead to gain for themselves a more glamorous (and usually more highly paid) role formulating policy and strategy. This is a short-sighted attitude. Achieving excellence (i.e. professionalism and cost effectiveness) in the delivery of the basic administrative tasks is important as an aim in itself, but it also helps the HR function in an organisation to gain and maintain the credibility and respect that are required in order to influence other managers in the organisation.

ACTIVITY 1.2

Each of the four types of HR objective is important and necessary for organisations in different ways. However, at certain times one or more can assume greater importance than the others. Can you identify types of situation in which each could become the most significant or urgent?

Delivering HRM objectives

The larger the organisation, the more scope there is to employ people to specialise in particular areas of HRM. Some, for example, employ employee relations specialists to look after the collective relationship between management and employees. Where there is a strong tradition of collective bargaining, the role is focused on the achievement of satisfactory outcomes from ongoing negotiations. Increasingly, however, employee relations specialists are required to provide advice about legal developments, to manage consultation arrangements and to preside over employee involvement initiatives.

Another common area of specialisation is in the field of training and development. Although much of this is now undertaken by external providers, there is still a role for in-house trainers, particularly in management development. Increasingly the term 'consultant' is used instead of 'officer' or 'manager' to describe the training specialist's role, indicating a shift towards a situation in which line managers determine the training *they* want rather than the training section providing a standardised portfolio of courses. The other major specialist roles are in the fields of recruitment and selection, health, safety and welfare, compensation and benefits and human resource planning.

In addition to the people who have specialist roles there are many other people who are employed as human resources or personnel generalists. Working alone or in small teams, they carry out the range of HR activities and seek to achieve all the objectives outlined above. In larger businesses generalists either look after all personnel matters in a particular division or are employed at a senior level to develop policy and take responsibility for HR issues across the organisation as a whole. In more junior roles, human resource administrators and assistants undertake many of the administrative tasks mentioned earlier. It is increasingly common for organisations to separate the people responsible for undertaking routine administration and even basic advice from those employed to manage case work, to develop policies and to manage the strategic aspects of the HR role. In some cases the administrative work is outsourced to specialist providers, while in others a **shared services model** has been established whereby a centralised administrative function is distinguished from decentralised teams of HR advisers working as part of management teams in different divisions. Figure 1.1 summarises the roles and objectives of HRM.

Most HR practitioners working at a senior level are now professionally qualified, having secured membership of the Chartered Institute of Personnel and Development (CIPD). The wide range of elective subjects which can now be chosen by those seeking qualification through the Institute's examinations has made it as relevant to those seeking a specialist career as to those who prefer to remain in generalist roles. However, many smaller businesses do not need, or cannot afford, HR managers at all. They may use consultants or the advisory services of university departments. They may use their bank's computer to process the payroll, but there is still a human resource dimension to their managers' activities.

ACTIVITY 1.3

Which of the various HR roles described above would you be most interested in undertaking? The generalist role, a specialist role or perhaps that of a consultant or subcontractor?

What are the main reasons for your choice?

Figure 1.1
HRM roles and
objectives

HRM mark 2: a distinctive approach to the management of people

The second meaning commonly accorded to the term 'human resource management' denotes a particular way of carrying out the range of activities discussed above. Under this definition, a 'human resource management approach' is something qualitatively different from a 'personnel management approach'. Commentators disagree, however, about how fundamental a shift is signified by a movement from personnel management to human resource management. For some, particularly those whose focus of interest is on the management of collective relationships at work, the rise of HRM in the last two decades of the twentieth century represented something new and very different from the dominant personnel management approach in earlier years. A particular theme in their work is the contention that personnel management is essentially *workforce centred*, while HRM is *resource centred*. Personnel specialists direct their efforts mainly at the organisation's employees; finding and training them, arranging for them to be paid, explaining management's expectations, justifying management's actions, satisfying employees' work-related needs, dealing with their problems and seeking to modify management action that could produce an unwelcome employee response. The people who work in the organisation are the starting point, and they are a resource that is relatively inflexible in comparison with other resources, like cash and materials.

Although indisputably a management function, personnel management is not totally identified with management interests. Just as sales representatives have to understand and articulate the aspirations of the customers, personnel managers seek to understand and articulate the aspirations and views of the workforce. There is always some degree of being in between management and the employees, mediating the needs of each to the other.

	Personnel management	Human resource management
Time and planning perspective	Short term, reactive, ad hoc, marginal	Long term, proactive, strategic, integrated
Psychological contract	Compliance	Commitment
Control systems	External controls	Self-control
Employee relations perspective	Pluralist, collective, low trust	Unitarist, individual, high trust
Preferred structures/ systems	Bureaucratic/mechanistic, centralised, formal defined roles	Organic, devolved, flexible roles
Roles	Specialist/professional	Largely integrated into line management
Evaluation criteria	Cost minimisation	Maximum utilisation (human asset accounting)

Figure 1.2
Personnel
versus HRM

HRM, by contrast, is directed mainly at management needs for human resources (not necessarily employees) to be provided and deployed. Demand rather than supply is the focus of the activity. There is greater emphasis on planning, monitoring and control, rather than mediation. Problem solving is undertaken with other members of management on human resource issues rather than directly with employees or their representatives. It is totally identified with management interests, being a general management activity, and is relatively distant from the workforce as a whole. David Guest (1987) emphasises the differences between the two approaches in his model illustrating 'stereotypes of personnel management and human resource management' (see Figure 1.2).

An alternative point of view, while recognising the differences, downplays the significance of a break between personnel and human resources management. Such a conclusion is readily reached when the focus of analysis is on what HR/personnel managers actually do, rather than on the more profound developments in the specific field of collective employee relations. Legge (1989 and 1995) concludes that there is very little difference in fact between the two, but that there are some differences that are important; first, that human resource management concentrates more on what is done to managers than on what is done by managers to other employees; second, that there is a more proactive role for line managers; and, third, that there is a top management responsibility for managing culture – all factors to which we return later in the book. From this perspective, human resource management can simply be seen as the most recent mutation in a long line of developments that have characterised personnel management practice as it evolved during the last century. Below we identify four distinct stages in the historical development of the personnel management function. HRM, as described above, is a fifth. On the companion website there is a journalist's view of contemporary HRM to which we have added some discussion questions.

THE EVOLUTION OF PERSONNEL AND HR MANAGEMENT

Theme 1: social justice

The origins of personnel management lie in the nineteenth century, deriving from the work of social reformers such as Lord Shaftesbury and Robert Owen. Their criticisms of the free enterprise system and the hardship created by the exploitation of workers by factory owners enabled the first personnel managers to be appointed and provided the first frame of reference in which they worked: to ameliorate the lot of the workers. Such concerns are not obsolete. There are still regular reports of employees being exploited by employers flouting the law, and the problem of organisational distance between decision makers and those putting decisions into practice remains a source of alienation from work.

In the late nineteenth and early twentieth centuries some of the larger employers with a paternalist outlook began to appoint welfare officers to manage a series of new initiatives designed to make life less harsh for their employees. Prominent examples were the progressive schemes of unemployment benefit, sick pay and subsidised housing provided by the Quaker family firms of Cadbury and Rowntree, and the Lever Brothers' soap business. While the motives were ostensibly charitable, there was and remains a business as well as an ethical case for paying serious attention to the welfare of employees. This is based on the contention that it improves commitment on the part of staff and leads potential employees to compare the organisation favourably vis-à-vis competitors. The result is higher productivity, a longer-serving workforce and a bigger pool of applicants for each job. It has also been argued that a commitment to welfare reduces the scope for the development of adversarial industrial relations. The more conspicuous welfare initiatives promoted by employers today include employee assistance schemes, childcare facilities and health-screening programmes.

Theme 2: humane bureaucracy

The second phase marked the beginnings of a move away from a sole focus on welfare towards the meeting of various other organisational objectives. Personnel managers began to gain responsibilities in the areas of staffing, training and organisation design. Influenced by social scientists such as F.W. Taylor (1856–1915) and Henri Fayol (1841–1925) personnel specialists started to look at management and administrative processes analytically, working out how organisational structures could be designed and labour deployed so as to maximise efficiency. The humane bureaucracy stage in the development of personnel thinking was also influenced by the **Human Relations School**, which sought to ameliorate the potential for industrial conflict and dehumanisation present in too rigid an application of these **scientific management** approaches. Following the ideas of thinkers such as Elton Mayo (1880–1949), the fostering of social relationships in the workplace and employee morale thus became equally important objectives for personnel professionals seeking to raise productivity levels.

Theme 3: negotiated consent

Personnel managers next added expertise in bargaining to their repertoire of skills. In the period of full employment following the Second World War labour became a scarce resource. This led to a growth in trade union membership and to what Allan Flanders, the leading industrial relations analyst of the 1960s, called 'the challenge from below'. Personnel specialists managed the new collective institutions such as joint consultation committees, joint production committees and suggestion schemes set up in order to accommodate the new realities. In the industries that were nationalised in the 1940s, employers were placed under a statutory duty to negotiate with unions representing employees. To help achieve this, the government encouraged the appointment of personnel officers and set up the first specialist courses for them in the universities. A personnel management advisory service was also set up at the Ministry of Labour, which still survives as the first A in ACAS (the Advisory, Conciliation and Arbitration Service).

Theme 4: organisation

The late 1960s saw a switch in focus among personnel specialists, away from dealing principally with the rank-and-file employee on behalf of management, towards dealing with management itself and the integration of managerial activity. This phase was characterised by the development of career paths and of opportunities within organisations for personal growth. This too remains a concern of personnel specialists today, with a significant portion of time and resources being devoted to the recruitment, development and retention of an elite core of people with specialist expertise on whom the business depends for its future. Personnel specialists developed techniques of manpower or workforce planning. This is basically a quantitative activity, boosted by the advent of information technology, which involves forecasting the likely need for employees with different skills in the future.

Theme 5: human resource management

This has already been explained in the previous pages.

Theme 6: a 'new HR'?

Some academic writers have recently begun to argue that we are now witnessing the beginning of a new sixth stage in the evolution of personnel/HR work. While there is by no means a clear consensus about this point of view, it is notable that leading thinkers have identified a group of trends which they believe to be sufficiently dissimilar, as a bundle, from established practices to justify, at the very least, a distinct title. Bach (2005, pp. 28–9) uses the term 'the new HR' to describe 'a different trajectory' which he believes is now clearly discernible. A number of themes are identified, including a global perspective and a strong tendency for issues relating to legal compliance to move up the HR management agenda and to occupy management time. Bach also sees as significant the increased prevalence of multi-employer networks which he calls 'permeable organizations'. Here, instead of employees having a single, readily defined employer, there may be a number of different employers, or at least more than one organisation which exercises a degree of authority over their work. Such is the case when organisational boundaries become blurred, as they have a tendency to in the case of public-private partnerships, agency working, situations where work is outsourced by one organisation to another, joint ventures and franchises, and where strong supply chains are established consisting of smaller organisations which are wholly or very heavily reliant on the custom of a single large client corporation.

In each of these cases 'the new HR' amounts to a change of emphasis in response to highly significant long-term trends in the business environment. It is therefore legitimate to question the extent to which it really represents anything genuinely 'new' as far as HR practice is concerned. However, in addition, Bach and others draw attention to another development which can be seen as more novel and which does genuinely represent 'a different trajectory'. This is best summarised as an approach to the employment relationship which views employees and potential employees very much as individuals or at least small groups rather than as a single group and which seeks to engage them emotionally. It is associated with a move away from an expectation that staff will demonstrate commitment to a set of corporate values which are determined by senior management and towards a philosophy which is far more customer focused. Customers are defined explicitly as the ultimate employers and staff are empowered to act in such a way as to meet their requirements. This involves encouraging employees to empathise with customers, recruiting, selecting and appraising them according to their capacity to do so. The approach now infuses the corporate language in some organisations to the extent that HR officers refer to the staff and line managers whom they 'serve' as their 'internal customers', a client group which they aim to satisfy and which they survey regularly as a means of establishing how far this aim is in fact being achieved. The practice of viewing staff as internal customers goes further still in some organisations with the use of HR practices that borrow explicitly from the toolkit of marketing specialists. We see this in the widespread interest in employer branding exercises (see Chapter 7) where an organisation markets itself in quite sophisticated ways, not to customers and potential customers, but to employees and potential employees.

Gratton (2004) shows how highly successful companies such as Tesco go further still in categorising job applicants and existing staff into distinct categories which summarise their principal aspirations as far as their work is concerned in much the same way that organisations seek to identify distinct market segments to use when developing, designing, packaging and marketing products and services. Such approaches aim to provide an 'employment proposition' which it is hoped will attract the right candidates, allow the appointment of highly effective performers, motivate them to provide excellent levels of service and subsequently retain them for a longer period of time.

Lepak and Snell (2007) also note a move in HR away from 'the management of jobs' and towards 'the management of people', which includes the development of employment strategies that differ for different groups of employees. Importantly this approach recognises the capacity that most people have to become emotionally engaged in their work, with their customers, with their colleagues and hence (if to a lesser extent) with their organisations. The employment relationship is not just a transactional one in which money is earned in exchange for carrying out a set of duties competently, but also a relational one which involves emotional attachments. The 'new HR' understands this and seeks to manage people accordingly.

ACTIVITY 1.4

Lynda Gratton (2004) reports that Tesco used the following five 'identities' to categorise its staff. The way that they are managed and the reward packages that are available to them can thus be tailored so as to be more appropriate to the needs and aspirations of each individual:

- work-life balancers

- want it all

- pleasure seekers
- live to work
- work to live

Which of these categories best describes you as far as your present employment is concerned? What about friends and members of your family? Choose any two of the categories and think about in what ways it would make sense to manage people in each group differently from one another.

HRM AND THE ACHIEVEMENT OF ORGANISATIONAL EFFECTIVENESS

For the past decade the theme that has dominated the HR research agenda has been the study of links between HR practices and organisational effectiveness. Throughout the book we make reference to this research in the context of different HR activities, but it is helpful briefly to set out at the start how what happens in the field of HR impacts on an organisation's ability to meet its objectives.

What those objectives are will vary depending on the type of organisation and its situation. For most businesses operating in the private sector the overriding long-term objective is the achievement and maintenance of competitive advantage, by which is meant a sustained period of commercial success vis-à-vis its principal competitors. For others, however, ensuring survival is a more pressing objective. In the public and voluntary sectors notions of competition and survival are increasingly present too, but here organisational effectiveness is primarily defined in terms of meeting a service need as cost efficiently as possible and to the highest achievable standard of quality. Meeting government-set targets is central to the operation of many public sector organisations, as is the requirement to ensure that the expectations of users are met as far as is possible. For all sizeable organisations there is also a need to foster a positive long-term corporate reputation. Developing such a reputation can take many years to achieve, but without care it can be lost very quickly with very damaging results. In particular organisations need to maintain a strong reputation for sound management in the financial markets. This enables them to raise money with relative ease when they need to and also helps to ensure that managers of investment funds and financial advisers see them or their shares as desirable places to put their clients' money. The maintenance of a positive reputation in the media is also an important objective as this helps to maintain and grow the customer base. In this context corporate ethics and social responsibility are increasingly significant because they are becoming more prominent factors in determining the purchasing decisions of consumers. The HR function should play a significant role in helping to achieve each of these dimensions of organisational effectiveness.

The contribution of the HR function to *gaining* competitive advantage involves achieving the fundamental aims of an organisation in the field of people management more effectively and efficiently than competitor organisations. These aims were discussed above – mobilising a workforce, maximising its performance, managing change effectively and striving to achieve excellence in administration.

The contribution of the HR function to *maintaining* competitive advantage involves recognising the significance of the organisation's people as an effective barrier preventing would-be rivals from expanding their markets into territory that the organisation holds. The term **human capital** is more and more used in this context to signify that the combined knowledge and experience of an organisation's staff is a highly significant source of competitive advantage largely because it is difficult for competitors to replicate easily. Attracting, engaging, rewarding, developing and retaining people effectively is thus vital. Failing to do so enables accumulated human capital to leak away into the hands of competitors, reducing the effectiveness of commercial defences and making it harder to maintain competitive advantage.

Fostering a positive reputation among would-be investors, financial advisers and financial journalists is also an aspect of organisational effectiveness to which the HR function makes a significant contribution. Key here is the need to reassure those whose job it is to assess the long-term financial viability of the organisation that it is competently managed and is well placed to meet the challenges that lie ahead in both the short and the longer term. The ability to attract and retain a strong management team is central to achieving this aspect of organisational effectiveness, as is the ability of the organisation to plan for the future by having in place effective succession planning arrangements and robust systems for the development of the skills and knowledge that will be key in the future. Above all, financial markets need to be assured that the organisation is stable and is thus a safe repository for investors' funds. The work of Stevens and his colleagues (2005) is helpful in this context. They conceive of the whole human resource contribution in terms of the management of risk, the aim being to ensure that an organisation 'balances the maximisation of opportunities and the minimisation of risks'.

Finally, the HR function also plays a central role in building an organisation's reputation as an ethically or socially responsible organisation. This happens in two distinct ways. The first involves fostering an understanding of and commitment to ethical conduct on the part of managers and staff. It is achieved by paying attention to these objectives in recruitment campaigns, in the criteria adopted for the selection of new employees and the promotion of staff, in the methods used to develop people and in performance management processes. The second relates to the manner in which people are managed. A poor ethical reputation can be gained simply because an organisation becomes known for treating its staff poorly. In recent years well-known fast food chains in the UK have suffered because of their use of zero hours contracts, while several large multinationals have had their reputations stained by stories in the media about the conditions under which their employees in developing countries are required to work.

DEBATES IN HRM

The world in which human resource managers exist and with which they interact is continually changing, generating new issues and conundrums to consider. While in most cases managers have a fair degree of choice about how to deal with new ideas and new sets of circumstances, the choices themselves are often difficult. Our final task in this opening chapter is to introduce readers to a number of these issues in general terms. All raise themes to which we will return at various stages later in the book.

In one way or another all the major debates that occupy HR professionals, analysts and commentators concern the appropriate response to the major trends which are evolving in our business environment. But people differ in their analysis of the extent and nature of these developments and this colours their ideas about whether or not radical **change** in the way that people are managed is or is not appropriate. Here we can usefully distinguish between three separate fields of debate.

The first is concerned with understanding and conceptualising the nature of current responses. How are organisations dealing with the issues that they face in terms of the management of their people? Are they developing new approaches that differ fundamentally from those that have been established for some time or are we witnessing a more steady, considered evolution of practice?

The second field of debate concerns what HR managers *should* be doing. Are new or radical changes in policy and practice necessary? Or is the correct response to environmental developments the further refinement of more familiar approaches? Further debate concerns the extent to which the answer to these questions is broadly the same for all employing organisations or whether it differs quite profoundly from industry to industry or firm to firm.

A third debate is oriented towards longer-term future developments. Many believe and have argued persuasively that we are currently witnessing changes in our business environment which are as fundamental and significant as those which accompanied the industrial revolution two hundred years ago. They further argue that the world of work which will emerge in future decades will be wholly different in major respects from that we currently inhabit. It follows that those organisations which 'see the future' most clearly and change accordingly stand to gain most. But are these predictions really accurate? Could the analysis on which they are built be faulty in key respects?

Of course it is also possible to ask rather different kinds of questions about the HR practices that are being, will be or should be developed, which in turn lead us to engage in various types of debate. Some, for example, focus exclusively on the requirements of the organisation and the search for competitive advantage. What can the HR function do that will maximise organisational growth, effectiveness and efficiency? However, many also like to think more broadly and to concern themselves with the impact of employment practice on the workforce and on society in more general terms. Hence we also engage in debates that are essentially ethical in nature or which have a prominent moral, sociological or political dimension.

Key environmental developments

The major trends in our contemporary **business environment** are well understood, well documented and uncontroversial. People differ, though, in their understanding of the speed of change and of the extent to which all organisations are or will be affected. As far as product markets are concerned the big trend is towards ever more intense competitive pressures, leading some to argue that we are now entering the era of hyper-competition (Sparrow 2003, p. 371). This is being driven by two major developments, the significance of which has increased considerably in recent years.

First, we are witnessing moves towards the globalisation of economic activity on a scale that has not been experienced before in human history. More and more the markets for the goods and products we sell are international, which means of course that competition for those markets as well as our established ones is also increasingly becoming international. Large organisations that were able to dominate national markets a decade or two ago (many owned and operated by governments) are now mainly privately owned and faced with vastly more competition from similar organisations based all over the world. This has led to consolidation through the construction of global corporations and strategic alliances whose focus in terms of people management is also international.

The second major antecedent of hyper-competition is technology, which moves forward at an ever-accelerating pace year by year. Developments in information technology, energy production, chemical engineering, laser technology, transportation and biotechnology are in the process of revolutionising the way that many industries operate. It is partly the sheer pace of change and the need for organisations to stay ahead of this very fast-moving game which drives increased competition. Being the first to develop and make efficient use of new technologies is the means by which many organisations maintain their competitive position and can thus grow and prosper.

But IT, and in particular the growth of e-business, is significant too because it has the potential vastly to increase the number of competitors that any one organisation faces. This is because it makes it much easier for customers and potential customers to compare what a particular organisation can offer in terms of price and quality with what others can offer.

What does this mean in practical terms from the point of view of the HR manager? First, it means that practices continually have to be developed which have the effect of enhancing an organisation's competitive position. Ways need to be found of improving quality and of bringing to market attractive new products and services, while at the same time ensuring that the organisation remains competitive in terms of its cost base. Second, it means that a good deal of volatility is the norm and that change, often of a profound nature, is something that people working in organisations must expect and be ready for. So a capacity for organisational flexibility has become central to the achievement and maintenance of competitive advantage. Third, there are direct practical outcomes. For example, HR managers have to learn how to manage an international workforce effectively and how best to attract, retain and develop and motivate people with those relatively scarce skills that are essential if an organisation is effectively to harness and deploy evolving technologies.

For the HR manager, however, unlike colleagues in other areas of management, responding to product market developments is only part of what is needed. Other major environmental trends are equally important and must also be understood and built into decision making. There are two areas that are particularly important:

- labour market trends
- the evolution of employment regulation

Developments in the labour market are significant partly in terms of the numbers of people and skills available, and partly in terms of attitudes towards work and the workplace. Major developments appear to be occurring in both these areas. Many industries, for example, have found themselves facing skills shortages in recent years. The impact varies from country to country depending on relative economic prosperity, but most organisations in the UK have seen a tightening of their key labour markets in recent years. Unemployment levels have remained low, while demographic trends have created a situation in which more older people are retiring than younger people are entering the job market. There are all kinds of implications. For a start, employers are having to make themselves more attractive to employees than has been necessary in recent years. No longer can they simply assume that people will seek work with them or seek to remain employed with them. In a tight labour market individuals have more choice about where and when they work, and do not need to put up with a working environment in which they are unhappy. If they do not like their jobs there are more opportunities for them to look elsewhere. So organisations are increasingly required to compete with one another in labour markets as well as in product markets. This has implications for policy in all areas of HRM, but particularly in the areas of reward, employee development and recruitment.

Labour market conditions along with other social trends serve to shape the attitudes of people towards their work. In order to mobilise and motivate a workforce, HR managers must be aware of how these are changing and to respond effectively. One of the most significant trends in recent years, for example, has been a reduced interest on the part of employees in joining trade unions and taking part in their activities. A more individualistic attitude now prevails in the majority of workplaces, people focusing on themselves and their own career development rather than standing in solidarity with fellow workers. Another well-documented trend is the increased desire for employees to achieve a better balance between their home and work lives and their increased willingness to seek out employers who can provide this.

The growth in the extent and complexity of employment regulation is a third area which HR managers are obliged to grasp and the elements of which they must implement in their organisations. Prior to 1970, with one or two exceptions, there was no statutory regulation of the employment relationship in the UK. An individual's terms and conditions of employment were those that were stated in the contract of employment and in any collective agreements. The law did not intervene beyond providing some basic health and safety protection, the right to modest redundancy payments and a general requirement on employers and employees to honour the contractual terms agreed when the employment began. Since 1970 this situation has wholly changed. The individual contract of employment remains significant and can be enforced in court if necessary, but there has been added to this a whole range of statutory rights which employers are obliged to honour. The most significant are in the fields of health and safety, equal pay, unlawful discrimination and unfair dismissal. Much recent new law such as that on working time, family-friendly rights, consultation and discrimination on grounds of sexual orientation, age and belief has a European origin, and a great deal more can be expected in the years ahead.

Debates about how HR managers are and should be responding to these various trends form the focus of much of what follows in this book and you will find a much more detailed treatment of some in other chapters. The international dimension, for example, is discussed in Chapter 4 and ethical matters in Chapter 30. We focus on the work-life balance in Chapter 31, on labour market trends in Part 2 and on regulatory matters in Part 5. Below we briefly set out the main contours of three specific debates that have a general relevance to many of the topic areas we discuss later.

The psychological contract

According to many, one consequence of these evolving environmental pressures is a significant and fundamental change in what has become known as 'the psychological contract'. This refers to the expectations that employees have about the role that they play and about what the employer is prepared to give them in return. Whereas a legal contract of employment sets out terms and conditions of employment, remuneration arrangements and the basic rules which are to govern the employment relationship, the psychological contract concerns broad expectations about what each party thinks it will gain from the relationship. By its nature the psychological contract is not a written document. Rather, it exists entirely within people's heads. But this has not prevented researchers from seeking to pin it down and to track the extent to which we are witnessing ongoing change in established psychological contracts.

While people disagree about the extent to which this change has in fact occurred, there is general agreement about the phenomenon itself and the notion that an 'old' psychological contract to which generations of employees have become accustomed is being superseded to some extent by a 'new' psychological contract which reflects the needs of the present business environment. From the employee perspective we can sum up the old psychological contract as follows:

> I will work hard for and act with loyalty towards my employer. In return I expect to be retained as an employee provided I do not act against the interests of the organisation. I also expect to be given opportunities for development and promotion should circumstances make this possible.

By contrast, the new psychological contract takes the following form:

> I will bring to my work effort and creativity. In return I expect a salary that is appropriate to my contribution and market worth. While our relationship may be short term, I will remain for as long as I receive the developmental opportunities I need to build my career.

A switch from the 'old' approach to the 'new' involves employers giving less job security and receiving less loyalty from employees in return. Instead, employees are given developmental opportunities and are expected to give the employer flexibility. The whole perception of the employment relationship on both sides is thus radically different. Moreover, moving from old psychological contracts towards new ones is a problematic process that involves managers 'breaching' the established deal. This is likely to lead to dissatisfaction on the part of employees who are affected and to some form of collective industrial action in unionised settings.

The big question is how far has a change of this nature actually occurred? Are we really witnessing a slow decline in the old psychological contract and its replacement by the new one, or have reports of its death been exaggerated? On this issue there is a great deal of disagreement. Many researchers claim to have found evidence of substantial change in many industries, particularly as regards reduced employee loyalty (e.g. Coyle-Shapiro and Kessler 2000, Maguire 2002). Yet others, notably Guest and Conway in their many studies conducted on behalf of the Chartered Institute of Personnel and Development (CIPD), have found relatively little evidence of any change in the state of the psychological contract. Their findings (e.g. Guest and Conway 2000 and 2001) suggest that while some change has occurred in the public sector, perceptions closer to the 'old' psychological contract remain a great deal more common than those associated with the 'new' approach.

It is difficult to reach firm conclusions about why these very marked differences of opinion exist. It is possible that the old psychological contract remains intact for most people, but that a significant minority, particularly managers and some public sector workers, have had to adjust to profound change. It is also possible that organisations have tried to move away from the old approach towards the new one, but have found it difficult to take their employees with them and have thus sought other methods of increasing their competitiveness. A third possibility, suggested by Atkinson (2003), is that the differences in the conclusions people reach about this issue derive from the methodologies they adopt when studying it. She argues that large-scale studies which involve sending questionnaires to employees have tended to report little change in the state of the psychological contract, while smaller-scale studies based on interviews with managers and trade union officials tend to report the opposite.

ACTIVITY 1.5

How would you characterise your current psychological contract at work? To what extent and in what ways does it differ from psychological contracts you have experienced in previous jobs or from those of your friends and family?

Best practice versus best fit

The debate between **best practice** and **best fit** is an interesting one of general significance which has consequences across the field of HRM. As well as being a managerial issue it concerns one of the most significant academic controversies in the HR field at present. At root it is about whether or not there is an identifiable 'best way' of carrying out HR activities which is universally applicable. It is best understood as a debate between two schools of thought, although in practice it is quite possible to take a central position which sees validity in both the basic positions.

Adherents of a best practice perspective argue that there are certain HR practices and approaches to their operation which will invariably help an organisation in achieving competitive advantage. There is therefore a clear link between HR activity and business performance, but the effect will only be maximised if the 'right' HR policies are pursued. A great deal of evidence has been published in recent years, using various methodologies, which appears to back up the best practice case (e.g. Pfeffer 1994; Huselid 1995; Wood and Albanese 1995; Delery and Doty 1996; Fernie and Metcalf 1996; Patterson *et al.* 1998; Guest and Conway 2000). While there are differences of opinion on questions of detail, all strongly suggest that the same basic bundle of human resource practices or general human resource management orientation tends to enhance business performance in all organisations irrespective of the particular product market strategy being pursued. According to David Guest this occurs through a variety of mechanisms:

> human resource practices exercise their positive impact by (i) ensuring and enhancing the competence of employees, (ii) by tapping their motivation and commitment, and (iii) by designing work to encourage the fullest contribution from employees. Borrowing from elements of expectancy theory (Vroom 1964, Lawler 1971), the model implies that all three elements should be present to ensure the best outcome. Positive employee behaviour should in turn impact upon establishment level outcomes such as low absence, quit rates and wastage, as well as high quality and productivity. (Guest 2000, p. 2)

The main elements of the 'best practice bundle' that these and other writers identify are those which have long been considered as examples of good practice in the HRM field. They include the use of the more advanced selection methods, a serious commitment to employee involvement, substantial investment in training and development, the use of individualised reward systems and harmonised terms and conditions of employment as between different groups of employees.

The alternative 'best fit' school also identifies a link between human resource management practice and the achievement of competitive advantage. Here, however, there is no belief in the existence of universal solutions. Instead, all is **contingent** on the particular circumstances of each organisation. What is needed is HR policies and practices which 'fit' and are thus appropriate to the situation of individual employers. What is appropriate (or 'best') for one will not necessarily be right for another. Key variables include the size of the establishment, the dominant product market strategy being pursued and the nature of the labour markets in which the organisation competes. It is thus argued that a small organisation which principally achieves competitive advantage through innovation and which competes in very tight labour markets should have in place rather different HR policies than those of a large firm which produces low-cost goods and faces no difficulty in attracting staff. In order to maximise competitive advantage, the first requires informality combined with sophisticated human resource practices, while the latter needs more bureaucratic systems combined with a 'low cost – no frills' set of HR practices.

The best fit or contingency perspective originated in the work of Joan Woodward and her colleagues at Imperial College in the 1950s. In recent years it has been developed and applied to contemporary conditions by academics such as Randall Schuler and Susan Jackson, John Purcell and Ed Lawler. In addition, a number of influential models have been produced which seek to categorise organisational contingencies and suggest what mix of HR practices is appropriate in each case. Examples are those of Miles and Snow (1978), Fombrun *et al.* (1984) and Sisson and Storey (2000) – a number of which we look at in more detail in Chapter 2.

To a great extent the jury is still out on these questions. Interestingly, however, some subfields in HRM are dominated by best practice thinking, while others broadly accept best fit assumptions. A good example of the former is employee selection (see Chapter 8), where for decades researchers have debated which of the various selection methods that can be used (interviews, psychometric tests, assessment centres, etc.) is 'best' in terms of its predictive validity. An example of the latter is the field of reward management (see Part 6) where no single best approach has yet to be identified, it being generally accepted that different situations require different types of reward package to be provided. When it comes to research on the HR function as a whole proponents of both the 'best practice' and 'best fit' perspectives can draw on bodies of empirical evidence to back up their respective positions and so the debate continues.

The future of work

Debates about what will happen in the future are inevitably speculative and impossible to prove one way or the other, but a great deal of attention and government research funding is currently being devoted to this issue. It matters a great deal from a public policy point of view because judgements about employers' human resource needs in the future must determine decisions about education and training now. Government actions in the fields of economic policy, employment legislation and immigration are also affected. We review these debates in detail in Chapter 34. Our purpose here is to summarise some of the key arguments that are put so that you can appreciate their relevance as you read our book.

A good starting point is the work of influential writers such as Charles Handy (1994 and 2001), Jeremy Rifkin (1995) and Susan Greenfield (2003). In different ways they have argued that the product market forces identified above will lead in future decades to the emergence of a world of work which is very different in many respects from that which most in western industrialised countries currently experience. Both the type of work we do and the nature of our contractual arrangements will, it is argued, change profoundly as we complete our journey out of the industrial era and into a new post-industrial age.

The first consequence will be a marked shift towards what is described as knowledge work. In the future, it is claimed, most people will be employed, in one way or another, to carry out tasks which involve the generation, interpretation, processing or application of knowledge. Automation and the availability of cheaper labour in developing countries will see further declines in much manufacturing activity, requiring the western economies to create wealth from the exploitation of scientific and technological advances. It follows that many more people will be employed for their specialist knowledge and that far fewer routine jobs will exist than is currently the case. Demand for professional and technical people will increase, while demand for manual and lower-skilled workers will decrease. It also means that competitive advantage from an employer's perspective will derive from the capacity to create and deploy knowledge more effectively than others can.

The second major claim that is made is that the 'job' as we have come to know it will become rarer and rarer. In the future many fewer people will occupy defined jobs in organisations. Instead we will tend increasingly to work on a self-employed basis carrying out specific, time-limited projects for organisations. This is inevitable, so the argument goes, in a highly volatile business climate. Organisations simply will not be able to offer long-term guarantees of work and so will be forced to stop offering contracts of employment in the way that they currently do. The future is therefore bleak for people who want job security, but bright for those who are happy working for many employers and periodically re-educating themselves for a new type of **career**.

In many respects these arguments are persuasive. They are based on a rational analysis of likely developments in the business environment as globalisation and technological advances further evolve. They remain, however, highly controversial and are increasingly subject to challenge by researchers who argue that change on this kind of scale is not currently happening and will not happen in the near future.

A prominent critic of the views expressed by the predictors of radical change is Peter Nolan (*see* Nolan 2001 and Nolan and Wood 2003), who argues that the case is often overstated to a considerable degree:

> Change is evident, to be sure, but the shifts in the patterns and rhythms of work are not linear, pre-determined by technology or, as some writers have uncritically assumed, driven by universal trends in market globalisation. (Nolan and Wood 2003, p. 165)

Instead, according to Nolan and his colleagues, we are witnessing the resolute continuation of established approaches and some reversal of trends that began to develop in the 1980s and 1990s but which have since petered out. Job tenure in the UK, for example, has risen significantly in recent years while the proportion of people employed on fixed-term contracts and a self-employed basis has either fallen or remained broadly stable. While we are seeing a slow growth in the proportion of people employed in professional and scientific roles (from 34 per cent to 37 per cent in the 1990s), there is no fall occurring in the number of lower-skilled jobs. Indeed, the proportion of people employed in relatively low-skilled jobs in the service sector is growing quickly. Critics of Handy and the other futurologists have thus identified a gap between a rhetoric which emphasises fundamental change and a reality which gives little support to the view that we are in the process of shaping a 'new world of work'.

These different conceptions of the future may well derive from a preference for a focus on different types of environmental development. A reading of the major contemporary product market trends can easily lead to predictions of radical change. The twin forces of technological advance and globalisation do indeed point to a transformation of many aspects of our lives. But trends in employment are equally determined by developments in the labour market and regulatory environments. These suggest a strong preference on the part of both employees and law makers for a continuation of traditional approaches towards employment.

WINDOW ON PRACTICE

Flexicurity in Denmark

Government intervention is commonly seen as a barrier blocking the creation of flexible labour markets such as those that it is argued are necessary if the western economies are to thrive in an increasingly volatile and knowledge-driven business environment. Labour market regulation serves to slow down progress towards a world of work in which most people are self-employed or employed on a series of short-term contracts for different organisations. In fact, as Madsen (2003) shows, the Danish experience appears to show that the opposite is the case.

Denmark has the highest level of employee turnover in Europe (30 per cent on average in recent years). It also has a very high level of job turnover, between 10 per cent and 15 per cent of its jobs disappearing each year and being replaced with new ones. Around a quarter of the Danish workforce finds itself unemployed for some portion of every year, while as many as 10 per cent of the country's people are employed on fixed-term contracts. The proportion of small and medium-sized enterprises is also the highest in Europe. Economically, Denmark is a success story. Inflation has been low for a decade, overall unemployment rates are well below those of other major EU economies and growth has been stronger. In short, Denmark appears to be a good deal further down the road to the kind of 'future world of work' envisaged by Charles Handy than the other EU countries.

The major reason for this appears to be the Danish social security system, which is very generous in comparison with those of other countries. It is relatively easy to dismiss people (although less easy than in the UK), but people who do find themselves out of work suffer a great deal less in financial terms than equivalents elsewhere. They are, however, obliged as a condition of receiving benefit to take part in government-sponsored retraining and educational programmes. It is this highly sophisticated and expensive unemployment benefit system that seems to have allowed Denmark to develop highly flexible labour markets. It means that people are more willing to take on insecure roles and that employers are less concerned than they are elsewhere to avoid redundancies at all costs.

A PHILOSOPHY OF HUMAN RESOURCE MANAGEMENT

The philosophy of human resource management that is the basis of this book has been only slightly modified since it was first put forward in 1979 (Torrington and Chapman 1979, p. 4). Despite all the changes in the labour market and in the government approach to the economy, this seems to be the most realistic and constructive approach, based on the earlier ideas of Enid Mumford (1972) and McCarthy and Ellis (1973). The original was:

Personnel management is most realistically seen as a series of activities enabling working man and his employing organisation to reach agreement about the nature and objectives of the employment relationship between them, and then to fulfil those agreements. (Torrington and Chapman 1979, p. 4)

Our definition for the fifth and sixth editions in 2002 and 2005 was:

Human resource management is a series of activities which: first enables working people and the organisation which uses their skills to agree about the objectives and nature of their working relationship and, secondly, ensures that the agreement is fulfilled. (Torrington, Hall and Taylor 2005, p. 14)

This remains our philosophy. Only by satisfying the needs of the individual contributor will the business obtain the commitment to organisational objectives that is needed for organisational success, and only by contributing to organisational success will individuals be able to satisfy their personal employment needs. It is when employer and employee – or business and supplier of skills – accept that mutuality and reciprocal dependence that human resource management is exciting, centre stage and productive of business success. Where the employer is concerned with employees only as factors of production, personnel management is boring and a cost that will always be trimmed. Where employees have no trust in their employer and adopt an entirely instrumental orientation to their work, they will be fed up and will make ineffectual the work of any HR function.

SUMMARY PROPOSITIONS

1.1 Human resource management is fundamental to all management activity.

1.2 It is possible to identify two distinct definitions of the term 'human resource management'. The first describes a body of management activities, while the second signifies a particular approach to carrying out those activities.

1.3 Human resource managers are concerned with meeting four distinct sets of organisational objectives: staffing, performance, change management and administration.

1.4 HRM activities are carried out in various ways through various forms of organisational structure. In some larger organisations HR generalists work alongside specialists in particular HR disciplines.

1.5 Human resource management can be characterised as one of the more recent in a series of incarnations that personnel practitioners have developed since the origins of the profession over 100 years ago.

1.6 The HRM function contributes to the achievement of different dimensions of organisational effectiveness. Prominent are the gaining and maintaining of competitive advantage, the fostering of a positive standing in financial markets and the development of a reputation for corporate social responsibility.

1.7 Most current debates about human resource management in general focus on the extent and nature of the responses needed in the face of developments in the business environment.

1.8 Three of the most prominent current debates focus on the nature of the psychological contract, the relative wisdom of the 'best fit' and 'best practice' approaches and predictions about the future of work.

1.9 The philosophy of human resource management in this book is that it is a series of activities which: first, enables working people and the business which uses their skills to agree about the nature and objectives of their working relationship; and, second, ensures that the agreement is fulfilled.

GENERAL DISCUSSION TOPICS

1 How do you understand the suggestion that the contract of employment is gradually changing to a contract for performance?

2 The philosophy of HRM set out in this chapter makes no reference to the customer. David Ulrich, a professor at Michigan Business School, believes that it is important to refocus HR activities away from the firm towards the customer so that suppliers, employees and customers are woven together into a value-chain team. What difference do you think that would make?

3 How far do you think it is possible to agree with both the 'best fit' and 'best practice' perspectives on HRM? In what ways are they compatible with each other?

FURTHER READING

British Journal of Industrial Relations (Vol. 41, No. 2).
The special edition, published in June 2003, was devoted to research on and debates about the future of work. Many leading writers in the field contributed articles which set out the first findings from a major national research project that has involved 22 universities.

Legge, K. (1995) *Human Resource Management: Rhetorics and Realities*. London: Macmillan.
This provides a rigorous discussion of the differences between personnel management and HRM, as well as introducing and considering a series of other debates about the nature of HRM and its purpose for organisations.

Sparrow, P. and Cooper, C. (2003) *The Employment Relationship: Key Challenges for HR*. London: Butterworth-Heinemann.
Bach, S. (2005) 'Personnel Management in Transition' in S. Bach (ed.), *Managing Human Resources: Personnel management in transition*. Oxford: Blackwell.
Two excellent introductions to the major issues facing HR managers in the current business environment. The psychological contract and the evolution of new organisational structures are particularly well covered by Sparrow and Cooper, globalisation and employment restructuring by Bach.

REFERENCES

Atkinson, C. (2003) 'Exploring the state of the psychological contract: the impact of research strategies on outcomes'. Paper presented to the CIPD Professional Standards Conference, Keele University, 2003.

Bach, S. (2005) 'Personnel Management in Transition' in S. Bach (ed.), *Managing Human Resources: Personnel management in transition*. Fourth Edition. Oxford: Blackwell.

Bridges, W. (1995) *Jobshift: How to prosper in a workplace without jobs*. London: Nicholas Brealey.

Coyle-Shapiro, J. and Kessler, I. (2000) 'Consequences of the psychological contract for the employment relationship: a large scale survey', *Journal of Management Studies*, Vol. 37, No. 7.

Delery, J. and Doty, D.H. (1996) 'Modes of Theorising in Strategic Human Resource Management: Tests of Universalistic, Contingency and Configurational Performance Predictions', *Academy of Management Journal*, Vol. 39, No. 4.

Fernie, S. and Metcalf, D. (1996) 'Participation, Contingent Pay, Representation and Workplace Performance: Evidence from Great Britain', *Discussion Paper 232*, Centre for Economic Performance, London School of Economics.

Fombrun, C., Tichy, N.M. and Devanna, M.A. (1984) *Strategic Human Resource Management*. New York: Wiley.

Gratton, L. (2004) *The Democratic Enterprise: Liberating your business with freedom, flexibility and commitment*. Harlow: Pearson Education.

Greenfield, S. (2003) *Tomorrow's People*. London: Penguin/Allen Lane.

Guest, D.E. (1987) 'Human resource management and industrial relations', *Journal of Management Studies*, Vol. 24, No. 5.

Guest, D.E. (1999) 'Human resource management: the workers' verdict', *Human Resource Journal*, Vol. 9, No. 3, pp. 5–25.

Guest, D.E. (2000) 'Human resource management, employee well-being and organisational performance', Paper given at the CIPD Professional Standards Conference, University of Warwick.

Guest, D.E. (2001) 'Human resource management: when research confronts theory', *International Journal of Human Resource Management*, Vol. 12, No. 7, pp. 1092–1106.

Guest, D.E. and Conway, N. (2000) *The Psychological Contract in the Public Sector*. London: CIPD.

Guest, D.E. and Conway, N. (2001) *Public and Private Sector Perceptions on the Psychological Contract*. London: CIPD.

Handy, C. (1994) *The Empty Raincoat: Making Sense of the Future*. London: Hutchinson.

Handy, C. (2001) *The Elephant and the Flea: Looking Backwards to the Future*. London: Hutchinson.

Huselid, M. (1995) 'The impact of Human Resource Management practices on Turnover, Productivity and Corporate Financial Performance', *Academy of Management Journal*, Vol. 38, No. 3.

Lawler, E.E. (1971) *Pay and Organizational Effectiveness. A Psychological View*. New York: McGraw-Hill.

Legge, K. (1989) 'Human resource management: a critical analysis', in J. Storey (ed.), *New Perspectives on Human Resource Management*. London: Routledge.

Legge, K. (1995) *Human Resource Management: Rhetorics and Realities*. London: Macmillan.

Lepak, D. and Snell, S.A. (2007) 'Employment sub-systems and the HR architecture' in P. Boxall, J. Purcell and P. Wright (eds), *The Oxford Handbook of Human Resource Management*. Oxford: Oxford University Press.

McCarthy, W.E.J. and Ellis, N.D. (1973) *Management by Agreement*. London: Hutchinson.

Madsen, P.K. (2003) 'Flexicurity through labour market policies and institutions in Denmark', in P. Auer and S. Cazes (eds), *Employment stability in an age of flexibility: Evidence from industrialised countries*. Geneva: ILO.

Maguire, H. (2002) 'Psychological contracts: are they still relevant?', *Career Development International*, Vol. 7, No. 3, pp. 167–80.

Miles, R.E. and Snow, C.C. (1978) *Organisational Strategy, Structure and Process*. New York: McGraw-Hill.

Mumford, E. (1972) 'Job satisfaction: a method of analysis', *Personnel Review*, Vol. 1, No. 3.

Nolan, P. (2001) 'Shaping things to come', *People Management*, 27 December.

Nolan, P. and Wood, S. (2003) 'Mapping the Future of Work', *British Journal of Industrial Relations*, Vol. 41, No. 2, pp. 165–74.

Patterson, M.G., West, M.A., Lawthom, R. and Nickell, S. (1998) *Impact of People Management Practices on Business Performance*. Issues in People Management No. 22. London: IPD.

Pfeffer, J. (1994) *Competitive Advantage Through People*. Boston: Harvard Business School Press.

Rifkin, J. (1995) *The End of Work: The decline of the global labour force and the dawn of the post market era*. New York: Putnam.

Sisson, K. and Storey, J. (2000) *The Realities of Human Resource Management: Managing the Employment Relationship*. Buckingham: Open University Press.

Sparrow, P.L. (2003) 'The Future of Work?', in D. Holman, T. Wall, C. Clegg, P. Sparrow and A. Howard (eds), *The New Workplace: a guide to the human impact of modern working practices*. Chichester: Wiley.

Sparrow, P.L. and Cooper, C.L. (2003) *The Employment Relationship: Key Challenges for HR*. London: Butterworth-Heinemann.

Stevens, J. (ed.) (2005) *Managing Risk: The Human Resources Contribution*. London: LexisNexis Butterworths.

Torrington, D.P. and Chapman, J.B. (1979) *Personnel Management*. Hemel Hempstead: Prentice Hall.

Torrington, D.P., Hall, L.A. and Taylor, S. (2002) *Human Resource Management* (5th edition). Harlow: Pearson Education.

Torrington, D.P., Hall, L.A. and Taylor, S. (2005) *Human Resource Management* (6th edition). Harlow: Pearson Education.

Vroom, V.H. (1964) *Work and Motivation*. New York: Wiley.

Wood, S. and Albanese, M. (1995) 'Can We Speak of High Commitment Management on the Shop Floor?', *Journal of Management Studies*, Vol. 32, No. 2.

An extensive range of additional materials, including multiple choice questions, answers to questions and links to useful websites can be found on the Human Resource Management Companion Website at **www.pearsoned.co.uk/torrington**.

STRATEGIC HUMAN RESOURCE MANAGEMENT

THE OBJECTIVES OF THIS CHAPTER ARE TO:

1 Clarify the use of the terms strategic human resource management and human resource strategy, and arrive at workable definitions of each

2 Explain the feasibility and nature of the link between business strategy and HR strategy

3 Evaluate three theoretical perspectives on the nature of HR strategy and show how each expresses a different view on how the contribution of people to the organisation might be understood and enhanced

There is a strong lobby propounding the view that human resources are *the* source of competitive advantage for the business, rather than, say, access to capital or use of technology. It is therefore logical to suggest that attention needs to be paid to the nature of this resource and its management as this will impact on human resource behaviour and performance and consequently the performance of the organisation. Indeed Boxall and Steeneveld (1999) argue that there is no need to prove the relationship between firm performance and labour management as it is self-evident that the quality of human resource management is a critical influence on the performance of the firm. It is not, therefore, surprising that the rhetoric of strategic human resource management has been readily adopted, especially as a strategic approach is considered to be one of the characteristics of HRM as opposed to personnel management, which is seen as operational. In the most recent Workplace Employment Relations Survey (WERS) it was found that 87 per cent of workplaces with a strategic plan included some issues relating to employment relations (broadly defined) (Kersley *et al*. 2006).

STRATEGIC HUMAN RESOURCE MANAGEMENT AND HUMAN RESOURCE STRATEGY

Our understanding of HR strategy has changed considerably since strategy first became the subject of great attention. We have moved from viewing strategy as a physical document to seeing it as an incremental process, affected by political influences and generating learning. Tyson's (1995) definition of human resource strategy is a useful starting point, although somewhat limited, as will be seen from our later discussion:

> the intentions of the corporation both explicit and covert, toward the management of its employees, expressed through philosophies, policies and practices. (Tyson 1995)

This definition is helpful because research on human resource strategy in the early 1980s tended to focus on seeking an HR strategy document in order to determine whether there was a strategic approach to HR and what that approach was. This was rather like searching for the Holy Grail. Not surprisingly few complete HR strategies were found and HR specialists berated themselves for having failed in this critical area. Gradually the thinking changed to encompass a view that HR strategy need not be written on a piece of paper or need not, indeed, be explicit, as the Tyson quotation illustrates. Further developments in thinking began to accept the idea that strategies are neither finished, nor complete, but rather incremental and piecemeal. There is compelling evidence to suggest that strategic HR tends to be issue based rather than the formulation of a complete and integrated strategy (for example, Grundy 1998; Hall and Torrington 1998). Strategic thinking, strategic decision making and a strategic orientation (for example, Hunt and Boxall 1998) were gradually understood as much more realistic expectations.

In parallel with this thinking there were developments in the general strategy literature which viewed strategy as a process which was not necessarily rational and top down, but a political and evolutionary process (*see*, for example, Mintzberg 1994). Mintzberg argues that strategy is 'formed' rather than 'formulated' and that any intended strategy is changed by events, opportunities, the actions of employees and so on – so that the realised strategy is different from the initial vision. Strategy, Mintzberg argues, can only be identified in retrospect and, as Boxall and Purcell (2003) suggest, is best seen in the ultimate behaviour of the organisation. Wrapped up in this view is also the idea that strategy is not necessarily determined by top management alone but can be influenced 'bottom up', as ideas are tried and tested in one part of the organisation and gradually adopted in a wholesale manner if they are seen to be applicable and successful. This is not to say that producing a strategy is an unhelpful act, and indeed research carried out by PriceWaterhouseCoopers indicated that those organisations with a written HR strategy generated 35 per cent greater revenues per employee than those without (Higginbottom 2002).

This leads on to the concept of strategy as learning both in content and in process (*see*, for example, Senge 1990; Pedler *et al.* 1991), which is supported by the notion of strategy as a process of change (*see*, for example, Hendry and Pettigrew 1992). Literature draws out the need to sense changes in the environment, develop a resultant strategy and turn this strategy into action. While the HR function has often found itself excluded from the strategy formation process, HR strategy has more often been seen in terms of the implementation of organisational strategies. However, implementation of HR strategy has been weak, at best. Among the qualities of the most successful organisations is the ability to turn strategy into action quickly (Ulrich 1998), in other words to implement the chosen strategy (Grensing-Pophel 1999), and Guest (1987) maintained that the capability to implement strategic plans is an important feature of successful HRM. However, a lack of attention to the implementation of HR strategy has been identified (Beaumont 1992; Lundy and Cowling 1996; Skinner and Mabey 1997), and the information that does exist suggests that this is a problematic area. Legge (1995) maintained that the evidence of implementation of HR strategies was patchy and sometimes contradictory, and Skinner and Mabey (1997) found that responsibility for implementation was unclear, with only 54 per cent of respondents, in organisations with an HR director, perceiving that the HR function played a major part in implementation. In their research Kane and Palmer (1995) found that the existence of an HR strategy was only a minor influence on the HR policies and procedures that were used. Frameworks such as the HR scorecard (Becker *et al.* 2001) are aimed, at least in part, at facilitating the management and implementation of HR architecture ('the sum of the HR function, the broader HR system, and the resulting employee behaviors', p. 1) as a strategic asset, and we look at this in more detail in Chapter 33.

One organisation where the HR function has had a major role to play in the successful implementation of HR strategy is Kwik-Fit Financial Services. The overriding strategic purpose was to make the organisation 'a fantastic place to work' and this led to initiatives focusing on improving the working environment and encouraging employees to bring their whole selves to work (Griffiths 2006). There are further details in a case study on the website **www.pearsoned.co.uk/torrington**.

THE LINK BETWEEN BUSINESS AND HR STRATEGY

The nature, desirability and feasibility of the link between business strategy and HR strategy is a consistent theme which runs through the strategy literature, although, as we shall discuss later, some theories suggest that implementing 'best practice' in HRM is

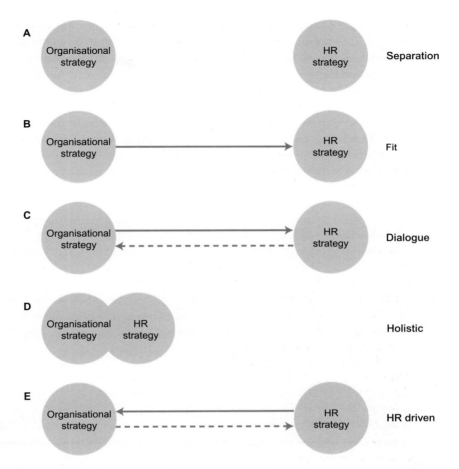

Figure 2.1
Potential
relationships
between
organisational
strategy and
HR strategy

even more important than this. Figure 2.1 is a simple model that is useful in visualising different ways in which this relationship may be played out and has relevance for the newer conceptions of strategy based on the resource-based view of the firm, as well as earlier conceptions.

In the *separation model* (A) there is no relationship at all, if indeed organisational and human resource strategy *does* exist in an explicit form in the organisation. This is a typical picture of twenty years ago, but it still exists today, particularly in smaller organisations.

The *fit model* (B) represents a growing recognition of the importance of people in the achievement of organisational strategy. Employees are seen as key in the implementation of the declared organisational strategy, and human resource strategy is designed to fit with this. Some of the early formal models of human resource strategy, particularly that proposed by Fombrun *et al.* (1984), concentrate on how the human resource strategy can be designed to ensure a close fit, and the same approach is used in the Schuler and Jackson example in Table 2.1.

This whole approach depends on a view of strategy formulation as a logical rational process, which remains a widely held view. The relationship in the fit model is exemplified by organisations which cascade their business objectives down from the senior management team through functions, through departments, through teams and so on. Functions, for example, have to propose a functional strategy which enables the organisational strategy to be achieved. Departments have to propose a strategy which enables the functional strategy to be achieved, and so on. In this way the HR function (as with any other) is required to respond to organisational strategy by defining a strategy which meets organisational demands.

The *dialogue model* (C) takes the relationship one step further, as it recognises the need for two-way communication and some debate. What is demanded in the organisation's strategy may not be viewed as feasible and alternative possibilities need to be reviewed. The debate, however, is often limited, as shown in the example in the Window on practice which follows.

WINDOW ON PRACTICE

In one large multinational organisation an objectives-setting cascade was put in place. This cascade allowed for a dialogue between the planned organisation strategy and the response of each function. In the organisation strategy there was some emphasis on people growth and development and job fulfilment. The HR Department's response included among other things an emphasis on line management involvement in these areas, which would be supported by consultancy help from the HR Department.

The top management team replied to this by asking the HR Department to add a strategic objective about employee welfare and support. The HR Department strongly argued that this was a line management responsibility, along with coaching, development and so on. The HR Function saw its customers as the managers of the organisation, not the employees. The result of the debate was that the HR Function added the strategic objective about employee welfare.

Although the approach in this case appeared two-way, the stronger of the parties was the management team, and they were determined that their vision was the one that would be implemented!

The holistic model and the HR-driven model (D and E) show a much closer involvement between organisational and human resource strategy.

The *holistic model* (D) represents the people of the organisation being recognised as the key to competitive advantage rather than just the way of implementing organisational strategy. In other words HR strategy is not just the means for achieving business strategy (the ends), but an end in itself. Human resource strategy therefore becomes critical and, as Baird *et al.* (1983) argued, there can be no strategy without human resource strategy. Boxall (1996) develops this idea in relation to the resource-based firm, and argues convincingly that business strategy can usefully be interpreted as more broad than a competitive strategy (or positioning in the marketplace). In this case business strategy can encompass a variety of other strategies including HRM, and he describes these strategies as the pieces of a jigsaw. This suggests mutual development and some form of integration, rather than a slavish response to a predetermined business strategy.

The *HR-driven model* (E) offers a more extreme form, which places human resource strategy in prime position. The argument here is that if people are the key to competitive advantage, then we need to build on our people strengths. Logically, then, as the potential of our employees will undoubtedly affect the achievement of any planned strategy, it would be sensible to take account of this in developing our strategic direction. Butler (1988/89) identifies this model as a shift from human resources as the implementors of strategy to human resources as a driving force in the formulation of the strategy. Again this model is a reflection of a resource-based strategic HRM perspective, and sits well with the increasing attention being given to the notion of 'human capital' where it is the collective nature and quality of the people in the organisation which provide the potential for future competitive advantage (*see*, for example, Lengnick-Hall and Lengnick-Hall 2003).

ACTIVITY 2.1

- Which of these approaches to human resource strategy most closely fits your organisation? (If you are a full-time student read one or two relevant cases in *People Management* and interpret these as 'your organisation'.)
- Why did you come to this conclusion?
- What are the advantages and disadvantages of the approach used?

THEORETICAL PERSPECTIVES OF STRATEGIC HUMAN RESOURCE MANAGEMENT

Three theoretical approaches to strategic HRM can be identified. The first is founded on the concept that there is 'one best way' of managing human resources in order to improve business performance. The second focuses on the need to align employment policies and practice with the requirements of business strategy in order that the latter will be achieved and the business will be successful. This second approach is based on the assumption that different types of HR strategies will be suitable for different types of business strategies. Third, a more recent approach to strategic HRM is derived from the resource-based view of the firm, and the perceived value of human capital. This view focuses on the quality of the human resources available to the organisation and their ability to learn and adapt more quickly than their competitors. Supporters of this perspective challenge the need to secure a mechanistic fit with business strategy and focus instead on long-term sustainability and survival of the organisation via the pool of human capital.

Universalist approach

The perspective of the universalist approach is derived from the conception of human resource management as 'best practice', as we discussed in Chapter 1. In other words it is based on the premise that one model of labour management – a high-commitment model – is related to high organisational performance in all contexts, irrespective of the particular competitive strategy of the organisation. An expression of this approach can be seen in Guest's theory of HRM, which is a prescriptive model based on four HR policy goals: strategic integration, commitment, flexibility and quality. These policy goals are related to HRM policies which are expected to produce desirable organisational outcomes.

Guest (1989) describes the four policy goals as follows:

- **Strategic integration** – ensuring that HRM is fully integrated into strategic planning, that HRM policies are coherent, and that line managers use HRM practices as part of their everyday work.

- **Commitment** – ensuring that employees feel bound to the organisation and are committed to high performance via their behaviour.

- **Flexibility** – ensuring an adaptable organisation structure, and functional flexibility based on multiskilling.

- **Quality** – ensuring a high quality of goods and services through high-quality, flexible employees.

Guest sees these goals as a package – all need to be achieved to create the desired organisational outcomes, which are high job performance, problem solving, change, innovation and cost effectiveness; and low employee turnover, absence and grievances.

Clarity of goals gives a certain attractiveness to this model – but this is where the problems also lie. Whipp (1992) questions the extent to which such a shift is possible, and Purcell (1991) sees the goals as unattainable. The goals are also an expression of human resource management, as opposed to personnel management, and as such bring us back to the debate about what human resource management really is and the inherent contradictions in the approach (Legge 1991, 1995). Ogbonna and Whipp (1999) argue that internal consistency within such a model is extremely difficult to achieve because of such contradictions (for example the tension between flexibility and commitment). Because the prescriptive approach brings with it a set of values, it suggests that there is only one best way and this is it. Although Guest (1987) has argued that there is no best practice, he also encourages the use of the above approach as the route to survival of UK businesses.

Pfeffer (1994) and Becker and Gerhart (1996) are well-known exponents of this view. While there is some support for this perspective, there remains some debate as to which particular human resource practices will stimulate high commitment. We consider this perspective in more depth in Chapter 11 on Strategic aspects of performance.

Falling somewhere between the universalist approach and the fit approach is the Harvard model of HRM. This model, produced by Beer *et al.* (1984), is analytical rather than prescriptive. The model, shown in Figure 2.2, recognises the different stakeholder interests that impact on employee behaviour and performance, and also gives greater emphasis to factors in the environment that will help to shape human resource strategic choices – identified in the **Situational factors** box. Poole (1990) also notes that the model has potential for international or other comparative analysis, as it takes into account different sets of philosophies and assumptions that may be operating.

Although Beer *et al.*'s model is primarily analytical, there are prescriptive elements leading to some potential confusion. The prescription in Beer *et al.*'s model is found in the **HR outcomes** box, where specific outcomes are identified as universally desirable.

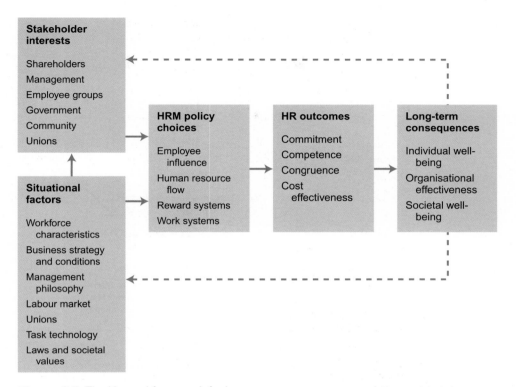

Figure 2.2 The Harvard framework for human resource management (Source: Adapted with permission of The Free Press, a Division of Simon & Schuster, Inc., from *Managing Human Assets* by Michael Beer, Bert Spector, Paul R. Lawrence, D. Quinn Mills, Richard E. Walton. New York: The Free Press. Copyright © 1984 by The Free Press.)

Fit or contingency approach

The fit or contingency approach is based on two critical forms of fit. The first is external fit (sometimes referred to as vertical integration) – that HR strategy fits with the demands of business strategy; the second is internal fit (sometimes referred to as horizontal integration) – that all HR policies and activities fit together so that they make a coherent whole, are mutually reinforcing and are applied consistently. One of the foundations of this approach is found in Fombrun *et al.* (1984), who proposed a basic framework for strategic human resource management, shown in Figures 2.3 and 2.4. Figure 2.3 represents the location of human resource management in relation to organisational strategy, and you should be able to note how the Fit model (B) is used (*see* Figure 2.1). Figure 2.4 shows how activities within human resource management can be unified and designed in order to support the organisation's strategy.

The strength of this model is that it provides a simple framework to show how selection, appraisal, development and reward can be mutually geared to produce the required type of employee performance. For example, if an organisation required cooperative team behaviour with mutual sharing of information and support, the broad implications would be:

- **Selection**: successful experience of teamwork and sociable, cooperative personality; rather than an independent thinker who likes working alone.

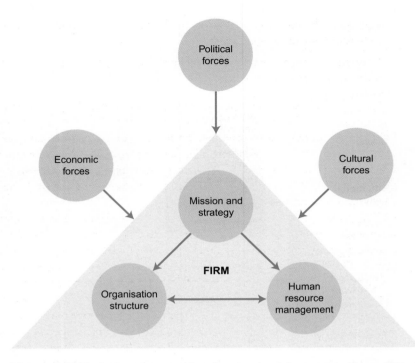

Figure 2.3 Strategic management and environmental pressures (Source: C. Fombrun, N.M. Tichy and M.A. Devanna (1984) *Strategic Human Resource Management*, p. 35. New York: John Wiley and Sons, Inc. © John Wiley and Sons Inc., 1984. Reprinted by permission of John Wiley and Sons, Inc.)

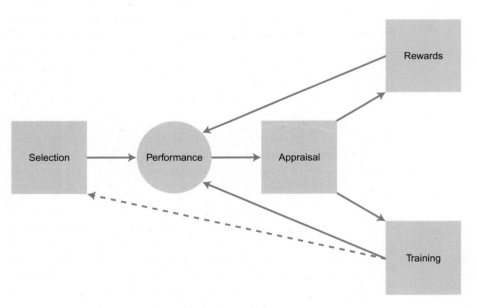

Figure 2.4 The human resource cycle (Source: C. Fombrun, N.M. Tichy and M.A. Devanna (1984) *Strategic Human Resource Management*, p. 41. New York: John Wiley and Sons, Inc. © John Wiley and Sons Inc., 1984. Reprinted by permission of John Wiley and Sons, Inc.)

- **Appraisal**: based on contribution to the team, and support of others; rather than individual outstanding performance.
- **Reward**: based on team performance and contribution; rather than individual performance and individual effort.

There is little doubt that this type of internal fit is valuable. However, questions have been raised over the model's simplistic response to organisation strategy. The question 'what if it is not possible to produce a human resource response that enables the required employee behaviour and performance?' is never addressed. So, for example, the distance between now and future performance requirements, the strengths, weaknesses and potential of the workforce, the motivation of the workforce and employee relations issues are not considered.

This model has been criticised because of its dependence on a rational strategy formulation rather than on an emergent strategy formation approach; and because of the nature of the one-way relationship with organisational strategy. It has also been criticised owing to its unitarist assumptions, as no recognition is made for employee interests and their choice of whether or not to change their behaviour.

Taking this model and the notion of fit one step further, human resource strategy has been conceived in terms of generating specific employee behaviours. In the ideal form of this there would be analysis of the types of employee behaviour required to fulfil a pre-determined business strategy, and then an identification of human resource policies and practices which would bring about and reinforce this behaviour. A very good example of this is found in Schuler and Jackson (1987). They used the three generic business strategies defined by Porter (1980) and for each identified employee role behaviour and HRM policies required. Their conclusions are shown in Table 2.1.

Similar analyses can be found for other approaches to business strategy, for example in relation to the **Boston matrix** (Purcell 1992) and the developmental stage of the organisation (Kochan and Barocci 1985). Some human resource strategies describe the behaviour of all employees, but others have concentrated on the behaviour of Chief Executives and senior managers; Miles and Snow (1984), for example, align appropriate managerial characteristics to three generic strategies of prospector, defender and analyser. The rationale behind this matching process is that if managerial attributes and skills are aligned to the organisational strategy, then a higher level of organisational performance will result. There is little empirical evidence to validate this link, but work by Thomas and Ramaswamy (1996) does provide some support. They used statistical analysis to investigate if there was a match between manager attributes and skills in organisations with either a defender or a prospector strategy in 269 of the Fortune 500 companies in the United States. They found an overall statistical relationship between manager attributes and strategy. Taking the analysis a step further they then compared 30 organisations which were misaligned with 30 which were aligned and found that performance in the aligned companies (whether prospector or defender) was statistically superior. While this work can be criticised, it does provide an indication of further research which can be developed to aid our understanding of the issues. Sanz-Valle *et al.* (1999) found some partial support for the Schuler and Jackson model in terms of the link between business strategy and HR practices, but they did not investigate the implications of this link for organisational performance. The types of strategies described above are generic, and there is more concentration in some organisations on tailoring the approach to the particular needs of the specific organisation.

Strategy	Employee role behaviour	HRM policies
1 Innovation	A high degree of creative behaviour	Jobs that require close interaction and coordination among groups of individuals
	Longer-term focus	Performance appraisals that are more likely to reflect longer-term and group-based achievements
	A relatively high level of co-operative, interdependent behaviour	Jobs that allow employees to develop skills that can be used in other positions in the firm
		Compensation systems that emphasise internal equity rather than external or market-based equity
	A moderate degree of concern for quality	Pay rates that tend to be low, but that allow employees to be stockholders and have more freedom to choose the mix of components that make up their pay package
	A moderate concern for quantity; an equal degree of concern for process and results	Broad career paths to reinforce the development of a broad range of skills
	A greater degree of risk taking; a higher tolerance of ambiguity and unpredictability	
2 Quality enhancement	Relatively repetitive and predictable behaviours	Relatively fixed and explicit job descriptions
	A more long-term or intermediate focus	High levels of employee participation in decisions relevant to immediate work conditions and the job itself
	A moderate amount of co-operative, interdependent behaviour	A mix of individual and group criteria for performance appraisal that is mostly short term and results orientated
	A high concern for quality	A relatively egalitarian treatment of employees and some guarantees of employment security
	A modest concern for quantity of output	Extensive and continuous training and development of employees
	High concern for process: low risk-taking activity; commitment to the goals of the organisation	
3 Cost reduction	Relatively repetitive and predictable behaviour	Relatively fixed and explicit job descriptions that allow little room for ambiguity
	A rather short-term focus	Narrowly designed jobs and narrowly defined career paths that encourage specialisation, expertise and efficiency
	Primarily autonomous or individual activity	Short-term results-orientated performance appraisals
	Moderate concern for quality	Close monitoring of market pay levels for use in making compensation decisions
	High concern for quantity of output	Minimal levels of employee training and development
	Primary concern for results; low risk-taking activity; relatively high degree of comfort with stability	

Table 2.1 Business strategies, and associated employee role behaviour and HRM policies

Source: R.S. Schuler and S.E. Jackson (1987) 'Linking competitive strategies with human resource management practices', *Academy of Management Executive*, No. 3, August. Reproduced with permission of the Academy of Management.

Many human resource strategies aim not just to target behaviour, but through behaviour change to effect a movement in the culture of the organisation. The target is, therefore, to change the common view of 'the way we do things around here' and to attempt to manipulate the beliefs and values of employees. There is much debate as to whether this is achievable.

We have previously recounted some of the concerns expressed about Fombrun *et al.*'s specific model; however, there is further criticism of the fit or matching perspective as a whole. Grundy (1998) claims that the idea of fit seems naive and simplistic. Ogbonna and Whipp (1999) argue that much literature assumes that fit can be targeted, observed and measured and there is an underlying assumption of stability. Given that most companies may have to change radically in response to the environment, any degree of fit previously achieved will be disturbed. Thus, they contend that fit is a theoretical ideal which can rarely be achieved in practice. Boxall (1996) criticises the typologies of competitive advantage that are used, arguing that there is evidence that high-performing firms are good 'all rounders'; the fact that strategy is a given and no account is taken of how it is formed or by whom; the assumption that employees will behave as requested; and the aim for consistency, as it has been shown that firms use different strategies for different sections of their workforce.

However, in spite of the criticisms of this perspective, it is still employed in both the academic and practitioner literature – see, for example, Holbeche's (1999) book entitled *Aligning Human Resources and Business Strategy*.

A further form of fit which we have not mentioned so far is cultural fit, and the Window on Practice, below, demonstrates this aspect.

WINDOW ON PRACTICE

The influence of national culture on human resource management strategies

Fields and his colleagues (2006) investigated whether, under similar conditions, organisations in different cultural contexts would strategically respond in a different manner. They compared US organisations with Hong Kong Chinese organisations and studied their strategic approach in conditions of uncertainty in the supply of qualified labour. They studied three aspects of HR relevant to this situation:

- training and development
- monitoring and assessment of employee performance, and
- staffing through an internal labour market

They found, as they expected, that in these conditions the Hong Kong Chinese companies increased their use of these three HRM strategies, but that the US companies decreased their use. They explain these different strategic approaches by reference to the cultural context.

You may wish to look ahead to the work of Hofstede, which we present in Chapter 4, before reading on.

Training and development (TD)

They suggest that more TD would be positively viewed by the more collective Chinese culture as a symbol that the organisation is fulfilling its moral obligation to employees, as a way to increase the value of each individual to the collective organisation, and as a reward. Each of these would be valued by Chinese employees, and would encourage them to remain with the organisation. Alternatively in the more individualistic US culture managers would be reluctant to invest in TD when labour supply is scarce as employees may take advantage of this and use it to find a better job elsewhere.

Emphasis on performance assessment (PA)

They suggest that in the Chinese culture, with greater power distance, greater PA may be viewed by employees as a positive symbol that managers are interested in them, and may act as a reminder of the employees' moral association with the organisation – thus encouraging employees to stay. Alternatively in the US culture with lower power distance, more PA would be viewed negatively. It may be seen as emphasising the difference between managers and employees, and as a way of tightening up the employment relationship, both of which may lead employees to seek employment elsewhere.

Internal labour market (IL)

Greater use of the IL might be viewed in a collectivist culture by the Chinese employees as evidence that they are valued by the organisaiton and thus may encourage retention. Alternatively in an individualistic culture employees may view this unfavourably as evidence of a subjective rather than objective (based on merit) approach to promotion, and managers may view it as a means by which employees can barter for better rewards in a tight labour market.

Source: Adapted from Fields, D., Chan, A., Aktar, S. and Blum, T. (2006) 'Human resource management strategies under uncertainty', *Cross Cultural Management: An International Journal*, Vol. 13, No. 2, pp. 171–86.

Resource-based approach

The resource-based view of the firm (Barney 1991) has stimulated attempts to create a resource-based model of strategic HRM (Boxall 1996). The resource-based view of the firm is concerned with the relationships between internal resources (of which human resources is one), strategy and firm performance. It focuses on the promotion of sustained competitive advantage through the development of human capital rather than merely aligning human resources to current strategic goals. Human resources can provide competitive advantage for the business, as long as they are unique and cannot be copied or substituted for by competing organisations. The focus is not just on the behaviour of the human resources (as with the fit approach), but on the skills, knowledge, attitudes and competencies which underpin this, and which have a more sustained impact on long-term survival than current behaviour (although this is still regarded as important). Briggs and Keogh (1999) maintain that business excellence is not just about 'best practice' or 'leapfrogging the competition', but about the intellectual capital and business intelligence to anticipate the future, today.

Barney states that in order for a resource to result in sustained competitive advantage it must meet four criteria, and Wright *et al.* (1994) demonstrate how human resources meet these. First, the resource must be *valuable*. Wright and his colleagues argue that this is the case where demand for labour is heterogeneous, and where the supply of labour is also heterogeneous – in other words where different firms require different competencies from each other and for different roles in the organisation, and where the supply of potential labour comprises individuals with different competencies. On this basis value is created by matching an individual's competencies with the requirements of the firm and/or the job, as individuals will make a variable contribution, and one cannot be substituted easily for another.

The second criterion, *rarity*, is related to the first. An assumption is made that the most important competence for employees is cognitive ability due to future needs for adaptability and flexibility. On the basis that cognitive ability is normally distributed in the population, those with high levels of this ability will be rare. The talent pool is not unlimited and many employers are currently experiencing difficulties in finding the talent that they require.

Third, resources need to be *inimitable*. Wright *et al.* argue that this quality applies to the human resource as competitors will find it difficult to identify the exact source of competitive advantage from within the firm's human resource pool. Also competitors will not be able to duplicate exactly the resource in question, as they will be unable to copy the unique historical conditions of the first firm. This history is important as it will affect the behaviour of the human resource pool via the development of unique norms and cultures. Thus even if a competing firm recruited a group of individuals from a competitor they would still not be able to produce the same outcomes in the new firm as the context would be different. Two factors make this unique history difficult to copy. The first is causal ambiguity – in other words it is impossible to separate out the exact causes of performance, as the sum is always more than the parts; and, second, social complexity – that the complex of relationships and networks developed over time which have an impact on performance is difficult to dissect.

Finally resources need to be *non-substitutable*. Wright and his co-authors argue that although in the short term it may be possible to substitute human resources with others, for example technological ones, in the long term the human resource is different as it does not become obsolete (like technology) and can be transferred across other products, markets and technologies.

Wright *et al.* noted that attention has often been devoted to leaders and top management in the context of a resource-based approach, and indeed Boxall (1996) contends that this approach provides the theoretical base on which to concentrate in the renewal and development of the critical resource of leaders in the organisation. However, Wright and his co-authors view all human resources in the organisation as the pool of capital. This sits well with the view of strategy as evolutionary and strategy being influenced from the bottom up as well as from the top down. Also it is likely that top managers are more easily identified for their contribution to the organisation and hence are more likely to be mobile, therefore, than other employees who may not be so easily identified.

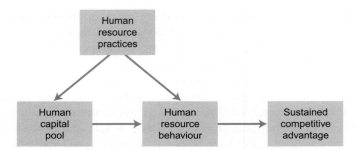

Figure 2.5 A model of human resources as a source of sustained competitive advantage
(Source: P. Wright, G. McMahon and A. McWilliams (1994) 'Human resources and sustained competitive advantage: a resource-based perspective', *International Journal of Human Resource Management*, Vol. 5, No. 2, p. 318. Reproduced with the permission of Taylor and Francis Ltd. *See* www.tandf.co.uk/journals.)

However, different segments of the human resource are viewed differently by organisations in terms of their contribution to competitive advantage, so for some organisations the relevant pool of human capital may not be the total pool of employees.

Whereas fit models focus on the means of competitive advantage (HR practices) the resource-based view focuses on the source (the human capital). Wright *et al.* argue that while the practices are important they are not the source of competitive advantage as they can be replicated elsewhere, and they will produce different results in different places because of the differential human capital in different places. The relationship between human capital, human resource practices and competitive advantage is shown in Figure 2.5.

Boxall (1996) argues that this theoretical perspective provides a conceptual base for asserting that human resources are a source of competitive advantage, and as such valued as generating strategic capability. Thus there is a case for viewing HR strategy as something more than a reactive matching process. Indeed Wright *et al.* argue that it provides the case for HR to be involved in the formulation of strategy rather than just its implementation. They suggest that it provides a grounding for asserting that not every strategy is universally implementable, and that alternatives may have to be sought or the human capital pool developed further, via human resource practices, where this is possible.

The importance of this perspective is underlined by the current emphasis on a firm's intangible assets. Numerous studies have shown that a firm's market value (the sum of the value of the shares) is not fully explained by its current financial results (*see*, for example, Ulrich and Smallwood 2002) or its tangible assets and the focus has moved to a firm's intangible assets such as intellectual capital and customer relationships – all of which are derived from human capital (*see*, for example, Schmidt and Lines 2002). This emphasis has resulted in a great deal of attention being paid to the evaluation of human capital through measuring, reporting and managing it. Human capital can be reported both internally and externally (as in the annual financial report, or similar), and Angela Baron from the CIPD has been reported as commenting that 'investors are demanding information on human capital' (Roberts 2002).

But human capital is loaned: 'human capital is not owned by the organization, but secured through the employment relationship' (Scarborough 2003a, p. 2) and because this is so, the strategy for the management of people is also critical. The government's White Paper, *Modernising Company Law*, suggested that the largest 1,000 companies should publish an annual operating and financial review (OFR), and experts believed this would need to include a review about the ways that employees are managed (*People Management* 2002). However this planned requirement has now been scrapped and a simpler report is now sufficient which meets the minimum demands of the EU Accounts and Modernisation Directive (EAMD) (Scott 2005). The report now required is entitled the 'Business Review', forms part of the Director's Report, and actually came into force in April 2005. The Business Review requires 'a balanced and comprehensive analysis of the business', and that human capital management issues should be included 'where material'. The scrapping of the OFR raised fears that human capital reporting would have less priority in the business; however the Business Review does apply in some form to all organisations except small firms. Angela Baron suggests that the better the information an organisation has on its human capital the more likely it is that business benefits will accrue (Manocha 2006), and it has been suggested that many companies which have prepared for the OFR will go ahead and produce the more extensive report. The Department for Business, Enterprise and Regulatory Reform (DBERR) has not discounted the possibility of the OFR being resurrected.

The perceived importance of people as an intangible asset is demonstrated in the action of Barclays Group who on their Investor's Day were keen to demonstrate not only their financial results but their people strategies and improvements in staff satisfaction which they believe have contributed to the results (Arkin and Allen 2002). The Barclays approach is covered in more detail in a case study on the website **www.pearsoned.co.uk/torrington**.

This approach has great advantages from an HR point of view. People in the organisation become the focus, their contribution is monitored and made more explicit, the way people are managed can be seen to add value and money spent on people can be seen as an investment rather than a cost. Some firms are using the balanced scorecard to demonstrate the contribution that human capital makes to firm performance, such as Norwich Union, and Scarborough (2003b) argues that this builds a bridge between the role of the HR function and the strategy of the firm. However, there are inbuilt barriers in the language of the resource-based view. One is the reference to people as 'human capital' which some consider to be unnecessarily instrumental. Another is the focus on 'firms' and 'competitive advantage' which makes it harder to see the relevance of this perspective for organisations in the public sector. There is also the issue of what is being measured and who decides this. The risk is that too much time is spent measuring and that not everything that is measured is of critical value to the organisation. So far, such measures appear very varied, although different firms will, of course, need to measure different things. Measures often appear to be taken without a coherent framework, as appears to be the case in the results documented by Scarborough and Elias (2002) for their 10 case study organisations. The balanced scorecard and the HR scorecard, however, appear to be useful mechanisms in this respect. The evaluation of human capital is considered in greater depth in Chapter 33.

Why does the theory matter?

It is tempting to think of these theories of strategic HRM as competing with each other. In other words one is right and the others are wrong. If this were the case HR managers/directors and board members would need only to work out which is the 'right' theory and apply that. This is, of course, a gross oversimplification, as each theory can be interpreted and applied in different ways, and each has advantages and disadvantages. It could be argued that different theories apply in different sectors or competitive contexts. For example Guest (2001) suggests that there is the possibility that a 'high performance/high commitment' approach might always be most appropriate in manufacturing, whereas strategic choice (which could be interpreted as choice to fit with business strategy) might be more realistic in the services sector. This could be taken one step further to suggest that different theories apply to different groups in the workforce.

Consequently, these three theories do not necessarily represent simple alternatives. It is also likely that some board directors and even HR managers are not familiar with any of these theories (*see*, for example, Guest and King 2001). In spite of that, organisations, through their culture, and individuals within organisations operate on the basis of a set of assumptions, and these assumptions are often implicit. Assumptions about the nature and role of human resource strategy, whether explicit or implicit, will have an influence on what organisations actually do. Assumptions will limit what are seen as legitimate choices.

Understanding these theories enables HR managers, board members, consultants and the like to interpret the current position of HR strategy in the organisation, confront current assumptions and challenge current thinking and potentially open up a new range of possibilities.

This chapter forms the underpinning for the other strategic chapters later in the book and links with key material in Chapter 3 on HR planning, Chapter 14 on Leadership and change, Chapter 32 on The changing HR function and Chapter 33 on IT and human capital measurement.

SUMMARY PROPOSITIONS

2.1 It is more helpful to focus on the concept of strategic HRM than on HRM strategy as the former directs us to consider strategic thinking and a strategic orientation, rather than a 'strategy' which is written down and exists as a physical entity.

2.2 The nature of the link between business strategy and HR strategy is critical and can be played out in a variety of ways.

2.3 Three theoretical perspectives on strategic HR management can be identified: universalist/best practice; contingency/fit; and the resource-based/human capital view.

GENERAL DISCUSSION TOPICS

1 Is it feasible to link business strategy with the management of people in organisations?

2 Human resource strategies can be stimulating to produce and satisfying to display, but how can we make sure that they are implemented?

FURTHER READING

Salaman, G., Storey, J. and Billsberry, J. (2005) *Strategic Human Resource Management: Theory and Practice: A Reader*. London: The Open University in association with Sage.

This is an excellent source book bringing together a variety of perspectives and divided into four sections: strategic human resource management and knowledge; strategic human resource management and business performance; the emergence of new organisational forms and relationships and strategic human resource management in practice. Each chapter is an article previously published, and is either produced in full or summarized. This means that some work is older than others, but the choice of chapters means that key and influential strategic works (for example Wright *et al.* 2001 referred to in this chapter) are grouped together.

Mayo, A. (2001) *The Human Value of the Enterprise*. London: Nicholas Brealey.

Mayo provides one approach to the measurement of human capital – the human capital monitor, which is based on people as assets, people's motivation and commitment and people's contribution to added value. There is advice on maximising human capital, motivation and commitment, innovation and learning and the challenges of mergers, acquisitions and alliances.

REFERENCES

Arkin, A. and Allen, R. (2002) 'Satisfaction guaranteed', *People Management*, Vol. 8, No. 21, October, pp. 40–2.

Baird, L., Meshoulam, I. and DeGive, G. (1983) 'Meshing human resources planning with strategic business planning: a model approach', *Personnel*, Vol. 60, Part 5 (Sept/Oct.), pp. 14–25.

Barney, J. (1991) 'Firm resources and sustained competitive advantage', *Journal of Management*, Vol. 17, No. 1, pp. 99–120.

Beaumont, P. (1992) 'The US human resource management literature: a review', in G. Salaman (ed.) *Human Resource Strategies*. London: Sage in association with OUP.

Becker, B. and Gerhart, B. (1996) 'The Impact of Human Resource Management on Organisational Performance: Progress and Prospects', *Academy of Management Journal*, Vol. 39, pp. 779–801.

Becker, B., Huselid, M. and Ulrich, D. (2001) *The HR Scorecard: Linking People, Strategy and Performance*. Boston: Harvard Business School Press.

Beer, M., Spector, B., Lawrence, P.R., Quinn Mills, D. and Walton, R.E. (1984) *Managing Human Assets*. New York: Free Press.

Boxall, P.F. (1992) 'Strategic human resource management: beginnings of a new theoretical sophistication?', *Human Resource Management Journal*, Vol. 2, No. 3.

Boxall, P.F. (1996) 'The strategic HRM debate and the resource-based view of the firm', *Human Resource Management Journal*, Vol. 6, No. 3, pp. 59–75.

Boxall, P. and Purcell, J. (2003) *Strategy and Human Resource Management*. Basingstoke: Palgrave Macmillan.

Boxall, P. and Steeneveld, M. (1999) 'Human Resource Strategy and competitive advantage: A longitudinal study of engineering consultancies', *Journal of Management Studies*, Vol. 36, No. 4, pp. 443–63.

Briggs, S. and Keogh, W. (1999) 'Integrating human resource strategy and strategic planning to achieve business excellence', *Total Quality Management*, July, p. 447.

Brown, D. (2002) 'Top-down and bottom-up', *People Management*, Vol. 8, No. 17, 29 August, p. 18.

Butler, J. (1988/89) 'Human resource management as a driving force in business strategy', *Journal of General Management*, Vol. 13, No. 4.

Fields, D., Chan, A., Aktar, S. and Blum, T. (2006) 'Human resource management strategies under uncertainty', *Cross Cultural Management: An International Journal*, Vol. 13, No. 2, pp. 171–86.

Fombrun, C., Tichy, N.M. and Devanna, M.A. (1984) *Strategic Human Resource Management*. New York: John Wiley and Sons.

Grensing-Pophel, L. (1999) 'Taking your "seat at the table" (the role of Human Resource Managers in companies)', *HRMagazine*, March, Vol. 44, No. 3, pp. 90–4.

Griffiths, J. (2006) 'Keep-fit scheme', *People Management*, Vol. 12, No. 7, 6 April, pp. 18–19.

Grundy, T. (1998) 'How are corporate strategy and human resources strategy linked?', *Journal of General Management*, Vol. 23, No. 3, Spring, pp. 49–72.

Guest, D. (1987) 'Human resource management and industrial relations', *Journal of Management Studies*, Vol. 24, No. 5.

Guest, D. (1989) 'Personnel and HRM: Can you tell the difference?', *Personnel Management* (January).

Guest, D. (2001) 'Human resource management: when research confronts theory', *International Journal of Human Resource Management*, Vol. 12, No. 7, pp. 1092–1106.

Guest, D. and King, Z. (2001) 'Personnel's Paradox', *People Management*, Vol. 17, No. 19, 27 September, pp. 24–9.

Hall, L. and Torrington, D. (1998) *The Human Resource Function: The Dynamics of change and development*. London: Financial Times Pitman Publishing.

Hendry, C. and Pettigrew, A. (1992) 'Patterns of strategic change in the development of Human Resource Management', *British Journal of Management*, Vol. 3, No. 3, pp. 137–56.

Higginbottom, K. (2002) 'Profits rise with a written HR strategy', *People Management*, Vol. 8, No. 25, 26 December, p. 9.

Holbeche, L. (1999) *Aligning Human Resources and Business Strategy*. Oxford: Butterworth-Heinemann. © Roffey Park Management Institute.

Hunt, J. and Boxall, P. (1998) 'Are top Human Resource Specialists strategic partners? Self-perceptions of a corporate elite', *International Journal of Human Resource Management*, Vol. 9, pp. 767–81.

Kane, B. and Palmer, I. (1995) 'Strategic HRM or managing the employment relationship?', *International Journal of Manpower*, Vol. 15, No. 5, pp. 6–16.

Kersley, B., Alpin, C., Forth, J., Bryson, A., Bewley, H., Dix, G. and Oxenbridge, S. (2006) *Inside the Workplace: Findings from the 2004 Workplace Employment Relations Survey*, London: Routledge.

Kochan, T.A. and Barocci, T.A. (1985) *Human Resource Management and Industrial Relations: Text, Readings and Cases*. Boston: Little Brown.

Legge, K. (1991) 'Human resource management: a critical analysis', in J. Storey (ed.) *New Perspectives on Human Resource Management*. London: Routledge.

Legge, K. (1995) *Human Resource Management: Rhetorics and realities*. Basingstoke: Macmillan.

Lengnick-Hall, M. and Lengnick-Hall, C. (2003) *Human Resource Management in the Knowledge Economy*. San Francisco: Berrett-Koehler Inc.

Lundy, O. and Cowling, A. (1996) *Strategic Human Resource Management*. London: Routledge.

Manocha, R. (2006) 'Review puts reporting back on agenda', *People Management*, Vol. 12, No. 1, 12 January, p. 9.

Miles, R.E. and Snow, C.C. (1984) 'Organisation strategy, structure and process', *Academy of Management Review*, Vol. 2, pp. 546–62.

Mintzberg, H. (1994) 'The fall and rise of strategic planning', *Harvard Business Review*, February.

Ogbonna, E. and Whipp, R. (1999) 'Strategy, culture and HRM: evidence from the UK food retailing sector', *Human Resource Management Journal*, Vol. 9, No. 4, pp. 75–90.

Pedler, M., Burgoyne, J. and Boydell, T. (1991) *The Learning Company*. Maidenhead: McGraw-Hill.

People Management (2002) 'Human Capital Review', *People Management*, Vol. 8, No. 15, 25 July, p. 9.

Pfeffer, J. (1994) *Competitive Advantage through People*. Boston: Harvard Business School Press.

Poole, M. (1990) 'Editorial: HRM in an international perspective', *International Journal of Human Resource Management*, Vol. 1, No. 1.

Porter, M. (1980) *Competitive Strategy*. New York: Free Press.

Purcell, J. (1991) 'The impact of corporate strategy on human resource management', in J. Storey (ed.) *New Perspectives on Personnel Management*. London: Routledge.

Purcell, J. (1992) 'The impact of corporate strategy on human resource management', in G. Salaman *et al.* (eds) *Human Resource Strategies*. London: Sage Publications.

Roberts, Z. (2002) 'CIPD task force to create new framework for external reporting of human capital' *People Management*, Vol. 8, No. 23, 21 November, p. 7.

Sanz-Valle, R., Sabater-Sánchez, R. and Aragón-Sánchez, A. (1999) 'Human Resource management and business strategy links: an empirical study', *International Journal of Human Resource Management*, Vol. 10, No. 4, pp. 655–71.

Scarborough, H. (2003a) *Human Capital – External Reporting Framework*. London: CIPD.

Scarborough, H. (2003b) 'Recipe for success', *People Management*, Vol. 9, No. 2, 23 January, pp. 32–5.

Scarborough, H. and Elias, J. (2002) *Evaluating Human Capital – Research Report*. London: CIPD.

Schmidt, J. and Lines, S. (2002) 'A measure of success', *People Management*, Vol. 8, No. 9, May, pp. 32–4.

Schuler, R.S. and Jackson, S.E. (1987) 'Linking competitive strategies with human resource management practices', *Academy of Management Executive*, No. 3 (August).

Scott, A. (2005) 'Scrapping OFRs "an astonishing U-turn"', *People Management*, Vol. 11, No. 24, 8 December, p. 10.

Senge, P. (1990) *The Fifth Discipline: The Art and Practice of the Learning Organization*. London: Century Business, Random House.

Skinner, D. and Mabey, C. (1997) 'Managers' perceptions of strategic HR change', *Personnel Review*, Vol. 26, No. 6, pp. 467–84.

Thomas, A. and Ramaswamy, K. (1996) 'Matching managers to strategy: further tests of the Miles and Snow typology', *British Journal of Management*, Vol. 7, pp. 247–61.

Tyson, S. (1995) *Human Resource Strategy*. London: Pitman.

Ulrich, D. (1998) 'A new mandate for human resources', *Harvard Business Review*, Jan.– Feb., pp. 125–34.

Ulrich, D. and Smallwood, N. (2002) 'Seven Up', *People Management*, Vol. 8, No. 10, May, pp. 42–4.

Whipp, R. (1992) 'Human resource management, competition and strategy: some productive tensions', in P. Blyton and P. Turnbull (eds) *Reassessing Human Resource Management*. California: Sage Publications.

Wright, P., McMahon, G. and McWilliams, A. (1994) 'Human Resources and sustained competitive advantage: a resource-based perspective', *International Journal of Human Resource Management*, Vol. 5, No. 2, May, pp. 301–26.

Wright, P., Dunford, B. and Snell, S. (2001) 'Human Resources and the Resource based View of the firm', *Journal of Management*, Vol. 27, pp. 701–21.

An extensive range of additional materials, including multiple choice questions, answers to questions and links to useful websites can be found on the Human Resource Management Companion Website at **www.pearsoned.co.uk/torrington**.

PLANNING: JOBS AND PEOPLE

THE OBJECTIVES OF THIS CHAPTER ARE TO:

1   Discuss the contribution and feasibility of HR planning

2   Explore the scope of HR planning

3   Explain an integrated HR planning framework

Planning for human resources has experienced a chequered history. In the 1960s and 1970s it was heralded as a critical tool for business success, as planning to get the right people in the right place at the right time was seen to be essential to achieving rapid growth. In the 1980s and 1990s planning was viewed as a suitable tool for managing downsizing and redundancies. On the other hand it has been argued that planning is no longer meaningful in an era of rapid and discontinuous change where it been recognised that strategies emerge rather than being precisely planned in advance. However, good planning still has an important contribution in supporting strategic HRM in this context (*see*, for example, Boxall and Purcell 2003; Stiles 2001).

THE CONTRIBUTION AND FEASIBILITY OF HR PLANNING

A useful starting point is to consider the different contributions that strategy and planning make to the organisation. A common view has been that they are virtually one and the same – hence the term 'strategic planning'. Henry Mintzberg (1994, p. 108) distinguished between *strategic thinking*, which is about synthesis, intuition and creativity to produce a not too precisely articulated vision of direction, and *strategic planning*, which is about collecting the relevant information to stimulate the visioning process and also programming the vision into what needs to be done to get there. It is helpful to look at human resource planning in the same way, and this is demonstrated in Figure 3.1. In more detail he suggests:

- **Planning as strategic programming** – planning cannot generate strategies, but it can make them operational by clarifying them; working out the consequences of them; and identifying what must be done to achieve each strategy.
- **Planning as tools to communicate and control** – planning can ensure coordination and encourage everyone to pull in the same direction; planners can assist in finding successful experimental strategies which may be operating in just a small part of the organisation.
- **Planners as analysts** – planners need to analyse hard data, both external and internal, which managers can then use in the strategy development process.
- **Planners as catalysts** – raising difficult questions and challenging the conventional wisdom which may stimulate managers into thinking in more creative ways.

Organisational and human resource planners make an essential contribution to strategic visioning. Sisson and Storey (2000) identify HR planning as 'one of the basic building blocks of a more strategic approach'. Starting with some ideas of Lam and Schaubroeck (1998) we identify four specific ways in which HR planning is critical to strategy, as it can identify:

- *gaps in capabilities* – lack of sufficient skills, people or knowledge in the business which will prevent the strategy being implemented successfully;
- *surpluses in capabilities* – providing scope for efficiencies and new ventures to capitalise on the skills, people and knowledge that are currently underused, in order to influence or shape the strategy;
- *poor utilisation of people* – suggesting inappropriate human resource practices that need to be altered;
- *developing a talent pool*.

Figure 3.1
Human
resource
strategic
visioning
and strategic
planning
(Source: After
Mintzberg 1994.)

Strategic planning	**Strategic visioning**	**Strategic planning**
Providing HR data, ideas	Defining a vision of the	Programme the vision –
Asking difficult questions	future (organisational	HR objectives targets
	and HR)	action plans

If you turn back to Chapter 2 and look again at the resource-based view of the firm you will see how these four aspects are crucial to sustaining competitive advantage through making the most of human resources.

Our environment of rapid and discontinuous change makes any planning difficult, and HR planning is especially difficult as people have free will, unlike other resources, such as finance or technology. The contribution and implementation of HR planning is likely to be enhanced if:

- plans are viewed as flexible and reviewed regularly, rather than being seen as an end point in the process;
- stakeholders, including all levels of manager and employee, are involved in the process. Surveys and focus groups are possible mechanisms, in addition to line manager representatives on the HR planning team;
- planning is owned and driven by senior managers rather than HR specialists, who need to facilitate the process;
- plans are linked to business and HR strategy;
- plans are user-friendly and not overly complex;
- it is recognised that while a comprehensive plan may be ideal, sometimes it may only be feasible to plan on an issue-by-issue basis.

WINDOW ON PRACTICE

Tony, the Personnel Manager, shouted at Ian, the Chief Executive: 'What do you mean, it wasn't agreed?'

'I mean it's the first I've heard that you need £22k for a new apprentice scheme.'
'Well, it was in the plan.'
'What plan?'
'The manpower plan, what other f*****g plan would I mean!'
'You didn't ask me for the money.'
'I asked you in the plan, and you didn't come back and say we couldn't have it.'
'I didn't come back and say you could – now let's start at the beginning – tell me why we need to spend it and what will happen if we don't.'

The conversation continued and finally Tony and Ian began to talk about the real issues. Ian never told Tony that he had filed the manpower plan unread, but he did tell him that he wanted next year's plan to be five pages of interpretation and recommendations and not 85 pages of figures.

THE SCOPE OF HUMAN RESOURCE PLANNING

Traditionally human resource planning, generally termed manpower planning, was concerned with the numbers of employees and the levels and types of skill in the organisation. A typical model of traditional manpower planning is shown in Figure 3.2. In this model the emphasis is on balancing the projected demand for and supply of labour, in order to have the right number of the right employees in the right place at the right time. The demand for manpower is influenced by corporate strategies and objectives, the environment and the way that staff are utilised within the business. The supply of manpower is projected from current employees (via calculations about expected leavers, retirements, promotions, etc.) and from the availability of the required skills in the labour market. Anticipated demand and supply are then reconciled by considering a range of options, and plans to achieve a feasible balance are designed.

As the world has moved on this model has been viewed as too narrow, being heavily reliant on calculations of employee numbers or potential employee numbers. It has also been criticised for giving insufficient attention to skills (Hendry 1994; Taylor 1998). In addition there has been an increasing recognition of the need to plan, not just for hard numbers, but for the **softer** issues of employee behaviour, organisation culture and systems; these issues have been identified as having a key impact on business success in the current environment.

Increasingly there is a need for organisations to integrate the process of planning for numbers and skills of employees; employee behaviour and organisational culture; organisation design and the make-up of individual jobs; and formal and informal systems. These aspects are all critical in terms of programming and achieving the vision. Each of these aspects interrelates with the others. However, reality has always been recognised as being a long way from identified best practice. Undoubtedly different

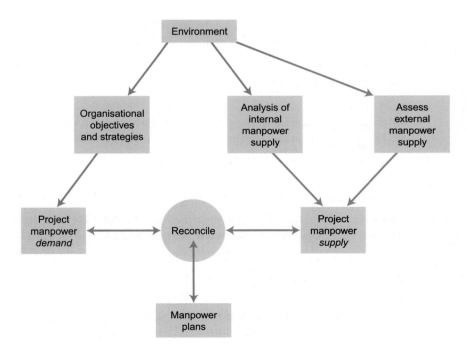

Figure 3.2
A model of traditional manpower planning

Figure 3.3
Integrated
human
resource
planning
framework

organisations will place different emphases on each of these factors, and may well plan each separately or plan some and not others.

The framework we shall use in this chapter attempts to bring *all* aspects of HR planning together, incorporating the more traditional approach to 'manpower planning', but going beyond this to include behaviour, culture, systems and so on. Our framework identifies 'where we want to be', translated from responses to the strategic vision; 'where we are now'; and 'what we need to do to make the transition' – all operating within the organisation's environment. The framework is shown in diagrammatic form in Figure 3.3. An alternative framework to use may be the HR scorecard (*see* Becker *et al.* 2001). Chapter 33 provides more details.

We shall now look in more depth at each of these four areas. The steps are presented in a logical sequence. In practice, however, they may run in parallel, and/or in an informal fashion, and each area may well be revisited a number of times.

ANALYSING THE ENVIRONMENT

In this chapter we refer to the environment broadly as the context of the organisation, and this is clearly critical in the impact that it has on both organisational and human resource strategy. Much strategy is based on a response to the environment – for example, what our customers now want or what competitors are now offering – or in anticipation of what customers will want or what they can be persuaded to want. In human resource terms we need to identify, for example, how difficult or easy it will be to find employees with scarce skills and what these employees will expect from an employer so that we can attract them. (*See* **www.pearsoned.co.uk/torrington** HRP Exercise, 3.1, note 1.) We shall be concerned with legislation which will limit or widen the conditions of employment that we offer, with what competitors are offering and with what training schemes are available locally or nationally.

Data on relevant trends can be collected from current literature, company annual reports, conferences/courses and contacts and networking. Over recent years considerable attention has been given to the need for companies to benchmark their activities, processes and outcomes against other 'successful' organisations. However much care needs to be taken to select the most appropriate benchmarks, and Denrell (2005) warns of how misleading it can be to look only at successful organisations, and recommends that unsuccessful organisations should be similarly explored. Looking at successes only may lead to the assumption that certain practices they use are critical to that success, and yet unsuccessful organisations may use similar practices. The key is understanding the context and considering the full picture of how organisations are differentiated. Table 3.1 gives examples of the many possible sources for each major area.

Trend area	Possible sources
Social	Census information CIPD journals News media *Social Trends* *General Household Survey* *Employment Gazette* Local papers
Demographics	*Labour Market Quarterly* Census information *Employment Gazette* Local council, Learning and Skills Councils
Political and legislative	News media *Proceedings of European Parliament* *Proceedings of British Parliament* *Hansard* *Industrial Relations Review and Report* *Industrial Law Journal* *IDS Brief*
Industrial and technological	*Employment Digest* Journals specifically for the industry *Financial Times* Employers' association Trade association
Competitors	Annual reports Talk to them!

Table 3.1
Sources of information on environment trends

WINDOW ON PRACTICE

The impact of demographics, legislation and pension reforms

Demographics, legislation and pension reforms have come together to create a very different environment for organisations than the one that existed in the 1980s and 1990s. The number of younger people in the population is reducing in proportion to the number of older people, as birth rates are lower than previously and people are living longer. This has an impact on many organisations. For example skills loss and shortages will require organisational planners to devise novel solutions. Currently EU workers (especially from Poland and Eastern Europe) are being recruited in the UK to compensate for skills shortages.

At a national level the Employment Equality (Age) Regulations came into force in 2006, introducing a default retirement age (DFA) of 65, preventing organisations from retiring people earlier (without a legitimate business aim for doing to). Employees will have the right to request to work beyond 65. Prior to this organisations could choose to have a much earlier retirement age, and in the 1980s and 1990s early retirement was widely used and viewed as a favourable means to downsize the organisation. Additional changes relating to pensions also form part of the context. The age at which individuals may claim their state pension is currently 65 for men and 60 for women (although these ages are gradually being equalised at 65), and it is predicted that this state retirement age will rise further in the future, in order to cope with the impact of the demographic changes. Furthermore changes in occupational pension schemes are resulting in less well-funded occupational pensions and the need for many employees to work longer to build up a better pension.

Given this environment one of the approaches organisations may need to employ is to delay retirement age even further (beyond 65), to encourage employees to stay on so that vital skills are retained for longer, or alternatively adopt a flexible retirement age rather than a mandatory age (employees being protected until they are 65 in any case). This is not just a UK phenomenon, and in the US Bovbjerg, Director of Education, Workforce and Income Security Issues (quoted in Geissler 2005), claims that barriers to older workers staying in employment such as social security rules, pensions rules and lack of flexible work need to be dismantled. Gomez *et al.* (2002) explore this in the Canadian context, making the point that a flexible retirement age will make HR planning much more difficult for companies particularly in respect of succession planning and planning for disability, medical and pension costs. There will be pressures on organisations to design the most appropriate jobs for older workers, to allow more flexibility pre-retirement, to offer a variety of employment options beyond retirement, and to plan to meet the needs of workers who feel forced to stay on at work due to inadequate pensions.

Once one has acquired and constantly updated data on the environment, a common method of analysis is to produce a map of the environment, represented as a wheel. The map represents a time in the future, say three years away. In the centre of the wheel can be written the core purpose of the organisation as it relates to people, or potential future strategies or goals. Each spoke of the wheel can then be filled in to represent a factor of the external environment, for example, potential employees, a specific local competitor, competitors generally, regulatory bodies, customers, government. From all the spokes the six or seven regarded as most important need to be selected.

These can then be worked on further by asking what demands each will make of the organisation, and how the organisation will need to respond in order to achieve its goals. From these responses can be derived the implications for human resource activities. For example, the demands of potential employees may be predicted as:

- We need a career, not just a job.
- We need flexibility to help with childrearing.
- We want to be treated as people and not as machines.
- We need a picture of what the organisation has in store for us.
- We want to be better trained.

And so on.

Managers then consider what the organisation would need to offer to meet these needs in order to meet a declared organisational goal or strategy. It is a good way of identifying human resource issues that need to be addressed. The analysis can also be fed back into identifying and clarifying the future vision or goals in human resource terms. Figure 3.4 gives an outline for the whole process. (For a worked example *see* **www.pearsoned.co.uk/torrington** HRP Exercise, 3.1, note 2.)

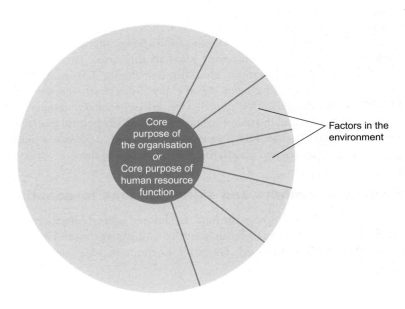

Individual factors in the environment

Demands from the factor	Responses from the organisation

Figure 3.4
Mapping the
environment

ACTIVITY 3.1

Draw a map of the external environment, for any organisation in which you are involved, for three to five years ahead. Individually, or as a group, brainstorm all the spokes in the wheel and select the six most important ones. Draw up a demands and responses list for each. Write a summary (one side of A4) of what you think your organisation's priorities should be in the people area over the next 3–5 years.

FORECASTING FUTURE HUMAN RESOURCE NEEDS

Organisation, behaviour and culture

There is little specific literature on the methods used to translate the strategic objectives of the organisation and environmental influences into qualitative or soft human resource goals. In general terms, they can be summed up as the use of managerial judgement. Brainstorming, combined with the use of structured checklists or matrices, can encourage a more thorough analysis. Organisation-change literature and corporate planning literature are helpful as sources of ideas in this area. Three simple techniques are a human resource implications checklist (*see* Figure 3.5), a strategic brainstorming exercise (Figure 3.6) and a behavioural expectation chart (*see* **www.pearsoned.co.uk/ torrington** HRP Exercise, 3.1, note 3). The HR scorecard may be a useful tool for this aspect of planning, and the use of **scenarios** may also be helpful (*see*, for example, Boxall and Purcell 2003; Turner 2002). Scenarios can be used to provide a picture of alternative organisational futures and alternative HR responses to these.

Employee numbers and skills (demand forecasting)

There is far more literature in the more traditional area of forecasting employee number demand based on the organisation's strategic objectives. Both objective and subjective approaches can be employed. Objective methods include statistical and work study approaches.

Corporate goal	Human resource implications in respect of:	Methods of achieving this
	New tasks?	
	For whom?	
	What competencies needed?	
	Relative importance of team/individual behaviour	
	Deleted tasks?	
	How will managers need to manage?	

Figure 3.5
The beginnings of a human resource implications checklist

Figure 3.6
Strategic
brainstorming
exercise

Managers write a corporate goal in the centre and brainstorm changes
that need to take place in each of the four areas, one area at a time

Statistical models generally relate employee number demand to specific organisational circumstances and activities. Models can take account of determining factors, such as production, sales, passenger miles, level of service. A simple model might relate people demand to production, using a constant relationship, without making any assumptions about economies of scale. In this model if output is to be doubled, then employees would also need to be doubled. (*See* **www.pearsoned.co.uk/torrington** HRP Exercise, 3.1, note 4.)

More complicated equations can be formulated which describe the way that a combination of independent factors is expected to affect the dependent employee demand. By inserting new values for the independent factors, such as new projected sales figures, we can work out the demand for employees from the equation. The equations can also be represented as graphs, making the relationships clear to see. These models can be adapted to take account of projected changes in utilisation, owing to factors such as the introduction of new technology, or alternative organisational forms, such as high-performance teams.

The work-study method is based on a thorough analysis of the tasks to be done, and the time each takes. From this the person-hours needed per unit of output can be calculated, and standards are developed for the numbers and levels of employees required. These are most useful when one is studying production work. They need to be checked regularly to make sure they are still appropriate. Work study is usually classified as an objective measure; however, it is often accepted that since the development of standards and the grouping of tasks is partly dependent on human judgement, it could be considered as a subjective method.

The most common subjective method of demand forecasting is managerial judgement (sometimes referred to as managerial opinion or the inductive method), and this can also include the judgements of other operational and technical staff, as well as all levels of managers. This method relies on managers' estimates of human resource demand based on past experience and on corporate plans. Managerial judgements can be collected from the 'bottom up' with lower-level managers providing estimates to go up the hierarchy for discussion and redrafting. Alternatively, a 'top-down' approach can be used with estimates made by the highest level of management to go down the hierarchy for discussion and redrafting. When this method is used it is difficult to cope with changes that are very different from past experiences. It is also less precise than statistical methods, but it is more comprehensive. Managerial judgement is a simple method, which can be applied fairly quickly and is not restricted by lack of data, particularly historical data, as are statistical techniques. However, managerial judgement is important even when statistical techniques are used. (*See* **www.pearsoned.co.uk/torrington** HRP Exercise, 3.1, note 5.)

- Introducing new materials or equipment, particularly new technology
- Introducing changes in work organisation, such as:
  - quality circles
  - job rotation
  - job enlargement
  - job enrichment
  - autonomous work groups
  - high-performance teams
  - participation
- Organisation development
- Introducing changes in organisation structure, such as:
  - centralisation/decentralisation
  - new departmental boundaries
  - relocation of parts of the organisation
  - flexible project structures
- Introducing productivity schemes, bonus schemes or other incentive schemes
- Encouraging greater staff flexibility and work interchangeability
- Altering times and periods of work
- Training and appraisal of staff
- Developing managers and use of performance management

Table 3.2
A range of methods to change employee utilisation

A specialised procedure for the collection of managerial opinions is based on the idea of the oracle at Delphi. A group of managers anonymously and independently answer questions about anticipated human resource demand. A compilation of the answers is fed back to each individual, and the process is repeated until all the answers converge.

The way that human resources are utilised will change the number of employees required and the necessary skills needed. There are many ways to change how employees are used, and these are shown in Table 3.2. Some methods are interrelated or overlap and would therefore be used in combination. (*See* **www.pearsoned.co.uk/torrington** HRP Exercise, 3.1, note 6.) Interconnections between most of these areas and soft human resources planning are also apparent.

WINDOW ON PRACTICE

Technology changes employee utilisation

In September 2006 Aviva insurance company announced 4,000 UK job losses. Whilst about 1,000 jobs would be offshored to India and about 500 outsourced, the majority of the jobs were not to be sourced elsewhere. Patrick Snowball who heads UK operations identified greater use of the Internet to purchase insurance as the reason for the job losses. He commented that 'I closed a call centre in Liverpool . . . because the phones were not ringing'.

Adapted from Felsted, A. and Taylor, A. (2006) 'Aviva says job cuts will save £250m annually', *Financial Times*, 15 September.

Whilst it could be argued that there will be a likely increase of IT jobs in the company, it seems very clear that technological advances have reduced employee demand in this area of employment.

ANALYSING THE CURRENT SITUATION AND PROJECTING FORWARD

Organisation, behaviour and culture

It is in this area that more choice of techniques is available, and the possibilities include the use of questionnaires to staff (*see* **www.pearsoned.co.uk/torrington** HRP Exercise, 3.1, note 7.), interviews with staff and managerial judgement. Focus groups are an increasingly popular technique where, preferably, the Chief Executive meets with, say, 20 representative staff from each department to discuss their views of the strengths and weaknesses of the organisation, and what can be done to improve. These approaches can be used to provide information on, for example:

- Motivation of employees.
- Job satisfaction.
- Organisational culture.
- The way that people are managed.
- Attitude to minority groups and equality of opportunity.
- Commitment to the organisation and reasons for this.
- Clarity of business objectives.
- Goal-focused and other behaviour.
- Organisational issues and problems.
- What can be done to improve.
- Organisational strengths to build on.

WINDOW ON PRACTICE

Jennifer Hadley is the Chief Executive of Dynamo Castings, a long-established organisation which had experienced rapid growth and healthy profits until the past three years. Around 800 staff were employed mostly in production, but significant numbers were also employed in marketing/sales and research/development. Poor performance over the last three years was largely the result of the competition who were able to deliver a quality product more quickly and at a competitive price. Dynamo retained the edge in developing new designs, but this consumed a high level of resources and was a lengthy process from research to eventual production. Most employees had been with the company for a large part of their working lives and the culture was still appropriate to the times of high profit where life had been fairly easy and laid back. Messages about difficult times, belt tightening and higher productivity with fewer people had been filtered down to employees, who did not change their behaviour but did feel threatened.

It was with some trepidation that Jennifer decided to meet personally with a cross-section of each department to talk through company and departmental issues. The first meeting was with research/development. As expected, the meeting began with a flood of concerns about job security. No promises could be given. However, the mid-point of the meeting was quite fruitful, and the following points, among others, became clear:

- development time could be reduced to one year from two if some production staff were involved in the development process from the very beginning;

- many development staff felt their career prospects were very limited and a number expressed the wish to be able to move into marketing. They felt this would also be an advantage when new products were marketed;

- staff felt fairly paid and would be prepared to forgo salary rises for a year or two if this would mean job security; they liked working for Dynamo and didn't want to move;

- staff were aware of the difficult position the company was in but they really didn't know what to do to make it any better;

- development staff wanted to know why Dynamo didn't collaborate with Castem Ltd on areas of mutual interest (Jennifer didn't know the answer to this one).

The meeting gave Jennifer not only a better understanding of what employees felt, but also some good ideas to explore. Departmental staff knew their problems had not been wiped away, but did feel that Jennifer had at least taken the trouble to listen to them.

Turnover figures, performance data, recruitment and promotion trends and characteristics of employees may also shed some light on these issues.

Data relating to current formal and informal systems, together with data on the structure of the organisation, also need to be collected, and the effectiveness, efficiency and other implications of these need to be carefully considered. Most data will be collected from within the organisation, but data may also be collected from significant others, such as customers, who may be part of the environment.

Current and projected employee numbers and skills (employee supply)

Current employee supply can be analysed in both individual and overall statistical terms. To gain an overview of current supply the following factors may be analysed either singly or in combination: number of employees classified by function, department, occupation job title, skills, qualifications, training, age, length of service, performance appraisal results. (*See* **www.pearsoned.co.uk/torrington** HRP Exercise, 3.1, note 8.)

Forecasting employee supply is concerned with predicting how the current supply of employees will change, primarily how many will leave, be internally promoted or transferred. These changes are forecast by analysing what has happened in the past, in terms of staff retention and/or movement, and projecting this into the future to see what would happen if the same trends continued. The impact of changing circumstances would also need to be taken into account when projecting analyses forward. Bell (1989)

provides an extremely thorough coverage of possible analyses, on which this section is based. Behavioural aspects are also important, such as investigating the reasons why staff leave, the criteria that affect promotions and transfers and changes in working conditions and in HR policy. Analyses fall broadly into two categories: analyses of staff leaving, and analyses of internal movements. The following calculations are the most popular forms of analysing staff leaving the organisation.

Annual labour turnover index

The annual labour turnover index is sometimes called the percentage wastage rate, or the conventional turnover index. This is the simplest formula for wastage and looks at the number of staff leaving during the year as a percentage of the total number employed who could have left.

$$\frac{\text{Leavers in year}}{\text{Average number of staff in post during year}} \times 100 = \text{percentage wastage rate}$$

(*See* **www.pearsoned.co.uk/torrington** HRP Exercise, 3.1, note 9.)

This measure has been criticised because it gives only a limited amount of information. If, for example, there were 25 leavers over the year, it would not be possible to determine whether 25 different jobs had been left by 25 different people, or whether 25 different people had tried and left the same job. Length of service is not taken into account with this measure, yet length of service has been shown to have a considerable influence on leaving patterns, such as the high number of leavers at the time of induction.

Stability index

The stability index is based on the number of staff who could have stayed throughout the period. Usually, staff with a full year's service are expressed as a percentage of staff in post one year ago.

$$\frac{\text{Number of staff with one year's service at date}}{\text{Number of staff employed exactly one year before}} \times 100 = \text{per cent stability}$$

(*See* **www.pearsoned.co.uk/torrington** HRP Exercise, 3.1, note 10.)

This index, however, ignores joiners throughout the year and takes little account of length of service.

Cohort analysis

A cohort is defined as a homogeneous group of people. Cohort analysis tracks what happens as some people leave a group of people with very similar characteristics who all joined the organisation at the same time. Graduates are an appropriate group for this type of analysis. A graph showing what happens to the group can be in the form of a survival curve or a log-normal wastage curve, which can be plotted as a straight line and can be used to make predictions. The disadvantage of this method of analysis is that it cannot be used for groups other than the specific group for which it was originally prepared. The information has also to be collected over a long time-period, which produces problems of availability and reliability of data.

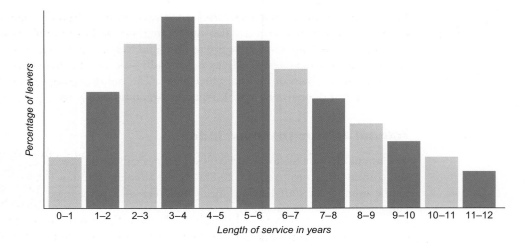

Figure 3.7
Census analysis: percentage of leavers with differing lengths of service

Half-life

The half-life is a figure expressing the time taken for half the cohort to leave the organisation. The figure does not give as much information as a survival curve, but it is useful as a summary and as a method of comparing different groups.

Census method

The census method is an analysis of leavers over a reasonably short period of time – often over a year. The length of completed service of leavers is summarised by using a histogram, as shown in Figure 3.7. (*See* **www.pearsoned.co.uk/torrington** HRP Exercise, 3.1, note 11.)

Retention profile

Staff retained, that is those who remain with the organisation, are allocated to groups depending on the year they joined. The number in each year group is translated into a percentage of the total number of individuals who joined during that year.

We move now to methods of analysing internal movements. These focus on either overall analyses of movement patterns in the organisation or succession planning, which has a more individual emphasis.

Analyses of internal movements

Movement patterns

Age and length of service distributions can be helpful to indicate an overall pattern of problems that may arise in the future, such as promotion blocks. They need to be used in conjunction with an analysis of previous promotion patterns in the organisation. (*See* **www.pearsoned.co.uk/torrington** HRP Exercise, 3.1, note 12.) An alternative is a stocks and flows analysis of the whole organisation or a part of it, such as a department.

The model is constructed to show the hierarchy of positions and the numbers employed in each. Numbers moving between positions, and in and out of the organisation over any time-period, can be displayed. The model displays visually promotion and lateral move channels in operation, and shows what happens in reality to enable comparison to be made with the espoused approach, but users need to recognise, and work within, the limitation that the structure of jobs will change more rapidly than in the past.

Individual succession analysis

On an individual basis many organisations pay special attention to analysing the likely succession into key roles of current high-potential employees. Originally the process was an informal approach to promotion with a short-term focus on who would be able to replace senior people if they left suddenly, so that disruption and dislocation were minimised (*see*, for example, Huang 2001). Such analyses have increasingly involved a range of proactive approaches to developing successors and talent in general, and we say more about this in the section on plans below.

ACTIVITY 3.2

1 Why do employees leave organisations?

2 What are the determinants of promotion in your organisation? Are they made explicit? Do staff understand what the determinants are?

3 What would be your criteria for promotion in your organisation?

RECONCILIATION, DECISIONS AND PLANS

We have already said that, in reality, there is a process of continuous feedback between the different stages of human resource planning activities, as they are all interdependent. On the soft side (organisation, behaviour and culture) there is a dynamic relationship between the future vision, environmental trends and the current position. Key factors to take into account during reconciliation and deciding on action plans are the acceptability of the plans to both senior managers and other employees, the priority of each plan, key players who will need to be influenced and the factors that will encourage or be a barrier to successful implementation.

On the hard side, feasibility may centre on the situation where the supply forecast is less than the demand forecast. Here, the possibilities are to:

- alter the demand forecast by considering changes in the utilisation of employees (such as training and productivity deals, or high-performance teams): by using different employees with higher skills; employing staff with insufficient skills and training them immediately; or outsourcing the work;

- alter the supply forecast by, say, reducing staff turnover, delaying retirement, or widening the supply pool by including EU nationals;

- change the company objectives, as lack of human resources will prevent them from being achieved in any case. Realistic objectives need to be based on the resources that are, and are forecast to be, available either internally or externally.

When the demand forecast is less than the internal supply forecast in some areas, the possibilities are to:

- consider and calculate the costs of overemployment over various timespans;
- consider the methods and cost of losing staff;
- consider changes in utilisation: work out the feasibility and costs of retraining, redeployment and so on;
- consider whether it is possible for the company objectives to be changed. Could the company diversify, move into new markets, etc.?

We have also noted the interrelationship between the soft and the hard aspects of planning. For example, the creation of high-performance teams may have implications for different staffing numbers, a different distribution of skills, alternative approaches to reward and a different management style. The relocation of a supplier's staff on to the premises of the company that they supply, in order to get really close to this customer, could have implications for relocation, recruitment, skills required and culture encouraged. The development of a learning organisation may have implications for turnover and absence levels, training and development provision, culture encouraged and approach to reward.

Once all alternatives have been considered and feasible solutions decided, specific action plans can be designed covering all appropriate areas of HRM activity. Whilst these have been grouped in separate sections, below, there is clearly potential overlap between the groups.

Human resource supply plans

Plans may need to be made concerning the timing and approach to recruitment or downsizing. For example, it may have been decided that in order to recruit sufficient staff, a public relations campaign is needed to promote a particular company image. Promotion, succession, transfer and redeployment and redundancy plans are also relevant here. Plans for the retention of those aged over 50 and flexible retirement plans are a key theme at present and we consider some examples of these in Chapter 24 on Equal opportunities and diversity. Increasingly there is the need to focus on plans for the development and retention of the talent pool, and given their continuing high profile we look at succession plans in more detail below.

Succession plans

From the 1980s onwards the more proactive and formal approaches to succession included careful analysis of the jobs to be filled, a longer-term focus, developmental plans for individuals who were identified as successors, and the possibility of cross-functional moves. This approach was typically applied to those identified as having high potential, and was generally centred on the most senior positions. Larger organisations would produce tables of key jobs on which were named immediate successors, probable longer-term successors and potential longer-term successors, all with attached development plans. Alternatively, high-potential individuals were identified with likely immediate moves, probable longer-term moves and possible longer-term moves. However, as Hirsh

(2000) points out, this model is appropriate to a stable environment and career structure, and the emphasis in current succession planning has changed yet again. The concentration is now on the need to build and develop a pool of talent, without such a clear view of how the talent will be used in the future, and this is associated with the current high profile of 'talent management', brought into focus by McKinsey's 'war for talent' (1997). Developing a talent pool is a more dynamic approach and fits well with the resource-based view of the firm. While the link to business strategy is emphasised, there is more recognition of individual aspirations and a greater opportunity for people to put themselves forward to be considered for the talent pool. Developing talent at different leadership levels in the organisation is considered important, and current debates focus on the definition of talent in terms of what it means and to whom it applies. Warren (2006) discusses the issue of inclusivity and whether organisations should focus on an elite of high-performing, high-potential individuals, or whether inclusivity should be more broadly defined. Much greater openness in succession planning is encouraged, and more consideration is given to the required balance between internal talent development and external talent. Simms (2003) provides an interesting debate on these issues, which is provided as Case study 3.2 at **www.pearsoned.co.uk/torrington**. Talent management is most closely associated with development activities and we return to this topic in Chapter 16 on Strategic aspects of development.

WINDOW ON PRACTICE

Succession planning at Astra Zeneca

Astra Zeneca have designed a new succession planning programme which replaces an older more complex Zeneca one, and an Astra one which reflected the competition rather than collaboration between local sites. The new programme was designed to bring the best out of both systems.

The business drivers for the new system were to:

- develop leadership capability to move a larger global business forward
- integrate the business culturally (Zeneca was UK based and demerged from ICI; Astra was Swedish)
- ensure a diverse, cross-functional base of talent
- develop the ability to lead cross-functional and cross-national teams

In the new system there is greater integration with business and strategic planning, and the focus is on identifying an international key talent pool rather than identifying successors to current jobs which may not exist in the future. Individuals in the pool are provided with challenging opportunities to foster their development. They are also made aware that they are valued and supported, and are involved in an open dialogue. While it is also necessary for future leaders to be identified and developed, they must be broadly based, come from diverse backgrounds and possess strategic capability.

Source: Summarised from: Industrial Relations Services (2002)
'The changing face of succession planning', *IRS Employment Review*, No. 756, July, pp. 37–42.

Organisation and structure plans

Organisation and structure plans may concern departmental existence, remit and structure and the relationships between departments. They may also be concerned with the layers of hierarchy within departments and the level at which tasks are done, and the organisational groups within which they are done. Changes to organisation and structure will usually result in changes in employee utilisation.

Employee utilisation plans

Any changes in utilisation that affect human resource demand will need to be planned. Some changes will result in a sudden difference in the tasks that employees do and the numbers needed; others will result in a gradual movement over time. Other plans may involve the distribution of hours worked, for example the use of annual hours contracts; or the use of functional flexibility where employees develop and use a wider range of skills. There are implications for communications plans as the employees involved will need to be consulted about the changes and be prepared and trained for what will happen. There will be interconnections with supply plans here: for example, if fewer employees will be needed, what criteria will be used to determine who should be made redundant and who should be redeployed and retrained, and in which areas?

Learning and development plans

There will be development implications from both the human resource supply and the utilisation plans. The timing of development can be a critical aspect. For example, training for specific new technology skills loses most of its impact if it is done six months before the equipment arrives. If the organisation wishes to increase recruitment by promoting the excellent development that it provides for employees, then clear programmes of what will be offered need to be finalised and resourced so that these can then be used to entice candidates into the organisation. If the organisation is stressing customer service or total quality, then appropriate development will need to be carried out to enable employees to achieve this.

Performance management and motivation plans

These plans may include the development or renewal of a performance management system; and ensuring that employees are assessed on objectives or criteria that are key to organisational success, and which may then be linked to reward. They may also include setting performance and quality standards; culture change programmes aimed at encouraging specified behaviour and performance; or empowerment or career support to improve motivation.

Reward plans

It is often said that what gets rewarded gets done, and it is key that rewards reflect what the organisation sees as important. For example, if quantity of output is most important for production workers, bonuses may relate to number of items produced. If quality is most important, then bonuses may reflect reject rate, or customer complaint rate. If managers are only rewarded for meeting their individual objectives there may be problems if the organisation is heavily dependent on teamwork.

Employee relations plans

These plans may involve unions, employee representatives or all employees. They would include any matters which need to be negotiated or areas where there is the opportunity for employee involvement and participation.

Communications plans

The way that planned changes are communicated to employees is critical. Plans need to include not only methods for informing employees about what managers expect of them, but also methods to enable employees to express their concerns and needs for successful implementation. Communications plans will also be important if, for example, managers wish to generate greater employee commitment by keeping employees better informed about the progress of the organisation.

Once the plans have been made and put into action, the planning process still continues. It is important that the plans be monitored to see if they are being achieved and if they are producing the expected results. Plans will also need to be reconsidered on a continuing basis in order to cope with changing circumstances.

SUMMARY PROPOSITIONS

3.1 Even in a context of rapid and discontinuous change HR planning still has a valuable contribution to make, but as human resource planning deals with people, planners need to plan for what is acceptable as well as what is feasible.

3.2 The scope of human resource planning covers not only numbers of people and skills, but also structure, culture, systems and behaviour.

3.3 An integrated framework which attempts to cover all aspects of HR planning involves:

- analysing the external environment and business strategy;
- analysing where do we want to be? (forecasting HR requirements);
- analysing where are we now? (defining the current HR position and projecting this forward);
- comparing the two and forming plans to bridge the gap.

3.4 Human resource planning is a continuous process rather than a one-off activity.

GENERAL DISCUSSION TOPICS

1 Discuss the proposition that traditional (numbers) human resource planning is only of interest to organisations in periods of growth when unemployment levels are low.

2 'It is worthwhile planning even if you have no strategy.' For what reasons might you agree or disagree with this statement?

FURTHER READING

Day, G. and Schoemaker, P. (2005) 'Scanning the Periphery', *Harvard Business Review*, November, pp. 135–48.
This article underlines the organisational importance of keeping a constant eye on peripheral features in an organisation's environment as well as its direct and close competitors. Examples are included of challenges different organisations have faced and there are practical suggestions about how organisations could improve their scanning of the peripheral environment. Included is a self-assessment tool to identify the need for an organisation to have peripheral vision, and to assess its capability for peripheral vision. The capability part encompasses an assessment of leadership orientation, knowledge management systems, strategy-making processes, organisational structure and incentives, and culture (values, beliefs and behaviours).

Pfeffer, J. and Sutton, R. (2006) 'The real Brain Teaser', *People Management*, Vol. 12, No. 8, pp. 28–30.
This article challenges the notion that identifying talent within organisations is unproblematic. The authors demonstrate how performance varies over time, that talent is determined by the standards of performance accepted at the time it is identified, and that talent is as much a product of effort training and environment as it is of innate ability. Thus talent can easily be missed.

McNeilly, M. (2002) 'Gathering information for strategic decisions', *Strategy and Leadership*, Vol. 30, No. 5, pp. 29–34.
Focuses on information gathering, making strategic decisions and taking action, and provides some useful tools for each of these three stages. Some interesting suggestions for making strategic decisions include scenario planning and acting out scenarios in advance.

Turner, P. (2002) *Strategic Human Resource Forecasting*. London: CIPD.
An excellent and detailed text which covers issues involved in forecasting, strategy and planning and the HR role in this. Turner includes a wide range of aspects of HR from employee numbers to employee relations and organisation design.

REFERENCES

Becker, B., Huselid, M. and Ulrich, D. (2001) *The HR Scorecard: Linking People, Strategy and Performance*. Boston: Harvard Business School Press.
Bell, D.J. (1989) *Planning Corporate Manpower*. London: Longman.
Boxall, P. and Purcell, J. (2003) *Strategy and Human Resource Management*. Basingstoke: Palgrave, Macmillan.
Denrell, J. (2005) 'Selection Bias and the Perils of Benchmarking', *Harvard Business Review*, 20 April, pp. 114–19.
Felsted, A. and Taylor, A. (2006) 'Aviva says job cuts will save £250m annually', *Financial Times*, 14 September.
Geissler, C. (2005) 'The Cane Mutiny – Managing a Graying Workforce', *Harvard Business Review*, October, pp. 31–42.
Gomez, R., Gunderson, M. and Luchak, A. (2002) 'Mandatory retirement: a constraint in transitions to retirement?', *Employee Relations*, Vol. 24, No. 4, pp. 403–22.
Hendry, C. (1994) *Human Resource Strategies for International Growth*. London: Routledge.
Hirsh, W. (2000) *Succession planning demystified*. Brighton: Institute for Employment Studies.
Huang, T.-C. (2001) 'Succession Management Systems and human resource outcomes', *International Journal of Manpower*, Vol. 22, No. 8, pp. 736–47.
Industrial Relations Services (2002) 'The changing face of succession planning', *IRS Employment Review*, No. 756, July, pp. 37–42.

Lam, S.S. and Schaubroeck, J. (1998) 'Integrating HR planning and organizational strategy', *Human Resource Management Journal*, Vol. 8, No. 3, pp. 5–19.

Michaels, E., Handfield-Jones, H. and Axelrod, B. (2001) *The War for Talent*. Harvard: McKinsey and Company Incorporated/Harvard Business School Publishing.

Mintzberg, H. (1994) 'The fall and rise of strategic planning', *Harvard Business Review*, Jan./Feb.

Simms, J. (2003) 'The generation game', *People Management*, Vol. 9, No. 9, 1 May, pp. 26–31.

Sisson, K. and Storey, J. (2000) *The Realities of Human Resource Management*. Buckingham: Open University Press.

Stiles, P. (2001) 'The impact of the board on strategy: an empirical examination', *Journal of Management Studies*, Vol. 38, No. 5, pp. 627–50.

Taylor, S. (1998) *Employee Resourcing*. London: IPD.

Turner, P. (2002) 'How to do HR forecasting and planning', *People Management*, Vol. 8, No. 6, March, pp. 48–9.

Warren, C. (2006) 'Curtain Call' *People Management*, Vol. 12, No. 6, 23 March, pp. 24–9.

An extensive range of additional materials, including multiple choice questions, answers to questions and links to useful websites can be found on the Human Resource Management Companion Website at **www.pearsoned.co.uk/torrington**.

CHAPTER 4

THE INTERNATIONAL DIMENSION

THE OBJECTIVES OF THIS CHAPTER ARE TO:

1   Define international HRM

2   Present an analysis of cultural differences in management

3   Review aspects of international communication and coordination

The main problem about understanding international HRM issues is that they evolve so rapidly; having worked out how to deal with one opportunity or challenge, you find that things have changed and your plans are obsolete. As one company chairman put it, 'You feel as if you are driving from one station to another, hoping to get on a train, only to find that the train has just left and has gone on another route and your ticket is no longer valid'. The problem may be difficult, but solutions have to be found as this is an area where HR really is centre stage:

> HR can add real value here. Enabling people to work most effectively in these changing, challenging contexts is still the ultimate competitive advantage of any organisation, and what it will take to survive and thrive in this new world. (Glanz and Hirsch 2006, p. 54)

Until the last quarter of the twentieth century, the term 'international' hardly appeared in HR/personnel thinking, which remained within the culture, politico/legal system and workforce of the country in which the business was based. With the exception of inescapably international businesses, like oil companies and shipping, any HR issues were likely to be limited to deciding such matters as what expenses a sales manager could claim for travelling abroad, and whether or not the technician who was also going could stay at the same hotel. The establishment of overseas subsidiaries brought another range of issues to do with expatriation and responsibility not just for the expatriated employee, but also for the employee's family. As subsidiaries grew they evolved into partner companies in an international business, with expatriation moving both ways, training and language issues became more important, and understanding cultural and national differences came to involve more than globe-trotting sales and technical people. The most recent evolutionary development of globalisation, which seeks to reduce the significance of national interests and emphasise the attachment to the whole business, is an intensification of the process we described in our opening chapter of changing from personnel management to human resource management. Personnel management is essentially *workforce centred*, while HRM is *resource centred*. Personnel management is preoccupied with managing the supply of people to the business. They are the 'given' of the situation. In contrast human resource management is preoccupied with managing the demand for human resources to meet the operational needs of the business, whether they be employees or not, whether they be the residents of the local community or not; whether they be citizens of the home country or not.

We first worked out this distinction in 1987, when HRM was still a novel idea that needed to be described. Some may regard it as simply a different way of describing the same thing: just playing with words. To a great extent it is the same thing because most of the things that HR people do remain the same, but the change in emphasis and approach is profound. It is rather surprising to realise that this now describes very precisely, if not completely, the world of international HRM, which is much more strategic than operational in its main focus.

An axiom about any form of international management is 'global thinking; local action'. This is not just a neat form of words, it sums up precisely the spread of understanding that international management activity requires, and everyone requires it. On our website (**www.pearsoned.co.uk/torrington**) we have some additional reading about the types of people who represent their businesses in other countries, but everyone in the business is affected by the international developments in management. Local action increasingly requires global thinking, or at least global understanding, by everyone who goes to work anywhere.

ACTIVITY 4.1

1 Think of where you work, or where you have worked, and identify three activities where global thinking influences local action. What are the local HR implications of this?

2 In the same situation what aspects of local action influence global thinking?

In international matters HR has a more significant strategic input than in domestic management. Global thinking in an international business is concerned with all the things that are different in doing business in more than one country at the strategic level, how the cultural differences between countries are understood and how the management of those differences can be coordinated effectively. The issues include how the cultural differences can be accommodated and how effective communication can be maintained across long distances, different time zones, different managerial assumptions, varying national norms and different languages. There are also differences in legislation, training methods, education systems, social security arrangements and pension provision. This is human resource management at its most intellectually demanding because of the deep understanding that is needed of so many complex issues.

> When you enter a company, differences in architecture, interior design, dress and behaviour and styles of interaction are immediately apparent. The styles of architecture and design may emphasize tradition or modernity and signal the importance of hierarchy or collegial relations. A telling clue would be the existence of an executive parking lot and dining rooms, of open office space or closed doors. Others include the dress code and forms of address (the use of first or last names, titles, spoken deference), and the ease of interaction between senior and junior members, or between peers. (Schneider and Barsoux 2003, p. 52)

Understanding these variations indicates the values that are held on crucial issues like the importance of rules and procedures, whether information flows easily or is jealously guarded by a few and how the role of manager is understood. Within a culture where we have grown up we develop this understanding by a protracted process of learning over decades. When trying to understand a different culture, the same level of learning is needed in a very short time.

Local action is informed by global thinking, but carried out quite separately as all action is local and has to be decided by referring to aspects of employment in one locality only. HRM deals with people who are employed within only one set of legal, cultural, demographic and physical conditions. A debug technician may be employed in Italy to do exactly the same job on exactly the same range of products as another employee of the same company in Iowa or Indonesia, but the terms and conditions of employment and social conventions and the accepted management practices will be totally different.

In other chapters we frequently mention aspects of local action in different contexts. Here we shall introduce the general topic and then deal with just two aspects of global thinking that are particularly important to international HRM.

INTERNATIONAL HUMAN RESOURCE MANAGEMENT

Europeans share a common heritage, no matter how bloodstained it may be, through fighting against each other in various combinations for a thousand years, throughout which time the Christian religion has been shared by all nationalities. North Americans stopped fighting each other on any big scale 150 years ago and share a common religious tradition with the Europeans, as well as sharing one of the European languages. Europe and North America also share the concept and practices of 'westernisation', but there is still regular misunderstanding between the two continents as well as between individual European countries. Contrasts become even starker when one moves to Arab countries, to India, to China or to South East Asia. This is just an illustration of the diversity that international HRM has to encompass.

WINDOW ON PRACTICE

At the Irish manufacturing subsidiary of a French company there are problems if managers in the subsidiary are not competent in the native language of the parent company.

Only three of the five local senior managers speak French, with various degrees of proficiency. As many of the managers in France speak English, everyday contact between the two countries is reasonable for even the non-French speakers in Ireland. However, all the documentation, from technical forms to invoices, is in French so it is exceptionally difficult and often impossible for those who do not speak French to extract the full meaning and nuances of any written communication.

The biggest problem is at meetings in France, which are conducted entirely in French. All five senior managers have to travel frequently to these meetings but most of what is said is lost on the two who do not speak French and their input is minimal. The effect of this is that the two managers lose the respect of their colleagues and their authority and confidence are undermined, leading to some serious errors and to stress in situations where clear thinking and constant dialogue between the two countries are required.

Towards the end of the twentieth century there grew a concern about the ever-increasing significance of the multinational company as the means whereby individual economies are integrated into a global economy, with a small number of very large companies accounting for a disproportionately large number of the people in employment.

Globalisation has become a dirty word, sparking demonstrations and being blamed for many of the ills in the developing world, yet human resource management in any business has to contend with the human resource implications of globalisation. There is always an HRM dimension to any strategic initiative, and international moves perhaps present the strongest case for the HRM specialist to be involved at the beginning in formulating the overall approach, simply because the HRM implications and opportunities are not all immediately obvious.

International HRM is a particular type of decentralisation and expansion of the HR role. As an organisation increases its international activities, it inevitably steps up the degree of decentralisation, but internationalisation is not simply a form of decentralisation. It is the most complex form of decentralising operations and involves types of difference – language, culture, economic and political systems, legislative frameworks, management styles and conventions – that are not found in organisational growth and diversification that stays within national boundaries.

In these circumstances human resource management logically follows, as well as helping to shape, the strategic direction set by the financial, marketing and operational decisions. In practice there may be a different pattern, as HR often remains one of the last centralising forces because of the importance of such features of management as equity, order, consistency and control.

Decentralisation is needed to empower subsidiaries, so that they become autonomous units within a corporate family instead of being overseas subsidiaries of a parent company. Some features, like recruitment and industrial relations negotiations, are almost entirely decentralised, so that there is little need for a coordinated, centrally driven policy.

Integration is expansion of the HR role to achieve the necessary coordination so that the business remains whole. New features are added, like advanced schemes of remuneration for expatriate employees, new forms of communication to ensure the necessary 'corporate glue'. Although nearly all recruitment and selection is decentralised, a new activity will develop in the recruitment, selection and training for an elite corps of international managers.

ACTIVITY 4.2

In the website material for this chapter (*see* **www.pearsoned.co.uk/torrington**), in what ways would you expect the make-up of the reward package for Willem to be different from that of Charles, and why?

Another way of describing this is the concept of convergence and divergence, which was first introduced to organisation theory by Kerr and colleagues (1960). This describes the process of extending the principle of homogeneity across products and services throughout the business in order to achieve efficiency in management and consistency for the customer. Initially the focus was on mass production, using the term 'Fordism', coined in the United States to describe the economic philosophy that prosperity and high corporate profits can be achieved by high wages that allow the workers to purchase the output they produce.

Henry Ford improved mass production methods and developed the assembly line by 1910. He sold large numbers of inexpensive automobiles and made a fortune, while his employees became the highest paid factory workers in the world. This idealist approach carried negative implications and Braverman (1974, 1994) argued that the type of managerial control of the production process that was needed was achieved by mono-polising judgement, knowledge and decision making with the effect that workers lose control of their work, the knowledge and their skill. This was applied not only to manual workers, but to most white collar employees ('the new middle class') as well. Marxists Antonio and Bonanno (2000) traced the development of Fordism and subsequent eco-nomic stages to globalisation, emphasising routinised and intensified labour to promote production. This has underpinned some of the large-scale protests against meetings of G8 heads of state in recent years. As the epitome of what the protesters object to, Fordism has now turned into 'McDonaldisation', a description of the reach of stand-ardised products and services into every part of the globe. A management perspective on convergence is a little more benign:

> Where organisations possess a strong corporate culture seen as vital to maintaining competitive advantage, this is likely to be translated into standardisation of operating methods, work organisation and employment policies. Although terms of employment may be set locally, there may . . . be corporate co-ordination exercised according to over-arching guiding principles embedded in corporate values. (Lucas *et al.* 2006)

Despite the apparent managerial benefits of convergence, a more divergent approach is also widely practised, for two powerful reasons. One reason is cultural variation, which is explored shortly, the other is labour market considerations. National labour markets operate in quite different ways, due to different institutions, legal frameworks, labour market conventions and national political and social factors. The pan-European 'super-jumbo' Airbus 380 may revolutionise air travel or not, but it will certainly have a significant effect – if it is ever built. In February 2007 the parent company EADS had to postpone announcing details of its restructuring plans because Britain, France, Germany and Spain could not agree on how to share the work. EADS Chief Executive Louis Gallois expected to reveal how it planned to restructure to save around £3.4 billion over the next three years. Mr Gallois urged the four countries to reach an agreement quickly, saying the workforce 'are eager to know how the future of their company, together with their own future, is being shaped'.

This type of analysis is one framework for considering international human resource management. Other members of management may deal with aspects of takeover and merger, global computer systems, technology transfer and international investment, but HR specialists will be concerned with such matters as comparative pay rates, perform-ance assessment, employee voice in the business, employee relocation and expatriation, cultural variation and communication.

CULTURAL DIFFERENCES IN MANAGEMENT

The history of the European Union in attempting to establish a supranational institution is one of constant, but reluctant recognition of the stubbornness of national differences and the accentuation of regional differences among, for instance, the Basques, the Flemish and the Scottish. The cultural diversity and intensity of feeling on national issues in a close-knit and economically developed region like Western Europe indicates the significance of cultural difference on a global scale. Nationality is important in human resource management because of its effect on human behaviour and the consequent constraints on management action.

Some things that initially appear specific to a particular national culture turn out to be understood and welcomed in almost all cultures. Westernisation and globalisation are prime targets for international terrorism because of the cultural values that are seen to undermine the social cohesion of other cultures, as well as the apparent reluctance of western governments to change their colonial assumptions and interference in the internal affairs of other countries. Despite that widespread hostility Italian pizza has been adopted in most countries of the world, and the expansion has been largely brought about by Pizza Hut, which is owned by Pepsi-Cola, an American company known for a drink that has also gone to every corner of the globe. Who would have expected that Muscovites would daily queue up outside the largest McDonald's in the world until it was overtaken by the branch in Beijing? Few brands are more obviously global than Microsoft.

Newspapers and magazines in social democracies and socialist republics frequently devote more space in twelve months to the British Royal Family than to any other topic, despite the fact that the institution is utterly British and theoretically alien to their political systems. Countless millions every day follow the fortunes of some very ordinary people in the fictional Australian setting of Ramsey Street, Erinsborough, and even more watch association football. The wide international acceptability of these things could suggest that we are all members of the global village with converging tastes and values. Yet certain facets of national culture remain deeply rooted and have a way of undermining that argument.

> It is difficult to prove that any given language determines management behaviour in specific ways. Nevertheless, it seems incontestable that the French have developed their language as a precision tool for analysis and conceptualisation; that the Japanese use their language as an emollient for creating an atmosphere conducive to harmonious interaction; and that the Americans use their version of English as a store of snappy neologisms to excite, distract and motivate. (Holden 1992)

HR professionals in businesses with an international dimension have a job that is forcing them to be more internationally minded almost daily, yet they do not always realise the impacts of different national cultures on management practices.

Cultural diversity in management is so extensive that anyone's brain hurts when trying to comprehend it and then trying to remember the details. For example, to the European, Israel is in the Middle East and has a government. To the Malaysian, Israel is in West Asia and has a regime. The cultural range is so great that there is a danger of international managers operating simply at the level of caricature, folklore and trivia, such as learning how to present one's business card to a Japanese person, or what it means when a German takes his jacket off.

Hofstede

One approach to understanding the maze of cultural diversity is the classic study by Geert Hofstede, first published in 1980 and then re-visited in 1984, 1988 and 1991. As with any original piece of work it has been criticised, but it remains the most convincing analysis. One of his critics acknowledges:

> The importance and value of Hofstede's work cannot be overstated . . . the criticisms levelled against him are dwarfed by the strengths of [his] work in comparing cultures and applying cultural analysis to practical management problems . . . The four dimensions tap into deep cultural values and allow significant comparisons to be made across national cultures. To ignore his findings would be inexcusable. (Tayeb 2003, p. 71)

Hofstede (1980) analysed 116,000 questionnaires administered to employees of IBM in seventy different countries and concluded that national cultures could be explained by four key factors.

1 **Individualism** This is the extent to which people expect to look after themselves and their family only. The opposite is collectivism, which has a tight social framework and in which people expect to have a wider social responsibility to discharge because others in the group will support them. Those of a collectivist persuasion believe they owe absolute loyalty to their group.

2 **Power distance** This factor measures the extent to which the less powerful members of the society accept the unequal distribution of power. In organisations this is the degree of centralisation of authority and the exercise of autocratic leadership.

3 **Uncertainty avoidance** The future is always unknown, but some societies socialise their members to accept this and take risks, while members of other societies have been socialised to be made anxious about this and seek to compensate through the security of law, religion or technology.

4 **Masculinity** The division of roles between the sexes varies from one society to another. Where men are assertive and have dominant roles these values permeate the whole of society and the organisations that make them up, so there is an emphasis on showing off, performing, making money and achieving something visible. Where there is a larger role for women, who are more service oriented with caring roles, the values move towards concern for the environment and the quality of life, putting the quality of relationships before the making of money.

Hofstede found some clear cultural differences between nationalities. A sample of scores on the four criteria are in Table 4.1.

These findings were then compared with the large-scale British study of organisations carried out in the 1970s (Pugh and Hickson 1976) and some unpublished analysis of MBA students' work at INSEAD, which suggested that there were clusters of national cultures that coincided with different organisational principles, when Hofstede's results were plotted against two of his dimensions: uncertainty avoidance and power distance. Hofstede argues (1991, pp. 140–6) that countries emphasising large power distance and strong uncertainty avoidance were likely to produce forms of organisation that relied heavily on hierarchy and clear orders from superiors: **a pyramid of people**.

In countries where there is small power distance and strong uncertainty avoidance there would be an implicit form of organisation that relied on rules, procedures and clear structure: **a well-oiled machine**.

Criterion	High	Low
Power distance	Mexico Philippines Venezuela Yugoslavia	Austria Denmark Israel New Zealand
Uncertainty avoidance	Belgium Greece Japan Portugal	Denmark Hong Kong Singapore Sweden
Individualism	Australia Canada Great Britain United States	Colombia Pakistan Peru Venezuela
Masculinity	Austria Italy Japan Venezuela	Denmark Norway Sweden Yugoslavia

Table 4.1
Cultural differences between nations

The implicit model of organisation in countries with small power distance and weak uncertainty avoidance was a reliance on ad hoc solutions to problems as they arose, as many of the problems could be boiled down to human relations difficulties: **a village market**.

The picture is completed by the fourth group of countries where there is large power distance and weak uncertainty avoidance, where problems are resolved by constantly referring to the boss who is like a father to an extended family, so there is concentration of authority without structuring of activities. The implicit model of organisation here is: **the family**. Table 4.2 shows which countries are in the different segments.

So now we have a classification of cultural diversity that helps us. Table 4.2 tells us that the implicit form of organisation for Britain is a village market, for France it is a pyramid of people, for Germany it is a well-oiled machine and for Hong Kong it is a family. If we can understand the organisational realities and detail in those four countries, then this can provide clues about how to cope in Denmark, Ecuador, Austria or Indonesia because they each share the implicit organisational form and implicit organisational culture of one of the original four.

ACTIVITY 4.3

Identify your country and its type from those shown in Table 4.2. If it is not there, pick one with which you are familiar.

1 Do you agree with Hofstede's description of the type of organisation that is implicit?

2 Think of examples of how that implicit type of organisation affects HR activities.

It is not quite as easy as that, because the clusters show only relative similarities and, inevitably, other studies do not entirely agree with Hofstede (for example, Ronen and Shenkar 1985), but there is sufficient agreement for us to regard the four-way classification as useful, if not completely reliable, although all the research material was gathered in the 1970s: there may have been radical changes since then.

Pyramid of people	Well-oiled machine	Village market	Family
Arab-speaking	Austria	Australia	East Africa
Argentina	Costa Rica	Britain	Hong Kong
Belgium	Finland	Canada	Indonesia
Brazil	Germany	Denmark	India
Chile	Israel	Ireland	Jamaica
Colombia	Switzerland	Netherlands	Malaysia
Ecuador		New Zealand	Philippines
France		Norway	Singapore
Greece		South Africa	West Africa
Guatemala		Sweden	
Iran		United States	
Italy			
Japan			
Korea			
Mexico			
Pakistan			
Panama			
Peru			
Portugal			
Salvador			
Spain			
Taiwan			
Thailand			
Turkey			
Uruguay			
Venezuela			
Yugoslavia			

Table 4.2
Clusters of
countries

Hofstede's second book produces a refinement of the uncertainty avoidance dimension: 'Confucian dynamism', or long-term versus short-term orientation. Later he used the term 'time orientation' instead. Management researchers are typically from Western Europe or the United States, with all the cultural bias that such an orientation involves. Working with the Canadian Michael Bond, Hofstede used a Chinese value survey technique in a fresh study and uncovered a cultural variable that none of the original, western, questions had reached. This was long-term orientation, and the highest scoring countries on this dimension were China, Hong Kong, Taiwan, Japan and South Korea. Singapore was placed ninth. Leaving out the special case of China, we see that the other five countries are those known as the 'Five Dragons' because of their dramatic rate of economic growth in the 1980s.

Hofstede argues that countries in the West have derived their culture largely from the three religions of Judaism, Christianity or Islam, all of which are centred on the assertion of truth that is accessible to true believers, whereas none of the religions of the East are based on the assertion that there is a truth that a human community can embrace.

> They offer various ways in which a person can improve him/herself, however these do not consist in believing but in ritual, meditation, or ways of living . . . What one does is important. (ibid., p. 171)

The 'Confucian' values found attached to this long-term orientation included perseverance, clearly maintained status differentials, thrift, and having a sense of shame. In many ways these values are valuable for business growth, as they put social value on entre-preneurial initiative, support the entrepreneur by the willing compliance of others seeking a place in the system, encourage saving and investment, and put pressure on those who do not meet obligations.

This suggests that international companies should consider the location of some of their strategic activities in the East. This idea was reflected in a comment from an expert on international human resource issues:

> Philips is establishing centres of competence . . . their centre for long-range technology development was recently moved from the United States to the Far East, where the time orientation was seen as more conducive to innovation that the 'quick fix' mentality of North America. (Evans *et al.* 1989, p. 116)

More recently there has been the widespread phenomenon of western companies locating their call centres outside the host country. This has been most common in Anglophone countries which can take advantage of the extensive facility with English as a first or second language in many countries.

A movement in the opposite direction has been by Japanese manufacturing into rural locations in the USA:

> Honda in Maryville, Ohio; Nissan in Smyrna, Tennessee and Mazda in Flat Rock, Michigan. Tennessee is considered particularly attractive because of its similarities, being non-union, having higher than average US productivity, a strong work ethic, racial homogeneity, and using courtesy to resolve conflicts. (Schneider and Barsoux 2003, p. 55)

Hofstede's work ignores all the countries of Russia and Eastern Europe, as well as the Republic of China. The globalisation of management is now more real than at any time previously, but our understanding of how different cultures alter the HRM process is still slight.

From a strategic perspective cultural diversity has many implications for human resource management. Hodgetts and Luthans (1991, p. 36) have selected some of these where the culture of a society can directly affect management approaches.

1 **The centralisation of decision making** In some societies (especially the pyramid of people type) all important decisions are taken by a small number of managers in senior positions. In other societies (like the village markets) decision making is more decentralised. In a joint venture between two dissimilar societies, not only will these differences of approach need to be recognised, but management systems will have to enable members of the two cultures to understand each other and work together.

2 **Rewards and competition** The level of financial rewards between countries can be a problem, when those in country A appear to receive much more money than those in country B for doing the same job, but a more subtle difference is the way in which rewards are disbursed. In some instances there is a culture favouring individual

recognition, whilst elsewhere there is a convention of group rewards. Similarly some societies encourage competition rather than cooperation, and in others the reverse applies.

3 Risk As Hofstede demonstrated in his first study, attitudes towards taking risks are a clear discriminator between cultures, with marked variations of uncertainty avoidance.

4 Formality The well-oiled machine cultures place great emphasis on clear procedures and strict rules, while pyramid of people cultures emphasise clear hierarchies and observance of rank. This contrasts strongly with the village market type societies where relationships are more informal and ad hoc action more likely.

5 Organisational loyalty In Japan there tends to be a strong sense of loyalty to one's employer, while in Britain and the United States there is a growing sense of identification with one's occupational group, rather than with a particular employer. The long-standing importance of professional bodies and the declining long-term reliability of corporations to look after one's career development have increased this loyalty to one's occupation rather than to one's employer.

6 Short or long-term orientation Hofstede's identification of an eastern predilection for the long-term is beginning to influence strategic decisions on where to locate those organisational activities for which long-term thinking is particularly appropriate.

Table 4.2 gives us a rough guide to similarities between national cultures and the classification gives us some route markings through the cultural maze. We also have the long-term orientation of Confucian dynamism, which can guide thinking on a number of strategic issues in international management.

INTERNATIONAL COMMUNICATION AND COORDINATION

Communicating across geographical, ethnic and national boundaries is a major challenge for HR people. Brandt and Hulbert (1976) studied organisational feedback in a number of multinational companies that had their headquarters in Europe, Japan and the United States. They found that the American organisations had many more feedback reports and meetings between headquarters and subsidiaries than their European or Japanese counterparts. In contrast, Pascale (1978) found that Japanese managers in Japan used face-to-face contacts more than American managers as well as more upwards and lateral communication. Japanese managers in America used communication in the same way as Americans.

Some barriers to effective international communication

There are various ways in which expectation determines communication content and all can impair the accuracy of message transmission. Several of these – the frame of reference, stereotyping and cognitive dissonance – are explained in the Part 1 Focus on skills. Such problems are compounded by geographical distance, cultural differences and subtleties of language.

The clearest example of contrasted frames of reference is when international expansion is by the route of acquisition. Employees in the acquired company will feel a greater sense of community with each other than with those who have acquired them. They will see corporate affairs from their own standpoint and will tend to be cautious in their behaviour and suspicious in their interpretation of what they hear from their new owners. Every acquisition has this problem, but international acquisition is beset by particular problems.

Despite all attempts to forge a common identity, companies in different countries will take pride in their own accomplishments and informally disparage the accomplishments of other national groups. As long as this stimulates healthy competition, rivalry can benefit the business, but it quickly becomes destructive, like the situation of the car assembly plant in Britain which constantly rejected and returned gear boxes made by the same company in Germany. National boundaries produce distorted ideas about the 'other' people, whose achievements are underestimated and undervalued in comparison with the achievements of your own group, which may be overestimated.

Among the stereotypes allegedly held by Anglo-Saxons are that Germans are thorough and unimaginative, the French are romantic and obsessed with status, the Chinese all look the same, Americans are loud and brash, the English are reserved and aloof, Arabs are fatalists, Spaniards are haughty, and so on.

Our review of culture was partly an account of national stereotypes and exemplifies the problem: we need to understand general differences in behaviour and attitude that are rooted in cultural diversity, otherwise we will be misunderstood in what we say and will misinterpret what we hear, but we must avoid the trap of assuming that all nationals conform precisely to a single model. Not all the Irish are talkative and not all the Scots are mean.

In dealing with foreigners, some well-informed stereotyping can avoid initial offence and misunderstanding, but it must give way to more sensitive behaviour as the other person is evaluated and better understood.

Cognitive dissonance does more than lead to misunderstanding; it can also distort or inhibit action. Not only do recipients of information find it difficult to understand, remember and take action, they will also grapple with the dissonance that the problematical new information presents. One of the ways in which they do this is to distort the message so that what they actually hear is what they expect to hear and can easily understand rather than the difficult, challenging information that is being put to them.

There are frequent problems with *language*. In Shell International there used to be a term to describe the purpose of certain types of meeting as 'flocking', which is a wonderfully precise term to express the nature and purpose of those particular gatherings that take place, yet French and German people have great difficulty in understanding the nuances of the term, because neither language has an equivalent that distinguishes between, for example, flocking and herding.

The problem of jargon is where a word or a phrase has a specialised meaning that is immediately understandable by those in the know, but meaningless or misleading to those who do not share the specialised knowledge. The Maslow hierarchy of human needs is by now quite well known in management circles. On one occasion a lecturer was describing the ideas that were implicit in this notion and was surprised some months later in an examination script to see that one of the students had heard not 'hierarchy' but 'high Iraqui'. The unfamiliarity of the word 'hierarchy' had been completely misinterpreted by that particular student, who had imposed her own meaning on the words because of the need to make sense of what she heard. Professor Eugene McKinna relates how he was lecturing on the same subject of motivation, describing job enlargement and job enrichment. After the lecture a puzzled student asked him, 'what exactly was the job in Richmond?'

The value of jargon in international management is that the jargon quickly becomes universally understood by the experts, no matter what their nationality. Botany, Medicine and Chemistry are fields where a specialist can probably understand a technical paper no matter what the language may be. Sheet music is covered in Italian words that have no neat translation and no need for translation as they are universally understood by musicians. Management is moving in that direction, with PC, salaryman, JIT, QWL, TQM, WLB and all the new language of computing.

A quite different aspect of communication for HR people in international business is disseminating information and other messages within the organisation to help develop corporate culture, a sense of collaboration across national boundaries in order to integrate the business, with members of the different units in the business understanding, for instance, why a company has been acquired in South America, even though it seems to threaten the livelihood of some parts of the parent organisation. Comprehensive communication can raise awareness of the wider market and the opportunities that are waiting to be grasped.

There is a need for constant communication throughout the business to disseminate information and to sustain changing values. The organisation must operate holistically. It is not the sum of its parts: the whole exists in every part, like the human body. If you are ill a doctor can obtain information about your illness from any part of you. A sample of your blood or the taking of your temperature is just as good wherever it comes from. If you are to be protected against cholera, which attacks the intestines, you have an injection in your arm. If you are about to be shot in the chest, your entire body will shiver in fear.

When a company is operating internationally, one logical main channel for communication could be the workflow pattern. If a washing machine is produced by manufacturing electronic components in California, sub-assemblies and wiring harnesses in Korea and final assembly in Scotland, there is an easy sequence to follow. Job instructions, guidance notes, queries, telephone calls, specifications, requisitions, authorisations, order forms are some of the many ways in which groups of people communicate with those before and after them in the workflow, or critically adjacent to the process, like the HR people. Among the most effective international communicators are airlines, as their entire business is moving not only customers but also staff constantly across national boundaries to different organisational outposts of the business: the business activity creates the communications. All international businesses require centralised, coordinated communications to create a common purpose and to share ideas and benefits, but those that do not have a natural workflow link across national boundaries will have this need more highly developed.

The communications management challenge for international human resource management is at two extremes. At one is the personal behaviour and skill of individual people in making themselves understood, persuading others to do things, negotiating agreements with people from different cultural backgrounds, overcoming language barriers, appreciating different frames of reference and developing heightened sensitivity to varying behavioural norms and conventions. Communication is an individual activity, reflecting personal style and the HRM requirement is for cultural awareness and perhaps language training. In this type of communication the manager is a skilled solo performer.

The other extreme is impersonal and systemic, more concerned with channels of communication than with individual behaviour, and more concerned with systematic distribution of carefully chosen information and the organisation of communications opportunities. In this type of communication the manager metaphorically writes the score and then conducts the orchestra.

Although the forms of communication are so different, they are also linked. Organisational communication is only as good as the quality of interpersonal communication that is taking place.

> consistent patterns of interaction begin to develop when a group of individuals, in response to certain characteristics and needs of the environment, create a system of patterned activities for the accomplishment of a specific task. The process by which these relationships are formed and maintained is interpersonal communication.
> (Baskin and Aronoff 1980, p. 7)

It is not practicable for employees to develop confidence in a communications system; they can only acquire confidence in what the system produces and in those other members of the organisation with whom they interact. That confidence is built by the substance of what people say and do, but also by a climate in which people feel encouraged to express ideas, make suggestions and question decisions they cannot understand. Communications and behaviour are so closely interlinked that everything influencing behaviour also influences communication.

Coordination

Managers working internationally give themselves major problems of coordination by adopting measures that they see as necessary for business success. On the one hand they have to encourage diversity of local action, so that what is done fits local circumstances. On the other hand their global thinking requires careful coordination as the way to synergy, so that the global business does more and better together than it could possibly achieve as a number of independent units.

Bartlett and Ghoshal (1989) described three conventional approaches to coordination that were used, stemming from the nationality of the parent company, the Japanese, the American and the European.

Japanese centralisation

The typical Japanese approach is for a strong headquarters group to keep for themselves all major decisions and frequently to intervene in the affairs of overseas subsidiaries. This appears to stem from their difficulty in dealing with foreigners:

> a major strategic challenge for Japanese firms is to accept that non-Japanese must somehow be given more direct responsibility and opportunity for promotion within the company at local level . . . there has to be letting-go from the centre. But this is no easy thing. For companies must overcome severe impediments associated with wariness, distrust and lack of knowledge about the world beyond Japan. (Holden 1994, p. 127)

American formalisation

The American approach is described as formalisation. Power is vested not in headquarters or in the managers of local companies, but in formal systems, policies and standards, so that it is the systems that drive the business. Many American businesses went international at the time that the use of control systems was being rapidly developed to cope with the large size of the businesses. The idea of delegation and holding others accountable by means of extensive computerised information systems seemed eminently suitable for operating the increasing number of overseas units, especially when one remembers the apparent unpopularity of overseas postings among American managers (e.g. Tung and Miller 1990).

European socialisation

In European companies the approach to coordination is described as socialisation. There has been a reliance on key, highly skilled and trusted individuals. These people were carefully selected and developed a detailed understanding of the company's objectives and methods. Their personal development included the establishment of close working relationships and mutual understanding with colleagues. Once groomed these key decision-makers were despatched to manage the subsidiaries, so that the headquarters and the subsidiaries were both strengthened.

> because it relies on shared values and objectives, it represents a more robust and flexible means of co-ordination. Decisions reached by negotiations between knowledgeable groups with common objectives should be much better than those made by superior authority or by standard policy. (Bartlett and Ghoshal 1989, p. 163)

These three different approaches worked best for companies headquartered in those three regions of the globe. As the world becomes smaller and companies become more diverse, with subsidiaries that are fully mature, more sophisticated methods are needed: companies are not international, but global. The influence of the parent company's national culture remains strong, but there is a cosmopolitan tendency gradually blurring some of the traditional boundaries. Before getting too excited about this we should remember the post-Hofstede research of Laurent (1989) that differences in values and beliefs tend to survive the growing homogeneity of business practices. He showed that French and American managers working in the same division of a large US oil company expressed more diverse views about the role of managers than French and American managers from different companies.

Increasing the range of coordination methods

Any management will benefit from considering additional methods of coordination. Some of our suggestions will fit well with their current practice, adding to their strength; others will not yet seem suitable, others will not seem suitable at all.

The first suggestion is summed up by using the word *evangelisation*, to describe winning the acceptance throughout the business of a common mission and a shared purpose. The need to win hearts and minds has been a thread in management thinking for many years, but it is particularly significant in the international or global business because of the number of barriers to be overcome in coordination, especially the barriers of language, culture, national boundaries and parochial self-interest. It is a remarkable management team who, for instance, will be able to commit themselves with enthusiasm to closing down their local operation on the grounds that the business as a whole will benefit if an operation in another country is developed instead.

Coordination by evangelisation works through **shared belief**. The beliefs may be interpreted in different ways and may produce varied behaviours, but there is the attempt to spread relatively simple doctrines to which members of the business subscribe and through which they are energised. Some readers of this book will have learned their catechism as children, or will know the Gettysburg Address by heart. Although this may seem inappropriate to the business world, in the 1970s a British company, Vitafoam, was established by a man who required his senior executives to copy out his annual policy statement by hand, three times, before handing it back to him. It is now common-place for companies to have mission statements, which come close to being unifying articles of faith.

Evangelisation also works through **parables**. We all love a good story and we learn from the message that the stories convey. Ed Schein (2004, pp. 237–42) identified 'stories and legends' as one of the key mechanisms for articulating and reinforcing the organisation's culture. The company house magazine partly serves the purpose of circulating the good news about heroic deeds in all parts of the company network. Better are the word of mouth exchanges and accounts of personal experience. Those who visit another country have to be fully exploited when they return. Returning expatriates have stories to tell to all members of the company to which they are coming back, not just to the senior managers conducting the debriefing. There are many problems in repatriation, but one of the best ways of getting re-established is to share one's overseas experience widely, with as many people as possible, covering the full range of their experiences. Occasional visitors to other branches of the business also need to be encouraged to tell their stories. They return with important technical understandings that need to be shared, but they also return with an awareness of the visited company which can contribute to the bonding between units. On a tedious flight between Istanbul and Singapore, an Australian businesswoman spent over an hour sorting through a large number of holiday snaps, explaining that she regarded them as the most important present she could bring back. Her male colleagues brought back photographs of machine parts, warehouse layout, operational equipment and production processes. These were used at important debriefing sessions with fellow managers. She brought back pictures of people and places, of food and mealtimes, of cluttered offices and what was put up on the office walls. These were handed round and explained in casual encounters over coffee, on the way to and from meetings and at dinner parties.

Evangelisation can use **apostles**, ambassadors sent out to preach the faith. These are those management role holders who are constantly on the move. Because of their frequent movement they know the worldwide organisation well and can describe one component to another, explaining company policy, justifying particular decisions and countering parochial thinking. They can also move ideas around ('In Seoul they are wondering about . . . what do think?') and help in the development of individual networks ('Try getting in touch with Oscar Jennings in Pittsburgh . . . he had similar problems a few weeks ago').

At times of crisis, apostles are likely to be especially busy, countering rumour and strengthening resolve. In mature companies apostles will have home bases in different regions, just as expatriates will move in various directions and not simply from the centre out, but before the business reaches maturity it will probably be important that most of the apostles come from headquarters and have personally met, and can tell stories about, the founder.

ACTIVITY 4. 4

From your own working experience what examples have you seen of evangelisation, parables and apostles as methods of coordination?

Coordination can be improved by the development and promulgation of *standards and norms*. Many British companies have sought the accreditation of BS 5750, the British Standard for quality, others claim to be equal opportunity employers. Global companies will wish to set standards for many aspects of their operation. Cynthia Haddock (1992) describes how Shell develop and maintain standards relating to alcohol and drug abuse. If standards are adopted throughout a global company, they become a form of coordination. Furthermore it is not necessary for all of them to be developed at the centre. Decentralised standard formulation can enable different parts of the global business to take a lead as a preliminary to universal adoption of the standard they have formulated: an excellent method of integration.

Few businesses will be able to develop universally applicable standards in all aspects of human resource management. Many manufacturing developments in Asia have occurred for the explicit reason that the area enables organisations to enjoy the benefits of low labour costs. It is most unlikely that the American/European/Japanese parent company would develop a company-wide standard on the level of pay rates in manufacturing. In contrast a company-wide standard set of terms and conditions for expatriate assignment would be much more feasible.

There is obvious scope for coordination through *systems*. Many global businesses are dominated by a single system, which reaches every part of the business. Any international airline has a ticketing and booking system which links thousands of computer terminals in order to operate the airline. The system is only useful if it provides the global link, and provision of the systems link constantly reinforces with all personnel the interrelationship of the airline's activities in all countries where it operates. Although that is a specialised example, all businesses have systems and they can be developed to avoid duplication and overlap, so that in one country a team develops a spare part retrieval system that is quickly adopted for use throughout the business, while in another country they concentrate on an aspect of accounting procedures or systematic advice on training opportunities.

A similar approach is to concentrate *capability* by encouraging the development of particular expertise in different locations, but for group-wide application and exploitation. Bartlett and Ghoshal (1989, p. 106) offer the intriguing example of how Teletext was developed by Philips. Because of an interest from the BBC, the British Philips subsidiary began work on the possibility of transmitting text and simple diagrams through a domestic television set. Within Philips generally it was regarded as 'a typical British toy – quite fancy but not very useful'. Despite little encouragement and sales that were initially disappointing, the British persisted. Ten years after starting work, there were three million Teletext receivers in use in Britain and Philips had established a world lead in a product for which there was initially only a British market.

SUMMARY PROPOSITIONS

4.1 International human resource management is a subject that still lacks an accepted definition and content. A central feature is convergence or divergence in HR policy and practice.

4.2 Much international management activity is through multinational companies and their policies of globalisation.

4.3 Understanding cultural diversity is crucial. Work by Hofstede has identified four distinguishing factors of national culture: individualism, power distance, uncertainty avoidance and masculinity. He later added a fifth: Confucian dynamism or time orientation.

4.4 Hofstede also concluded that organisations within certain cultures had one of four dominant value systems, so that they would resemble a pyramid of people, a well-oiled machine, a village market or a family.

4.5 Problems of communication in any international business are made more difficult by different frames of reference, stereotyping, cognitive dissonance and language.

4.6 Traditional forms of coordination can be roughly stereotyped as Japanese centralisation, American formalisation or European socialisation.

4.7 More particular forms of coordination include evangelisation, standards and norms, systems and locating capability.

GENERAL DISCUSSION TOPICS

1 Multinational companies tend to be unpopular with social activists, who mount demonstrations against their apparent greed and serious impact on some of the societies in which they operate. What are the arguments for and against this point of view?

2 Can an HRM manager from one culture carry out a line management role working in a different culture?

3 Have you come across examples of American formalisation, Japanese centralisation and European socialisation? How do they conflict? What is the practical implication of these variations?

FURTHER READING

Tayeb, M. (2003) *International Management: Theories and Practices*. Harlow: Prentice Hall. This provides a recent general treatment of international management. It has five chapters on culture, two on communication and three on managing employees in different cultures and contains a very well-informed chapter on international HRM by P.S. Budhwar.

Trompenaars, F. and Hampden-Turner, C. (1998) *Riding the Waves of Culture: Understanding Cultural Diversity in Business*, 2nd edn. New York: McGraw-Hill.

This is a major work on culture. It sets out the findings of the authors' extensive research, but also includes much practical advice.

Dowling, P.J., Welch, D.E. and Schuler, R.S. (1999) *International Dimensions of Human Resource Management*. Cincinnati: South Western College Publishing.
Texts on international human resource management are very varied and usually selective, and concentrate on one or two aspects at the expense of others (like this chapter). One exception is this book.

Lucas, R., Lupton, B. and Mathieson, H. (2006) *Human Resource Management in an International Context*. London: CIPD.
This is a valuable recent edited text on international HRM.

Mead, R. (1990) *Cross-Cultural Management Communication*. Chichester: Wiley.
This is useful on communication.

Smethurst, S. (2006) 'Worldly Pursuit', *People Management*, 29 June, pp. 40–3.
This describes some of the courses available in international management.

CIPD guide, *International Management Development*.
This can be downloaded from **www.cipd.co.uk/training/td/MLD**.

WEB LINKS

The International Labour Organisation is at **www.ilo.org**

Another international body is the World Federation of Personnel Management Associations at **www.wfpma.com**

A selection of national bodies is:

Australian Human Resources Institute at **www.ahri.com.au**

British Chartered Institute of Personnel and Development at **www.cipd.co.uk**

Hong Kong Institute of Human Resource Management at **www.hkihrm.org**

Japanese Society for Human Resource Management at **www.jshrm.org**

United States Society for Human Resource Management at **www.shrm.org**

REFERENCES

Antonio, R.J. and Bonanno, A. (2000) 'A New Global Capitalism? From "Americanism and Fordism" to "Americanization-globalization",' *American Studies*, Vol. 41, Nos 2–3, pp. 33–77.
Bartlett, C.A. and Ghoshal, S. (1989) *Managing Across Borders*. London: Random House.
Baskin, O.W. and Aronoff, C.E. (1980) *Interpersonal Communication in Organizations*. Santa Monica, California: Goodyear Publishing.
Beardwell, I. *et al.* (2004) *Human Resource Management: A Contemporary Approach*. Harlow, England: Prentice Hall.
Brandt, W.K. and Hulbert, J.M. (1976) 'Patterns of Communication in the Multinational Company', *Journal of International Business Studies*, Spring, pp. 57–64.
Braverman, H. (1974) *Labour and Monopoly Capital: the Degradation of Work in the Twentieth Century*. New York: Monthly Review Press.
Braverman, H. (1994) 'The Making of the US Working Class', *Monthly Review*, November.
Dowling, P.J., Welch, D.E. and Schuler, R.S. (1999) *International Dimensions of Human Resource Management*. Cincinnati: South Western College Publishing.
Evans, P., Doz, Y., Laurent, A. (1989) *Human Resource Management in International Firms*. London: Macmillan.

Glanz, E. and Hirsch, M.S. (2006) 'Leading in the Level Playing Field', *People Management*, 6 April, p. 54.

Haddock, C. (1992) 'How Shell's Organisation and HR Practices Help it to be Both Global and Local', in Torrington, D.P., *International Human Resource Management*. London: Prentice Hall International.

Hodgetts, R.M. and Luthans, F. (1991) *International Management*. New York: McGraw-Hill.

Hofstede, G. (1980) *Culture's Consequences: International Differences in Work-Related Values*. Beverly Hills, California: Sage Publications.

Hofstede, G. (1991) *Cultures and Organizations: Software of the Mind*, London: McGraw-Hill.

Holden, N.J. (1992) 'Management Language and Euro-Communications: 1992 and Beyond', in Berry, M. (ed.) *Cross-Cultural Communication in Europe*. Proceedings of Conference on Cross-Cultural Communication, Helsinki. Turku: Institute for European Studies.

Holden, N.J. (1994) 'NEC: International HRM with Vision', in Torrington, D.P., *International Human Resource Management*. London: Prentice Hall International.

Kerr, C., Dunlop, J., Myers, C. and Harbison, F. (1960) *Industrialisation and Industrial Management*. Boston, Massachusetts: Harvard University Press.

Laurent, A. (1989) 'A cultural view of organisational change', in P. Evans, Y. Doz and A. Laurent (eds) *Human Resource Management in International Firms*. London: Macmillan.

Lucas, R., Lupton, B. and Mathieson, H. (2006) *Human Resource Management in an International Context*. London: CIPD.

Mead, R. (1990) *Cross-Cultural Management Communication*. Chichester: Wiley.

Pascale, R.T. (1978) 'Communication and Decision Making Across Cultures: Japanese and American Comparisons', *Administrative Science Quarterly*, March, pp. 91–110.

Pugh, D.S. and Hickson, D.J. (1976) *Organisational Structure in its Context*. Farnborough: Saxon House.

Ronen, S. and Shenkar, O. (1985) 'Clustering Countries on Attitudinal Dimensions: A Review and Synthesis', *Academy of Management Review*, Vol. 10, No. 3, pp. 435–54.

Schein, E.H. (2004) *Organizational Culture and Leadership*. San Francisco: Jossey-Bass.

Schneider, S.C. and Barsoux, J.-L. (2003) *Managing Across Cultures*, 2nd edn. Harlow, England: Pearson Education.

Tayeb, M. (2003) *International Management: Theories and Practices*. Harlow, England: Prentice Hall.

Trompenaars, F. and Hampden-Turner, C. (1998) *Riding the Waves of Culture: Understanding Cultural Diversity in Business*, 2nd edn. New York: McGraw-Hill.

Tung, R.L. and Miller, E.L. (1990) 'Managing in the Twenty-first Century: The Need for Global Orientation', *Management International Review*, Vol. 30, 1990/1991, pp. 5–18.

An extensive range of additional materials, including multiple choice questions, answers to questions and links to useful websites can be found on the Human Resource Management Companion Website at **www.pearsoned.co.uk/torrington**. On the website there is also some material about managing the cosmopolitans, which explains the different types of international employee.

INTERACTIVE SKILL 1: FACE-TO-FACE SKILLS

It is not by luck that the most successful self-help book ever published, Dale Carnegie's *How to Win Friends and Influence People*, sold no fewer than 16,000,000 copies over seventy years. The ability to influence people is an ambition of most human beings and is fundamental to HR management. Professor Tom Lupton was the second Director of Manchester Business School and a distinguished industrial relations academic. On one occasion he was addressing the national conference of the Institute of Personnel Management on the importance of personnel people being involved in strategy because, 'otherwise all you have left is selling it to the lads'. Yet that is precisely where skill is really needed: not working out what to do, but getting people to share that understanding and then making it happen. The latest theoretical explanation of this is in the concept of social intelligence (Goldman 2006). The core expertise of HR specialists is skill in interaction and handling of face-to-face situations effectively is essential throughout human resource management. As well as being articulate and receptive in any face-to-face situation, HR specialists need to develop their skills in various types of encounter.

The recruiter has to be effective in the highly specialised interaction of the selection interview, where the task is to find out relevant information about an applicant on which to base a judgement as to whether or not that person would match the skills, experience and attitudes required in the job to be filled. That information will only come from an applicant who has confidence in the interviewer's integrity and who volunteers the information, responding willingly and helpfully to the questions that are posed.

The industrial relations manager, in contrast, needs to be an effective negotiator, explaining a position that those on the other side of the table may not appreciate and who have themselves a position which the industrial relations manager may not appreciate. Common ground has to be established, differences clarified and possibilities for reconciling those differences explored.

Both interactions have things in common, but they require different skills. Each Part of this book is rounded up by focusing on an interaction central to the theme of the Part. Understanding that interaction helps with understanding the other activities that have been reviewed.

Our objectives in this introductory Focus on skills are to:

1 Explain what makes for effectiveness in interaction

2 Explain the different types of interaction

3 Review the fundamental skills of (a) setting the tone, (b) listening, (c) questioning and (d) feedback

There is also a brief case study, typical examination questions and some suggested weblinks.

Effectiveness in interaction

In the remainder of this Focus on skills we concentrate on methods, including the need to understand non-verbal behaviour. We all reveal our feelings by what we do as well as in what we say. Someone blushing is obviously embarrassed and someone crying is clearly distressed, but there are a host of other signs or *tells* that indicate what a person is feeling. The person who is able to read these signals has a great advantage in interactions. The term 'tell' comes from the study of poker players, who are as anxious to conceal their own hand as they are to guess what is in someone else's (Caro 1994). It is an interesting feature of human behaviour that we all lie when we think it will help us socially. Those of you who are outraged by that comment because of your personal honesty and integrity, remember the word 'socially' in the above sentence. As H.G. Wells said a century ago:

> The social contract is . . . a vast conspiracy of human beings to lie and humbug themselves and one another for the general good. Lies are the mortar that bind the savage individual man into the social masonry. (*Love and Mr Lewisham*, 1900)

A contemporary, albeit light-hearted, treatment of this need to lie in order to maintain the fabric of social relationships is in King (2007).

Effective face-to-face people are likely to have some basic qualities. *Poise* enables a person to be at ease in a wide variety of social situations, often enjoying them, and able to talk with different types of people in a relaxed and self-confident way. This self-confidence comes partly from the feedback of willing responses constantly provided by other people.

Another element of poise is knowing what you are talking about, so we demonstrate our poise much more in situations with which we are familiar than we do in strange circumstances. There is less fear of what the other may say and less apprehension about appearing naive. Questions, and even criticism, are easier to deal with and are often wanted, so stimulating the interchange.

Poise is often associated with maturity, due to a person having succeeded in developing a rounded view of themselves without feeling too much anxiety about the possible adverse opinions of others. The process of acquiring poise can be accelerated by the experience of meeting a variety of people from differing backgrounds.

A necessary adjunct to poise is the quality of being *responsive* to the needs, feelings and level of understanding in other people. This prevents poise from becoming too egocentric. The teacher, for instance, will be looking for signs of misunderstanding in the student so that the message can be restated or clarified, and the market research interviewer will be looking for signals that the question has been accurately construed, or that it needs elaboration. Responsiveness can also include offering rewards, like friendliness, warmth, sympathy and helpfulness as features of general style or as part of a relationship with other participants. These not only sustain and strengthen the relationship, but may also be held back as a means of trying to get one's own way.

There are certain general problems that impair effectiveness. They mostly concern ways in which people tend to hear what they expect to hear rather than what they are being told.

The *frame of reference* is the standpoint from which a person views an issue, and understanding of the issue will be shaped by that perspective rather than any abstract 'reality'. It is a set of basic assumptions or standards that frame our behaviour. These are developed through childhood conditioning, through social background, education and through our affiliations. Differences in the frames of reference held by participants in interactions present inescapable problems. Can Israelis and Arabs ever really understand each other? How can those who manage and direct ever appreciate the point of view of those who are managed and directed?

The frame of reference on any particular matter is largely determined by opinions developed within a group with which we identify, as few of us alter our opinions alone. We both follow and help to shape opinion in our group, and most of us are in a number of such reference groups. Because of this, complexities arise: some people can be vociferously anti-union as citizens and voters in general elections, yet support a union of which they are members at their workplace.

The *stereotype* is the standardised expectation we have of those who have certain dominant characteristics: typical stereotypes are that all Scots are mean, all shop stewards are disruptive, women are more caring than men, and that men are more aggressive than women. The behaviour of some people in a category makes us expect all in that category to behave in the same way. This is obviously invalid, but is a tendency to which we are prone. We must always listen to what people are actually saying to us rather than hearing what we think a person of that type *would say*.

Making use of stereotypes is necessary at the start of working relationships; it is not feasible to deal with every individual we meet as being a void until we have collected enough information to know how to treat them, so we always try to find a pigeon-hole in which to put someone. We begin conversations with a working stereotype, so that, for example, we stop someone in the street to ask directions only after we have selected a person who looks intelligent and sympathetic. If we are giving directions to a stranger we begin our explanation having made an assessment of their ability to understand quickly, or their need for a more detailed, painstaking explanation. The stereotype becomes a handicap only when we remain insensitive to new information enabling us to develop a fuller and more rational appraisal of the individual with whom we are interacting.

Being aware of the dangers of stereotyping others, and trying to exercise self-discipline, can reduce the degree to which you misunderstand other people, but you still have the problem that your respondents will put *you* into a stereotype and hear what you say in accordance with whatever their predetermined notion may be.

Cognitive dissonance is the difficulty we all have in coping with behaviour that is not consistent with our beliefs. Such behaviour will make us uncomfortable and we will try to cope with the dissonance in various ways in order to reduce the discomfort. Either we persuade ourselves that we believe in what we are doing, or we avoid the necessary behaviour. We all interpret or decode words that we hear in order to make sense of them. If we decode the words we hear in a way that does not agree with what we believe, then we tend to reinterpret them in a way that we can believe.

Different types of interaction

Meetings are needed to make decisions, to overcome misunderstanding and to develop ideas. Interviews are used for selection, discipline, appraisal, counselling, problem solving and grievance handling. Managers 'put things across' in selling, persuasion, presentation and negotiation.

It is helpful to group interactions into four broad types: enquiry, exposition, joint problem solving and conflict resolution, as indicated in Figure 1.1.

Enquiry is that group of situations where the HR specialist needs to find things out from someone else, with the selection interview being the classic example. What needs to be found out may be factual information, attitudes, feelings, levels of understanding or misunderstanding. The main skill is in types of questioning.

Enquiry	**Exposition**
Selection	Presentation
Attitude survey	Lecture
Health screening	Briefing
Joint problem solving	**Conflict resolution**
Appraisal	Negotiation
Counselling	Arbitration
Discipline	Mediation

Figure 1.1
Four categories
of interaction

Exposition is almost the direct opposite. Instead of finding things out, the HR person is trying to convey information, to develop in the other person a level of knowledge and understanding, acceptance of an argument or agreement with a proposition. Although some questioning is often an integral part of exposition, the main skill is in clear articulation, fluency, good organisation of material and effective illustration.

Joint problem solving is a different type of activity as it involves developing an exchange in which both parties work together to unravel a problem or understand a situation which neither fully understands beforehand. It is not one person transferring an 'answer' to another, but both trying to understand together something which they can only partly understand alone. The skills involve some questioning and explanation, but also careful listening and feedback.

Joint problem solving assumes that both parties trust each other and see a common interest in helping the other. *Conflict resolution* begins without that mutual confidence, as the parties have interests that inevitably conflict and they are not likely fully to trust each other. The skills here are first those of presentation and then listening, questioning and feedback.

A very specialised skill is that of *chairing*, which is dealt with at the end of the book.

Fundamental skills in setting the tone

Any interaction begins by someone setting the tone of what is to follow. A shop assistant who says, 'Can I help you', or the strangely common, 'Are you all right *there*?' is trying to set a tone of knowledgeable helpfulness to a customer that might eventually result in a sale. It is the inclusion of the apparently superfluous 'there' that is puzzling. Of course you are there; where else would you be? Presumably the reason is to make the question less blunt, avoiding the implication that you are not all right. The HR specialist will set the tone of a selection interview, for instance, by explaining what is to happen and providing other contextual information that will enable the candidate to engage in the process constructively. There will also be a process of conveying more subtle messages to say, 'I'm in charge; I know what I'm doing; you can trust me'. In other interactions the way of setting the tone is different, but some features are common:

- Speak first.
- Smile, looking confident and relaxed (much easier said than done).
- Have brief, harmless exchanges that enable the parties to speak to each other without the answers mattering (weather, travel problems, etc.), but always react appropriately to answers.
- Explain your understanding of what is to happen.
- Check that that is understood and accepted.

Fundamental skills in listening

Tone of voice

Different feelings express themselves in different voice characteristics. Possible meanings for various characteristics are tabulated overleaf:

97

Characteristic	Probable meaning
Monotone voice	Boredom
Slow speed, low pitch	Depression
High voice, emphasis	Enthusiasm
Ascending tone	Astonishment
Abrupt speech	Defensiveness
Terse speed, loud tone	Anger
High pitch, drawn-out speech	Disbelief

Giving attention

Inclining the body towards the other person is a signal of attentiveness, so our posture should be inclined forward and facing the other squarely with an open posture: folded arms can be inhibiting.

Eye contact is crucial to good listening, but is a subtle art:

> Effective eye contact expresses interest and a desire to listen. It involves focusing one's eyes softly on the speaker and occasionally shifting the gaze from his face to other parts of the body, to a gesturing hand, for example, and then back to the face and then to eye contact once again. Poor eye contact occurs when a listener repeatedly looks away from the speaker, stares at him constantly or blankly, or looks away as soon as the speaker looks at the listener. (Bolton 1987, p. 36)

The distinction between 'focusing one's eyes softly' and staring is vital, though difficult to describe, and competence in eye contact is never easy to establish. It is one of the most intimate ways of relating to a person and many managers fear that the relationship may become too close.

We also show *physical responses* in our attentiveness. First we have to avoid distracting the other person by physical behaviour that is unrelated to what is being said; fiddling with a pen, playing with car keys, scrutinising our fingernails, wringing our hands, brushing specks of dust off our sleeves are a few typical behaviours that indicate inattention. Skilled listeners not only suppress these, they also develop minor gestures and posture variants that are directly responsive to what the other is saying.

Being silent helps you to listen by providing space for incoming messages, but it also provides opportunities to observe the other person and to think about what is being said. Most people are uncomfortable with silence and try to fill it with inconsequential chat, but this interferes with listening. Silence still has to be attentive and the longer the silence, the harder it is to be attentive: think of the last lecture you attended and how hard it was to maintain attentiveness.

Fundamental skills in questioning

Closed questions seek precise, terse information and are useful when you want clear, straightforward data. Most encounters feature closed questioning at some point.

Open-ended questions avoid terse replies by inviting respondents to develop their opinions without the interviewer prescribing what the answer should be. The question does little more than introduce a topic to talk about. The main purpose of such questions is to obtain the type of deeper information that the closed question misses, as the shape of the answer is not predetermined by the questioner. You are informed not simply by the content of the answers, but by what is selected and emphasised.

Indirect questions take an oblique approach on a difficult matter. A blunt 'Did you like that job?' almost suggests you didn't, or at least raises the suspicion that the interviewer thinks you didn't; it is a bit like the shop assistant avoiding being too blunt. Put indirectly as 'What gave you the most satisfaction in that job?' it has the merit of concentrating on the work rather than the person.

The *probe* is a form of questioning to obtain information that the respondent is trying to conceal. When the questioner becomes aware that the respondent is doing so he or she has to make an important, and perhaps difficult, decision: whether to respect the candidate's unwillingness and let the matter rest, or to persist with the enquiry. Reluctance is quite common in selection interviews where a candidate may wish to gloss over an aspect of the recent employment history. The most common sequence for the probe takes the following form: (a) direct questions, replacing the more comfortable open-ended approach ('What were you doing in the first six months of 2006?'). Careful phrasing may avoid a defensive reply, but those skilled at avoiding unwelcome enquiries may still deflect the question, leading to (b) supplementaries, which reiterate the first question with different phrasing ('Yes, I understand about that period. It's the first part of 2006 that I'm trying to get clear: after you came back from Belgium and before you started with Amalgamated Widgets'). Eventually this should produce the information the questioner needs. (c) Closing. If the information has been wrenched out like a bad tooth and the interviewer looks horrified or sits in stunned silence, then the candidate will feel badly put down. The interviewer needs to make the divulged secret less awful than the candidate had feared, so that the interview can proceed with reasonable confidence ('Yes, well you must be glad to have that behind you'). It may be that the interviewer will feel able to develop the probe by developing the answer by a further question such as 'And how did that make you feel?' or 'And how did you react to that? It must have been a terrible blow.' It is only reasonable to do this if the resultant exchange adds something useful to the questioner's understanding of the client: simple nosiness is not appropriate.

WINDOW ON (MAL) PRACTICE

One rather dubious version of the probe is to offer an exaggerated explanation for something being avoided. In the imaginary situation described above the selector might do this:

Selector: Yes, I understand about that period. It's the first part of 2006 that I'm trying to get clear: after you came back from Belgium and before you started with Amalgamated Widgets. You weren't in prison or anything, were you?

Candidate: Oh no. I had a nervous breakdown.

The explanation offered by the selector is so appalling that the candidate rushes to offer a less appalling explanation. This is not recommended, but it is interesting to know about. It might happen to you one day.

Some common lines of questioning should be avoided because they can produce an effect that is different from what is intended.

Leading questions ('Would you agree with me that . . . ?') will not necessarily produce an answer that is informative, but an answer in line with the lead that has been given.

Multiple questions give the candidate too many inputs at one time ('Could you tell me something of what you did at university, not just the degree, but the social and sporting side as well, and why you chose to backpack your way round the world? You didn't travel on your own, did you?'). This sort of questioning is sometimes adopted by interviewers who are trying very hard to efface themselves and let the respondent get on with the talking. However helpful the interviewer intends to be, the effect is that the candidate will usually forget the later parts of the question, feel disconcerted and ask, 'What was the last part of the question?' By this time the interviewer has also forgotten, so they are both embarrassed.

Taboo questions are those that do not respect the reasonable personal privacy of the other person. Some questions have to be avoided, especially in selection interviews, as they could be interpreted as biased. It is at least potentially discriminatory, for instance, to ask women how many children they have and what their husbands do for a living. Questions about religion or place of birth should also be avoided. Some questions may do no more than satisfy the idle curiosity of the questioner. If there is no point in asking them, they should not be put.

Fundamental skills in feedback

As well as listening, it is necessary to provide feedback to demonstrate that you have received and understood what you are being told.

In *reflection*, the listener picks up and re-states the content of what has just been said. In a difficult situation the listener picks out the emotional overtones of a statement and 'reflects' them back to the respondent without any attempt to evaluate them. The interviewer expresses neither approval nor disapproval, neither sympathy nor condemnation.

At a more prosaic level, there is *summary and re-run* to show you are listening and providing the opportunity for any misunderstanding to be pointed out. In appraisal, for instance, the respondent will produce lots of information in an interview and you will be selecting that which is to be retained and understood. From time to time you interject a summary sentence or two with an interrogative inflection. This shows that you are listening, gives the respondent the chance to correct any false impressions and reinforces the key points that are being retained. It is also a useful way of making progress, as the interjection is easily followed by another open-ended question – 'Now perhaps we can turn to . . .'.

The standard method in both reflection and summary is *paraphrasing*, by which the listener states the essence of what has been said. This is done concisely, giving the speaker a chance to review what has been said and, perhaps, to correct it.

We all respond positively when a listener shows *interest* in what is being said. If it is possible also to agree with what is being said, the reinforcement of the respondent will be greater.

The most common form of *affirmation* in feedback is the head nod, and many public speakers look for head nods (not to be confused with nodding off) as a way of judging the supportive mood of the audience. Other ways of affirming involve the use of the eyes. These are too subtle and individual to describe, but we each have a repertoire of signals to indicate such reactions as encouragement, surprise and understanding. When the eyes are part of a smile, there will be stronger reward to the talker. There are also words and phrases: 'Really?' 'Go on . . .', 'Yes . . .', 'Of course . . .', 'My word . . .', 'You were saying . . .'.

Interaction contains a variety of noises that are ways of feeding back to the other party. They are impossible to reproduce in words but are usually variations of a theme of 'Mmm . . .' and they form a part of the exchanges that is inarticulate yet meaningful, keeping things going without interrupting.

SUMMARY PROPOSITIONS

1.1 Interactive skills are a fundamentally important aspect of all managerial work.

1.2 Effectiveness in interaction is aided by poise and being responsive to others, as well as by understanding the effects of the frame of reference, stereotyping and cognitive dissonance.

1.3 The basic types of interaction can be categorised as enquiry, exposition, joint problem solving and conflict resolution. A specialised skill is chairing.

1.4 Listening skills include tone of voice, giving attention, eye contact, physical responses and being silent.

1.5 The main types of question are closed, open ended, indirect and the probe. Inappropriate questions are leading, multiple and taboo.

1.6 Methods of feedback include reflection, summary and re-run, paraphrasing, showing interest, affirmation and using appropriate noises.

GENERAL DISCUSSION TOPICS

1 What are the advantages of face-to-face conversation compared with a combination of e-mail, fax, text messages and telephone calls? To what extent is videoconferencing adequate as an alternative to meeting face to face?

2 If a central part of HRM is getting things done by other people, what is the difference between telling them what to do and asking them to do things? In what sort of situations would each approach be appropriate?

FURTHER READING

Argyle, M. (1994) *The Psychology of Interpersonal Behaviour*. Harmondsworth, Middlesex: Penguin Books.
This classic was first published in 1967 and remains the ideal introduction to understanding the dynamics of interpersonal skills.

Collett, P. (2003) *The Book of Tells*. London: Doubleday.
A comprehensive explanation of non-verbal behaviours that reveal a person's true feelings. The author is a social psychologist who combines research at the Oxford University Department of Experimental Psychology with acting as resident psychologist for the television programme *Big Brother*.

Glass, L. (1992) *He Says, She Says*. London: Piatkus.
This shows the differences in communication behaviour between men and women, which lead to such extensive misunderstanding of motives. The author explains differences in body language, voice tone, speech patterns and even choice of words.

WEB LINKS

www.cipd.co.uk takes you to the Chartered Institute of Personnel and Development, which is the professional body for HR people. The site has a wealth of information, not only on qualification courses, but on all aspects of human resource management.

www.shrm.org is a similar site for the Society of Human Resource Management in the United States.

www.peoplemanagement.co.uk is the website for the monthly journal, published by CIPD.

The book's companion website, **www.pearsoned.co.uk/torrington**, contains more practical advice on interaction techniques.

REFERENCES

Bolton, R. (1987) *People Skills*. Brookvale, New South Wales: Simon & Schuster.
Carnegie, D. (2006) *How to Win Friends and Influence People*. London: Vermilion.
Caro, M. (1994) *The Body Language of Poker*. Secaucus, New Jersey: Carol Publishing Group.
Goldman, D. (2006) *Social Intelligence: The New Science of Human Relationships*. London: Hutchinson.
King, B. (2007) *The Lying Ape*. Cambridge: Icon Books.

REVIEW OF PART 1

The early chapters of this book indicated that many controversial incidents in human life have what might be called an HR dimension. If someone fails in a job, was the right person chosen in the first place? Was the 'right' person unfairly rejected? If a train crashes with serious loss of life, was the driver properly trained and supervised? Are employees effectively disciplined when they make mistakes, or does the manager concerned avoid the issue for fear of jeopardising a working relationship? And so they go on, issues of fitting people to jobs and jobs to people, issues of training, appraisal, motivation, payment and many more. All go to the core of human resource management, yet the role of the human resource manager is not directly to manage these situations, but to ensure they are managed and to enable other people to manage them well.

The challenge for HRM people is thus, somehow or other, to get the job done by other people, not all of whom will welcome assistance and guidance because they are quite sure of their own ability to deal with the matters. Furthermore, they may well outrank the HR people and disparage HR expertise, although the latter problem seems to be getting less common.

The human resource manager needs to understand the range and potential of human resource management, its traditions, its problems and its expertise, so as to adopt a perspective on any situation (as in the case study that follows) that is realistic and fit for the purpose.

Advice from HR will always be strengthened when based on sound analysis, so expertise in planning methods and the ability to use this quickly and appropriately is a necessary part of the HR manager's toolkit.

Any business with an international dimension has a much greater range of HR challenges, particularly cultural diversity, communication and coordination. Because human resource management deals with such a variety of situations and people, a skill that is even more important is that of being effective in face-to-face interaction. This is where advice works or is disregarded, where the 'right' person is spotted and selected or lost to a competitor, where the disgruntled employee is brought back on board or the union agreement is sealed, and so on. When the business has to deal with barriers of culture, language and basic management assumptions, the challenges are intensified. Human resource management is one of the great tasks of getting things done through other people.

Part 1

CASE STUDY PROBLEM

You have just been appointed to replace the personnel manager in an organisation where members of the Board felt that HR practice had become over-preoccupied with fashionable ideas and was not meeting the needs of the business and the people who worked there. They have asked you to:

1 Review the ways in which human resource management is being conducted across the entire business, within the line as well as by the HR specialists.

2 Identify aspects of best practice that are currently being employed by leading-edge HR practitioners in other organisations and which would be relevant to your situation.

3 Draft proposals for a programme of strategic initiatives to enhance human resource management throughout the business.

On investigation you find:

1 A scheme of employee involvement in management decision making has foundered because of resistance from two unions with members in the organisation, whose representatives were excluded from discussions about the proposals; and by reservations held by a number of senior managers, who felt that the scheme had not been properly thought through and that it was too radical a development.

2 The concept of performance management has been introduced at the same time as moves to empower line managers. Many line managers feel that empowerment means no more than taking the blame for things that go wrong, and many of their subordinates feel that they are now cut off from the centralised, expert services of the HR function.

3 A case for the Investors in People award was turned down because what actually happened in practice did not match what the policy statement claimed.

4 Members of the HR function say that they have lost credibility and job satisfaction by a series of grandiose schemes that were not fully developed and which could not be fully implemented in a short time.

Required

Produce outline proposals for the Board to consider, setting out what you would do in the first six months and in the following 12 months to deal with this situation and what you expect to achieve in that time. Include any resource implications of your proposals.

Locate the organisation in a real context, either in a company or other organisation with which you are familiar or in a particular industry that interests you.

RESOURCING

The first major activity of the human resource specialist is to find and bring in the people that the business needs for its success. These people may not be employees; they may be consultants or subcontractors. They may be temporary, full time, part time or occasional, and the working relationship between the business and its people is the contract, which sums up the features of that relationship so that both parties know where they stand. Nearly always there is a face-to-face meeting between the parties to agree terms before the relationship begins. The process of 'coming to terms' is one of mutual assessment. Many prospective employees reject a prospective employer by deciding not to apply for a post, or by discontinuing their application. Employers usually choose between many, and often feel there are too few applicants. Once recruited, people have to be retained within the business by a series of strategies that sustain their interest and motivation as well as keeping the focus of their activities within an evolving organization and a changing business context. Contracts end as well as begin, and we have to be sure that the arrangements to end the contract are as sound as those for it to start.

The whole resourcing process is symbolised by the mutual assessment that takes place in the selection interview: 'Is this person right for us?' and 'Is this job and situation right for me?' The answers to those questions have major implications for both parties. The uncertainty about whether or not the right answers are found at the interview is why we have to examine resourcing so closely.

REWARD

INTRODUCTION

EMPLOYEE RELATIONS

EMERGING ISSUES

RESOURCING

DEVELOPMENT

PERFORMANCE

Strategy
Contracts
Recruitment
Selection
Retention
Ending the contract
Skills

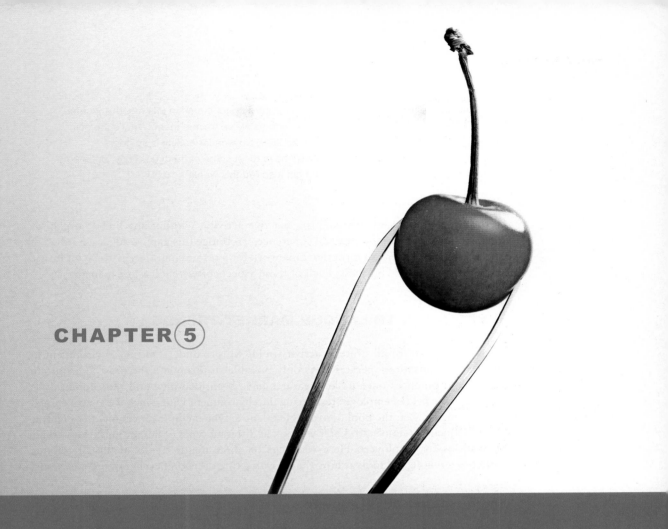

CHAPTER ⑤

STRATEGIC ASPECTS OF RESOURCING

THE OBJECTIVES OF THIS CHAPTER ARE TO:

1   Review key contemporary labour market trends

2   Describe different ways in which labour markets can be usefully analysed

3   Explain different types of flexible working

4   Debate the merits of moving towards a higher degree of organisational flexibility

5   Assess different strategies to use in order to mobilise a workforce

'Angela's leaving – quick, we must make sure to get the ad in this month's journal.'

'It's hopeless – they all leave just as soon as we've trained them. What's the point?'

'It's not my fault – we just can't get the staff. No wonder quality is so poor.'

'That's it. The results are so bad we'll have to let some of them go. Tony, draw up a shortlist of possibles and we'll try and get it sorted this week.'

All too often employee resourcing is a reactive activity, without any link to organisational strategy and without internal coherence. To bridge this gap we suggest a range of aspects which together can form the framework for a resourcing strategy to facilitate the future direction of the business. Each of these aspects offers choices for managers.

RESPONDING TO LABOUR MARKET TRENDS

The starting point for all strategic activity in HRM is to understand the environment in which an organisation operates. It is only possible to formulate the most appropriate policies and practices once its key features have been identified and their importance grasped. In the field of employee resourcing the environment with which we are concerned is the labour market, the pool of available talent in which employers compete to recruit and subsequently retain staff. Later we look at different types of labour market and their implications for employers. Here we focus on three major trends in the UK labour market as a whole and look at how they are affecting decision making in organisations.

Demographic developments

In 2006 the UK's population numbered 60.5 million, of whom just over half (30.71 million) were officially classed as economically active (CIPD 2006a, p. 8). Both figures are projected to rise during the coming decades. The overall population is increasing, despite falling birth rates, because of lengthening life expectancy and substantial net immigration (Blanchflower *et al*. 2007). The number of people who are economically active is increasing largely because of women spending a greater proportion of their lives in paid work than has been the case historically. Over the longer term, however, the proportion of the population that is of working age is likely to shrink in comparison with the total population as more and more people live longer after reaching retirement age. This process has already begun in countries such as Japan and Germany, with significant implications for the provision of care and pensions for the growing number of elderly people. In the UK there are currently 21 people over the age of 65 for every 100 people of working age. After 2010 this number will start to rise significantly. By 2030 more than a quarter of the population will be over 65. The coming years will therefore see a substantial change in the age profile of the workforce, as the population as a whole gets older and a greater proportion of young people remain in full-time education for longer.

There are two major implications for employers. First, because their numbers will fall, it will be progressively harder to recruit and retain the more talented younger workers. Organisations that have sought to resource their organisations by recruiting and training new graduates or school leavers will either have to work a good deal harder at competing for them or have to bring in older people in their place. Second, there are implications for the capacity of the state to provide a reasonable level of pension for so many retired people. Increasingly, therefore, people are likely to look at the nature of the occupational pension being provided by employers when deciding on their career options. Organisations offering good, well-communicated pension benefits will be better placed than others to attract and retain the employees they need.

WINDOW ON PRACTICE

Global demographic trends vary considerably from region to region. According to United Nations statistics, many major European countries can expect to see an overall fall in their populations over the next fifty years. The biggest projected falls are in Eastern Europe. Russia, for example, can anticipate a fall in its population of 30 per cent before 2050, while the highest figure of all (a 52 per cent population fall) is projected in Estonia. Substantial population falls are also predicted for Italy (22 per cent), Switzerland (19 per cent) and Poland (15 per cent). These figures partly reflect low birth rates, but also the likelihood that more people will emigrate from than immigrate into these economies.

Where birth rates are high and where the likelihood of net immigration is also relatively high, population rates are projected to increase. One such country is the United States of America, where fertility rates (i.e. number of children born per couple) are currently running at 2.11 and around two million immigrants settle each year (many illegally). As a result, the US population will overtake that of the EU in the 2030s, passing 400 million by 2050.

Diversity

According to the most recent government figures 88 per cent of men and 77 per cent of women of working age are either in work or actively seeking work in the UK (Office for National Statistics 2006, pp. 87 and 94). Increased female participation in the workforce has been one of the most significant social trends over recent decades. In 1980 the employment rate for women of working age was 59 per cent, since when the figure has risen steadily, while that for men has declined somewhat. This has happened as more women with young children have opted to work while more men have taken early retirement. As a result there has been some decline in the number of workplaces where women are heavily outnumbered by men and an increase in the number where men are outnumbered by women. Although the vast majority of management posts are still held by men, we have also seen a substantial increase in the number of women occupying such positions – another trend that is going to continue in the years ahead. Despite these developments there remain many areas of work which are dominated by either men or women and a continued substantial **gender gap** in overall pay levels (women's average salary is 83 per cent of that for men). A trend which has been identified in many surveys is the growth in the number of part-time workers in the UK. They now account for over a quarter of the total workforce and over 80 per cent of them are women.

Representation of ethnic minorities has also increased over recent years. In the early 1980s around 4.5 per cent of employees came from ethnic minorities. Twenty-five years on the figure is 8 per cent. Whereas in 1980 two-thirds of workplaces employed no one from an ethnic minority, nearly half now do (Millward *et al.* 2000, p. 43, Kersley *et al.* 2006, p. 30). Increases in representation have occurred across the industrial sectors. Taken together, these various trends mean that the workforce is steadily becoming more diverse in its make-up. While there remains a strong degree of segregation in terms of the types of work performed, the trend is towards heterogeneity at all organisational levels. There are a number of important implications for human resource managers:

- In order to attract and retain the best employees it is necessary to take account of the needs of dual-career families. The law now requires employers to offer a measure of support, recent measures being those on parental leave, the right to time off for family emergencies, and the right to request flexible working, but there is a great deal more that can be done. Career-break entitlements, crèches and job-share schemes are the most common initiatives. (See Chapter 31 for more on work-life balance issues.)

- There is a heightened need for awareness of the possibility of discrimination against any group which is underrepresented in the workplace. The perception of inequity, however justifiable in practice, is all that is needed for staff turnover rates to increase and for an employer to gain a poor reputation in its labour markets. Employers are required to pay more serious attention to the issues of sexual and racial harassment in a workplace characterised by diversity than in one which is less heterogeneous. It is advisable to have written policies covering such matters and to ensure that line managers are fully aware of the developing law on harassment.

Skills and qualifications

The third major development in the labour market is the changing occupational structure, leading to a greater demand for skilled staff. In recent decades the chief job growth areas have been in the managerial and professional occupations, and in service industries such as retailing, security and catering. By contrast there has been an ongoing decline in demand for people to work in the manufacturing and agricultural sectors (Office for National Statistics 2006, p. 7). While technical skills are not required for all the new jobs, social skills are necessary, as is the ability to work effectively without close supervision.

The past two decades have also seen a strong increase in demand for graduates. Over 400,000 now graduate from universities in the UK every year, including 260,000 with first degrees. Unemployment among this group is considerably lower than for the rest of the population whatever the economic conditions, indicating a capacity on the part of employers to absorb the growing numbers into their labour forces. However, despite the increasing numbers of people gaining formal qualifications at all levels, there remain skills shortages. When the economy is performing well these can be significant.

The annual CIPD Labour Turnover Survey for 2006 reported that 82 per cent of employers had had problems filling vacancies (CIPD 2006b, p. 3), mainly due to a lack of required specialist skills and/or experience. In particular, there are too few people with high-level IT and scientific qualifications entering the labour market and far too many people lacking basic numeracy and literacy skills. It is estimated that 16 per cent of adults in the UK are not capable of passing a GCSE English examination, while as many as 29 per cent lack basic skills in mathematics (National Literacy Trust 2007).

Policy initiatives are in place to improve skills levels at both ends of the scale, but it will take a number of years before the effects are apparent in the labour market. Until then employers have to devise strategies to deal with skills shortages in key areas. One approach is simply to work harder at recruiting and retaining employees. Another is to find ways of reducing reliance on the hard-to-recruit groups by reorganising work and dividing tasks up differently so that people with particular skills spend 100 per cent of their time undertaking the duties for which only they are qualified. A third response is to look overseas for recruits interested in working in the UK. Where skills shortages are particularly acute there is also the possibility of relocating one or more organisational functions abroad. Finally, of course, it is possible to recruit people without the required skills and to provide the necessary training and development opportunities.

ANALYSING LABOUR MARKETS

While the general trends outlined above have significant implications for employers, more important for individual organisations are developments in the particular labour markets which have relevance to them. An understanding of what is going on in these can then form the basis of decision making across the employee resourcing field. There are several different ways in which labour markets vary.

Geographical differences

For most jobs in most organisations the relevant labour market is local. Pay rates and career opportunities are not so great as to attract people from outside the district in which the job is based. The market consists of people living in the 'travel to work area', meaning those who are able to commute within a reasonable period of time. In determining rates of pay and designing recruitment campaigns there is a need to compare activities with those of competitors in the local labour market and to respond accordingly. Skills shortages may be relieved by increases in the local population or as a result of rival firms contracting. New roads and improved public transport can increase the population in the travel to work area, with implications for recruitment budgets and the extent to which retention initiatives are necessary. For other jobs, usually but not always those which are better paid, the relevant labour market is national or even international. Here different approaches to recruitment are necessary and there is a need to keep a close eye on what a far larger number of rival employers are doing to compete for staff.

Tight versus loose

A tight labour market is one in which it is hard to recruit and retain staff. Where the labour market is loose, there are few problems finding people of the required calibre. Labour market conditions of this type clearly vary over time. The higher the rate of unemployment in an area, the looser the labour market will be. However, some labour markets always remain tight whatever the economic conditions simply because there are insufficient numbers of people willing or able to apply for the jobs concerned. In recent years, even at the depths of the recessions of the 1980s and 1990s, it has been difficult to find good IT staff and effective sales people.

A number of researchers have looked at the responses of employers faced with either loose or tight labour markets. Windolf (1986) identified four types of approach used in the UK and Germany which varied depending not only on the tightness of the market, but also on the capacity of the organisation to respond intelligently to the situation. He found that many organisations with high market power (that is, faced with a relatively loose labour market) made little effort at all in the employee resourcing field. They simply took the opportunity to spend as little as possible on recruitment and selection and waited for people to come to them. When there was a vacancy it tended to be filled by a similar person to the one who had left, thus maintaining the status quo. According to Windolf, the more intelligent organisations took the opportunity afforded by favourable labour market conditions to seek out people with the capacity to innovate and who would develop their roles proactively. All available recruitment channels were used, leading to the development of a richly diverse and creative workforce. A similar dichotomy was identified in the case of tight labour markets. Here many organisations simply 'muddled through', finding people where they could, giving them training and hoping that they would stay long enough to give a decent return on the investment. By contrast, the more intelligent organisations were looking at restructuring their operations, introducing flexible working patterns and devising ways of reducing their reliance on people who were difficult to recruit.

Occupational structure

Labour markets also differ according to established behavioural norms among different occupational groups. The attitudes of people to their organisations and to their work vary considerably from profession to profession, with important implications for their employers. A useful model developed by Mahoney (1989) illustrates these differences. He identifies three distinct types of occupational structure: craft, organisation career and unstructured. In craft-oriented labour markets, people are more committed over the long term to their profession or occupation than they are to the organisation for which they work. In order to develop a career they perceive that it is necessary for them to move from employer to employer, building up a portfolio of experience on which to draw. Remaining in one organisation for too long is believed to damage or at least to slow down career prospects. Examples include teaching, where there is often a stronger loyalty to the profession as a whole than towards the employing institution. By contrast, an organisation-career occupation is one in which progress is primarily made by climbing a promotion ladder within an organisation. People still move from employer to employer, but less frequently, and will tend to stay in one organisation for as long as their careers are advancing. Mahoney's third category, the unstructured market, consists of lower-skilled jobs for which little training is necessary. Opportunities for professional advancement are few, leading to a situation where people move in and out of jobs for reasons which are not primarily career related.

To an extent employers can seek to influence the culture prevailing among members of each type of occupational group. There is much to be gained in terms of employee retention, for example, by developing career structures which encourage craft-oriented workers to remain for longer than they otherwise would. However, a single employer can have limited influence of this kind. It is therefore necessary to acknowledge the constraints associated with each labour market and to manage within them. Different areas of HR activity have to be prioritised in each case. It is necessary to work harder at retaining people in craft-oriented labour markets than in those which are organisation oriented, because people will be more inclined to stay with one employer in the latter than in the former. Recruitment and selection will be different too. Where career advancement is generally achieved within organisations, as in banking or the civil service, there is a good case for giving a great deal of attention to graduate recruitment. It is worth spending large sums to ensure that a good cohort is employed and subsequently developed because there is likely to be a long period in which to recoup the investment. The case is a good deal weaker in craft-oriented labour markets where there is less likelihood of a long association with individual employees.

Generational differences

Within the constraints of age discrimination law, employee resourcing practices should also be adapted to take account of variations in the age profile of those whom the organisation is seeking to employ. While it is clearly wrong to assert that everyone of a certain age shares the same attitudes and characteristics, significant if broad differences between the generations can be identified. Sparrow and Cooper (2003), in their review of recent research in this area, argue that there are good reasons for believing that the workforce of the future (i.e. made up of young people currently in full-time education) will have decidedly different 'work values' from those of the current workforce. This is because the shared experiences which shape the attitudes and expectations of each generation are different. Evidence suggests that future employees will be less trusting of organisations, more inclined to switch jobs, and more prepared to relocate, and indeed emigrate, than is the case today.

Research on generational differences from a management perspective remains underdeveloped, but a number of writers have put forward interesting ideas. Both Eisner (2004) and Zemke *et al.* (2000), for example, identify four groups defined by their dates of birth. They go on to argue that each must be treated rather differently if they are to be successfully managed. The four categories are Veterans or Traditionalists (born before and during the Second World War), Baby Boomers (late 1940s and 1950s), Generation X (1960s and 1970s) and a group labelled 'Nexters' or Generation Y (born after 1980). Some of the points made about each are as follows:

- Veterans are attracted to workplaces which offer stability and which value experience.
- Boomers place a high value on effective employee participation.
- Xers enjoy ambiguity and are at ease with insecurity.
- Nexters are wholly intolerant of all unfair discrimination.
- Boomers do not object to working long hours.
- Xers require a proper 'work-life balance'.
- Veterans are loyal to their employers and are less likely to look elsewhere for employment opportunities than younger colleagues.
- Xers are strongly resistant to tight control systems and set procedures.
- Nexters, being serious minded and principled, prefer to work for ethical employers.
- Xers and Nexters work more easily with new technology than veterans and boomers.

Where a workforce is dominated by a particular age group, it makes sense to manage the workers in a way with which they feel comfortable. Organisational performance as well as turnover rates improve as a result. Similarly, where a recruitment drive is aimed at a particular age group, it is important to give out appropriate messages about what the organisation is able to offer.

ACTIVITY 5.1

Eisner and Zemke and his colleagues developed their theories of intergenerational difference in the context of labour markets in the USA. Their analysis is based on the idea that successive generations of Americans have been shaped by shared formative influences.

In what ways has the historical experience of these generational groups differed in the UK or in other EU countries?

What implications might such differences have from an employer's perspective?

FLEXIBLE RESOURCING CHOICES

Understanding the dynamics of the organisational environment is only one part of taking a strategic approach to employee resourcing. Having gained an understanding one must decide how the organisation can best interact with its environment to maximise its performance. One set of key choices concerns the extent to which the organisation can aspire to flexibility and in what ways this can be achieved. Three types of flexibility are often identified in the literature: numerical flexibility, temporal flexibility and functional flexibility. A fourth type, financial flexibility, is discussed in Chapter 28.

Numerical flexibility

Numerical flexibility allows the organisation to respond quickly to the environment in terms of the numbers of people employed. This is achieved by using alternatives to traditional full-time, permanent employees. The use, for example, of short-term contract staff, staff with rolling contracts, staff on short-term, government-supported training schemes, outworkers, and so on, enables the organisation to reduce or expand the workforce quickly and cheaply.

Atkinson is one of a number of commentators who has described the way in which firms may develop flexibility in their approach to employment, as shown in Figure 5.1. The flexible firm in this analysis has a variety of ways of meeting the need for human resources. First are core employees, who form the primary labour market. They are highly regarded by the employer, well paid and involved in those activities that are unique to the firm or give it a distinctive character. These employees have improved career prospects and offer the type of flexibility to the employer that is so prized in the skilled craftworker who does not adhere rigidly to customary protective working practices.

There are then two peripheral groups: first, those who have skills that are needed but not specific to the particular firm, like typing and word processing. The strategy for these posts is to rely on the external labour market to a much greater extent, to specify

THE FLEXIBLE FIRM

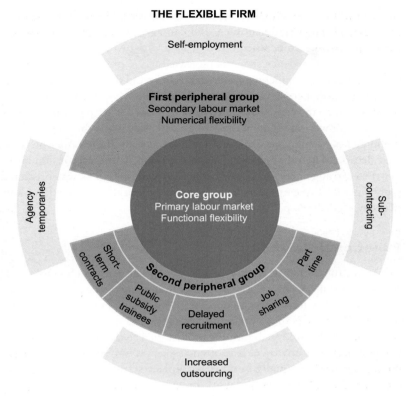

Figure 5.1
Atkinson's
model of the
flexible firm
(Source:
J. Atkinson (1984)
'Manpower
strategies
for flexible
organisations',
*Personnel
Management*,
August. Used with
the permission of
the author.)

a narrow range of tasks without career prospects, so that the employee has a job but not a career. Some employees may be able to transfer to core posts, but generally limited scope is likely to maintain a fairly high turnover, so that adjustments to the vagaries of the product market are eased.

The second peripheral group is made up of those enjoying even less security, as they have contracts of employment that are limited, either to a short-term or to a part-time attachment. There may also be a few job sharers and many participants on government training schemes find themselves in this category. An alternative or additional means towards this flexibility is to contract out the work that has to be done, either by employing temporary personnel from agencies or by subcontracting the entire operation.

A slightly different version of the peripheral workforce is created when the organisation boundary is adjusted by redefining what is to be done in-house and what is to be contracted out to various suppliers.

Temporal flexibility

Temporal flexibility concerns varying the pattern of hours worked in order to respond to business demands and employee needs. Moves away from the 9–5, 38-hour week include the use of annual hours contracts, increased use of part-time work, job sharing and flexible working hours. For example, an organisation subject to peaks and troughs of demand (such as an ice cream manufacturer) could use annual hours contracts so that more employee hours are available at peak periods and less are used when business is slow. Flexitime systems can benefit the employer by providing employee cover outside the 9–5 day and over lunchtimes, and can also provide employee benefits by allowing personal demands to be fitted more easily around work demands.

The research evidence suggests increased usage of all forms of temporal flexibility in recent years. Longer opening hours in retailing and the growth of the leisure sector mean that many more people now work in the evening (17 per cent) and at night (6 per cent) than used to be the case. The proportion of jobs that are part time also continues to rise, albeit at a slower rate than in the 1970s and 1980s, while the length of the working week for higher-paid full-time workers has increased by three hours on average during the past decade. There has also been some growth in the use of annual hours contracts, but these arrangements have not become as widespread as was predicted a decade ago. Only 6 per cent of employers have chosen to adopt this approach for some of their staff (Kersley *et al.* 2006, p. 79).

Functional flexibility

The term 'functional flexibility' refers to a process in which employees gain the capacity to undertake a variety of tasks rather than specialising in just one area. Advocates of such approaches have been influenced by studies of Japanese employment practices as well as by criticisms of monotonous assembly-line work. Horizontal flexibility involves each individual employee becoming multiskilled so that he or she can be deployed as and where required at any time. It is often associated with shop-floor manufacturing work, but can be applied equally in other workplace settings. Vertical flexibility entails gaining the capacity to undertake work previously carried out by colleagues higher up or lower down the organisational hierarchy.

The primary purpose of functional flexibility initiatives is to deploy human resources more efficiently. It should mean that employees are kept busy throughout their working day and that absence is more easily covered than in a workplace with rigidly defined demarcation between jobs. Another source of efficiency gains arises because employees are more stretched, fulfilled and thus productive than is the case in a workplace with narrowly defined jobs. Despite its potential advantages research suggests that employers in the UK have been less successful than competitors elsewhere in Europe at developing functional flexibility. According to Blyton (1998, p. 748), this is primarily because of a reluctance to invest in the training necessary to support these new forms of working. By contrast, Reilly (2001, p. 132) points to employee resistance and the increased likelihood of errors occurring when functional flexibility programmes are introduced. It could also simply be a reflection of increased specialisation as jobs become more technically complex and rely to a greater extent on specific expert knowledge. Either way, according to the Workplace Employment Relations Survey, there has been a decline in formal multiskilling programmes during recent years. In 2004 only 19 per cent of workplaces reported that at least three-fifths of their core employees were trained to do more than one job, compared with 29 per cent in 1998 (Kersley *et al.* 2006, p. 92).

Debates about flexibility

The growth in flexible working arrangements combined with their promotion by governments since the 1990s has led to the development of robust debates about their desirability and usage in practice. As much controversy has centred on the Atkinson model of the flexible firm as on the rather different elements that go to make it up. There has been a continuing debate, for example, about whether the model of core and periphery is a description of trends or a prescription for the future. Two streams of research have flowed from these interpretations. The first concerns the extent to which the model has been adopted in practice, the second focuses on the advantages and disadvantages of the model as a blueprint for the future organisation of work.

Evidence on the first of these questions is patchy. There is no question that rhetoric about flexibility and the language of flexibility is increasingly used. The flexible firm model appears to be something that managers aspire to adopt, but the extent to which they have actually adopted it is questionable. In many organisations the drive for economies of scale means that far from becoming more flexible, organisations are just as likely to introduce bureaucratic systems and standardised practices in response to competitive pressures. And yet we also have seen for a long period now increased use of part-time workers, consultants, subcontractors, agency workers and of moves towards multiskilling. Karen Legge's (1995) conclusion that flexibility is used in a pragmatic and opportunistic way rather than as a strategic HRM initiative thus seems to hold true today.

On the question of the desirability of flexibility a number of views have been expressed. The theoretical advantages for organisations arise from productivity gains. In different ways each type of flexibility aims to deploy employee time and effort more efficiently so that staff are only at work when they need to be and are wholly focused on achieving organisational objectives throughout that time. However, the extent to which this is achieved in practice is not clear. Many writers equate the term 'flexibility' with 'insecurity' and argue that the consequences for organisations in terms of staff commitment and willingness to work beyond contract are damaging. Staff turnover is likely to increase in response to the introduction of flexible working practices, while recruitment of talented people will be harder too. In short it is plausibly argued that the flexible firm model, at least as far as the 'peripheral' workforce is concerned, is incompatible with best practice approaches to HRM which seek to increase employees' commitment. Sisson and Storey (2000, p. 83) make the further observation that too much 'hollowing out' can impair organisational learning and lead to the loss of expertise, a loss from which it is difficult to recover. These unintended consequences, it is argued, can worsen rather than improve an organisation's competitive position. Others (*see* Heery and Salamon 2000, Burchell *et al.* 2002) see too much flexibility as having damaging longer-term economic consequences. For example, it can lead to a reduced willingness on the part of employers to invest in training, the absence of which creates skills shortages that hold back economic development. It can also lead to a situation in which managers exploit the vulnerability of peripheral workers by intensifying their work to an unacceptable degree. Finally, it can be argued that in dividing people into 'core' and 'peripheral' groups, flexible firms perpetuate inequality in society more generally and that this leads to poverty, crime, family breakdown and political alienation. Fudge and Owens (2007) label the new types of work 'precarious' and point to the fact that in the majority of cases it is carried out by women who are much less likely than men to enjoy the benefits associated with long-term, full-time, stable, pensionable employment associated with an income which is sufficient to sustain a household.

WINDOW ON PRACTICE

Tuselmann (1996) argues that a high degree of interdependence exists between the different forms of flexibility, that there are costs and benefits of each, and that organisations choose an optimal mix dependent on their market conditions and the country in which they operate. He suggests that a high degree of functional flexibility may be generally inconsistent with a high degree of numerical or financial flexibility. It has been argued that while Britain pursues numerical flexibility, in an unregulated and decentralised labour market, there is a greater emphasis in other parts of Europe on functional flexibility. In particular Germany has successfully followed this route within a highly regulatory framework with a high degree of centralisation and industrial relations consensus. Tuselmann notes that this framework also constrains organisations' pursuit of numerical, temporal and financial flexibility, and that as Germany experiences increasing competitive pressures, their model of labour flexibility is at a crossroads.

There are other balances in resourcing strategy that can be addressed, for example the balance between numbers of permanent staff employed and the hours that each employee works. In November 1993 Volkswagen in Germany announced that in their current poor financial situation they were employing too many people. In order to avoid redundancies they agreed with the workforce that hours would be reduced by 20 per cent so that they worked a four-day week, and that wages would be reduced by 10 per cent. There is a good deal of emphasis in Europe on reducing the working week to help reduce redundancies, unemployment and absence levels, and to improve family life.

ACTIVITY 5.2

What evidence can you find in your organisation to support a more flexible approach to resourcing? What were the driving forces behind these changes?
   How have employees responded and why?

READY MADE OR HOME GROWN?

Organisations have a choice whether to depend extensively on the talent available in the external labour market or to invest heavily in training and development and career systems to exploit the potential in the internal labour market. Some organisations thrive despite having high levels of staff turnover, while others thrive on the development of employees who remain with the organisation in the long term. The emphasis on either approach, or a balance between the two, can be chosen to support organisational strategy.

Sonnenfield *et al.* (1992) propose a model which relates entry and exit of staff with promotion and development of staff in the organisation. One axis of the model is supply flow. They argue that, strategically, organisations that focus on internal supply tend to see people as assets with a long-term development value rather than costs in terms of annual expenditure. The other axis is labelled the assignment flow, which describes the basis on which individuals are assigned new tasks in the organisation. The criteria for allocation may be in terms of individual contribution to organisational performance, or on group contribution – which Sonnenfield *et al.* identify as factors such as loyalty, length of service and support of others. They argue that, strategically, organisations that emphasise individual contribution expect individuals to provide value on a continuous basis, whereas those that emphasise group contribution see employees as having intrinsic value.

The model proposed describes the combination of these two aspects of resourcing and results in four typical 'career systems' as shown in Figure 5.2. In each box alongside the career system label (academy, club, baseball team and fortress) Sonnenfield *et al.* identify the strategic organisation model and the competitive strategy which are most likely to drive each career system. They also identify the likely orientation of the human resource function. In this chapter we are concerned with the characteristics of the career systems, which are discussed below.

Academies

In academies there is a heavy emphasis on individual contribution, in terms of reward and promotion. They are characterised by stability and low turnover of staff, with many employees remaining until retirement. There is an emphasis on development and often competition for promotion and barriers to leaving the organisation. Examples of typical industries where academies operate are pharmaceuticals and automobiles.

Figure 5.2
A typology of
career systems
(Source: J.A.
Sonnenfield *et al.*
(1992) 'Strategic
determinants
of managerial
labour markets',
*Human Resource
Management*,
Vol. 27, No. 4.
Copyright © 1992
John Wiley and
Sons, Inc.
Reproduced with
permission of
John Wiley and
Sons, Inc.)

Clubs

Again there is a heavy emphasis on the internal labour market, but promotion in clubs is more likely to be based on loyalty, length of service, seniority and equality than on individual contribution. There is an emphasis on staff retention. Sectors where this type of system is likely to operate include public bodies, although the introduction of competitive forces will mean that a different career system may be appropriate.

Baseball teams

Organisations characterised as baseball teams use external labour sources at all levels to seek the highest contributors. There is an emphasis on recruitment to maintain staffing levels. Employees will tend to identify with their profession rather than the organisation, and examples given are advertising, accountancy and legal firms.

Fortresses

Fortress organisations are concerned with survival and cannot afford to be concerned with individuals, in terms of either reward or promotion. They are more likely to depend on external recruitment, often for generalists who meet the needs of a retrenchment or turnaround situation. Examples given are publishing, retailing and the hotel sector.

ACTIVITY 5.3

Which of the four career systems in the Sonnenfield *et al.* model typifies your organisation? What characteristics lead you to this conclusion?

How does this career systems strategy fit with your organisational strategy and organisational mission (either explicitly stated or implicit)?

SUMMARY PROPOSITIONS

5.1 A strategic approach to resourcing requires that account is taken of the changes taking place in the labour market.

5.2 Individual labour markets vary in key respects. These too need to be taken into account when formulating resourcing policy.

5.3 Models incorporating numerical, temporal and functional flexibility have been influential determinants of HRM thinking in recent years, leading to their adoption in many organisations.

5.4 The extent to which increased flexibility is evidence of a strategic approach to employee resourcing is a matter of debate. The extent to which such approaches are desirable in the long term is also open to question.

5.5 Organisations have strategic choices concerning the use they make of their internal and external labour market.

GENERAL DISCUSSION TOPICS

1 In times of high unemployment, many employers still continue to experience skills shortages. What steps can employers take to alleviate this situation? What steps might the government take?

2 Discuss the claim that flexible resourcing strategies should be welcomed by the individual as they provide new areas of opportunity rather than a threat.

FURTHER READING

Brown, P., Green, A. and Lauder, H. (2001) *High Skills: globalization, competitiveness and skill formation*. Oxford: Oxford University Press.
The authors draw on the results of a large international study to compare and contrast the different approaches being used around the globe to promote skills acquisition and to create a high-skill labour force. Their analysis focuses in particular on the impact of economic globalisation on skills development.

IRS (2002) 'Internal applicants – handle with care', IRS Employment Review, 25 March.
This article focuses on the practical implications that arise when organisations opt to recruit and promote staff internally rather than sourcing new people from the external labour market. The article draws on a study by researchers at the Institute of Employment Studies to set out best practice guidelines.

Pollert, A. (1988) 'The flexible firm: fixation or fact?' *Work, Employment and Society*, Vol. 2, No. 3, pp. 281–316.
Although published some years ago, this article is the best and most coherent critique of Atkinson's model of the flexible firm and the management trends it has influenced for two decades.

REFERENCES

Atkinson, J. (1984) 'Manpower strategies for flexible organisations', *Personnel Management*, August.

Blanchflower, D.G., Saleheen, J. and Shadforth, C. (2007) 'The Impact of Recent Migration from Eastern Europe on the UK Economy'. London: Bank of England.

Blyton, P. (1998) 'Flexibility', in M. Poole and M. Warner (eds) *The IEBM Handbook of Human Resource Management*. London: Thomson.

Burchell, B., Ladipo, D. and Wilkinson, F. (2002) *Job Insecurity and Work Intensification*. London: Routledge.

Chartered Institute of Personnel and Development (2006a) *Labour Market Outlook: Quarterly Survey Report*, Autumn. London: CIPD.

Chartered Institute of Personnel and Development (2006b) *Recruitment, Retention and Turnover. Annual Survey Report 2006*. London: CIPD.

Eisner, S.P. (2004) 'Managing Generation Y', *SAM Advanced Management Journal*, Vol. 70, No. 4, pp. 4–15.

Fudge, J. and Owens, R. (2007) 'Precarious Work, Women and the New Economy: The Challenge to Legal Norms', in J. Fudge and R. Owens (eds) *Precarious Work, Women and the New Economy*. Oxford: Hart Publishing.

Heery, E. and Salamon, J. (eds) (2000) *The Insecure Workforce*. London: Routledge.

Hibbett, A. and Meager, N. (2003) 'Key indicators of women's position in Britain', *Labour Market Trends*, October.

IRS (2002) 'Internal applicants – handle with care', *IRS Employment Review*, 25 March.

Kersley, B., Alpin, C., Forth, J., Bryson, A., Bewley, H., Dix, G. and Oxenbridge, S. (2006) *Inside the Workplace: Findings from the 2004 Workplace Employment Relations Survey*. Abingdon: Routledge.

Legge, K. (1995) *Human Resource Management: Rhetorics and realities*. Basingstoke: Macmillan.

Mahoney, T.A. (1989) 'Employment Compensation Planning and Strategy', in L. Gomez-Mejia (ed.) *Compensation and Benefits*. Washington, DC: BNA.

Millward, N., Bryson, A. and Forth, J. (2000) *All Change at Work? British employment relations 1980–1998, as portrayed by the Workplace Industrial Relations Survey series*. London: Routledge.

National Literacy Trust (2007) Key literacy statistics. Available at **www.literacytrust.org.uk/database/stats/keystatsadult.html**.

Office for National Statistics (2006) *Labour Market Review*. Basingstoke: Palgsave Macmillan.

Reilly, P. (2001) *Flexibility at Work: Balancing the interests of employer and employee*. Aldershot: Gower.

Sisson, K. and Storey, J. (2000) *The Realities of Human Resource Management: Managing the Employment Relationship*. Buckingham: Open University Press.

Sonnenfield, J.A. *et al.* (1992) 'Strategic determinants of managerial labour markets', *Human Resource Management*, Vol. 27, No. 4, reprinted in G. Salaman *et al.* (eds) *Human Resource Strategies*. London: Sage.

Sparrow, P. and Cooper, C. (2003) *The Employment Relationship: Key Challenges for HR*. London: Butterworth-Heinemann.

Tuselmann, H.-J. (1996) 'The path towards greater labour flexibility in Germany: hampered by past success?', *Employee Relations*, Vol. 18, No. 6, pp. 26–47.

Windolf, P. (1986) 'Recruitment, Selection and Internal Labour Markets in Britain and Germany', *Organizational Studies*, Vol. 7, No. 3, pp. 235–54.

Zemke, R., Raines, C. and Filipczak, B. (2000) *Generations at Work*. New York: AMACOM.

An extensive range of additional materials, including multiple choice questions, answers to questions and links to useful websites can be found on the Human Resource Management Companion Website at **www.pearsoned.co.uk/torrington**.

CHAPTER ⑥

CONTRACTS, CONTRACTORS AND CONSULTANTS

THE OBJECTIVES OF THIS CHAPTER ARE TO:

1 Review the major duties and rights which derive from the contract of employment

2 Describe the range of hours and shift patterns specified in contracts

3 Evaluate the advantages and disadvantages associated with different approaches to temporal flexibility

4 Examine the reasons for growth in atypical contractual arrangements and of regulation in this area

5 Debate the advantages and disadvantages of employing consultants

6 Assess the trend towards more outsourcing of activities traditionally carried out in-house

Although a great deal is written about 'psychological contracts' and 'contracts for performance', the association between employer and employee remains at base a legal relationship governed by 'a contract of employment'. Whatever expectations employers and employees have of one another when the employment begins, the basic terms and conditions will be agreed and understood at the start and may, if necessary, be enforced in a court. In law the existence of such a contract confers on both parties important obligations as well as giving the employee access to significant legal rights which are not available to people who work under different contractual arrangements.

Employment contracts are very varied, and in recent years all industrialised countries have seen a trend away from what are usually described as being 'traditional' arrangements in which employees are employed on an open-ended basis for 38 hours or so over a 5-day standard 'working week' towards a variety of different alternative types of contract. In some industrial sectors we have seen a move away from employment altogether as people have chosen, or been required, to switch to self-employment or agency working. These developments have given employers more options in terms of how they resource their organisations and there is evidence that some are making use of the outermost ring of Atkinson's flexible firm model (*see* Chapter 5) to a greater extent than they were previously. The more consultants, specialist employment agencies and outsourcing specialists that exist and the more effective the services they provide, the more they are considered to provide a viable alternative to the more traditional forms of employment.

CONTRACTS OF EMPLOYMENT

As far as the law is concerned over 80 per cent of people who work in the UK are employees. This means that they have a contract of employment with their employer, with the duties and privileges that that implies. The employer may be an individual, as with most small businesses, or the contract may be with a large corporation. Throughout this book we use terms like 'organisation' and 'business' more or less interchangeably and 'employer' is the legal term to describe the dominant partner in the employment relationship. This derives from the old notion of a master and servant relationship and indicates that the employee (or servant) has obligations to the employer or master and vice versa. In contrast, those who are self-employed or subcontractors have greater autonomy, but no one standing between them and legal accountability for their actions.

The law makes an important distinction between the two groups, employees having access to a wider range of legal rights than non-employees. While some areas of employment law apply to all workers, others only apply to employees. Non-employees are deemed to be working under 'a contract for services' rather than 'a contract of service' as is the case for employees. In 2007 the main statutory rights that applied to each were those shown in Table 6.1.

In addition to the statutory rights conferred by Acts of Parliament, a range of common law duties are owed by employers to employees and vice versa which do not apply in the case of other forms of relationship. The major obligations are as follows:

1 Owed by employers to employees:
- a general duty of care
- a duty to pay agreed wages

Employment rights which apply to all workers	Employment rights which apply only to employees
Equal pay for equal work	Right to a statement of terms and conditions of employment
Non-discrimination on grounds of sex, race, religious belief, sexual orientation, age and disability	Right to an itemised pay statement
Right not to have unauthorised deductions from pay	Statutory Sick Pay
Basic health and safety rights	Time off for public duties
Minimum wage	Nine months' maternity pay
Working time regulations	Trade union rights
Data protection rights	Minimum notice periods
Time off to care for dependants	Fixed-term workers regulations
Part-time workers regulations	Statutory Maternity Pay (after six months' service)
Nine months' maternity leave	Additional maternity leave
	Unfair dismissal rights (after one year's service)
	Parental leave (after one year's service)

Table 6.1 Access to statutory employment rights

- a duty to provide work
- a duty not to treat employees in an arbitrary or vindictive manner
- a duty to provide support to employees
- a duty to provide safe systems of work

2 Owed by employees to employers:
- a duty to cooperate
- a duty to obey reasonable/lawful instructions
- a duty to exercise reasonable care and skill
- a duty to act in good faith

3 Owed by employers to employees and vice versa:
- to maintain a relationship of mutual trust and confidence

4 Owed by employees and ex-employees:
- duty of fidelity

A contract of employment, contrary to common perception, need not exist in written form. It is much more satisfactory for both parties if there is documentary evidence of what terms and conditions have been offered and accepted, but a contract of employment exists whether agreed verbally on the telephone or sealed with no more than a handshake. Where there is any doubt about whether someone is an employee or not, the courts look at the evidence presented to them concerning the reality of the existing relationship between the two parties. If they consider, on balance, that it is governed by a 'contract of service' rather than a 'contract for services', they will consider the worker to be an employee and entitled to the full range of rights outlined above.

125

WINDOW ON PRACTICE

A case heard in the House of Lords illustrates the importance of employee status. Mrs Carmichael and a colleague were employed as tour guides at a power station run by National Power PLC. They started working for the company on a casual basis in 1989, undertaking about four hours work each week as and when they were needed. By 1995 they each were working around 25 hours a week, so they decided to ask for written particulars of their terms and conditions of employment. The company refused on the grounds that they were casual workers and not employees. The women won their case in the lower courts, but the company decided to appeal right up to the House of Lords. At this stage the women lost their case on the grounds that there was no mutuality of obligation. They could, and indeed had, turned down requests to work without suffering any disciplinary action. They were therefore not employees and not entitled to the rights associated with full employment status.

An employment contract comes into existence when an unambiguous offer of employment is made and is unconditionally accepted. Once agreed neither side can alter the terms and conditions which govern their relationship without the agreement of the other. An employer cannot therefore unilaterally cut employees' pay, lengthen their hours of work, reduce their holiday entitlement, change their place of work or move them to another kind of work. To do so the employer either has to secure the employees' agreement (by offering some kind of sweetener payment) or has to ensure that the right to make adjustments to terms and conditions is written into the contract by means of flexibility clauses. Where an employer forces changes through without securing the agreement of employees directly, or in many cases through negotiation with union representatives, legal action may follow. An employee may simply bring a claim for breach of contract and ask that the original contract be honoured. In such circumstances compensation may or may not be appropriate. Alternatively, where the employer's breach is serious or where it is one of the implied duties listed above that has not been honoured, employees are entitled to resign and claim constructive dismissal in an Employment Tribunal, in which case their situation is treated as if they had actually been dismissed (*see* Chapter 10). Table 6.2 provides a checklist for preparing a contract of employment.

WORKING PATTERNS

Aside from payment arrangements, for full-time workers the pattern of hours which they are expected to work is the most important contractual issue. The total number of hours worked by the average full-time worker in the UK fell substantially for much of the past 150 years, but started to rise again in the 1990s (Harkness 1999). In 1850 the normal working week was established as 60 hours spread over six days of 10 hours each. Now, the average number of hours worked each week by full-time workers, including paid and unpaid overtime, is 45 hours for men and 40 hours for women (Walling 2007, p. 40). Interestingly, in the last five or six years there is evidence that people have started

Table 6.2 Checklist for preparing a contract of employment

1 Name of employer; name of employee.	**6** Arrangements for holidays and holiday pay, including means whereby both can be calculated precisely.	**10** Disciplinary rules and procedure.
2 Date on which employment began.	**7** Terms and conditions relating to sickness, injury and sick pay.	**11** Arrangements for handling employee grievances.
3 Job title.	**8** Terms and conditions of pension arrangements.	**12** (Where applicable) Conditions of employment relating to trade union membership.
4 Rate of pay, period and method of payment.	**9** Length of notice due to and from employee.	
5 Normal hours of work and related conditions, such as meal-breaks.		

working rather fewer hours again, the number working in excess of 45 hours a week falling by 20 per cent (Office for National Statistics 2006).

A return to the downward trend in terms of hours worked may be a direct response to new regulation in this area. The European Union's Working Time Directive was introduced into UK law in 1998 as a health and safety initiative (*see* Chapter 22). Among other measures, it seeks to ensure that no one is required to work more than an average of 48 hours a week against their will. In some countries legislation limiting working hours is primarily seen as a tool for reducing unemployment. In recent years the most extreme example of such regulation has been the 'loi Aubry' which was introduced in 2000 in France limiting people to an average working week of only 35 hours (EIRR 1998). In the view of many economists, however, such laws tend to reduce productivity over the long term because they limit the capacity of highly productive people to put their skills at the disposal of the national economy. For this reason during the French presidential election of 2007 President Nicholas Sarkozy argued that he would be happier if 35 hours was the minimum number of hours that people worked rather than the maximum.

ACTIVITY 6.1

Would you like to see legislation passed in the UK limiting to 35 the number of hours in a week that each person can work? What would be the main arguments for and against the introduction of such legislation?

The past two decades have also seen some increase in the proportion of the working population engaged in shiftworking. This is nothing new in the manufacturing sector where the presence of three eight-hour shifts has permitted plants to work round the clock for many years. Recently, however, there has been a substantial rise in the number of service-sector workers who are employed to work shifts. Over 32 per cent of workplaces now employ shiftworkers, their numbers being most heavily concentrated in health and social work, hotels and restaurants, and the energy and water industries (Kersley *et al.* 2006, p. 79). They, unlike most factory-based staff, are not generally paid additional shift payments to reward them for working unsocial hours. The change has come about because of moves towards 'a 24-hour society' which have followed on from globalisation, the emergence of e-commerce and consumer demand. Each year more and more people are reported to be watching TV and making phone calls in the early hours of the morning, while late-night shopping has become the norm for a third of adults in the UK. Banks, shops, airports and public houses are now round-the-clock operations. The result is a steadily increasing demand for employees to work outside the standard hours of 9–5, Monday to Friday, a trend long established in the USA, where fewer than a third of people work the standard weekday/daytime shift (IDS 2000, p. 1).

While some people remain attached to the 'normal' working week and would avoid working 'unsocial hours' wherever possible, others like the flexibility it gives them, especially where they are rewarded with shift premia for doing so. Shiftworking particularly appeals to people with family responsibilities as it permits at least one parent to be present at home throughout the day. Several types of distinct shift pattern can be identified, each of which brings with it a slightly different set of problems and opportunities.

Part-timer shifts require employees to come to work for a few hours each day. The most common groups are catering and retail workers employed to help cover the busiest periods of the day (such as a restaurant at lunchtime) and office cleaners employed to work early in the morning or after hours in the evening. This form of working is convenient for many and clearly meets a need for employers seeking people to come in for short spells of work.

Permanent night shifts create a special category of employee set apart from everyone else. They work full time, but often have little contact with other staff who leave before they arrive and return after they have left. Apart from those working in 24-hour operations, the major categories are security staff and maintenance specialists employed to carry out work when machinery is idle or when roads are quiet. There are particular problems from an HR perspective as they are out of touch with company activities and may be harder to motivate and keep committed as a result. Some people enjoy night work and maintain this rhythm throughout their working lives, but for most such work will be undertaken either reluctantly or for relatively short periods. Night working is now heavily regulated under the Working Time Regulations 1998.

Double day shifts involve half the workforce coming in from early in the morning until early afternoon (an early shift), while the other half work from early afternoon until 10.00 or 11.00 at night (a late shift). A handover period occurs between the two shifts when everyone is present, enabling the organisation to operate smoothly for 16–18 hours a day. Such approaches are common in organisations such as hospitals and hotels which are busy throughout the day and evening but which require relatively few people to work overnight. Rotation between early and late shifts permits employees to take a 24-hour break every other day.

Three-shift working is a well-established approach in manufacturing industry and in service-sector organisations which operate around the clock. Common patterns are 6–2, 2–10 and 10–6 or 8–4, 4–12 and 12–8. A further distinction can be made between discontinuous three-shift working, where the plant stops operating for the weekend, and continuous three-shift working, where work never stops. Typically the workforce rotates between the three shifts on a weekly basis, but in doing so workers suffer the consequences of a 'dead fortnight' when normal evening social activities are not possible. This is avoided by accelerating the rotation with a 'continental' shift pattern, whereby a team spends no more than three consecutive days on the same shift.

Split shifts involve employees coming into work for two short periods twice in a day. They thus work on a full-time basis, but are employed on part-timer shifts to cover busy periods. They are most commonly used in the catering industry so that chefs and waiting staff are present during meal times and not during the mornings and afternoons when there is little for them to do. Drawbacks include the need to commute back and forth from home to work twice and relatively short rest-periods in between shifts in which staff can wind down. For these reasons split shifts are unpopular and are best used in workplaces which provide live-in accommodation for staff.

Compressed hours shifts are a method of reducing the working week by extending the working day, so that people work the same number of hours but on fewer days. An alternative method is to make the working day more concentrated by reducing the length of the midday meal-break. The now commonplace four-night week on the night shift in engineering was introduced in Coventry as a result of absenteeism on the fifth night being so high that it was uneconomic to operate.

WINDOW ON PRACTICE

Since 1999 the banking group Lloyds TSB has operated a 'work options scheme' to help it recruit and retain effective performers. It aims to help employees to find ways of meeting both their work and home obligations without having to compromise one or the other. According to the group's website, the major options offered are:

- reduced hours
- working less than a full-time schedule by job sharing
- two individuals sharing the duties of a full-time position
- variable hours
- varying the start and finish time of a standard day
- compressed work week
- working a full working week in fewer than five days a week
- tele-working
- working at home or off-site for up to three days a week.

In 2005 the bank conducted a review of the scheme which involved surveying employees to establish their level of satisfaction with the flexible working opportunities they received in practice. An overall satisfaction rating of 67 per cent was recorded. As a result the bank decided to retain the scheme but put in place plans to communicate its benefits more effectively to staff and managers.

Sources: **www.lloydstsbjobs.com/pages/whatrweroffer.html** and IDS (2006a).

FLEXIBLE WORKING HOURS

Another way of dealing with longer operating hours and unpredictable workloads is to abandon regular, fixed hours of working altogether. This allows an organisation to move towards the 'temporal flexibility' we discussed in Chapter 5. The aim is to ensure that employees are present only when they are needed and are not paid for being there during slack periods. However, there are also advantages for employees. Three types of arrangement are reasonably common in the UK: flexitime, annual hours and zero-hours contracts.

Flexitime

A flexitime system allows employees to start and finish the working day at different times. Most systems identify core hours when everyone has to be present (for example 10–12 and 2–4) but permit flexibility outside those times. Staff can then decide for themselves when they start and finish each day and for how long they are absent at lunchtime. Some systems require a set number of hours to be worked every day, while others allow people to work varying lengths of time on different days provided they complete the quota appropriate for the week or month or whatever other settlement period is agreed. This means that someone can take a half-day or full day off from time to time when they have built up a sufficient bank of hours.

There are great advantages for employees working under flexitime. Aside from the need formally to record time worked or to clock in, the system allows them considerable control over their own hours of work. They can avoid peak travel times, maximise the amount of time they spend with their families and take days off from time to time without using up holiday entitlement. From an employer's perspective flexitime should reduce the amount of time wasted at work. In particular, it tends to eliminate the frozen 20-minute periods at the beginning and end of the day when nothing much happens. If the process of individual start-up and slowdown is spread over a longer period, the organisation is operational for longer. Moreover, provided choice is limited to a degree, the system encourages staff to work longer hours at busy times in exchange for free time during slack periods.

Annual hours

Annual hours schemes involve an extension of the flexitime principle to cover a whole year. They offer organisations the opportunity to reduce costs and improve performance by providing a better match between working hours and a business's operating profile. Unlike flexitime, however, annual hours systems tend to afford less choice for employees.

Central to each annual hours agreement is that the period of time within which full-time employees must work their contractual hours is defined over a whole year. All normal working hours contracts can be converted to annual hours; for example, an average 38-hour week becomes 1,732 annual hours, assuming five weeks' holiday entitlement. The principal advantage of annual hours in manufacturing sectors, which need to maximise the utilisation of expensive assets, comes from the ability to separate employee working time from the operating hours of the plant and equipment. Thus we have seen the growth of five-crew systems, in particular in the continuous process industries. Such systems are capable of delivering 168 hours of production a week by rotating five crews. In 365 days there are 8,760 hours to be covered, requiring 1,752 annual hours from each shift crew, averaging just over 38 hours for 46 weeks. All holidays can be rostered into 'off' weeks, and 50 or more weeks of production can be planned in any one year without resorting to overtime. Further variations can be incorporated to deal with fluctuating levels of seasonal demand.

The move to annual hours is an important step for a company to take and should not be undertaken without careful consideration and planning. Managers need to be aware of all the consequences. The tangible savings include all those things that are not only measurable but capable of being measured before the scheme is put in. Some savings, such as reduced absenteeism, are quantifiable only after the scheme has been running and therefore cannot be counted as part of the cost justification. A less tangible issue for both parties is the distance that is introduced between employer and employee, who becomes less a part of the business and more like a subcontractor. Another problem can be the carrying forward of assumptions from the previous working regime to the new. One agreement is being superseded by another and, as every industrial relations practitioner knows, anything that happened before, which is not specifically excluded from a new agreement, then becomes a precedent.

Zero hours

A zero-hours contract is one in which individuals are effectively employed on a **casual** basis and are not guaranteed any hours of work at all. Instead they are called in as and when there is a need. This has long been the practice in some areas of employment, such as nursing agencies and the acting profession, but it has recently been used to some extent in other areas, such as retailing, to deal with emergencies or unforeseen circumstances. Such contracts allow employers to cope with unpredictable patterns of business, but they make life rather more unpredictable for the individuals involved. The lack of security associated with such arrangements makes them an unattractive prospect for many.

ACTIVITY 6.2

What types of job would you regard as most appropriate for the following variations of the conventional 9-to-5 working pattern?

- Shift working
- Part-time working
- Job sharing
- Flexible hours
- Compressed hours
- Annual hours

What types of job would not be suitable for each of these?

ATYPICAL CONTRACTUAL ARRANGEMENTS

Recent decades have seen the growth of contractual arrangements that differ from the permanent, open-ended, full-time, workplace-based form of employment that has always been regarded as representing the norm. There has always been considerable disagreement about the significance of these trends. For some they mark the 'beginning of the end' for jobs as we have come to experience them over the past 100 years, while for others they represent a modest adjustment of traditional practices in response to evolving labour market developments and to industrial restructuring. Either way they have important implications for the effective management of people.

Contracts of limited duration

Contracts of employment vary in all manner of ways. One of the most important distinctions relates to their length. Here it is possible to identify three basic forms:

- **Permanent**: This is open ended and without a date of expiry.
- **Fixed term**: This has a fixed start and finish date, although it may have provision for notice before the agreed finish date.
- **Temporary**: Temporary contracts are for people employed explicitly for a limited period, but with the expiry date not precisely specified. A common situation is where a job ends when a defined source of funding comes to an end. Another is where someone is employed to carry out a specified task, so that the expiry date is when the task is complete. The employer is obliged to give temporary workers an indication in writing at the start of their employment of the expected duration of the job.

Around half of all employers in the UK, including a good majority of public sector bodies, employ some people on a fixed-term basis or make use of agency temps. In 2005 a total of 1.4 million people worked under some form of non-permanent contract, which is 5.6 per cent of all employees (Office of National Statistics 2006). This is appreciably more than the 5 per cent who were employed on such a basis in the 1980s, but represents a substantial fall over the past few years; in 1998 the figure was close to 1.8 million. As unemployment has fallen and the economy has grown employers have found that they have to offer permanent positions if they are to attract effective employees. Although only around a quarter of temporary staff now claim that they would prefer a permanent job, in the mid-1990s this figure was close to half.

Some of the reasons for employing people on a temporary or fixed-term basis are obvious. Retail stores need more staff immediately before Christmas than in February and ice cream manufacturers need more people in July than November, so both types of business have seasonal fluctuations. Nowadays, however, there is the additional factor of flexibility in the face of uncertainty. Will the new line sell? Will there be sustained business after we have completed this particular contract? In the public sector fixed-term employment has grown with the provision of funds to carry out one-off projects, while the signing of time-limited service provision agreements with external private-sector companies has also become a great deal more common.

Often temporary staff are needed to cover duties normally carried out by a permanent employee. This can be due to sickness absence or maternity leave, or it may occur when there is a gap between one person resigning and another taking up the post. Another common approach is to employ new starters on a probationary basis, confirming their appointments as permanent when the employer is satisfied that they will perform their jobs successfully.

Some argue (e.g. Geary 1992) that managers have a preference for temporary staff because the use of such people gives them a greater degree of control over labour. This control derives from the fact that many temporary staff would dearly love to secure greater job security in order to gain access to mortgages and to allow them to plan their future lives with greater certainty. As a result temporary workers are often keenest to impress and will work beyond their contract in a bid to gain permanent jobs. Their absence levels also tend to be low. Because they work under the constant, unspoken threat of dismissal, they feel the need to behave with total compliance to avoid this. Managers sometimes take advantage of such a situation and push people into working harder than is good for them.

The law on the employment of fixed-term workers has changed in recent years and this may well in part account for the reduction in their numbers. Until October 1999 it was possible to employ staff on fixed-term contracts which contained clauses waiving the right to claim unfair dismissal. This meant that the employer could terminate the relationship by failing to renew the contract whether or not there was a good reason for doing so. It was thus possible substantially to avoid liability for claims of unfair dismissal by employing people on a succession of short contracts. For fixed-term contracts entered into after October 1999 waiver clauses no longer apply. Henceforth employers who do not renew a fixed-term contract have had to be able to justify their decision just as they do with any other dismissal, if they want to avoid court action. Temporary and fixed-term workers also gained a number of further rights via the Employment Act 2002 which implemented the EU's Fixed-term Work Directive. This seeks to ensure that temporary employees enjoy the same terms and conditions as permanent employees undertaking equivalent roles, that employers inform them of permanent vacancies and allow them access to training opportunities. The new law also seeks to limit the number of times that an employer can renew a fixed-term contract without making it permanent without good reason. Since 2006 people who have been employed on a temporary basis for four years or more are entitled to permanent contracts unless the employer can objectively justify less favourable treatment. They are also now entitled to redundancy payments when they are laid off.

A special type of contract is that for apprenticeship. Although this is not seen as a contract of employment for the purpose of accumulating employment rights, it is a form of legally binding working relationship that pre-dates all current legislative rights in employment, and the apprentice therefore has additional rights at common law relating to training. An employer cannot lawfully terminate an apprentice's contract before the agreed period of training is complete, unless there is closure or a fundamental change of activity in the business to justify redundancy.

Part-time contracts

At one time part-time working was relatively unusual and was scarcely economic for the employer as the national insurance costs of the part-time employee were disproportionate to those of the full-timer. The part-time contract was regarded as an indulgence for the employee and only a second-best alternative to the employment of someone full time. This view was endorsed by lower rates of pay, little or no security of employment and exclusion from such benefits as sick pay, holiday pay and pension entitlement. The situation has now wholly changed.

Since the 1960s the proportion of the employed workforce on part-time contracts has increased dramatically. Around a quarter of us (seven million) now work on a part-time basis, compared to just 9 per cent in 1961. Between 1992 and 2006 the number of full-time jobs in the UK increased by 10 per cent, while the rate of increase in part-time jobs

Country	1985	2005	Country	1985	2005
Australia	20.4	27.3	Japan	16.6	25.8
Belgium	11.5	18.1	Luxemburg	7.2	14.0
Canada	17.1	18.3	Netherlands	19.5	35.7
France	11.7	13.6	UK	19.7	23.6
Germany	13.4	21.8	USA	14.7	12.8
Greece	5.9	6.1	EU Average	12.9	18.0
Ireland	8.1	18.7	OECD average	14.6	16.3
Italy	7.9	14.7			

Table 6.3
Proportion
of the total
workforce
working part
time

Source: OECD 2007.

was 23 per cent. Here too, however, there has been a modest reduction in the most recent years, the figure peaking in 2004. Table 6.3 shows that this proportion is greater than that in most other countries, although there is some difficulty in making precise comparisons because the definition of what constitutes a part-time job varies somewhat from country to country. Whatever the definition used, however, it is clear that the number of part-timers across the world has steadily grown over recent decades. Only in the USA has the number declined of late.

Women account for four-fifths of all part-time workers in the UK, 44 per cent of all female workers being employed on a part-time basis and only 11 per cent of men. Male part-timers are overwhelmingly in the 16–19 and over 65 age groups, suggesting that full-time work is the preference for most men between leaving school and retiring. In the case of women the age pattern is markedly different. Around a quarter of women work on a part-time basis in their twenties, but this figure rises to 40 per cent for women aged 30–34 and to 50 per cent for those aged 35–39. After that the proportion declines some-what until close to retirement. Among women, therefore, part-time work appears very frequently to be undertaken during the time that their children are at school and that it is the preference for many. Among women with dependent children who work part time, government statistics report that 94 per cent do not want a full-time job (Labour Market Trends 2003).

Many part-timers work short shifts and sometimes two will share a full working day. Others will be in positions for which only a few hours within the normal day are required or a few hours at particular times of the week. Retailing is an occupation that has considerable scope for the part-timer, as there is obviously a greater need for counter personnel on Saturday mornings than on Monday mornings. Also many shops are now open for longer periods than would be normal hours for a full-time employee, so that the part-timer helps to fill the gaps and provide the extra staffing at peak periods. Catering is another example, as is market research interviewing, office cleaning, clerical work and some posts in education.

Unjustified discrimination against part-time workers has effectively been outlawed in the UK since 1994 when it was held by the courts potentially to amount to indirect dis-crimination on grounds of sex. Since 2000, however, statute has required that all part-timers and full-timers are treated equally. The Part-time Workers (Prevention of Less Favourable Treatment) Regulations provide that part-time workers are to be given the same pay per hour and the same terms and conditions of employment as full-time col-leagues undertaking the same or similar work. All benefits must also be provided to part-timers on a pro-rata basis. Moreover, the regulations state that employers cannot subject workers to a detriment of any kind simply because they work part time. This means, for example, that both part-time and full-time workers must be given equal access to training. It also means that the fact that an employee works part time should not be taken into account when deciding who is to be made redundant. Unlike other forms of direct discrimination, however, in the case of part-timers employers can seek to justify their actions on objective grounds.

ACTIVITY 6.3

Table 6.3 shows that the proportion of people who work part time varies very considerably in different countries. In most there has been an increase in recent years, but the rate of increase has been far more pronounced in some countries than others. Only in the USA has there been a decline in part-time working over the past twenty years. How can these very varied international trends be explained?

Distance working

In the quest for greater flexibility many employers are beginning to explore new ways of getting work done which do not involve individuals working full time on their premises. Working overseas, selling in the field and home-working are the most obvious types of distance working, but advances in information technology have led to increased interest in the concepts of teleworking and tele-cottaging. The term *tele* is the Greek for distant, which is familiar to us in words such as telegram and television.

The total number of UK workers who either are based at home or work mainly from home is just over 3 million (around 8 per cent of the total workforce). But a large proportion of these people are self-employed (Office for National Statistics 2006, p. 25). Despite the possibilities for such arrangements deriving from new technologies, only around 200,000 employees in the UK are based mainly at home, a further 380,000 being mobile workers who use their home as their base (IDS 2005, p. 2).

The main advantage, for both the employer and the employee, is the flexibility that teleworking can provide, but the employer also benefits from reduced office accommodation costs and potential increases in productivity. Employees avoid the increasingly time-consuming activity of commuting to work and can manage their own workload around their home responsibilities and leisure interests. But there is a downside too. Many find working from home all the time to be a rather isolating experience and miss the social life and sense of belonging to a community of colleagues that comes with traditional employment.

The main problem for employers, aside from fostering staff morale, commitment and a sense of corporate identity, is the need to maintain a reasonable degree of management control when the workforce is so geographically diffused. Drawing up an appropriate job specification is thus particularly important in the case of teleworking jobs. It is important to set out clearly defined parameters of action, criteria for decisions and issues which need reference back. Person specifications are also crucial since in much distance working there is less scope for employees to be trained or socialised on the job. In addition, 'small business' skills are likely to be needed by teleworkers, networkers, consultants and subcontractors.

Attention also needs to be given to the initial stages of settling in distance workers. Those off-site need to know the pattern of regular links and contacts to be followed. Those newly recruited to the company need the same induction information as regular employees. In fact, those working independently with less supervision may need additional material, particularly on health and safety. Heightened team-building skills will also be needed to encompass staff who are working on a variety of different contracts and at different locations.

The final key aspect of employing distance workers is the need for a close link between pay and performance. Managers must be able to specify job targets and requirements accurately and to clarify and agree these with the employees concerned. Where a fee rather than a salary is paid, the onus is on the manager to ensure the work has been completed satisfactorily.

Self-employment

In the UK 3.7 million people are self-employed, which is around 13 per cent of the total workforce. The proportion is somewhat higher in London and the south-east than elsewhere in the country because that is where the industries which employ most self-employed people are most common. Weir (2003) shows that demand for the services of self-employed people is lowest in manufacturing and in the public services. By contrast there are many more opportunities for self-employment in the construction, retailing, property, business services and personal services industries. Three-quarters of self-employed people work for themselves or in partnership with one other person and they are heavily concentrated in skilled trades and professional services occupations. They also tend to be a good deal older than average workers, as many as 31 per cent of older workers employing themselves.

The 1980s saw a substantial growth in the number of self-employed people. The growth slowed down in the 1990s, but started increasing again after 2002. There is some debate about the reasons for these patterns. Lindsay and Macaulay (2004) have examined the data in some detail. One possibility they consider is a response to changes in taxation which were made in the early years of the twenty-first century aimed at assisting small businesses. Another is a change in the way that the government gathers the statistics, but detailed examination of the trends suggests that neither of these is a plausible explanation. What seems to be happening is that people are in a better position than they were to set up their own businesses because of rises in house prices during this time. People are leaving employment and are using their houses as collateral to raise the necessary finance. The particular growth in self-employment that can be observed occurring in the finance industry appears to result from large redundancy payments made as finance houses have restructured in order to compete more effectively internationally.

What is clear is that most employed people earn considerably more than most self-employed people (Weir 2003, p. 449). While around 17 per cent of self-employed people earn well in excess of the national average, the big majority earn substantially less. Some running fledgling businesses struggle to earn anything at all. Some of these earnings figures may be subject to some under-reporting for tax avoidance reasons, but they firmly dispel the myth that self-employment is a route to affluence and an easy life. Many more self-employed people work longer hours for less reward than those employed by organisations.

Increasing the proportion of the workforce that is hired on a self-employed basis has both attractions and drawbacks for employers. While self-employed people typically cost more per hour to employ, they only need to be paid for the time they actually spend completing a job or can simply be paid a set fee for the completion of a project irrespective of how long it takes. The fact that they can be asked to tender for work in competition with others tends to further reduce costs, as does the fact that a self-employed person manages their own taxation and pension arrangements. So overall there are often major savings to be made in replacing certain jobs in an organisation with self-employed people. Moreover, as was shown at the start of this chapter, huge swathes of employment rights such as unfair dismissal and paid maternity leave apply only to employees and not to those employed on a subcontracted basis. The negative implications derive from the inevitable fact that a self-employed person is not obliged to work exclusively for one employer or even to work uniquely in the interests of any one organisation. The relationship is thus more distant and conditional on external influences for its continuance. This can mean that only the minimum acceptable levels of quality are achieved in practice and that the contribution made by the worker to longer-term business development is severely limited. An employer can buy a self-employed person's expertise, but cannot draw on the full range of their energies and commitment as is possible in the case of well-managed employees to whom a longer-term commitment has been made and with whom a closer personal relationship has been forged.

CONSULTANTS

Some management consultants are self-employed people who have gained considerable experience over some years and are in a position to sell their expertise to organisations for a fee. Many more are employed by larger firms which also provide a range of other business services. These tend to be younger people who have substantial, specialist, technical knowledge of particular areas of business activity. Consultants offer advice about issues faced by organisations, but they are also in a position to carry out research, to design new policies and procedures, and to brief or train staff in their effective use. Nowadays a lot of their work involves selling already developed IT products to clients and assisting them to put these into operation. In the HR field this is true of consultancies that specialise in job evaluation and in the provision of personnel information systems.

In many ways consultants thus provide a service analogous to that of an accountant, a lawyer or a financial adviser. However the service is packaged, organisations are being invited to buy their professional expertise and to apply it (or not) as they see fit. Substantial demand for such services over recent years has meant that consultancy has grown into a major multi-billion pound international industry employing hundreds of thousands of highly qualified people, many of whom are in a position to charge their clients upwards of £3,000 per day. Yet, despite their having been a fixture on the management scene for decades, there remains considerable cynicism about consultancy as a trade (*see* the poem overleaf entitled 'The Business Consultant'). The following quotation from the leading industrialist Lord Weinstock is born of disappointing experiences:

> Consultants are invariably a waste of money. There has been the occasional instance where a useful idea has come up, but the input we have received has usually been banal and unoriginal, wrapped up in impressive sounding but irrelevant rhetoric. (Caulkin 1997)

WINDOW ON PRACTICE

The Business Consultant

Of all the businesses, by far,
Consultancy's the most bizarre.
For, to the penetrating eye,
There's no apparent reason why,
With no more assets than a pen,
This group of personable men
Can sell to clients more than twice
The same ridiculous advice,
Or find, in such a rich profusion,
Problems to fit their own solution.
The strategy that they pursue –
To give advice instead of do –
Keeps their fingers on the pulses
Without recourse to stomach ulcers,
And brings them monetary gain,
Without a modicum of pain.
The wretched object of their quest,
Reduced to cardiac arrest,
Is left alone to implement
The asinine report they've sent.
Meanwhile the analysts have gone
Back to client number one,
Who desperately needs their aid
To tidy up the mess they made.
And on and on – ad infinitum –
The masochistic clients invite 'em.
Until the merciful reliever
Invokes the company receiver.
No one really seems to know
The rate at which consultants grow.
By some amoeba-like division?
Or chemobiologic fission?
They clone themselves without an end
Along their exponential trend.
The paradox is each adviser,
If he makes his client wiser,
Inadvertently destroys
The basis of his future joys.
So does anybody know
Where latter-day consultants go?
('Bertie Ramsbottom')

Source: *The Bottom Line* (1985). London: Century Hutchinson.
Reprinted by permission of Ralph Windle.

The use of consultants is thus a matter about which managers are very divided. In some companies, and increasingly in public-sector organisations, they are employed regularly and found to offer a useful if expensive service. Elsewhere it appears almost to be a matter of policy to resist their blandishments and to tap into alternative sources of advice. The best approach, as with all major purchasing decisions, is to employ them only in situations where there is a good business case for doing so and where they are likely to add value. The most likely scenario is where the organisation needs specialist advice and cannot gain access to it through its internal resources. In the HR field an example would be the need to develop a competitive employment package for an individual who is being sent on long-term expatriate assignment to a country with which people within the organisation are largely unfamiliar. It makes sense in such a situation to take advice from someone who has technical knowledge of the tax systems, pay rates and living standards in that country. Another common situation in which consultants are employed in the HR field is to administer psychometric selection tests to candidates applying for jobs and then to interpret and provide feedback on the results. However, there can also be other reasons for their employment, as Duncan Wood (1985) found in his interviews with well-established HR consultants:

- To provide specialist expertise and wider knowledge not available within the client organisation.
- To provide an independent view.
- To act as a catalyst.
- To provide extra resources to meet temporary requirements.
- To help develop a consensus when there are divided views about proposed changes.
- To demonstrate to employees the impartiality/objectivity of personnel changes or decisions.
- To justify potentially unpleasant decisions.

ACTIVITY 6.4

What HR problems currently facing your organisation do you think might best be approached by using outside consultants? Why? How would you specify the requirements? What HR problems currently facing your organisation would you not remit to outside consultants? Why not?

The likelihood of securing a positive outcome when employing consultants depends on two conditions being present. First, it is essential that the consultant is given very clear instructions both about the nature of the issue or problem that they are being asked to advise about, and about what the client expects of them. Second, they should only be employed once it has first been established that they are likely to be able to provide knowledge and ideas that cannot be sourced in-house, and that the costs associated with their employment are justified.

WINDOW ON PRACTICE

Typical views about using outside consultants

A Favourable views

1 The HR manager knows what to do, but proposals are more likely to be implemented if endorsed by outside experts.
2 The outsider can often clarify the HR manager's understanding of an issue.
3 Specialist expertise is sometimes needed.
4 The HR manager has insufficient time to deal with a particular matter on which a consultant could work full time.
5 The consultant is independent.
6 Using consultants can be cheaper than employing your own full-time, permanent specialists.

B Less favourable views

1 The HR function should contain all the necessary expertise.
2 In-house HR specialists know what is best for the company.
3 Other members of the organisation are prejudiced against the use of outside advisers.
4 Using consultants can jeopardise the position of the HR specialists and reduce their influence.

OUTSOURCING

Consultants are mainly employed to give advice or to carry out a defined project. In employing them an organisation is effectively subcontracting part of its management process. But organisations can and do subcontract out to specialist service providers a great deal more than in the past. The outsourcing of functions which could either be or were previously carried out in-house has become much more common in recent years. It is a trend that creates its own momentum because the more outsourcing that occurs, the bigger and better the providers become, making it an increasingly viable proposition for more organisations. According to the most recent Workplace Employment Relations Survey 86 per cent of organisations subcontract a service of some kind (Kersley *et al.* 2006, p. 106).

Of particular interest to readers of this book is the strong trend that can now be discerned towards the outsourcing (either in whole or in part) of activities that have traditionally been carried out by the HR function in organisations. You will find further information and discussion exercises about this on our companion website www.pearsoned.co.uk/torrington.

According to Colling (2005) the organisational functions which are most commonly out-sourced by UK organisations are ancillary services such as cleaning, catering, security, transportation and buildings maintenance. There is nothing new about organisations subcontracting such functions to external providers, but there is clearly an increased trend in that direction. Twenty years ago most larger corporations and the entire public sector managed these ancillary services themselves, employing their own people to carry them out. This is less and less true. Increasingly managers are keen to focus all their energies on their 'core business activities', by which they mean those activities which are the source of competitive advantage and which determine the success or failure of their organisations. There is thus a desire to minimise the amount of management time and effort which is spent carrying out more marginal activities. The decision to outsource is made easier by the fact that specialist security, cleaning and catering companies are often in a position to provide a higher-quality standard of service at a lower cost than can be achieved by in-house operations. This is because for them the provision of ancil-lary services is the core business and they have the expertise, up-to-date equipment, and staff to run highly efficient operations. Moreover, their size means that they can benefit from economies of scale that are not available to the far smaller locally run operations.

The nature and standard of services that the external company provides are deter-mined by the service level agreement that is signed. This will usually follow on from a competitive tendering exercise in which providers of outsourced services compete with one another to secure a three- or five-year contract. If the standards of service fall short of those set out in the agreement, the purchasing organisation is then able to look else-where, and can in any case sign a new agreement with a different provider at the end of the contract. This should ensure that high standards are maintained, but the evidence suggests that outsourcing frequently disappoints in practice. Reilly (2001, p. 135) lists all manner of problems that occur due to poor communication, differences of opinion about the service levels being achieved and different interpretations of terms in the con-tract. These occur because it will always be in the interests of the providing company to keep its costs low and in the interests of the purchasing company to demand higher standards of service and value for money.

In practice the theoretical advantages of outsourcing thus often fail to materialise. Serious cost savings are often difficult to achieve, largely because the Transfer of Under-takings laws require existing staff to be retained by the new service provider on their existing terms and conditions, yet standards of service may actually decline. Loss of day-to-day control means that problems take longer to rectify because complaints have to be funnelled through to managers of the providing company and cannot simply be addressed on the spot. It is also hard in practice to replace one contractor with another, as well as being costly, because there are a limited number of companies that are both viable over the long term and interested in putting in a bid. So great care has to be taken when adopting this course of action. Expectations need to be managed and deals should only be signed with providers who can demonstrate a record of satisfactory service achieved in comparable organisations.

These potential obstacles have not stopped a number of large corporations from out-sourcing large portions of their HR functions in recent years. The service level agree-ments that are signed typically involve a specialist provider taking over responsibility for the more routine administrative tasks that are traditionally carried out by in-house HR teams. These include payroll administration, the maintenance of personnel databases, the provision of intranet services which set out HR policies, recruitment administration and routine training activities. Such arrangements enable the organisation to dispense with the services of junior HR staff and to retain small teams of more senior people to deal with policy issues, sensitive or confidential matters and union negotiations.

ACTIVITY 6.5

Make a list of all the major activities carried out by your organisation's HR function. Which of these could realistically be outsourced and which could not and why?

WINDOW ON PRACTICE

In 2005 IRS carried out a survey that focused in depth on the practice of outsourcing all or part of the recruitment function. The main finding was that the majority of employers surveyed had not contracted out any part of recruitment and did not intend to do so. Only 22 per cent had taken the step of outsourcing a recruitment activity that had previously been undertaken in-house.

Of those who did not outsource recruitment 49 per cent said it was because they considered recruitment too important an activity to entrust to an external provider, while 45 per cent contended that it would not be cost-effective to take such a step and 35 per cent stated that outsourcing recruitment 'would not add value'.

Interestingly, achieving cost savings was one of the most common reasons given by respondents whose organisations had outsourced a recruitment activity. But the more common reasons were the ability the new arrangement gave them to speed up recruitment (63 per cent), to gain access to greater expertise (44 per cent), to help make HR more strategic (39 per cent) and to make recruitment more flexible and responsive (34 per cent).

Source: IRS 2005.

SUMMARY PROPOSITIONS

6.1 The law distinguishes between 'employees' and 'workers', the former enjoying a wider range of statutory and contractual rights than the latter.

6.2 Once a contract is established its terms cannot be broken by either party without the consent of the other.

6.3 Patterns of work vary considerably. The traditional Monday to Friday, 9–5 pattern is increasingly giving way to new shift patterns and contractual arrangements.

6.4 In recent years we have seen a growth in the number of 'atypical contracts', such as those which provide work on a temporary or fixed-term basis.

6.5 New technologies allow a greater proportion of people to work from home. This development brings all manner of new challenges for HR managers.

6.6 The use of outside consultants to undertake HR activities is rising.

6.7 Larger organisations and public-sector bodies are increasingly outsourcing functions that are not considered to be 'core' to their operations. This includes some HR activities.

GENERAL DISCUSSION TOPICS

1 What are the advantages and disadvantages of part-time working for the employer and for the employee? In what ways do the age and domestic situation of the employee alter the answer?

2 The chapter indicates some of the problems in employing consultants and specialist outsourcing companies. How can these be overcome?

3 What is the future for teleworking?

FURTHER READING

Beynon, H., Grimshaw, D., Rubery, J. and Ward, K. (2002) *Managing Employment Change: The New Realities of Work.* Oxford: Oxford University Press.

This provides a critical perspective on many of the trends introduced in this chapter. The authors draw on seven case studies of UK organisations to explore why employment restructuring is occurring and its consequences.

Colling, T. (2005) 'Managing human resources in the networked organisation', in S. Bach (ed.) *Managing Human Resources: Personnel Management in Transition,* 4th edn. Oxford: Blackwell.

This article gives an excellent summary of research into the increased use of outsourcing and new forms of subcontracting in the UK and the implications of the trend for HR practice. The author explores all the problematic issues and presents useful case study evidence.

Incomes Data Services (IDS) publications.

Incomes Data Services regularly publish studies focusing on different types of contractual arrangement which draw on the experiences of larger UK employers. Recent publications have covered *Teleworking,* IDS Study 729 (May 2002), *Outsourcing HR Administration,* IDS Study 746 (Spring 2003), *Homeworking,* IDS Study 793 (March 2005), *Annual Hours,* IDS Study 815 (February 2006), *Flexitime Schemes,* IDS Study 822 (May 2006) and *Flexible Working,* IDS Study 834 (November 2006).

REFERENCES

Caulkin, S. (1997) 'The great consultancy cop-out', *Management Today,* February, pp. 32–8.

Colling, T. (2005) 'Managing human resources in the networked organisation', in S. Bach (ed.) *Managing Human Resources: Personnel Management in Transition,* 4th edn. Oxford: Blackwell.

European Industrial Relations Review (EIRR) (1998) 'Making way for the 35-hour working week', *EIRR 294.* London: Eclipse Group Ltd.

Geary, J.F. (1992) 'Employment flexibility and human resource management: the case of three electronics plants', *Work, Employment and Society*, Vol. 4, No. 2, pp. 157–88.

Harkness, S. (1999) 'Working 9–5?', in P. Gregg and J. Wadsworth (eds) *The State of Working Britain*. Manchester: Manchester University Press.

IDS (2000) *24-hour society*, IDS Focus 93. London: Incomes Data Services Ltd.

IDS (2003) *Outsourcing HR Administration*, IDS Study 746. London: Incomes Data Services Ltd.

IDS (2005) *Homeworking*, IDS Study 793, March. London: Incomes Data Services.

IDS (2006a) *Flexible Working*, IDS Study 834, November. London: Incomes Data Services.

IDS (2006b) *Annual Hours*, IDS Study 815, February. London: Incomes Data Services.

IDS (2006c) *Flexitime Schemes*, IDS Study 822, May. London: Incomes Data Services.

IRS (2005) 'Outsourcing recruitment: a minority pursuit?', *IRS Employment Review* 830, 26 August.

Kersley, B., Alpin, C., Forth, J., Bryson, A., Bewley, H., Dix, G. and Oxenbridge, S. (2006) *Inside the Workplace: Findings from the 2004 Workplace Employment Relations Survey*. Abingdon: Routledge.

Labour Market Trends (2003) 'Employment: full-time, part-time and temporary workers', *Labour Market Trends*, November, p. S26.

Lindsay, C. and Macaulay, C. (2004) 'Growth in self-employment in the UK', *Labour Market Trends*, October.

Lloyds TSB (2003) **www.lloydstsbjobs.com**.

Office for National Statistics (2006) *Labour Market Review*. Basingstoke: Palgrave Macmillan.

Organisation for Economic Co-operation and Development (2007) *OECD Factbook 2007*. Paris: OECD, p. 40.

Reilly, P. (2001) *Flexibility at Work*. Aldershot: Gower.

Walling, A. (2007) 'Understanding statistics on full-time/part-time employment', *Economic & Labour Market Review*, Vol. 1, No. 2, February.

Weir, G. (2003) 'Self-employment in the UK labour market', *Labour Market Trends*, September, pp. 441–51.

Windle, R. (1985) *The Bottom Line*. London: Century-Hutchinson.

Wood, D. (1985) 'The uses and abuses of personnel consultants', *Personnel Management*, October, pp. 40–7.

An extensive range of additional materials, including multiple choice questions, answers to questions and links to useful websites can be found on the Human Resource Management Companion Website at **www.pearsoned.co.uk/torrington**.

RECRUITMENT

THE OBJECTIVES OF THIS CHAPTER ARE TO:

1 Identify alternative courses of action to take when an employee leaves an organisation

2 Explain the role played by job descriptions and person specifications in the recruitment process

3 Compare and contrast the major alternative recruitment methods

4 Assess developments in recruitment advertising and internet recruitment

5 Introduce the concept of employer branding

6 Clarify the need for control and evaluation procedures in recruitment

7 Assess different approaches to shortlisting

There is always a need for replacement employees and those with unfamiliar skills that business growth makes necessary, and with the Institute for Employment Research (2006) now estimating that UK employers will be creating an additional 1.3 million jobs before 2014, it is clear that effective recruitment will remain a central HR objective for the foreseeable future. Recruitment is also an area in which there are important social and legal implications, but perhaps most important is the significant part played in the lives of individual men and women by their personal experience of recruitment and the failure to be recruited. Virtually everyone reading these pages will know how significant those experiences have been in their own lives.

WINDOW ON PRACTICE

On graduating from university, Howard was employed as a management trainee by a large bank and was soon assigned to taking part in interviews of prospective graduate recruits, which he found interesting and a boost to his ego. After two years in the bank a programme of reorganisation led to Howard being out of a job. It was seven months before he was employed again and he had undergone many disappointments and frustrations. His new post was again in recruitment and he wrote himself a short homily on a postcard which he kept propped up on his desk. It said:

> When you turn someone down, remember:
>
> First, what the experience of rejection can do to a person.
> Second, that the rejected person may be a customer.
> Third, you may want to recruit that person later.

Over three million people are recruited by employers in the UK each year. It can be a costly and difficult process when skills are in short supply and labour markets are tight. In such circumstances the employer needs to 'sell' its jobs to potential employees so as to ensure that it can generate an adequate pool of applicants, but even then for some groups of staff it is getting harder to find people who are both willing and able to fill the vacancies that are available. According to the CIPD annual survey of recruitment practice, the vast majority of respondents report experiencing recruitment difficulties, particularly when it comes to finding appropriate management and professional staff (CIPD 2006, pp. 6–7). This means that the time taken to fill vacancies is increasing as are the costs associated with recruitment. However, as Barber (1998) points out, it is important that employers do not consider the recruitment process to be finished at the point at which a pool of applications has been received. It continues during the shortlisting and interviewing stages and is only complete when an offer is made and accepted. Until that time there is an ongoing need to ensure that a favourable impression of the organisation as an employer is maintained in the minds of those whose services it wishes to secure. That said, it is also important to avoid overselling a job in a bid to secure the services of talented applicants. Making out that the experience of working in a role is going to be more interesting or exciting than it really will be is an easy trap to fall into, but ultimately it is counterproductive because it raises unrealistic expectations. These then get quickly dashed, leading to unnecessary demotivation and, quite possibly, an early resignation. You will find further information and discussion exercises about realistic recruitment on our companion website **www.pearsoned.co.uk/torrington**.

DETERMINING THE VACANCY

Is there a vacancy? Is it to be filled by a newly recruited employee? These are the first questions to be answered in recruitment. Potential vacancies occur either through someone leaving or as a result of expansion. When a person leaves, there is no more than a prima facie case for filling the vacancy thus caused. There may be other ways of filling the gap. Vacancies caused by expansion may be real or imagined. The desperately pressing need of an executive for an assistant may be a plea more for recognition than for assistance. The creation of a new post to deal with a specialist activity may be more appropriately handled by contracting that activity out to a supplier. Recruiting a new employee may be the most obvious tactic when a vacancy occurs, but it is not necessarily the most appropriate. Listed below are some of the options, several of which we discussed in Chapters 5 and 6:

- Reorganise the work
- Use overtime
- Mechanise the work
- Stagger the hours
- Make the job part time
- Subcontract the work
- Use an agency

ACTIVITY 7.1

Can you think of further ways of avoiding filling a vacancy by recruiting a new employee? What are the advantages and disadvantages of the methods you have thought of? For what types of job with which you are familiar would each of your methods, and those listed above, be most appropriate?

If your decision is that you are going to recruit, there are four questions to determine the vacancy:

1 What does the job consist of?
2 In what way is it to be different from the job done by the previous incumbent?
3 What are the aspects of the job that specify the type of candidate?
4 What are the key aspects of the job that the ideal candidate wants to know before deciding to apply?

The conventional HR approach to these questions is to produce job descriptions and personnel specifications. Methods of doing this are well established. Good accounts are provided by Pearn and Kandola (1988), Brannick and Levine (2002) and IRS (2003a). The approach involves breaking the job down into its component parts, working out what its chief objectives will be and then recording this on paper. A person specification listing the key attributes required to undertake the role can then be derived from the job description and used in recruiting the new person. An example of a job description is given in Figure 7.1.

Job title: SENIOR SALES ASSISTANT

Context
The job is in one of the thirteen high-technology shops owned by 'Computext'
Location: Leeds
Supervised by, and reports directly to, the Shop Manager
Responsible for one direct subordinate: Sales Assistant

Job summary
To assist and advise customers in the selection of computer hardware and software, and to arrange delivery and finance where appropriate.
Objective is to sell as much as possible, and for customers and potential customers to see 'Computext' staff as helpful and efficient.

Job content
Most frequent duties in order of importance

1 Advise customers about hardware and software.
2 Demonstrate the equipment and software.
3 Organise delivery of equipment by liaising with distribution department.
4 Answer all after-sales queries from customers.
5 Contact each customer two weeks after delivery to see if they need help.
6 Advise customers about the variety of payment methods.
7 Develop and keep up to date a computerised stock control system.

Occasional duties in order of importance

1 Arrange for faulty equipment to be replaced.
2 Monitor performance of junior sales assistant as defined in job description.
3 Advise and guide, train and assess junior sales assistant where necessary.

Working conditions
Pleasant, 'business-like' environment in new purpose-built shop premises in the city centre. There are two other members of staff and regular contact is also required with the Delivery Department and Head Office. Salary is £18,000 p.a. plus a twice-yearly bonus, depending on sales. Five weeks' holiday per year plus statutory holidays. A six-day week is worked.

Other information
There is the eventual possibility of promotion to shop manager in another location depending on performance and opportunities.

Performance standards
There are two critically important areas:

1 Sales volume. Minimum sales to the value of £700,000 over each six-month accounting period.
2 Relations with customers:
   – Customers' queries answered immediately.
   – Customers always given a demonstration when they request one.
   – Delivery times arranged to meet both customer's and delivery department's needs.
   – Complaints investigated immediately.
   – Customers assured that problem will be resolved as soon as possible.
   – Customers never blamed.
   – Problems that cannot be dealt with referred immediately to Manager.

Figure 7.1
Job description for a senior sales assistant

An alternative approach which allows for more flexibility is to dispense with the job description and to draw up a person specification using other criteria. One way of achieving this is to focus on the characteristics or competences of current job holders who are judged to be excellent performers. Instead of asking 'What attributes are necessary to undertake this role?' this second method involves asking 'What attributes are shared by the people who have performed best in the role?' According to some (for example Whiddett and Kandola 2000), the disadvantage of the latter approach is that it tends to produce employees who are very similar to one another and who address problems with the same basic mindset (corporate clones). Where innovation and creativity are wanted it helps to recruit people with more diverse characteristics.

INTERNAL RECRUITMENT

Vacancies, of course, are often filled internally. Sometimes organisations advertise all vacancies publicly as a matter of course and consider internal candidates along with anyone from outside the organisation who applies. This approach is generally considered to constitute good practice and is widely used in the UK's public sector. However, many organisations prefer to invite applications from internal candidates *before* they look to their external labour markets for new staff (Newell and Shackleton 2000, pp. 116–17; CIPD 2006, p. 8). There are considerable advantages from the employer's perspective. First it is a great deal less expensive to recruit internally, there being no need to spend money on job advertisements or recruitment agencies. Instead a message can simply be placed in a company newsletter or posted on its intranet or staff noticeboards. Further cost savings and efficiency gains can be made because internal recruits are typically able to take up new posts much more quickly than people being brought in from outside. Even if they have to work some notice in their current positions, they are often able to take on some of their new responsibilities or undergo relevant training at the same time. The other advantage stems from the fact that internal candidates, as a rule, are more knowledgeable than new starters coming in from other organisations about what exactly the job involves. They are also more familiar with the organisation's culture, rules and geography, and so take less time to settle into their new jobs and to begin working at full capacity.

Giving preference to internal recruits, particularly as far as promotions are concerned, has the great advantage of providing existing employees with an incentive to work hard, demonstrate their commitment and stay with the organisation when they might otherwise consider looking for alternative employment. The practice provides a powerful signal from management to show that existing employees are valued and that attractive career development opportunities are available to them. Failing to recruit internally may thus serve to put off good candidates with potential from applying for the more junior positions in an organisation.

The main disadvantage of only advertising posts internally stems from the limited field of candidates that it permits an organisation to consider. While it may mean that someone who 'fits in well' is recruited, it may also very well mean that the best available candidate is not even considered. Over the long term the organisation can thus end up being less well served than it would have been had internal candidates been required to compete with outside people for their posts. For this reason internal recruitment sits uneasily with a commitment to equal opportunities and to the creation of a diverse workforce. Talented candidates from under-represented groups are not appointed because they never get to know about the vacancies that the organisation has.

It is also important to note that the management of internal recruitment practices is difficult to carry out effectively in practice. Research carried out by the Institute of Employment Studies (2002) shows that serious problems often occur when internal candidates fail to be selected. This is because they tend to enter the selection process with higher expectations of being offered the position than is the case with external candidates. Bitterness, antipathy and low morale are thus likely to follow. Moreover, failed internal candidates are considerably more likely to pursue claims of unfair discrimination following a selection process than external candidates. For these reasons it is essential that great care is taken when managing internal recruitment to ensure that the approach taken is both fair and seen to be fair. Giving honest, full, accurate and constructive feedback to failed candidates is an essential part of the process.

METHODS OF RECRUITMENT

Once an employer has decided that external recruitment is necessary, a cost-effective and appropriate method of recruitment must be selected. There are a number of distinct approaches to choose from, each of which is more or less appropriate in different circumstances. As a result most employers use a wide variety of different recruitment methods at different times. In many situations there is also a good case for using different methods in combination when looking to fill the same vacancy. Table 7.1 sets out the usage of different methods reported in a recent CIPD survey of 802 UK employers (CIPD 2006).

It is interesting to compare the figures in Table 7.1 with those reported in surveys of how people actually find their jobs in practice. These repeatedly show that informal methods (such as word of mouth and making unsolicited applications) are as common as, if not more common than, formal methods such as recruitment advertising. In 2002, the Labour Force Survey asked over a million people how they had obtained their current job. The results are shown in Table 7.2.

Table 7.1 Usage of various methods of recruitment by 803 organisations in 2006

Advertisements in local press	79%
Recruitment agencies	76%
Corporate website	75%
Specialist journals and trade press	66%
Jobcentre Plus	51%
Word of mouth/speculative applications	49%
Employee referral scheme	47%
National newspaper advertisements	45%
Education liaison	37%
Apprentices/work placements/secondments	36%
Commercial job-board Internet sites	16%
Posters/billboards	10%
Radio/TV	7%
Other	11%

Source: Table compiled from data in CIPD (2006) *Recruitment, Retention and Turnover: Annual Survey Report.* London: CIPD.

	Men	Women
Hearing from someone who worked there	30%	25%
Reply to an advertisement	25%	31%
Direct application	14%	17%
Private employment agency	10%	10%
Job centre	9%	8%
Other	12%	9%

Table 7.2
Methods of
obtaining a job

Source: *Labour Market Trends* (2002) 'Labour market spotlight', August.

THE RECRUITMENT METHODS COMPARED

All the various methods of recruitment have benefits and drawbacks, and the choice of a method has to be made in relation to the particular vacancy and the type of labour market in which the job falls. A general review of advantages and drawbacks is given in Table 7.3.

ACTIVITY 7.2

We have seen the significance of informal methods of recruitment whereby new employees come as a result of hearing about a vacancy from friends, or putting their names down for consideration when a vacancy occurs. Employees starting employment in this way present the employer with certain advantages as they come knowing that they were not wooed by the employer: the initiative was theirs. Also they will probably have some contacts in the company already that will help them to settle and cope with the induction crisis. What are the drawbacks of this type of arrangement?

RECRUITMENT ADVERTISING

In order to assist them in drafting advertisements and placing them in suitable media, many employers deal with a recruitment advertising agency. Such agencies provide expert advice on where to place advertisements and how they should be worded and will design them attractively to achieve maximum impact. Large organisations often subcontract all their advertising work to an agency with whom a mutually acceptable service-level agreement has been signed.

Recruitment advertising companies (as opposed to headhunters and recruitment consultants) are often inexpensive because the agency derives much of its income from the commission paid by the journals on the value of the advertising space sold, the bigger agencies being able to negotiate substantial discounts because of the amount of business they place with the newspapers and trade journals. A portion of this saving is then passed on to the employer so that it can easily be cheaper *and* a great deal more effective to

Table 7.3 Advantages and drawbacks of traditional methods of recruitment

Job centres

Advantages:
(a) Applicants can be selected from nationwide sources with convenient, local availability of computer-based data.
(b) Socially responsible and secure.
(c) Can produce applicants very quickly.
(d) Free service for employers.

Drawbacks:
(a) Registers are mainly of the unemployed rather than of the employed seeking a change.
(b) Produces people for interview who are not genuinely interested in undertaking the job.

Commercial employment agencies and recruitment consultancies

Advantages:
(a) Established as the normal method for filling certain vacancies, e.g. secretaries in London.
(b) Little administrative chore for the employer.

Drawbacks:
(a) Can produce staff who are likely to stay only a short time.
(b) Widely distrusted by employers.
(c) Can be very expensive.

Management selection consultants

Advantages:
(a) Opportunity to elicit applicants anonymously.
(b) Opportunity to use expertise of consultant in an area where employer will not be regularly in the market.

Drawbacks:
(a) Internal applicants may feel, or be, excluded.
(b) Cost.

Executive search consultants ('headhunters')

Advantages:
(a) Known individuals can be approached directly.
(b) Useful if employer has no previous experience in specialist field.
(c) Recruiting from, or for, an overseas location.

Drawbacks:
(a) Cost.
(b) Potential candidates outside the headhunter's network are excluded.
(c) Recruits remain on the consultant's list and can be hunted again.

Visiting universities

Advantages:
(a) The main source of new graduates from universities.
(b) Rated by students as the most popular method.

Drawbacks:
(a) Need to differentiate presentations from those of other employers.
(b) Time taken to visit a number of universities (i.e. labour intensive).

Schools and the Careers Service

Advantages:
(a) Can produce a regular annual flow of interested enquirers.
(b) Very appropriate for the recruitment of school-leavers, who seldom look further than the immediate locality for their first employment.

Drawbacks:
(a) Schools and the advisers are more interested in occupations than organisations.
(b) Taps into a limited potential applicant pool.

work with an agent providing this kind of service. The HR manager placing, say, £50,000 of business annually with an agency will appreciate that the agency's income from that will be between £5,000 and £7,500, and will expect a good standard of service. The important questions relate to the experience of the agency in dealing with recruitment, as compared with other types of advertising, the quality of the advice they can offer about media choice and the quality of response that their advertisements produce.

In choosing where to place a recruitment advertisement the aim is to attract as many people as possible with the required skills and qualifications and to reach people who are either actively looking for a new job or thinking about doing so. The need is therefore to place the advertisement where job seekers who are qualified to take on the role are most likely to look. Except in very tight labour markets, where large numbers of staff are required at the same time, there is no point in placing a recruitment advertisement outside a newspaper or journal's recruitment pages. In some situations newspaper readership figures are helpful when deciding where to advertise. An example would be where there are two or more established trade journals or local newspapers competing with one another, both of which carry numerous recruitment advertisements. Otherwise readership figures are unimportant because people tend to buy different newspapers when job searching than they do the rest of the time. It is often more helpful to look at the share of different recruitment advertising markets achieved by the various publications, as this gives an indication of where particular types of job are mostly advertised. In the UK in recent years the *Guardian* newspaper has gained and sustained a 40 per cent market share of national recruitment advertising. For many jobs in the media, education and the public sector it is now established as the first port of call for job seekers. This has been achieved by cutting rates to less than half those charged by other national newspapers. For the more senior private sector jobs, however, the established market leaders are the *Daily Telegraph*, the *Sunday Times* and the *Financial Times*. While recruitment advertising agents are well placed to advise on these issues, it is straightforward to get hold of information about rates charged by different publications and their respective market shares. Good starting points are the websites of British Rate and Data (**www.brad.co.uk**), which carries up-to-date information about thousands of publications, and the National Readership Survey (**www.nrs.co.uk**) which provides details of readership levels among different population groups. Table 7.4 reviews the advantages and drawbacks of various methods of job advertising.

Drafting the advertisement

The decision on what to include in a recruitment advertisement is important because of the high cost of space and the need to attract attention; both factors will encourage the use of the fewest number of words. Where agencies are used they will be able to advise on this, as they will on the way the advertisement should be worded, but the following is a short checklist of items that must be included.

- Name and brief details of employing organisation
- Job role and duties
- Training to be provided
- Key points of the personnel specification or competency profile
- Salary
- Instructions about how to apply

Many employers are coy about declaring the salary that will accompany the advertised post. Sometimes this is reasonable as the salary scales are well known and inflexible, as in much public sector employment. Elsewhere the coyness is due either to the fact that

Table 7.4 The advantages and drawbacks of various methods of job advertising

Internal advertisement

Advantages:
- (a) Maximum information to all employees, who might then act as recruiters.
- (b) Opportunity for all internal candidates to apply.
- (c) If an internal candidate is appointed, there is a shorter induction period.
- (d) Speed.
- (e) Cost.

Drawbacks:
- (a) Limit to number of applicants.
- (b) Internal candidates not matched against those from outside.
- (c) May be unlawful if indirect discrimination. (See Chapter 23.)

Vacancy lists outside premises

Advantage:
- (a) Economical way of advertising, particularly if premises are near a busy thoroughfare.

Drawbacks:
- (a) Vacancy list likely to be seen by few people.
- (b) Usually possible to put only barest information, like the job title, or even just 'Vacancies'.

Advertising in the national press

Advantages:
- (a) Advertisement reaches large numbers.
- (b) Some national newspapers are the accepted medium for search by those seeking particular posts.

Drawbacks:
- (a) Cost.
- (b) Much of the cost 'wasted' in reaching inappropriate people.

Advertising in the local press

Advantages:
- (a) Recruitment advertisements more likely to be read by those seeking local employment.
- (b) Little 'wasted' circulation.

Drawback:
- (a) Local newspapers appear not to be used by professional and technical people seeking vacancies.

Advertising in the technical press

Advantage:
- (a) Reaches a specific population with minimum waste.

Drawbacks:
- (a) Relatively infrequent publication may require advertising copy six weeks before appearance of advertisement.
- (b) Inappropriate when a non-specialist is needed, or where the specialism has a choice of professional publications.

Internet

Advantages:
- (a) Information about a vacancy reaches many people.
- (b) Inexpensive once a website has been constructed.
- (c) Speed with which applications are sent in.
- (d) Facilitates online shortlisting.

Drawbacks:
- (a) Can produce thousands of unsuitable applications.
- (b) Worries about confidentiality may deter good applications.

the employer has a general secrecy policy about salaries and does not want to publicise the salary of a position to be filled for fear of dissatisfying holders of other posts, or does not know what to offer and is waiting to see 'what the mail brings'. All research evidence, however, suggests that a good indication of the salary is essential if the employer is to attract a useful number of appropriate replies (*see* Barber 1998, pp. 42–3).

ACTIVITY 7.3

Table 7.5 contains phrases about the value in pay terms of 12 different jobs. Try putting them in rank order of actual cash value to the recipient. Then ask a friend to do the same thing and compare your lists.

1	*c.*£60,000 + bonus + car + benefits
2	from *c.*£35k
3	£30,000–£40,000 + substantial bonus + car
4	You will already be on a basic annual salary of not less than £40,000
5	Six-figure remuneration + profit share + benefits
6	*c.*£60,000 package
7	Attractive package
8	Substantial package
9	£50,000 OTE, plus car and substantial benefits
10	£ excellent + benefits
11	£ Neg.
12	*c.*£60k package + banking benefits

Table 7.5
Phrases from a quality newspaper about salary

E-RECRUITMENT

The use of the Internet for recruitment purposes is, along with the substantial recent growth in international recruitment, the most striking recent development in the field, but its practical significance remains a question of debate. When the Internet first became widely used ten or fifteen years ago it was often predicted that it would revolutionise the recruitment industry. In the future, it was argued, most of us would find out about jobs through web searches. It now appears that these predictions greatly overstated the influence that the Internet would have. Incomes Data Services came to the following conclusion having carried out an extensive survey of approaches used by UK organisations:

> Although the significance of online recruitment is growing, it has to be remembered that the medium is not appropriate for all jobs or for all candidates. There are still some people who are not comfortable using a computer and even 'web savvy' applicants may be deterred by the perceived impersonal nature of online recruitment . . . There is, therefore, still a role for conventional advertising, particularly when recruiting locally or for hard-to-fill jobs. Ultimately, many employers may seek to combine online and traditional approaches to maximise their chances of securing the best candidate. (IDS 2006, p. 2)

Internet recruitment takes two basic forms. The first is centred on the employer's own website, jobs being advertised alongside information about the products and services offered by the organisation. The second approach makes use of the growing number of cyber-agencies which combine the roles traditionally played by both newspapers and employment agents. They advertise the job and undertake shortlisting before they send on a selection of suitable CVs to the employer.

For employers the principal attraction is the way that the Internet allows jobs to be advertised inexpensively to a potential audience of millions. According to Frankland (2000) the cost of setting up a good website is roughly equivalent to that associated with advertising a single high-profile job in a national newspaper. Huge savings can also be made by dispensing with the need to print glossy recruitment brochures and other documents to send to potential candidates. The other big advantage is speed. People can respond within seconds of reading about an opportunity by emailing their CV to the employer. Shortlisting can also be undertaken quickly with the use of CV-matching software or online application forms.

In principle e-recruitment thus has a great deal to offer. In practice, however, there are major problems which may take many more years to iron out. A key drawback is the way that employers advertising jobs tend to get bombarded with hundreds of applications. This occurs because of the large number of people who read the advertisement and because it takes so little effort to email a copy of a pre-prepared CV to the employer concerned. In order to prevent 'spamming' of this kind it is necessary to make use of online shortlisting software which is able to screen out unsuitable applications. Such technologies, however, are not wholly satisfactory. Those which work by looking for key words in CVs inevitably have a 'hit and miss' character and can be criticised for being inherently unfair. The possibility that good candidates may not be considered simply because they have not chosen a particular word or phrase is strong. The same is true of online application systems which include a handful of 'killer' questions designed to sift out unsuitable candidates at a very early stage. The tendency is for people who have a somewhat unconventional career background simply to be disregarded when, in fact, they may have the required talent or potential to do an excellent job.

The alternative is to require candidates to apply online by completing a pschyometric test. This approach has the advantage of deterring candidates who are not prepared to invest the time and effort required to complete the forms, but is unreliable in important respects – there is no guarantee that the test is in fact being completed by the candidate, nor is it completed within a standard, pre-determined time limit. Other problems concern fears about security and confidentiality which serve to deter people from submitting personal details over the web:

> Everybody should be familiar with the fear of using a credit card on-line even though good e-commerce sites have secure servers that enable these transactions to take place safely. The job-seeker's equivalent of this is 'how safe is it to put my CV on-line?' Although the figures prove that plenty of people have overcome this fear (there are an estimated 4.5 million CVs on-line), horror stories of candidates' CVs ending up on their employer's desktop aren't entirely without foundation. (Weekes 2000, p. 35)

Criticisms have also been made about poor standards of ethicality on the part of cyber-agencies. As with conventional employment agents there are a number who employ sharp practices such as posting fictional vacancies and falsely inflating advertised pay rates in order to build up a bank of CVs which can be circulated to employers on an unsolicited basis. Some cyber-agencies also copy CVs from competitors' sites and send them on to employers without authorisation. Over time, as the industry grows, professional standards will be established and a regulatory regime established, but for the time being such problems remain.

The fact that there are so many drawbacks alongside the advantages explains why so many employers appear to use the Internet for recruitment while rating it relatively poorly. When asked to rank recruitment methods in terms of their effectiveness very few employers place the Internet at the top of the list (only 7 per cent according to a 2003 CIPD survey). While employers rank the Internet highly vis-à-vis other methods in terms of its cost effectiveness, they are much less convinced when asked about the quality of applicants and the ability of web-based advertising to source the right candidates (IRS 2005, p. 45). Established approaches such as newspaper advertising and education liaison are much more highly rated and are thus unlikely to be replaced by e-recruitment in the near future. However, over the longer term, technological developments and increased web usage may improve the effectiveness of e-recruitment considerably. In 2007 it was announced by Ofcom (the telecommunications regulatory body) that over half of adults in the UK have broadband Internet connections at home, while many more can access the web speedily at work, in a library, job centre, educational institution or Internet café. Ultimately it is likely that one or two very well-funded job sites will emerge from the current mass and will be in a position to command substantial shares of the market. We may then have a situation in which anyone seeking a new job in a particular field will make a familiar website rather than the newspaper or journal their first port of call.

WINDOW ON PRACTICE

In 2000 an unemployed 53-year-old electronics manager called David Hall took part in a project commissioned by Wynnwith, an established recruitment company. He spent three months unsuccessfully looking for a job using the services of 12 well-known cyber-agencies. He registered with each, giving full details of his background and skills. At the end of the period he concluded that 'these sites appear to offer little more than pretty coloured graphics and empty promises about job opportunities'. He was offered one interview during the 12 weeks, for a role that was unsuitable given his experience. Of the hundreds of job opportunities emailed to him, he reckoned that only 5 per cent matched his capabilities. Among his criticisms were the following:

- the same jobs were advertised week after week
- very little information was provided about most vacancies
- salary levels were inflated to make jobs more appealing
- he received no feedback on applications that failed
- he was concerned that his CV was being circulated without his consent
- his emails were often not acknowledged

Source: 'Online Recruitment Study' at **www.wynnwith.com**.

RECRUITING OVERSEAS

As labour markets have tightened, skills shortages have become more acute and as employers have found it harder to recruit UK-based staff at a level of salary that is affordable, they have increasingly been looking overseas as a major source of staff. The accession of ten new countries to the EU in 2004 greatly assisted in this respect, permitting, according to official estimates, over half a million people to come into the UK to work by the end of 2006 (Blanchflower *et al*. 2007).

Citizens of EU countries that joined the Union prior to January 2007 are permitted to work in the UK without a permit; this includes countries such as Poland and Hungary which have become major sources of staff for UK employers in recent years. People from countries acceding in 2004, however, must in most cases register with the government under its Worker Registration Scheme and then apply for a residence permit after completing a years' continuous service with a UK employer. Work permits are not required by people coming from countries in the European Economic Area (EEA) but not in the EU (such as Norway and Switzerland), citizens of British Overseas Territories (e.g. Gibraltar) or people from Commonwealth states whose parents or grandparents were born in the UK. Spouses of UK citizens who retain an overseas nationality can also work in the UK without a permit. For people who do not fall into one of these categories there are complex rules which will determine whether or not they can receive a work permit and for how long they are able to stay in the UK to work thereafter. Different rules apply, for example, to students studying in the UK, to spouses of people with work permits, and to people from overseas who have qualifications that are in short supply in the UK. At the time of writing (2007) a new streamlined system for granting work permits and rights of residence is being developed by the government and will soon be implemented. It will be points based, making it a great deal easier for someone in their early twenties with a higher degree, and a high existing salary, to obtain a permit than someone who is older, poorer and less highly educated. Low-skilled workers from outside the EU will effectively have no possibility of entering the UK legally to work, except on a temporary basis in very limited situations.

Running large-scale overseas recruitment campaigns is expensive and it is an activity that has to be planned carefully if it is to yield effective results. Over recent years, as demand for overseas workers has increased, a number of well-run agencies with a high level of knowledge and experience of specific labour markets have become established, and many employers have used them. Others, particularly NHS Trusts and larger recruiters of skilled workers, have developed their own competence in this area and recruit directly. IDS (2005) gives the following sound advice:

- Recruit in countries where skills and qualifications are comparable with those in the UK. This reduces the length of time it takes for each new migrant worker to adapt and begin performing at a high level.

- Recruit in countries with relatively high unemployment and relatively low wages vis-à-vis the UK. Elsewhere workers will have a great deal less motivation to move to the UK.

- Meet potential candidates face to face before employing them. Do not rely on telephone interviews or the opinion of an agency. This typically involves flying managers out to an overseas destination to run intensive interview days or assessment centres.

- Ensure that candidates have strong communication skills and a sufficient level of competence in the English language before recruiting them.
- Ensure that appropriate accommodation is provided when the new recruits first arrive in the UK along with support systems so that they feel welcome and become effective quickly.

It is also important to be aware of the various ethical issues associated with overseas recruitment. Care must be taken, for example, to ensure equal treatment with UK nationals so that neither group perceives that the other is being given favourable treatment by their employers. Another major ethical issue relates to the recruitment of 'key workers' such as doctors and nurses in developing countries where they are in short supply. In recent years a number of governments have rightly complained that the NHS is robbing local health providers of the staff they need to help ensure the health of their own people.

EMPLOYER BRANDING

In recent years considerable interest has developed in the idea that employers have much to gain when competing for staff by borrowing techniques long used in marketing goods and services to potential customers. In particular, many organisations have sought to position themselves as 'employers of choice' in their labour markets with a view to attracting stronger applications from potential employees. Those who have succeeded have often found that their recruitment costs fall as a result because they get so many more unsolicited applications (*see* Taylor 2002, p. 449).

Central to these approaches is the development over time of a positive '**brand image**' of the organisation as an employer, so that potential employees come to regard working there as highly desirable. Developing a good brand image is an easier task for larger companies with household names than for those which are smaller or highly specialised, but the possibility of developing and sustaining a reputation as a good employer is something from which all organisations stand to benefit.

The key, as when branding consumer products, is to build on any aspect of the working experience that is distinct from that offered by other organisations competing in the same broad applicant pool. It may be relatively high pay or a generous benefits package, it may be flexible working, or a friendly and informal atmosphere, strong career development potential or job security. This is then developed as a 'unique selling proposition' and forms the basis of the employer branding exercise. The best way of finding out what is distinct and positive about working in your organisation is to carry out some form of staff attitude survey. Employer branding exercises simply amount to a waste of time and money when they are not rooted in the actual lived experience of employees because people are attracted to the organisation on false premises. As with claims made for products that do not live up to their billing, the employees gained are not subsequently retained, and resources are wasted recruiting people who resign quickly after starting.

Once the unique selling propositions have been identified they can be used to inform all forms of communication that the organisation engages in with potential and actual applicants. The aim must be to repeat the message again and again in advertisements, in recruitment literature, on Internet sites and at careers fairs. It is also important that existing employees are made aware of their employer's brand proposition too as so much recruitment is carried out informally through word of mouth. Provided the message is accurate and provided it is communicated effectively over time, the result will be a 'leveraging of the brand' as more and more people in the labour market begin to associate the message with the employer.

WINDOW ON PRACTICE

Like many fast food chains, Burger King and McDonald's have found it hard to recruit managers to run their restaurants. Such workplaces have long suffered from a poor image in the labour market and lose out as a result in the recruitment of graduates and junior managerial staff, many of whom would prefer to work pretty well anywhere else. Burger King reversed its fortunes to a great extent during 2002 and 2003 by running a shrewd recruitment advertising campaign rooted in an employer branding exercise. The advertisements were strikingly designed and printed in colour to attract attention. A small corporate logo was featured in one corner, but this was dwarfed by slogans which set out what made working as a Burger King manager distinct. The focus was on the following:

• The fact that the job was never dull

• The career development opportunities that were available to ambitious people

• The relatively attractive salary package on offer

In the week after the first advertisement was placed in a local paper two hundred people phoned for further details leading to the appointment of eight new managers. The company's equivalent old-style advertisement had only yielded twenty applicants, none of whom were considered appointable.

McDonald's has also developed a bold approach to its recent recruitment campaigns, making good use of the employer branding concept in a bid to rid itself of the image as a bad employer to work for. As the leading organisation in the fast food market the company has had to suffer the ignomany of seeing the term 'McJob' being included in the Oxford English Dictionary and being defined as a job which is badly paid, unstimulating and having few prospects. It has, however, sought to turn this notoriety to its advantage by running recruitment campaigns which flag up the positive aspects of a career with McDonald's (flexibility, fast career prospects, etc.) while incorporating the slogan 'Not bad for a McJob?' In addition the company has revamped its selection procedures so that would-be staff at all levels experience a day working in a restaurant before they are offered a job. This has the twin advantages of ensuring that they know what to expect and do not accept a job on false premises, while also helping recruiters to make better-informed judgement about their suitability.

Sources: IRS (2003b) and IRS (2006).

CONTROL AND EVALUATION

The HR manager needs to monitor the effectiveness of advertising and all other methods of recruitment, first, to ensure value for money and, second, to ensure that the pool of applicants produced by the various methods is suitable.

Wright and Storey (1994, p. 209) suggest that information on the following should be collected:

- Number of initial enquiries received which resulted in completed application forms.
- Number of candidates at various stages in the recruitment and selection process, especially those shortlisted.
- Number of candidates recruited.
- Number of candidates retained in organisation after six months.

There is also a good case for monitoring the numbers of men and women who are successful at each stage of the process and the numbers of people from different ethnic minorities. Where an imbalance becomes apparent the organisation can then take remedial action.

There needs, however, to be more information than this in order to get to the more intangible questions, such as 'Did the best candidate not even apply?' The most important source of information about the quality of the recruitment process is the people involved in it. Do telephonists and receptionists know how to handle the tentative employment enquiry? What did they hear from applicants in the original enquiries that showed the nature of their reaction to the advertisement? Is it made simple for enquirers to check key points by telephone or personal visit? Is there an unnecessary emphasis on written applications before anything at all can be done? Useful information can also be obtained from both successful and unsuccessful applicants. Those who have been successful will obviously believe that recruitment was well done, while the unsuccessful may have good reason to believe that it was flawed. However, those who are unsuccessful sometimes ask for feedback on the reasons. If a recruiter is able to give this, it is also a simple development to ask the applicant for comment on the recruitment process.

CORRESPONDENCE

If an organisation is to maximise its chances of recruiting the best people to the jobs it advertises it must ensure that all subsequent communication with those who express an interest is carried out professionally. The same is true of casual enquirers and those who find out about possible vacancies informally through word of mouth. Failing to make a positive impression may well result in good candidates losing interest or developing a preference for a rival organisation which takes greater care to project itself effectively in its labour markets. Providing information to would-be candidates who express an interest is the first step. This is often seen as unnecessary and costly, but it should be seen as the organisation's opportunity to sell itself as an employer to its potential applicant pool. The following are commonly provided:

- a copy of the relevant job description and personnel specification;
- a copy of the advertisement for reference purposes;

- a copy of any general recruitment brochure produced by the organisation;
- the staff handbook or details of a collective agreement;
- details of any occupational pension arrangements;
- general information about the organisation (e.g. a mission statement, annual report or publicity brochures).

It is also essential to have some method of tracking recruitment, either manually or by computer, so that an immediate and helpful response can be given to applicants enquiring about the stage their application has reached. Moreover, it is necessary to ensure that all applicants are informed about the outcome of their application. This will reduce the number of enquiries that have to be handled, but it is also an important aspect of public relations, as the organisation dealing with job applicants may also be dealing with prospective customers. Many people have the experience of applying for a post and then not hearing anything at all. Particularly when the application is unsolicited, HR managers may feel that there is no obligation to reply, but this could be bad business as well as disconcerting for the applicant. Standard letters ('I regret to inform you that there were many applications and yours was not successful . . .') are better than nothing, but letters containing actual information ('out of the seventy-two applications, we included yours in our first shortlist of fifteen, but not in our final shortlist of eight') are better. Best of all are the letters that make practical suggestions, such as applying again in six months' time, asking if the applicant would like to be considered for another post elsewhere in the organisation, or pointing out the difficulty of applying for a post that calls for greater experience or qualifications than the applicant at that stage is able to present.

ACTIVITY 7.4

Recruiters are interested in the job to be done, so that they concentrate on how the vacancy fits into the overall structure of the organisation and on the type of person to be sought. Applicants are interested in the work to be done, as they want to know what they will be doing and what the work will offer to them. Think of your own job and list both types of feature.

The job to be done:

1
2
3
4
5

The work that is offered:

1
2
3
4
5

How does your listing of features in the second list alter the wording of advertisements and other employment documentation?

SHORTLISTING

Shortlisting of candidates can be difficult in some instances because of small numbers of applicants and in other instances because of extremely large numbers of applicants. Such difficulties can arise unintentionally when there is inadequate specification of the criteria required or intentionally in large-scale recruitment exercises such as those associated with an annual intake of graduates.

In such circumstances it is tempting for the HR department to use some form of arbitrary method to reduce the numbers to a more manageable level. Examples include screening people out because of their age, because of their handwriting style or because their work history is perceived as being unconventional in some way. No doubt there are other whimsical criteria adopted by managers appalled at making sense of 100 or so application forms and assorted curricula vitae. Apart from those that are unlawful, these criteria are grossly unfair to applicants if not mentioned in the advertisement, and are a thoroughly unsatisfactory way of recruiting the most appropriate person.

It is far more satisfactory to have in place a fair and objective system for shortlisting candidates which produces the best group of alternative candidates to move forward to the interview stage. This can be achieved in one of three basic ways – which can be used separately or in combination. The first involves using a panel of managers to undertake shortlisting, reducing the likelihood that individual prejudices will influence the process. A number of distinct stages can be identified:

- **Stage 1:** Panel members agree essential criteria for those to be placed on the shortlist.
- **Stage 2:** Using those criteria, selectors individually produce personal lists of, say, ten candidates. An operating principle throughout is to concentrate on who can be included rather than who can be excluded, so that the process is positive, looking for strengths rather than shortcomings.
- **Stage 3:** Selectors reveal their lists and find their consensus. If stages 1 and 2 have been done properly the degree of consensus should be quite high and probably sufficient to constitute a shortlist for interview. If it is still not clear, they continue to:
- **Stage 4:** Discuss those candidates preferred by some but not all in order to clarify and reduce the areas of disagreement. A possible tactic is to classify candidates as 'strong', 'possible' or 'maverick'.
- **Stage 5:** Selectors produce a final shortlist by discussion, guarding against including compromise candidates: not strong, but offensive to no one.

The second approach involves employing a scoring system as advocated by Roberts (1997) and Wood and Payne (1998). As with the panel method, the key shortlisting criteria are defined at the start of the process (e.g. three years' management experience, a degree in a certain discipline, current salary in the range of £20,000–£30,000, evidence of an ability to drive change, etc.). The shortlister then scores each CV or application form received against these criteria awarding an A grade (or high mark) where clear evidence is provided that the candidate matches the criteria, a B grade where there is some evidence or where the candidate partially meets the criteria and a C grade where no convincing evidence is provided. Where a structured application form has been completed by the candidates, this process can be undertaken quickly (two or three minutes per application) because a candidate can be screened out whenever, for example, more than one C grade has been awarded.

The third approach involves making use of the software systems on the market which shortlist candidates electronically. The different types of system and some of the drawbacks were described above in the section on e-recruitment. Despite the problems, such systems can be useful where the criteria are very clearly and tightly defined, and where an online application form is completed which makes use of multiple-choice answers. Such forms can be scored speedily and objectively, the candidate being given feedback on whether or not they have been successful. Only those who make the 'right' choices when completing the online questionnaire are then invited to participate in the next stage of the recruitment process.

SUMMARY PROPOSITIONS

7.1 Alternatives to filling a vacancy include reorganising the work; using overtime; mechanising the work; staggering the hours; making the job part time; subcontracting the work; using an employment agency.

7.2 Recent trends indicate a greater use by employers of recruitment agencies and executive consultants, open days, recruitment fairs, etc. Relocation constraints have also prompted a move towards the use of regional as opposed to national recruitment advertising.

7.3 Advertising agencies and specialist publications provide a wealth of information to ensure that advertisements reach the appropriate readership.

7.4 E-recruitment provides great potential advantages for employers but is not seen as being especially effective at present.

7.5 Employer branding involves actively selling the experience of working for an organisation by focusing on what makes the experience both positive and distinct.

7.6 Increasing the amount of information provided to potential applicants reduces the number of inappropriate applications.

7.7 Care with shortlisting increases the chances of being fair to all applicants and lessens the likelihood of calling inappropriate people for interview.

GENERAL DISCUSSION TOPICS

1 What are the advantages and disadvantages of graduate recruitment fairs from an employer's point of view?

2 Why is it that the national newspapers which sell the fewest copies (broadsheets) dominate the market for recruitment advertising in the UK, while the more popular tabloids carry virtually none at all?

3 Can you improve on the suggestions for shortlisting that the chapter contains?

FURTHER READING

Barber, A.E. (1998) *Recruiting Employees: Individual and Organizational Perspectives*. Thousand Oaks, Cal.: Sage.

Taylor, S. and Collins, C. (2000) 'Organizational Recruitment: Enhancing the Intersection of Research and Practice', in C. Cooper and E. Locke (eds) *Industrial and Organizational Psychology*. Oxford: Blackwell.

Academic research on recruitment as opposed to selection processes is relatively undeveloped and there remain many central issues that have not been rigorously studied. In the USA the gap has been filled to some extent in recent years. The best summary and critique of this work is provided by Barber (1998). Taylor and Collins (2000) provide a shorter treatment with an additional practical focus.

Chartered Institute of Personnel and Development

CIPD commissions a large survey each year on recruitment and selection issues which tracks all the major trends and provides authoritative evidence about employer practices. The institute's journal, *People Management*, also publishes a very useful supplement each July reviewing developments in the recruitment industry.

Edwards, M. (2005) 'Employer and Employee Branding: HR or PR?', in S. Bach (ed.) *Managing Human Resources: Personnel Management in Transition*. Oxford: Blackwell.

This is one of the first serious analyses of academic thinking on the emerging concept of employer branding.

REFERENCES

Barber, A.E. (1998) *Recruiting Employees: Individual and Organizational Perspectives*. Thousand Oaks, Cal.: Sage.

Blanchflower, D.G., Saleheen, J. and Shadforth, C. (2007) 'The Impact of Recent Migration from Eastern Europe on the UK Economy'. London: Bank of England.

Brannick, M.T. and Levine, E.L. (2002) *Job Analysis: Methods, research and applications for human resource management in the new millennium*. Thousand Oaks, Cal.: Sage.

Chartered Institute of Personnel and Development (2003) *Recruitment and Retention 2003: survey report*. London: CIPD.

Chartered Institute of Personnel and Development (2006) *Recruitment, Retention and Turnover: Annual Survey Report 2006*. London: CIPD.

Edwards, M. (2005) 'Employer and Employee Branding: HR or PR?', in S. Bach (ed.) *Managing Human Resources: Personnel Management in Transition*. Oxford: Blackwell.

Frankland, G. (2000) 'If you build it, they will come', *People Management*, 16 March, p. 45.

IDS (2003) *Recruitment Practices*, IDS Study No. 751, June. London: Incomes Data Services.

IDS (2005) *Recruiting Foreign Workers*. IDS Study 807, October (pp. 7–16). London: Incomes Data Services.

IDS (2006) *Online Recruitment*. IDS Study 819, April. London: Incomes Data Services.

Institute for Employment Research (2006) *Working Futures 2004–2014: National Report*. Warwick: Institute for Employment Research.

Institute of Employment Studies (2002) *Free, fair and efficient? Open internal job advertising* (W. Hirsh, E. Pollard and P. Tamkin). Brighton: IES.

IRS (2003a) 'Job descriptions and person specifications', *IRS Employment Review*, No. 776, 23 May.

IRS (2003b) 'Better recruitment processes', *IRS Employment Review*, No. 780, 18 July.

IRS (2005) 'Online recruitment in the UK: 10 years older and wiser', *IRS Employment Review*, No. 822, 29 April, pp. 42–8.

IRS (2006) 'Building a McReputation to aid recruitment and retention', *IRS Employment Review*, No. 853, 18 August.

Labour Market Trends (2002) 'Labour market spotlight', August.

Newell, S. and Shackleton, V. (2000) 'Recruitment and selection', in S. Bach and K. Sisson (eds), *Personnel Management: A Comprehensive Guide to theory and practice*. Oxford, Blackwell.

Pearn, M. and Kandola, R. (1988) *Job Analysis: A practical guide for managers*. London: IPM.

Roberts, G. (1997) *Recruitment and Selection*. London: IPD.

Taylor, S. (2002) *People Resourcing*. London, CIPD.

Weekes, S. (2000) 'Hire on the wire', *Personnel Today*, 2 May, pp. 31–5.

Whiddett, S. and Kandola, B. (2000) 'Fit for the job?', *People Management*, 25 May, pp. 30–4.

Wood, R. and Payne, T. (1998) *Competency Based Recruitment and Selection: A Practical Guide*. Chichester: Wiley.

Wright, M. and Storey, J. (1994) 'Recruitment', in I. Beardwell and L. Holden (eds) *Human Resource Management*. London: Pitman.

An extensive range of additional materials, including multiple choice questions, answers to questions and links to useful websites can be found on the Human Resource Management Companion Website at **www.pearsoned.co.uk/torrington**.

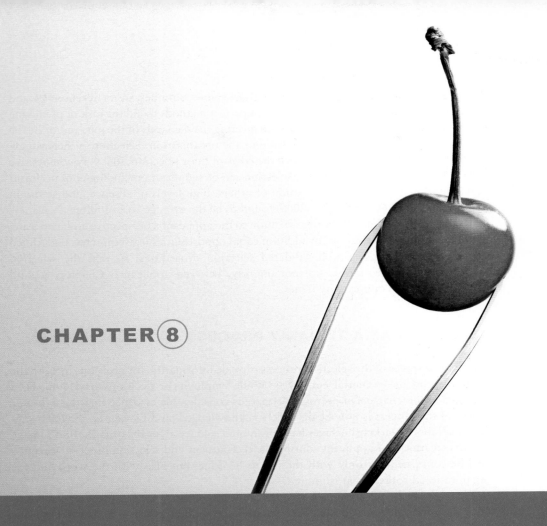

CHAPTER 8

SELECTION METHODS AND DECISIONS

THE OBJECTIVES OF THIS CHAPTER ARE TO:

1 Explain the importance of viewing selection as a two-way process

2 Examine the development and use of selection criteria

3 Evaluate the range of selection methods that are available (interviewing will be dealt with in detail in the interactive skills section of the focus on skills at the end of part 2) and consider the criteria for choosing different methods

4 Review approaches to selection decision making

5 Explain how selection procedures can be validated

While the search for the perfect method of selection continues, in its absence HR and line managers continue to use a variety of imperfect methods to aid the task of predicting which applicant will be most successful in meeting the demands of the job, and/or be the best fit with the work group and culture of the organisation. Selection is increasingly important as more attention is paid to the costs of poor selection, in a very competitive market for talent. The costs of poor selection can be significant, including poor performance, additional training, demotivation of others, high levels of absence, and so on, in addition to the £3,600 the CIPD (2006) found to be the average cost of filling a vacancy. This context has promoted greater attention to the applicant's perspective and increasing use of technology in selection. In addition equal opportunities legislation has underlined the importance of using well validated selection procedures, so that the selection process discriminates fairly, and not unfairly, between applicants. Chapters 23 and 24 deal with equal opportunity issues.

SELECTION AS A TWO-WAY PROCESS

The various stages of the selection process provide information for decisions by both the employer and the potential employee. While employment decisions have long been regarded as a management prerogative there is considerable evidence that the two-way nature of the process is now being widely acknowledged, and Lievens *et al.* (2002) suggest that labour market shortages have promoted a concern for the organisation's image and the treatment of applicants during the recruitment and selection process. We must also be concerned not only with the job to be done, but also with the work and the organisational context that is offered.

Throughout the selection process applicants choose between organisations by evaluating the developing relationship between themselves and the prospect. This takes place in the correspondence from potential employers; in their experience of the selection methods used by the employer; and in the information they gain on interview. Applicants will decide not to pursue some applications. Either they will have accepted another offer, or they will find something in their dealings with the organisation that discourages them and they withdraw. When large numbers of candidates withdraw it may be because the information provided by the organisation was sufficiently detailed, accurate and realistic that they were able to make a wise decision that they were not suited to the organisation and that time would be wasted by continuing. On the other hand, it might be that potentially admirable recruits were lost because of the way in which information was presented, lack of information, or the interpretation that was put on the 'flavour' of the correspondence.

The frame of reference for the applicant is so different from that of the manager in the organisation that the difference is frequently forgotten. It would not be unrealistic to suggest that the majority of applicants have a mental picture of their application being received by the company and immediately being closely scrutinised and discussed by powerful figures. The fact that the application is one element in a varied routine for the recipient is incomprehensible to some and unacceptable to many. The thought that one person's dream is another's routine is something the applicant cannot cope with.

If they have posted or emailed an application with high enthusiasm about the fresh prospects that the new job would bring, they are in no mood for delay and they may quickly start convincing themselves that they are not interested, because their initial euphoria has not been sustained. If candidates get as far as interview they will also be influenced by recruiter behaviour in deciding whether to accept a job offer, if one is made. Papadopoulou *et al.* (1996), for example, demonstrated that candidates were influenced by the recruiter's ability to supply adequate and accurate information, as this is what they had expected from the interview. In addition they were influenced by the way the recruiter managed the interaction, as well as the content, so the recruiter's control of the interaction, their listening ability and in particular their ability/willingness to allow the candidate to present themselves effectively are all important.

Some of the points that seem to be useful about interacting with the candidate are:

1 Reply, meaningfully, fast. The printed postcard of acknowledgement is not a reply, neither is the personal letter or email which says nothing more than that the application has been received. Web-based selection can speed things up considerably, and we look at this in more detail later in the chapter.

2 Conduct correspondence in terms of what the applicants want to know. How long will they have to wait for an answer? If you ask them in for interview or assessment centre, how long will it take, what will it involve, do you defray expenses, can they park their car, how do they find you, etc.?

3 Interviewers should be trained to ensure that they have not only full knowledge of the relevant information, but also the skills to manage the interaction effectively.

SELECTION CRITERIA AND THE PERSON SPECIFICATION

Unless the criteria against which applicants will be measured are made explicit, it is impossible to make credible selection decisions. It will be difficult to select the most appropriate selection procedure and approach, and it will be difficult to validate the selection process. Selection criteria are typically presented in the form of a person specification representing the ideal candidate, and cover such areas as skills, experience, qualifications, education, personal attributes, special attributes, interests and motivation (IRS 2003). Although the IRS found that person specifications were used by three-quarters of the organisations in their study, Lievens *et al.* (2002) challenge the use of traditional person specifications as jobs become less defined and constantly change. Three perspectives can be used to determine selection criteria – organisational fit, team/functional fit and job fit.

Fit with the organisation

The organisational criteria are those attributes that an organisation considers valuable in its employees and that affect judgements about a candidate's potential to be successful within an organisation. For example, the organisation may be expanding and innovating and require employees who are particularly flexible and adaptable. Previously, these organisational criteria were rarely made explicit and they were often used at an intuitive level. However, Townley (1991) argues that organisations are increasingly likely to focus on more general attitudes and values than narrow task-based criteria. Barclay (1999) explains how fit with the organisation is often expressed in terms of personality, attitudes, flexibility, commitment and goals, rather than the ability to do the specific job for which the person is being recruited. Such organisational criteria are important where jobs are ill-defined and constantly changing. There are also some groups who are recruited into the organisation rather than into specific jobs or even a specific function – new/ recent graduates, for example, and, here again, organisation criteria are important.

Functional and team fit

Between the generality of the organisational criteria and the preciseness of job criteria there are functional criteria, such as the definition of appropriate interpersonal skills for all members of the HR department. Criteria may also be important when the new appointee will have to fit into a pre-existing work team. For a useful discussion of person/group fit *see* Werbel and Johnson 2001.

Individual job criteria

Individual job criteria contained in job descriptions and person specifications are derived from the process of job analysis. Although it is reasonably easy to specify the factors that should influence the personnel specification, the process by which the specification is formed is more difficult to describe. Van Zwanenberg and Wilkinson (1993) offer a dual perspective. They describe 'job first – person later' and 'person first – job later' approaches. The first starts with analysing the task to be done, presenting this in the form of a job description and from this deriving the personal qualities and attributes or competencies that are necessary to do the task. The difficulty here is in the translation process and the constant change of job demands and tasks. The alternative approach suggested by van Zwanenberg and Wilkinson starts with identifying which individuals are successful in a certain job and then describing their characteristics. There is also a trend towards making the person specification appropriate for a broad band of jobs rather than one particular job.

In addition to, or sometimes instead of, a person specification, many organisations are developing a competency profile as a means of setting the criteria against which to select. Competencies have been defined as underlying characteristics of a person which result in effective or superior performance; they include personal skills, knowledge, motives, traits, self-image and social role (*see* Boyatzis 1982). The advantage of competencies is that they can be used in an integrated way for selection, development, appraisal and reward activities; and also that from them behavioural indicators can be derived against which assessment can take place. For a fuller discussion of the nature and role of competencies, *see* Chapter 17. Woodruffe (2000) and Whiddett and Hollyforde (2003) provide useful practical sources of information on how to use competencies in the selection process. It should be noted, however, that using competencies as the only selection criterion is considered to be limiting and unhelpful (*see*, for example, Brittain and Ryder (1999) and Whiddett and Kandola (2000)).

ACTIVITY 8.1

Write a brief job description and a person specification for the anti-rape detective job as described in Case study 8.1 at www.pearsoned.co.uk/torrington.

CHOOSING SELECTION METHODS

It is unusual for one selection method to be used alone. A combination of two or more methods is generally used, and the choice of these is dependent upon a number of factors:

1 **Selection criteria for the post to be filled.** For example, group selection methods and assessment centre activities would be most useful for certain types of job, such as managerial, professional, supervisory and those who will be part of self-managing teams.

2 **Acceptability and appropriateness of the methods.** For the candidates involved, or likely to be involved, in the selection. The use, for example, of intelligence tests may be seen as insulting to applicants already occupying senior posts.

3 **Abilities of the staff involved in the selection process.** This applies particularly in the use of tests and assessment centres. Only those staff who are appropriately qualified by academic qualification and/or attendance on a recognised course may administer psychological tests.

4 **Administrative ease.** For administrative purposes it may be much simpler, say, to arrange one or two individual interviews for a prospective candidate than to organise a panel consisting of four members, all needing to make themselves available at the same time. Web-based testing may save much administrative time, particularly when there are large numbers of candidates.

5 **Time factors.** Sometimes a position needs to be filled very quickly, and time may be saved by using telephone or video-based interviews, or organising individual interviews rather than group selection methods, which would mean waiting for a day when all candidates are available.

6 **Accuracy.** Accuracy in selection generally increases in relation to the number of appropriate selection methods used (*see*, for example, IRS 2002a).

7 **Cost.** Tests may cost a lot to set up but once the initial outlay has been made they are reasonably cheap to administer. Assessment centres involve an even greater outlay and continue to be fairly expensive to administer. Interviews, on the other hand, cost only a moderate amount to set up in terms of interviewer training and are fairly cheap to administer. For the costlier methods great care needs to be taken in deciding whether the improvement in selection decision making justifies such costs.

SELECTION METHODS

In Chapter 7 on recruitment we considered the shortlisting process and the sifting of applications. We go on to look at selection methods in more detail, many of which may be used at different stages in the selection process, including shortlisting and sifting. We deal with interviews in depth in the interactive skills section at the end of Part 2 of the book.

Application forms

For a long time the application form was not suitable for use as a selection tool as it was a personal details form, which was intended to form the nucleus of the personnel record for the individual when they began work. As reservations grew about the validity of interviews for employment purposes, the more productive use of the application form was one of the avenues explored for improving the quality of decisions.

Forms were considered to act as a useful preliminary to employment interviews and decisions, either to present more information that was relevant to such deliberations, or to arrange such information in a standard way. This made sorting of applications and shortlisting easier and enabled interviewers to use the form as the basis for the interview itself, with each piece of information on the form being taken and developed in the interview. While there is heavy use of CVs for managerial and professional posts, many organisations, especially in the public sector, require both – off-putting to the applicant but helpful to the organisation in eliciting comparable data from all applicants.

The application form has been extended by some organisations to take a more significant part in the employment process. One form of extension is to ask for very much more, and more detailed, information from the candidate.

Another extension of application form usage has been in weighting, or biodata. Biodata have been defined by Anderson and Shackleton (1990) as 'historical and verifiable pieces of information about an individual in a selection context usually reported on application forms'. Biodata are perhaps of most use for large organisations filling fairly large numbers of posts for which they receive extremely high numbers of applications. This method is an attempt to relate the characteristics of applicants to characteristics of a large sample of successful job holders. The obvious drawbacks of this procedure are, first, the time that is involved and the size of sample needed, so that it is only feasible where there are many job holders in a particular type of position. Second, it smacks of witchcraft to the applicants who might find it difficult to believe that success in a position correlates with being, inter alia, the first born in one's family. Such methods are not currently well used and Taylor (2005) notes their controversial nature and perceived unfairness. In addition the 1998 Data Protection Act prohibits the use of an automated selection process (which biodata invariably are) as the *only* process used at any stage in the procedure.

Generally, application forms are used as a straightforward way of giving a standardised synopsis of the applicant's history. This helps applicants present their case by providing them with a predetermined structure, it speeds the sorting and shortlisting or sifting of applications either by hand or elecronically and it guides the interviewers as well as providing the starting point for personnel records. There remain concerns about the reliability of applications forms and CVs and this issue is dealt with in Case study 8.2 at **www.pearsoned.co.uk/torrington**. Application forms are increasingly available electronically; this not only speeds up the process but also enables 'key word' searches of the data on the forms (for alternative ways in which this may be carried out *see* Mohamed *et al.* (2001)), but there are questions about the legality of this method when used alone. Initial sifting of electronic applications often includes a variety of methods including material from an application form as shown in the Woolworths examples in the Window on Practice.

WINDOW ON PRACTICE

Multiple method interactive screening at Woolworths

Receiving a large number of CVs for a wide range of jobs Woolworths designed their interactive screening process to deal professionally and speedily with this volume. There are two stages in the interactive screening process: the first stage consists of biographical, competency and expectation matching, and the second comprises telephone screening.

First stage

Biographical screening

This comprises a series of questions to check for required qualifications, experience and education. In addition there are 'killer questions' which are so crucial that if an inappropriate response is received the candidate is advised that their application is unlikely to be successful, although it is their choice if they wish to continue. Feedback is always given anyway at the end of this biographical exploration, where they may be advised to perhaps consider applying for a different job.

Competency screening

Candidates are asked behavioural questions about their previous experiences to check whether their behaviours and attitudes match with the competency framework appropriate to the role for which they are applying.

Expectation Matching

Candidates are asked questions about what they expect or desire from a career with Woolworths. These are matched against the reality of the role and mismatches are followed up in the second stage of screening.

Second stage

From the first stage candidates are assessed as A (great candidate), B (possible) and C (not suitable). Telephone interviews with A candidates aim to hook them in and invite them to the next selection event, whereas with B candidates the interview will be more exploratory.

Woolworths maintain that screening has produced a greater quality of candidates for the next stage in selection process, an assessment centre, and note that the conversion rate has increased to 40 per cent.

Source: Summarised from Suff, R. (2005a) 'First-line filter: screening candidates for selection', *Employment Review*, No. 837, 16 December, pp. 44–8.

Self-assessment and peer assessment

There is increasing interest in providing more information to applicants concerning the job. This may involve a video, an informal discussion with job holders or further information sent with the application form. This is often termed giving the prospective candidate a 'realistic job preview' (Wanous 1992), enabling them to assess their own suitability to a much greater extent and some organisations have taken the opportunity to provide a self-selection questionnaire on the company website. Another way of achieving this is by asking the candidates to do some form of pre-work. This may also involve asking them questions regarding their previous work experiences which would relate to the job for which they are applying.

WINDOW ON PRACTICE

Job experience day at Pret à Manger

Pret à Manger have reduced staff turnover from 130 per cent (not high for the industry) to 98 per cent. They put this down to the use of a job experience day, which candidates have to do after an initial interview, but before they are granted a further competency-based interview.

Applicants do a day's work for which they are paid and they receive guidance and mentoring from an existing team member who is assigned to them for the day. But the aim is to enable applicants to work across a wide range of tasks with a wide range of team members. During the day the candidate also has an interview with the shop manager.

Team members who would be the applicant's future colleagues assess the applicant on competencies relevant to the job and then vote at the end of the day as to whether they would employ the applicant. The manager does not get a vote but can lobby for or against any candidate.

The success rate for the day is around 50 per cent. Pret à Manger have found this a good way of sifting large numbers of applicants and at the same time developing team commitment to new recruits.

Source: Summarised from L. Carrington (2002) 'At the cutting edge',
People Management, Vol. 8, No. 10, 16 May, pp. 30–1.

WINDOW ON PRACTICE

Using self-assessment realistic job previews for expatriate assignments

Caligiuri and Phillips (2003) carried out a field experiment using a self-assessment realistic job preview tool for potential expatriates in a multinational oil and energy company based in the USA. Candidates who had expressed interest were given the preview which explained the challenges and difficulties of expatriate assignments. There was a control group of candidates who did not receive these details. Information provided related to personality characteristics needed, family considerations and career considerations. All candidates were asked to complete a questionnaire prior to the self-assessment and then after the self-assessment which assessed self-efficacy (their expectation that they were capable of doing the expatriate assignment), ability to make an informed decision, and level of interest in the assignment.

The self-assessment resulted in increased self-efficacy and increased ability to make an informed decision, but interestingly the level of interest in doing the assignment was unchanged. The authors argue that impact of self-assessments is to enhance candidates' commitment to do the job (if selected) and prepare them for it by developing appropriate expectations, rather than providing an opportunity for candidates to deselect themselves.

Source: summarised from P. Caligiuri and J. Phillips (2003) 'An application of self-assessment realistic job previews to expatriate assignments', *International Journal of Human Resource Management*, Vol. 14, No. 7, pp. 1102–16.

Telephone interviewing

Telephone interviews can be used if speed is particularly important, and if geographical distance is an issue, as interviews with appropriate candidates can be arranged immediately. CIPD (2006) report that 56 per cent of organisations use this method of selection, a figure which has doubled since 2003, and probably reflects their use as one of a combination of screening tools, as well as a test of telephone manner, where required. Murphy (2005) reports similar figures and growth from an IRS survey. There is evidence that telephone interviews are best used as a part of a structured selection procedure, rather than alone – generally in terms of pre-selection for a face-to-face interview. However, they may also have an important role when selecting for jobs in which telephone manner is critical such as call centre and contact centre staff. There may be problems such as lack of non-verbal information, and difficulties getting hold of the applicant. However, positive aspects have been reported, such as concentration on content rather than the person. From an applicant perspective telephone interviews can be daunting, if they have no experience of them, and Murphy (2005) refers to and replicates checklists for organizations and candidates in the most effective use of such interviews.

WINDOW ON PRACTICE

One large employer requests CVs from applicants, and, on the basis of these, invites a selected number to take part in a telephone interview. A date and time are given and an idea of the questions that will be asked so that the candidate can prepare. The interview takes about 15–20 minutes, and time is allowed for the candidate to ask questions of the interviewer as well. Candidates are also told in advance of the telephone interview that if they are successful at this stage they will be invited to a one-day assessment centre on a specified date. After the telephone interview candidates are notified in writing whether or not they will move on to the assessment centre stage of the selection procedure.

ACTIVITY 8.2

What are the advantages of using telephone interviews of the type described in the Window on Practice above? For what types of job would you use this approach to selection?

Testing

The use of tests in employment procedures is surrounded by strong feelings for and against. Those in favour of testing in general point to the unreliability of the interview as a predictor of performance and the greater potential accuracy and objectivity of test data. Tests can be seen as giving credibility to selection decisions. Those against them either dislike the objectivity that testing implies or have difficulty in incorporating test evidence into the rest of the evidence that is collected. Questions have been raised as to the relevance of the tests to the job applied for and the possibility of unfair discrimination and bias. Also, some candidates feel that they can improve their prospects by a good interview performance and that the degree to which they are in control of their own destiny is being reduced by a dispassionate routine.

Tests remain heavily used, and the key issue debated currently is the extent to which tests should be administered over the web. CIPD (2006) with a larger sample found 75 per cent of organisations using general ability tests, 72 per cent of organisations using literacy/ numeracy tests and 60 per cent using personality tests, all of which had increased from previous years, and Murphy (2006) in an IRS survey found similar results. Testing is more likely to be used for management, professional and graduate jobs – although as testing on the web becomes more common it is likely to be used for a wider range of jobs.

Tests are chosen on the basis that test scores relate to, or correlate with, subsequent job performance, so that a high test score would predict high job performance and a low test score would predict low job performance.

WINDOW ON PRACTICE

Online testing at B&Q

B&Q have been using online psychological testing for managers, and this is being extended to all managerial and shop floor appointments. The system cost £12,000 to install and it is expected that costs will be recouped by the end of the first year of full use. B&Q have introduced this in a context of a growing company in a competitive recruitment market, and the tests are open to anyone who can access the website (www.diy.com). Tests are assessed as they are completed and feedback is immediately given to candidates to tell them if they can progress to the next stage of the selection procedure. B&Q argue that this approach avoids bias which may be present when initially assessing CVs. If candidates do not have online access a telephone test is available as an alternative.

Source: E. Davidson (2003) 'You can do it', *People Management*, Vol. 9, No. 4, 20 February, pp. 42–3.

Critical features of test use

Validity

Different types of validity can be applied to psychological tests. Personnel managers are most concerned with predictive validity, which is the extent to which the test can predict subsequent job performance. Predictive validity is measured by relating the test scores to measures of future performance, such as error rate, production rate, appraisal scores, absence rate or whatever criteria are important to the organisation. Sometimes performance is defined as the level of the organisation to which the individual has been promoted – so the criteria here are organisational rather than job specific. If test scores relate highly to future performance, however defined, then the test is a good predictor.

Reliability

The reliability of a test is the degree to which the test measures consistently whatever it does measure. If a test is highly reliable, then it is possible to put greater weight on the scores that individuals receive on the test. However, a highly reliable test is of no value in the employment situation unless it also has high validity.

Use and interpretation

Tests need to be used and interpreted by trained or qualified testers. Test results, especially personality tests, require very careful interpretation as some aspects of personality will be measured that are irrelevant to the job. The British Psychological Society (BPS) can provide a certificate of competence for occupational testing at levels A and B. Both the BPS and CIPD have produced codes of practice for occupational test use. It is recommended that tests are not used in a judgemental, final way, but to stimulate discussion with the candidate based on the test results and that feedback is given to candidates. The International Test Commission also provide guidelines on computer-based and Internet-delivered testing and their website is included at the end of this Part of the book. In addition it is recommended in the CIPD code that test data alone should not be used to make a selection decision (which could contravene the 1998 Data Protection Act), but should always be used as part of a wider process where inferences from test results can be backed up by other sources. Norm tables and the edition date of a test are also important features to check. For example Ceci and Williams (2000) warn that intelligence is a relative concept and that the norm tables change over time – so using an old test with old norm tables may be misleading.

Problems with using tests

A number of problems can be incurred when using tests.

1 In the last section we commented that a test score that was highly related to performance criteria has good validity. The relationship between test scores and performance criteria is usually expressed as a correlation coefficient (r). If $r = 1$ then test scores and performance would be perfectly related; if $r = 0$ there is no relationship whatsoever. A correlation coefficient of $r = 0.4$ is comparatively good in the testing world and this level of relationship between test scores and performance is generally seen as acceptable. Tests are, therefore, not outstanding predictors of future performance.

2 Validation procedures are very time consuming, but are essential to the effective use of tests. There are concerns that with the growth of web testing, new types of tests, such as emotional intelligence tests, are being developed without sufficient validation (Tulip 2002).

3 The criteria that are used to define good job performance in developing the test are often inadequate. They are subjective and may account to some extent for the mediocre correlations between test results and job performance.

4 Tests are often job specific. If the job for which the test is used changes, then the test can no longer be assumed to relate to job performance in the same way. Also, personality tests only measure how individuals see themselves at a certain time and cannot therefore be reliably reused at a later time.

5 Tests may not be fair as there may be a social, sexual or racial bias in the questions and scoring system. People from some cultures may, for example, be unused to 'working against the clock'.

6 Increasingly organisations are using competencies as a tool to identify and develop the characteristics of high performance. However, as Fletcher (1996) has pointed out, it is difficult to relate these readily to psychological tests. Rogers (1999) reports research which suggests the two approaches are compatible – but there is little evidence to support this so far.

WINDOW ON PRACTICE

Ensuring tests are 'fair and reasonable' and free from ethnic or sexual bias

Indirect discrimination would result when a test unfairly and unjustifiably disadvantages one race or sex compared with another, and test results need to be monitored to show that this is not happening. Organisations need to be able to demonstrate that the test has been developed or tailored and assessed in relation to the job content and person specification. Alternative means of taking the test also need to be developed when the use of tests would disadvantage a disabled person.

Source: Summarised from M. Palmer (2002) 'Very testing testing',
People Management, Vol. 8, No. 1, 10 January, pp. 18–19.

ACTIVITY 8.3

In what ways could you measure job performance for the following?

- A data input clerk
- A mobile plumber
- A call centre operator
- A supervisor

Types of test for occupational use

Aptitude tests

People differ in their performance of tasks, and tests of aptitude (or ability) measure an individual's potential to develop in either specific or general terms. This is in contrast to attainment tests, which measure the skills an individual has already acquired. When considering the results from aptitude tests it is important to remember that a simple relationship does not exist between a high level of aptitude and a high level of job performance, as other factors, such as motivation, also contribute to job performance.

Aptitude tests can be grouped into two categories: those measuring general mental ability or general intelligence, and those measuring specific abilities or aptitudes.

General intelligence tests

Intelligence tests, sometimes called mental ability tests, are designed to give an indication of overall mental capacity. A variety of questions are included in such tests, including vocabulary, analogies, similarities, opposites, arithmetic, number extension and general information. Ability to score highly on such tests correlates with the capacity to retain new knowledge, to pass examinations and to succeed at work. However, the intelligence test used would still need to be carefully validated in terms of the job for which the candidate was applying. And Ceci and Williams (2000) note that intelligence is to some extent determined by the context – so an individual's test score may not reflect capacity to act intelligently. Indeed practical intelligence, associated with success in organisations, may be different from the nature of intelligence as measured by tests (Williams and Sternberg 2001). Examples of general intelligence tests are found in IDS (2004).

Special aptitude tests

There are special tests that measure specific abilities or aptitudes, such as spatial abilities, perceptual abilities, verbal ability, numerical ability, motor ability (manual dexterity) and so on. An example of a special abilities test is the Critical Reasoning Test developed by Smith and Whetton (*see* IDS 2004).

Trainability tests

Trainability tests are used to measure a potential employee's ability to be trained, usually for craft-type work. The test consists of the applicants doing a practical task that they have not done before, after having been shown or 'trained' how to do it. The test measures how well they respond to the 'training' and how their performance on the task improves. Because it is performance at a task that is being measured, these tests are sometimes confused with attainment tests; however, they are more concerned with potential ability to do the task and response to training.

Attainment tests

Whereas aptitude tests measure an individual's potential, attainment or achievement tests measure skills that have already been acquired. There is much less resistance to such tests of skills. Few candidates for a secretarial/administrative post would refuse to take a keyboard speed test, or a test on 'Word', 'PowerPoint' or 'Excel' software before interview. The candidates are sufficiently confident of their skills to welcome the opportunity to display them and be approved. Furthermore, they know what they are doing and will know whether they have done well or badly. They are in control, whereas they feel that the tester is in control of intelligence and personality tests as the candidates do not understand the evaluation rationale. Attainment tests are often devised by the employer.

Personality tests

The debate still rages as to the importance of personality for success in some jobs and organisations. The need for personality assessment may be high but there is even more resistance to tests of personality than to tests of aptitude, partly because of the reluctance to see personality as in any way measurable. There is much evidence to suggest that personality is also context dependent, and Iles and Salaman (1995) also argue that personality changes over time. Both of these factors further complicate the issue. Personality tests are mainly used for management, professional and graduate jobs, although there is evidence of their use when high-performance teams are developed.

Theories of human personality vary as much as theories of human intelligence. Jung, Eysenck and Cattell, among others, have all proposed different sets of factors/traits which can be assessed to describe personality. Based on research to date Robertson (2001) argues that it is now possible to state that there are five basic building blocks of personality: extroversion/introversion; emotional stability; agreeableness; conscientiousness and openness to new experiences. Myers–Briggs is a well used personality test; for details *see* McHenry (2002).

It is dangerous to assume that there is a standard profile of 'the ideal employee' (although this may fit nicely with theories of culture change) or the ideal personality for a particular job, as the same objectives may be satisfactorily achieved in different ways by different people. Another problem with the use of personality tests is that they rely on an individual's willingness to be honest, as the socially acceptable answer or the one best in terms of the job are seemingly easy to pick out, although 'lie detector' questions are usually built in. Ipsative tests (as opposed to normative tests)* seek to avoid the social desirability problem by using a different test structure – but other problems arise from this approach. Heggestad *et al.* (2006) suggest that in their pure form ipsative tests are inappropriate for selection and that in their partial form they might be just as susceptible to faking as normative tests.

WINDOW ON PRACTICE

A different type of personality test: Waves

Smethurst (2006) reports on a new type of test which has been developed by Saville Consulting. There are two key differences between this and previous personality tests. The first is that both normative and ipsative questions are used, and the second is that talent and motivation are assessed together in a single test rather than in separate questionnaires.

Source: Summarised from S. Smethurst (2006) 'The window test',
People Management, Vol. 12, No. 2, 26 January, pp. 28–30.

---

* Ipsative tests require the candidate to make a *choice*, usually between two statements or adjectives, rather than allowing the candidate to answer, for example, 'true' or 'false' or give a rating of 'to what extent' they agree an item applies to themselves, as in a normative test.

Dalen *et al.* (2001) did show that tests are manipulable but not sufficiently for the candidate to match an ideal profile, and that such manipulation would be exposed by detection measures within the test. There is a further problem that some traits measured by the test will not be relevant in terms of performance on the job. There is at the time of writing an interest in emotional intelligence – tests measure self-awareness, self-motivation, emotional control, empathy and the ability to understand and inspire others.

WINDOW ON PRACTICE

Online testing: the case for and against

CIPD (2006) reports that 25 per cent of respondents to its survey used online tests and there is much interest in developing this area. Tests can be used in one of three different ways:

- uncontrolled – anyone can register to use them on the open Internet;
- controlled – the candidate needs first to be registered by the organisation using the test, and their identity must be checked;
- supervised – as above, and a qualified tester from the organisation also logs on and ensures that time limits and other requirements are met.

For:

- Cheaper in the long run
- Immediate analysis
- Immediate feedback to candidate
- Can be used for wider range of (lower-paid) jobs
- Speeds processes and helps to retain potential candidates
- Good for company image
- Can use a wider range of different tests – e.g. video scenarios, followed by 'what would you do next?'
- Can be convenient for applicants

Against:

- Worries over confidentiality and security of personal data
- Appears cold and impersonal
- Open to misuse – who is actually completing the test?
- Can encourage the rapid development of new tests which are not properly validated

Group selection methods and assessment centres

Group methods

The use of group tasks to select candidates is not new – the method dates back to the Second World War – but such measures have gained greater attention through their use in assessment centres. Plumbley (1985) describes the purpose of group selection methods as being to provide evidence about the candidate's ability to:

- get on with others;
- influence others and the way they do this;
- express themselves verbally;
- think clearly and logically;
- argue from past experience and apply themselves to a new problem;
- identify the type of role they play in group situations.

These features are difficult on the whole to identify using other selection methods and one of the particular advantages of group selection methods is that they provide the selector with examples of behaviour on which to select. When future job performance is being considered it is behaviour in the job that is critical, and so selection using group methods can provide direct information on which to select rather than indirect verbal information or test results. The increasing use of competencies and behavioural indicators, as a way to specify selection criteria, ties in well with the use of group methods.

There is a range of group exercises that can be used including informal discussion of a given topic, role plays and groups who must organise themselves to solve a problem within time limits which may take the form of a competitive business game, case study or physical activity.

Group selection methods are most suitable for management, graduate and sometimes supervisory posts. One of the difficulties with group selection methods is that it can be difficult to assess an individual's contribution, and some people may be unwilling to take part.

ACTIVITY 8.4

To what extent does a person's behaviour on these group selection tasks accurately reflect behaviour on the job? Why?

Assessment centres

Assessment centres incorporate multiple selection techniques, and group selection methods outlined above form a major element, together with other work-simulation exercises such as in-basket tasks, psychological tests, a variety of interviews and presentations. Assessment centres are used to assess, in depth, a group of broadly similar applicants, using a set of competencies required for the post on offer and a series of behavioural statements which indicate how these competencies are played out in practice. Even assuming that the competencies for the job in question have already been identified, assessment centres require a lengthy design process to select the appropriate activities so

Day One Times	Activity	Who is involved
9.30–10.00	Introduction to centre	All
10.00–10.45	General discussion – given topics	All
10.45–11.15	Coffee	
11.15–12.00	General intelligence test	All
12.00–12.30	One-to-one interviews (30 mins each)	Candidates A, B, C
12.30–1.30	Lunch	
1.30–2.00	One-to-one interviews (30 mins each)	Candidates B, E, C
2.00–2.45	Spatial reasoning test	All
2.45–3.15	Coffee	
3.15–4.00	Personality test	All
4.00–4.30	One-to-one interviews (30 mins each)	Candidates C, F, D

Day Two Times	Activity	Who is involved
9.30–10.15	Verbal reasoning test	All
10.15–10.45	One-to-one interviews (30 mins each)	Candidates D, A, F
10.45–11.15	Coffee	
11.15–12.00	Critical thinking test	All
12.00–12.30	One-to-one interviews (30 mins each)	Candidates E, B, A
12.30–1.30	Lunch	
1.30–3.00	In-tray exercise	All
3.00–3.30	Coffee	
3.30–4.00	One-to-one interviews (30 mins each)	Candidates F, D, E

Figure 8.1
An example of the scheduling of events – based on an assessment centre for a professional post (central government)

Note: Based on six candidates (A, B, C, D, E, F) and three assessors.

that every competency will be measured via more than one task. Assessment centres have been proven to be one of the most effective ways of selecting candidates – this is probably due, as Suff (2005b) notes, to the use of multiple measures, multiple assessors and predetermined assessment criteria.

A matrix is usually developed to show how the required competencies and the activities link together. In terms of running the centre sufficient well-trained assessors will be needed, usually based on the ratio of one assessor for two candidates to ensure that the assessor can observe each candidate sufficiently carefully. Lists of competencies and associated behaviours will need to be drawn up as checklists and a careful plan will need to be made of how each candidate will move around the different activities – an example of which is found in Figure 8.1. Clearly candidates will need to be very well briefed both before and at the start of the centre.

At the end of the procedure the assessors have to come to agreement on a cumulative rating for each individual, related to job requirements, taking into account all the selection activities. The procedure as a whole can then be validated against job performance rather than each separate activity. The predictive validities from such procedures are not very consistent, but there is a high 'face validity' – a feeling that this is a fairer way of selecting people. Reliability can also be improved by the quality of assessor training, careful briefing of assessors and a predetermined structured approach to marking. The chief disadvantages of these selection methods are that they are a costly and time-consuming procedure, for both the organisation and the candidates. The time commitment is extended by the need to give some feedback to candidates who have been through such a long procedure which involves psychological assessment – although feedback is still not always available for candidates. There is evidence of increasing use of assessment centres and CIPD (2006) reports that 48 per cent of organisations in its survey used such centres for selection. Some organisations have been improving their centres (*see* IRS 2002b) by making the activities more connected or by using longer simulations or scenarios which are a reflection of real-life experience on the job, and are carrying out testing separately from the centre. Some are assessing candidates against the values of the company rather than a specific job, in view of the rapid change in the nature of jobs, and others, such as Britvic, are running a series of assessment centres which candidates must attend, rather than only one. A helpful text relating competency profiles and assessment centre activities is Woodruffe (2000) and IDS (2005) provides examples of different company experiences.

Work sampling/portfolios

Work sampling of potential candidates for permanent jobs can take place by assessing candidates' work in temporary posts or on government training schemes in the same organisation. For some jobs, such as photographers and artists, a sample of work in the form of a portfolio is expected to be presented at the time of interview. Kanter (1989) suggests that managers and professionals should also be developing portfolios of their work experiences and achievements as one way of enhancing their employability.

References

One way of informing the judgement of managers who have to make employment offers to selected individuals is the use of references. Candidates provide the names of previous employers or others with appropriate credentials and then prospective employers request them to provide information. Reference checking is increasing as organisations react to scandals in the media and aim to protect themselves from rogue applicants (IRS 2002c). There are two types: the factual check and the character reference.

The factual check

The factual check is fairly straightforward as it is no more than a confirmation of facts that the candidate has presented. It will normally follow the employment interview and decision to offer a post. It simply confirms that the facts are accurate. The knowledge that such a check will be made – or may be made – will help focus the mind of candidates so that they resist the temptation to embroider their story.

The character reference

The character reference is a very different matter. Here the prospective employer asks for an opinion about the candidate before the interview so that the information gained can be used in the decision-making phases. The logic of this strategy is impeccable: who knows the working performance of the candidate better than the previous employer? The wisdom of the strategy is less sound, as it depends on the writers of references being excellent judges of working performance, faultless communicators and – most difficult of all – disinterested. The potential inaccuracies of decisions influenced by character references begin when the candidate decides who to cite. They will have some freedom of choice and will clearly choose someone from whom they expect favourable comment, perhaps massaging the critical faculties with such comments as: 'I think references are going to be very important for this job' or 'You will do your best for me, won't you?'

Other methods

A number of other less conventional methods such as physiognomy, phrenology, body language, palmistry, graphology and astrology have been suggested as possible selection methods. While these are fascinating to read about there is little evidence to suggest that they could be used effectively. Thatcher (1997) suggests that the use of graphology is around 10 per cent in Holland and Germany and that it is regularly used in France; in the UK he found nine per cent of small firms (with fewer than 100 employees), one per cent of medium-sized firms (100–499 employees) and five per cent of larger firms used graphology as a selection method. In 1990 Fowler suggested that the extent of use of graphology is much higher in the UK than reported figures indicate, as there is some reluctance on the part of organisations to admit that they are using graphology for selection purposes. There are also concerns about the quality of graphologists – who can indeed set themselves up with no training whatsoever. The two main bodies in this field in the UK are the British Institute of Graphology and the International Graphology Association and both these organisations require members to gain qualifications before they can practise.

WINDOW ON PRACTICE

It is interesting to contrast different approaches to selection in different countries. Bulois and Shackleton (1996) note that interviews are the cornerstone of selection activity in both Britain and France, but that they are consciously used in different ways. In Britain they argue that interviews are increasingly structured and criterion referenced, whereas in France the approach tends to be deliberately unstructured and informal. They note that in France the premise is that 'the more at ease the candidates are, the higher the quality of their answer', whereas in Britain they characterise the premise as 'the more information you get about an individual, the better you know him/her and the more valid and reliable your judgement is' (p. 129). Tixier (1996), in a survey covering the EU (but excluding France), Switzerland, Sweden and Austria, found that structured interviews were favoured in the UK, Scandinavia, Germany and Austria. This contrasted with Italy, Portugal, Luxembourg and Switzerland where unstructured styles were preferred.

Bulois and Shackleton identify selectors in Britain as more aware of the limitations of interviews and as attempting to reduce the subjectivity by also carrying out assessment centres and psychological tests; whereas in France these methods were identified as unnatural, tedious and frustrating. Interviews are much more likely to be supplemented by handwriting analysis in France – both methods being identified as valuable, flexible and cheap sources of information. Shackleton and Newell (1991) report that handwriting analysis was used in 77 per cent of the organisations that they surveyed in France compared with 2.6 per cent of the organisations they surveyed in the UK.

Both culture and employment legislation clearly have an influence on the selection methods adopted in any country and the way in which they are used.

ACTIVITY 8.5

Design an assessment centre for the anti-rape detective job as described in Case 8.1 on the companion website **www.pearsoned.co.uk/torrington**.

FINAL SELECTION DECISION MAKING

The selection decision involves measuring the candidates individually against the selection criteria defined in the person specification, and not against each other. A useful tool to achieve this is the matrix in Figure 8.2. This is a good method of ensuring that every candidate is assessed against each selection criterion and in each box in the matrix the key details can be completed. The box can be used whether a single selection method was used or multiple methods. If multiple methods were used and contradictory information is found against any criterion, this can be noted in the decision-making process.

When more than one selector is involved there is some debate about how to gather and use the information and judgement of each selector. One way is for each selector to assess the information collected separately, and then for all selectors to meet to discuss assessments. When this approach is used, there may be some very different assessments, especially if the interview was the only selection method used. Much heated and time-consuming debate can be generated, but the most useful aspect of this process is sharing the information in everyone's matrix to understand how judgements have been formed. This approach is also helpful in training interviewers.

An alternative approach is to fill in only one matrix, with all selectors contributing. This may be quicker, but the drawback is that the quietest member may be the one who has all the critical pieces of information. There is a risk that all the information may not be contributed to the debate in progress. Iles (1992), referring to assessment centre decisions, suggests that the debate itself may not add to the quality of the decision, and that taking the results from each selector and combining them is just as effective.

Selection criteria	Candidate 1	Candidate 2	Candidate 3	Candidate 4
Criterion a				
Criterion b				
Criterion c				
Criterion d				
Criterion e				
General comments				

Figure 8.2
A selection decision-making matrix

VALIDATION OF SELECTION PROCEDURES

We have already mentioned how test scores may be validated against eventual job performance for each individual in order to discover whether the test score is a good predictor of success in the job. In this way we can decide whether the test should be used as part of the selection procedure. The same idea can be applied to the use of other individual or combined selection methods.

The critical information that is important for determining validity is the selection criteria used, the selection processes used, an evaluation of the individual at the time of selection and current performance of the individual.

Unfortunately we are never in a position to witness the performance of rejected candidates and compare this with those we have employed. However, if a group of individuals are selected at the same time, for example, graduate trainees, it will be unlikely that they were all rated equally highly in spite of the fact that they were all considered employable. It is useful for validation purposes if a record is made of the scores that each achieved in each part of the selection process. Test results are easy to quantify, and for interview results a simple grading system can be devised.

Current performance includes measures derived from the job description, together with additional performance measures:

1 **Measures from the job description:** quantitative measures such as volume of sales, accuracy, number of complaints and so on may be used, or qualitative measures such as relations with customers and quality of reports produced.

2 **Other measures:** these may include appraisal results, problems identified, absence data and, of course, termination.

Current performance is often assessed in an intuitive, subjective way, and while this may sometimes be useful it is no substitute for objective assessment.

Selection ratings for each individual can be compared with eventual performance over a variety of time periods. Large discrepancies between selection and performance ratings point to further investigation of the selection criteria and methods used. The comparison of selection rating and performance rating can also be used to compare the appropriateness of different selection criteria, and the usefulness of different selection methods.

ACTIVITY 8.6

How would you validate the selection process for the anti-rape detective job as described in Case 8.1 on the companion website www.pearsoned.co.uk/torrington?

SUMMARY PROPOSITIONS

8.1   Selection is a two-way process. The potential employer and the potential employee both make selection decisions.

8.2   A combination of selection methods is usually chosen, based upon the job, appropriateness, acceptability, time, administrative ease, cost, accuracy and the abilities of the selection staff. Different countries often have a different view on which methods are most appropriate.

8.3   The most well-used selection methods are application forms, interviews (including those conducted by video and telephone), tests, group selection procedures, assessment centres and references. There is increasing use of the Internet in applying many of these methods.

8.4   A procedure for selection decision making needs to be agreed which can integrate all the selection information available.

8.5   Selection methods should be validated. A simple system is better than no system at all.

GENERAL DISCUSSION TOPICS

1 It could be argued that the selection process identifies candidates who are competent in the selection process rather than candidates who are most competent to perform the job on offer. Discuss this in relation to all forms of selection.

2 'It is unethical and bad for business to make candidates undergo a selection assessment centre without providing detailed feedback and support.' Discuss.

FURTHER READING

International Journal of Selection and Assessment, Vol. 11, No. 2/3, June/September 2003.
This is a special edition of the journal and it is devoted to the role of technology in shaping the future of staffing and assessment. Contains some highly relevant articles, including, for example, using technology in the recruiting, screening and selection process; applicant and recruiter reactions to technology; Internet-based personality testing and privacy in Internet-based selection systems.

IRS (2002) 'Of good character: supplying references and providing access', *Employment Review*, No. 754, 24 June, pp. 34–6.
Second of a two-part series on references – this one concentrating on providing references and employee access to references about them. Useful to read this in conjunction with No. 752, 27 May, entitled 'The check's in the post' which focuses on the legal position and on the content and nature of references.

Murphy, N. (2006) 'Voyages of discovery: carrying out checks on job applicants', *IRS Employment Review*, No. 850, 7 July, pp. 42–8.
This article reports the results of a survey into employer practices to check the background details of applicants, and is much broader than reference seeking from previous employers. It covers the type of information that is checked on, together with the mechanisms used.

Murphy, N. (2005) 'Selecting graduates: doing it on-line, on time', *IRS Employment Review*, No. 836, 2 December, pp. 42–5.

This article provides a very good insight into the stages of the selection process for fast-track candidates in the Civil Service, and demonstrates how online tools have been designed to reflect the real nature of the job being applied for and how such tools integrate with an assessment centre. An example from Cadbury Schweppes is also included.

REFERENCES

Anderson, N. and Shackleton, V. (1990) 'Staff selection decision making into the 1990s', *Management Decision*, Vol. 28, No. 1.

Barclay, J. (1999) 'Employee Selection: a question of structure', *Personnel Review*, Vol. 28, No. 1/2, pp. 134–51.

Boyatzis, R. (1982) *The Competent Manager*. Chichester: John Wiley.

Brittain, S. and Ryder, P. (1999) 'Get complex', *People Management*, 25 November, pp. 48–51.

Bulois, N. and Shackleton, V. (1996) 'A qualitative study of recruitment and selection in France and Britain: the attitudes of recruiters in multinationals', in I. Beardwell (chair), *Contemporary Developments in Human Resource Management*. Paris: Editions ESKA, pp. 125–35.

Caligiuri, P. and Phillips, J. (2003) 'An application of self-assessment realistic job previews to expatriate assignments', *International Journal of Human Resource Management*, Vol. 14, No. 7, pp. 1102–16.

Carrington, L. (2002) 'At the cutting edge', *People Management*, Vol. 8, No. 10, pp. 30–1.

Ceci, S. and Williams, W. (2000) 'Smart Bomb', *People Management*, 24 August, pp. 32–6.

CIPD (2006) *Recruitment and Retention 2006*. London: CIPD.

Dalen, L., Stanton, N. and Roberts, A. (2001) 'Faking personality questionnaires in selection', *Journal of Management Development*, Vol. 20, No. 8, pp. 729–41.

Davidson, E. (2003) 'You can do it', *People Management*, Vol. 9, No. 4, 20 February, pp. 42–3.

Fletcher, C. (1996) 'Mix and match fails to work on competencies', *People Management*, September.

Fowler, A. (1990) 'The writing on the wall', *Local Government Chronicle*, 26 January, pp. 20–8.

Heggestad, E., Morrison, M., Reeve, C. and McCloy, R.A. (2006) 'Forced-choice assessments of personality for selection: evaluating issues of normative assessment and faking resistance', *Journal of Applied Psychology*, Vol. 91, No. 1, pp. 9–24.

Iles, P. (1992) 'Centres of excellence? Assessment and development centres, managerial competence and human resource strategies', *British Journal of Management*, Vol. 3, pp. 79–90.

Iles, P. and Salaman, G. (1995) 'Recruitment, selection and assessment', in J. Storey (ed.) *Human Resource Management: A critical text*. London: Routledge.

Incomes Data Services (2004 update) *IDS Study Plus: Psychological Tests*, No. 770, Spring. London: IDS.

Incomes Data Services (2005) *Assessment Centres*, IDS Study No. 800, June. London: IDS.

IRS (2002a) 'Psychometrics: the next generation', *Employment Review*, No. 744, 28 January, pp. 36–40.

IRS (2002b) 'Focus of attention', *Employment Review*, No. 749, 15 April, pp. 36–41.

IRS (2002c) 'The check's in the post', *Employment Review*, No. 752, 27 May, pp. 34–42.

IRS (2003) 'Setting the tone: job descriptions and person specifications', *Employment Review*, No. 776, 23 May, pp. 42–8.

Kanter, R.M. (1989) *When Giants Learn to Dance*. New York: Simon and Schuster.

Lievens, F., van Dam, K. and Anderson, N. (2002) 'Recent trends and challenges in personnel selection', *Personnel Review*, Vol. 31, No. 5, pp. 580–601.

McHenry, R. (2002) 'The Myers–Briggs Response', *People Management*, Vol. 8, No. 24, 5 December, p. 34.

Mohamed, A., Orife, J. and Wibowo, K. (2001) 'The legality of a key word search as a personnel selection tool', *Personnel Review*, Vol. 24, No. 5, pp. 516–22.

Murphy, N. (2005) 'Got your number: using telephone interviewing', *IRS Employment Review*, No. 832, 30 September, pp. 43–5.

Murphy, N. (2006) 'Testing the waters: employers' use of selection assessments', *IRS Employment Review*, No. 852, 4 August, pp. 42–8.

Palmer, M. (2002) 'Very testing testing', *People Management*, Vol. 8, No. 1, 10 January, pp. 18–19.

Papadopoulou, A., Ineson, E. and Williams, D. (1996) 'The graduate management trainee pre-selection interview', *Personnel Review*, Vol. 25, No. 4, pp. 21–37.

Plumbley, P.R. (1985) *Recruitment and Selection*, 4th edn. London: Institute of Personnel Management.

Robertson, I. (2001) 'Undue diligence', *People Management*, Vol. 7, No. 23, 22 November, pp. 42–3.

Rogers, G. (1999) 'All round vision', *People Management*, 2 July.

Shackleton, V. and Newell, S. (1991) 'Management selection: a comparative survey of methods used in top British and French companies', *Journal of Occupational Psychology*, Vol. 64, pp. 23–36.

Sigman, A. (2002) 'Body of evidence', *People Management*, Vol. 8, No. 5, 7 March, pp. 48–9.

Smethurst, S. (2006) 'The window test', *People Management*, Vol. 12, No. 2, 26 January, pp. 28–30.

Suff, R. (2005a) 'First-line filter: screening candidates for selection', *Employment Review*, No. 837, 16 December, pp. 44–8.

Suff, R. (2005b) 'Centres of attention', *IRS Employment Review*, No. 816, 28 January, pp. 42–8.

Taylor, S. (2005) *Employee Resourcing*. London: IPD.

Thatcher, M. (1997) 'A test of character', *People Management*, 15 May.

Tixier, M. (1996) 'Employers' recruitment tools across Europe', *Employee Relations*, Vol. 18, No. 6, pp. 67–78.

Townley, B. (1991) 'Selection and appraisal: reconstituting social relations?', in J. Storey (ed.) *New Perspectives in Human Resource Management*. London: Routledge.

Tulip, S. (2002) 'Personality trait secrets', *People Management*, Vol. 8, No. 17, pp. 34–8.

van Zwanenberg, N. and Wilkinson, L.J. (1993) 'The person specification – a problem masquerading as a solution?', *Personnel Review*, Vol. 22, No. 7, pp. 54–65.

Wanous, J.P. (1992) *Organisational Entry: Recruitment, Selection, Orientation and Socialisation of Newcomers*. Reading, Mass.: Addison-Wesley.

Werbel, J. and Johnson, D. (2001) 'The use of person-group fit for employment selection: a missing link in person-environment fit', *Human Resource Management*, Vol. 40, No. 3, pp. 227–40, Fall.

Whiddett, S. and Hollyforde, S. (2003) *The competencies handbook*. London: IPD.

Whiddett, S. and Kandola, B. (2000) 'Fit for the job?', *People Management*, 25 May.

Wilkinson, L.J. and van Zwanenberg, N. (1994) 'Development of a person specification system for managerial jobs', *Personnel Review*, Vol. 23, No. 1, pp. 25–36.

Williams, W. and Sternberg, R. (2001) *Success for Managers*. London: Lawrence Erlbaum Associates.

Woodruffe, C. (2000) *Development and Assessment Centres: Identifying and assessing competence*, 3rd edn. London: IPD.

An extensive range of additional materials, including multiple choice questions, answers to questions and links to useful websites can be found on the Human Resource Management Companion Website at **www.pearsoned.co.uk/torrington**.

CHAPTER ⑨

STAFF RETENTION

THE OBJECTIVES OF THIS CHAPTER ARE TO:

1 Examine recent trends in job tenure and turnover in the UK

2 Assess the arguments for and against investing resources in staff turnover reduction programmes

3 Outline the main reasons for voluntary resignations

4 Set out how staff turnover can be costed

5 Explore some approaches which improve staff retention rates

The last three chapters focused on the processes used to mobilise a workforce: activities which are often expensive and time consuming. It is estimated that the costs associated with recruiting and training a new employee average between half and one and a half times the annual salary for the post in question, depending on the approaches used (Branham 2005, p. 3). In this chapter we consider the most important way in which human resource managers seek to reduce the time and money spent on these activities, namely by trying to ensure that people choose not to leave an organisation voluntarily in the first place.

The extent of interest in employee retention issues varies over time as labour markets become successively tighter and looser depending on economic conditions. In recent years, as unemployment has fallen, making it harder to recruit staff with the necessary skills and attitudes, the subject has again moved up the HRM agenda. This has led to the publication of several new books and articles exploring how organisations can ensure that they have the best chance of retaining the people they employ. The authors tend to take one of two distinct perspectives on the subject. The first focuses on the organisation as a whole, tracking staff turnover rates over time, benchmarking the figures against industry or regional averages and developing organisational policy aimed at improving retention generally. The second, illustrated in work by Hiltrop (1999), Woodruffe (1999), Williams (2000), Cappelli (2000), Larkan (2006) and Clayton (2006), concentrates primarily on retaining high-performing key players. Each of these authors uses the expression 'the war for talent' to illustrate the significance and difficulty faced by those competing for the services of individuals who have the capacity to make a real difference to an organisation's competitive position. While the methods put forward to reduce turnover are similar in each case, the second group advocate more sophisticated retention practices aimed specifically at those whose talents are the most scarce.

ACTIVITY 9.1

Employee retention becomes an important item on the HRM agenda when organisations are faced with skills shortages. When labour is in reasonably good supply leavers can easily be replaced by new starters. Aside from working harder at retaining staff, what alternative approaches could be adopted to help staff an organisation when the skills it requires are in short supply?

TURNOVER RATES AND TRENDS

In recent years there has been a mismatch between the rhetoric about job tenure and the reality. Much mileage continues to be made by some consultants, academics and management gurus out of the claim that 'there are no longer any jobs for life', suggesting that the length of time we spend working for organisations has fallen substantially in recent years. In fact this is a misleading claim. All the available evidence strongly suggests that job tenure has been broadly stable for several decades. The most comprehensive study to be published in recent years was carried out by Gregg and Wadsworth (1999). Their

Year	Male job tenure	Female job tenure	Average tenure
1975	6 years, 6 months	3 years, 7 months	4 years, 9 months
1985	7 years, 2 months	3 years, 10 months	5 years, 6 months
1990	6 years	3 years, 9 months	4 years, 4 months
1995	6 years, 10 months	4 years, 6 months	5 years, 7 months
1998	5 years, 9 months	4 years, 4 months	4 years, 10 months

Table 9.1
Job tenure
in the UK
1975–1998

Source: Compiled from data in P. Gregg and J. Wadsworth (1999) 'Job tenure, 1975–98', in P. Gregg and
J. Wadsworth (eds) *The State of Working Britain*. Manchester: Manchester University Press, p. 115.

detailed analyses of data from the New Earnings Survey, the General Household Survey
and the British Labour Force Survey showed that relatively little actually changed in
terms of worker retention during the latter part of the twentieth century. This is illustrated in Table 9.1 which shows how average job tenure rates fluctuated for men and
women between 1975 and 1998 while the overall tenure rate for the UK as a whole
remained stable. What happened over this period is that male tenure rates fell as men in
their fifties and early sixties took early retirement or accepted redundancy packages,
while job tenure among women rose. Gregg and Wadsworth's study showed that
the biggest increase has been among women with children. In 1975, on average, they
remained in a job for 20 months; the figure in 1998 was 46 months. This reflects the
greater propensity of women during this period to return to work following maternity
leave and the improved career opportunities available to them. Other fluctuations are
readily explained by economic conditions.

Staff turnover always rises when the economy is strong and jobs are plentiful because
there are more opportunities available for people to change employers. Conversely, during recessions staff turnover falls because relatively few attractive permanent positions
are advertised.

These trends appear to have continued in the first decade of the twenty-first century.
While there has been no comprehensive study carried out more recently along the lines
of Gregg and Wadsworth's work, the statistics that have been published point to continuity rather than to either reduced or increased job tenure. OECD statistics show that
average job tenure among *permanent employees* in the UK remained steady at or around
eight years from 1992 until 2002 (Auer *et al.* 2004, p. 3), Labour Force Survey data
confirming that long periods of job tenure remain the norm for a substantial portion of
the working population (see Table 9.2). People tend to move from employer to employer
early on in their careers, often staying in one employment for just a few months. But
once they find a job (or an employer) that they like, the tendency is to remain for several
years. 'Jobs for life' have, in truth, always been a relative rarity, but the evidence

Length of service	% of the workforce
1 month–2 years	27
2–5 years	24
5–8 years	13
8–12 years	9
Over 12 years	24

Table 9.2
Job tenure in
the UK among
permanent
employees

Source: Adapted from DTI 2006, p. 4.

suggests that they remain a reality for many employees, despite the predictions of the management gurus. Over a third of employees have already been in their current jobs for over eight years.

The overall figures mask substantial differences between tenure and turnover rates in different industries. Studies undertaken annually by the Chartered Institute of Personnel and Development persistently show retailing and catering to be the sectors with the highest turnover levels, with rates averaging over 40 per cent in recent years. By contrast the most stable workforces are to be found in the public services, where reported annual turnover rates are only 10 or 11 per cent (CIPD 2006, p. 26). Rates also vary from region to region and over time, being highest when and where average pay levels are highest and unemployment is low, and between different professions. As a rule, the more highly paid a person is, the less likely they are to switch jobs, but there remain some highly paid professions such as sales where turnover is always high. It is also interesting to observe how much more inclined younger workers are to switch jobs than their older colleagues. Macaulay (2003) calculated what proportion of employees had completed more than a year's service with their employer. For the over-fifties the figure was 86 per cent, for the 18–24 age group it was only 51 per cent.

ACTIVITY 9.2

Why do you think staff turnover rates are so much higher in some industries than others? Make a list of the different factors you consider may account for variations.

WINDOW ON PRACTICE

The length of time that employees remain in their jobs, or at least with the same employers, varies considerably from country to country. Auer *et al.* (2006) analysed the proportion of staff who had less than a year's service in the OECD countries and the proportion who had completed more than ten years' service. The country with the most shorter-term employees is the USA, where 24.5 per cent have less than a year's service, while only 26.2 per cent have been with their employers for more than ten years. At the other end of the scale is Greece, where only 9.8 per cent have less than a year's service and as many as 52 per cent have over ten years' service. High rates of job stability are also common in Italy, Belgium and Portugal. By contrast relatively low stability rates are found in the UK, Denmark and Ireland.

THE IMPACT OF STAFF TURNOVER

There is some debate about the level which staff turnover rates have to reach in order to inflict measurable damage on an employer. The answer varies from organisation to organisation. In some industries it is possible to sustain highly successful businesses with turnover rates that would make it impossible to function in other sectors. Some chains of fast food restaurants, for example, are widely reported as managing with turnover rates in excess of 300 per cent. This means that the average tenure for each employee is only four months (Ritzer 1996, p. 130; Cappelli 2000, p. 106), yet the companies concerned are some of the most successful in the world. By contrast, in a professional services organisation, where the personal relationships established between employees and clients are central to ongoing success, a turnover rate in excess of 10 per cent is likely to cause damage to the business.

There are sound arguments that can be made in favour of a certain amount of staff turnover. First, it is fair to say that organisations need to be rejuvenated with 'fresh blood' from time to time if they are to avoid becoming stale and stunted. This is particularly true at senior levels, where new leadership is often required periodically to drive change forward. More generally, however, new faces bring new ideas and experiences which help make organisations more dynamic. Second, it is possible to argue that a degree of turnover helps managers to keep firmer control over labour costs than would otherwise be the case. This is particularly true of organisations which are subject to regular and unpredictable changes in business levels. When income falls it is possible to hold back from replacing leavers until such time as it begins to pick up again. In this way organisations are able to minimise staffing budgets while maintaining profit levels during leaner periods. Redundancy bills are also lower in organisations with relatively high staff turnover because they are able to use natural wastage as the main means of reducing their workforce before compulsory lay-offs are needed. Third, it can be plausibly argued that some employee turnover is 'functional' rather than 'dysfunctional' because it results in the loss of poor performers and their replacement with more effective employees.

The arguments against staff turnover are equally persuasive. First are the sheer costs associated with replacing people who have left, ranging from the cost of placing a recruitment advertisement, through the time spent administering and conducting the selection process, to expenses required in inducting and training new employees. On top of these there are less easily measurable losses sustained as a result of poorer performance on the part of less experienced employees. For larger organisations employing specialist recruiters these costs can add up to millions of pounds a year, with substantial dividends to be claimed from a reduction in staff turnover levels by a few percentage points. The second major argument in favour of improving staff retention results from a straightforward recognition that people who leave represent a lost resource in whom the organisation has invested time and money. The damage is all the greater when good people, trained and developed at the organisation's expense, subsequently choose to work for competitors. Finally, it is argued that high turnover rates are symptomatic of a poorly managed organisation. They suggest that people are dissatisfied with their jobs or with their employer and would prefer to work elsewhere. It thus sends a negative message to customers and helps create a poor image in the labour market, making it progressively harder to recruit good performers in the future.

We may thus conclude that the case for seeking to reduce staff turnover varies from organisation to organisation. Where replacement employees are in plentiful supply, where new starters can be trained quickly and where business levels are subject to regular fluctuation it is possible to manage effectively with a relatively high level of turnover. Indeed, it may make good business sense to do so if the expenditure required to increase employee retention is greater than the savings that would be gained as a result. In other situations the case for taking action on turnover rates is persuasive, particularly where substantial investment in training is required before new starters are able to operate at maximum effectiveness. Companies which achieve turnover rates below their industry average are thus likely to enjoy greater competitive advantage than those whose rates are relatively high.

TURNOVER ANALYSIS AND COSTING

There is little that an organisation can do to manage turnover unless there is an understanding of the reasons for it. Information about these reasons is notoriously difficult to collect. Most commentators recommend exit interviews (that is, interviews with leavers about their reasons for resigning), but the problem here is whether the individual will feel able to tell the truth, and this will depend on the culture of the organisation, the specific reasons for leaving and support that the individual will need from the organisation in the future in the form of references. Despite their disadvantages, exit interviews may be helpful if handled sensitively and confidentially – perhaps by the HR department rather than the line manager. You will find further information and discussion exercises about them on our companion website **www.pearsoned.co.uk/torrington**. In addition, analyses of turnover rates between different departments and different job groups may well shed some light on causes of turnover. Attitude surveys can also provide relevant information.

WINDOW ON PRACTICE

It is very easy for an organisation to get itself into a vicious circle of turnover if it does not act to stem a retention problem. Modest turnover rates can rapidly increase as the pressures on remaining staff become greater, leading to serious operational difficulties. As soon as more than one or two people leave an established team, more is demanded of those left to carry the burden. First, there may be a sizeable time gap between leavers resigning and new starters coming into post. Then there is the period when the new people are learning their jobs, taking more time to accomplish tasks and needing assistance from more established employees. The problem can be compounded with additional pressure being placed on managers and HR specialists faced with the need to recruit people quickly, leading to the selection of people who are not wholly suited to the jobs in question. The result is greater turnover as people respond by looking for less pressured job opportunities elsewhere.

Problems of this kind were faced by the Japanese engineering company, Makita. It addressed the issue by increasing its induction programme from half a day to four weeks and by taking a good deal more care over its recruitment and selection processes. The result was a reduction in turnover levels from 97 per cent in 1997 to 38 per cent in 1999.

Source: IDS (2000) *Improving Staff Retention*, IDS Study No. 692, July, pp. 14–17.

People leave jobs for a variety of different reasons, many of which are wholly outside the power of the organisation to influence. One very common reason for leaving, for example, is retirement. It can be brought forward or pushed back for a few years, but ultimately it affects everyone. In many cases people leave for a mixture of reasons, certain factors weighing more highly in their minds than others. The following is one approach to categorising the main reasons people have for voluntarily leaving a job, each requiring a different kind of response from the organisation.

Outside factors

Outside factors relate to situations in which someone leaves for reasons that are largely unrelated to their work. The most common instances involve people moving away when a spouse or partner is relocated. Others include the wish to fulfil a long-term ambition to travel, pressures associated with juggling the needs of work and family and illness. To an extent such turnover is unavoidable, although it is possible to reduce it somewhat through the provision of career breaks, forms of flexible working and/or childcare facilities.

Functional turnover

The functional turnover category includes all resignations which are welcomed by both employer and employee alike. The major examples are those which stem from an individual's poor work performance or failure to fit in comfortably with an organisational or departmental culture. While such resignations are less damaging than others from an organisation's point of view they should still be regarded as lost opportunities and as an unnecessary cost. The main solution to the reduction of functional turnover lies in improving recruitment and selection procedures so that fewer people in the category are appointed in the first place. However, some poorly engineered change management schemes are also sometimes to blame, especially where they result in new work pressures or workplace ethics.

Push factors

With push factors the problem is dissatisfaction with work or the organisation, leading to unwanted turnover. A wide range of issues can be cited to explain such resignations. Insufficient development opportunities, boredom, ineffective supervision, poor levels of employee involvement and straightforward personality clashes are the most common precipitating factors. Organisations can readily address all of these issues. The main reason that so many fail to do so is the absence of mechanisms for picking up signs of dissatisfaction. If there is no opportunity to voice concerns, employees who are unhappy will inevitably start looking elsewhere.

Pull factors

The opposite side of the coin is the attraction of rival employers. Salary levels are often a factor here, employees leaving in order to improve their living standards. In addition there are broader notions of career development, the wish to move into new areas of work for which there are better opportunities elsewhere, the chance to work with particular people, and more practical questions such as commuting time. For the employer losing people as a result of such factors there are two main lines of attack. First, there is a need to be aware of what other employers are offering and to ensure that as far as possible this is matched – or at least that a broadly comparable package of pay and opportunities is offered. The second requirement involves trying to ensure that employees appreciate what they are currently being given. The emphasis here is on effective communication of any 'unique selling points' and of the extent to which opportunities comparable to those offered elsewhere are given.

What are the most common reasons?

Taylor and his colleagues (2002) interviewed 200 people who had recently changed employers about why they left their last jobs. They found a mix of factors at work in most cases but concluded that push factors were a great deal more prevalent than pull factors as causes of voluntary resignations. Very few people appear to leave jobs in which they are broadly happy in search of something even better. Instead the picture is overwhelmingly one in which dissatisfied employees seek alternatives because they no longer enjoy working for their current employer.

Interestingly this study found relatively few examples of people leaving for financial reasons. Indeed more of the interviewees took pay cuts in order to move from one job to another than said that a pay rise was their principal reason for switching employers.

Other factors played a much bigger role:

- dissatisfaction with the conditions of work, especially hours;
- a perception that they were not being given sufficient career development opportunities;
- a bad relationship with their immediate supervisor.

This third factor was by far the most commonly mentioned in the interviews, lending support to the often stated point that people leave their managers and not their organisations.

Branham (2005), drawing on research undertaken by the Saratoga Institute, reached similar conclusions. His seven 'hidden reasons employees leave' are as follows:

- the job or workplace not living up to expectations;
- a mismatch between the person and the job;
- too little coaching and feedback;
- too few growth and advancement opportunities;
- feeling devalued and unrecognised;
- stress from overwork and work-life imbalance;
- loss of trust and confidence in senior leaders.

 You will find further information and discussion exercises about the issue of trust and its link to employee retention on our companion website **www.pearsoned.co.uk/torrington**.

ACTIVITY 9.3

Think about jobs that you or members of your family have left in recent years. What were the key factors that led to the decision to leave? Was there one major factor or did several act together in combination?

Costing

When deciding what kind of measures to put in place in order to improve staff retention generally or the retention of particular individuals, organisations need to balance the costs involved against those that are incurred as a direct result of voluntary resignations. Although it is difficult to cost turnover accurately, it is possible to reach a fair estimate by taking into account the range of expenses involved in replacing one individual with another. Once a figure has been calculated for a job, it is relatively straightforward to compute the savings to be gained from a given percentage reduction in annual turnover rates. Figure 9.1 shows the approach to turnover costing recommended by Hugo Fair (1992).

Costing turnover each year permits organisations to state with some confidence how much money is being saved as a result of ongoing staff turnover reduction programmes. It can also be used as a means of persuading finance directors of the case for investing money in initiatives which can be shown to improve retention. An example of an organisation which has done this is Positive Steps Oldham, a not-for-profit company set up when two local careers service organisations merged (see IDS 2005). The new organisation employs 205 people and at the time it was formed had an overall staff turnover rate of 38 per cent. Over a three-year period, as a result of various targeted initiatives,

Enter number of employees	_____ (a),
Enter average weekly wage	£ _____ (b),
Multiply (a) × (b)	£ _____ (c),
Multiply (c) × 52	£ _____ (d) = *Total paybill*
Enter current turnover rate	___%___ (e),
Multiply (e) × (a)	_____ (f) = *Staff loss p.a.*
Enter average number of days to replace	_____ (g),
Multiplier rate for overtime/temps.	_____ (h),
Multiply (b) × (h)	£ _____ (i),
Multiply (f) × (g) × [(i)/5]	£ _____ (j) = Immediate cover costs
Preparation and interview time per applicant (days)	_____ (k),
Shortlisted applicants per position	_____ (l),
Enter average manager weekly wage	£ _____ (m),
Multiply (f) × (k) × (l) × [(m)/5]	£ _____ (n) = Interview time costs
Enter average recruitment fees	___%___ (o),
Multiply (d) × (e) × (o)	£ _____ (p) = Recruitment fee costs
Length of induction training (days)	_____ (q),
Frequency of this training (p.a.)	_____ (r),
Multiply [(b)/5] × (q) × [(f) + (r)]	£ _____ (s) = Induction training cost
Duration of learning curve (months)	_____ (t),
Enter non-productive element	___%___ (u),
Multiply (d) × (e) × [(t)/12] × (u)	£ _____ (v) = Non-productive costs
Multiply (t) × (u) (months)	£ _____ (w),
Multiply (d) × (e) × (h) × [(w)/12]	£ _____ (x) = Continuing cover costs
Multiply (g) × [(b)/5] × (f)	£ _____ (y) = Salary savings
Add (j) + (n) + (p) + (s) + (v) + (x) − (y)	£ _____ (z) = *Turnover cost p.a.*
Potential cost saving	
Enter expected turnover reduction	___%___ (1),
Multiply (z) × [(1)/(e)]	£ _____ (2) = Labour turnover savings
Enter reduction in replacement time	___%___ (3),
Multiply (j) × (3)	£ _____ (4) = Added cover savings
Add (2) + (4)	£ _____ (5) = *Total savings p.a.*

Figure 9.1
A sample form for costing labour turnover

Source: H. Fair (1992) *Personnel and Profit: The pay-off from people*, p. 41. London: IPM. Used with permission of CIPD Publications.

turnover fell to a much more healthy 14 per cent. Not only did this make the organisation much more effective, it also substantially reduced overheads. The company model for calculating turnover costs includes direct and indirect costs along the lines put forward by Fair in Figure 9.1. At Positive Steps Oldham it was estimated that around £20,000 a year was saved by more than halving turnover.

STAFF RETENTION STRATEGIES

The straightforward answer to the question of how best to retain staff is to provide them with a better deal, in the broadest sense, than they perceive they could get by working for alternative employers. Terms and conditions play a significant role, but other factors are often more important. For example, there is a need to provide jobs which are satisfying, along with career development opportunities, as much autonomy as is practicable and, above all, competent line management. Indeed, at one level, most of the practices of effective human resource management described in this book can play a part in reducing turnover. Organisations which make use of them will enjoy lower rates than competitors who do not. Below we look at six measures that have been shown to have a positive effect on employee retention, focusing particularly on those practices which are not covered in any great depth elsewhere in the book.

Pay

There is some debate in the retention literature about the extent to which raising pay levels reduces staff turnover. On the one hand there is evidence to show that, on average, employers who offer the most attractive reward packages have lower attrition rates than those who pay poorly (Gomez-Mejia and Balkin 1992, pp. 292–4), an assumption which leads many organisations to use pay rates as their prime weapon in retaining staff (Cappelli 2000, pp. 105–6; IRS 2000a, p. 10; IRS 2000b, p. 9). On the other, there is questionnaire-based evidence which suggests that pay is a good deal less important than other factors in a decision to quit one's job (Bevan *et al*. 1997, p. 25; Hiltrop 1999, p. 424). The consensus among researchers specialising in retention issues is that pay has a role to play as a satisfier, but that it will not usually have an effect when other factors are pushing an individual towards quitting. Raising pay levels may thus result in greater job satisfaction where people are already happy with their work, but it will not deter unhappy employees from leaving. Sturges and Guest (1999), in their study of leaving decisions in the field of graduate employment, summed up their findings as follows:

> As far as they are concerned, while challenging work will compensate for pay, pay will never compensate for having to do boring, unstimulating work. (Sturges and Guest 1999, p. 19)

Recent research findings thus appear to confirm the views expressed by Herzberg (1966) that pay is a 'hygiene factor' rather than a motivator. This means that it can be a cause of dissatisfaction at work, but not of positive job satisfaction. People may be motivated to leave an employer who is perceived as paying badly, but once they are satisfied with their pay additional increases have little effect.

The other problem with the use of pay increases to retain staff is that it is an approach that is very easily matched by competitors. This is particularly true of 'golden handcuff' arrangements which seek to tie senior staff to an organisation for a number of years by paying substantial bonuses at a defined future date. As Cappelli (2000, p. 106) argues, in a buoyant job market, recruiters simply 'unlock the handcuffs' by offering equivalent signing-on bonuses to people they wish to employ.

It is important that employees do not perceive their employers to be treating them inequitably. Provided pay levels are not considerably lower than those paid by an organisation's labour market competitors, other factors will usually be more important contributors towards high turnover levels. Where the salaries that are paid are already broadly competitive, little purpose is served by increasing them further. The organisation may well make itself more attractive in recruitment terms, but the effect on staff retention will be limited. Moreover, of course, wage costs will increase.

There is potentially more to be gained from enhancing benefits packages, because these are less easily imitated or matched by competitors. Where particular benefits, such as staff discounts, holiday entitlements or private healthcare schemes, are appreciated by staff, they are more likely to have a positive effect on staff turnover than simply paying higher base wages. Potentially the same is true of pension schemes, which are associated with relatively high levels of staff retention. However, the research evidence suggests that except for older employees who have completed many years of service, most pension schemes are not sufficiently valued by staff to cause them to stay in a job with which they are dissatisfied (Taylor 2000). Arguably, the best way of using benefits to keep a lid on staff turnover is to move towards flexible schemes such as those discussed in Chapter 29. An employer who allows individual employees to choose how they make up their own remuneration package will generally be more attractive than one who only offers a 'one size fits all' set of benefits.

While pay rates and benefit packages may play a relatively marginal role in the retention of good people, reward in the broader sense plays a more significant role. If employees do not find their work to be 'rewarding' in the broadest sense of the word, they will be much more likely to start looking for alternative jobs. Making work rewarding is a good deal harder for managers to achieve because different people find different aspects of their work to be rewarding. There is thus a need to understand what makes people tick and to manage them as individuals accordingly. Getting this right is difficult, but achieving it is worthwhile from the point of view of retaining people. It is far harder for would-be competitors to imitate the effective motivation of an individual than it is for them to increase the salary that a person is paid.

ACTIVITY 9.4

The case for arguing that pay rates have a relatively minor role to play in explaining individual resignations rests partly on the assumption that other elements of the employment relationship are more important. It is argued that people will 'trade in' high pay in order to secure other perceived benefits and that consequently low-paying employers can retain staff effectively.

What other factors do you think employees consider to be more important than pay? What role can the HRM function play in helping to develop these?

Managing expectations

For some years research evidence has strongly suggested that employers benefit from ensuring that potential employees gain a 'realistic job preview' before they take up a job offer. The purpose is to make sure that new staff enter an organisation with their eyes wide open and do not find that the job fails to meet their expectations. A major cause of job dissatisfaction, and hence of high staff turnover, is the experience of having one's high hopes of new employment dashed by the realisation that it is not going to be as enjoyable or stimulating as anticipated.

Several researchers have drawn attention to the importance of these processes in reducing high turnover during the early months of employment (e.g. Wanous 1992, pp. 53–87; Hom and Griffeth 1995, pp. 193–203). The need is to strike a balance at the recruitment stage between sending out messages which are entirely positive and sending out those which are realistic. In other words, it is important not to mislead candidates about the nature of the work that they will be doing.

Realistic job previews are most important when candidates, for whatever reason, cannot know a great deal about the job for which they are applying. This may be because of limited past experience or it may because the job is relatively unusual and not based in a type of workplace with which job applicants are familiar. An example quoted by Carroll *et al.* (1999, p. 246) concerns work in nursing homes, which seems to attract people looking to undertake a caring role but who are unfamiliar with the less attractive hours, working conditions and job duties associated with the care assistant's role. The realistic job preview is highly appropriate in such a situation as a means of avoiding recruiting people who subsequently leave within a few weeks.

The importance of unmet expectations as an explanation for staff turnover is also stressed by Sturges and Guest (1999, pp. 16 and 31) in their work on the retention of newly recruited graduates. Here the problem is one of employers overselling graduate careers when competing with others to secure the services of the brightest young people:

> False impressions are given and a positive spin put on answers to questions so as to deter able applicants from taking up alternative offers. As a result, graduates start work confident in the belief that their days will be filled with interesting work, that they will be treated fairly and objectively in terms of performance assessment, that their career development will be fostered judiciously, and that their working lives will in some way be 'fun' and 'exciting'. That is fine if it really can be guaranteed. Unfortunately such is often not the case, and unsurprisingly it leads to early dissatisfaction and higher turnover rates than are desirable. (Jenner and Taylor 2000, p. 155)

A solution, aside from the introduction of more honest recruitment literature, is to provide periods of work experience for students before they graduate. A summer spent working somewhere is the best possible way of finding out exactly what a particular job or workplace is really like. The same argument can be deployed in support of work experience for young people who are about to leave school in order to enter the job market.

Induction

Another process often credited with the reduction of turnover early in the employment relationship is the presence of effective and timely induction. It is very easy to overlook in the rush to get people into key posts quickly and it is often carried out badly, but it is essential if avoidable early turnover is to be kept to a minimum. Gregg and Wadsworth (1999, p. 111) show in their analysis of 870,000 workers starting new jobs in 1992 that as many as 17 per cent had left within three months and 42 per cent within 12 months. No doubt a good number of these departures were due either to poorly managed expectations or to ineffective inductions.

Induction has a number of distinct purposes, all of which are concerned with preparing new employees to work as effectively as possible and as soon as is possible in their new jobs. First, it plays an important part in helping new starters to adjust emotionally to the new workplace. It gives an opportunity to ensure that they understand where things are, who to ask when unsure about what to do and how their role fits into the organisation generally. Second, induction provides a forum in which basic information about the organisation can be transmitted. This may include material about the organisation's purpose, its mission statement and the key issues it faces. More generally a corporate induction provides a suitable occasion to talk about health and safety regulations, fire evacuation procedures and organisational policies concerning matters like the use of telephones for private purposes. Third, induction processes can be used to convey to new starters important cultural messages about what the organisation expects and what employees can expect in return. It thus potentially forms an important stage in the establishment of the psychological contract, leaving new employees clear about what they need to do to advance their own prospects in the organisation. All these matters will be picked up by new starters anyway in their first months of employment, but incorporating them into a formal induction programme ensures that they are brought up to speed a good deal more quickly, and that they are less likely to leave at an early date.

There is no 'right' length for an induction programme. In some jobs it can be accomplished effectively in a few days, for others there is a need for some form of input over a number of weeks. What is important is that individuals are properly introduced both to the organisation and to their particular role within it. These introductons are usually best handled by different people. Organisational induction, because it is given to all new starters, is normally handled centrally by the HR department and takes place in a single place over one or two days. Job-based induction takes longer, will be overseen by the individual's own line manager and will usually involve shadowing colleagues. The former largely takes the form of a presentation, while the latter involves the use of a wider variety of training methods. IRS (2000c, pp. 10–12) draws attention to the recent development of web-based training packages which allow new employees to learn about their organisations and their jobs at their own pace, when they get the opportunity.

Family-friendly HR practices

Labour Force Survey statistics show that between 5 per cent and 10 per cent of employees leave their jobs for 'family or personal reasons' (IRS 1999, p. 6), while Hom and Griffeth (1995, p. 252) quote American research indicating that 33 per cent of women quit jobs to devote more time to their families – a response given by only one per cent of men. To these figures can be added those quoted by Gregg and Wadsworth (1999,

p. 116) which show average job tenure among women with children in the UK to be over a year shorter than that of women without children and almost two years shorter than that of men. These statistics suggest that one of the more significant reasons for voluntary resignations from jobs is the inability to juggle the demands of a job with those of the family. They indicate that there is a good business case, particularly where staff retention is high on the agenda, for considering ways in which employment can be made more family friendly.

WINDOW ON PRACTICE

IRS (2000c, p. 11) describes an original approach taken to the induction of staff at a large Novotel Hotel in London. Unusually for the hotel industry the induction programme here lasts for three weeks. It includes some job shadowing of experienced staff, but also consists of several days spent in a training room learning about the hotel's main services and learning how to deal with difficult customers. A variety of training techniques are used including quizzes, games, discussion forums and role play exercises. The management saw their retention rates increase by 12 per cent after the introduction of the new programme.

As a result of legislation under the Working Time Regulations 1998, the Employment Relations Act 1999, the Employment Act 2002 and the Work and Families Act 2006, UK employers are now obliged by law to provide the following as a minimum floor of rights:

- nine months' leave for all employees paid according to a formula set out in the regulations;
- an additional three months' unpaid maternity leave for employees;
- reasonable paid time off for pregnant employees to attend ante-natal clinics;
- specific health and safety measures for workers who are pregnant or have recently given birth;
- four weeks' paid holiday each year in addition to eight bank holidays;
- a total of three months' unpaid parental leave for mothers and fathers on the birth or adoption of a child;
- reasonable unpaid time off for employees to deal with family emergencies such as the sickness of a child or dependent relative;
- consideration of reasonable requests by parents of young children and with caring responsibilities for adults to work flexibly;
- two weeks' paid paternity leave for new fathers.

Many employers, however, have decided to go a good deal further down this road than is required by law. The most common example is the provision of more paid maternity leave and the right, where possible, for mothers to return to work on a part-time or job-share basis if they so wish. Crèche provision is common in larger workplaces, while others offer childcare vouchers instead. Career breaks are offered by many public sector employers, allowing people to take a few months off without pay and subsequently to return to a similar job with the same organisation. Flexitime systems such as those described in Chapter 6 are also useful to people with families and may thus serve as a retention tool in some cases. In the USA the literature indicates growing interest in 'elder care' arrangements (Lambert 2000) aimed specifically at providing assistance to those seeking to combine work with responsibility for the care of elderly relatives. An example in the UK is the 'granny crèche' established by Peugeot for employees at its plant in Coventry. You can read much more about these and other work-life-balance initiatives in Chapter 31.

Training and development

There are two widely expressed, but wholly opposed, perspectives on the link between training interventions and employee turnover. On the one hand is the argument that training opportunities enhance commitment to an employer on the part of individual employees, making them less likely to leave voluntarily than they would if no training were offered. The alternative view holds that training makes people more employable and hence more likely to leave in order to develop their careers elsewhere. The view is thus put that money spent on training is money wasted because it ultimately benefits other employers.

Green *et al.* (2000, pp. 267–72) report research on perceptions of 1,539 employees on different kinds of training. They found that the overall effect is neutral, 19 per cent of employees saying that training was 'more likely to make them actively look for another job' and 18 per cent saying it was less likely to do so. However, they also found the type of training and the source of sponsorship to be a significant variable. Training which is paid for by the employer is a good deal less likely to raise job mobility than that paid for by the employee or the government. Firm-specific training is also shown in the study to be associated with lower turnover than training which leads to the acquisition of transferable skills. The point is made, however, that whatever the form of training, an employer can develop a workforce which is both 'capable and committed' by combining training interventions with other forms of retention initiative.

The most expensive types of training intervention involve long-term courses of study such as an MBA, CIPD or accountancy qualification. In financing such courses, employers are sending a very clear signal to the employees concerned that their contribution is valued and that they can look forward to substantial career advancement if they opt to stay. The fact that leaving will also mean an end to the funding for the course provides a more direct incentive to remain with the sponsoring employer.

Improving the quality of line management

If it is the case that many, if not most, voluntary resignations are explained by dissatisfaction on the part of employees with their supervisors, it follows that the most effective means of reducing staff turnover in organisations is to improve the performance of line managers. Too often, it appears, people are promoted into supervisory positions without adequate experience or training. Organisations seem to assume that their managers are capable supervisors, without recognising that the role is difficult and does not usually come naturally to people. Hence it is common to find managers who are 'quick to critise but slow to praise', who are too tied up in their own work to show an interest in their subordinates and who prefer to impose their own solutions without first taking account of their staff's views. The solution is to take action on various fronts to improve the effectiveness of supervisors:

- select people for line management roles following an assessment of their supervisory capabilities;
- ensure that all newly appointed line managers are trained in the art of effective supervision;
- regularly appraise line managers on their supervisory skills.

This really amounts to little more than common sense, but such approaches are the exception to the rule in most UK organisations.

WINDOW ON PRACTICE

In 2006 the Chartered Institute of Personnel and Development's annual survey on recruitment and retention matters asked employers to state what steps they were currently taking to address staff retention. The range of initiatives was extensive and broadly appropriate given what the research evidence tells us are the principal reasons for voluntary resignations. The top ten initiatives were as follows:

10 better recognition of employee efforts (20%)

 9 offering coaching and mentoring (21%)

 8 improving work-life balance (30%)

 7 improving benefits (31%)

 6 improving employee involvement (32%)

 5 improving line management HR skills (33%)

 4 increasing pay (34%)

 3 improving selection techniques (38%)

 2 increasing learning and development opportunities (45%)

 1 improving induction processes (49%)

SUMMARY PROPOSITIONS

9.1 Staff turnover tends to decrease in recessions and increase during economic booms.

9.2 Contrary to much popular perception, average job tenure has not reduced substantially over the past thirty years.

9.3 Retention rates vary very considerably between industries and between different regions.

9.4 While there are arguments that can be deployed in favour of modest staff turnover, it is generally agreed that too great a rate is damaging for an organisation.

9.5 In planning retention initiatives it is important both to analyse the causes of turnover and to calculate the current costs associated with each voluntary resignation.

9.6 Specific programmes which lead to improved retention include flexible benefits, better induction, the effective management of expectations, family-friendly initiatives, training opportunities and the improvement of line management in organisations.

GENERAL DISCUSSION TOPICS

1 What are the main reasons for the trends in job tenure illustrated in Table 9.1?

2 Staff turnover is generally low during recessions, but it increases substantially in firms which get into financial difficulty. What factors account for this phenomenon?

3 Think about your own experiences at work or those of close friends and family. What were the key factors that affected decisions to leave a particular job? What, if anything, could the employer have done to ensure that no resignation took place?

FURTHER READING

Chartered Institute of Personnel and Development (annual) *Recruitment, Retention and Turnover Survey*. London: CIPD.
Confederation of British Industry (annual) *Absence and Labour Turnover Survey*. London: CBI.
Each year the CIPD and the CBI carry out major surveys looking at staff turnover across the UK. They report the labour turnover rates among different groups as well as estimates of turnover costs. Many smaller surveys covering specific employee groups (like graduates) or particular industries are also published annually. *IRS Employment Review* always carries a number of 'benchmarking turnover' articles towards the end of the year which report the key findings from all these surveys.

Hom, P. and Griffeth, R. (1995) *Employee Turnover*. Cincinnati, Ohio: South Western College Publishing.
This is by far the best source of information about academic research on turnover and staff retention issues. It is now out of print, but the same authors' more recent book, Griffeth, R. and Hom, P. (2001) *Retaining Valued Employees*, Thousand Oaks, Cal.: Sage, is widely available.

Taylor, S. (2002) *The Employee Retention Handbook*. London: CIPD.
This is a useful source of information about UK research on the topic. It contains chapters focusing on measuring and costing turnover, identifying the causes of turnover and several looking at different strategies for improving retention rates.

REFERENCES

Auer, P., Berg, J. and Coulibaly, I. (2004) *Is a stable workforce good for the economy? Insights into the tenure-productivity-employment relationship*. Geneva: International Labour Organisation.

Bevan, S., Barber, L. and Robinson, D. (1997) *Keeping the Best: a practical guide to retaining key employees*. Brighton: Institute for Employment Research.

Branham, L. (2005) *The Seven Hidden Reasons Employees Leave*. New York: The American Management Association.

Cappelli, P. (2000) 'A market-driven approach to retaining talent', *Harvard Business Review*, January/February, pp. 103–11.

Carroll, M., Marchington, M., Earnshaw, J. and Taylor, S. (1999) 'Recruitment in small firms: processes, methods and problems', *Employee Relations*, Vol. 21, No. 3, pp. 236–50.

Chartered Institute of Personnel and Development (2006) Recruitment, *Retention and Turnover: Annual Survey Report 2006*. London: CIPD.

Clayton, G. (2006) 'Key skills retention and motivation: the war for talent still rages and retention is the high ground', *Industrial and Commercial Training*, Vol. 38, No. 1, pp. 37–45.

Department of Trade and Industry (2006) *Collective Redundancies – Employer's Duty to Notify the Secretary of State. Full Regulatory Impact Assessment*. London: DTI.

Fair, H. (1992) *Personnel and Profit: The pay-off from people*. London: IPM.

Gomez-Mejia, L. and Balkin, D. (1992) *Compensation, Organizational Strategy and Firm Performance*. Cincinnati, Ohio: South Western College Publishing.

Green, F., Felstead, A., Mayhew, K. and Pick, A. (2000) 'The impact of training on labour mobility: individual and firm-level evidence from Britain', *British Journal of Industrial Relations*, Vol. 38, No. 2.

Gregg, P. and Wadsworth, J. (1999) 'Job tenure, 1975–98', in P. Gregg and J. Wadsworth (eds) *The State of Working Britain*. Manchester: Manchester University Press.

Griffeth, R. and Hom, P. (2001) *Retaining Valued Employees*. Thousand Oaks, Cal.: Sage.

Herzberg, F. (1966) *Work and the Nature of Man*. Cleveland, Ohio: World Publishing.

Hiltrop, J.-M. (1999) 'The quest for the best: human resource practices to attract and retain talent', *European Management Journal*, Vol. 17, No. 4, pp. 423–31.

Hom, P. and Griffeth, R. (1995) *Employee Turnover*. Cincinnati, Ohio: South Western College Publishing.

IDS (2000) *Improving Staff Retention*, IDS Study No. 692, July.

IDS (2005) *Positive Steps Oldham halves employee turnover*, IDS Study 807, October, pp. 17–22.

IRS (1999) 'Benchmarking labour turnover: annual guide 1999/2000', *Employee Development Bulletin*, No. 118, October.

IRS (2000a) 'Employee Retention 1 – the tools and techniques', *Employee Development Bulletin*, No. 128, pp. 6–10, August.

IRS (2000b) 'Retention 2 – effective methods', *Employee Development Bulletin*, No. 129, pp. 6–16, September.

IRS (2000c) 'Improving retention and performance through induction', *Employee Development Bulletin*, No. 130, pp. 10–16, October.

Jenner, S. and Taylor, S. (2000) *Recruiting, Developing and Retaining Graduate Talent*. London: Financial Times/Prentice Hall.

Labour Market Trends (2001) 'Length of time continuously employed by occupation and industry', February.

Lambert, S. (2000) 'Added benefits: The link between work-life benefits and organizational citizen behavior', *Academy of Management Journal*, Vol. 43, No. 5, pp. 801–15.

Larkan, K. (2006) *The Talent War: How to find and retain the best people for your company*. New York: Marshall Cavendish.

Macaulay, C. (2003) 'Job mobility and job tenure in the UK', *Labour Market Trends*, November.

Ritzer, G. (1996) *The Macdonaldisation of Society: an investigation into the changing character of contemporary social life*, revised edn. Thousand Oaks, Cal.: Pine Forge.

Sturges, J. and Guest, D. (1999) *Shall I Stay or Should I go?* Warwick: Association of Graduate Recruiters.

Taylor, S. (2000) 'Occupational pensions and employee retention: debate and evidence', *Employee Relations*, Vol. 22, No. 3, pp. 246–59.

Taylor, S. (2002) *The Employee Retention Handbook*. London: CIPD.

Wanous, J.P. (1992) *Recruitment, Selection, Orientation and Socialization of Newcomers*. Reading, Mass.: Addison Wesley.

Williams, M. (2000) *The War for Talent*. London: CIPD.

Woodruffe, C. (1999) *Winning the Talent War*. Chichester: Wiley.

An extensive range of additional materials, including multiple choice questions, answers to questions and links to useful websites can be found on the Human Resource Management Companion Website at **www.pearsoned.co.uk/torrington.**

CHAPTER (10)

ENDING THE CONTRACT

THE OBJECTIVES OF THIS CHAPTER ARE TO:

1 Outline the framework in which the law of unfair dismissal operates

2 Set out the major reasons for which an employer can and cannot lawfully dismiss employees

3 Explain the concept of 'reasonableness' in unfair dismissal cases and its significance

4 Review the law on dismissals on grounds of capability, misconduct and redundancy

5 Describe the operation of the law of constructive dismissal and the law of wrongful dismissal

In the last chapter we looked at situations in which employees decide to end their contracts of employment by giving their employers notice. Here we focus on circumstances when the contract is brought to an end by the employer through a dismissal of one kind or another, something that over a million employees experience in the UK each year (Knight and Latreille 2000). In some cases employees are happy to leave (or at least not unhappy) such as when they are retiring or when they are due to receive a large redundancy payment. More common, however, are situations where the person dismissed is distinctly unhappy about the contract being brought to an end. When someone perceives that they have been treated unfairly in terms of the reason for, or the manner of, their dismissal they can take their case to an employment tribunal. In practice, between five per cent and ten per cent of all dismissed workers who qualify do bring such claims, leaving the Employment Tribunal Service to deal with 30,000–40,000 cases each year (see ETS 2006). If someone wins their case they may ask to be reinstated, but will usually settle for a compensation payment. The size of such awards is not generally substantial (around £8,500 on average), but occasionally people are awarded larger sums. Whatever the final outcome there are often additional legal costs for the employer to bear, not to mention the loss of a great deal of management time. An organisation's reputation as a good employer can also be damaged by adverse publicity arising from such cases. Employers generally take careful account of the requirements of the law when dismissing employees. The alternative is to run the risk of being summoned to an employment tribunal and possibly losing the case. To a great extent the law therefore effectively determines practice in the field of dismissal.

In the UK there are three forms of dismissal claim that can be brought to a tribunal. Rights associated with the law of wrongful dismissal are the longest established. A person who claims wrongful dismissal complains that the way that they were dismissed breached the terms of their contract of employment. Constructive dismissal occurs when someone feels forced to resign as a direct result of their employer's actions. In this area the law aims to deter employers from seeking to avoid dismissing people by pushing them into resignation. The third category, unfair dismissal, is by far the most common. It is best defined as a dismissal which falls short of the expectations of the law as laid down in the Employment Rights Act 1996. You will find some practical case study exercises relating to unfair dismissal law on our companion website **www.pearsoned.co.uk/torrington**.

UNFAIR DISMISSAL

The law of unfair dismissal dates from 1971, since when it has been amended a number of times. Although amendments and the outcomes of leading cases have made it more complex than it was originally, the basic principles have stood the test of time and remain in place. The latest major changes were contained in the Statutory Dispute Resolution Regulations which came into effect in 2004 (DTI 2003). Their aim was to reduce the number of claims being brought before employment tribunals by providing strong incentives for employers and employees to make use of internal disciplinary and grievance procedures first. These regulations also adjusted the position of the law in respect of dismissals that are for justified reasons but which are carried out using an incomplete or deficient procedure. At the time of writing (March 2007) the future of the 2004 regulations is in some doubt and it is likely that significant further reform may soon be introduced (see the Window on Practice box).

In most circumstances the right to bring a claim of unfair dismissal applies to employees who have completed a year's continuous service with their employer on the date their contract was terminated. This allows the employer a period of 12 months to assess whether or not an individual employee is suitable before the freedom to dismiss is restricted. For a number of years until 1999 the time limit was two years. In reducing the period, the government brought an additional 2.8 million people within the scope of unfair dismissal law (DTI 1999). Until recently people who were over the age of 65 or 'the normal retiring age' in a particular employment had no right to bring an unfair dismissal case to an employment tribunal. This restriction was removed as part of the introduction of age discrimination law in October 2006. At the time of writing, however (March 2007), it remains lawful for an employer to retire people mandatorily at the age of 65 provided a prescribed procedure is followed.

The one-year restriction on qualification applies except where the reason for the dismissal is one of those listed below which are classed as 'automatically unfair' or 'inadmissible'. A further requirement is that the claim form is lodged at the tribunal office before three months have elapsed from the date of dismissal. Unless there are circumstances justifying the failure to submit a claim before the deadline, claims received after three months are ruled out of time.

Before a case comes to tribunal, officers of the Advisory, Conciliation and Arbitration Service (ACAS) will often try to help the parties reach a settlement. The papers of all cases lodged with the employment tribunals' offices are sent to ACAS with a view to conciliation taking place ahead of a tribunal hearing. As a result the majority of cases either get settled or are withdrawn without the need for the parties to attend a full hearing.

When faced with a claim of unfair dismissal, and where it is not disputed that a dismissal took place, an employment tribunal asks two separate questions:

1 Was the reason for the dismissal one which is classed by the law as legitimate?

2 Did the employer act reasonably in carrying out the dismissal?

Where the answer to the first question is 'no', there is no need to ask the second because the dismissed employee will already have won his or her case. Interestingly the burden of proof shifts as the tribunal moves from considering the first to the second question. It is for the employer to satisfy the tribunal that it dismissed the employee for a legitimate reason. The burden of proof then becomes neutral when the question of reasonableness is addressed.

ACTIVITY 10.1

Consider the working activities of some of your colleagues (and perhaps your own working activities). What examples are there of behaviour that you feel justify dismissal? Make a list of your ideas and check them when you have finished this chapter and see how many might be classified by a tribunal as unfair dismissals.

Automatically unfair reasons

Certain reasons for dismissal are declared in law to be inadmissible or automatically unfair. Where the tribunal finds that one of these was the principal reason for the dismissal, they find in favour of the claimant (i.e. the ex-employee) whatever the circumstances of the case. In practice, therefore, there is no defence that an employer can make to explain its actions that will be acceptable to the tribunal. Some of these relate to other areas of employment law such as non-discrimination, working time and the minimum wage, which are discussed in more detail elsewhere in this book. The list of automatically unfair reasons for dismissal has grown steadily in recent years as new employment rights have come on to the statute book; in 2007 it was as follows:

- dismissal for a reason relating to pregnancy or maternity;
- dismissal for a health and safety reason (e.g. refusing to work in unsafe conditions);
- dismissal because of a spent conviction;
- dismissal for refusing to work on a Sunday (retail and betting workers only);
- dismissal for a trade union reason;
- dismissal for taking official industrial action (during the first 12 weeks of the action);
- dismissal in contravention of the part-time workers or fixed-term employees' regulations;
- dismissal for undertaking duties as an occupational pension fund trustee, employee representative, member of a European Works Council or in connection with jury service;
- dismissal for asserting a statutory right (including rights exercised under the Employment Rights Act, as well as those connected with the Working Time Regulations, the National Minimum Wage Regulations, the Public Interest Disclosure Act and the Information and Consultation of Employees Regulations; the right to request flexible working, the right to time off for dependents, the right to adoptive, parental or paternity leave, the right to be accompanied at disciplinary and grievance hearings and the claiming of working tax credits);
- dismissal for a reason connected with the transfer of an undertaking (i.e. when a business or part of a business changes hands or merges with another organisation) in the absence of a valid economic, technical or organisational reason;
- dismissals that take place before the completion of the disciplinary and dismissal procedures (DDPs) required by the Dispute Resolution Regulations 2004.

The requirement to have completed a year's continuous service only applies in the case of the last two dismissal scenarios on this list. Under the Dispute Resolution Regulations 2004 a dismissal must be found unfair, irrespective of the circumstances, whenever an employer dismisses an employee with over a year's service *without* first having initiated the following basic three-step procedure:

- Step 1: The employer sends the employee a letter setting out the nature of the circumstances that may lead to the employee's dismissal.
- Step 2: The employer invites the employee to a meeting to discuss the issue at which both parties put their views across. After the meeting the employer informs the employee about the outcome. If it is to dismiss, then the right of appeal is confirmed.
- Step 3: The employee exercises their right to appeal and a further meeting is held for this purpose.

In exceptional cases of gross misconduct employers are permitted to omit stage 2 of this procedure. This does not, however, make the dismissal fair, it just means that it is not automatically unfair. A failure to investigate properly or hold a hearing would mean that such a dismissal would usually be found to have been carried out unreasonably.

WINDOW ON PRACTICE

In 2002 the government decided to bring forward measures aimed at reducing the number of cases that the Employment Tribunal Service was required to handle each year. A consequence of the proliferation of new employment rights that have been introduced in recent years has been a substantial increase in the case load and hence an additional cost to the Treasury. The employment tribunal system costs over £100 million a year to operate. The proposals that were originally brought forward were heavily criticised at the time and were modified following an extensive consultation exercise. But significant changes were included in the Employment Act 2002 and were subsequently brought into effect via the 2004 Statutory Dispute Resolution Regulations.

In the case of dismissals the new regulations created a new minimum procedure which employers had to follow whenever they dismissed anyone with over a years' service – whatever the circumstances. They were even to apply when a fixed-term contract comes to an end where there is no anticipation of future employment on either side. The consequence of failing to follow the basic procedure was a finding that the dismissal was automatically unfair – i.e. unfair in law whatever the particular circumstances of the case. At the same time the regulations gave ex-employees a strong incentive to attend disciplinary hearings and to appeal against the outcomes internally by making a portion of the compensation that is payable dependent on their having done so.

In the case of legal action that does not relate to a straight dismissal (e.g. discrimination claims, claims for unpaid wages, working time issues, and constructive dismissals) the 2004 regulations required that the employee or ex-employee raised their complaint internally, perhaps using a formal grievance procedure, before they were able to bring it to an employment tribunal. Here too financial incentives were introduced to encourage cooperation by employers, the aim being to try to get disputes settled in the workplace without the need for formal legal action.

At the time of writing (March 2007) a report commissioned by the government into the operation of the 2004 regulations has been published. Written by Michael Gibbons of the Better Regulation Commission and a team of lawyers, employers and trade union representatives, the report is highly critical of the 2004 regulations, although supportive of their aims. It concludes that they have not met their objectives in practice and have, at the same time, tended to deter people with genuine cases from pursuing them in the employment tribunal. It proposes their wholesale abolition and replacement with less formal mechanisms aimed at persuading the parties to settle disputes locally, with or without the assistance of ACAS conciliation officers. In particular it suggests that tribunals themselves can provide financial incentives by taking account of the efforts made to settle disputes ahead of hearings in the awards they make and by requiring claimants to make a contribution to the legal costs incurred by employers more frequently than they do at present.

On receiving the Gibbons Report the government launched a further consultation exercise about whether or not the 2004 regulations should be repealed and what should be put in their place. Further significant legislation in this area is thus likely to be brought forward in 2008 or 2009.

Potentially fair reasons

From an employer's perspective it is important to be able to satisfy the tribunal that the true reason for the dismissal was one of those reasons classed as potentially fair in unfair dismissal law. Only once this has been achieved can the second question (the issue of reasonableness) be addressed. The potentially fair grounds for dismissal are as follows:

- Lack of capability or qualifications: if an employee lacks the skill, aptitude or physical health to carry out the job, then there is a potentially fair ground for dismissal.
- Misconduct: this category covers the range of behaviours that we examine in considering the grievance and discipline processes: disobedience, absence, insubordination and criminal acts. It can also include taking industrial action.
- Redundancy: where an employee's job ceases to exist, it is potentially fair to dismiss the employee for redundancy.
- Statutory bar: when employees cannot continue to discharge their duties without breaking the law, they can be fairly dismissed. Most cases of this kind follow disqualification of drivers following convictions for speeding, or for drunk or dangerous driving. Other common cases involve foreign nationals whose work permits have been terminated.
- Some other substantial reason: this most intangible category is introduced in order to cater for genuinely fair dismissals for reasons so diverse that they could not realistically be listed. Examples have been security of commercial information (where an employee's husband set up a rival company) or employee refusal to accept altered working conditions.
- Dismissals arising from official industrial action after 12 weeks have passed.
- Dismissals that occur on the transfer of an undertaking where a valid ETO (economic, technological or organisational) reason applies.
- Mandatory retirements which follow the completion of the procedures set out in the Employment Equality (Age) Regulations 2006 (see Chapter 23).

Determining reasonableness

Having decided that potentially fair grounds for the dismissal exist, the tribunal then proceeds to consider whether the dismissal is fair in the circumstances. The test used by the tribunal in reaching decisions about the fairness of a dismissal is that of the reasonable employer. Tribunal members are not required to judge cases on the basis of what they would have done in the circumstances or what the best employers would have done. Instead they have to ask themselves whether what the employer did in the circumstances of the time fell within a possible band of reasonable responses. In practice this means that the employer wins the case if it can show that the decision to dismiss was one that a reasonable employer *might* conceivably have taken.

In assessing reasonableness tribunals always take a particular interest in the procedure that was used. They are also keen to satisfy themselves that the employer has acted broadly consistently in its treatment of different employees and that it has taken into account any mitigating circumstances that might have explained a deterioration in an employee's conduct or performance. In addition, they are required to have regard to the size and resources of the employer concerned. Higher standards are thus expected of a large PLC with a well-staffed HR department than of a small owner-managed business employing a handful of people. The former, for example, might be expected to give two or three warnings and additional training before dismissing someone on grounds of incapability. One simple warning might suffice in a small business which relied heavily on an acceptable level of performance from the individual concerned.

The significance attached to procedure has varied over the years. Until 1987 employers were able to argue successfully that although the procedure used was deficient in some respects, the outcome was not affected. This changed following the judgment of the House of Lords in the case of *Polkey* v. *AE Dayton Services* (1987). Henceforth, tribunals were obliged to find dismissals unfair where the employer had not completed a proper procedure before making the final decision to dismiss. In 2004 the law changed again, but the extent to which this has occurred has only become clear more recently as a result of evolving case law. The current position is that the employer must only dismiss once the basic two or three-step procedure set out in the 2004 Dispute Resolution Regulations has been completed. A failure to do so renders the dismissal automatically unfair. However, beyond that, procedural deficiencies can be defended on the grounds that they made no difference to the outcome. In other words, a dismissal would have occurred whether or not the employers' own established procedures were or were not carried through to the letter.

In this book we have separated the consideration of discipline from the consideration of dismissal in order to concentrate on the practical aspects of discipline (putting things right) rather than the negative aspects (getting rid of the problem). The two cannot, however, be separated in practice and the question of dismissal needs to be reviewed in the light of the material in Chapter 25.

WINDOW ON PRACTICE

In 1999 the Employment Appeal Tribunal made a landmark decision in the case of *Haddon* v. *Van den Bergh Foods* only to be overturned a few months later in another case. Mr Haddon was dismissed in extraordinary circumstances when he failed to return to work after having attended a ceremony at which he had been presented with a long service award. Rather than completing the last few hours of his shift, he decided to take the time off. This was contrary to the workplace rules; so he was fired. When the case came to an employment tribunal Mr Haddon lost on the grounds that the employer's decision, though harsh, fell within the band of reasonable responses open to an employer in the circumstances. He appealed to the EAT, who took the opportunity not only to overturn the original decision, but also to hold that the long-established 'band of reasonable responses' test was unhelpful. Instead, they suggested that tribunals should simply make a general judgment about whether or not an employer had acted reasonably, taking into account their own opinion about what is appropriate.

For a few months the new ruling stood and tribunals began to use it in order to find in favour of ex-employees in many more cases than had been their practice previously. In March 2000, the EAT (with a new chairman) overturned its own decision in Haddon's case, putting back the band of reasonable responses test in the case of *Midland Bank* v. *Madden* (IRS 2000a). It argued that only a higher court, such as the Court of Appeal or the House of Lords, could discard the test, so it must remain until this occurs.

Lack of capability or qualifications

A common reason for dismissal is poor performance on the part of an employee. The law permits dismissals for this reason. It also allows employers to determine for themselves what constitutes an acceptable level of performance in a job, provided of course that a consistent approach is followed between different employees. However, such dismissals are only considered to be reasonable (and hence fair in law) if the employee concerned has both been formally warned about their poor performance at least once and given a reasonable opportunity to improve. Formality in this context means that a formal hearing has been held at which the employee has been entitled to be represented and after which there has been a right of appeal to a more senior manager.

The employer will always need to demonstrate the employee's unsuitability to the satisfaction of the tribunal by producing evidence of that unsuitability. This evidence must not be undermined by, for instance, giving the employee a glowing testimonial at the time of dismissal or by the presence of positive appraisal reports on the individual's personal file. Lack of skill or aptitude is a fair ground when the lack can be demonstrated and where the employer has not contributed to it by, for instance, ignoring it for a long period. Redeployment to a more suitable job is also an option employers are expected to consider before taking the decision to dismiss.

The requirement on employers to warn an employee formally that their performance is unsatisfactory at a meeting at which they have the opportunity to answer back, and the subsequent requirement to give the employee concerned support during a reasonable period in which they have an opportunity to improve, means that dismissals on grounds of poor performance can take several weeks or months to carry through. Moreover, during this time relationships can become very strained because formal action has been taken and a formal warning given. For these reasons managers often seek to avoid dismissing in line with the expectations of the law, instead seeking to dress up poor performance dismissals as redundancies or cases of gross misconduct. However, employment tribunals are very aware of this tendency and always find dismissals that occur in such circumstances to be unfair.

WINDOW ON PRACTICE

Dr Al-Tikriti was a senior registrar employed by the South Western Regional Health Authority. The practice of the authority was to allow registrars three attempts at passing the examination of the Royal College of Pathologists. Dr Al-Tikriti failed on the third attempt and was subsequently dismissed. He claimed that the dismissal was unfair on the grounds that he had had insufficient training to pass the exams. The tribunal, having heard evidence from the Royal College, decided that the training had been adequate and found the dismissal to have been fair

Source: *Al-Tikriti* v. *South Western RHA* (1986).

Another aspect of employee capability is health. It is potentially fair to dismiss someone on the grounds of ill health which renders the employee incapable of discharging the contract of employment. Even the most distressing dismissal can be legally admissible, provided that it is not too hasty and that there is consideration of alternative employment. Employers are expected, however, to take account of any medical advice available to them before dismissing someone on the grounds of ill health. Companies with occupational health services are well placed to obtain detailed medical reports to help in such judgements but the decision to terminate someone's employment is ultimately for the manager to take and, if necessary, to justify at a tribunal. Medical evidence will be sought and has to be carefully considered but dismissal remains an employer's decision, not a medical decision.

Normally, absences through sickness have to be frequent or prolonged in order for dismissal on the grounds of such absence to be judged fair, although absence which seriously interferes with the running of a business may be judged fair even if it is neither frequent nor prolonged. In all cases the employee must be consulted and effectively warned before being dismissed.

In the leading case of *Egg Stores* v. *Leibovici* (1977) the EAT set out nine questions that have to be asked to determine the potential fairness of dismissing someone after long-term sickness:

(a) how long has the employment lasted; (b) how long had it been expected the employment would continue; (c) what is the nature of the job; (d) what was the nature, effect and length of the illness; (e) what is the need of the employer for the work to be done, and to engage a replacement to do it; (f) if the employer takes no action, will he incur obligations in respect of redundancy payments or compensation for unfair dismissal; (g) are wages continuing to be paid; (h) why has the employer dismissed (or failed to do so); and (i) in all the circumstances, could a reasonable employer have been expected to wait any longer?

A different situation is where an employee is frequently absent for short spells. Here too it is potentially reasonable to dismiss, but only after proper consideration of the illnesses and after warning the employee of the consequences if their attendance record does not improve. Each case has to be decided on its own merits. Medical evidence must be sought and a judgement reached about how likely it is that high levels of absence will continue in the future. The fact that an employee is wholly fit at the time of his or her dismissal does not mean that it is necessarily unfair. What matters is the overall attendance record and its impact on the organisation.

In another leading case, that of *International Sports Ltd* v. *Thomson* (1980), the employer dismissed an employee who had been frequently absent with a series of minor ailments ranging from althrugia of one knee, anxiety and nerves to bronchitis, cystitis, dizzy spells, dyspepsia and flatulence. All of these were covered by medical notes. (While pondering the medical note for flatulence, you will be interested to know that althrugia is water on the knee.) The employer issued a series of warnings and the company dismissed the employee after consulting its medical adviser, who saw no reason to examine the employee as the illnesses had no connecting medical theme and were not chronic. The Employment Appeals Tribunal held that this dismissal was fair because proper warning had been given and because the attendance record was deemed so poor as not to be acceptable to a reasonable employer. This position was confirmed by the Court of Appeal in *Wilson* v. *The Post Office* (2000) where it was held to be quite acceptable, in principle, for an employer to dismiss someone simply because of a poor absence record.

The law on ill-health dismissals was affected in important ways by the passing of the Disability Discrimination Act 1995. In Chapter 23 we look at this important piece of legislation in detail. Here it is simply necessary to state that dismissing someone who is disabled according to the definition given in the Act, without first considering whether adjustments to working practices or the working environment would allow them to continue working, is unlawful. Reasonable adjustments might well include tolerance of a relatively high level of absence, especially where the employer is large enough to be able to cope perfectly well in the circumstances. Employers are well advised to pay particular attention to disability discrimination issues when dismissing people on the grounds of ill health because the level of compensation that can be awarded by tribunals in such cases is considerably higher than it is for unfair dismissal.

WINDOW ON PRACTICE

In 1998 Mr Kirker, a man with a visual impairment, was selected for redundancy by managers at British Sugar PLC. The selection criteria included assessments of competence and potential, on both of which measures he scored poorly because of his disability. He took his case to an employment tribunal and won. It was ruled that in dismissing him, the employer had unlawfully discriminated on grounds of disability. Had it not been for the visual impairment, he would have been retained.

There are no limits on the amount of compensation that can be awarded in disability discrimination cases, so the tribunal can make an award based on their estimate of the true level of financial loss suffered by the individual concerned. In Mr Kirker's case the figure was £103,146. British Sugar subsequently lost their appeal to the Employment Appeal Tribunal.

Source: *British Sugar* v. *Kirker* [1998] IRLR 624.

Misconduct

The law expects employers to make a distinction between two classes of misconduct when dismissing employees or considering doing so.

1 Gross misconduct. This occurs when an employee commits an offence which is sufficiently serious to justify summary dismissal. To qualify, the employee must have acted in such a way as to have breached either an express term of their contract or one of the common law duties owed by an employee to an employer (see Chapter 6). In practice this means that their actions must be 'intolerable' for any reasonable employer.

2 Ordinary misconduct. This involves lesser transgressions, such as minor breaches of rules and relatively insignificant acts of disobedience, insubordination, lateness, forgetfulness or rudeness. In such cases the employer is deemed by the courts to be acting unreasonably if it dismisses as a result of a first offence. The dismissal would only be fair if, having been formally warned at least once, the employee failed to improve his/her conduct.

Employers have a wide degree of discretion when it comes to deciding what exactly does and does not constitute gross misconduct, and this will vary from workplace to workplace. For example, a distinction can be made between uttering an obscene swear word in front of colleagues (ordinary misconduct) and swearing obscenely to a customer (gross misconduct). While much depends on the circumstances, the tribunals also look carefully at an employer's established policies on matters of conduct:

> Where the disciplinary rules spell out clearly the type of conduct that will warrant dismissal then a dismissal for this reason may be fair. Conversely, if the rules are silent or ambiguous as to whether particular conduct warrants dismissal, a dismissal for a first offence may be unfair. It is important, therefore, for employers to set out in writing what standards of conduct they expect, to make clear what will be regarded as 'sackable misconduct', and to ensure that everyone is aware of these rules. (Duggan 1999, p. 178)

The second key principle in misconduct cases concerns procedure. Whether the individual is dismissed summarily for gross misconduct or after a number of warnings for ordinary misconduct, the tribunals look to see if a reasonable procedure has been used. This basic requirement is unaffected by the Dispute Resolution Regulations (2004) which clearly state that employers are required to adhere to basic procedures. However, these regulations do permit employers to dispense with the need for a disciplinary hearing in 'extreme' cases of gross misconduct. We look in more detail at disciplinary procedures in Chapter 25. Here it is necessary to note the main questions that an employment tribunal asks when faced with such cases:

1 Was the accusation thoroughly, promptly and properly investigated by managers before the decision was made to dismiss or issue a formal warning?

2 Was a formal hearing held at which the accused employee was given the opportunity to state their case and challenge evidence brought forward by managers?

3 Was the employee concerned permitted to be represented at the hearing by a colleague or trade union representative?

4 Was the employee treated consistently when compared with other employees who had committed similar acts of misconduct in the past?

Only if the answers to all these questions is 'yes' will a tribunal find a dismissal fair. They do not, however, expect employers to adhere to very high standards of evidence gathering such as those employed by the police in criminal investigations. Here, as throughout employment law, the requirement is for the employer to act reasonably in all the circumstances, conforming to the principles of natural justice and doing what it thought to be right at the time, given the available facts.

Conversely, if an employee is found guilty by court proceedings, this does not automatically justify fair dismissal; it must still be procedurally fair and reasonable. A theft committed off duty and away from the workforce is not necessarily grounds for dismissal; it all depends on the nature of the work carried out by the employee concerned. For example, it might well be reasonable to dismiss members of staff with responsibility for cash if they commit an offence of dishonesty while off duty.

On the other hand, evidence that would not be sufficient to bring a prosecution may be sufficient to sustain a fair dismissal. Clocking-in offences will normally merit dismissal. Convictions for other offences like drug handling or indecency will only justify dismissal if the nature of the offence will have some bearing on the work done by the employee. For someone like an instructor of apprentices it might justify summary dismissal, but in other types of employment it would be unfair, just as it would be unfair to dismiss an employee for a driving offence when there was no need for driving in the course of normal duties and there were other means of transport for getting to work.

WINDOW ON PRACTICE

In the past few years employment tribunals have had to come to grips with a new type of dismissal case, situations in which people are dismissed for downloading and storing pornographic images from the Internet. Tribunals have had to consider whether or not such actions constitute gross misconduct (leading to summary dismissal without notice), or whether they should be considered as ordinary misconduct, in which case summary dismissal for a first offence would be regarded as being unfair.

Cases have been decided in different ways depending on the clarity of established rules and procedural matters. In *Parr* v. *Derwentside District Council* (1998), Mr Parr was summarily dismissed having been caught by his employers accessing pornography from his computer while at work. He claimed that he had visited the site concerned by accident, had got himself stuck in it and had subsequently 'revisited it only because he was disturbed by the prospect that entry could easily be made by children'. His claim for unfair dismissal failed because the employers had used a fair procedure and because they were able to show that Mr Parr had broken established codes of conduct.

$\rightarrow$

By contrast, in *Dunn* v. *IBM UK Ltd* (1998), a summary dismissal occurring in similar circumstances was found to fall outside the 'band of reasonable responses'. In this case the employers were found not to have investigated the matter properly and not to have convened a fair disciplinary hearing, the whole matter having been handled far too hastily. Moreover, there was no company policy on Internet usage for Mr Dunn to have broken and he was unaware that he had done anything that would be construed as gross misconduct. He won his case, but had his compensation reduced by 50 per cent on the grounds that he was partly responsible for his own dismissal.

In a third case, *Humphries* v. *VH Barnett & Co* (1998), a tribunal stated that in normal circumstances the act of accessing pornography from the Internet while at work should not be construed as gross misconduct unless such a policy was made clear to employees and established as a workplace rule. However, in this case, the tribunal decided that the pictures downloaded were so obscene that Mr Humphries could be legitimately treated as having committed an act of gross misconduct.

Source: IDS (1999), 'Downloading pornography', *IDS Brief 637*, May.

Redundancy

Dismissal for redundancy is protected by compensation for unfair redundancy, compensation for genuine redundancy and the right to consultation before the redundancy takes place:

An employee who is dismissed shall be taken to be dismissed by reason of redundancy if the dismissal is attributable wholly or mainly to:

(a) the fact that his employer has ceased, or intends to cease, to carry on the business for the purposes of which the employee was employed by him, or has ceased, or intends to cease, to carry on that business in the place where the employee was so employed,

or

(b) the fact that the requirements of that business for employees to carry out work of a particular kind, or for employees to carry out work of a particular kind in the place where he was so employed, have ceased or are expected to cease or diminish.

Source: Employment Rights Act 1996, s. 139(1).

Apart from certain specialised groups of employees, anyone who has been continuously employed for two years or more is guaranteed a compensation payment from an employer, if dismissed for redundancy. The compensation is assessed on a sliding scale relating to length of service, age and rate of pay per week. If the employer wishes to escape the obligation to compensate, then it is necessary to show that the reason for dismissal was something other than redundancy. The inclusion of age in the criteria for calculating redundancy payments remained, despite the introduction of age discrimination law in 2006.

Although the legal rights relating to redundancy have not altered for 35 years, there have been persistent problems of interpretation, different courts reaching different decisions when faced with similar sets of circumstances (*see* IRS 2000b). In 1999 the House of Lords provided some long-needed clarification of key issues in the cases of *Murray et al.* v. *Foyle Meats Ltd*, where it was decided that tribunals should look at the actual facts of someone's working situation rather than at their written contractual terms when deciding whether or not their jobs were redundant. In so doing it confirmed that the practice of 'bumping', where the employer dismisses a person whose job is remaining to retain the services of another employee whose job is disappearing, is acceptable under the statutory definition. The questions laid out by the Employment Appeals Tribunal (EAT) in *Safeway* v. *Burrell* (1997) are thus now confirmed as those that tribunals should ask when considering these cases:

1 Has the employee been dismissed?

2 Has there been an actual or prospective cessation or diminution in the requirements for employees to carry out work of a particular kind?

3 Is the dismissal wholly or mainly attributable to the state of affairs?

The employer has to consult with the individual employee before dismissal takes place, but there is also a separate legal obligation to consult with recognised trade unions or some other body of employee representatives where no union is recognised. If 20 or more employees are to be made redundant, then the employer must give written notice of intention to any recognised unions concerned and the Department for Business, Enterprise and Regulatory Reform (DBERR) at least 30 days before the first dismissal. If it is proposed to make more than 100 employees redundant within a three-month period, then 90 days' advance notice must be given. Having done this, the employer has a legal duty to consult on the redundancies. There is no obligation to negotiate with employees, merely to explain, listen to comments and reply with reasons. Employees also have the right to reasonable time off with pay during their redundancy notice so that they can seek other work.

One of the most difficult aspects of redundancy for the employer is the selection of who should go. The traditional approach provides that people should leave on a last-in-first-out basis, or LIFO, as this provides a rough-and-ready justice with which it is difficult to argue. In recent years, however, an increasing number of employers are using a mix of other criteria, including skill, competence and attendance record. A third approach involves drawing up a new post-redundancy organisation structure and inviting everyone to apply for the jobs that will remain. All three approaches are widely used and have been considered acceptable as far as the law is concerned provided they are carried out objectively and consistently. However, some commentators question whether or not LIFO is compatible with age discrimination law on the grounds that it inevitably involves favouring older employees over younger colleagues and is not always objectively justifiable.

Increasingly, employers are trying to avoid enforced redundancy by a range of strategies, such as not replacing people who leave, early retirement and voluntary redundancy. They also increasingly seek to make the management of redundancy more palatable by appointing redundancy counselling or outplacement services. Sometimes this is administered by the HR department, but many organisations use external services. Contrary to some popular perception there is no legal requirement to offer such services or to ask for volunteers before carrying through a programme of compulsory redundancies.

Some other substantial reason

As the law of unfair dismissal has evolved since 1971 the most controversial area has been the category of potentially fair dismissals known as 'some other substantial reason'. Many commentators see this as a catch-all or dustbin category which enables employers to dismiss virtually anyone provided a satisfactory business case can be made. All manner of cases have been successfully defended under this heading including the following: dismissals resulting from personality clashes, pressure to dismiss from subordinates or customers, disclosure of damaging information, the dismissal of a man whose wife worked for a rival firm, and the dismissal of a landlord's wife following her husband's dismissal on grounds of capability.

The majority of cases brought under this heading, however, result from business reorganisations where there is no redundancy. These often occur when the employer seeks to alter terms and conditions of employment and cannot secure the employee's agreement. Such circumstances can result in the dismissal of the employee together with an offer of re-employment on new contractual terms. Such dismissals are judged fair provided a sound business reason exists to justify the changes envisaged. It will usually be necessary to consult prior to the reorganisation but the tribunal will not base its judgment on whether the employee acted reasonably in refusing new terms and conditions. The test laid down in *Hollister* v. *The National Farmers' Union* (1979) by the Court of Appeal merely requires the employer to demonstrate that the change would bring clear organisational advantage.

Written statement of reasons

The Employment Rights Act 1996 (s. 92) gives employees the right to obtain from their employer a written statement of the reasons for their dismissal if they are dismissed after completing a year's continuous service. If asked, the employer must provide the statement within 14 days. If it is not provided, the employee can complain to an employment tribunal that the statement has been refused and the tribunal will award the employee two weeks' pay if they find the complaint justified. The same right applies where a fixed-term contract is not renewed after having expired. The employee can also complain, and receive the same award, if the employer's reasons are untrue or inadequate, provided that the tribunal agrees.

Such an award is in addition to anything the tribunal may decide about the unfairness of the dismissal, if the employee complains about that. The main purpose of this provision is to enable the employee to test whether there is a reasonable case for an unfair dismissal complaint or not. Although the statement is admissible as evidence in tribunal proceedings, the tribunal will not necessarily be bound by what the statement contains. If the tribunal members were to decide that the reasons for dismissal were other than stated, then the management case would be jeopardised.

CONSTRUCTIVE DISMISSAL

When the conduct of the employer causes an employee to resign, the ex-employee may still be able to claim dismissal on the grounds that the behaviour of the employer constituted a repudiation of the contract, leaving the employee with no alternative but to resign. The employee may then be able to claim that the dismissal was unfair. It is not sufficient for the employer simply to be awkward or whimsical; the employer's conduct must amount to a significant breach, going to the root of the contract, such as physical assault, demotion, reduction in pay, change in location of work or significant change in duties. The breach must, however, be significant, so that a slight lateness in paying wages would not involve a breach, neither would a temporary change in place of work.

Some of the more interesting constructive dismissal cases concern claims that implied terms of contract have been breached, such as the employer's duty to maintain safe systems of working or mutual trust and confidence.

WINDOW ON PRACTICE

In 1994 a former manager of an off-licence called Mrs Gullyes won a case of constructive dismissal. She argued successfully that her employer had breached an implied term of her contract and that this had led directly to her resignation.

At the time of her resignation, Mrs Gullyes had been employed as a branch manager for four years – a job she carried out with conspicuous success. As a result she had been promoted into a manager's role in a larger branch with severe staffing problems. She accepted the new post with some reluctance after agreeing with the company that she could transfer again if things did not work out.

She found the new job hard from the start, finding herself working 76 hours a week and gaining insufficient help from other members of staff. After a few months she went away on holiday, returning to find that two of her staff had been transferred to other branches in her absence. At this point she requested a transfer herself and was refused. She resigned and brought a claim of constructive dismissal.

Mrs Gullyes won her case by arguing that the company had breached its common law duty to provide adequate support to her in the new job. The case was appealed to the EAT, where she won again.

Sources: L. Macdonald (1998) 'Termination of Employment: Breach of contract, constructive dismissal and wrongful dismissal', *Personnel Manager's Fact Finder*. London: Gee Publishing and *Whitbread PLC/Thresher* v. *Gullyes* (1994).

Constructive dismissal, like unfair dismissal, dates from 1971. It too only applies to employees who have completed a year's continuous service. The cases are harder for employees to win and easier for employers to defend because of the need to establish that a dismissal has taken place, before issues of reasonableness in the circumstances are addressed. The burden of proof is on the employee to show that they were forced into resigning as a result of a repudiatory breach on the part of the employer.

COMPENSATION FOR DISMISSAL

Having found in favour of the applicant in cases of unfair or constructive dismissal, the tribunal can make two types of decision: either they can order that the ex-employee be re-employed or they can award some financial compensation from the ex-employer for the loss that the employee has suffered. Originally it was intended that re-employment should be the main remedy, although this was not previously available under earlier legislation. In practice, however, the vast majority of ex-employees (over 98 per cent) want compensation.

Tribunals will not order re-employment unless the dismissed employee wants it, and tribunals can choose between reinstatement or re-engagement. In reinstatement the old job is given back to the employee under the same terms and conditions, plus any increments, etc., to which the individual would have become entitled had the dismissal not occurred, plus any arrears of payment that would have been received. The situation is just as it would have been, including all rights deriving from length of service, if the dismissal had not taken place. The alternative of re-engagement will be that the employee is employed afresh in a job comparable to the last one (usually in a different department), but without continuity of employment. The decision as to which of the two to order will depend on assessment of the practicability of the alternatives, the wishes of the unfairly dismissed employee and the natural justice of the award taking account of the ex-employee's behaviour.

Tribunals currently calculate the level of compensation under a series of headings. First is the basic award which is based on the employee's age and length of service. It is calculated in the same way as statutory redundancy payments, and like them has not been changed following the introduction of age discrimination law:

- half a week's pay for every year of service below the age of 22;
- one week's pay for every year of service between the ages of 22 and 41;
- one and a half weeks' pay for every year of service over the age of 41.

The basic award is limited, however, because tribunals can only take into account a maximum of 20 years' service when calculating the figure to be awarded. A maximum weekly salary figure is also imposed by the Treasury. This was £310 in 2007. The maximum basic award that can be ordered is therefore £9,300. In many cases, of course, where the employee has only a few years' service the figure will be far lower. In addition a tribunal can also order compensation under the following headings:

- Compensatory awards take account of loss of earnings, pension rights, future earnings loss, etc. The maximum level in 2007 was £60,600.
- Additional awards are used in cases of sex and race discrimination and also when an employer fails to comply with an order of reinstatement or re-engagement. In the former case the maximum award is 52 weeks' pay, in the latter 26 weeks' pay.
- Special awards are made when unfair dismissal relates to trade union activity or membership. They can also be used when the dismissal was for health and safety reasons.

A tribunal can reduce the total level of compensation if it judges the individual concerned to have contributed to his or her own dismissal. For example, a dismissal on grounds of poor work performance may be found unfair because no procedure was followed and consequently no warnings given. This does not automatically entitle the ex-employee concerned to compensation based on the above formulae. If the tribunal judges the ex-employee to have been 60 per cent responsible for his or her own dismissal the compensation will be reduced by 60 per cent. Reductions are also made if an ex-employee is judged not to have taken reasonable steps to mitigate his or her loss.

ACTIVITY 10.2

In what circumstances do you think a dismissed employee might welcome reinstatement or re-engagement, and in what circumstances might the employer welcome it?

WRONGFUL DISMISSAL

In addition to the body of legislation defining unfair and constructive dismissal there is a long-standing common law right to damages for an employee who has been dismissed wrongfully.

Cases of wrongful dismissal are taken to employment tribunals where the claim is for less than £25,000; otherwise they are taken to the county court. These cases are concerned solely with alleged breaches of contract. Employees can thus only bring cases of wrongful dismissal against their employers when they believe their dismissal to have been unlawful according to the terms of their contract of employment. Wrongful dismissal can, therefore, be used when the employer has not given proper notice or if the dismissal is in breach of any clause or agreement incorporated into the contract. This remains a form of remedy that very few people use, but it could be useful to employees who do not have sufficient length of service to claim unfair dismissal and whose contracts include the right to a full disciplinary procedure. There may also be cases where a very highly paid employee might get higher damages in an ordinary court than the maximum that the tribunal can award.

WINDOW ON PRACTICE

In order to bring a claim of unfair dismissal ex-employees must have been employed continuously for at least 12 months by the organisation concerned when they are dismissed. As a result it is common for employers to dismiss people after 11 months' service in the belief that they will never have to justify their actions in court. However, such approaches can backfire, as was shown in the case of *Raspin* v. *United News* (1999). Here the applicant brought a case of wrongful dismissal, basing the claim on the presence in the contract of employment of a disciplinary procedure. The Employment Appeals Tribunal decided that had the employer fulfilled its contractual duties and dismissed the employee using the procedure, the date of the dismissal would have occurred after 12 months' service had been completed. In assessing compensation the matter was thus treated as if it was an unfair dismissal claim.

NOTICE

An employee qualifies for notice of dismissal on completion of four weeks of employment with an employer. At that time the employee is entitled to receive one week's notice. This remains constant until the employee has completed two years' service, after which it increases to two weeks' notice, thereafter increasing on the basis of one week's notice per additional year of service up to a maximum of 12 weeks for 12 years' unbroken service with that employer. These are minimum statutory periods. If the employer includes longer periods of notice in the contract, which is quite common with senior employees, then they are bound by the longer period.

The employee is required to give one week's notice after completing four weeks' service and this period does not increase as a statutory obligation. If an employee accepts a contract in which the period of notice to be given is longer, then that is binding, but the employer may have problems of enforcement if an employee is not willing to continue in employment for the longer period.

Neither party can withdraw notice unilaterally. The withdrawal will be effective only if the other party agrees. Therefore, if an employer gives notice to an employee and wishes later to withdraw it, this can be done only if the employee agrees to the contract of employment remaining in existence. Equally, employees cannot change their minds about resigning unless the employer agrees.

Notice exists when a date has been specified. The statement 'We're going to wind up the business, so you will have to find another job' is not notice: it is a warning of intention.

SUMMARY PROPOSITIONS

10.1 Of the many dismissals that take place in a year, a minority are reported to tribunals and a small minority are found in favour of the ex-employee.

10.2 The main grounds on which an employee can be dismissed without the likelihood of an unfair dismissal claim are lack of capability, misconduct, redundancy, statutory bar, some other substantial reason and fair mandatory retirement.

10.3 If an employee is dismissed on one of the above grounds, the dismissal must still be procedurally acceptable and fair in the circumstances.

10.4 An employee who resigns as a result of unreasonable behaviour by the employer can claim constructive dismissal and, if successful, have their case treated as if they had in fact been dismissed.

10.5 Minimum notice periods, in most cases amounting to a week for every year of service, must be given when terminating employees' contracts.

GENERAL DISCUSSION TOPICS

1 If you were dismissed in circumstances that you regarded as legally unfair, would you prefer to seek satisfaction through ACAS conciliation or through a tribunal hearing? Why?

2 In some countries a dismissal cannot be made until *after* a tribunal hearing, so that its 'fairness' is decided before it takes effect. What do you see as the benefits and drawbacks of that system?

3 What changes would you make in the criteria for dismissal on the grounds of misconduct?

FURTHER READING

Collins, H. (1992) *Justice in Dismissal: The Law of Termination of Employment*. Oxford: Oxford University Press.

Dickens, L., Jones, M., Weekes, B. and Hant, M. (1985) *Dismissed: A Study of Unfair Dismissal and the Industrial Tribunal System*. Oxford: Blackwell.

Many of the best scholarly critiques of unfair dismissal law were published some years ago, but they remain the best source of arguments about how the law might be reformed. These two works make major contributions to the literature.

Rojot, J. (2001) 'Security of employment and employability', in R. Blanpain and C. Engels (eds) *Comparative Labour Law and Industrial Relations in Industrialized Market Economies*. The Hague: Kluwer.

There is a huge variety of different laws regulating dismissal in different countries. In the USA most states retain the doctrine of 'employment at will', placing no general statutory restrictions on the right of an employer to dismiss. In the Netherlands, by contrast, employers cannot generally dismiss without first getting the approval of a government officer. This book provides a good account of the various systems in use around the globe.

IDS (2005) *Unfair Dismissal*. London: Incomes Data Services.

Yew, J. (2005) *Dismissals, Law and Practice*. London: The Law Society.

These are the two most comprehensive and current guides to the law of unfair dismissal. Both review the leading cases and deal with all the practical aspects of dismissing people lawfully.

REFERENCES

DTI (1999) *The Unfair Dismissal and Statement of Reasons for Dismissal (variation of qualifying period) Order 1999 – regulatory impact assessment*. London: Department of Trade and Industry.

DTI (2003) *Statutory Dispute Resolution Procedures*. London: Department of Trade and Industry.

Duggan, M. (1999) *Unfair Dismissal: Law, practice & guidance*. Welwyn Garden City: CLT Professional Publishing.

Employment Tribunal Service (2006) *Annual Report*. London: HMSO.

IDS (1999) 'Downloading pornography', *IDS Brief*, No. 637, May.

IRS (2000a) 'Range of reasonable responses test is not wrong', *Industrial Relations Law Bulletin*, No. 638, April.

IRS (2000b) 'The (re)definition of redundancy', *Industrial Relations Law Bulletin*, No. 633, January.

Knight, K.G. and Latreille, P.L. (2000) 'Discipline, dismissals and complaints to employment tribunals', *British Journal of Industrial Relations*, Vol. 38, No. 4, p. 533.

Macdonald, L. (1998) 'Termination of Employment: Breach of contract, constructive dismissal and wrongful dismissal', *Personnel Manager's Fact Finder*. London: Gee Publishing.

LEGAL CASES

Al-Tikriti v. *South Western RHA* (1986).

British Sugar v. *Kirker* [1998] IRLR 624.

Dunn v. *IBM UK Ltd* (1998) IDS Brief 637, May 1999.

Egg Stores v. *Leibovici* [1977] ICR 260.

Haddon v. *Van den Bergh Foods* [1999] IRLR 672, EAT.

Hollister v. *The National Farmers' Union* [1979] ICR 542.

Humphries v. *VH Barnett & Co* (1998) IDS Brief 637, May 1999.

International Sports Ltd v. *Thomson* [1980] IRLR 340.

Midland Bank v. *Madden* [2000] IRLR 288.

Murray et al. v. *Foyle Meats Ltd* [1999] IRLR 562.

Parr v. *Derwentside District Council* (1998) IDS Brief 637, May 1999.

Polkey v. *AE Dayton Services* [1987] ICR 142.

Raspin v. *United News* [1999] IRLR 9.

Safeway v. *Burrell* [1997] IRLR 200.

Whitbread PLC/Thresher v. *Gullyes* [1994] EAT 478/92.

Wilson v. *The Post Office* [2000] IRLR 834.

An extensive range of additional materials, including multiple choice
questions, answers to questions and links to useful websites can be
found on the Human Resource Management Companion Website at
www.pearsoned.co.uk/torrington.

INTERACTIVE SKILL 2: SELECTION INTERVIEWING

Central to all resourcing is the selection interview, which is also one of the most familiar and forbidding encounters of working life. Most people have had at least one experience of being interviewed as a preliminary to employment and few people enjoy it. HR specialists have a critical role in selection interviewing, carrying out many of the interviews and encouraging good interviewing practice in others by example, support and training.

In this Focus on skills our objectives are to:

1 Review the varieties of selection interview and its purpose

2 Explain interview strategy and consider the number of interviews and interviewers

3 Explain interview structure and the five key aspects of method

Varieties of selection interview

There are various practices in selection interviewing. At one extreme we read of men seeking work in the docks of Victorian London and generally being treated as if they were in a cattle market. They had to queue up in a series of gangways, similar to those used today to corral cattle at market, and had to vie with each other for the attention of the foreman hiring labourers for the day. Some of the older men apparently used to dye their hair in a pathetic attempt to appear younger and fitter than they really were and thereby catch the foreman's eye. At the opposite extreme we hear of people being telephoned by complete strangers and being offered handsome contracts to work in Hollywood studios.

There is a range of employee participation in the employment process which correlates with the type of work. There are working situations where the amount of discussion between the parties is limited to perfunctory exchanges about trade union membership, hours of work and rates of pay: labourers on building sites and extras on film sets being two examples. As interviews move up the organisational hierarchy there is growing equilibrium, with the interviewer becoming more courteous and responsive to questions from the applicant, who will probably be described as a 'candidate' or someone who 'might be interested in the position'. For the most senior positions it is less likely that people will be invited to respond to vacancies advertised in the press, although equality legislation is leading to more senior positions being openly advertised. It is more likely that individuals will be approached, either directly or through consultants, and there will be an elaborate ritual in which each party tries to persuade the other to declare an interest first.

Another indication of the variety of employment practice is in the titles used. The humblest of applicants seek 'jobs' or 'vacancies', while the more ambitious are looking for 'places', 'posts', 'positions', 'openings' or 'opportunities'. The really high-flyers seem to need somewhere to sit down, as they are offered 'seats on the board', 'professorial chairs' or 'places on the front bench'.

The purpose of the selection interview

The interview is a controlled conversation with a purpose. There are more exchanges in a shorter period related to a specific purpose than in an ordinary conversation. In the selection interview the purposes are:

- to collect information in order to predict how well the applicants would perform in the job for which they have applied, by measuring them against predetermined criteria;

- to provide candidates with full details of the job and organisation to facilitate their decision making;

- to conduct the interview in such a way that candidates feel that they have been given a fair hearing.

The selection interview has been extensively criticised as being unreliable, invalid and subjective, but this criticism is about the decisions made and ignores the importance of the interview as a **ritual** in the employment process. Recent comprehensive analysis of selection interview effectiveness, however, concludes that their validity is now much greater than previously believed (McDaniel *et al*. 1994 and Judge 2000), provided that the interview is structured.

Handling this most crucial of encounters is a key skill for personnel and other managers as the interview has a number of important advantages which cannot be provided by any other means. It cannot be bettered as a means of exchanging information and meeting the human and ritual aspects of the employment process.

Exchanging information

The interview is a flexible and speedy means of exchanging information, over a broad range of topics. The employer has the opportunity to sell the company and explain job details in depth. Applicants have the chance to ask questions about the job and the company in order to collect the information they need for their own selection decision. The interview is also the logical culmination of the employment process, as information from a variety of sources, such as application forms, tests and references, can be discussed together.

Human and ritual aspects

In an interview some assessment can be made of matters that cannot be approached in any other way, such as the potential compatibility of two people who will have to work together. Both parties need to meet before the contract begins, to 'tune in' to each other and begin the process of induction. The interview is valuable in that way to both potential employee and potential employer. It gives interviewees the feeling that they matter, as another person is devoting time to them and they are not being considered by a computer. Also, giving applicants a chance to ask questions underlines their decision-making role, making them feel less helpless in the hands of the all-powerful interviewer. Selection interviewing has important ritual elements, as the applicant is seeking either to enter, or to rise within, a social system. This requires the display of deferential behaviours:

> upward mobility involves the presentation of proper performances and . . . efforts to move upward . . . are expressed in terms of sacrifices made for the maintenance of front. (Goffman 1974, p. 45)

At the same time those who are already inside and above display their superiority and security, even unconsciously, in contrast with the behaviour of someone so obviously anxious to share the same privileged position. Reason tells us that this is inappropriate at the beginning of the twenty-first century as the books are full of advice to interviewers not to brandish their social superiority, but to put applicants at their ease and to reduce the status differentials. This, however, still acknowledges their superiority as they are the ones who take the initiative; applicants are not expected to help the interviewer relax and feel less apprehensive. Also the reality of the situation is usually that of applicant anxious to get in and selector choosing among several. Status differentials cannot simply be set aside. The selection interview is at least partly an initiation rite, not as elaborate as entry to commissioned rank in the armed forces, nor as whimsical as finding one's way into the Brownie ring, but still a process of going through hoops and being found worthy in a process where other people make all the rules.

233

ACTIVITY 2.1

For a selection interview in which you recently participated, either as selector or as applicant, consider the following:

1 What were the ritual features?

2 Were any useful ritual features missing?

3 Could ritual have been, in any way, *helpfully* reduced?

No matter what other means of making employment decisions there may be, the interview is crucial, and when worries are expressed about its reliability, this is not a reason for doing away with it: it is a reason for conducting it properly.

Interview strategy

The approach to selection interviewing varies considerably from the amiable chat in a bar to the highly organised, multi-person panel.

Frank and friendly strategy

By far the most common is the approach which has been described as frank and friendly. Here the interviewer is concerned to establish and maintain rapport. This is done in the belief that if interviewees do not feel threatened, and are relaxed, they will be more forthcoming in the information that they offer. It is straightforward for both interviewer and interviewee and has the potential advantage that the interviewees will leave with a favourable impression of the business.

Problem-solving strategy

A variation of the frank and friendly strategy is the problem-solving approach. It is the method of presenting the candidate with a hypothetical problem and evaluating the answer.

These are sometimes called situational interviews. The questions asked are derived from the job description and candidates are required to imagine themselves as the job holder and describe what they would do in a variety of hypothetical situations. This method is most applicable to testing elementary knowledge, such as the colour coding of wires in electric cables or maximum dosages of specified drugs. It is less effective to test understanding and ability.

There is no guarantee that the candidate would actually behave in the way suggested. The quick thinker will score at the expense of those who can take action more effectively than they can answer riddles. A useful analysis and commentary on situational interviews is in Latham *et al.* (1980).

Biographical strategy

Similar to the problem-solving strategy is the biographical method. The focus is on the candidate's past behaviour and performance, which is a more reliable way of predicting future performance than asking interviewees what they would do in a certain situation. Candidates are requested to describe the background to a situation and explain what they did and why; what their options were; how they decided what to do; and the anticipated and real results of their action. The success of this method depends on in-depth job analysis, and preferably competency analysis, in order to frame the best questions. Bearing in mind the importance of structure in selection interviewing, the biographical approach is an excellent method.

Stress strategy

In the stress approach the interviewer becomes aggressive, disparages the candidates, puts them on the defensive or disconcerts them by strange behaviour. The advantage of the method is that it may demonstrate a necessary strength or a disqualifying weakness that would not be apparent through other methods. The disadvantages are that evaluating the behaviour under stress is problematic, and those who are not selected will think badly of the employer. The likely value of stress interviewing is so limited that it is hardly worth mentioning, except that it has spurious appeal to many managers, who are attracted by the idea of injecting at least some stress into the interview 'to see what they are made of', or 'to put them on their mettle'. Most candidates feel that the procedures are stressful enough, without adding to them.

Number of interviews and interviewers

There are two broad traditions governing the number of interviewers. One says that effective, frank discussion can only take place on a one-to-one basis, so candidates meet one interviewer, or several interviewers, one at a time. The other tradition is that fair play must be demonstrated and nepotism prevented so the interview must be carried out, and the decision made, by a panel of interviewers. Within this dichotomy there are various options.

The individual interview

The individual interview gives the greatest chance of establishing rapport, developing mutual trust and is the most efficient deployment of time in the face-to-face encounter, as each participant has to compete with only one other speaker. It is usually also the most satisfactory method for the candidate, who has to tune in to only one other person instead of needing constantly to adjust to different interviewers. The candidate can more readily ask questions, as it is difficult to ask a panel of six people to explain the workings of the pension scheme, and it is the least formal type of interview. The disadvantages lie in the reliance the organisation places on the judgement of one of its representatives, although this can be mitigated by a series of individual interviews, and the ritual element is largely missing. Candidates may not feel they have been 'done' properly. A sole interview with the line manager is very popular in the selection of blue-collar staff, being used in a third of all interviews. It is less popular for white-collar and management staff.

Sequential interviews

Sequential interviews are a series of individual interviews. The series most often consists of just two interviews for blue- and white-collar staff, but more than two for managerial staff. The most frequent combination is an interview with the line manager and one with a representative of the HR department. For managerial posts this will be extended

235

to interviews with other departmental managers, top managers and significant prospective colleagues. Sequential interviews can give the employer a broader picture of the candidate and they also allow the applicant to have contact with a greater number of potential colleagues. However, for the advantages of sequential interviews to be realised there is a need for effective organisation and for all interviews to be held on the same day. It is important that all interviewers meet beforehand to agree on the requirements of the post and to decide how each will contribute to the overall theme. Immediately following the interviews a further meeting needs to take place so that the candidates can be jointly evaluated. One disadvantage of the method is the organisation and time that it takes from both the employer's and the candidate's point of view. It requires considerable commitment from the candidate who may have to keep repeating similar information and whose performance may deteriorate throughout the course of the interviews due to fatigue.

Panel interviews

The panel interview method has the specious appeal of sharing judgement and may appear to be a way of saving time in interviewing as all panel members are operating at once. It is also possible to legitimise a quick decision, always popular with candidates, and there can be no doubt about the ritual requirements being satisfied. Panel interviews reduce the likelihood of personal bias in interviewing, particularly in guarding against possible infringements of legal requirements.

WINDOW ON (MAL)PRACTICE

We have said above that panel interviews reduce the likelihood of personal bias. Perhaps we should have written 'reduce but do not eliminate personal bias', as indicated by the situation following a panel interview to select a senior manager for a public corporation. After the interview and after the decision had been made, the HR manager was tidying up the papers in the room and found a scrap of paper on which a member of the panel had scribbled, 'looks like a good screw'. The HR manager decided that this was not a case of a panel member relieving boredom by examining the structure of the table round which the members had been sitting.

They can also ensure the candidate is acceptable to the whole organisation, and allow the candidate to get a good feel for the business and its culture. The drawbacks lie in the tribunal nature of the panel. They are not having a conversation with the candidates; they are sitting in judgement upon them and assessing the evidence they are able to present in response to the panel's requests. There is little prospect of building rapport and developing discussion, and there is likely to be as much interplay between members of the panel as there is between the panel and the candidate.

Panel interviews tend towards over-rigidity and give ironic point to the phrase, 'it is only a formality'. They are ritualistically superb, but dubious as a useful preliminary to employment. However, the benefits of the panel interview can be increased, and the disadvantages reduced, if the interviewers are properly trained and the interview well organised, thoroughly planned and made part of a structured selection process.

ACTIVITY 2.2

In your organisation how many interviews and interviewers are used? How effective is this approach and why? In what ways could the approach be improved?

The selection interview sequence

Preparation

We assume that the preliminaries of job analysis, recruitment and shortlisting are complete and the interview is now to take place. The first step in preparation is for the interviewers to brief themselves. They will collect and study a job description or similar details of the post to be filled, a candidate specification or statement of required competencies and the application forms or curricula vitae of the candidates.

If there are several people to be interviewed the interview timetable needs greater planning than it usually receives. The time required for each interview can be determined beforehand only approximately. A rigid timetable will weigh heavily on both parties, who will feel frustrated if the interview is closed arbitrarily at a predetermined time and uncomfortable if an interview that has 'finished' is drawn out to complete its allotted timespan. However, the disadvantages of keeping people waiting are considerable and underrated.

WINDOW ON PRACTICE

Barbara Trevithick applied for a post as personnel officer at a hospital and was invited for interview at 2.00 p.m. On arrival she was ushered into a small, windowless room where four other people were waiting. At 2.20 a secretary came in and asked Mr Brown to come with her. At 3.00 Mr Jones was called for. At 3.45 the remaining three candidates went out in search of the secretary to ask what the remaining timetable for the day was to be. The secretary replied that she did not know but the panel members had just gone to the canteen for a cup of coffee. By now Barbara had figured out that her surname was the last in alphabetical order. Miss Mellhuish was called for interview at 4.10 and Miss Roberts left because her last train home to Scotland was due in 20 minutes. Barbara Trevithick went in for interview at 4.45 to find that two members of the panel 'had had to leave', so she was interviewed by the two surviving members: a personnel officer and a nursing officer. At the close of the interview she asked when the decision would be made and was told that the two interviewers would have to consult with their two absent colleagues in the morning. Three weeks later Barbara rang to ask the outcome, as she had not received a letter, to be told that Mr Brown had been appointed and 'I'm surprised they didn't tell you, as it was offered to him that afternoon, after the coffee break'.

The experience of Barbara Trevithick reflects the thinking of some selectors that candidates are supplicants waiting on interviewers' pleasure, they have no competing calls on their time and a short period of waiting demonstrates who is in charge. There are flaws in this reasoning. Most candidates will have competing calls on their time, as they will have taken time off to attend and have earmarked the anticipated interview time to fit in a busy schedule. Some may have other interviews to go to. An open-ended waiting period can be worrying, enervating and a poor preliminary to an interview. If the dentist keeps you waiting you may get distressed, but when the waiting is over you are simply a passive participant and the dentist does not have the success of the operation jeopardised. The interview candidate has, in a real sense, to perform when the period of waiting is over and the success of the interaction could well be jeopardised.

The most satisfactory timetable is the one that guarantees a break after all but the most voluble candidates. If candidates are asked to attend at hourly intervals, for example, this would be consistent with interviews lasting between 40 and 60 minutes. This would mean that each interview began at the scheduled time and that the interviewers had the opportunity to review and update their notes in the intervals. The whole plan can still go wrong if one or more candidates fail to turn up.

Reception

Candidates arrive on the premises of their prospective employer on the lookout for every scrap of evidence they can obtain about the business, what it looks like, what the people look like and what people say. A candidate is likely to meet at least one and possibly two people before meeting the interviewer. First will be the commissionaire or receptionist. There is frequently also an emissary from the HR department to shepherd them from the front door to the waiting-room. Both are valuable sources of information, and interviewers may wish to prime such people so that they can see their role in the employment process and can be cheerful, informative and helpful.

The candidate will most want to meet the interviewer, the unknown but powerful figure on whom so much depends. Interviewers easily forget that they know much more about the candidates than the candidates know about them, because the candidates have provided a personal profile in the application form.

Interviewers do not reciprocate. To bridge this gap it can be very useful for interviewers to introduce themselves to the candidate in the waiting-room, so that contact is made quickly, unexpectedly and on neutral territory. This makes the opening of the interview itself rather easier.

Candidates wait to be interviewed. Although there are snags about extended, open-ended waiting periods, some time is inevitable and necessary to enable candidates to compose themselves. It is a useful time to deal with travelling expenses and provide some relevant background reading about the employing organisation.

Setting

The appropriate setting for an interview has to be right for the ritual and right from the point of view of enabling a full and frank exchange of information. It is difficult to combine the two. Many of the interview horror stories relate to the setting in which it took place. A candidate for a post as Deputy Clerk of Works was interviewed on a stage while the panel of 17 sat in the front row of the stalls, and a candidate for a Headteacher post came in to meet the interview panel and actually moved the chair on which he was to sit. He only moved it two or three inches because the sun was in his eyes, but there was an audible frisson and sharp intake of breath from the members of the panel.

Remaining with our model of the individual interviewer, here are some simple suggestions about the setting:

- The room should be suitable for a private conversation.
- If the interview takes place across a desk, as is common, the interviewer may wish to reduce the extent to which the desk acts as a barrier, inhibiting free flow of communication.
- All visitors and telephone calls should be avoided, as they do not simply interrupt: they intrude and impede the likelihood of frankness.
- It should be clear to the candidates where they are to sit.

Interview structure

There are several important reasons why the employment interview should be structured, making use of the application or CV:

- The candidate expects the proceedings to be decided and controlled by the interviewer and will anticipate a structure within which to operate.
- It helps the interviewer to make sure that they cover all relevant areas and avoid irrelevancies.
- It looks professional.
- Structure can be used to guide the interview and ensure that it makes sense.
- It assists the interviewer in using the time available in the most effective way.
- The application form can be used as a memory aid by the interviewer when making notes directly after the interview or during it.
- It makes it easier to compare candidates.

The interview

There are several different ways to structure the interview. We recommend the form set out in Table 2.1. This divides activities and objectives into three interview stages: opening, middle and closing. While there are few, if any, alternative satisfactory ways for conducting the beginning and the end of the interview, the middle can be approached from a number of different angles, depending on the circumstances.

The interviewer needs to work systematically through the structure that has been planned but not too rigidly. Interviewers should abandon their own route whenever the candidate chooses one that seems more promising.

The opening of the interview is the time for mutual preliminary assessment and tuning in to each other. A useful feature of this phase is for the interviewer to sketch out the plan or procedure for the interview and how it fits in the total employment decision process. It is also likely that the application form will provide an easy, non-controversial topic for these opening behaviours.

One objective is for the two parties to exchange words so that they can adjust their receiving mechanism to be mutually intelligible. It also provides an opportunity for both to feel comfortable in the presence of the other. Interviewers able to achieve these two

Stage	Objectives	Activities
Opening	To put the candidate at ease, develop rapport and set the scene	Greet candidate by name Introduce yourself Explain interview purpose Outline how purpose will be achieved Obtain candidate's assent to outline
Middle	To collect and provide information	Ask questions within a structure that makes sense to the candidate, such as biographical, areas of the application form, or competencies identified for the job Listen Answer questions Summarise interview
Closing	To close the interview and confirm future action	Check candidate has no more questions Indicate what happens next and when

Table 2.1
Interview structure: a recommended pattern

objectives may then succeed in developing a relationship in which candidates trust the interviewer's ability and motives so that they will speak openly and fully. This is known as 'rapport', which was dealt with in the Part 1 Focus on skills. The interviewer's effectiveness will greatly depend on their being skilled at this process.

We are working on the assumption that candidates will behave in a reasonably genuine way, provided the interviewer can convince them that the process is fair. Some candidates do not and such people have been labelled as 'white collar psychopaths', although it has to be said that they are rare. They are very good at presenting themselves as being exactly what the interviewer is looking for. Not only are they manufacturing the truth about their experience, the trait (or psychopathic tendency) that drives them causes them to wreak havoc once they are appointed. A New York psychologist cites the example of 'Ron' who was appointed to a sales post in a pharmaceuticals company:

> Ron fiddled his sales figures, charged call girls to the company and nearly succeeded in using his charm to get his new boss fired when he was questioned about his behaviour. Psychopaths are motivated by three things: thrill-seeking, game-playing and hurting people. Once inside the organization they build networks of influence that make it very difficult to get rid of them and can help them join the management fast track. (Paul Babiak, quoted in *Financial Times*, 12 January 2004)

For the middle of the interview the biographical approach is the simplest. It works on the basis that candidates at the time of the interview are the product of everything in their lives that has gone before. To understand the candidate the interviewer must understand the past and will talk to the candidate about the episodes of his or her earlier life, education and previous employment.

The advantage of this is that the objectives are clear to both interviewer and interviewee, there is no deviousness or 'magic'. Furthermore, the development can be logical and so aid the candidate's recall of events. Candidates who reply to enquiries about their choice of A level subjects will be subconsciously triggering their recollection of contemporaneous events, such as the university course they took, which are likely to come next in the interview. The biographical approach is the simplest for the inexperienced interviewer to use as discussion can develop from the information provided by the candidate on the application form. Some version of sequential categories, such as employment, education and training, seems the most generally useful, but it will need the addition of at least two other categories: the work offered and the organisational context in which it is to be done. The middle of the interview can be structured by systematically working through items of the job description or the person specification. Increasingly, where competencies have been identified for the job, these are used as the basis of the structure.

In the preparatory stage of briefing, the interviewer will also prepare notes on two elements to incorporate in their plan: key issues and checkpoints.

Key issues will be the two or three main issues that stand out from the application form for clarification or elaboration. This might be the nature of the responsibilities carried in a particular earlier post, the content of a training course, the reaction to a period of employment in a significant industry or whatever else strikes the interviewer as being productive of useful additional evidence.

Checkpoints are matters of detail that require further information: grades in an examination, dates of an appointment, rates of pay, and so forth.

At the close of the interview the explanation of the next step needs especial attention. The result of the interview is of great importance to the candidates and they will await the outcome with anxiety. Even if they do not want the position they will probably hope to have it offered. This may strengthen their hand in dealings with another prospective employer, or with their present employer, and will certainly be a boost to their morale. The great merit of convention in the public sector is that the chosen candidate is told before the contenders disperse: the great demerit is that they are asked to say yes or no to the offer at once.

In the private sector it is unusual for an employment offer to be made at the time of the interview, so there is a delay during which the candidates will chafe. Their frustration will be greater if the delay is longer than expected and they may start to tell themselves that they are not going to receive an offer, in which case they will also start convincing themselves that they did not want the job either! It is important for the interviewer to say as precisely as possible when the offer will be made, but ensuring that the candidates hear earlier rather than later than they expect, if there is to be any deviation.

The interviewer will need to call into play certain key aspects of method.

1 Some data can be collected by simple observation of the candidate. Notes can be made about dress, appearance, voice, height and weight, if these are going to be relevant, and the interviewer can also gauge the candidate's mood and the appropriate response to it by the non-verbal cues that are provided. The study of body language has achieved great popularity in the last twenty years, largely because of its alleged potential for interpreting the thoughts and intentions of members of the opposite sex in social situations. Although the available books are designed for a popular market, they are usually sound and contain useful advice for the selection interviewer.

2 The remainder of the evidence will come from listening to what is said, so the interviewer has to be very attentive throughout; not only listening to the answers to questions, but also listening for changes in inflection and pace, nuances and overtones that

provide clues on what to pursue further. The amount of time that the two spend talking is important, as an imbalance in one direction or the other will mean that either the candidate or the interviewer is not having enough opportunity to hear information.

Being silent and deliberately leaving verbal lulls in face-to-face situations provide the opportunity for the other person to say more, perhaps more than was initially intended. Silence still has to be attentive and the longer the silence, the harder it is to be attentive.

3 In order to have something to hear, the interviewer will have to direct the candidate. This, of course, is done by questioning, encouraging and enabling the candidate to talk, so that the interviewer can learn. The art of doing this depends on the personality and style of the interviewer who will develop a personal technique through a sensitive awareness of what is taking place in the interviews.

The selection interviewer needs to distinguish between different types of question. In the Part 1 Focus on skills we explained the difference in nature and usage of various questioning methods.

4 The best place for the interviewer to make notes is on the application form or CV. In this way they can be joined to information that the candidate has already provided and the peculiar shorthand that interviewers use when making notes during interviews can be deciphered by reference to the form and the data that the note is embellishing. It also means that the review of evidence after the interview has as much information as possible available on one piece of paper. An alternative is to record notes on the interview plan where the structure is based on job description, person specification or competencies. Interviewers are strangely inhibited about note taking, feeling that it in some way impairs the smoothness of the interaction. This apprehension seems ill-founded as candidates are looking for a serious, businesslike discussion, no matter how informal, and note taking offers no barrier, provided that it is done carefully in the form of jottings during the discussion, rather than pointedly writing down particular comments by the candidate which make the interviewer seem like a police officer taking a statement.

5 Data exchange marks a change of gear in the interview. Rapport is necessarily rather rambling and aimless, but data exchange is purposeful and the interviewer needs to control both the direction and the pace of the exchanges. Candidates will be responsive throughout to the interviewer's control, and the better the rapport the more responsive they will be. Skilled interviewers close off areas of discussion and open fresh ones. They head off irrelevant reminiscences and probe where matters have been glossed over. They can never abandon control. Even when the time has come for the candidates to raise all their queries, they will do this at the behest of the interviewer and will look to him or her constantly for a renewal of the mandate to enquire by using conversational prefixes such as, 'Can I ask you another question?', 'If it's not taking up your time, perhaps I could ask . . . ?', 'I seem to be asking a lot of questions, but there was just one thing . . .'

6 Closing the interview can be as skilful as opening it. Most of the suggestions so far have been to encourage a response, but it is easy to nod and smile your way into a situation of such cosy relaxation that the respondent talks on and on . . . and on. A surprising number of interviewers have great difficulty closing. These methods can help:

- *Braking* slows the rate of talking by the candidate by working through a series of steps. You will seldom need to go beyond the first two or three, but five are described in case you have to deal with a really tough case. (a) One or two closed questions to clarify specific points may stem the tide. (b) The facial expression changes with the brow furrowed to indicate mild disagreement, lack of understanding or professional anxiety. The reassuring nods stop and the generally encouraging, supportive behaviours of reward are withdrawn. (c) Abstraction is when the eyes glaze over, showing that they belong to a person whose attention has now shifted away from the respondent and towards lunch. (d) To look at one's watch during a conversation is a very strong signal indeed, as it clearly indicates that time is running out. Other, milder ways of looking away are: looking for your glasses, looking at your notes or looking at the aircraft making a noise outside the window. A rather brutal variant is to allow your attention to be caught by something the respondent is wearing, a lapel badge, a tie, a ring or piece of jewellery, maybe. Putting on your glasses to see it more clearly is really going too far! (e) If all else fails, you simply have to interrupt.

- *Closing* requires the interview to end smoothly. Future action is either clarified or confirmed. Also, candidates take a collection of attitudes away with them, and these can be influenced by the way the interview is closed. There is a simple procedure. (a) First signal, verbal plus papers. The interviewer uses a phrase to indicate that the interview is nearing its end ('Well now, I think we have covered the ground, don't you? There isn't anything more I need to ask you. Is there anything further you want from me?'). In this way you signal the impending close at the same time as obtaining the candidate's confirmation. There is additional emphasis provided by some paper play. A small collection of notes can be gathered together and stacked neatly, or a notebook can be closed. (b) Second signal, the interviewer confirms what will happen next ('There are still one or two people to see, but we will write to you no later than the end of the week'). (c) The final signal is to stand up: the decisive act to make the close. By standing up the interviewer forces the candidate to stand as well and there remain only the odds and ends of handshakes and parting smiles.

PRACTICAL EXERCISE IN SELECTION INTERVIEWING

For this exercise you need a cooperative, interested relative, or a very close friend, who would welcome interview practice.

1 Follow the sequence suggested in Table 2.1 to give your partner practice in being interviewed for a job, and giving yourself practice in interviewing and note taking.

2 After the interview, discuss your mutual feelings about the process around questions such as:

Selector	Did you ever feel you were being misled? When? Why?
	Did you feel the interview got out of your control? When? Why?
	How could you have avoided the problem?
	How was your note taking?
	What, if anything, made you bored or cross?
	What did you find most difficult?
	How comprehensive are the data you have collected?
Candidate	Were you put at your ease?
	Were you at any time inhibited by the selector?

Did you ever mislead the selector? When? How?

Did the selector ever fail to follow up important points? When? Which?

Were you in any way disconcerted by the note taking?

Has the selector got a comprehensive set of data about you, so that you could feel any decision made about you would be soundly based?

What did you think of the interview experience?

3 Now swap roles.

SUMMARY PROPOSITIONS

2.1 Despite criticisms and shortcomings, the selection interview remains a central feature of the recruitment and selection process.

2.2 Typical interview strategies are frank and friendly, problem solving, behavioural event and stress.

2.3 Aspects of interview preparation are timetabling, reception and deciding the right setting.

2.4 Features of the interview itself are the opening for preliminary mutual assessment; data gathering, involving a logical sequence, key issues and checkpoints; and the closure, which prepares candidates for the next step in the process.

2.5 The main types of questions are closed, open ended, probes and reflection. Questions to avoid are leading, multiples or taboo questions.

GENERAL DISCUSSION TOPICS

1 Our examination of the selection interview assumes that the candidate is seeking to become an employee. How would the interview be different if the candidate was being interviewed with a view to becoming a freelance consultant doing work for the organisation rather than being an employee in it?

2 'HR are constantly wanting to "involve me" in their recruitment and selection of staff. I'm too busy to spend time doing that. I want HR to do their job properly and send the people through to me when everything is sorted out and a new recruit is ready to start.' How do you react to that comment from an operations manager in an airline?

FURTHER READING

Anderson, N. and Shackleton, V. (1993) *Successful Selection Interviewing*. Oxford: Blackwell.
Newell, S. and Shackleton, V. (2000) 'Recruitment and Selection', in S. Bach and K. Sisson (eds) *Personnel Management: A Comprehensive Guide to Theory and Practice*. Oxford: Blackwell.
Both of these books provide full treatment of the selection interview in all its forms.

Brewster, C. and Tyson, S. (eds) (1991) *International Comparisons in Human Resource Management*. London: Pitman.
Lawler, J.J., Zaidi, M.A. and Atriyanandana, V. (1989) 'Human Resources Strategies in South East Asia: the Case of Thailand', in A. Nedd, G.R. Ferris and K.M. Rowland (eds) *Research in Personnel and Human Resources Management*, Supplement 1. Greenwich, Conn.: JAI Press, pp. 201–23.
Tan, K.H. (1995) *Planning, Recruiting and Selecting Human Resources*. Shah Alam, Malaysia: Federal Publications.
Each of these works provides research findings on interview validity.

McDaniel, M.A., Whetzel, D.A., Schmidt, F.L. and Maurer, S.D. (1994) 'The validity of the employment interviews', *Journal of Applied Psychology*, Vol. 79, No. 19, pp. 599–616.

Smith, M. (2002) 'Personnel Selection Research', *International Journal of Organizational and Occupational Psychology*.

Williamson, L.G. *et al.* (1996) 'Employment Interview on Trial', *Journal of Applied Psychology*, Vol. 82, No. 6.

Selection interviewing varies considerably across different cultures. This Focus on skills and most of the available literature is rooted in Anglo-American practice. Some insights into practice in other situations can be found in the three works given above.

WEB LINKS

Apart from material on the companion website for this book, plenty of material from consultants can be reached.

www.thedevco.com (the Development Company).

www.bps.org.uk (British Psychological Society).

www.opp.co.uk (Oxford Psychologists Press).

www.shlgroup.com/uk (Saville and Holdsworth, test developer/supplier).

www.psl.net (test developer).

www.intest.com is the website of the International Test Commission which has provided guidelines on computer-based and Internet-delivered testing

REFERENCES

Babiak, P. (2004) quoted in Butcher, S., 'When the ideal applicant is too good to be true', *Financial Times*, 12 January 2004, p. 12.

Billsberry, J. (2000) *Finding and Keeping the Right People*, London: Pearson Education.

Goffman, E. (1974) *The Presentation of Self in Everyday Life*. London: Penguin Books.

Judge, T. (2000) 'The Employment Interview: A Review of Recent Research', *Human Resource Management*, Vol. 10, No. 4.

Latham, G., Saari, L.M., Pursell, E.D. and Campion, M.A. (1980) 'The Situational Interview', *Journal of Applied Psychology*, Vol. 65, No. 4, pp. 422–7.

McDaniel, M.A., Whetzel, D.A., Schmidt, F.L. and Maurer, S.D. (1994) 'The validity of the employment interview', *Journal of Applied Psychology*, Vol. 79, No. 19, pp. 599–616.

REVIEW OF PART 2

> 'Angela's leaving – quick, we must make sure to get the ad in this month's journal.'
>
> 'It's hopeless – they all leave just as soon as we've trained them. What's the point?'
>
> 'It's not my fault – we just can't get the staff. No wonder quality is so poor.'
>
> 'That's it. The results are so bad we'll have to let some of them go. Tony, draw up a shortlist of possibles and we'll try to get it sorted this week.'

That hypothetical conversation was in a business that clearly had not even the most basic grasp of HR realities and the last six chapters have been taken up with how best to avoid that sort of unsatisfactory situation. With any staffing situation there is potentially the basic question, should we recruit an employee to do this work, should we reorganise things to cover the duties with existing personnel, or should we contract the work out to a supplier, a subcontractor or a consultant, or do we appoint an interim manager? Answers to that question come from the facts of the particular situation in the context of the resourcing strategy and the plans that have been developed along the lines outlined in Chapter 3.

Whenever a new employee is to be recruited a further set of actions is triggered to decide the method of approach to the labour market, including an assessment of which labour market you are working in, the approach that is best to use, specifying the vacancy for the benefit of the potential applicants as well as to guide the selectors, and working up a shortlist of people from among whom you hope to select.

Various methods of selection can be used to get as close as possible to the ideal match between the work that is being offered and the person best suited to do the job in its particular context. Central to that is the face-to-face situation of the selection interview, where the two-way discussion needs to ensure that the selected person is the most suitably equipped for the job and for the organisational position and the culture in which it is set, as well as making sure that that same person will derive from the appointment the satisfactions and rewards of the psychological contract that the post provides.

After being appointed employees need to be retained as long as they are doing what is required of them, so work has to be done to ensure that their expectations of the employment contract continue to be met. Eventually employees leave and HR people need to understand the various ways in which the contract can be terminated with as little difficulty as possible. It would be unrealistic to suggest that every termination leaves the ex-employee content, but the level of any discontent can always be reduced by treating matters thoroughly, fairly, with consideration and, of course, within the law.

We close this review with a metaphor or parable slightly abridged from the original by Jon Billsberry:

A gardener wakes up one morning to find that, overnight, thieves have stolen the ornamental pot containing a number of plants that formed the centrepiece in a prize-winning border. The BBC programme *Gardener's World* is due to visit in a few months to film the garden in full bloom, so he has to do something about it. He needs to find a replacement.

Looking at the border, he realises that he has several options. His initial reaction is to rush to the garden centre to purchase another ornamental pot, replant it in a similar fashion and thereby re-create what had existed. But he pauses; he has a 'development opportunity'. Could he make things even better? Have the thieves done him a favour? That pot had always been a bit of a problem, it had come with the garden and had always seemed such a formidable, if impressive, thing. Now the pot's gone, the other plants in the border seem much more prominent and much more attractive. Perhaps, rather than finding another centrepiece, he could replace the pot with something that helps the others stand out even more. Eventually he chooses this option and decides to buy some smaller shrubs that will enhance the other plants in the border. His choice is limited by the nature of the soil and the sunlight, so he carries out a lot of analysis to identify suitable plants.

Where to buy the plants? He has several options, but as time is tight, he decides to get in the car and go straight to his local garden centre which he knows has the sort of shrubs he is looking for. At the garden centre his choice of plants is easy as he knows exactly what he is looking for. He also buys the right fertiliser and compost to ensure that the new plants bed in properly.

Before planting the shrubs he spends a lot of time preparing the border and getting the conditions just right. When the new plants are in he waters them daily and keeps predatory birds away. He continues to tend the new plantings carefully to make sure they develop in the way he wants to complement the other plants in the border.

When the *Gardener's World* team come to film the producer says that the border is much different from when he saw it before, but just as good; perhaps even better. (Based on Billsberry (2000), pp. 225–6)

You are the Human Resources Manager for a large insurance company with 2,000 employees based in a large city in the north of England and your company has just taken over another insurance company in the south of England which currently employs 1,100 staff. Both firms have a long history and to some extent cover the same insurance markets, although the company in the south of England covers two fairly large specialist areas which are not covered in the north. This was one of the reasons for the takeover, as such specialist staff require a long training and need to acquire high levels of expertise. There are 300 staff in the south who are dedicated to these specialist insurance services.

The takeover did not go smoothly as there was resistance from the southern company, and now it is complete there is considerable uneasiness. Only three years ago the southern company was party to a merger with another local firm and as a result 20 per cent of staff were made redundant. There had been promises of a bright future after these difficult times.

For financial and pragmatic reasons it has been decided that the southern office will close almost immediately and all staff will be located in newly built offices 15 miles out of the northern city. Many of the southern staff are alarmed at the idea of moving and equally alarmed that they may not be invited to move due to another round of redundancies. This especially applies to those who are over 50, who will expect to find it difficult to find another job despite the 2006 legislation on age discrimination. The northern staff are divided in their views about the move out of the city centre. Those who live on the western side of the city where the new offices are located are generally delighted to be able to work near to home in an exclusive part of the county. Staff who live on the other side of the city are concerned – some are not happy to travel long distances each day, and for a variety of reasons do not want to move to the other side of the city. Some would like to move, but find that the difference in house prices is too great. Many are disappointed that they will no longer work in the city centre, which is something they had valued. Redundancy is not a possibility which was seriously considered by the northern staff.

The required profile is broadly as set out in the following table:

A	Senior and middle management	35
B	Professional/junior management	1,700 (to include 300 specialist staff)
C	Clerical/administrative	600
D	Manual/ancillary	65

	Northern	Southern	Total
A	30	20	50
B	1,400	700	2,100
(there are no specialist professional staff in the north and 300 in the south)			
C	540	370	910
D	30	10	40

Current staffing

In terms of staffing demand it has been estimated that a total staffing of 2,400 is required for the next three-year period with hopes of some increase after this period, based on growth.

The reduction in the number of professional/junior management staff required reflects a general reduction of all types of professional staff due to the economies of scale and more sophisticated IT use. The only professional staff group to increase in size is the IT group.

The reduction in clerical/administrative staff is due largely to the use of more sophisticated IT systems.

The increase in the number of manual/ancillary staff is due to the move to a much larger site with substantial grounds, including a range of on-site facilities due to a non-city centre location.

You are informed that staffing levels and the move should be complete in six months' time and that, as HR Manager, you are to have a high-profile role. You have initially been asked for a recommended strategy and plan to achieve the target resourcing figures with the least possible disruption and damage to morale.

Required

1 What information would you gather before putting your proposal together?

2 What issues would you address in the proposal?

3 What options are there for achieving the target, what impact might each have, and which would you recommend and why?

PART ③

PERFORMANCE

It is no good having all the right people all in the right place, but not delivering the goods. It has been suggested that there is a general change of emphasis in attitude to the contract between the parties, away from a contract _of_ employment towards a contract _for_ performance. We all have to perform effectively. A large part of achieving effective performance is getting the organisational processes right, but within the organisational framework there are the teams, groups and individuals who do the work. Also within that framework we have to understand what it is that motivates people to perform and deploy leadership skills that match those motivations. A key feature is the nature of leadership and how it is carried out effectively, especially in situations requiring change.

Performance management is an idea that has been developed to coordinate several features, especially targets, training, appraisal and payment, in order to deliver effectiveness. Within that sequence is the hardest type of meeting most managers ever have to handle: the appraisal interview. Also included here is the management of absence or of attendance. Are you managing processes which encourage people to attend or are you dealing with the problem of people being absent? It is not simply an alternative way of wording the question.

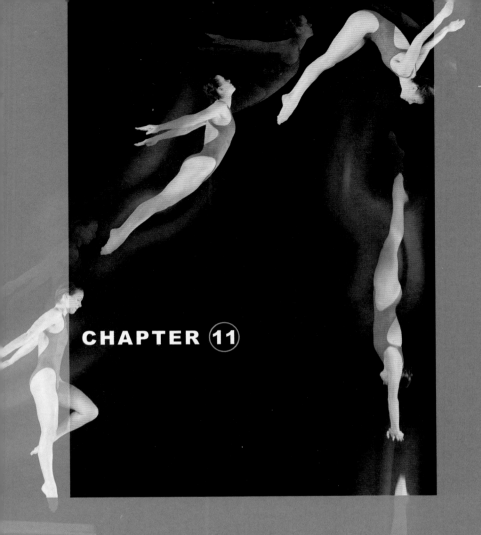

CHAPTER ⑪

STRATEGIC ASPECTS OF PERFORMANCE

THE OBJECTIVES OF THIS CHAPTER ARE TO:

1   Identify a changing perspective on performance

2   Review some major influences on our current thinking about performance

3   Examine the research which links human resource policies and practices with internal and external measures of company performance

4   Explore the mechanisms which link HR policies and practices and performance

5   Identify the direction of current thinking on the link between HRM and performance

6   Review, briefly, a range of performance initiatives

In our opening chapters we described the shift in emphasis away from the contract of employment towards the contract for performance. Even before the development of Taylor's scientific management methods a century ago, getting the most out of the workforce has always been a predominant management preoccupation, and the management literature is full of studies on the topic. Psychologists have studied motivation and leadership, ergonomists have dismantled and reconstructed every aspect of the physical environment in which people work, industrial relations specialists have pondered power relationships and reward, while sociologists discussed the design of organisations and their social structure, and operations experts have looked for ways to engineer process improvements. In 2001, Caulkin asserts:

> more than 30 studies in the US and UK leave no room for doubt; how organizations manage and develop people has a powerful – perhaps the most powerful – effect on overall performance, including the bottom line. (Caulkin 2001, p. 32)

A CHANGE IN PERSPECTIVE: FROM EMPLOYMENT TO PERFORMANCE

The traditional HRM approach to enhancing individual performance has centred on the assessment of past performance and the allocation of reward – rewards were provided in exchange for performance. This has been powerfully influenced by the industrial relations history, as trade unions have developed the process of collective bargaining and negotiation.

The prime purpose of trade unions has always been to improve the terms and working conditions of their members; the union has only one thing to offer in exchange for improvements in terms and conditions, that is, some opportunity for improvement in productivity or performance. With the steadily increasing influence of unions in most industrial countries through most of the twentieth century, it was inevitable that performance improvement was something of direct interest only to management. Performance therefore became stereotyped as something of no intrinsic interest to the person doing the work.

The influence of trade unions has altered and collective bargaining does not dominate the management agenda as much as it used to. This is the most significant feature in the general change in attitudes about what we go to work for. Managements have been gradually waking up to this fact and realising the scope for integration in a way that was previously unrealistic. Not only is it possible to say, 'Performance is rewarded', one can now begin to say, 'Performance *is* a reward'. The long-standing motivational ideas of job enlargement, job enrichment, and so forth, become more cogent when those at work are able to look for the satisfaction of their needs not only in the job, but also in their performance at the job.

Although it may seem like playing with words, this subtle shift of emphasis is fundamental to understanding the strategic approach to performance.

WINDOW ON PRACTICE

Mavis has worked in a retail store for 18 years and has recently attended a training course in customer care. She says:

I always regarded the customer as some sort of enemy; we all did. In our coffee breaks we chatted away about the customer from hell, who was never satisfied, or who always put you down. Also I used to feel that I had to grin and bear it in trying to be nice to these enemies in order to earn commission.

Since the course I feel much more in control and have more self-respect. I really feel that most customers will respond positively if I approach them in the right way. It is my performance that largely affects how they behave. I actually enjoy what I am doing most of the time (and I never thought I'd say that!), because I can see myself doing a bit of good as well as selling more than I used to.

INFLUENCES ON OUR UNDERSTANDING OF PERFORMANCE

The Japanese influence

In the 1980s the success of Japanese companies and the decline of western organisations encouraged an exploration and adoption of Japanese management ideas and practices in order to improve performance. Thurley (1982) described the objectives of personnel policies in Japan as performance, motivation, flexibility and mobility. Delbridge and Turnbull (1992) described type 'J' organisations (based on Japanese thinking) as characterised by commitment, effort and company loyalty. A key theme in Japanese thinking appears to be people development and continuous improvement, or 'kaizen'.

Much of this thinking and the specific management techniques used in Japan, such as JIT (just in time), have been adopted into UK organisations, often in an uncritical way and without due regard for the cultural differences between the two nations. It is only where the initiatives are developed *and modified* for their location that they appear to succeed.

The American literature

Key writers from the American 'excellence' school, Peters and Waterman (1982), identified eight characteristics that they found to be associated with excellent companies – all American. These companies were chosen as excellent on the basis of their innovativeness and on a set of financial indicators, compared on an industry-wide basis. The characteristics they identified included such factors as a bias for action (rather than an emphasis on bureaucracy or analysis) and using a simple form with lean staff (meaning a simple organisation structure and small HQ staffing).

Peters and Waterman identified a shift from the importance of strategy and structural factors to style, systems, staff and skills (from the hard 's's to the soft 's's). In a follow-on book Peters and Austin (1985) identify four key factors related to excellence as concern for customers, innovation, attention to people and leadership.

However, there are problems with the research methodology used; for example, no comparison was made with companies not considered to be excellent. We do not, therefore, know whether these principles were applied to a greater extent in excellent organisations. In addition, a number of the companies quoted have experienced severe problems since the research was carried out, and there remains the problem of the extent to which we can apply the results to UK organisations.

Whatever the reservations, the influence of this work on strategic thinking about performance remains profound. Even the use of the term 'excellence' means that there is a change of emphasis away from deadpan, objective terms such as profitability, effectiveness, value added and competitive advantage towards an idea that may trigger a feeling of enthusiasm and achievement. 'Try your best' becomes 'Go for it'.

More recently there has been considerable quantitative research in the USA that aims to identify HR practices which lead to high organisational performance, for example Huselid (1995) and Pfeffer (1998). The HR practices identified are termed 'high performance work practices' and have encouraged similar investigations in the UK to determine 'high commitment work practices'.

HRM and the strategy literature

The HRM strategy literature provides different ways to understand the contribution of HR policies and practices to organisational performance. We noted in Chapter 2 that three distinct approaches to HR strategy can be identified. The universalist or best practice approach presupposes that certain HR policies and practices will always result in high performance, and the question is to identify exactly what these are. The contingency or fit approach suggests that different HR policies and practices will be needed to produce high performance in different firms depending on their business strategy and environment. Finally the resource-based view of the firm suggests that neither of these approaches is sufficient, but that every organisation and its employees should be considered as unique and that the set of HR policies and practices that will result in high performance will also be unique to that firm. From this perspective no formula can be applied, and the way that people processes contribute to organisational performance can only be understood within the context of the particular firm. These three perspectives have resulted in different investigational approaches to understanding the impact of people management on organisational performance, as will become clear in the following section.

DO PEOPLE-MANAGEMENT PROCESSES CONTRIBUTE TO HIGH PERFORMANCE?

The investigations to date have had a dual purpose, the first being to seek to establish a link between people-management practices and organisational performance. In other words, does the way that people are managed affect the bottom line? The second one follows logically from this, and is: If the answer to the first question is yes, then which particular policies and practices result in high performance? Both these questions are usually investigated in parallel. A variety of different definitions of performance have been used in these studies. These range from bottom line financial performance (profitability), through productivity measures, to measurement of outcomes such as wastage, quality and labour turnover (which are sometimes referred to as internal performance outcomes). Sometimes the respondent's perception of performance is used, on the basis that bottom line figures can be influenced by management accounting procedures. The studies have generally used large datasets and complex statistical analysis to determine relationships.

Some researchers argue that the performance effects of HR policies and practices are multiplicative rather than additive, and this is often termed the 'bundles' approach (*see*, for example, MacDuffie 1995), and this highlights an emphasis on internal rather than external fit. In other words, a particular set of mutually reinforcing practices is likely to have more impact on performance than applying one or just some of these in isolation. This is sometimes referred to as complementarity. Pfeffer (1998), for example, identifies seven critical people-management policies: emphasising employment security; recruiting the 'right' people; extensive use of self-managed teams and decentralisation; high wages solidly linked to organisational performance; high spending on training; reducing status differentials; and sharing information; and he suggests that these policies will benefit *every* organisation. In the UK the Sheffield Enterprise Programme (Patterson *et al.* 1997) has studied 100 manufacturing organisations over 10 years (1991–2001) and used statistical techniques to identify which factors affect profitability and productivity. It has been reported that aspects of culture, supervisory support, concern for employee welfare, employee responsibility, and training were all important variables in relation to organisational performance. Also in the UK, Wood and de Menezes (1998) identify a bundle of HR practices which they term high-commitment management, and these comprise recruitment and selection processes geared to selecting flexible and highly committed individuals; processes which reward commitment and training by promotion and job security; and the use of direct communication and teamwork.

This avenue of work has a very optimistic flavour, suggesting not only that people-management practices are related to high organisational performance, but that we can identify the innovative and sophisticated practices that will work best in combination. On a practical level there are problems because different researchers identify different practices or 'bundles' associated with high performance (*see*, for example, Becker and Gerhard 1996), and the results overall have been patchy and inconclusive. Guest *et al.* (2003) address these issues by suggesting that it is the internal fit of practices that is important, rather than the exact practices that are in the bundle.

There have been many criticisms of this approach, partly based on the methods used – which involve, for example, the view of a single respondent as to which practices are in place, with no account taken of how the practices are implemented. A further confusion is that some studies are at establishment level, some at corporate level, some are sector based and some are cross-sector. Each of these approaches has inbuilt problems and creates extreme difficulties for any meta-analysis of the studies so far. A further problem is causality. It could be that profitable firms use best practice people-management methods, because they can afford to do so since they are profitable, rather than that such methods lead to profitability. A further issue concerns the conflict between different aspects of the bundle. Such contradictions are, for example, between individualism and teamwork and between a strong culture and adaptability. Lastly, this approach ignores the business strategy of the organisation.

The work we have described so far comes from a universalist/best practice perspective; an alternative way forward is to use the contingency or fit point of view (*see*, for example, the work of Wright and Snell 1998), asking the question, 'Which people-management policies create high performance in which different organisational circumstances?' This approach does bring the integration with business strategy to the fore, and draws attention to sectoral differences; for example Guest (2001) has suggested that 'high performance work practices' may be effective in producing high performance in manufacturing rather than services. However, it fails to provide a more useful way forward.

Attempting to model all the different factors that influence the appropriate set of HR policies and practices that lead to high performance is an extremely complex, if not impossible, task. In addition to this Purcell *et al.* (2000) argue that the speed of change poses a real problem for the fit approach.

In summary, the extent to which all the statistical work that has been done proves the relationship between people-management practices and organisational performance continues to be hotly contested. Reviewing the academic literature Richardson and Thompson (1999) come to the conclusion that the evidence indicates a positive relationship between innovative and sophisticated people-management practices and better business performance. Guest *et al.* (2003), however, recognise that although the statistical work so far provides some associations between people management and organisational performance there is a lack of convincing evidence. Guest (2000), Hall (2002) and particularly Purcell (1999) all provide detailed expositions of the problems with the above approaches. The situation is further confused by the fact that organisations often apply differing HR practices to different groups of employees. For example Melián-González and Veranco-Tacoronte (2006) found that the value and the uniqueness of jobs were two factors that influenced the application of differing practices.

Purcell (1999) suggests that a more useful approach is to focus on the resource-based view of the firm, which is the third perspective on HR strategy that we considered in Chapter 2. From this perspective each organisation is a unique and complex whole, so we need to look beyond lists of HR policies and practices to explain organisational performance. We also need to consider long-term performance capability and not just short-term performance improvements. From this perspective Paauwe and Richardson (2001) argue that the move to longitudinal studies and case study work is useful, and suggest that organisational context and institutional arrangements need greater attention; Becker and Gerhard (1996) suggest that it is more likely to be the architecture of the system, not just a group of HR practices, that results in high performance, and Purcell suggests that it is how practices are implemented and change is managed that makes the difference. Hutchinson *et al.* (2000) term this 'idiosyncratic fit'. The work of Purcell and his colleagues from Bath University, which forms part of the CIPD's research in this area, attempts to address some of the deficits in large-sample statistical work. They have investigated 12 case study organisations on a longitudinal basis, collecting the employees' view and concentrating on the line manager's role in implementation.

 They collected data on 11 HR policy/practice areas identified from previous research as being linked to high organisational performance. In testing the link between people management and performance this study differs from others in that the measures taken were ones that were the most meaningful to each organisation. (The issue of performance measurement and its varying nature is addressed in Case 11.1 on the companion website, **www. pearsoned.co.uk/torrington**). Also each of the organisations was visited twice over a two-and-a-half-year period so comparisons could be made over time. Their results are not clear-cut, but a major conclusion is that it is the way policies are implemented and the role of line managers which are critical. They also acknowledge that it is difficult to disentangle the performance impact of HR policies from the performance impact of changing environmental circumstances and other changes such as technology. They do argue, however, that those organisations with a 'big idea', which expresses what the organisation stands for and what it is trying to achieve, were more able to sustain their performance over the longer term. For example the big idea in Jaguar is quality and in Nationwide it is mutuality. They also found that such big ideas have five characteristics in high-performing organisations:

- **Embedded** – in policies and practices
- **Connected** – connects relationships with customers, values, culture and the way people are managed
- **Enduring** – stable, long-lasting values which survive even in difficult times
- **Collective** – acts as corporate glue
- **Measured and managed** – often through the use of balanced scorecard type approaches

For further information on the balanced scorecard *see* Chapter 33.

HOW DO HR POLICIES AND PRACTICES AFFECT PERFORMANCE?

If we accept that there is sufficient evidence to claim that HR policies and practices do affect company performance (although some studies, for example Lahteenmaki and Storey 1998 do not support this) then we need to understand better the processes which link these HR practices to business performance. As Purcell *et al.* (2000) point out, 'what remains unclear is what is actually happening in successful organisations to make this connection' (p. 30). Job satisfaction was for a long time seen as key and some evidence was produced to support this (*see*, for example, Patterson *et al.* 1997). However, more generally, connections between this and organisational performance did not prove fruitful and the focus moved to commitment (Guest 2002) in mediating the impact of HR policies and practices on business performance. In addition to commitment researchers have also identified motivation as the mediating mechanism and some identify trust and morale. Purcell and his colleagues (2003) give equal prominence to job satisfaction and motivation and commitment. In their model HR policies and practices are seen to impact on employee ability/skills, motivation and incentive (in that people can be motivated to use their ability productively via intrinsic and extrinsic rewards) and opportunity. In turn these three factors have an impact on commitment, individual motivation and job satisfaction, all of which have an impact on employee discretionary behaviour which in turn impacts on performance. Their 'People and Performance' model is displayed in Figure 11.1.

WINDOW ON PRACTICE

Some findings from the People and Performance research

In relation to HR practices they found that:

- job influence, career opportunities, job challenge, involvement in management decisions, training and line manager respect all influence employee motivation;
- job influence, career opportunities, job challenge and teamworking all influence job satisfaction;
- training, career opportunities, job challenge, management leadership, performance appraisal, work-life balance and communication on organisational performance all influence commitment.

Source: Summarised from Purcell, J., Kinnie, N., Hutchinson, S., Rayton, B. and Swart, J. (2003) *Understanding the People Performance Link: Unlocking the black box*, Research report. London: CIPD.

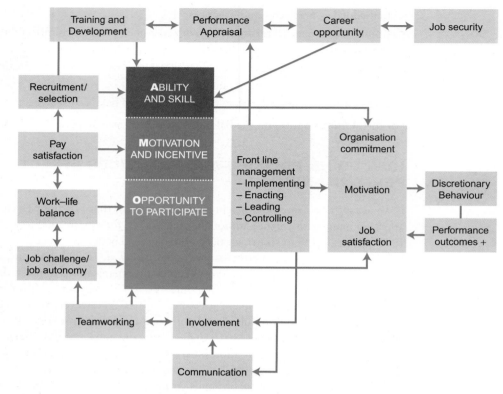

Figure 11.1
The People and Performance model (Source: Purcell, J., Kinnie, N., Hutchinson, S., Rayton, B. and Swart, J. (2003) *Understanding the People and Performance Link: Unlocking the Black Box.* London: CIPD.)

The search continues to explain better the mediating variables which encourage employees to perform at a high level, but as you will see from this chapter there is much overlap between the key mediating variables proposed to date and the idea that there is an 'answer' to be found may well be an illusion.

The Window on practice below gives an example of satisfaction being used as an explanatory variable, and given the prominence of commitment and motivation we will consider these in more detail next. We conclude this section with some key themes of current enquiry in explaining how HR policies and practice impact on employee performance.

WINDOW ON PRACTICE

Khilji and Wang (2006) propose that the inconclusive findings in relating HRM practices to performance are a consequence of both methodological weaknesses and the failure of researchers to distinguish between intended and implemented practices.

They set out to explore the disparity between intended and implemented HR practices, the impact of this on employee satisfaction and the impact of employee satisfaction on performance. The work was carried out in the banking sector in

Pakistan, and involved 12 of the 18 banking companies in the country. Of these 12 some were multinationals and some were local companies. Every company was following a growth strategy.

The research first involved interviews with senior and HR managers to identify intended HR practices, and they found that all of the banks had, in terms of intention, adopted a number of very similar HR practices, which is not surprising given similar strategies. The practices included those relating to recruitment, training and development, performance evaluation, rewards and compensation and job design.

Following this they interviewed managers and non-managers to explore implemented HR practices. They classified implementation on each practice as low, medium or high. Many employees criticised weak implementation and in some cases they were not even aware that the practice was being pursued. Only if 80 per cent or more of interviewees provided a description of a practice similar to that which was intended was implementation classified as high.

A questionnaire was then distributed to employees to assess the satisfaction they felt with the implementation of intended practices.

Three measures of organisational performance were taken one year later (to allow for the time lag) and these were: percentage increase in profits; percentage increase of market share; and percentage increase of deposit base. These were appropriate measures given the growth strategy all had adopted.

The researchers found that satisfaction with HR practices was higher for both local and international companies where HR practices were implemented as intended. The lack of difference between local companies and multinationals leads the researchers to suggest that this reflects a desire of employees to converge towards new forms of HRM, even though many of the HR practices would not appear to run counter to the high power distance* and high uncertainty avoidance* that characterise the culture in Pakistan. They found that that level of satisfaction did have a positive impact on the measures of actual organisational performance.

Source: Adapted from Khilji, S. and Wang, X. (2006) '"Intended" and "implemented"'
HRM: the missing linchpin in strategic human resource management research',
International Journal of Human Resource Management, Vol. 17, No. 7, pp. 1171–89.
* For definitions refer to Chapter 4.

Commitment

Commitment has been described as:

- **Attitudinal commitment** – that is, loyalty and support for the organisation, strength of identification with the organisation (Porter 1985), a belief in its values and goals and a readiness to put in effort for the organisation.
- **Behavioural commitment** – actually remaining with the company and continuing to pursue its objectives.

Walton (1985) notes that commitment is *thought* to result in better quality, lower turnover, a greater capacity for innovation and more flexible employees. In turn these are seen to enhance the ability of the organisation to achieve competitive advantage. Iles, Mabey and Robertson (1990) add that some of the outcomes of commitment have been identified as the industrial relations climate, absence levels, turnover levels and individual performance. Pfeffer (1998) and Wood and Albanese (1995) argue that commitment is a core variable, and Guest (1998, p. 42) suggests that:

> The concept of organizational commitment lies at the heart of any analysis of HRM. Indeed the whole rationale for introducing HRM policies is to increase levels of commitment so that other positive outcomes can ensue.

Marchington and Zagelmeyer (2005) suggest that most studies explaining an HRM-performance link use some variant of the high commitment model. Hence we see the adoption of the terms 'high commitment work practices' and 'high commitment management' and their linkage with high performance. Meyer and Allen (1997) argue that there is not a great deal of *evidence* to link high commitment and high levels of organisational performance.

Some authors, however, have argued that high commitment could indeed reduce organisational performance. Cooper and Hartley (1991) suggest that commitment might decrease flexibility and inhibit creative problem solving. If commitment reduces staff turnover, this may result in fewer new ideas coming into the organisation. Staff who would like to leave the organisation but who are committed to it in other ways, for example through high pay and benefits, may stay, but may not produce high levels of performance.

As well as the debate on the value of commitment to organisational performance, there is also the debate on the extent to which commitment can be managed, and how it can be managed. Guest (1992) suggests that commitment is affected by: personal characteristics; experiences in job role; work experiences; structural factors; and personnel policies. This suggests there is a limit to the extent to which commitment can be manipulated.

More recently the emphasis on commitment is being downplayed as new areas of understanding are opening up, and old ones are being revisited.

Motivation

Until the 1980s performance was usually construed as the output of a combination of ability and motivation, given appropriate resources, and hence motivating others became a key part of most management skills training. The word motivation is generally used to reflect the effort or drive that an individual puts into an activity. In spite of more recent attention to commitment, motivation is still considered to be an important influence on performance. It is not our purpose here to recount any motivation theories in detail (for this *see* texts such as Huczynski and Buchanan 2007; Mullins, 2006; Fulop and Linstead 1999; or Hollyforde and Whiddett 2002), but below we identify some of the key concepts addressed in motivation theories and suggest how HR policies and practice can influence motivation and potentially performance. Some theories of motivation emphasise the needs that individuals are motivated to fulfil (such as an adequate standard of living, recognition for good work, social activity and so on) and these are referred to as content theories of motivation. If work is constructed as an opportunity for these needs to be fulfilled then greater effort at work is predicted. Other theories explore the process of motivation. We draw on both types of theories here.

- **Importance of the work itself.** Maslow (1943), Herzberg (1968) and Hackman and Oldham (1976), for example, all underline the way in which individuals are motivated to seek and may achieve satisfaction through their jobs. Herzberg, for example, identifies how opportunities for achievement, recognition, responsibility, autonomy, challenging tasks and opportunities for development may all be motivational. There are clear possibilities for HR policies and practice in this area. For example this would include policies on job design, empowerment, training and development and career development.

- **Social needs are important.** Maslow (1943), Mayo (1953) and McClelland (1971), among others, highlight the need for affiliation as a motivational factor. These needs are likely to be met by policies to incorporate teamwork and involvement generally.

- **Reward cannot be ignored.** For most employees pay is important, if not a sufficient motivator. Maslow (1943) recognizes the need to have sufficient money for basic needs, and Herzberg (1968) suggests that whilst pay may not motivate per se it does have the ability to demotivate if not sufficient. So policies which ensure that pay and benefits are comparable with, or greater than, competitors are likely to have some motivational value.

- **Expectancy has an impact on motivation.** Vroom's (1964) expectancy theory of motivation recognises that in the process of motivation the extent to which the individual feels he or she can realistically achieve the target will have an influence on whether he or she is motivated even to try, so policies which enable individuals to agree targets would be appropriate. Communication, empowerment and involvement policies would have some impact here.

- **Different people are motivated by different things.** Expectancy theory, previously mentioned, also identifies that different individuals value different things and hence have different motivational needs. In the process of motivation, only those things that the individual values will spur them to act. So, for example, policies on work-life balance and time flexibility will be motivational for some people, whilst for others promotion policies may have more impact. Policies which enable managers to really get to know those who work for them would be appropriate here as well.

- **Social context influences motivation.** Recent work in the area of motivation suggests that motivations are socially or culturally determined, and this reinforces the issues identified in the point above.

- **The influence of the line manager is key.** McGregor (1960) argued that workers were basically motivated to be responsible and perform well. He suggested that if you treat people as responsible and self-motivated then they will act in a responsible and motivated manner. On the other hand if managers treat employees as if they are irresponsible and are basically work shy then they will act as such. The role of the line managers is increasingly seen as key and we discuss this in more detail below.

We have indicated how HR policies and practice can tap into employees' motivation, but, just as with commitment, there is a limit to which individual motivation can be manipulated. For example, some people have less internal energy and drive than others and less need for growth. Also, individuals with high levels of energy and drive may satisfy these outside the work environment. While we may try to motivate people externally the greatest power for motivation comes from within and is therefore under the control of the individual rather than another. The best we can say is that managers can enhance employees' motivation by the way they treat them, and at worst managers may neutralise the motivational energy in their followers. There will always be some factors on which managers and organisations have no impact whatsoever.

CURRENT DIRECTIONS IN HRM-PERFORMANCE THINKING

We have identified a number of problematic aspects of the research to date in understanding the HRM-performance link. These have led to some slight changes in direction in order to develop our understanding of the issues. Key themes of interest are focused on exploring the discrepancy between intended and implemented HRM practices and the key role of the line manager; investigating the sustainability of high-performance work practices, and exploring alternative mediating variables. Underpinning each of these is a focus on understanding employee perceptions in relation to HRM, an area which has until recently been widely neglected (*see*, for example, Boselie *et al*. 2005). Hope Hailey *et al*. (2005) suggest that their research demonstrates the need to incorporate the employee voice into conceptual models of the HRM-performance link, and Kinnie *et al*. (2005) propose that 'the fulcrum of the HRM-performance causal chain is the employees' reactions to HR practices as experienced by them' and they go on to say that this is what drives discretionary behaviour.

In considering the employee view we are cognisant of the impact that line managers have on this, particularly in view of the continuing trend to devolve HR activities to the line, which we discuss in more detail in Chapter 32. Employees are influenced not so much by the way policies are intended to operate but by the way they are actually implemented (Kinnie *et al*. 2005) as this affects the meaning and sense that employees make of these policies and will affect their behaviour and performance (Hutchinson and Purcell 2003). It is therefore critical that line managers buy into and understand HR policies and implement them appropriately and fairly. As Richardson and Thompson (1999) suggest, there is a need to know if the HR practices 'are . . . pursued by managers with equity, vigour and belief'.

Research however suggests that line managers often have differing interpretations of HR policies as they are often not precisely defined, and that the managers themselves are not adequately prepared for implementation (*see*, for example, Renwick 2003). Lack of consistency and perceived access to, and fairness of, policies as implemented by line managers are likely to damage employee attitudes, behaviours and performance, and employee dissatisfaction with policies has been shown to have a greater impact, in terms of lowering commitment, than the absence of policies (Purcell *et al*. 2003). Purcell and his colleagues provide an example of two Tesco stores each operating the same Tesco HRM policies but with very different performance levels. In this particular case the line manager's role was identified as key in the way the policies were delivered and the consequent impact on employees and their performance.

The employee view is highly relevant not only in understanding how implementation of HR policies may vary from intention and the line manager's role in this, but also in understanding the response to policies that are implemented as intended. Increasing attention is being given to the sustainability of high-performance work practices. High-performance work practices vary in their nature, and some approaches have been criticised as a form of work intensification, and whilst these practices may provide short-term gains they do not provide a sustainable approach to increasing performance. In parallel with this there is a growing body of knowledge which until recently has not been reflected in the HRM-performance research, and this focuses on happiness and well-being. Such concepts are attracting considerable general attention of late. Guest (2002) argues that such concepts need to be built into the HRM-performance relationship and there is some evidence of their integration (*see*, for example, Peccei 2004). For example there is currently greater interest in practices such as work-life balance and support for physical and mental well-being, the argument being that such practices improve performance. Case study 11.2, 'BT launches UK's biggest mental health drive', on the companion website, **www.pearsoned.co.uk/torrington** focuses on well-being and aspects of performance. However an alternative school of thought suggests that the combination of work-life balance practices and high-performance practices is contradictory. The combination of these practices therefore remains a challenge.

MAJOR PERFORMANCE INITIATIVES

We have previously considered some HR policies and practices that have been identified as related to high performance, and have noted the idea of using practices in bundles. Many of the popular performance initiatives that companies have adopted represent similar (but not the same) bundles of HR policies and practices, and we now turn to these. There are many small initiatives every day that help to improve performance, but we are concentrating here on major strategic initiatives although the labels may, of course, mean different things in practice in different organisations. Interestingly, Guest and King (2001) found that many senior managers were not aware of the research on performance, and it is therefore unclear what is informing senior managers' choice of performance initiatives.

This brings us to the concern that too many initiatives in the same organisation will give conflicting messages to employees, particularly when they are introduced by different parts of the business. There may, for example, be contradictions between the messages of total quality management ('right first time') and those of the learning organisation type of approach ('it's OK to make mistakes as long as you learn from them').

The performance research to date focuses very much on the individual, but we agree with Caulkin (2001) who suggests that organisations also need to develop the capability of the organisation as a whole, and to this end we include in Table 11.1 three levels of initiative depending on the primary focus: organisational, team or individual. Some of them cover some of the same ground, and it would be surprising to find them in the same business at the same time. In Chapter 14 on Leadership and change we discuss the introduction of practices such as these into the organisation.

ACTIVITY 11.1

1 Identify the main performance initiatives in your organisation.

2 What/who is the source of each initiative?

3 In what ways do they mutually support each other, and in what ways do they conflict?

Table 11.1 Some major performance initiatives

Organisational focus	Learning organisation
	Knowledge management
	Organisational development
	Investors in people
	Total quality management (TQM)
	Performance culture
	Lean production
	Business process re-engineering
	Just in time (JIT)
	Standards: e.g. ISO9000
	Customer care/orientation
Individual focus	Performance management
	Performance-related pay
	Self-development/continuous development
	Empowerment
	Involvement and Engagement
	Physical and mental well-being initiatives
Team focus	High-performance teams
	Cross-functional teams
	Self-regulating teams

SUMMARY PROPOSITIONS

11.1 Central to understanding management interest in performance is understanding the subtle change in attitudes: not only is performance rewarded, performance is also a reward.

11.2 In the UK views of performance improvement have been influenced by the US literature, the Japanese experience and the HRM strategy literature.

11.3 There has been considerable research effort devoted to investigating the link between a bundle of people-management practices and organisational performance, and some would argue that the link has been successfully demonstrated.

11.4 Much less clear are the processes by which the link is made, for example how, why and in what context? Commitment, motivation and job satisfaction are currently seen to have a key role.

11.5 Attention is currently focused on the extent to which intended HR practices are implemented, the role of the line manager in this, and on the long-term impact of high-performance HR practices.

11.6 Underpinning these issues is the recognition that the employee perspective is missing from much HRM-performance research and this is beginning to receive more attention.

GENERAL DISCUSSION TOPICS

1 'Motivation, commitment, and job satisfaction are basically one and the same thing, and it is unhelpful to separate them out as mediating variables in the HRM-performance relationship. A better approach would be to use the catch-all "attitudes and feelings".' What are the arguments for and against this statement?

2 Can commitment, empowerment and job flexibility be pursued together? If yes, how can this be achieved? If no, why not – what are the alternatives?

FURTHER READING

Godard, J. (2004) 'A Critical Assessment of the High-Performance Paradigm', *British Journal of Industrial Relations*, Vol. 42, No. 2, pp. 349–78.
This paper presents an excellent analysis of the nature of the high-performance paradigm before exploring the problematic aspects. Godard goes on to consider the implication of high-performance working for employees and unions, before applying a political economy approach to understanding the limitations of high-performance working.

Purcell J., Kinnie, N. and Hutchinson, S. (2003) 'Open minded', *People Management*, Vol. 9, No. 10, 15 May, pp. 30–3.
A useful summary of the Bath research to date, if you can't afford or haven't time to read the full report – provided in the reference list below (Purcell *et al.* 2003). Displays the whole people and performance model and discusses the importance of implementation of policies. Provides some detail on the importance of the 'big picture' and the five key attributes of this.

Truss, C. (2003) 'Complexities and controversies in linking HRM with organizational outcomes', *Journal of Management Studies*, Vol. 38, No. 8, pp. 1121–48.
An excellent critique of the quantitative approach to establishing the link between people policies and organisational performance. Useful case study of Hewlett-Packard which demonstrates that even high-performing companies do not necessarily follow best practice in all areas of people management. The approach taken in this research is different in that it tracks back from high performance and looks at the people management processes which contribute to this.

REFERENCES

Becker, B. and Gerhard, B. (1996) 'The impact of human resource management on organizational progress and prospects', *Academy of Management Journal*, Vol. 39, No. 4, pp. 779–801.

Boselie, P., Dietz, G. and Boon, C. (2005) 'Commonalities and contradictions in HRM and Performance research', *Human Resource Management Journal*, Vol. 15, No. 4, pp. 67–94.

Caulkin, S. (2001) 'The time is now', *People Management*, Vol. 7, No. 17, 30 August, pp. 32–4.

Cooper, J. and Hartley, J. (1991) 'Reconsidering the case for organisational commitment', *Human Resource Management Journal*, Vol. 3, Spring, pp. 18–32.

Delbridge, R. and Turnbull, P. (1992) 'Human resource maximisation: The management of labour under just-in-time manufacturing systems', in P. Blyton and P. Turnbull (eds) *Reassessing Human Resource Management*. Beverly Hills: Sage.

Fulop, L., Linstead, S. and Dunford, R. (1999) 'Leading and managing', in L. Fulop and S. Linstead, *Management. A Critical Text*. South Yarra: Macmillan Business.

Guest, D. (1992) 'Right enough to be dangerously wrong; an analysis of the "In search of excellence" phenomenon', in G. Salaman *et al.* (eds) *Human Resource Strategies*. London: Sage.

Guest, D. (1998) 'Beyond HRM: Commitment and the contract culture', in P. Sparrow and M. Marchington (eds) *Human Resource Management: The New Agenda*. London: Financial Times Pitman Publishing.

Guest, D. (2000) 'Human Resource Management, employee well-being and organizational performance'. Paper presented at the CIPD Professional Standards Conference, 11 July.

Guest, D. (2001) 'Human resource management: when research confronts theory', *International Journal of Human Resource Management*, Vol. 12, No. 7, pp. 1092–1106.

Guest, D. (2002) 'Human Resource Management, corporate performance and employee well-being; building the worker into HRM', *Journal of Industrial Relations*, Vol. 44, No. 3, pp. 335–58.

Guest, D. and King, Z. (2001) 'Personnel's Paradox', *People Management*, Vol. 17, No. 19, 27 September, pp. 24–9.

Guest, D., Michie, J., Conway, N. and Sheehan, M. (2003) 'Human Resource management and corporate performance in the UK', *British Journal of Industrial Relations*, Vol. 41, No. 2, pp. 291–314.

Hackman, J. and Oldham, G. (1976) 'Motivation through the design of work; test of a theory', *Organisational Behaviour and Human Performance*, Vol. 16, pp. 250–79.

Hall, L. (2002) 'HRM practices and employee and organisational performance: a critique of the research and Guest's model'. Paper presented to Manchester Metropolitan University Business School Performance and Reward conference, 11 April.

Herzberg, F. (1968) 'One more time. How do you motivate employees?', *Harvard Business Review*, Vol. 46, pp. 53–62.

Hollyforde, S. and Whiddett, S. (2002) *The Motivation Handbook*. London: CIPD.

Hope Hailey, V., Farndale, E. and Truss C. (2005) 'The HR department's role in organisational performance', *Human Resource Management Journal*, Vol. 15, No. 3, pp. 49–66.

Huczynski, A. and Buchanan, A. (2007) *Organisational Behaviour*, 6th edn. Harlow: FT Prentice-Hall.

Huselid, M. (1995) 'The impact of human resource management practices on turnover, productivity and corporate financial performance', *Academy of Management Journal*, Vol. 38, No. 3, pp. 635–73.

Hutchinson, S., Purcell, J. and Kinnie, N. (2000) 'Evolving high commitment management and the experience of the RAC call center', *Human Resource Management Journal*, Vol. 10, No. 1, pp. 63–78.

Iles, P., Mabey, C. and Robertson, I. (1990) 'Human resource management practices and employee commitment. Possibilities, pitfalls and paradoxes', *British Journal of Management*, Vol. 1, pp. 147–57.

Johnson, R. (1999) 'Case 2: Holiday Inn Mayfair', in A. Baron and R. Collard, 'Realising our assets', *People Management*, 14 October.

Khilji, S. and Wang, X. (2006) '"Intended" and "implemented" HRM: the missing linchpin in strategic human resource management research', *International Journal of Human Resource Management*, Vol. 17, No. 7, pp. 1171–89.

Kinnie, N., Hutchinson, S., Purcell, J., Rayton, B. and Swart, J. (2005) 'Satisfaction with HR practices and commitment to the organization: why one size does not fit all', *Human Resource Management Journal*, Vol. 15, No. 4, pp. 9–29.

Lahteenmaki, S. and Storey, J. (1998) 'HRM and company performance: the use of measurement and the influence of economic cycles', *Human Resource Management Journal*, Vol. 8, No. 2, pp. 51–65.

McClelland, D.C. (1971) *Motivational Trends in Society*. Morristown, NJ: General Learning Press.

MacDuffie, J. (1995) 'Human resource bundles and manufacturing performance: organizational logic and flexible production systems in the world auto industry', *Industrial and Labor Relations Review*, Vol. 48, No. 2, pp. 197–221.

McGregor, D. (1960) *The Human Side of Enterprise*. New York: McGraw-Hill.

Marchington, M. and Zagelmeyer, S. (2005) 'Foreword: linking HRM and performance – a never ending search?', *Human Resource Management Journal*, Vol. 15, No. 4, pp. 3–8.

Maslow, A. (1943) 'A theory of human motivation', *Psychological Review*, Vol. 50, pp. 370–96.

Mayo, E. (1953) *The problems with an industrialized civilization*. New York: Macmillan.

Melián-González, S. and Veranco-Tacoronte, D. (2006) 'Is there more than one way to manage human resources in companies', *Personnel Review*, Vol. 35, pp. 29–50.

Meyer, J. and Allen, N. (1997) *Commitment in the workplace: theory, research and application*. London: Sage.

Mullins, L. (2006) *Management and Organisational Behaviour*, 5th edn. Harlow: Financial Times Pitman Publishing.

Paauwe, J. and Richardson, R. (2001) 'Editorial introduction: HRM and performance: confronting theory and reality', *International Journal of Human Resource Management*, Vol. 12, No. 7, pp. 1085–91.

Patterson, J., West, M., Lawthom, R. and Nickell, S. (1997) *The Impact of People Management Practices on Business Performance*. London: IPD.

Peccei, R. (2004) 'Human Resource Management and the search for the Happy Workplace'. Inaugural Address to the Erasmus Research Institute of Management, Erasmus University, Rotterdam, 15 January.

Peters, T. and Austin, N. (1985) *A Passion for Excellence*. New York: Harper and Row.

Peters, T. and Waterman, R. (1982) *In Search of Excellence*. New York: Harper and Row.

Pfeffer, J. (1998) *The Human Equation*. Boston: Harvard Business School Press.

Porter, M. (1985) *Competitive Advantage*. New York: Free Press.

Purcell, J. (1999) 'Best practice and best fit: chimera or cul-de-sac?', *Human Resource Management Journal*, Vol. 9, No. 3, pp. 26–41.

Purcell, J., Kinnie, N., Hutchinson, S. and Rayton, B. (2000) 'Inside the box', *People Management*, 26 October.

Purcell, J., Kinnie, N., Hutchinson, S., Rayton, B. and Swart, J. (2003) *Understanding the People Performance Link: Unlocking the black box*, Research report. London: CIPD.

Renwick, D. (2003) 'HR managers: Guardians of employee wellbeing?', *Personnel Review*, Vol. 132, No. 3, pp. 341–59.

Richardson, R. and Thompson, M. (1999) *The Impact of People Management Practices – A Review of the Literature*. London: IPD.

Thurley, K. (1982) 'The Japanese model: practical reservations and surprising opportunities', *Personnel Management*, February.

Vroom, V. (1964) *Work and Motivation*. Chichester: John Wiley.

Walton, R.E. (1985) 'From control to commitment in the workplace', *Harvard Business Review*, March–April, pp. 77–84.

Wood, S. and Albanese, M. (1995) 'Can we speak of high commitment management on the shop floor?', *Journal of Management Studies*, Vol. 32, No. 2, pp. 215–47.

Wood, S. and de Menezes, L. (1998) 'High commitment management in the UK: evidence from the Workplace Industrial Relations Survey and employers' manpower and skills practices survey', *Human Relations*, Vol. 51, No. 4, pp. 485–515.

Wright, P. and Snell, S. (1998) 'Towards a unifying framework for exploring fit and flexibility in strategic human resource management', *Academy of Management Review*, Vol. 23, No. 4, pp. 756–72.

An extensive range of additional materials, including multiple choice questions, answers to questions and links to useful websites can be found on the Human Resource Management Companion Website at **www.pearsoned.co.uk/torrington**.

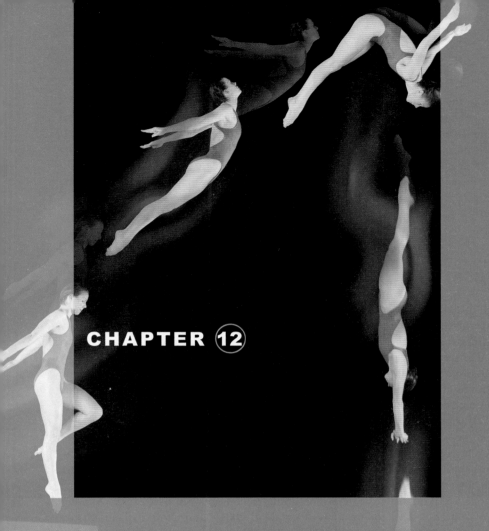

CHAPTER ⑫

ORGANISATIONAL PERFORMANCE: KNOWLEDGE AND LEARNING

THE OBJECTIVES OF THIS CHAPTER ARE TO:

1   Review the nature of organisational initiatives and processes which focus on organisational performance

2   Explore the concepts of learning organisations and organisational learning

3   Explain the concept and practice of knowledge management

There was a time when performance was seen primarily in terms of individual motivation and performance. The focus has now shifted to emphasise performance of the organisation as a whole. While some performance variations are the result of individual differences, ultimate organisational performance can also be significantly affected by systems, processes, structures and culture. These are outside the control of the individual employee, but can be implemented and controlled to some extent by managers. The focus of this chapter is on the whole organisation and its performance, although it is inevitable that within this individual performance and team performance issues will play a part.

ORGANISATIONAL PERFORMANCE 'INITIATIVES'

The word 'initiative' may appear inappropriate, as approaches to improving organisational performance may be seen as long-term and permanent changes in the philosophy of the organisation and the way that it is managed. We use the word 'initiative' as this is usually the term used for packaging such ideas and presenting them to managers. These 'initiatives' generally involve a variety of organisational change measures, which may be structural, processual and/or cultural. Culture, in particular, has a high profile. How many times have you heard that organisations are attempting to develop a 'quality culture', a 'learning culture' or a 'knowledge-centric culture'?

Many of these initiatives overlap; for example, similarities between business process re-engineering (BPR) and total quality management (TQM), and between TQM and learning organisations have been pointed out, although there are contradictions here too. Much current research and literature demonstrates the similarity between learning organisations and knowledge management. Similar concepts are used, such as 'communities of practice' (*see*, for example, Ortenblad 2001); and similar dilemmas are addressed, such as how to embed individual knowledge and learning into organisational systems and processes. Some of the same researchers investigate both areas, others link the two areas explicitly together (*see*, for example, Wang and Ahmed 2003; Easterby-Smith and Lyles 2005), conferences span both areas, for example the 2001 event in a series of conferences on organisational learning was entitled 'Organizational Learning and Knowledge Management: New Directions' (Vince *et al.* 2002), and in 2006 a special issue of the journal *The Learning Organization* focused on 'Facilitating Organizational Learning and Knowledge Management'.

The term 'initiative' may also be misleading in that some organisations may display characteristics of these organisational performance strategies without ever consciously trying to implement such a strategy. A good example of this is provided by Jones (2001) who, in research on organisational twinning, claims that he might have 'discovered' a learning organisation. He suggests that members of the organisation may not have heard the term 'learning organisation', but the way that the organisation was led and managed provided the suitable conditions for a learning organisation to happen naturally. This is an interesting contrast to organisations which employ the rhetoric of a learning organisation but which in practice are quite different. In all of these performance initiatives, it is unfortunate that the way they have been applied does not always live up to the ideals that are promulgated.

LEARNING ORGANISATIONS

The interest in learning organisations has been stimulated by the need to be competitive, as learning is considered to be the only way of obtaining and keeping a competitive edge. Edmonson and Moingeon (1998, p. 9) put it very well when they say:

> To remain viable in an environment characterized by uncertainty and change, organizations and individuals alike depend upon an ability to learn.

While the concept of organisational learning has been explored for some time, the concept of the learning organisation is a comparatively recent notion reflected in the literature since the late 1980s. Pedler *et al.* (1989) suggested that the concept of the learning organisation was a response to poor organisational performance. In other words they saw it as a way of overcoming

> sluggishness, an excess of bureaucracy and over-control, of organisations as straitjackets frustrating the self-development efforts of individual members and failing to capitalise upon their potential.

In 1987 Pedler, Boydell and Burgoyne carried out a project entitled 'Developing the Learning Company' and interviewed staff in organisations which were pursuing learning company strategies. They asked why these strategies had been adopted, and found such reasons as the need to improve quality; the wish to become more people oriented in relation to both staff and customers; the need to encourage 'active experimentation' and generally to cope with competitive pressures in order to survive. They defined the learning organisation, which they identify as a 'dream' rather than a description of current practice, as:

> an organisation which facilitates the learning of all its members and continually transforms itself.

There continues to be little empirical evidence of organisations that have transformed themselves like this, and in 1999 Sloman suggested that the concept of the learning organisation was in terminal decline. Part of the problem, he argues, is that there is such confusion over the concept and, as Stewart (2001) notes, a lack of tangible practices to implement. While Burgoyne (1999) and many others, such as Popper and Lipshitz (2000), concur with the extent of confusion, Burgoyne claims that there is still considerable interest in the idea from both organisations and academics, and that our understanding of the concept needs to be developed. He recognises that much of the early thinking about the learning organisation was naive, and suggests that, as the concept is developed, organisations will have more success with it. In particular, he describes the idea of becoming a learning organisation as one grand project, as 'utopian and unrealistic', and he recognises the value of a more incremental approach.

Easterby-Smith and Araujo (1999) note that a number of different disciplines have made a contribution to the debate on organisational learning and learning organisations, producing a plurality of perspectives. Part of the confusion, though, lies in the practices adopted by organisations under the banner of a learning organisation, rather than in the fundamental ideas. For example Yeo (2005) refers to nine different theoretical positions on the learning organisation. Academics and theorists may place different emphases on different aspects, but these are mutually supportive rather than conflicting. There is a common thread of a holistic approach and that organisational learning is greater than the sum of individual learning in the organisation. Different organisations appear to have been inspired by some aspects of this approach and, having adopted these, they see themselves as learning organisations. In essence they have taken some steps towards their goal, and have certainly improved the level of learning going on in the organisation, but have taken a partial rather than a holistic approach. A further confusion lies in the difference between the nature of organisational learning and the learning organisation, which we consider in the following section.

Organisational Learning and the Learning Organisation

The study of *organisational learning* is based on the detached observation of individual and collective learning processes in the organisation. The approach is critical and academic, and the focus is the nature and processes of learning, whereas Easterby-Smith and Araujo (1999) suggest that the study of *learning organisations* is focused on 'normative models for creating change in the direction of improved learning processes'. Much of the research on learning organisations has been produced by consultants and organisations that are involved in the process. In other words the data come from an action learning perspective and are produced by interested parties, giving, inevitably, a positive spin to what is produced. This is not to say that the learning organisation perspective is devoid of theory. The study of learning organisations often focuses on organisational learning mechanisms, and these can be seen as a way of making the concept of organisational learning more concrete, and thus linking the two perspectives. Popper and Lipshitz (1998) describe organisational learning mechanisms as the structural and procedural arrangements that allow organisations to learn, in other words:

> that is to collect, analyse, store, disseminate and use systematically information that is relevant to their and their members' performance.

These issues are well reflected in Pedler *et al.*'s (1991) model of the learning organisation, which we will describe shortly. Easterby-Smith and Araujo (1999) argue that the literature on the learning organisation draws heavily on the concepts of organisational learning, from a utilitarian perspective, and there is some commonality in the literature, as Argyris and Schon (1996) suggest. It is generally agreed that there is a lack of critical research from both perspectives.

Organisational and individual learning

Although some pragmatic definitions of learning organisations centre on more and more individual learning, learning support and self-development, organisational learning is more than just the sum of individual learning in the organisation. It is only when an individual's learning has an impact on and interrelates with others that organisation members learn together and gradually begin to change the way things are done.

WINDOW ON PRACTICE

The difference between individual and organisational learning

Brian learns from the last research project team he ran that it would be much more effective if a member of the marketing department were fully involved at an early stage. Therefore he includes a marketing specialist from the outset on the next project team and finds that this reduces the time needed for the project team and results in less hassle towards the end of the project. Brian and the organisation have gained from this learning, but if only Brian learns this lesson the learning will be lost when he leaves the organisation. If, however, Brian discusses the idea with colleagues, or if there is heated debate at the beginning of the project team due to resistance to marketing specialists being included, and/or if there is some appraisal at the end of the project, there is some chance that others may learn from being involved in this experience. Others may feel that marketing specialists should be involved from the outset, may request that this happens, may apply it to other teams, and the new practice may become the way that the organisation operates. In this second scenario, if Brian leaves the organisation, he may take his learning with him, but the organisation also retains the learning as it has become embedded in the way that the organisation operates.

In this way mutual behaviour change is achieved which increases the collective competence, rather than just individual competence. Argyris and Schon (1978) see such learning as a change in the 'theory in use' (that is, the understanding, whether conscious or unconscious, that determines what we actually *do*) rather than merely a change in the 'espoused' theory (what we *say* we do). In other words the often unspoken rules of the organisation have changed. The question of how individual learning feeds into organisational learning and transformation, and how this is greater than the sum of individual learning, is only beginning to be addressed. Viewing the organisation as a process rather than an entity may offer some help here. Another perspective is that of viewing the organisation as a living organism. Pedler *et al.* (1991) make a useful start with their company energy flow model, shown in Figure 12.1.

Argyris and Schon (1978) describe different levels, or loops, of organisational learning, which others have developed. These levels are:

- **Level 1: Single loop learning.** Learning about *how* we can do better, thus improving what we are currently doing. This is seen as learning at the operational level, or at the level of rules.

Figure 12.1
The energy
flow model
(Source:
M. Pedler,
J. Burgoyne and
T. Boydell (1991)
*The Learning
Company.*
Maidenhead:
McGraw-Hill.
Copyright © 1991
McGraw-Hill
Europe.
Reproduced with
the permission
of McGraw-Hill
Book Company,
Europe.)

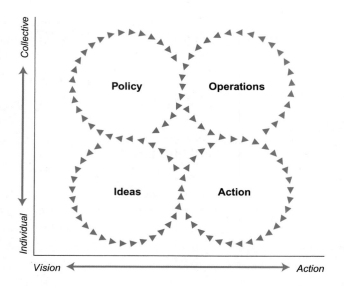

- **Level 2: Double loop learning.** A more fundamental level, which is concerned with '*why*' questions in relation to what we are doing rather than with doing the same things better, that is, questioning whether we should be *doing different things*. This level is described as developing knowledge and understanding due to insights, and can result in strategic changes and renewal.

- **Level 3: Triple loop learning.** This level of learning is the hardest of all to achieve as it is focused on the purpose or principles of the organisation, challenging whether these are appropriate, and is sometimes described as learning at the level of will or being.

All these levels of organisational learning are connected, as shown in Figure 12.2.

What are the characteristics of learning organisations?

There are many different approaches to describing the characteristics of a learning organisation, and we shall briefly consider three of these. First, we look at the approach of Pedler *et al.* (1991), who identify 11 characteristics of a learning organisation, grouped into five general themes.

Strategy

Two characteristics within this theme are suggested, first that a *learning approach to strategy* should be taken. Strategy formation, implementation, evaluation and improvement are deliberately structured as learning experiences by using feedback loops. Second, *participative policy making* infers that this is shared with all in the organisation, and even further, that suppliers, customers and the total community have some involvement. The aim of the policy is to 'delight customers', and the differences of opinion and values that are revealed in the participative process are seen as productive tensions.

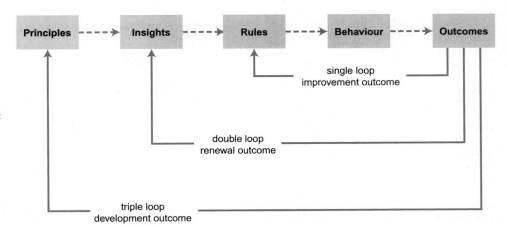

Figure 12.2
Three levels of organisational learning (Source: Adapted from J. Swieringa and A. Wierdsma (1992) *Becoming a Learning Organisation.* Wokingham: Addison-Wesley.)

Looking in

Four characteristics are suggested within this theme – the first being *informating* which involves using technology to empower and inform employees, and to ensure information is made widely available. They note that such information should be used to provide understanding about what is going on in the company, and so stimulate learning, rather than being used to reward, punish or control. Second, there is *formative accounting and control* which involves designing accounting, budgeting and reporting systems to assist learning. Third, there is *internal exchange* which involves all internal units seeing themselves as customers and suppliers of each other. Fourth, they identify *reward flexibility*, which implies that the question of why some receive more money than others is a debate to be brought out into the open. They recommend that alternatives are discussed and tried out, but recognise that this is the most difficult of the 11 characteristics to put into practice.

Structures

Enabling structures suggest that roles are loosely structured in line with the needs of internal customers and suppliers, and in a way that allows for personal growth and experimentation. Internal boundaries can be flexible. For example, project groups and transient structures help to break down barriers between units, provide mechanisms for spreading new ideas and encourage the idea of change.

Looking out

Boundary workers as environmental scanners implies that part of the role of all workers in contact with suppliers, customers and neighbours of the organisation should be to participate in data collection. A second feature in this theme is *inter-company learning*, which entails joining with customers, suppliers and possibly competitors in training experiences, research and development and job exchanges. They also suggest that benchmarking can be used to learn from other companies.

Learning opportunities

First, a *learning climate* is important, that is, one that encourages experimentation and learning from experience, questioning current ideas, attitudes and actions and trying out new ideas. Mistakes are allowed because not all new ideas will work. There is a focus on continuous improvement, and the involvement of customers, suppliers and neighbours in experimentation is suggested. A learning climate suggests that feedback from others is continually requested, is made available and is acted upon. Second, *self-development opportunities for all* requires resources and facilities for self-development for employees at all levels in the organisation, and coaching, mentoring, peer support, counselling, feedback and so on must be available to support individuals in their learning.

ACTIVITY 12.1

Which of the 11 dimensions identified by Pedler *et al.* (1991) are currently being pursued in your organisation, or any organisation with which you are familiar? How is this being done?

Apart from 'reward flexibility', which of the 11 would be the most difficult for this organisation to pursue? What are the barriers, and how might they be overcome?

Peter Senge (1990) takes a slightly different perspective. In his book about the art and practice of a learning organisation he identified five vital dimensions in building organisations which can learn, which he refers to as disciplines:

1 **Systems thinking.** This is an understanding of the interrelatedness between things, seeing the whole rather than just a part and concentrating on processes. In terms of organisational actions it suggests that connections need to be constantly made and that there must be consideration of the implications that every action has elsewhere in the organisation.

2 **Personal mastery.** This underlines the need for continuous development and individual self-development.

3 **Mental models.** This is about the need to expose the 'theories in use' in the organisation. These can block change and the adoption of new ideas, and can only be confronted, challenged and changed if they are brought to the surface rather than remaining unconscious.

4 **Shared visions.** This is expressing the need for a common purpose or vision which can inspire members of the organisation and break down barriers and mistrust. Senge argues that such a vision plus an accurate view of the present state results in a creative tension which is helpful for learning and change.

5 **Team learning.** Teams are seen as important in that they are microcosms of the organisation, and the place where different views and perspectives come together, which Senge sees as a productive process.

Senge acknowledges that he presents a very positive vision of what organisations can do, and recognises that without the appropriate leadership this will not happen. He goes on to identify three critical leadership roles: designer, teacher and steward. As designer the leader needs to engage employees at all levels in designing the vision, core purpose and values of the organisation: design processes for strategic thinking and effective learning processes. As teacher the leader needs to help all organisation members gain more insight into the organisational reality, to coach, guide and facilitate, and help others bring their theories into use. As steward the leader needs to demonstrate a sense of personal commitment to the organisation's mission and take responsibility for the impact of leadership on others.

Bob Garratt (1990) concentrates on the role that the directors of an organisation have in encouraging a learning organisation and in overcoming learning blocks. He suggests:

- the top team concentrate on strategy and policy and hold back from day-to-day operational issues;
- thinking time is needed for the top team to relate changes in the external environment to the internal working of the organisation;
- the creation of a top team, involving the development and deployment of the strengths of each member;
- the delegation of problem solving to staff close to the operation;
- acceptance that learning occurs at all levels of the organisation, and that directors need to create a climate where this learning flows freely.

Clearly, a learning organisation is not something that can be developed overnight and has to be viewed as a long-term strategy.

Easterby-Smith (1990) makes some key points about encouraging experimentation in organisations in relation to flexible structures, information, people and reward. We have discussed flexibility and information in some detail. In respect of people he argues that organisations will seek to select those who are similar to current organisation members. The problem here is that such a strategy, in reinforcing homogeneity and reducing diversity, restrains the production of innovative and creative ideas. He sees diversity as a positive stimulant and concludes that organisations should therefore select some employees who would not normally fit their criteria, and especially those who would be likely to experiment and be able to tolerate ambiguity. In relation to the reward system he notes the need to reinforce rather than punish risk taking and innovation.

Critique

The initial idealism of the learning organisation concept has been tempered by experiences, and more pragmatic material is gradually being developed. Popper and Lipshitz (2000) have identified four conditions under which organisational learning is likely to be productive. These are in situations where there is:

1 **Valid information** – that is, complete, undistorted and verifiable information.

2 **Transparency** – where individuals are prepared to hold themselves open to inspection in order to receive valid feedback. This reduces self-deception, and helps to resist pressures to distort information.

3 **Issues orientation rather than a personal orientation** – that is, where information is judged on its merits and relevance to the issue at hand, rather than on the status or attributes of the individual who provides the information.

4 Accountability – that is, 'holding oneself responsible for one's own actions and their consequences and for learning from these consequences'.

In a different approach Burgoyne (1999) provides a list of nine things that need to happen for continuous learning to become a reality.

There remains a wide range of concerns regarding the concept of the learning organisation. Hawkins (1994) notes the evangelistic fervour with which learning organisations and total quality management (TQM) are recommended to the uninitiated and fears that the commercialisation of these ideas means that they become superficial. He argues that an assumption may be made that all learning is good whatever is being learned, whereas the value of learning lies in where it is taking us and, as Stewart (2001) points out, learning is neither objective nor neutral. Learning should be seen as the means rather than the end in itself. Learning to be more efficient at what is being done does not necessarily make one more effective; it depends on the appropriateness of the activity itself. It is not surprising therefore that there is a lack of evidence linking learning organisation strategies with financial performance (*see*, for example, Sonsino 2002).

WINDOW ON PRACTICE

Is organisational learning capability related to performance outcomes?

Increasing investigation of this relationship has only produced contradictory findings. For example Bhatnagar and Sharma (2005), in an Indian context found organisational learning capability to be related to the firm's profit, but not its turnover, and Bhatnagar (2006) in a different study found that the relationship was with financial turnover rather than profit. Prieto and Revilla (2006) in a Spanish context found organisational learning capability to be related to measures of non-financial performance (including measures of job satisfaction) and not directly related to financial performance, although non-financial performance was related to financial performance. In the USA Kiedrowski (2006) carried out a study with a control group and found that although an organisational learning intervention over five years showed a positive relationship with improved job satisfaction in one large department of a bank, the control departments (with no intervention) showed similar improvements in job satisfaction.

Part of the difficulty here may be that almost all these studies used different methods of measuring organisational learning capability.

Nor does the literature cover adequately the barriers to becoming a learning organisation – for example, the role of politics within the organisation. If learning requires sharing of information, and information is power, then how can individuals be encouraged to let go of the power they have? There has also been a lack of attention to emotion, ethics and human irrationality. Harris (2002), for example, demonstrates how the potential for learning in her retail bank case studies was constrained by the overwhelming desire to maintain continuity in the organisation. Other qualitative work concentrating on employee perceptions has found that some employees exclude themselves from being part of a learning organisation, apparently feeling no need to develop further (Dymock and McCarthy 2006).

In particular, both Senge (1990) and Garratt (1990) have high expectations of the leaders of organisations. To what extent are these expectations realistic, and how might they be achieved? The literature of learning organisations has a clear unitarist perspective – the question of whether employees desire to be involved in or united by a vision of the organisation needs to be addressed. The question of willing participation was also raised by Harris when she found that contractors were unwilling to share their learning when leaving the organisation, even though this expectation was built into their contracts. For a useful critique of the assumptions behind learning organisations, see Coopey (1995). In addition, the full complexity of the ideas implicit in the words 'learning organisation' requires more explanation.

The problems in implementing learning organisation prescriptions has led Sun and Scott (2003) to suggest that attention needs to refocus on organisational learning in order really to understand how individual learning can be transformed into collective learning, and they suggest some useful ways forward. An alternative development is that of the 'living company' which extends the learning organisation concept, and this is the subject of Case 12.1 on this book's companion website, **www.pearsoned.co.uk/torrington**. Another focus has been the more recent attention to knowledge management which is generally presented in a more practical/applicable manner, and yet as we have previously suggested has some similar foundations to the learning organisation.

KNOWLEDGE MANAGEMENT

Knowledge and its perceived value

Knowledge is increasingly viewed as a critical organisational resource which provides competitive advantage, and as Gourlay (2006) demonstrates, it has a particular importance for multinational companies (MNCs). As the speed of change gets faster organisations increasingly need innovations, new ideas and new ways of doing things to keep ahead of the competition, and they constantly need to know what their competitors and customers are doing. Increasing organisational knowledge is seen to underpin this. In addition knowledge-based organisations, such as consultancies and finance companies, are growing. The growth of knowledge work and the increasing number of knowledge workers has been well reported. Examples of knowledge workers are research and development staff, legal, IT, accounting and other professionals. But, although the prevalence of knowledge work still accounts for only a minority of workers in the UK (Nolan 2001), it would be a mistake to see knowledge as relevant just to such a narrow range of staff (*see*, for example, Evans 2003). We take the view in this chapter that knowledge is important for everyone in the organisation.

There are many different perspectives in the literature on what constitutes knowledge, and for an academic debate about the nature of knowledge *see* Tsoukas and Vladimirou (2001). At a simple level we can say that data are raw facts, that analysis and contextualisation of raw data so that they become something meaningful produce information, and that knowledge is more than information in that it has been reflected on and processed to the extent that it can be applied and is with the person who needs to apply it. Explicit knowledge, sometimes referred to as operational knowledge, or the 'know what' type of knowledge, can be codified and stored for others to access. Examples here might be competitors' price changes, new competitor products, customer buying patterns and changes in employment legislation.

However, most knowledge is more complex than this, it is something which resides in a person's head and we are often unaware of what we know until we come to use it. This is usually referred to as tacit knowledge, or the 'know how' type of knowledge. This is made up of our accumulated experiences about how things are done, how problems can be solved, what works, what doesn't and in what contexts and under what conditions. An example of this might be a fireman who during a fire would be able to work out when a backdraught would be likely to occur and could then make sure the immediate area is clear of people. Working this out involves a series of decision processes about the current conditions of the fire and comparing this with previous experiences when backdraughts have occurred. This is usually done intuitively. For anyone else to use this knowledge it needs to be made explicit, which is recognised by many as difficult, and by some as unachievable. Knowledge management initiatives may cover either or both types of knowledge.

WINDOW ON PRACTICE

We have just cited changing employment legislation as an example of explicit knowledge which could easily be written down and shared. But an experienced lawyer would bring deeper and more detailed tacit knowledge to enhance this.
For example, from past experiences and case law he or she may have some feel for the way new regulations will be interpreted, or the stance that different judges may take on such regulations.

Knowledge in itself is not enough as it has to be accessed, applied appropriately and used to enhance the organisation's ability to achieve its objectives. Thus for knowledge to be of value it needs to be turned into action. Given this, it is not surprising that attention has been focused on how to generate knowledge, how to share knowledge and how to reuse it – in other words knowledge management.

ACTIVITY 12.2

Think of an activity in which you are skilled, where you will have a high level of tacit knowledge. You could even think of riding a bike or crossing a busy road.
Try to write down all the comparisons and decisions that you make when applying your knowledge to the task in hand.

MANAGING KNOWLEDGE

Knowledge management has been variously defined and the term is ambiguous. In this chapter we will use a definition suggested by Scarbrough and Swan (2001):

> defined broadly and inclusively to cover a loosely connected set of ideas, tools and practices centring on the communication and exploitation of knowledge in organisations. (p. 3)

Our understanding of what knowledge is will have implications for the way we try to manage it. Early approaches to knowledge management focused on IT systems as a means of codifying an individual's knowledge, storing it and making it available to others in the organisation. This somewhat simplistic approach was based on the concept that knowledge is an abstract objective truth which can be easily recorded and manipulated, separately from the person who created the knowledge. The resultant activity led to a proliferation of organisational databases, search programmes, yellow pages type directories, intranets and extranets. An example of an extranet is provided by Hunter *et al.* (2002) in the context of a legal firm which offered professional knowledge in this format to valued clients as part of the service that they paid for. While this may be useful for the explicit knowledge referred to above, and is the focus of much research work in the area, it has very limited value.

WINDOW ON PRACTICE

Kermally (2002) provides a case study of 'ResearchNet' demonstrating a simple knowledge-sharing mechanism which demonstrates how explicit knowledge can be effectively shared without IT.

The marketing department of this company wanted to collect external information relevant to its operations. To do this all marketing staff were asked to put Post-it® notes on the departmental notice board of any information they came across which they felt was relevant. Every week a coordinator would collate the information and produce a short report for discussion. This process then spread to other departments. Kermally suggests this was a useful approach as it involved all staff, used resources effectively, was a meaningful activity, and hence motivational, and was evolutionary.

Source: Summarised from S. Kermally (2002) *Effective Knowledge Management*.
Chichester: John Wiley.

The alternative perspective is that knowledge is personal and socially constructed. In other words, knowledge is an ongoing interpretation of the external world, as suggested by Blackler (2000):

> knowledge to be . . . pragmatic, partial, tentative and always open to revision – it is no more, and no less, than a collective interpretation. (p. 61)

This perspective suggests that codifying knowledge and using IT systems to store and share it is inadequate. Instead attention needs to be focused on 'communities of interest' – in other words the way in which individuals with a common interest network to share knowledge and spark off new ideas. A second focus is on the way that knowledge becomes embedded into systems, processes and culture within the organisation. This perspective requires that individuals need to be willing to share their knowledge, and since knowledge is power, there can be no assumptions that individuals will comply. To this end encouraging and perhaps facilitating various types of networking would be more appropriate. Trust in the organisation is critical here as sharing knowledge may involve admitting to failures and what has been learned from them and giving bad news. Project write-ups and reports may also be used in trying to make tacit knowledge explicit, especially when individuals holding the knowledge may leave the organisation. An example of this is a Department Head in a university who was aware that a valued member of staff teaching a very specialist area was about to retire and instigated a project to document their teaching content and methods so that their particular knowledge would not be lost to the university.

WINDOW ON PRACTICE

Using knowledge as a competitive differentiator at Atlantis Systems

Atlantis used knowledge management principles to support internal change management process in the company in 2004 after suffering difficult financial times following the terrorist attacks of 9/11.

The methods of knowledge management encouraged at Atlantis are:

- Democratisation of knowledge: every employee has the ability to influence the company's direction

- Iterative improvement – each employee strives to move beyond best practice in their daily activities, by capturing ideas for improvement as they go about their daily tasks

- Rewards and recognition: Employees are rewarded for contributing to the collective knowledge base of the company

- Bring the customer into the improvement process by having them contribute to the knowledge base of the company

- Flattening the hierarchy so people are free to talk to each other

Source: Melnick, B. (2006) 'Using knowledge as a competitive differentiator at Atlantis Systems', *Knowledge Management Review*, Vol. 9, No. 4, September/October, p. 4.

Kermally identifies a range of knowledge management initiatives, based on Nonaka and Takeuchi's (1995) model of how organisational knowledge can be created. Kermally suggests that to develop knowledge through *socialisation* activities such as brainstorming, informal meetings, conversations, coaching, mentoring, interacting with customers, on-the-job training and observation may be helpful; to develop knowledge through *externalisation*, databases, exchange of best practices, building models, after-action reviews and master classes would also be helpful; for a *combined approach*, conferences, publications and electronic libraries are suggested; and for knowledge *internalisation*, feedback from customers, facilitation skills and development counselling would be helpful.

WINDOW ON PRACTICE

Knowledge management at Thames Water

Lank and Windle (2003) report an interview with Peter Hemmings, Director of Knowledge Management at Thames Water, on the progress that the company is making. Hemmings explains that Thames Water's strategy for knowledge management rests on four key building blocks:

- Making knowledge visible
- Increasing knowledge intensity
- Creating a knowledge infrastructure
- Developing a knowledge culture

He suggests that cross-boundary knowledge-sharing communities are critical in achieving this strategy. These communities focus on groups of professionals who share knowledge on common interests, say, bidding, negotiations and contracts or the avoidance of water diversion and loss. Each community is initiated with a facilitator and they start by designing the remit of the group: this includes writing a mission statement, terms of membership, and how the group will use the organisation's electronic 'tea rooms'. Thereafter the communities manage themselves and decide which issues they need to concentrate on. In addition Thames Water has developed an internal electronic directory to help people find needed expertise and people with shared business interests. Knowledge sharing is explicitly encouraged in the company value statements and reinforced through training.

Source: Summarised from E. Lank and I. Windle (2003) 'Catch me if you can', *People Management*, Vol. 9, No. 2, 6 February, pp. 40–2.

The barriers to knowledge management have been variously identified as the culture of the organisation, the risk of admitting to failure, lack of incentive to change, resistance to ideas and learning from other contexts, internal competition and individual reward practices. Factors identified as encouraging knowledge management are an organisation which engenders trust and openness, a knowledge-centric culture, defined roles and responsibilities in knowledge management, support through the performance management system (such as targets about sharing knowledge and team/organisational rewards), building on informal practices which already exist.

WINDOW ON PRACTICE

Knowledge sharing across organisational boundaries

Reporting on a two-year study of six knowledge-intensive firms Swart and Kinnie (2003) found that it was as important for these firms to share knowledge with other firms as to share knowledge within their own organisation. Some of these companies work closely with fellow suppliers of a client to form a network in order to provide an integrated service or product. This demands a lot of trust as it requires commercially sensitive information to be shared with other companies which, at other times, may be their competitors. Such hybrid teams will often involve the client. This poses a dilemma as such teams can develop a strong identity, and result in members becoming isolated from their employer. This may inhibit the sharing of knowledge within the employing company.

Source: Summarised from J. Swart and N. Kinnie (2003) 'Free Transfer', *People Management*, Vol. 9, No. 4, 20 February, pp. 38–40.

It has been suggested that organisations need to make all their knowledge management activities explicit in order to justify the investment made and demonstrate the organisation's commitment to knowledge. Strategies for making knowledge management explicit are the subject of Case 12.2 at **www.pearsoned.co.uk/torrington**.

WINDOW ON PRACTICE

Knowledge sharing across organisational boundaries

Dana and his colleagues (2005) investigated knowledge management practices in high-technology knowledge-intensive companies in the Silicon Valley (USA), Singapore, The Netherlands and Israel. To do this they used the Knowledge Practices Survey Instrument (KPSI) and found no statistical differences between the four regions, suggesting that such firms, no matter where they are located, tend to display similar knowledge management practices, beliefs, values and norms regardless of national context. Questions were asked about the perceived importance of different knowledge management activities and current practices. Key current practices were found to be:

- a propensity for experimentation
- collective sharing of knowledge
- collective decision making

The four areas where practice falls to a greater extent behind perceived importance are:

- flow of knowledge within the organisation

- openness and trust

- learning processes

- tacit knowledge transfer

In follow-up interviews employees saw a discrepancy between what top management was promoting and actual practice. The difference between importance and actual practice was explained by respondents as being due to the sense of urgency that affected the operation of the companies.

Source: Summarised from Dana, L., Korot, L. and Tovstiga, G. (2005) 'A cross-national comparison of knowledge management practices', *International Journal of Manpower*, Vol. 26, No. 1, pp. 10–22.

Roles in knowledge management

Evans (2003) notes that there is still much confusion about the responsibility for and accountabilities in knowledge management, and Lank (2002) suggests three new organisational roles intended to promote knowledge management:

- **The knowledge architects.** Lank suggests that these are senior, strategic roles such as Chief Knowledge Officer and involve, among other things, working out which knowledge is critical and how it will be shared, how technology could be used, how people will be trained, how they will be rewarded for collaborative working.

- **The knowledge facilitators.** These are the people who run processes to help knowledge flow, for example company journalists who write up customer case studies and project reviews; librarians who develop indexes for storage and retrieval of information; information service providers who provide an internal consultancy service to find and deliver information to staff – including external and internal information; webmasters who develop the company intranet; and learning facilitators who can facilitate post-event reviews to elicit lessons learned.

- **The knowledge aware.** These include all employees, who have a responsibility to share their own expertise and knowledge, who will participate in post-event reviews, and who act to reinforce the value of collaboration.

There are two critical roles missing here – the line manager and the HR specialist. MacNeil (2003) makes a convincing case for the importance of the line manager in knowledge management which she suggests has been overlooked to date. She identifies the line manager's contribution as creating a positive learning climate, encouraging open exchange, reinforcing that making mistakes is acceptable and that it is helpful to share errors. She does, however, note that there are questions about the extent to which line managers have the skills to facilitate knowledge management.

Given a broader understanding of knowledge as outlined above, then knowledge management is inevitably bound up with human resource management in overcoming barriers and in proactively supporting knowledge management. HR professionals may, for example, utilise facilitation skills in supporting knowledge management, or they align human resource activities with knowledge management needs.

Knowledge management and human resource management

MacNeil (2003) goes on to suggest that there has been a lack of research on the links between HRM and knowledge management, yet Lengnick-Hall and Lengnick-Hall (2003) suggest that knowledge facilitator is a key HR role. They suggest that HR has a key role in:

> developing the motivation, competencies, value orientation, and knowledge of the firm's strategic intent to use knowledge to enhance organisational capabilities. (p. 90)

In more detail they recommend that HR managers need to design organisational structures and processes that promote knowledge diffusion, contribute to designing user-friendly systems for accessing knowledge and training people in their use, develop a knowledge-centric culture, provide mechanisms for people to share knowledge – for example allowing teams to work together long enough to develop knowledge together and then move people around the organisation to cross-fertilise.

Scarbrough and Carter (2000) asked their sample of researchers in the knowledge management area what implications their work had for HRM, and found that:

- 27 per cent claimed there were implications for recruitment and selection policy;
- 63 per cent claimed there were implications for training and development in the workplace;
- 27 per cent claimed there were implications for rewards and appraisal;
- 77 per cent claimed there were implications for organisational and cultural change policy and practice.

At a strategic level Scarbrough and Carter identify five different perspectives in the work on knowledge management and draw out the implications that each has for HRM:

- **Best practice perspective.** Encouraging employees to share knowledge and cooperate with knowledge management initiatives. If commitment is required in order that individuals are prepared to share their knowledge and remain with the organisation then 'best practice' HRM will be important to generate that commitment. (*See* Chapter 2 for a reminder of this approach.)
- **Knowledge work perspective.** Managing knowledge work and knowledge workers. Such workers may have distinctive needs in terms of motivation, job challenge, autonomy, careers and so on. These will need to be addressed by HR policies. For further depth on this issue *see* Beaumont and Hunter (2002).
- **Congruence perspective.** Increasing performance by aligning HRM and knowledge management practices. For a reminder of this *see* the fit model of HR strategy in Chapter 2.
- **Human and social capital perspective.** This involves the development of human and social resources in the organisation. This both underpins the success of knowledge management initiatives and mobilises longer-term capabilities. This perspective is based on the resource-based view of the firm that we explored in Chapter 2.
- **Learning perspective.** This perspective incorporates two different approaches. First is the notion of communities of learning, discussed above, which draws attention to the

way tacit knowledge is developed and shared in practitioner groups. Second, there is organisational learning which focuses on how learning can be embedded in organisational routines and processes to improve organisational performance.

SUMMARY PROPOSITIONS

12.1 There is an increasing emphasis on organisational performance and the factors that affect it. Systems, structures, processes, resources and culture will all have an impact on organisational performance.

12.2 The concentration on the learning organisation has not fulfilled its potential and it is suggested that further investigation into the process of organisational learning would be helpful.

12.3 Knowledge management is an alternative way forward which is packaged in a more user-friendly way, but is not without significant problems.

GENERAL DISCUSSION TOPICS

1 'Knowledge management is nothing other than learning organisation strategies presented in a more user-friendly way.' To what extent would you support this statement, and why?

2 'Learning organisations are dreams which can never come true.' Discuss why you agree or disagree with this statement.

FURTHER READING

Alvesson, M. and Karreman, D. (2001) 'Odd couple: making sense of the curious concept of knowledge management', *Journal of Management Studies*, Vol. 38, No. 7, pp. 995–1018.
In complete contrast to the following suggested reading, this is theoretical and conceptual analysis of the subject of knowledge management. It is, however, quite accessible and thought provoking. Alvesson and Karreman, among other issues, identify the contradiction of putting knowledge and management together; suggest the possibility that trying to manage knowledge may reduce its value; identify the potential that knowledge management has for control; and question the assumption that knowledge is always a good thing.

Collinson, C. (2006) 'Avoiding the typical barriers to effective KM', *Knowledge Management Review*, Vol. 4, No. 4, pp. 16–19.
And in the same issue:
Kishore, K., Singh, M. and Sidu, G. (2006) 'Identifying and overcoming barriers to sharing', pp. 6–7.
Both of these articles provide practical examples of what gets in the way of effective knowledge management.

Funes, M. and Johnson, N. (1998) *Honing your knowledge skills*. Oxford: Butterworth Heinemann.
A useful collection of skills aimed at enabling the individual to be a better knowledge manager. There is some background on the role of knowledge management and then sections which explain practical skills, tools and techniques that can be applied. For example there are sections

on gathering data, creating knowledge frameworks, developing intuition and the use of IT. User-friendly style and format, although some of the tools themselves can be complex.

Thomas, K. and Allen, S. (2006) 'The learning organization: a meta-analysis of themes in literature', *The Learning Organization*, Vol. 13, No. 2, pp. 123–39.
An interesting approach to interpreting the literature, which is based on quantitative analysis of themes and sub-themes. Using this technique, the authors find five key themes present in the literature: Learning; Structure; Shared vision; Knowledge management; and Strategy. From this they identify sub-themes which they combine to form a causal model. This article is interesting not only from the analytical perspective, but also in proving a synthesis of the learning organisation and knowledge management. The discussion of the differences between organisational learning and the learning organisation is another reason for this recommendation.

REFERENCES

Argyris, C. and Schon, D.A. (1978) *Organisational Learning*. Reading, Mass.: Addison-Wesley.

Argyris, C. and Schon, D.A. (1996) *Organisation Learning II: Theory, Method and Practice*. Reading, Mass.: Addison-Wesley.

Beaumont, P. and Hunter, L. (2002) *Managing Knowledge Workers: Research Report*. London: CIPD.

Bhatnagar, J. (2006) 'Measuring organizational learning capability in Indian Managers and establishing firm performance linkage: An empirical analysis', *The Learning Organisation*, Vol. 13, No. 5, pp. 416–33.

Bhatnagar, J. and Sharma, A. (2005) 'The Indian perspective of strategic HR roles and organizational learning capability', *International Journal of Human Resource Management*, Vol. 16, No. 9, pp. 1711–39.

Blackler, F. (2000) 'Collective wisdom', *People Management*, Vol. 6, No. 13, 22 June, p. 61.

Burgoyne, J. (1999) 'Design of the times', *People Management*, 3 June, pp. 38–44.

Coopey, J. (1995) 'The learning organisation, power, politics and ideology', *Management Learning*, Vol. 26, No. 2, pp. 193–213.

Dana, L., Korot, L. and Tovstiga, G. (2005) 'A cross-national comparison of knowledge management practices', *International Journal of Manpower*, Vol. 26, No. 1, pp. 10–22.

Dymock, D. and McCarthy, C. (2006) 'Towards a learning organization? Employee Perceptions', *The Learning Organization*, Vol. 13, No. 5, pp. 525–36.

Easterby-Smith, M. (1990) 'Creating a learning organisation', *Personnel Review*, Vol. 19, No. 5, pp. 24–8.

Easterby-Smith, M. and Araujo, L. (1999) 'Organisational Learning: Current debates and opportunities', in M. Easterby-Smith, J. Burgoyne and L. Araujo (eds), *Organisational Learning and the Learning Organisation*. London: Sage.

Easterby-Smith, M. and Lyles, M. (eds) (2005) *The Blackwell Handbook of Organisational Learning and Knowledge Management*. Oxford: Blackwell.

Edmonson, A. and Moingeon, B. (1998) 'From organizational learning to the Learning Organisation', *Management Learning*, Vol. 29, pp. 5–20.

Evans, C. (2003) *Managing for Knowledge: HR's strategic role*. Oxford: Butterworth Heinemann.

Garratt, B. (1990) *Creating a Learning Organisation*. Hemel Hempstead: Director Books.

Gourlay, S. (2006) 'Knowledge management and international human resource management', in T. Edwards and C. Rees (eds), *International Human Resource Management*. Harlow: Prentice Hall Financial Times.

Harris, L. (2002) 'The learning organization – myth or reality? Examples from the UK retail banking industry', *The Learning Organisation*, Vol. 9, No. 2, pp. 78–88.

Hawkins, P. (1994) 'Organisational learning; Taking stock and facing the challenge', *Management Learning*, Vol. 25, No. 1.

Hunter, L., Beaumont, P. and Lee, M. (2002) 'Knowledge management practice in Scottish law firms', *Human Resource Management Journal*, Vol. 12, No. 2, pp. 4–21.

Jones, M. (2001) 'Sustainable organizational capacity building: is organizational learning the key?', *International Journal of Human Resource Management*, Vol. 12, No. 1, pp. 91–8.

Kermally, S. (2002) *Effective Knowledge Management*. Chichester: John Wiley.

Kiedrowski, P. (2006) 'Quantitative assessment of a Senge learning organisaiton intervention', *The Learning Organisation*, Vol. 13, No. 4, pp. 369–83.

Lank, E. (2002) 'Head to head', *People Management*, Vol. 8, No. 4, pp. 46–9.

Lank, E. and Windle, I. (2003) 'Catch me if you can', *People Management*, Vol. 9, No. 2, 6 February, pp. 40–2.

Lengnick-Hall, M. and Lengnick-Hall, C. (2003) *Human Resource Management in the Knowledge Economy*. San Fransisco: Berrett-Koehler Inc.

MacNeil, C. (2003) 'Line managers: facilitators of knowledge sharing in teams', *Employee Relations*, Vol. 25, No. 3, pp. 294–307.

Melnick, B. (2006) 'Using knowledge as a competitive differentiator at Atlantis Systems', *Knowledge Management Review*, Vol. 9, No. 4, September/October, p. 4.

Nolan, P. (2001) 'Shaping things to come', *People Management*, Vol. 7, No. 25, 27 December, pp. 30–1.

Nonaka, I. and Takeuchi, H. (1995) *The Knowledge-Creating Company: How Japanese companies create the dynamics of innovation*. Oxford: Oxford University Press.

Ortenblad, A. (2001) 'On differences between organizational learning and learning organisation', *The Learning Organisation*, Vol. 8, No. 3, pp. 125–33.

Pedler, M., Boydell, T. and Burgoyne, J. (1989) 'Towards the learning company', *Management Education and Development*, Vol. 20, Pt 1.

Pedler, M., Burgoyne, J. and Boydell, T. (1991) *The Learning Company*. Maidenhead: McGraw-Hill.

Popper, M. and Lipshitz, R. (1998) 'Organisational learning mechanisms: A cultural and structural approach to organizational learning', *Journal of Applied Behavioural Science*, Vol. 34, pp. 161–78.

Popper, M. and Lipshitz, R. (2000) 'Organisational Learning', *Management Learning*, Vol. 31, No. 2, pp. 181–96.

Prieto, I. and Revilla, E. (2006) 'Learning capability and business performance: a non-financial and financial assessement', *The Learning Organisation*, Vol. 13, No. 2, pp. 166–85.

Scarbrough, H. and Carter, C. (2000) *Investigating Knowledge Management: Research Report*. London: CIPD.

Scarbrough, H. and Swan, J. (2001) 'Explaining the diffusion of knowledge management: the role of fashion', *British Journal of Management*, Vol. 12, pp. 3–12.

Senge, P. (1990) *The Fifth Discipline: The art and practice of the learning organisation*. London: Century Business, Random House.

Sloman, M. (1999) 'Seize the Day', *People Management*, Vol. 5, No. 10, 20 May, p. 31.

Sonsino, S. (2002) 'How convincing is the evidence that learning organizations generate better financial returns?', *People Management*, Vol. 8, No. 12, p. 65.

Stewart, D. (2001) 'Reinterpreting the learning organisation', *The Learning Organisation*, Vol. 8, No. 4, pp. 141–52.

Sun, Y. and Scott, J. (2003) 'Explore the divide – organisational learning and learning organisation', *The Learning Organisation*, Vol. 10, No. 4, pp. 202–15.

Swart, J. and Kinnie, N. (2003) 'Free Transfer', *People Management*, Vol. 9, No. 4, 20 February, pp. 38–40.

Swieringa, J. and Wierdsma, A. (1992) *Becoming a Learning Organisation*. Wokingham: Addison-Wesley.

Tsoukas, H. and Vladimirou, E. (2001) 'What is organisational knowledge?', *Journal of Management Studies*, Vol. 38, No. 7, pp. 973–93.

Vince, R., Sutcliffe, K. and Olivera, F. (2002) 'Organisational Learning: New Directions', *British Journal of Management*, Vol. 13, special edition, pp. S1–S6.

Wang, C. and Ahmed, P. (2003) 'Organisational Learning: a critical review', *The Learning Organisation*, Vol. 10, No. 1, pp. 8–17.

Yeo, R. (2005) 'Revisiting the roots of learning organization: A synthesis of the learning organization literature', *The Learning Organization*, Vol. 12, No. 4, pp. 368–82.

An extensive range of additional materials, including multiple choice questions, answers to questions and links to useful websites can be found on the Human Resource Management Companion Website at **www.pearsoned.co.uk/torrington**.

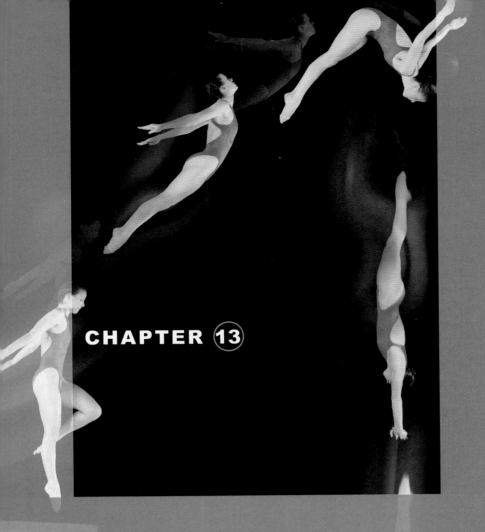

CHAPTER (13)

EMPLOYEE PERFORMANCE MANAGEMENT

THE OBJECTIVES OF THIS CHAPTER ARE TO:

1 Clarify the nature and purpose of performance management and performance appraisal

2 Explain the stages of a typical performance management system

3 Review how team performance and individual performance management can be integrated

4 Review the implementation of performance management systems

5 Explore the contribution of 360-degree/multi-rater feedback

Managing individual performance in organisations has traditionally centred on assessing performance and allocating reward, with effective performance seen as the result of the interaction between individual ability and motivation.

Increasingly, it is recognised that planning and enabling performance have a critical effect on individual performance, with performance goals and standards, appropriate resources, guidance and support from the individual's manager all being central.

The words 'performance management' are sometimes used to imply organisational targets, frameworks like the balanced scorecard, measurements and metrics, with individual measures derived from these. This meaning of performance management has been described by Houldsworth (2004) as a harder 'performance improvement' approach compared with the softer developmental and motivational approaches to aligning the individual and the organisation, which she suggests equates to good management practice. We adopt this as a very helpful distinction and in this chapter focus on the softer approach to employees and teams, covering aspects of the organisational measurement approach in Chapter 33 on Information technology and human capital measurement.

PERFORMANCE MANAGEMENT AND PERFORMANCE APPRAISAL

Appraisal systems

Traditionally performance appraisal systems have provided a formalised process to review employee performance. They are centrally designed, usually by the HR function, requiring each line manager to appraise the performance of their staff, usually each year. This normally requires the manager and employee to take part in a performance review meeting. Elaborate forms are often completed as a record of the process, but these are not living documents, they are generally stored in the archives of the HR department, and the issue of performance is often neglected until the next round of performance review meetings.

What is being appraised varies and might cover personality, behaviour or job performance, with measures being either quantitive or qualitative. Qualitative appraisal is often an unstructured narrative on the general performance of the appraisee, although some guidance might be given as to the areas on which the appraiser should comment. The problem with qualitative appraisals is that they may leave important areas unappraised, and that they are not suitable for comparison purposes.

Coates (1994) argues that what is actually measured in performance appraisal is the extent to which the individual conforms to the organisation. Some traditional appraisal was based on measures of personality traits that were felt to be important to the job. These included traits such as resourcefulness, enthusiasm, drive, application and other traits such as intelligence. One difficulty with these is that everyone defines them differently. Raters, therefore, are often unsure of what they are rating, leaving more scope for bias and prejudice. Another problem is that since the same scales are often used for many different jobs, traits that are irrelevant to an appraisee's job may still be measured.

Other approaches link ratings to behaviour and performance on the job. So performance may be reviewed against key aspects of the job or major headings on the job description. Behaviourally anchored rating scales (BARS) and behavioural observation scales (BOS) are specific methods of linking ratings with behaviour at work, although evidence suggests that these are not widely used (Williams 2002).

Another method of making appraisal more objective is to use the process to set job objectives over the coming year and, a year later, to measure the extent to which these objectives have been met. The extent to which the appraisee is involved in setting these objectives varies considerably. When a competency profile has been identified for a particular job, it is then possible to use this in the appraisal of performance. Many appraisal systems combine competency assessment with assessment against objectives or job accountabilities. IRS (2005b) report that 89 per cent of their respondents that used appraisals measured employees against objectives or goals, with 56 per cent measuring against competencies and 53 per cent measuring against pre-set performance standards, as might be used in a harder approach to performance improvement.

Lastly, performance may be appraised by collecting primary data via various forms of electronic surveillance system. There are increasing examples of how activity rates of computer operators can be recorded and analysed, and how the calls made by telephone sales staff can be overheard and analysed. Sewell and Wilkinson (1992) describe a Japanese electronics plant where the final electronic test on a piece of equipment can indicate not only faults but the individual operator responsible for them. On another level some companies test the performance of their sales staff by sending in assessors acting in the role of customer (Newton and Findlay 1996), often termed 'mystery shoppers'.

In a recent survey (IRS 2005a) 146 of the 154 respondents used appraisal, and of the 146 mixed size, but mainly large companies, 91 per cent appraised all employees. But while performance appraisal has gradually been applied to wider groups of employees, beyond managers and professionals, there are also concerns that appraisal systems are treated as an administrative exercise, are ineffective, and do little to improve performance of employees in the future.

WINDOW ON PRACTICE

Performance Appraisal (PA) for non-managers

Brown and Heywood (2005) in their analysis of the Australian Workplace Industrial Relations survey found that 70 per cent of establishments had formal appraisal for non-managerial workers. They found that PA was more likely to be used when workers had greater control over their own productivity; and that such practices were, not surprisingly, more likely to be used in larger organisations, and in organisations where there were complementary HR practices such as incentive-based pay and formal training. They also found that PA was more likely to be used for non-managerial workers when there was a lower rather than higher union density. Interestingly a key finding was that for non-manual workers, appraisal was more likely to be used when employees were expected to have shorter tenure and the authors argue that this may be so as PA can facilitate the payment of more immediate short-term rewards for performance, which are important if deferred rewards, such as promotion, are unlikely.

Source: Summarised from Brown, M. and Heywood, J. (2005) 'Performance Appraisal systems: Determinants and change', *British Journal of Industrial Relations*, Vol. 43, No. 4, pp. 659–79.

A further problem with such systems is the lack of clarity of purpose. The Employment Studies Institute (IRS 2001) suggests that appraisal is a victim of its own expectations, in that it is expected to deliver in too many areas. Systems may focus on development, identifying future potential, reward, identifying poor performers, or motivation. In systems where appraisal results were linked to reward the manager was placed in the position of an assessor or judge. Alternatively some systems focused on support or development, particularly in the public sector. These provided a better opportunity for managers to give constructive feedback, for employees to be open about difficulties, and for planning to improve future performance. Many systems try to encompass both approaches; for example in the IRS survey (IRS 2005b) 92 per cent of companies used appraisal to determine training and development needs (mainly formally), and 65 per cent used the system either formally or informally to determine pay, with 43 per cent using it formally or informally to determine bonuses. However, as these approaches conflict, the results are typically unsatisfactory.

WINDOW ON PRACTICE

Applicability of appraisal in different cultural settings

The way that an appraisal process is used may be affected by the cultural context in which it takes place. For example, Varma *et al.* (2005) compare the use of performance appraisal in manufacturing organisations in the USA and India using statistical analysis. They found that interpersonal affect (the like–dislike relationship between supervisor and subordinate) appeared to have no impact in performance appraisal rating given in the USA but that in India supervisors inflated the rating of low performers. They suggest that this may be due to local cultural norms and a collectivist Indian culture as opposed to an individualistic US culture, and a greater concern in India for positive relationships.

Another example is an event experienced by one of the present authors when running a course on Performance Appraisal in the Czech Republic some time after the Velvet Revolution. Managers on the course said that the use of performance appraisal would be entirely unacceptable at that time as workers would associate it with what had gone before under the communist regime. Apparently every year a list of workers was published in order of the highest to the lowest performer. Whilst this list was claimed to represent work performance the managers said that in reality it represented degrees of allegiance to the communist party and was nothing to do with work performance.

The effectiveness of appraisal systems hinges on a range of different factors. Research by Longenecker (1997) in the USA sheds some light on this. In a large-scale survey and focus groups he found that the three most common reasons for failure of an appraisal system were: unclear performance criteria or an ineffective rating instrument (83 per cent); poor working relationships with the boss (79 per cent); and that the appraiser lacked information on the manager's actual performance (75 per cent). Other problems were a lack of ongoing performance feedback (67 per cent) and a lack of focus on management development/improvement (50 per cent). Smaller numbers identified problems with the process, such as lack of appraisal skills (33 per cent) and the review process lacking structure or substance (29 per cent).

Ownership of the system is also important. If it is designed and imposed by the HR function there may be little ownership of the system by line managers. Similarly, if paperwork has to be returned to the HR function it may well be seen as a form-filling exercise for someone else's benefit and with no practical value to performance within the job. There is an increasing literature indicating that appraisal can have serious negative consequences for the employee and IRS (2005b) found that whilst 40 per cent of respondents in their survey reported no negative consequences, 30 per cent had negative impacts for the organisation, the individual or a relationship, and were able to explain specific incidents where this had happened. Political manipulation of the appraisal process is increasingly being recognised as problematic.

More fundamentally Egan (1995) argues that the problem with appraisal not only relates to poor design or implementation, but is rooted deeply in the basic reaction of organisational members to such a concept. There is an increasing body of critical literature addressing the role and theory of appraisal. These debates centre on the underlying reasons for appraisal (*see*, for example, Barlow 1989; Townley 1989, 1993; Newton and Findlay 1996) and the social construction of appraisal (*see*, for example, Grint 1993). This literature throws some light on the use and effectiveness of performance appraisal in organisations.

Performance management systems

While many appraisal systems are still in existence and continue to be updated, performance management systems are increasingly seen as the way to manage employee performance, and have incorporated the appraisal/review process into this. In the Focus on skills at the end of Part 3 we consider the performance appraisal interview in the context of either an appraisal or a performance management system. Clark (2005) provides a useful definition of performance management, stating that the essence of it is:

> Establishing a framework in which performance by human resources can be directed, monitored, motivated and refined, and that the links in the cycle can be audited.
> (p. 318)

Bevan and Thompson (1992) found that 20 per cent of the organisations they surveyed had introduced a performance management system. Armstrong and Baron (1998a) report that 69 per cent of the organisations they surveyed in 1997 operated a formal process to measure manager performance. Such systems are closely tied into the objectives of the organisation, so that the resulting performance is more likely to meet organisational needs. The systems also represent a more holistic view of performance. Performance appraisal or review is almost always a key part of the system, but is integrated with *performance planning*, which links an individual's objectives to business objectives to ensure that employee effort is directed towards organisational priorities: support for *performance delivery* (via development plans, coaching and ongoing review) to enable employee effort to be successful, and that performance is *assessed* and successful performance *rewarded and reinforced*.

The conceptual foundation of performance management relies on a view that performance is more than ability and motivation. It is argued that clarity of goals is key in enabling the employee to understand what is expected and the order of priorities. In addition goals themselves are seen to provide motivation, and this is based on goal-setting theory originally developed by Locke in 1968 and further developed with practical applicability (Locke and Latham 1990). Research to date suggests that for goals to be motivating they must be sufficiently specific, challenging but not impossible and set participatively. Also the person appraised needs feedback on future progress.

The other theoretical base of performance management is expectancy theory, which states that individuals will be motivated to act provided they expect to be able to achieve the goals set, believe that achieving the goals will lead to other rewards and believe that the rewards on offer are valued (Vroom 1964). Given such an emphasis on a link into the organisation's objectives it is somewhat disappointing that Bevan and Thompson found no correlation between the existence of a performance management system and organisational performance in the private sector. Similarly, Armstrong and Baron (1998a) report from their survey that no such correlation was found. They do report, however, that 77 per cent of organisations surveyed regarded their systems as effective to some degree and Houldsworth (2003), using the Henley and Hay Group survey of top FTSE companies and public sector respondents, reports that 68 per cent of organisations rated their performance management effectiveness as excellent. While Houldsworth *et al.* (2005) propose that performance management practice is now more sophisticated and better received by employees, we suggest that it still remains an act of faith.

Some performance management systems are development driven and some are reward driven. Whereas in the 1992 IPD survey 85 per cent of organisations claimed to link performance management to pay (Bevan and Thompson 1992), Armstrong and Baron (1998a) found that only 43 per cent of survey respondents reported such a link. However, 82 per cent of the organisations visited had some form of performance-related pay (PRP) or competency-based pay, so the picture is a little confusing. They suggest that a view is emerging of performance management which centres on 'dialogue', 'shared understanding', 'agreement' and 'mutual commitment', rather than rating for pay purposes. To this end organisations are increasingly suggesting that employees take more ownership of performance management (*see* Scott 2006 for a good example) and become involved in collecting self-assessment evidence throughout the year (IDS 2005). While these characteristics may feature in more sophisticated systems, Houldsworth (2003) reports that 77 per cent of organisations link performance assessments with pay, and it appears that many organisations are trying to achieve both development and reward outcomes. She also contrasts systems driven by either performance development or performance measurement, finding that the real experience of developmental performance management is that it is motivational, encourages time spent with the line manager, encourages two-way communication and is an opportunity to align roles and training with business needs. Alternatively, where there is a measurement focus, performance management is seen as judgemental, a chance to assess and get rid of employees, emphasises control and getting more out of staff, raises false expectations and is a way to manage the salaries bill. (*See* Table 13.1.)

Table 13.1 Characteristics of performance management systems

- Top-down link between business objectives and individual objectives (compared with performance appraisal where there may be no objectives, or objectives not explicitly linked to business objectives)
- Line manager driven and owned (rather than being owned by the HR function, as typically with performance appraisal)
- A living document where performance and development plans, support and ongoing review are documented as work progresses, and prior to annual review (rather than an archived document retrieved at appraisal time to compare achievement with intentions)
- Performance is rewarded and reinforced

ACTIVITY 13.1

Think of the performance appraisal or performance management system at your place of work.

1 To what extent does it focus on development and to what extent does it focus on reward?

2 How, and how well, are each of these purposes achieved? Explain why this is.

3 What would you do to improve the system, and what impacts would these actions have?

STAGES IN A PERFORMANCE MANAGEMENT SYSTEM

Figure 13.1 shows a typical performance management system, including both development and reward aspects, the main stages of which are discussed below.

Business mission, values, objectives and competencies

There is an assumption that before it is able to plan and manage individual performance the organisation will have made significant steps in identifying the performance required of the organisation as a whole. In most cases this will involve a mission statement so that performance is seen within the context of an overriding theme. In addition many organisations will identify the strategic business objectives that are required within the current business context to be competitive and that align with the organisation's mission statement.

Many organisations will also identify core values of the business and the key competencies required. Each of these has a potential role in managing individual performance.

Figure 13.1
Stages of a typical performance management system

Figure 13.2
An objective-
setting cascade

Organisational objectives are particularly important, as it is common for such objectives to be cascaded down the organisation in order to ensure that individual objectives contribute to their achievement (for an example of an objective-setting cascade, *see* Figure 13.2).

Planning performance: a shared view of expected performance

Individual objectives derived from team objectives and an agreed job description can be jointly devised by manager and employee. These objectives are outcome/results oriented rather than task oriented, are tightly defined and include measures to be assessed. The objectives are designed to stretch the individual, and offer potential development as well as meeting business needs. It is helpful to both the organisation and the individual if objectives are prioritised. Many organisations use the 'SMART' acronym for describing individual objectives or targets:

- Specific
- Measurable
- Appropriate
- Relevant
- Timed

It is clearly easier for some parts of the organisation than others to set targets. There is often a tendency for those in technical jobs, such as computer systems development, to identify purely technical targets, reflecting the heavy task emphasis they see in their jobs. Moving staff to a different view of how their personal objectives contribute to team and organisational objectives is an important part of the performance management process. An objective for a team leader in systems development could be:

To complete development interviews with all team members by end July 2007 (written March 2007).

Clearly, the timescale for each objective will need to reflect the content of the objective and not timescales set into the performance management system. As objectives are met, managers and their staff need to have a brief review meeting to look at progress in all objectives and decide what other objectives should be added, changed or deleted. Five or six ongoing objectives are generally sufficient for one individual to work on at any time. A mix of objectives about new developments and changes as well as routine aspects of the job is generally considered to be appropriate.

The critical point about a *shared* view of performance suggests that handing out a job description or list of objectives to the employee is not adequate. Performance expectations need to be understood and, where possible, to involve a contribution from the employee. For example, although key accountabilities may be fixed by the manager, they will need to be discussed. Specific objectives allow for and benefit from a greater degree of employee input as employees will have a valid view of barriers to overcome, the effort involved and feasibility. Expressing objectives as a 'what' statement rather than a 'how' statement gives employees the power to decide the appropriate approach once they begin to work on the issue. Incorporating employee input and using 'what' statements are likely to generate a higher degree of employee ownership and commitment. However, difficulties have been experienced with purely 'what' objectives as there may be appropriate and inappropriate ways of achieving an objective. For example, a manager with an objective to ensure that another department agrees to a plan of action could achieve this in different ways. The manager may pressure susceptible members of the other department and force agreement through without listening to the other department's perspective. This may alienate the other department and damage future good relations. Alternatively the manager could adopt a collaborative approach so that the needs of both departments are met, providing a sound basis for future cooperation between the departments. More sophisticated systems now incorporate the 'how' as well (*see* IDS 2003).

Planning the support, development and resources necessary for employees to achieve their objectives is imperative. Without this support it is unlikely that even the most determined employees will achieve the performance required.

Concerns have been expressed over restricting the objectives to those which specify output targets, and there is now evidence of increasing use of input targets, such as developing a critical competency which is valued by the organisation and relevant to the achievement of objectives. Williams (2002) argues that as individuals cannot always control their results it is important to have behavioural targets as well as output targets. It is also recommended that there is a personal development plan which would again underpin the achievement of objectives.

Delivering and monitoring performance

While the employee is working to achieve the performance agreed, the manager retains a key enabling role. Organising the resources and off-job training is clearly essential. So too is being accessible. There may well be unforeseen barriers to the agreed performance which the manager needs to deal with, and sometimes the situation will demand that the expected performance needs to be revised. The employee may want to sound out possible courses of action with the manager before proceeding, or may require further information. Sharing 'inside' information that will affect the employee's performance is often a key need, although it is also something that managers find difficult, especially with sensitive information. Managers can identify information sources and other people who may be helpful.

Ongoing **coaching** during the task is especially important as managers guide employees through discussion and by constructive feedback. They can refer to practical job experiences to develop the critical skills and competencies that the employee needs, and can provide job-related opportunities for practice. Managers can identify potential role models to employees, help to explain how high achievers perform so well, and oil the organisational wheels.

ACTIVITY 13.2

1 Do managers actively support employee performance in your organisation? If they do, by what means do they do this and how effective is it? If they do not, why not, and what is the impact of this?

Or

2 Think of any organisation in which you have had some involvement:

- How has individual performance been supported?
- How effective was/is this?
- How would you improve the way in which performance was/is supported?

Employees carry out ongoing reviews to plan their work and priorities and also to advise the manager well in advance if the agreed performance will not be delivered by the agreed dates. Joint employee/manager review ensures that information is shared. For example, a manager needs to be kept up to date on employee progress, while the employee needs to be kept up to date on organisational changes that have an impact on the agreed objectives. Both need to share perceptions of how the other is doing in their role, and what they could do that would be more helpful.

These reviews are normally informal, although a few notes may be taken of progress made and actions agreed. They need not be part of any formal system and therefore can take place when the job or the individuals involved demand, and not according to a pre-set schedule. The review is to facilitate future employee performance, providing an opportunity for the manager to confirm that the employee is 'on the right track', redirecting him or her if necessary. They thus provide a forum for employee reward in terms of recognition of progress. A 'well done' or an objective signed off as completed can enhance the motivation to perform well in the future. During this period evidence collection is also important. In the Scottish Prison Service (IDS 2003) line managers maintain a performance monitoring log of their team members' positive and negative behaviours in order to provide regular feedback and to embed the practice of ongoing assessment. Employees are expected to build up a portfolio of evidence of their performance over the period to increase the objectivity of reviews and to provide an audit trail to back up any assessment ratings. It is also during this part of the cycle that employees in many organisations can collect 360-degree feedback to be used developmentally and as part of an evidence base.

Formal performance review/assessment

Regular formal reviews are needed to concentrate on developmental issues and to motivate the employee. Also, an annual review and assessment is needed, of the extent to which objectives have been met – and this may well affect pay received. In many organisations, for example Microsoft and AstraZeneca, employees are now invited to prepare an initial draft of achievement against objectives (IDS 2003). Some organisations continue to have overall assessment ratings which have to conform to a forced distribution, requiring each team/department to have, say, 10 per cent of employees on the top point, 20 per cent on the next point, and so on, so that each individual is assessed relative to others rather than being given an absolute rating. These systems are not popular and Roberts (2004) reports how staff walked out in a part of the Civil Service over relative assessment; AstraZeneca does not encourage its managers to give an overall rating to staff at all as its research suggested that this was demotivating (IDS 2003). Research by the Institute for Employment Studies (IRS 2001) found that review was only seen as fair if the targets set were seen as reasonable, managers were seen to be objective and judgements were consistent across the organisation.

Some organisations encourage employees to give upward feedback to their managers at this point in the cycle. For further details of this stage in the process *see* the Focus on skills at the end of Part 3.

Reward

Many systems still include a link with pay, but Fletcher and Williams (1992) point to some difficulties experienced. Some public and private organisations found that the merit element of pay was too small to motivate staff, and sometimes seen as insulting. Although performance management organisations were more likely than others to have merit or performance-related pay (Bevan and Thompson 1992), some organisations have regretted its inclusion. Armstrong and Baron (1998a) report that staff almost universally disliked the link with pay, and a manager in one of their case study companies reported that 'the whole process is an absolute nightmare' (p. 172). Clark (2005) provides a good discussion of the problems with the pay link and we include a detailed discussion of performance related pay in Chapter 28.

There are other forms of reward than monetary and the Institute for Employment Studies (IRS 2001) found that there was more satisfaction with the system where promotion and development, rather than money, were used as rewards for good performance.

WINDOW ON PRACTICE

Performance management at Orange

To meet a very competitive environment and the convergence of a number of businesses Orange recognised that it needed to make its performance management process more robust. There were a number of concerns with the existing system including the five-point ratings scale; executives feeling that HR owned the process;

employees feeling that objective setting often did not support the business; and some feelings of lack of support and direction.

The new system has five core principles:

- one clear cascade process for objectives

- reward should stay linked to performance

- a balance between 'what' and 'how' objectives

- process needs to be owned by the business

- performance should be clearly and consistently differentiated across the ratings

The design of the system was led by senior representatives of the core businesses and a decision was made to keep the best parts of the current system and incorporate 'snippets of good stuff' from elsewhere, rather than looking for a 'best practice' model used elsewhere to implement.

The five-point ratings scale was kept but the labels attached to each point were changed to demonstrate that the mid-point was a good place to be (which was used previously when employees had met their objectives and were doing a good job, and which had caused disagreements). The new scale ranged from 'unacceptable' (one); 'getting there' (two); 'great stuff' (three, the mid-point); 'excellent' (four) to 'exceptional' (five). The distribution curve used to ensure consistent ratings was abandoned in favour of 'calibration' which takes place at various levels and involves managers sharing the ratings they have given to those who report directly to them with other managers at their level, providing justification for their ratings and being prepared to explore and discuss their views. Objective setting is now linked into the balanced scorecard approach they have adopted with Vice Presidents' objectives being set at the same time (and published on the intranet) and cascaded down the organisation. Objectives are weighted to ensure prioritisation and staff must have two or three behavioural ('how' or input) objectives. Orange has a profit-sharing scheme for non-managers called 'success share', and now performance ratings are used to determine the proportion received by each individual. For managers the bonus scheme has altered giving senior managers more flexibility to allocate rewards for each point on the five-point scale, without having to manipulate ratings.

Source: Summarised from R. Johnson (2006) 'Orange Blossoms', *People Management*, Vol. 12, No. 21, 26 October, pp. 56–60.

INDIVIDUAL VERSUS TEAM PERFORMANCE MANAGEMENT

There is one key aspect of employee performance management which we have yet to touch upon and that is how organisations can use performance management to support team performance as well as individual performance. This is a critical balancing act in most cases as, if managers and employees are not mindful in their objective setting, development, review and reward process, there can be conflicts built into performance management activity causing employees' pursuit of individual objectives to damage the performance of the team they are in and vice versa. The complications that can arise and the way they are best dealt with will depend very much on the type of team(s) to which the employee belongs and the individual circumstances. Below we consider different types of team situations and the challenges these bring for performance management, and how both individual performance and team performance can best be enhanced at the same time.

It is generally agreed that team working has increased but this may take many forms. First, let us look at the situation where an employee has a base role in a departmental team, such as the 'training team', 'contracts team', 'schools marketing team' for example, reflecting where that person is placed in the organisation and who their line manager is. If this is the only team to which the employee belongs then it is highly likely that he or she will agree individual performance management objectives with the team leader which relate to the employee's role in the achievement of the team's objectives. One of those individual objectives may of course focus on collegiality or support to other members of the functional team.

However many employees will at the same time be members of other teams, perhaps ongoing cross-functional teams or time-limited cross-functional problem-solving teams. The objectives for this cross-functional team may be owned elsewhere in the organisation. One danger in such a situation is that if the employee does not have at least one objective relating to his or her role in this second team then this aspect of his or her job may suffer as effort is prioritised on areas that purely relate to his or her home team. This will be especially so if any kind of reward is attached to achievement of objectives. So neglect of a part of the employee's job relating to the second team is the first potential problem. The remedy to this is fairly straightforward, but easily overlooked. An objective relating to the contribution the employee makes to the second team needs to be included (an input objective), or alternatively an objective relating to the achievement of one or more objectives of the second team (an output objective). An example of the first may concern the team role the employee is required to play in that second team, perhaps focusing on strengthening it, if it is not well developed, or concern the skills that are needed in that team given its stage of development, or concern the extent to which the employee is collaborative in his or her work with the team. An example of the second may concern, say, the team delivering on a target date, to the standard agreed, or other output targets it has agreed.

The second potential problem is that the employee's individual objectives may actually conflict with the objectives of the second team of which he or she is a part. This conflict may be political in nature, where the home team leader agrees an objective with an individual that he or she should influence the second team to, for example, plan in a certain amount of training, before the roll-out of a new IT system. However if roll-out is to commence on the target date agreed by the second team, fitting in this training may be extremely difficult, if not impossible. The employee in this situation may not be able to win, either he or she fails to achieve his or her individual objective or the second team of which he or she is a part fails to achieve one of its objectives.

Van Vijfeijken *et al.* (2006) provide another example of potential conflict in relation to the operation of management teams, where the employee (this time a departmental head) has individual objectives relating to the achievement of the department's objectives, but is also part of the organisation's management team which has its own set of objectives. The researchers identified potential conflicts between the individual objectives of different department heads in the management team, and also between any individual head's goals and the team goals. An example here might be that a department head of marketing has an objective relating to cost reductions in their department, whereas a management team goal may concern an extensive marketing campaign to launch a new product. There is a great deal written about how such management teams need to distance themselves from their department (*see*, for example, Garratt 1990) and operate in the interests of the organisation as a whole. This is clearly difficult if the department head has individual objectives relating to the department, which will drive monetary or other rewards. Such contradictions need to be openly aired at an early stage, but this is often not the case, due to lack of awareness, inertia or politicking.

We turn now to consider permanent self-managed teams or the like. Often in such teams all performance management objectives are team based, with the whole team needing to pull together to achieve these objectives effectively. In such teams there may in addition be individual input objectives such as skills development. These teams are more likely to fit the classical definition of a team. Moxon (1993) defines a team as having a common purpose; agreed norms and values which regulate behaviour; members with interdependent functions; and a recognition of team identity. Katzenbach and Smith (1993) and Katzenbach (1997) have also described the differences that they see between teams and work groups, and identify teams as comprising individuals with complementary skills, shared leadership roles, mutual accountability and a specific team purpose, amongst other attributes. In organisations this dedication only happens when individuals are fully committed to the team's goals. This commitment derives from an involvement in defining how the goals will be met and having the power to make decisions within teams rather than being dependent on the agreement of external management. These are particularly characteristics of self-managing teams.

The problems most likely to occur with team objectives in this setting are peer pressure and social loafing (*see*, for example, Clark 2005). Peer pressure can be experienced by an individual, such as for example, the pressure not to take time off work when feeling ill, as this may damage achievement of objectives; or pressure to work faster, make fewer mistakes and so on. This pressure is likely to be much greater when rewards are attached to the achievement of team objectives. Individuals will vary in the competitiveness and in the value they place on monetary rewards and this may cause a pressure for all. Social loafing occurs in a situation where one or more team members rely on the others to put in extra effort to achieve objectives, to cover for their own lack of effort. It works when some members are known to be conscientious or competitive or to care deeply about the rewards available, and there are others who are likely to be less concerned and who know the conscientious team members will make sure by their own efforts that the objectives are achieved.

IMPLEMENTATION AND CRITIQUE OF PERFORMANCE MANAGEMENT

Performance management needs to be line driven rather than HR driven, and therefore mechanisms need to be found to make this happen. The incorporation of line managers alongside HR managers in a working party to develop the system is clearly important as it not only takes account of the needs of the line in the system design, but also demonstrates that the system is line led. Training in the introduction and use of the system is also ideally line led, and Fletcher and Williams (1992) give us an excellent example of an organisation where line managers were trained as 'performance management coaches' who were involved in departmental training and support for the new system. However, some researchers have found that line managers are the weak link in the system (*see*, for example, Hendry *et al*. 1997). The Department of Trade and Industry (DTI) (*see* IRS 2001) notes that any system is only as good as the people who operationalise it. See Case 13.1 at **www.pearsoned.co.uk/torrington** which deals with the introduction of a performance management system.

WINDOW ON PRACTICE

Fletcher and Williams (1992) report on a scheme that was introduced by training a series of nominated line manager coaches from each department of an organisation. They had then to take the message back to their colleagues and train them, tailoring the material to their department (Personnel/Training providing the back-up documentation). These were serving line managers who had to give up their time to do the job. Many of them were high-flyers, and they have been important opinion leaders and influencers – though they themselves had to be convinced first. Their bosses could refuse to nominate high-quality staff for this role if they wished, but they would subsequently be answerable to the Chief Executive. This approach was taken because it fits with the philosophy of performance management (i.e. high line-management participation), and because it was probably the only way to train all the departmental managers in the timescale envisaged.

Source: Summarised from C. Fletcher and R. Williams (1992)
Performance Management in the UK: Organisational Experience. London: IPM, p. 133.

Bevan and Thompson (1992) found incomplete take-up of performance management, with some aspects being adopted and not others. They noted that there was a general lack of integration of activities. This is rather unfortunate as one of the key advantages of performance management is the capacity for integration of activities concerned with the management of individual performance. This problem is still apparent. Hendry *et al*. (1997) reported the comments of Phil Wills from GrandMet, that there is still little understanding of what an integrated approach to performance management means. While alignment is critical, some organisations do not understand whether their HR processes are aligned or pulling in different directions. Williams (2002) suggests that there is still confusion over the nature of performance management.

Performance management seems to suffer from the same problems as traditional appraisal systems. Armstrong and Baron (1998a) report, for example, that over half the respondents to their survey feel that managers give their best ratings to people that they like (p. 202), and over half the managers surveyed felt that they had not received sufficient training in performance management processes (p. 203). They also report (1998b) that the use of ratings was consistently derided by staff and seen as subjective and inconsistent. Performance ratings can be seen as demotivating, and forced distributions are felt to be particularly unfair. Yet Houldsworth (2003) found 44 per cent of the Henley and Hay Group survey sample did this.

In terms of individual objective setting linked to organisational performance objectives, there are problems when strategy is unclear and when it evolves. Rose (2000) also reports a range of problems, particularly the fact that SMART targets can be problematic if they are not constantly reviewed and updated, although this is a time-consuming process. Pre-set objectives can be a constraining factor in such a rapidly changing business context, and they remind us of the trap of setting measurable targets, precisely because they are measurable and satisfy the system, rather than because they are most important to the organisation. He argues that a broader approach which assesses the employee's accomplishments as a whole and the contribution to the organisation is more helpful than concentrating on pre-set objectives. Williams (2002) also notes that there is more to performance than task performance, such as volunteering and helping others. He refers to this as contextual performance; it is sometimes referred to as collegiate behaviour.

A further concern with SMART targets is that they inevitably have a short-term focus, yet what is most important to the organisation is developments which are complex and longer term, which are very difficult to pin down to short-term targets (*see*, for example, Hendry *et al.* 1997). In this context systems which also focus on the development of competencies will add greater value in the longer term. Armstrong and Baron (1998b) do note that a more rounded view of performance is gradually being adopted, which involves the 'how' as well as the 'what', and inputs such as the development of competencies. There is, however, a long way to go adequately to describe performance and define what is really required for organisational success.

For an in-depth example of performance management in the Scottish Prison Service *see* Case 13.2 at **www.pearsoned.co.uk/torrington**.

360-DEGREE FEEDBACK

The term 360-degree feedback, a very specific term used to refer to multi-rater feedback, is increasingly being used within performance management systems and as a separate development activity.

The nature of 360-degree feedback

This approach to feedback refers to the use of the whole range of sources from which feedback can be collected about any individual. Thus feedback is collected from every angle on the way that the individual carries out his or her job: from immediate line manager; peers; subordinates; more senior managers; internal customers; external customers; and from individuals themselves. It is argued that this breadth provides better feedback than relying on the line manager only, who will only be able to observe the individual in a limited range of situations, and Atwater and his colleagues (2002) suggest that 360-degree feedback provides a better way to capture the complexities of performance. Hogetts *et al.* (1999) report that more than 70 per cent of United Parcels Service employees found that feedback from multiple sources was more useful in developing self-insight than feedback from a single source. Individuals, it is argued, will find feedback from peers and subordinates compelling and more valid (*see*, for example, Borman 1997 and Atwater *et al.* 2001), and Edwards and Ewen (1996, p. 4) maintain that:

> No organizational action has more power for motivating employee behaviour change than feedback from credible work associates.

Such all-round feedback enables the individual to understand how he or she may be seen differently (or similarly) by different organisational groups, and how this may contrast with the individuals own views of his or her strengths and weaknesses. This provides powerful information for the development of self-awareness. While 360-degree feedback may be collected using informal methods, as shown in the Window on practice box on Humberside Tec, the term itself is a registered trade mark, and refers to a very specific method of feedback collection and analysis which was devised in the United States (*see* Edwards and Ewen 1996, p. 19), and they suggest that 'simplistic, informal approaches to multi-source assessment are likely to multiply rather than reduce error'. However, informal approaches to 360-degree feedback are sometimes used quite successfully as an alternative to a survey questionnaire and statistical analysis.

WINDOW ON PRACTICE

Using an informal approach to 360-degree feedback at Humberside Tec

Storr (2000) reports on a 360-degree feedback process which is quite different from the survey approach. It is a process which has gradually been built up from upward appraisal for team leaders, has been piloted, and has gradually become standard. The process is owned by the appraisees, and is different because it is carried out face to face rather than using a paper system, and by all raters at the same time in a group-based approach for 90 per cent of individuals. It is a dialogue rather than a survey, and the only rule is that every individual must carry out at least one per year. The purpose of the system is to 'improve performance and enable people to learn and grow' (p. 38). Each group has a trained facilitator who supports both appraisers and appraisees. Different individuals have reacted differently to the approach, as might be expected: one individual saw it as empowerment, and many found that there was a great advantage in seeing the world from other people's point of view. Storr reports on one individual who received similar feedback from the group to that which she had received previously, from her manager, but hearing it from the six members of the group had a much stronger effect on her. Individuals often used their first experience of the process in a general way to ask the group what they should start doing, stop doing, continue doing or do differently. Over time, however, individuals began to ask more specific questions.

Source: Summarised from F. Storr (2000) 'This is not a circular', *People Management*, 11 May, pp. 38–40.

ACTIVITY 13.3

Think of your current or previous role, in paid employment or any other capacity, and:

1 Identify one or two critical incidents (such as making a presentation or attending an important meeting for the first time).

2 Identify a longer-term activity you have been involved in (such as a project group or working party).

For both of these identify who could have provided you with constructive feedback, and why, and what specific questions you would have asked of them.

Now think ahead. What plans can you make to incorporate feedback into an upcoming one-off or longer-term activity?

The formal process is a survey approach which involves the use of a carefully constructed questionnaire that is used with all the contributors of feedback. This questionnaire may be bought off the peg, providing a well-tested tool, or may be developed internally, providing a tool which is more precisely matched to the needs of the organisation. Whichever form is used, the essence is that it is based on behavioural competencies (for a more detailed explanation of these *see* Chapter 17), and their associated behaviours. Contributors will be asked to score, on a given scale, the extent to which the individual displays these behaviours. Using a well-designed questionnaire, distributed to a sufficient number of contributors and employing appropriate sophisticated analysis, for example specifically designed computer packages which are set up to detect and moderate collusion and bias on behalf of the contributors, should provide reliable and valid data for the individual. The feedback is usually presented to the individual in the form of graphs or bar charts showing comparative scores from different feedback groups, such as peers, subordinates, customers, where the average will be provided for each group, and single scores from line manager and self. In most cases the individual will have been able to choose the composition of the contributors in each group, for example which seven subordinates, out of a team of 10, will be asked to complete the feedback questionnaire. But beyond this the feedback will be anonymous as only averages for each group of contributors will be reported back, except for the line manager's score. The feedback will need to be interpreted by an internal or external facilitator, and done via a face-to-face meeting. It is generally recommended that the individual will need some training in the nature of the system and how to receive feedback, and the contributors will need some training on how to provide feedback. The principle behind the idea of feedback is that individuals can then use this information to change their behaviours and to improve performance, by setting and meeting development goals and an action plan.

Reported benefits include a stronger ownership of development goals, a climate of constructive feedback, improved communication over time and an organisation which is more capable of change as continuous feedback and improvement have become part of the way people work (Cook and Macauley 1997). Useful texts on designing and implementing a system include Edwards and Ewen (1996) from the US perspective and Ward (1995) from the UK perspective. A brief 'how to do it guide' is Goodge and Watts (2000).

Difficulties and dilemmas

As with all processes and systems there needs to be clarity about the purpose. Most authors distinguish between developmental uses, which they identify as fairly safe and a good way of introducing such a system, and other uses, such as to determine pay awards. There seems to be an almost universal view that using these data for pay purposes is not advisable, and in the literature from the United States there is clearly a concern about the legal ramifications of doing this. Ward (1998) provides a useful framework for considering the different applications of this type of feedback, and reviews in some detail other applications such as using 360-degree feedback as part of a training course to focus attention for each individual on what he or she needs to get out of the course. Other applications he suggests include using 360-degree feedback as an approach to team building, as a method of performance appraisal/management, for organisation development purposes and to evaluate training and development. Edwards and Ewen (1996) suggest that it can be used for nearly all HR systems, using selection, training and development, recognition and the allocation of job assignments as examples.

Most approaches to 360-degree feedback require rater confidentiality as well as clarity of purpose, and this can be difficult to maintain with a small team, so raters may feel uncomfortable about being open and honest. In their research Pillutla and Ronson (2006) demonstrate how peer evaluations may be biased and warn against recruitment, reward and promotion decisions being made on this basis. The dangers of collusion and bias need to be eliminated, and it is suggested that the appropriate software systems can achieve this, but they are of course expensive, as are well-validated off-the-peg systems.

Follow-up is critical and if the experience of 360-degree feedback is not built on via the construction of development goals and the support and resources to fulfil these, the process may be viewed negatively and may be demotivating. There is an assumption that the provision of such feedback will motivate the individuals receiving it to develop and improve their performance, but Morgan and Cannan (2005) found very mixed results in their Civil Service research. One-third of their respondents were not motivated to act on the feedback and in this case felt that the 360-degree process was an isolated act with lack of follow-up, depending heavily on the proactivity of the individuals involved, with little support.

London *et al.* (1997) report concerns about the way systems are implemented, and that nearly one-third of respondents they surveyed experienced negative effects. Atwater and his colleagues (2002) found some negative reactions such as reduced effort, dissatisfaction with peers who provided the feedback and a lower commitment to colleagues. Fletcher and Baldry (2001) note that there are contradictions in the results from 360-degree feedback so far, and they suggest that further research is needed on how feedback affects self-esteem, motivation, satisfaction and commitment. The DTI (2001) suggested that sufficient resources need to be devoted to planning a system and that it should be piloted before general use. Clearly, 360-degree feedback needs to be handled carefully and sensitively and in the context of an appropriate organisational climate so that it is not experienced as a threat. The DTI (2001) suggested that there needs to be a climate of openness and trust for 360-degree feedback to work. Atwater *et al.* (2002) suggest that to counteract any negative effects it is important to prepare people for making their own ratings and on how they can provide honest and constructive feedback to others, ensure confidentiality and anonymity of raters, make sure the feedback is used developmentally and owned by the person being rated (for example that person may be the only one to receive the report), provide post-feedback coaching and encouragement and encourage people to follow up the feedback they have received.

WINDOW ON PRACTICE

Johnson (2001) reports on the merger between two pharmaceuticals companies – UniChem from the UK and Alliance Sante from France to form Alliance UniChem. In an attempt to focus managers from diverse cultures on a single vision the HR department concentrated on all aspects of performance management, in particular 360-degree feedback which was felt to be a pragmatic and practical tool. Four key values were identified: excellence, service, innovation and partnership, and competencies were drawn up to reflect these. The process had to be introduced very sensitively as 360-degree feedback was virtually unheard of in three countries covered by the company – Italy, Spain and Portugal, and in France it was seen very much as an American tool and regarded with considerable suspicion.

The most senior managers went through the process first, and it was then piloted in different countries. The tool was developed to be used in five different languages, and the customised package adopted came with development activities for each competency, and coaching sessions to ensure that feedback was not interpreted without analysis and support. The whole process formed part of a self-development programme.

Source: Summarised from R. Johnson (2001) 'Doubled entente',
People Management, Vol. 7, No. 9, 3 May, pp. 38–9.

SUMMARY PROPOSITIONS

13.1 Employee performance management systems incorporate appraisal activity, but include other aspects such as a link to organisational objectives, an emphasis on ongoing review, motivation, coaching and support, and reinforcement/reward for performance achieved.

13.2 There is a conflict in many appraisal and performance management systems as managers frequently have a dual role as assessor and developer.

13.3 Current trends in sophisticated appraisal activity include greater employee ownership, emphasis on the 'how' as well as the 'what', emphasis on evidence collection from both manager and employee, and upward feedback to the line manager as well as downward feedback to the employee.

13.4 Most employee performance management systems focus on the individual, but there is a need to ensure that team contributions are not neglected and more importantly that team and individual goals do not conflict.

13.5 360-degree feedback is increasingly being used to provide individuals with a basis for changing behaviour and improving performance. It is important to use this process developmentally rather than linking it directly to pay awards.

GENERAL DISCUSSION TOPICS

1 In what ways is the concept of performance management different from the way in which management has been traditionally practised? What are the advantages and disadvantages for employees and employers?

2 360-degree feedback may have many advantages, but there is the argument that it can never really work because of the built-in biases, such as marking a boss well because you're due for a pay rise; marking yourself low so that you can be happily surprised by others' evaluations; marking peers down to make oneself look better. Discuss as many built-in biases as you can think of, and suggest how they might be tackled and whether substantive improvements could be made.

FURTHER READING

Cunneen, P. (2006) 'How to improve performance management', *People Management*, Vol. 12, No. 1, pp. 42–3.
Some brief and well-focused guidance for implementing a performance management system.

Kuvaas, B. (2006) 'Performance Appraisal satisfaction and employee outcomes: mediating and moderating roles of work motivation', *International Journal of Human Resource Management*, Vol. 17, No. 3, pp. 504–22.
And
Poon, J. (2004) 'Effects of performance appraisal politics on job satisfaction and turnover intention', *Personnel Review*, Vol. 33, No. 3, pp. 322–34.
These articles reflect a stream of research connecting looking at the outcomes of appraisal from the employee perspective, in particular focusing on job satisfaction, intention to quit and commitment. Comparing both articles provides an interesting country comparison, with savings banks being investigated in Norway by Kuvaas and a cross-sector study of part-time MBA students in Malaysia being carried out by Poon.

Nurse, L. (2005) 'Performance appraisal, employee development and organizational justice: exploring the linkages', *International Journal of Human Resource Management*, Vol. 16, No. 7, pp. 1176–94.
An interesting article which explores different ways in which performance appraisal (PA) contributes to organisational justice, which is a topic of increasing interest. Nurse identifies the way that PA contributes to procedural justice (fairness of the process by which PA decisions are made); distributive justice (fairness of the outcomes and rewards from PA) and interactional justice. The research was carried out with a cross-section of organisations in Barbados.

Swinburne, P. (2001) 'How to use feedback to improve performance', *People Management*, Vol. 7, No. 11, 31 May, pp. 46–7.

Short but extremely helpful and full of practical detail. Excellent guidelines on the dos and don'ts of giving feedback and some very useful tips for receiving feedback.

REFERENCES

Armstrong, M. and Baron, A. (1998a) *Performance Management – The New Realities*. London: IPD.

Armstrong, M. and Baron, A. (1998b) 'Out of the Tick Box', *People Management*, 23 July, pp. 38–41.

Atwater, L., Waldman, D. and Brett, J. (2002) 'Understanding and optimising multi-source feedback', *Human Resource Management*, Vol. 41, No. 2, Summer, pp. 193–208.

Audit Commission (2002) *Performance Breakthrough: improving performance in public sector organizations*. London: The Audit Commission.

Barlow, G. (1989) 'Deficiencies and the perpetuation of power: latent functions in management appraisal', *Journal of Management Studies*, Vol. 26, No. 5, pp. 499–518.

Bevan, S. and Thompson, M. (1992) 'An overview of policy and practice', *Personnel Management in the UK: an anaylsis of the issues*. London: IPM.

Borman, W. (1997) '360° ratings: an analysis of assumptions and a research agenda for evaluating their validity', *Human Resource Management Review*, Vol. 7, Autumn, pp. 247–68.

Brown, M. and Heywood, J. (2005) 'Performance Appraisal systems: Determinants and change', *British Journal of Industrial Relations*, Vol. 43, No. 4, pp. 659–79.

Clark, G. (2005) 'Performance Management Strategies', in G. Salaman, J. Storey and J. Billsberry (eds), *Strategic Human Resource Management: Theory and Practice*. London: The Open University in association with Sage.

Coates, G. (1994) 'Performance appraisal as icon: Oscar winning performance or dressing to impress?', *International Journal of Human Resource Management*, No. 1, February.

Cook, S. and Macauley, S. (1997) 'How colleagues and customers can help improve team performance', *Team Performance Management*, Vol. 3, No. 1.

DTI (2001) *360 degree feedback: Best practice guidelines* (Prof C. Farrell).

Edwards, M.R. and Ewen, A.J. (1996) *360 Degree Feedback*. New York: Amacom, American Management Association.

Egan, G. (1995) 'A clear path of peak performance', *People Management*, 18 May, pp. 34–7.

Fletcher, C. and Baldry, C. (2001) 'Multi-source feedback systems: a research perspective', in I. Robertson and C. Cooper (eds), *Personnel Psychology and HRM*. Chichester: John Wiley and Sons Ltd.

Fletcher, C. and Williams, R. (1992) *Performance Management in the UK: Organisational experience*. London: IPM.

Garratt, B. (1990) *Creating a Learning Organisation*. Hemal Hempstead: Director Books.

Goodge, P. and Watts, P. (2000) 'How to manage 360° feedback', *People Management*, 17 February, pp. 50–2.

Grint, K. (1993) 'What's wrong with performance appraisals? – a critique and a suggestion', *Human Resource Management Journal*, Vol. 3, No. 3, pp. 61–77.

Hendry, C., Bradley, P. and Perkins, S. (1997) 'Missed a motivator?', *People Management*, 15 May, pp. 20–5.

Hendry, C., Woodward, S., Bradley, P. and Perkins, S. (2000) 'Performance and rewards: cleaning out the stables', *Human Resource Management Journal*, Vol. 10, No. 3, pp. 46–62.

Hogetts, R., Luthans, F. and Slocum, J. (1999) 'Strategy and HRM initiatives for the '00s: environment redefining roles and boundaries, linking competencies and resources', *Organizational Dynamics*, Autumn, p. 7.

Houldsworth, E. (2003) 'Managing Individual performance', paper presented to the CIPD National Conference, Harrogate, 22–24 November 2003.

Houldsworth, E. (2004) 'Managing Performance', in D. Rees and R. McBain (eds), *People Management: Challenges and Opportunities*. Basingstoke: Macmillan.

Houldsworth, E., Jirasinghe, D. and Everall, K. (2005) 'How can HR get the measure of performance management?', *People Management*, Vol. 11, No. 16, 11 August, p. 48.

Hurley, S. (1998) 'Application of team-based 360° feedback systems', *Team Performance Management*, Vol. 4, No. 5.

IDS (2003) *IDS Studies: Performance Management*, No. 748, April, London: IDS.

IDS (2005) *IDS Studies: Performance Management*, No. 796, April, London: IDS.

IRS (2001) 'Performance appraisal must try harder', *IRS Employment Trends*, No. 724, March, pp. 2–3.

IRS (2005a) 'Appraisals (1): not living up to expectations', *IRS Employment Review*, No. 828, 29 July, pp. 9–15.

IRS (2005b) 'Appraisals (2): learning from practice and experience', *IRS Employment Review*, No. 829, 12 August, pp. 13–17.

Johnson, R. (2001) 'Doubled entente', *People Management*, Vol. 7, No. 9, 3 May, pp. 38–9.

Johnson, R. (2006) 'Orange Blossoms', *People Management*, Vol. 12, No. 21, 26 October, pp. 56–60.

Katzenbach, J.R. (1997) 'The myth of the top management team', *Harvard Business Review*, November–December, pp. 82–91.

Katzenbach, J.R. and Smith, D.K. (1993) 'The discipline of teams', *Harvard Business Review*, March–April.

Locke, E. (1968) 'Towards a theory of task performance and incentives', *Organisational Behaviour and Human Performance*, Vol. 3, No. 2, pp. 157–89.

Locke, E. and Latham, G. (1990) *A Theory of Goal Setting and Task Performance*. Englewood Cliffs, NJ: Prentice-Hall.

London, M., Smither, J. and Adsit, D. (1997) 'Accountability: the achilles heel of multi-source feedback', *Group and Organizational Dynamics*, Vol. 22, No. 2, pp. 162–84.

Longenecker, C. (1997) 'Why managerial performance appraisals are ineffective: causes and lessons', *Career Development International*, Vol. 2, No. 5.

Mabey, C. and Salaman, G. (1995) *Strategic Human Resource Management*. Oxford: Blackwell.

Morgan, A. and Cannan, K. (2005) '360° feedback: a critical enquiry', *Personnel Review*, Vol. 34, No. 6, pp. 663–80.

Moxon, P. (1993) *Building a Better Team*. Aldershot: Gower in association with ITD.

Newton, T. and Findlay, P. (1996) 'Playing God? – the performance of appraisal', *Human Resource Management Journal*, Vol. 6, No. 3, pp. 42–58.

Pillutla, M. and Ronson, S. (2006) 'Survival of the similar', *People Management*, Vol. 12, No. 6, 23 March, pp. 36–7.

Roberts, Z. (2004) 'Q&A: "We must move on"', *People Management*, Vol. 10, No. 10, 20 May, pp. 16–17.

Rose, M. (2000) 'Target Practice', *People Management*, 23 November, pp. 44–5.

Scott, A. (2006) 'Intensive care', *People Management*, Vol. 12, No. 9, 4 May, pp. 14–15.

Sewell, G. and Wilkinson, B. (1992) 'Someone to watch over me: surveillance, discipline and the just-in-time process', *Sociology*, Vol. 26, pp. 271–89.

Storr, F. (2000) 'This is not a circular', *People Management*, 11 May, pp. 38–40.

Townley, B. (1989) 'Selection and appraisal: reconstituting social relations', in J. Storey (ed.), *New Perspectives on Human Resource Management*. London: Routledge.

Townley, B. (1993) 'Performance appraisal and the emergence of management', *Journal of Management Studies*, Vol. 30, No. 2, pp. 27–44.

Varma, A., Pichler, S. and Srinivas, E. (2005) 'The role of interpersonal affect in performance appraisal: evidence from two samples – the US and India', *International Journal of Human Resource Management*, Vol. 16, No. 11, pp. 2029–44.

van Vijfeijken, H., Kleingeld, A., van Tuijl, H. and Algera, J. (2006) 'Interdependence and fit in team performance management', *Personnel Review*, Vol. 35, No. 1, pp. 98–117.

Vroom, V. (1964) *Work and Motivation*. Chichester: John Wiley.

Ward, P. (1995) 'A 360 degree turn for the better', *People Management*, 9 February.

Williams, R. (2002) *Managing Employee Performance*. London: Thompson Learning.

An extensive range of additional materials, including multiple choice questions, answers to questions and links to useful websites can be found on the Human Resource Management Companion Website at **www.pearsoned.co.uk/torrington**.

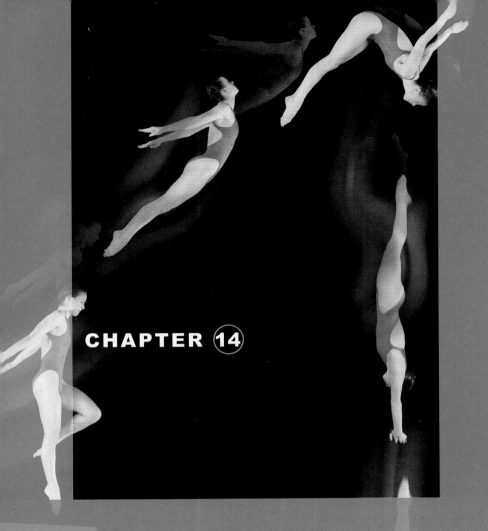

CHAPTER (14)

LEADERSHIP AND CHANGE

THE OBJECTIVES OF THIS CHAPTER ARE TO:

1   Introduce a working definition which reflects the general nature of leadership

2   Examine the trait approach to leadership

3   Examine the style (behavioural) and contingency approaches to leadership

4   Explore the nature of heroic and post-heroic leadership

5   Present a traditional view of the process of leading change and contrast this with a learning perspective

6   Relate approaches to organisational change and leadership style

Leadership is one of the most loaded and misunderstood words in management. Individual managers are often seduced by concepts of leadership that show them to be knights in shining armour with superhuman qualities and (this is the really dangerous bit) adoring followers. The followers rarely have that view of their managers. Similarly change is often presented in terms of how leaders can push or drive change through using change levers and the force of their personality. Change is often seen as something which is done to employees rather than something which employees participate in, seeking opportunities to improve the way they work and to use their skills and abilities to the full.

We must not, however, underestimate the importance of leadership. There are indeed sometimes needs for individual leaders who have outstanding personal qualities and who achieve extraordinary change in their business. Sometimes more subtle leadership qualities are more important, and there are infinitely more roles which call on different and more modest leadership skills, which can be learned and which are equally important, even if they do not merit shining armour and a white charger.

Understanding of both leadership and change was well developed in the second half of the twentieth century and it is this work which is the basis of our understanding and analysis today. The one major addition of recent years has been an appreciation of the impact of the changing circumstances of contemporary business and the role of women. All of the twentieth-century studies and theories were based on two complementary assumptions; first, the business norm was of large, stable organisations steadily getting bigger; second, management was almost exclusively a male activity, with male norms. This led to explanations and suggestions based on those two givens. We now see a weakening of both these assumptions. Effective businesses are not necessarily large, growing organisations and there are many more women in the workforce and in management positions within it. Although charismatic leaders (a predominantly male concept) are still needed in some situations, empowering leaders are increasingly required. Although leading change clearly retains value, a learning approach to change brings another dimension to the achievement of change. We reach this at the close of the chapter, but we can only get there by starting further back.

LEADERSHIP AND MANAGEMENT

Northouse (2006) suggests that there are four components that characterise leadership: that leadership is a process; it involves influence; it occurs within a group context; and it involves goal attainment. This corresponds with Shackleton's (1995) definition, which we shall use as a working definition for the remainder of the chapter:

> Leadership is the process in which an individual influences other group members towards the attainment of group or organizational goals. (Shackleton 1995, p. 2)

This definition is useful as it leaves open the question of whether leadership is exercised in a commanding or a facilitative manner. It does suggest, however, that the leader in some way motivates others to act in such a way as to achieve group goals.

The definition also makes no assumptions about who the leader is; it may or may not be the nominal head of the group. Managers, therefore, may or may not be leaders, and leaders may or may not be managers. Some authors distinguish very clearly between the nature of management and the nature of leadership but this draws on a particular perspective, that of the transformational leader, and we will consider this in the section on whether the organisation needs heroes. This is a school of thought that concentrates on the one leader at the top of the organisation, which is very different from organisations and individuals who use the terms manager and leader interchangeably with nothing more than a vague notion that managers should be leaders. Indeed, any individual may act as a manager one day and a leader the next, depending on the situation. In addition we should not assume that leadership is always a downwards process, as sometimes employees and managers lead upwards (Hollington 2006).

The flow of articles on leadership continues unabated, but it would be a mistake to think that there is an ultimate truth to be discovered; rather, there is a range of perspectives from which we can try to make sense of leadership and motivation. Grint (1997) puts it well when he comments that

> What counts as leadership appears to change quite radically across time and space.
> (p. 3)

In the following three sections we will look at three questions which underlie virtually all the work on leadership. First, what are the traits of a leader, or an effective leader? Second, what is the 'best' leadership style or behaviour? Third, if different styles are appropriate at different times, what factors influence the desired style?

WHAT ARE THE TRAITS OF LEADERS AND EFFECTIVE LEADERS?

Trait approaches, which were the earliest to be employed, seek to identify the traits of leaders – in other words what characterises leaders as opposed to those who are not leaders. These approaches rest on the assumption that some people were born to lead due to their personal qualities, while others are not. It suggests that leadership is only available to the chosen few and not accessible to all. These approaches have been discredited for this very reason and because there has been little consistency in the lists of traits that research has uncovered. However, this perspective is frequently resurrected.

Kilpatrick and Locke (1991), in a meta-analysis, did seem to find some consistency around the following traits: drive to achieve; the motivation to lead; honesty and integrity; self-confidence, including the ability to withstand setbacks, standing firm and being emotionally resilient; cognitive ability; and knowledge of the business. They also note the importance of managing the perceptions of others in relation to these characteristics. Northouse (2006) provides a useful historical comparison of the lists of traits uncovered in other studies. Perhaps the most well-known expression of the trait approach is the work relating to charismatic leadership. House (1976), for example, describes charismatic leaders as being dominant, having a strong desire to influence, being self-confident and having a strong sense of their own moral values. We will pick up on this concept of leadership in the later section on heroes.

In a slightly different vein Goleman (1998) carried out a meta-analysis of leadership competency frameworks in 188 different companies. These frameworks represented the competencies related to outstanding leadership performance. Goleman analysed the competencies into three groups: technical, cognitive and emotional, and found that, in terms of the ratios between the groups, emotional competencies 'proved to be twice as important as the others'. Goleman goes on to describe five components of emotional intelligence:

- **Self-awareness:** this he defines as a deep understanding of one's strengths, weaknesses, needs, values and goals. Self-aware managers are aware of their own limitations.

- **Self-regulation:** the control of feelings, the ability to channel them in constructive ways. The ability to feel comfortable with ambiguity and not panic.

- **Motivation:** the desire to achieve beyond expectations, being driven by internal rather than external factors, and to be involved in a continuous striving for improvement.

- **Empathy:** considering employees' feelings alongside other factors when decision making.

- **Social skill:** friendliness with a purpose, being good at finding common ground and building rapport. Individuals with this competency are good persuaders, collaborative managers and natural networkers.

Goleman's research is slightly different from previous work on the trait approach, as here we are considering what makes an effective leader rather than what makes a leader (irrespective of whether they are effective or not). It is also different in that Goleman refers to competencies rather than traits. There is a thorough discussion of competencies in Chapter 17; it is sufficient for now to say that competencies include a combination of traits and abilities, among other things. There is some debate over whether competencies can be developed in people. The general feeling is that some can and some cannot. Goleman maintains that the five aspects of emotional intelligence can be learned and provides an example in his article of one such individual. In spite of his argument we feel that it is still a matter for debate, and as many of the terms used by Goleman are similar to those of the previous trait models of leadership, we have categorised his model as an extension of the trait perspective. To some extent his work sits between the trait approach and the style approach which follows. It is interesting that a number of researchers and writers are recognising that there is some value in considering a mix of personality characteristics and behaviours, and in particular Higgs (2003) links this approach to emotional intelligence.

Rajan and van Eupen (1997) also consider that leaders are strong on emotional intelligence, and that this involves the traits of self-awareness, zeal, resilience and the ability to read emotions in others. They argue that these traits are particularly important in the development and deployment of people skills. Heifetz and Laurie (1997) similarly identify that in order for leaders to regulate emotional distress in the organisation, which is inevitable in change situations, the leader has to have 'the emotional capacity to tolerate uncertainty, frustration and pain' (p. 128). Along the same lines Goffee (2002) identifies that inspirational leaders need to understand and admit their own weaknesses (within reason); sense the needs of situations; have empathy and self-awareness.

ACTIVITY 14.1

Think of different leaders you have encountered – in particular those that were especially effective or ineffective:

1 What differences can you identify in terms of their traits (personal characteristics)?

2 What differences can you identify in terms of their behaviour?

3 Are the trait and behaviour lists connected in any way? If so how?

4 Which of these two approaches – trait or behaviour – do you find more useful in helping you to understand the nature of effective leadership?

WHAT IS THE 'BEST WAY TO LEAD'? LEADERSHIP STYLES AND BEHAVIOURS

Dissatisfaction with research on leadership that saw leadership as a set of permanent personal characteristics that describe the leader led to further studies that emphasised the nature of the leadership process – the interaction between leader and follower – aiming to understand how the leaders *behave* rather than what they *are*. The first such studies sought to find the 'best' leadership style; from this perspective leadership comprises an ideal set of behaviours that can be learned. Fulop *et al.* (1999) suggest that Douglas McGregor's (1960) work, *The Human Side of Enterprise*, can be understood from this perspective. McGregor argued that American corporations managed their employees as if they were work-shy, and needed constant direction, monitoring and control (theory 'x'), rather than as if they were responsible individuals who were willing and able to take on responsibility and organise their own work (theory 'y'). McGregor argued that the underlying assumptions of the manager determined the way he or she managed the employees and this in turn determined how the employees would react. Thus if employees were managed as if they operated on theory 'x' then they would act in a theory 'x' manner; conversely if employees were managed as if they operated on theory 'y' then they would respond as theory 'y' employees would respond. The message was that management style should reinforce theory 'y' and thus employees would take on responsibility, be motivated by what they were doing and work hard. Although the original book was written over forty years ago, this approach is being revisited (*see*, for example, Heil *et al.* 2000) and it fits well with the empowering or post-heroic approach to leadership that we discuss later in the chapter. Another piece of research from the style approach is that by Blake and Mouton (1964), who developed the famous 'Managerial Grid'. The grid is based on two aspects of leadership behaviour. One is concern for production, that is, task-oriented behaviours such as clarifying roles, scheduling work,

Table 14.1 Blake and Mouton's four leadership styles

High concern for people Low concern for production **Country Club management**	High concern for people High concern for production **Team management**
Low concern for people Low concern for production **Impoverished management**	Low concern for people High concern for production **Authority-compliance management**

Source: Adapted from R.R. Blake and J.S. Mouton (1964) *The Managerial Grid*. Houston, Texas: Gulf Publishing.

measuring outputs; the second is concern for people, that is, people-centred behaviour such as building trust, camaraderie, a friendly atmosphere. These two dimensions are at the heart of many models of leadership. Blake and Mouton proposed that individual leaders could be measured on a nine-point scale in each of these two aspects, and by combining them in grid form they identified the four leadership styles presented in Table 14.1.

Such studies, which are well substantiated by evidence, suggest that leadership is accessible for all people and that it is more a matter of learning leadership behaviour than of personality characteristics. Many leadership development courses have therefore been based around this model. However, as Northouse (2006) argues, there is an assumption in the model that the team management style (high concern for people and high concern for production; sometimes termed 9,9 management) is the ideal style; and yet this claim is not substantiated by the research. This approach also fails to take account of the characteristics of the situation and the nature of the followers.

WINDOW ON PRACTICE

A large organisation adopted the Managerial Grid as the framework for its leadership development programme. The programme was generally well accepted and successful application of the team management style was seen to be connected to future promotions. Most managers, on leaving the programme, set out to display 9,9 leadership behaviours. However, this had unexpected and undesirable consequences. Not only were team members daunted by their managers suddenly displaying a different style, but sometimes the 9,9 style was not appropriate in the circumstances in which it was used. The organisation eventually discontinued the programme due to the damage that it was causing.

Much of the recent work on the notion of transformational/heroic leadership, and empowering/post-heroic leadership, similarly assumes that what is being discussed is the one best way for a leader to lead, and we return to this leadership debate later on.

DO LEADERS NEED DIFFERENT STYLES FOR DIFFERENT SITUATIONS?

WINDOW ON PRACTICE

Goffee and Jones (2006) highlight the situational nature of leadership by using examples of key figures. They identify how Winston Churchill was an inspirational wartime leader but when this time and place were gone his 'bulldog' style was not well suited to leading the reconstruction of post-war Britain. As an alternative they name Nelson Mandela who is someone who could offer leadership across a wide range of contexts, adjusting from leading whilst in a prison cell on Robben Island to leading from Union House in Pretoria when he was released and was elected President of South Africa.

Source: Goffee, R. and Jones, G. (2006) 'The Lizard Kings',
People Management, Vol. 12, No. 2, 26 January, pp. 32–4.

A variety of models, sometimes termed contingency models, have been developed to address the importance of context in terms of the leadership process, and as a consequence these models become more complex. Many, however, retain the concepts of production-centred and people-centred behaviour as ways of describing leadership behaviour, but use them in a different way. Hersey and Blanchard (1988) developed a model which identified that the appropriate leadership style in a situation should be dependent on their diagnosis of the 'readiness', that is, developmental level or maturity, of their followers. The model is sometimes referred to as 'situational leadership', and works on the premise that leaders can 'adapt their leadership style to meet the demands of their environment' (Hersey and Blanchard 1988, p. 169). Readiness of followers is defined in terms of ability and willingness. Level of ability includes the experience, knowledge and skills that an individual possesses in relation to the particular task at hand; and level of willingness encompasses the extent to which the individual has the motivation and commitment, or the self-confidence, to carry out the task. Having diagnosed the developmental level of the followers, Hersey and Blanchard suggest, the leader then adapts his or her behaviour to fit. They identify two dimensions of leader behaviour: task behaviour, which is sometimes termed 'directive'; and relationship behaviour, which is sometimes termed 'supportive'. Task behaviour refers to the extent to which leaders spell out what has to be done. This includes 'telling people what to do, how to do it, when to do it, where to do it, and who is to do it' (Hersey 1985, p. 19). On the other hand, relationship behaviour is defined as 'the extent to which the leader engages in two-way or multi-way communication. The behaviours include listening, facilitating and supporting behaviours' (ibid.). The extent to which the leader emphasises each of these two types of behaviour results in the usual two-by-two matrix. The four resulting styles are identified, as shown in Table 14.2.

There is an assumption that the development path for any individual and required behaviour for the leader is to work through boxes 1, 2, 3 and then 4 in the matrix.

Table 14.2 Hersey and Blanchard's four styles of leadership

High relationship behaviour Low task behaviour Followers are able, but unwilling or insecure **Supportive (participating) style (3)**	High relationship behaviour High task behaviour Followers are unable, but willing or confident **Coaching (selling) style (2)**
Low relationship behaviour Low task behaviour Followers are both able and willing or confident **Delegation style (4)**	Low relationship behaviour High task behaviour Followers are unable and unwilling or insecure **Directing (telling) style (1)**

Source: Adapted from P. Hersey and K.H. Blanchard (1988) *Management of Organizational Behavior: Utilizing Human Resources*, 5th edn. Englewood Cliffs, NJ: Prentice-Hall International. © Copyright material, adapted and reprinted with the permission of Center for Leadership Studies, Escondido, CA92025.

Hersey and Blanchard produced questionnaires to help managers diagnose the readiness of their followers.

Other well-known contingency models include Fielder's (1967) contingency model where leadership behaviour is matched to three factors in the situation: the nature of the relationship between the leader and members, the extent to which tasks are highly structured and the position power of the leader. The appropriate leader behaviour (that is, whether it should be task oriented or relationship oriented) depends on the combination of these three aspects in any situation. Fielder's model is considered to be well supported by the evidence. The research was based on the relationship between style and performance in existing organisations in different contexts. For a very useful comparison of contingency models *see* Fulop *et al.* (1999).

WINDOW ON PRACTICE

Hilary Walmsley (1999) reports some of her work as a consultant with BUPA. One of the aims of the exercise she was involved in was to:

> raise individuals' awareness of their own management styles and encourage them to stop and think about which approach to adopt rather than automatically respond to every challenge in a similar way. (p. 48)

She recounts the experiences of Brian Atkins, General Manager of BUPA's Gatwick Park and Redwood Hospitals, as an illustration of this learning process. On joining the hospital group, which was undergoing a critical phase of change, in 1990, Atkins consciously used an authoritative leadership style, at the directive and controlling end of the spectrum. Once the hospital was soundly on course for recovery he began to use a more empowering and facilitative style. Atkins describes modern managers as 'style travellers', and suggests that they need to be skilled at using different styles, even though they may naturally prefer one approach. Walmsley notes that managers are tempted to use the same styles out of habit, and are often unaware of alternative styles they could use.

Table 14.3 Six leadership styles reported by Goleman

Coercive style	Leader demands immediate compliance
Authoritative style	Leader mobilises people towards a vision
Affiliative style	Leader creates emotional bonds and harmony
Democratic style	Leaders use participation to build consensus
Pacesetting style	Leader expects excellence and self-direction from followers
Coaching style	Leader develops people for the future

Source: Reprinted by permission of *Harvard Business Review*. Adapted from 'Leadership that gets results', by D. Goleman, March–April, pp. 80 and 82–3. Copyright © 2000 by the Harvard Business School Publishing Corporation; all rights reserved.

Goleman (2000) reports the results of some research carried out by Hay/McBer who sampled almost 20 per cent of a database of 20,000 executives. The results were analysed to identify six different leadership styles, which are shown in Table 14.3, but most importantly Goleman reports that 'leaders with the best results do not rely on only one leadership style' (p. 78).

Goleman goes on to consider the appropriate context and impact of each style, and argues that the more styles the leader uses the better. We have already reported Goleman's work on emotional intelligence, and he links this with the six styles by suggesting that leaders need to understand how the styles relate back to the different competencies of emotional intelligence so that they can identify where they need to focus their leadership development.

ACTIVITY 14.2

For each of Goleman's six styles think of a leader you have worked with, or know of. For each of these individuals write a list of the behaviours that they use. Then consider the impact that these behaviours have on followers.

Do the behaviours have the same impact on all followers? If not, why not?

In a less mechanistic vein Goffee and Jones (2006) suggest that what works for one leader will not necessarily work for another. Whilst adaptability of styles to suit different contexts is key, aspiring leaders need to discover what it is about themselves that they can mobilize in a leadership situation. Given this perspective leadership appears very personal.

One of the differences between the contingency models we have just discussed and the 'best' style models is the implications for development. The Blake and Mouton model suggests leaders can be developed to lead in the one best way. The Hersey and Blanchard model, and most other contingency models, stress the flexibility of the leader – to learn to lead differently with different employees depending on their needs; hence the leader should learn many styles and learn to diagnose the needs of their employees. Fielder's model, however, emphasises matching the leader to the context (a selection decision), rather than developing leaders in the context.

DO WE REALLY NEED HEROES?

A different approach to understanding leadership is transformational leadership, which focuses on the leader's role at a strategic level, so there is a concentration on the one leader at the top of the organisaton. There is a wide range of literature in this vein, most of it written in the 1980s. Since that time the academic literature may have moved on but the image of the transformational leader still remains widely attractive. While this is a different approach it links back to our original three questions about leadership. Transformational leadership shows elements of the trait approach, as leaders are seen to 'have' charisma, which sets them apart as extraordinary and exceptional, and they are also seen to use a set of 'ideal' behaviours, with the assumption in many writings that this is the 'best' approach.

The leader is usually characterised as a hero, although Steyrer (1998) proposes that there are other charismatic types such as the father figure, the saviour and the king. Such leaders appear to know exactly what they are doing and how to 'save' the organisation from its present predicament (and consequently such leadership is found more often when organisations are in trouble). Leaders involve followers by generating a high level of commitment, partly due to such leaders focusing on the needs of followers and expressing their vision in such a way that it satisfies these needs. They communicate high expectations to followers and also the firm belief that followers will be able to achieve these goals. In this way the leader promotes self-confidence in the followers and they are motivated to achieve more than they ordinarily expect to achieve. In terms of behaviours, perhaps the most important is the vision of the future that the leader offers and that he or she communicates this and dramatises this to the followers. Such leaders are able to help the followers make sense of what is going on and why as well as what needs to be done in the future. It is from this perspective that the distinction between management and leadership is often made. Bennis and Nanus (1985), for example, suggest leadership is path finding while management is path following; and that leadership is about doing the right thing whereas management is about doing things right. Kotter (1990) identified leaders as establishing a direction (whereas managers plan and budget); leaders align people with the vision (whereas managers organise things); leaders motivate and inspire (whereas managers control and solve problems); and leaders encourage change (whereas managers encourage order and predictability). Other writers analysing leadership from this perspective include Tichy and Devanna (1986) and Bass (1985), and there is a wide research base to support the findings. The approach does have a great strength in taking followers' needs into account and seeking to promote their self-confidence and potential, and the idea of the knight in shining armour is very attractive and potentially exciting – Tichy and Devanna, for example, present the process of such leadership as a three-act drama. However, in spite of the emphasis on process there is also an emphasis on leadership characteristics which harks back to the trait approach to leadership, which has been characterised as elitist. There is also the ethical concern of one person wielding such power over others.

Maybe we should ask whether organisations really require such leaders. A very different conception of leadership is now offered as an alternative, partly a reaction to the previous approach, and partly a response to a changing environment. This is termed empowering or post-heroic leadership, and could be described as the currently favoured ideal way to lead.

WINDOW ON PRACTICE

Goffee and Jones (2006) provide an excellent example of leadership by someone lower down in the organisation. They met Marcia, who was a cleaning supervisor in a large New York office block. She had the ability to read people from different cultures, and although often brash was able to use humour to great effect, not tolerating slovenly cleaning. She managed in unpromising circumstances to forge a high-performing team as members knew she demanded that the job be done well but at the same time she cared about them.

Source: Goffee, R. and Jones, G. (2006) 'The Lizard Kings',
People Management, Vol. 12, No. 2, 26 January, pp. 32–34.

Fulop *et al.* (1999) identify factors in a rapidly changing turbulent environment which by the 1990s dilute the appropriateness of concentrating on the one leader at the top of the organisation. These factors include: globalisation making centralisation more difficult; technology enabling better sharing of information; and change being seen as a responsibility of all levels of the organisation – not just the top. They also note a dissatisfaction with corporate failures, identify few transformational leaders as positive role models, suggest that such a model of male authoritarian leadership is less relevant, and in particular that the macho leader with all the answers does not necessarily fit well with the encouragement of creativity and innovation. In addition they suggest that increasing teamwork and an increasing emphasis on knowledge workers mean that employees will be less responsive now to a transformational leader. The emphasis has therefore moved away from understanding the traits and style of the one leader at the top of the organisation who knows how to solve all the organisation's problems, to how empowering or post-heroic leaders can facilitate many members of the organisation in taking on leadership roles. In this context Applebaum *et al.* (2003) comment that female leadership styles are more effective in today's team-based consensually driven organisations. Many commentators speak of leaders with integrity and humility, the ability to select good people and to remove barriers so they can fulfil their potential and perform (*see*, for example, Collins 2003; Alimo-Metcalfe and Alban-Metcalfe 2002).

The leader becomes a developer who can help others identify problems as opportunities for learning, and who can harness the collective intelligence of the organisation, and Fulop *et al.* (1999) note that this means in practice that they encourage the development of a learning organisation. Senge (1990), who is a protagonist of the learning organisation (*see* Chapter 12 for further details), sees the leader's new roles in encouraging a learning organisation as designer, teacher and steward, rather than a traditional charismatic decision maker. He suggests that leaders should *design* the organisation in terms of vision, purpose, core values and the structures by which these ideas can be translated into business decisions. However, he also suggests that the leader should involve people at all levels in this design task. It is the role of the leader not to identify the right strategy, but to encourage strategic thinking in the organisation, and to design effective learning processes to make this happen. The leader's role as a *teacher* is not to teach people the correct view of reality, but to help employees gain more insight into the current reality. The leader therefore coaches, guides and facilitates. As a *steward* the leader acts as a servant in taking responsibility for the impact of his or her leadership on others, and in the sense that he or she overrides his or her own self-interest by personal commitment to the organisation's larger mission. To play this role effectively, Senge suggests, the leader will need many new skills, in particular vision-making skills – a never-ending sharing of ideas and asking for feedback. Skills that will encourage employees to express and test their views of the world are also key. These involve actively seeking others' views, experimenting, encouraging enquiry and distinguishing 'the way things are done' from 'the way we think things are done'.

WINDOW ON PRACTICE

The role that leaders play in the organisation in the twenty-first century is seen by some as very different from the hero roles of the past, and leaders are no longer expected always to know the solutions to problems.

Williams (2000), who talks about enabling and empowering leadership, suggests that 'twenty first century leaders are not expected to be all-knowing gurus and peddlers of panaceas' (p. 113). However, they are expected to know the right questions to ask, as Heifetz and Laurie (1997) suggest: 'leaders do not need to know all the answers. They do need to know the right questions' (p. 124).

Building on this a speaker from Henley Management College (Radio 4, 25 February 2001) argued that leaders need to be able to admit that they do not know all the answers, and that there was a paradox in leadership, as leaders need to display both boldness and humility.

Taking this one step further Anne Atkinson (Radio 4, 29 November 2000), speaking in relation to the tussle over who won the American presidential election, described the leader as a servant, arguing that the best leaders are unwilling leaders and do not seek power, but instead have a desire to benefit the people they lead.

These ideas take us some way from the charismatic and transformational view of the leader.

This changing perspective on leadership is well demonstrated by a survey on leadership skills reported by Rajan and van Eupen (1997). The research is based on interviews with 49 top business leaders, 50 HR directors and a postal questionnaire of 375 companies in the service sector. They asked what were the most important leadership skills during the period 1995–7 and compared the results with those of a similar survey conducted in the late 1980s. They found that the key skill was seen to be inspiring trust and motivation followed by visioning skills and ability, willingness and self-discipline to listen in 1995–7 compared with strategic thinking followed by entrepreneurial skills and originality in the late 1980s. The change in skills base reflects very well the change in the idealised leadership role and the increasing importance of facilitative people-related skills. They also note the prediction that the future will require an equal balance of traditionally masculine and feminine personality traits.

Higgs (2003) argues that leaders need a combination of skills and personality: envisioning, engaging, enabling, enquiring and developing skills are needed, together with authenticity, integrity, will, self-belief and self-awareness.

From a slightly different perspective Heifetz and Laurie (1997) propose six guiding principles of post-heroic leadership, and they conclude that leadership is about learning and that the idea of having a vision and aligning people to this is bankrupt. The idea of one leader at the top creating major changes in order to solve a one-off challenge is no longer appropriate, as organisations now face a constant stream of adaptive challenges, and leadership is required of many in the organisation, not just one person at the top. They argue that employees should be allowed to identify and solve problems themselves and learn to take responsibility. The role of the leader is to develop collective self-confidence. As Grint (1997) puts it, 'the apparent devolvement (or desertion – depending on your perspective) of responsibility has become the new standard in contemporary models of leadership' (p. 13). For further discussion on the devolution of responsibility *see* Case 14.1 on this book's companion website **www.pearsoned.co.uk/torrington**.

These visions of leadership are very attractive but they do require a dramatic change in thinking for both leaders and followers. For leaders there is the risk of giving away power, learning to trust employees, developing new skills, developing a different perspective of their role and overriding self-interest. For followers there is the challenge of taking responsibility – which some may welcome, but others shun. Yet, if sustained competitive advantage is based on human capital and collective intelligence, it is difficult to relegate this perspective to 'just an ideal'.

While empowering leaders have been shown to fit with the current climate we may sometimes need heroic leaders. Kets de Vries (2003) makes the point that heroic leadership will never die as change makes people anxious and we need heroic leaders to calm them down, but since no one can live up to the expectations of heroic leaders, they will eventually become a disappointment. We conclude with the thought that there is no one best way – different leaders and different leader behaviours are needed at different times. For an example of a mixed approach to leadership *see* Case 14.2 on the companion website, **www.pearsoned.co.uk/torrington**, about Tim Smit of the Eden Project.

LEADERSHIP AND CHANGE

We are all now familiar with the mantra that change is a constant in our world and that its pace is increasing. Inevitably therefore leaders will find themselves leading, promoting, encouraging and stimulating change as a key part of their role. In this last part of the chapter we will briefly review the nature of organisational change, explain a traditional perspective on managing and leading change and contrast this with a learning perspective suggested by Binney and Williams (2005). We will then link these two perspectives back to perspectives on the nature of leadership.

There is a good deal of literature identifying the drivers for change (*see*, for example, Greenhalgh 2001), such as competitor behaviour, customer expectations, or a change of technology, with distinctions being made as to whether the drivers are external or internal. Other distinctions are made as to whether the change is proactive or reactive. A distinction is also made between change that is revolutionary and that which is evolutionary or incremental. It is sometimes suggested that transformational change is equivalent to revolutionary change, but we suggest that evolutionary change can equally be transformational. However, underlying all of this is the fundamental reason for change, which is organisational survival and competitiveness in the complex and global world which we have created.

The nature of change has also been hotly debated and the emphasis has increasingly been on transformational change. Change may involve movements in organisational shape, size, structure, rewards, values, beliefs, systems, procedures, roles, responsibilities, culture, tasks and behaviour. Whilst transformational change may involve all of these it is generally agreed that transformational change is more than this and involves fundamentally new ways of understanding what the organisation is for and is doing. Beckhard (1992), for example, suggested that transformational change may involve the organisation's shape, structure or nature, but more than this requires a re-examination of the organisation's mission and a vision of a different future state of the organisation. As Binney and Williams (2005) suggest transformational change is about the change in mental models of what the organisation is about, sometimes referred to as change in the organisational paradigm.

All change, no matter how small, presents a challenge to leaders and followers alike. For leaders there is the challenge of making the required changes happen in reality, and for followers there is the challenge of coping with changes over which they often have no control and for which they have potentially no desire. Such changes invariably involve them in engaging in new activities, behaviours and thinking, and the even more difficult task of letting go and unlearning old activities, behaviours and thinking. In trying to understand how employees cope with change, in an effort to then manipulate this, managers have used models from other parts of the social sciences. An example is the Kubler-Ross change curve (1997) which tracks the stages an individual generally experiences when coping with loss, a model that was developed in the context of bereavement.

In addition to this there has been a long-running school of thought which proposes that leaders can plan and manage change given the right processes and tools to use. There is a variety of models in the literature but most focus on such stages as:

- identify the need for change
- define our current state
- vision the future desired state
- identify the gap
- diagnose capacity for change including barriers and how they can be overcome
- plan actions and behaviours needed to close the gap
- implement required actions
- manage the transition
- constantly reinforce changes, sustain momentum and measure progress

More details on such processes are readily available in the literature; *see*, for example, Hayes (2007) and Walton (1999).

However this approach to change relies on a rational view of the organisation, and as Binney and Williams (2005) suggest a model of the organisation as a machine. They outline the limitations of such an approach, including: unintended consequences of change, its messiness, the gap in perceptions between leaders and followers, the fact that visions often do not inspire. They also point out the assumption that change is something which is done to organisations, rather like the assumption that leadership is done to followers rather than with them (Goffee and Jones 2006). Eriksson (2004) highlights the legitimate role of emotion in the implementation of change and draws our attention to the work of Kanter (1983) who identifies change as exhilarating when done by us and disturbing when done to us. There is an assumption that employee resistance to change is a characteristic of the individual psyche that, ultimately, has to be overcome, rather than that resistance stems from legitimate reasons and is partly a result of the way that change is conceived and led in the organisation.

Research by Les Worrall and Cary Cooper (2006) provides us with a managerial/employee perspective on change, rather than that of the leader(s) at the top of the organisation. They suggest that change is reaching epidemic proportions. In their survey they found that 90 per cent of managers were affected by change (97 per cent in the public sector), compared with 83 per cent five years earlier. In addition over half the managers were affected by three or more forms of change (increased from 45 per cent). Managers felt that changes were a result of cost reductions and created work intensification and increased pressure to perform. This had negatively affected their morale (61 per cent), sense of job security (56 per cent) motivation (51 per cent), sense of employee well-being (48 per cent) and loyalty (47 per cent). Managers felt they were subject to greater top-down control, and greater scrutiny, and felt overloaded with insufficient time and resources to do their job at the standard they felt appropriate. Absence levels were significantly higher in those organisations with cost-cutting programmes, and larger proportions of managers reported insomnia, persistent headaches, appetite problems, muscular tension, constant tiredness and other symptoms, and the researchers suggest that such levels of change are literally making managers ill. Such problems interestingly did not apply to the same extent to directors, and in addition they felt much more positively about the changes taking place, reporting lower levels of stressors.

In a different study, Eriksson (2004) found that change programmes resulted in employees exhibiting signs of depression and experiencing feelings of failure.

The above create real concerns about the leadership of change, and Binney and Williams (2005) propose a way to reconceptualise change, based on the metaphor of the organisation as a living system rather than a machine. They suggest that this perspective helps us see organisations as adaptive (as behaviour and thinking shift of their own accord in response to the pressure of events); as self-organising (to achieve an equilibrium); as interdependent with their environment (interacting in complex ways); and as dynamic.

They propose that this perspective suggests change is natural, if painful, and that the challenge is to release the potential for change rather than drive it. In addition they identify the need for some stability as well as change. They suggest that this perspective encourages the view that managers cannot control change, and that the problem with a vision for the future is that it denigrates the present and the past of the organisation. A good example of this is the town of Crewe. Much effort and money is being put in to regenerate and develop the town, but whilst there are newcomers who feel this is an excellent change programme, there are many people who have been brought up in the town who feel that the changes are unnecessary and are spoiling things. The living organism approach also suggests that trying to copy excellence elsewhere is a fruitless task, as is a change consultant or chief executive telling people to change; changes, they suggest, emerge and the key is seeing the new pattern, drawing attention to it and reinforcing it. The acceptance that the future is unknowable and unpredictable is important, as is the need for leaders to recognise that they are also part of the problem, and acknowledge that people are not rational and that feelings and emotion are legitimate. They characterise this approach to change as a learning approach rather than a leading approach, but

Figure 14.1 Leaning into the future (Source: Binney, G. and Williams, C. (2005) 'The myth of managing change', in G. Salaman, J. Storey and J. Billsberry (eds), *Strategic Human Resource Management: Theory and Practice – A Reader*. London: Sage/Open University, p. 317.

recognise that both perspectives add value in a change situation; in order to reflect this they propose the concept of 'leaning into the future'. Figure 14.1 summarises their thinking.

If you look back to the characteristics of empowering leadership you will be able to see the commonality between this and the learning approach to change suggested by Binney and Williams (2005).

ACTIVITY 14.3

Explore the similarities and differences between the empowering approach to leadership and the learning approach to change.

WINDOW ON PRACTICE

Leadership and change

Hope (2006) explains how Lady Marie Stubbs turned round the inner London school after its previous Head, Philip Lawrence was murdered. Stubbs set out to make the children feel valued, first by physically transforming the building and second by welcoming them back to the school individually. Another way she approached this was to break down the division between teachers and pupils. For example, instead of locking the pupils out and the staff in at break times, she opened the school and created an atrium that students could use, with staff presence, and played music that the pupils would relate to. In the same vein she secured the part-time use of games pitches at Harrow Public School. She consulted the pupils on changes and gave them responsibility, such as handling reception for school visitors, focused on their aspirations and believed in them.

Edwards (2006) explains how Greg Dyke led the BBC. Whilst having a vision for the corporation Dyke constantly asked staff how he could improve, and really listened to their views. He worked on the basis that he wanted to demonstrate to staff that he cared about them, as people work better if they are valued than if they are afraid. He was not afraid to be himself, and to admit mistakes and say sorry where this was appropriate. He made an effort to look at things from the point of view of the staff, and considered their interests – persuading them that the changes were in their best interests rather than just telling them what to do. He made a great effort to be accessible to staff and when he left thousands of staff across the country staged protests.

Sources: Hope, K. (2006) 'Lessons Learnt', *People Management*, Vol. 12, No. 6, 23 March, pp. 30–1.
Edwards, C. (2006) 'On being Gregarious', *People Management*, Vol. 12, No. 8, 20 April, pp. 32–4.

ACTIVITY 14.4

Identify the similarities and differences in the approaches of Stubbs and Dyke.
   How would you describe their approach to leadership and their approach to change?

SUMMARY PROPOSITIONS

14.1   Leadership is a process where one person influences a group of others to achieve group or organisational goals – leadership is thus about motivation.

14.2   The trait model of leadership, although often discredited, continues to play a part in our understanding of leadership.

14.3 Behavioural models are more helpful than earlier models as they concentrate on what leaders do rather than on what they are.

14.4 Some behavioural models offer a 'one best way' of leadership, but more sophisticated models take account of contingency factors such as maturity of followers and the nature of the task.

14.5 Models of transformational leadership treat the leader as a hero who can (single-handedly) turn the organisation around and deliver it from a crisis.

14.6 Empowering and post-heroic leadership models conceptualise the leader as teacher and facilitator, who involves many in the leadership task.

14.7 Change is ever present in today's world. A rational approach to change is enhanced by supplementing this with a learning approach to change which generates higher levels of involvement of employees.

14.8 A learning approach to change sits well with empowering post-heroic leadership styles.

GENERAL DISCUSSION TOPICS

1 Do we need leaders at all? Discuss what alternatives there might be.

2 Consider the four types of charismatic leader identified by Steyrer (1998): hero, father figure, missionary and saviour. Discuss the ways in which the types of leader are similar or different.

3 Read Binney and Williams (2005) and the advantages and disadvantages of their concept of a learning approach to change.

FURTHER READING

IDS (2003) *IDS Studies: Leadership Development*, No. 753. London: Incomes Data Services.
A useful book outlining the work of five case study organisations, in terms of their conception of leadership, what prompted their leadership development programmes and an outline of the programmes themselves. The case organisations are the Dixons group, the Inland Revenue, Novartis Pharmaceuticals, Portsmouth City Council and Skipton Building Society.

Goffee, R. and Jones, G. (2006) *Why Should Anyone be led by you?* Harvard: Harvard Business School Press.
And
Goffee, R. and Jones, G. (2006) 'This time it's personal', *People Management*, Vol. 12, No. 21, 26 October, pp. 28–33.
Goffee and Jones combine sound concepts and practical advice on leadership, in the thought-promoting book and article. They identify the context where the hierarchy is long enough to get things done, and that the challenge facing many leaders is to enable highly talented followers to perform to their best. They recognise that leadership, as well as being non-hierarchical, is situational and relational. In meeting the leadership challenge, they suggest, leaders need to know themselves and show who they are to a sufficient extent; they need to be prepared to take personal risks; they need to be sensitive to context and re-write this; they need to be authentic, but conform sufficiently; and they need to manage the social distance between themselves and their followers.

REFERENCES

Alimo-Metcalfe, B. and Alban-Metcalfe, J. (2002) 'The great and the good', *People Management*, Vol. 8, No. 1, 10 January, pp. 32–4.

Applebaum, S., Audet, L. and Miller, J. (2003) 'Gender and leadership? Leadership and gender? A journey through the landscape of theories', *Leadership and Organisation*, Vol. 24, No. 1, pp. 43–51.

Arkin, A. (1997) 'The secret of his success', *People Management*, 23 October, pp. 27–8.

Bass, B.M. (1985) 'Leadership: Good, Better, Best', *Organisational Dynamics*, Winter, pp. 26–40.

Beckhard, R. (1992) 'A model for the executive management of organizational change', in G. Salaman (ed.), *Human Resource Strategies*. London: Sage.

Bennis, W.G. and Nanus, B. (1985) *Leaders: the strategies for taking charge*. New York: Harper and Row.

Binney, G. and Williams, C. (2005) 'The Myth of Managing change', in G. Salaman, J. Storey and J. Billsberry (eds), *Strategic Human Resource Management; Theory and Practice; A Reader*. London: Sage.

Blake, R.R. and Mouton, J.S. (1964) *The Managerial Grid*. Houston, Texas: Gulf Publishing.

Buchanan, D. and Huczynski, A. (1997) *Organisational Behaviour*. London: Prentice Hall.

Collins, J. (2003) 'From good to great', presentation to the CIPD National Conference, Harrogate, 22–24 November.

Edwards, C. (2006) 'On being Gregarious', *People Management*, Vol. 12, No. 8, 20 April, pp. 32–4.

Eriksson, C. (2004) 'The effects of change programmes on employee emotions', *Personnel Review*, Vol. 33, No. 1, pp. 110–26.

Fielder, F.E. (1967) *A Theory of Leadership Effectiveness*. New York: McGraw-Hill.

Fulop, L. and Linstead, S. (1999) *Management. A Critical Text*. South Yarra: Macmillan Business.

Fulop, L., Linstead, S. and Dunford, R. (1999) 'Leading and managing', in L. Fulop and S. Linstead, *Management. A Critical Text*. South Yarra: Macmillan Business.

Goffee, R. (2002) 'Send out the right signals', *People Management*, Vol. 8, No. 21, 24 October, pp. 32–8.

Goffee, R. and Jones, G. (2006) 'The Lizard Kings', *People Management*, Vol. 12, No. 2, 26 January, pp. 32–4.

Goleman, D. (1998) 'What makes . . . a leader?', *Harvard Business Review*, Nov.–Dec., pp. 93–102.

Goleman, D. (2000) 'Leadership that gets results', *Harvard Business Review*, March–April, pp. 78–90.

Greenhalgh, L. (2001) 'Managers Face up to the new era', *Mastering Management*, Series 23, London: Financial Times.

Grint, K. (1997) 'Introduction', in K. Grint (ed.), *Leadership*. Oxford: Oxford University Press.

Hayes, J. (2007) *The Theory and Practice of Change Management*, 2nd edn. Basingstoke: Palgrave Macmillan.

Heifetz, R. and Laurie, D. (1997) 'The work of leadership', *Harvard Business Review*, Jan.–Feb., pp. 124–34.

Heil, G., Bennis, W. and Stephens, D.C. (2000) *Douglas McGregor, revisited: managing the human side of the enterprise*. New York: Wiley.

Hersey, P. (1985) *Situational Selling*. Escondido, Calif.: Centre for Leadership Studies.

Hersey, P. and Blanchard, K.H. (1988) *Management of Organizational Behavior: Utilizing Human Resources*, 5th edn. Englewood Cliffs, NJ: Prentice-Hall International.

Higgs, M. (2003) 'How can we make sense of leadership in the 21st century?', *Leadership and Organisation Development Journal*, Vol. 24, No. 5, pp. 273–84.

Hollington, S. (2006) 'How to lead your boss', *People Management*, Vol. 12, No. 24, 7 December, pp. 44–5.

Hollyforde, S. and Whiddett, S. (2002) *The Motivation Handbook*. London: CIPD.

Hope, K. (2006) 'Lessons Learnt', *People Management*, Vol. 12, No. 6, 23 March, pp. 30–1.

House, R. (1976) 'A 1976 theory of charismatic leadership', in J. Hunt and L. Larson (eds), *Leadership: the Cutting Edge*. Carbondale, Ill.: Southern Illinois University Press.

Kakabadse, A., Myers, A., McMahon, T. and Spony, G. (1997) 'Top management styles in Europe: Implications for business and cross-national teams', in K. Grint (ed.), *Leadership*. Oxford: Oxford University Press.

Kanter, R.M. (1983) *The Change Masters*. New York: Simon and Schuster.

Kets de Vries, M. (2003) 'The dark side of leadership', *Business Strategy Review*, Vol. 14, No. 3, pp. 25–8.

Kilpatrick, S. and Locke, E. (1991) 'Leadership: Do Traits Matter?', *Academy of Management Executive*, Vol. 5, No. 2, pp. 48–60.

Kotter, J. (1990) *A Force for change: How leadership differs from management*. New York: Free Press.

Kubler-Ross, E. (1997) *On Death and Dying*. Washington DC: Touchstone.

McClelland, D.C. (1971) *Motivational Trends in Society*. Morristown, NJ: General Learning Press.

McGregor, D. (1960) *The Human Side of Enterprise*. New York: McGraw-Hill.

Mullins, L. (1999) *Management and Organisational Behaviour*, 5th edn. Harlow: Financial Times Pitman Publishing.

Northouse, P. (2006) *Leadership – Theory and Practice*, 4th edn. California: Sage.

Rajan, A. and van Eupen, P. (1997) 'Take it from the top', *People Management*, 23 October, pp. 26–9.

Senge, P. (1990) *The Fifth Discipline: The art and practice of the learning organisation*. London: Century Business, Random House.

Shackleton, V. (1995) *Business Leadership*. London: Routledge.

Steyrer, J. (1998) 'Charisma and the Archetypes of leadership', *Organisation Studies*, Vol. 19, No. 5, pp. 807–28.

Tichy, N. and Devanna, M. (1986) *The Transformational Leader*. New York: Wiley.

Vroom, V. (1964) *Work and Motivation*. Chichester: John Wiley.

Walmsley, H. (1999) 'A suitable ploy', *People Management*, 8 April, pp. 48–50.

Walton, J. (1999) *Strategic Human Resource Development*. Harlow: Financial Times/Prentice Hall.

Williams, M. (2000) *The war for talent: Getting the best from the best*. London: CIPD.

Worrall, L. and Cooper, C. (2006) 'Short Changed', *People Management*, Vol. 12, No. 13, 29 June, pp. 36–8.

An extensive range of additional materials, including multiple choice questions, answers to questions and links to useful websites can be found on the Human Resource Management Companion Website at **www.pearsoned.co.uk/torrington**.

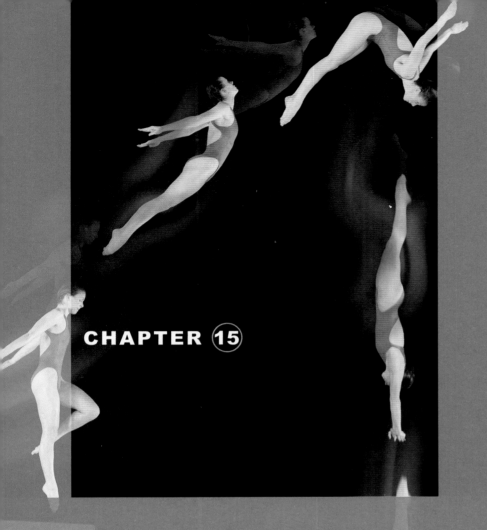

MANAGING ABSENCE AND ATTENDANCE

THE OBJECTIVES OF THIS CHAPTER ARE TO:

1   Review the national context on employee absence

2   Identify the impact of absence on the organisation

3   Explore the process of absence from work and absence causation

4   Discuss methods by which long- and short-term absence can
be minimised

For organisations to achieve their optimum performance the extent to which employees are absent from their place of work clearly needs to be minimised. Absence has always been a matter of concern to all employers, and methods for reducing it have frequently focused on disciplinary or punitive measures. More recently absence has been framed in a more positive discourse, and the focus is now on what organisations can do to promote attendance and rehabilitation of employees with long-term absence.

THE NATIONAL CONTEXT

The CIPD (2006) found a level of 3.5 per cent sickness absence (defined as the percentage of working time missed, and often referred to as the headline rate) from a survey they carried out in early 2006 with responses from 1,083 public sector and private sector organisations. This represents eight days' absence per employee per year. CIPD commented that this is a reduction on the figure of 3.7 per cent reported by a similar survey in the previous year. Other surveys produce fairly similar figures; for example the CBI survey (CBI/AXA 2006) reports a rate of 3.1 per cent (equating to 6.6 days lost per person per year). Whilst this is the lowest figure found since the CIPD absence surveys began in 2000, it is, for two reasons, difficult to argue yet that there is a clear downward trend in absence rates. First, the rate in the CIPD surveys has fluctuated up and down, as in the CBI survey. Second, while the methodology of the CIPD survey remains constant the actual organisations responding each year are not necessarily the same, within either the CIPD or CBI surveys. In addition, the Engineering Employers Federation (EEF) (2005) report that absence has become a bigger problem since their survey in 2003, with the rate increasing from 2 per cent to 3.6 per cent, yet it reduced again the following year (EEF 2006). Bevan of the Work Foundation (Silcox 2006) concludes that absence has remained broadly at the same level for the past 30 years with small fluctuations due to unemployment and the wider economic cycle.

WINDOW ON PRACTICE

Comparative absence figures

Lokke and her colleagues (2007) used data from the European Employee Index. The data were collected from employees, randomly selected, in 2004. Days absence per employee in 2004 were as follows: Denmark: 2.8; Norway: 3.5; Sweden 3.9; Finland 4.6 In each country absence in the public sector was higher than in the private sector, except for Sweden where there were no differences.

It is interesting to compare these figures with British data for the same year where the CBI reports 6.8 working days lost per employee (CBI/AXA 2005) and the CIPD reports 8.4 (CIPD 2005). The differences might, however, be explained by the respondents used, as the British surveys collect data from managers in organisations about their employees, rather than directly from employees themselves. In addition the TUC (2005) report European comparisons based on figures produced by the University of Surrey. These indicate that short-term absence in Britain is lower than in any other country, apart from Denmark; and that long-term absence is lower than others except for Ireland, Austria and Germany.

There is a clear message that comparative figures are difficult to produce as so much depends on sources and methods.

Sources: Lokke, A., Eskildsen, J. and Jensen, T. (2007) 'Absenteeism in the Nordic Countries', *Employee Relations*, Vol. 29, No. 1, pp. 16–29.
TUC (2005) *Countering an urban legend: sicknote Britain?* London: TUC.
CBI/AXA (2005) *Who cares wins; Absence and labour turnover 2005.* London: CBI/AXA.
CIPD (2005) *Absence Management: A survey of policy and practice.* London: CIPD.

In terms of the patterns of absence most surveys report that absence is higher in larger than in smaller organisations, which is likely to be why the CBI figures are generally lower than the ones from the CIPD, as the CBI sample includes a higher proportion of smaller organisations. Public sector absence is usually found to be higher than that in the private sector: for example in 2006 the CIPD found the public sector absence rate to be 4.3 per cent. Reviewing the Labour Force Survey, the General Household Survey and employer surveys, Barham and Leonard (2002) found that absence does tend to be concentrated in some groups of people rather than others: in addition to higher rates in the public sector they found higher rates for women, full-time workers and those aged under 30. They also found differences by occupational group, with managers, professionals and administrative professionals having lower levels than other groups. The CBI found that sickness absence was higher among manual workers, and this to some extent must reflect the nature of job demands. The CIPD (2006) found that absence levels were highest in the food, drink and tobacco sector, local and central government and the health sectors; and lowest in media and publishing, the voluntary sector, and the hotel, restaurant and leisure sector. These sectors do change to some extent each year.

The CBI reports that absence costs the UK economy around £13 billion per year and it constantly asserts that around 13 per cent of all absence is not genuine, whilst unions point to the efforts that workers often make to attend work even when ill (*see*, for example, TUC 2005). Big sporting events, such as the World Cup, often attract attention in terms of their impact on absence levels, but organisations can use these events to their advantage given some thought. Smethurst (2006) reports on how Prudential and Egg responded to the World Cup by offering more flexible working over the period, with incentive schemes and themed competitions to incorporate interest in the event.

At a national level the government has an interest in reducing absence and loss of employment due to sickness. Roberts (2003) reports that while there are 1.46 million people claiming unemployment pay, there are 2.7 million people out of work claiming long-term sickness and disability benefits. Roberts goes on to explain how this situation has stimulated a focus on how society manages long-term sickness and rehabilitation. The government has an interest in reducing NHS costs and Invalidity Benefit costs, and the Department for Work and Pensions has arranged a two-year series of job rehabilitation pilot studies. The pilots will test three different approaches, healthcare interventions, workplace interventions and combined interventions, and the aim is to learn which approaches are most successful. The Welfare Reform Bill proposes a variety of measures designed to encourage and enable welfare claimants back to work (for brief details *see*, for example, Brockett 2006; Griffiths 2006).

WINDOW ON PRACTICE

International approaches to long-term absence

James and his colleagues (2002) explain how different countries have enacted legislation in respect of sickness absence. For example, in Sweden employers must ensure that they have assessed rehabilitation needs at an early stage, and are then obliged to put any relevant rehabilitation measures in place. In the Netherlands employers must submit a report on any employee who is unable to work within 13 weeks of the start of the absence. They are required to submit this to a social security agency and must produce a 'work resumption plan'. In New South Wales, Australia, where workers have been absent for 12 weeks employers must establish a work rehabilitation programme, and if there are more than 20 people employed, they must appoint a rehabilitation coordinator and prepare plans for return to work.

Source: Summarised from P. James, I. Cunningham and P. Dibben (2002) 'Absence management and the issues of job retention and return to work', *Human Resource Management Journal*, Vol. 12, No. 2, pp. 82–94.

THE ORGANISATIONAL CONTEXT

Barham and Leonard (2002) question the accuracy of data in absence surveys. They argue that given the low response rates to such surveys, there is no evidence to suggest that the survey findings are representative of the whole population. In addition the CIPD found that much management absence is not recorded. It is likely that respondents are those with better absence information. On this basis they argue that absence costs to the organisation are underestimated.

The CIPD found that over 90 per cent of organisations in their survey considered absence to be a significant cost to the organisation, but less that half monitored this cost. The average cost was reported to be £598 per year per employee. Barham and Leonard (2002) suggest that estimating the costs of absence is complicated, and that the estimate needs to include not only the direct costs (i.e., paying salary and benefits for a worker who is not there), but also indirect costs such as organising replacement staff, overall reductions in productivity and administrative costs. Bevan (2002), reporting research from the Employment Studies Institute, suggests that there are virtually no robust data on direct and indirect costs of absence and that most employers under-estimate the true costs of sickness absence, particularly in respect of long-term sickness. Costing currently does not distinguish between short-term and long-term sickness. Using case study research Bevan reports that long-term sickness costs account for between 30 per cent and 70 per cent of absence costs. He goes on to argue, on the basis of this research, that even the most sophisticated companies are not well equipped to calculate such costs.

Statutory Sick Pay (SSP) changes in 1994 have given absence costs a higher profile as the burden has been passed to the employer, although there were compensatory mechanisms in place and direct costs to the employer are increased and are more prominent.

Traditionally employers have concentrated on short-term absence, and while long-term absence accounts for only around 20 per cent of absence incidents it can represent more than 40 per cent of total working time lost, according to the CBI, although figures do vary. CIPD (2006) found that long-term absence was most significant in the public sector where it accounts for 25 per cent of absence, compared with 17 per cent in manufacturing, 16 per cent in not-for-profit organisations and 12 per cent in private services. Reducing such absence is increasingly seen as having the potential to create significant costs savings. Cost is not the only factor in influencing organisations to attend to long-term absence, and we have already mentioned government interest in this. In addition, the Disability Discrimination Act 1995 requires employers to provide reasonable adjustments to enable disabled workers to continue in employment, and the term 'disabled' extends to those suffering from long-term ill health. It has been argued that employers have a more explicit duty of care to their employees due to UK and EU legislation, and there is a growing concern for the well-being of employees, partly due to fear of litigation.

In summary the evidence suggests that absence levels in the UK are decreasing to a small extent, but that there is insufficient evidence as yet to conclude how our absence rates compare with the rest of Europe. Long-term sickness generates proportionately greater costs and problems than short-term sickness and it is appropriate that the focus on this has increased significantly in recent years.

PROCESS AND CAUSES OF ABSENCE

The CIPD found the most frequently stated causes of absence are minor illness for short-term absence and back pain and minor illness (for manual workers) and stress and minor illness (for non-manual workers). For long-term illness the most frequent causes for manual workers are back pain and musculo-skeletal injuries; and for non-manual workers stress remains the greatest, and an increasing cause. The increase in stress as a cause may well be partly due to the fact that this is now a more legitimate reason for non-attendance than previously. Case 15.1 on this book's companion website at **www.pearsoned.co.uk/torrington** focuses on stress as a reason for absence. It is important to bear in mind that recorded causes of absence in organisations will be those causes which employees perceive the organisation to view as legitimate.

The causes of absence are complex and interrelated and a process approach is generally agreed to be the most useful way of understanding absence behaviour, although there are criticisms that such models are not supported by the evidence. One of the most widely quoted models is from Rhodes and Steers (1990) and in our view this is the most useful of the process models. For an alternative model *see* Nicholson (1977).

The Rhodes and Steers model (*see* Figure 15.1) not only includes content information on the causes of absence but also incorporates a range of interdependent processes. In essence the model focuses on attendance motivation and the ability to attend in terms of resulting attendance behaviour.

Rhodes and Steers suggest that *attendance motivation* is directly affected by two factors: *satisfaction with the job* and *pressure to attend*. Pressure to attend may result from such factors as market conditions. Examples include the likelihood that there will be redundancies at their workplace and how easy it would be to get another job; incentives to attend, such as attendance bonuses; work-group norms on what is acceptable in the

Figure 15.1
The Rhodes
and Steers
process model
of attendance
(Source:
S. Rhodes and
R. Steers (1990)
*Managing
Employee
Absenteeism*,
Reading, Mass.:
Addison Wesley.)

work group and the effects of absence on other group members; personal work ethic producing internal pressure to attend based on beliefs about what is right; and commitment to the organisation through an identification with the beliefs and values of the organisation and an intention to remain with the organisation. On this basis threat of redundancies, attendance bonuses, team structures where team members have to cover the workload of an absent member, a personal ethic about the need to attend work wherever possible, and feelings of loyalty to the organisation should all promote the motivation to attend.

Rhodes and Steers suggest that satisfaction with the job is determined by the *job situation* and moderated by *employee values and job expectations*. Factors in the job situation are identified as job scope and level of responsibility and decision making; role stress such as work overload, underload, difficult working conditions or hours; work-group size; leadership style of their immediate manager, particularly the openness of the relationship and how easy it is to discuss and solve problems jointly; strength of relationships with co-workers; and the opportunity for promotion. On this basis higher levels of responsibility and the opportunity to make decisions in relation to job demands, balanced workload and good working conditions, small work group size, an open relationship with immediate manager, good relationships with colleagues and the opportunity for promotion should all improve attendance motivation.

However job satisfaction is moderated by the values and expectations of the employee. Such values and expectations are shaped by both personality and personal characteristics and life experiences, but can also change during the course of one's life. The extent to which the job matches up with expectations and values will have a bearing on job satisfaction; a close match is more likely to lead to satisfaction than a mismatch.

Personality and personal characteristics influence expectations and values and job satisfaction. We have previously referred to the influence of age and sex on absence rates. Length of service has also been identified as having an influence. However, none of these relationships is clear-cut, and different pieces of research often produce different findings. There is most evidence for suggesting that younger workers and female workers have the highest rates of absence, and it is argued that younger workers value free time to a greater extent than older workers.

This brings us to the last influence on attendance, which is the *ability to attend*. This influence is interposed between attendance motivation and actual attendance. For example an employee could be highly motivated to attend, but may have insurmountable transportation difficulties, family or domestic responsibilities, or may be genuinely ill. In these cases motivation to attend does not result in attendance.

MANAGING FOR ATTENDANCE

The complex interrelationship of the causes of absence needs to be taken into account in its management. Many organisations have introduced policies for managing absence that focus on minimising short-term rather than long-term absence. The role of sickness in long-term absence has been given little priority in the past, as has the issue that short-term absence, if badly handled, can lead to long-term absence. Typically long-term absence and short-term absence require different approaches. Attendance management policies need to take into account causes of absence, which may be identified by patterns of absence and by enabling individuals to be open about why they are not at work. Measures range from proactive methods intended to reduce the risk of ill health; measures intended to reduce spells of absence and those intended to reduce the length of absence. Typically there is a mix of processes both to discourage absence and positively to encourage attendance, but these work differently with those on long- and short-term sickness absence.

Whatever approach is chosen, there is a great need for consistency in the construction and implementation of absence management policies and procedures, not only in terms of ensuring fairness and as a support for any disciplinary action taken, but also in terms of providing employees with clear expectations about how absence will be tackled, and promoting an attendance culture. While different approaches work in different sectors and with different types of staff, there is a strong argument that the policies themselves need to be consistent in any organisation, to encourage employee acceptance and line manager support. For example Dunn and Wilkinson (2002) report the difficulties that a line manager in a production company experienced due to the fact that manufacturing staff were subject to more stringent absence procedures than other staff in the company.

Lack of consistency in implementation also weakens any policy and procedures. The role of the line manager is key and there is much emphasis on giving the line manager ownership of absence and attendance issues, with support from HR. Whatever policies and procedures are set up it is critical that the line manager feels ownership of these and applies them in practice. James and his colleagues (2002) found that two-thirds of their interviewees in a long-term absence management study noted that there were problems in the way that line managers carried out their responsibilities. Managers frequently did not follow the guidelines in matters such as ongoing contact with absent employees, and consequently HR did not know what was going on and often had to step in and manage cases. James and his colleagues found that managers' behaviour resulted from time pressures, lack of awareness of what the procedure was and lack of training.

WINDOW ON PRACTICE

Managing absence at HBOS

Mary McFadzean (2003) reports on a pilot project at HBOS which encouraged HR to look at absence from a different perspective. The project was intended to test two theories: first, that much absence had non-medical causes and therefore could be tackled by HR and, second, that absence could be reduced without buying in any extra resources.

To introduce the project workshops were held with HR members and best practice guidelines were made available, HR advisers were then encouraged to go out and talk to managers about absence. The best practice model included an emphasis on finding the underlying cause of absence in terms of social or work-related issues, based on the belief that this is the root cause of much absence, and if issues are not dealt with they will gradually produce medical symptoms. The skill was therefore in getting beyond the symptoms on the medical note to understand the underlying cause of absence. Once the underlying cause was understood then temporary or permanent changes could be made to help, such as reducing targets, hours and responsibilities or changing work patterns.

HBOS promoted an absence champion network in its first-tier approach which would adopt the best practice principles provided by HR, and would receive up-to-date information on absence and target cases for intervention (over 20 days' absence for long-term absence and four periods in a year for short-term absence). HR received consistent management information, and progress was monitored in all cases. A health provider network was also set up, as a second-tier approach (for long-term absence), to target high-risk areas and the two top causes of absence. Individuals were referred after 10 days' absence in these cases, and the health provider network included a psychologist and a physiotherapist. Treatment was considered justified if there was deemed to be an 80 per cent chance of return to work. HBOS feel that rehabilitation back into work needs to become part of the business culture.

The project was only carried out in some areas and performance was measured against control groups. HBOS saved 21,000 days over the six-month period (6,000 headcount) and £880,000. Short-term absence was reduced by 35 per cent, but there was no impact on long-term absence, which continues to creep up.

Source: Summarised from M. McFazdean (2003) 'Managing Absence',
paper presented at the CIPD National Conference, Harrogate, 22–24 October.

It has been found that some measures to manage absence actually increase absence, so monitoring any new policies and procedures is critical. In terms of implementing a new absence strategy, the advice given by Huczynski and Fitzpatrick (1989) still holds good. The ALIEDIM process they suggest comprises the following stages:

- Assess the absence problem
- Locate the absence problem
- Identify and prioritise absence causes
- Evaluate the current absence control methods
- Design the absence control programme
- Implement the absence control programme
- Monitor the effectiveness of the absence control programme

 The mix of policies and methods chosen will be specific to the needs of the individual organisation, and Case 15.2 on the book's companion website, **www.pearsoned.co.uk/ torrington** explains the mix chosen by Newry and Mourne Police Unit in Ireland. Below are some of the most frequently used approaches to managing absence. Some are most appropriate for short-term absence, and some better suited to long-term absence, others meet the needs of both.

Accurate records

Managing absence is almost impossible without an accurate picture of current absence levels and patterns, which requires identification of areas of high absence and the most common reasons for absence in the organisation. The CIPD (2006) found that 60 per cent of those organisations reporting a reduction in absence said that this was due to improved monitoring. However, such data collection is more often reported in the public sector and manufacturing industry than in the rest of the private sector. The HSE (Silcox 2005a) in a bid to aid employers has produced a new computerised absence recording and management tool, SART, which it hopes will also encourage employers to record such data in a more consistent manner. Prior to its review of absence Carlsberg-Tetley (IDS 2001) did not have an accurate picture of sickness absence. Although some records were kept, absence was inconsistently measured and recorded, so there was no reliable information about level of absence and patterns. This was their first task in tackling absence. They decided to adopt the 'Bradford factor' method for scoring absence where both frequency of absence spells and absence duration are used but with the weight being given to the former. The Bradford factor formula, devised by Bradford University, is shown in Figure 15.2. For further information on statistics see IDS (2005).

Absence score = (spells of absence × spells of absence) × duration of absence

Figure 15.2 The Bradford factor formula for scoring absence
(Note: The score is usually calculated over a year.)

WINDOW ON PRACTICE

Absence data at Brakes

AHP (Active Health Partners) who manage absence and attendance for Brakes receive weekly updates from the payroll in order to update their absence data and produce reports. These reports are available to managers and include:

- details of who is absent and their expected return
- individual data for each employee including: days lost; absence rate, longest absence spell; number of absence spells; any Monday and Friday absences
- department breakdowns
- details relating to those employees most frequently absent
- reasons for absence overall
- trend reports
- number of accidents

This information is regularly discussed, typically weekly at the conference call between all managers in a region.

Source: IDS (2005) 'Brakes', *Absence Management*, No. 801, November, London: IDS.

Absence reports are frequently produced by HR and sent to line managers – and such reports will often include details of employees where trigger points have been hit and where intervention is required by the line manager. However, Dunn and Wilkinson (2002) found that the attention line managers gave to these reports varied, and some managers never even looked at the reports, because they did not agree that this was the best way to manage staff. As one manager commented, 'I know my staff well enough not to need these reports . . . at the end of the day it all comes down to good management and knowing your staff'. Some managers argued that the reports were of little use because the employees they managed often worked long hours (beyond contract) and came in at weekends. It was felt that to punish such employees, who were clearly committed to the company, because they had reached certain absence levels was unreasonable, and would be counter-productive.

Absence review and trigger points

In order to focus attention on those with less satisfactory absence records many organisations identify trigger points in terms of absence spells or length, or Bradford factor scores which indicate that action is needed when an individual's absence record hits the trigger. Such policies for reviewing absence appear to be critical in absence reduction, and the CIPD (2006) reports that 67 per cent of organisations reporting a decrease in absence levels put this down to tightened policies for reviewing absence. The HBOS Window on practice above describes the trigger points that they use. However, such trigger points may be well known to employees, and Connex (IDS 2001) found that some employees were able to manipulate the system and regularly have absence levels just below the trigger point. To overcome this some organisations have a rolling year, rather than, say, a calendar year or a financial year, against which absence levels are assessed – on the grounds that it will be much more difficult for employees to keep track of their absence levels and manipulate the system. In fact Dunn and Wilkinson (2002) found organisations where the trigger system was avoided because it was felt that it would encourage employees to take off time until they were just under the trigger limit.

Some organisations have absence review groups, such as the absence champion network at HBOS, and the safety, health and absence unit at HM Customs and Excise (IDS 2001). While the role of these groups varies, they are frequently used to review all absences and identify those who have hit trigger points which will then require intervention, such as an absence review meeting with the employee.

Absence targets and benchmarking

Many organisations have absence targets phrased in terms of a reduction on current absence levels or a lower absence level to attain. However, the CIPD (2006) found that although 80 per cent of the organisations it surveyed believed that absence levels could be reduced, less than half of these had set targets for this, and only around 37 per cent benchmarked their absence levels against other organisations. An alternative approach, used by some organisations, is to give managers absence targets for their group, and tie this into their performance review and performance payments. This is the approach used in Connex (IDS 2001). Such overall and local targets need to be carefully used, however, so as not to give the impression to employees that absence is not allowed.

ACTIVITY 15.1

We have noted that some organisations link improvements in absence levels in their departments to managers' performance assessments and performance-related pay.

1 What are the potential advantages of this approach?

2 What are the potential problems?

3 How else might managers be encouraged to treat absence levels as a key priority?

Training and support for line managers

Most organisations recognise that line managers play a key role in making absence procedures work and in reducing absence levels, and training is usually available when a new absence system is introduced. Connex (IDS 2001) has introduced a creative form of training. The company takes managers to an employment tribunal to view an absence-related case so that managers will understand the consequences of not dealing fairly and consistently with employees when they have to deal with similar situations at work. HM Customs and Excise (IDS 2001) uses training videos showing role plays of return to work interviews (*see* below). These demonstrate that such a meeting is not about accusation or recrimination. The idea is that managers watch the video with their team of supervisory staff and then discuss the issues that arise.

However, there is evidence that further training is needed. Both James *et al.* (2002) and Dunn and Wilkinson (2002) found managers who could not understand how 'sickness' could be managed, were scared of dealing with the situation and were embarrassed about asking personal questions about an employee's state of health.

Absence notification procedures

Many organisations specify that when employees phone in as absent they must phone themselves, rather than asking another person to phone on their behalf. Many also specify that the employee must speak to their direct line manager or nominated representative. This means that such a telephone conversation can be the first stage of the absence management process. The conversation is welfare based and the intention is that the manager is able to ask about the nature of the problem and the anticipated date of return to work. Brakes (IDS 2005), interestingly, outsources potential absence reporting calls to a nurse helpline. The nurse gives confidential advice on how to manage symptoms but makes no recommendation about whether the individual should attend work or not. The nurse does, however, make a record of the call and notifies the appropriate line manager and also informs the line manager when the individual is ready to return to work. Apparently managers appreciate this burden being removed and concentrate their attention on those employees whose absence level has reached a trigger point.

Some organisations, such as First Direct (IDS 2001), make every effort to offer alternative work. For example, a telephone operator who cannot do telephone work with a sore throat may be able to do other work, and managers are asked to bear this in mind when employees phone in sick and to try to encourage the employees to come in, where appropriate, to carry out other tasks. This telephone conversation is also seen as an important tool in reducing the length of the absence.

Better understanding of the causes of absence

Analysis of absence data can show the primary causes of absence in any particular organisation and this may help employers develop absence management methods relevant to the most frequent causes. However, as we have said, the reasons employees give for absence will be those that the organisation considers legitimate, and further investigation may be necessary.

Organisations can encourage individuals to be open about the real cause for their absence, for example a minor illness may be used as an excuse to cover for caring responsibilities, a stressful working environment or alcohol or drug problems. However, this is easier said than done. The London Borough of Brent (IRS 2002b) has decided that the next stage in its efforts to tackle long-term absence is to try to unpick the causes of such absence. The employer has a feeling that the explanation may be partly related to issues of stress and the nature and organisation of the work. Helping employees to feel they can trust the employer sufficiently to admit the real cause of absence means that absence can then effectively be tackled by providing the appropriate form of support. Another key tool is risk assessment, so, for example, some organisations will assess the risk of back pain or stress and then training can be provided to meet identified needs.

The CIPD (2006) found that organisations used risk assessments, training, staff surveys, policy development, flexible working, employee assistance programmes, focus groups and changes in work organisation as methods to identify and reduce stress. The HSE encourage the use of focus groups for stress identification and management and more details and examples can be found in Silcox (2005b).

WINDOW ON PRACTICE

Risk assessments for stress

Stress accounts for a large proportion of sickness absence in the NHS, and researchers from the Institute of Work, Health and Organisations at Nottingham University studied five groups of hospital staff working under pressure: nurses, healthcare assistants, technical and professional staff, catering staff and clerical/reception staff. The aim was to measure and tackle stress at work. The intervention began with risk assessment, and a well-being questionnaire was used to gather employee feelings about tiredness and exhaustion. Employees were asked to identify not only causes of stress but also changes to management practice which would provide a solution. One of the examples provided is the catering team who identified causes as peak-time high workloads, poorly maintained equipment and inadequate training. Resultant interventions included regular equipment maintenance, additional peak-time staff and regular team briefings.

Source: Summarised from HSE (2002b) *Interventions to control stress at work in hospital staff*, HSE Contract Research Paper No. 435.

Ongoing contact during absence

Maintaining contact during absence is considered by many organisations as a method of reducing length of absence, demonstrating to the employee that the organisation is interested in them, and maintaining employee motivation. In some organisations it is the line manager who will keep in touch, and in others, such as Walter Holland and Son (IDS 2001), there are liaison officers who fulfil this role. Contact may be by telephone, and with longer periods of absence may involve home visits. For a useful summary of a wide range of methods of keeping in touch with employees who are off sick see Silcox (2005c). The Employers Organisation for Local Government (EO) (HSE 2002a) suggests that more effort should be made to keep in touch with employees after operations, partly to keep them up to date, but also to see if it is possible for them to come back to work on light duties or on a part-time basis. In working out its policy of visits, Bracknell Forest Council (IRS 2002a) pays due attention to the requirements of the Human Rights Act 1998. The council recommends one visit per month in working hours and considers this is reasonable in terms of the need to demonstrate 'respect for private and family life', and the wish to avoid putting pressure on employees to return to work too early.

Return to work interviews and formal absence reviews

Return to work interviews are increasingly used as a key part of attendance procedures, and CIPD (2006) reports that these were used by 81 per cent of organisations in 2006 compared with 57 per cent in 2000. CIPD also reports that these interviews are regarded as the most effective way of managing short-term absence. For some organisations these interviews are mandatory, even following a single day's absence, but there is frequently some flexibility about the nature of the interview depending on the circumstances. In general the purposes of such interviews are identified as to: welcome the employee back and update them on recent events; check that the employee is well enough to resume normal duties and whether any further organisational support is needed; reinforce the fact that the employee has been missed and that attendance is a high priority in the organisation; and review the employee's absence record. Dunn and Wilkinson (2002) found managers in their research who said that there was not time to concentrate on return to work interviews, as the practicalities of getting the job done were more critical. They also found a view among line managers that they were just so glad to get the employee back that they did not want to 'rock the boat'. Where formal absence reviews are held these need to be handled with sensitivity and tact, and care needs to be taken so that the interview does not become recriminatory or accusatory.

Use of disciplinary procedures

If someone is genuinely ill and unable to work as a result, disciplinary action whether threatened or real is unlikely to bring about a return to work. It would not be desirable from the point of view of the employee or the employing organisation were this to be the case. There are, however, situations in which people who are too ill to work have to be dismissed. This is never a pleasant task, but it often falls to the HR manager to carry it out. The key is to make sure that the dismissal is carried out in a legally sound manner. This issue is covered in greater detail in Chapters 10 and 25, so it is only necessary here to summarise the main points:

1 Dismissing someone who is unable to work because of ill health is potentially fair under unfair dismissal law.

2 It is necessary to warn the individual concerned that he or she may be dismissed if he or she does not return to work and to consult with the individual ahead of time to establish whether a return in the foreseeable future is feasible.

3 It is necessary to act on whatever medical advice is available.

4 In larger organisations, except where a person's job is very specialised or senior, it is normally considered reasonable to refrain from dismissing a sick employee for at least six months.

5 In any case no dismissal should occur if the employee falls under the definition of 'disabled' as set out in the Disability Discrimination Act 1995. In these cases an employee should only be dismissed once the employer is wholly satisfied that no reasonable adjustments could be made to accommodate the needs of the sick employee so as to allow them to return to work.

Where someone is persistently absent for short periods of time, the course of action taken will depend on whether or not there is a genuine underlying medical condition which explains most of the absences. If so, the matter should be handled in the same way as cases of long-term absence due to ill health outlined above. If not, then it is feasible for the employer to take a tougher line and to threaten disciplinary action at an earlier stage. It is quite acceptable in law to dismiss someone whose absence record is unacceptably high, provided the individual has been warned ahead of time and given a fair opportunity to improve his or her attendance. It is also necessary to treat different employees in a consistent fashion. Taking disciplinary action in the form of issuing a formal warning is therefore credible and likely to be successful.

Absence levels and performance assessments

Some organisations have communicated to employees the message that attendance levels are a measure of their performance so they are included in annual assessments. Dunn and Wilkinson (2002) found that in the three retail companies in their case sample, employees were assessed via a separate rating category on their absence levels. In addition employees with unacceptable absence levels would not be put forward for transfers or promotion. At HBOS (IDS 2005) line managers have a key performance objective relating to employee absence, reflecting their enhanced roles in managing absence.

Attendance bonus and rewards

Some organisations pay bonuses direct to employees on the basis of their attendance records. For example Richmondshire District Council (Silcox 2005d) have adopted a scheme where staff receive an additional day's leave for 100 per cent attendance in the previous year. The council found that, coupled with other absence management measures, absence was reduced from 10 days to 8 days in the first year. The council argue not only that this is a cost saving, but that an anticipated day's holiday is much easier to manage than an unanticipated day's sickness absence. Connex (IDS 2001) will pay a quarterly attendance bonus of £155 at the end of each 13-week period for full attendance and an additional lump sum of £515 if an employee has had no sickness absence during a full calendar year. In addition Connex sends out letters commending employees for improving their absence record. The company considers that its absence scheme is a success as 80 per cent of eligible employees now qualify for payments. However, some managers do not support attendance bonuses as they feel that employees are already paid to turn up, and they are effectively being paid twice. Connex also found managers who felt that attendance bonuses were a signal to employees that managers cannot control the work environment themselves and that they have relinquished all responsibility for managing absence. On the other hand, Dunn and Wilkinson (2002) found that managers felt attendance bonuses were unfair as they penalised those employees who were genuinely ill. A further problem is that such rewards may encourage employees to come into work when they are genuinely ill which is not good for either the individual or the organisation. Such rewards therefore remain controversial.

ACTIVITY 15.2

In terms of your own organisation consider the approaches by which sickness absence is minimised in terms of proactive ill-health prevention methods, discouragement of sickness absence, and encouragement of attendance:

1 Where is the emphasis in terms of approach?

2 Why do you think this is so?

3 Is this the most appropriate approach? Why?

4 To what extent are different employee groups treated differently?

5 Why do you think this is so?

6 Is this the most appropriate approach? Why?

Occupational health support, health promotion and well-being

A number of organisations carry out pre-employment screening to identify any potential health problems at this stage. Others screen employees for general fitness and for potential job hazards, such as working with radiation, or VDUs. General screening may involve heart checks, blood tests, eye tests, well-woman/man clinics, ergonomics and physiotherapy, and discussions about weight and lifestyle, such as smoking, drinking and fitness levels. The value of such screening is that problems can be identified at an early stage so that the impact on sickness absence will be minimised. In some organisations positive encouragement will be given to employees to follow healthy lifestyles, such as healthy eating, giving up smoking, taking up exercise routines. Increasing numbers of employers offer exercise classes and or an on-site gym, or alternatively pay for gym membership. Healthier canteen menus are appearing, and healthier snacks in some vending machines. However the CIPD (2006) found that barriers to such well-being initiatives were lack of resources, lack of senior management buy-in, and lack of employee buy-in, especially in manufacturing and production. The government has provided some funding (together with other organisations) for nine health promotion projects in England, and a good example of one of these is the 'Be Active 4 life' Programme at Exeter City Council which will be evaluated soon after the time of writing by a team from Loughborough University. Details of this project and the eight others are provided by Silcox (2005e).

For long-term absence the CIPD (2006) reported that the involvement of occupational health professionals was seen to be the most effective management tool, although HSE (2002c) shows that only one in seven workers has the benefit of comprehensive occupational health support. However, such support does not have to be in-house and can be purchased: this is the course followed by the London Borough of Brent (IRS 2002b).

Physiotherapists, counsellors and psychologists are often employed, and the occupational health role may include remedial fitness training and exercise therapy for those recovering from an illness. Stress counselling is increasingly being provided and if this is offered as part of an employee assistance programme can reduce the liability in stress-related personal injury cases. Also training in stress management may be offered.

James and his colleagues (2002) found that the role of occupational health workers was ambiguous and problematic. Their respondents suggested that while occupational health professionals worked on behalf of the employer, they tended to see themselves as representing employee interests. They also found that employees were very sceptical about visiting occupational health workers as they saw it as the first step in the termination of their employment.

Changes to work and work organisation

Many employers appear to offer flexible working hours, part-time work and working from home. Employers also sometimes consider offering light duties or redeployment. However, James and his colleagues (2002) found that operational factors often limited what was possible. In the three manufacturing organisations they visited it was not always feasible to offer light duties or make adjustments to the workplace. They also found that other departments were reluctant to accept someone who was being redeployed after sickness, partly because they felt the employee might have lost the work habit, and also because there might be problems with pay if the levels of the old and new job differed. They also noted that there might be no budget to pay for adaptations to equipment or to purchase further equipment.

WINDOW ON PRACTICE

Flexible working cuts sickness absence

People Management reports that the London Borough of Merton has halved its sickness absence rate and improved productivity by introducing flexible working as part of a work-life balance pilot project. The flexible patterns of work involved a compressed working week, working from home, career breaks, job sharing and special leave including compassionate leave. Keith Davis, the Assistant Chief Executive, explained that the management style had to change from managing attendance to managing output, and significant training was required. The council plans to roll out the scheme over the entire council.

Source: Summarised from *People Management* (2002) 'Flexible working cuts sickness absence', *People Management*, Vol. 8, No. 1, 10 January, p. 1.

Practical support

There are many ways in which the employer can provide practical support to minimise sickness absence. Many organisations have experienced frustrations while employees are on waiting lists for diagnostic procedures and operations. In order to speed up medical treatment that employees need some organisations are prepared to pay the medical costs for employees where there is a financial case to do this, for example the Corporation of London (Silcox 2005f). Training in areas such as stress management and time management may help employees minimise feelings of stress, childcare support may simplify childcare arrangements, and phased return to work after a long-term absence is also a useful strategy. For more details on phased return to work and some examples *see* Silcox (2005g).

SUMMARY PROPOSITIONS

15.1 Employee absence continues to be a major problem for both the country and business in terms of direct costs and lost performance.

15.2 The most often reported cause of short-term absence is minor illness; however, back pain for manual workers and stress for non-manual workers are the leading causes of long-term absence.

15.3 It is important to understand the true nature of the causation of absence, as remedies can only be developed with this knowledge. The causation of absence can result from a complex interrelationship of factors.

15.4 Typical attendance management policies include absence monitoring and reporting, absence review and trigger points, training and support for line managers, absence notification procedures, better understanding of the causes of absence, risk assessments, ongoing contact during absence, return to work interviews and absence review interviews, use of disciplinary procedure, absence-influenced performance assessments, absence bonus and rewards, occupational health support, changes to work and work organisation, and practical support. The mix of policies and processes used needs to be tailored to the needs of the organisation.

GENERAL DISCUSSION TOPICS

1 'If we gave employees longer holidays and more flexibility in the hours that they worked it would reduce the conflict between personal responsibilities/interests and work responsibilities. This reduction in conflict would reduce unplanned absence from work.' To what extent do you agree with this statement and why?

2 To what extent do you consider that absence statistics underestimate the extent of absence in the UK, and why?

3 It could be argued that encouraging employees to engage in exercise and keep fit will improve their work motivation and sense of well-being, and that this would reduce absence. To what extent do you agree with this notion?

FURTHER READING

Evans, A. and Walters, M. (2002) *From Absence to Attendance*. London: CIPD.
A thorough text which covers absence measuring and monitoring; understanding the causes of absence; absence management policies; the disciplinary and legal framework of absence management; and developing and implementing absence management strategies.

James, P., Cunningham, I. and Dibben, P. (2006) 'Job retention and return to work of ill and injured workers: Towards an understanding of the organizational dynamics', *Employee Relations*, Vol. 28, No. 3, pp. 290–303.

This paper proposes a conceptual framework of policies and practices appropriate to the effective management of long-term ill and injured workers and makes some assessment of UK current practices in relations to this framework.

Johns, G. (2001) 'Contemporary research on absence from work: correlates, causes and consequences', in I. Robertson and C. Cooper, *Personnel Psychology and HRM*. Chichester: John Wiley and Sons Ltd.

A useful chapter which provides a wide range of perspectives on understanding the nature of absence from work. Johns considers process and decision models, the withdrawal model, demographic models, the medical model, the stress model, social and cultural models, the conflict model, the deviance model and the economic model. An awareness of such a range of perspectives is useful as it provides a context against which to understand any one approach to absence.

Robson, F. (2006) 'How to manage absence effectively', *People Management*, Vol. 12, No. 17, pp. 44–5.

This is a brief and well-focused summary of how to improve absence management.

Silcox, S. (2005) 'Absence essentials: the why and wherefores of sick notes', *IRS Employment Review*, No. 850, 7 July, pp. 18–21.

This interesting article explains the current sickness certification system and explores the role of the GP in this. The GP perspective is outlined and the tensions between this and the government's proposed welfare reforms aimed at reducing long-term absence from work and the numbers receiving invalidity benefit.

REFERENCES

Barham, C. and Leonard, J. (2002) 'Trends and sources of data on sickness absence', *Labour Market Trends*, April, pp. 177–85.

Bevan, S. (2002) 'Counting the cost of absence', *IRS Employment Review*, No. 739, pp. 46–7.

Brockett, J. (2006) 'Government aiming to get one million welfare claimants back into the workplace', *People Management*, Vol. 12, No. 14, 13 July, p. 10.

CBI/AXA (2005) *Who cares wins; Absence and labour turnover 2005*. London: CBI/AXA.

CBI/AXA (2006) *Absence minded; absence and labour turnover in 2006. The lost billions: addressing the cost of absence*. London: Confederation of British Industry.

CIPD (2005) *Absence Management: A survey of policy and practice*. London: CIPD.

CIPD (2006) *Employee Absence 2006*. London: CIPD.

Dunn, C. and Wilkinson, A. (2002) 'Wish you were here: managing absence', *Personnel Review*, Vol. 31, No. 2, pp. 228–46.

EEF (2005) *Absence and Labour turnover survey: EEF 2005 Survey of Absence costs*. London: EEF.

EEF (2006) *EEF Sickness absence and rehabilitation survey, 2006*. London: EEF.

Griffiths, J. (2006) 'Road to Recovery', *People Management*, Vol. 12, No. 14, 13 July, pp. 16–17.

HSE (2002a) *Initiative Evaluation Report: Back in Work*, HSE Research Report No. 441.

HSE (2002b) *Interventions to control stress at work in hospital staff*, HSE Contract Research Paper No. 435.

HSE (2002c) *Survey of the use of occupational health support*, HSE Research Report No. 445.

Huczynski, A.A. and Fitzpatrick, M.J. (1989) *Managing Employee Absence for a Competitive Edge*. London: Pitman.

IDS (2001) *Absence Management*, No. 702, January. London: IDS.

IDS (2005) *Absence Management*, No. 810, November, London: IDS.

IRS (2002a) 'Tackling long-term absence in local government (1): Bracknell Forest Borough Council', *Employment Review*, No. 762, 21 October, pp. 42–6.

IRS (2002b) 'Tackling long-term absence (2): London Borough of Brent', *IRS Employment Review*, No. 763, 11 November, pp. 44–6.

James, P., Cunningham, I. and Dibben, P. (2002) 'Absence management and the issues of job retention and return to work', *Human Resource Management Journal*, Vol. 12, No. 2, pp. 82–94.

Lokke, A., Eskildsen, J. and Jensen, T. (2007) 'Absenteeism in the Nordic Countries', *Employee Relations*, Vol. 29, No. 1, pp. 16–29.

McFadzean, M. (2003) 'Managing Absence', paper presented at the CIPD National Conference, Harrogate, 22–24 October.

Nicholson, N. (1977) 'Absence behaviour and attendance motivation: a conceptual synthesis', *Journal of Management Studies*, Vol. 14, pp. 231–52.

People Management (2002) 'Flexible working cuts sickness absence', Vol. 8, No. 1, 10 January, p. 13.

Rhodes, S. and Steers, R. (1990) *Managing Employee Absenteeism*. Reading, Mass.: Addison Wesley.

Roberts, Z. (2003) 'Get well sooner', *People Management*, Vol. 9, No. 7, 3 April, pp. 10–11.

Silcox, S. (2005a) 'Making progress towards an absence-recording standard', *IRS Employment Review*, No. 820, 25 March, pp. 18–19.

Silcox, S. (2005b) 'Absence essentials: using focus groups in stress management', *IRS Employment Review*, No. 832, 30 September, pp. 21–4.

Silcox, S. (2005c) 'Absence Essentials: Maintaining Contact', *IRS Employment Review*, No. 818, 25 February, pp. 23–4.

Silcox, S. (2005d) 'Attendance incentives are on the HR agenda once again', *IRS Employment Review*, No. 832, 30 September, pp. 18–20.

Silcox, S. (2005e) 'Exeter City Council wants its employees to "Be Active 4 Life"', *IRS Employment Review*, No. 836, 2 December, pp. 19–21.

Silcox, S. (2005f) 'Corporation of London tackles long-term absence', *IRS Employment Review*, No. 834, 28 October, pp. 19–21.

Silcox, S. (2005g) 'Absence essentials: phased return to work', *IRS Employment Review*, No. 828, 29 July, pp. 18–21.

Silcox, S. (2006) 'The CBI and EEF agree that absence is falling', *IRS Employment Review*, No. 850, 7 July, pp. 22–3.

Smethurst, S. (2006) 'Sporting Chance', *People Management*, Vol. 12, No. 13, 29 June, pp. 32–4.

TUC (2005) *Countering an urban legend: sicknote Britain?* London: TUC.

An extensive range of additional materials, including multiple choice questions, answers to questions and links to useful websites can be found on the Human Resource Management Companion Website at **www.pearsoned.co.uk/torrington**.

INTERACTIVE SKILL 3: APPRAISAL INTERVIEWING

Throughout the first years of the twenty-first century the British government ran various programmes within its civil service departments to manage performance by setting specific targets by which senior civil servants' performance would be judged and rewarded. This is a common enough feature of employment outside the Civil Service, however varied its effectiveness, but novel in government service. In the middle of 2006 a survey by the Prime Minister's Delivery Unit cast doubt on the impact of this policy. The survey assessed four of the largest Departments of State: Education and Science, Constitutional Affairs, Home Office, Work and Pensions. On a four-point scale, with 4 at the top, they all scored 2 for managing performance and even less well for providing value for money. In a foreword to the document the Prime Minister said the departments needed to transform the way they deliver services to meet growing public expectations and that government ministers could not 'micro-manage' services. Most people would probably say, 'Thank God for that!', but it is a common cry in business circles as well, with senior managers confidently inhabiting the sunlit uplands of strategy formulation and therefore being far to busy to 'micro-manage' performance.

This Focus on skills is firmly on a crucial act of micro-management: appraising performance <u>face to face.</u> We open with an examination of the performance appraisal process, with particular reference to the appraisal interview. We have seen how effective performance may be that of the organisation as a complete entity, that of a managed team within that framework or that of an individual person. We have also seen the place of leadership and motivation in producing a situation where effective performance is likely. Face-to-face appraisal is crucial within the whole complex process of achieving an effective focused performance. In conversations with our colleagues, our bosses and perhaps our customers or clients, we move forward in our understanding of how we are doing. Usually it is an erratic sequence of a word here, an observation there, a complaint, an argument, an explanation of why something failed or was brilliantly successful. As we build up our understanding of who we are, where we want to be, what we want to do and how we can make progress towards whatever our goals may be, we piece together the products of dozens of such inputs. There are occasional landmark conversations, which crystallise our thinking. These are most likely to be appraisal interviews, and they are landmarks because of their relative formality and their official nature and because they are dedicated solely to bringing our personal performance up to an even higher level than it is already.

The objectives of this Focus on skills are:

1 To explain the purpose and nature of the appraisal interview

2 To suggest a model sequence for conducting appraisal interviews

The appraisal interview

The novelist, the textbook writer, the popular vocalist, the newspaper editor, the sculptor or painter, the athlete or the owner of a corner shop all have in common the fact that their performance is measurable in an absolute way by numbers. When Madonna releases an album or writes a book for children, she can see the effectiveness of her performance in the irrefutable logic of the numbers sold. When Paula Radcliffe runs a race the effectiveness of that performance is measured in the time taken. The measure of both performances can then be compared with that of competitors. There are no mitigating circumstances. The writer may feel that the publisher should have done a better job or that the reviewers were incompetent, but that has no weight compared with the inescapable fact of the numbers. The shop owner may grumble about local authority planners or about unfair competition from the local hypermarket, but that explanation will not stop customers from drifting away.

Most working people do not have that same absolute measure for their own personal performance, which is all part of a more general, corporate endeavour. Individual effectiveness is not measurable by an indicator of customer appreciation, as so many other members of the corporate body contribute to the effectiveness or ineffectiveness of any individual's activity. The inexorable logic of the marketplace or other external arena has to be replaced by internal measures, mediated by managerial judgement. This is tricky.

Appraising performance is not a precise measurement but a subjective assessment. It has a long history of being damned for its ineffectiveness at the same time as being anxiously sought by people wanting to know how they are doing. It is difficult to do, it is frequently done badly with quite serious results, as we explored in Chapter 13, but on the rare occasions when it is done well it can be invaluable for the business, and literally life transforming for the appraisee. It is probably the most demanding and skilful activity for any manager to undertake and is dreaded by both appraisers and appraisees (Carroll and Schneier 1982; Grint 1993). Recent research about appraising the performance of British school teachers found that the appraisal itself was often accompanied by long periods of sickness absence due to stress. To a great extent this centred on the difficulty of appropriate criteria, particularly where

> headteachers link capability to personal qualities such as 'open-minded and prepared to adapt and take on new skills' or 'attitude' or where generalised descriptions such as 'unable to do the job properly' or 'not meeting standards' are offered. Measurement is also inevitably imprecise when it is subjective, making the judgement difficult to substantiate and prone to challenge. This leads to the risk that the yardsticks of acceptable performance chosen are those that can best be justified rather than those that are most important. (Torrington *et al.* 2003)

A selection of comments by those taking CIPD examinations underlines the point:

1 I cannot bring myself to tell people that they are less than brilliant because I would tie myself up in knots trying to justify it. However well-designed the scheme is it all boils down to people wanting to know if they are good or better than average. If you don't tell them that, they will interpret something you said to mean what they want to hear. Otherwise they will have you for infringing their human rights or discriminating against them. (from a large retail grocery company)
2 We have had approximately one new scheme per year over the last six years. These have ranged from a blank piece of paper to multi-form exercises, complete with tick boxes and a sentence of near death if they were not complete by a specified date. (from an international motor manufacturer)
3 Our scheme is not objective and has become a meaningless ritual. It is not a system of annual appraisal; it is an annual handicap. (from a public corporation)

With reactions like this, it makes the appraisal interview sound even more suspect than the selection interview, as we saw in the Part 2 Focus on skills. If it is so difficult to get right, why does it survive? Why persist with something that was described 15 years ago as an idea whose time had *gone* (Fletcher 1993)?

One might just as well ask why marriage survives despite its extensive failure and the innumerable personal tragedies it produces. Why do teachers grade students' work? Why do we all seek advice? Why do audiences applaud? Why do wives and husbands seek the views of their spouses on the prospective purchase of a new suit/dress/shirt/hat? The reason is simple: we all seek approval and confirmation that we are doing the right thing, and most of us yearn to advise or direct what other people should do.

At work these basic human drives are classified into activities including objective setting, counselling, coaching or feedback on performance. They all have in common the feature of one person meeting face to face with another for a discussion focused on the performance of only one of them. It may initially seem strange that we use the performance appraisal interview as an example of the problem-solving approach to interaction, as so much individual performance is not problematic. The point is that the interactive approach involved is *joint* in a way that is distinct from enquiry or exposition, and it is a process of jointly finding out ways in which the performance might be enhanced.

There are appraisal schemes in all areas of employment. Once installed, schemes are frequently modified or abandoned, and there is widespread management frustration about their operation. Despite the problems, the potential advantages of appraisal are so great that organisations continue to introduce them and appraisal can produce stunning results. Here is an extract from another set of examination answers:

> I have had [an] annual appraisal for three years. Each time it has been a searching discussion of my objectives and my results. Each interview has set me new challenges and opened up fresh opportunities. Appraisal has given me a sense of achievement and purpose that I had never previously experienced in my working life. (from an insurance company)

In Chapter 13 we considered the place of the interview in the overall performance management process with the comment:

> What is appraised varies and might cover personality, behaviour or job performance, with the measures being either quantitative or qualitative. Qualitative appraisal is often an unstructured narrative on the general performance of the appraisee, although some guidance might be given on the areas about which the appraiser should comment. The problem with qualitative appraisals is that they may leave important areas unappraised, and that they are not suitable for comparison purposes.

It is this tendency for qualitative appraisal to be unstructured, avoiding awkwardness and being unsuitable for comparison that we have to try and reduce. There are two difficulties: the first is the potential lack of the *systematic* reporting that is looked for in attempts at management control of, and information about, the process; the second is that qualitative appraisal interviewing is not easy and requires a high level of *mutual trust* between appraiser and appraisee. How many appraisees are appraised by a paragon in whom they can trust?

Frances Storr describes an approach to performance appraisal that seeks to take out almost all the formality; it includes the appraisees choosing their own appraisers and usually the feedback is face to face, with virtually no form filling:

> its purpose is stated clearly: to improve performance and enable people to learn and grow. We emphasise that appraisal is as much about celebrating people's achievements, as it is about helping them to identify areas in which they can improve. Within that framework it is up to individuals to decide how they will carry out their own 360 degree appraisal. In more than 90 per cent of cases, feedback is given face to face, with people talking to their appraisers as a group. Any written material . . . belongs to the appraisee, with the result that the appraisal has become a dialogue rather than a survey. (Storr 2000, p. 39)

ACTIVITY 3.1

To what extent can the benefits of both approaches be created in a single scheme? Who should conduct the appraisal interview?

Appraisal is valueless unless the general experience of it is satisfactory. Appraisees have to find some value in the appraisal process itself and see tangible outcomes in follow-up. Appraisers have to find the appraisal process not too arduous and have to see constructive responses from appraisees. When general experience of appraisal is satisfactory, it becomes an integral part of managing the organisation and modifies the management process.

Who does the appraisal?

Individuals are appraised by a variety of people, including their immediate superior, their superior's superior, a member of the HR department, themselves, their peers or their subordinates. Sometimes, assessment centres are used to carry out the appraisal.

There are, however, many problems for those carrying out the appraisal. For example:

- **Prejudice**: the appraiser may actually be prejudiced against the appraisee, or be anxious not to be prejudiced; either could distort the appraiser's judgement.

- **Insufficient knowledge of the appraisee**: appraisers often carry out appraisals because of their position in the hierarchy rather than because they have a good understanding of what the appraisee is doing.

- **The 'halo effect'**: the general likeability (or the opposite) of an appraisee can influence the assessment of the work that the appraisee is doing.

- **The problem of context**: the difficulty of distinguishing the work of appraisees from the context in which they work, especially when there is an element of comparison with other appraisees.

Problems for both the appraiser and the appraisee include:

- **The paperwork**: documentation soon gets very cumbersome in the attempts made by scheme designers to ensure consistent reporting.

- **The formality**: although appraisers are likely to try to avoid stiff formality, both participants in the interview realise that the encounter is relatively formal, with much hanging on it.

ACTIVITY 3.2

Think of jobs where it is difficult to disentangle the performance of the individual from the context of the work. How would you focus on the individual's performance in these situations?

WINDOW ON PRACTICE

In 1997 the Secretary of State for Education issued guidance to schools and local education authorities about capability procedures to deal with the problem of school teachers who did not perform satisfactorily. This degree of formality for dealing with performance is very rare outside schools and produced major problems. Teachers who were 'put on procedure' found that so humiliating that they rarely improved and usually spent long periods of absence from school suffering from stress. Throughout the education system there was a preference for informal arrangements to deal with this very difficult issue.

Among the other common problems, which often cause appraisal schemes to fail, are:

- **Outcomes are ignored**: follow-up action for management to take, although agreed in the interview, fails to take place.
- **Everyone is 'just above average'**: most appraisees are looking for reassurance that all is well, and the easiest way for appraisers to deal with this is by stating or inferring that the appraisee is doing at least as well as most others, and better than a good many. It is much harder to deal with the situation of presenting someone with the opinion that they are average; who wants to be average?
- **Appraising the wrong features**: sometimes behaviours other than real work are evaluated, such as time-keeping, looking busy and being pleasant, because they are easier to see.

The appraisal interview style

The different styles of appraisal interview were succinctly described fifty years ago by the American psychologist Norman Maier (1958). His threefold classification remains the most widely adopted means of identifying the way to tackle the interview. The *problem-solving* style has been summarised as:

> The appraiser starts the interview by encouraging the employee to identify and discuss problem areas and then consider solutions. The employee therefore plays an active part in analysing problems and suggesting solutions, and the evaluation of performance emerges from the discussion at the appraisal interview, instead of being imposed by the appraiser upon the employee. (Anderson 1993, p. 102)

This is certainly the most effective style provided that both the appraiser and appraisee have the skill and ability to handle this mode. This Focus on skills is based on this style, but it is not the only style. Maier's alternatives included, first, *tell and sell*, where the appraiser acts as judge, using the interview to tell the appraisee the result of the appraisal and how to improve. This 'ski instructor' approach can be appropriate when the appraisees have little experience and have not developed enough self-confidence to analyse their own performance. *Tell and listen*, the second alternative, still casts the appraiser in the role of judge, passing on the outcome of an appraisal that has already been completed and listening to reactions. Both of these approaches could sometimes change the assessment, as well as enabling the two people to have a reasonably frank exchange.

Pryor (1985) offers a reappraisal of Maier's three styles, particularly the usefulness of tell and sell and tell and listen. He suggests that they can be effectively adapted to the needs of appraisees with little experience who require less participation in the appraisal interview.

It is tempting to identify the problem-solving approach as 'the best', because it appears to be the most civilised and searching, but not all appraisal situations call for this style, not all appraisees are ready for it and not all appraisers normally behave in this way.

The appraisal interview sequence

Certain aspects of the appraisal interview are the same as those of the selection interview discussed in the Part 2 Focus on skills. There is the inescapable fact that the appraiser determines the framework of the encounter, there is a need to open in a way that develops mutual confidence as far as possible and there is the use of closed and open-ended questions, reflection and summarising. It is also a difficult meeting for the two parties to handle:

> The appraisal interview is a major problem for both appraisers and appraisees. The appraiser has to have a degree of confidence and personal authority that few managers have in their relationship with all those whom they have to appraise. The most contentious aspect of many appraisal schemes is the lack of choice that appraisees have in deciding who the appraiser should be. Interview respondents regularly cite the interview as something that they dread. (Torrington 1994, p. 149)

For the appraisee there are concerns about career progress, job security, the ongoing working relationship with the appraiser and the basic anxieties relating to self-esteem and dealing with criticism.

The fundamental difference between selection and appraisal that every appraiser has to remember is that the objective is to reach an understanding that will have some impact on the future performance of the appraisee: it is not simply to formulate a judgement by collecting information, as in selection. A medical metaphor may help. A surgeon carrying out hip replacements will select patients for surgery on the basis of enquiring about their symptoms and careful consideration of the evidence. The surgeon asks the questions, makes the decision and implements that decision. A physician examining a patient who is overweight and short of breath may rapidly make the decision that the patient needs to lose weight and take more exercise. It is, however, not the physician but the patient who has to implement that decision. The physician can help with diet sheets, regular check-ups and terrifying advice; the real challenge is how to get the patient to respond.

The easy part of appraisal is sorting out the facts. The difficult bit is actually bringing about a change in performance. The interview, like the discussion in the physician's consulting rooms, is crucial in bringing about a change of attitude, fresh understanding and commitment to action.

Preparation

The appraiser should brief the appraisee on the form of the interview, possibly asking for a self-appraisal form to be completed in advance. To some extent this is establishing rapport, with the same objectives, and makes the opening of the eventual interview easier.

Asking for the self-appraisal form to be completed will only be appropriate if the scheme requires this. As we have seen, self-appraisal gives the appraisee some initiative, ensures that the discussion will be about matters which the appraisee can handle and on 'real stuff'.

The appraiser has to review all the available evidence on the appraisee's performance, including reports, records or other material regarding the period under review. Most important will be the previous appraisal and its outcomes.

Most of the points made in the Part 2 Focus on skills about preparing for the selection interview apply to appraisal as well, especially the setting. Several research studies (e.g. Anderson and Barnett 1987) have shown the extremely positive response of appraisees who felt that the appraiser had taken time and trouble to ensure that the setting and supportive nature of the discussion was considerate of the appraisee's needs.

Interview structure

A recommended structure for a performance appraisal interview is shown in Figure 3.1. Alternative frameworks can be found in Anderson (1993, pp. 112–13) and Dainow (1988).

Rapport is unusual because it attempts to smooth the interaction between two people who probably have an easy social relationship, but now find themselves ill at ease. This is not the sort of conversation they are used to having together, so they have to find new ground-rules. The appraisal interview itself may be easier to introduce and handle if, as generally recommended, there are mini-reviews throughout the year. This should ensure that there are no surprises, and the two people concerned get used to having performance-focused meetings, however informal. This type of review happens in some companies, but some appraisers find it difficult. There is still the problem of appraisee reaction to the tentative presentation of things they are not doing properly. A minority will misconstrue comments to focus on the good at the expense of the not so good, while a different minority will do the exact opposite: demoralised collapse at facing a suspended sentence. The majority will obviously react sensibly and most appraisees will have the simple guts to face up to issues that are problematic.

The opening of the interview itself still needs care. The mood needs to be light, but not trivial, as the appraisee has to be encouraged towards candour rather than gamesmanship.

1	**Purpose and rapport**	Agree purpose with appraisee Agree structure for meeting Check that pre-work is done
2	**Factual review**	Review of known facts about performance in previous period. Appraiser reinforcement.
3	**Appraisee views**	Appraisee asked to comment on performance over the last year. What has gone well and what has gone less well; what could be improved; what they liked; what they disliked; possible new objectives.
4	**Appraiser views**	Appraiser adds own perspective, asks questions and disagrees, as appropriate, with what appraisee has said.
5	**Problem solving**	Discussion of any differences and how they can be resolved.
6	**Objective setting**	Agreeing what action should be taken, and by whom.

Figure 3.1
Structure for a performance appraisal interview

ACTIVITY 3.3

What do you think of the following openings to appraisal interviews heard recently?

(a) 'Well, here we are again. I'm sure you don't like this business any more than I do, so let's get on with it.'

(b) 'Now, there's nothing to worry about. It's quite painless and could be useful. So just relax and let me put a few questions to you.'

(c) 'I wonder if I will end up conning you more than you will succeed in conning me.'

(d) 'Right. Let battle commence!'

Factual review is reviewing aspects of the previous year's work that are unproblematic. The appraiser should begin by reviewing the main facts about the performance, without expressing opinions about them but merely summarising them as a mutual reminder, perhaps reviewing previous objectives set and including the outcome of the previous appraisal. This will help to key in any later discussion by confirming such matters as how long the appraisee has been in the job, any personnel changes in the period, turnover figures, training undertaken, and so forth.

The appraiser will still be doing most, but not all, of the talking, and can isolate those aspects of performance that have been disclosed which are clearly satisfactory, mention them and comment favourably. This will develop rapport and provide the basic reassurance that the appraisee needs in order to avoid being defensive. The favourable aspects of performance will to some extent be *discovered* by the factual review process. It is important that 'the facts speak for themselves' rather than appraiser judgement being offered. Not, for instance:

Well, I think you are getting on very well. I'm very pleased with how things are going generally.

That sort of comment made at this stage would have the appraisee waiting for 'but . . .' as the defences have not yet been dismantled. A different approach might be:

> Those figures look very good. How do they compare with . . . ? That's X per cent up on the quarter and Y per cent on the year . . . That's one of the best results in the group. You must be pleased with that . . . How on earth did you do it?

This has the advantage of the evidence, including that collected throughout the year as we suggested earlier, being there before the eyes of both parties, with the appraiser pointing out and emphasising. It is also specific rather than general, precise rather than vague. This type of approach invariably raises the question from appraisers about what to do in a situation of poor performance. Appraising stars is easy; what about the duds? The answer is that all appraisees have some aspects of their performance on which favourable comment can be made, and the appraisal process actually identifies strengths that might have been previously obscured by the general impression of someone who is not very good. The appraiser may discover something on which to build, having previously thought the case was hopeless. If there is not some feature of the performance that can be isolated in this way, then the appraiser probably has a management or disciplinary problem that should have been tackled earlier.

The appraiser then asks for the *appraisee's views* on things that are not as good as they might be in the performance, areas of possible improvement and how these might be addressed. These will only be offered by the appraisee if there has been effective positive reinforcement in the previous stages of the interview. People can only acknowledge shortcomings about performance when they are reasonably sure of their ground. Now the appraisee is examining areas of dissatisfaction by the process of discussing them with the appraiser, with whom it is worth having the discussion, because of the appraiser's expertise, information and 'helicopter view'. There are three likely results of debating these matters:

- some will be talked out as baseless;
- some will be shown to be less worrying than they seemed when viewed only from the single perspective of the appraisee, and ways of dealing with them become apparent;
- some will be confirmed as matters needing attention.

This stage in the interview is fraught with difficulties for the manager, and is one of the reasons why an alternative style is sometimes preferred:

> some employees prefer to be told rather than invited to participate . . . the manager receives extra pay and status for making decisions, so why should the manager expect them to do his or her job as well? (Wright and Taylor 1984, p. 110)

These, however, are problems to be recognised and overcome: they are not reasons for not bothering to try.

Appraiser views can now be used in adding to the list of areas for improvement. In many instances there will be no additions to make, but usually there are improvement needs that the appraisee cannot, or will not, see. If they are put at this point in the interview, there is the best chance that they will be understood, accepted and acted upon. It is not possible to guarantee success. Demoralised collapse or bitter resentment is always a possibility, but this is the time to try, as the appraisee has developed a basis of reassurance and has come to terms with some shortcomings that he or she had not already recognised.

The appraiser has to judge whether any further issues can be raised and if so, how many. None of us can cope with confronting all our shortcomings, all at the same time, and the appraiser's underlying management responsibility is to ensure that the appraisee is not made less competent by the appraisal interview. There is also a fundamental moral responsibility not to use a position of organisational power to damage the self-esteem and adjustment of another human being.

Problem solving is the process of talking out the areas for improvement that have been identified, so that the appraisee can cope with them. Underlying causes are uncovered through further discussion. Gradually huge problems come into clearer and less forbidding perspective, perhaps through being analysed and broken up into different components. Possibilities for action, by both appraiser and appraisee, become clear.

These central stages of the interview, factual exchange, appraisee views, appraiser views and problem solving, need to move in that sequence. Some may be brief, but none should be omitted and the sequence should not alter.

The final stage of the encounter is to agree what is to be done: **objective setting**. Actions need to be agreed and nailed down, so that they actually take place. One of the biggest causes of appraisal failure is with action not being taken, so the objectives set must be not only mutually acceptable, but also deliverable. It is likely that some action will be needed from the appraiser as well as some from the appraisee.

Making appraisal work

There are many reports of businesses installing an appraisal system only to find that they have to change it or completely abandon it after only a short time. Others battle on with their systems, but recognise that they are ineffective or inadequate or disliked. What can be done to encourage the system to work as effectively as possible?

Effectiveness will be greater if all involved are clear about what the system is for. The personnel manager and senior managers need to work out what they want the appraisal system to achieve and how it fits in with the other HR activities that feed into it and are fed by it, such as career planning, training and HR planning. Those who have to operate the system also have to appreciate its objectives, otherwise they are just filling in forms to satisfy the irksome HR people, as we saw at the opening of this Focus on skills. Finally, those whose performance is to be appraised will answer questions and contribute ideas with much greater constructive candour if they understand and believe in the purposes of the scheme.

It is vital that the system is visibly owned by senior and line management in the business, and that it is not something that is done for the HR department. This may mean, for example, that appraisal forms are kept and used within the department and only selected types of data are fed through to the HR function or other departments. Ideally, the form itself should be a working document used by appraiser and appraisee throughout the year.

The more 'open' the appraisal system is, that is, the more feedback appraisees are given about their appraisal ratings, the more likely appraisees are to accept rather than reject the process. Similarly, the greater the extent to which appraisees participate in the system, the greater the chance of gaining their commitment, subject to the reservation already made: not all appraisees are ready and willing to participate, and not all organisational cultures support participative processes.

The involvement of both appraisers and appraisees in the identification of appraisal criteria has already been noted. Stewart and Stewart (1977) suggest that these criteria must be:

1 Genuinely related to success or failure in the job.

2 Amenable to objective, rather than subjective judgement, and helpful if they:
   (a) are easy for the appraiser to administer;
   (b) appear fair and relevant to the appraisee;
   (c) strike a fair balance between catering for the requirements of the present job while at the same time being applicable to the wider organisation.

Appraisers need training in how to appraise and how to conduct appraisal interviews. Appraisees will also need some training if they have any significant involvement in the process. An excellent performance appraisal system is of no use at all if managers do not know how to use the system to best effect.

The appraisal system needs to be administered so that it causes as few problems as possible for both parties. Form filling should be kept to a minimum, and the time allocated for this activity should be sufficient for it to be done properly, but not so much that the task is seen as unimportant and of low priority.

Appraisal systems need to be supported by follow-up action. Work plans agreed by appraiser and appraisee need to be monitored to ensure that they actually take place, or that they are modified in accordance with changed circumstances or priorities. Training needs should be identified and plans made to meet those needs. Other development plans may involve the HR department in arranging temporary transfers or moves to another department when a vacancy arises. In order to do this, it is vital that appraisal forms are not just filed and forgotten. Peter Goodge and Philip Watts are consultants working in the field of 360-degree feedback and one of their suggestions demonstrates the importance of follow-up:

> We suggest that organizations should spend 20 per cent of the project's budget on the assessment and 80 per cent on the subsequent development support.
> (Goodge and Watts 2000, p. 51)

SUMMARY PROPOSITIONS

3.1   Performance appraisal has a poor track record, but it has considerable potential, when done well.

3.2   Among the problems of appraisal are prejudice, insufficient knowledge by the appraiser of the appraisee, the halo effect, the problem of context, the paperwork, the ignoring of outcomes, appraising the wrong features and the tendency for everyone to be appraised as just above average.

3.3   Three approaches to the appraisal interview are problem solving, tell and sell and tell and listen.

3.4   Features of the interview itself are the opening for preliminary mutual assessment; factual review; appraisee views on performance; appraiser views, to add perspective; problem solving; and objective setting.

3.5   Appraisers must follow up on interviews, making sure that all agreed action (especially that by the management) takes place.

3.6   Training in appraisal is essential for appraisers and for appraisees.

GENERAL DISCUSSION TOPICS

1   'What right does he have to ask me questions about my motivation and objectives? I come here to do a job of work and then go home. What I want to do with my life is my business.' How would you react to that comment by someone who had just emerged from an appraisal interview?

2   In what situations have you seen outstanding individuals depress the performance of a team where the other people were demoralised by the dominance of that individual? How do you cope with this?

FURTHER READING

Fletcher, C. (1999) *Appraisal: routes to improved performance*. London: CIPD.
Lowry, D. (2002) 'Performance management', in J. Leopold (ed.), *Human Resources in Organisations*. London: Prentice Hall.
The appraisal interview has not been the subject of much research in recent years, but the above reviews provide practical suggestions.

Redman, T. and McElwee, G. (1993) 'Upward appraisal of lecturers: lessons from industry', *Education and Training*, Vol. 35, No. 2, pp. 20–5.
Redman, T., Snape, E., Thompson, D. and Kaching Yan, F. (2000) 'Performance appraisal in the National Health Service', *Human Resource Management Journal*, Vol. 10, No. 1, pp. 1–16.
Torrington, D.P., Earnshaw, J.M., Marchington, L. and Ritchie, M.D. (2003) *Tackling Underperformance in Teachers*. London: Routledge Falmer.
Recent studies of appraisal in specific professional contexts include the above, Redman and McElwee (1993) on further education and Redman *et al*. (2000) on the National Health Service.

WEB LINKS

The book's website contains practical exercises in appraisal interviewing. General information about aspects of performance can be found at:

www.hrmguide.co.uk/hrm/chap10

www.som.cranfield.ac.uk (the Performance Management Association)
Trade unions, some employers and most public bodies provide information about the performance management arrangement on their websites. One example of general interest is at:

www.governyourschool.co.uk
Consultancy firms provide information about their particular approach. A selection of interesting sites (without any assessment of the value of their products) is:

www.hrwigwam.co.uk

www.targetimprovement.co.uk

www.openview.hp.com/solutions

www.hse.gov.uk (the Health and Safety Executive)

www.managingabsence.org.uk (a site supported by government and industry partners)

www.statistics.gov.uk (the National Statistics site)

www.cbi.org.uk (the Confederation of British Industry)

www.leadersdirect.com (an American site of the Self Renewal Group)

www.audit-commission.gov.uk (Best Value Performance Plan Toolkit from the Audit Commission)

www.apse.org.uk (Association for Public Service Excellence)

www.performance-appraisals.org (an American business site)

www.dti.gov.uk (Department of Trade and Industry)

www.employment-studies.co.uk (the Institute of Employment Studies site)

www.acas.org.uk (Advisory, Conciliation and Arbitration Service)

REFERENCES

Anderson, G.C. (1993) *Managing Performance Appraisal Systems*. Oxford: Blackwell.

Anderson, G.C. and Barnett, J.G. (1987) 'The characteristics of effective appraisal interviews', *Personnel Review*, Vol. 16, No. 4.

Carroll, S.J. and Schneier, C.E. (1982) *Performance Appraisal and Review Systems*. Glenview, Ill.: Scott Foresman.

Dainow, S. (1988) 'Goal-oriented appraisal', *Training Officer*, January, pp. 6–8.

Fletcher, C. (1993) 'Appraisal: an idea whose time has gone?', *Personnel Management*, September, Vol. 25, No. 9, pp. 34–8.

Goodge, P. and Watts, P. (2000) 'How to Manage 360 degree feedback', *People Management*, February, pp. 50–2.

Grint, K. (1993) 'What's wrong with performance appraisals? A critique and a suggestion', *Human Resource Management*, Vol. R, No. 3, pp. 61–77.

Maier, N.R.F. (1958) *The Appraisal Interview: Objectives, methods and skills*. New York: John Wiley.

Pryor, R. (1985) 'A fresh approach to performance appraisal', *Personnel Management*, June.

Stewart, V. and Stewart, A. (1977) *Practical Performance Appraisal*. Aldershot: Gower.

Storr, F. (2000) 'This is not a Circular', *People Management*, May, pp. 38–40.

Torrington, D.P. (1994) 'Sweets to the sweet: performance-related pay in Britain', *International Journal of Employment Studies*, Vol. 1, No. 2, pp. 149–64.

Torrington, D.P., Earnshaw, J.M., Marchington, L. and Ritchie, M.D. (2003) *Tackling Underperformance in Teachers*. London: Routledge Falmer.

Wright, P.L. and Taylor, D.S. (1984) *Improving Leadership Performance*. Hemel Hempstead: Prentice Hall International.

REVIEW OF PART 3

Delivering performance lies at the core of human resource management. Reverting to the philosophy of human resource management set out at the beginning of the book:

> Human resource management is a series of activities which: first enables working people and the organisation which uses their skills to agree about the objectives and nature of their working relationship and, second, *ensures that the agreement is fulfilled* . . .

The words in italics describe the HR role in performance management. HR people do not personally lead groups outside the HR function, nor do they manage performance directly, but they do ensure that all these activities are carried out and they have a responsibility to ensure that the activities are understood, valued and carried out as effectively as possible. If they can deliver those three requirements – that the processes are understood, valued and carried out effectively – then they make a major contribution to the bottom-line performance referred to above.

A piece of contemporary history illustrates how significant the management of performance can be. When Britain and the United States invaded Iraq in 2003 there was a great deal of speculation about Iraq's possession of weapons of mass destruction. A BBC journalist, Andrew Gilligan, claimed that a British government document on this issue had been 'sexed up' to strengthen the case for war. This allegation was denied by government ministers.

Subsequently the BBC broadcast a television programme in which another journalist, John Ware, stated that Gilligan had previously been 'hauled over the coals' by his superiors for using loose language. Andrew Gilligan was outraged about this statement that had been broadcast by John Ware without any reference to him first. He also said that the interview referred to was with his manager:

> It was a meeting to say how well I had done in Iraq and I was criticized over one matter. It was 95 per cent praise. In no sense could it be described as a hauling over the coals. (The Times, 22 January 2004, p. 1)

He also said that he had checked with his manager, who agreed that he had not been hauled over the coals. This whole issue became one that caused intense interest and imperilled the government, but it illustrates how important running performance management in general, and the appraisal interview in particular, is; making adverse comments about someone's performance without their having the chance to explain or rebut can lead to serious difficulties. Although we have emphasised the importance of setting critical comments in the broader context of more favourable judgements, it is always important to ensure that the criticisms are understood and accepted.

We have said earlier that conducting an appraisal interview is one of the hardest things any manager has to do. For HR specialists managing the surrounding process, the task is not so daunting, but it has to be done very thoroughly indeed.

Bakersfield University

Bakersfield (new) University is in a process of change in order to promote more effective service delivery to its customers within tight budget constraints. Teaching staff have increasingly taken on higher teaching hours as the staff to student ratio has increased from 1 : 18 to 1 : 28 over the past 12 years. The decrease in staff numbers has been managed through the non-replacement of leavers and a limited level of early retirement. In addition to taking on increased teaching loads staff have been exhorted to engage themselves in commercial work and in research to a much greater extent and to complete PhDs. The staff have increasingly felt under pressure, but have on the whole been dedicated workers. Those staff who were most seriously disillusioned by the changes taking place were generally those opting for early retirement, although this process also meant that much expertise was suddenly lost to many departments.

The pressure of work seems set to increase and the goodwill and relatively high performance of staff are increasingly at risk. In the current circumstances departments have found it difficult to recognise the good work of staff by promotion, which had been the traditional approach. Many department heads have tried to deal with this by holding out the hope of future promotion and by recognition of a good job done. Some department heads were more effective in this than others.

The university as a whole has decided to put two major schemes into place in relation to staff performance: first, a staff appraisal scheme and, second, an individual performance-related pay scheme. Standard forms were produced for all departments to use and guidelines were produced relating to the purpose and frequency of appraisal. All departments conformed in terms of carrying out the appraisals, but there were great differences in how this was handled in different departments. Those heads who had experience of successful systems elsewhere, or who were enthusiastic about this change, carried out the appraisals in a more thorough and committed way, and did try to integrate them into the running of the department and link them to departmental goals. Other heads failed to do this, and some were positively against the system as they saw it as impinging on academic freedom, and in any case had never seen themselves as true managers.

The reaction of staff was mixed, often depending on their past employment experiences and length of time employed by the university. In general staff were resistant and sceptical. The culture of the university had been easygoing with staff able to 'do their own thing', and relied on to focus on work that was important for the university and to organise themselves in a conscientious manner. Those who had come to the university from industry had been attracted by the opportunity to control the nature and content of their own work. The new system was perceived as wresting control away from the individual and as an indication that they were not trusted.

There were disparate reactions to the individual performance pay scheme. Department heads were each allocated a small pot of money to distribute as they saw fit between their staff. There were only two months between the announcement of the availability of this money and the date for distribution. Some department heads announced its availability and others never mentioned it. Some made allocations based on performance appraisal results and others made a separate judgement – perhaps allocating money only to someone who was highly valued and who had threatened to leave, but who was not necessarily the best performer. Others shared the money, in different amounts, between the top three high performers and one other shared the money out equally between all staff in the department. Most heads of department allocated the money without any consultation, indeed the heads never got together to talk about the new system and how to handle it. A small number of heads quickly formed a senior staff panel to judge the allocation and one head devised a peer assessment panel.

Staff reactions were mixed. Some were pleased that at last there was potential monetary recognition for the extra effort they had put in. But those who only found out about the system after the money had been allocated to others were angry. Some of the staff who had received the money were so embarrassed about it that they kept it secret. Union representatives complained about the 'shady' process in many departments. Only three heads announced the criteria which had been used to allocate the money. There were complaints about the timescale – but this was improved by the immediate announcement in the university's newsletter of a similar pot of money being made available for the following year. Many objected on principle, though, to the idea of individual performance pay and felt that it undermined the teamwork that was necessary for the department to run effectively. A number argued that if there was to be such pay next year, it should relate directly to the performance appraisal results, and hence became more concerned that these were carried out more thoughtfully.

Staff morale was damaged by these events and the university, which is aware that it mishandled these issues, is anxious to improve matters as quickly as possible.

Required

1 What were the main problems with the approach adopted by the university authorities?

2 What options does the university have for next year? What are the advantages and disadvantages of each?

3 Which option would you recommend, and how would you implement it?

PART 4

DEVELOPMENT

Having set up appropriate methods of organisation and systems to ensure performance, we now have to consider in more detail the ways in which people acquire skill, knowledge and effectiveness in their capacity to perform.

One feature of development is the national framework within which vocational skills can be acquired. Here the individual employer relies on the provision of the education system and the arrangements of professional and other bodies, which specify the appropriate standards for vocational competence. Individuals are developed further within the business, especially in management development, where the skills and knowledge needed tend to be much more specific to the organisation within which they are employed where the methods of development are geared to the ongoing processes of the business.

Individually we are all interested in our own careers. It is now unlikely that anyone will spend more than a few years with a single employer, especially at the start of their working life, so career development is something that we take on as our responsibility rather than as solely the responsibility of our employer.

A crucial part of all individual development is the coaching interaction, whereby a competent performer can become excellent with the skilled and benign assistance of a coach who can hone the performance of the protégé and help improve self-confidence and effectiveness in social situations. Associated with this is the skill of presentation, which is a requirement of all in management positions, especially HR specialists.

CHAPTER 16

STRATEGIC ASPECTS OF DEVELOPMENT

THE OBJECTIVES OF THIS CHAPTER ARE TO:

1   Review the role of training and development and skills in the UK

2   Analyse the link between business strategy and HRD strategy and the various ways that this can be played out

3   Examine the need to align HRD strategy with other aspects of HR strategy, and the influence of the external labour market

4   Explore the range of HRD roles and stakeholders

WINDOW ON PRACTICE

First Monday of the month again – Board meeting. This was the opportunity I'd been waiting for – with some trepidation. My function had produced firm proposals on a new training and development strategy which I was to present to the Board. Development for all was the theme, with key competencies being identified at each level of the organisation and everyone being entitled to six days' off-job training per year, plus coaching on the job to meet individual development goals. A real step in the right direction at last. All I had to do was to get the Board's backing and we'd be off.

I began to present the scheme, complete with user-friendly overheads, information packs for employees and a manager guidance and support package. My colleagues listened intently, for about 5 minutes, then all hell broke loose.

'So what's going to happen to production when they're all off swanning around training – we're understaffed anyway?' – that was Gary, the Production Manager.

Brian from Marketing chipped in next: 'They'll be poached as soon as they're trained if word gets out about this – we'll be doing it for nothing'.

But worst of all was Karen, the MD: 'Why are you proposing this anyway? Granted we desperately need some skills training for those new machines and to encourage flexibility – but we didn't ask for all this. How will it improve business performance? What are we going to get out of all the money this is going to cost us?'

I had hoped more of Karen. She was usually very supportive when I came up with training proposals to solve business problems – well crises would be a better word – we did what I suggested and it usually worked.

This time my words fell on stony ground – no one was interested.

Where do we go from here??????

(Extract from the diary of Len Hodge, Human Resource Director)

ACTIVITY 16.1

Before you read on . . .

- What went wrong in the Board meeting?
- Why do you think that the directors reacted as they did?
- What could Len have done differently to improve his chances of success?
- Where does Len go from here?

There seems to be general agreement that training and development is a good thing, and that it increases productivity, but the question is 'how much?' It is even difficult to show a causal link between HR development and organisational performance, partly because such terms are difficult to define precisely, and partly because the payoff from development may not be seen in the short term. It is also difficult to tie down performance improvements to the development itself and to understand the nature of the link. For example, is performance better because of increased or different HR development, because the reward package has improved or because we have a clearer set of organisational and individual objectives? If there is a link with HR development initiatives, is it that employees have better skills, or that they are better motivated, or that they have been selected from a more able group of candidates attracted to the organisation as it offers a high level of development?

In spite of these difficulties it is important to identify the contribution of HR development to business success, and wider measures for assessing business success, beyond the standard financial indicators, make this more feasible, as, for example, suggested by Kaplan and Norton (1992) and discussed in Chapter 33. While the search for 'evidence' goes on, the current climate encourages high levels of attention to HR development, which is increasingly seen not only as a route to achieving business strategy, but also as a means of building core competence over the longer term to promote organisational growth and sustained competitive advantage. Global competition and a fast pace of change have emphasised the importance of the human capital in the organisation, and the speed and ways in which they learn. A Green Paper produced by the Department for Education and Employment (1998) stated that 'investment in human capital will be the foundation of success in the 21st century'. Nationally the emphasis on qualifications is increasing and Case 16.1 on this book's companion website, **www.pearsoned.co.uk/torrington**, focuses on the development of directors from this perspective.

In addition, levels and sophistication of training and development have received considerable attention in the context of the 'new psychological contract' and the need to promote employability, which we discuss in more detail in Chapter 19. There is some evidence that employee demand for training and development is increasing and that unions are beginning to engage in bargaining for development. Opportunities for training and development may be a vital tool in recruitment and retention, and considered to be a reward when promotion or monetary rewards are less available. However, Stewart and Tansley (2002) found significant structural and cultural barriers to formal and informal learning in organisations; in particular lack of time was identified as an issue.

THE NATIONAL PICTURE AND STRATEGY

Employee development has traditionally been seen as a cost rather than an investment in the UK, although this is certainly changing in some organisations. It has been argued that UK organisations give little support to training and development compared with our European partners (*see*, for example, Handy 1988; Constable and McCormick 1987 for keystone reports). This lack of investment in training and development has been identified as a major factor in Britain's economic performance, and it has been argued that without such investment we will be trapped in a low-wage, low-skills economy (Rainbird 1994; Keep and Mayhew 1999), with the emphasis on competing on price rather than quality. In recent years in the UK there has been a governmental focus on measures to increase our skills levels and reduce skills gaps, which we review in more detail in the following chapter. Despite these efforts, and some evidence from the Workplace Employment Relations Survey (WERS) that training for core employees has increased between 1998 and 2004 (Kersley *et al.* 2006), evidence of skills gaps remains (*see*, for example, Phillips 2006). Our national training framework is voluntarist, with the government's role limited to *encouraging* training rather than intervening, as in many other countries. High levels of skills are seen as critical in promoting high performance and wealth as a country.

WINDOW ON PRACTICE

Access to training: an international comparison with the USA

Finegold and his co-researchers (Finegold *et al.* 2005) investigated the access to training of temporary workers. They found that less than 25 per cent of these workers took part in training and that educated and experienced individuals were more likely to be offered training. Lower-skilled individuals were, however, more likely to accept training when offered it. For temporary office staff, formal training was associated with significant wage growth in the following year. However there was no such association for blue-collar workers. On-job skill development was associated with greater wage growth for both office and blue-collar temporary staff.

Source: Finegold, D., Levenson, A. and Van Buren, M. (2005), 'Access to training and its impact on temporary workers', *Human Resource Management Journal*, Vol. 15, No. 2, pp. 66–85.

Alternatively it has been argued that it is not a lack of investment in training that is the problem but the way such investment is distributed, that is, who it is spent on and the content of the training. It is generally agreed that training spend is unevenly distributed. For example Stevens (2001) argues that it is the people at the lower end of the hierarchy that miss out on training, and Westwood (2001) reports that:

> Access to workforce development is unequal with managers and professionals or those with a degree up to five times more likely to receive work based training than people with no qualification and/or unskilled jobs. (p. 19)

Thomson (2001) explains that broader development is concentrated on those at the beginning of their careers and those in more senior and specialist posts, rather than part-timers and those with fewer qualifications to begin with. The WERS survey found that professionals, associated professionals, managers and those with most qualifications receive most training rather than low-skilled workers (Kersley *et al.* 2006). In the aerospace and pharmaceuticals businesses, defined as high-skills sectors, Lloyd (2002) found a conflict of interests between employees' desire for training and development and managerial short-term aims, lack of accreditation of skills, structured development focused on key employees, access to training being dependent on individual initiative, senior managers viewing training as a minor issue to be dealt with by lower-level managers and insufficient resources. She suggests that there was under-investment and lack of support for flexibility and employability. Westwood (2001) concludes that while we do not do as much training as in Europe, we do spend a lot of money on training that doesn't last very long and on the people who may not need it. In terms of training content there is evidence to suggest that much training is related to induction and particularly health and safety, as demonstrated in the WERS survey, and it has been argued that this does nothing to drive the development of a knowledge-based economy (*see*, for example, Westwood 2001). In addition there is considerable ongoing evidence that employees in small organisations are at a disadvantage in terms of access to training. In the construction industry overall low levels of apprenticeships and a heavy reliance on contingent (temporary) workers were found, particularly in smaller organisations (Forde and MacKenzie 2004), and evidence from the WERS survey suggests that the highest levels of training are in the public sector and larger organisations, particularly those employing high levels of professional employees.

Some view the solution to this problem as increasing state intervention, as many view voluntarism as having a limited effect (*see*, for example, Sloman 2001). It is argued that potential intervention would not mean a return to the levy system, where employers were forced to make an annual payment relative to profits which they could recoup by providing evidence that the equivalent money had been spent of training. But, for example, statutory rights for paid study leave and employer tax credits, and funding mechanisms to create a demand-led system, could be introduced.

A demand-led approach is currently receiving much attention, but there are subtle differences in how this is interpreted. The Leitch Review (Leitch 2006) provides a useful starting point in differentiating between a supply-led and a demand-led training system. He characterises the supply-driven approach as being based on ineffectively articulated collective employer views of training needed and a central system of provision planned by the government to meet these needs, and predict future needs. He suggests that employers and individuals find it difficult to articulate their needs partly due to the profusion of bodies to which they are asked to input, that this approach results in too little investment by employers, too little responsibility being taken by individuals for their own training and a qualifications system divorced from the needs of the workplace. In contrast he suggests a demand-led system is about directly responding to demand rather than planning supply. To achieve this suppliers (such as colleges of further education) only receive funding as they attract customers (rather than being given block funding in advance, based on estimated demand), driving them to respond flexibly and immediately to employer demand. He suggests this approach, as used in Employer Training Pilots (which we discuss in the following chapter), leads to training provision which is more relevant, reflects the needs of customer, and is likely to produce higher completion rates and better value for money.

Keep (2006) identifies current problems for demand-led and employer-led training in terms of the mismatch between employer needs and training provision. For example he suggests that colleges offer longer-term accredited courses as these attach Learning and Skills Council funding in response to government targets, whilst employers may be seeking short uncertificated courses. Such a mismatch is addressed in the recommendations of the Leitch Review, and we highlight the principles and mechanisms proposed to achieve Leitch's 2020 vision for the UK being a world leader in skills in the following chapter. If these mechanisms are effective, training supply should be much more reactive to the real needs of employers; however the limitations of this approach are that such a reactive approach focuses on current and short-term needs at the expense of anticipating and preparing for future needs, and does not address the structure of jobs in this country.

There is, however, a subtly different school of thought in relation to the supply/demand debate which suggests the problem lies with the demand side of the equation rather than the supply side. In other words the problem is not with government initiatives and measures to encourage training, development and learning but with the way that skills are used and jobs are constructed, and hence the employer demand for training, development and learning. In speaking of the Learning and Skills Councils (LSCs), Stevens (2002) says that he is less concerned with what the LSCs can do to encourage learning than with 'whether the UK can generate enough jobs for people who have learnt and can learn' (p. 44). Lloyd (2002) suggests that the country cannot solve its problems just by developing skills, as it is critical to change the structure of jobs:

> All this suggests that we still have a situation in which the majority of organizations are using a reactive strategy: training only in response to the immediate short-term demands of the business, rather than being considered a strategic issue. (Ashton 2003, p. 23)

This implies that training and development needs to be considered at a strategic level in the business, but also, and perhaps more challenging, that employers need to change their business strategies to focus on quality rather than cost. Lloyd (2005), however, in the context of research in the fitness industry suggests that even this may not be enough to shift the low-skills equilibrium, and that amongst other things, customer expectations in this country need to be higher.

ORGANISATIONAL STRATEGY AND HR DEVELOPMENT STRATEGY

For training and development to be effective in terms of business success there is a well-rehearsed argument that it should be linked upfront with business strategy, and the WERS survey (Kersley *et al.* 2006) did find evidence that there was more training in organisations with a strategic plan that covered employee development. McClelland's research (1994) is one of many studies showing that organisations generally do not consider development issues to be part of their competitive strategy formulation, but those that do so identified it to be of value in gaining as well as maintaining competitive advantage. Miller (1991), writing specifically of management development, points to a lack of fit between business strategy and development activity. Miller makes the point that although at the organisational level it is difficult to identify quantitatively the direct impact of strategic investment in development, this impact is well supported by anecdotal evidence and easily demonstrated at the macro-level.

Those organisations that do consider HR development at a strategic level usually see it as a key to *implementing* business strategy in a reactive way. Luoma (2000) categorises this approach as a 'needs-driven' approach, where the purpose of the HR development

| Environment condition | | | |
Stable	Unstable growth	Unstable decline	Competitive
Content Environment scanning skills	Environment scanning skills	Stakeholder relations skills	Competitive strategy development
Understanding sources of stability (e.g. geographically isolated product market, state of technology)	Industry analysis skills	Executive retention skills	Competitor analysis
	Sales, marketing	Understanding competitor environment	Marketing/cost control (dependent on competitive strategy)
	Financial control		
	Creative thinking	Negotiating skills	
Defence strategies	Team building	Diversification skills (technology, human resources)	Industry analysis (dependent on competitive strategy)
Industrial relations skills (but depends on source of stability)	Organisation structure skills		
	Forecasting techniques		
Process Slow pace but 'eventful'	Fast-moving	Medium pace	High pressure
Modest emphasis on individual development	High pressure	Co-operative environment	Competitive
	Intense	Reactive	
Non-competitive but 'aggressive'	Team-oriented		
	Proactive		
Reactive			

Table 16.1 Linking management development to strategic situations

Source: P. Miller (1991) 'A strategic look at management development', *Personnel Management*, August, p. 47. Reproduced with permission of the author.

strategy is to identify and remedy skill deficiencies in relation to the organisational strategy. Luoma suggests that in many articles this is 'implicitly referred to as the only way of managing strategic HRD'. Miller, for example, has demonstrated how management development can be aligned with the strategic positioning of the firm, and this can be seen as coming within the broad remit of such approaches as a needs-driven approach. He has produced a matrix demonstrating how development content and processes can reflect stable growth, unstable growth, unstable decline and competitive positions, as shown in Table 16.1. He offers the model as suggestive, only, of the 'possibilities in designing strategically-oriented management development programmes'.

Luoma (2000), however, identifies a second approach to HR development strategy which is an 'opportunistic approach', where the impetus is external rather than internal. This would include applying leading ideas on development to the organisation in a more general way, rather than specifically in relation to meeting the current business objectives. Such ideas may be developed from benchmarking, case studies, networking and the academic and practitioner press. Such ideas could include content and method, for example the development of a corporate university, and the concept of developing non-employees who perhaps work for suppliers or who are contracted to the organisation. The abilities thus developed may indeed be relevant in achieving business objectives, but they may also be relevant in developing abilities and behaviours which may be the source of future competitiveness. Thus they may also be a means of achieving culture change and/or facilitating the strategy process itself by constructing it as a learning process. In this approach the learning potential of all employees will be emphasised, and the HR development strategy may meet reactive needs in the implementation of business strategy, but may also be proactive in influencing the formation of future business strategy.

The third approach to the strategy link suggested by Luoma is based on the concept, which we discussed in Chapter 2, of organisational capability as the key to sustained competitive advantage, the resource-based view of the firm. This approach is proactive in that it focuses on the desired state of the organisation as defined in its future vision. Within this would come the interest in anticipatory learning, which has been attracting some interest, where future needs are predicated and development takes place in advance.

ACTIVITY 16.2

How can future development needs, say, five years out, be anticipated?

With a group of colleagues/students, brainstorm future needs for your own organisation, or the university/college which you attend.

Of paramount importance, therefore, is the ability to learn. Watkins (1987) suggests that development for strategic *capability*, rather than just targeting development on achieving business objectives, needs to reinforce an entrepreneurial and innovative culture in which learning is part of everyday work. He identifies the importance of acting successfully in novel and unpredictable circumstances and that employees acquire a 'habit of learning, the skills and learning and the desire to learn'. Within this same perspective Mayo (2000) suggests that the intangible assets of the organisation are increasing in proportion to the value of tangible assets. He recognises that developing intellectual capital may be an 'act of faith', or one of budgetary allocation, and suggests that the most useful measures to track such investments are individual capability, individual motivation, the organisational climate and work-group effectiveness. While he recognises the value of competency frameworks in respect of individual development he does point out that these neglect such features as experience and the networks and range of personal contacts, both of which are key to the development of core organisational competencies which are in turn key to developing uniqueness.

In a slightly different but compatible approach McCracken and Wallace (2000) develop a redefinition of strategic HR development, based on an initial conception by Garavan (1991). They suggest nine characteristics of a strategic approach to HR development, which are that:

- HR development shapes the organisation's mission and goals, as well as having a role in strategy implementation.

- Top management are leaders rather than just supporters of HR development.

- Senior management, and not just HR development professionals, are involved in environmental scanning in relation to HR development.

- HR development strategies, policies and plans are developed, which relate to both the present and future direction of the organisation, and the top management team are involved in this.

- Line managers are not only committed and involved in HR development, but involved as strategic partners.
- There is strategic integration with other aspects of HRM.
- Trainers not only have an expanded role, including facilitation and acting as organisational change consultants, but also lead as well as facilitate change.
- HRD professionals have a role in influencing the organisational culture.
- There is an emphasis on future-oriented cost effectiveness and results, in terms of evaluation of HR development activity.

They suggest that each of these aspects needs to be interrelated in an open system. In the following sections we will address some of these characteristics in more detail; however it is worth bearing in mind that changing learning patterns and HR development roles both place challenges on the alignment of learning and development with business needs (for more details *see* Hirsh and Tamkin 2005).

THE EXTERNAL LABOUR MARKET AND HR STRATEGIC INTEGRATION

The external availability of individuals with the skills and competencies required by the organisation will also have an impact on employee development strategy. If skilled individuals are plentiful, management has the choice of whether, and to what extent, it wishes to develop staff internally. If skilled individuals are in short supply, internal development invariably becomes a priority. Predicting demographic and social changes is critical in identifying the extent of internal development required and also who will be available to be developed. In-depth analysis may challenge traditionally held assumptions about who will be developed, how and to what extent. For example, the predicted shortage of younger age groups in the labour market, coupled with a shortage of specific skills, may result in a strategy to develop older rather than younger recruits. This poses potential problems about the need to develop older workers some of whom may learn more slowly. What is the best form of development programme for employees with a very varied base of skills and experiences? Another critical issue is that of redeployment of potentially redundant staff and their development to provide skills that are in short supply.

Prediction of skills availability is critical, as for some jobs the training required will take years rather than months. Realising in January that the skills required in August will not be available in the labour market is too late if the development needed takes three years!

The external labour market clearly has a big impact on employee development strategy, so it is important that there is effective integration between HR development strategy, other aspects of human resource strategy and overall organisational strategy. Currently many skills gaps are being covered by the recruitment of immigrant workers with valued skills and who employers often consider to work very willingly and very hard. However Philpott and Davies (2006) warn that if employers see the immigrant labour force as a quick fix for skills shortages this may undermine employers' efforts to develop the existing workforce.

Where there is a choice between recruiting required skills or developing them internally, given a strategic approach, the decision will reflect on the positioning of the organisation and its strategy. In Chapter 5 we looked at this balance in some depth and you may find it helpful to re-read this. A further issue is that of ensuring a consistency between the skills criteria used for recruitment and development.

From a slightly different perspective, the impact of the organisation's development strategy on recruitment and retention, either explicit or implicit, is often underestimated. There is increasing evidence to show that employees and potential employees are more interested in development opportunities, especially structured ones, than in improvements in financial rewards. Development activity can drive motivation and commitment, and can be used in a strategic way to contribute towards these. For these ends, publishing and marketing the strategy is key, as well as ensuring that the rhetoric is backed up by action. There is also the tricky question of access to and eligibility for development. If it is offered only very selectively, it can have the reverse of the intended impact.

However, not all employees see the need for, nor the value of, development and this means that reward systems need to support the development strategy, a topic to which we return in Chapter 26. If we want employees to learn new skills and become multi-skilled, it is skills development we need to reward rather than the job that is currently done. If we wish employees to gain vocational qualifications, we need to reflect this in our recruitment criteria and reward systems. Harrison (1993) notes that these links are not very strong in most organisations.

Other forms of reward, such as promotions and career moves, also need to reflect the development strategy; for example, in providing appropriate, matrix, career pathways if the strategy is to encourage a multifunctional, creative perspective in the development of future general management. Not only do the pathways have to be available, they also have to be used, and this means encouraging current managers to use them for their staff. In Chapter 19 we explore such career issues more fully.

Finally, an organisation needs to reinforce the skills and competencies it wishes to develop by appraising *those* skills and competencies rather than something else. Developmentally based appraisal systems can clearly be of particular value here. Mabey and Iles (1993) note that a strategic approach to development differs from a tactical one in that a consistent approach to assessment and development is identified with a common skills language and skills criteria attached to overall business objectives. They also note the importance of a decreasing emphasis on subjective assessment. To this end many organisations have introduced a series of development centres, similar to the assessment centres discussed in Chapter 8, but with a clear outcome of individual development plans for each participant related to their current levels of competence and potential career moves, and key competencies required by the business.

TRAINING AND DEVELOPMENT ROLES

Salaman and Mabey (1995) identify a range of stakeholders in strategic training and development, each of which will have different interests in, influence over and ownership of training and development activities and outcomes. They identify senior managers as the *sponsors* of training and development, who will be influenced by professional, personal and political agendas; and business planners as the *clients* who are concerned about customers, competitors and shareholders. Third, they identify *line managers* who are responsible for performance, coaching and resources; and fourth, *participants* who are influenced by their career aspirations and other non-work parts of their lives. HRM staff are identified as *facilitators* who are concerned with best practice, budget credibility and other HR strategy. Lastly, training specialists are identified as *providers*, who are influenced by external networks, professional expertise and educational perspectives. The agendas of each of these groups will overlap on some issues and conflict on others. We have already noted how McCracken and Wallace (2000) have redefined the roles of top managers, line managers and HR professionals so that they are all more proactively involved in HRD strategy. Sloman (2006) defines the role of trainer in a service-led, knowledge-driven economy as 'that of a people developer, and [it] is about supporting, accelerating and directing learning that meets the organisation's needs and that are appropriate to the learner and the context' (p. 35).

Most organisational examples suggest that the formation of training and development strategy is not something that should be 'owned' by the HR/HRD function. The strategy needs to be owned and worked on by the whole organisation, with the HR/HRD function acting in the roles of specialist/expert and coordinator. The function may also play a key role in translating that strategy into action steps. The actions themselves may be carried out by line management, the HR/HRD function or outside consultants. Stewart and Tansley (2002) suggest that the immediate and medium-term contribution of HRD professionals should focus on developing the competence and motivation of managers to manage learning and development. They confirm that such professionals need to act as facilitators and not instructors, and have a focus on the process and design of development rather than its content. There is a debate about where the training and development function should be located in order best to fulfil its role; and the balance between central specialists concentrating on strategic activities and local specialists integrated into departments needs to be appropriate to the organisational context. Hirsh and Tamkin (2005) provide an informed discussion of the central/local tension.

Involvement of line management in the delivery of the training and development strategy can have a range of advantages. Top management have a key role in introducing and promoting strategic developments to staff, for example creating an organisation-wide competency identification programme; setting up a system of development centres or introducing a development-based organisational performance management system. Only if management carry out this role can employees see and believe that there is a commitment from the top. At other levels line managers can be trained as trainers, assessors and advisers in delivering the strategy. This is a mechanism not only for getting them involved, but also for tailoring the strategy to meet the real and different needs of different functions and departments.

External consultants may be used at any stage. They may add to the strategy development process, but there is always the worry that their contribution comes down to an offering of their ready-packaged solution, with a bit of tailoring here and there, rather than something which really meets the needs of the organisation. It is useful to have an outside perspective, but there is an art in defining the role of that outside contribution.

In delivery, external consultants may make a valuable contribution where a large number of courses have to be run over a short period. The disadvantages are that they can never really understand all the organisational issues, and that they may be seen as someone from outside imposing a new process on the organisation.

WINDOW ON PRACTICE

One large organisation had a well-established training function and on an annual basis they sat down to plan the year ahead. They would plan how many of what types of course would be needed, depending on the demand in the previous year and the availability of appropriate staff. New courses would be introduced where a need had been identified and they were piloted. Course evaluation data (collected mainly from participants, but sometimes from their managers) were used to inform course demand and course structure and content.

Individuals were booked on training courses following discussion with their manager regarding their individual needs. There were often problems resulting from long waiting lists and individuals being nominated for courses for which they were not eligible (defined by the nature of their job) – it appeared that individuals sometimes nominated themselves and the manager rubber-stamped this.

Some years later, after efforts on the part of general management and training and development management to employ a more strategic approach to the business, the picture was very different. Performance management had been introduced as the cornerstone of people management, resulting from a multifunctional, high-level working party. A course was devised and delivered in chunks of one and two days and this was delivered to all staff, with slightly differing versions for managers and non-managers. The course was an integrating mechanism for all people management activities and most importantly it promoted a cohesive style and philosophy of people management that the organisation felt was critical in the achievement of its business objectives. Not only was senior general management involved in the initial stages of the course, but key line managers were involved in delivering the subsequent modules.

WINDOW ON PRACTICE

Holden and Livian (1992) compared some strategic aspects of training across 10 European countries.*

Training as a recruitment strategy

All 10 countries identified training as being used in recruitment strategy. In eight (not including Germany and Sweden) training for new recruits was seen as the most popular method (from a list of 11) of attracting recruits.

Knowledge of investment in training

Although all organisations had increased expenditure on training over the previous year, many were unclear about the actual money spent as a proportion of wages. However, this varied by country. The three highest – Sweden (44 per cent of organisations did not know), Denmark (42 per cent of organisations did not know) and the UK (38 per cent of organisations did not know) – compare markedly with the lowest, France, where only 2 per cent of organisations did not know. This no doubt reflects the French taxation system, where a tax is levied if the organisation does not spend 1.2 per cent of the paybill on training.

Actual investment in training

In only Sweden and France do more than a quarter of the organisations surveyed spend above 4 per cent of the paybill on training. With the exception of France, the majority of organisations in each of the other countries spent less than 2 per cent of their paybill on training.

Time spent on training

Only some 10 per cent of organisations provided over 10 days' training per year – the exception to this being Spain, where 29 per cent of organisations provided this level of training. In all countries the amount of time for managerial training was greater than that for other groups of employees.

* The countries surveyed were Switzerland, Denmark, Germany, Spain, Finland, Italy, Norway, Netherlands, Sweden and the UK.
Source: Summarised from L. Holden and Y. Livian (1992) 'Does strategic training policy exist? Some evidence from ten European countries', *Personnel Review*, Vol. 21, No. 1, pp. 12–23.

 Case 16.2 on this book's companion website, **www.pearsoned.co.uk/torrington**, focuses on the changing roles of training and development specialists.

SUMMARY PROPOSITIONS

16.1 There is currently a voluntarist approach to training and development in the UK, which means that employers make their own choices about the extent to which they train. The government attempts to influence what organisations do by a range of supply-side initiatives.

16.2 HR development strategy needs to focus on the organisation's strategy and objectives and involves identifying the skills and competencies required to achieve this, now and in the future. HR development strategy may also be opportunistic and proactive and may influence the development of organisational strategy.

16.3 It is important that HR development strategy is reinforced by, and reinforces, other HR strategy, and the context of the external labour market will be an influencing factor in how these strategies are framed.

16.4 The HR/HRD function does not own HR development strategy – it must be owned by the organisation as a whole.

GENERAL DISCUSSION TOPICS

1 Both the UK as a whole and organisations themselves would benefit if the government adopted an interventionist approach to training.
- Do you agree or disagree? Why?
- How might this intervention be shaped?

2 What opportunities are there for development strategy and reward strategy to be mutually supportive?

Think of examples (real or potential) where reward strategies undermine development strategies.

FURTHER READING

Grieves, J. (2003) *Strategic Human Resource Development*. London: Sage.
A thoughtful approach to strategic human resource development which considers its roots in organisational development and which rises above the level of training programmes. The book presents an ethical approach to change management and reviews the role of culture, the consultancy relationship and strategic HRD interventions.

Heaton, I. and Suff, P. (2006) *Learning and Development*. London: CIPD.
This is a very useful training resource providing a good section on a strategic approach, credibility and working with stakeholders. There is other more operational material and some useful case studies to illustrate key messages. It is not cheap but would make a useful organisational purchase.

Wright, P. and Geroy, G. (2001) 'Changing the mindset: the training myth and the need for world-class performance', *International Journal of Human Resource Management*, Vol. 12, No. 4, pp. 586–600.
An interesting article which challenges the link between training and productivity. The article argues that training is used instead of addressing the problems of poor management, job design and physical aspects of the job. The authors argue that training is often not applied due to cultural barriers and the fact that it is too narrowly focused on current jobs. They suggest that training should be more broadly based on developing capability and that the training function needs to reinvent itself and have a broader-based approach rather than concentrating on skills development.

REFERENCES

Ashton, D. (2003) 'Training Trends: Past, Present and Future', in CIPD (ed.), *Reflections: New Developments in Training*. London: CIPD.
Constable, R. and McCormick, R.J. (1987) *The Making of British Managers*. London: BIM.
Department for Education and Employment (1998) *The LEARNING Age: A Renaissance for a New Britain*, Green Paper, Cm. 3790. London: HMSO.

Finegold, D., Levenson, A. and Van Buren, M. (2005) 'Access to training and its impact on temporary workers', *Human Resource Management Journal*, Vol. 15, No. 2, pp. 66–85.

Forde, C. and MacKenzie, R. (2004) 'Cementing skills: training and labour use in UK construction', *Human Resource Management Journal*, Vol. 14, No. 3, pp. 74–88.

Garavan, T. (1991) 'Strategic Human Resource Development', *Journal of European Industrial Training*, Vol. 11, No. 9, pp. 17–30.

Handy, C. (1988) *Making Managers*. London: Pitman.

Harrison, R. (1993) *Human Resource Management: Issues and Strategies*. Wokingham: Addison Wesley.

Hirsh, W. and Tamkin, P. (2005) 'Piece by piece: How do organizations align their training and development with business needs?', *People Management*, Vol. 11, No. 24, 8 December, pp. 32–4.

Holden, L. and Livian, Y. (1992) 'Does strategic training policy exist? Some evidence from ten European countries', *Personnel Review*, Vol. 21, No. 1, pp. 12–23.

Journal of Management Education and Development (1994) 'Anticipatory learning: learning for the twenty-first century', Vol. 12, No. 6.

Kaplan, R. and Norton, D. (1992) 'The balanced scorecard – measures that drive performance', *Harvard Business Review*, January–February, pp. 71–9.

Keep, E. (2006) 'Live and Learn', *People Management*, Vol. 12, No. 15, 27 July, p. 7.

Keep, E. and Mayhew, K. (1999) 'The assessment: knowledge, skills and competitiveness', *Oxford Review of Economic Policy*, Vol. 15, No. 1, pp. 1–15.

Kersley, B., Alpin, C., Forth, J., Bryson, A., Bewley, H., Dix, G. and Oxenbridge, S. (2006) *Inside the Workplace: Findings from the 2004 Workplace Employment Relations Survey*, London: Routledge.

Leitch, S. (2006) *Leitch Review of Skills: Prosperity for all in the Global economy: Final Report*. London: HMSO, December.

Lloyd, C. (2002) 'Training and development deficiencies in "high skill" sectors', *Human Resource Management Journal*, Vol. 12, No. 2, pp. 64–81.

Lloyd, C. (2005) 'Competitive strategy and skills: working out the fit in the fitness industry', *Human Resource Management Journal*, Vol. 15, No. 2, pp. 15–34.

Luoma, M. (2000) 'Investigating the link between strategy and HRD', *Personnel Review*, Vol. 29, No. 6.

Mabey, C. and Iles, P. (1993) 'Development practices: succession planning and new manager development', *Human Resource Management Journal*, Vol. 3, No. 4.

McClelland, S. (1994) 'Gaining competitive advantage through strategic management development', *Journal of Management Development*, Vol. 13, No. 5, pp. 4–13.

McCracken, M. and Wallace, M. (2000) 'Towards a Redefinition of Strategic HRD', *Journal of European Industrial Training*, Vol. 24, No. 5, pp. 281–90.

Mayo, A. (2000) 'The role of development in the growth of intellectual capital', *Personnel Review*, Vol. 29, No. 4.

Miller, P. (1991) 'A strategic look at management development', *Personnel Management*, August, pp. 46–9.

Phillips, L. (2006) 'UK's IT skills gap remains wide', *People Management*, Vol. 12, No. 23, 23 November, p. 12.

Philpott, J. and Davies, G. (2006) 'No turning back', *People Management*, Vol. 12, No. 18, 14 September, pp. 26–30.

Rainbird, H. (1994) 'Continuing training', in K. Sisson (ed.), *Personnel Management in Britain*. Oxford: Blackwell.

Salaman, G. and Mabey, C. (1995) *Strategic Human Resource Management*. Oxford: Blackwell Business.

Sloman, M. (2001) 'Sharing the power of learning', in CIPD (ed.), *The Future of Learning for Work*. London: CIPD.

Sloman, M. (2006) 'Just your cup of tea', *People Management*, Vol. 12, No. 24, 7 December, pp. 34–6.

Stevens, J. (2001) 'Training from the top down', *People Management*, Vol. 7, No. 11, 31 May, p. 53.

Stevens, J. (2002) 'Balancing Act', *People Management*, Vol. 8, No. 25, 26 December, p. 44.

Stewart, J. and Tansley, C. (2002) *Training in the Knowledge Economy*. London: CIPD.

Thomson, A. (2001) 'Too much apple pie', *People Management*, Vol. 7, No. 9, 3 May, p. 49.

Watkins, J. (1987) 'Management development policy in a fast-changing environment: the case of a public sector service organisation', *Management Education and Development*, Vol. 18, Pt 3, pp. 181–93.

Westwood, A. (2001) 'Drawing a line – who is going to train our workforce?' in CIPD (ed.), *The Future of Learning for Work*. London: CIPD.

An extensive range of additional materials, including multiple choice questions, answers to questions and links to useful websites can be found on the Human Resource Management Companion Website at **www.pearsoned.co.uk/torrington**.

CONTEXT, COMPETENCE AND COMPETENCIES

THE OBJECTIVES OF THIS CHAPTER ARE TO:

1   Outline key aspects of the national training framework and proposed changes in the Leitch Review

2   Identify the characteristics of NVQs and analyse their strengths and weaknesses

3   Identify the characteristics of behavioural competencies and analyse their strengths and weaknesses

In the UK the national training framework is constantly changing in an attempt to improve the skills base. The latest thinking is encapsulated in the Leitch Report which we discuss at the start of this chapter. The Leitch Report uses National Vocational Qualification (NVQ) levels (NVQs or equivalents) as the measure of existing and targeted skills. These qualifications and the competences they represent have become the language of our skills since they were introduced in 1987 as a vehicle for skills improvement.

The words competence, competency and competencies pervade much of the HRM literature, and it is argued that they provide a sound basis for the integration of HRM activities. The terms however are often used confusingly, so we will start with some definitions. The word 'competence' (plural 'competences') relates to the ability to carry out a specific task, and it is this interpretation of competence that forms the foundation for NVQs, referred to above, which could be described as job standards. The concept is therefore output, or performance based. In contrast the word 'competency' and its plural 'competencies' refer to behaviour (*see*, for example, Whiddett and Hollyforde 1999, p. 5) rather than task achievement, and there is general agreement that this concept is based on the work of Boyatzis (1982). There is a third definition, with which we are not concerned in this chapter, and that is the core competence of the organisation, which relates to the foundation for competitive advantage. Before exploring competence and competencies in more detail we first outline the context in terms of the changing national training framework.

NATIONAL TRAINING FRAMEWORK

We referred in the last chapter to government initiatives intended to encourage the extent and nature of employer training and development in order to narrow the skills gap, and improve British industrial performance. In this section we explain the Leitch Report (2006) and then briefly review four government initiatives/bodies highlighting any consequences of the Report for them. The UK training framework is complex and based on a number of reports and papers, and comprises implementing bodies and a range of specific initiatives. The framework constantly evolves, sometimes dramatically but most often in smaller changes as, for example, individual initiatives or bodies are introduced, changed or abandoned. Harrison (2005) provides a useful table listing many of the reports, bodies and initiatives. There is continued concern that our approach to skills training is confusing, and that whilst large amounts of money are being spent by the government the money is not used as effectively as it could be, with information overload resulting from too many initiatives and bodies involved (EEF 2006). The Leitch Review, published as we write this text, proposes some significant developments in order to attain the proposed skills targets in 2020.

The Leitch Review of Skills: Prosperity for all in the global economy – world-class skills

The following sections are summarised from the Final Report of the Leitch Review published in December 2006:

Purpose of the Review

The purpose of the review was to identify the UK's optimal skills mix for 2020 to maximise economic growth, productivity and social justice, to set out how responsibilities should be balanced for achieving that skills profile and to consider the policy framework required to support it.

Vision for 2020

The vision is for the UK to become a world leader in skills by 2020 with reference to the top quartile of the 31 leading industrial countries that make up the OECD (Organisation for Economic Cooperation and Development). This will require the almost doubling of skills attainment, and the targets include:

- 95 per cent of adults to achieve basic literacy and numeracy (compared with 85 per cent for literacy and 79 per cent for numeracy in 2005);
- more than 90 per cent of adults to achieve NVQ/NVQ equivalent level 2 (compared with 69 per cent in 2005);
- moving the balance of intermediate skills from level 2 to level 3 (this will mean a further 1.9 million level 3 completions and increase the number of apprentices to 500,000 per year);
- more than 40 per cent of adults to achieve level 4 (compared with 29 per cent in 2005).

Principles

Leitch proposed that delivery of the vision should be underpinned by the following principles:

- Shared responsibility for skill development between employers, the individual and the government.
- The focus should be on economically valuable skills which should where possible be portable so as to encourage labour mobility.
- Skills should be demand led, meeting the needs of employers and individuals rather than being centrally planned.
- The framework must adapt and respond to future market needs as they arise.
- Existing structures to be built upon (rather than swept away), and improved through simplification and rationalisation, as continuity is important.

Main recommendations

- Progress is best measured by increased adult skill attainment at all levels, with the government increasing the share of gross domestic product (GDP) allocated to education and skills, together with additional investment by employers and individuals.
- Train to Gain and Individual Learner Accounts should be the route for all public funding for vocational skills by 2010.

- Employer voice to be strengthened, and employers' ability to better articulate skill needs to be improved via a new Commission for Employment and Skills to channel views, as well as rationalising existing bodies.

- A voluntary employer 'pledge' to be launched reflecting a commitment to train all eligible employees to level 2, with a statutory entitlement to be introduced if progress is insufficient by 2010.

- Increase employer involvement in level 3 and 4 qualifications in the workplace, increasing apprenticeships, extending Train to Gain to higher levels, and improving engagement between employers and universities.

- Increase people's aspirations and awareness of skills, via sustained awareness programmes and a new universal adult careers service.

- Create a new integrated employment and skills service, based on existing structures, to include basic skills programmes for the unemployed and a network of employer-led Employment and Skills Boards.

The review recommends that the government must now decide the detailed next steps. To what extent the recommendations of this review will help simplify and clarify the skills system in the UK remains to be seen as employers react to changes being made.

Learning and Skills Councils (LSCs)

As a result of the 1999 White Paper *Learning to Succeed* the LSCs have replaced the old Training and Education Councils (TECs). They are responsible for planning and funding all post-16 education and training, except for the university sector. The LSC, set up in 2001, has produced a national workforce development strategy in response to three key objectives (*see* Sanderson 2002): to stimulate demand from employers and individuals for education and training; to improve the responsiveness and flexibility of providers better to meet business needs; and to provide better labour market intelligence. However, evidence suggests that employers are not able clearly to differentiate LSCs from TECs (CIPD 2003). The same survey reports that most employers contact LSCs about qualifications, such as NVQs. The EEF (2006) proposes that the LSC be amalgamated with the Sector Skills Development Agency (SSDA).

Sector Skills Councils (SSCs) and the SSDA

SSCs have taken over from the old National Training Organisations (NTOs) and they are generally amalgamations of the old NTOs covering a wider range of sectors and drawing in more employers. The SSCs have to apply to be licensed by the SSDA before they can operate, and are funded and supported by this body. SSCs are employer-led independent organisations. Twenty-five have been licensed at the time of writing, compared with 70 NTOs, covering around 85 per cent of the workforce, and Terry Watts, Chief Executive of Proskills, the SSC for the process and manufacturing sector, comments that the SSCs are working with the government to increase representation to 100 per cent (Phillips 2006). Like the old NTOs, SSCs are empowered to set occupational standards (on which NVQs are based); promote training which will help to reduce skills shortages; and lobby on behalf of employers. However there are concerns from the CIPD and some of the SSCs that the agenda for SSCs is driven too much by the government rather than the needs of employers (Phillips 2006).

Train to Gain/ Employer Training Pilots

Employer Training Pilots (ETPs) were experimented with as a means of encouraging training by rewarding employers with state funding for giving employees time off for training. The pilots proved very successful and are now been expanded under the banner 'Train to Gain', as the pilot scheme is phased out.

Train to Gain is accessed through the LSCs, which via a broker offer advice to employers on their skills needs and match this up with appropriate provision from training providers and the further education (FE) sector. The aim is for advice to be flexible and tailored to the business, and that solutions be negotiated in a similar manner between the employer and the provider. Train to Gain is targeted on smaller employers and low-skill sectors of the economy with a broadly consistent approach in each of the nine LSC regions, but with room for some adaptability. Brokers are charged with proactively contacting 'hard to reach' employers and to focus on the attainment of level 2 qualifications and basic numeracy and literacy, but also to go beyond this in terms of level. Some elements of provision under Train to Gain will be state funded, broadly level 2 qualifications and basic skills, and in addition there is funding for wages costs for these qualifications for employers with a staffing of under 50.

The brokers are independent and impartial advisers and organisations which have won contracts from the LSC via a competitive tendering process. An independent review of Employer Training Pilots (where brokers were similarly used) by the Small Business Council in 2005 indicated that employers valued the contribution of brokers.

The target for Train to Gain is that 53,000 employers will be engaged in 2007–8 and in each successive year to 2010. The costs will be £399 million for provision in 2007–8, £36 million for brokerage costs and £38 million for wages costs. The approach is demand led as training providers do not receive any funding until an employee begins training.

For businesses with 5,000 or more employees, the National Employer Service of the LSC will provide brokerage.

Investors in People (IiP)

Compared with many government initiatives IiP has had a long-lasting impact since being introduced in 1991, although since then there have been several major revisions. More recent versions are increasingly less prescriptive and have more emphasis on outcomes rather than the process by which the business achieves IiP recognition. In addition they have attempted to simplify the framework and make it more user friendly. There are now three principles: plan, do and review, and there are 10 criteria in total set against the three principles in the latest framework applied from January 2006 onwards. In the original framework organisations needed to go through a range of internal processes in order to meet the standard and provide a portfolio of evidence to be assessed by IiP UK, which may or may not result in accreditation. The aim of these processes was to ensure that the appropriate training and development policies and procedures exist to meet business goals, and more generally to promote a culture where this linkage is a key part of the way the organisation operates. The current approach is more flexible, providing more opportunities to build on existing organisational processes; assessment no longer requires huge amounts of paperwork, as assessors now take on the responsibility of collecting mainly verbal evidence by interviewing a range of employees in relation to the standard. Whilst major revisions to the standard have generally been received as improvements the process of moving from an existing to a revised standard may be challenging and problematic for organisations and advisers/assessors alike (*see*, for example, Collins and Smith 2004).

IDS (2006) provides a helpful analysis of how the 2006 standard differs from what has gone before. In terms of content the new standard incorporates more attention on employee involvement, for example in setting objectives for their own work and perhaps in providing input to more strategic issues. It also pays more attention to continuous development as there is now a requirement for organisations to address any deficiencies found in their assessment when they are accredited. Third, there is greater focus on the organisation's responsibility to ensure that managers have the resources and capabilities needed to perform in line with the standard; there is also a requirement to look at the actual performance of managers. The framework has been extended in two distinct ways. First, a 'profile' framework has been developed in which four levels of achievement against the standard are identified rather than just the base level in the main standard. The second way in which the standard has been extended is by the provision of three specialised modules intended to be used as development tools, and against which employers can apply to be assessed. These three modules are leadership and management; recruitment and selection; and work-life balance. In addition in 2004 the 'Investors in People Champion' status was introduced, for which accredited IiP employers could apply. To achieve Champion status organisations need to be outstanding in terms of how they have used IiP to improve organisational performance; to disseminate good IiP practice and learning (for example in visiting other organisations to promote IiP); to excel in one or more organisational aspects of IiP (and to be capable, say, of running a best practice seminar on this); and to inspire enthusiasm for continuous improvement.

The IiP standard is developed and promoted by Investors in People UK, a public body representing employers, training organisations and unions. The initial targets set for the number of employers seeking and achieving the IiP recognised status are proving to have been very ambitious. However, by 2006 37,000 employers have been accredited and this covers well over one-quarter of UK employees (IDS 2006). A commitment to IiP requires significant time and effort, and the benefits from gaining recognition of IiP status have been debated. Some studies have found an increase in commitment to HR development, a belief in the value of the process and perceived performance gains (*see*, for example, Alberga *et al*. 1997); other studies have found significant benefits, although organisations themselves found it difficult to identify these (Down and Smith 1998). There is a tendency in the IiP process to focus on formal qualifications, such as NVQs, and for the significance of informal development to be neglected (*see*, for example, Ram 2000).

Some studies show that organisations struggle with the bureaucracy of the approach, and Ram also found considerable evidence that the standard is sought for its 'stamp of approval' rather than because of a genuine commitment to improving training; and Down and Smith also argue convincingly that it is those organisations that have most to gain from pursuing the standard that are least likely to attempt to do this. In a study of a hospital trust Grugulis and Bevitt (2002) found that most of the soft HR initiatives employed had existed before accreditation. Hammond (2001) reports research carried out by Hoque, who found that a substantial minority of accredited workplaces did not adopt best practice. Although he also found that training is generally better in accredited organisations, they were still characterised by a lack of training opportunities. It will be interesting to see how evaluation of the new 2006 IiP standard in practice compares with this research on the earlier frameworks.

COMPETENCES AND NVQS

Characteristics and benefits of NVQs

The vehicle for this attempted revolution has been an array of National Vocational Qualifications (NVQs), which have brought together a wide and unstructured range of previous vocational qualifications and are heavily promoted by the LSCs and the Department for Education and Employment. Now vocational qualifications either are completed directly by the NVQ competence route itself, or, if they are of a different nature, will be identified as equivalent to a specific NVQ level. NVQs have been developed for all occupational areas, and within each occupation there are potentially eight (initially five) levels of NVQ with level 1 relating to basic and routine work and levels 5, 6, 7 and 8 relating to the most complex tasks. There are standards for the management occupation at levels 2, 3, 4 and 5.

The basic idea of training for competence is that it should be criterion related, directed at developing the ability of trainees to perform specific tasks directly related to the job they are in or for which they are preparing, expressed in terms of performance outcomes and specific indicators. It is a reaction against the confetti-scattering approach to training as being a good thing in its own right, concerned with the general education of people dealing with general matters. The design of the standards themselves was initially somewhat complex, but revisions have tried to simplify this. The management standards, for example, have undergone two major revisions in 1997 and 2004 (with assessments against the 2004 standards beginning around a couple of years after the standard was developed). Each standard is first divided into job roles. For example in the updated (2004) level 3 management standards, four mandatory job roles are identified with 11 optional roles, as shown in Table 17.1. To achieve the level 3 qualification candidates have to be satisfactorily assessed against all mandatory roles and three of the optional roles.

In the United Kingdom, competence standards have been developed in line with other aspects of change in education, such as experiential learning, problem-based learning,

Table 17.1 Level 3 management standards

Key roles: Mandatory
A2	Manage your own resources and professional development
B6	Provide leadership for your own area of responsibility
D6	Allocate and monitor the progress and quality of work in your area of responsibility
E6	Ensure health and safety requirements are met in your area of responsibility

Optional roles
B11	Promote equality of opportunity and diversity in your area of responsibility
C2	Encourage innovation in your area of responsibility
C5	Plan change
C6	Implement change
D1	Develop productive working relationships with colleagues
D3	Recruit, select and keep colleagues
D7	Provide learning opportunities for colleagues
E1	Manage a budget
F1	Manage a project
F6	Monitor and solve customer service problems
F8	Work with others to improve customer service

the national curriculum and GCSEs, as an attempt to develop the ability of learners to *do* rather than to *know*. This introduces greater flexibility into the learning process, so that career aspirants are not restrained by the elitist exclusiveness of either educational institutions or professional associations. The standards are designed so that the vast majority of work can be done 'on the job' with maybe small inputs from educational providers. Where this route is not possible the standards can be completed as part of a 'course'. Wherever they are done the individual's completed portfolio of work has to be assessed by a qualified and accredited assessor.

The principles of competencies leading to national vocational qualifications are:

1 **Open access.** There should be no artificial barriers to training, such as that it is available only to people who are members of a professional body, such as the Chartered Institute of Personnel and Development or the Law Society, or those in a particular age group. There are no previous qualifications required in order to embark on the NVQ process.

2 There is a focus on what people can **do**, rather than on the process of learning. Master's degree students in a university typically cannot graduate in less than 12 months. With competence-based qualifications, you graduate when you can demonstrate competence, however long or short a period it takes you to achieve the standard.

3 **National** vocational qualifications, which are the same wherever the training takes place, so that the control is in the hands of the awarding body rather than the training body, and there is only one strand of qualification for each vocational area: no multiplication of rival qualifications. The overall control is with the National Council for Vocational Qualifications (NCVQ).

4 The feature of performance **standards** as the basis of assessment; not essays or written-up case studies, but practical demonstrations in working situations, or replicas, of an ability to do the job at a specified standard. Although training schemes are littered with euphoria about excellence, the competence basis has only one standard. The only degree of differentiation between trainees is the length of time taken to complete the qualification.

5 **Flexibility and modularisation.** People must be able to transfer their learning more or less at will between 'providers', so that they are not tied to a single institution or by needless regulations about attendance. Candidates can stop and start their work towards the standard as it suits their personal or work needs, and they can begin on any element of the standard and complete the elements in any order. This means that standards can be worked on in line with business demands.

6 **Accreditation of prior experience and learning.** You can accredit prior learning, no matter how you acquired it. If you have been able to acquire a competence by straightforward experience or practice at home, and if you can reach the performance standard, you can receive the credit for it. If prior experience enables you to demonstrate competence, you can receive credit for that as well.

7 Flexibility in assessment is partly achieved by the **portfolio** principle, as you accumulate evidence of your competence from your regular, day-to-day working and submit it for assessment as appropriate. For further details of how technology can be used to enhance portfolio compilation, *see* Case 17.1 at **www.pearsoned.co.uk/ torrington**.

8 The standards to be achieved are determined by designated **standards-setting bodies some of which are SSCs**, which involve or consult with employers, practitioners and professional bodies, so that vocational standards are decided by those in charge of the workplace instead of by those in charge of the classroom. The standards-setting body for the management and leadership standards is the Management Standards Organisation (**www.management-standards.org.uk**).

9 **Assessment.** Written examinations are not regarded as being always the most appropriate means of assessing competence. Assessment of whether or not the learner has attained the appropriate standard must be by a **qualified assessor**, who becomes qualified by demonstrating competence according to two units of the scheme produced by the Training and Development Lead Body. Assessment may be partly by portfolio (*see* 7 above), but has to be **work based**. Originally assessment was to be in the workplace, but that proved impracticable to implement in every case.

10 **General National Vocational Qualifications (GNVQs)** are school or college based and take the place of BTec and similar qualifications.

The general intention is that NVQs should run alongside traditional academic qualifications at undergraduate level.

The standards have strong support from some quarters as we have already stated, but there have been fewer reports of the benefits of pursuing the standards. Winterton and Winterton (1999) report that organisations adopting the management standards have been able to identify gaps in competence, identify competence development targets, develop a coherent structure for training and development and identify clearer criteria for human resource planning and career progression. In our own studies, again in relation to the management standards, it was found that participants developed self-confidence in their managerial role, became better organised and were motivated to focus on improvement (Hall and Holman 1996). Most critically, we found that following the standards was a rite of passage for those who were new to the managerial world (Holman and Hall 1996).

Problematic aspects of NVQs

NVQs have had a rough ride since the concept was first introduced, coming under some heavy criticism and not being extensively taken up. Revisions of the standards have aimed to address problems, but this has not always been achieved satisfactorily. However research on the use of the standards inevitably relates to earlier versions, and it will be some time before we see the impact of the changes made in 2004 as there is a time lag before assessments can be made against these and then a further time lag before researchers can investigate how the process has worked.

One of the most common reservations about NVQs is the laborious nature of assessment. In our own studies (Hall and Holman 1996) we found that candidates were heavily engaged in a 'paper chase' to gather evidence of their competence, and this seemed to take over from the importance of the learning process and what was being learned. It is also very difficult to ensure a satisfactory quality of assessment, where so much depends on a large number of individual assessors.

NVQs have developed an entire vocabulary to bring the concept into action, and this causes difficulties (*see*, for example, Priddley and Williams 2000). Initially one of the key terms is 'range indicators' and at a meeting of 50 HR practitioners, no one could produce a definition that the rest of the group could accept. These indicators have now been dropped, as have performance criteria, and in the latest review of the management standards the 'elements of performance' have also been dropped to avoid duplication where these appeared against many different roles. However the framework remains complex. You will have noticed the numbers and letters in Table 17.1. These refer to a full list of roles from which a selection is made appropriate to the level of NVQ an individual is aiming to achieve. Group A is about Managing self and personal skills; B is about Providing direction; C about Facilitating change; D about Working with people; E about Using resources; and F about achieving results.

In the 2004 version of the management standards there are both mandatory and optional units at each level so that the qualification itself gives only a partial indication of areas of competence.

In relation to the management standards in particular there is a criticism that the standards are reductionist. In other words, because the standards try to spell out the detail of what management entails, the complexity of management gets lost as it is difficult to specify this in the structure and language of the standards. A related criticism is that the functional approach (*see*, for example, Stewart and Hamblin 1992), used to identify what management is (that is, through specifying management activities), is a narrow and partial approach. The early management standards were also criticised for being an incomplete representation of management, and yet in our research we found that those following the pre-1997 standard had not recognised any omissions, for example ethics and politics.

A lack of attention to learning and cognitive processes has also been identified (for example by Holman and Thorpe 1993), as the emphasis is on doing rather than thinking and understanding. The qualifications require candidates to demonstrate that they can competently perform actions but neglect an explanation of why such actions may be appropriate. Grugulis (2003) identifies this as a 'Taylorist separation between conception and execution' (p. 462). The new management standards have gone some way to broaden the focus by including indications of knowledge within each standard as well as performance standards.

It has also been argued that following the standards rubber-stamps the level of competence already achieved, rather than stimulating further development.

From their introduction in 1987 until 2006, 6.1 million NVQ/SNVQ awards have been made. In 2005–6, 662,000 awards were made, and currently there is a year-on-year increase in qualifications, although the increase is decreasing gradually. However this has not always been the case; for example, in 2001–2 there was a five per cent drop in the number of all vocational qualifications awarded: in this period 408,000 were awarded compared with 428,000 in 2000–1 (DfEE 2003). However awards of traditional vocational qualifications continue to outstrip NVQs, especially at higher levels, and these are increasingly important. There were 1.2 million vocational awards made outside NVQs themselves. These are reported awards which only made up about 60 per cent of all non-NVQ awards. So it appears that the goal of NVQs taking over from traditional qualifications has not been achieved. The figures reported in this paragraph are from (DfEE 2007) unless otherwise stated.

BEHAVIOURAL COMPETENCIES

Characteristics of behavioural competencies

The key piece of research on competencies is by Richard Boyatzis, who carried out a large-scale intensive study of 2,000 managers, holding 41 different jobs in 12 organisations. He defines a competency as: 'an underlying characteristic of a person which results in effective and/or superior performance in a job' (Boyatzis 1982, p. 21).

Competency may be a trait, which is a characteristic or quality that a person has, such as efficacy, which is the trait of believing you are in control of your future and fate. When you encounter a problem, you then take an initiative to resolve the problem, rather than wait for someone else to do it.

Competency may be a motive, which is a drive or thought related to a particular goal, such as achievement, which is a need to improve and compete against a standard of excellence.

Competency may be a skill, which is the ability to demonstrate a sequence of behaviour that is functionally related to attaining a performance goal. Being able to tune and diagnose faults in a car engine is a skill, because it requires the ability to identify a sequence of actions, which will accomplish a specific objective. It also involves being able to identify potential obstacles and sources of help in overcoming them. The skill can be applied to a range of different situations. The ability to change the sparking plugs is an ability only to perform that action.

Competency may be a person's self-image, which is the understanding we have of ourselves and an assessment of where we stand in the context of values held by others in our environment. For example: 'I am creative and innovative. I am expressive and I care about others.' In a job requiring routine work and self-discipline, that might modify to: 'I am creative and innovative. I am too expressive. I care about others and lack a degree of self-discipline.'

Competency may be a person's social role, which is a perception of the social norms and behaviours that are acceptable and the behaviours that the person then adopts in order to fit in. It may be a body of knowledge.

If these are the elements of competency, some of them can be developed, some can be modified and some can be measured, but not all.

Threshold competencies	
Use of unilateral power	Using forms of influence to obtain compliance.
Accurate self-assessment	Having a realistic or grounded view of oneself, seeing personal strengths and weaknesses and knowing one's limitations.
Positive regard	Having a basic belief in others; that people are good; being optimistic and causing others to feel valued.
Spontaneity	Being able to express oneself freely or easily, sometimes making quick or snap decisions.
Logical thought	Placing events in causal sequence; being orderly and systematic.
Specialised knowledge	Having usable facts, theories, frameworks or models.
Developing others	Helping others to do their jobs, adopting the role of coach and using feedback skills in facilitating self-development of others.

Table 17.2
The seven threshold competencies identified by Richard Boyatzis

Source: R. Boyatzis (1982) *The Competent Manager*. New York: John Wiley.

Boyatzis makes a further distinction of the threshold competency, which is: 'A person's generic knowledge, motive, trait, self-image, social role, or skill which is essential to performing a job, but is not causally related to superior job performance', such as being able to speak the native tongue of one's subordinates. Table 17.2 summarises these elements.

Competencies are required for superior performance and are grouped in clusters, shown in Table 17.3. The goal and action management cluster relates to the requirement to make things happen towards a goal or consistent with a plan. The leadership cluster relates to activating people by communicating goals, plans and rationale and stimulating interest and involvement. The human resource management cluster relates to managing the coordination of groups of people working together towards the organisation's goals. The focus on others cluster relates to maturity and taking a balanced view of events and people. The directing subordinates cluster relates to providing subordinates with information on performance, interpreting what the information means to the subordinates, and placing positive or negative values on the interpretation.

The Boyatzis framework is set out at some length because of its influence. It is the basis of the work carried out by many consultants in the training field. It has, however, suffered criticism. Academics were sceptical about the methods of investigation, and practitioners found the framework too complex to translate into action. Boyatzis may be slipping into history, but his work remains an invaluable point of reference because of the way it demonstrates the scale and complexity of the management job. Subsequently tailor-made competency frameworks have come thick and fast from the training and development specialists, and most large companies have produced such a framework. Most frameworks have clusters of competencies, like the Boyatzis model, and within each of the competencies within the cluster a list of behavioural indicators is usually attached. *See* Figure 17.1 for an example. Some frameworks include level definitions encapsulating the simplicity or sophistication of the way that the competency is displayed whilst others include positive and negative behaviours in relations to a competency, as shown in the following two Windows on Practice.

Management competency clusters	
The goal and action management cluster	Concern *with impact*: Being concerned with symbols of power to have impact on others concerned about status and reputation. *Diagnostic use of concepts*: Identifying and recognising patterns from an assortment of information by bringing a concept to the situation and attempting to interpret events through that concept. *Efficiency orientation*: Being concerned to do something better. *Proactivity*: Having a disposition towards taking action to achieve something.
The leadership cluster	*Conceptualisation*: Developing a concept that describes a pattern or structure perceived in a set of facts: the concept emerges from the information. *Self-confidence*: Having decisiveness or presence; knowing what you are doing and feeling you are doing it well. *Use of oral presentations*: Making effective verbal presentations in situations ranging from one to one to several hundred people (plus threshold competency of logical thought).
The human resource management cluster	*Use of socialised power*: Using forms of influence to build alliances, networks, coalitions and teams. *Managing group process*: Stimulating others to work effectively in group settings (plus threshold competencies of accurate self-assessment and positive regard).
The focus on others cluster	*Perceptual objectivity*: Being able to be relatively objective avoiding bias or prejudice. *Self-control*: Being able to inhibit personal needs or desires in the service of organisational needs. *Stamina and adaptability*: Being able to sustain long hours of work and have the flexibility and orientation to adapt to changes in life and the organisational environment.
The directing subordinates cluster	*Threshold competencies* of developing others, spontaneity and use of unilateral power.

Table 17.3
The five clusters of management competencies by Richard Boyatzis (1982)

Source: R. Boyatzis (1982) *The Competent Manager*. New York: John Wiley.

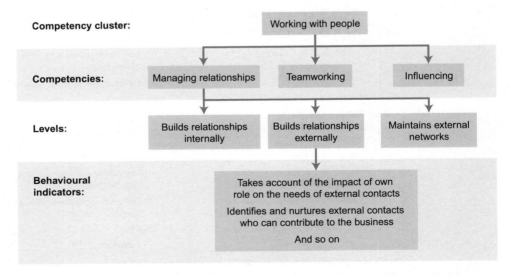

Figure 17.1
Typical content of a competency framework

(Source: This material is adapted from *The Competencies Handbook* by S. Whiddett and S. Hollyforde (1999), p. 14, with the permission of the Chartered Institute of Personnel and Development, CIPD House, Camp Road, London, SW19 4UX.)

WINDOW ON PRACTICE

An example of behavioural skills with level definitions from Connexions

Working with others

The ability to work constructively within a group/team environment

Level definitions	Examples of actions demonstrated at each level
Stage Three – Contributes to organisational success by defining, planning and implementing strategies for the future and building strategic relationships and alliances – Manages and allocates available resources, including financial, capital and people to best meet current and future requirements (2 of 4)	– Is able to recognise opportunities for organisation-wide networking – Develops and maintains strategic partnerships and alliances – Understands the strategic implications of working within different cultures (3 of 4)
Stage Two – Able to transfer knowledge – Challenges procedures – Develops best practice – Provides leadership to others (4 of 6)	– Builds confidence in others to take further responsibility – Provides constructive feedback to others on performance and impact on others – Maximises networking opportunities (3 of 7)
Stage One – Uses information to improve systems – Regularly acts on own initiative – Takes responsibility for own actions and decisions	– Understands team goals and objectives and works proactively for team success – Shares knowledge, skills and experience openly and honestly – Volunteers to work in projects or sub-committees – Helps others to achieve goals (4 of 10)
Foundation stage – Takes responsibility for own actions and decisions – Understands fundamental principles and applications – Refers to others for guidance – Follows procedures and processes	– Responsive, open and friendly in manner – Considers and relates well to all kinds of people – Personally enthusiastic, positive and approachable – Owns up to responsibility, even if mistakes happen – resilient (4 of 9)

Source: Connexions Cheshire and Warrington, but a national framework.

WINDOW ON PRACTICE

A sample competency from the Police Force

Respect for Race and Diversity – A

Behaviour category

Considers and shows respect for the opinions, circumstances and feelings of colleagues and members of the public, no matter what their race, religion, position, background, circumstances, status or appearance.

Understands other people's views and takes them into account. Is tactful and diplomatic when dealing with people, treating them with dignity and respect at all times. Understands and is sensitive to social, cultural and racial differences.

Positive indicators

- Sees issues from other people's viewpoints
- Is polite and patient when dealing with people, treating them with respect and dignity
- Shows understanding and sensitivity to people's problems, vulnerabilities and needs
- Makes people feel valued by listening to and supporting their needs and interests
- Understands what offends and adapts own actions accordingly
- Respects confidentiality wherever appropriate

(this is a selection from a full list of 13)

Negative indicators

- Does not consider other people's feelings
- Does not encourage people to talk about personal issues
- Makes situations worse with inappropriate remarks, language or behaviour
- Is thoughtless and tactless when dealing with people
- Is dismissive and impatient with people
- Does not respect confidentiality
- Uses humour inappropriately

(this is a selection from a full list of 11)

Source: Police (Cheshire Constabulary). However, these are national competencies.

Case 17.2 on this book's companion website at **www.pearsoned.co.uk/torrington** concentrates on Goleman's emotional intelligence competencies which we discussed in Chapter 14 on leadership. It is interesting to note that in the 2004 version of the management and leadership NVQ standards there are lists of behaviours supplementing each unit.

Advantages of behavioural competencies

Behavioural competencies are often seen as a way of expressing what is valued by the organisation as well as what characteristics have been seen to result in superior performance. In addition they are seen to provide a critical mechanism for the integration of human resource practices which is considered essential to a strategic approach to HR. Thus, once a competency framework has been researched and designed it can be used in recruitment, selection, training, performance management and reward. In this way employees are given consistent messages about what is valued and what is expected of them. Westminster City Council, for example has introduced a competency framework (CIPD 2006) which Tony Reynolds, Organisation Development Manager, describes as 'a golden thread running through the people management process' (p. 12) and that 'they are the behaviours we want to recruit, develop, manage and reward' (p. 12) However, in practice this link is often weak; for example Abraham and his colleagues (2001) found organisations willing to identify a set of managerial competencies that described a successful manager, but did not place a corresponding emphasis on including these competencies in their performance appraisal. A further advantage of competency frameworks is that, as they can be expressed as behaviours, they are more easily measurable, and thus can be used explicitly in all HR processes. This means, for example, that in a development centre, assessors can be trained in how to observe a long list of behaviours. In the centre itself each assessor can then check the behaviours of the candidates under observation to record how many times that particular behaviour is displayed.

Problematic aspects of behavioural competencies

Criticisms of the approach have been focused around the complex process required to research the appropriate competencies for the organisation, and perhaps more importantly, the fact that such competencies, due to the research process itself, will be inevitably backward looking rather than future oriented. Antonacopoulou and FitzGerald (1996), for example, found that competency work focused on what managers do now rather than what is needed to perform effectively in the future. Hayes *et al.* (2000) also note that a competency framework may not include every aspect that is critical to superior performance, and also that while one set of competencies may result in high performance this does not necessarily mean that such performance may not be achieved via a different set of competencies. Whiddett and Kandola (2000) similarly argue that processes *solely* based on competencies are flawed and that a wider perspective needs to be taken. Without the wider perspective the scope for encouraging and using diversity may be diminished. In terms of performance management they also highlight that changes in behaviour may be due to factors other than competencies, and this, of course, has implications for development. A similar perspective is taken by Brittain and Ryder (1999) who suggest that organisations need to take into account the fact that a person's behaviour is not necessarily consistent, and may be affected by the environment and the situation. Salaman and Taylor (2002) suggest that there are five inherent weaknesses where organisations limit themselves to a behavioural competency approach for managers including: marginalisation of the cultural, social and organisational context, the fact that such frameworks emphasise a narrow set of behaviours and attitudes with a lack of emphasis on the long-term processes of management development, and that competencies are founded on the questionable assumption that managers behave rationally and are achievement driven.

ACTIVITY 17.2

Research the use of behavioural competencies in your own organisation (if they are used), or one with which you are familiar.

1 What are the advantages of their use?

2 What are the disadvantages?

3 Compare views, if you can, from members of the HR function, line managers elsewhere, and other professionals.

SUMMARY PROPOSITIONS

17.1 The Leitch Review (2006) proposes UK skills targets for 2020 and the principles (especially the importance of employer-led principles) which should be a foundation for their achievement. Targets are measured in terms of NVQ achievements.

17.2 Skills development and the achievement of NVQs is supported by a national skills framework which includes: Investors in People, Sector Skills Councils and Learning and Skills Councils, Train to Gain and Individual Learning Accounts.

17.3 NVQs measure and accredit competence (plural: competences) and are concerned with job standards and output, and are focused on the ability of trainees to perform specific tasks directly related to the work they are doing or which they are preparing to do.

17.4 Ever since they were initially proposed, NVQs have been continually criticised, mainly because of queries about assessment, bureaucracy, generality and the quality of the standards, although improvements have resulted from major reviews.

17.5 Competency (plural: competencies) refers to behaviour, that is, input. Behavioural competencies are applauded as an integrative mechanism for HR processes. Problems with behavioural competencies are that they are backward, not forward looking, and are limiting and misleading if they are used alone.

GENERAL DISCUSSION TOPICS

1 The Boyatzis approach to competency-based management training has been criticised as being too complicated. To what extent do you agree and why?

2 What are the differences between skill, competence and competency?

FURTHER READING

Harrison, R. (2005) *Learning and Development*. London: CIPD.
Chapter 2, 'The National Framework for workforce development', is an excellent overview of the government's vision for national vocational education and training, and its implementation. The chapter explains the development of the current approach and also addresses emerging concerns.

Smith, A., Boocock, G., Loan-Clarke, J. and Whittaker, J. (2001) 'IIP and SMEs: awareness, benefits and barriers', *Personnel Review*, Vol. 31, No. 1, pp. 62–85.
The bureaucracy that has to be dealt with to achieve IiP status and the time that needs to be devoted to this have been viewed as barriers for small and medium-sized enterprises (SMEs) and this article considers the significance of IiP to the SME sector. A quantitative and qualitative study was undertaken which addressed the levels of awareness, interest in and commitment to IiP; triggers for IiP commitment; inhibitors to IiP; and the benefits of IiP.

REFERENCES

Abraham, S., Karns, L., Shaw, K. and Mena, M. (2001) 'Managerial competencies and the managerial performance appraisal process', *Journal of Management Development*, Vol. 20, No. 10, pp. 842–52.

Alberga, T., Tyson, S. and Parsons, D. (1997) 'An evaluation of the Investors in People Standard', *Human Resource Management Journal*, Vol. 7, No. 2, pp. 47–60.

Antonacopoulou, E. and FitzGerald, L. (1996) 'Reframing competency in management development', *Human Resource Management Journal*, Vol. 6, No. 1, pp. 27–48.

Berry, A.J. (1990) 'Masters or subjects?', *British Academy of Management Newsletter*, No. 5, February.

Boyatzis, R.E. (1982) *The Competent Manager*. New York: John Wiley.

Brewis, J. (1996) 'The "making" of the "competent" manager: Competency development, personal effectiveness and Foucault', *Management Learning*, Vol. 27, No. 1, pp. 65–86.

Brittain, S. and Ryder, P. (1999) 'Get complex', *People Management*, 25 November, pp. 48–51.

CIPD (2003) *Training and Development 2003*. London: CIPD.

CIPD (2006) 'Competency work pays off for council', *People Management*, Vol. 12, No. 13, 29 June, p. 12.

Collins, L. and Smith, A. (2004) 'Understanding the new Investors in People standard – lessons from experience', *Personnel Review*, Vol. 33, No. 5, pp. 583–604.

DfEE (2000) *Vocational Qualifications in the UK 1998/9*, Statistical Bulletin No. 05/00. London: HMSO.

DfEE (2003) *Vocational Qualifications in the UK 2001/02*, Statistical Bulletin No. 02/03. London: HMSO.

DfEE (2007) *Vocational Qualifications in the UK 2005/06*, Statistical Bulletin No. 05/07. London: HMSO.

Down, S. and Smith, D. (1998) 'It pays to be nice to people – Investors in People: the search for measurable benefits', *Personnel Review*, Vol. 27, No. 2.

EEF (2006) *Learning to Change: Why the UK skills system must do better*. Birmingham: EEF.

Grugulis, I. (2003) 'The contribution of National Vocational Qualifications to the Growth of Skills in the UK', *British Journal of Industrial* Relations, Vol. 41, No. 3, pp. 457–75.

Grugulis, I. and Bevitt, S. (2002) 'The impact of Investors in People: a case study of a hospital trust', *Human Resource Management Journal*, Vol. 12, No. 3, pp. 44–60.

Hall, L. and Holman, D. (1996) 'A competent experience?', *Organisations and People*, Vol. 3, No. 1, pp. 9–14.

Hammond, D. (2001) 'IIP companies "fail to implement best practice"', *People Management*, Vol. 7, No. 8, 19 April, p. 6.

Harrison, R. (2005) *Employee Development*. London: CIPD.

Hayes, J., Rose-Quirie, A. and Allinson, C. (2000) 'Senior managers' perceptions of the competencies they require for effective performance: implications for training and development', *Personnel Review*, Vol. 29, No. 1.

Holman, D. and Hall, L. (1996) 'The rites and wrongs of competence', *British Journal of Management*, Vol. 7, No. 2, pp. 191–202.

Holman, D. and Thorpe, R. (1993) 'MCI Management Competencies', paper presented at the Conference of the British Academy of Management, September.

IDS (2006) *Investors in* People, IDS HR Studies, No. 816, February.

Institute of Manpower Studies (1994) *National and Scottish Vocational Qualifications: Early indications of employers' take-up and use*. Poole, Dorset: BEBC.

Leitch S. (2006) *Leitch Review of Skills: Prosperity for all in the Global economy: Final Report*, London: HMSO, December.

Merrick, N. (2003) 'Happy Returns?', *People Management*, Vol. 9, No. 5, 6 March, pp. 16–17.

Phillips, L. (2006) 'Surveying the damage', *People Management*, Vol. 12, No. 18, 14 September, pp. 16–17.

Priddley, L. and Williams, S. (2000) 'Cognitive styles: enhancing the developmental component in National Vocational Qualifications', *Personnel Review*, Vol. 29, Issue 2.

Ram, M. (2000) 'Investors in People in small firms: Case study evidence from the businesses services sector', *Personnel Review*, Vol. 29, No. 1.

Robinson, P. (1996) *Rhetoric and Reality: Britain's new vocational qualifications*. London: London School of Economics, Centre for Economic Performance.

Salaman, G. and Taylor, S. (2002) 'Competency's consequences – changing the character of managerial work', paper presented at the ESRC Critical Management Studies Seminar: Managerial Work, The Judge Institute of Management, Cambridge.

Sanderson, B. (2002) 'The grand plan', *People Management*, Vol. 8, No. 22, 7 November, p. 51.

Spellman, R. (2002) 'Raising the standard', *People Management*, Vol. 8, No. 8, 18 April, p. 23.

Stewart, J. and Hamblin, B. (1992) 'Competence-based qualifications: the case for established methodologies', *Journal of European Industrial Training*, Vol. 16, No. 10, pp. 91–6.

Whiddett, S. and Hollyforde, S. (1999) *The Competencies Handbook*. London: IPD.

Whiddett, S. and Kandola, B. (2000) 'Fit for the job?', *People Management*, 25 May, pp. 30–4.

Whittaker, J. (1998) 'Pass notes', *People Management*, October, pp. 36–40.

Winterton, J. and Winterton, R. (1999) *Developing Managerial Competence*. London: Routledge.

An extensive range of additional materials, including multiple choice questions, answers to questions and links to useful websites can be found on the Human Resource Management Companion Website at **www.pearsoned.co.uk/torrington**.

CHAPTER 18

LEARNING AND DEVELOPMENT

THE OBJECTIVES OF THIS CHAPTER ARE TO:

1   Explore four perspectives on the nature of learning and consider the implications that each has for development provision and support

2   Review some of the practical characteristics of learning and development

3   Explain the various methods of addressing learning and development needs

4   Investigate the nature of evaluation in this context

There has been a considerable shift in the way that individual development is understood and characterised. We have moved from identifying training needs to identifying learning needs, the implication being that development is owned by the learner with the need rather than by the trainer seeking to satisfy that need. This also has implications for who identifies the needs and the way that those needs are met. Current thinking suggests that needs are best developed by a partnership between the individual and the organisation, and that the methods of meeting these needs are not limited only to formal courses, but to a wide range of on-the-job development methods and distance/e-learning approaches. Whilst a partnership approach is considered ideal the phrase 'self-development' is an important one in our development lexicon, indicating the growing emphasis on the individual having ownership of and taking responsibility for their own development. There has also been a shift in the type of skills that are the focus of development activity. Hallier and Butts (1999) for example identify a change from an interest in technical skills to the development of personal skills, self-management and attitudes. Lastly, while the focus on development for the current job remains high, there is greater pressure for development which is also future oriented. These shifts reflect the changes that we have already discussed in terms of global competition, fast and continuous change and the need for individuals to develop their employability in an increasingly uncertain world.

THE NATURE OF LEARNING

For the purpose of this text we consider the result of learning to be changed or new behaviour resulting from new or reinterpreted knowledge that has been derived from an external or internal experience. There are broadly four theoretical approaches or perspectives to understanding the nature of learning, and the training and development that organisations carry out reflect the explicit or implicit acceptance of one or more perspectives. We will look at each perspective, in the evolutionary order in which they became important. There is no right or wrong theory – each has strengths and weaknesses.

The **behaviourist** perspective is the earliest which, reflecting the label, concentrates on changes in observable behaviour. Experiments with animals formed the foundation of this theory, for example the work of Skinner, Watson and Pavlov. Researchers sought to associate rewards with certain behaviours in order to increase the display of that behaviour. The relevance of this for organisations today may be seen for example in telesales training where employees are taught to follow a script and calls are listened to, to ensure that the script is followed. Reward or punishment follows depending on behaviour. Trainers are not interested in what is going on in the heads of employees, they merely want them to follow the routine to be learned. This approach has also been used for a range of interpersonal skills training. One American company, for example plays video sequences to trainees portraying the 'correct' way to carry out, say, a return to work interview. Trainees then practise copying what they have seen and are given cue cards to use when carrying out that particular interpersonal event. The problems with the perspective are that it is overtly manipulative, simplistic and limited. It may produce only temporary changes in behaviour and increase cynicism.

Cognitive approaches are based on an information-processing perspective and are more concerned with what goes on in the learner's head. This is a more technical perspective and maps out the stages of learning such as: expectancy to learn (motivation); attention and perception required; experience is coded (meaning is derived); meaning is stored in long-term memory; meaning is retrieved when needed; learning is applied; feedback is received (which may supply reinforcement). The strengths of this perspective are that it stresses the importance of learner motivation and individual needs, it recognises that the individual has some control over what is learned and it identifies feedback as an important aspect of learning. The weaknesses are that it assumes learning is neutral and unproblematic and it is a purely rational approach that ignores emotion. From this perspective useful development activities would be seen as formal courses offering models and ideas with lots of back-up paperwork. Activities to improve learning motivation are also important, for example helping employees to recognise their own development needs and providing rewards for skills development. Mechanisms for providing feedback to employees are also key.

The third perspective is based on **social learning theory**, in other words learning is a social activity and this is based on our needs as humans to fit in with others. In organisations this happens to some extent naturally as we learn to fit in with things such as dress codes, behaviour in meetings and so on. Fitting in means that we can be accepted as successful in the organisation, but it is not necessary that we internalise and believe in these codes. Organisations often use role models, mentors and peer support, and 'buddies', to intensify our natural will to fit in. The disadvantages of this perspective are that it ignores the role of choice for the individual and it is based, to some extent, on a masquerade.

The **constructivist** perspective is a development of the information-processing perspective, but does not regard learning as a neutral process: it is our perception of our experiences that count; there is no 'objective' view. This perspective accepts that in our dealings with the world we create 'meaning structures' in our heads and these are based on our past experiences and personality. New information and potential learning need to fit with these meaning structures in some way, which means that a similar new experience will be understood differently by different people. We tend to pay attention to things which fit with our meaning structures and ignore or avoid things that don't fit. As humans we are also capable of constructing and reconstructing our meaning structures without any new experiences. These meaning structures are mainly unconscious and therefore we are not aware of the structures which constrain our learning. We are generally unaware of how valid our meanings sets are, and they are deeply held and difficult to change. Making these structures explicit enables us to challenge them and to start to change them. This perspective recognises that learning is a very personal and potentially threatening process. We develop mechanisms to protect ourselves from this threat, and thus protect ourselves from learning. The implication of this is that learning support needs to encourage introspection and reflection, and providing the perspectives of others (for example as in 360-degree feedback, outdoor courses or relocations) may assist in this process.

PRACTICAL CHARACTERISTICS OF LEARNING AND DEVELOPMENT

Learning from experience

A significant amount of work has been done which helps us understand how managers, and others, learn from their experiences. Kolb *et al.* (1984) argue that it is useful to

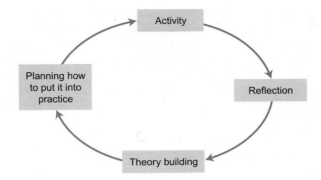

Figure 18.1
The learning
cycle

combine the characteristics of learning, which is usually regarded as passive, with those of problem solving, which is usually regarded as active. From this combination Kolb *et al.* developed a four-stage learning cycle, which was further developed by Honey and Mumford (1989).

The four stages, based on the work of both groups of researchers, are shown in Figure 18.1.

WINDOW ON PRACTICE

Gwen is a management trainer in a large organisation running a number of in-house management courses. She has just moved into this position from her role as section leader in the research department; the move was seen as a career development activity in order to strengthen her managerial skills.

Gwen is working with her manager to learn from her experiences. Here is an extract from her learning diary based on the learning cycle:

Activity – I've had a go at running three sessions on my own now, doing the input and handling the questions.

Reflection – I find the input much easier than handling questions. When I'm asked a question and answer it I have the feeling that they're not convinced by my reply and I feel awkward that we seem to finish the session hanging in mid-air. I would like to be able to encourage more open discussion.

Theory building – If I give an answer to a question it closes off debate by the fact that I have 'pronounced' what is 'right'. If I want them to discuss I have to avoid giving my views at first.

Planning practice – When I am asked a question rather than answering it I will say to the group: 'What does anyone think about that?' or 'What do you think?' (to the individual who asked) or 'What are the possibilities here?' I will keep encouraging them to respond to each other and reinforce where necessary, or help them change tack by asking another question.

Each of these four stages of the learning cycle is critical to effective learning, but few people are strong at each stage and it is helpful to understand where our strengths and weaknesses lie. Honey and Mumford designed a questionnaire to achieve this which identified individuals' learning styles as 'activist', 'reflector', 'theorist' and 'pragmatist', and explain that:

- **Activists** learn best from 'having a go', and trying something out without necessarily preparing. They would be enthusiastic about role-play exercises and keen to take risks in the real environment.

- **Reflectors** are much better at listening and observing. They are effective at reflecting on their own and others' experiences and good at analysing what happened and why.

- **Theorists'** strengths are in building a concept or a theory on the basis of their analysis. They are good at integrating different pieces of information, and building models of the way things operate. They may choose to start their learning by reading around a topic.

- **Pragmatists** are keen to *use* whatever they learn and will always work out how they can apply it in a real situation. They will plan how to put it into practice. They will value information/ideas they are given only if they can see how to relate them to practical tasks they need to do.

Understanding how individuals learn from experience underpins all learning, but is particularly relevant in encouraging self-development activities. Understanding our strengths and weaknesses enables us to choose learning activities which suit our style, and gives us the opportunity to decide to strengthen a particularly weak learning stage of our learning cycle. While Honey and Mumford adopt this dual approach, Kolb firmly maintains that learners *must* become deeply competent at all stages of the cycle. There has been considerable attention to the issue of matching and mismatching styles with development activities: *see*, for example, Hayes and Allinson (1996), who also consider the matching and mismatching of trainer learning style with learner learning style.

ACTIVITY 18.1

1 If you have not already done so obtain the Honey and Mumford questionnaire and work out your learning style(s).

2 Select your weakest style and try to identify two different learning activities which fit with this style, but that you would normally avoid.

3 Seek opportunities for trying out these learning activities. If you practise these activities on a regular basis this should help you strengthen the style you are working on.

4 Log your experiences and in particular what you have learned about these 'new' learning activities.

Learner type	Planned learning score	Emergent learning score
Sage	High	High
Warrior	High	Low
Adventurer	Low	High
Sleeper	Low	Low

Table 18.1
Planned and
emergent
learning

Source: Adapted from D. Megginson (1994) 'Planned and emergent learning: A framework and a method',
Executive Development, Vol. 7, No. 6, pp. 29–32.

Planned and emergent learning

From a different, but compatible, perspective, David Megginson characterises learners by
the extent to which they plan the direction of their learning and implement this (planned
learning), and the extent to which they are able to learn from opportunistic learning
experiences (emergent learning). Megginson (1994) suggests that strengths and weaknesses in these two areas will influence the way individuals react to self-development.
These two characteristics are not mutually exclusive, and Megginson combines them to
identify four learning types, as shown in Table 18.1.

Warriors are those who are strong at planning what they want to learn and how, but
are less strong at learning from experiences they had not anticipated. They have a clear
focus on what they want to learn and pursue this persistently. On the other hand
Adventurers respond to and learn from opportunities that come along unexpectedly,
they are curious and flexible. However, they tend not to plan and create opportunities
for themselves. *Sages* are strong on both characteristics, and *Sleepers* display little
of either characteristic at present. To be most effective in self-development activities
learners need to make maximum use of both planned and emergent learning. For a
further explanation of this model also *see* Megginson and Whitaker (1996).

ACTIVITY 18.2

Consider your development over the past year: do you feel that your strengths are in
planning your learning or in learning opportunistically?
    Choose your weaker approach, and identify how you could strengthen this.

Learning curves

The idea of the learning curve has been promulgated for some time, and was developed
in relation to technical skills development. The general idea was that we tend to learn a
new task more rapidly at first, so that the learning curve is steep, and then gradually
plateau after we have had significant experience. A slightly different shape of learning is
more relevant to personal skills development: the curve is less likely to be smooth, or it

Increase in skill
development

Time

Figure 18.2 The reality of learning progress

may not even be curved. Ideally our learning would be incremental, improving bit by bit all the time; in reality, however, learning is usually characterised by a mix of improvements and setbacks. Although, with persistence, our skills gradually increase, in the short term we may experience dips. These dips are demotivating but they are a necessary part of learning. Developing personal skills usually requires us to try out a new way of doing things. This is risky because, although the skills we are developing may be quite personal to us, we usually have to experiment with new ways of doing things in public. Understanding that sometimes things get worse before they get better helps to carry us through the dips. Figure 18.2 shows the reality of learning progress.

Identifying learning and training needs

The 'systematic training cycle' was developed to help organisations move away from ad hoc non-evaluated training, and replace it with an orderly sequence of training activities, but this approach has been less prominent of late. Harrison (2005) contests that such a cycle is not necessarily the most appropriate to use as it falls far short of the messy world of practice, and does not focus adequately on learning. Sloman (2001) argues that it may have fitted the 1960s mood for rationality and efficiency, but it is somewhat mechanical and fits less well with our faster pace of continuous change. In spite of this the cycle does retain some value, and we describe an adaptation of such a model to make it more applicable to today's environment. The model is set within an external environment and within an organisation strategy and an HR development strategy. Even if some of these elements are not made explicit, they will exist implicitly. Note that the boundary lines are dotted, not continuous. This indicates that the boundaries are permeable and overlapping. The internal part of the model reflects a systematic approach to learning and to training. Learning needs may be identified by the individual, by the organisation or in partnership, and this applies to each of the following steps in the circle. This dual involvement is probably the biggest change from traditional models where the

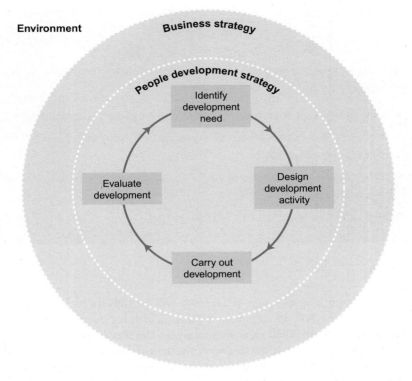

Figure 18.3 A systematic model of learning and training

steps were owned by the organisation, usually the trainers, and the individual was con-sidered to be the subject of the exercise rather than a participant in it, or the owner of it. The model that we offer does not exclude this approach where appropriate, but is intended to be viewed in a more flexible way. The model is shown in Figure 18.3.

There are various approaches to analysing needs, the two most traditional being a problem-centred approach and matching the individual's competency profile with that for the job that person is filling. The problem-centred approach focuses on any perform-ance problems or difficulties, and explores whether these are due to a lack of skills and, if so, which. The profile comparison approach takes a much broader view and is perhaps most useful when an individual, or group of individuals, are new to a job. This latter approach is also useful because strategic priorities change and new skills are required of employees, as the nature of their job changes, even though they are still officially in the same role with the same job title. When a gap has been identified, by whatever method, the development required needs to be phrased in terms of a learning objective, before the next stage of the cycle, planning and designing the development, can be undertaken. For example, when a gap or need has been identified around team leadership, appropriate learning objectives may be that learners, by the end of the development, will be able 'to ask appropriate questions at the outset of a team activity to ascertain relevant skills and experience, and to check understanding of the task' or 'to review a team activity by involving all members in that review'.

ACTIVITY 18.3

Write learning objectives for the following individuals who are experiencing problems in their performance:

1 Tina, who always dominates meetings, and neglects the contribution of others.

2 Brian, who has never carried out a selection interview before, and is very unsure of how to go about this.

3 Mark, who feels he has lots of contributions to make at meetings, but never actually says anything.

4 Sara, who can never get to meetings on time.

The planning and design of learning will be influenced by the learning objectives and also by the HR development strategy, which for example may contain a vision of who should be involved in training and development activities, and the emphasis on approaches such as self-development and e-learning. Once planning and design have been specified the course, or coaching or e-learning activity, can commence, and should be subject to ongoing monitoring and evaluated at an appropriate time in the future to assess how behaviour and performance have changed.

METHODS OF LEARNING AND DEVELOPMENT

Off-job methods: education and training courses

Educational courses undertaken during a career are frequently done on a part-time basis leading to a diploma or master's degree with a management or business label, and/or qualification for a professional body. It is considered that such courses provide value for both the employer and the participant – and MBA study is a popular route. For advantages of such a course for the employee *see*, for example, Baruch and Leeming (2001). An alternative approach to qualification is the NVQ route which we discussed in the previous chapter, which is more closely tied to on-job experiences and not concerned with 'education'.

In addition there are consultancy courses. Varying from a half-day to several weeks in length, they are run by consultants or professional bodies for all comers. They have the advantage that they bring together people from varying occupational backgrounds and are not, therefore, as introspective as in-house courses and are popular for topical issues. They are, however, often relatively expensive and superficial, despite their value as sources of industrial folklore, by which we mean the swapping of experiences among course members.

The most valuable courses of this type are those that concentrate on specific skills or knowledge, such as developing time management, interviewing or disciplinary skills, or being introduced to a new national initiative. This short-course approach is probably the only way for individuals to come to terms with some new development, such as a change in legislation, because they need not only to find an interpretation of the development, but also to share views and reactions with fellow employees to ensure that their own feelings are not idiosyncratic or perverse.

In-house courses are often similar in nature to the consultancy courses, and are sometimes run with the benefit of some external expertise. In-house courses can be particularly useful if the training needs to relate to specific organisational procedures and structures, or if it is geared to encouraging employees to work more effectively together in the organisational environment. The drawbacks of in-house courses are that they suffer from a lack of breadth of content, and there is no possibility of learning from people in other organisations.

Alternatively, there are outdoor-type courses (sometimes known as Outward Bound, after the organisation that pioneered them). Outdoor courses attempt to develop skills involved in working with and through others, and aim to increase self-awareness and self-confidence through a variety of experiences, including outdoor physical challenges. Courses like these continue to be increasingly used, and their differential value is assumed to hinge on their separation from the political, organisational environment. A natural, challenging and different environment is assumed to encourage individuals to forsake political strategising, act as their raw selves and be more open to new ideas. Burleston and Grint (1996), based on ethnographic research into outdoor programmes, found that while most participants did gain from the experience, the idea of providing a de-politicised environment is a naive hope rather than a reality. Ibbetson and Newell (1999) did find, however, that non-competitive outdoor programmes were more effective in meeting teambuilding objectives than competitive programmes. More recently learning experiences based on drama have increasingly been used; in these participants are engaged in improvisation through role play and exercises. For a fascinating insight into the variety of forms this may take *see* Monks *et al.* (2001). There are other forms of simulation in addition to role play, such as games and computer simulations; for a good discussion of definitions and outcomes of such approaches *see* Feinstein *et al.* (2002).

One of the major concerns with these different types of off-job courses and activities is the difficulty of ensuring transfer of learning back to the workplace. As part of their research on the contribution of off-job courses to managers Longenecker and Ariss (2002) asked managers what helped them retain what they had learned and transfer it to the workplace. Developing goals/plans for implementing new skills was most frequently identified. In addition managers said that it helped to review materials immediately after the programme; be actively involved in the learning itself; make a report to peers/superiors on what they had learned; review material and development plans with their mentor/manager; and include development goals in performance reviews. It is generally agreed that a supportive climate helps transfer (for example line manager interest and involvement, and development having a high priority in the organisation). Santos and Stewart (2003), for example, found that transfer was more likely if reward such as promotion or pay was attached to developmental behaviour change, and also where there was a helpful management climate in terms of pre- and post-course briefings and activities. Currently there are number of more creative approaches where experiential job-related activities are included on courses, as shown in the Window on practice.

WINDOW ON PRACTICE

Experiential activities

Brockett (2006) explains how EDF Energy aims to improve customer service via experiential course activities for engineers, dispatch and call-centre workers. During the course participants play the roles of guests at a sixtieth birthday party. Cake, music and decorations accompany this. Half-way though the party there is a surprise power cut represented by a blackout and audio recording of family members becoming distressed and stumbling about in the dark. The aim was to let course members experience what their customers experience when they have a power cut so that they can better understand the effect that it has on people's lives. Performance improvements followed in terms of repair times, accuracy of estimated repair times and increase in commendations letters from the public. This suggests that an experience, especially in the shoes of the customer, can have a powerful impact on employee perceptions and behaviours.

Phillips (2006) provides an example of BUPA care staff in a retirement home. As part of a 'Personal Best' programme aimed at improving customer service staff took the role of residents so as to see life through their customers' eyes. So, for example, they were fed puréed food and were hoisted in a mechanical sling from a chair into a bed. As a result staff behaviour towards residents has changed, for example explaining the hoisting procedure to residents and doing it more slowly.

Sources: Brockett, J. (2006) 'Energy firm gets party vibe', *People Management*, Vol. 12, No. 10, 18 May, p. 12; Phillips, L. (2006) 'BUPA Stars', *People Management*, Vol. 12, No. 22, 9 November, pp. 30–2.

In relation to MBAs Martin and Pate (2001) found, surprisingly, that a poor transfer climate did not affect transfer, but willingness to apply what was learned was related to the individual's positive feelings about the company and his or her intended continuance there.

While courses are no longer viewed as the key means of developing staff, they still have an important role to play, and in Interactive skill 4, in the Focus on skills at the end of Part 4, we therefore explore presentation as well as coaching skills.

Learning on the job

Manager coaching and other internal and external coaching

The line manager's role in learning and development has increased with the devolution of HR tasks. Coaching is an informal approach to individual development based on a close relationship between the individual and one other person either internal or external to the organisation. The coach is often the immediate manager, who is experienced in the task, but there is increasing use of external coaches, especially for more senior managers, or specially trained internal coaches, and 'coaching' has become very much a professional occupation with its own code of ethical practice. We will look at this in more detail, but first we explore the coaching role of the line manager.

The manager as coach helps trainees to develop by giving them the opportunity to perform an increasing range of tasks, and by helping them to learn from their experiences. Managers work to improve the trainee's performance by asking searching questions, actively listening, discussion, exhortation, encouragement, understanding, counselling and providing information and honest feedback. The manager coach is usually in a position to create development opportunities for the trainee when this is appropriate. For example, a line manager can delegate attendance at a meeting, or allow a trainee to deputise, where this is appropriate to the individual's development needs. Alternatively a line manager can create the opportunity for a trainee to join a working party or can arrange a brief secondment to another department. Coaches can share 'inside' information with the individual they are coaching to help them understand the political context in which they are working. For example, they are able to explain who will have most influence on a decision that will be made, or future plans for restructuring within a department.

Skilled coaches can adapt their style to suit the individual they are coaching, from highly directive at one end of the scale to non-directive at the other. The needed style may change over time, as the trainee gains more confidence and experience. A useful text on the practical skills of coaching is Pemberton (2006). In an exploratory study Carroll and Gillen (2001) found a variety of barriers to line manager acceptance of a teaching/ coaching role, in particular lack of interpersonal competence, lack of time, performance pressures, and a feeling that the teaching role was not valued and was the role of the HR department. This same article also provides some excellent material on what makes an effective coach. The CIPD (2006) found that competing business pressures and lack of internal skills and experience were the greatest barriers to coaching, and IDS (2006a) suggests that in view of the emphasis in coaching on honest self-reflection, there will be barriers in organisations where the culture is not one of openness and honesty. They also point out that coaching has been seen as a remedial tool but that it probably has more to offer as a development opportunity for turning good performers into excellent ones.

There has been an increasing trend to broaden the concept of coaching in terms of both content and who carries out the coaching. Many organisations are now providing or arranging intensive training for designated internal coaches who operate broadly in the organisation, just in a coaching role. This is quite different from the basic training line managers are likely to receive. External executive coaching is often provided by consultancies and specialist coaching organisations. IDS (2006a) provides an excellent range of case studies demonstrating the different ways in which organisations are using coaching. Various forms of coaching may include career coaching, performance coaching, skills coaching, business coaching and life coaching. Given the increasing professionalisation of coaching it is not surprising that the quality of the coaching experience is receiving attention. Supervision of practice is increasingly being used in a way that is similar to supervision for counsellors, which involves regular meetings with a more experienced practitioner to explore their client relationships and reflect on practice. A CIPD study carried out by the Bath Consultancy Group (Arney 2006) found that nearly half the coaches received regular supervision, and that it was a fast growing practice.

Such individual supervision is carried out with a mind to client confidentiality; however there is also a growing trend for group supervision of coaches and also for organisations wanting to collect common themes discussed in coaching sessions as these can be used to inform organisational thinking (Arney 2006). Both these approaches put client confidentiality at greater risk.

WINDOW ON PRACTICE

Group supervision at PricewaterhouseCoopers

Group supervision has been used for internal coaches for some time and involves sessions of three hours every month led by an external facilitator with experience of coaching supervision and a background in psychology or psychotherapy.

Coaches present a case with the emphasis on the work of the coach and the coaching relationship rather than the individual client. In order to protect confidentiality real names are not disclosed. It is an opportunity for an individual coach to get reactions from others about their own practice, and also to reflect on approaches that others take. So the aim is to encourage constant learning and reflection, through making one's work open to scrutiny.

Source: Summarised from E. Arney (2006) 'Insider's Guide', *People Management*, Vol. 12, No. 23, 23 November, pp. 40–2.

WINDOW ON PRACTICE

Coaching at the Medical Research Council (MRC) and Unilever

Hall (2006) reports on the arrangement that external coaching company 'Laughing Phoenix' has made with the (MRC) which involves coaching the 30 most senior HR professionals. One of the conditions of the agreement was that the company would feed back recurring themes to the MRC so that they could align coaching with the wider business picture. Unilever has contacted internal coaches regularly to 'harvest some of the intelligence they had gathered from their clients', again keen to pick up recurring themes, helping the organisation know which areas to tackle and help the coaches understand the context of their work .

Source: Hall, L. (2006) 'Inside Job', *People Management*, Vol. 12, No. 16, 10 August, pp. 34–6.

The emphasis on coaching is underlined by the recently released CIPD journal, *Coaching at Work*, and the development of the institute's coaching standards. The number of organisations aiming to develop a coaching culture reached 80 per cent in the 2006 CIPD survey, with 79 per cent already using some coaching activities, and Lehane (2005) provides some guidance on getting started on this. Useful ideas for developing a coaching culture include making coaching part of conversations, day to day; shifting the power to the learner; integrating external and internal coaching resources; the focus on continuous improvement in coaching activities making this a valued and natural part of a manager's job; and shifting the emphasis from individual coaching to team coaching (Clutterbuck and Megginson 2005). Concerns for quality are being addressed, for example by a kitemarking scheme for coaching and mentoring qualifications, launched by the European Coaching and Mentoring Council (*see* **www.emccouncil.org**), and the British Psychological Society now has a specialist interest group focused on coaching.

Mentoring

Mentoring offers a wide range of advantages for the development of the mentee or protégé, coaching as described above being just one of the possible benefits of the relationship. The mentor may occasionally be the individual's immediate manager, but usually it is a more senior manager in the same or a different function. Kram (1983) identifies two broad functions of mentoring, the first of which is the career function, including those aspects of the relationship that primarily enhance career advancement, such as exposure and visibility and sponsorship. The second is the psychosocial function, which includes those aspects of the relationship that primarily enhance a sense of competence, clarity of identity and effectiveness in the managerial role. More recently Fowler and O'Gorman (2005) on the basis of research with both mentors and mentees, describe eight individual mentoring functions which are: personal and emotional guidance; coaching; advocacy; career development facilitation; role modelling; strategies and systems advice; learning facilitation; and friendship, whilst Arnold (1997) found that the most common advantages of mentoring were perceived as role modelling and counselling. There is evidence that mentoring does benefit both parties (*see*, for example, Johnson *et al.* 1999), and Broadbridge (1999) suggests that mentors can gain through recognition from peers, increased job satisfaction, rejuvenation, admiration and self-satisfaction. The drawbacks to mentoring that were revealed in Broadbridge's research include the risk of over-reliance, the danger of picking up bad habits, the fact that the protégé may be alienated from other sources of expertise and the sense of loss experienced when a mentor leaves. In addition, the difficulty of dealing with conflicting views in such an unequal relationship was identified. Perceived benefits, however, considerably outweighed any drawbacks. Megginson (2000) identifies the issue of dysfunctional mentoring, and the danger of assuming that mentoring is unquestionably good.

Managers are also seen as responsible for developing talent, and while a mentor/protégé relationship might not naturally occur, mentorship may be encouraged or formalised. For example, there are systems where all new graduates are attached to a mentor as soon as they join the organisation. The difficulties of establishing a formal programme include the potential mismatch of individuals, unreal expectations on both sides and the time and effort involved.

WINDOW ON PRACTICE

Mentoring at Fifteen

Liam Black, Director of Fifteen (Jamie Oliver's project to turn disadvantaged youngsters into cooks) initiated a structured programme to turn six members of staff into qualified mentors able to support the more vulnerable youngsters to aid retention. The staff are from different companies run by Olliver and are not directly working with the youngsters. The six are working towards a Certificate in Workplace Mentoring from the Oxford School of Coaching and Mentoring (accredited by John Brookes University), which is suitably tailored to their work-based needs. The programme is a six-month blended learning package and the mentors will work with the youngsters setting goals, developing coping strategies and building their often non-existent self-esteem.

Cottee, P. (2006) 'Oliver's Army', *People Management*, Vol. 12, No. 19, 28 September, pp. 44–5.

WINDOW ON PRACTICE

Tony Stott and Jenny Sweeney (1999) report on a structured mentoring scheme with a difference at Shell. While Shell runs a very flexible mentoring scheme appropriate for many different types of employee and purposes, it recognises the importance of the design of the scheme and good administration. The authors suggest that there are five critical elements in a good scheme:

- **A database.** Although the scheme is based on natural selection, that is, a mutual decision between a potential mentor and a new recruit, the database appears to be critical, in order to track the flow of mentees and the availability of mentors. Copies of mentor biographies are available for new recruits to read.

- **Mentor support.** Mentors are trained in their role and in recognising the limits of their abilities. There is also a support mechanism for mentors, and mentors meet to share their experiences.

- **Training.** Both mentors and mentees are trained, and this forms a key part of the induction programme for new recruits, with information on reasons for using mentoring, roles and expectations.

- **Resource materials.** These include websites for mentors. Guidance booklets for mentees are also produced.

- **Evaluation.** Shell found that a non-bureaucratic scheme, which gives ownership to the participants, was appreciated.

Source: Summarised from T. Stott and J. Sweeney (1999) 'More than a match', *People Management*, June, pp. 45–8.

Peer relationships

Although mentor-protégé relationships have been shown to be related to high levels of career success, not all developing individuals have access to such a relationship, and even formal schemes are often reserved for specific groups such as new graduate entrants. Supportive peer relationships at work are potentially more widely available to the individual and offer a number of benefits for the development of both parties. The benefits that are available depend on the nature of the peer relationship, and Kram and Isabella (1985) have identified three groups of peer relationships, which are differentiated by their primary development functions. These can be expressed on a continuum from 'information peer', based primarily on information sharing, through 'collegial peer', based on career strategising, giving job-related feedback and friendship, to 'special peer', based on emotional support, personal feedback, friendship and confirmation. Most of us benefit from one or a number of peer relationships at work but often we do not readily appreciate their contribution towards our development. Peer relationships most often develop on an informal basis and provide mutual support. Some organisations, however, formally appoint an existing employee to provide such support to a new member of staff through their first 12–18 months in the organisation. These relationships may, of course, continue beyond the initial period. The name for the appointed employee will vary from organisation to organisation, and sometimes the word 'buddy', 'coach' or 'mentor' is used – which can be confusing! Cromer (1989) discusses the advantages of peer relationships organised on a formal basis and the skills and qualities sought in peer providers, which include accessibility, empathy, organisational experience and proven task skills.

ACTIVITY 18.4

Consider each significant peer relationship that you have at work. Where does each fit on the continuum of relationships described above, and what contributions does it make towards your development?

If you are in full-time education consider the contribution that each of your relationships (whether at university, home or work) has to your development.

Self-development

Natural learning is learning that takes place on the job and results from an individual's everyday experience of the tasks to be undertaken. Natural learning is even more difficult to investigate than coaching, mentoring or peer relationships, and yet the way in which we learn from everyday experiences, and our level of awareness of this, is very important for our development. To some extent self-development may be seen as a conscious effort to gain the most from natural learning in a job, and to use the learning cycle as a framework. Self-development can be focused in specific skills development, but often extends to attitude development and personal growth.

ACTIVITY 18.5

The video *Groundhog Day* can be viewed as a journey of self-development. Watch the video and answer the following questions:

- How did Phil's attitudes change and how was this reflected in his behaviour?
- What do you think Phil learned?
- How did he learn it?
- Why is personal development so difficult?

The emphasis in self-development is that each individual is responsible for, and can plan, his or her own development, although he or she may need to seek help when working on some issues. Self-development involves individuals in analysing their strengths, weaknesses and the way in which they learn, primarily by means of questionnaires and feedback from others. This analysis may initially begin on a self-development course, or with the help of a facilitator, but would then be continued by the individual back on the job. From this analysis individuals, perhaps with some help at first, plan their development goals and the way in which they will achieve them, primarily through development opportunities within the job. When individuals consciously work on self-development they use the learning cycle in a more explicit way than in natural learning. They are also in a better position to seek appropriate opportunities and help, in their learning, from their manager.

Many of the activities included in self-development are based on observation, collecting further feedback about the way they operate, experimenting with different approaches and in particular reviewing what has happened, why and what they have learned. Self-development, however, is not a quick fix as it requires a long-term approach and careful planning and, as Stansfield (1996) suggests, attention needs to be paid to the 'scaffolding' which supports the self-development process. To this end she suggests that extensive briefing and explanation of the theoretical underpinning of the self-development are both important. In addition she suggests direct skill development concerning the role, importance and nature of peer feedback, and further support in tracking personal learning needs to ensure a more rigorous learning journey. Woodall (2000) also notes difficulties around the support structure for self-development, and identifies confusion in terminology as unhelpful. Confusion in terminology is also raised by Antonacopoulou (2000), who highlights a much neglected influence on self-development – that the individuals themselves have to be capable of taking on this responsibility.

Self-development groups

Typically, in self-development groups a group of individuals is involved in a series of meetings where they jointly discuss their personal development, organisational issues and/or individual work problems. Groups may begin operating with a leader who is a process expert, not a content expert, and who therefore acts as a facilitator rather than, but not to the complete exclusion of, a source of information. The group itself is the primary source of information and may operate without outside help as its members' process skills develop. The content and timings of the meetings can be very flexible, although meetings will require a significant level of energy and commitment if they are to operate well.

Self-development groups can be devised in a variety of contexts. They can be part of a formal educational course, for example a Diploma in Management Studies, where a group of managers from different organisations come together to support their development; they may constitute the whole of a self-development 'course'; or they can be an informal support group within an organisation. However the group originates, it is important that the members understand what every member hopes to get out of the group, the role of the facilitator (if there is one), the processes and rules that the group will operate by and how they agree to interact.

Learning logs

Learning logs are a mechanism for learning retrospectively as they encourage a disciplined approach to learning from opportunistic events. The log may be focused around one particular activity and is usually designed to encourage the writer to explain what happened, how he or she has reflected on this, what conclusions he or she has made and what future learning actions he or she wishes to make. Alternatively logs can be used in the form of a daily or weekly diary.

ACTIVITY 18.6

Identify a management skills area that you need to develop. (You may find it particularly helpful to choose an interpersonal area, for example, assertiveness, influencing others, presentation, being more sociable, contributing to meetings, helping others.)

Keep a learning diary over the next few weeks, logging anything that is relevant to your development area. Use the framework which Gwen used in a previous example (see Window on practice box at the beginning of this chapter).

At the end of the period review what you have learned in your development area and also what you have learned about the learning cycle.

Learning contracts

There is increasing use of learning contracts, sometimes used within more formalised self-development groups; on other management courses; as part of a mentoring or coaching relationship; or in working towards a competency-based qualification. These contracts are a formal commitment by the learner to work towards a specified learning goal, with an identification of how the goal might be achieved. They thus promote a proactive approach to learning. Boak (1991) has produced a very helpful guide to the use of such contracts and suggests that they should include:

- an overall development goal;
- specific objectives in terms of skills and knowledge;
- activities to be undertaken;
- resources required;
- a method of assessment of learning.

The value that individuals gain from learning contracts is dependent on their choosing to participate, their identification of the relevant goal and the importance and value they ascribe to achieving it. Only with commitment will a learning contract be effective, because ultimately it is down to the individual learner manager to make it happen.

WINDOW ON PRACTICE

David wanted to improve his influencing skills and has sent the following draft learning contract to his manager for discussion:

Goal

To improve my influencing skills with both peers and more senior managers.

Specific objectives

- To prepare for influencing situations.
- To try to understand better the perspective of the other.
- To identify the interpersonal skills required – probably active listening, reflecting, summarising, stating my needs, collaboration (but maybe more).
- To be able to identify that I have had more influence in decisions made.

Activities

- Watch a recommended video on influencing skills.
- Re-read my notes from the interpersonal skills course I attended.
- Watch how others in my department go about influencing.
- Ask other people (supportive ones) how they go about it.
- Identify possible influencing situations in advance, and plan for what I want and what might happen.
- Reflect back on what happened, and work out how to do better next time.
- Ask for feedback.

Resources

- Video.
- Notes.
- The support of others.

Assessment

- I could ask for feedback from colleagues and my manager.
- My own assessment may be helpful.
- Make a log over time of decisions made and my originally preferred outcome.

e-learning and blended learning

As technology enables interesting and interactive presentation of distance learning materials, there is evidence of considerable enthusiasm on the part of organisations to pursue this approach to development, and take advantage of the opportunities it presents. CIPD (2003) reports that one of the most significant changes in training over the last five years is the increased use of e-learning, although it is still most heavily used by IT staff. However, by 2006 only a quarter of respondents to the Learning and Development CIPD survey said that it had significantly altered learning and training offerings. E-learning can be defined as 'learning that is delivered, enabled or mediated by electronic technology' (Sloman and Rolph 2003, p. 1). While e-learning has been characterised as requiring high investment in terms of hardware, software and design time, it has also been characterised as cost effective in the long run, with the ability to provide speedy and flexible training. IDS (2006b) identifies the main advantages of e-learning as flexible access across time and place; flexible use of content; consistent delivery; sustainable and easy to update; value for money and of the moment, being particularly useful for the launch of new products. Hammond (2001), for example, describes the case of Cisio which is constantly launching new IT-based products. The company has moved from 90 per cent classroom-based training for its sales representatives to 80 per cent online training so that the large numbers of representatives can experience training immediately the product is launched. Channel Four (Cooper 2001) has a strategy to replace much of its classroom teaching activity with interactive learning, and the London Emergency Services are using virtual reality training to prepare employees for emergency events. Prickett (1997) reports how Hendon Police Training College uses virtual reality to prepare officers to deal with siege and hostage situations. Sloman and Rolph (2003) found that e-learning has been implemented in a variety of ways, from being introduced as a sweeping ambitious change to small incremental changes to the organisation's approach to training, and from a mandatory change to an offer to volunteers. They also report that key barriers are the computer literacy of employees and access to the appropriate equipment.

However enthusiasm from the organisation is not sufficient, and there has been much evidence of employees being unwilling to use e-learning. There was much initial euphoria about what e-learning could contribute, but increasingly it has been recognised that motivating learners is critical and most organisations now have much more realistic expectations of what e-learning can achieve, and often have to improve and re-launch e-learning solutions before they bed in, as for example in Hilton Hotels (Smethurst 2006). The support provided may well be critical, as may the way that such methods are introduced and used.

WINDOW ON PRACTICE

E-learning for leadership development at Barclays

In order to focus more on leadership abilities in promotion decisions Barclays wanted to provide leadership development which was available to all, regardless of age, gender, grade and geographical location. They produced a leadership development portal called 'Take the Lead', which could be used on a voluntary basis. Shortly after the initial launch the offering was re-launched making it more interactive and engaging and accessible, with dedicated 'learning laptops' that could be borrowed. An incentive was also offered in the form of a qualification in conjunction with Nottingham University Business School. Before this they had found that take-up in the UK was lower than elsewhere, with e-learning not being regarded as a first-choice approach to learning. To encourage use of the website news articles were published every two weeks, and managers in the appropriate grades were specifically targeted with 'teaser' postcards asking, for example, whether they were serious about their development. In addition testaments were given by managers of different levels of authority. Target managers also received brochures about the re-launch, their line managers received information packs, and e-learning featured in the in-house magazine. Email reminders were sent to participants who had not logged on to the portal for some months and learning logs were automatically produced when an individual completed a module with the suggestion that he or she should discuss with his or her manager how best to utilise these newly developed skills in his or her job. 'Take the Lead' is gradually becoming a more blended approach. Modules can be completed in any order according to job needs and good use is made of Barclays case studies.

Source: Summarised from IDS (2006b) *E-Learning*, HR Studies, No. 818, London: IDS.

E-learning covers a wide variety of approaches from using CD-roms to the company intranet and the Internet. More sophisticated approaches do not confine e-learning to interactive learning at a distance. Increasingly, synchronous learning is used where all participants log on at the same time, with a tutor or facilitator being available. Individuals can progress through material alone or network with others to complete a task and use chat rooms and have a dialogue with the tutor. Videoconferencing can also be used to bring participants together at the same time. For example, some MBAs have been delivered via videoconferencing rather than classroom-based teaching, and further details of this are provided in Cases 18.1 and 18.2 on this book's companion website at **www.pearsoned.co.uk/torrington**. The concept of blended learning also has had much appeal recently, but this term can be interpreted in different ways. Some use it to indicate the blending of e-learning with face-to-face learning experiences, while others use it more broadly to indicate 'a range of ways that e-learning can be delivered when combined with multiple additional routes that support and facilitate learning' (Sloman and Rolph 2003, p. 6).

WINDOW ON PRACTICE

Hills and Francis (1999) suggest that computer-based learning is a solitary activity, and that social contact and interaction were a necessary ingredient in learning. They assessed the use of their local computer-based training centres in Lloyds TSB, and found that some were used much more than others. The extent of use was not related to geographical accessibility, but instead to the support provided by the centre administrator, before, during and after learning sessions, and also the support of local managers.

Blended learning is increasingly used to indicate a blend of any approaches to learning, and there is evidence that learning and training now involve a much wider range of activities (CIPD 2006), while Pickard (2006) reports on the blended learning approach at the Department for Work and Pensions which integrates self-managed learning, coaching and e-learning.

WINDOW ON PRACTICE

Julie Scumming at AXA

Clarke (2006) recounts a very inventive learning experience at AXA, highly job based and involving a variety of activities. The exercise started with a Christmas card from a fictitious employee Julie Scumming. Posters followed announcing her arrival and then her fictitious husband entered the offices, shouting. After this there were diary entries on the intranet from both Julie and from her boss which staff began to follow, and picked up the story that Julie was a devout Christian and who felt she was being discriminated against and bullied by her boss and peers. Dummy tabloid articles were circulated, a stand-up row in the canteen was performed by actors. Sticky notes were put on computers saying not to get 'stuck like Julie', and an Advent calendar counted down the days to the main event which was a tribunal hearing for managers. When the tribunal panel retired to consider their verdict actors acted out scenes which had led up to the tribunal. Meanwhile employees could log on to discussion forums to express their views about the case, and there was a poll about the anticipated results. Involvement in all of this was voluntary but many staff participated. The objective was to raise awareness about discrimination issues. Responses to questionnaires after the event demonstrated that managers were more aware of religious discrimination issues.

Source: Clarke, E. (2006) 'Julie Diligent', *People Management*, Vol. 12, No. 14, 13 July, pp. 32–43.

EVALUATION OF TRAINING AND DEVELOPMENT

One of the most nebulous and unsatisfactory aspects of the training job is evaluating its effectiveness, yet it is becoming more necessary to demonstrate value for money. Whilst Campbell (2006) estimates that employer, public and individual spend on workforce training and development in the UK nears £30 billion each year, Phelps (2002) suggests there is no satisfactory return on investment calculation to prove its value, and that we remain unsure whether training breeds success or success breeds training. Evaluation is straightforward when the output of the training is clear to see, such as reducing the number of dispatch errors in a warehouse or increasing someone's typing speed. It is more difficult to evaluate the success of a management training course or a programme of social skills development, but the fact that it is difficult is not enough to prevent it being done.

A familiar method of evaluation is the post-course questionnaire, which course members complete on the final day by answering vague questions that require them to assess aspects of the course using only such general terms as 'good', 'very good' or 'outstanding'. The drawbacks with such questionnaires are, first, that there is a powerful halo effect, as the course will have been, at the very least, a welcome break from routine and there will probably have been some attractive fringe benefits such as staying in a comfortable hotel and enjoying rich food. Second, the questionnaire tends to evaluate the course and not the learning, so that the person attending the course is assessing the quality of the tutors and the visual aids, instead of being directed to examine what has been learned.

Hamblin (1974), in a much-quoted work, identified five levels of evaluation: (1) evaluating the training, as in the post-course questionnaire above; (2) evaluating the learning, in terms of how the trainee now behaves; (3) evaluating changes in job performance; (4) evaluating changes in organisation performance; and (5) evaluating changes in the wider contribution that the organisation now makes. Perhaps the most well-referenced approach to evaluation is Kirkpatrick (1959) who suggested four levels of evaluation, somewhat similar to Hamblin: (1) reaction level; (2) learning level (have the learning objectives been met?); (3) behaviour (how has the individual's behaviour changed back in the job?); and (4) results and impact on the bottom line (what is the impact of training on performance?).

WINDOW ON PRACTICE

Demonstrating the value of learning, training and development

The CIPD Learning and Development Survey (CIPD 2006) found that nine in ten respondents used some form of evaluation in an effort to identify the value of learning, training and development activities. Of these:

- 98 per cent evaluate to Kilpatrick level 1
- 73 per cent to Kilpatrick level 2
- 62 per cent to Kilpatrick level 3
- 36 per cent to Kilpatrick level 4
- and only 18 per cent look at the full return on their investment.

Source: CIPD (2006) *Learning and Development: Annual Survey Report 2006*. London: CIPD.

Bramley (1996) suggests that performance effectiveness can be measured at individual, team and organisational levels, and that changes in behaviour, knowledge, skills and attitudes need to be considered. He makes the worthwhile point – as do others – that the criteria for evaluation need to be built into development activities from the very beginning, and not tagged on at the end. Lingham and his co-researchers (2006) provide a good example of how this can be done in practice. They describe an action research project where evaluation was built in from the outset and involved collaboration between organisational leaders, trainers, participants and evaluators. A four-phase approach was used:

- Phase 1: Design of training programme (organisational leaders, trainers and evaluators agree design and methods to obtain feedback from participants after the initial runs of the training programme).
- Phase 2: Launch and evaluation of initial programme (training conducted and agreed methods used to collect participants' views).
- Phase 3: Feedback and design of evaluation instrument (organisational leaders, trainers and evaluators meet to review feedback and field notes and adapt the training programme where necessary. A survey instrument designed for evaluation of future iterations of the programme).
- Phase 4: Ongoing training and evaluation (training programme conducted with new design/content, evaluation survey used and results fed back into Phase 3. (adapted from Lingham *et al*. 2006)

Problems with evaluation persist and in the 2006 CIPD survey 80 per cent of respondents reported that their training activities are delivering greater value to the business than they are able to demonstrate. There is always a need, however, to assess value for money, and this is generally worked out on a payback basis, which focuses attention on the short term. Lee (1996) suggests a 'pay-forward' approach to assessing value for money and this concept appears to be more consistent with the nature of training and development strategy and interventions than a payback approach, as the outcome may only be observed in the long term.

While organisations may desire a measure of the impact of training on the organisation, in practice this appears to be rarely achieved. Sadler-Smith *et al*., for example, found in their study (1999) that the reasons for evaluating training were more often operational than strategic, and they state that evaluation information was used 'mostly for feedback to individuals, and to inform the training process, and less for return on investment decisions' (p. 369).

SUMMARY PROPOSITIONS

18.1 There are four perspectives on learning: behaviourist, cognitive, social and constructivist. Each has different implications for the approach taken to training and development.

18.2 The emphasis has moved from training to learning, with individuals taking ownership of their own learning needs. To be effective learners we need to understand the nature of learning and our own strengths and weaknesses.

18.3 The emphasis on formal development programmes is declining in favour of greater interest in approaches to on-the-job development, such as coaching, mentoring, peer relationships and self-development.

18.4 There has been an upsurge of interest in e-learning. However, the extent to which employees take advantage of such opportunities will be affected by the context and the support available. E-learning is increasingly being blended with other forms of learning.

18.5 Evaluation of development is critical but difficult. It is most effective when built into the design of the development activity rather than tagged on at the end.

GENERAL DISCUSSION TOPICS

1 If learning is an individual process, why is so much training done in groups? What are the implications of moving towards more individualised learning?

2 Discuss the view that the role of the trainer/facilitator is critically important in the effectiveness of a training programme.

FURTHER READING

Hawkins, P. and Schwenk, G. (2006) *Coaching Supervision – Maximising the potential of Coaching, A Change Agenda*. London: CIPD.
This is a full report of the research carried out by the Bath Consultancy Group, and is a fascinating read providing an assessment of current practice, with examples of good practice and guidelines for managers.

Jarvis, J. and Lane, D. (2006) *The Case for Coaching: Making evidence based decisions on coaching*. London: CIPD.
A combined approach from academics and professionals makes this well-researched book both interesting and informative, and includes coaching by a range of different practitioners.

Passmore, J. (ed.) (2006) *Excellence in Coaching: The Industry Guide*. London: Kogan Page.
A combination of contributions from both academics and practitioners provides expertise in a range of areas relevant to coaching.

Reynolds, J., Caley, L. and Mason, R. (2002) *How do People Learn? A Research report*. London: CIPD.
This research report covers the background context to learning in today's organisations and considers the four theoretical perspectives on learning. The report also covers practical aspects of learning and e-learning. This report has been summarised by Jennifer Schramm (2002) in *The change agenda: How do people learn?* London: CIPD.

Tulip, S. (2006) 'Lighting the Way', *People Management*, Vol. 12, No. 18, 14 September, p. 44.
This is a very useful summary of coaching trends.

Thorne, K. (2003) *Blended Learning*. London: Kogan Page.
A useful, broadly based handbook which explains how to get the best out of combining innovative and technological advances offered by e-learning with the best of traditional approaches to learning. Thorne considers the high-level support required for such approaches and the involvement of

stakeholders, and also provides practical design solutions. A range of case studies shows, in particular, the various ways in which different approaches to learning can be combined.

REFERENCES

Antonacopoulou, E. (2000) 'Employee development through self-development in three retail banks', *Personnel Review*, Vol. 29, No. 4.

Arney, E. (2006) 'Insider's Guide', *People Management*, Vol. 12, No. 23, 23 November, pp. 40–42.

Arnold, J. (1997) 'Mentoring in early career', *Human Resource Management Journal*, Vol. 7, No. 4, pp. 61–70.

Baruch, Y. and Leeming, A. (2001) 'The added value of MBA studies – graduates' perceptions', *Personnel Review*, Vol. 30, No. 5, pp. 589–601.

Bee, F. and Bee, R. (1994) *Training Needs Analysis and Evaluation*. London: IPM.

Boak, G. (1991) *Developing Managerial Competencies. The management learning contract approach*. London: Pitman.

Bramley, P. (1996) *Evaluating Training*. London: IPD.

Broadbridge, A. (1999) 'Mentoring in retailing: a tool for success?', *Personnel Review*, Vol. 28, No. 4.

Brockett, J. (2006) 'Energy firm gets party vibe', *People Management*, Vol. 12, No. 10, 18 May, p. 12.

Burleston, L. and Grint, K. (1996) 'The deracination of politics: outdoor management development', *Management Learning*, Vol. 27, No. 2, pp. 187–202.

Campbell, M. (2006) 'Demonstrating the value of learning, training and development', in *Latest Trends in Learning, Training and Development: Reflections on the 2006 Learning and Development Survey*. London: CIPD.

Canning, R. (1996) 'Enhancing the quality of learning in human resource development', *Journal of European Industrial Training*, Vol. 20, No. 2, pp. 3–10.

Carroll, S. and Gillen, D. (2001) 'Exploring the teaching function of the managerial role', *Journal of Management Development*, Vol. 21, No. 5, pp. 330–42.

CIPD (2003) *Training and Development 2003: Survey Report*. London: CIPD.

CIPD (2006) *Learning and Development: Annual Survey 2006*. London: CIPD.

Clarke, E. (2006) 'Julie Diligent', *People Management*, Vol. 12, No. 14, 13 July, pp. 32–43.

Clutterbuck, D. and Megginson, D. (2005) *Making coaching work: Creating a Coaching Culture*. London: CIPD.

Cooper, C. (2001) 'Connect Four', *People Management*, February.

Cottee, P. (2006) 'Oliver's Army', *People Management*, Vol. 12, No. 19, 28 September, pp. 44–45.

Cromer, D.R. (1989) 'Peers as providers', *Personnel Administrator*, Vol. 34, Pt 5, pp. 84–6.

Feinstein, A., Mann, S. and Corsum, D. (2002) 'Charting the experiential territory – Clarifying definitions and uses of computer simulations, games and role plays', *Personnel Review*, Vol. 21, No. 10, pp. 732–44.

Fowler, J. and O'Gorman, J. (2005) 'Mentoring functions: A Contemporary view of the perceptions of mentees and mentors', *British Journal of Management*, Vol. 16, pp. 51–7.

Hall, L. (2006) 'Inside Job', *People Management*, Vol. 12, No. 16, 10 August, pp. 34–6.

Hallier, J. and Butts, S. (1999) 'Employers' discovery of training: self-development, employability and the rhetoric of partnership', *Employee Relations*, Vol. 21, No. 1.

Hamblin, A.C. (1974) *Evaluation and Control of Training*. Maidenhead: McGraw-Hill.

Hammond, D. (2001) 'Reality Bytes', *People Management*, January.

Harrison, R. (1997) *Employee Development*. London: IPD.

Harrison, R. (2005) *Learning and Development*. London: IPD.

Hayes, J. and Allinson, C.W. (1996) 'The implications of learning styles for training and development: a discussion of the matching hypothesis', *British Journal of Management*, Vol. 7, pp. 63–73.

Hills, H. and Francis, P. (1999) 'Interaction Learning', *People Management*, July.

Honey, P. and Mumford, A. (1989) *A Manual of Learning Opportunities*. Maidenhead: Peter Honey.

Ibbetson, A. and Newell, S. (1999) 'A comparison of a competitive and non-competitive outdoor management development programmes', *Personnel Review*, Vol. 28, No. 1/2.

IDS (2006a) *Coaching in the Workplace*. HR Studies No. 831, October. London: IDS.

IDS (2006b) *E-Learning*. HR Studies, No. 818. London: IDS.

Johnson, S., Geory, G. and Griego, O. (1999) 'The Mentoring Model theory: dimensions in mentoring protocols', *Career Development International*, Vol. 4, No. 7.

Kirkpatrick, D. (1959) 'Techniques for evaluating training programmes', *Journal of the American Society of Training Directors*, Vol. 13.

Kolb, D.A., Rubin, I.M. and McIntyre, J.M. (1984) *Organization Psychology*, 4th edn. Englewood Cliffs, NJ: Prentice-Hall.

Kram, K.E. (1983) 'Phases of the mentor relationship', *Academy of Management Journal*, Vol. 26, No. 4.

Kram, K.E. and Isabella, L.A. (1985) 'Mentoring alternatives: the role of peer relationships in career development', *Academy of Management Journal*, Vol. 28, No. 1.

Lee, R. (1996) 'The pay-forward view of training', *People Management*, pp. 30–2.

Lehane, S. (2005) 'Whistle while you work', *People Management*, Vol. 11, No. 25, 29 December, pp. 32–3.

Lingham, T., Richley, B. and Rezania, D. (2006) 'An evaluation system for training programs: a case study using a four-phase approach', *Career Development International*, Vol. 11, No. 4, pp. 334–51.

Longenecker, C. and Ariss, S. (2002) 'Creating competitive advantage through effective management education', *Personnel Review*, Vol. 21, No. 9, pp. 640–54.

Martin, G. and Pate, J. (2001) 'Company-based education programmes: what's the pay off for employers?', *Human Resource Management Journal*, Vol. 11, No. 4, pp. 55–73.

Megginson, D. (1994) 'Planned and Emergent Learning: A framework and a method', *Executive Development*, Vol. 7, No. 6, pp. 29–32.

Megginson, D. (2000) 'Current issues in mentoring', *Career Development International*, Vol. 5, No. 4/5.

Megginson, D. and Whitaker, V. (1996) *Cultivating Self-development*. London: IPD.

Monks, K., Barker, P. and Mhanachain, A. (2001) 'Drama as an opportunity for learning and development', *Personnel Review*, Vol. 20, No. 5, pp. 414–23.

Mumford, A. (1994) *How Managers Develop Managers*. Aldershot: Gower.

O'Hara, S., Webber, T. and Murphy, W. (2001) 'The joy of sets', *People Management*, 8 Feb., pp. 30–4.

Paauwe, J. and Williams, R. (2001) 'Seven key issues for management development', *Journal of Management Development*, Vol. 20, No. 2, pp. 90–105.

Pemberton, C. (2006) *Coaching to Solutions: A Manager's toolkit for Performance delivery*. Oxford: Butterworth-Heinemann.

Phelps, M. (2002) 'Blind faith', *People Management*, Vol. 8, No. 9, 2 May, p. 51.

Phillips, L. (2006) 'BUPA Stars', *People Management*, Vol. 12, No. 22, 9 November, pp. 30–2.

Pickard, J. (2006) 'Suits Ewe', *People Management*, Vol. 12, No. 12, 15 June, pp. 36–7.

Prickett, R. (1997) 'Screen savers', *People Management*, 26 June, pp. 36–8.

Sadler-Smith, E., Down, S. and Field, J. (1999) 'Adding value to HRD: evaluation, Investors in People and small firm training', *Human Resource Development International*, Vol. 2, No. 4, pp. 369–90.

Sadler-Smith, E., Down, S. and Lean, J. (2000) ' "Modern" learning methods: rhetoric and reality', *Personnel Review*, Vol. 29, No. 4.

Santos, A. and Stewart, M. (2003) 'Employee perceptions and their influence on training effectiveness', *Human Resource Management Journal*, Vol. 13, No. 1, pp. 27–45.

Sloman, M. (2001) 'Hardier laurels, please', *People Management*, Vol. 7, No. 25, 27 December, p. 39.

Sloman, M. and Rolph, J. (2003) *E-learning: The learning curve – The change agenda*. London: CIPD.

Smethurst, S. (2006) 'Staying Power', *People Management*, Vol. 12, No. 7, 6 April, pp. 34–6.

Stansfield, L. (1996) 'Is self-development the key to the future?', *Management Learning*, Vol. 27, No. 4, pp. 429–45.

Stott, T. and Sweeney, J. (1999) 'More than a match', *People Management*, June, pp. 45–8.

Woodall, J. (2000) 'Corporate support for work-based management development', *Human Resource Management Journal*, Vol. 10, No. 1, pp. 18–32.

An extensive range of additional materials, including multiple choice questions, answers to questions and links to useful websites can be found on the Human Resource Management Companion Website at **www.pearsoned.co.uk/torrington**.

CAREER DEVELOPMENT

THE OBJECTIVES OF THIS CHAPTER ARE TO:

1 Explain and critique how and why careers are changing

2 Introduce some definitions of career and career development

3 Review some of the models and theories which help us understand the concept

4 Explore practical ways in which individuals can manage and enhance their careers, especially continuous professional development

5 Explore the types of support the organisation can provide for career development and management

WINDOW ON PRACTICE

In a survey of business school graduates in Austria, Mayrhofer and his colleagues (2005) found that whilst many preferred the idea of an organisational career, the majority (56 per cent) preferred post-organisational careers. Post-organisational careers were defined by the researchers as any of the following:

- Self-employment: working in the stable and limited field of their own expertise but outside an organisation, operating as either a self-employed professional or an entrepreneur. Typically such workers have several customers and these customers do not change frequently.

- Free-floating professionals: also working in their domain of expertise but having a close relationship with one customer at a time, but of limited duration and possibly with a rapid change of customers.

- Chronic flexibility: working as free-floating professionals above, but also dealing with several customers at a time.

In a very different context, Mallon (1998) reports on research with 24 ex-managers of one branch of the public sector who now had portfolio careers, and through in-depth biographical interviews set out to understand how they account for their career move. From the data she grouped the participants into three categories: 'refugees', 'missionaries' and 'reluctant missionaries'.

There were only two managers classified as 'refugees' and both were unexpectedly made compulsorily redundant, from senior positions. Since then they had not reconciled themselves to any alternative form of working other than full-time employment. One found a new job, after a year, in which she hopes to remain until retirement, the other still looks for jobs, but having been unsuccessful so far is developing his portfolio of work. Two others Mallon classified as 'ex-refugees'. Both experienced redundancy, both found other work, but both have since chosen the portfolio route. Their explanation for this centred around growing disillusionment with the 'employment' world, stimulated by their bitter experiences of redundancy.

Mallon identified five of her respondents as 'missionaries'. All left voluntarily and two of these never felt that they fitted in the 'employed world'. Three made very well-planned decisions to move to a portfolio, reducing hours with their current employer in order to gradually build up work elsewhere, for example. These three felt that there were no further challenges in the organisation for them, they talked about 'new' careers, and about taking control for themselves. They clearly felt pulled by other opportunities.

The final, largest group, 'reluctant missionaries', were somewhere in between. Two were offered the choice between a different job or redundancy, and chose to leave, others felt a growing dissatisfaction with the organisation and being out of step with the organisation, and one felt that dismissal was looming. However, although these individuals were pushed into action they did report factors which pulled them towards a portfolio approach, such as integrity, time for childcare and doing the type of work that they wanted to do. Others fled the organisation because they felt their position was untenable but, at the time, they had no idea what they were going to do next, and their decision to go portfolio was a pragmatic response to the situation that they were in.

Sources: Summarised from Mayrhofer W., Steyrer J., Meyer, M., Strunk, G., Schiffinger, M. and Iellatchitch, A. (2005) 'Graduates' career aspirations and individual characteristics', *Human Resource Management Journal*, Vol. 15, No. 1, pp. 38-56; and adapted from M. Mallon (1998) 'The portfolio career; pushed or pulled to it?', *Personnel Review*, Vol. 27, No. 5.

There is a considerable body of literature indicating that the foregoing examples are typical of a general and substantial move from long-term organisationally based careers to individually managed portfolio, boundaryless, post-organisational or protean (driven by desire for self-fulfilment) careers.

HOW AND WHY ARE CAREERS CHANGING?

Many writers over the past decade have provided a picture of dramatic change in the nature of careers that are possible in today's society. The traditional career within a single organisation, characterised by hierarchical progression, managed on a planned basis by the organisation, is gone, it is argued (*see*, for example, Arthur and Rousseau 1996a; Adamson *et al.* 1998). Organisations now have flatter structures and need to be flexible, fluid and cost effective in the face of an uncertain and unpredictable future. Thus they can no longer offer long-term career progression in return for loyalty, commitment and adequate performance, which was an unwritten deal and part of the traditional psychological contract.

Kanter (1989), for example, suggests that managers can no longer rely on the organisation for their career future and must learn to manage themselves and their work independently, as many professionals do. In particular, they must build portfolios of their achievements and skills, develop networks, make a 'name' for themselves and market themselves within the relevant industry sector rather than just within their current organisation. In a different sense Handy (1994) uses the words 'portfolio career' to mean 'exchanging full time employment for independence', which is expressed in the collection of different pieces of work done for different clients. Individuals starting off a portfolio career often continue to do some work for their previous organisation (on a fee-paying basis) and add to this a network of other clients. Arthur *et al.* (2005) describe the 'boundaryless career' as one which includes moves between organisations, non-hierarchical moves within organisations where there are no norms of progress or success, and moves into different careers as well as employment outside the organisation. Post-organisational careers (sometimes called post-corporate) were defined in the Window on Practice at the opening of this chapter; and protean careers, involving reinvention of the self and discovery, have probably best been described by Hall (2004) who identifies such as career as bound up with the development of the self, driven by the individual's values and self-fulfilment.

There is some debate, however, about whether portfolio and associated careers are liberating or exploitative (*see*, for example, Smeaton 2003), and the extent to which individuals have sought such careers or found them to be the only alternative may have some influence on their perceptions of this. Interestingly Fenwick (2006) in a study of nurses and adult educators who had become portfolio workers, found that such careers were simultaneously liberating and exploitative, partly due to individual desires for both contingency and stability.

The evidence to support the reality that careers have fundamentally changed is 'shaky at best' (Mallon 1998) and Guest and McKenzie-Davey (1996), for example, found the traditional organisation and the traditional career 'alive and well' (pp. 22–3), with the hierarchy still used for motivation and progression. However, there is increasing evidence over the past five or so years that professionals, in particular, are moving into self-employment or agency work (*see*, for example, Purcell *et al.* 2005). As yet there remains insufficient research into the extent to which new career patterns are developing, for whom, and the mechanisms by which individuals are pulled or pushed into them.

WINDOW ON PRACTICE

Explaining the rise in social workers moving into agency work

Kilpatrick and Hoque (2006) investigated the increasing popularity of agency work for social workers in a tight jobs market where plenty of permanent jobs are available. The authors explored whether this movement was due to the lure of the benefits of portfolio careers (the 'free agent perspective') or whether the move could be explained by a desire to escape from, or adjust to, the deteriorating conditions in public organisations. They found that the move to agency work from permanent employment (or at the beginning of professional employment) was voluntary. They suggest that this is not surprising, given the scarcity and demand for their skills, and the limited risk therefore taken. In interviews social workers talked about flexibility and personal control as an agency worker so that they could integrate work and non-work activities more effectively. Others spoke of the opportunities to learn new things in new areas of work and not be stuck in one specialism. Whilst some mentioned the better pay levels, there was a recognition that loss of benefits such as sick pay, pensions and so on, often balanced this out. They identified problems, such as being potentially marginalised due to the fact that they were not a permanent part of the organisation, and that sometimes they might get the less interesting and more onerous tasks to do. Others identified the loss of training and limited supervision as a disadvantage for their career development. So, whilst benefits of agency working were identified, disadvantages were too, and the researchers found other explanations accounting for the move to this type of employment, which focused on escape from the prevailing work conditions of a permanent contract. The respondents reported limitations in job mobiliy when on a

→

permanent contract (being restricted to current specialism), the feeling of being 'burnt out' and having increased case loads and administrative burdens, and the uncertainty created by constant restructurings. Agency work enabled professionals to have some control over the assignments they chose to do and there was also a feeling expressed that if they did not like an assignment they could easily leave if they wished. Such workers felt they could distance themselves from the organisation in terms of politics, targets and audit, and were in a better position simply to do their job and leave, rather than feeling obliged to put in unpaid discretionary time. The authors found that 'Quite often, going agency represented not so much a liberation from the toil of permanent employment but "the lesser of two evils"', and concluded that moves to agency work are in large part a reaction to deteriorating conditions at work and an increasingly rigid employment system.

Source: Kilpatrick, I. and Hoque, K. (2006) 'A retreat from permanent employment? Accounting for the rise of professional agency work in UK public services', *Work, Employment and Society*, Vol. 20, No. 4, pp. 649–66,

Some argue that the contradictions between the above views are a result of people being in transition (*see*, for example, Burke 1998a), whereas King (2003) suggests that the 'new career' may be reflected in people's expectations rather than their labour market experiences. Another explanation may be that temporary work and contract work are spread more evenly across different sectors (*see*, for example, Burke 1998b), and have therefore become more visible. Let us not forget that the traditional psychological contract was never available to everyone. Smithson and Lewis (2000) argue that public perceptions of increasing insecurity may have more to do with the characteristics of those whom the insecurity now affects, such as graduates and professional staff, than with an increase in the phenomenon. Similarly, different groups have different sets of expectations and subjective feelings of job insecurity. Younger workers accept insecurity, almost as the norm (*see*, for example, Smithson and Lewis 2000), but older workers feel the psychological contract has been violated. Older workers may have the same expectations as before but realise that the employer is no longer going to fulfil their part of the bargain (*see*, for example, Herriot *et al*. 1997; Thomas and Dunkerley 1999).

A different explanation for these contradictory findings is that organisations project the image of a stable and predictable internal career structure, because it is in their interests to do so, whatever the reality. Adamson *et al*. (1998) suggest that it is in the organisation's interests to maintain the illusion of such career structures so as to retain high-performance employees. It could also be argued that such structures are useful in recruiting highly skilled employees, for whom career structures are likely to continue. Purcell *et al*. (2003) also showed that positive perceptions of career advancement opportunities are one of the most powerful determinants of employee commitment. However, if this is an illusion such a strategy may well backfire.

If the psychological contract between employer and employee now needs to be renegotiated, this does not mean abandoning the concept of career, rather, the idea of a new psychological contract is developing. Many articles identify a 'new psychological contract' in which the deal between employer and staff is different but still mutually beneficial. Employees offer high productivity and total commitment while with their

Employee offers	Employer offers
Loyalty	Security
Commitment	Future career
Adequate performance	To look after the employee

Table 19.1
The old psychological contract

Employee offers	Employer offers
Continuous learning	Employability
Keep pace with change	Tools and environment to achieve this
Commitment to organisational success	Opportunities for assessment
Manage their own career	Opportunities for development
High productivity	Care

Table 19.2
The new psychological contract

Source: Based on R.H. Waterman, J.A. Waterman and B.A. Collard (1994) 'Toward a career-resilient workforce', *Harvard Business Review*, July–August.

employer, and the employer offers enhanced *employability* rather than long-term employment. The offer of employability centres on enabling employees to develop skills that are in demand, and allows them opportunities to practise these and keep up to date. This equips the employee with the skills and experiences needed to obtain another appropriate job when he or she is no longer needed by their present employer (*see*, for example, Waterman *et al.* 1994). The differences between the old psychological contract and the new, as they relate to careers, are shown in Tables 19.1 and 19.2. King (2003) found that graduates rated the offer of employability as of most importance in career terms, and they still expected the organisation to provide a career for them; she argues that the picture presented is one of lip service and a less than whole-hearted commitment to the concept of the 'new career'.

However, a further contradiction is apparent in the literature: the assumption that the 'new psychological contract' supplants the old when the original contract is violated, but the degree to which this happens is debatable (*see*, for example, Doherty *et al.* 1997). Herriot (1998) argues that the new psychological contract is just more rhetoric, and that in reality there are many different new deals, and Sparrow (1996) suggests that the solution to the fragmentation of the old psychological contract is a series of layered individualised career contracts. King also suggests that the organisation should not adopt an either/or career approach, but aim to offer both internal careers and employability support.

WINDOW ON PRACTICE

The implications of supporting employability

Benson (2006) investigated a company which had introduced employability activities in the form of 100 per cent reimbursement of tuition fees for a range of development activities as a constructive reaction to a period of downsizing and instability. The aim was to develop well-trained employees but also to put them in a better position in the jobs market. As the CEO commented:

We cannot guarantee anyone a job, but we are nonetheless obliged to provide employees with reasonable opportunities to re-establish themselves, ideally on more favourable conditions, in the event of job loss.

Overall it was found that the activities reduced the intention to quit and increased commitment to the organisation. However in the group that studied degree courses the intention to quit was only reduced if the individual was subsequently promoted internally.

This is a good example of the importance of offering employability support and internal careers in parallel.

Source: Benson, G. (2006) 'Employee development, commitment and intention to turnover: a test of "employability" policies in action', *Human Resource Management Journal*, Vol. 16, No. 2, pp. 173–91.

DEFINITIONS AND IMPORTANCE OF CAREER DEVELOPMENT

A career can be defined as the pattern or sequence of work roles of an individual. Traditionally, the word applied only to those occupying managerial and professional roles, but increasingly it is seen as appropriate for everyone in relation to their work roles. Also, the word career has been used to imply upward movement and advancement in work roles. As we have noted, many organisations no longer offer a traditional career, or only offer it to a selected few. Enforced redundancies, flatter structures, short-term contracts, availability of part-time rather than full-time work, all break the idealised image of career. We now recognise other moves as legitimate expressions of career development, including development and extension within the job itself, lateral moves and the development of portfolio work. Career can also be conceptualised more broadly in terms of 'the individual's development in learning and work throughout life' (Collin and Watts 1996), and thus includes voluntary work and other life experiences. Indeed Adamson *et al*. (1998) go so far as to say that a good curriculum vitae may

no longer be one with an impressive list of job titles of increasing seniority, but rather a rich cv (e.g. one which includes a variety of work and non-work activities). (p. 256)

Male careers are becoming increasingly similar to the traditional fragmented pattern of women's careers (Goffee and Nicholson 1994), and many men are generally keener to develop careers which take account of personal and family needs, including children's education, partner's career and quality of life. Career development is no longer a stand-alone issue and needs to be viewed in the context of the life and development of the whole person and not just the person as employee.

We view career development as something experienced by the individual (sometimes referred to as the *internal* career), and therefore not necessarily bounded by one organisation. This also means that the responsibility for managing a career is with the individual, although the organisation may play a key facilitating and supporting role.

The primary purpose of career development is to meet the current and future needs of the organisation and the individual at work, and this increasingly means developing employability. On this basis Walton (1999) argues that it is increasingly difficult to disentangle career development from general training and development. We could make a strong case for the value of self-development here. Career success is seen through the eyes of the individual, and can be defined as individual satisfaction with career through meeting personal career goals, while making a contribution to the organisation. Although in this chapter we prioritise the needs of the individual, in Chapter 3 we prioritise the needs of the organisation when we review replacement and succession planning.

We have given priority to the individual in career development, but it is worth noting the general benefits career development provides for the organisation:

- It makes the organisation attractive to potential recruits.
- It enhances the image of the organisation, by demonstrating a recognition of employee needs.
- It is likely to encourage employee commitment and to reduce staff turnover.
- It is likely to encourage motivation and job performance as employees can see some possible movement and progress in their work.
- Perhaps most importantly it exploits the full potential of the workforce.

Before looking at how individuals can manage their career development with organisational support, we need to review some of the concepts underlying the notion of career.

UNDERSTANDING CAREERS

Career development stages

Many authors have attempted to map out the ideal stages of a successful career and in this section we loosely use the five stages outlined by Greenhaus and Callanan (1994). Few careers follow such an idealised pattern, and even historically such a pattern did not apply for all employees. However, the stage approach offers a useful framework for understanding career experiences, if we use it flexibly as a tool for understanding careers rather than as a normative model.

Stage 1: occupational choice: preparation for work

This first stage involves developing an occupational self-image and will of course reappear for those who wish to change career later in life The key theme is a matching process between the strengths/weaknesses, values and desired lifestyle of the individual and the requirements and benefits of a range of occupations. One of the difficulties that can arise at this stage is a lack of individual self-awareness. There are countless tests available to help identify individual interests, but these can only complete part of the picture, and need to be complemented by structured exercises, which help people look at themselves from a range of perspectives. Other problems involve individuals limiting their choice due to social, cultural, gender or racial characteristics. Although we use role models to identify potential occupations, and these extend the range of options we consider, this process may also close them down. Another difficulty at this stage is gaining authentic information about careers which are different from the ones pursued by family and friends.

Stage 2: organisational entry

This stage involves the individual in both finding a job which corresponds with his or her occupational self-image, and starting to do that job. Problems here centre on the accuracy of information that the organisation provides, so that when the individual begins work expectations and reality may be very different. Recruiters understandably 'sell' their organisations and the job to potential recruits, emphasising the best parts and neglecting the downside. Applicants often fail to test their assumptions by asking for the specific information they really need. In addition, schools, colleges and universities have, until recently, only prepared students for the technical demands of work, ignoring other skills that they will need, such as communication skills, influencing skills and dealing with organisational politics. To aid organisational entry, Wanous (1992) has suggested the idea of realistic recruitment with the emphasis on providing accurate information, to which we refer in Chapter 8. Pazy and his colleagues (2006) also demonstrate how information-free interventions can be beneficial in this respect. They provided a decision-making tool to a random selection of candidates eight months prior to their joining the Technical School of the Israeli air force so that they could use this for occupational choice decisions. The candidates who had been introduced to the tool had significantly lower turnover during the programme and a lower turnover six months after the programme. The authors suggest that the tool enabled the trainees to make better career choices and also made trainees aware of self-determination in their career.

ACTIVITY 19.1

Think of three different jobs in your organisation (or any organisation with which you are familiar) which have been/may be recruited externally. If a 'realistic recruitment' approach were adopted:

- What information would you give to the candidates about each job and the organisation so that a balanced picture was presented?
- What methods would you use to communicate this information?

Stage 3: early career – establishment and achievement

The establishment stage involves fitting into the organisation and understanding 'how things are done around here'. Thorough induction programmes are important, but more especially it is important to provide the new recruit with a 'real' job and early challenges rather than a roving commission from department to department with no real purpose, as is often found on trainee schemes. Feedback and support from the immediate manager are also key. This has implications, for example for the design of graduate training programmes.

The achievement part of this stage is demonstrating competence and gaining greater responsibility and authority. It is at this stage that access to opportunities for career development becomes key. Development within the job and opportunities for promotion and broadening moves are all aided if the organisation has a structured approach to career development, involving career ladders, pathways or matrices, but not necessarily hierarchical progression. Feedback remains important, as do opportunities and support for further career exploration and planning. Organisations are likely to provide the most support for 'high fliers' who are seen as the senior management of the future and who may be on 'fast track' programmes.

Stage 4: mid-career

Mid-career may involve further growth and advancement or the maintenance of a steady state. In either case it is generally accompanied by some form of re-evaluation of career and life direction. A few will experience decline at this stage. For those who continue to advance, organisational support remains important. Some people whose career has reached a plateau will experience feelings of failure. Organisational support in these cases needs to involve the use of lateral career paths, job expansion, development as mentors of others, further training to keep up to date and the use of a flexible reward system.

Stage 5: late career

The organisation's task in the late career stage is to encourage people to continue performing well. This is particularly important as some sectors are experiencing skills shortages and there are moves by some companies to allow individuals to stay at work after the state retirement age. Demographics indicate that in the UK we have an ageing labour force, and the 'early retirement' culture of the 1980s and early 1990s, when many retired at around the ago of 50, has all but disappeared, although subtle pressures to retire early probably remain. In addition there is also a pressure on individuals to work longer to improve their pensions and the 2006 Age Discrimination Act prohibits organisations from retiring anyone under 65 without good reason and provides a statutory right for individuals to request to remain working after the age of 65.

WINDOW ON PRACTICE

Portfolio working in late career

It has been suggested that using flexible working and adopting portfolio careers are mechanisms for retaining older workers in employment. Platman (2004) reports on research into portfolio careers for men and women in the 50-plus age range in the media industry where portfolio work/freelancing has been a common form of employment for some time. Such careers are thought to be particularly attractive because they avoid an imposed retirement threshold, and leave individuals free to negotiate a different relationship, doing as little or as much work as they wish, choosing their own mix of clients and assignments. The researcher investigated the views of both client employers and the freelancers. For the client this group of freelancers was attractive due to its flexibility, affordability and 'instant' knowledge. Older freelancers often used their own equipment, had a broader grasp of the issues and a more sophisticated approach. On the other hand such freelancers were seen to bring historical 'baggage' and may work in outdated ways.

Freelancers mainly landed contracts through informal networking, and being very adaptable in what they would do. They focused on meeting project delivery deadlines, in spite of any health or personal problems and most felt that fees offered should be accepted unless they felt strongly that the work was being undervalued. A constant source of concern was gaining further work from the client employer. This often resulted in their accepting assignments they didn't want as a refusal often cut off the work supply. This severely limited their freedoms as freelancers, although there were times when work-life integration went well, and they did feel they had some self-determination even though this wasn't as much as they desired. The intensification of the media industry affected freelancers too and faster turnarounds were required with little more compensation, and there was a feeling that increasingly their experience was not valued. Many freelancers found it difficult to work for much younger client employers who provided guidance which they felt inappropriate, and they felt increasingly out of step with their younger clients. Keeping up with skills and technology was a demand on time and money and the informal networks providing the work gradually reduced with age.

In summary such work did allow them the freedom to maintain employment and to pick and choose what they did to some extent. but they were vulnerable to client demand, and found they needed to be very adaptable to meet others' needs.

Even given the limitations the freelancers felt that this was the best, if not the only, form of working available to them at this stage in their career.

Source: Platman, K. (2004) '"Portfolio careers" and the search for flexibility in later life', *Work, Employment and Society*, Vol. 18, No. 3, pp. 573–99.

Despite the stereotypes that abound defining older workers as slower and less able to learn, evidence suggests that the over-50s can be valuable employees who perform well if managed appropriately. Greenhaus and Callanan point out that the availability of flexible work patterns, clear performance standards, continued training and the avoidance of discrimination are helpful at this stage, combined with preparation for retirement. Portfolio careers can be a particularly attractive option at this stage. Organisations are sometimes unwilling to invest in the over-50s as, from an economic perspective, there is less time for payback. However as retirement is delayed and protean careers increase ongoing learning is even more important, rather than less. Greller (2006) found no differences between the employed 50–70 age group and other age groups in terms of the hours spent on professional development (work-related-knowledge skills development and the development of career opportunities) and also found that time spent was associated with career motivation (as for other age groups). Interestingly, though, they found that the initiative for most activities for the 50–70 age group came from the people themselves rather than from organisation.

ACTIVITY 19.2

If you had a high degree of choice in terms of your career stages would you prefer to:

1 Remain with one organisation for life, or move around?

2 Stay with one occupation/profession for life or change your occupation/profession once or twice?

3 Have hierarchical job moves with more responsibility in the same area, or have the opportunity to move into new areas without increasing your responsibility level?

4 Retire as soon as you can, or work for as long as you can?

Identify the reasons for your choice, and consider its advantages and disadvantages. How likely do you think it is that you will be able to fulfil your choice?

Career balance

Much of the original work done on describing career stages was carried out by analysing the experiences of those who were both male and white, so the analyses are clearly inadequate for our contemporary world of work and we still lack satisfactory explanations of career development that can embrace the full variety of ethnic backgrounds, gender and occupational variety.

There is considerable evidence that women and those from racial minorities limit their career choices, both consciously and unconsciously, for reasons other than their basic abilities and career motives. Social class identity may have the same impact. Employers need at least to be aware of such forces and ideally would explore such constraints with their employees to encourage individual potential to be exploited to the full.

The acceptance of such idealised career development stages as described above, particularly in an era of work intensification, leaves little room for family and other interference in career development, and until recently there has been no place in career development and even in the thinking about careers for those who do not conform to the stages outlined. There are hopeful signs of increasing recognition that career and life choices need to be explored in unison. There has also been little recognition of the commercial environment and the impact that this has on career development stages for many individuals. Considerable attention is being paid, currently, to the concept of work-life balance where aspects of work are combined with other life choices and Dickmann *et al.* (2006), for example, note that this is a significant factor in career planning for growing numbers of both female and male managers. However Hirsh (2003) warns that:

If employees want to get on they should seek qualifications and training, greater responsibility and varied work experiences. They should not work reduced hours, take career breaks, work from home or get ill. (p. 7)

451

We devote Chapter 31 to this issue, and Rabinowitz (2007) provides a useful review of recent books which focus on work, family and life interfaces.

INDIVIDUAL CAREER MANAGEMENT

If we identify a career as the property of the individual, then clearly the responsibility for managing this rests on the individual, who should identify career goals, adopt strategies to support them and devise plans to achieve the goal.

Many research studies highlight the role of luck in relation to career decisions (*see* Bright *et al.* 2005 for a useful summary), and Pringle and Gold (1989) found a lack of career planning in their sample of 50 'achieving' men and women managers. Only around a quarter of people had plans for the future and many identified luck, opportunity or being in the right place at the right time as the reason they had achieved promotions. However, Dickmann and his colleagues (2006) note that individuals are increasingly focused on developing their 'career capital' as they seek to enhance their position in the jobs market, but this does not mean that they necessarily involved themselves in planning and setting career goals.

We suggest that planning is an essential ingredient of individual career management even if only to provide a framework for decisions about the opportunities that arise through identifying priorities. We also argue that the more individuals attempt to manage their career, the more likely it is that opportunities will arise that they can use constructively. Similarly the more proactive an individual is in identifying and meeting his or her career-related development needs the better he or she will able to grasp opportunities when they arise.

Identifying a short-or medium-term career goal is probably the best way to start. A career goal will be specific to the individual, such as to become an internal senior organisational consultant by the age of 35. The range of strategies that a person may adopt in pursuit of his or her goal can be described in more general terms. The list below describes the type of strategies, identified from a review of the literature by Gould and Penley (1984), and they relate to career improvement/promotion within the organisation.

- **Creating opportunities.** This involves building the appropriate skills and experiences that are needed for a career in the organisation. Developing those skills that are seen as critical to the individual's supervisor and department are most useful, as is exercising leadership in an area where none exists at present.

- **Extended work involvement.** This necessitates working long hours, both at the workplace and at home, and may also involve a preoccupation with work issues at all times.

- **Self-nomination/self-presentation.** Individuals who pursues this strategy will communicate the desire for increased responsibility to their managers. They will also make known their successes, and build an image of themselves as someone who achieves things.

- **Seeking career guidance.** This involves seeking out a more experienced person, either within the organisation or without, and looking for guidance or sponsorship. The use of mentor relationships would come into this category.

- **Networking.** Networking involves developing contacts both inside and outside the organisation to gain information and support.

- **Interpersonal attraction.** This strategy builds the relationship with one's immediate manager on the basis that he or she will have an impact on career progression. One form of this is 'opinion conformity'; that is, sharing the key opinions of the individual's manager, perhaps with minor deviations. Another is expressed as 'other enhancement', which may involve sharing personal information with one's manager and becoming interested in similar pursuits.

More recently Siebert and colleagues (2001) suggest that career success hinges on who you know as well as what you know, and often on the relationship between the two. In their research they found that it was better to have a large network of contacts and weaker ties, rather than a smaller network with stronger ties, which generally disadvantages women.

There is evidence however, that individuals are generally not good at career self-management, as demonstrated by Sturges *et al.* (2002). Nevertheless, they did find that informal career support, perhaps in terms of mentoring, did reinforce self-management activities. This supports the partnership approach to career development. From a slightly different angle, Yarnall (1998) found that career education for employees helps them extract support from the business. In the 2003 career management survey by CIPD (2003, the most recent at the time of writing) 95 per cent of respondents felt that individuals will be expected to take responsibility for their own careers in the future and 90 per cent felt that they must be offered organisational support to do this. Arguing that the public sector seems to depend more on individuals to drive their own careers Hirsh (2003) suggests that this may be related to the lower effectiveness of the public sector.

ACTIVITY 19.3

What general types of career strategy would be appropriate for:

- organisational entry?

- late career?

Compare your views with those of people you know who are in each of these career stages.

Inter-organisational and post-organisational careers and career change

So far we have tended to focus on career moves within the organisation, but many people desire the next career move to be to another organisation or into a new type of career. The concept of a personal career agent has emerged for top-flight executives and for further details on this *see* Case 19.1 on this book's companion website at **www. pearsoned.co.uk/torrington**. However, most us of need to rely on our own skills and effort to make a career move. Arthur and Rousseau (1996b) suggest that individuals need to develop career resilience, which they define as bouncing back from disruptions to one's career, and Waterman *et al.* (1994), in an article on the career-resilient workforce, suggest that individuals need to:

- make themselves knowledgeable about relevant market trends;
- understand the skills and knowledge needed in their area and anticipate future needs;
- be aware of their own strengths and weaknesses;
- have a plan for increasing their performance and employability;
- respond quickly to changing business needs;
- move on from their current employer when a win/win relationship is no longer possible.

Career self-management is increasingly the label used to describe the way that individuals need to approach their careers in all contexts, and there is an increasing literature on this. Hesketh (2001) suggests that career goal setting based on self-knowledge and career clarity will lead to more effective career self-management and Chiaburu and others (2006) identify 'job mobility preparedness' and 'developmental feedback-seeking' as key career self-management behaviours which support the development of career networks, coping with career challenges and adapting to changes in the organisation and its environment. The same researchers identify that a proactive personality is positively related to career self-management behaviours, and suggest that self-managing individuals are more adept at understanding organisational and environmental changes, and are more likely than those who do not adopt career self-management behaviour to seek out relevant career information and support. Finally, King (2004) defines and identifies three groups of key behaviours. She identifies 'positioning' behaviours in which individuals make sure they have the contacts, the skills and the experience to achieve their career goal; 'influence' behaviours where individuals make active efforts to influence key gatekeepers who make decisions relating to career progress; and 'boundary management' behaviours, which are concerned with balancing the demands of work and non-work.

In particular, moving into a different type of career is very difficult for many of us and so we conclude this section by discussing why this is so difficult and what steps might be taken to improve one's chances of success. Drummond and Chell (2001) use two case studies to illustrate some of the issues which embed us in our career. They explain, using Becker's theory of side bets, how other interests influence our choice of career in addition to the work itself, for example the likelihood of high earnings, status, travel and so on. If these desires are fulfilled but we are dissatisfied with our career we may find ourselves trapped. They also show how we use self-justification to defend the careers choices we have made and to stick with them, failure or problems being attributed to external causes. They suggest that decisions made early in life are hard to reverse and that the more we stick with what we have done and the more we rationalise this, the more likely we are to stick with it in the future. Ibarra (2002) also uses case studies to illustrate how individuals try to make the change but fail, because of the way they go about it, and also because of our natural fear of change. There are cases where dramatic changes were attempted and failed, either because they turned out to be the same as before (moving to a new job in a new organisation, but finding the nature of the work just the same) or because they just did not work (as in a new start-up business that could not make sufficient profit). Not only is self-knowledge important, Ibarra argues, but much of this needs to be gained from real experiences. Planning to change and using advisers is insufficient. She suggests that working identity, as a practice, is necessarily a process of experimenting, testing, and learning about our possible selves. (p. 43)

Her advice is to try out new activities on a small scale before making a major commitment to a new career path, for example trying out additional work at the evenings or weekends, or on the basis of temporarily reduced hours, sabbatical or extended holidays, and maybe working on a voluntary basis. She also suggests developing new networks and reference groups in areas where we may be interested to work, as these people will not only provide information and possible opportunities but also a support network when different types of work are begun. Third, she suggests that we to seek out or create triggers and catalysts for change. For example, one may use redundancy as an opportunity to be free to try something different.

Continuous Professional Development (CPD)

CPD is an umbrella term referring to professional learning and development which is linked to either a licence to practise or professional accreditation, and is relevant whether an individual practises his or her profession within or outside an organisation. Many professions have schemes to ensure appropriate standards for different levels of membership and also to ensure that the professional keeps up to date and continues to develop after accreditation. Examples include architects, surveyors and human resource professionals. In early 1992 CPD became a part of the membership requirements for the CIPD, and was associated with record keeping and the production of evidence. However Floodgate (2006) explains how the focus has changed from the early assessment and policing approach. She suggests that there has been a move from compliance to commitment and from enforcement to encouragement in the approach of the CIPD to CPD, suggesting that this approach is no longer about documentation but about reflecting on experiences and building on these insights. This change of approach is reflected, according to Floodgate, in an approach to upgrading which asks a series of questions that allow individuals to express in their own ways the value gained from their learning and the reasoning behind learning that they plan to undertake.

Interestingly, research by Rothwell and Arnold (2005) involving CIPD branch members found that the drivers for CPD were primarily organisational, that is, dependent on the nature of their job and the perceived benefits to the employer, but following this enhanced employability and career prospects were seen as the most valuable reason for completing CPD. Of least value was the expectation of a reward linked to this. However whilst CPD was valued and the degree of value was associated with degree of CPD activities, valuing CPD did not always lead to CPD actions for the respondents to this survey. In addition the authors argue that just because CPD is carried out, there is no guarantee that anything is learned. And Hirsh and Jackson (2004) make the point that CPD may well be carried out by the people who need it least rather than the people who need it most.

There is some evidence that women are more likely to involve themselves in CPD. This was found in the above study and in a study by Rowold and Schilling (2006), who investigated 'career-related continuous learning'. This is a slightly broader concept than CPD, and defined by them as self-initiated, discretionary, planned, proactive activities carried out for the purpose of career development and being related to improving career options and aspirations. It is interesting that they found that such careeer-related learning was not related to career planning or career exploration activity. This supports the idea that CPD is more about loyalty to the profession, rather than a calculated way to get ahead.

ORGANISATIONAL SUPPORT FOR CAREER DEVELOPMENT

Although career management is primarily the individual's responsibility, organisations can and should support this. This will be relevant whether careers are offered internally or whether employability is promoted, although the support may be different. Most organisations still see career management as optional rather than essential, its future orientation makes it slip down the business agenda, and there is always a tension between individual and organisational needs (Hirsh 2003). Successful career management is dependent on resolving these differences. CIPD (2003) argues that the factors contributing to effective career management are using career management activities valued by employees; training line managers and HR staff in career management; line managers taking career management seriously; commitment of senior managers; a formal written career management strategy; integration with overall HR and business strategy. Based on the 2003 CIPD study Hirsh notes that the main barriers to career management are practical rather than philosophical and involve lack of time and resources, career management being seen as peripheral and lack of senior management commitment. Organisations can help individuals with:

- **Career exploration** – providing tools and help for self-diagnosis and supplying organisational information.
- **Career goal setting** – providing a clear view of the career opportunities available in the business, making a wider range of opportunities available to meet different career priorities.
- **Career strategies and action planning** – providing information and support; what works in this organisation; what's realistic; when considering working for other organisations may be appropriate.
- **Career feedback** – providing an honest appraisal of current performance and career potential. Organisations can make this contribution through the activities discussed below.

 Case 19.2 on this book's companion website at **www.pearsoned.co.uk/torrington** focuses on different ways that one organisation supports career development in the restaurant sector.

Career strategy

Although a career strategy is critical, less than a half of the organisations responding to the 2003 CIPD careers survey reported that a written career strategy existed, and only one-quarter of respondents had a career strategy that covered *all* employees. Most organisations concentrate on senior managers and key staff that the organisation wishes to retain. There appeared to be little support for traditionally disadvantaged groups such as part-time workers, those returning after long-term sickness absence or a career break, women returning to work after bearing children and workers over the age of 50.

Career pathways and grids

A career path is a sequence of job roles or positions, related via work content or abilities required, through which an individual can move. Publicised pathways can help people to identify a realistic career goal within the organisation. Traditional pathways were normally presented as a vertical career ladder, emphasising upward promotion within a function, and focusing on full-time jobs meant that career progress for the majority was halted early on in their careers. This inflexibility tended to stifle cross-functional moves and emphasised progression via management rather than equally through development of technical expertise.

There is now increasing use of alternative approaches, often designed in the form of a grid, with options at each point, so that upwards, lateral, diagonal and even downwards moves can be made. These grids may also be linked into grids for other parts of the business, thereby facilitating cross-functional moves. Ideally, positions are described in behavioural terms, identifying the skills, knowledge and attitudes required for a position rather than the qualifications needed or age range anticipated. However, as organisations continue to change more and more rapidly even such a matrix may prove to be too rigid and career opportunities may need to be expressed in terms of groups of roles, and be fluid enough to integrate newly developed and unexpected types of roles.

Not only do career routes need to be carefully communicated to employees, they also need to reflect reality, and not just present an ideal picture of desirable career development. Managers who will be appointing staff need to be fully apprised of the philosophy of career development and the types of move that the organisation wishes to encourage. It is important that the organisation reinforces lateral moves by developing a payment system that rewards the development of skills and not just the organisation level.

Fast-track programmes

Fast-track programmes have been considered as a way of developing and retaining high performers. However, problems have been found with such accelerated progress. Hall (1999) reports that although individuals on such programmes perform well early on, they tend to experience derailment later in their career. He proposed four reasons for this. First, that moving through the organisation so quickly means that they have never been in one place long enough to develop a network of learning support. Second, that in their rapid progress they will have alienated a lot of people on the way. Third, that they have never been in one position long enough to experience failure and setbacks and learn how to deal with these, and, finally, this means that they have not received sufficient developmental feedback, which is critical to career success. Iles (1997) suggests that to make such careers more sustainable there needs to be greater emphasis on developing empowerment skills and more developmental feedback.

Career conversations

The lack of opportunity to discuss career options is frustrating for employees, and to discover the nature of helpful career conversations Hirsh and her colleagues (2001) asked individuals to explain positive career conversations in terms of where they took place, who was involved, how they were conducted and the impact that they had. They found that only around one-fifth of the discussions took place with the individual's line manager and many more had conversations with other managers in the organisation, and some with specialist advisers or HR. Around half the discussions took place informally, outside the remit of, say, an appraisal, development centre, mentoring, coaching, or any other formal system, and of these 40 per cent were unplanned. It was key that discussions were held with people who were trusted and open, prepared to be frank about the individual's skills and potential and who were genuinely interested in the individual. Around three-quarters of these conversations appeared to result in some form of career action. Hirsh and her colleagues note that these findings differ from current ideas of best practice, which are to discuss one's career with one's line manager in an appraisal context.

Managerial support

In spite of the above findings managerial support remains critical, not only in terms of appointing new staff, but also in terms of supporting the career development of their current staff. Direct feedback on current performance and potential is vital, especially in identifying strengths and weaknesses, and what improvement is required. The immediate manager is in a good position to refer the individual to other managers and to introduce them into a network which will support their career moves. In addition the manager is in the ideal position to provide job challenges and experiences within the current job which will equip the incumbent with the skills needed for the desired career move.

Unfortunately, managers often do not see these responsibilites as part of their job and see them as belonging to the HR department, and Hirsh notes that managers often need to be cajoled by HR to play their part. Yarnall (1998) found low levels of support from managers, but also found that employees participating in self-development career initiatives did encourage management support. Managers often feel constrained by their lack of knowledge about other parts of the organisation, and often withdraw from giving accurate feedback about career potential, particularly when they know that what they have to say is not what the individual wishes to hear. CIPD (2003) notes that there appears to be a lack of training for line managers to support them in their career development role. It also found that the most common career goals explored by line managers concerned short-term promotions and projects within the organisation, at the expense of more complex issues such as lateral moves, secondments, work-life balance and career flexibility. Managers are also sometimes tempted, in their own interests, to hold on to good employees rather than encourage them to develop elsewhere.

ACTIVITY 19.4

As a member of the HR function pursuing an organisational philosophy of flexible career moves and continuous career development, how would you:

- encourage managers to adopt this philosophy?
- prepare them for the skills they will need to use?

What other career development support could immediate managers give in addition to the suggestions made above?

Career counselling

Occasionally immediate managers will be involved in career counselling, drawing out the strengths, weaknesses, values and interests of their staff. In many cases, however, those who seek such counselling would prefer to speak in confidence to someone independent of their work situation. In these circumstances a member of the HR department may act as counsellor. In more complex cases, or those involving senior members of staff, professionals external to the organisation may be sought. This is also more likely to be the case if the career counselling is offered as part of an outplacement programme resulting from a redundancy.

Career workshops

Career workshops are usually, but not always, conducted off-site, and offered as a confidential programme to help individuals assess their strengths and weaknesses, values and interests, identify career opportunities, set personal career goals and begin to develop a strategy and action plan. Career goals will not necessarily be restricted to the current employing organisation – and one objective of the workshop is often to broaden career perspectives. Workshops may last 2–3 days, and normally involve individual paper-and-pencil exercises, group discussions, one-to-one discussions and private conferences with tutors. For some people these can be quite traumatic events as they involve whole-life exploration, and often buried issues are confronted which have been avoided in the hurly-burly of day-to-day life. The most difficult part for many individuals is keeping the momentum going after the event by continuing the action planning and self-assessment of progress.

Self-help workbooks

As an alternative to a workshop there are various self-help guides and workbooks which can assist people to work through career issues by presenting a structure and framework. Organisations such as Lifeskills provide a range of workbooks appropriate for different stages of career development.

Career centres

Career centres within organisations can be used as a focal point for the provision of organisational and external career information. The centre may include a library on career choices and exploration, information on organisational career ladders and grids, current opportunities, self-help workbooks and computer packages. Such centres appear to be relatively common in large organisations, yet CIPD (2003) reports that participants do not consider them to be very useful.

Assessment and development centres

Assessment centres for internal staff have traditionally taken the form of pass/fail assessment for a selected group of high-potential managers at a specific level. They were focused on organisational rather than individual needs. Recently changes to some of these centres have moved the focus to the individual, with fewer limitations on who is allowed to attend. These 'development centres' assess the individual's strengths and weaknesses and provide feedback and development plans so that each can make the most of his or her own potential. The outcome is not pass/fail but action plans for personal and career development.

Whatever career activities are in place in the organisation it is important to ensure that:

- There is a clear and agreed careers philosophy communicated to all in the organisation.
- Managers are supported in their career development responsibilities.
- Career opportunities are communicated to staff.
- There is an appropriate balance between open and closed internal recruitment.
- The reasons for the balance are explained.
- There are rewards for knowledge, skills and attitude development, as well as for progression to a higher organisational level.
- Attention is given to career development within the current job.

Although all of these activities focus on careers within an organisation, most are still appropriate for employers providing development leading to employability rather than long-term employment. Waterman *et al.* (1994) stress that employers need to move to an adult/adult relationship with their employees from that of parent/child, be prepared to share critical organisational information and let go of the old notion of loyalty, thus accepting that good employees will leave. Hiltrop (1996) provides a good range of suggestions for managing the changing psychological contract.

ACTIVITY 19.5

1 What are the advantages and disadvantages of open and closed internal recruitment?

2 In which circumstances might it be appropriate to give a greater emphasis to closed recruitment?

3 In which circumstances might it be appropriate to give a greater emphasis to open recruitment?

Perhaps the most outstanding challenge is to come to terms with the facts that careers have changed due to a changing organisational structure and competitive demands; that individuals in our current labour market have a greater say in their career and how it relates to their whole life; and that alternative career profiles are equally legitimate. It is a sad reflection that in most research career development activities are not found to have a high profile (*see*, for example, Atkinson 2000).

SUMMARY PROPOSITIONS

19.1 The context of careers is changing from long-term careers in one organisation with upward movement to careers that are characterised by disruption, movement between employers and the development of portfolios of work. There is a school of thought that suggests this trend is overstated.

19.2 Careers are owned by individuals and the primary responsibility for managing them falls to the individual; organisations have a role in supporting and encouraging this.

19.3 Theories of career development include career stage theories. Although these were developed in an era of more stable career structures they still have interpretive value if used in a flexible manner.

19.4 Individuals need to manage their own careers and aim to become career resilient, so that they have developed the skills and knowledge to overcome career setbacks. Continuous professional development is an important part of this.

19.5 Organisations can support and encourage individual career management by providing flexible and realistic career grids, honest feedback, opportunities for individual career exploration and planning.

GENERAL DISCUSSION TOPICS

1 What is the career management challenge for the early twenty-first century? What appropriate strategies and actions might there be for employers and employees?

2 'No matter how much we encourage individuals to plan their careers, at the end of the day it comes down to opportunity and chance.'

Do you think that this comment is a fair reflection of the way in which individuals manage their careers?

FURTHER READING

Fugate, M., Kinicki, A. and Ashforth, B. (2004) 'Employability: A psycho-social construct, its dimensions, and applications', *Journal of Vocational Behaviour*, Vol. 65, pp. 14–38.

A conceptual paper which attempts to unpick the meaning of 'employability'. The conclusions of the authors are that employability represents an active and proactive adaptability in relation to the world of work, and that it has three dimensions: career identity; personal adaptability and social and human capital. It is not the easiest of reads, but it does present some interesting and useful ideas.

Hirsh, W. and Rolph, J. (2003) 'Snakes and Ladders', *People Management*, Vol. 9, No. 9, 1 May, pp. 36–7.

An extremely useful summary of the CIPD 2003 survey report, *Managing Employee Careers*, together with some brief material from CIPD's *Reflections: Trends and Issues in Career Management*. If you do not have time to read the full reports this is an accessible and informative alternative.

King, Z. (2004) *Career Management: A CIPD Guide*. London: CIPD.
A very practical guide incorporating a range of career development activities; integrating career management with other aspects of HR; and supporting the career development of specific groups of employees.

Megginson, D. and Whitaker, V. (2007) *Continuous Professional Development*. London: CIPD.
The latest edition of this useful handbook focusing on CPD from the Institute's perspective.

Quigley, N. and Tymon, W. (2006) 'Towards an integrated model of intrinsic motivation and career self-management', *Career Development International*, Vol. 11, No. 6, pp. 522–43.
This paper provides a useful review of the context of career self-management and proposes a model focused on four components of intrinsic motivation: meaningfulness; competence; choice; and progress, which they suggest can contribute to career self-management.

REFERENCES

Adamson, S., Doherty, N. and Viney, C. (1998) 'The meanings of career revisited: Implications for theory and practice', *British Journal of Management*, Vol. 9, pp. 251–9.

Arthur, M. (1994) 'The boundaryless career', *Journal of Organisational Behaviour*, Vol. 15, pp. 295–306.

Arthur, M. and Rousseau, D. (1996a) 'A career lexicon for the 21st century', *Academy of Management Executive*, Vol. 10, No. 4, pp. 28–39.

Arthur, M. and Rousseau, D. (1996b) *The Boundaryless Career: A New Employment Principle for a New Organisational Era*. Oxford: OUP.

Arthur, M., Khapova, S. and Wilderom, C. (2005) 'Career success in a boundaryless career world', *Journal of Organisational Behaviour*, Vol. 26, No. 2, pp. 177–202.

Ball, B. (1997) 'Career Management competencies – the individual perspective', *Career Development International*, Vol. 2, No. 2.

Benson, G. (2006) 'Employee development, commitment and intention to turnover: a test of "employability" policies in action', *Human Resource Management Journal*, Vol. 16, No. 2, pp. 173–91.

Bright, J., Pryor, R. and Harpham, L. (2005) 'The role of chance events in career decision making', *Journal of Vocational Behaviour*, Vol. 66, pp. 561–76.

Burke, R. (1998a) 'Correlations of job insecurity amongst recent business school graduates', *Employee Relations*, Vol. 20/1, No. 2, pp. 92–100.

Burke, R. (1998b) 'Changing career rules: clinging to the past or accepting the new reality?', *Career Development International*, Vol. 3, No. 1.

Chiaburu, D., Baker, V. and Pitariu, A. (2006) 'Beyond being proactive: what (else) matters for career self-management behaviours?', *Career Development International*, Vol. 11, No. 7, pp. 619–23.

CIPD (2003) *Managing Employee Careers – Issues, Trends and Prospects, Survey Report, June 2003*. London: CIPD.

Collin, A. and Watts, A. (1996) 'The death and transfiguration of career – and of career guidance?', *British Journal of Guidance and Counselling*, Vol. 24, No. 3, pp. 385–98.

Dickmann, M., Harris, H. and Wilson, F. (2006) 'A wing and a prayer', *People Management*, Vol. 12, No. 1, pp. 39–41.

Doherty, N., Viney, C. and Adamson, S. (1997) 'Rhetoric or reality – shifts in the philosophy and practice of graduate career management?', *Career Development International*, Vol. 2, No. 4.

Drummond, H. and Chell, E. (2001) 'Life's chances and choices: A study of entrapment in career decisions with reference to Becker's side bet theory', *Personnel Review*, Vol. 30, No. 2, pp. 186–202.

Fenwick, T. (2006) 'Contradictions in portfolio careers: work design and client relations', *Career Development International*, Vol. 11, No. 1, pp. 66–79.

Floodgate, J. (2006) 'Perpetual Motion', *People Management*, Vol. 12, No. 1, p. 49.

Goffee, R. and Nicholson, N. (1994) 'Career development in male and female managers – convergence or collapse?', in M.J. Davidson and R.J. Burke (eds), *Women in Management: Current Research Issues*. London: Paul Chapman.

Gould, S. and Penley, L. (1984) 'Career strategies and salary progression: a study of their relationships in a municipal bureaucracy', *Organisational Behaviour and Human Performance*, Vol. 34, pp. 244–65.

Greenhaus, J.H. and Callanan, G.A. (1994) *Career Management*. London: Dryden Press.

Greller, M. (2006) 'Hours invested in professional development during later career as a function of career motivation and satisfaction', *Career Development International*, Vol. 11, No. 6, pp. 544–59.

Guest, D. and McKenzie-Davey, K. (1996) 'Don't write off the traditional career', *People Management*, February.

Hall, D. (2004) 'The protean career: a quarter century journey', *Journal of Vocational Behaviour*, Vol. 65, No. 1, pp. 1–13.

Hall, D.T. (1999) 'Accelerate executive development at your peril', *Career Development International*, Vol. 4, No. 4, pp. 237–9.

Hall, D.T. and Nougaim, K. (1968) 'An examination of Maslow's need hierarchy in an organisational setting', *Organisational Behaviour and Human Performance*, Vol. 13, pp. 12–35.

Handy, C. (1994) *The Empty Raincoat: Making Sense of the Future*. London: Hutchinson.

Herriot, P. (1998) 'The role of the HRM function in building a new proposition for staff', in P. Sparrow and M. Machington (eds), *Human Resource Management: The New Agenda*. London: Financial Times/Pitman.

Herriot, P. and Pemberton, C. (1996) 'Contracting careers', *Human Relations*, Vol. 49, No. 6, pp. 757–90.

Herriot, P., Manning, W. and Kidd, J. (1997) 'The content of the psychological contract', *British Journal of Management*, Vol. 8, pp. 151–62.

Hesketh, B. (2001) 'Adapting vocational psychology to cope with change', *Journal of Vocational Behaviour*, Vol. 59, pp. 203–12.

Hiltrop, J.-M. (1996) 'Managing the changing psychological contract', *Employee Relations*, Vol. 18, No. 4, pp. 36–49.

Hirsh, W. (2003) 'Career management – meeting the challenge?', in CIPD (ed.) *Reflections: Trends and Issues in Career Management*. London: CIPD.

Hirsh, W. and Jackson, C. (2004) *Managing Careers in Large Organisations*. London: The Work Foundation.

Hirsh, W., Jackson, C. and Kidd, J. (2001) 'A word with the wise', *People Management*, Vol. 7, No. 12, 4 June, pp. 42–6.

Ibarra, H. (2002) 'How to stay stuck in the wrong career', *Harvard Business Review*, December, pp. 40–7.

IDS (2000) *Work-life Balance*, IDS Study 698, November. London: IDS.

Iles, P. (1997) 'Sustainable high-potential career development: a resource-based view', *Career Development International*, Vol. 2, No. 7.

Kanter, R.M. (1989) *When Giants Learn to Dance*. New York: Simon and Schuster.

Kilpatrick, I. and Hoque, K. (2006) 'A retreat from permanent employment? Accounting for the rise of professional agency work in UK public services', *Work, Employment and Society*, Vol. 20, No. 4, pp. 649–66.

King, Z. (2003) 'New or traditional careers? A study of UK graduates' perceptions', *Human Resource Management Journal*, Vol. 13, No. 1, pp. 5–26.

King, Z. (2004) 'Career self-management: Its nature, causes and consequences', *Journal of Vocational Behaviour*, Vol. 65, pp. 112–33.

Mallon, M. (1998) 'The portfolio career; pushed or pulled to it?', *Personnel Review*, Vol. 27, No. 5.

Mayrhofer, W., Steyrer, J., Meyer, M., Strunk, G., Schiffinger, M. and Iellatchitch, A. (2005) 'Graduates' career aspirations and individual characteristics', *Human Resource Management Journal*, Vol. 15, No. 1, pp. 38–56.

Pazy, A., Ganzach, Y. and Davidov, Y. (2006) 'Decision-making training for occupational choice and early turnover: a field experiment', *Career Development International*, Vol. 11, No. 1, pp. 80–91.

Platman, K. (2004) ' "Portfolio careers" and the search for flexibility in later life', *Work, Employment and Society*, Vol. 18, No. 3, pp. 573–99.

Pringle, J.K. and Gold, U.O'C. (1989) 'How useful is career planning for today's managers?', *Journal of Management Development*, Vol. 8, No. 3, pp. 21–6.

Purcell, J., Kinnie, N., Hutchinson, S., Rayton, B. and Swart, J. (2003) *Understanding the people and performance link: Unlocking the black box*. London: CIPD.

Purcell, J., Purcell, K. and Tailby, S. (2005) 'Temporary Work Agencies: Here today, gone tomorrow?', *British Journal of Industrial Relations*, Vol. 42, No 4, pp. 705–25.

Rothwell, A. and Arnold, J. (2005) 'How HR professionals rate "continuing professional development" ', *Human Resource Management Journal*, Vol. 15, No. 3, pp. 18–32.

Schein, E. (1978) *Career Dynamics: Matching individual and organisation needs*. Reading, Mass.: Addison-Wesley.

Siebert, S., Kraimer, M. and Liden, R. (2001) 'A social capital theory of career success', *Academy of Management Journal*, Vol. 44, No. 2, pp. 219–37.

Smeaton, D. (2003) 'Self-employed workers: calling the shots or hesitant independents? A consideration of the trends', *Work, Employment and Society*, Vol. 17, No. 2, pp. 379–91.

Smithson, J. and Lewis, S. (2000) 'Is job insecurity changing the psychological contract?', *Personnel Review*, Vol. 29, No. 6.

Sparrow, P. (1996) 'Transitions in the psychological contract: some evidence from the banking sector', *Human Resource Management Journal*, Vol. 6, No. 4.

Sturges, J., Guest, D., Conway, N. and MacKenzie Davey, K. (2002) 'A longitudinal study of the relationship between career management and organisational commitment among graduates in the first ten years at work', *Journal of Organisational Behaviour*, Vol. 23, pp. 731–48.

Thomas, R. and Dunkerley, D. (1999) 'Careering downwards? Middle managers' experiences in the downsized organisation', *British Journal of Management*, Vol. 10, pp. 157–69.

Walton, J. (1999) *Strategic Human Resource Development*. Harlow: Financial Times Prentice Hall.

Wanous, J.P. (1992) *Recruitment, Selection, Orientation and Socialisation of Newcomers*. Wokingham: Addison-Wesley.

Waterman, R.H., Waterman, J.A. and Collard, B.A. (1994) 'Toward a career-resilient workforce', *Harvard Business Review*, July–August.

Yarnall, J. (1998) 'Line managers as career developers: rhetoric or reality?', *Personnel Review*, Vol. 27, No. 5.

An extensive range of additional materials, including multiple choice questions, answers to questions and links to useful websites can be found on the Human Resource Management Companion Website at **www.pearsoned.co.uk/torrington**.

INTERACTIVE SKILL 4: COACHING AND PRESENTATION

A central function of HRM is to enable people to learn. There are many ways to do this, especially with the development of technical aids, but here we concentrate on the face-to-face learning situations of coaching and presentation. Many people visualise teaching as a process in which someone who knows instructs someone who does not; but coaching is enabling people to learn by a process that goes beyond simple instruction. Learners frequently have to discover for themselves, as this is the only way in which they will understand, and they frequently need the assistance of a coach to be a sounding board for their uncertainties, to point out things about their performance which they try to ignore and to be a wise counsellor in times of difficulty or lack of confidence.

The objectives of this Focus on skills are to:

1 Review various approaches to learning
2 Describe different types of learner
3 Explain coaching
4 Explain features of presentation

Approaches to learning

Different types of learning require fundamentally different methods and approaches by the teacher. Teaching a person to do something is different from teaching someone to understand something, and understanding something intellectually is different from understanding and changing how you interact with other people.

One detailed classification was shown in the CRAMP taxonomy (ITRU 1976), developed after a study of the work of the Belbins (Belbin and Belbin 1972) and following an earlier analysis by Bloom (1956). This system divides all learning into five basic types.

1 *Comprehension* is where the learning involves knowing how, why and when certain things happen, so that learning has only happened when the learner understands: not simply when the learner has memorised. Examples include having enough understanding of how German grammar works to be able to get the words of a sentence in the right order, or knowing enough of the law of employment to decide whether or not someone has been dismissed unfairly.

2 *Reflex learning* is involved when skilled movements or perceptual capacities have to be acquired, involving practice as well as knowing what to do. Speed is usually important and the task needs constant repetition to develop the appropriate synchronisation and coordination. Among the examples in normal working life are driving a fork-lift truck, spot welding, fault-finding and typing. One of the most widespread in management circles is the use of a keyboard.

3 *Attitude development* is enabling people to develop the capacity to alter their attitudes and improve their social skills. Much customer care training has this as its basis, as dealing with customers requires people to be confident of their own ability to deal with others, shedding some of their feelings of insecurity and discovering how they are able to elicit a positive response. This can partly be achieved by the process of 'scripting', whereby staff have a set formula to follow. We are all familiar with making a telephone call which brings a response along the lines of, 'Good morning, Bloggs, Blenkinsop, Huggins and Scratchit. Mandy speaking. How may I help you?' The woodenness of that method can be overcome by enabling people to develop positive attitudes about themselves and their relationships with others, so that they can cope effectively with other people in a variety of situations, including the telephone.

4 *Memory training* enables trainees to remember how to handle a variety of given situations. Pharmacists learn by rote a series of maximum dosages, for example, and an office messenger will need to remember that all invoices go to Mr Brown and all cheques to Mrs Smith. Anyone who is good with figures has probably at some time learned their multiplication tables. Doing this is a chore, yet it is fundamental to any facility with numbers. Police officers remember the registration numbers of cars better than most of us, and we all need to remember telephone numbers and PINs. Memory training is distinguished from comprehension because understanding is not

necessary, only recall, and it is worth referring back to the example above of under-standing German grammar. Learning grammatical rules by rote does not enable one to use that knowledge, because understanding is also required. Learning your PIN does not require any understanding at all.

5 **Procedural learning** is similar to memory training except that the drill to be followed does not have to be memorised, but located and understood. An example is the procedure to be followed in shutting down a plant at Christmas, or dealing with a safety drill.

This classification is given the acronym CRAMP. Most forms of training involve more than one type of learning, so that the apprentice vehicle mechanic will need to under-stand how the car works as well as practising the skill of tuning an engine, and the learner driver needs to practise the skill of coordinating hands, feet and eyes in driving as well as knowing the procedure to follow if the car breaks down.

Broadly speaking, comprehension-type learning is best approached by a method that teaches the whole subject as an entity rather than splitting it up into pieces and taking one at a time. Here the lecture or training manual is typically used. Attitude change is often handled by group discussion, but reflex learning is best handled by part methods, which break the task down into sections, each of which can be studied and practised separately before being put together as a complete performance, just as a tennis player will practise the serve, the smash, the forehand, the backhand and other individual strokes before playing a match in which all are used. Memory training and procedural learning may take place either by whole or by part methods.

In this Focus on skills we are concentrating on comprehension-type learning (C) through presentation and attitude development (A) through coaching. In previous edi-tions we have provided guidance on other forms of teaching. Readers with a need to study reflex learning, memorisation and procedural learning will find the material on our companion website **www.pearsoned.co.uk/torrington**.

ACTIVITY 4.1

1 Think of things that you have learned in the recent past and identify whether the learning was comprehension, reflex, attitude development, memorisation or procedural.

2 How would you classify learning for the following?

Swimming	Selection interviewing
Calorie counting in a diet	Learning Russian
Parenting	Running a business
Safe lifting	Preparing for retirement

Types of learner

Learners differ according to their prior knowledge, the quality and nature of their pre-vious education and their age. Most of the learning carried out under the aegis of HRM is by adults, so we need some understanding of how learners differ. An excellent analysis has been produced by Robert Quinn (1988) based on earlier work by Dreyfus *et al.* (1986). It also appears in Quinn's work on management skills (Quinn *et al.* 2002). He

467

believes that mastery of an activity involves a learning process over an extended period and that the capacity to learn evolves at the same time. The inference of this is that our approach to organising facilities for others to learn will be influenced by how far their learning capacity has developed. There are five stages:

1 *The novice* learns facts and rules without criticism or discussion, accepting that there are ways of doing things that others have devised, and that's that.

2 *The advanced beginner* goes a little further by being able to incorporate the lessons of experience, so that understanding begins to expand and embellish the basic facts and rules. As you begin working in an organisation, aspects of cultural norms gradually become apparent that are just as important as the basic rules. You find out the subtleties of the dress code and working relationships and extend competence by trying out very slight departures from the rigidity of the rules.

3 *Competency* represents a further development of confidence and a reduced reliance on absolute rules by recognising a wider variety of cues from the working context. There is a greater degree of learning by trial and error, experimenting with new behaviours. It is not abandoning the rules, but being able to use them more imaginatively and with an interpretation that suits one's own personal strengths and inclinations.

4 *Proficiency* is where the learner transcends analysis and begins to use intuition:

Calculation and rational analysis seem to disappear. The unconscious, fluid, and effortless performance begins to emerge, and no one plan is held sacred. You learn to unconsciously 'read' the evolving situation. You notice cues and respond to new cues as the importance of the old ones recedes. (Quinn *et al.* 1990, p. 315)

5 *Expert* describes those rare people who produce a masterly performance simply by doing what comes naturally, because all the learning has fused together to develop a capacity based on having in their heads 'multidimensional maps' of the territory' that are unknown to other people; they are thus able to meet effortlessly the contradictions of organisational life.

This is a neat and helpful model, although it could also be an excuse for sloppy thinking and an inability to see that there has been a sea change that undermines the expert's certainties. HR students have ground into them the risks of snap judgements in selection interviewing ('I can tell as soon as they come through the door') and there will always be a temptation for established managers to take short cuts on the basis of their assumed expertise without realising that the rules have been changed and they are now playing the wrong game.

WINDOW ON PRACTICE

David teaches a teacher-training course which has a mixture of students. Most are recent graduates with little working experience but well-developed study skills. A minority are a little older, usually mothers with growing children, who have experience, but whose study skills are rusty. He finds that the mature students tend to dominate discussion at the beginning of the course, as they constantly relate everything to their own experience and circumstances, while the recent graduates feel at a loss and put down. After a few weeks the younger students become more assertive in discussion as they gain confidence from their developing understanding, and the mature students are less dominant because they are beginning to question some of the taken-for-granted certainty of their earlier opinions. Mutual respect gradually develops and both groups learn from each other. David classifies the recent graduates as novices rapidly becoming advanced beginners and the mature students as competents who have to revert to being novices in order to move on to proficiency.

Coaching

This section of the Focus on skills follows on particularly from Chapter 19, where we saw the importance of informal discussion in enabling people to make career choices, as well as the difficulty many have in making such choices and in finding the confidence and resolve to make necessary changes. Coaching is not teaching people how to do things, but helping them to do even better things that they have already learned. Janice Caplan has described it this way:

> Coaching is about enhancing and developing the performance of an individual . . .
> Coaching . . . is a way of learning that is highly personal, flexible and individualized.
> (Caplan 2003, p. ix)

Coaching is as important for the competent, proficient or expert as it is for the advanced beginner, and it is important for novices, even though they are still acquiring the basics. The more expert a person becomes, the more important a coach becomes to hone performance, to take a broad view of the context in which the learner's career is developing and how it may proceed. Although coaching is a skill, it is not simply an encounter that has to be managed, like most of the skills described in these Focus chapters, it is a skill in managing a relationship.

WINDOW ON PRACTICE

In 2005 the British sporting public was hungry for success in tennis. Wimbledon annually stages the world's greatest tennis tournament and winning is the greatest achievement in a player's career, yet it was over seventy years since a British man had won the title. A young Scot, Andy Murray, suddenly emerged as the great hope of British tennis. He was young, skilled and with a great competitive temperament, who had been coached by his mother, but he needed a different coach to take him forward to international success. He needed someone with international experience as well as

469

personal authority, who could take the already-acquired skill of this fiery young man and develop it, and him, to greater international achievement. Brad Gilbert was an experienced coach. He took on the coaching of Andy Murray, whose accomplishments soon began to increase. Brad Gilbert was not personally as good a player as Andy Murray, but had a breadth of international experience and expertise that provided exactly the right complement to Andy's youth, talent and temperament.

Coaching is a part of the job of every manager, but it is an approach being used increasingly in business circles to bring on the effectiveness of people at all levels. As long ago as 1994 Clutterbuck and Wynne made a comment combining mentoring and coaching:

> They represent an increasing trend towards helping the individual take charge of his or her own learning: the primary driver . . . becomes the employee; the coach or mentor is available to give guidance, insight and encouragement. (p. 156)

Currently there is great enthusiasm for coaching to be seen as a central feature of the managerial role so that every manager is expected to act as a coach to those for whom the manager has direct line responsibility. Coaching takes the place of supervision and instruction to the extent that the manager concentrates on developing the skills and capacities of the individual members of his or her team, enabling them to perform rather than directing their performance. This is a nice distinction that takes account of changes in the types of jobs that people have and the moves towards flexible rather than hierarchical organisation structures. The reality is rarely so clear cut, as managers have to combine coaching with direction. Not all managers like the coaching role. As was pointed out in Chapter 18, Carroll and Gillen (2001) identified various barriers to line manager acceptance of a teaching or coaching role, including lack of interpersonal competence, lack of time, performance pressures, a feeling that the teaching role was not valued and should be done by the HR department. The article also provides material on what makes an effective coach.

Other members of the business may be involved in coaching on particular aspects of the learner's work. Janice Caplan identifies a coaching style of management as having three elements, role model, interim and directive:

> to enable, encourage and facilitate so that staff have a stronger sense of control over their own work and their own time, and so that they identify their own options and solutions to problems . . . The manager also needs to act as a role model of the desired . . . behaviours. Nonetheless, there may be times when the manager will still need to be more directive. (Caplan 2003, p. 20)

Before considering the appropriate qualities of a coach, we note the important concept of the career anchor, identified by Edgar H. Schein, one of the founding fathers of organisational psychology during his thirty years as Sloan Fellows Professor of

Management at MIT. The Career Anchor is something that is so important to a person's self-estimate that it will be abandoned only reluctantly, and then only if it can be replaced by something else equally rewarding. Schein described career anchors as much broader than motivation, and as including the following:

- self-perceived talents and abilities;
- self-perceived motives and needs;
- self-perceived attitudes and values.

Our perception of ourselves in these areas comes from direct experiences of work, from successes, from self-diagnosis and from feedback. The conclusions that we draw both drive and constrain future career development. Career anchors can identify a source of personal stability in the person which has determined past choices and will probably determine future choices.

The problematic aspect of career anchors is the accuracy of the individual's self-perceptions, and the question of what happens in mid-career to those who feel their attitudes and values are changing. Schein acknowledges that career anchors are learned rather than reflecting latent abilities and are the sorts of things that people are reluctant to abandon. Not only do we all need to identify and understand what our anchors are in order to make sure we are doing the right thing, we also need to appreciate that there are things that we shall continue to need even if we make a career change.

Among the anchors most widely found are technical/functional competence, managerial competence and security. Those who are confident of their technical competence in their job and enjoy those aspects of their duties will move to a job with a lower technical component very reluctantly. For those anchored to managerial competence the exercising of managerial responsibility is an end in itself, and technical/functional jobs just a way of getting there. They are likely to possess three key competences: analytical competence to solve problems characterised by incomplete information in areas of uncertainty; interpersonal competence to influence and control; and emotional resilience, with the ability to be stimulated rather than paralysed by crises. They will readily move away from technical specialisation if they can maintain, or enhance their managerial role. Security and stability is an anchor for those who seek this above all else.

Any coach needs to identify these anchors for individuals they are coaching. If a coach can spot the anchors correctly, he or she has a very good chance of establishing trust, especially if the person being coached has never really worked out what his or her anchors are, nor heard of the concept. If a coach guesses the anchors wrongly, or has strong views on what they should be, then coaching becomes very difficult (Schein, 1990, 2004).

Anchors can move, and certainly change over time. The person who is technically anchored at 30 may be managerially anchored at 40 and security/stability anchored at 50, but that is a stereotypical assumption only. Coaches have to work out the anchors for each individual at the time when the coaching conversation takes place, not yesterday or last year.

The qualities of the coach

Coaching is usually a one-to-one activity, for which the coach needs various qualities.

1 *Trust.* As the coach will often need to deal with what are usually very private aspects of someone's life, it is first necessary that the learner has absolute trust in the coach's

471

integrity and commitment to the coaching. The interpersonal chemistry has to be completely correct between the two of them. They will probably argue, may have flaming rows and not speak to each other for days. Learners will, for instance, usually be highly skilled performers with a shrewd knowledge of their job and a fair understanding of what they can and cannot do. A coach may need to challenge some part of that self-confidence, which the learner will then be anxious about, because that seems to be removing one of the things that the learner has previously relied on – a career anchor – and there will be a disagreement. It will not be easy for a learner to abandon something that has previously been an anchor, but it will probably not happen unless there is a grounded belief in the coach's trustworthiness.

2 *Respect.* Closely allied to trust and the next requirement of expertise is *mutual* respect. The learner needs to feel that the coach is worthy of respect because he or she is trustworthy, is expert in the job of the learner, is proficient at the job of coaching, has a great deal of broader experience, is good at explaining things and explaining the right things. These 'things' have to be strong enough to overwhelm other possible thoughts about the coach, such as 'has-been', 'past-it', 'couldn't hack it at the sharp end', 'the job is not like it was in his day'. Coaches are nearly always older than learners, so there may be a temptation for ambitious learners to have such thoughts. Equally the coach must have respect for the learner: no condescension or patronising behaviour, but a real respect for the learner's skill, accomplishments and ambitions.

3 *Job expertise.* The coach needs to *know how* to do the learner's job at least as well as the learner; this is not the same as *being able to do* the job as well as the learner. The person training the novice usually has to be expert at actually doing the job of the learner; the coach enhancing the skill of someone who is proficient does not need that particular level of ability, as long as there is the understanding. It is often important that the coach is *not* as practically skilled; otherwise coaching may become 'watch me; do this' instead of 'listen to what I say and then work out how to do better'.

WINDOW ON PRACTICE

England won the Rugby World Cup in 2004 and much of the credit for this victory went to Clive Woodward (who soon became Sir Clive). Subsequently he left his job as rugby coach, saying that he would like to try his approach in another sport, perhaps soccer. Despite one or two opportunities he never succeeded in this area. Notwithstanding his apparent effectiveness in motivating sportsmen, he appeared not able to succeed when outside his own job expertise.

4 *Listening.* Coaches have to be very sensitive and conscientious listeners. The coaching relationship has many similarities with performance appraisal, in that the coach can only work to improve what the learner is able to acknowledge and understand. There will be a lot of explanation and even simple instruction, but the starting point will usually be in the learner's head. The learner will ask questions, express frustrations or describe a problem that the coach may believe to be the wrong problem. All the time the coach listens with close attention and works on understanding the questions,

what lies behind the frustrations and why the wrong problem has been identified – and what makes the coach so sure it is the wrong problem anyway?

School teachers sometimes say that gifted teachers are able to develop children's understanding almost entirely by getting them to ask the right questions. Coaches who can do this with adults are on the way to being outstanding, although the method has to be rather more subtle and not manipulative. Focus on skills Part 1 had some advice on this, especially reflection and reflecting and summarising.

5 *Evaluating.* The coach listens to the learner, listens to what other people say and can probably study aspects of the learner's performance, so that there is a collection of information to process. The coach needs to be able to evaluate all of these data dispassionately but effectively, having the advantage of a degree of objectivity which the learner cannot hope to have, and assembling it in a way that will make a constructive contribution to the coaching process.

6 *Challenging.* However true it may be that talking a problem through should enable a learner to solve whatever the career block may be, it is also true that few of us can do this with everything. We always tend to construe a situation in a way that puts us in the right. There will be times when the coach simply has to confront the learner with a different interpretation of what is going on and challenge the learner to accept the validity of criticism. Some coaches who are not the direct line manager say that it is not their role to do that, and that challenging should be left to the manager, but that is just shirking the responsibility. A coach cannot just do the nice, agreeing things with lots of understanding smiles and sympathetic nods of support. The coach is in a privileged position, being trusted by the learner to provide help, including guidance on what is wrong, however reluctant they may be to hear it.

7 *Practical help.* A part of the coaching relationship will be for the coach to provide straightforward practical suggestions: 'Have you thought of . . . ?', 'Have you spoken to . . . ?', 'Would it help if I went through it with you . . . ?', 'No, that simply won't work'.

It might well be thought that all of these great qualities are to be found in any competent manager, so that the learner automatically has the line manager as coach. However, not all managers have all these qualities particularly well developed, and there are advantages in the coach being outside the line. The act of talking with a 'supportive outsider' can be a help to managers in unravelling and evaluating the mixed messages they are hearing in the workplace, where custom and practice are lagging behind policy, which – in turn – appears to be out of line with organisational culture. However, a line manager may well be suspicious of supportive outsiders who appear to be giving messages that contradict what the manager is saying. After all, coaching is not quite the same as counselling, where an outsider has a better justification.

The solution to this dilemma seems to be to acknowledge that all managers need to adopt a coaching mode of working with individual members of their department, but that other supportive *insiders* could be called upon to act as individual mentors, where there is a good working relationship or prior familiarity between prospective coach and prospective learner. Clutterbuck and Megginson (2005, pp. 54–7), quoting from earlier work by Clutterbuck and Gover (2004) suggest there are seven stages in the coaching process:

1 Identify the need

2 Gather evidence

3 Motivate and set targets

4 Plan how to achieve

5 Create opportunities to practice

6 Observe and give feedback

7 Support through the setbacks

Presentation

The skill of presentation is required mainly for explanations leading to comprehension, the C of the CRAMP acronym explained earlier. Much training takes this form, as people simply have to be told about things. Induction is partly experiential, in that a person is shown round and given a workspace and so forth, but much of it simply has to be known and understood. In the last ten years there has been a plethora of guides and self-help books on how to make an effective presentation. HR people constantly have to present on such matters as explaining a change of policy, clarifying details of a new trade union agreement or setting out the implications in a change of employment legislation. There may be presentations on career prospects in the business at careers conventions, pitching to a senior management group for an improvement in the budget, 'selling' the advantages of a new performance-related pay scheme, or explaining to a small group of job applicants the details of the post for which they have applied.

Objectives

As with almost every aspect of management, the starting point is the objective. What are you aiming to achieve? What do you want the listeners to do, to think or to feel? Note that the question is not 'What do you want to say?' The objective is in the response of the listeners. That starting point begins the whole process with a focus on results and payoff, turning attention away from ego. It also determines tone. If your objective is to inform, you will emphasise facts. If you aim to persuade, you will try to appeal to emotion as well as to reason.

The material

What is to be said or, more accurately, what should members of the audience go away having understood and remembered?

> Organise your material with an introduction that previews, a body that develops, and a conclusion that reviews. When you organize the body of your presentation, start by sorting out the theme. The theme is a planning device that holds together the various ideas you want to discuss. If the theme of your presentation is informative, then the body should provide facts. If the theme is persuasive, the body should develop persuasive arguments. (Fandt 1994, p. 159)

In the introduction the speaker establishes rapport with the audience. Apart from gaining their attention, the speaker will include here an answer to the unspoken question: is it going to be worth our while listening? Is this person worth listening to? The person who is worth listening to is someone who looks at the audience and looks friendly, knowledgeable and, above all, enthusiastic. A useful format for the introduction is to explain what the members of the audience will know or be able to do at the end. It is also helpful to sketch out the framework of what is to come, so that people can follow it more readily. But stick to what you promise. If you say there are going to be five points, the audience will listen for five to make sure that they have not missed one.

Having secured the attention of the listeners, you now have them waiting not just for what you say next, but with a framework in their heads of what they will hear, so they will be able to locate their understanding within that framework. The main body of the presentation is the message that is to be conveyed, the development of the argument and the build-up of what it is that the audience should go away having understood and remembered.

The main body will need to be effectively organised. This will not only help members of the audience to maintain attention, but also discipline the speaker to avoid rambling, distracting irrelevance or forgetting. The most common methods are:

- *Chronological sequence*, dealing with issues by taking the audience through a series of events. A presentation to an employment tribunal often follows this pattern.

- *Known to unknown, or simple to complex.* The speaker starts with a brief review of what the audience already know or can easily understand and then develops to what they do not yet know or cannot yet understand. The logic of this method is to ground the audience in something they can handle so that they can make sense of the unfamiliar. This is the standard method of organising teaching sessions.

- *Problem to solution* is almost the exact opposite of simple to complex. A problem is presented and a solution follows. The understanding of the audience is again grounded, but this time grounded in an anxiety that the speaker is about to relieve.

- *Comparison* is a method of organisation which compares one account with another. Selling usually follows this path, as the new is compared with the old.

Whatever the method of organisation for the material, the main body will always contain a number of key thoughts or ideas. This is what the speaker is trying to plant in the minds of the audience: not just facts, which are inert, but the ideas which facts may well illustrate and clarify. The idea that inflation is dangerously high is only illustrated by the fact that it is at a particular figure in a particular month.

The ideas in a presentation can be helpfully linked together by a device that will help audience members to remember them and to grasp their interdependence. One method is to enshrine the ideas in a story. If the story is recalled, the thoughts are recalled with it, as they are integral to the structure. Another method is to use key words to identify the points that are being made, especially if they have an alliterative or mnemonic feature, such as 'People Produce Prosperity'. In a lecture it is common to provide a framework for ideas by using a drawing or system model to show the interconnection of points.

Facts, by giving impact, keep together the framework of ideas that the speaker has assembled. They clarify and give dimension to what is being said. The danger is to use too many, so that the audience are overwhelmed by facts and figures which begin to bemuse them. If the presentation is to be accompanied by a hand-out, facts may be usefully contained in that, so that they can be referred to later, without the audience having to remember them.

Humour is the most dangerous of all aids to the speaker. If the audience laugh at a funny story, the speaker will be encouraged and may feel under less tension, but how tempting to try again and end up 'playing for laughs'. Laughter is a most seductive human reaction, but too many laughs are even more dangerous than too many facts. What will the audience remember, the joke, or what the joke was intended to illustrate? Attempted humour is also dangerous for the ineffective comedian. If you tell what you think is a funny story and no one laughs, you have made a fool of yourself (at least in your own eyes) and risk floundering.

Very few people speak effectively without notes. Although there is a tendency to marvel at those who can, relying solely on memory risks missing something out, getting a fact wrong or drying up completely. Notes follow the pattern of organisation you have established, providing discipline and limiting the tendency to ramble. It is both irritating and unhelpful for members of an audience to cope with a speaker who wanders off down a blind alley, yet this is very common. When an amusing anecdote pops up in your brain, it can be almost irresistible to share it.

There are two basic kinds of notes: headlines or a script. Headlines are probably the most common, with main points underlined and facts listed beneath. Sometimes there will also be a marginal note about an anecdote or other type of illustration. The alternative, the script, enables the speaker to try out the exact wording, phrases and pauses to achieve the greatest effect. The script will benefit from some marking or arrangement that will help you to find your place again as your eyes constantly flick from the page to the audience and back again. This can be underlining or using a highlighter. When using a script it is important not to make the reading too obvious. Head down, with no eye contact and little light and shade is a sure-fire way of turning off the attention of the audience. Public figures increasingly use electronic prompters which project the script progressively through the presentation on to a glass screen some way in front of the speaker. By this means the script can be spoken with little break in eye contact with the audience. This will be too ambitious for most HR people, but the important thing is that the words should be *spoken* rather than *read*.

There are many variations of these basic methods of organising the material, so that one approach is to use varying line length, while another is to use rows of dots to indicate pause or emphasis.

Some people like to have their notes on small cards, so that they are unobtrusive, but this is difficult if the notes are more than headlines. Standard A4 paper should present no problem, if the notes are not stapled, are well laid out and can be handled discreetly. Never forget to number the pages or cards, as the next time you speak they may slip off your lap moments before you are due to begin.

Most presentations benefit from using visual aids. You may use a model, a sample or even a person ('Here is our trainee of the month'), but mostly you will use visual images. Blackboards still exist and white boards are fairly common. Flip charts and overhead projector acetates are widely used. The most rapidly growing type of visual image in presentation is that from a computer, projected on a screen, usually using a PowerPoint package. PowerPoint is so good that it can be dangerous. One problem is its relative sophistication technically. It has to be operated by someone who knows what he or she is doing and has confidence in being able to manage the computer rather than being managed by it. Every reader will have had experience of a presenter being baffled by a technical glitch that held up the presentation and knocked the presenter's confidence sideways. If the computer is being managed by someone other than the presenter, there is the potential difficulty of presenter and operator not always being coordinated.

WINDOW ON PRACTICE

In 2006 a newly-appointed vice chancellor of a British university was giving his first major address to a large audience, using a PowerPoint presentation which he controlled with a remote, although technical staff at the side of the hall had overall control. At one point he went back to a previous page, then went forward to the wrong page without realising it. Technical staff corrected the mistake at the same time as he noticed it. He then corrected it without realising they had spotted it. Confusion and uncertainty persisted for several minutes. At the subsequent lunch the muddle was discussed more extensively than the content of the address.

The rationale for visual aids is that we remember what we see for longer than we remember what we are told, and we can sometimes understand what we see better than we can understand what we hear. Too much displayed material can obscure rather than illuminate what is being said. Television news provides a good example of how much can be used. The dominant theme is always the talking head with frequently intercut pieces of film. Very seldom do words appear on the screen and then usually as extracts from a speech or report, where a short sentence or passage is regarded as being especially meaningful. The other situation in which words and numbers appear is when facts are needed to illustrate an idea, so that ideas such as football scores or a change in the value of the US dollar almost always have the figures shown on the screen to clarify and illustrate. Seldom, however, will more than two or three numbers be displayed at the same time. Speakers need to remember the size of what they are displaying as well as its complexity. Material has to be big enough for people to read and simple enough for them to follow. Material also has to be timed to coincide with what is being said.

PowerPoint is a most seductive toy for the presenter. The box of tricks is enormous and too many people give a show, with clever figures dancing across the screen and other distractions. We must always remember what the purpose of the presentation is; clever or spectacular forms of display can become what people remember rather than the message that is to be conveyed. Television news is again an illustration. Between programmes there may be all manner of clever visual entertainment in brief clips. Once the news report begins there are no such fancy tricks.

SUMMARY PROPOSITIONS

4.1 A useful classification of types of learning is CRAMP: comprehension, reflex learning, attitude development, memory training, procedural learning.

4.2 Selecting the right approach to learning is helped by identifying the learner as being at one of these stages: novice, advanced beginner, competent, proficient or expert.

4.3 Coaching is an approach to learning that concentrates on enhancing the already-established competence, proficiency or expertise of the learner, using the skilled listening and evaluation of the coach as an aid.

4.4 Presentation is the main method used for comprehension-type learning, with a presenter aiming to convey information and understanding to the learner.

GENERAL DISCUSSION TOPICS

1 There is an old saying, 'You can lead a horse to water, but you cannot make it drink.' How true is this of training and development in general and coaching in particular, and what are the HR implications?

2 Another saying is, 'What I hear I forget, what I see I can understand and what I do I know.' The relevance of that to job instruction is easy in relation to manual skills, but what are the implications for aspects of training and development dealing with values and attitudes such as, for example, racist or sexist behaviour?

3 Why do students attend lectures where information is presented to them, rather than reading that information presented in a book?

FURTHER READING

Hawkins, P. and Schwenk, G. (2006) *Coaching Supervision – Maximising the potential of Coaching. A Change Agenda*. London: CIPD.

Jarvis, J. and Lane, D. (2006) *The Case for Coaching: Making evidence based decisions on coaching*. London: CIPD.

Both the above recent publications by CIPD include solid research evidence to produce a thorough assessment of current practice, including examples of good practice and guidelines for managers.

Fandt, P.M. (1994) *Management Skills: Practice and Experience*. St Paul, Minn.: West Publishing.

Quinn, R.E. (1988) *Beyond Rational Management: Mastering the paradoxes and competing demands of high performance*. San Francisco: Jossey-Bass.

Quinn, R.E., Faerman, S.R., Thompson, M.P. and McGrath, M.R. (2002) *Becoming a Master Manager*. New York: John Wiley.

Material on management skills is everywhere, but in this context the above works are especially helpful.

Yate, M. and Sander, P. (2003) *The Ultimate Business Presentations Book*. London: Kogan Page. Presentation is also preached very widely. This excellent recent import from the United States covers the ground very thoroughly and readably.

WEB LINKS

On the book's Companion website, **www.pearsoned.co.uk/torrington**, there is supplementary material on handling group discussion as a form of learning. This is the usual method for social skills training and attitude development. There is also material on job instruction and reflex learning.

Other useful websites are:

www.lsc.gov.uk (Learning and Skills Council).

www.mmu.ac.uk/academic/studserv/learningsupport/studyskills/presentations (Manchester Metropolitan University).

www.spokenwordltd.com/coaching (Spoken Word Ltd, providing teaching and coaching in spoken word skills).

www.emccouncil.org is the site for the European Coaching and Mentoring Council which has recently launched a kitemarking scheme for coaching and mentoring qualifications.

REFERENCES

Belbin, E. and Belbin, R.M. (1972) *Problems in Adult Retraining*. London: Heinemann.

Bloom, B.S. (1956) *Taxonomy of Educational Objectives: The cognitive domain*. London: Longman.

Caplan, J. (2003) *Coaching for the Future*. London: CIPD.

Carroll, S. and Gillen, D. (2001) 'Exploring the teaching function of the managerial role', *Journal of Management Development*, Vol. 21, No. 5, pp. 330–42.

Clutterbuck, D. and Gover, S. (2004) *The Effective Coach Manual*. Burnham: Clutterbuck Associates.

Clutterbuck, D. and Megginson, D. (2005) *Making Coaching Work*. London: CIPD.

Clutterbuck, D. and Wynne, B. (1994) 'Mentoring and Coaching', in A. Mumford (ed.) *Handbook of Management Development*, 4th edn. Epping, Essex: Gower Press.

Fandt, P.M. (1994) *Management Skills: Practice and Experience*. St Paul, Minn.: West Publishing.

Hardingham, A. (1999) 'Moments of Clarity', in *People Management in Perspective*, London: IPD.

ITRU (Industrial Training Research Unit) (1976) *Choose an Effective Style: A self-instructional approach to the teaching of skills*. Cambridge: ITRU Publications.

Quinn, R.E. (1988) *Beyond Rational Management: Mastering the paradoxes and competing demands of high performance*. San Francisco: Jossey-Bass.

Quinn, R.E., Faerman, S.R., Thompson, M.P. and McGrath, M.R. (2002) *Becoming a Master Manager*. New York: John Wiley.

Schein, E.H. (1990) *Career Anchors*. San Diego, Cal.: University Associates.

Schein, E.H. (2004) *Organizational Culture and Leadership*, 3rd edn. New York: Wiley Publishers.

REVIEW OF PART 4

It is a long time since Lord Weinstock, as Chairman of GEC, asked all his senior managers to tell him how they were going to save money, starting with management development. He can perhaps be forgiven for his shortsightedness as he was an accountant, and HR people tend to view the world differently from accountants. The thinking behind his request, however, lies in the difficulty that training and development so often faces: does it work; is it worth the money? At the time of Lord Weinstock's comment a Director of Training in a different multinational business explained to one of the authors how his objective was to establish in the organisation 'a learning community within, but separate from, grim commercial pressures of the bottom line'. There is always the lurking suspicion that training is an escape from real life into a realm of chat and putting the world to rights. We all know that that is a total misrepresentation, but the suspicions remain. Another problem is the question of who should pay for it. Governments typically want employers to pay for training, while employers expect governments to pay for it, especially if those being trained at great expense are not going to remain for long with their current employer.

In Part 4 we have considered the strategic questions in development and the ways in which we can understand how people learn and how they develop. The more specific chapters have dealt first with competence, a word that has taken on new potency in the last twenty years by concentrating on particular things that a person can do, and with approaches to learning and development. All this is a far cry from chat and putting the world to rights at a training centre in a converted stately home somewhere. Then we have considered the development of careers and the way in which individuals take control of their own destiny within the constraints imposed, but using the benefits provided, by their employer.

CASE STUDY PROBLEM

Micropower

Micropower is a rapidly growing computer software firm, specialising in tailor-made solutions for business. Increasingly, training for other businesses in their own and other software packages has occupied the time of the consultants. Micropower sees this as a profitable route for the future and such training is now actively sold to clients. Consultants both sell and carry out the training. As an interim measure, to cope with increasing demand, the firm is now recruiting some specialist trainers, but the selling of the training is considered to be an integral part of the consultant's role.

Micropower has just issued a mission statement which accentuates 'the supply of and support for sophisticated computer solutions', based on a real understanding of business needs. The firm considers that it needs to be flexible in achieving this and has decided that multiskilling is the way forward.

All consultants need to sell solutions and training at all levels, and be excellent analysts, designers and trainers. Some 200 consultants are now employed; most have a degree in IT and most joined the firm initially because of their wish to specialise in the technical aspects of software development, and they spent some years almost entirely in an office-based position before moving into a customer contact role. A smaller proportion were keen to concentrate on systems analysis, and were involved in customer contact from the start.

In addition there are 300 software designers and programmers who are primarily office based and rarely have any customer contact. It is from this group that new consultants are appointed. Programmers are promoted to two levels of designer and those in the top level of designer may then, if their performance level is high enough, be promoted to consultant. There is some discontent among designers that promotion means having to move into a customer contact role, and there are a growing number who seek more challenge, higher pay and status, but who wish to avoid customer contact. Another repercussion of the promotion framework is that around a quarter of the current consultants are not happy in their role. They are consultants because they valued promotion more than doing work that they enjoyed. Some have found the intense customer contact very stressful, feel they lack the appropriate skills, are not particularly comfortable with their training role and are unhappy about the increasing need to 'sell'.

Required

1 What immediate steps could Micropower take to help the consultants, particularly those who feel very unhappy, perform well and feel more comfortable in their new roles?

2 In the longer term how can Micropower reconcile its declared aim of multiskilling with a career structure which meets both organisational and employee needs?

3 What other aspects of human resource strategy would support and integrate with the development strategy of multiskilling?

4 Micropower wishes to develop a competency profile for the consultant role. How would you recommend that the firm progress this, and how might the profile be used in the widest possible manner in the organisation?

PART 5

EMPLOYEE RELATIONS

All jobs have the potential to be alienating, making the job holder indifferent or hostile both to the job and to the management, who are seen as responsible for obliging the employee to continue doing the job.

Employee relations is largely concerned with preventing or alleviating that type of alienation. Because the issues are often collective, concerning a number of people in a similar situation, many procedures incorporate the recognition of trade unions and ways of making that recognition productive for both parties. Even where trade unions are not recognised, there is still a need for the employee voice to be heard, partly because they want to be heard and partly because the management of the business need to be well aware of the feelings and reactions from the people who are doing the work. Working safely in a healthy environment is included under this heading as there is a legal obligation to involve employee representatives in monitoring management arrangements for safe working. Safe working is ultimately a matter of employees working safely because they understand and follow the practices that are provided for their personal safety.

Two parallel chapters, on diversity and equality, deal with the issue of people being treated fairly, not only because we all want to be fair in the way we do things, but also because there is a strong social justice theme to consider, as well as significant legal requirements. Furthermore, people who feel they are managed with due respect for their diversity and recognition of their equality are more likely to be resourceful humans than those who do not sense that respect and recognition.

There are always points of disagreement between managers and the managed and here we consider two rather 'heavy' areas: grievance and discipline. Few managers like to participate in grievance and discipline processes, but they are very interesting and provide the opportunity for major change and improvement for the manager who handles them well.

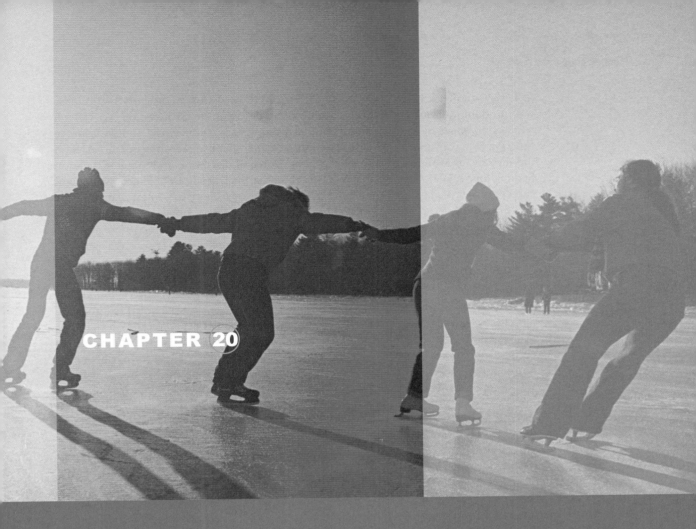

STRATEGIC ASPECTS OF EMPLOYEE RELATIONS

THE OBJECTIVES OF THIS CHAPTER ARE TO:

1 Explain the decline of trade unions in recent decades

2 Review developments in the fields of collective bargaining and industrial action

3 Account for the substantial and ongoing increase in the extent of employment regulation

4 Explore the implications of these trends for the study of employment relations

5 Identify the major strategic choices that employers face in the employee relations field

6 Contrast prevalent approaches to the management of employee relations in different countries

When we surveyed the activities and priorities of HR specialists in the early 1980s, there was no doubt about the pre-eminence of employee relations as being the activity on which they spent most of their time and as being most central to the human resource function (Mackay and Torrington 1986, pp. 149, 161). Only in recruitment and selection did they feel that they had a slightly greater degree of discretion and scope in decision making (pp. 146–8). Twenty-five years on, the situation has wholly changed. Nowadays surveys of HR managers always show that employee relations issues are well down their lists of current and perceived future priorities (e.g. IRS 2006a, pp. 8–12). The emphasis is overwhelmingly on recruitment, staff retention, organisational restructuring, development and absence management, along with the HR implications associated with the introduction of new technologies and, in particular, legislation. The main reason appears to be a widespread perception that employee relations in UK organisations are in a healthy state. The 2004 Workplace Employment Relations (WER) Survey found that 93 per cent of HR managers believed their own organisations' employment relations climate to be either 'good' or 'very good', while only one per cent saw it as being poor (Kersley *et al.* 2006, p. 277), suggesting that the pressures placed on many workforces to become more efficient and flexible are not in the main leading to overt forms of conflict. Employee relations is not therefore seen as an organisational problem. Interestingly the WER Survey also found that a majority of employees were positive about the employee relations climate in their own organisations, although theirs was a less enthusiastic endorsement (16 per cent characterised the climate as being 'poor' or 'very poor'). Employee relations activities may not be as significant to HR practitioners as they once were, but they remain important. A poor employee relations climate can easily develop, while a good one is not created or maintained automatically; ongoing action on the part of managers is required.

ACTIVITY 20.1

What do you think are the main reasons for the fall in the perceived importance of employee relations activities? What would need to happen for the position to be reversed?

KEY TRENDS IN EMPLOYEE RELATIONS

The past thirty years have witnessed a sea change in the UK employee relations scene. Most of the once well-established norms in British industry have been abandoned or have withered away as the nature of the work that we do and the types of workplace in which we are employed have evolved. To an extent, cultural change has accompanied this structural change too, creating a world of work in which employee attitudes towards their employers and employer attitudes towards their employees have developed in new directions. As we demonstrate throughout this book, ongoing change of one kind or another has affected and continues to affect most areas of HRM activity, but it is in the field of employee relations that the most profound transformations have occurred.

That said, it is important to appreciate that change in this field proceeds at a different pace in different places. There remain many workplaces, particularly in the public sector and in the former public sector corporations, in which more traditional models of employee relations continue to operate despite attempts by successive governments to change them. What we now have, therefore, is a far greater variety of approaches in place across the different industrial sectors than was the case in past decades.

Trade union decline

The most significant and fundamental trend is the decline in the number of people joining trade unions and taking part in trade union activity. In the UK membership levels reached a historic peak in 1979, when it was recorded that over 13 million people (58 per cent of all employees) were members of listed trade union organisations. In almost every year since then the number has declined as people have let their membership lapse, older members have retired and younger people have not replaced them. By 2005 membership among employees stood at just 6.4 million and represented just 26.2 per cent of the working population (DTI 2006, p. 1). The rate of decline has reduced somewhat in recent years, some unions reporting modest increases in their membership levels, but trade union density (i.e. the percentage of employees in membership) has fallen year on year for all but two of the past thirty years.

Because the decline started in 1979 at the time that Margaret Thatcher was first elected prime minister, the actions of her governments have frequently been cited as a major source of the trade unions' decline. While it is true that a series of hostile employment Acts passed on to the statute books in the 1980s did not help the union cause, the extent to which these directly impacted on union decline was limited. The only full-frontal legal attack on the ability of unions to recruit members came in the form of regulations which made it impossible to sustain closed shop agreements whereby membership of a specific trade union was a necessary pre-condition of employment in certain workplaces. This was a major reform, affecting over five million employees who worked in closed shops (Dunn and Gennard 1984), but it did not lead directly to a great number of resignations from unions. Membership decline may have been partly precipitated by legislation of the 1980s and early 1990s which sought to reduce the number of strikes by making it harder for a union to press its demands through industrial action, but there is little evidence to support this. The view that 'anti-union' legislation can be blamed for membership decline in the UK is thus unconvincing, especially as the substantial downward trend in the number of trade unionists was and still is an international trend (*see* Vissa 2002).

The main cause of trade union decline has less to do with the employment policy of governments than with the kind of industrial restructuring that has occurred across the developed world. Established industries with union membership, such as mining, shipbuilding and heavy manufacturing, have declined. The jobs lost have been replaced by those in the service sector, in call centres, hospitality, tourism and retailing, where union membership is much rarer. The size of the average workplace has declined too, and this has reduced the propensity of employees to join a union. There are fewer large factories employing thousands on assembly and many more small-scale office and hi-tech manufacturing operations. Management styles in small workplaces, even when part of a much larger group, inevitably tend to be more ad hoc and personal. Grievances, disputes and requests for a pay rise are thus discussed and settled in face-to-face meetings or informally between people who know each other well, without the need to involve a trade union. Moreover, in the private services sector the proliferation of small workplaces means that alternative employment is readily available for suitably qualified people. When receptionists, shopworkers, sales executives, call-centre staff or IT people are dissatisfied with their work, their workplace or their managers, they can simply look for another job and resign. They do not need to move house to find work and are unlikely, in the present economic climate, to suffer any decline in income. Their jobs thus matter less to them than was the case in the days of the steel town, the mining village or the city suburb in which one big employer provided the lion's share of all employment. In short, there is now less need to join a union because there are other ways of resolving problems at work and relieving discontent. Union members no longer enjoy the substantially higher wages and greater levels of job security that they used to, so the economic incentive for non-members to join is less strong too (Metcalf 2005).

By 2004 49 per cent of UK workplaces employing over 25 people stated that they employed no union members at all (Kersley *et al.* 2006, p. 110), while in tens of thousands more unions have no influence of any significance. For most employees, therefore, the norm is now to work in a non-union workplace. However, this is not true in the public sector, where union density remains high (64 per cent) and collective bargaining with full union recognition is still near universal. The same is true in the utility firms and in the transportation and education sectors. As a result, employee relations has come to be characterised by a far greater variety of forms than had been the case throughout much of the past century, traditional approaches continuing to decline:

> What we find, therefore, is a marked split between the public sector, where traditional industrial relations appears to have survived, albeit with some adaptations, and a private sector which, with the exception of a declining set of large establishments, is predominantly non-union and without worker representation. . . . Management appears to be firmly in the driving seat, controlling the direction of employment relations.
> (Guest 2001, p. 99)

Whether continued trade union decline is inevitable produces diverse views. From a trade union perspective there are grounds for pessimism, despite years of new initiatives aimed at recruiting new members in the private sector. The proportion of younger people who choose to join unions has declined dramatically, suggesting that they do not see membership of a collective employee body as necessary or desirable. In 1991 as many as 37 per cent of people in the 25–34 age group were union members (Waddington 2003, p. 239). Ten years later, union density among the under 30s had fallen to just 16 per cent, compared with 34 per cent among those over the age of 30 (Freeman and Diamond 2003, p. 29). The second reason to anticipate further decline in the future relates to the continued growth of industries which have not traditionally been unionised. With the exception of some jobs in the public sector, the fastest-growing professions are all ones that have very low rates of union density (e.g. technicians, consultants, software engineers, nursery nurses, hairdressers and beauticians). These factors lead Metcalf (2005) to calculate that 'long run union density will be around 20%, implying a rate of 12% in the private sector'.

The alternative view rests first of all on the observation that trade unions have been through periods of steep decline before and have later recovered. Kelly (1998) shows how union membership declined steeply during the 1920s and early 1930s, density falling as low as 22 per cent in 1933, only to recover again afterwards. His theory of 'long waves' in industrial relations leads him to conclude that workers will only ever put up with so much 'exploitation and domination' by employers, before beginning to unite to fight back. Others take heart from research which shows that many employees in the non-union sectors (including young people) are neither strongly opposed to unions, nor unwilling to countenance joining a union in the future. Fifty per cent of those asked in a poll in 2001 said that they would be either 'very likely' or 'fairly likely' to join if one were available at their workplace (Charlwood 2003, p. 52), while positive attitudes to unions appear to be just as common among non-members as they are among members (Prowse and Prowse 2006). These figures suggest that unions could create a renaissance for themselves if they could find more effective ways of organising and marketing themselves in the private services sector. You will find an article and some discussion exercises focusing on the prospects for trade union revival on our companion website, **www.pearsoned.co.uk/torrington.**

WINDOW ON PRACTICE

Trade unions face a major problem in recruiting members in what are known as 'dispersed sectors' in which people are scattered across the country in small workplaces, working in small teams less than half a dozen strong or even alone. Traditional approaches involving communication from the union hierarchy through local shop stewards is clearly inappropriate for these groups. New methods such as the use of mobile phone text alerts thus have to be harnessed.

Despite the difficulties some of the larger unions have enjoyed some modest successes in recent years by setting up special sections for people working in these dispersed occupations. IRS (2003) gives several interesting examples. The GMB union has recently started targeting professional boxers, London minicab drivers and workers in the sex industry, while the Transport and General Workers Union has signed up over 2,000 childcare workers in private nurseries. However, the biggest success story is probably Amicus's (now Unite) clergy and church workers' section which has over 2,500 members and recently succeeded in persuading the Church of England to recognise the right of clergymen not to be unfairly dismissed.

Collective bargaining and industrial action

A major consequence of the decline in trade union membership has been a simultaneous decline in the number of employees whose terms and conditions are determined through collective bargaining (i.e. negotiation with a union or unions). Here, too, dramatic changes have occurred over recent decades. We have moved from a position in which a large majority of people worked in establishments which recognised trade unions, to one in which a large majority do not. In 1970 over 80 per cent of the UK workforce was covered by collective agreements. Thirty-five years later, the figure was just 35.3 per cent (DTI 2006, p. 12).

Table 20.1 Average number of working days lost due to strikes

1970–1974	14.1 million
1975–1979	11.6 million
1980–1984	10.5 million
1985–1989	3.9 million
1990–1994	824,000
1995–1999	594,000
2000–2005	651,000

Source: Adapted from R. Taylor (1993) *The Trade Union Question in British Politics*. Oxford: Blackwell; and R. Beardsmore (2006a) 'Labour disputes in 2005', *Labour Market Trends*, June. London: HMSO.

Profound changes have also occurred within the sectors that remain covered by collective agreements, and continue to do so. Over several decades we have seen the breaking down of the system of national collective bargaining established in the middle years of the twentieth century. Agreements of this kind are now very rare outside the public sector whereas once they were the norm. They involve terms and conditions being agreed at industry level between representatives of the relevant unions and an employers association, resulting in an agreement to which all operating in the industry agree to adhere. One by one arrangements of this kind have collapsed as collective bargaining, where it continues at all, increasingly takes place at the level of the organisation or the individual workplace. In 1960, according to Brown *et al.* (2003), 60 per cent of UK employees were covered by industry-level collective agreements. By 1980 the proportion had fallen to 43 per cent and by 2004 to only seven per cent. These remaining agreements are largely in the public sector and are themselves under robust attack from government ministers who see local bargaining as a more efficient and fairer way of distributing public money.

Another significant change in employee relations has been the very marked decline in the incidence of industrial action in recent years. Contrary to commonly held perceptions, UK workers have never been more prone to take industrial action than their counterparts in other countries, but the 1970s and early 1980s did see the loss of millions of days' work as a result of strikes, not to mention the fall of at least two governments in the wake of major disputes. The position is now wholly transformed. The UK's strike rate has been below the average for both the European Union and the OECD countries in every year except one since 1992 (Beardsmore 2006b), while the subject has long ceased to be one which influences voting patterns. The number of stoppages varies from year to year. In 2002, for example, there was a marked increase due to a long-running dispute in the fire service, but the overall trend has been downwards for over a decade. The number of working days lost to strikes each year is now a fraction of what it was thirty years ago (*see* Table 20.1). Some argue that we can expect to see an increase in the incidence of industrial action over coming years in the public sector as employees respond to government attempts to restructure services and reduce the costs associated with providing generous occupational pensions. Industrial action in the private sector, by contrast, is generally expected to remain rare and restricted to specific sectors (IRS 2006b).

The rise of employment law

Until the 1960s there was no such thing as employment law in Britain. With the exception of basic protection for child workers and some health and safety regulations, the state 'kept its distance' from the relationship between employers and employees. This became known as the principle of voluntarism and it meant that the UK differed very markedly from most other industrialised countries. All workers and employers, it was argued, were free to enter into whatever contractual relationship they preferred and it was not for the state to determine people's terms and conditions or to set minimum standards. All the courts did was provide a mechanism for contracts of employment to be enforced when one side or the other breached them or sought to change them unilaterally without the consent of the other party. Protection from injustices perpetrated by managers and abuse of power was provided by trade unions and through collective agreements.

Over the past forty years this position has wholly reversed. In 1965 the first major piece of modern employment legislation was introduced – a right for redundant workers to receive payments by way of compensation. In the years since a major new field of legal practice has been created as the law has intervened more and more in the regulation of the employment relationship. As trade unions have declined in size and influence, the law has stepped in to provide a minimum floor of rights and to deter employers from acting without proper employee relations procedures. In recent years many developments have originated at European level, but UK governments have pushed the agenda forward on their own account too.

Unfair dismissal law dates from 1971, sex discrimination law from 1975 and race discrimination law from 1976. Since 1974 we have had comprehensive health and safety law together with a government inspectorate to enforce it. Regulations relating to 'transfers of undertakings' were introduced in 1981, when it also became a formal requirement to consult collectively when making redundancies. The past ten years have seen an astonishing quickening of the pace. We now have disability discrimination law, a national minimum wage, restrictions on working time, compulsory union recognition, a host of new family-friendly measures, extensive data protection law and measures preventing discrimination against people employed on fixed-term and part-time contracts. In 2003 new regulations outlawing discrimination on grounds of sexual orientation and religion or belief were introduced, and there were significant improvements to the rights of people with family responsibilities. In 2004 new workplace dispute resolution measures came into force and in 2005 significant new obligations were introduced in the field of information and consultation. Age discrimination legislation was introduced in 2006 and 2007 saw a major extentsion of maternity and other family-friendly rights.

Employment tribunals now oversee nearly one hundred separate areas of jurisdiction (i.e. distinct types of claim that an aggrieved employee, ex-employee or job applicant can bring before them). In addition there are some thirty or forty separate types of claim rooted in the laws of contract, trust or tort that can be taken to the county courts. Around 100,000 claims are lodged with the Employment Tribunal Service each year, leading the government to reform procedures and adjust remedies so as to discourage parties from pursuing cases they are unlikely to win.

Given the acceleration of developments in the field of employment law, it is not surprising that its implementation by organisations now comes so much higher up HR managers' agendas than more traditional employee relations concerns (IRS 2006a). Two-thirds of HR specialists claim to spend in excess of 20 per cent of their time 'dealing with employment law issues', while a quarter report that over 40 per cent of their working days are spent in this way (CIPD 2002). In the vast majority of workplaces the nature of the relationship that is established between employers and employees, and the rules that govern it, owe far more to the requirements of employment law than to the demands of trade unions. This represents a total transformation from the position that prevailed a generation ago.

ACTIVITY 20.2

Why do you think employment practice in the UK moved from being unregulated to being so highly regulated in thirty years? Do you agree that we now have 'too much' employment law? If so, which statutes would you like to see kept and which repealed?

STRATEGIC CHOICES

Most organisations in the UK do not have a clearly identifiable employee relations strategy which their managers can readily articulate. At no point have managers at senior levels determined what the general approach or philosophy of the organisation should be towards the relationship it has with its employees, either individually or collectively. While it may be possible to identify the operation of a clear management style or the presence of definable employee relations culture, these have not in most cases been shaped in a deliberate or coherent manner by managers (Blyton and Turnball 2004: 121). Instead, pragmatism reigns and employee relations issues only receive serious attention at senior levels when problems arise (Keenoy 1992, p. 97).

The reason for this is that there is often only limited scope for individual managers or teams of managers, however senior, to determine the nature of the employment relationships in an organisation. Whereas a reward strategy or an employee development strategy can be thought through, devised and then introduced by managers with relative ease, altering, let alone shaping the direction of employee relations is far harder to achieve. This is because the nature of the employment relationship in an organisation is controlled to a considerable extent by the attitudes, outlook and responses of employees. While managers can often readily get employees to *do* what they want them to, they cannot do more than influence their hearts and minds. As a result, even if a strategic approach to employee relations is developed, there is no guarantee that it will be successfully implemented and the extent of its success will always be difficult to measure objectively and accurately.

Moreover, the defining characteristics of the employment relationship in most organisations are heavily determined by the nature of the work that is being carried out and the way that it is organised. For example, a new manufacturing plant which mass produces goods via assembly lines is inevitably going to develop different kinds of employment relationships with its staff than would be the case in a new shop, hotel, hospital or government department. Different types of workplace develop clearly differentiated cultures derived from the complexity of work that they carry out, the nature of customer interactions, the extent of competition and the nature of the skills and qualifications their staff possess. Once established, workplace cultures are difficult to change, and this means that the nature of established employment relationships is difficult to change too.

Despite these difficulties, it can be strongly argued that organisations are more effective when their senior managers do think strategically about the employment relationship and develop policies and practices which help them to achieve clearly articulated objectives. There are strategic choices to be made in the field of employee relations and it is better that these should be considered and rational, rather than determined in an ad hoc, inconsistent and reactive fashion.

Management control

It would be a great deal easier for organisations if their employees had an innate desire to come to work on time every day and carry out their duties in a highly efficient fashion and were always happy to accept change. If this were the case there would hardly be a need to employ managers at all, while terms such as 'industrial conflict' would never have been invented. But, of course, the real world is very different. Employees and their employers share some interests in common, but what they aim to get from their relationship also varies considerably. There is thus an ever-present need, from a management perspective, to supervise what employees are doing and, more generally, to exercise a degree of control over a workplace. However, the nature of the control that is exercised varies from organisation to organisation, and this is largely a matter determined by management.

The central choice is between the two fundamentally different control strategies identified by Friedman (1977); 'direct control' and 'responsible autonomy'. The former involves close supervision by managers who determine what work is done, when and by whom. Employees are required to do what they are told and are not given any meaningful day-to-day influence over the way their work is organised or performed. Hard work is rewarded, while disciplinary sanctions are conspicuously used to deter recalcitrant behaviour. This is a model of control that is often seen as being similar to that used in the armed forces, although its origins lie as much in the ideas of F.W. Taylor (*see* Chapter 1) and the school of scientific management which sought to organise work in the way that an engineer might design a machine. Responsible autonomy, by contrast, is both subtler and a great deal more pleasant from the employees' point of view. It is also believed by many managers to be more desirable because it leads to less conflict with staff, and more cost effective because less management time needs to be spent supervising the activities of others. Here the organisation sets the objectives, communicating clearly to its staff what it wants them to achieve, but it allows employees as much autonomy as is practicable to decide how and when they meet these objectives.

Labour-market orientation

In Chapter 5 we looked in detail at the strategic choices available to organisations when interacting with their labour markets. We noted that in recent years most labour markets have tightened, making it harder for employers to recruit and retain good performers. Staff who are unhappy now have more alternative employment opportunities open to them and can thus either switch employers, or credibly threaten to do so if they find that their objectives from an employment relationship are not being met. For an employer seeking to respond effectively employee relations practices have a great deal to contribute because of the major role they play in influencing job satisfaction.

One strategic choice that many employers have taken in response to tightening labour market conditions has been to seek status as an 'employer of choice' or even as *the* employer of choice in their industry. This involves making themselves more attractive to prospective employees than competitor organisations, the aim being to secure and then to hold on to the services of high performers. Positioning an organisation as an employer of choice can be expensive in the short term, but over time dividends are reaped because fewer people are required, and those that are employed help ensure that the organisation meets its objectives more effectively and efficiently than its rivals. Sustained competitive advantage thus results. It follows that employers seeking to achieve employer of choice status, or simply aiming to recruit and retain more effectively, need to develop employee relations strategies that increase the chances that employees are satisfied and decrease the likelihood of dissatisfaction.

Taylor (2001, p. 15) drawing on the work of Michael White and Stephen Hill states that contemporary research into what employees want to achieve from the employment relationship consistently reports a desire, above other possibilities, for the following:

- an interesting job
- employment security
- a feeling of positive accomplishment
- influence over how their job gets done

This strongly suggests that there are substantial long-term dividends to be gained by employers who develop sophisticated employee relations strategies. Effective employee involvement practices are central as are approaches to supervision which combine responsible autonomy with strong positive feedback mechanisms. Involving employees in the management of change is particularly important so as to minimise perceptions of insecurity. Above all an employer of choice requires an employee relations strategy which is built around a view of employees as individuals with different personalities, attributes and ambitions. A traditional approach which views employees as a mass group of people with identical aspirations is unlikely to deliver jobs which individuals find interesting or fulfilling.

Not all labour markets are tight, and while they have tightened considerably over the long term in most parts of the UK, it is important to recognise that there are areas of high unemployment both in this country and overseas. Moreover, in all countries, there are groups of people who lack sufficient basic skills or whose skills have become obsolete. In such conditions employers are not required to become employers of choice in order to recruit and retain effective staff. People may prefer jobs which are interesting, secure and satisfying, and may desire a degree of influence over how they do their jobs, but management do not have to provide such employment for reasons of commercial necessity. Where competitive pressures require organisations to minimise costs in order to survive and prosper, a rather different employee relations strategy is appropriate. Policies are likely to be highly standardised, employee involvement limited and few formal opportunities for positive feedback provided. Jobs are designed first and foremost around the need of the organisation to maximise its efficiency rather than the needs or aspirations of employees. In such conditions employers are often tempted to avoid legal obligations, taking short cuts with health and safety for example, and may permit managers at the local level to take a somewhat 'flexible' approach when interpreting written policy.

In between these two extreme types of employee relations strategy there are a variety of other possibilities. Shore *et al.* (2004), for example, refer to employee relations strategies adopted by US companies which differentiate between 'core' and 'non-core' employees, the purpose of which is to ensure that the former are retained while maximum efficiency is extracted from the latter. They also describe employee relations strategies which vary from division to division within a corporation depending on the particular business strategy being pursued.

Management style

So far we have only discussed strategic choices in employee relations as they affect the individual employment relationship. Debates about what is usually termed 'management style' relate to the different approaches employers choose to take as far as the collective employment relationship is concerned. How does an employer wish to view its relationship with its employees as a group? Does it wish to engage with them through representatives whom they appoint or elect? Does it wish to establish formal mechanisms for consultation or negotiation? What is its approach to possible trade union recognition?

One of the best-known typologies of management style is that developed by Purcell and Sisson (1983) following extensive research into the different approaches favoured by employers. These are summarised in Table 20.2. Their categories are useful, although some organisations do not fit easily into any one of them. Most large, long-established companies will be in one of the last three; most public sector organisations will be in category 4; and many newer businesses will be in some version of category 2. Smaller organisations tend to take the 'traditional' approach, having no considered employee relations strategy in place.

Table 20.2 Categories of management styles in employee relations

Style	Characteristics
[1] Traditional	Fire-fighting approach. Employee relations not important until there is trouble. Low pay. Hostile to trade unions. Authoritarian. Typical in small, owner-managed businesses.
[2] Paternalist	Unions regarded as unnecessary because of employer's enlightenment. High pay. Concentration on encouraging employee identification with business objectives.
[3] Consultative	Union participation encouraged through recognition. Problem-solving, informal approach to employee relations. Emphasis on two-way communications.
[4] Constitutional	Similar to consultative, but emphasis on formal agreements to regulate relationship between two powerful protagonists.
[5] Opportunistic	Large company devolving responsibility for employee relations to subsidiaries, with no common approach but emphasis on unit profitability.

Source: J. Purcell and K. Sisson (1983) 'Strategies and practice in the management of industrial relations', in G.S. Bain (ed.), *Industrial Relations in Britain*. Oxford: Blackwell, pp. 112–18.

ACTIVITY 20.3

Which of the five categories in Table 20.2 most closely fits your establishment? Does the category vary for different groups of employees?

It is also possible to view management styles in terms of the extent and nature of collective employee participation in decision making. Below we set out seven categories of consent, in which there is a steadily increasing degree of involvement. We begin with a category in which there is straightforward and unquestioning acceptance of management authority, and then move through various stages of increasing participation in decision making and the necessary changes in management style as the power balance alters and the significance of bargaining develops and extends to more and more areas of organisational life.

1 **Normative.** We use this term in the sense of Etzioni (1961), who described 'normative' organisations as those in which the involvement of individuals was attributable to a strong sense of moral obligation. Any challenge to authority would imply a refutation of the shared norms and was therefore unthinkable. Many of the exercises in corporate culture are construed by some as strategies to develop this type of consent, with strong emphasis on commitment and the suppression of views opposed to managerial orthodoxy.

2 **Disorganised.** In organisations that are not normative there may be collective consent simply because there is no collective focus for a challenge; disorganised consent is where there may be discontent but consent is maintained through lack of employee organisation to articulate and endorse the dissatisfaction. A Victorian sweatshop would come into this category.

3 **Organised.** When employees organise it is nearly always in trade unions and the first collective activities are usually those dealing with general grievances. It is very unlikely that there will be any degree of involvement in the management decision-making processes. Employees simply consent to obey instructions as long as grievances are dealt with.

4 **Consultative.** Consultation is a stage of development beyond initial trade union recognition, even though some employers consult with employees before – often as a means of deferring – trade union recognition. This is the first incursion into the management process as employees are asked for an opinion about management proposals before decisions are made, even though the right to decide remains with the management.

5 **Negotiated.** Negotiation implies that both parties have the power to commit and the power to withhold agreement, so that a decision can only be reached by some form of mutual accommodation. No longer is the management retaining all decision making for itself; it is seeking some sort of bargain with employee representatives, recognising that only such reciprocity can produce what is needed.

6 **Participative.** When employee representatives reach the stage of participating in the general management of the business in which they are employed, there is a fundamental change in the control of that business, even though this may initially be theoretical rather than actual. Employee representatives take part in making the decisions on major strategic issues such as expenditure on research, the opening of new plants and the introduction of new products. In arrangements for participative consent there is a balance between the decision makers representing the interests of capital and those representing the interests of labour, though the balance is not necessarily even.

7 **Controlling.** If the employees acquire control of the organisation, as in a workers' cooperative, then the consent is a controlling type. This may sound bizarre, but there will still be a management apparatus within the organisation to which employee collective consent will be given or from which it will be withheld.

All of the above categories require some management initiative to sustain collective consent. In categories 1 and 2 it may be exhortation to ensure that commitment is kept up, or information supplied to defer organisation. In each subsequent category there is an increasing bargaining emphasis, which becomes progressively more complex. The implication is that there is a hierarchy of consent categories, through which organisations steadily progress. Although this has frequently been true in the past, it is by no means necessary.

UNION RECOGNITION AND DERECOGNITION

The single most important strategic decisions that managers may have to take in the employee relations sphere concern trade union recognition:

- Whether or not to recognise a trade union, and if so about what form the recognition should take.
- Whether or not to resist a trade union campaign for recognition.
- Whether or not to derecognise a union with an established presence in the workplace.

As we explained above, over time trade union membership in the UK as a whole has declined in recent decades, as has the extent of trade union recognition. But unions still retain a presence of some kind in 36 per cent of workplaces employing over ten people, and in 18 per cent they have the majority of employees in membership. Unions are formally recognised in 30 per cent of workplaces overall, but in as many as 67 per cent of those employing over 500 people (Kersley *et al.* 2006, pp. 111 and 119). Moreover, since 1999 there has been an increase in the number of recognition agreements that have been established, caused mainly by the introduction of laws which can force employers to recognise in certain circumstances. The issue of trade union recognition thus remains a live one for substantial numbers of UK employers.

WINDOW ON PRACTICE

Surveys focusing on employee attitudes consistently find that employees who are members of unions tend to be a good deal less satisfied with their work and with their pay than colleagues who are not union members. To many commentators this is a paradox. If a union is effective, surely it will serve to improve the experience of working, and if it is ineffective why would people join it in the first place?

Several possible explanations can be advanced. According to Guest and Conway (2004) there are two principal explanations. The first is that because managers are hostile to unions, they respond negatively and this creates dissatisfaction among staff. The second is that unions have the effect of raising expectations among members and then, in practice, fail to deliver greatly improved terms and conditions or job security. Bryson *et al.* (2004) advance a different explanation from their analysis of the data. They suggest that union members are less satisfied than non-members simply because dissatisfied people are more likely to join unions than those who are satisfied. They therefore reject the suggestion that unions cause dissatisfaction in any way.

Defining recognition

Section 178 of the Trade Union and Labour Relations (Consolidation) Act 1992 contains the established legal definition of recognition as being a situation in which, either via a formal written agreement or through custom and practice, employers engage in collective bargaining with union representatives about some or all of the following matters:

- Terms and conditions of employment, or the physical conditions in which any workers are required to work.
- Engagement or non-engagement, or termination or suspension of employment or the duties of employment of one or more workers.
- Allocation of work or the duties of employment as between workers or groups of workers.
- Matters of discipline.
- The membership or non-membership of a trade union on the part of a worker.
- Facilities for officials of trade unions.

The decision to recognise or to withdraw recognition from a trade union has implications far beyond the terms of the agreement itself. Once recognised, the union gains a raft of defined legal rights to exercise on behalf of its members. First, there is the right to be consulted before redundancies are made or before a business is transferred to new owners. Recognised unions also have consultation rights in the fields of health and safety and occupational pensions, and are empowered to conclude workplace agreements with employers concerning the working time and parental leave regulations. Second, officials of recognised unions and union-appointed learning representatives have a right to reasonable paid time off work in order to carry out their duties and for training purposes. Union health and safety representatives enjoy these rights as well as others giving them access to office facilities. Third, recognised unions have the right to receive information from managers to enable them to engage in meaningful collective bargaining. Finally, the Transfer of Undertakings Regulations 2006 require that union recognition continues and collective agreements remain in force after the transfer of an undertaking to new ownership, provided that the transferred undertaking retains 'an identity distinct from the remainder of the transferee's undertaking'.

A range of other rights such as protection from discrimination on trade union grounds, the right to accompany an employee at a serious disciplinary or grievance hearing, and the right to organise lawful industrial action apply to unions and their members irrespective of whether or not they are formally recognised. However, these rights are conditional on the union concerned being accepted as an independent body by the Certification Officer who has the responsibility of maintaining the official list of trade unions.

ACTIVITY 20.4

What do you think should be the main criteria used to establish whether a body should or should not be granted the status of a trade union?

Traditionally the Certification Officer has placed a great deal of importance on independence from management, ensuring that staff associations that are limited to specific companies cannot qualify. Is this fair?

The cases for and against union recognition

When a trade union has recruited a number of members in an organisation, it will seek recognition from the employer in order to represent those members. If the employees want that type of representation, they will not readily cooperate with the employer who refuses. In extreme cases this can generate sufficient antagonism to cause industrial action in support of recognition. In such situations the employer may be forced to grant partial recognition or even concede the demand for full negotiating rights over a whole range of issues. Alternatively refusal may lead to a situation in which the employer is forced to recognise the union under the terms of the Employment Relations Act 1999 (*see* below).

However, there are also positive reasons for considering recognising trade unions, relating to the benefits that can flow as a result: there are employee representatives with whom to discuss, consult and negotiate so that communication and working relationships can be improved:

> There are a number of reasons why employers should choose to work with, rather than against, unions at the workplace. Firstly, management may regard trade union representatives as an essential part of the communication process in larger workplaces. Rather than being forced to establish a system for dealing with all employees, or setting up a non-union representative forum, trade unions are seen as a channel which allows for the effective resolution of issues concerned with pay bargaining or grievance handling. It is also the case that reaching agreement with union representatives, in contrast to imposing decisions, can provide decisions with a legitimacy which otherwise would be lacking. It can also lead to better decisions as well. (Marchington and Wilkinson 2002, p. 425)

There are also various arguments that can be put for resisting the recognition of a trade union. Employers are often apprehensive about the degree of rigidity in employment practice that union aims for security of employment appear to imply, and they therefore consider to what extent collective consent can be achieved by other means, provided that the management work hard at both securing and maintaining that consent. Managers also tend to perceive unions as being resistant to necessary change, the result of recognition being a reduction in their ability to respond quickly and flexibly to market pressures and opportunities.

Forms of trade union recognition

Union recognition comes in various shapes and forms. It may be 'partial', in which case the range of topics subject to negotiation is limited, or it may be 'full', covering pay, conditions and all employer policies relating to the employment relationship. The irreducible minimum is assistance by a union representative for members with grievances, but the extent to which matters beyond that are recognised as being a subject of bargaining depends on the type of management regime that is in place. It also depends on the possible existence of other agreements that could take some matters out of the scope of local recognition. A feature of some collective agreements is an acceptance that certain matters are potentially subject to negotiation with the recognised union (e.g. pay and redundancy), while in other areas the union has the right only to be consulted or informed.

The second fundamental decision to be taken in respect of recognition concerns the number of unions to be recognised and the type of bargaining to be adopted. There are three basic alternatives:

1   **Multi-union bargaining** involves the recognition of several different unions, each of which negotiates separately on behalf of different groups of workers. Sometimes this leads to a situation in which the separate groups are employed on different sets of terms and conditions. Such an approach has traditionally been common in large public sector organisations such as the National Health Service, although union mergers in recent years have tended to reduce the overall number that are recognised. As a rule different unions will represent different 'bargaining groups' such as unskilled manual workers, skilled manual grades and white-collar workers.

2   **Single-table bargaining** is a situation in which a number of unions are recognised, but where only one set of negotiations takes place over terms and conditions at a time. The full range of issues is thus determined for all groups of staff around a single table. It is usual for such arrangements to be associated with 'single-status' practices or har-monised terms and conditions, so that all workers enjoy the same basic entitlements as regards matters such as holiday, pensions, hours and sick pay.

3   **Single-union bargaining** is principally associated with situations in which only one union seeks recognition. However, it can also occur where an employer rejects multi-union bargaining and agrees instead only to recognise one union. These are popularly known as 'sweetheart' or 'new style' agreements and have been the subject of some controversy. They are typically found on greenfield sites and in businesses of techno-logical sophistication, their essential novelty being the closeness and extent of the working relationship between management and union. Union officials find that they have less freedom of action on some matters than their members expect, but also find they are involved in the full range of human resource management questions, not simply the familiar terrain of collective bargaining. The agreements are also frequently accompanied by 'no strike' clauses, which supposedly remove the need for industrial action by providing for independent arbitration in situations where management and union fail to reach agreement. Single-status arrangements also often feature in single-union deals.

From a management perspective it is preferable, if possible, to conclude a partnership agreement with the union or unions which have been recognised. Such approaches have been actively encouraged by the government in recent years because they are believed to constitute good practice and to increase prospects for national economic growth. Partnership deals represent an attempt to move away from the traditional, adversarial, low-trust form of union–management relationship towards one which is characterised by high trust and a willingness to engage in joint problem solving. Communication and consultation are watchwords, so that employees and their representatives are kept fully aware of the factors affecting management decision making and are themselves involved as far as is possible.

The third major way in which collective bargaining arrangements differ is in their level. Three approaches are commonly identified:

•   multi-employer bargaining
•   single-employer bargaining
•   workplace bargaining

All can operate within the same organisation at the same time with different matters being determined at different levels. However, in most organisations which recognise trade unions the most important decisions are taken in one forum.

Multi-employer bargaining involves negotiations over basic pay and conditions of employment taking place at industry or national level through the auspices of employers associations. The result is the presence of industry norms, the same rates of pay and agreements on hours being honoured by all employers in a particular industry. Once common in the UK, this approach is now largely restricted to the public sector, but it remains common in many European countries. Most bargaining in the UK therefore takes place within organisations either at employer level, or in multi-site operations at the level of the workplace. The former is better where core terms and conditions are standardised across the organisation. It is also the more efficient approach as it ties up less managerial time than is the case where each workplace carries out its own negotiations.

ACTIVITY 20.5

What do you think are the main reasons for the breaking up of so many industry-level collective agreements in the UK over recent decades? Why have they survived in other countries such as Denmark and Italy?

Derecognition

Derecognition of trade unions is often seen in published literature as being redolent of fundamentally undesirable 'macho' approaches to employee relations. Outright derecognition against the stated wishes of the workforce is rare in the UK, but by no means unknown (Millward *et al.* 2000, pp. 103–4, Kersley *et al.* 2006, p. 121). The majority of episodes relate to specific grades of employees rather than the entire workforce, while in other cases partial derecognition has occurred where the scope of matters covered by collective bargaining is narrowed. Such situations often accompany moves by employers to establish personal employment contracts and/or to move towards pay rises based on individual performance or contribution. The result is the retention of collective bargaining machinery, but a tendency for it to be used more and more rarely in important decision making. In recent years some employers have threatened to derecognise their unions if they refuse to adjust established adversarial approaches and enter into partnership agreements. A well-documented example is the negotiation that occurred between USDAW (the shopworkers' union) and Tesco in 1999 leading to the signing of one of the largest and most controversial new-style union deals (Blyton and Turnball 2004, p. 252).

It could be argued that partial derecognition of this kind ultimately leads to full derecognition as fewer staff see any particular advantage in joining the union. Over time the union becomes so numerically weak that there is no longer a persuasive case for its continued recognition – even over the limited range of issues for which it retains bargaining rights. In such circumstances there is a good case for accepting that the union is no longer performing a useful representative function and that employees' interests might thus be better served with the introduction of other forms of collective or individual involvement.

Trade union recognition law

Since 2000 there has been in place a formal legal route which unions can use as a means of forcing employers to recognise them and to bargain with them in good faith about the pay and conditions of the workers they represent. The new law was introduced as part of the Employment Relations Act 1999 and is highly complex. A central role is played by the Central Arbitration Committee (CAC), a statutory body which is independent of government, to which union recognition claims are sent. The CAC is required to consider the claim and to seek voluntary agreement between the parties. Where this cannot be established it can require management either to recognise the union or to organise a ballot of the workforce concerned. The law applies in all organisations employing more than 20 people where there is no existing collective bargaining arrangement in place.

Where it can be shown that over 50 per cent of the workers in the defined bargaining group are members of the union/unions bringing the claim, the CAC will order recognition unless there is evidence to suggest that sufficient members may not want their union to be recognised or where the panel is persuaded that it would not be in the interests of good industrial relations to require recognition without first organising a ballot. Where the union concerned shows that over 10 per cent of the bargaining group are members and produces evidence to suggest that a ballot for recognition stands a good chance of succeeding the CAC will order that a ballot should take place. In most cases the evidence required will be in the form of a petition of workers in the defined bargaining group.

The direct impact of the recognition law has been relatively slight. Only 450 claims had been made to the CAC by the end of 2005, and in the vast majority of cases these were withdrawn without the need for a formal recognition order to be made. But the introduction of the procedure has led many more employers to enter into voluntary negotiations and to establish recognition agreements on their own terms before the unions that represent their staff need to force the issue by making a claim to the CAC. It is impossible to know exactly how many new agreements have originated as a result of the new law, but 2,000 or so were recorded in the first five years following its introduction.

WINDOW ON PRACTICE

While some managers clearly see advantages in recognising trade unions, and particularly in concluding partnership deals, others take a radically different view and take quite radical steps to resist union recruitment and recognition campaigns. According to Gregor Gall (2005) this is a major explanation for the failure of trade unions to develop a meaningful presence in larger private services companies despite the presence of genuine grievances among staff.

One of his case studies concerns the online retailer Amazon, where the Graphical, Paper and Media Union (GPMU) sought recognition in 2001. According to the union officers involved, the company deployed a variety of tactics to ensure that the vote on recognition went against the union. These included instituting pay rises and some promotions, setting up a works council, ending compulsory overtime and improving canteen facilities (i.e. dealing with grievances), but also involved issuing anti-union leaflets and T-shirts to staff and sacking four union members. The union became concerned about the fairness of the ballot, and so urged its members to spoil their ballot papers. The outcome, however, on a 90 per cent turnout was an 80 per cent vote against recognition. Only 15 per cent of the workforce voted in favour, 5 per cent spoiling their ballot papers.

You can read about other similar failed attempts by unions to establish recognition in service sector companies in Gregor Gall's very interesting article.

THE STUDY OF EMPLOYEE RELATIONS

The profound changes in the employee relations world outlined at the beginning of this chapter have had, and continue to have, important implications for those whose job it is to study and conduct research into this area of organisational life. Until recently most of this work continued to be carried out within a frame of reference founded on the assumption that union membership and collective bargaining were the norm. The questions asked and the research undertaken focused for the most part on trade union organisation, forms of bargaining, industrial conflict and resolution, and the 'assaults' on established UK employment practices by employers and government. Since 1997 a great deal of attention has been given to the operation of the new institutions that have been set up to provide trade unions with a method of forcing employers to recognise them when they have sufficient support in the workforce, and to other measures introduced by the Blair Government aimed at fostering partnership agreements between employers and employee representatives. The focus for many thus remains the formal, collective aspects of the employment relationship and the prospects of a revival in the fortunes of trade unions. The continued, widespread use of the term 'non-union firm', when such employers have constituted the large majority for many years, illustrates the lasting influence of this long-established frame of reference.

Mike Emmott of the Chartered Institute of Personnel and Development (CIPD 2005, p. 15) goes as far as to argue that academic thinking in the field has 'little energy left' and that nowadays 'few managers look to the literature for inspiration about how to manage better'. He goes on to call for an adjustment in emphasis away from institutions and towards relationships, suggesting that the concept of employee engagement 'is an idea whose time has come'.

Increasingly academics specialising in this field are also looking at employee relations from new perspectives and are asking different kinds of questions in their research. Some have firmly argued that the time has come for industrial relations specialists 'to move on' and focus on the lived reality of working in contemporary workplaces in which trade unions and collective bargaining are either peripheral or wholly irrelevant:

> the search for the familiar – committees, procedures and so on – could blind the discipline to the relative sociological marginality of many of these new forms. Whereas collective bargaining in 1968 was a central social institution comparable to supermarket shopping today in its impact on the economy and ordinary people's lives, these new institutions are of far lesser significance . . . The danger is that we cling to one small log that is being washed downstream by a mighty river of socio-economic change. The log is worth grasping, clearly, but Industrial Relations needs to address the encircling current too. (Ackers and Wilkinson 2003, pp. 13–14)

We are thus now witnessing a very interesting period in the development of employee relations as an academic discipline. Prominent figures in the field are directing their minds to different types of issues and the development of new paradigms. Guest (2001), for example, has argued that developments in the state of the psychological contract between employers and employees (*see* Chapter 1) might provide a good focus for the study of employee relations in the future, while Rubery and Grimshaw (2003) make a good case for focusing on a wider range of employment institutions beyond those which derive from union recognition and collective bargaining. Their comparative studies look at regulatory practices in the areas of training, pay determination, working time, retirement, downsizing and employee involvement.

Edwards (2005) argues that academic researchers need to broaden their frame of reference and that greater emphasis should be placed on contextual issues (i.e. the causes of the trends that are observed), on comparing different international systems of industrial relations and on gender relations in the workplace. Sisson (2005) gives a robust defence of contemporary academic research in employee relations, but also sets out an extensive and wide-ranging agenda for the future. His list of 'major issues' includes managing diversity, organisational learning, employee voice and corporate social responsibility alongside institutional concerns relating to organisational structure and industrial conflict.

INTERNATIONAL PERSPECTIVES

Employee relations, more than other areas of HRM practice, varies considerably from country to country. Although there has been some convergence recently due to increased global competition and new technologies, substantial differences remain. Different countries have seen different responses to the same environmental pressures (*see* Bamber and Lansbury 1998 for a summary of these). In industrialised countries comparative studies reveal the continued effect of different industrial relations traditions on contemporary practice. They also identify the importance of historical experience and institutional differences in explaining the observed variations. The major dimensions across which national systems vary are as follows:

- high union membership and low union membership;
- single-employer bargaining and multi-employer bargaining;
- interventionist government role and non-interventionist role;
- adversarial tradition and consensual (or social partnership) tradition;
- autocratic management style and involving management style.

ACTIVITY 20.6

Making reference to our description of employee relations trends above, consider in which ways the UK employee relations system has evolved along each of these dimensions in recent years.

Clearly, of course, there is a great deal of variation within as well as between national systems in all the above areas. It is also true that things do not remain static over time and that prevailing norms within any country evolve in new directions. However, it remains the case that certain approaches remain associated with particular countries. In Japan, for example, union membership is high and management practices relatively autocratic, but the unions themselves are enterprise based and there is a consensual tradition. In Germany and the Scandinavian countries the social partnership approach is well established, but here it is associated with industry-based unions, national-level bargaining, extensive employee involvement in decision making and heavy government intervention. Hence employers are obliged by law to consult and share decision making with their workforces through works councils (*see* Chapter 21). In France, by contrast, union membership is notoriously low, but the unions maintain a role in negotiating terms and conditions because they are empowered to do so in law. The government is further involved through the setting of minimum standards in areas such as training provision, holiday entitlements, wages, hours of work, health insurance and pensions. Government intervention is also extensive in the Eastern European countries, but here union membership remains relatively high, while bargaining is often carried out at industry level. The main practical implications associated with this variation in approach are for multinational organisations. They have an understandable impulse to strengthen their corporate culture by taking a standard approach to employee relations management across their operations, but also have to take account of local conditions. For them, success comes when they find ways of creating a company-wide, international strategy which is adaptable to the requirements of the various countries in which they operate. Employee relations considerations thus play a major role in determining which countries are chosen as the locations for their operations. They can also contribute to decisions about plant closures when retrenchment is deemed necessary.

WINDOW ON PRACTICE

Trade unions in Eastern European countries have experienced a rocky ride in recent years. Membership has fallen greatly and they have often found it difficult to maintain a meaningful presence in even the largest companies. According to Frantisek Stasek (2005), the president of the Czech print-workers union, the problem stems from several factors.

First, many people associate the unions with the past communist regime, under which membership was compulsory, but union activity was restricted to 'dispersing welfare and holiday benefits' and leaders were seen as fully paid up collaborators with the regime. Second, since the Velvet Revolution in 1989 Czech unions have lost many of their most effective leaders to politics and business, hampering their effectiveness in the workplace. Finally, privatisation, the introduction of western technologies, industrial relocation and the splitting of the country into two republics (Czech and Slovak) have had a disorientating effect.

Stasek argues that the powerlessness of unions is having a negative effect as companies are able to downsize, cut benefits, dismiss people and preside over unsafe working conditions with relative ease.

SUMMARY PROPOSITIONS

20.1 Since 1979 trade union membership and the significance of collective bargaining have both declined.

20.2 Increasingly it is the requirements of the law more than the demands of employees that shape the rules which govern employment relationships.

20.3 Most employers do not have a definable employee relations strategy. They make strategic choices when required to by events.

20.4 It is possible to identify seven categories of consent to illustrate variations in the level and type of collective employee involvement.

20.5 There is a great deal of debate at present about the future direction of employee relations as a field of academic study.

20.6 Despite some convergence in recent years, national employee relations systems remain very different from one another in important respects.

GENERAL DISCUSSION TOPICS

1 To what extent do you agree with the proposition that the decline of trade unions in the form that they have traditionally taken is inevitable?

2 What kind of employee relations strategy and management style would you prefer your own employer to adopt and why?

3 Why do you think national employee relations systems remain so different in an era of globalisation?

FURTHER READING

Boeri, T., Brugiavani, A. and Calmfors, L. (eds) (2001) *The Role of Unions in the Twenty First Century*. Oxford: OUP.

Gospel, H. and Wood, S. (eds) (2003) *Representing Workers: Union recognition and membership in Britain*. London: Routledge.

Fernie, S. and Metcalf, D. (eds) (2005) *Trade Unions: Resurgence or Demise?* London: Routledge. There is no shortage of excellent scholarly writing on recent trends in employee relations, and in particular on the position of trade unions. An up-to-date summary of UK-based research is provided by the authors contributing to the books edited by Gospel and Wood (2003) and Fernie and Metcalf (2005). For an international perspective Boeri, Brugiavani and Calmfors (2001) provide a good starting point.

Millward, N., Bryson, A. and Forth, J. (2000) *All Change at Work?* London: Routledge.

Kersley, B., Alpin, C., Forth, J., Bryson, A., Bewley, H., Dix, G. and Oxenbridge, S. (2006) *Inside the Workplace: Findings from the 2004 Workplace Employment Relations Survey*. Abingdon: Routledge. It is impossible seriously to study trends in employment relations in the UK without taking account of the findings of the vast Workplace Employee Relations Surveys which are undertaken periodically. The most recent survey was conducted in 2004. The findings of this and the four previous versions are extensively summarised in the above books.

CIPD (2005) *What is Employee Relations?* London: CIPD.

Sisson, K. (2005) 'Responding to Mike Emmott: What "industrial relations" suggests should be at the heart of "employee relations"', **www.buira.org.uk**. A vigorous and highly informative debate has recently been conducted between Mike Emmott of the Chartered Institute of Personnel and Development (CIPD) and Professor Keith Sisson of Warwick University about the future direction of employee relations both as an area of professional practice and as a subject for academic study. These two papers provide an excellent introduction to the debate as well as being interesting assessments in their own right.

REFERENCES

Ackers, P. and Wilkinson, A. (2003) 'Introduction: The British Industrial Relations Tradition – Formation, Breakdown, and Salvage', in P. Ackers and A. Wilkinson (eds), *Understanding Work and Employment: Industrial Relations in Transition*. Oxford: OUP.

Bamber, G. and Lansbury, R. (1998) 'An introduction to international and comparative employment relations', in G. Bamber and R. Lansbury (eds), *International and Comparative Employment Relations*, 3rd edn. London: Sage.

Beardsmore, R. (2006a) 'Labour disputes in 2005', *Labour Market Trends*, June. London: HMSO.

Beardsmore, R. (2006b) 'International comparisons of labour disputes in 2004', *Labour Market Trends*, April. London: HMSO.

Blyton, P. and Turnball, P. (2004) *The Dynamics of Employee Relations*. Basingstoke, Palgrave Macmillan.

Boeri, T., Brugiavani, A. and Calmfors, L. (eds) (2001) *The Role of Unions in the Twenty First Century*. Oxford: OUP.

Brown, W., Marginson, P. and Walsh, J. (2003) 'The management of pay as the influence of collective bargaining diminishes', in P. Edwards (ed.), *Industrial Relations: Theory and Practice*, 2nd edn. Oxford: Blackwell.

Bryson, A., Cappellari, L. and Lucifora, C. (2004) 'Does union membership really reduce job satisfaction?', *British Journal of Industrial Relations*, Vol. 42, No. 3, pp. 439–59.

Charlwood, A. (2003) 'Willingness to unionize amongst non-union workers', in H. Gospel and S. Wood (eds), *Representing Workers: union recognition and membership in Britain*. London: Routledge.

CIPD (2002) *Employment Law: Survey Report*. London: CIPD.

CIPD (2005) *What is Employee Relations?* London: CIPD.

DTI (2006) *Unions in 2005.* London: DTI.

Dunn, S. and Gennard, J. (1984) *The Closed Shop in British Industry.* London: Macmillan.

Edwards, P. (2005) 'The challenging but promising future of industrial relations: developing theory and method in context-sensitive research', *Industrial Relations Journal*, Vol. 36, No. 4, pp. 264–82.

Etzioni, A. (1961) *A Comparative Analysis of Complex Organisations.* New York: Free Press.

Freeman, R. and Diamond, W. (2003) 'Young workers and trade unions', in H. Gospel and S. Wood (eds), *Representing Workers: union recognition and membership in Britain.* London: Routledge.

Friedman, A. (1977) *Industry and Labour: Class struggle at work and monopoly capitalism.* London: Macmillan.

Gall, G. (2005) 'Union organising in the "new economy" in Britain', *Employee Relations*, Vol. 27, No. 2, pp. 208–25.

Gospel, H. and Wood, S. (eds) (2003) *Representing Workers: Union recognition and membership in Britain.* London: Routledge.

Guest, D. (2001) 'Industrial Relations and Human Resource Management', in J. Storey (ed.), *Human Resource Management: A Critical Text*, 2nd edn. London: Thomson Learning.

Guest, D. and Conway, N. (2004) 'Exploring the paradox of unionised worker dissatisfaction', *Industrial Relations Journal*, Vol. 35, No. 2, pp. 102–21.

IRS (2003) 'Part of the union', *IRS Employment Review*, No. 764, November. London: IRS.

IRS (2006a) 'HR Prospects 2006', *IRS Employment Trends*, No. 847. London: IRS.

IRS (2006b) 'Waiting for the backlash', *IRS Employment Trends*, No. 848. London: IRS.

Keenoy, T (1992) 'Constructing control', in J.F. Hartley and G.M. Stephenson (eds), *Employment Relations: The Psychology of Influence and Control at Work.* Oxford: Blackwell (pp. 91–110).

Kelly, J. (1998) *Rethinking Industrial Relations: mobilization, collectivism and long waves.* London: Routledge.

Kersley, B., Alpin, C., Forth, J., Bryson, A., Bewley, H., Dix, G. and Oxenbridge, S. (2006) *Inside the Workplace: Findings from the 2004 Workplace Employment Relations Survey.* Abingdon: Routledge.

Mackay, L.E. and Torrington, D.P. (1986) *The Changing Nature of the Personnel Function.* London: IPM.

Marchington, M. and Wilkinson, A. (2002) *People Management & Development.* London: CIPD.

Metcalf, D. (2005) 'Trade unions: resurgence or perdition? An economic analysis', in S. Fernie and D. Metcalf (eds), *Trade Unions: Resurgence or Demise?* London: Routledge.

Millward, N., Bryson, A. and Forth, J. (2000) *All Change at Work?* London: Routledge.

Prowse, P.J. and Prowse, J.M. (2006) 'Are non-union workers different to their union colleagues? Evidence from the public sevices', *Industrial Relations Journal*, Vol. 37, No. 3, pp. 222–41.

Purcell, J. and Sisson, K. (1983) 'Strategies and practice in the management of industrial relations', in G.S. Bain (ed.), *Industrial Relations in Britain.* Oxford: Blackwell.

Rubery, J. and Grimshaw, D. (2003) *The Organization of Employment: An International Perspective.* Basingstoke: Palgrave Macmillan.

Shore, L.M., Porter, L.W. and Zahra, S.A. (2004) 'Employer-oriented strategic approaches to the employee-organization relationship', in J.A. Coyle-Shapiro, L.M. Shore, S.M. Taylor and L.E. Tetrick (eds), *The Employment Relationship: Examining psychological and contextual perspectives.* Oxford: Oxford University Press.

Sisson, K. (2005) 'Responding to Mike Emmott: What "industrial relations" suggests should be at the heart of "employee relations"', **www.buira.org.uk**.

Stasek, F. (2005) 'Employee relations in the Czech Republic – past, present and future, *Employee Relations*, Vol. 27, No. 6, pp. 581–91.

Taylor, R. (1993) *The Trade Union Question in British Politics*. Oxford: Blackwell.

Taylor, R. (2001) *The Future of Employement Relations*. ESCR Future of Work Seminar Series.

Vissa, J. (2002) 'Why fewer workers join unions in Europe: a social custom explanation of membership trends', *British Journal of Industrial Relations*, Vol. 40, No. 3, pp. 403–30.

Waddington, J. (2003) 'Trade union organization', in P. Edwards (ed.), *Industrial Relations: Theory and Practice*. Oxford: Blackwell.

An extensive range of additional materials, including multiple choice questions, answers to questions and links to useful websites can be found on the Human Resource Management Companion Website at www.pearsoned.co.uk/torrington.

CHAPTER 21

EMPLOYEE INVOLVEMENT

THE OBJECTIVES OF THIS CHAPTER ARE TO:

1 Introduce the main methods used by employers to involve employees in decision making

2 Assess the extent of information sharing and its purpose

3 Outline the major ways in which employers are legally obliged to consult with employees

4 Set out the case for formal and informal consultation with employees and their representatives

5 Explore situations in which co-determination occurs in UK and overseas organisations

It is quite possible to run a successful business without involving employees in management activities to any meaningful extent, but the chances of sustained sucess are higher when employees are involved. The same is true of organisations in the public and voluntary sectors. Objectives are more effectively and efficiently achieved if employees have some say in decision-making, especially as it affects their own areas of work. This is for two principal reasons:

1 Managers may be paid more than their staff, have bigger offices and drive more expensive cars, but that does not mean that they always know best. There is no fount of wisdom exclusive only to managers. Ultimately it is for managers to make decisions and to be held accountable, and these can be tough to make. But the chances that they will make the right decision are enhanced if they listen to the views of others and allow their own ideas to be subjected to a degree of scrutiny and constructive criticism. Moreover, involvement allows managers to tap into the ideas and suggestions of staff. The best new ideas often originate from people lower down organisational hierarchies because they are closest to the operational coalface and often to customers.

2 Employees like being involved. They appreciate having their opinions listened to and acted upon, particularly in matters that directly concern their day-to-day activities. The chances of their being positively satisfied with their work are thus greatly improved if they are genuinely able to be involved. The knock-on effects include lower staff turnover, lower levels of absence, the ability to attract more recruits and higher levels of performance. The effective management of change is especially enhanced by employee involvement because people are always happier to support what they helped to create.

Employee involvement activity comes in many different forms. It can be formal or informal, direct or indirect, one-off or sustained over time, central to an organisation's core business or relatively peripheral. In recent years the number and extent of such programmes has increased. This is partly due to the requirements of the law and partly because they have a part to play in many of the more common, contemporary human resource management initiatives we have discussed elsewhere in this book – becoming an 'employer of choice', 360-degree appraisal, employee engagement, knowledge management and total quality management (TQM) programmes.

Our aim in this chapter is to discuss the major forms employee involvement takes, to set out the legal obligations, explore the difficulties that can be experienced in the implementation of initiatives and to evaluate their contribution to the achievement of an organisation's objectives.

TERMINOLOGY

A variety of labels are used to describe employee involvement initiatives singly and collectively. While some writers have sought to make distinctions between them, there is no generally accepted usage. Hence you will read not just about 'involvement', but also about 'employee participation', 'industrial democracy', 'empowerment' and, in the most recent literature, about 'employee voice'. Each of these terms differs subtly and suggests a different perspective, but all to a greater or lesser extent are used to describe a situation in which employees are given, gain or develop a degree of *influence* over what happens in an organisation. The extent and nature of that influence, however, varies considerably.

Marchington and Wilkinson (2000, p. 343) helpfully distinguish between the major categories of involvement with their 'escalator' model. The focus here is on the extent of influence. At the bottom of the escalator are organisations where there is no involvement at all, managers taking all decisions without taking any meaningful account of what employees might think. By contrast, at the top of the escalator are organisations or parts of organisations which are controlled by employees rather than by a distinct group of managers. Employee control is very rare in the UK at the level of the organisation, although there are one or two examples of companies which are communally owned and run by staff in a partnership arrangement. However, a substantial degree of control is much more often exercised by employees at the level of an individual department or team within a larger organisation.

WINDOW ON PRACTICE

Loch Fyne Oysters is an example of a very successful company which is owned by its employees.

Based at the head of Loch Fyne in Argyll, the company runs the largest oyster farm in the UK, a mussel farm, a smokehouse for the processing of salmon, a world-famous restaurant and a shop. Products are sold to retailers, hotels and restaurants in 22 countries. The company employs 120 people and has a turnover of £11 million. It was founded in 1977 by a local landowner and a biologist, Johnnie Noble and Andy Lane, who built it up steadily over 25 years. When Mr Noble died suddenly in 2003 at a time when the company needed an injection of funds, it was put on the market. The company would have been taken over by a large corporation had Andy Lane not found a way of securing the necessary funds while also transferring ownership to the employees.

This was achieved by entering into an agreement with the Baxi Trust which invested £2 million to buy 50 per cent of the shares, with the promise of a 7 per cent return for 15 years. The shares are held in an employee trust. Each year a number are purchased using the company's profits and distributed among staff with more than three years' service. Further shares are also purchased by the trust each year, so that over time the company will become owned in its entirety by its staff. No one is permitted to own more than 5 per cent of the company, while two board members are elected by the staff. Loch Fyne Oysters is run like any other company, except that there is necessarily more emphasis placed on communicating, consulting and involving employees in decision making. Openness with staff, together with increased development opportunities, has led to improved customer service, increased staff morale and a substantial improvement in productivity.

In between 'no involvement' and 'employee control', there are three further stages, each in turn representing a deepening of the extent of involvement. The first is 'communication', signalling a very limited degree of involvement. At this stage employer and employees simply exchange information. Managers disclose defined classes of information, ensuring that employees are aware of the decisions they are taking, the economic situation and their objectives. Employees are also given an opportunity to respond, to voice concerns or put their own ideas forward. But decision making remains exclusively in the management realm. The next step up the escalator is 'consultation'. Here information is exchanged, often through formalised channels. Decision making is still the responsibility of managers, but full and proper consideration is given to the views expressed by staff (or their elected representatives) before key decisions are taken. Finally, a further step up the escalator takes us to co-determination or joint decision making. This is relatively rare in a formal sense in the UK, although it happens informally all the time. But it is very common indeed in Northern European countries where the law requires the agreement of a works council before significant decisions affecting employment can be taken.

At each of these stages involvement initiatives can be either direct or indirect in nature. The term 'direct involvement' relates to situations in which managers enter into a dialogue with, consult with or co-determine decisions with employees as individuals. People thus have a direct input in some shape or form. By contrast, the term 'indirect employee involvement' refers to a situation in which employers take account of employee views through the filter of a representative institution. This may be a trade union, or it may be another kind of body such as a works council, a working party or a consultative committee. Either way, direct involvement is restricted to representatives of the workforce as a collective group.

Academic research into employee involvement often encompasses payment arrangements such as profit sharing and employee share ownership schemes which are referred to as types of 'financial participation'. These help to develop a community of interest between employers and their staff and can lead to situations in which individual employees cast votes at annual general meetings. We will discuss them in Chapter 29. The remainder of this chapter will focus on the major information-sharing, consultation and co-determination initiatives.

INFORMATION SHARING

According to the 2004 Workplace Employment Relations Survey formal systems of communication between managers and employees are present in the vast majority of UK organisations (Kersley *et al.* 2006, p. 135). In many cases, however, the communication is carried out at the local level (e.g. line managers meeting with employees individually), there being no formal mechanisms provided for more senior managers to communicate directly with their staff or vice versa. Moreover, where a degree of formality is reported it can be limited simply to the posting of important data on noticeboards or ad hoc circulation of information by e-mail. As a result, a substantial minority of UK employees are reported to believe that they are not kept informed about what their companies are doing (45 per cent) or are not even given sufficient information to do their jobs effectively (35 per cent) (ORC International 2004, cited by IRS 2005a).

The extent to which the disclosure of information by managers can be regarded as a form of employee involvement is debatable. After all, merely being told about an organisation's plans or its financial results does not in any way give employees influence. Nonetheless it can help to make employees feel a sense of involvement or at least of inclusion in the circle of those 'in the know'. It also enables employees, either individually or collectively, to exercise informal influence locally, simply because they are in a position to develop and articulate credible alternative approaches to those their immediate line managers would otherwise impose. Alternatively they are in a position to help improve or refine their strategies. It is often rightly stated that 'knowledge is power' and it therefore follows that spreading relevant knowledge beyond the ranks of management to employees is an empowering activity. This is why managers will frequently hold back information from their staff while also letting it be known that they are doing so. Except in a crisis situation in which there is a need to promote calm and keep everyone focused on their jobs, often no conceivable damage would be done to the organisation by disclosing the information; labelling it 'confidential' and refusing to disclose it serves to enhance managers' own sense of personal authority and power.

However reluctant line managers may be to share information to which they are privy, there is substantial evidence to back up the view that regular, extensive information sharing has positive outcomes for organisations. This occurs because it improves levels of commitment among staff (*see* Peccei *et al*. 2005) and because in a practical sense it helps everyone to clarify what their role is in the wider organisation. It thus enhances communication and coordination across divisions. It also helps to prevent false understanding developing among staff thanks to the inevitable 'rumour mills' that operate in all organisations.

Two-way communication, by contrast, especially when it takes the form of a formal exercise, clearly falls into the category of employee involvement. Staff are being asked to respond to a suggested new approach, asked their opinion, being invited to make suggestions for improvements or given an opportunity to point out flaws in current systems or management thinking. Provided the exercise is not merely cosmetic, and that the views of staff are given serious consideration, influence is gained. The following are some of the most common methods of information sharing.

Team briefing

Team briefing is an initiative that attempts to do a number of different things simultaneously. It provides authoritative information at regular intervals, so that people know what is going on, the information is geared to achievement of production targets and other features of organisational objectives, it is delivered face to face to provide scope for questions and clarification, and it emphasises the role of supervisors and line managers as the source of information:

> Team briefings are often used to cascade information or managerial messages throughout the organisation. The teams are usually based round a common production or service area, rather than an occupation, and usually comprise between four and fifteen people. The leader of the team is usually the manager or supervisor of the section and should be trained in the principles and skills of how to brief. The meetings last for no more than 30 minutes, and time should be left for questions from employees. Meetings should be held at least monthly or on a regular pre-arranged basis. (Holden 1997, p. 624)

With goodwill and managerial discipline, team briefing can be a valuable contributor to employee involvement, as it deals in that precious commodity, information. Traditionally, there has perhaps been a managerial view that people doing the work are not interested in anything other than the immediate and short term and that the manager's status partly rests on knowing what others do not know. For this reason all the managers and supervisors in the communications chain have to be committed to making it a success, as well as having the training that Holden refers to above.

Team briefing gets easier once it is established as a regular event. The first briefing will probably go very well and the second will be even better. It is important that management enthusiasm and commitment do not flag just as the employees are getting used to the process.

> During economic recessions there is a boost to the team briefing process because so many managements have so much bad news to convey. When you are losing money and profitability, there is a great incentive to explain to the workforce exactly how grim the situation is, so that they do not look for big pay rises. Whatever the economic climate, team briefing continues to be used widely and was found to operate in a majority of organisations featured in the 2004 WER Survey. (Kersley *et al.* 2006, p. 135)
>
> Sometimes, instead of cascading information down a management hierarchy, senior managers in larger organisations like to brief larger groups of employees about significant developments directly. Roadshows or 'interactive executive sessions' of this kind are common and are seen by managers as being almost as effective a means of passing information to employees as more conventional forms of team-briefing. (IRS 2005, p. 11)

Quality circles

Originating in Japanese firms, quality circles comprise small groups of employees (10–15 maximum) who meet regularly to generate ideas aimed at improving the quality of products and services and of organisational productivity. They can also be used as problem-solving groups and as a means by which employee opinion is transmitted to senior management. Some quality circles consist of staff who work together within a team or organisational function, others are cross-functional and focus on interdepartmental issues.

> These sorts of practice have several objectives, such as to increase the stock of ideas within an organisation, to encourage co-operative relations at work, and to legitimise change. These practices are predicated on the assumption that employees are recognised as a (if not the) major source of competitive advantage for organisations, a source whose ideas have been ignored in the past or who have been told that 'they are not paid to think'. (Marchington 2001, p. 235)

Not only, therefore, are quality circles a potential source of useful ideas for improving systems and saving costs. They also give people a welcome opportunity to contribute their thoughts and experience. A general positive impact on employee attitudes should thus result.

News sheets

Another common form of employee involvement occurs through the regular publication of in-house journals or news sheets either in paper or electronic form. On one level they simply provide a means by which information concerning finances, policy and proposed change can be transmitted by managers to employees. This is a limited form of employee involvement which does little more than improve the extent to which employees are informed about what is going on elsewhere in their organisations. This will engender a perception of greater involvement and belonging, but does not directly involve employees in any type of decision making. For that to occur the news sheet must be interactive in some way. It may, for example, be used as a means by which employees are consulted about new initiatives, or may provide a forum through which complaints and ideas are voiced.

Attitude surveys

Regular surveys of employee opinion are very useful from a management point of view, particularly where there are no unions present to convey to management an honest picture of morale and commitment in the organisation. In order to be effective (that is, honest), responses must be anonymous, individuals stating only which department they work in so that interdepartmental comparisons can be made. It also makes sense to ask the same questions in the same format each time a survey is carried out, so that changes in attitude and/or responses to initiatives can be tracked over time.

The major problems with attitude surveys are associated with situations in which they reveal serious problems which are then not properly addressed. This can easily lead to cynicism and even anger on the part of the workforce. The result is a poorer employee relations climate than would have been the case had no survey taken place. It is counter-productive to involve employees if their contribution is subsequently ignored, yet this appears to happen in many of the organisations where regular surveys are conducted. IRS (2005b) found that the main reasons employers in their sample gave for carrying out employee surveys were to 'take the pulse of the organisation' and to 'demonstrate commitment to employee views'. Only a minority subsequently used the information gathered to shape decision making, even in the HR arena.

Suggestion schemes

A common system of formal bottom-up communication employed by organisations involves encouraging staff to make suggestions as to how practices and processes could be improved to make them more effective, efficient or safe. Employees are often best placed to observe in detail what happens operationally on the front-line because they have the greatest level of interaction on a day-to-day basis with customers, equipment and organisational procedures. Managers often only become aware of problems when their employees report them, and without such reports can have no opportunities for improving things. So it makes sense to encourage staff to put forward suggestions; and having a formal scheme enhances the chances that they will do so. IDS (2005a) describes several types of scheme and draws together from these examples some good practice points. IDS argues that employees should be be recognised financially or otherwise when they make a suggestion which is taken up, that systems for submitting ideas should be as uncomplicated as possible, that feedback should be given to all who submit ideas, that past suggestions should be revisited periodically and that schemes must be regularly publicised to remind staff of their existence. IDS also found that organisations are increasingly benefiting from schemes which operate electronically. Suggestions are submitted via e-mail or a form placed on an intranet and filed systematically by an evaluator. Feedback is then given electronically and the successes of the whole scheme publicised regularly through e-mail bulletins sent to all staff.

ACTIVITY 21.1

Despite plenty of evidence that demonstrates how beneficial two-way information sharing can be for organisations, only a minority of non-union employers operate formal systems. Why do you think this is? What are the likely consequences? What arguments would you use to persuade a team of managers of the need to listen to the views of staff and to take them seriously?

CONSULTATION

After information sharing, the next step up the 'employee involvement escalator' is consultation. Here employees are asked either directly, or through representatives to express views which management take into account when making decisions. Such processes fall short of negotiation or co-determination because there is no ultimate expectation of agreement if the views of staff and management diverge. In some organisations regular meetings are held to enable consultation to take place about a wide range of issues. In others consultation exercises take place irregularly and focus on specific areas such as organisational restructuring or policy changes. Consultation is generally regarded as a hallmark of good management. An employer who fails to consult properly, particularly at times of significant change, is likely to be perceived as being unduly autocratic. The result will be dissatisfaction, low levels of motivation, higher staff turnover and poorer levels of customer service. Moreover, consultation has important advantages as a means by which good ideas are brought forward and weak ones challenged.

In workplaces where unions are recognised it is usual for consultation to take place over a range of issues through permanent consultative institutions. The joint consultative committee (JCC) is the most common form, being a forum in which managers and staff representatives meet on a regular basis. In more traditional unionised organisations JCCs are kept distinct from negotiating forums – despite the fact that the membership is often the same. A clear divide is thus established between areas which are to be the subject of negotiation (typically terms and conditions of employment) and matters which are the subject of consultation such as health and safety or training. In recent years as partnership agreements have become more common (*see* Chapter 20), there has been a shift from negotiation towards consultation, the aim being to downplay the adversarial nature of the union–employer relationship and to widen the range of topics about which both sides can engage constructively.

JCCs are only found in 14 per cent of UK workplaces employing over ten people, but they are present in a majority of those employing over two hundred (Kersey *et al.* 2006, pp. 126–7). It is unusual for the very largest workplaces not to have some form of consultative forum which meets periodically, although in some multi-site corporations formal consultation with employee representatives is restricted to the corporate level and does not take place in individual workplaces. JCCs are four times as common in union workplaces than in those where unions are not recognised (Kersley *et al.* 2006, p. 127), suggesting that they are mostly still used in parallel with collective bargaining machinery. However, some researchers (e.g. Marchington 1989 and Kelly 1998) have argued that they are used in some workplaces as a substitute for collective bargaining or as a means of discouraging the development of a union presence. Managers in such workplaces believe that unions are less likely to gain support and request recognition if the employer keeps the staff informed of issues that affect them and consults with them before taking decisions. Consultative forums in non-union firms also provide a means whereby managers can put their case effectively without the presence of organised opposition.

From a management perspective, the great danger is that people come to believe that management is not genuinely interested in hearing their views or in taking them on board. Rose (2001, p. 391) refers to this approach as 'pseudo-consultation' in which managers are really doing little more than informing employees about decisions that have already been taken. Cynicism results because there is perceived to be an attempt on the part of managers to use consultative forums merely as a means of legitimising their decisions. They can say that consultation has taken place, when in truth it has not. Pseudo-consultation typically involves assembling employees in large groups with senior managers present. The management message is then put across strongly and a short time is given for others to respond. In such situations employees have no time to give proper consideration to the proposals and are likely to feel too intimidated to articulate criticisms. The result is often worse in terms of employee morale and engagement with the changes than would have been the case had no consultation been attempted.

Even where managers genuinely intend to undertake meaningful consultation, they can very easily create an impression that it is no more than a 'pseudo' exercise. It is therefore important to avoid the approaches outlined in the above paragraph. Employees should be informed of a range of possible ways forward (not just the one favoured by management) and invited to consider them in small groups. The results of their deliberations can then be fed back to senior managers and given proper consideration. In this way the appearance of pseudo-consultation, as well as the reality, can be avoided.

WINDOW ON PRACTICE

IRS (2006) describe how a marketing company called BI increased its profitability and halved its staff turnover, in part by introducing a range of employee involvement initiatives. The early years had seen company revenues decline markedly, leading to a pay freeze and staff turnover of 60 per cent.

In 2004, following the appointment of a new chief executive and HR director, a wide range of measures were introduced to tackle these problems. Improving employee involvement was a priority, to signal very clearly the adoption of a new management style, to promote a positive culture and to encourage staff to identify problems and possible solutions. The initiatives included the following:

- weekly e-mail bulletins to staff from senior managers explaining major developments;
- annual letters to staff from the MD thanking them and setting out key achievements;
- quarterly company meetings at which all staff are briefed about financial matters and strategy;
- an intranet site updated daily with fresh information about the company's activities;
- monthly meetings at which the HR director talks in confidence to 10 randomly selected employees about their concerns;
- regular meetings of a 'people forum' at which representatives from each team are consulted about developments.

As a result of these involvement activities many changes were made to operational processes and also to HR practices. Hours of work were made more flexible, and staff discouraged from working more hours than was necessary. A scheme was also introduced to allow people to trade some of their salary for additional holiday.

THE LEGAL DUTY TO CONSULT

In most Western European countries it has long been the case that employers must consult formally with representatives of their workforce about significant matters which affect employment prospects and practices. A legal requirement to consult at certain times has thus become a part of European employment regulation and has accordingly found its way into UK employment law. In this context the term 'consultation' means formally talking to employee representatives with a view to reaching agreement. There is no obligation on employers to negotiate or to conclude any formal deal, but an attempt must be made in good faith. The major examples are as follows.

Redundancy

Where an employer proposes to make 20 or more people redundant there is an obligation to consult when formal proposals are drawn up. Where a union or unions are recognised, consultation must be with their representatives. In non-union organisations the obligation is to consult with representatives chosen by all relevant sections of the affected workforce. The aim of the consultation is to find ways of avoiding redundancies and/or to mitigate the consequences. Consultation should take place over issues such as the proposed selection procedure, the method used to determine the pool of affected employees and the basis on which redundancy payments are to be calculated.

Transfer of undertakings

The same regulations covering redundancies apply in transfer of undertakings cases (namely, situations in which one organisation is taken over by another, usually as a result of a sale). Consultation is a requirement placed on both the transferor and transferee companies. The duty to consult extends to representatives of employees whose work or conditions will be directly affected by the transfer. There is a more general duty to inform representatives of other workers about the reasons for the transfer and its longer-term implications.

Health and safety

Under the Health and Safety (Consultation with Employees) Regulations 1996 employers have a general duty to consult with worker representatives about all health and safety matters. Here too the obligation is to consult with trade union appointed safety representatives wherever a union is formally recognised. In other organisations employers can either consult with the workforce directly or set up a health and safety committee to which employee representatives are elected. There are specific duties to consult 'in good time' on the introduction of any measure (e.g. new technology or working arrangement) which substantially affects health and safety, and on procedural arrangements for managing health and safety issues.

Pensions

Recognised unions must be consulted where an employer proposes that its occupational pension should 'contract out' of the State Earnings Related Pension Scheme (*see* Chapter 29). They also have the right to receive on request information concerning a pension scheme's rules and membership numbers, as well as copies of its accounts and actuarial valuations.

Workplace agreements

Two recent pieces of legislation originating in Europe provide employers with the opportunity to determine their local application via workplace agreements. These are the Working Time Regulations 1998 and the Maternity and Parental Leave etc. Regulations 1999 (as they apply to parental leave). In both cases the basic rights are set out together with a 'default scheme' which contains more detailed rules on their application. However, employers are permitted to develop their own local rules to replace the government's default scheme, provided these are agreed through a formal workplace agreement. Where unions are recognised this can be achieved using established collective bargaining machinery. Otherwise the employer needs either to secure the explicit agreement of a majority of employees or to arrange for representatives to be elected to a consultative forum.

European Works Councils

Since 2001 European Works Councils (or an equivalent type of body) have to be set up in all 'community scale undertakings', defined as organisations which employ over 1,000 people in the European Union and including at least 150 in two EU states. The major requirements are as follows:

- Councils must have between three and 30 members.
- These individuals must be elected to the council by the workforce.

- Council meetings are to be held annually and at such meetings the management are obliged to give reports concerning progress, prospects, the financial situation and plans relating to sales, production, employment, investment and/or the corporate structure.

- Special meetings are to be held in 'exceptional' circumstances when, for example, large-scale redundancies or plant relocations are being contemplated.

- Councils have the right to be informed and consulted about 'any measure liable to have a considerable effect on employees' interests'.

- Only matters that are 'community scale' need be discussed. There is no legal requirement to cover affairs affecting employees in only one EU country.

The Information and Consultation Regulations

A new EU directive extending information and consultation rights was agreed in March 2002, its aim being to extend some of the principles associated with European Works Councils to all workplaces employing 50 or more people. It has been introduced into UK law in three stages.

Since 2005 workplaces employing over 150 staff have had to comply. The requirement was extended to those employing over 100 in 2007 and to those employing over 50 in 2008.

The regulations require that workers in qualifying workplaces should regularly receive information from their employers and be consulted on all issues which affect their interests, these being defined as anything which affects employment prospects, changes in work organisation or substantial changes in terms and conditions of employment. However, there is no need to negotiate, still less to establish, formal arrangements of this kind unless 10 per cent of the staff employed in a workplace formally request their establishment.

Employers and employee representatives are free to establish arrangements that suit local circumstances. Where there are existing consultation arrangements in place changes only need be introduced following a ballot of employees, following the same rules as exist currently for union recognition (i.e. a majority vote including at least 40 per cent of the electorate). The regulations set out the default arrangements that apply where management and workforce are unable to reach agreement about another system. The major features are as follows:

- Appointment to an information and consultation committee is via election, a secret ballot of all employees being held.

- The maximum number of representatives is 25, one person being elected for every 50 employees.

- Management are required to *provide information* to the committee in three areas:
  - (a) the recent and probable development of the undertaking's activities and economic situation;
  - (b) the situation, structure and probable development of employment; – and
  - (c) about any threats to employment and decisions likely to lead to substantial changes in work organisation or contractual relations.

- Management are required to *consult* the committee on items (b) and (c) above, namely employment and work organisation.

Once established, the committee itself determines how and in what way, if any, it wants to move away from the default scheme – this can be achieved if management and a majority of members agree. You will find further information and discussion exercises about the Information and Consultation Regulations on this book's companion website **www.pearsoned.co.uk/torrington**.

ACTIVITY 21.2

The UK government is known to have opposed the extension of works councils beyond community-scale undertakings and sought, with other countries, to block the Information and Consultation Directive. Why do you think this might have been? What arguments could be put for and against requiring all substantial UK employers to operate works councils?

CO-DETERMINATION

In the UK, important decision making in organisations is nearly always the preserve of managers. Decisions in the employment area are often taken after extensive and genuine consultation, or after negotiation with union representatives, but anything approaching serious co-determination with employees is very rare indeed. Nevertheless, it must be pointed out that at the level of the individual team, a degree of informal co-determination is common. Indeed, in recent years it has become more common as organisations have tended to de-layer, reducing the number of managers and levels of hierarchy. Increasingly employees and team leaders have found themselves 'empowered' to take decisions for themselves that once they would have had to refer to a manager. It is important not to overestimate the significance of this trend, as any discretion that is given operates within tightly defined boundaries. What gets done is still determined by managers, but there is greater flexibility about when and how exactly it gets done.

The limitations are well illustrated by the following findings from the 2004 Workplace Employment Relations Survey (Kersley *et al.* 2006, pp. 89–90):

- 72 per cent of workplaces employ people to work in 'formally designated teams';
- 83 per cent of these teams are given responsibility for products or services;
- in 61 per cent of these teams members jointly decide how work is done;
- in 66 per cent of these teams tasks are rotated among members;
- in only 6 per cent of these teams are team members able to choose their own leader.

Elsewhere in Europe the extent of co-determination at the level of the team and of individual empowerment varies from country to country. In southern European nations such as France, Italy and Spain managers at the local level tend to guard their autonomy more tightly than typical British line managers. Co-determination at the local level over day-to-day workplace activities is thus rarer than in the UK. In northern Europe, by contrast, a far greater degree of team-based autonomy is common. The best-known examples of teams assuming responsibility and decision-making authority are in the

Scandinavian countries. The approach involves organising a workforce into small groups of about a dozen members, who are mutually supportive and who operate with minimal supervision. Management set performance targets (often after consultation) and allocate tasks, but it is for the team itself to decide exactly how these are to be achieved. The team organises its own activities, appoints its own leaders and works out for itself how to overcome problems. Teamworking can thus be characterised as a form of worker control, even though it operates within heavily prescribed limits. Managers refrain from giving day-to-day supervision, but are on hand to give advice or more direct assistance where necessary. Disciplining staff, for example, is a task carried out by managers and not by team members. Teamworking is often associated with situations in which several regionally based teams compete with each other to meet or exceed performance targets. Team-based remuneration then accounts for a proportion of the total pay received.

While practice varies at the local team level across Europe, at the level of the organisation co-determination is a great deal more established and widespread in most countries than is the case in the UK. It occurs through two distinct mechanisms:

1 through the legal empowerment of works councils or enterprise committees

2 by reserving places on executive boards for worker directors

Both approaches are famously used in Germany, where co-determination over employment matters is standard practice in organisations of any size. In the UK most of the activities described in this book are the preserve of managers, while in Germany they are decided jointly between managers and workforce representatives. German managers cannot impose any decision relating to changing workplace rules, disciplinary procedures, working hours, holidays, bonus payments, overtime arrangements, health and safety matters, training or selection methods without first securing the agreement of their organisation's works council. Moreover, their autonomy to make decisions about any changes relating to the nature of the work their employees do or the physical environment in which it is performed is subject to them first consulting with the works council and taking its objections and suggestions into account. In addition the law requires that managers share a great deal of financial and planning information with works councils that goes well beyond the employment sphere (Budd 2004, p. 129). Seats are also reserved on the supervisory boards of German companies for workforce representatives. In the case of companies employing more than 500 people, a third of the seats are reserved. Where over 2,000 are employed, half the seats are taken by worker representatives. You will find further information and discussion exercises about variations in the way employee relations is managed internationally on our companion website, **www.pearsoned.co.uk /torrington.**

ACTIVITY 21.3

In many European companies works councils or enterprise committees tend to be dominated by trade unions, even where a majority of the staff are not members. Why do you think this is? What do you think are the major advantages and disadvantages of trade union representatives also acting as works council members or worker directors?

SUMMARY PROPOSITIONS

21.1 Genuine employee involvement serves to increase commitment and to improve decision making in organisations.

21.2 Information sharing is common in the UK. Team briefing, news sheets and suggestion schemes are the most common mechanisms adopted.

21.3 The use of formal consultation processes is common in larger UK organisations. Joint Consultative Committees are found in most unionised workplaces.

21.4 Employers are obliged by law to consult collectively with their employees about specific employment-oriented issues, and where there is sufficient demand, about a wide variety of such issues.

21.5 Co-determination at the level of the organisation or workplace is rare in the UK, but common in many other EU countries.

21.6 Co-determination at the level of teams is increasing in the UK, but is limited in the extent to which it empowers employees.

GENERAL DISCUSSION TOPICS

1 Why do you think employers in the UK are more reluctant to involve employee representatives in strategic decision making than is the case in a country such as Germany?

2 How far do you agree with the view that information sharing barely constitutes employee involvement at all?

3 In what ways would you like to see increased or decreased employee involvement in your organisation, and why?

FURTHER READING

IDS (2005) *Information and Consultation Arrangements*, IDS Study No. 790. London: IDS.
An excellent summary of good practice and legal obligations which is particularly informative about the practical consequences of the Information and Consultation with Employees Regulations. Seven detailed case studies are provided to illustrate the approaches taken by some major UK companies.

Dundon, T. *et al.* (2005) 'The management of voice in non-union organisations: managers' perspectives', *Employee Relations*, Vol. 27, No. 3, pp. 307–19.
In this article Tony Dundon and his colleagues explore the views of managers about the role played by consultative fora in seven non-union organisations. They conclude that commentators have often been too hasty to dismiss these practices as inconsequential or ineffective.

Storey, J. (ed.) (2005) *Adding Value through Information and Consultation*. Basingstoke: Palgrave Macmillan/Open University.
Harley, B., Hyman, J. and Thompson, P. (2005) *Participation and Democracy at Work: Essays in Honour of Harvie Ramsay*. Basingstoke: Palgrave Macmillan.

Two books of articles by leading academic researchers which between them cover every aspect of informing, consulting and involving employees.

REFERENCES

Budd, J. (2004) *Employment with a Human Face*. Ithaca, NY: Cornell University Press.

Dundon, T., Wilkinson, A., Marchington, M. and Ackers, P. (2005) 'The management of voice in non-union organisations: managers' perspectives', *Employee Relations*, Vol. 27, No. 3, pp. 307–19.

Harley, B., Hyman, J. and Thompson, P. (2005) *Participation and Democracy at Work: Essays in Honour of Harvie Ramsay*. Basingstoke: Palgrave Macmillan.

Holden, L. (1997) 'Employee Involvement', in I. Beardwell and L. Holden (eds), *Human Resource Management*, 2nd edn. London: Pitman.

IDS (2005a) *Suggestion Schemes*, IDS Study No. 812. London: IDS.

IDS (2005b) *Information and Consultation Arrangements*, IDS Study No. 790. London: IDS.

IRS (2005a) 'Dialogue or monologue: is the message getting through?', *IRS Employment Review* No. 834, October. London: IRS.

IRS (2005b) 'More questions than answers? Employee surveys revealed', *IRS Employment Review* No. 820, March. London: IRS.

IRS (2006) 'BI bounces back with culture of employee engagement', *IRS Employment Review* No. 839. January. London: IRS.

Kelly, J. (1998) *Rethinking Industrial Relations: mobilization, collectivism and long waves*. London: Routledge.

Kersley, B., Alpin, C., Forth, J., Bryson, A., Bewley, H., Dix, G. and Oxenbridge, S. (2006) *Inside the Workplace: Findings from the 2004 Workplace Employment Relations Survey*. Abingdon: Routledge.

Marchington, M. (1989) 'Joint consultation in practice', in K. Sisson (ed.), *Personnel Management in Britain*. Oxford: Blackwell.

Marchington, M. (2001) 'Employee Involvement at Work', in J. Storey (ed.) *Human Resource Management: A Critical Text*, 2nd edn. London: Thomson Learning.

Marchington, M. and Wilkinson, A. (2000) 'Direct Participation', in S. Bach and K. Sisson (eds), *Personnel Management*, 3rd edn., Oxford: Blackwell, p. 343.

Peccei, R., Bewley, H., Gospel, G. and Willman, P. (2005) 'Is it good to talk? Information disclosure and organisational performance in the UK', *British Journal of Industrial Relations*, Vol. 43, No. 1, pp. 11–39.

Rose, E. (2001) *Employee Relations*. London: Financial Times/Prentice Hall.

Storey, J. (ed.) (2005) *Adding Value through Information and Consultation*. Basingstoke: Palgrave Macmillan/Open University.

An extensive range of additional materials, including multiple choice questions, answers to questions and links to useful websites can be found on the Human Resource Management Companion Website at **www.pearsoned.co.uk/torrington**.

CHAPTER 22

HEALTH, SAFETY AND WELFARE

THE OBJECTIVES OF THIS CHAPTER ARE TO:

1 Define the terms health, safety and welfare and the role they play in HRM

2 Explain the framework of criminal law in the health and safety field and its enforcement

3 Assess the increased role played by the civil law in health and safety management, particularly in respect of stress at work

4 Outline the major methods available to improve emotional welfare among staff

5 Identify the major processes used to prevent physical injuries from occurring in the workplace

6 Describe the role that can be played by an occupational health function

There is always a conflict between the needs of the employer to push for increased output and efficiency and the needs of the employee to be protected from the hazards of the workplace. In the mid-nineteenth century these tensions centred almost entirely on the long hours and heavy physical demands of the factory system. In the opening years of the twenty-first century the tensions are more varied and more subtle, but concern about them remains as great, being expressed by employers, employees, trade unions, government agencies and campaign groups. As international competitive pressures become greater and employers respond by giving employees incentives to work harder and faster there is an inevitable temptation to cut corners with safety and a greater tendency for employees to suffer from stress-related illnesses.

Increasingly, aspects of protection are being provided by statute, much new legislation having a European origin. The most recent major addition is the body of measures contained in the Working Time Regulations 1998 which aim to reduce the number of hours we work each week, while also guaranteeing everyone a minimum period of paid holiday each year. In addition some aspects result from the initiatives of managements, employees and their representatives. No matter what the source of the initiative or the nature of the concern, the human resource manager is often the focus of whatever action has to be taken.

HRM AND HEALTH, SAFETY AND WELFARE

The development of health, safety and welfare provision is to a large extent interrelated with the development of human resource management itself. As mentioned in Chapter 1, one of the early influences on the development of the profession was the growth of industrial welfare workers at the beginning of the twentieth century. Enlightened employers gradually began to improve working conditions for employees and the industrial welfare worker was often concerned in implementing these changes. Much of this work was carried out voluntarily by employers, although not necessarily from altruistic motives alone. Another influence was that of the 'human relations school', in particular the work of Elton Mayo at the Hawthorne plant of the Western Electric Company. Here there was an employee counselling programme, which operated from 1936 to 1955. It was found that such a programme was beneficial for both the mental health of the employees and their work.

More recently the state has stepped in by requiring employers to take reasonable steps to protect the health and safety of employees and by providing an inspectorate charged with helping to ensure that they do so in practice. Some aspects of welfare provision, particularly in respect of safety, such as limitations on the hours of work of children, were enshrined in the law from as early as the 1840s. But it is only since the passing of the Health and Safety Act 1974 that a comprehensive regime covering all workplaces has been in place. During the 1980s and 1990s health and safety at work increasingly became subject to European Union directives and regulations, the result being greater complexity and more extensive obligations for employers. Except in workplaces with particularly high safety risks where a specialised function has been established, the human resource department has taken on the role of advising managers on the organisation's legal obligations.

The importance of health, safety and welfare from the employees' point of view is clear because their lives and futures are at risk. Health and safety has thus been given increasing emphasis by the trade unions in recent years and has been covered more extensively in the media. Two major developments in recent years are discernible:

1 A shift in emphasis from concern about the prevention of physical injury towards a focus on mental health and work-related stress.

2 The development of the view that employers should take steps not just to prevent injury and unnecessary stress, but actively to seek to promote healthy lifestyles in a more general sense.

A convincing business case for addressing these issues has been articulated in the human resource management press, while the Health and Safety Executive campaigns vigorously to raise awareness of its validity among employers. The business case is based on three propositions:

- Illness and injury which is work related leads to avoidable absence.

- Serious injury and illness can lead to litigation and substantial compensation being paid out by employing organisations.

- A poor reputation for safety and welfare makes it harder for an organisation to recruit, retain and motivate its staff.

The number of serious injuries sustained at work by UK employees fluctuates substantially each year. The level has dropped considerably since the 1970s with the fall in manufacturing employment, but the total number remains much higher than it should be. In the year to April 2006, for example, 212 people lost their lives in the UK as a result of accidents sustained at work, mostly as result of falls and motor vehicle accidents (HSC 2006). It is further estimated that around 5,000 people die each year from cancers caused by working conditions (mainly resulting from the inhalation of chemicals, fumes and dusts). In addition, over two million people are reported by the Health and Safety Executive to suffer from some form of work-related illness each year (HSE 2006). In 2004–5 35 million working days were lost in the UK due to injuries and illnesses sustained at work, a third of these being due to stress, depression or anxiety (HSC 2005). The total cost to employers runs to several billion pounds a year, including the costs associated with the early retirement of around 30,000 employees forced to give up work on grounds of ill health. If the number of incidents were reduced by only a small percentage, employers would thus save a considerable amount of money and trouble.

The reason that the numbers remain so high is the continual conflict between health, safety and welfare considerations and other business priorities. Leach (1995) reports a line manager who had previously been a safety officer as saying: 'I think in general managers don't see [health and safety issues] [being] as important as . . . other issues [on which they would take disciplinary action]. I mean you do take short cuts, I do myself. I mean I am not practising a lot of what I used to preach, there's no doubt about it. Managers know it is a part of their job, but I don't think they personally see [health and safety offences] as an offence as such.' You will find further information and discussion exercises about encouraging higher standards of health and safety management on our companion website, **www.pearsoned.co.uk/torrington**.

ACTIVITY 22.1

How convincing do you find the business case for the maintenance of a high level of health and safety? What additional arguments, other than those outlined here, could be deployed either for or against its validity in different workplaces?

HEALTH AND SAFETY LAW

In the area of health and safety legislative intervention has existed continuously for well over a century, longer than for any other matter we consider. Prior to 1974 the principal statutes were the Factories Act 1961, the Offices, Shops and Railway Premises Act 1963 and the Fire Precautions Act 1971. These three Acts, along with others relating to specific industries, were all brought up to date by the Health and Safety at Work etc. Act 1974 which remains the major statute governing the law in this area. In addition there are a host of health and safety regulations primarily extending the Health and Safety Act to expand specific areas of the legislation, the most significant of which are the Control of Substances Hazardous to Health (COSHH) Regulations 1988 and the series of 'daughter directives' issued by the EU concerning matters such as the manual handling of heavy loads, use of visual display units (VDUs) and use of carcinogens and biological agents. In addition there are specific sets of regulations covering matters such as violence at work, fire precautions, ventilation, the provision of sanitary facilities, safety signs and noise at work. In 1998 a major new piece of legislation came into UK law in the form of the Working Time Regulations which also have an EU origin. Many of the regulations are supplemented by Health and Safety Commission codes of practice which are not themselves legally enforceable, but which define the standard against which the authorities judge employers' actions.

The reason that EU directives have increased so rapidly in this area is that the Single European Act 1987 added another article to the Treaty of Rome. This allowed health and safety directives to be accepted by a qualified majority vote as a move towards harmonising EU health and safety legislation.

Health and safety law can be neatly divided into two halves, representing its criminal and civil spheres. The first is based in statute and is policed both by the Health and Safety Executive and by local authority inspectorates. The second relies on the common law and allows individuals who have suffered injury as a result of their work to seek damages against their employers. The former is intended to be preventative, while the latter aims to compensate individuals who become ill as a result of their work.

WINDOW ON PRACTICE

For many people the risk of suffering from violence and highly unpleasant verbal abuse is a day-to-day occupational hazard, and hence a major health and safety issue. NHS workers are such a group. According to the latest statistics 12 per cent claim to have experienced physical violence at the hands of patients or their relatives

→

in the past year, the problems being concentrated in mental health services and in the ambulance service. A further 25 per cent claim to have been verbally harassed by patients and their relatives, while 15 per cent report bullying and abuse from other staff. Work-related stress is thus common, as is absence for stress-related reasons. While health and safety training is regularly received by NHS workers, it appears that only half of them have undertaken specific training in how to handle violent and aggressive encounters.

Source: IRS 2006a.

Criminal law

Health and safety inspectors potentially wield a great deal of power, but their approach is to give advice and to issue warnings except where they judge that there is a high risk of personal injury. They visit premises without giving notice beforehand in order to inspect equipment and make sure that the appropriate monitoring procedures are in place. They have a general right to enter premises, to collect whatever information they require and to remove samples or pieces of equipment for analysis.

Where they are unhappy with what they find, inspectors issue **improvement notices** setting out recommended improvements and requiring these to be put in place by a set date. In the case of more serious lapses, where substantial risk to health is identified, the inspectors issue **prohibition notices** which prevent employers from using particular pieces of equipment until better safety arrangements are established. Breach of one of these statutory notices is a criminal offence, as is giving false information to an inspector. Over a thousand prosecutions are brought each year for non-compliance with a Health and Safety Executive Order, leading to fines of up to £20,000.

Prosecutions are also brought after injuries have been sustained where it can be shown that management knew of risks and had not acted to deal with them. Where fatalities result and an employer is found guilty of committing corporate manslaughter, fines of several hundred thousand pounds are levied. Moreover, in some cases custodial sentences have been given to controlling directors held to have been individually liable. A well-publicised case occurred in 1994 when the manager of an adventure company based at Lyme Bay, Dorset was given a three-year prison sentence and fined £60,000 following the deaths of four teenagers. In recent years the government has come under pressure following rail accidents to create a new more clearly drawn offence of 'corporate killing'. This would extend criminal responsibility beyond directors to anyone acting in 'a management role' and could lead to their disqualification from such work.

Lack of resources has led the Health and Safety Executive to place less stress on 'negative' enforcement and more on 'positive' encouragement. The focus in the last few years has been on developing partnership approaches and giving advice to employers, the aim being to recruit them to the cause of effective safety management. The most recent initiatives involve using the promise of rewards as well as the threat of punishments to help encourage compliance (IRS 2005a). But this 'light touch' approach has been criticised by unions and safety specialists who argue that it is only 'the threat of getting caught' that acts as a genuine deterrent to employers and that this requires more inspections and more investigations (Boyd 2003; IRS 2005b).

The Health and Safety at Work etc. Act 1974

This Act is the source of most health and safety law in the UK, under which more detailed sets of regulations are periodically issued. Its main purposes are as follows:

- to secure the health, safety and welfare of people at work;
- to protect the public from risks arising from workplace activities;
- to control the use and storage of dangerous substances;
- to control potentially dangerous environmental emissions.

The Act places all employers under a general duty 'to ensure, as far as is reasonably practicable, the health, safety and welfare at work' of all workers. In addition there are specific requirements to maintain plant and equipment, to provide safe systems of working, to provide a safe and healthy working environment, to consult with trade union safety representatives, to maintain an accident reporting book and to post on a noticeboard a copy of the main provisions contained in the 1974 Act. Where hazardous substances or equipment are in use, there is a further requirement to train people properly in their use and to have safe arrangements for their 'handling, transport and storage'. Where more than five workers are employed, employers are expected to have a written health and safety policy which must be kept up to date and made available to all staff.

In the case law, judges have interpreted the phrase 'as far as is reasonably practicable' relatively narrowly. Employers are expected to undertake formal risk assessments and to compare the level of risk against the costs involved in making a workplace safer. Wherever there is risk identified improvements must be made unless it would be unreasonable, for example on grounds of excessive cost, to expect an employer to do so.

The management of the organisation carries the prime responsibility for implementing the policy it has laid down; it also has a responsibility under the Act for operating the plant and equipment in the premises safely and meeting all the Act's requirements whether these are specified in the policy statement or not. A duty is also placed on employees while they are at work to take reasonable care for the safety of themselves and others, as well as their health, which appears a more difficult type of responsibility for the individual to exercise. The employee is, therefore, legally bound to comply with the safety rules and instructions that the employer promulgates and can be prosecuted for failing to do so. Employers are also fully empowered to dismiss on the grounds of misconduct employees who refuse to obey safety rules, especially if the possibility of such a dismissal is explicit in the disciplinary procedure.

Under the 1974 Act recognised trade unions have the right to appoint safety representatives who have specific duties and with whom managers are obliged to consult. Their role is to investigate complaints from staff about health and safety matters, to carry out their own inspections, to liaise with HSE inspectors and to attend meetings of health and safety committees. Managers are not permitted to prevent a representative from carrying out an inspection, but may be present during the process. Safety representatives are legally entitled to reasonable paid time off work to carry out their duties and to undertake necessary training, as well as to have facilities such as a noticeboard, telephone access, secure filing and photocopying. In 1993 new legislation gave safety representatives protection from victimisation, while case law has determined that managers cannot decide who is appointed to the role or for how long they remain in post.

The First Aid Regulations 1981

These regulations place employers under a general duty to provide adequate first aid equipment and facilities. The accompanying code of practice sets out what should be kept in a first aid box and what supplementary equipment is required in different types of workplace. In low-risk environments it is recommended that there should be one person with first aid training for every 50–100 employees, rather more being needed in high-risk workplaces such as construction sites and chemical plants.

The Control of Substances Hazardous to Health (COSHH) Regulations 1988

These comprise 19 regulations and four approved codes of practice. The purpose of the legislation is to protect all employees who work with any substances hazardous to their health, by placing a requirement on their employer regarding the way in which and extent to which such substances are handled, used and controlled. The regulations apply to all workplaces, irrespective of size and nature of work. They therefore apply equally to a hotel as to a chemical plant, and in firms of a handful of employees as well as major PLCs. The regulations place a responsibility for good environmental hygiene not only on the employer, but on employees too. All substances are included, except for asbestos, lead, materials producing ionising radiations and substances underground, all of which have their own legislation (*see* Riddell 1989). The regulations require employers to focus on five major aspects of occupation in respect of hazardous substances. These are:

- Assessing the risk of substances used, and identifying what precautions are needed. This initial assessment of substances already in use, and those that are intended for use, is a major undertaking in terms of both the number of substances used and the competency of the assessor. Cherrie and Faulkner (1989) report that one employer in their survey used over 25,000 different substances!

- Introducing appropriate measures to control or prevent the risk. These may include: removing the substance, by changing the processes used, substituting the substance or controlling the substance where this is practical. Examples include totally or partially enclosing the process, increasing ventilation and instituting safer systems of work and handling procedures.

- Ensuring that control measures are used, that procedures are observed and that equipment involved is regularly maintained. Where necessary, exposure of employees to the substance should be monitored. This particularly applies where there could be serious health hazards were the measures to fail or be suboptimal. Records of monitoring should be made and retained.

- Health surveillance. Where there is a known adverse effect of a particular substance, regular surveillance of the employees involved can identify problems at an early stage. When this is carried out, records should be kept and these should be accessible to employees.

- Employees need to be informed and trained regarding the risks arising from their work and the precautions that they need to take.

The Management of Health and Safety at Work Regulations 1992

These regulations implemented the EU's Framework and Temporary Workers Directives. The Framework Directive is an umbrella directive, in a similar way that the

Health and Safety at Work Act is an umbrella act. Additional rules known as 'daughter directives' covering specific areas have been issued within the framework of this directive. The following examples apply to workplaces generally. Others apply to specific industries such as construction, mining and chemicals.

- The Workplace (Health, Safety and Welfare) Regulations 1992 set out minimum design requirements, including provision of rest and no-smoking areas.
- The Provision and Use of Work Equipment Regulations 1992 set minimum standards for the safe use of machines and equipment.
- The Personal Protective Equipment at Work Regulations 1992 require employers to provide appropriate protective equipment, and workers to use this correctly.
- The Manual Handling Operations Regulations 1992 require employers to reduce the risk of injury by providing lifting equipment where appropriate and training in lifting.
- The Health and Safety (Display Screen Equipment) Regulations 1992 require employers to provide free eye tests, glasses where appropriate, regular breaks, appropriate training and organisation of equipment to reduce strain.
- The Protection of Pregnant Workers Directive 1994 was implemented in 1994 via a range of UK Acts and regulations. The major measures are now incorporated into the Employment Relations Act 1999. The most important element is that requiring employers to offer alternative work to a pregnant employee or to one who has recently given birth where there are identifiable health and safety risks.

The Health and Safety (Consultation with Employees) Regulations 1996

These regulations require employers to consult collectively with their employees about health and safety matters irrespective of whether a trade union is recognised. Consultation is defined as discussing issues with employee representatives, listening to their views and taking these into account when decisions are being made which have health and safety implications. Where trade unions are recognised the regulations require that their representatives are consulted. In situations where there are no recognised unions the employer must consult with employees as individuals directly or must make arrangements for employees to elect health and safety representatives. Elected representatives have the same rights to paid time off for training and to information disclosure as trade union appointed safety representatives.

The Working Time Regulations 1998

These regulations comprise the most significant recent addition to UK health and safety law. Like the other legislative instruments described above, they are enforced by officers of the Health and Safety Executive, but complaints can also be taken directly to employment tribunals by individuals whose employers deny them the various rights set out in the regulations.

The law on working time originates in the EU's Working Time Directive 1993. This was agreed by the Council of Ministers via qualified majority voting, with the UK government voting against. Moves were subsequently made to challenge the legality of its imposition in the UK on the grounds that it was essentially a social issue, and thus inapplicable in the UK, and not about health and safety at all. Predictably the government's case was turned down by the European Court of Justice, leading to the rather hurried introduction of the new regulations in October 1998.

In 2006 the basic entitlements apply to all workers whether or not they work under a contract of employment. They are:

- a working week limited to a maximum of 48 hours;
- four weeks' paid annual leave per year (in addition to bank holidays);
- a limitation on night working to eight hours in any one 24-hour period;
- 11 hours' rest in any one 24-hour period;
- an uninterrupted break of 24 hours in any one seven-day period;
- a 20-minute rest break in any shift of six hours or more;
- regular free health assessments to establish fitness for night working.

There are more restrictive, additional regulations relating to those aged between 16 and 18, while other groups such as transport workers, junior doctors and people who determine their own working time are excluded from the 48-hour week. Further complexity derives from the way the regulations permit more than 48 hours to be worked in some weeks and more than eight hours on some nights provided that the average number of hours worked over a 17-week period does not breach these limits. Individuals can agree with their employers in writing that they are excluded from the right to the 48-hour maximum working week, but all must be permitted to opt back into the scheme with reasonable notice if they so wish.

The regulations set out the basic rights, but they also allow for locally agreed variation on detailed matters through the mechanism of **workplace agreements**. Where trade unions are recognised, these can be drawn up and agreed through existing collective bargaining machinery. Where unions are not recognised a workplace agreement can be established in one of two ways:

- The employer can draw up the text before asking employees to sign their approval. Once over half of the employees' signatures in a workplace are obtained, the agreement becomes valid.
- The employer can arrange for representatives of employees to be elected to negotiate on behalf of everyone. An existing health and safety committee, provided it is properly elected, can fulfil this function.

It is likely that the EU will seek to tighten these regulations in future years. It is generally agreed that they have had an insufficient impact on the UK's 'long hours culture' in their first years of operation because so many people either opt out or remain unaware of their rights under the regulations. Further restrictions will thus be necessary if the directive's health and safety objectives are to be met. So far, however, the government has successfully resisted attempts at the EU level to end opt-out arrangements and many of the other exemptions that mean some professions are not covered by parts of the regulations. You will find further information about these debates and some discussion exercises on our companion website, **www.pearsoned.co.uk/torrington**.

Bans on smoking in most workplaces have now been implemented across the whole of the UK. This followed an acceptance on the part of ministers that organisations such as the British Medical Association (2002) were correct in asserting that at least 1,000 people in the UK die each year as a result of passive smoking (i.e. breathing in other people's cigarette smoke), many of whom have contracted lung cancer while working in bars and clubs where smoking is highly prevalent. Many thousands more suffer from respiratory conditions caused or made worse by passive smoking at work. In England a ban on smoking in enclosed public spaces was introduced in the summer of 2007. Substantial fines can be levied by the health and safety authorities if employers fail to comply with the regulations by taking the appropriate preventative measures.

ACTIVITY 22.2

Devise a health and safety policy for your organisation. Include information about:

- General policy on health and safety.
- Specific hazards and how they are to be dealt with.
- Management responsibility for safety.
- How the policy is to be implemented.

Or:

Obtain the Health and Safety Policy from any organisation and assess the policy in the light of these four points.

Civil law

While distinct in origin and nature from the criminal sanctions, civil cases relating to health and safety are often brought alongside criminal proceedings in connection with the same incident. When someone is seriously injured or suffers ill health as a direct result of their work the health and safety authorities will bring a criminal prosecution, while the injured party will sue for damages in the civil courts. Most claims are brought under the law of negligence, the injured party alleging that their employer acted negligently in allowing him or her to become injured. It is also possible in certain circumstances to sue for damages under the law of contract by claiming that an employer is guilty of breaching its duty of care (*see* Chapter 6) or of breaching its statutory duties.

Whatever the nature of the claim, the courts have to be satisfied that the employer failed to act reasonably and that the injury or illness was sustained 'during the course of employment'. Central here, as in the criminal law, are the notions of foreseeability and risk assessment. Cases often hinge on what the employer knew at the time the injury was sustained and whether or not reasonable precautions in the form of training or the provision of equipment had been taken. Employers can thus defend themselves effectively by satisfying the court that little else could have been done by any reasonable employer to prevent the accident from occurring. Importantly the principle of vicarious liability applies in this field, as in sexual harassment (*see* Chapter 23). This means that the employer is legally liable for the negligent actions of employees when they are at work. If one employee causes another to become injured, the claim is therefore brought against the employer and not the fellow employee who was responsible.

There are a number of defences open to employers which can result in no award being made or in reduced damages. These include situations in which an accident was not foreseeable (for example if someone was struck by a piece of masonry during exceptionally heavy winds), where the employee voluntarily assumed a risk despite being warned of possible danger, and where an injury which originated outside the workplace was worsened as a result of working. Most significant of all are situations where the employee is found to have contributed to their own injury in some way. This can happen where illnesses derive from lapses of concentration, professional misjudgement or simply stupid behaviour in the face of dangerous conditions. An example is the extraordinary case of *Jones* v. *Lionite Specialities (Cardiff) Ltd* (1961) where an employee fell into a tank of noxious liquid and died. The court held that he was wholly to blame as he had put himself at risk in order to take big whiffs of the liquid's vapour 'to which he had taken a liking'.

MANAGING STRESS AND EMOTIONAL WELFARE

Workplace stress is the welfare topic which has received the most coverage in recent years. It is also a source of litigation which has led to particularly high amounts of damages being paid to those who have sustained illnesses brought on directly as a result of work-related strain. An out-of-court settlement worth £175,000 was agreed following the High Court ruling in the landmark case of *Walker* v. *Northumberland County Council* (1995). Here a social work manager who had returned to work following a nervous breakdown was given inadequate support and an increased workload leading to a further breakdown. The court held that this amounted to a breach of the implied duty of care, because the second illness had been clearly foreseeable. In *Ingram* v. *Worcester County Council* (2000), a settlement of £203,000 was reached after a warden responsible for the regulation of travellers' sites suffered a single breakdown after having been subjected to physical and verbal abuse from site residents. The fact that he had been undermined in his efforts by senior council officials and had suffered 'prolonged and unremitting stress' led to the finding that the duty of care had been breached (*see* IRS 2000a, p. 4).

Until recently there were fewer successful personal injury claims based on stress and lower amounts of damages awarded to victorious applicants. This trend followed the guidance given by the Court of Appeal in four linked cases heard in February 2002. The Court overturned the judgments of lower courts in three of the cases and reduced the damages that had been awarded in the fourth. They made the following important points in their judgment:

- Employers are not obliged to make searching enquiries to establish whether an individual is at risk.
- Employees who stay in stressful jobs voluntarily are responsible for their own fate if they subsequently suffer stress-based illnesses.
- There must be indications of impending harm arising from workload in order for an employer to take action.
- The employer is only in breach where the risk is foreseeable 'bearing in mind the size of the risk, the gravity of the harm, the costs of preventing it and the justification of running the risk'.
- There are no occupations which should be regarded as intrinsically dangerous to mental health.
- Employers who offer confidential counselling services with access to treatment are unlikely to be found in breach.
- The illness must clearly be caused by breach of duty and not just by occupational stress.
- Damages must be reduced to take account of pre-existing disorders or the chance that the claimant would have fallen ill anyway.

Thanks to these rulings, employers were able to take a tougher line on stress-related absences and the management of these issues for much of 2002 and 2003. However, the respite was short-lived because in 2003 the Health and Safety Executive announced that its inspectors would soon be adding stress-related illnesses to their list of checks when visiting employer premises and that the first improvement notices concerning stressful working environments had been served. The Executive's guidance makes it clear that employers are now expected to treat stress like any other health hazard, and that there is consequently 'a legal duty to take reasonable care to ensure that health is not placed at risk through excessive and sustained levels of stress arising from the way people deal with each other at their work or from the day-to-day demands placed on their workforce' (Willey 2003, p. 414).

A further development was the landmark ruling by the House of Lords in the case of *Majrowski* v. *Guy's and St Thomas's NHS Trust* (2006) where it was established that the Protection from Harassment Act 1997 applies just as much to bullies in a workplace as it does in cases involving disputes between neighbours or the activities of animal rights protestors. The test is that a harasser must have knowingly caused serious distress or alarm on at least two occasions. As a result substantial sums by way of damages can be awarded to people who suffer breakdowns due to the manner that they have been treated by managers or colleagues. The precedent was used in July 2006 by Helen Green in a well-publicised High Court victory over Deutsche Bank in which damages of £828,000 were awarded following two breakdowns caused by bullying co-workers.

ACTIVITY 22.3

'Some argue that highly paid jobs are inevitably going to be stressful and that people know this when they apply for them. It follows that it is as much their fault as it is that of their employer if they subsequently find they can't cope with the pressure. They should not therefore be entitled to claim compensation in the courts.'

To what extent do you agree with this view and why?

Stress at work is not a new idea, although it was originally viewed in terms of executive stress (*see* Levinson 1964), and seen only to apply to those in senior management positions. The literature on the subject of stress at work is large (for example, Roney and Cooper 1997; Jex 1998; Macdonald 1999). It is defined by Ganster and Murphy (2000) as a form of 'strain' provoked in response to situational demands labelled 'stressors' which occur 'when jobs are simultaneously high in demands and low in control':

Stressors generally mean environmental factors that cause the individual to muster a coping response because they pose threat or harm. In the work domain examples of such stressors are high workloads, requirements for working fast and meeting strict deadlines, conflicting demands and interruption . . . Problems are seen to arise when exposure to such demands is chronic and elicits a strong enough pattern of responses to strain the individual's physical and mental resources. (Ganster and Murphy 2000, p. 36)

The incidence of chronic stress is often seen as a 'by-product' of management initiatives adopted in many countries, including the UK, in the past twenty years. These include delayering, downsizing, the intensification of work, increased monitoring of staff, moves towards greater flexibility at work and competitive tendering. Each has placed increased burdens on staff groups who have had to accept lower job security, greater levels of responsibility and longer hours of work. The inability to reconcile such demands with family life is a further cause of strain. The results are twofold:

- adverse health conditions (such as heart disease, high blood pressure, ulcers, depression and panic attacks);
- behavioural consequences (such as insomnia, anxiety, poor concentration and increased consumption of alcohol, tobacco and other substances).

Both can lead to increased rates of absence, high staff turnover, low levels of job satisfaction and the sustenance of a low-trust employee relations environment.

Stress and its consequences are often caused by a combination of strains originating in and outside work. A person who is normally able to cope well with the demands of a stressful job may cease to do so when home-based problems come to the fore, the major culprits being bereavement, debt and marital breakdown. There is thus a good business case for employers to provide formal mechanisms for emotional support, quite aside from the strong ethical case. The following are examples of available approaches.

Someone to talk to/someone to advise

A person to talk to could be the individual's manager, or the human resource manager, but it is often more usefully someone who is distinct from the work itself. Occupational health nurses, welfare officers or specialised counsellors are the sort of people well placed to deal with this area. There are two benefits that come from this, the first being advice and practical assistance. This would be relevant, for example, if the individual had financial problems, and the organisation was prepared to offer some temporary assistance. Alternatively, the individual could be advised of alternative sources of help, or referred, with agreement, to the appropriate agency for treatment. The second benefit to be gained is that of having someone just listen to the individual's problem without judging it, in other words, counselling. The types of work-related problems that employees may need to be counselled on are competence, underwork, overwork, and uncertainty about the future and relationships at work. Counselling aims to provide a supportive atmosphere to help people to find their own solution to a problem. Sometimes organisations formalise these approaches by establishing an Employee Assistance Programme (EAP) or subscribing to specialised counselling services (*see* below under Occupational health services).

Reorganisation of work

This is a preventive measure involving reorganisation of those aspects of work that are believed to be affecting the mental health of employees. This may include changes that could be grouped as 'organisational development', such as job rotation and autonomous work groups. Eva and Oswald (1981) suggest greater control over the speed and intensity of work, an increase in the quality of work and a reduction in unsocial hours.

Individually based training and development programmes would also be relevant here. Specifically for the executive, there is growing use of the 'managerial sabbatical'. Some American companies have begun to give a year off after a certain number of years' service in order to prevent 'executive burnout'. In the UK, the John Lewis Partnership has a programme allowing six months away from work.

Recent research studies persistently show that stress at work can be substantially reduced by giving employees greater control over exactly when, where and how they carry out their jobs (*see* Silcox 2006). The evidence suggests that employees who perceive themselves to exercise little control over their jobs have much higher rates of sickness than those who say that they exercise high levels of control. Moreover, increasing the extent of employee control appears to have positive effects on performance and reduces employee turnover rates too.

Positive health programmes

Positive health programmes display a variety of different approaches aimed at relieving and preventing stress and associated problems, and promoting healthy lifestyles. There is increasing activity in terms of healthy eating and no-smoking campaigns and support, together with the provision of resources for physical activity. Corporate wellness programmes have been in place for a longer period in the USA, where the prime motivation was the reduction of medical costs (most employers covering these costs as a benefit for their employees). In the UK the programmes are more often seen as an employee benefit in themselves, with the hope that providing them will also encourage higher productivity and reduce absence levels. However, Mills (1996) argues that although there is a weak positive relationship between healthier lifestyles and the bottom line, there is little evidence that health promotion programmes are actually working. He argues that only a small number of employees are affected by such programmes and that these are likely to be those who already have healthier lifestyles. Mills suggests that blue-collar employees, who have the least control over their working lives, also tend to have less healthy lifestyles and are more resistant to health promotions. He suggests that all three factors are interrelated and connected in a complex manner with employee motivation. If Mills is right, this presents a challenge to organisations and suggests at the very least that they should evaluate positive health programmes as well as investigating the impact of the prevailing management style.

Some approaches to corporate wellness include the use of yoga and meditation. Others, such as 'autogenic training', are based on these principles, but are presented in a new guise. Autogenic training is developed through exercises in body awareness and physical relaxation which lead to passive concentration. It is argued that the ability to achieve this breaks through the vicious circle of excessive stress, and that as well as the many mental benefits, there are benefits to the body including relief of somatic symptoms of anxiety, and the reduction of cardiovascular risk factors (Carruthers 1982). Another approach is 'chemo feedback', which is geared towards the connection between stress and coronary heart disease, high blood pressure and strokes. Chemo feedback (Positive Health Centre 1985) is designed as an early warning system to pick up signs of unfavourable stress. The signs are picked up from the completion of a computerised questionnaire together with a blood test. This approach, like others such as the Occupational Stress Indicator (*see* IRS 2000b, pp. 13–16), is being offered as a 'stress-audit' tool for use on a company-wide basis.

WINDOW ON PRACTICE

An example of a wide-ranging positive health programme is the one provided by the professional services firm Ernst and Young for its 100,000 employees. Here the view is taken that a healthy workforce is necessary if a high-performance culture is to be created and maintained. The jobs their people are employed to do can be highly stressful and there is little that can be done to change this, so the firm believes it should take active steps to help them develop the necessary 'physical and emotional robustness' to handle the pressure.

Initiatives include the following:

- an intranet site giving advice about health and healthy living;
- an occupational health service and employee assistance programme provided by BUPA;
- access to complementary therapies such as reflexology, manicure, chiropractice and massage;
- regular health assessments offered to all employees;
- two annual health promotions focusing on different issues (e.g. stress, healthy eating, etc.);
- the provision of healthy dishes in staff restaurants;
- company sports days;
- subsidised gym membership;
- stress management training.

Source: IDS 2006.

MANAGING PHYSICAL WELFARE

There are a number of ways in which managerial responsibility can be discharged to implement the organisation's health and safety policy statement and to ensure compliance with legal requirements.

Making the work safe

Making the work safe is mainly in the realm of the designer and production engineer. It is also a more general management responsibility to ensure that any older equipment and machinery that is used is appropriately modified to make it safe, or removed. The provision of necessary safety wear is also a managerial responsibility – for example, making sure goggles and ear protectors are available.

Enabling employees to work safely

Whereas making the work safe is completely a management responsibility, the individual employee may contribute by his or her own negligence, working unsafely in a safe situation. The task of managers is twofold; first, the employee must know what to do; second, this knowledge must be translated into action: the employee must comply with the safe working procedures that are laid down. To meet the first part of the obligation management need to be scrupulous in communication of drills and instructions and the analysis of working situations to decide what the drills should be. That is a much bigger and more difficult activity than can be implied in a single sentence, but the second part of getting compliance is more difficult and more important. Employee failure to comply with clear drills does not absolve the employer and the management. When an explosion leaves the factory in ruins it is of little value for the factory manager to shake his head and say: 'I told them not to do it.' We examine the way to obtain compliance shortly, in the course of our discussion about training and other methods of persuasion.

In larger organisations the initiative on safe working will be led by the professionals within the management team. They are the safety officer, the medical officer, the nursing staff and the safety representatives. Although there is no legal obligation to appoint a safety officer, more and more organisations are making such appointments. One reason is to provide emphasis on and focus for safety matters. The appointment suggests that the management mean business, but the appointment itself is not enough. It has to be fitted into the management structure with lines of reporting and accountability which will enable the safety officer to be effective and which will prevent other members of management becoming uncertain of their own responsibilities – perhaps to the point of thinking that they no longer exist. Ideally, the safety officers operate on two fronts: making the work safe and ensuring safe working, although this may require an ability to talk constructively on engineering issues with engineers as well as being able to handle training and some industrial-relations-type arguments.

The medical officer (if one is appointed) will almost certainly be the only medically qualified person and can therefore introduce to the thinking on health and safety discussions a perspective and a range of knowledge that is both unique (in that organisation) and relevant. Second, the medical officer will probably carry more social status than the managers dealing with health and safety matters and he or she will be detached from the management in their eyes and his or her own. Doctors have their own ethical code, which is different from that of the managers. They are authoritative advisers to management on making the work safe and can be authoritative advisers to employees on working safely. They are invaluable members of the safety committee and potentially important features of training programmes. Occupational nurses also deal directly with working safely and often play a part in safety training, as well as symbolising care in the face of hazard.

Safety training and other methods of persuasion

Safety training has three major purposes: (1) employees should be told about and understand the nature of the hazards at the place of work; (2) employees need to be made aware of the safety rules and procedures; and (3) they need to be persuaded to comply with them. The first of these is the most important, because employees sometimes tend to modify the rules to suit their own convenience. Trainers cannot, of course, condone the short cut without implying a general flexibility in the rules, but they need to be aware of how employees will probably respond. In some areas the use of short cuts by skilled employees does not always mean they are working less safely, but there are many areas where compliance with the rules is critical, for example, the wearing of safety goggles.

Safety training needs to be carried out in three settings: at induction, on the job and in refresher courses. A variety of different training techniques can be employed, including lectures, discussions, films, role playing and slides. These methods are sometimes supplemented by poster or other safety awareness campaigns and communications, and disciplinary action for breaches of the safety rules. Management example in sticking to the safety rules no matter what the tempo of production can also set a good example.

Research by Pirani and Reynolds (1976) indicated that the response to a variety of methods of safety persuasion – poster campaigns, film shows, fear techniques, discussion groups, role playing and disciplinary action – was very good in the short term (over two weeks) but after four months the initial improvement had virtually disappeared for all methods except role playing. From this it can be concluded that: first, a management initiative on safety will produce gratifying results in the obeying of rules, but a fresh initiative will be needed at regular and frequent intervals to keep it effective; and, second, the technique of role playing appears to produce results that are longer lasting.

Embedding a safety culture

Exhortation from management and training initiatives play a significant part in improving safety in a workplace, but they are increasingly recognised as being insufficient. Most accidents occur because employees act unsafely. What is really required, therefore, is the embedding of a safety culture (or climate) so that everyone behaves in a safe manner without consciously thinking about doing so.

So far in this chapter we have made a clear distinction between emotional and stress-based illnesses derived from work and physical injuries sustained at work. In fact the two are closely linked as occupational stress is a significant cause of physical injury. When people become stressed and tired they tend to make mistakes and pay less attention to safety matters than they would in other circumstances (Clarke and Cooper 2004). It follows that significant progress towards the creation of a safety culture can be made by reducing stressors and improving satisfaction among workers. Policy, procedure and training interventions play a role, but unless employees have a positive attitude towards their work, are clear about what they should be doing and are able to work at a pace and in a manner which enables them to work without undue stress, no genuine, long-lasting culture of safety can be sustained.

WINDOW ON PRACTICE

One of the most influential books about safety systems published in recent years is Scott Sagan's *The Limits of Safety: Organizations, Accidents and Nuclear Weapons* (1993). Sagan examines the systems employed in the US defence services to ensure that nuclear weapons cannot be deployed accidentally. In the process he examines critically rival theories of safety and rather alarmingly concludes that a nuclear accident is likely to occur one day because the safety systems employed are insufficiently robust. His argument, however, has wider significance and can be applied equally well to safety in the workplace (*see* Edwards and Wajcman 2005, ch. 7).

Sagan starts by outlining the four core principles of High Reliability Organisational Theory:

- safety is prioritised by leaders of organisations;
- complex systems are designed with 'redundancy features' meaning that there are back-up safety systems;
- mistakes are eliminated through trial and error as organisations learn from past mistakes;
- decisions are taken at an appropriate level and are decentralised as far as possible.

He goes on to show how in practice even the most apparently reliable systems based on these principles can be compromised because systems are unduly opaque and because there are always other priorities which compete with safety. Organisational politics tends to undermine the decentralisation of decision making, while a culture of blame and secrecy gets in the way of effective organisational learning.

OCCUPATIONAL HEALTH SERVICES

Occupational health and welfare is a broad area which includes both physical and emotional well-being. The medical officer, occupational health nurse and welfare officer all have a contribution to make here. In a broader sense so do the dentist, chiropodist and other professionals when they are employed by the organisation. The provision of these broader welfare facilities is often found in large organisations located away from centres of population, especially in industrial plants, where the necessity of at least an occupational health nurse can be clearly seen.

In terms of physical care the sorts of facility that can be provided are:

- Emergency treatment, beyond immediate first aid, of injuries sustained at work.
- Medical, dental and other facilities, which employees can use and which can be more easily fitted into the working day than making appointments with outside professionals.
- Immediate advice on medical and related matters, especially those connected with work.
- Monitoring of accidents and illnesses to identify hazards and danger points, and formulating ideas to combat these in conjunction with the safety officer.
- On-site medical examinations for those joining the organisation.
- Regular medical examinations for employees.
- Input into health and safety training courses.
- Regular screening services (e.g. cervical cancer screening).

Employee Assistance Programmes (EAPs) have become reasonably common in recent years as a means of providing both practical and emotional support for employees. Counselling forms a major part of their activity, although the remit goes well beyond problems that people may be experiencing in the workplace. Any source of stress (financial worries, bereavements, relationship breakdowns, etc.) can lead to absence and diminished performance at work. EAPs are the main formal method used to provide support at difficult times. Not only are they valued by employees and thus likely to improve recruitment and retention, they also can pay for themselves by helping to save organisations money that would otherwise be lost paying people who are absent or performing below par. It is also possible to subscribe to specialist EAPs which employees are able to call confidentially and free of charge. An example is the cancer information service offered by the charity CancerBACUP (*see* IRS 2006b). It reckons that 500,000 employees in the UK suffer from some form of cancer at any one time and that around 10 per cent have close friends or relatives with the disease. Their helplines are staffed by specialist cancer nurses. They also have an e-mail-based information service and provide educational information.

SUMMARY PROPOSITIONS

22.1 Occupational welfare is the 'well-being' of people at work, encompassing occupational health and safety.

22.2 The history of human resource management is interrelated with the concept of welfare. Many HR managers find this association a disadvantage when trying to develop the authority and status of personnel management.

22.3 The legal framework for health and safety includes both the criminal and the civil law. The former is policed by health and safety inspectors; the latter provides a vehicle for those who suffer illness or injury as a result of their work to claim damages.

22.4 The Health and Safety at Work etc. Act 1974 is a major piece of UK legislation in this field. The efforts of the EU to ensure harmonisation of health and safety resulted in a major surge of new legislation in the 1990s.

22.5 The period since the 1980s has seen increasing interest in occupational health and welfare, particularly related to stress, alcoholism and counselling.

GENERAL DISCUSSION TOPICS

1 'Good health is good business.' Discuss.

2 To what extent and by what processes can organisations reduce stress for employees who are members of dual-career families?

3 How can an organisation utilise training and development to foster a culture that is receptive to health and safety?

FURTHER READING

Special Edition of *Employee Relations*, Summer 2006.
The third issue of the journal *Employee Relations* in 2006 (Vol. 28, No. 3) was edited by Professor Phil James of Middlesex University. It was devoted to articles examining occupational health and safety issues from an employee relations perspective.

Ganster, D.C. and Murphy, L. (2000) 'Workplace Interventions to Prevent Stress-Related Illness: Lessons from Research and Practice', in C. Cooper and E. Locke (eds), *Industrial and Organizational Psychology: Linking Theory with Practice*. Oxford: Blackwell.

These authors provide an excellent summary of research and effective practice on the subject of stress-related illnesses. They conclude by suggesting a best practice approach to stress prevention.

Stranks, J. (2005a) *A Manager's Guide to Health and Safety at Work*, 8th edn. London: Kogan Page.

Stranks, J. (2005b) *Health and Safety Law*, 5th edn. London: Prentice Hall.

Jeremy Stranks is the most prolific writer on health and safety issues. He has written dozens of handbooks explaining the law and setting out the most recent guidance on reducing ill health and injuries in the workplace. Two of the most recent editions of his handbooks are listed above.

REFERENCES

Boyd, C. (2003) *Human Resource Management and Occupational Health and Safety*. London: Routledge.

British Medical Association (2002) *Towards Smoke-Free Public Places*. London: BMA.

Carruthers, M. (1982) 'Train the mind to calm itself', *General Practitioner*, 16 July.

Cherrie, I. and Faulkner, C. (1989) 'Will the COSHH regulations improve occupational health?', *Safety Practitioner*, February, pp. 6–7.

Clarke, S. and Cooper, C. (2004) *Managing the Risk of Workplace Stress: Health and Safety Hazards*. London: Routledge.

Edwards, P. and Wajcman, J. (2005) *The Politics of Working Life*. Oxford: Oxford University Press.

Eva, D. and Oswald, R. (1981) *Health and Safety at Work*. London: Pan Books.

Ganster, D.C. and Murphy, L. (2000) 'Workplace Interventions to Prevent Stress-Related Illness: Lessons from Research and Practice', in C. Cooper and E. Locke (eds), *Industrial and Organizational Psychology: Linking Theory with Practice*. Oxford: Blackwell.

HSC (2005) *Health and Safety Statistics*. London: The Health and Safety Commission/National Statistics.

HSC (2006) *Statistics of fatal injuries*. London: The Health and Safety Commission/National Statistics.

HSE (2006) *Occupational Health Statistics Bulletin 2005/6*. London: The Health and Safety Executive.

IDS (2006) *Employee Health and Well-being*, IDS Study No. 823, June. London: IDS.

IRS (2000a) '£203,000 award for single breakdown', *Employee Health Bulletin*, No. 13, February.

IRS (2000b) 'Stress auditing – the OSI', *Employee Health Bulletin*, No. 16, August.

IRS (2003) 'Cold comfort in safety record', *IRS Employment Review*, January, p. 41.

IRS (2005a) 'HSE plans to involve business', *IRS Employment Review*, No. 834, October.

IRS (2005b) 'We're listening, HSE tells stakeholders', *IRS Employment Review*, No. 838, December.

IRS (2006a) 'NHS violence fell in 2005 but still affected one in three staff', *IRS Employment Review*, No. 850, July.

IRS (2006b) 'Providing assistance for employees with cancer', *IRS Employment Review*, No. 840, February.

Jex, S.M. (1998) *Stress and Job Performance: Theory, Research and Implications for Managerial Practice*. Thousand Oaks, Calif.: Sage.

Leach, J. (1995) 'Devolution of personnel activities – the reality', MA dissertation, Manchester Metropolitan University.

Levinson, H. (1964) *Executive Stress*. New York: Harper & Row.

Macdonald, L. (1999) *Sensitive Issues in Employment*. Dublin: Blackhall.

Mills, M. (1996) 'Body and soul', *People Management*, 2 September, pp. 36–8.

Nykodym, N. and George, K. (1989) 'Stress busting on the job', *Personnel*, July, pp. 56–9.

Pirani, M. and Reynolds, J. (1976) 'Gearing up for safety', *Personnel Management*, February.

Positive Health Centre (1985) *Chemo Feedback*. London: Positive Health Centre.

Riddell, R. (1989) 'Why COSHH will hit hard on health and safety', *Personnel Management*, September, pp. 46–9.

Roney, A. and Cooper, C. (eds) (1997) *Professionals on Workplace Stress*. Chichester: Wiley.

Sagan, S. (1993) *The Limits of Safety: Organizations, Accidents and Nuclear Weapons*. Princeton: Princeton University Press.

Silcox, S. (2006) 'The business case for using HSE stress standards', *IRS Employment Review*, No. 844, April.

Willey, B. (2003) *Employment Law in Context*, 2nd edn. London: Financial Times/Prentice Hall.

LEGAL CASES

Green v. *Deutsche Bank* (2006).

Ingram v. *Worcester County Council* (2000) (in IRS 2000a).

Jones v. *Lionite Specialities (Cardiff) Ltd* (1961) 105 SJ 1082.

Majrowski v. *Guy's and St Thomas's NHS Trust* (2006).

Walker v. *Northumberland County Council* [1995] 1 All ER 737; [1995] IRLR 35.

An extensive range of additional materials, including multiple choice questions, answers to questions and links to useful websites can be found on the Human Resource Management Companion Website at **www.pearsoned.co.uk/torrington**.

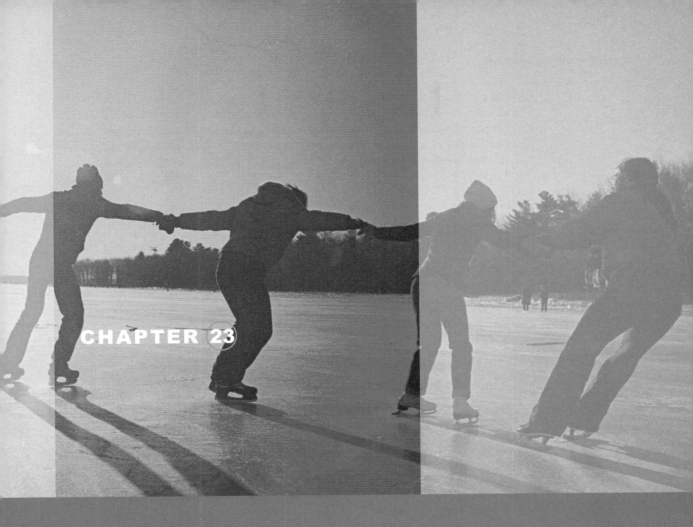

CHAPTER 23

EQUALITY: THE LEGAL FRAMEWORK

THE OBJECTIVES OF THIS CHAPTER ARE TO:

1 Review the key legal requirements in the areas of discrimination

2 Explain the core principles of discrimination law

3 Distinguish between direct and indirect discrimination

4 Explain the importance of harassment in discrimination law

5 Set out the major defences deployed by employers in discrimination cases

An important part of employment law in the UK is concerned with deterring employers from discriminating unfairly at any stage in their relationship with an individual worker. It is an area of law which is well established but which has also developed in new directions more recently. At present there are specific statutes making it unlawful to discriminate on the following grounds:

- sex;
- marital status;
- race;
- national origin;
- ethnicity;
- disability;
- sexual orientation;
- religion or belief;
- age;
- union membership or non-membership;
- that individuals are part-time workers;
- that individuals are fixed-term workers;
- that individuals are ex-offenders whose convictions are spent.

Discrimination law operates rather differently in the case of each of the above grounds, providing a greater degree of protection, for example, to those discriminated against on the grounds of sex or race than to union members or ex-offenders. In some cases the law allows employers to discriminate on certain grounds provided their action can be objectively justified, while in others the grounds for defence are very limited.

In recent years the UK has had to amend and extend its discrimination laws in order to comply with new European directives which establish a common framework across all member states in respect of discrimination on grounds of sex, race, sexual orientation, religion or belief, disability and age. This process was completed in December 2006 with the introduction of the final statutes relating to age discrimination. Most of UK discrimination law thus now falls within the boundaries of European competence, the European Court of Justice being the final court of appeal.

In the next chapter we look more generally at employment policy on equality issues and at the practices associated with the effective management of diversity. You will find some case study exercises on the practicalities of managing discrimination issues lawfully on our companion website, **www.pearsoned.co.uk/torrington**.

ACTIVITY 23.1

What other grounds, aside from those currently covered by the law, would you consider should be covered by discrimination law? Are there any that are currently covered that you think should not be?

DISCRIMINATION ON GROUNDS OF SEX OR MARITAL STATUS

The two major Acts of Parliament that govern sex discrimination matters in the UK are the Equal Pay Act 1970 and the Sex Discrimination Act 1975. Both originally came into effect more than thirty years ago, and have been subsequently amended in important ways. Sex discrimination is an area of law which has long been one of EU competence, so appeals can be made to the European Court of Justice. UK law can also be challenged in the European courts if it is considered that it fails to comply in some way with Article 141 of the Treaty of Amsterdam (formerly Article 119 of the Treaty of Rome) or with EU directives in the sex discrimination field.

The Equal Pay Act 1970

The Equal Pay Act 1970 was the first legislation promoting equality at work between men and women. Although passed in 1970, it only came into force in December 1975. It was subsequently amended, and its scope extended, by the Equal Pay (Amendment) Regulations 1983 and by the Sex Discrimination Act 1986. The Act is solely concerned with eliminating unjustifiable differences between the treatment of men and women in terms of their rates of pay and other conditions of employment. It is thus the vehicle that is used to bring a case to tribunal when there is inequality between a man's contract of employment and that of a woman. In practice the majority of cases are brought by women and concern discriminatory rates of payment, although there have been some important cases brought by men focusing on aspects of pension provision. The Act, as amended in 1983, specifies three types of claim that can be brought. These effectively define the circumstances in which pay and other conditions between men and women should be equal:

- **Like work:** where a woman and a man are doing work which is the same or broadly similar – for example where a woman assembly worker sits next to a male assembly worker, carrying out the same range of duties.

- **Work rated as equivalent:** where a man and a woman are carrying out work which, while of a different nature, has been rated as equivalent under a job evaluation scheme. We cover this aspect of equal pay in greater detail in Chapter 27.

- **Work of equal value:** where a man and a woman are performing different tasks but where it can be shown that the two jobs are equal in terms of their demands, for example in terms of skill, effort and type of decision making.

In order to bring a case the applicant must be able to point to a comparator of the opposite gender with whom he or she wishes to be compared. The comparator must be employed by the same employer and at an establishment covered by the same terms and conditions. When an equal value claim is brought which an employment tribunal considers to be well founded, an 'independent expert' may be appointed to carry out a job evaluation exercise in order to establish whether or not the two jobs being compared are equal in terms of the demands they make.

Employers can employ two defences when faced with a claim under the Equal Pay Act. First, they can seek to show that a job evaluation exercise has been carried out which indicates that the two jobs are not like, rated as equivalent or of equal value. To succeed the job evaluation scheme in use must be both analytical and free of sex bias (*see*

Chapter 27). Second, the employer can claim that the difference in pay is justified by 'a genuine material factor not of sex'. For this to succeed, the employer has to convince the court that there is a good business reason for the unequal treatment and that there has thus been no sex discrimination. Examples of genuine material factors that have proved acceptable to the courts are as follows:

- different qualifications (e.g. where a man has a degree and a woman does not);
- performance (e.g. where a man is paid a higher rate than a woman because he works faster or has received a higher appraisal rating);
- seniority (where the man is paid more because he has been employed for several years longer than the woman);
- regional allowances (where a man is paid a London weighting, taking his pay to a higher rate than that of a woman performing the same job in the Manchester branch).

The courts have ruled that differences in pay explained by the fact that the man and woman concerned are in separate bargaining groups, by the fact that they asked for different salaries on appointment or because of an administrative error are not acceptable genuine material factor defences. It is possible to argue that a difference in pay is explained by market forces, but evidence has to be produced to satisfy the court that going rates for the types of work concerned are genuinely different and that it is therefore genuinely necessary to pay the comparator at a higher rate.

In 2003 a questionnaire system was introduced to provide a vehicle for people who believe that they may have grounds for bringing a claim formally to ask their employers whether they are being paid less than a named comparator and, if this is the case, to give reasons. Legal action can then follow (or be threatened) if the reasons given are unsatisfactory. When someone wins an equal pay claim that person is entitled to receive up to six years' back pay to make up the difference between their salary and that of their comparator.

WINDOW ON PRACTICE

Ms Smith was taken on to work for a company as a stockroom manager at a salary of £50 a week. After a few months she discovered that her predecessor (a man) had been paid £60 a week for doing the same job. As there was no suitable male comparator currently employed by the firm, she decided to bring an equal pay case using her predecessor as her male comparator. The European Court of Justice decided that this was acceptable under the terms of Article 119 of the Treaty of Rome. Ms Smith thus won her case.

In a more recent case, a woman who had been employed in a senior role resigned and was subsequently replaced by a man who was paid a considerably higher salary. She brought an equal pay claim against her former employer citing her successor as the male comparator. This too was ruled acceptable under the terms of the European Treaties.

Sources: *Macarthy's Ltd* v. *Smith* (1980), *Diocese of Hallam Trustees* v. *Connaughton* (1995).

The Sex Discrimination Act 1975

The Sex Discrimination Act also came into force in December 1975 and was designed to complement the Equal Pay Act 1970 by dealing primarily with non-contractual forms of sex discrimination such as employee selection, the provision of training opportunities, promotion, access to benefits and facilities and dismissal. It also applies outside the workplace, so case law that relates to events which have nothing at all to do with employment can be the source of important precedents. The Act covers all workers whether or not they serve under contracts of employment or are employed and all job applicants. The only groups excluded are ministers of religion, soldiers who may serve in front-line duties and people employed to work abroad. It thus remains permissible for firms recruiting employees to work in Saudi Arabia exclusively to select men. The Act applies equally to men and women, and also protects people from unfair discrimination on the grounds that they are married.

There are now four headings under which claims are brought: direct discrimination, indirect discrimination, sex or sexual harassment and victimisation, the way the law works in each case being rather different.

Direct discrimination

Direct discrimination is straightforward. It occurs simply when an employer treats someone unfavourably and when sex or marital status is an important factor in this decision. In judging claims the courts use the 'but for' test, asking whether the woman would have received the same treatment as a man (or vice versa) but for her sex. Examples of direct sex discrimination include advertising for a man to do a job which could equally well be done by a woman, failing to promote a woman because she is pregnant or dismissing a married woman rather than her single colleague because she is known to have a working husband.

If an employer is found to have discriminated *directly* on grounds of sex or marital status, except in one type of situation, there is no defence. The courts cannot, therefore, take into account any mitigating circumstances or make a judgment based on the view that the employer acted reasonably. Once it has been established that direct discrimination has occurred, proceedings end with a victory for the applicant.

The one exception operates in the area of recruitment, where it is possible to argue that certain jobs have to be reserved for either women or men. For this to be acceptable the employer must convince a court that it is a job for which there is a 'genuine occupational qualification'. The main headings under which such claims are made are as follows:

- **authenticity** (e.g. acting or modelling jobs);
- **decency** (e.g. lavatory or changing room attendants);
- **personal services** (e.g. a counsellor engaged to work in a rape crisis centre).

Direct discrimination on grounds of pregnancy or maternity is assumed automatically to constitute unlawful sex discrimination. This means that there is no defence of reasonableness whatever the individual circumstances. It is thus unlawful to turn down a job application from a well-qualified woman who is eight months pregnant, irrespective of her intentions as regards the taking of maternity leave.

Indirect discrimination

Indirect discrimination is harder to grasp, not least because it can quite easily occur unintentionally. It occurs when a 'provision, criterion or practice' is set or operated which has the effect, in practice, of disadvantaging a significantly larger proportion of one sex than the other. In other words, if substantially fewer women than men can comply with the condition, even if it is applied in exactly the same way to both men and women, it is potentially unlawful. A straightforward example is a job advertisement which specifies that applicants should be taller than 5 feet 10 inches. This is indirectly discriminatory because a substantially smaller proportion of women are able to comply than men.

Indirect discrimination differs from direct discrimination in that there is a defence that an employer can deploy. An employer can objectively justify the condition or requirement they have set 'on grounds other than sex', in which case it may be lawful. An example might be a job for which a key requirement is the ability to lift heavy loads. It is reasonable in such circumstances for the employer to restrict recruitment to people who are physically able to comply, for example by including a test of strength in selection procedures. The fact that more men than women will be able to do so does not make the practice unlawful, provided the lifting requirement is wholly genuine. In judging cases of this kind the tribunal has to decide whether or not the provision, criterion or practice constitutes 'a proportionate means of achieving a legitimate aim'. If they decide it does, the employer wins, if not the employee wins.

It is not sufficient for the employer to show that the practice was convenient or administratively desirable – that does not amount to objective justification – to form the basis of an acceptable defence it must be shown to be genuinely necessary for the achievement of a legitimate business objective.

WINDOW ON PRACTICE

The Commission for Equality and Human Rights

Employer actions in the area of discrimination are policed to some extent by the Commission for Equality and Human Rights (CEHR) which is required to keep the legislation under review, to conduct formal investigations into employer actions where it has reason to suspect there has been a contravention of the law, to issue codes of practice and to provide legal assistance to employees who consider themselves to be victims of unfair discrimination. On occasions the CEHR itself represents employees before employment tribunals. It also brings its own test cases in a bid to push back the frontiers of the law

The CEHR began operating in October 2007, replacing three well-established commissions – the Equal Opportunities Commission, the Commission for Racial Equality and the Disability Rights Commission. However, its remit extends much further than those of the commissions it replaced to encompass fields covered by the Human Rights Act 1998 as well as discrimination law.

Sex or sexual harassment

Sex or sexual harassment is defined as unwanted conduct of a sexual nature or based on sex, which affects the dignity of men and women at work. It can be physical or verbal in nature, leading *either* to material detriment (i.e. it affects promotion, pay, access to training, etc.) *or* to the creation of an intimidating or humiliating work environment.

Although the law applies equally to men and women, the vast majority of cases are brought by women. The employer's liability in harassment cases arises from the application of the doctrine of *vicarious liability*, under which employers are held responsible for the commitment of civil wrongs by employees when they are at work. The doctrine also plays an important role in health and safety law, as we saw in Chapter 22.

In judging cases the courts focus on the reaction of the victim and do not apply any general definitions of what types of conduct do and do not amount to unlawful harassment. Hence conduct which may not offend one person in the slightest can be found to constitute sexual harassment when directed at someone else who is deeply offended.

For an employer the only valid defences relate to the notion of vicarious liability. An employer can, for example, claim ignorance of the incident of which the victim is complaining or can claim that vicarious liability does not apply because it occurred away from the workplace and outside office hours. Finally the employer can defend itself by showing that all reasonable steps were taken to prevent the harassment from occurring or continuing. In order to succeed here, the employer needs to produce evidence to show that initial complaints were promptly acted upon and that appropriate action, such as disciplining the perpetrators or moving them to other work, was taken.

Victimisation

In the field of sex discrimination the term 'victimisation' means the same as it does in other areas of employment law. An employer victimises workers if it disadvantages them in any way simply because they have sought to exercise their legal rights or have assisted others in doing so. An employee would thus bring a claim of victimisation to a tribunal if he or she had been overlooked for promotion having recently successfully settled an equal pay claim. Importantly victimisation covers situations in which someone threatens to bring an action or plans to do so even if no case is ultimately brought.

Positive discrimination

Positive sex discrimination involves directly or indirectly discriminating in favour of women in situations where they are underrepresented – usually at senior levels in an organisation or in occupational groups which are male dominated. Such practices are unlawful under UK law when they involve actively discriminating against men who are better qualified to fill the positions concerned. However, it is lawful to take positive action aimed at encouraging and supporting women provided it stops short of actually discriminating in their favour. It is thus acceptable to include an equal opportunities statement in a job advertisement as a means of indicating that the organisation welcomes applications from women. Similarly employers can design and offer training courses tailored specifically for women. As long as men are not prevented from participating, such action is lawful.

Dress codes

In relation to dress codes, a tribunal will only find valid a claim of sex discrimination if the applicant or applicants can be shown to have suffered a detriment as a result of the condition being imposed. Merely treating members of the two sexes differently is not in itself sufficient to constitute unlawful indirect discrimination. For this reason it is acceptable in principle for employers to impose different dress codes on male and female staff, provided the same broad 'standard of conventionality' is applied.

It is thus lawful, as far as sex discrimination law is concerned, to insist that male employees wear business suits at work while permitting women more choice about their attire. Over the years, however, tribunals have adapted their interpretation of the term 'standards of conventionality' to reflect changing social norms. As a result sex discrimination claims have been successfully won by men who wish to retain their long hair tied in a pony-tail and women who wish to wear trousers at work.

Transsexuals

Whereas homosexuals have had great difficulty over the years in persuading the courts that they have rights under sex discrimination law, transsexuals have been protected for some years. It is therefore unlawful to discriminate against someone on the grounds that he or she is a medically defined transsexual. The rights of people undergoing gender reassignment are now specifically protected by the Sex Discrimination (Gender Reassignment) Regulations 1999.

ACTIVITY 23.2

The only situation in UK law when positive discrimination can occur is in the selection of parliamentary candidates. Here it is lawful for political parties to draw up 'all-women shortlists' to help ensure that a reasonable number of female candidates are elected to represent safe seats. Many commentators, however, argue that unless employers are permitted generally to discriminate positively in favour of minority or under-represented groups a truly equal society will never be created (*see* Fredman 2002). The problem, it is argued, is that discrimination law aims to promote 'equality of opportunity' rather than 'equality of outcome', and this is not sufficient to bring about radical social change. Some go as far as to argue that employers should be required to discriminate positively in certain circumstances.

What is your view about positive discrimination? Should the law be changed or should it remain as it is? Justify your answer.

RACE DISCRIMINATION

UK race discrimination law is governed by the Race Relations Act 1976 and subsequent amendments. This area of law became one of European competence in 2003, but the principles established in the 1976 Act have not changed, and they remain very similar to those set out in the Sex Discrimination Act described above. The law applies to all workers except those recruited to work overseas or in private households. The 'direct' and 'indirect' forms of discrimination are defined in the same way as in sex discrimination law, as are the terms 'victimisation', 'positive discrimination' and 'harassment'. The Commission for Equality and Human Rights plays the same facilitating role, while legal precedents from the sex discrimination arena can apply in that of race discrimination and vice versa. There is, however, no equivalent law to that contained in the Equal Pay Act operating in the field of race discrimination.

Importantly the Act extends beyond discrimination on grounds of race to embrace the notions of nationality and ethnic and national origin. It is thus as unlawful for an employer to discriminate against someone because they are French or American as it is to treat someone less favourably because of their racial origins. The term 'ethnicity' was defined by Lord Fraser in the case of *Mandla* v. *Lee* (1983) as applying to a distinct group within the population sharing the following essential characteristics:

- a long history of which the group is conscious as distinguishing it from other groups, and the memory of which keeps it alive;
- a cultural tradition of its own, often but not necessarily associated with religious observance;
- a common geographical origin, or descent from a small number of common ancestors;
- a common language, not necessarily peculiar to the group;
- a common literature peculiar to the group;
- a common religion different from that of neighbouring groups or from the general community surrounding it;
- being a minority or being an oppressed or a dominant group within a larger community.

According to this definition, merely practising a minority religion is an insufficient basis to constitute being of distinct ethnic origin. There also has to be a shared and long history of distinctiveness. As a result, until the introduction of law preventing discrimination based on religion in 2003, unless a religious group was ethnically distinct, its members could lawfully be treated less well because of their faith.

Genuine occupational qualifications (now known as genuine occupational requirements), as in sex discrimination law, permit discrimination on grounds of race at the recruitment stage for one or two kinds of job. The main grounds are authenticity and the provision of personal services to members of a particular racial community. In the case of race discrimination the defence of authenticity extends to employers of people to work in ethnic restaurants.

Most cases involving indirect discrimination under the Race Relations Act concern requirements being set for a high standard of English or for specific UK-based qualifications. As in sex discrimination law, it is necessary to be able to show objectively that these are necessary for the jobs in question. The courts will not allow employers to set conditions such as these unless it can be shown that there really is a *need* for such a condition (i.e. a proportionate means of achieving a legitimate aim). For example, in the case of *Hampson* v. *Department of Education and Science* (1990) a teacher was able to show that the requirement to have completed a three-year training course before being appointed to a teaching post in the UK unfairly discriminated against people of Chinese origin who had qualified in Hong Kong. She was successful because she was able to convince the Court of Appeal that her two-year qualification followed by eight years' classroom experience made her well qualified to teach in Britain.

A fine line has to be trodden when recruiting people from overseas countries because there is a need to stay on the right side of both the Race Relations Act 1976 and the more recent Asylum and Immigration Act 1996. The former makes it unlawful to treat an overseas application unfavourably in any way, while the latter makes it a criminal offence to employ someone who does not have the right of residence in the UK or a valid work permit. Great care is thus called for in handling such matters.

WINDOW ON PRACTICE

A race discrimination case with important implications was brought by two women in 1996.

This case concerned the appearance at a private function of Mr Bernard Manning in the guise of a comedian. The audience consisted of 400 men who were treated to a routine consisting in large part of racially and sexually offensive jokes. Two of the waitresses employed by the hotel at the function were black. Bernard Manning noticed them and made a number of remarks directed at them during his routine.

The two women sued the hotel group which employed them on the grounds that it was vicariously liable and that they had been allowed to suffer racial harassment. The employer contested this, saying that it could not be liable for offensive remarks made by someone who was not an employee – indeed was not even a guest in the hotel and thus had no contractual relationship with it at all.

The women won their claim, successfully arguing that the hotel's management had failed to take action to prevent the harassment from occurring by removing them from the function at the earliest possible time.

Source: *Burton* v. *De Vere Hotels Ltd* (1996).

DISABILITY DISCRIMINATION

The Disability Discrimination Act (1995) came into force in December 1996, since when several thousand cases have been lodged with employment tribunals. It replaced the Disabled Persons (Employment) Act 1944, which was widely criticised for being ineffective, only eight successful prosecutions having been brought during its fifty-year existence. In 2007 the role played by the Disability Rights Commission, like those of the other statutory commissions, was taken over by the Commission for Equality and Human Rights which now has the task of promoting the interests of disabled people and policing the actions of employers.

Disability discrimination became a field of European competence in 2006. This has had major consequences for countries which did not have established law in this area, but for the UK only relatively minor adjustments were necessary to bring the law into line with EU requirements.

While it shares some features in common with established legislation on sex and race discrimination, disability discrimination law is different in important respects The most significant is the restriction of protection to direct discrimination and victimisation. There are no provisions equivalent to those on indirect discrimination in the Sex Discrimination and Race Relations Acts. The key words are as follows:

An employer discriminates against a disabled person if for a reason which relates to the disabled person's disability, he treats him less favourably than he treats or would treat others to whom that reason does not or would not apply. (Disability Discrimination Act 1995, s. 5(1))

The Act is thus concerned with preventing an employer from discriminating directly against an individual worker or job applicant who suffers from a disability. There is no specific prohibition on the setting of requirements for use in recruitment or promotion processes which might be held to discriminate against disabled people in general. It is thus lawful to list 'good record of health' as a desirable characteristic in a person specification – that alone cannot constitute discrimination under the terms of the Act. Employers only invite tribunal claims at the point that they actually discriminate against an individual.

However, this does not mean that employers can safely use language in job advertisements which could deter disabled people, because the advertisement can later be used by a rejected applicant as evidence in support of a disability discrimination claim. Newspapers and employment agencies which knowingly publish advertisements which are discriminatory may also face fines of up to £5,000 if successfully prosecuted.

The other important difference between direct discrimination on grounds of disability and that on grounds of sex or race is the existence of defences which an employer can employ. Essentially, 'less favourable treatment' is permitted if it is for a good reason. An example of this might be a typist who is required to type at a certain speed due to valid job demands. If a person with arthritis in their hands, who could only type at a much lower speed, applied for this job, that person could lawfully be rejected on the grounds of his or her disability provided the potential employer had first explored whether any adjustment in the working environment could be made to overcome the mismatch. Discrimination is thus permitted if no 'reasonable adjustment' can be made to allow the person concerned to perform the job satisfactorily. Employers are nonetheless under a duty to consider reasonable adjustments in any situation in which 'a provision, criterion or practice puts the disabled individual at a substantial disadvantage'.

Since 2004 a distinction has been made between treating somebody less favourably 'because they are disabled' and treating somebody less favourably 'for a reason related to their disability'. There is now no defence that can be deployed in the former case, the established defence relating to reasonable adjustment remaining in the latter.

There are two key issues which the courts are required to rule on when determining cases brought under the Disability Discrimination Act:

- What does and what does not constitute a disability for the purposes of the Act.
- What is and what is not 'a reasonable adjustment' for an employer to make in order to accommodate the needs of a disabled person.

The first issue is decided with reference to the words used in the Act. These define someone as disabled if she or he has 'a physical or mental impairment which has a substantial and long term adverse affect on their ability to carry out normal day to day activities'. The term 'impairment' is taken by the courts to mean any kind of a loss of a key bodily function such as the ability to hear, see, walk or write. It also covers conditions involving loss of memory and incontinence. An impairment is 'substantial' if it is more than minor or trivial, while 'long term' is defined as a condition which has lasted or *might reasonably* be expected to last for 12 months or more.

The words 'normal day to day activities' have been the source of much confusion and litigation. This is because the courts have taken the phrase very much at face value. It is thus the case that someone is not disabled – and is thus not protected by the Act – if his or her condition stops him or her from climbing mountains or playing football, as these are not considered to be 'normal day to day activities'. It has to be an impairment which severely restricts someone's ability to carry out basic, commonplace tasks in the household or workplace.

However, provided the symptoms are serious in their impact, virtually all medical conditions can potentially be accepted as 'disabilities' for the purposes of the Disability Discrimination Act. This includes mental illnesses as well as those with physical symptoms. Hence the definition of disability in the Act has been found by the courts to encompass severe depression, bulimia and ME, as well as asthma, speech impairments and severe back pain. Severe facial disfigurement is also included as a relevant condition. The only exceptions are a few conditions with socially undesirable symptoms which have specifically been excluded. These include alcoholism, drug addiction, exhibitionism, kleptomania and pyromania. Hay fever is also excluded. Importantly it is irrelevant whether or not an individual has recovered from the disability.

Discriminating against someone on the grounds that he or she has suffered from a condition in the past amounts to unlawful discrimination, provided the discrimination met the definition set out in the Act. The fact that someone can live and work normally because he or she is receiving treatment for a condition, for example in the form of drugs or psychiatric counselling, does not mean that that person has ceased to be disabled under the terms of the Act. It is thus unlawful to discriminate against such an individual on these grounds without an objectively justifiable reason.

WINDOW ON PRACTICE

In 1997 a Mr Quinlan was dismissed from his job as an assistant working at a garden centre after seven days because he refused to carry out the heavy lifting work that formed a part of the job. He would not do this because he had had open heart surgery some ten years previously and had been told that lifting heavy weights might injure his health. He brought a claim to a tribunal under the Disability Discrimination Act arguing that it would have been reasonable for the employer to omit from his work the requirement to lift heavy weights, and that his dismissal was thus unlawful.

He lost his case on the grounds that he was not disabled under the terms of the Act. This was because lifting heavy weights was not found to constitute 'a normal day to day activity'. He could only have succeeded had his illness not allowed him to lift everyday objects. There was no consideration given to questions of reasonable adjustment, because the Disability Discrimination Act was found not to apply to Mr Quinlan in the first place.

(*Quinlan* v. *B&Q plc* (1997) Employment Appeals Tribunal 1386/97).
Source: L. Macdonald (1998) 'Discrimination', *Personnel Manager's Factfinder*. London: Gee Publishing.

The burden of proof in disability discrimination cases passes to the employer to satisfy the tribunal that no reasonable adjustments could be made to accommodate the needs of a disabled person. The courts thus assume that adjustments are possible unless the employer can show that it would be unreasonable to expect them to be made. There are no general rules here, because the courts are obliged in reaching their judgments to take account of the size and resources of the employer concerned. The large PLC is thus expected to make bigger adjustments in response to the demands of the Act than the owner of a small corner shop.

It is expected that employers consider making adjustments to the physical working environment, working arrangements and working conditions. Minor building alterations are clearly covered; so unless the employer is very small and is unable to afford to make them, it would be expected that disabled toilets and/or wheelchair ramps would be installed to accommodate a disabled person. Other examples would include changing taps to make them easier to switch on, altering lighting for people with restricted vision and allocating specific parking spaces. However, the concept of 'reasonable adjustment' goes a great deal further, encompassing changes in all kinds of working practices. It is thus expected that employers reorganise duties, allocate ground-floor offices to wheelchair users, adjust working hours for a disabled person or allow someone to work from home if these changes would allow an individual disabled person to be employed. Of particular importance is the requirement to permit disabled people a greater amount of sick leave than other employees. Hence, as was shown in Chapter 9, it is no longer possible to dismiss a chronically ill employee on grounds of incapability, without first considering whether reasonable adjustments could be made to allow that person to continue working. The courts expect to see evidence that the employer has given serious consideration to a request for adjustments and that no request is turned down without a proper investigation having first taken place.

When applicants win their cases at tribunal, there are three possible outcomes:

1 The tribunal issues a declaration affirming the complainant's rights (e.g. preventing an employer from making someone redundant).

2 The tribunal makes a recommendation (e.g. requiring a doorway to be widened to accommodate a wheelchair).

3 The tribunal makes a compensatory award.

In the case of the third outcome, there are no statutory limits on the compensation that can be paid, allowing the courts to fully recompense people for any past or estimated future losses they may have incurred.

DISCRIMINATION ON GROUNDS OF SEXUAL ORIENTATION

The Equality (Sexual Orientation) Regulations 2003 gave effect to EU law which seeks to protect people from discrimination on grounds of their sexual orientation. For many years test cases had been brought in a bid to establish rights of this kind using sex discrimination law. Occasionally applicants were successful, but almost all these rulings were subsequently overturned by the higher courts. The principle that such discrimination is unlawful has now been established in statute, but aspects of the 2003 regulations are controversial, and there are significant outstanding issues that will have to be addressed by the courts as more cases come through the system and are decided by the higher courts. Research suggests that discrimination against people on grounds of their sexual orientation is common in the UK, so there are good reasons for anticipating substantial numbers of claims being brought to employment tribunals in the coming years.

All workers and job applicants are covered by the regulations. Former employees are also explicitly covered and could bring a claim, for example, were a discriminatory job reference to be written. Four types of claim can be brought, reflecting the standard approach to discrimination law which is now being developed in the statutes. The meanings of these terms are the same as for sex discrimination law (*see* above):

- direct discrimination;
- indirect discrimination;
- harassment;
- victimisation.

Harassment claims are relatively common under the 2003 regulations, as this is the major form of discrimination suffered by gay and lesbian people. It is thus important for employers to put relevant policies in place and to take a very firm line with staff who perpetrate harassment of this kind if they wish to avoid a day in court defending their actions.

One of the most interesting issues the government had to wrestle with when drawing up the regulations was how to define the term 'sexual orientation'. After consulting extensively it was decided to define the term narrowly and specifically as meaning 'a sexual orientation towards persons of the same sex, persons of the opposite sex, or persons of the same sex and the opposite sex'. Importantly, the regulations make it unlawful to discriminate against someone 'on grounds of sexual orientation' and not simply because of their sexual orientation. This means that treating someone unfavourably because a relative is gay or because the person has gay friends is as unlawful as discriminating against someone because that person is gay or perceived to be so. Discriminating against people because they are not gay is also equally unacceptable under the regulations. It remains to be seen how the courts will deal with situations in which someone claims to be in a gay relationship in order to gain access for a partner to a benefit of some kind (e.g. a staff discount scheme) but where the employer claims that this person is not in fact in a gay relationship.

As is the case with existing law on sex and race discrimination, it is permissible to discriminate against people on grounds of sexual orientation where there is a 'genuine occupational requirement'. It is thus lawful in principle to refuse to employ someone, or to promote him or her, if the job concerned is only suitable for someone of a particular sexual orientation. However, the guidance notes issued by the government and ACAS suggest only two types of genuine occupational requirement that might apply:

- Counselling/support services related to sexual matters.
- Some roles in religious organisations.

A major source of complaint, and of litigation, over the years has been differential treatment given to heterosexual and homosexual people in the field of employee benefits. Pension scheme rules are the biggest issue, particularly widows' pensions and survivors' payments under life assurance terms, but some staff discount schemes have similarly been restricted to spouses and heterosexual partners. While the 2003 regulations made it unlawful for an employer to favour heterosexual partners over homosexual partners in the operation of any type of scheme, it remained possible to restrict benefits to married people. This was hugely criticised at the time the regulations were passed because gay people were unable to marry and thus could still lawfully be treated less favourably in this important area. The advent in 2004 of civil partnerships (equivalent to marriages from a legal rights perspective) was thus an important step towards achieving complete equality between heterosexual and homosexual workers.

DISCRIMINATION ON GROUNDS OF RELIGION OR BELIEF

The Employment Equality (Religion and Belief) Regulations also came into force in December 2003 and derive directly from the European Union's Equal Treatment Framework Directive. Their structure and content is the same as for sexual orientation, although the practical issues that they throw up are different. They had the effect of righting some anomalies in existing UK law, under which discrimination *purely* on grounds of religious belief was lawful except in Northern Ireland. Religious groups who do not share a common ethnicity are thus now protected from unfair discrimination.

The government stated from the outset that its intention was to define the term 'religion or belief' narrowly. However, the definition that appears in the regulations allows plenty of room for interpretation. The wording used is 'any religion, religious belief or philosophical belief'. Specifically excluded are 'philosophical or political beliefs unless those beliefs are similar to a religious belief'. The aim is to try to avoid a situation arising in which, for example, a member of a neo-nazi group could make use of the law to protect themselves from discrimination on grounds of their politics but, in the process, the regulations also ensure that people with pacifist or vegetarian convictions, or indeed those committed to any political creed, fall outside their protection. The explanatory notes issued alongside the regulations state that courts should take a number of factors into account when deciding whether or not a 'belief' falls within the purview of these regulations. In particular, there should be evidence of collective worship, 'a clear belief system' and a 'profound belief affecting way of life or view of the world'. It will not be long before cases of discrimination on grounds of political belief start coming through European court systems and the European Court of Justice may well interpret the term 'religion and belief' more broadly than the UK government has chosen to.

As elsewhere in discrimination law the regulations on religion or belief permit direct discrimination to occur only where a post carries with it a genuine occupational requirement (GOR). This is likely to be one of the major areas in which the case law evolves over time as there are a number of obvious and common situations in which GORs will be an issue. The regulations permit GORs *both* where 'being of a particular religion is a genuine and determining occupational requirement for the job' *and* where 'the employer has an ethos based on religion or belief'. It is pretty clear therefore that a GOR would apply in the case of clerical roles, such as a hospital chaplain or a Christian outreach worker, but what about posts in denominational schools? More interesting is the case of organisations which do not have a religious purpose, but which claim to run themselves in accordance with a particular religious ethos. There are, for example, Christian medical practices, Islamic businesses and Jewish law firms which currently only employ members of a particular religious group, at least in senior roles.

For most employers, however, the most important practical consequence of the 2003 regulations was a need to review policy on time off for religious holidays. Refusing to allow someone to take a day off to observe a Sabbath or religious festival constitutes indirect discrimination because the organisation has a rule in place which indirectly discriminates against members of certain religious groups. This means that it is only permissible to refuse time off if the rule can be objectively justified. In other words, there must be a credible business reason advanced for refusing requests. In its guidance ACAS states that where it would be possible to accommodate the request, and where sufficient notice has been given, it will normally be expected that employers should grant it. Examples of where it would be reasonable to refuse would be where a large proportion of the workforce wanted to take the same day off, making it impossible to continue operating or where the dates coincide with a very busy period.

ACTIVITY 23.3

An organisation operates a chain of petrol stations which are open 24 hours a day, 365 days a year. Because working on Christmas Day is unpopular among staff it has long been the practice to require everyone employed in a customer-service role to work one eight-hour shift between 11.00 pm on 24 December and 7.00 am on the morning of 26 December. As a result, managers have not had to choose who does and who does not have a break over the Christmas period. This year, however, a new member of staff complains that his request to take annual leave on 25 December has been turned down. He is a devout Christian and intends to attend his church twice on Christmas Day. He says he will resign and bring a tribunal case if he is not granted the leave he has requested.

What is the legal position in this situation? What would happen if the employee did take his case to an employment tribunal? What advice would you give this organisation?

AGE DISCRIMINATION LAW

The final element of the EU's Equal Treatment Framework Directive to be implemented in the UK was the outlawing of age discrimination. The relevant legislation was introduced in two tranches in October and December 2006.

In terms of its basic structure and scope, age discrimination law follows the same approach as has been established for the other types of discrimination law that fall within the area of European competence (i.e. sex, race, disability, sexual orientation and religion or belief). It also extends beyond the world of employment to the activities of trade unions, professional bodies and institutions of further and higher education. However, like disability discrimination law but unlike the other areas, there is a defence that employers can deploy when faced with claims of *direct* as well as *indirect* discrimination on grounds of age. The defence is one of objective justification (i.e. the employer needs to show that its discrimination amounted to 'a proportionate means of achieving a legitimate aim'. So provided there are strong and genuine business reasons, employers can continue to discriminate aginst people because of their age.

The consultation document issued by the government ahead of the regulations labels these 'exceptional circumstances', but goes on to list situations which appear commonplace:

- health, safety and welfare reasons;
- facilitation of employment planning;
- encouraging or rewarding loyalty;
- the need for a reasonable period for employment prior to retirement.

The biggest issue of all in the field of age discrimination is mandatory retirement, and here the government has had little option but to introduce quite complex and radical changes in order to comply with the principles of the EU's Equal Treatment Framework Directive. Effectively a new potentially fair reason for dismissal has been created permitting employers mandatorily to retire someone at the age of 65 or later provided a standard procedure has first been followed. This involves writing to employees at least six months ahead of the date at which mandatory retirement is due to occur informing them of their right 'to request' an extension to their contracts beyond that date. If they wish to, employees in this position can then make a formal request to which the employer must give full consideration in good faith. There is some debate among lawyers as to whether in practice this will mean that good reasons need to be given for turning requests down. In time, as cases come before the tribunals, we will discover whether this is necessary to comply with the law or whether the employer simply has to follow the bare bones of the procedure in order to mandatorily retire fairly in law.

Either way, the new regulations clearly bring people over the age of 65 within the remit of unfair dismissal law for the first time. So employers will have to take great care when handling older employees whose performance has fallen below the required standard. Dismissal without first giving warnings and looking for ways to improve performance may now be found to constitute not just unfair dismissal (with limited compensation available), but also unlawful age discrmination (with unlimited potential compensation).

TRADE UNION DISCRIMINATION

The freedom to join a trade union and take part in its lawful activities is generally regarded as a fundamental human right. It is included in both the European Convention on Human Rights and the founding conventions of the International Labour Organisation. Although this freedom is not couched in the language of positive rights, it is in practice difficult for a UK employer lawfully to discriminate against people simply because they have joined a union or have taken part in union activities. These rights are long established, but are now found in the Trade Union and Labour Relations (Consolidation) Act 1992. In 1990, equivalent rights were extended to people who do not wish to join a union or become involved in its activities. There are three basic rights:

- the right not to be dismissed for a trade union reason;
- the right not to suffer action short of dismissal for a trade union reason;
- the right not to be refused a job on trade union grounds.

The first two of these protect people who take part (or refuse to take part) 'in the activities of an independent trade union at an appropriate time'. The protection, however, only extends to employees (i.e. people working under a contract of service) and does not apply in the police and armed services. In the case of dismissals, because trade union reasons are regarded as 'automatically unfair', there is no qualifying period of service. Full rights thus apply from the first day someone is employed at a particular establishment.

In order to gain the protection of the law in this area the organisation an individual joins or with which he or she becomes involved must be one which has been listed as an independent trade union by the Certification Officer. Moreover, the activities in which the individual engages must be authorised by the trade union concerned and must, if they take place during work time, be carried out with the consent of the employer. Industrial action is not included in the definition of 'the activities of an independent trade union at an appropriate time', but is the subject of other protective legislation.

Discrimination against prospective employees at the recruitment stage simply because they are or are not union members has been an unlawful practice since 1990. In the Employment Relations Act 1999 rights in this area were extended to cover any discrimination occurring as a result of an individual's past involvement in trade union activity. The aim was to prevent groups of employers from maintaining blacklists of individuals perceived to be union troublemakers.

PART-TIME WORKERS

Discriminating against a female part-time worker has long been taken by the courts to constitute indirect sex discrimination because the vast majority of part-time workers are female. Since 2000, however, it has not been necessary for part-time workers (of either gender) to use sex discrimination law to protect themselves. The Part-time Workers (Prevention of Less Favourable Treatment) Regulations 2000 were introduced to ensure that the UK complied with the EU's Part-Time Workers Directive. They now seek to ensure that part-time workers (not just employees) are treated equally with full-time workers in all aspects of work, the key features being as follows:

- Part-time workers who believe that they are being treated less favourably than a comparable full-time colleague can write to their employer asking for an explanation.
- This must be given in writing within 14 days.
- Where the explanation given by the employer is considered unsatisfactory, the part-time worker may ask an employment tribunal to require the employer to affirm the right to equal treatment.
- Employers are required under the regulations to review their terms and conditions and to give part-timers pro rata rights with those of comparable full-timers.
- There is a right not to be victimised on account of enforcing rights under the Part-time Workers Regulations.
- Any term or condition of employment is covered by the regulations, as is any detriment caused as a result of failure to be promoted or given access to training. It is also now unlawful to select someone for redundancy simply because he or she works part-time.

There are a number of problems with the new regulations, including the absence of a statutory authority to enforce the third of the above points. One of the more complex issues involves how the term 'part-time worker' should be defined, because it is used differently in different workplaces. In some organisations someone working 35 hours a week is employed on a 'part-time contract' because full-time hours are 40 per week. Elsewhere, where everyone works 35 hours, such a worker would be regarded as a full-timer. The regulations simply state that a worker is part-time if he or she works fewer hours in a week than are worked by recognised full-timers. This obviously poses difficulties for organisations which do not employ people to work a set number of hours a week, or for whom patterns of hours vary considerably over the course of a year. There is also a need for part-time workers who consider themselves to have been less favourably treated to name a comparator employed in a broadly similar job who is employed on a full-time basis in the same employment. Where none exists it is effectively impossible to bring a claim.

FIXED-TERM WORKERS

The EU's Fixed-term Work Directive (brought into UK law via the Employment Act 2002) includes a range of important provisions designed to improve the position of the many employees who are employed on temporary contracts. The general requirement is that a fixed-term employee should not be treated less favourably than a comparable permanent employee unless less favourable treatment can be objectively justified. This has meant an end to the common practice of avoiding making redundancy payments when fixed-term contracts finish by including a waiver clause in the contract of employment. The statute extends to fixed-term employees the right to receive statutory sick pay (SSP) in the same way as permanent staff and also requires employers to inform fixed-term employees about permanent vacancies in the organisation.

However, the most significant change is the restriction on the employment of people on successive fixed-term contracts. In the past employers commonly used this device to give themselves numerical flexibility and, many would argue, to extract greater effort out of people who were in constant fear of the consequences of non-renewal. Employment of people on successive fixed-term contracts is now limited to four years unless further extensions can be objectively justified. It thus remains acceptable to extend a fixed-term contract beyond four years if the money to fund the post is limited or if a specific project is clearly coming to an end within a short period of time. However, in other situations, after four years the law treats all fixed-term contracts as if they were permanent.

The law gives fixed-term employees the right to ask for a written statement of reasons from their employer if they are being treated unfavourably as well as a statement that their contract has become permanent after four years. Where employers fail to honour these rights or to give satisfactory explanations, complaints can be taken to an employment tribunal.

EX-OFFENDERS

Another group who are given some measure of legal protection from discrimination at work are ex-offenders whose convictions have been 'spent'. The relevant legislation is contained in the Rehabilitation of Offenders Act 1974 which sets out after how many years different types of criminal conviction become spent and need not be acknowledged by the perpetrator. In the field of employment, protection from discrimination extends to dismissal, exclusion from a position and 'prejudicing' someone in any way in their employment. In other words, employers cannot dismiss people, fail to recruit them or hold them back in their occupations simply because they are known or discovered to have a former conviction. Failing to disclose the conviction can also be no grounds for discrimination. Moreover, no one (the individual concerned or anyone else) is under any obligation to tell anyone else about the conviction once it has been spent. Effectively, the slate is wiped clean, allowing the ex-offender to live and work as if no conviction had been received.

The rehabilitation periods set out in the Act vary depending on the type of sentence that has been received. The tariff is as follows:

- imprisonment of over 30 months: never spent
- imprisonment of 6 to 30 months: ten years
- less than 6 months' imprisonment: seven years
- fine or community service order: five years
- detention in a detention centre: three years
- conditional discharge: one year
- absolute discharge: six months

The time runs from the date of the conviction, the times being cut in half for those who are under the age of 18 at this time. It is the sentence imposed that is relevant to the Act and not the sentence actually served.

Numerous jobs and occupations are excluded from the terms of the Act. Organisations which employ people to work in these positions are entitled to know about spent convictions and can lawfully discriminate against individuals on these grounds. The list includes all jobs which involve the provision of services to minors, employment in the social services, nursing homes and courts, as well as employment in the legal, medical and accountancy professions.

At the time of writing the government is proposing to make a series of relatively minor amendments to the law on the rehabilitation of offenders, but no date has been given for their introduction.

SUMMARY PROPOSITIONS

23.1 Discrimination law has grown rapidly in recent years, extending to new grounds such as age, sexual orientation and religion or belief.

23.2 Equal pay law requires men and women to be paid the same wage for doing work which is the same or which can be shown to be of equal value unless the employer can justify a difference on grounds other than sex.

23.3 In much discrimination legislation an important distinction is made between direct and indirect discrimination. The former relates to a situation in which someone is discriminated against because of a personal characteristic, the latter relates to the setting of a requirement by an employer with which fewer of one group can comply than another.

23.4 Harassment claims can be brought against any employer who allows a worker to be subjected to treatment which intimidates or humiliates the victim for reasons related to his or her sex, sexual orientation, race or disability.

23.5 The Disability Discrimination Act 1995 requires employers to consider making reasonable adjustments to working conditions to accommodate the needs of a disabled person before dismissing him or her or failing to offer him or her a job.

23.6 Limited protection from discrimination is given in law to trade union members, employees who do not engage in union activity, part-time workers, fixed term-workers and ex-offenders whose convictions are spent.

GENERAL DISCUSSION TOPICS

1 How far do you think that UK discrimination law is effective in achieving its aims? What could be done to make it more effective?

2 It is sometimes argued that the UK should restructure discrimiunation law so that a single Equality Act offers the same protection to people who suffer from discrimination at work on all the different grounds discussed in this chapter (*see* Hepple *et al*. 2000). What would be the advantages and disadvantages of such a move from an employer perspective?

FURTHER READING

Bowers, J. and Moran, E. (2002) 'Justification in sex discrimination law: breaking the taboo', *Industrial Law Journal*, Vol. 31, No. 4, pp. 307–20.
Gill, T. and Monaghan, K. (2003) 'Justification in sex discrimination law: taboo upheld', *Industrial Law Journal*, Vol. 32, No. 2, pp. 115–22.
An interesting debate was carried out in 2002 and 2003 in the pages of the *Industrial Law Journal* about whether or not there is a good case for allowing employers grounds for justifying direct sex discrimination in certain defined circumstances. This view was advanced by Bowers and Moran in 2002 and robustly rebutted a few months later by Gill and Monaghan.

Department for Business, Enterprise and Regulatory Reform (DBERR)
IRS Employment Review (Industrial Relations Services)
The best way of keeping up to date with this fast-evolving area of law is to visit the DBERR website (**www.berr.gov.uk**). There is extensive coverage there of new discrimination law on the equality and employment pages. It is also possible to download research commissioned by the DBERR looking at the background to new laws and their impact. Any significant new case law is reported fortnightly in *IRS Employment Review*.

Fredman, S. (2002) *Discrimination Law*. Oxford: OUP.
This provides an excellent and thoughtful summary of the principles behind the law, the purposes it serves and the major critiques that are advanced. It also draws extensively on the experience of other countries.

REFERENCES

Fredman, S. (2002) *Discrimination Law*. Oxford: OUP.

Hepple, B., Coussey, M. and Choudhury, T. (2000) *Equality: A New Framework: Report of the Independent Review of the Enforcement of UK Anti-Discrimination Legislation*. Oxford: Hart Publishing.

IRS (1993) 'Dress and Personal Appearance at Work', *IRS Law Bulletin*, No. 469, pp. 2–13.

Macdonald, L. (1998) 'Discrimination', *Personnel Manager's Factfinder*. London: Gee Publishing.

LEGAL CASES

Burton v. *De Vere Hotels Ltd* [1996] IRLR 596.

Diocese of Hallam Trustees v. *Connaughton* (1995) (EAT 1128/95).

Hampson v. *Department of Education and Science* [1990] IRLR 302.

Macarthy's Ltd v. *Smith* [1980] IRLR 209–10.

Mandla et al. v. *Lee et al.* [1983] IRLR 209.

Quinlan v. *B&Q plc* (1997) (EAT 1386/97).

Rewcastle v. *Safeway plc* (1989) (EAT 22482/89).

An extensive range of additional materials, including multiple choice questions, answers to questions and links to useful websites can be found on the Human Resource Management Companion Website at **www.pearsoned.co.uk/torrington**.

CHAPTER 24

EQUAL OPPORTUNITIES AND DIVERSITY

THE OBJECTIVES OF THIS CHAPTER ARE TO:

1 Review the current employment experiences of the members of some socially defined minority groups

2 Analyse the differing approaches to achieving equality for those groups, in particular contrasting the more traditional equal opportunities approach with the management of diversity approach

3 Explore the implications which managing diversity has for organisations

In today's period of globalisation and demographic changes the workforce is becoming increasingly diverse and it is more than ever important for organisations to develop equal opportunity and diversity strategies to attract and retain talent to improve workforce performance and so retain and promote their competitive position. Legislation, voluntary codes of practice and equality initiatives have resulted in some progress towards equality of treatment for minority groups, but there remains inescapable evidence of continuing discrimination. More recent approaches under the banner of management of diversity include the economic and business case for equality, the valuing and managing of diversity in organisations, culture change and the mainstreaming of equality initiatives. Such approaches are partly a response to the insufficient progress from the equal opportunities route, yet there is only limited evidence that they have made a difference. Diversity approaches offer some useful perspectives and practices, although the underlying concepts also raise some issues and concerns.

CURRENT EMPLOYMENT EXPERIENCES OF SOCIALLY DEFINED MINORITY GROUPS

CIPD (2006a) notes that the UK labour force has gradually become more diverse particularly in terms of gender, age, race and ethnicity, sexual orientation, and political and religious beliefs. In choosing these groups we have clearly been selective, and indeed British Telecom have identified as many as 12 aspects of difference between employees (Liff 1999). It should also be noted that CIPD (2003) provides a much broader definition of diversity, going beyond social category diversity, as above, to include informational diversity (differences in terms of education, tenure and functional background) and value diversity (which includes differences in personality and attitudes).

We have therefore been selective in the groups we have chosen to discuss specifically in this initial section: women, racial/ethnic minorities, disabled people, older people and individuals who are lesbian, gay, bisexual or transsexual.

Women

If **participation** in the labour force is an indication of decreasing discrimination then recent figures are encouraging. From 1971 to 2005 the female participation rate in employment increased from 56.8 per cent to 70 per cent, compared with the male participation rate which is slowly falling, and now at 79 per cent (ONS, 2006) based on the spring 2005 Labour Force Survey. These trends are predicted to continue. Much of this increase has been due to the replacement of full-time jobs with part-time jobs, and indeed the same article reports that around 50 per cent of women are in part-time jobs compared with around one-sixth of men. Hakim (1993) concludes that only an increase in full-time employment is likely to have a wider impact on women's opportunities at work and elsewhere.

Some of the more obvious signs of discrimination, such as in recruitment advertising, may have disappeared, and there is some evidence to suggest that women are beginning to enter some previously male-dominated occupations. For example, women have now been ordained as priests in the Church of England, and are plumbers and builders but not without deep and continuing debate. Similarly men are beginning to enter some previously female-only occupations, such as midwifery. However, there remains a high degree of subtle, for example in access to training and support for development and promotion, and not-so-subtle discrimination, as in the continued **gender segregation** in terms of both type and level of work undertaken. The EOC (2007) reports that only 10 per cent of FTSE directors, only 20 per cent of MPs, and 26 per cent of top civil servants are women. And historical evidence shows these figures do not always follow an upward trend. Higginbottom and Roberts (2002) report that the EOC found only 28 per cent of elected councillors, 12 per cent of elected council leaders, and 10 per cent of local authority chiefs were women. The majority of managers and administrators are men and most women remain in three occupational groups: clerical and secretarial, personal and protective services such as catering, caring, cleaning and selling occupations (Thair and Risden 1999). These occupations are often characterised by part-time work, and poor pay, and are in a mainly narrow range of industrial sectors. Part-time workers are often described as part of the secondary labour market with pay, conditions and employment rights being vastly inferior to those of full-time permanent workers, although legislation now provides for some equalisation.

WINDOW ON PRACTICE

Gender segregation at Deloitte Touche

McCracken (2000) reports how Deloitte Touche were good at recruiting women and felt they had achieved equal opportunities, but they were finding that women were leaving at a much higher rate than men and few women were made partners. On investigating the situation they found that women were leaving, not for domestic reasons as they had anticipated, but due to the male-dominated culture. Men were assigned high-visibility assignments in manufacturing, financial services, acquisitions and mergers, whereas women were offered assignments in non-profit organisations, healthcare and retail. They also found that women were genuinely assessed on their performance levels, but that men were also assessed on their potential, which women missed out on.

Deloitte Touche made efforts to change these practical features of working life and also tried to promote work-life balance. Having identified the real problems in achieving equality they found that more women partners were coming through and that money was being saved as they were losing fewer talented women.

Summarised from: D. McCracken (2000) 'Winning the talent war for women: sometimes it takes a revolution', *Harvard Business Review*, November–December, pp. 159–65.

Pay differentials between men and women have narrowed very little except for a hike of women's pay upwards when the Equal Pay Act 1970 came into force in 1975. According to the Annual Survey of Hours and Earnings 1997–2006 (Dobbs 2007) the mean hourly rate for full-time women is 17.2 per cent lower than that for men, having increased from around 30 per cent lower prior to the Equal Pay Act. However, if over-time is included the current gap widens as men work a greater number of hours. Remembering that around 50 per cent of women work part-time, the same survey shows

Table 24.1 Barriers to the achievement of gender-based equal pay

Starting pay is frequently individually negotiated	As men usually have higher previous earnings this means they can negotiate a higher starting rate
Length of service	Men generally have longer service and fewer career breaks, and while this may result in greater experience early in a career it is less of a performance-influencing factor as general length of service increases
Broadbanding	There is a lack of transparency in such systems and there is a lack of structured progression, managers are likely to have high levels of discretion and may be unaware of biases
Lack of equal access to bonus payments	There is evidence that appraisal ratings and assessments discriminate unfairly against minority groups
Market allowances not evenly distributed	Such allowances are more likely to be given to men
Different pay structures and negotiating bodies	As some jobs are done primarily by women and some primarily by men, direct comparisons are harder to make
Job evaluation	Such schemes often perpetuate old values and may be subject to managerial manipulation

Source: Based primarily on material in IDS (2004) 'Employers move on equal pay', *IDS Report*, No. 897, January, pp. 10–18.

that the median hourly rate of part-timers (women and men) is 37 per cent less than that for full-timers, with overtime excluded. While some progress has been made towards equal pay and the gap continues to slowly narrow, these factors still remain as barriers to be overcome. The abolition of the wages councils has not helped in this respect, but the minimum wage has provided some limited support. IDS (2004) identifies a range of unintentional consequences of pay systems which prove to be a barrier to achieving equal pay, and these are shown in Table 24.1.

Racial and ethnic groups

In spite of the legislation evidence of discrimination continues to exist. The CRE (2006) based on Labour Force Survey data reports that the gap between whites and racial and ethnic minority groups was 15.4 per cent in spring 2005. This picture of **comparative level of unemployment** has barely changed over the last 18 years, although there has been some improvement since 2003. There are differences between the different ethnic groups. In addition, there is continued **segregation in the labour market**, with ethnic minority male employees being employed in the hotel, catering and repairs and distribution sectors, and manufacturing industry, to a much greater extent than their white counterparts. But for construction the reverse is true. Segregation also occurs vertically. In the Civil Service for example, the CRE (2006) reports that 3.3 per cent of senior staff were from ethnic minority groups compared with 9.7 per cent of administrative staff, with little change since 2003. Samir Sharma OBE, Chair of the Runnymede Trust, commented that 'there is still a sea of white faces in the boardrooms of Europe' (EOR 2000). Racial discrimination may also happen less blatantly. Rana (2003) reports on a project designed to understand why ethnic minority managers are underrepresented in senior levels of local government. The researchers found that in 360-degree feedback results the line managers' assessments of ethnic minority employees were less favourable for each individual than all other assessments, which were generally similar. This discrepancy did not occur when considering the ratings of white employees. In terms of **pay**, non-white workers are also comparatively disadvantaged, with ethnic minority male workers as a whole group earning a median of 50p less per hour than white males (CRE 2006). However Indian males earned 41p more per hour than white males, so when treating ethnic minority workers as a group the statistics can hide a wide range of difference.

WINDOW ON PRACTICE

The Guardian (4 November 2000) contained the following report:

The IT industry is often considered to be one which is more open to the employment of different racial groups. But while the workforce may look more diverse the top jobs are still mostly filled by white people. The article goes on to report the experiences of two non-white IT directors. The first, Rene Carayol, is Chief Executive of an e-business consultancy, and comments that he is shocked by the racial prejudice that he encounters. For example, when Rene and the team are visiting new offices, people who have not met them before look around the team for the white faces to work out who is the boss. He comments that it takes some time for people to get used to working with him, and feels that it took him longer to rise to his present position due to his race.

The second, Sarabjit Ubhey, Head of Operational Control at BUPA, identifies the glass ceiling above which there are few senior non-white IT people. She feels that the fundamental problem is awareness, pointing out, for example, that when social/networking events are held at a pub Muslims cannot be present. This, in addition to making them feel excluded, hinders their career progression.

Source: Adapted from R. Woolnough (2000) 'Racism reinforces the glass ceiling',
The Guardian, 4 November, p. 31.

Disabled people

Woodhams and Danieli (2000) point out that people who have a disability face common barriers to full integration into society and yet are a very varied group in that impairments can vary in severity, stability and type. Based on the Labour Force Survey in spring 2005 there are 6.9 million people in the UK who have a current long-term health problem or disability which has a substantial adverse impact on their day-to-day activities and affects the work they can do (ONS 2005). People with a disability are more likely to be unemployed than their able-bodied counterparts, and once unemployed they are likely to remain so for a longer period (EOR 2003). The economic activity rate for disabled people is 55 per cent compared with 84 per cent for non-disabled people, and 50 per cent of disabled people are in employment compared with 80 per cent of non-disabled people (ONS 2005). Hammond (2002) notes that the media have a particularly poor reputation for employing disabled people. This is particularly unfortunate as this is a missed opportunity to create visible and influential role models.

Choice of job is often restricted for people with a disability, and where they do find work it is likely to be in low-paid, less attractive jobs. People with a disability are overrepresented in plant and machine operative jobs and in the personal and protective services, and are underrepresented in professional and managerial jobs (Skills and Enterprise Network 2000). Periods of high general unemployment exacerbate these problems.

Employers traditionally have had a wide range of concerns regarding the employment of disabled people, including worries about general standards of attendance and health, safety at work, eligibility for pension schemes and possible requirements for alterations to premises and equipment. The two ticks disability symbol is a government initiative and can be used by employers to demonstrate their commitment to employing disabled people. Employers who use the symbol make five commitments to action: a guaranteed job interview for disabled applicants, regular consultation with disabled employees, retaining employees if they become disabled during their employment, improving knowledge about disability for key employees, reviewing these commitments and planning ahead. However Dibben *et al.* (2001) note that the symbol appeared to have only a limited effect on support for disabled employees or potential employees.

WINDOW ON PRACTICE

The case of Val Milnes

Glover reports the experiences of Val Milnes in seeking employment after recovering from a skiing accident, which left her paralysed from the chest down. After being dismissed by her current employer six months after the accident, she began to look for work when she had been through a rehabilitation process. Her experiences of seeking employment are salutary. Little support was made in most organisations to enable her to compete on a 'level playing field', and she comments that HR professionals did not help. In terms of finding locations and carrying out interviews Val was constantly put at a disadvantage. She felt that on many occasions she was interviewed as a matter of procedure and as a way of complying with the two ticks symbol; and that there was no intention to consider her for employment. She suggests some very practical steps that employers could take to make people with a disability feel more welcome.

Source: Summarised from C. Glover (2003) 'Ticked off', *People Management*, Vol. 8, No. 2, 24 January, pp. 38–9.

Age

Due to the Voluntary Code of Practice on Age Discrimination and a range of government campaigns, the awareness of age discrimination has increased. However from its baseline survey (CIPD 2005a) the CIPD reports that age discrimination remained a significant problem, with 59 per cent of respondents reporting that they had been disadvantaged at work due to age, although the number of people, aged 55 and over, who thought they had been passed over for promotion due to age had halved since 1995. And the Department for Work and Pensions (DWP 2006) reports that whilst the employment of older workers has increased over the last 10 years, employment rates still fall with age.

Evidence suggests that line managers have negative perceptions of older workers, seeing them as less able to cope with change, training or technology and less interested in their careers, more likely to be sick and to cost more money to employ. Philpott (2003) reports that in a survey of 600 retired people, two-fifths believe they had suffered discrimination in some way, age discrimination being the most frequent form. He goes on to argue that there are fewer older people in the workforce, not because they prefer to retire, but because they feel they have been discriminated against.

Given that by 2010 almost 40 per cent of the working population will be over 45 (Higginbottom 2002) and the current shortage of many skills, there is a critical problem for organisations. Older workers are also seen to be more loyal and conscientious, to have better interpersonal skills, to be more efficient in the job and their experience in the job counteracts any age-related factors lowering productivity; older workers are generally more satisfied with their jobs and have fewer accidents and a better absence record; and in any case there is considerable variation within individuals. Older workers also have lower turnover rates which saves the organisation money. However CIPD (2005a) found that 68 per cent of workers anticipated going part-time at the end of their careers and yet only 34 per cent of organisations surveyed offered this to all older workers.

On the basis of their research Snape and Redman (2003) argue that discrimination for being too young is at least as common as that for being too old. Both forms of discrimination adversely affected commitment to the organisation, and hence, it could be argued, performance.

Improvements are to be expected due to the pressure of skills and the impact of the Age Discrimination Act 2006, but it is too soon to assess this at the time of writing.

Sexuality

Lesbian, gay and bisexual discrimination is the most difficult to identify due to the fact that group membership is more easily concealed, usually due to the anticipation of discrimination. It is therefore difficult to quantify the extent to which these groups experience active discrimination. The protection now given to transsexuals means that they are not forced to offer historical information on their gender, but transsexuals in transition clearly cannot keep this confidential, and will need support and protection from harassment (Higginbottom 2002). Most employers have been slow to include sexual orientation in their diversity management initiatives (Ward 2003).

Wilson (2000) in an article reporting three case studies found that in two of the three organisations sexuality other than the heterosexual norm was not considered acceptable in the culture. In one engineering company, the researcher was told that you would have to be very discreet if you were gay, and that one gay person, who had not 'come out', had left the organisation. In the second, a professional partnership, the researcher was told that sexuality was 'under wraps'. Only in the third, a media organisation, were different sexual orientations considered acceptable.

In a TUC survey carried out at the end of 1998 (EOR 1999b), 44 per cent of the 440 gay, lesbian and bisexual respondents said they had experienced discrimination at work due to their sexuality. Forms of discrimination reported ranged from verbal abuse to dismissal. Even in jobs where employees feel sufficiently comfortable to disclose their sexuality, there is considerable discrimination in the terms and benefits they receive, although legislation is beginning to change this situation.

Some progress has been made: for example Stonewall (Stonewall 2007), which used the Workplace Equality Index for the first time in 2005, found improvements by the time of the 2007 Index.

In summary

Although some of the more blatant aspects of discrimination have been significantly improved, there remain considerable discrimination and inequality in respect of minority groups in the workplace. To some extent we are only just beginning to understand the causes and nature of more subtle forms of discrimination which are the root of inequality. We now turn to the theoretical debate which underpins different organisational approaches to tackling discrimination.

DIFFERENT APPROACHES TO EQUALITY

There has been a continuing debate concerning the action that should be taken to alleviate the disadvantages that minority groups encounter. One school of thought supports legislative action, which we considered in detail in the previous chapter, and this approach is generally referred to as the equal opportunities, or liberal, approach. The other argues that this will not be effective and that the only way to change fundamentally is to alter the attitudes and preconceptions that are held about these groups. This second perspective is embodied in the managing diversity approaches. The initial emphasis on legislative action was adopted in the hope that this would eventually affect attitudes. A third, more extreme, radical approach, which enjoys less support, comes from those who advocate legislation to promote positive or reverse discrimination to compensate for a history of discrimination against specified groups and to redress the balance more immediately. In the UK, legislation provides for positive action, such as special support and encouragement, for disadvantaged groups, but not positive or reverse discrimination (discriminating in their favour). The labels 'equal opportunities' and 'management of diversity' are used inconsistently, and to complicate this there are different perspectives on the meaning of managing diversity, so we shall draw out the key differences which typify each of these approaches, and offer some critique of their conceptual foundations and efficacy.

The equal opportunities approach

The equal opportunities approach seeks to influence behaviour through legislation so that discrimination is prevented. It has been characterised by a moral and ethical stance promoting the rights of *all* members of society. The approach, sometimes referred to as the liberal tradition (Jewson and Mason 1986), concentrates on the equality of opportunity rather than the equality of outcome found in more radical approaches. The approach is based on the understanding that some individuals are discriminated against, for example in the selection process, due to irrelevant criteria. These irrelevant criteria arise from assumptions based on the stereotypical characteristics attributed to them as members of a socially defined group, for example that women will not be prepared to work away from home due to family commitments; that a person with a disability will have more time off sick. As these assumptions are not supported by any evidence, in respect of any individual, they are regarded as irrelevant. The equal opportunities approach therefore seeks to formalise procedures so that relevant, job-based criteria are used (using job descriptions and person specifications), rather than irrelevant assumptions. The equal opportunities legislation provides a foundation for this formalisation of procedures, and hence procedural justice. As Liff (1999) points out, the use of systematic rules in employment matters which can be monitored for compliance is 'felt fair'. In line with the moral argument, and emphasis on systematic procedures, equal opportunities is often characterised as a responsibility of the HR department.

The rationale, therefore, is to provide a 'level playing field' on which all can compete on equal terms. Positive action, not positive discrimination, is allowable in order that some may reach the level at which they can compete equally. For example British Rail has given members of minority groups extra coaching and practice in a selection test for train drivers, as test taking was not part of their culture so that, when required to take a test, they were at a disadvantage.

Equal opportunities approaches stress disadvantaged groups, and the need, for example, to set targets for those groups to ensure that their representation in the workplace reflects their representation in wider society. Targets are needed in occupations where they are underrepresented, such as firefighters, police officers and in the armed forces, where small numbers of ethnic minorities are employed (*see* IDS 2006 for an air force example) or senior management roles where there are small numbers of women. These targets are not enforceable by legislation, as in the United States, but organisations have been encouraged to commit themselves voluntarily to improvement goals, and to support this commitment by putting in place measures to support disadvantaged groups such as special training courses and flexible employment policies.

Differences between socially defined groups should be glossed over, and the approach is generally regarded as one of 'sameness'. That is, members of disadvantaged groups should be treated in the same way as the traditional employee (white, male, young, able-bodied and heterosexual), and not treated differently due to their group membership, unless for the purpose of providing the 'level playing field'.

Problems with the equal opportunities approach

There is an assumption in the equal opportunities approach that equality of outcome will be achieved if fair procedures are used and monitored. In other words, if this is done it will enable any minority groups to achieve a fair share of what employment has to offer. Once such minority groups become full participating members in employment, the old stereotypical attitudes on which discrimination against particular social groups is based will gradually change, as the stereotypes will be shown to be unhelpful.

The assumption that fair procedures or procedural justice will lead to fair outcomes has not been borne out in practice, as we have shown. In addition there has been criticism of the assumption that once members of minority groups have demonstrated their ability to perform in the organisation this will change attitudes and beliefs in the organisation. This is a naive assumption, and the approach has been regarded as simplistic. Liff (1999) argues that attitudes and beliefs have been left untouched. Other criticisms point out that the legislation does not protect all minority groups (although it is gradually being extended); and there can be a general lack of support within organisations, partly because equality objectives are not linked to business objectives (Shapiro and Austin 1996). Shapiro and Austin, among others, argue that equal opportunities has often been the concern of the HR function, and Kirton and Greene (2003) argue that a weak HR function has not helped. The focus of equal opportunities is on formal processes and yet it is it not possible to formalise everything in the organisation. Recent research suggests that this approach alienated large sections of the workforce (those not identified as disadvantaged groups) who felt that there was no benefit for themselves, and indeed that their opportunities were damaged. Others felt that equal opportunities initiatives had resulted in the lowering of entry standards, as in the London Fire and Civil Defence Authority (EOR 1996). Shapiro and Austin argue that this creates divisions in the workforce. Lastly, it is the individual who is expected to adjust to the organisation, and 'traditional equal opportunities strategies encourage a view that women (and other groups) have a problem and need help' (Liff 1999, p. 70).

Such regulation under the Conservative government was also seen to undermine competitiveness (Dickens 2006), although more recently the Labour government has introduced some re-regulation.

In summary the equal opportunities approach is considered simplistic and to be attempting to treat the symptoms rather than the causes of unfair discrimination.

The management of diversity approach

The management of diversity approach concentrates on individuals rather than groups, and includes the improvement of opportunities for *all* individuals and not just those in minority groups. Hence managing diversity involves everyone and benefits everyone, which is an attractive message to employers and employees alike. Thus separate groups are not singled out for specific treatment. Kandola and Fullerton (1998, p. 4), who are generally regarded as the main UK supporters of a managing diversity approach, express it this way:

> The basic concept of managing diversity accepts that the workforce consists of a diverse population of people consisting of visible and non-visible differences . . . and is founded on the premis that harnessing these differences will create a productive environment in which everyone feels valued, where all talents are fully utilized and in which organizational goals are met.

And (1998, p. 11) they contest, in addition, that:

> if managing diversity is about an individual and their contribution . . . rather than about groups it is contradictory to provide training and other opportunities based solely on people's perceived group membership.

The CIPD (2005b, p. 2) suggests the central theme of diversity as:

> valuing everyone as individuals – as employees, customers, clients and extending diversity beyond what is legislated about to looking at what's positively valued.

So the focus is on valuing difference rather than finding a way of coping fairly with it. Whereas the equal opportunities approach minimised difference, the managing diversity approach treats difference as a positive asset. Liff (1996), for example, notes that from this perspective organisations should recognise rather than dilute differences, as differences are positive rather than negative.

WINDOW ON PRACTICE

At Zurich Financial Services we believe that managing diversity is about valuing people as individuals. The scope of this definition includes age, colour, disability, ethnicity, economic status, family/marital status, nationality, religious beliefs, sexual orientation, spent convictions, part-time working, political opinion/affiliation and gender reassignment . . . It also embraces the range of individual skills, educational qualifications, work experience and background, languages and other relevant attributes and experiences that differentiate us; all differences can result in varying experiences, values, and ways of thinking, behaving, communicating and working.

Source: CIPD (2005b) *Managing Diversity: Linking Theory and Practice to business performance.* London: CIPD.

This brings us to a further difference between the equal opportunities approach and the managing diversity approach which is that the managing diversity approach is based on the economic and business case for recognising and valuing difference, rather than the moral case for treating people equally. Rather than being purely a cost, equal treatment offers benefits and advantages for the employer if it invests in ensuring that everyone in the organisation is valued and given the opportunities to develop his or her potential and make a maximum contribution. The practical arguments supporting the equalisation of employment opportunities are thus highlighted. CIPD (2006a) suggests that business benefits can be summed up in three broad statements: that diversity enhances customer relations and market share; that it enhances employee relations and reduces labour costs; and that it improves workforce quality and performance in terms of diverse skills, creativity, problem solving and flexibility.

For example, a company that discriminates, directly or indirectly, against older or disabled people, women, ethnic minorities or people with different sexual orientations will be curtailing the potential of available talent, and employers are not well known for their complaints about the surplus of talent. The financial benefits of retaining staff who might otherwise leave due to lack of career development or due to the desire to combine a career with family are stressed, as is the image of the organisation as a 'good' employer and hence its attractiveness to all members of society as its customers. A relationship between a positive diversity climate and job satisfaction and commitment to the organisation has also been found (Hicks-Clarke and Iles 2000). Although the impact on performance is more difficult to assess, it is reasonable to assume that more satisfied and committed employees will lead to reduced absence and turnover levels. In addition, the value of different employee perspectives and different types of contribution is seen as providing added value to the organisation, particularly when organisational members increasingly reflect the diverse customer base of the organisation. This provides a way in which organisations can better understand, and therefore meet, their customer needs. The business case argument is likely to have more support from managers as it is less likely to threaten the bottom line. Policies that do pose such a threat can be unpopular with managers (Humphries and Rubery 1995).

Managing diversity highlights the importance of culture. The roots of discrimination go very deep, and in relation to women Simmons (1989) talks about challenging a system of institutional discrimination and anti-female conditioning in the prevailing culture, and the Macpherson Report (1999) identifies institutional racism as a root cause of discrimination in the police force. Culture is important in two ways in managing diversity: first, organisational culture is one determinant of the way that organisations manage diversity and treat individuals from different groups. Equal opportunity approaches tended to concentrate on behaviour and, to a small extent, attitudes, whereas management of diversity approaches recognise a need to go beneath this, as the CIPD (2005b) points out that diversity requires 'a mutual respect, obligation to and appreciation of others, irrespective of difference' (p. 17). So changing the culture to one which treats individuals as individuals and supports them in developing their potential is critical, although the difficulties of culture change make this a very difficult task.

Second, depending on the approach to the management of diversity, the culture of different groups within the organisation comes into play. For example, recognising that men and women present different cultures at work, and that this diversity needs to be managed, is key to promoting a positive environment of equal opportunity, which goes beyond merely fulfilling the demands of the statutory codes. Masreliez-Steen (1989) explains how men and women have different perceptions, interpretations of reality, languages and ways of solving problems, which, if properly used, can be a benefit to the whole organisation, as they are complementary. She describes women as having a collectivist culture where they form groups, avoid the spotlight, see rank as unimportant and have few but close contacts. Alternatively, men are described as having an individualistic culture, where they form teams, 'develop a profile', enjoy competition and have many superficial contacts. The result is that men and women behave in different ways, often fail to understand each other and experience 'culture clash'. However, the difference is about how things are done and not about what is achieved. However, we must be aware that here we have another stereotypical view which simplifies reality.

The fact that women have a different culture, with different strengths and weaknesses, means that women need managing and developing in a different way, needing different forms of support and coaching. Women more often need help to understand the value of making wider contacts and how to make them. Attending to the organisation's culture suggests a move away from seeing the individual as the problem, and requiring that the individual needs to change because he or she does not fit the culture. Rather, it is the organisation that needs to change so that traditional assumptions of how jobs are constructed and how they should be carried out are questioned, and looked at afresh. As Liff (1999) comments, the sociology of work literature shows how structure, cultures and practices of organisations advantage those from the dominant group by adapting to their skills and lifestyles. This is the very heart of institutional discrimination, and therefore difficult to address as these are matters which are taken for granted and largely unconscious. The trick, as Thomas (1992) spells out, is to identify 'requirements as opposed to preferences, conveniences or traditions'. This view of organisational transformation rather than individual transformation is similar to Cockburn's (1989) 'long agenda' for equality, as she discusses changing cultures, systems and structures.

Finally, managing diversity is considered to be a more integrated approach to implementing equality. Whereas equal opportunities approaches were driven by the HR

Aspect	Equal opportunities	Managing diversity
Purpose	Reduce discrimination	Utilise employee potential to maximum advantage
Approach	Operational	Strategic
Case argued	Moral and ethical	Business case – improve profitability
Whose responsibility	HR/personnel department	All managers
Focuses on	Groups	Individuals
Perspective	Dealing with different needs of different groups	Integrated
Benefits for employees	Opportunities improved for disadvantaged groups, primarily through setting targets	Opportunities improved for all employees
Focus on management activity	Recruitment	Managing
Remedies	Changing systems and practices	Changing the culture
Monitoring success	Changed processes	Business outcomes

Table 24.2
Major differences between 'equal opportunities' approaches and 'management of diversity' approaches

function, managing diversity is seen to be the responsibility of all managers. And, as there are business reasons for managing diversity it is argued that equality should not be dealt with as a separate issue, as with equal opportunities approaches, but integrated strategically into every aspect of what the organisation does; this is often called mainstreaming.

Table 24.2 summarises the key differences between equal opportunities and managing diversity.

Problems with the managing diversity approach

While the management of diversity approach was seen by many as revitalising the equal opportunities agenda, and as a strategy for making more progress on the equality front, this progress has been slow to materialise. In reality, there remains the question of the extent to which approaches have really changed in organisations. Redefining equal opportunities in the language of the enterprise culture (Miller 1996) may just be a way of making it more palatable in today's climate, and Liff (1996) suggests that retitling may be used to revitalise the equal opportunities agenda.

It has been pointed out by Kirton and Greene (2003) that only a small number of organisations are ever quoted as management of diversity exemplars, and EOR (1999b) notes that even organisations which claim to be managing diversity do not appear to have a more diverse workforce than others, and neither have they employed more minority groups over the past five years.

Apart from this there are some fundamental problems with the management of diversity approach. The first of these is its complexity, as there are differing interpretations, which we have so far ignored, and which focus on the prominence of groups or individuals. Miller (1996) highlights two different approaches to the management of diversity. The first is where individual differences are identified and celebrated, and where prejudices are exposed and challenged via training. The second, more orthodox, approach is where the organisation seeks to develop the capacity of all. This debate between group and individual identity is a fundamental issue:

> Can people's achievements be explained by their individual talents or are they better explained as an outcome of their gender, ethnicity, class and age? Can anything meaningful be said about the collective experience of all women or are any generalisations undermined by other cross-cutting ideas? (Liff 1997, p. 11)

The most common approach to the management of diversity is based on individual contribution, as we have explained above, rather than group identity, although Liff (1997) identifies different approaches with different emphases. The *individualism* approach is based on dissolving differences. In other words, differences are not seen as being distributed systematically according to membership of a social group, but rather as random differences. Groups are not highlighted, but all should be treated fairly and encouraged to develop their potential. The advantage of this approach is that it is inclusive and involves all members of the organisation. An alternative emphasis in the management of diversity is that of *valuing differences* based on the membership of different social groups. Following this approach would mean recognising and highlighting differences, and being prepared to give special training to groups who may be disadvantaged and lack self-confidence, so that all in the organisation feel comfortable. Two further emphases are *accommodating* and *utilising* differences, which she argues are most similar to equal opportunity approaches where specific initiatives are available to aid identified groups, but also where these are also genuinely open for all other members of the organisation. In these approaches talent is recognised and used in spite of social differences, and this is done, for example, by recognising different patterns of qualifications and different roles in and out of paid work. Liff's conclusion is that group differences cannot be ignored, because it is these very differences which hold people back.

There is a further argument that if concentration on the individual is the key feature, then this may reduce our awareness of social-group-based disadvantage (Liff 1999) and may also weaken the argument for affirmative action (Liff 1996). The attractive idea of business advantage and benefits for all may divert attention from disadvantaged groups and result in no change to the status quo (*see*, for example, Ouseley 1996). Young (1990) argues that if differences are not recognised, then the norms and standards of the dominant group are not questioned.

On the other hand, a management of diversity approach may reinforce group-based stereotypes, when group-based characteristics are identified and used as a source of advantage to the organisation. For example it has been argued, in respect of women, that as these differences were treated previously as a form of disadvantage, women may be uncomfortable using them to argue the basis for equality. Others argue that a greater recognition of perceived differences will continue to provide a rationale for disadvantageous treatment.

In addition to this dilemma within managing diversity approaches, the literature provides a strong criticism of the business case argument, which has been identified as contingent and variable (Dickens 1999). Thus the business case is unreliable because it will only work in certain contexts. For example, where skills are easily available there is less pressure on the organisation to promote and encourage the employment of minority groups. Not every employee interacts with customers so if image and customer contact are part of the business case this will apply only to some jobs and not to others. Also some groups may be excluded. For example, there is no systematic evidence to suggest that disabled customers are attracted by an organisation which employs disabled people. UK managers are also driven by short-term budgets and the economic benefits of equality may only be reaped in the longer term. Indeed as Kirton and Greene (2003) conclude, the business case is potentially detrimental to equality, when, for example, a cost–benefit analysis indicates that pursuing equality is not an economic benefit.

The CIPD (2006a) argues that the evidence of performance improvements resulting from diversities is scanty and identifies the need to go beyond the rhetoric of the business case for diversity and to conduct more systematic research, and monitoring to demonstrate the outcomes of diversity policies. It also points to the importance of a conducive environment in gaining benefits. Furthermore it recites problems which can result from a more diverse workforce; these include increased conflict, often resulting in difficulties in coming up with solutions, and poorer internal communication, with increased management costs due to these issues.

In terms of implementation of a diversity approach there are also difficulties. We have identified above the complexity of some of the varying ideas which come under the banner of diversity and this in itself is a barrier to implementation. Foster and Harris (2005) in their research in the retail sector found that it was a concept that lacked clarity for line managers in terms both of what it is and of how to implement it within anti-discrimination laws, and some were concerned that it may lead to feelings of unfairness and claims of unequal treatment.

There are also concerns about whether diversity management, which originated in the USA, will travel effectively to the UK where the context is different, especially in terms of the demographics and the history of equality initiatives. Furthermore, there are concerns about whether diversity can be managed at all, as Lorbiecki and Jack (2000) note:

> the belief that diversity management is do-able rests on a fantasy that it is possible to imagine a clean slate on which memories of privilege and subordination leave no mark (p. 528)

and they go on to say that the theories do not take account of existing power differentials.

Lastly, managing diversity can be seen as introspective as it deals with people already in the organisation, rather than with getting people into the organisation – managing rather than expanding diversity (Donaldson 1993). Because of this Thomas (1990) suggests that it is not possible to *manage* diversity until you actually have it.

Equal opportunities or managing diversity?

Are equal opportunities and managing diversity completely different things? If so, is one approach preferable to the other? For the sake of clarity, earlier in this chapter we characterised a distinct approach to managing diversity which suggests that it is different from equal opportunities. Miller (1996) identifies a parallel move from the collective to the individual in the changing emphasis in personnel management as opposed to HRM.

However, as we have seen, managing diversity covers a range of approaches and emphases, some closer to equal opportunities, some very different.

Much of the management of diversity approach suggests that it is superior to and not compatible with the equal opportunities approach (*see* Kandola *et al.* 1996). There is, however, increasing support for equal opportunities and managing diversity to be viewed as mutually supportive and for this combination to be seen as important. Dickens (2006) suggests that social justice and economic efficiency are increasingly being presented as complementary, although there is so far a lack of guidance as to how this can be done in practice. To see equal opportunities and management of diversity as *alternatives* threatens to sever the link between organisational strategy and the realities of internal and external labour market disadvantage.

While recognising that legislation on its own cannot change attitudes, Dickens (2006) suggests that this is an important intervention, not only symbolically, but also as the market tends to produce discrimination rather than equality. In a similar vein Woodhams and Lupton (2006) underline the value of legislation in setting minimum standards.

IMPLICATIONS FOR ORGANISATIONS

Conceptual models of organisational responses to equal opportunities and managing diversity

A conceptual model of organisational responses to achieving equality, concentrating on perceived rationale and the differing contributions of equality of opportunity and managing diversity, has been developed by LaFasto (1992). This is shown in Figure 24.1.

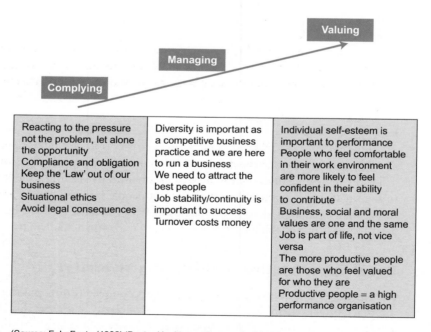

Figure 24.1
Conceptual model of diversity

(Source: F. LaFasto (1992) 'Baxter Healthcare Corporation', in B.W. Jackson, F. LaFasto, H.G. Schultz and D. Kelly, 'Diversity', *Human Resource Management*, Vol. 31, Nos 1 and 2, Spring/Summer, p. 28. Reproduced with permission of John Wiley and Sons, Inc. Copyright © 1992 John Wiley and Sons, Inc.)

An alternative framework is proposed by Jackson *et al.* (1992) who, concentrating on culture, identify a series of stages and levels that organisations go through in becoming a multicultural organisation.

Level 1, stage 1: the exclusionary organisation

The exclusionary organisation maintains the power of dominant groups in the organisation, and excludes others.

Level 1, stage 2: the club

The club still excludes people but in a less explicit way. Some members of minority groups are allowed to join as long as they conform to predefined norms.

Level 2, stage 3: the compliance organisation

The compliance organisation recognises that there are other perspectives, but does not want to do anything to 'rock the boat'. It may actively recruit minority groups at the bottom of the organisation and make some token appointments.

Level 2, stage 4: the affirmative action organisation

The affirmative action organisation is committed to eliminating discrimination and encourages employees to examine their attitudes and think differently. There is strong support for the development of new employees from minority groups.

Level 3, stage 5: the redefining organisation

The redefining organisation is not satisfied with being anti-racist and so examines all it does and its culture to see the impact of these on its diverse multicultural workforce. It develops and implements policies to distribute power among all groups.

Level 3, stage 6: the multicultural organisation

The multicultural organisation reflects the contribution and interests of all its diverse members in everything it does and espouses. All members are full participants of the organisation and there is recognition of a broader social responsibility – to educate others outside the organisation and to have an impact on external oppression.

ACTIVITY 24.1

Think of five organisations that you know or have read about and plot where they are on each of the two frameworks we have reviewed. Explain the evidence and examples you have used in order to support where you have located them in the frameworks.

Equal opportunities and managing diversity: strategies, policies and plans

Kersley *et al.* (2006) found that 73 per cent of organisations in the Workplace Employee Relations (WER) Survey had equal opportunities or diversity policies or a statement, and this compares with 64 per cent in 1998. The public sector were more likely to have such policies (97 per cent, a level unchanged from the last survey) and larger organisations were more likely to have policies than smaller ones, which means that 88 per cent of the labour force are in organisations where such a policy exists. In addition the existence of a policy was more likely in organisations where there was union recognition. Organisations were more likely to have a policy if they had an employment relations specialist (even allowing for size), a finding confirmed by Woodhams and Lupton (2006) who found that the existence of an HR specialist in small firms increased the likelihood of a policy existing. Clearly the existence of policy or statement depends on the nature of organisations surveyed. It would also be a mistake to assume that all policies cover all potentially disadvantaged groups (*see*, for example, EOR 1999b), and there is evidence that as legislation begins to cover new groups these are more likely to be covered. Whilst the CIPD (2006b) found that 93 per cent of organisations which responded to its survey did have a diversity policy, the disadadvantaged groups covered by these were very variable, and many did not cover all the groups for whom there is legislative protection.

In the WER Survey the existence of a policy was positively associated with the existence of processes aimed at preventing discrimination such as job evaluation and monitoring of recruitment, selection, promotion and pay. However these activities were still only carried out by a minority of such organisations. Despite the prevalence of policies there is always the concern that having a policy is more about projecting the right image than about reflecting how the organisation operates. For example, Hoque and Noon (1999) found that having an equal opportunities statement made no difference to the treatment of speculative applications from individuals who were either white or from an ethnic minority group and that 'companies with ethnic minority statements were more likely to discriminate *against* the ethnic minority applicant'. The Runnymede Trust (2000) in a survey on racial equality found that the way managers explained their equal opportunities policy was different from employee views about what happened in practice. Creegan *et al.* (2003) investigated the implementation of a race equality action plan and found a stark difference between paper and practice. Line managers who were responsible for implementing the plan were operating in a devolved HR environment and so had to pay for advice, training and support from HR. The consequence of this was that in order to protect their budgets they were reluctant to seek help. Employees felt that there was no ownership of the strategy or the plan within the organisation by senior or

ACTIVITY 24.2

Consider the equal opportunities policy in your own organisation, or another with which you are familiar.

1 To what extent does practice match policy?

2 Explore the reasons for the achievement of a match or mismatch.

middle managers. Woodhams and Lupton (2006) found a disconnection between policy and practice in small organisations, and that whilst the presence of an HR specialist meant policies were more likely, this seemed to have no effect on implementation.

A process for managing diversity

Ross and Schneider (1992) advocate a strategic approach to managing diversity that is based on their conception of the difference between seeking equal opportunity and managing diversity. The difference, as they see it, is that diversity approaches are:

- internally driven, not externally imposed;
- focused on individuals rather than groups;
- focused on the total culture of the organisation rather than just the systems used;
- the responsibility of all in the organisation and not just the HR function.

Their process involves the following steps:

1 Diagnosis of the current situation in terms of statistics, policy and culture, and looking at both issues and causes.

2 Setting aims which involve the business case for equal opportunities, identifying the critical role of commitment from the top of the organisation, and a vision of what the organisation would look like if it successfully managed diversity.

3 Spreading the ownership. This is a critical stage in which awareness needs to be raised, via a process of encouraging people to question their attitudes and preconceptions. Awareness needs to be raised in all employees at all levels, especially managers, and it needs to be clear that diversity is not something owned by the personnel function.

4 Policy development comes after awareness raising as it enables a contribution to be made from all in the organisation – new systems need to be changed via involvement and not through imposition on the unwilling.

5 Managing the transition needs to involve a range of training initiatives. Positive action programmes, specifically designed for minority groups, may be used to help them understand the culture of the organisation and acquire essential skills; policy implementation programmes, particularly focusing on selection, appraisal, development and coaching; further awareness training and training to identify cultural diversity and manage different cultures and across different cultures.

6 Managing the programme to sustain momentum. This involves a champion, not necessarily from the HR function, but someone who continues in his or her previous organisation role in addition. Also the continued involvement of senior managers is important, together with trade unions. Harnessing initiatives that come up through departments and organising support networks for disadvantaged groups are key at this stage. Ross and Schneider also recommend measuring achievements in terms of business benefit – better relationships with customers, improvements in productivity and profitability, for example – which need to be communicated to all employees.

Ellis and Sonnenfield (1994) make the point that training for diversity needs to be far more than a one-day event. They recommend a series of workshops which allow time for individuals to think, check their assumptions and reassess between training sessions. Key issues that need tackling in arranging training are ensuring that the facilitator has the appropriate skills; carefully considering participant mix; deciding whether the training should be voluntary or mandatory; being prepared to cope with any backlash from previously advantaged groups who now feel threatened; and being prepared for the fact that the training may reinforce stereotypes. They argue that training has enormous potential benefits, but that there are risks involved.

 While the ideal may be for organisations to work on all aspects of diversity in an integrated manner, the reality is often that organisations will target specific issues or groups at different times. Case 24.1 on this book's companion website, **www.pearsoned.co.uk/ torrington**, is focused on improving diversity practice for people with disabilities.

WINDOW ON PRACTICE

Age equality at Derby City Council

Platman (2002) reports that in Derby City Council potential applicants would phone to find out if there was any point in applying for a particular job, expecting that their older age would rule them out. The Council felt that age discrimination restricted the pool of applicants and that they had to get rid of signals that age was not valued. They now have a code of practice which centres on dignity at work, and this applies to both councillors and employees. The aim of the code is to ensure that ageist behaviour, attitudes and language are avoided. The intention is to put across the message that the Council values the experience of older employees, and older employees are now specifically encouraged to apply for further training and promotions.

Source: Summarised from K. Platman (2002) 'Matured Assets', *People Management*, Vol. 8, No. 24, 5 December, pp. 40–2.

Changing culture is clearly a key part of any process for managing diversity. In 1995 Her Majesty's Inspectorate of Constabulary (HMIC) stressed the business case for diversity in the police force. The police force, over a number of years, has made considerable efforts to increase the recruitment and promotion of members of ethnic minorities (*see*, for example, EOR 1997). It began to tackle the issues of why individuals from different ethnic backgrounds would not even apply to the police for a career (for example, they may be seen, within some ethnic groups, as traitors for doing so). Some progress was made but the Macpherson Report (1999) highlighted the issue of institutional racism, and further efforts were made to reduce discrimination. However, in 2004 there was still clear evidence of discriminatory cultures and attitudes, as evidenced by the television programme about the racist attitudes of new recruits into Manchester police. On Radio 4 on 20 January 2004 the Ali Desai case was discussed and it was argued that the metropolitan police service were racist in the way that they applied discipline to officers, picking up on smaller issues for racial minority groups than for white officers. The changes required to manage diversity effectively should not be underestimated.

Case study 24.2 on the companion website considers the achievement of an ethnic mix on some MBA courses.

WINDOW ON PRACTICE

Arriva: dramatic results on diversity

Arriva embarked on a diversity programme in 2003 and claims that it has stimulated a change in workforce profile and reduced employee turnover. This is a key outcome as one of the drivers behind the programme was to become an employer of choice in response to predicted demographic and legislative changes, recruitment challenges, and a need to reflect the broader community in order to stay ahead in business. The company was aware for example that it was a traditional white male environment, with bus driving, for example, being seen as man's job. Arriva began by setting up a diversity committee made up of senior leaders from across the businesses to review progress and measures of success. In addition a Diversity Best Practice Forum was set up with responsibility for delivering the diversity agenda. Diversity behaviours were included in management and leadership competencies and individuals at all levels have objectives linked to diversity.

Training was a key part of the company's approach to diversity and was accomplished in two phases. The first was very innovative, and a drama-based training organisation started off the programme, called Managing and Valuing Difference. They prepared by researching what actually happened in the business and identified current key issues relating to diversity. Scenarios were then acted out and participants were encouraged to be involved by interactive exercises and discussions. The aim was to create an understanding in the workforce of diversity and the business case for it, to help people appreciate the differences in others and to create a situation where people felt able to challenge unacceptable behaviour. The second part of the training involved Arriva staff who volunteered to be trained as facilitators and the use of video scenarios. This second part of the training addressed 'Valuing and welcoming difference'.

In addition it was decided to extend flexible working and to strengthen the role of minority groups. For example there was a women's networking event attended by the chief executive with a view to encouraging, developing and retaining women in senior management. A recruitment monitoring process was also introduced to help decide how to allocate resources on diversity. For example in one part of the business it might be to target underrepresented groups and produce a tailored approach to recruitment advertising, whilst in another it may be to have greater involvement in the local community. Open days have been held to encourage the recruitment of women bus drivers where existing women drivers also attend to share their views. Two-part application forms are used so that any personal data is separate from the application form and cannot bias shortlisting, and the use of male and female mentors has proved successful.

Source: Adapted from Wolff, C. (2007) 'Arriva; dramatic results on diversity', *Equal Opportunities Review*, No. 160, pp. 5–11, January.

ACTIVITY 24.3

Prepare a strategy for managing diversity which would be appropriate for your organisation, or one with which you are familiar.

SUMMARY PROPOSITIONS

24.1 The essence of much HR work is to discriminate between individuals. The essence of equality is to avoid unfair discrimination. Unfair discrimination often results from people being treated on the basis of limited and prejudiced understanding of the groups to which they belong rather than on the basis of an assessment of them as individuals. People are not always aware when they are discriminating unfairly.

24.2 Legislation can have only a limited effect in achieving equality, and does not change attitudes, beliefs and cultures and structures. Organisations and their cultures, processes and structures are founded on the needs of the majority group and individuals from other groups are expected to adapt to this norm. This explains why progress towards equality of opportunity has been very slow.

24.3 Equal opportunities approaches highlight the moral argument for equal treatment, whereas managing diversity highlights the business case.

24.4 Actual changes in practice relating to equalising opportunity are taking place very slowly, and only long-term organisational transformation is likely to support equality.

24.5 Equal opportunities approaches and the management of diversity are best viewed, not as alternatives, but as complementary approaches which need to be interrelated.

GENERAL DISCUSSION TOPICS

1 Discuss Liff's (1997) question:

'Can people's achievements be explained by their individual talents or are they better explained as an outcome of their gender, ethnicity, class and age? Can anything meaningful be said about the collective experience of all women or are any generalisations undermined by other cross-cutting ideas?' (p. 11)

2 Which is preferable – the UK approach or the US approach to equal opportunities? What are the implications of each for all members of the organisation?

FURTHER READING

Benschop, Y. (2001) 'Pride, prejudice and performance: relations between HRM, diversity and performance', *International Journal of Human Resource Management*, Vol. 12, No. 7, pp. 1166–81.

This a very illuminating article which presents the experience of the impact of workforce diversity in two case study organisations. The findings indicate that an organisation's strategy for diversity influences how employees perceive and understand diversity and the impact that it has on performance.

Fagan, C., Rubery, J., Grimshaw, D., Smith, M., Hebson, G. and Figueiredo, H. (2005) 'Gender mainstreaming in the enlarged European Union: recent developments in the European employment strategy and Social Inclusion Process', *Industrial Relations Journal*, Vol. 36, No. 6, pp. 568–91. Provides some excellent data comparing progress in the UK with that in other members of the EU in relation to employment rates and gender gaps.

Kirton, G. and Greene, A. (2004) 'The discourse of diversity in unionized contexts: views from trade union equality officers', *Personnel Review*, Vol. 35, No. 4, pp. 431–48.

Mattis, M. (2001) 'Advancing women in business organisations', *Journal of Management Development*, Vol. 20, No. 4, pp. 371–88. This article examines the role of key players such as middle and first-line managers in supporting gender diversity initiatives. A wide range of case examples are used and the article provides a range of practical activities to support gender diversity.

Phillips, T. (2007) *Fairness and Freedom: Final Report of the Equalities Review*. London: HMSO. Specifically the section on employment, Chapter 3, which discusses the idea of employment penalties.

REFERENCES

CIPD (2003) *Diversity: Stacking up the evidence, Executive Briefing*. London: CIPD.

CIPD (2005a) *Tackling Age Discrimination in the workplace: Creating a new age for all*. London: CIPD.

CIPD (2005b) *Managing Diversity: Linking Theory and Practice to business performance*. London: CIPD.

CIPD (2006a) *Managing Diversity: Measuring Success*. London: CIPD.

CIPD (2006b) *Diversity in Business: How much progress have employers made? First findings*. London: CIPD.

Cockburn, C. (1989) 'Equal Opportunities: the long and short agenda', *Industrial Relations Journal*, Vol. 20, No. 3, pp. 213–25.

CRE (2006) *Employment and Ethnicity*, Factfile 1. Manchester: CRE.

Creegan, C., Colgan, F., Charlesworth, R. and Robinson, G. (2003) 'Race equality policies at work: employee perceptions of the "implementation gap" in a UK local authority', *Work, Employment and Society*, Vol. 17, No. 4, pp. 617–40.

Cully, M., Woodland, S., O'Reilly, A. and Dix, G. (1999) *Britain at Work: As depicted by the 1998 Workplace Employee Relations Survey*. London: Routledge.

Dibben, P., James, P. and Cunningham, I. (2001) 'Senior management commitment to disability', *Personnel Review*, Vol. 30, No. 4, pp. 454–67.

Dickens, L. (1999) 'Beyond the business case: a three pronged approach to equality action', *Human Resource Management Journal*, Vol. 9, No. 1, pp. 9–19.

Dickens, L. (2006) 'Re-regulation for gender equality: from "either/or" to "both"', *Industrial Relations Journal*, Vol. 37, No. 4, pp. 299–309.

Dobbs, C. (2007) 'Patterns of Pay: results of the Annual Survey of Hours and Earnings, 1997–2006', *Economic and Labour Market Review*, Vol. 1, No. 2, February, pp. 44–51.

Donaldson, L. (1993) 'The recession: a barrier to equal opportunities?', *Equal Opportunities Review*, No. 50, July–August.

DWP (2006) Department Report at **www.dwp.gov.uk/publications/dwp/2006/dr06/targets**.

Ellis, C. and Sonnenfield, J.A. (1994) 'Diverse approaches to managing diversity', *Human Resource Management*, Vol. 33, No. 1, Spring, pp. 79–109.

Equal Opportunities Commission (2007) *Sex and power: who runs Britain?* Manchester: EOC.

Equal Opportunities Review (1996) 'Ethnic minorities in the fire service', No. 68, July–August.

Equal Opportunities Review (1997) 'Ethnic minorities in the police service', No. 73.

Equal Opportunities Review (1998) 'Tackling Age bias: code or law?', No. 80, July–August.

Equal Opportunities Review (1999a) 'BT: Championing women in a man's world', No. 84, March–April, pp. 14–20.

Equal Opportunities Review (1999b) 'Equal Opportunities Policies: An EOR survey of employers', No. 87, September–October.

Equal Opportunities Review (2000) 'Businesses urged to shape up on race', No. 90, March–April.

Equal Opportunities Review (2002) 'Trends in female employment', No. 112, December, pp. 19–22.

Equal Opportunities Review (2003) 'Economic activity rates of disabled people and ethnic minorities', No. 121, September, pp. 7–8.

Foster, C. and Harris, L. (2005) 'Easy to say, difficult to do: diversity in retail management', *Human Resource Management Journal*, Vol. 15, No. 3, pp. 4–17.

Glover, C. (2003) 'Ticked off', *People Management*, Vol. 8, No. 2, 24 January, pp. 38–9.

Hakim, C. (1993) 'The myth of rising female employment', *Work, Employment and Society*, Vol. 7, No. 1, March, pp. 121–33.

Hammond, D. (2002) 'TV industry tackles inequality', *People Management*, Vol. 8, No. 15, 25 July, p. 9.

Hicks-Clarke, D. and Iles, P. (2000) 'Climate for diversity and its effects on career and organizational attitudes and perceptions', *Personnel Review*, Vol. 29, No. 3.

Higginbottom, K. (2002) 'The wonder years', *People Management*, Vol. 8, No. 24, 5 December, pp. 14–15.

Higginbottom, K. and Roberts, Z. (2002) 'EOC urges local authorities to confront lack of senior women', *People Management*, Vol. 8, No. 12, 13 June, p. 7.

Hoque, K. and Noon, M. (1999) 'Racial discrimination in speculative applications: new optimism six years on?', *Human Resource Management Journal*, Vol. 9, No. 3, pp. 71–82.

Humphries, J. and Rubery, J. (1995) *Research Summary of the Economics of Equal Opportunity*. Manchester: EOC.

IDS (2004) 'Employers move on equal pay', *IDS Report*, No. 897, January, pp. 10–18.

IDS (2006) *Promoting Race Equality*. IDS HR Studies No. 825. London: IDS.

Institute of Personnel and Development (1997) *Managing Diversity: A Position paper*. London: IPD.

Itzin, C. and Phillipson, C. (1993) *Age Barriers at Work: Maximising the potential of mature and older people*. London: Metropolitan Authorities Recruitment Agency.

Jackson, B.W., LaFasto, F., Schultz, H.G. and Kelly, D. (1993) 'Diversity', *Human Resource Management*, Vol. 31, Nos 1 and 2, Spring/Summer, pp. 21–34.

Jewson, N. and Mason, D. (1986) 'The theory and practice of equal opportunities policies: liberal and radical approaches', *Sociological Review*, Vol. 34, No. 2, pp. 307–34.

Kandola, P. and Fullerton, J. (1994, 2nd edn 1998) *Managing the Mosaic*. London: IPD.

Kandola, R., Fullerton, J. and Mulroney, C. (1996) *1996 Pearn Kandola Survey of Diversity Practice Summary Report*. Oxford: Pearn Kandola.

Kersley, B., Alpin, C., Forth, J., Bryson, A., Bewley, H., Dix, G. and Oxenbridge S. (2006) *Inside the Workplace: Findings from the 2004 Workplace Employment Relations Survey*. London: Routledge.

Kirton, G. and Greene, A. (2003) *The dynamics of managing diversity: a critical approach*. Oxford: Butterworth Heinemann.

LaFasto, F. (1992) 'Baxter Healthcare Corporation', in B.W. Jackson, F. LaFasto, H.G. Schultz and D. Kelly, 'Diversity', *Human Resource Management*, Vol. 31, Nos 1–2, Spring/Summer.

Liff, S. (1996) 'Managing diversity: new opportunities for women?', *Warwick Papers in Industrial Relations* No. 57. Coventry: IRU, Warwick University.

Liff, S. (1997) 'Two routes to managing diversity: individual differences or social group characteristics?', *Employee Relations*, Vol. 19, No. 1, pp. 11–26.

Liff, S. (1999) 'Diversity and Equal Opportunities: room for a constructive compromise?', *Human Resource Management Journal*, Vol. 9, No. 1, pp. 65–75.

Lorbiecki, A. and Jack, G. (2000) 'Critical turns in the evolution of diversity management', *British Journal of Management*, Vol. 11, pp. S17–S31.

McCracken, D. (2000) 'Winning the talent war for women: sometimes it takes a revolution', *Harvard Business Review*, November–December, pp. 159–65.

Macpherson of Cluny, Sir William (1999) *The Stephen Lawrence Inquiry. A Report by Sir William Macpherson of Cluny.* London: HMSO.

Masreliez-Steen, G. (1989) *Male and Female Management.* Sweden: Kontura Group.

Miller, D. (1996) 'Equality management – towards a materialist approach', *Gender, Work and Organisation*, Vol. 3, No. 4, pp. 202–14.

Newman, J. and Williams, F. (1995) 'Diversity and change, gender, welfare and organisational relations', in C. Itzin and J. Newman, *Gender, Culture and Organisational Change.* London: Routledge.

Ng, C. and Chiu, W. (2001) 'Managing Equal Opportunities for women: sorting the friends from the foes', *Human Resource Management Journal*, Vol. 11, No. 1, pp. 75–88.

ONS (2005) *Labour Force Survey Spring 2005.* London: HMSO.

ONS (2006) 'Working Lives: Half women's jobs are part-time' at **www.statistics.gov.uk/cci/ nugget.asp?id=1654**.

Ouseley, H. (1996) quoted in S. Overell, 'Ouseley in assault on diversity', *People Management*, 2 May, pp. 7–8.

People Management (2002) 'Call for women in senior roles', Vol. 8, No. 23, 21 November, p. 11.

Philpott, J. (2003) 'Time to tackle age-old problem', *People Management*, Vol. 9, No. 13, June, p. 22.

Platman, K. (2002) 'Matured Assets', *People Management*, Vol. 8, No. 24, 5 December, pp. 40–2.

Rana, E. (2003) 'Council appraisals discriminate', *People Management*, Vol. 9, No. 2, 23 January, p. 11.

Ross, R. and Schneider, R. (1992) *From Equality to Diversity – a business case for equal opportunities.* London: Pitman.

Runnymede Trust (2000) *Moving on up? Racial Equality and the Corporate Agenda, A Study of the FTSE 100 companies.* London: Central Books.

Shapiro, G. and Austin, S. (1996) 'Equality drives total quality', *Occasional Paper*. Brighton: Brighton Business School.

Simmons, M. (1989) 'Making equal opportunities training effective', *Journal of European Industrial Training*, Vol. 13, No. 8, pp. 19–24.

Singer, M. (1993) *Diversity-based Hiring.* Aldershot: Avebury.

Skills and Enterprise Network (2000) *Labour Market and Skills Trends.* Sheffield: DfEE.

Snape, E. and Redman, T. (2003) 'Too old or too young? The impact of perceived age discrimination', *Human Resource Management Journal*, Vol. 13, No. 1, pp. 78–89.

Stonewall (2007) *Workplace Equality Index.* London: Stonewall.

Thair, T. and Risden, A. (1999) 'Women in the labour market: results from the Spring 1998 Labour Force Survey', *Labour Market Trends*, March.

Thomas, R.R. (1990) 'From affirmative action to affirming diversity', *Harvard Business Review*, March–April.

Thomas, R.R. (1992) 'Managing diversity: a conceptual framework', in S. Jackson (ed.) *Diversity in the Workplace*. New York: Guildford Press.

Trades Union Congress (2000) *Qualifying for Racism*. London: TUC.

Ward, J. (2003) 'How to address sexual orientation', *People Management*, Vol. 9, No. 21, 23 October, pp. 62–3.

Wilson, E. (2000) 'Inclusion, exclusion and ambiguity – the role of organizational culture', *Personnel Review*, Vol. 29, No. 3.

Wolff, C. (2007) 'Arriva; dramatic results on diversity', *Equal Opportunities Review*, No. 160, January, pp. 5–11.

Woodhams, C. and Danieli, A. (2000) 'Disability and diversity – a difference too far?', *Personnel Review*, Vol. 29, No. 3.

Woodhams, C. and Lupton, B. (2006) 'Gender-based equal opportunities policy and practice in small firms: the impact of HR professionals', *Human Resource Management Journal*, Vol. 16, No. 1, pp. 74–97.

Woolnough, R. (2000) 'Racism reinforces the glass ceiling', *The Guardian*, 4 November, p. 31.

Young, I.M. (1990) *Justice and the Politics of Difference*. Princeton, NJ: Princeton University Press.

An extensive range of additional materials, including multiple choice questions, answers to questions and links to useful websites can be found on the Human Resource Management Companion Website at **www.pearsoned.co.uk/torrington**.

GRIEVANCE AND DISCIPLINE

THE OBJECTIVES OF THIS CHAPTER ARE TO:

1 Examine the nature and explain the place of grievance and discipline in the employment contract

2 Review the Milgram experiments with obedience and use them to explain our response to authority

3 Explain the framework of organisational justice in the business

4 Explain grievance and discipline procedures

Grievance and discipline are awkward words nowadays. They sound rather solemn and forbidding, more suitable for a nineteenth-century workhouse than a twenty-first-century business. But consider these two press reports:

> Michael Mitchell, 58, the Director General of Railways at the Department of Transport, appeared at Peterborough Magistrates' Court accused of attacking and swearing at Peter Etherington as he served vegetables to diners on a GNER King's Cross to Newcastle service in June last year. (*The Times*, 7 July 2006, p. 17)
>
> [Helen Green, 36,] a city secretary who endured a campaign of harassment at the hands of her co-workers, including mocking and offensive remarks and having raspberries blown at her, has won more than £800,000 compensation . . . She told a High Court judge: 'This was not playful, it was malicious. It was vicious.' (*The Times*, 2 August 2006, p. 3)

Both of these cases indicate the importance of managements taking employee grievances seriously, otherwise there will be recourse to the courts, where the costs will be substantial and the publicity grievous.

In 2004, under the terms of the 2002 Employment Act, the Dispute Resolution Regulations were issued, which give employees the right to take a grievance directly to a tribunal without necessarily going through internal procedures. Mordsley and Aylott (2006) have analysed recent EAT decisions to conclude that:

- There is no requirement to comply with any internal procedures.
- Employees do not have to ask for a meeting to discuss the complaint.

The employee must still advise the employer of the complaint, but does not need to set out the full basis of it until invited to a meeting with the employer. This is a further reason for employers to take complaints seriously and to ensure that their internal procedures are effective and fully respected.

We use the words grievance and discipline as technical terms to describe the breakdown of mutual confidence between employer and employee, or between managers and managed. When someone starts working at an organisation there are mutual expectations that form the basis of the forthcoming working relationship. We explained in the opening chapter of this book how the maintenance of those mutual expectations is the central purpose of human resource management. Apart from what is written in the contract of employment, both parties will have expectations of what is to come. Employees are likely to expect, for instance, a congenial working situation with like-minded colleagues, opportunities to use existing skills and to acquire others, work that does not offend their personal value system, acceptable leadership and management from those more senior and opportunities to grow and mature. Employers will have expectations such as willing participation in the team, conscientious and imaginative use of existing skills and an ability to acquire others, compliance with reasonable instructions without quibbles, acceptance of the authority of those placed in authority and a willingness to be flexible and accept change.

That working relationship is sometimes going to go wrong. If the employee is dissatisfied, then there is potentially a grievance. If the employer is dissatisfied, there is the potential for a disciplinary situation. The two complementary processes are intended to find ways of avoiding the ultimate sanction of the employee quitting or being dismissed, but at the same time preparing the ground for those sanctions if all else fails.

Usually, the authority to be exercised in a business is impersonalise̶d̶ ̶t̶h̶r̶o̶u̶g̶h̶ f roles in order to make it more effective. If a colleague mentions to you that you have overspent your budget, your reaction might be proud bravado unless you knew that the colleague had a role such as company accountant, internal auditor or financial director. Everyone in a business has a role. Most people have several roles and each confers some authority. The canteen assistant who tells you that the steak and kidney pudding is off is more believable than the managing director conveying the same message. Normally in hospitals people wearing white coats and a stethoscope are seen as being more author-itative than people in white coats without a stethoscope.

Dependence on role is not always welcome to those in managerial positions, who are fond of using phrases like, 'I know how to get the best out of people' or 'I have a loyal staff'. This may partly be due to their perception of their role being to persuade the reluctant and command the respect of the unwilling by the use of personal leadership qualities, and it is indisputable that some managers are more effective with some groups of staff than with others, as we saw in Chapter 14, but there is more to it than personal skill: we are predisposed to obey those who outrank us in any hierarchy.

THE MILGRAM EXPERIMENTS WITH OBEDIENCE

Obedience is the reaction expected of people by those in authority positions, who pre-scribe actions which, but for that authority, might not necessarily have been carried out. Stanley Milgram (1974) conducted a classic and controversial series of experiments to investigate obedience to authority and highlighted the significance of obedience and the power of authority in our everyday lives. His work remains a standard explanation of how we all behave.

Subjects were led to believe that a study of memory and learning was being carried out which involved giving progressively more severe electric shocks to a learner who gave incorrect answers to factual questions. If the learner gave the correct answer the reward was a further question; if the answer was incorrect there was the punishment of a mild electric shock. Each shock was more severe than the previous one. The 'learner' was not actually receiving shocks, but was a member of the experimental team simulating progressively greater distress, as the shocks were supposedly made stronger. Eighteen different experiments were conducted with over 1,000 subjects, with the circumstances between experiments varying. No matter how the variables were altered the subjects showed an astonishing compliance with authority even when delivering 'shocks' of 450 volts. Up to 65 per cent of subjects continued to obey throughout the experiment in the presence of a clear authority figure and as many as 20 per cent continued to obey when the authority figure was absent.

Milgram was dismayed by his results:

> With numbing regularity good people were seen to knuckle under to the demands of authority and perform actions that were callous and severe. Men who are in everyday life responsible and decent were seduced by the trappings of authority, by the control of their perceptions, and by the uncritical acceptance of the experimenter's definition of the situation into performing harsh acts. (1974, p. 123)

Our interest in Milgram's work is simply to demonstrate that we all have a predilection to obey instructions from authority figures, even if we do not want to. He points out that the act of entering a hierarchical system (such as any employing organisation) makes people see themselves acting as agents for carrying out the wishes of someone else, and this results in these people being in a different state, described as the agentic state. This is the opposite to the state of autonomy when individuals see themselves as acting on their own. Milgram then sets out the factors that lay the groundwork for obedience to authority.

1 Family. Parental regulation inculcates a respect for adult authority. Parental injunctions form the basis for moral imperatives, as commands to children have a dual function. 'Don't tell lies' is a moral injunction carrying a further implicit instruction: 'And obey me!' It is the implicit demand for obedience that remains the only consistent element across a range of explicit instructions.

2 Institutional setting. Children emerge from the family into an institutional system of authority: the school. Here they learn how to function in an organisation. They are regulated by teachers, but can see that the head teacher, the school governors and central government regulate the teachers themselves. Throughout this period they are in a subordinate position. When, as adults, they go to work it may be found that a certain level of dissent is allowable, but the overall situation is one in which they are to do a job prescribed by someone else.

3 Rewards. Compliance with authority is generally rewarded, while disobedience is frequently punished. Most significantly, promotion within the hierarchy not only rewards the individual but also ensures the continuity of the hierarchy.

4 Perception of authority. Authority is normatively supported: there is a shared expectation among people that certain institutions do, ordinarily, have a socially controlling figure. Also, the authority of the controlling figure is limited to the situation. The usher in a cinema wields authority, which vanishes on leaving the premises. Where authority is expected it does not have to be asserted, merely presented.

5 Entry into the authority system. Having perceived an authority figure, an individual must then define that figure as relevant to the subject. The individual not only takes the voluntary step of deciding which authority system to join (at least in most of employment), but also defines which authority is relevant to which event. The fire fighter may expect instant obedience when calling for everybody to evacuate the building, but not if asking employees to use a different accounting system.

6 The overarching ideology. The legitimacy of the social situation relates to a justifying ideology. Science and education formed the background to the experiments Milgram conducted and therefore provided a justification for actions carried out in their name. Most employment is in realms of activity regarded as legitimate, justified by the values and needs of society. This is vital if individuals are to provide willing obedience, as it enables them to see their behaviour as serving a desirable end.

Managers are positioned in an organisational hierarchy in such a way that others will be predisposed, as Milgram demonstrates, to follow their instructions. Managers put in place a series of frameworks to explain how they will exact obedience: they use *discipline*. Because individual employees feel their relative weakness, they seek complementary frameworks to challenge the otherwise unfettered use of managerial disciplinary power: they may join trade unions, but they will always need channels to present their *grievances*.

In later work Milgram (1992) made an important distinction between obedience and conformity, which had been studied by several experimental psychologists, most notably Asch (1951) and Abrams *et al.* (1990). Conformity and obedience both involve abandoning personal judgement as a result of external pressure. The external pressure to conform is the need to be accepted by one's peers and the resultant behaviour is to wear similar clothes, to adopt similar attitudes and adopt similar behaviour. The external pressure to obey comes from a hierarchy of which one is a member, but in which certain others have more status and power than oneself.

> There are at least three important differences . . . First, in conformity there is no explicit requirement to act in a certain way, whereas in obedience we are ordered or instructed to do something. Second, those who influence us when we conform are our peers (or equals) and people's behaviours become more alike because they are affected by example. In obedience, there is . . . somebody in higher authority influencing behaviour. Third, conformity has to do with the psychological need for acceptance by others. Obedience, by contrast, has to do with the social power and status of an authority figure in a hierarchical situation. (Gross and McIlveen 1998, p. 508)

In this chapter we are concerned only with discipline and grievance within business organisations, but it is worth pointing out that managers are the focal points for the grievances of people outside the business as well, but those grievances are called complaints. You may complain *about* poor service, shoddy workmanship or rudeness from an employee, but you complain *to* a manager.

HR managers make one of their most significant contributions to business effectiveness by the way they facilitate and administer grievance and disciplinary issues. First, they devise and negotiate the procedural framework of organisational justice on which both discipline and grievance depend. Second, they are much involved in the interviews and problem-solving discussions that eventually produce solutions to the difficulties that have been encountered. Third, they maintain the viability of the whole process which forms an integral part of their work: they monitor to make sure that grievances are not overlooked and so that any general trend can be perceived, and they oversee the disciplinary machinery to ensure that it is not being bypassed or unfairly manipulated.

Grievance and discipline handling is one of the roles in HRM that few other people want to take over. Ambitious line managers may want to select their own staff without HR intervention or by using the services of consultants. They may try to brush their HR colleagues aside and deal directly with trade union officials or organise their own management development, but grievance and discipline is too hot a potato.

The requirements of the law regarding explanation of grievance handling and the legal framework to avoid unfair dismissal combine to make this an area where HR people must be both knowledgeable and effective. That combination provides a valuable platform for influencing other aspects of management. The HR manager who is not skilled in grievance and discipline is seldom in a strong organisational position.

Everything we have said so far presupposes both hierarchy and the use of procedures. You may say that we have already demonstrated that hierarchy is in decline and that there is a preference for more flexible, personal ways of working than procedure offers. Why rely on Milgram's research, which is now over thirty years old? Surely we have moved on since then? Our response is simply that hierarchical relationships continue, although deference is in decline. We still seek out the person 'in authority' when we have a grievance and managers readily refer problems they cannot resolve to someone else with a more appropriate role. Procedures may be rigid and mechanical, but they are reliable and we use them even if we do not like them.

WINDOW ON PRACTICE

At the end of the twentieth century school teaching in Britain saw the widespread introduction of procedures to deal with teacher capability. Research (Torrington *et al.* 2003) showed that these procedures were generally ineffective in restoring capability and effectiveness for teachers who had lost their way, because of the general reluctance by head teachers to use procedures rather than personal leadership in finding solutions. The result was that heads used an inordinate amount of time in dealing with situations and 'incapable' teachers were extremely distressed and frequently ill because matters were never properly dealt with.

WHAT DO WE MEAN BY DISCIPLINE?

Discipline is regulation of human activity to produce a controlled performance. It ranges from the guard's control of a rabble to the accomplishment of lone individuals producing spectacular performance through self-discipline in the control of their own talents and resources.

The Advisory, Conciliation and Arbitration Service (ACAS) has produced a code of practice relating to disciplinary procedures which makes precisely this point:

> Disciplinary procedures should not be viewed primarily as a means of imposing sanctions [but] . . . as a way of helping and encouraging improvement amongst employees whose conduct or standard of work is unsatisfactory. (ACAS 2000, p. 6)

First, there is managerial discipline in which everything depends on the leader from start to finish. There is a group of people who are answerable to someone who directs what they should all do. Only through individual direction can that group of people produce a worthwhile performance, like the person leading the community singing in the pantomime or the conductor of an orchestra. Everything depends on the leader.

Second, there is team discipline, where the perfection of the performance derives from the mutual dependence of all, and that mutual dependence derives from a commitment by each member to the total enterprise: the failure of one would be the downfall of all. This is usually found in relatively small working groups, like a dance troupe or an autonomous working group in a factory.

Third, there is self-discipline, like that of the juggler or the skilled artisan, where a solo performer is absolutely dependent on training, expertise and self-control. One of

Figure 25.1
Three forms
of discipline

the few noted UK researchers working in the field of discipline concludes that self-discipline has recently become much more significant, as demonstrated in the title of his work, 'Discipline: towards trust and self-discipline' (Edwards 2000).

Discipline is, therefore, not only negative, producing punishment or prevention. It can also be a valuable quality for the individual who is subject to it, although the form of discipline depends not only on the individual employee but also on the task and the way it is organised. The development of self-discipline is easier in some jobs than others and many of the job redesign initiatives of recent years have been directed at providing scope for job holders to exercise self-discipline and find a degree of autonomy from managerial discipline. Figure 25.1 shows how the three forms are connected in a sequence or hierarchy, with employees finding one of three ways to achieve their contribution to organisational effectiveness. However, even the most accomplished solo performer has at some time been dependent on others for training and advice, and every team has its coach.

ACTIVITY 25.1

Note three examples of managerial discipline, team discipline and self-discipline from your own experience.

Managers are not dealing with discipline only when they are rebuking latecomers or threatening to dismiss saboteurs. As well as dealing with the unruly and reluctant, they are developing the coordinated discipline of the working team, engendering that *esprit de corps* which makes the whole greater than the sum of the parts. They are training the new recruit who must not let down the rest of the team, puzzling over the reasons why A is fitting in well while B is still struggling. Managers are also providing people with the equipment to develop the self-discipline that will give them autonomy, responsibility and the capacity to maximise their powers. The independence and autonomy that self-discipline produces also bring the greatest degree of personal satisfaction, and often the largest pay packet. Furthermore the movement between the three forms represents a declining degree of managerial involvement. If you are a leader of community singing, nothing can happen without your being present and the quality of the singing depends on your performance each time. If you train jugglers, the time and effort you invest pays off a thousand times, while you sit back and watch the show.

In employment there has long been an instinctive tendency to put discipline together with punishment, however limited this notion may be. The legislation on unfair dismissal is to most managers the logical final point of disciplinary procedures, yet it covers dismissal on the grounds of capability and ill health as well as more obvious forms of indiscipline. Because of this general feeling that disciplinary procedures imply disobedience, there is an emerging trend to have separate procedures to cover capability, so as to avoid the stigma, but being unsatisfactory in any way is difficult for many people to cope with:

> None of the teachers . . . believed they were 'perfect teachers' but they refused to equate imperfection with incapability . . . [for example] 'It was unsatisfactory and obviously I wanted to be satisfactory and above, but it wasn't poor, it wasn't incapability material.' (Torrington 2006, p. 391)

No matter how hard one tries, the prefix 'in-' causes problems. To be indisciplined is unwelcome (and does not actually appear in the dictionary): to be incapable is even worse.

WHAT DO WE MEAN BY GRIEVANCE?

We can distinguish between the terms dissatisfaction, complaint and grievance as follows:

- **Dissatisfaction.** Anything that disturbs an employee, whether or not the unrest is expressed in words.
- **Complaint.** A spoken or written dissatisfaction brought to the attention of a manager or other responsible person.
- **Grievance.** A complaint that has been formally presented to an appropriate management representative or to a union official.

This provides a useful categorisation by separating out grievance as a formal, relatively drastic step, compared with simply complaining. It is much more important for management to know about dissatisfaction. Although nothing is being expressed, the feeling of hurt following failure to get a pay rise or the frustration about shortage of materials can quickly influence performance.

Much dissatisfaction never turns into complaint, as something happens to make it unnecessary. Dissatisfaction evaporates with a night's sleep, after a cup of coffee with a colleague, or when the cause of the dissatisfaction is in some other way removed. The few dissatisfactions that do produce complaint are also most likely to resolve themselves at that stage. The person hearing the complaint explains things in a way that the dissatisfied employee had not previously appreciated, or takes action to get at the root of the problem.

Grievances are rare since few employees will openly question their superior's judgement, whatever their private opinion may be, and fewer still will risk being stigmatised as a troublemaker. Also, many people do not initiate grievances because they believe that nothing will be done as a result of their attempt. Tribunal hearings since the 2004 regulations, already referred to, were introduced have often found great difficulty in deciding when a complaint becomes a grievance.

HR managers have to encourage the proper use of procedures to discover sources of dissatisfaction. Managers in the middle may not reveal the complaints they are hearing, for fear of showing themselves in a poor light. Employees who feel insecure, for any reason, are not likely to risk going into procedure, yet the dissatisfaction lying beneath a repressed grievance can produce all manner of unsatisfactory work behaviours from apathy to arson. Individual dissatisfaction can lead to the loss of a potentially valuable employee; collective dissatisfaction can lead to industrial action.

In dealing with complaints it is important to determine what lies behind the complaint as well as the complaint being expressed; not only verifying the facts, which are the *manifest* content of the complaint, but also determining the feelings behind the facts: the *latent* content. An employee who complains of the supervisor being a bully may actually be expressing something rather different, such as the employee's attitude to any authority figure, not simply the supervisor who was the subject of the complaint.

ACTIVITY 25.2

Think of an example from your own experience of dissatisfaction causing inefficiency that was not remedied because there was no complaint. Why was there no complaint?

THE FRAMEWORK OF ORGANISATIONAL JUSTICE

The organisation requires a framework of justice to surround the employment relationship so that managers and supervisors, as well as other employees, know where they stand when dissatisfaction develops. An illustration of this is in Figure 25.2.

Organisation culture and management style

The culture of an organisation affects the behaviour of people within it and develops norms that are hard to alter and which provide a pattern of conformity. If, for instance, everyone is in the habit of arriving ten minutes late, a 'new broom' manager will have a struggle to change the habit. Equally, if everyone is in the habit of arriving punctually,

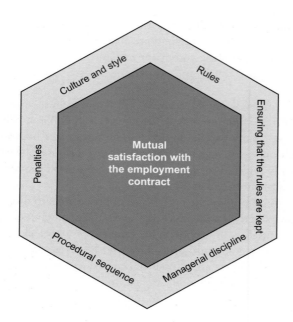

Figure 25.2
The
framework of
organisational
justice

then a new recruit who often arrives late will come under strong social pressure to conform, without need for recourse to management action. Culture also affects the freedom and candour with which people discuss dissatisfactions with their managers without allowing them to fester.

The style of managers in handling grievances and discipline reflects their beliefs. The manager who sees discipline narrowly as being punishment, and who regards grievances as examples of subordinates getting above themselves, will behave in a relatively autocratic way, being curt in disciplinary situations and dismissive of complaints. The manager who sees disciplinary problems as obstacles to achievement that do not necessarily imply incompetence or ill will by the employee will seek out the cause of the problem. That problem may then be revealed as one requiring firm, punitive action by the manager, or it may be revealed as a matter requiring management remedy of a different kind. The manager who listens out for complaints and grievances, gets to the bottom of the problems and finds solutions will run little risk of rumbling discontent from people obsessed by trivial problems.

Rules

Every workplace has rules; the difficulty is to have rules that people will honour. Some rules come from legislation, such as the tachograph requirement for HGV drivers, but most are tailored to meet the particular requirements of the organisation in which they apply. For example, rules about personal cleanliness are essential in a food factory but less stringent in a garage.

Rules should be clear and readily understood; the number should be sufficient to cover all obvious and usual disciplinary matters. To ensure general compliance it is helpful if rules are jointly determined, but it is more common for management to formulate the rules and for employee representatives eventually to concur with them. Employees should have ready access to the rules through the employee handbook and noticeboard, and the HR manager will always try to ensure that the rules are known as well as published.

Rules can be roughly grouped into various types:

1 **Negligence** is failure to do the job properly and is different from incompetence because of the assumption that the employee can do the job properly, but has not.

2 **Unreliability** is failure to attend work as required, such as being late or absent.

3 **Insubordination** is refusal to obey an instruction, or deliberate disrespect to someone in a position of authority. It is not to be confused with the use of bad language. Some of the most entertaining cases in employment tribunals have involved weighty consideration of whether or not colourful language was intended to be insubordinate.

4 **Interfering with the rights of others** covers a range of behaviours that are socially unacceptable. Fighting is clearly identifiable, but harassment or intimidation may be more difficult to establish.

5 **Theft** is another clear-cut aspect of behaviour that is unacceptable when it is from another employee. Theft from the organisation should be supported by very explicit rules, as stealing company property is regarded by many offenders as one of the perks of the job. How often have you taken home a box of paper clips or a felt tip pen without any thought that you were stealing from the employer?

6 **Safety offences** are those aspects of behaviour that can cause a hazard.

The value of rules is to provide guidelines on what people should do, as the majority will comply. It is extremely difficult to apply rules that do not command general acceptance.

WINDOW ON PRACTICE

In a recent discussion with a group of senior managers, employees identified the following as legitimately taken at will:

- paper clips, pencils, disposable pens, spiral pads, local telephone calls, plain paper, computer disks, adhesive tape, overalls and simple uniform.

Among the more problematic were:

- **Redundant or shop-soiled stock.** One DIY store insisted that the store manager should personally supervise the scrapping of items that were slightly damaged, to ensure that other items were not slightly damaged on purpose.

- **Surplus materials.** One electricity supplier had some difficulty in eradicating the practice of surplus cable and pipe being regarded as a legitimate perquisite of fitters at the end of installation jobs, as they suspected their engineers were using the surplus for private work. Twelve months later the level of material requisition had declined by 14 per cent.

Ensuring that the rules are kept

It is not sufficient just to have rules; they are only effective if they are observed. How do we make sure that employees stick to the rules?

1 **Information** is needed so that everyone knows what the rules are. Written particulars may suffice in an employment tribunal hearing, but most people conform to the behaviour of their colleagues, so informal methods of communication are just as important as formal statements.

2 **Induction** can make the rules coherent and reinforce their understanding. Rules can be explained, perhaps with examples, so that people not only know the rules but also understand why they should be obeyed.

3 **Placement or relocation** can avoid the risk of rules being broken, by placing a new recruit with a working team that has high standards of compliance. If there are the signs of disciplinary problems in the offing, then a quick relocation can put the problem employee in a new situation where offences are less likely.

4 **Training** increases awareness of the rules, improving self-confidence and self-discipline. There will be new working procedures or new equipment from time to time, and again training will reduce the risk of safety offences, negligence or unreliability.

5 **Reviewing the rules periodically** ensures that they are up to date, and also ensures that their observance is a live issue. If, for instance, there is a monthly staff council meeting, it could be appropriate to have a rules review every 12 months. The simple fact of the rules being discussed keeps up the general level of awareness of what they are.

6 **Penalties** make the framework of organisational justice firmer if there is an understanding of what penalties can be imposed, by whom and for what. It is not feasible to have a fixed scale, but neither is it wise for penalties to depend on individual managerial whim. This area has been partially codified by the legislation on dismissal, but the following are some typical forms of penalty:

(a) **Rebuke.** The simple 'Don't do that' or 'Smoking is not allowed in here' or 'If you're late again, you will be in trouble' is all that is needed in most situations, as someone has forgotten one of the rules, had not realised it was to be taken seriously, or was perhaps testing the resolution of the management. Too frequently, managers are reluctant to risk defiance and tend to wait until they have a good case for more serious action rather than deploy their own, there-and-then authority.

(b) **Caution.** Slightly more serious and formal is the caution, which is then recorded. This is not triggering the procedure for dismissal, it is just making a note of a rule being broken and an offence being pointed out.

(c) **Warnings.** When managers begin to issue warnings, great care is required because unfair dismissal legislation has made the system of warnings an integral part of disciplinary practice, which must be followed if the employer is to succeed in defending a possible claim of unfair dismissal at tribunal. For the employer to show procedural fairness there should normally be a formal oral warning, or a written warning, specifying the nature of the offence and the likely outcome if the offence is repeated. It should also be made clear that this is the first, formal stage in the procedure. Further misconduct could then warrant a final written warning containing a statement that further repetition would lead to a penalty such as suspension or dismissal. All written warnings should be dated, signed and kept on record for an agreed period. The means of appeal against the disciplinary action should also be pointed out.

(d) **Disciplinary transfer or demotion.** This is moving the employee to less attractive work, possibly carrying a lower salary. The seriousness of this is that it is public, as the employee's colleagues know the reason. A form of disciplinary transfer is found on assembly lines, where there are some jobs that are more attractive and carry higher status than others. Rule breakers may be 'pushed down the line' until their contempt is purged and they are able to move back up.

(e) **Suspension.** This tactic has the benefit of being serious and is not as long lasting as demotion. The employer has a contractual obligation to provide pay, but not to provide work, so it is easy to suspend someone from duty with pay either as a punishment or while an alleged offence is being investigated. If the contract of employment permits, it may also be possible to suspend the employee for a short period without pay.

The important general comment about penalties is that they should be appropriate in the circumstances. Where someone is, for instance, persistently late or absent, suspension would be a strange penalty. Also penalties must be within the law. An employee cannot be demoted or transferred at managerial whim, and unpaid suspension can only be imposed if the contract of employment allows it.

Procedural sequence

This is the clear, unvarying logic of procedure, which should be well known and trusted. Procedure makes clear, for example, who does and who does not have the power to dismiss. The dissatisfied employee, who is wondering whether or not to turn a complaint into a formal grievance, knows who will hear the grievance and where an appeal could be lodged. This security of procedure, where step B always follows step A, is needed by managers as well as by employees, as it provides them with their authority as well as limiting the scope of their actions.

Managerial discipline

This preserves general respect for the justice framework by managers exercising self-discipline in how they work within it. With very good intentions some senior managers maintain an 'open door' policy with the message: 'My door is always open . . . call in any time you feel I can help you'. This has many advantages and is often necessary, but it has danger for matters of discipline and grievance if it encourages people to bypass middle managers. There is also the danger that employees come to see the settlement of their grievances as being dependent on the personal goodwill of an individual rather than on the business logic or their human and employment rights.

Managers must be consistent in handling discipline and grievance issues. Whatever the rules are, they will be generally supported only as long as they deserve support. If they are enforced inconsistently they will soon lose any moral authority, and will be obeyed only because of employees' fear of penalties. Equally, the manager who handles grievances quickly and consistently will enjoy the support of a committed group of employees.

The other need for managerial discipline is to test the validity of the discipline assumption. Is it a case for disciplinary action or for some other remedy? There is little purpose in suspending someone for negligence when the real problem is lack of training. Many disciplinary problems disappear under analysis, and it is sensible to carry out the analysis before making a possibly unjustified allegation of indiscipline.

GRIEVANCE PROCEDURE

Managers who believe that it introduces unnecessary rigidity into the working relationship often resent the formality of the grievance procedure: 'I see my people all the time. We work side by side and they can raise with me any issue they want, at any time they want . . .'. The problem is that many people will not raise issues with the immediate superior that could be regarded as contentious, in just the same way that managers frequently shirk the rebuke as a form of disciplinary penalty. Formality in procedure provides a structure within which individuals can reasonably air their grievances and avoids the likelihood of managers dodging the issue when it is difficult. It avoids the risk of inconsistent ad hoc decisions, and the employee knows at the outset that the matter will be heard and where it will be heard. The key features of grievance procedure are fairness, facilities for representation, procedural steps and promptness.

1 **Fairness** is needed, to be just, but also to keep the procedure viable. If employees develop the belief that the procedure is only a sham, then its value will be lost and other means will be sought to deal with grievances. Fairness is best supported by the obvious even-handedness of the ways in which grievances are handled, but it will be greatly enhanced if the appeal stage is either to a joint body or to independent arbitration, as the management is relinquishing the chance to be judge of its own cause.

2 **Representation** can help the individual employee who lacks the confidence or experience to take on the management singlehandedly. A representative, such as a union official, has the advantage of having dealt with a range of employee problems and may be able to advise the aggrieved person whether the claim is worth pursuing. There is always the risk that the presence of the representative may produce a defensive management attitude that is affected by a number of other issues on which the manager and union official may be at loggerheads. Therefore the managers involved in hearing the grievance have to cast the representative in the correct role for the occasion.

3 **Procedural steps** should be limited to three. There is no value in having more just because there are more levels in the management hierarchy. This will only lengthen the time taken to deal with matters and will soon bring the procedure into disrepute. The reason for advocating three steps is that three types of management activity are involved in settling grievances. Nevertheless, it is quite common for there to be more than three steps where there is a steep hierarchy, within which there may be further, more senior, people to whom the matter could be referred. The reason for there being more steps has nothing to do with how to process grievances but is purely a function of the organisation structure.

- The first step is the *preliminary*, when the grievance is lodged with the immediate superior of the person with the complaint. In the normal working week most managers will have a variety of queries from members of their departments, some of which could become grievances, depending on the manager's reaction. Mostly the manager will either satisfy the employee or the employee will decide not to pursue the matter. Sometimes, however, a person will want to take the issue further. This is the preliminary step in procedure, but it is a tangible step as the manager has the opportunity to review any decisions made that have caused the dissatisfaction, possibly enabling the dissatisfied employee to withdraw the grievance. In our experience it is rare for matters to be taken any further unless the subject of the grievance is something on which company policy is being tested.

- The *hearing* gives the complainant the opportunity to state the grievance to a more senior manager, who is able to take a broader view of the matter than the immediate superior and who may be able both to see the issue more dispassionately and to perceive solutions that the more limited perspective of the immediate superior obscured. It is important for the management that the hearing should finalise the matter whenever possible, so that recourse to appeal is not automatic. The hearing should not be seen by the employees as no more than an irritating milestone on the way to the real decision makers. This is why procedural steps should be limited to three.
- If there is an *appeal*, this will usually be to a designated more senior manager, and the outcome will be either a confirmation or a modification of the decision at the hearing.

4 **Promptness** avoids the bitterness and frustration that comes from delay. When an employee 'goes into procedure', it is like pulling the communication cord in a train. The action is not taken lightly and is in anticipation of a swift resolution. Furthermore, the manager whose decision is being questioned will have a difficult time until the matter is resolved. The most familiar device to speed things up is to incorporate time limits between the steps, specifying that the hearing should take place no later than, say, four working days after the preliminary notice and that the appeal should be no more than five working days after the hearing. This gives time for reflection and initiative by the manager or the complainant between the stages, but does not leave time for the matter to be forgotten.

Where the organisation has a collective disputes procedure as well as one for individual grievances, there needs to be an explicit link between the two so that individual matters can be pursued with collective support if there is not a satisfactory outcome. An outline grievance procedure is in Figure 25.3.

DISCIPLINARY PROCEDURE

Procedures for discipline are very similar to those for grievance and depend equally on fairness, promptness and representation. There are some additional features.

Authorisation of penalties

The law requires that managers should not normally have the power to dismiss their immediate subordinates without reference to more senior managers. Whatever penalties are to be imposed, they should only be imposed by people who have that specific authority delegated to them. Usually this means that the more serious penalties can only be imposed by more senior people, but there are many organisations where such decisions are delegated to the HR department.

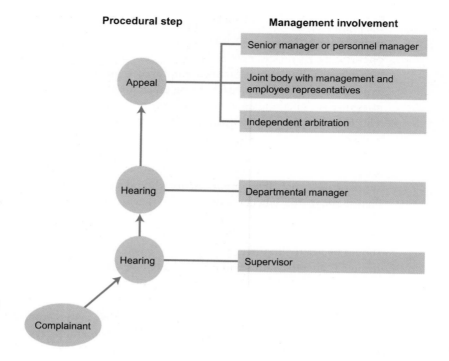

Figure 25.3
Outline
grievance
procedure

Investigation

The procedure should also ensure that disciplinary action is not taken until it has been established that there is a problem that justifies the action. The possibility of suspension on full pay is one way of allowing time for the investigation of dubious allegations, but the stigma attached to such suspensions should not be forgotten.

Information and explanation

If disciplinary action is possible, the person to be disciplined should be told of the complaint, so that an explanation can be made, or the matter denied, before any penalties are decided. If an employee is to be penalised, then the reasons for the decision should be explained to make sure that cause and effect are appreciated. The purpose of penalties is to prevent a recurrence. An outline disciplinary procedure is in Figure 25.4.

ARE GRIEVANCE AND DISCIPLINE PROCESSES EQUITABLE?

For grievance and discipline processes to work they must command support, and they will only command support if they are seen as equitable, truly just and fair. At first it may seem that concern for the individual employee is paramount, but the individual cannot be isolated from the rest of the workforce. Fairness should therefore be linked to the interests that all workers have in common in the business, and to the managers who must also perceive the system as equitable if they are to abide by its outcomes.

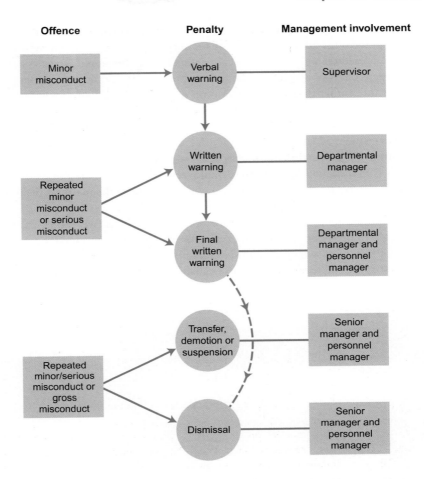

Figure 25.4
Outline
disciplinary
procedure

Procedures have a potential to be fair in that they are certain. The conduct of employee relations becomes less haphazard and irrational: people 'know where they stand'. The existence of a rule cannot be denied and opportunities for one party to manipulate and change a rule are reduced. Procedures also have the advantage that they can be communicated. The process of formalising a procedure that previously existed only in custom and practice clarifies the ambiguities and inconsistencies within it and compels each party to recognise the role and responsibility of the other. By providing pre-established avenues for responses to various contingencies, procedures make it possible for the response to be less random and so more fair. The impersonal nature of procedures offers the possibility of removing hostility from the workplace, since an artificial social situation is created in which the ritual displays of aggression towards management are not seen as personal attacks on managers.

The achievement of equity may not match the potential. Procedures cannot, for instance, impart equity to situations that are basically unfair. Thus attempting to cope with an anomalous pay system through a grievance procedure may be alleviating symptoms rather than treating causes. It is also impossible through a grievance procedure to overcome accepted norms of inequity in a company, such as greater punctuality being required of manual employees than of white-collar employees.

A further feature of procedural equity is its degree of similarity to the judicial process. All procedures adopt certain legalistic mechanisms, such as the right of individuals to be represented and to hear the case against them, but some aspects of legalism, such as burdens of proof and strict adherence to precedent, may cause the application of standard remedies rather than the consideration of individual circumstances.

There is a nice irony in the fact that equity is best achieved when procedures are not used. Procedure is there in the background and expresses principles for fair and effective management of situations. All the time that the **principles** are followed and the framework for organisational justice is observed, procedure is not invoked. The advantage of this is that individuals, whether employees or managers, are not named and shamed so that matters are much easier to deal with. Only when the matter is dealt with badly does the procedural step come closer.

The existence of the procedure becomes the incentive rather than the means for action to be taken: it is not an excuse for inaction. It is accepted that some employment situations require naming and shaming first, with possible remedial action following. In most sports there is on-the-spot penalising of players for breaking the rules.

WINDOW ON PRACTICE

The 'red-hot stove' rule of discipline offers the touching of a red hot stove as an analogy for effective disciplinary action:

1 The burn is immediate. There is no question of cause and effect.

2 You had warning. If the stove was red-hot, you knew what would happen if you touched it.

3 The discipline is consistent. Everyone who touches the stove is burned.

4 The discipline is impersonal. People are burned not because of who they are, but because they touch the stove.

ACTIVITY 25.3

Think of an attempt at disciplinary action that went wrong. Which of the features of the red-hot stove rule were missing?

Notions of fairness are not 'givens' of the situation; they are socially constructed and there will never be more than a degree of consensus on what constitutes fairness. Despite this, the procedural approach can exploit standards of certainty and consistency, which are widely accepted as elements of justice. The extent to which a procedure can do this will depend on the suitability of its structure to local circumstances, the commitment of those who operate it and the way in which it reconciles legalistic and bargaining elements.

SUMMARY PROPOSITIONS

25.1 The authority of managers to exercise discipline in relation to others in the organisation is underpinned by a general predilection of people to obey commands from those holding higher rank in the hierarchy of which they are members.

25.2 The exercise of that discipline is limited by the procedural structures for grievance and discipline.

25.3 Grievance and discipline handling are two areas of human resource management that few other people want to take over, and provide HR managers with some of their most significant contributions to business effectiveness.

25.4 Discipline can be understood as being managerial, team or self-discipline, and the three types are connected hierarchically.

25.5 Dissatisfaction, complaint and grievance form another hierarchy. Unresolved employee dissatisfaction can lead to the loss of potentially valuable employees. In extreme cases it can lead to industrial action.

25.6 Grievance and disciplinary processes both require a framework of organisational justice.

25.7 The procedural framework of disciplinary and grievance processes is one of the keys to their being equitable.

25.8 Effective management of both discipline and grievance is achieved by following the principles of the procedures without invoking them in practice.

GENERAL DISCUSSION TOPICS

1 Do you think Milgram's experiments would have had a different outcome if the subjects had included women as well as men?

2 What examples can individual members of the group cite of self-discipline, team discipline and managerial discipline?

3 'The trouble with grievance procedures is that they encourage people to waste a lot of time with petty grumbles. Life at work is rarely straightforward and people should just accept the rough with the smooth.'

What do you think of that opinion?

FURTHER READING

Torrington, D.P., Earnshaw, J.M., Marchington, L. and Ritchie, M.D. (2003) *Tackling Underperformance in Teaching*. London: Routledge.

This is a report on research regarding teachers' alleged lack of capability. The results, including a number of case studies, are really an object lesson in how *not* to deal with a problem. The reader will easily work out how the matters *should* have been dealt with. Whether they would actually have done any better is debatable. Handling misconduct is easy; handling lack of capability is much more difficult.

REFERENCES

Abrams, D., Wetherell, M., Cochrane, S., Hogg, M.A. and Turner, J.C. (1990) 'Knowing what to think by knowing who you are: Self categorization and norm formation', *British Journal of Social Psychology*, Vol. 29, pp. 97–119.

Advisory, Conciliation and Arbitration Service (2000) *Code of Practice on Disciplinary Practice and Grievance Procedures at Work*. London: HMSO.

Asch, S.E. (1951) 'Effect of group pressure upon the modification and distortion of judgements', in H. Guetzkow (ed.), *Groups, Leadership and Men*. Pittsburgh, Penn.: Carnegie Press.

Edwards, P. (2000) 'Discipline: towards trust and self-discipline', in S. Bach and K. Sisson (eds), *Personnel Management*, 3rd edn. Oxford: Blackwell.

Gross, R. and McIlveen, R. (1998) *Psychology: A New Introduction*. London: Hodder & Stoughton.

Milgram, S. (1974) *Obedience to Authority*. London: Tavistock.

Milgram, S. (1992) *The Individual in a Social World*, 2nd edn. New York: Harper & Row.

Mordsley, B. and Aylott, C. (2006) 'A Grievance By Any Other Name', *People Management*, 13 July, p. 19.

Torrington, D.P., Earnshaw, J.M., Marchington, L. and Ritchie, M.D. (2003) *Tackling Underperformance in Teachers*. London: Routledge.

Torrington, D.P. (2006) 'Procedures as a way of handling capability problems in the teaching profession and implications for more general application', *Employee Relations*, Vol. 28, No. 4, pp. 311–25.

An extensive range of additional materials, including exercises, a case study, multiple choice questions, answers to questions and links to useful websites can be found on the Human Resource Management Companion Website at **www.pearsoned.co.uk/torrington**.

INTERACTIVE SKILL 5: GRIEVANCE AND DISCIPLINARY INTERVIEWING

In concluding this Part we pick up on the theme of Chapter 25 by considering grievance and disciplinary interviewing. This type of interactive skill falls into the fourth category of face-to-face situations that we described in the first of our Focuses on skills, namely conflict resolution (*see* Figure 1.1).

We said earlier that the appraisal interview was the hardest aspect of management for any manager to undertake. The subject of this Focus is the least popular of all management activities: talking to people when things have gone wrong. Reading most books on management you might think that things never go wrong. The writing has such an upbeat tone that it is *entirely* positive, enthusiastic, visionary, forward looking and all the other qualities that are so important. Sometimes, however, things really do go wrong and have to be sorted out. The sorting out involves at some point a meeting between a dissatisfied manager and an employee who is seen as the cause of that dissatisfaction, or between a dissatisfied employee and a manager representing the employing organisation that is seen as the cause of the employee's dissatisfaction. Procedures, as described in Chapter 25, can do no more than force meetings to take place: it is the meetings themselves that produce answers.

The objectives of this Focus on skills are:

1 To review concepts of discipline and grievance

2 To examine the nature of interviewing in grievance and discipline

3 To outline an approach to grievance and discipline interviewing by suggesting model sequences

The concepts of discipline and grievance

Many present-day views of discipline are connected with the idea of punishment: a disciplinarian is one seen as an enforcer of rules, a hard taskmaster or martinet. To discipline schoolchildren is usually to punish them by keeping them in after school or chastising them. Disciplinary procedures in employment are usually drawn up to provide a preliminary to dismissal, so that any eventual dismissal will not be viewed as unfair by a tribunal. This background makes a problem-solving approach to discipline difficult for a manager, as there is always the sanction in the background making it unlikely that the employee will see the manager's behaviour as being authentic. There will always be a feeling somewhere between outright conviction and lingering uncertainty that a manager in a disciplinary interview is looking for a justification to punish rather than looking for a more constructive solution. The approach of this Focus on skills is based on the more accurate notion of discipline implied in its derivation from the Latin *discere*, to learn and *discipulus*, learner. In disciplinary interviews the manager is attempting to modify the working behaviour of a subordinate, but the modification does not necessarily involve punishment.

The idea of grievance similarly has problems of definition and ethos. In the last chapter we used the convenient scale of dissatisfaction–complaint–grievance as an explanation, but that is a convenient technical classification. The general sense of the word is closer to the dictionary definitions which use phrases such as 'a real or imaginary wrong causing resentment' or 'a feeling of injustice, of having been unfairly treated'. Notions of resentment and injustice seem too heavy for situations where the basic problem is that the maintenance crew have fallen down on the job or the central heating is not working properly. Where we have unresolved problems about our jobs (even when we are deeply worried by them) we are often reluctant to construe our feelings as 'having a grievance'. We just want to get more information, or an opportunity for training, or a chance to talk to someone a bit more senior. Very few people indeed want to be seen to be grumbling. Customers are generally reluctant to grumble about the service they receive, because it is too much trouble, because no one would listen, or just because they do not want to make a fuss; yet they can simply walk away. Compared with customers, employees are much less inclined to complain, or even to point out problems, for fear of being categorised as a nuisance.

Despite the difficulties, our aim here is to formulate an approach to the interview that achieves an adjustment in attitude, with the changed attitude being confirmed by subsequent experience. Either the manager believes that the employee's subsequent working behaviour will be satisfactory, or the employee believes that his or her subsequent experience in employment will be satisfactory. The conflict of interest between the parties is resolved and the interview only succeeds when there is that confirmation.

In his profound and simple book of 1960, Douglas McGregor advocated an approach to management based on the strategy of *integration and self-control*. He regarded forms and procedures as having little value and emphasised the importance of social inter-action as well as the difficulty of achieving any change in people's interactive behaviour:

> Every adult human being has an elaborate history of past experience in this field and additional learning is profoundly influenced by that history. From infancy on, his ability to achieve his goals and satisfy his needs – his 'social survival' – has been a function of his skills in influencing others. Deep emotional currents – unconscious needs such as those related to dependency and counterdependency – are involved. He has a large 'ego investment' and his knowledge and skill in this area, and the defences he has built to protect that investment are strong and psychologically complex. (McGregor 1960, p. 75)

Just as we set grievance and discipline alongside each other in the last chapter, sim-ilarly we examine here the grievance/disciplinary encounter in the same framework, as both are trying to tackle dissatisfaction where resolution of the problem is not straight-forward. If Jim sets fire to the Plant Director's office and admits to the police that he did it for a lark because he was bored, then any disciplinary interview ought not be too difficult. If Joe is not working as well as he used to, but nobody quite knows why and he refuses to say anything about it to anyone, then there is the less straightforward situation with which the approach of this Focus on skills might help.

ACTIVITY 5.1

What grievance or disciplinary incidents can you recall where the situation was not clear-cut and where an interview with a manager produced a resolution to the problem that was effective, although quite different from what had been anticipated by the manager at the beginning of the interview?

The nature of grievance and disciplinary interviewing

Many grievance or discipline interviews are simple: giving information, explaining work requirements and delivering rebukes, but from time to time every manager will need to use a problem-solving approach, involving sympathy, perception, empathy and the essential further feature that some managers provide only with reluctance: time. The method will be analytical and constructive; not only for the interviews built in to the grievance and discipline procedure, but also for interviews that avoid recourse to the rigid formality of procedure. We see such interviews as one of the means towards *self-discipline* and *autonomy* of employees, reducing the need for supervision. The sequence we advocate has discipline and grievance intertwined for much of the process but diverging in the interview itself (*see* Figure 5.1).

As we have shown in the previous chapter, a grievance may be expressed only in manifest form, requiring interviewing to understand its latent content in order that appropriate action is taken to remove the underlying dissatisfaction. Discipline

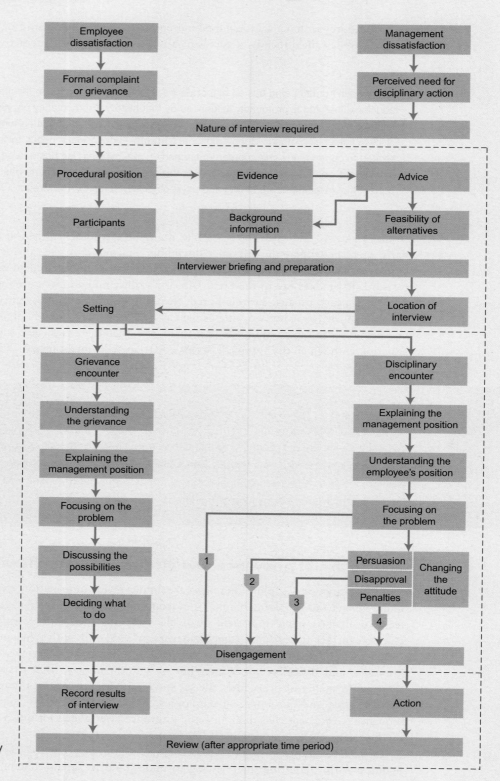

Figure 5.1
The grievance
and disciplinary
interviews

problems will have underlying reasons for the unsatisfactory behaviour and these need to be discovered before solutions to the problems can be attempted.

The discipline and grievance sequence

Preparation

The first requirement is to check the procedural position and to ensure that the impending interview is appropriate. In a grievance situation, for instance, is the employee pre-empting the procedure by taking the matter to the wrong person or to the wrong point in the procedure? This is most common when the first-line supervisor is being bypassed, either because the employee or the representative feels that it would be a waste of time, or perhaps because the supervisor is unsure of the appropriate action and is conniving at the side-stepping of the procedure. It is also possible that the supervisor knows what to do but is shirking the responsibility or the potential unpopularity of what has to be done.

In disciplinary matters even more care is needed about the procedural step, as the likelihood of penalties may already have been set up by warnings, thus reducing the scope for doing anything else in the impending interview apart from imposing a further penalty. In most cases we believe that interviews will precede procedure, so the parties to the interview are less constrained by procedural rules. In these situations the manager will be at pains to establish that the interview is informal and without procedural implications. Alternatively the interview may be one where the likelihood of a move into procedure is so remote that the manager will be at pains to avoid any such reference, for fear of the complainant taking fright.

Who will be there? Here there are similar procedural considerations. In procedure there is the likelihood of employee representation; out of procedure that is less likely, even though the employee may feel anxious and threatened without it. If the manager is accompanied in the interview, the employee may feel even more insecure, and it is doubtful how much can be achieved informally unless the employee feels reasonably secure and able to speak frankly.

What are the facts that the interviewer needs to know? In grievance it will be necessary to know the subject of the grievance and how it has arisen. This type of information will have been filtered through the management hierarchy and perhaps modified in the process, so it needs to be considered carefully and any additional background information collected.

Disciplinary interviews always start at the behest of the management so the manager will again need to collect evidence and consider how it may have been interpreted by intermediaries. This evidence will include some basic details about the interviewee, but mainly it will be information about the aspects of the working performance that are unsatisfactory and why. Too often this information exists only in opinions that have been offered and prejudices that are held. This provides a poor basis for a constructive interview, so the manager needs to ferret out details, with as much factual corroboration as possible, and should try to make a shrewd guess about the interviewee's perspective on the situation.

It is almost inevitable that the interviewee will start the interview defensively, expecting to be blamed for something and therefore ready to refute any allegations, probably deflecting blame elsewhere. The manager needs to anticipate the respondent's initial reaction and be prepared to deal with the reaction as well as with facts that have been collected. Unless the interview is at an early, informal stage, the manager also needs to know about earlier warnings, cautions or penalties that have been invoked.

For both types of interview there will be more general information that is required. Not just the facts of the particular grievance or disciplinary situation, but knowledge to give a general understanding of the working arrangements and relationships, will be required. Other relevant data may concern the employee's length of service, type of training, previous experience, and so forth.

Most managers approaching a grievance or disciplinary interview will benefit from advice before starting. It is particularly important for anyone who is in procedure to check the position with someone such as a personnel officer before starting, as management ability to sustain any action will largely depend on maintaining consistency with what the management has done with other employees previously. The manager may also have certain ideas of what could be done in terms of retraining, transfer or assistance with a domestic problem. The manager needs to verify the feasibility of such actions before broaching them with an aggrieved employee or with an employee whose work is not satisfactory.

Where is the interview to take place? However trivial this question may seem it is included for two reasons. First, because we have seen a number of interviews go sadly awry because the parties arrived at different places; this mistake seems to happen more often with this type of encounter than with others. Second, because there may be an advantage in choosing an unusually informal situation, or an unusually formal location, according to the manager's assessment. A discussion over a pie and a pint in the local pub may be a more appropriate setting for some approaches to grievance and disciplinary problems, although they are seldom appropriate if the matter has reached procedure. Also employees frequently mistrust such settings, feeling that they are being manipulated or that the discussion 'does not count' because it is out of hours or off limits. If, however, one is trying to avoid procedural overtones, this can be a way of doing it.

Unusual formality can be appropriate in the later stages of procedure, especially in disciplinary matters, when proceedings take on a strongly judicial air. An employee is not likely to take seriously a final warning prior to probable dismissal if it is delivered over a pint in a pub. The large, impressive offices of senior managers can provide appropriate settings for the final stages of procedure.

ACTIVITY 5.2

What incidents have you experienced or heard about where the location of the interview was clearly unsuitable for the nature of the encounter?

The grievance interview

The first step in the grievance interview is for the manager to be clear about what the grievance is; a simple way of doing this is to state the *subject* of the grievance and get confirmation from the employee that it is correct. The importance of this lies in the probability that the manager will have a different perspective on the affair from the employee, particularly if it has got beyond the preliminary stage. A supervisor may report to a superior that Mr X has a grievance and 'will not take instructions from me', but when the interview begins Mr X may state his grievance as being that he is unwilling to work on Saturday mornings. In other situations it might be the other way round, with the supervisor reporting that Mr X will not work Saturday mornings and Mr X saying in the interview that he finds the style of his supervisor objectionable. Even where there is no such confusion, an opening statement and confirmation of the subject demonstrate that the two parties are talking about the same thing.

Having clarified or confirmed the subject of the grievance, the manager will then invite the employee to state the case, explaining the nature and reasons for the dissatisfaction. This enables the employee to explain why he or she is aggrieved, citing examples, providing further information and saying not just 'what' but also 'why'. Seldom will this be done well. The presentation of a case is not an easy task for the inexperienced, and few aggrieved employees are experienced at making a case of this type. Furthermore, there is the inhibition of questioning the wisdom of those in power and some apprehension about the outcome. Because of this the manager will need to ask questions after the declaration of the case in order to fill in the gaps that have been left by the employee and to clarify some points that were obscure in the first telling. As a general rule it seems better to have an episode of questioning after the case has been made, rather than to interrupt on each point that is difficult. Interruptions make a poorly argued case even more difficult to sustain. There may, however, be disguised pleas for assistance that provide good opportunities for questioning to clarify: 'I'm not very good with words, but do you see what I'm getting at?', 'Do you see what I mean?' or 'Am I making myself clear?' Among the communication ploys that the manager will need at this stage could be the method of *reflection* that was mentioned briefly in our first Focus on skills. Its application in this context is described more fully by Beveridge:

> a selective form of listening in which the listener picks out the emotional overtones of a statement and 'reflects' these back to the respondent without making any attempt to evaluate them. This means that the interviewer expresses neither approval nor disapproval, neither sympathy nor condemnation. Because the respondent may be in an emotional state, sympathy is liable to make him feel resentful and angry. Any attempt to get the respondent to look objectively and rationally at his problem at this stage is also likely to fail; he is still too confused and upset to be able to do this and will interpret the very attempt as criticism. (Beveridge 1968, p. 121)

After all the necessary clarification has been obtained the manager will restate the employee's grievance, together with an outline of the case that has been presented, and will ask the employee to agree with the summary or to correct it. By this means the manager is confirming and demonstrating an understanding of what the grievance is about and why it has been brought. This is not agreeing with it or dismissing it; all that has happened is that the grievance is now understood.

This phase of the interview can be summarised in sequential terms, as in the table.

Manager	Employee
1 States subject of grievance	
	2 Agrees with statement
	3 States case
4 Questions for clarification	
5 Restates grievance	
	6 Agrees or corrects

The grievance is now understood

The next phase is to set out the management position on the grievance. This is not the action *to be taken* but the action that *has been taken*, with the reasons for the action; this phase may include an explanation of company policy, safety rules, previous grievances, supervisory problems, administrative methods and anything else which is needed to make clear why the management position has been what it has been. The manager will then invite the employee to question and comment on the management position to ensure that it is understood and the justifications for it are understood, even if they are not accepted. The objective is to ensure that the parties to the discussion see and understand each other's point of view.

The management position is now understood

Setting out the two opposed positions will have revealed a deal of common ground. The parties will agree on some things, though disagreeing on others. In the third phase of the interview the manager and employee sort through what they have discussed and identify the points of disagreement. At this stage the points on which they agree can be ignored, as the need now is to find the outer limits. This is very similar to the differentiation stage in negotiation, which is explained in the Part 6 Focus on skills.

Points of disagreement are now in focus

As a preliminary to taking action in the matter under discussion, various possibilities can be put up for consideration. It is logical that the employee's suggestions are put first. Probably this has already been done either explicitly or implicitly in the development of the case. If, however, specific suggestions are invited at this stage they may be different ones, as the aggrieved employee now understands the management position and is seeing the whole matter clearly following the focusing that has just taken place. Then the manager can put forward alternatives or modifications, and such alternatives may include, or be limited to, the suggestion that the grievance is mischievous and unfounded so that no action should be taken. Nevertheless, in most cases there will be some scope for accommodation even if it is quite different from the employee's expectation. Once the alternative suggestions for action are set out, there is time for the advantages and disadvantages of both sets to be discussed.

Alternatives have now been considered

A grievance interview is one that falls short of the mutual dependence that is present in negotiation, so that the decision on action is to be taken by the manager alone; it is not a joint decision even though the manager will look for a decision that all parties find acceptable. In bringing a grievance the employee is challenging a management decision and that decision will now be confirmed or it will be modified, but it remains a management decision.

Before making the decision the manager may deploy a range of behaviours to ensure that the decision is correct. It may be useful to test the employee's reaction by thinking aloud, 'Well, I don't know, but it looks to me as if we shall have to disappoint you on this one . . .'. There may be an adjournment for a while to seek further advice or to give the employee time to reflect further, but the manager has to decide and then explain the decision to the employee, not simply deciding and announcing, but supporting the decision with explanation and justification in the same way that the employee developed the case for the grievance at the beginning. There may be employee questions, the employee may want time to think, but eventually the management decision will have to be accepted, unless there is some further procedural step available.

Management action is now clear and understood.

The disciplinary interview

Discipline arises from management dissatisfaction rather than employee dissatisfaction with the employment contract, so the opening move is for a statement of why such dissatisfaction exists, dealing with the *facts* of the situation rather than managerial feelings of outrage about them. This shows that the manager sees the interview as a way of dealing with a problem of the working situation and not (at least not yet) as a way of dealing with a malicious or indolent employee. If an employee has been persistently late for a week, it would be unwise for a manager to open the disciplinary interview by saying, 'Your lateness this week has been deplorable' as the reason might turn out to be that the employee has a seriously ill child needing constant attendance through the night. Then the manager would be embarrassed and the potential for a constructive settlement of the matter would be jeopardised. An opening factual statement of the problem, 'You have been at least twenty minutes late each day this week . . .', does not prejudge the reasons and is reasonably precise about the scale of the problem. It also circumscribes management dissatisfaction by implying that there is no other cause for dissatisfaction: if there is, it should be mentioned.

Now the manager needs to know the explanation and asks the employee to say what the reasons for the problem are, perhaps also asking for comments on the seriousness of the problem itself, which the employee may regard as trivial but the manager regards as serious. If there is such dissonance it needs to be drawn out. Getting the employee's reaction is usually straightforward, but the manager needs to be prepared for one of two other types of reaction. Either there may be a need to probe because the employee is reluctant to open up, or there may be angry defiance. Disciplinary situations are at least disconcerting for employees and frequently very worrying, surrounded by feelings of hostility and mistrust, so that it is to be expected that some ill feeling will be pent up and waiting for the opportunity to be vented.

First possible move to disengagement

If the employee sees something of the management view of the problem and if the manager understands the reasons for the problem, the next step is to seek a solution. A disciplinary problem is as likely to be solved by management action as by employee action. If the problem is lateness, one solution would be for the employee to catch an earlier bus, but another might be for the management to alter the working shift to which the employee is assigned. If the employee is disobeying orders, one solution would be for him or her to start obeying them, but another might be for the employee to be moved to a different job where orders are received from someone else. Some managers regard such thinking as unreasonable, on the grounds that the contract of employment places obligations on individual employees that they should meet despite personal inconvenience. However, the point is not how people *should* behave, but how they do. Can the contract of employment be enforced on an unwilling employee? Not if one is seeking such attitudes as enthusiasm and cooperation, or behaviour such as diligence and carefulness. The disenchanted employee can always meet the bare letter rather than the spirit of the contract.

The most realistic view of the matter is that many disciplinary problems require some action from both parties, some require action by the employee only and a small proportion require management action only. The problem-solving session may quickly produce the possibility for further action and open up the possibility of closing the interview.

This simple, logical approach outlined so far may not be enough, due to the unwillingness of employees to respond to disciplinary expectations. They may not want to be punctual or to do as they are instructed, or whatever the particular problem is. There is now a test of the power behind management authority. Three further steps can be taken, one after the other, although there will be occasions when it is necessary to move directly to the third.

Second possible move to disengagement: persuasion

A first strategy is to demonstrate to employees that they will not achieve what they want, if their behaviour does not change:

> 'You won't keep your earnings up if you don't meet targets.'
> 'It will be difficult to get your appointment confirmed when the probationary period is over if . . .'.

By such means employees may see the advantages of changing their attitude and behaviour. If they are convinced, there is a strong incentive for them to alter, because they believe it to be in their own interests.

Third possible move to disengagement: disapproval

Another strategy is to suggest that continuing the behaviour will displease those whose goodwill the employee wishes to keep:

> 'The Management Development Panel are rather disappointed . . .'.
> 'Some of the other people in the department feel that you are not pulling your weight.'

A manager using this method needs to be sure that what is said is both true and relevant. Also the manager may be seen by the employee as shirking the issue, so it may be appropriate to use a version of 'I think this is deplorable and expect you to do better'.

We asked for a restraint from judgement in the early stages of the interview, until the nature of the problem is clear. The time for judgement has now come, with the proper deployment of the rebuke or the caution.

Fourth possible move to disengagement: penalties

When all else fails or is clearly inappropriate, as with serious offences about which there is no doubt, penalties have to be invoked. In rare circumstances there may be the possibility of a fine, but usually the first penalty will be a formal warning as a preliminary to possible dismissal. In situations that are sufficiently grave summary dismissal is both appropriate and possible within the legal framework.

Disengagement

We have indicated possible moves to disengagement at four different points in the disciplinary interview. Now we come to a stage that is common to both grievance and disciplinary encounters from the point of view of describing the process, although the nature of disengagement will obviously differ. The manager now needs to think of the working situation that will follow. In a grievance situation can the employee now accept the decision that has been made? Are there faces to be saved or reputations to be restored? What administrative action is to be taken? In closing a disciplinary interview, the manager will aim for the flavour of disengagement to be as positive as possible so that all concerned put the disciplinary problem behind them. Where the outcome of the interview is to impose or confirm a dismissal, then the manager will be exclusively concerned with the fairness and accuracy with which it is done, so that the possibility of tribunal hearings is reduced, if not prevented. It can never be appropriate to close an interview of either type leaving the employee humbled and demoralised.

WINDOW ON PRACTICE

The American Eric Harvey has reduced what he calls 'positive discipline' to three simple steps:

1 Warn the employee orally.

2 Warn the employee in writing.

3 If steps 1 and 2 fail to resolve the problem, give the employee a day off, with pay (Harvey 1987).

A similar, very positive, approach was outlined in a seminal paper by Huberman in 1967.

SUMMARY PROPOSITIONS

5.1   Grievance and disciplinary interviews are central to the process of sorting things out when there is a management/employee problem, but most managers dislike such interviews intensely.

5.2   Grievance and disciplinary interviews are one of the means whereby people at work achieve self-discipline and autonomy, reducing the need for supervision and reducing the need for recourse to the formality of procedure.

5.3   The steps in conducting a grievance interview are first to understand the nature of the grievance, to explain the management position, to focus on the problem, to discuss possibilities and then to decide what to do.

5.4   The disciplinary interview starts the other way around, first explaining the management position, then understanding the employee's position and focusing on the problem. If that does not produce a satisfactory result, the manager may have to move through three more steps: persuasion, showing disapproval or invoking penalties.

GENERAL DISCUSSION TOPICS

1   Do individual grievance and disciplinary procedures weaken trade union organisation in a workplace by enabling the management to deal with employees individually rather than having to face the potential strength of collective action and representation?

2   In 1791 Edmund Burke, a British statesman, said, 'He that wrestles with us strengthens our nerves, and sharpens our skill. Our antagonist is our helper.' Do trade union officials help HR managers by strengthening their nerves and sharpening their skill?

FURTHER READING

Bouwen, R. and Salipante, P.F. (1990) 'Behavioural analysis of grievances', *Employee Relations*, Vol. 12, No. 4, pp. 27–32.
Hook, C.M., Rollinson, D.J., Foot, M. and Handley, J. (1996) 'Supervisor and manager styles in handling discipline and grievance', *Personnel Review*, Vol. 25, No. 3, pp. 20–34.
These recent studies cover behaviour in discipline and grievance interviewing.

Edwards, P.K. (2000) 'Discipline: towards trust and self-discipline?', in S. Bach and K. Sisson (eds), *Personnel Management: A comprehensive guide to theory and practice.* Oxford: Blackwell, pp. 317–37.
Redman, T. and Wilkinson, A. (2001) *Contemporary Human Resource Management.* Harlow, Essex: Pearson Education, pp. 177–92.
These studies provide further background and discussion of the place of interviewing in employment relations processes.

Borg, J. (2004) *Persuasion: the art of influencing people.* Harlow, Essex: Pearson Education.
This is a rather different book, popular in style but with solid content on this particular aspect of discipline and grievance handling.

WEB LINKS

www.eoc.org.uk (the website of the Equal Opportunities Commission)

www.cre.gov.uk (the website of the Commission for Racial Equality)

www.cehr.org.uk (the website for the Commission for Equality and Human Rights)

www.cipd.co.uk/training (the website of the Chartered Institute of Personnel and Development)

REFERENCES

Beveridge, W.E. (1968) *Problem-Solving Interviews*. London: Allen and Unwin.

Harvey, E.L. (1987) 'Discipline versus punishment', *Management Review*, March, pp. 25–9.

Huberman, J.C. (1967) 'Discipline without punishment', *Harvard Business Review*, May, pp. 62–8.

McGregor, D. (1960) *The Human Side of Enterprise*. Maidenhead: McGraw-Hill.

REVIEW OF PART 5

Part 5 has dealt with aspects of management that centre on a basic conflict of interest between those who employ and those who are employed. To a great extent that is a feature of all management, but here it is most apparent. The grievance or disciplinary interview both illustrates and symbolises that division, but also illustrates how the conflict can often be resolved and does not have to be destructive. Various forms of collective consent can be negotiated, employees can be involved, teams briefed and unions recognised. Health hazards can be modified and stressful working conditions alleviated. The extent to which people are disadvantaged or have their dignity affronted through discrimination can be lessened. When there is a real problem of dissatisfaction with the employment or psychological contract, that problem can be tackled through policy, procedure or face to face.

In 1776 Adam Smith, in his *Wealth of Nations*, made a sly comment about universities:

> The discipline of colleges and universities is in general contrived, not for the benefit of the students, but for the interest, or more properly speaking, for the ease of the masters.

All readers of this book, as well as its authors, will know that is certainly not true for all universities in the twenty-first century even if it may have been true in the eighteenth, but it remains a useful homily to underpin the management of employee relations, illustrated by part of a true story about an industrial dispute. In a small factory in Lancashire production was halted because of an unofficial strike. Attempts to solve the problem failed and the strike lingered on despite the fact that the strikers were not eligible for strike pay and were experiencing considerable hardship. One day the pickets heard that 'a man from London' was coming. Hopes rose for a breakthrough. Soon after 11.00 am the General Manager drove to the station, returning with a passenger. Both went in to the offices to emerge after an hour with the Works Manager and the Production Manager. All four got into the car and drove out. The car and two passengers returned at 4.00 pm: the man from London had obviously been returned to the station after a lengthy lunch. The following day it emerged that the meeting had not been about the strike at all, but to discuss replacement company cars for the Works and Production Managers. The strike continued for six more weeks and the plant closed completely seven months later.

Industrial disputes at British Airways, 1997–2007

British Airways is an international company by any standards and, by 1990, was the world's most popular and most profitable airline, although this position was compromised after the events of September 2001, which had such a disastrous effect on air travel.

Because of its extensive network and the salient position of Heathrow as the world's busiest airport, it was relatively straightforward for BA to become the most popular airline, but achieving high profitability was more difficult. There was overstaffing and the need for radical measures:

> The organisation had a bureaucratic style of management, damaging industrial relations and a poor reputation for customer service . . . There was a drastic reduction in staff numbers from 60,000 to 38,000. This was achieved by a combination of voluntary severance and natural wastage. (Hopfl 1993, p. 117)

In order to maintain market leadership the airline embarked on a famous programme of staff training to develop commitment to customer service, and the quality of service to the customer improved markedly, so that British Airways was able to maintain its premier position despite ever-increasing competition.

There were, however, mounting problems with the staff as the pressure on margins continued. In 1996 a strike by pilots was narrowly averted, but 1997 brought one stoppage and the threat of another.

On 9 July a 72-hour strike by cabin staff began. It was an official stoppage called by the Transport and General Workers Union following protracted negotiations and a ballot among its members working for the airline. According to British Airways only 142 cabin crew formally joined the strike, but 1,500 (compared with a normal daily average of 120) reported sick – a novel strategy! The number that reported for work as usual was 834.

The management reaction was to announce that all strikers would forfeit travel perks and promotion prospects for three years. Film was also taken of strikers on picket lines. The threats were later withdrawn and the filming was stopped. The situation was complicated by the existence of a rival union, Cabin Crew 89, which had broken away from the TGWU in 1989. This union, known as CC89, supported the management position and all its members worked normally through the stoppage.

Another interesting feature of the dispute was reported by *The Times*:

During the past few years, BA, like many companies in Britain, has appointed middle and senior managers who fear for their jobs. To get on, they believe, they must show they are tough. I have heard these 'performance managers' brusquely warning vacillating staff that if they follow their union and refuse to work, they will 'face the consequences.' This has irked the cabin crew far more than the dispute over pay and conditions. They no longer feel part of a team and believe they are being bullied. (Elliott 1997, p. 41)

As usual, the dispute moved on to talks to find a resolution, but BA had lost many flights and its reputation was as severely dented as its financial position. The share price dropped from 763p to 583p before recovering to 635p, and there were varying reports about how many millions of pounds the dispute was costing.

Four years later the terrorist attack on the World Trade Center in New York badly affected full-service airlines, especially those with transatlantic services like BA. Competition from low-cost airlines and anxiety about a war in Iraq added to the pressure, so cost-cutting had to slice even deeper. One method introduced was Automated Time Recording (ATR) that kept a tighter control on hours worked. Many check-in and engineering staff were alarmed at this innovation, fearing that it might lead to a reduction in flexibility about working hours, which was a major attraction for many who relied on this to fit in with their domestic arrangements. They were also angered by senior managers using terms such as 'feather-bedding' and making comments about high absenteeism in the summer. On 18 July 2003, on one of the busiest weekends of the year, BA's operations at Heathrow were paralysed by a wildcat strike by check-in and other ground staff. It was expected to cost the airline £100 million.

Two years later British Airways was again badly hit by industrial action of a different nature. A dispute over restructuring plans at Gate Gourmet, the catering supplier to British Airways at Heathrow airport, resulted in unofficial strike action in August 2005 and the dismissal of hundreds of workers involved. BA ground staff at Heathrow took 'sympathy' action, which was also not authorised by the trade union concerned – the Transport and General Workers' Union (TGWU). This resulted in the cancellation of more than 700 flights at one of the busiest times of the year.

Gate Gourmet is one of the world's largest providers of in-flight meals, but had not made a profit since 2000 due to falling revenues in the face of increased cost competition in the airline sector and rising oil prices, which had squeezed catering services and budgets. The UK firm lost £22 million in 2004 and was expected to make a bigger loss in 2005.

Around 1,000 baggage handlers and loading staff at Heathrow refused to work to express their support for the sacked Gate Gourmet workers. Both groups belonged to the same union, and were colleagues until the meals business was outsourced by BA in 1997. The walkout by BA staff led to the cancellation of hundreds of flights and stranded 100,000 passengers. The disruption was estimated to have cost the company up to £   million.

By 2007 there was more trouble: this time it was cabin crew who were prepared to go to extreme lengths to express their dissatisfaction with aspects of BA management. In January an astonishing 96 per cent of over 8,400 staff voted to support industrial action by striking the following month. This time the inevitable talks produced an agreement that seemed to satisfy both sides after dealing with staffing levels, sickness absence and pension provision.

At long last the malaise appeared to be at an end and the share price had revived to 572p by the beginning of February. BA was, of course, unusual among British airlines in having such a high level of active trade union membership and some alarm was caused elsewhere in the airline industry when it was revealed that a part of the agreement was for the Chief Executive, Willie Walsh, to meet regularly with union representatives in the future. Leaders of other airline businesses denounced this as 'a dangerous precedent', 'a deplorable example' and 'a reward for union militancy'.

Required

1 Do you think it is inevitable that the pressures of international competition drive companies into a situation where unilateral managerial decision making must prevail and there is simply no time for the consultation and compromise that is involved in union negotiation?

2 This case provides an excellent example of the problems that can arise from having two unions representing the same group of employees and competing with each other for membership. How would you have tried to deal with this situation in 1997 – not back in 1989?

3 How accurate do you regard Harvey Elliott's views to be as a general comment on current management practice?

4 'Informal arrangements for flexible manning, made by supervisors individually with employees, are better than electronic or similar controls.' Do you agree or disagree?

Sources: Elliott, H. (1997) 'BA is Plunging towards Disaster', *The Times*, 10 July; Hopfl, H. (1993) 'Culture and Commitment: British Airways', in D. Gowler, K. Legge and C. Clegg (eds), *Case Studies in Organizational Behaviour and Human Resource Management*, 2nd edn. London: Paul Chapman Publishing, pp. 117–25.

PART ⑥

REWARD

Reward is clearly central to the employment relationship. While there are plenty of people who enjoy working and who claim that they would not stop working even if they were to win a large sum in a lottery, most of us work in large part because it is our only means of earning the money we need to sustain us and our families in the style to which we are accustomed. How much we are paid and in what form is therefore an issue which matters hugely to us. These questions are also central for the human resource management function because money spent on salaries, benefits and other forms of reward typically accounts for well over half an organisation's total costs. For commercial organisations it is thus a major determinant of both profitability and competitive advantage. In the public sector the cost of rewarding staff is determined by and, in turn helps determine, the level of taxes that we pay.

For these reasons, to a greater extent than is the case in other areas of HR practice, the management of reward is heavily constrained by the financial position of the organisation. The aim is thus to design competitive reward packages which serve to attract, retain and motivate staff, while at the same time keeping a lid on the costs so as to ensure the organisation's commercial and financial viability. This is not an easy task, and it is made harder because of the great significance that employees themselves attach to their pay, and particularly to the level of pay they receive vis-à-vis other people. Getting it wrong has major, negative consequences, because it can demotivate in quite serious ways, leading to the departure of good performers, higher absence levels, less effort and the deterioration of the organisation's employee relations climate. Over time, of course, these too serve to reduce an organisation's effectiveness and damage its financial performance.

In this part of the book we explore all the major elements that make up the reward package. In Chapter 27 we will look at how salaries are determined and at how organisations go about deciding how much each employee should be paid in comparison to others. In Chapter 28 our focus is on incentives and bonus payments of one kind or another and in Chapter 29 on pensions and benefits. Before these, in Chapter 26 we ask more general questions about reward practices and consider what factors need to be taken into account when developing a coherent reward strategy.

CHAPTER 26

STRATEGIC ASPECTS OF REWARD

THE OBJECTIVES OF THIS CHAPTER ARE TO:

1 Set out the different elements that can make up a reward package

2 Explain the concept of 'total reward' and explore the reasons for its increasing prominence

3 Define the term 'reward strategy'

4 Assess the major objectives managers have when determining reward systems

5 Consider the main employee objectives from a reward package

6 Evaluate the major alternative methods of setting base pay rates

7 Introduce the different elements that make up a reward package

8 State the significance of equity in designing and maintaining effective reward systems

While employers have been paying employees with money for centuries, it is only quite recently that organisations in the UK and in many other countries have begun to develop identifiable 'reward strategies' which seek to help achieve defined organisational objectives and priorities. The reason, as was explained in Chapter 20, is that until the 1980s in the private sector, and much more recently in the public sector, the prevalent industrial relations system tended to restrict the freedom of manoeuvre that managers had to design and develop payment packages that helped them to meet their objectives. Collective bargaining with trade unions was the method used to determine the pay and conditions that most people received, much of it carried out at a national or industry level. Managers in many organisations were thus restricted to deciding who should be employed on which grade, how they should progress up the grade hierarchy, what should be paid by way of an annual increment and how much overtime they worked. This system of multi-employer bargaining declined steeply during the 1980s and 1990s, so that by 2004 only 36 per cent of public sector employees and just one per cent of those employed in the private sector had their pay determined by such arrangements (Kersley *et al.* 2006, p. 184). The breaking down of this long-established system has enabled organisations to innovate by introducing payment systems which reward individual skills, effort and performance to a far greater degree. Much greater flexibility has been achieved in the provision of benefits, while rigid grade hierarchies have tended to be replaced by approaches which give managers much more say in how much an individual job is worth and how annual pay rises should be determined. The result has been a great deal of experimentation, some examples of which have proved more successful than others, and much more variety of practice across industries.

Over the last twenty years reward management has also attracted the keen interest of consultants and academic researchers leading to the publication of hundreds of books and thousands of articles about the effectiveness of different systems and approaches. We thus have a good deal of robust research evidence available on which to base practice in organisations. There remains, however, according to Armstrong *et al.* (2005, p. 4) a worrying 'knowing-doing gap' resulting in the promulgation of reward practices in organisations which are known by students of reward to be highly problematic and a failure on the part of managers to adopt approaches which the research shows are a great deal more effective. Moreover, to a great degree we are still at the experimentation stage with some approaches, and this means that fierce debates rage among commentators about the effectiveness, efficiency and fairness of systems which aim to enhance individual effort, encourage skills acquisition, reward specific employee behaviours and try to establish an identity of interest between employers and their staff.

TOTAL REWARD

A variety of different terms are used to describe the rewards that are given by an employer in return for the work carried out by workers. In previous editions of this book we have used the term 'payment', but this is often nowadays seen as being too narrow in scope because many of the rewards that people take from their work do not take a monetary form. 'Compensation' is a term widely used in the American literature, yet the idea of compensation is that it involves making amends for something that has caused loss or injury. Do we want to suggest that work necessarily causes loss or injury?

'Remuneration' is a more straightforward word which means exactly the same as payment but has five more letters and is misspelled (as renumeration) more often than most words in the human resource manager's lexicon. 'Reward' is not a perfect term to use because it suggests a special payment for a special act, but it is the best available for describing the whole range of elements which combine to make work 'rewarding' and worthwhile rather than 'unrewarding' and thankless.

For the most part we will be focusing in this Part of the book on transactional or tangible rewards, by which we mean those which are financial in nature. But it is important to remember that employees also value the intangible (or relational) rewards which they gain from coming to work, to all of which we have made extensive reference in earlier chapters. These include opportunities to develop both in terms of career and more generally as a human being, the social life which is associated with working in communal settings, recognition from managers and colleagues for a job well done and for the effort expended, and more generally from a sense of personal achievement. Increasingly the opportunity to work flexibly so as to achieve a better 'work-life balance' is discussed in this context too (*see* Chapter 31). The trend towards viewing reward policies and practices as extending well beyond the realms of payment has led to widespread interest in the concept of 'total reward' which involves managers viewing the way that they reward employees in the round, taking equal account of both the tangible and intangible ingredients that together help to make work and jobs 'rewarding' in the widest sense of the word. The idea is effectively illustrated in graphical form by Armstrong and Brown (2006, p. 25) in their model adapted from work by the Towers Perrin reward consultancy (*see* Figure 26.1). Here four distinct categories of rewards are identified, the implication being that each has equal potential significance as a source of reward from the employee perspective.

Figure 26.1 Categories of reward

The change in perspective away from a narrow focus on payment towards a broader focus on 'total reward' has come about largely because of developments in the commercial environment. Year on year, organisations operating in the private sector are facing greater competitive pressure in their product markets leading them to search for ways of reducing their costs while retaining or improving the levels of quality they achieve. In the public sector competitive forces increasingly play a role too, but here pressures to keep costs down come primarily from taxpayers seeking good value for their money. The trouble is that these pressures are being faced simultaneously with tighter labour market conditions, making it difficult for employers to recruit, retain and motivate the staff they need without substantially increasing pay levels. Organisations are embracing a variety of responses to this conundrum. One involves employing fewer, but more highly paid people to carry out existing work more efficiently. Another involves keeping a lid on payment levels while simultaneously looking for other ways of rewarding staff effectively. It is this latter approach which has led managers to think about the 'total reward' package that they offer.

As a rule managing the tangible, financial components is relatively unproblematic provided basic principles are adhered to and the correct technical decisions are made. While they enable organisations to secure a degree of competitive advantage in their labour markets, these tangible parts of a total reward package are readily imitated by competitors. It is much harder, in practice, to replicate intangible rewards. Over the longer term it is thus in the interests of organisations to improve the perceived value of the intangible elements, but that is a great deal harder both to achieve and to evaluate. Moreover, several important intangible rewards are 'intrinsically' rather than 'extrinsically' motivating, and by definition cannot be directly provided by managers. These are terms used by psychologists to distinguish between sources of positive motivation which are external to individuals and *given* to them by their employer, such as money or praise, and those which are internally generated. An example of intrinsic motivation is someone putting a great deal of effort into a project at work simply because he or she finds it interesting or enjoyable. The result may be very considerable satisfaction on the part of the employee concerned, but this has not resulted directly from any management action. All managers can do is try to create and sustain a culture in which individual employees can achieve intrinsic motivation and hence experience work which is rewarding.

ACTIVITY 26.1

How far do you agree with the proposition that managers should think in terms of 'total reward' as a means of recruiting, retaining and motivating their staff? Are praise and career development as important as pay? Would you trade some of your pay for greater recognition and development opportunities?

WINDOW ON PRACTICE

Total reward at the Crown Prosecution Service

In 2006 the Crown Prosecution Service (CPS) launched a new reward system which was heavily influenced by the 'total reward' concept. Until 1996 when responsibility for reward management was devolved, the CPS's 8,500 staff were paid on standard terms and conditions which were negotiated nationally for civil servants working across all government departments. After devolution incremental changes were introduced that aimed to meet the particular needs of the CPS, culminating in this major overhaul. Labelled 'Invest', the new approach aims to underpin the Service's evolving agenda.

The first priority for the CPS is to successfully manage a major programme of expansion. New responsibilities taken over from the police require that the CPS employs 300 new lawyers and 500 new administrators. 'Invest' is designed to increase the attractiveness of a career within the CPS and to help retain staff more effectively. An explicit objective of the service is to make itself 'an employer of choice' for lawyers and people seeking a career in public administration. A second aim is substantially to improve performance. The CPS has as its central corporate objective a mission to become recognised as 'a world-class prosecution authority'. This requires cultural change and the acquisition by staff of a range of new skills and attributes.

The new strategy aims to meet these objectives in a number of ways. First, a job evaluation system has been introduced to ensure that each job is fairly graded according to the skills its holders require and the responsibilities they shoulder. Second, a new performance appraisal system has come into effect to strengthen links between pay and individual effort and contribution. The existing civil service benefits package has been enhanced with new elements such as childcare services and a counselling service, the whole package being promoted with greater coherence at the recruitment stage. A major element is enhanced training and development opportunities for staff, allowing easier career progression within the service. Employees are sponsored to attain professional qualifications, while e-learning packages have also been developed to support career development. Finally flexible working initiatives have been developed, including a great deal more home-working, which aim to meet the needs of both the Service and its employees. In the future it is intended to introduce long-service awards and to recognise individual achievements with formal letters of recognition from senior managers.

Source: Suff 2006.

REWARD STRATEGIES

A major current feature of the literature and rhetoric about remuneration systems has been a concern with defining and refining reward strategies. While different writers have different ideas about what exactly constitutes a strategic approach to the management of reward, most agree that it is primarily about aligning an organisation's payment arrangements and wider reward systems with its business objectives. This means developing systems which enhance the chances that an organisation's employees will seek actively to contribute to the achievement of its goals. So if improved quality of service is the major business objective, this should be reflected in a payment system which rewards front-line staff who provide the best standards of service to customers. Alternatively, if increased productivity is sought, then an approach which rewards efficiency would be more appropriate. But choices in this area are not always as straightforward as this because organisations are obliged to compete with one another for good staff as well as for customers. And as Charles Cotton points out in the most recent CIPD survey of reward practices, 'respondents report that employees are becoming just as discerning as their customers in what they want from their employer' (CIPD 2007, p. 33). The tighter the labour market becomes, the harder it is to recruit and retain the best-qualified people, and the more pressure there is placed on employers to develop rewards packages that suit employees as much as they suit their own needs.

The extent to which organisations have taken full advantage of the opportunity to develop identifiable reward strategies since the disintegration of national-level, multi-employer bargaining has long been an area of contention. Moves in this direction by some prominent employers and the growth of specialist reward consultancies specialising in work of this kind has led some analysts to hail the dawn of a new era in reward management practice. Armstrong and Murlis (1998, pp. 12–14), for example, go so far as to argue that present-day practice is characterised by an acceptance of a 'new pay philosophy' in which decisions about payment levels and packages 'flow from the overall strategy' of the organisation. According to their view reward policy now increasingly underpins employer objectives and promotes change by rewarding 'results and behaviour consistent with the key goals of the organisation'. By contrast, academic researchers have tended to take issue with this assessment, often quite stridently. While they agree that major developments have occurred in pay determination over recent decades, they dispute the claims made about the extent of change and question how far organisations are taking a long-term strategic approach to the management of pay. Smith (1993) and Thompson (1998), in particular, have argued that managers are just as short-termist and reactive when making decisions about pay as they always were. Changes are introduced for damage limitation reasons, to respond to immediate recruitment difficulties or in response to government initiatives rather than as a means of aligning practices with organisational goals. Kessler (2001) and Poole and Jenkins (1998) also report considerable gaps in many organisations between the rhetoric and reality of strategic activity in pay management. Despite some examples of the development of genuinely original approaches in some larger private sector organisations, there is little evidence generally of the adoption of strategic principles as far as reward is concerned across most UK organisations. More recent surveys of reward practice back up this assessment, only 35 per cent of respondents to the CIPD's 2007 survey claiming to have a reward strategy (CIPD 2007, p. 6). The percentage was higher in the latest IRS survey (at 45 per cent), but only 18 per cent of their respondents had an identifiable written reward strategy, leading the authors to conclude that there is 'more talk of reward strategies, but little action' (IRS 2006, p. 28).

So what does a written reward strategy look like? According to Armstrong and Brown (2006, p. 34) there are four key components. First of all there needs to be a 'statement of intentions' setting out, in general terms, what the reward strategy of the organisation is seeking to achieve and which reward initiatives have been chosen in order to achieve these core objectives. Second, these ideas are expanded through a more detailed 'rationale' which explains the objectives in greater depth and shows how the various elements of the organisation's reward policy support the achievement of those objectives. In effect this amounts to a statement of the business case that underpins the strategy. To that end the rationale should include costings, a statement of the benefits that will accrue and an indication of the means that will be used to evaluate its success. The third element is an explanation of the guiding principles or values that have been used in developing the initiatives and that will be used to adapt them in the future. Typically this will include statements which deal with ethical issues or which reiterate a commitment to core principles such as equality between men and women, fair dealing or rewarding exceptional individual performance. The final component is an implementation plan, setting out exactly what initiatives are being brought forward and when, who has responsibility for their introduction and what their cost will be.

Later in this chapter and in those which follow we will be exploring the major alternative initiatives available to employers when developing their reward strategies. However, before we can get to this stage we first need to consider the major objectives that employers and employees have as far as their reward package is concerned. While meeting each of these effectively is a prerequisite for the long-term success of any reward strategy, the significance of different objectives varies over time because of changing environmental conditions and also varies between organisations. There are also several different alternative means available of meeting each objective.

Employer objectives

Reward strategies and the initiatives developed as part of those strategies should be judged according to their ability to meet certain core objectives.

Attracting staff

The reward package on offer must be sufficiently attractive vis-à-vis that of an organisation's labour market competitors to ensure that it is able to secure the services of the staff it needs. The more attractive the package, the more applications will be received from potential employees and the more choice the organisation will have when filling its vacancies. Attractive packages thus allow the appointment of high-calibre people and often mean that organisations are able to fill vacancies more quickly than is the case with a reward offering which is either unattractive or poorly communicated. However, what is 'attractive' in total reward terms in one labour market will be less attractive in others because people vary in what they are looking for. There is thus a need to establish what the target market values most and to tailor the offering accordingly.

Retaining staff

The costs associated with recruiting and developing people, as well as the growing significance of specialist organisational knowledge in creating value and maintaining competitive advantage, mean that retaining effective performers is a central aim of reward strategy in many organisations, particularly those competing in knowledge-intensive industries where highly qualified people are in short supply. This requires a package which is attractive enough to prevent people from becoming dissatisfied and looking elsewhere for career development opportunities. It may also involve the development of policies which reward seniority so as to provide an incentive for staff to stay when they might otherwise consider applying for alternative work.

Motivating staff

Aside from helping to ensure that effective performers are recruited and retained, in more general terms it is necessary that the reward package they are given serves to motivate positively and does not demotivate. The question of the extent to which money ever can positively motivate has long been debated by occupational psychologists, many of whom accept that the power of monetary reward to motivate is very limited, at least over the longer term. What is not in doubt, however, is the very considerable power of poorly designed or implemented reward practices to demotivate, particularly when they are perceived by staff to be inequitable in some shape or form. Ultimately the aim must be to reward people in such a way as to create the conditions in which they are prepared to work hard to help achieve their employer's objectives and, if possible, to demonstrate discretionary effort. Employers who want their workforces to be positively engaged with their work, to participate in continuous improvement programmes and to work beyond contract when required must have in place a reward package which does not demotivate and which, as far as is possible, motivates positively. In this regard, the total reward concept referred to above has plenty to offer as it incorporates intrinsic motivators alongside extrinsic motivators.

Driving change

Pay can be used specifically as one of a range of tools underpinning change management processes. The approach used is to tie higher base pay, bonuses or promotion to the development of new behaviours, attitudes or skills gained by employees. Pay works far more effectively than simple exhortation because it provides a material incentive to those whose natural inclination is to resist change. It also sends out a powerful message to employees indicating the seriousness of the employer's intentions as regards proposed or ongoing changes. The use of pay in this way is sometimes criticised because it serves to enhance management control in a very conspicuous way. Sociologists in particular tend to be uneasy about the capacity of payment systems to reinforce the position of powerful groups in organisations and in society generally at the expense of those who are relatively powerless. Examples are the use by employers of individualised reward packages which undermine the power of trade unions to organise and resist effectively and systems which have the effect of increasing the pay of predominantly male groups vis-à-vis those which are predominantly female.

Corporate reputation

Aside from the aim of developing and maintaining a reputation as a good employer in the labour market, organisations are increasingly concerned to establish a positive corporate reputation more generally. For some the notion of 'prestige' is something they aim for as part of a business strategy that seeks to produce high-quality, high-value added or innovative goods or services. For others the maintenance of an ethical reputation is important in order to attract and retain a strong customer base. Either way delivery is significantly linked in part to the organisation's reputation as an employer. Paying poorly or having in place policies which are perceived as operating unfairly serves to undermine any reputation gained for being either a prestigious organisation or one which acts ethically and in a socially responsible manner.

Affordability

The above objectives are all desirable for organisations and form the basis of their reward strategies. But in this field of HR activity there is a major restriction in the shape of affordability which serves to limit what can be done at any time. The extent to which a particular objective is affordable also varies over time and tends to be unpredictable as so much depends on the current financial performance of the organisation. If money were no object organisations would develop 'ideal' reward packages which paid above market rates to ensure that the best people were recruited and retained and which linked pay both to individual and collective achievement so as to maximise effort and performance. But the real world is not like this except, some would argue, when it comes to developing pay packages for senior executives, so tough choices inevitably have to be made when devising reward strategies. Organisational objectives have to be prioritised and decisions made about how limited resources are best to be deployed so as to maximise the positive impact of reward management interventions on the organisation's performance.

Employee objectives

You might think that employees have only one objective as far as reward is concerned, namely to maximise the amount that they earn. Indeed some theorists further argue that employees are primarily interested in maximising the amount they earn while also minimising the effort they put in to achieve these earnings. This was one of the assumptions about worker behaviour that underlay scientific management thinking in the early twentieth century (*see* Steers *et al.* 1996, pp. 25–28). In fact for most employees aims are more diverse and more subtle, particularly when the full range of elements that make up a total reward package are taken into consideration.

Purchasing power

The absolute level of weekly or monthly earnings determines the standard of living of the recipient, and will therefore be the most important consideration for most employees. How much can I buy? Employees are rarely satisfied about their purchasing power, and the annual pay adjustment will do little more than reduce dissatisfaction, even if it exceeds the current level of inflation. Enhanced satisfaction only occurs when a pay rise is given which surpasses expectations. It is important to remember, however, that surveys of employee satisfaction invariably show that while a good majority of employees are dissatisfied with the level of their pay, most are satisfied or very satisfied with other aspects of their jobs (*see* Kersley *et al.* 2005, p. 33).

Fairness

Elliott Jacques (1962) averred that every employee had a strong feeling about the level of payment that was fair for the job. In most cases this is a rough, personalised evaluation of what is appropriate, bearing in mind the going market rate and personal contribution vis-à-vis that of fellow employees. The employee who feels underpaid is likely to demonstrate the conventional symptoms of withdrawal from the job: looking for another, carelessness, disgruntlement, lateness, absence and the like. Perhaps the worst manifestation of this is among those who feel the unfairness but who cannot take a clean step of moving elsewhere. They then not only feel dissatisfied with their pay level, but also feel another unfairness too: being trapped in a situation they resent. Those who feel they are overpaid (as some do) may simply feel guilty, or may seek to justify their existence in some way by trying to look busy. That is not necessarily productive.

Rights

A different aspect of relative income is that concerned with the rights of the employee to a particular share of the company's profits or the nation's wealth. The employee is here thinking about whether the division of earnings is providing fair shares of the Gross National Product. The focus is often on the notion of need – the idea that people have a right to a greater share because they or their families are suffering unjustly. These are features of many trade union arguments and part of the general preoccupation with the rights of the individual.

Recognition

Most people have an objective for their payment arrangements, that their personal contribution is recognised. This is partly seeking reassurance, but is also a way in which people can mould their behaviour and their career thinking to produce progress and satisfaction. It is doubtful if financial recognition has a significant and sustained impact on performance, but providing a range of other forms of recognition while the pay packet is transmitting a different message is certainly counterproductive.

Composition

How is the pay package made up? The growing complexity and sophistication of payment arrangements raises all sorts of questions about pay composition. Is £400 pay for 60 hours' work better than £280 for 40 hours' work? The arithmetical answer that the rate per hour for the 40-hour arrangement is marginally better than that for 60 hours is only part of the answer. The other aspects will relate to the individuals, their circumstances and the conventions of their working group and reference groups. Another question about composition might be: is £250 per week plus a pension better than £270 per week without? Such questions do not produce universally applicable answers because different groups of employees tend to have different priorities. For example, younger staff tend to be more interested in maximising cash earnings than older colleagues who tend to be more interested in indirect forms of payment such as pension arrangements. Those in mid-career who have mortgages to pay off are likely to be interested in overtime rates and in systems which allow them to trade holiday entitlement or other benefits for cash. For second-income earners in a family cash is often less significant than flexible working arrangements, childcare vouchers or crèche facilities.

ACTIVITY 26.2

Which of the above objectives do you consider to be most important to you? How far do you think priorities in this area change with age?

SETTING BASE PAY

One of the most important decisions in the development of reward strategies concerns the mechanism or mechanisms that will be used to determine the basic rate of pay for different jobs in the organisation. There are, of course, restrictions on management action in this area provided by the law. Since 1999 the UK has had a National Minimum Wage (£5.35 an hour in 2007) to which workers over the age of 22 are entitled; a lower minimum rate is set for those aged 18–22. Equal pay law is a further way in which the state intervenes, providing a mechanism for employees to complain when they consider their pay to be unjustifiably lower than that paid to a colleague of the opposite sex. Moreover, in many countries incomes policies are operated as tools of inflation control. These restrict the amount of additional pay that people can receive in any one year while remaining in the same job. While formal incomes policies were abandoned in the UK after the 1970s, similar thinking continues to underpin government decision making in the area of public sector pay (Thorpe 2000, pp. 34–5).

A further restriction on management action is the nature of the product markets in which their organisations operate. The extent of this influence varies according to how important labour costs are in deciding product cost, and how important product cost is to the customer. In a labour-intensive and low-technology industry such as catering, there will usually be such pressure on labour costs that the pay administrator has little freedom to manipulate pay relationships. In an area such as magazine printing, the need of the publisher to get the product out on time is so great that labour costs, however high, may be of relatively little concern. In this situation the pay negotiators have much more freedom of manoeuvre.

It is possible, notwithstanding the above restrictions, to identify four principal mechanisms for the determination of base pay. They are not entirely incompatible, although one tends to be used as the main approach in most organisations.

External market comparisons

In making external market comparisons the focus is on the need to recruit and retain staff, a rate being set which is broadly equivalent to 'the going rate' for the job in question. The focus is thus on **external relativities**. Research suggests that this is always a major contributing factor when organisations set pay rates, but that it increases in significance higher up the income scale. Some employers consciously pay over the market rate in order to secure the services of the most talented employees. Others 'follow the market', by paying below the going rate while using other mechanisms such as flexibility, job security or longer-term incentives to ensure effective recruitment and retention. In either case the decision is based on an assessment of what rate needs to be paid to compete for staff in different types of labour market. Going rates are more significant for some than for others. Accountants and craftworkers, for instance, tend to identify with an external employee grouping. Their assessment of pay levels is thus greatly influenced by the going rate in the trade or the district. A similar situation exists with jobs that are clearly understood and where skills are readily transferable, particularly if the employee is to work with a standard piece of equipment. Driving heavy goods vehicles is an obvious example, as the vehicles are common from one employer to another, the roads are the same, and only the loads vary. Other examples are secretaries, switchboard operators and computer operators. Jobs that are less sensitive to the labour market are those that are organisationally specific, such as much semi-skilled work in manufacturing, general clerical work and nearly all middle-management positions.

There are several possible sources of intelligence about market rates for different job types at any one time. A great deal of information can be found in published journals such as the pay bulletins issued by Incomes Data Services (IDS) and Industrial Relations Services (IRS), focusing on the hard-to-recruit groups such as computer staff. More detailed information can be gained by joining one of the major salary survey projects operated by firms of consultants or by paying for access to their datasets. Information on specific types of job, including international packages for expatriate workers, is collected by specialised consultants and can be obtained on payment of the appropriate fee. White (2000, pp. 44–5) identifies a range of other sources of UK pay data including the Confederation of British Industry's Pay Databank and the Office of Manpower Economics. In addition there are more informal approaches such as looking at pay rates included in recruitment advertisements in papers, at job centres and on web-based job-board sites. New staff, notably HR people, often bring with them a knowledge of pay rates for types of job in competitor organisations and can be a useful source of information. Finally, it is possible to join or set up salary clubs. These consist of groups of employers, often based in the same locality, who agree to share salary information for mutual benefit.

Internal labour market mechanisms

Just as there is a labour market of which the company is a part, so there is a labour market within the organisation which also needs to be managed so as to ensure effective performance. According to Doeringer and Piore (1970) there are two kinds of internal labour market: the enterprise and the craft. The enterprise market is so called because the individual enterprise defines the boundaries of the market itself. Such will be the market encompassing manual workers engaged in production processes, for whom the predominant pattern of employment is one in which jobs are formally or informally ranked, with the jobs accorded the highest pay or prestige usually being filled by promotion from within and those at the bottom of the hierarchy usually being filled only from outside the enterprise. It is, therefore, those at the bottom that are most sensitive to the external labour market. Doeringer and Piore point out that there is a close parallel with managerial jobs, the main ports of entry being from management trainees or supervisors, and the number of appointments from outside gradually reducing as jobs become more senior. This modus operandi is one of the main causes of the problems that redundant executives face.

Recent American research has stressed the importance of this kind of internal labour market in determining pay rates. Here the focus is on **internal differentials** rather than external relativities. An interesting metaphor used is that of the sports tournament in which an organisation's pay structure is likened to the prize distribution in a knock-out competition such as is found, for example, at the Wimbledon Tennis Championships. Here the prize money is highest for the winner, somewhat lower for the runner-up, lower again for the semi-final losers and so on down the rounds. The aim, from the point of view of the tournament organisers, is to attract the best players to compete in the first round, then subsequently to give players in later rounds an incentive to play at their peak. According to Lazear (1995, pp. 26–33), the level of base pay for each level in an organisation's hierarchy should be set according to similar principles. The level of pay for any particular job is thus set at a level which maximises performance lower down the hierarchy among employees competing for promotion. The actual performance of the individual receiving the pay is less important.

The second type of internal labour market identified by Doeringer and Piore is the craft market, where barriers to entry are relatively high – typically involving the attainment of a formal qualification. However, once workers are established in the market, seniority and hierarchy become unimportant as jobs and duties are shared among the individuals concerned. Such arrangements are usually determined by custom and practice, but are difficult to break down because of the vested interests of those who have successfully completed their period of apprenticeship. Certain pay rates are expected by those who have achieved the required qualification and it is accepted by everyone that this is a fair basis for rewarding people.

Job evaluation

We assess job evaluation in some detail in the next chapter. Here it is necessary only to define the term and identify it as one of the four principal mechanisms of pay determination. Job evaluation involves the establishment of a system which is used to measure the size and significance of all jobs in an organisation. It results in each job being scored with a number of points, establishing in effect a hierarchy of all the jobs in the organisation ranging from those which require the most knowledge and experience and which carry a great deal of responsibility (i.e. senior management and specialist professional jobs) to those which require least knowledge and experience and require the job-holder to carry relatively low levels of responsibility. Each job is then assimilated to an appropriate grade and payment is distributed accordingly.

The focus is thus on the relative worth of jobs within an organisation and on comparisons between these rather than on external relativities and comparisons with rates being paid by other employers. Fairness and objectivity are the core principles, an organisation's wage budget being divided among employees on the basis of an assessment of the nature and size of the job each is employed to carry out. Usage of job evaluation has increased in recent years. It is currently used by just over half of public sector organisations in the UK and by 15 per cent of companies operating in the private sector (CIPD 2007, p. 10).

Collective bargaining

The fourth approach involves determining pay rates through collective negotiations with trade unions or other employee representatives. Thirty years ago this was the dominant method used for determining pay in the UK, negotiations commonly occurring at industry level. The going rates for each job group were thus set nationally and were adhered to by all companies operating in the sector concerned. Recent decades have seen a steady erosion of these arrangements, collective bargaining being decentralised to company or plant level in the manufacturing sector, where it survives at all. Meanwhile the rise of service sector organisations with lower union membership levels has ensured that collective bargaining arrangements now cover only a minority of UK workers. According to Kersley *et al.* (2006, p. 180) only 40 per cent now have any of their terms and conditions determined in this way, collective bargaining over any kind of issue continuing in only 27 per cent of workplaces. The experience of many other countries is similar, but there remain regions such as Eastern Europe and Scandinavia where collective bargaining remains the major determinant of pay rates. Where separate clusters of employees within the same organisation are placed in different bargaining groups and represented by different unions, **internal relativities** become an issue for resolution during bargaining.

In carrying out negotiations the staff and management sides make reference to external labour market rates, established internal pay determination mechanisms and the size of jobs. However, a host of other factors come into the equation too as each side deploys its best arguments. Union representatives, for example, make reference to employee need when house prices are rising and affordable accommodation is hard to find. Both sides refer to the balance sheet, employers arguing that profit margins are too tight to afford substantial rises, while union counterparts seek to gain a share of any increased profits for employees. However good the case made, what makes collective bargaining different from the other approaches is the presence of industrial muscle. Strong unions which have the support of the majority of employees, as is the case in many public sector organisations, are able to ensure that their case is heard and taken into account. They can thus 'secure' a better pay deal for their members than market rates would allow.

ACTIVITY 26.3

Which of the four mechanisms outlined above do you think is usually most efficient for setting the following?

- Base pay
- Annual cost of living increases
- Executive remuneration packages
- Bonus schemes

THE ELEMENTS OF PAYMENT

Once the mechanisms for determining rates of pay for jobs in an organisation have been settled, the second key strategic decision relates to the make-up of the pay package. Here there is a great deal of potential choice available. What is included and to what extent are matters which should be decided with a view to supporting the organisation's

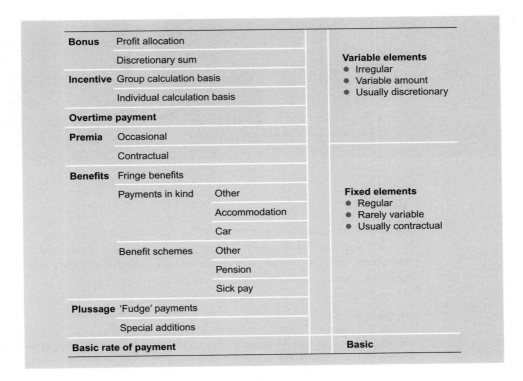

Figure 26.2
The potential
elements of
payment

objectives and encouraging the necessary attitudes and actions on the part of employees. The payment of an individual will be made up of one or more elements from those shown in Figure 26.2. Fixed elements are those that make up the regular weekly or monthly payment to the individual, and which do not vary other than in exceptional circumstances. Variable elements can be varied by either the employee or the employer.

Basic rate

The irreducible minimum rate of pay is the basic. In most cases this is the standard rate also, not having any additions made to it. In other cases it is a basis on which earnings are built by the addition of one or more of the other elements in payment. Some groups of employees, such as operatives in the footwear industry, have little more than half of their earnings in basic, while primary and secondary schoolteachers have virtually all their pay in this form. In the UK as many as 60 per cent of employees receive no additional payments at all beyond their basic pay (Grabham 2003, p. 398).

Plussage

Sometimes the basic has an addition to recognise an aspect of working conditions or employee capability. Payments for educational qualifications and for supervisory responsibilities are quite common. There is also an infinite range of what are sometimes called 'fudge' payments, whereby there is an addition to the basic as a start-up allowance, mask money, dirt money, and so forth.

ACTIVITY 26.4

If your employer offered you a 'remuneration package', which could be made up from any of the items in Figure 26.2 provided that the total cost was no more than £X, what proportion of each item would you choose and why? Does your answer suggest ideas for further development of salary policies?

Benefits

Extras to the working conditions that have a cash value are categorised as benefits and can be of great variety. Some have already been mentioned; others include luncheon vouchers, subsidised meals, discount purchase schemes and the range of welfare provisions such as free chiropody and cheap hairdressing.

Premia

Where employees work at inconvenient times – or on shifts or permanently at night – they receive a premium payment as compensation for the inconvenience. This is for inconvenience rather than additional hours of work. Sometimes this is built into the basic rate or is a regular feature of the contract of employment so that the payment is unvarying. In other situations shift working is occasional and short-lived, making the premium a variable element of payment. Shift premia are received by 11 per cent of UK workers (Grabham 2003, p. 399), accounting on average for around 6 per cent of their total pay (Office for National Statistics 2006, p. 9).

Overtime

It is customary for employees working more hours than are normal for the working week to be paid for those hours at an enhanced rate, usually between 10 and 50 per cent more that the normal rate according to how many hours are involved. Seldom can this element be regarded as fixed. No matter how regularly overtime is worked, there is always the opportunity for the employer to withhold the provision of overtime or for the employee to decline the extra hours. Overtime is earned by over a quarter of the UK workforce, more than two-thirds of the recipients being men (Grabham 2003, p. 398; Office for National Statistics 2006, p. 9). It is particularly associated with less-well-paid manual work. Where overtime is paid it tends to account for a major portion of an individual's gross pay (18.2 per cent on average in 2006).

Incentive

Incentive is here described as an element of payment linked to the working performance of an individual or working group, as a result of prior arrangement. This includes most of the payment-by-results schemes that have been produced by work study, as well as commission payments to salespeople, skills-based pay schemes and performance-related pay schemes based on the achievement of agreed objectives. The distinguishing feature is that the employee knows what has to be done to earn the payment, though he or she may feel very dependent on other people, or on external circumstances, to receive it. Forty-four per cent of employees in the private sector, compared with only 19 per cent in the public sector receive a portion of their pay via some sort of incentive (Kersley *et al.* 2006, p. 190). Around 10 per cent of pay on average takes this form (Office for National Statistics 2006, p. 9).

Bonus

A different type of variable payment is the gratuitous payment by the employer that is not directly earned by the employee: a bonus. The essential difference between this and an incentive is that the employee has no entitlement to the payment as a result of a contract of employment and cannot be assured of receiving it in return for a specific performance. The most common example of this is the Christmas bonus.

We include profit sharing under this general heading although the ownership of shares confers a clear entitlement. The point is that the level of the benefit cannot be directly linked to the performance of the individual. Rather, it is linked to the performance of the business. In some cases the two may be synonymous, with one dominant individual determining the success of the business, but there are very few instances like this, even in the most feverish imaginings of tycoons. Share ownership or profit sharing on an agreed basis can greatly increase the interest of the employees in how the business is run and can increase their commitment to its success, but the performance of the individual is not directly rewarded in the same way as in incentive schemes.

THE IMPORTANCE OF EQUITY

Whatever methods are used to determine pay levels and to decide what elements make up the individual pay package, employers must ensure that they are perceived by employees to operate equitably. It has long been established that perceived inequity in payment matters can be highly damaging to an organisation. Classic studies undertaken by J.S. Adams (1963) found that a key determinant of satisfaction at work is the extent to which employees judge pay levels and pay increases to be distributed fairly. These led to the development by Adams and others of **equity theory** which holds that we are very concerned that rewards or 'outputs' equate to our 'inputs' (defined as skill, effort, experience, qualifications, etc.) and that these are fair when compared with the rewards being given to others. Where we believe that we are not being fairly rewarded we show signs of 'dissonance' or dissatisfaction which leads to absence, voluntary turnover, on-job shirking and low-trust employee relations. It is therefore important that an employer not only treats employees equitably in payment matters but is *seen* to do so too.

While it is difficult to gain general agreement about who should be paid what level of salary in an organisation, it is possible to employ certain clear principles when making decisions in the pay field. Those that are most important are the following:

- a standard approach for the determination of pay (basic rates and incentives) across the organisation;
- as little subjective or arbitrary decision making as is feasible;

- maximum communication and employee involvement in establishing pay determination mechanisms;
- clarity in pay determination matters so that everyone knows what the rules are and how they will be applied.

These are the foundations of procedural fairness or 'fair dealing'. In establishing pay rates it is not always possible to distribute rewards fairly to everyone's satisfaction, but it should always be possible to distribute rewards using procedures which operate equitably. You will find further information and discussion exercises about the way people perceive their pay and talk about it on this book's companion website, www.pearsoned.co.uk/torrington.

WINDOW ON PRACTICE

Attitudes towards payment arrangements vary radically between countries. In a survey in Singapore 1,500 respondents were asked to pick three of the following five factors which they believed would have a significant impact on wage determination: wages in the same industry, wages in a different industry, union representation, government influence and productivity. The proportion of respondents identifying the five factors as significant were:

- Productivity   33.5%
- Government   29.1%
- Wages in the same industry   27.1%
- Unions   18.3%
- Wages in a different industry   14.8%

The same survey demonstrated that the main cause of differences between individual perspectives was the quality and quantity of information that they had received from their employers about their businesses.

Source: D.P. Torrington and Tan Chwee Huat (1994) *Human Resource Management for South East Asia*. Singapore: Simon & Schuster.

SUMMARY PROPOSITIONS

26.1 Until relatively recently many employers in the UK were greatly restricted in their capacity to design reward strategies which met their priorities by the prevailing system of multi-employer or industry-level collective bargaining. The experimentation that followed the disintegration of this system has led to both successful and unsuccessful outcomes.

26.2   Simultaneous competition in product and labour markets has led employers increasingly to think in terms of 'total reward' when developing reward strategies. This involves incorporating all management initiatives which may have the effect of adding value to the experience of working in an organisation.

26.3   In payment matters employees are principally concerned with purchasing power, fairness and recognition of effort and skills. Employers are concerned with recruitment, retention, motivation and minimising the wage budget. Employers are restricted in pay matters by the law and the realities of their product markets.

26.4   There are four main alternative methods of setting base pay rates: external labour market comparisons, internal labour market mechanisms, job evaluation and collective bargaining.

26.5   The main elements of payment are basic rate, plussage, benefits, premia, overtime, incentives and bonus.

26.6   Procedural equity is essential to the design of successful payment systems.

GENERAL DISCUSSION TOPICS

1 Can payment ever be truly fair?

2 The chapter lists employer and employee objectives in relation to payment. What changes or additions would you make to these lists?

3 Do you think it is possible to identify 'best practice' in payment policy? What elements would you consider should make up any such package?

FURTHER READING

Chartered Institute of Personnel and Development.
The Chartered Institute of Personnel and Development (CIPD) carries out a big annual survey of reward management policy and practice which is published in February each year. It can be downloaded from the institute's website. In addition it publishes the results of other research projects that focus on reward. Two recent examples are the report of a symposium held in 2005 at which academics and practitioners who specialise in reward matters met to discuss developments in the field (Armstrong *et al.* 2005) and a series of papers by John Purcell and Sue Hutchison (2006–7) summarising their research on the role played by line managers in the implementation of reward initiatives.

Kessler, I. (2005) 'Remuneration Systems', in S. Bach (ed.), *Managing Human Resources: Personnel Management in Transition*, 4th edn. Oxford: Blackwell.
This excellent chapter assesses the recent research into all major aspects of reward strategy and policy that has been undertaken in the UK. All aspects are discussed, including regulatory developments and the ever-present search for links between reward practice and improved organisational performance.

Thorpe, R. and Homan, G. (2000) *Strategic Reward Systems*. London: Financial Times/Prentice Hall. Several of the chapters in this volume take forward the main points made in the present chapter. Many contain case study examples which illustrate the problems organisations face putting pay strategy into action in practice.

REFERENCES

Adams, J.S. (1963) 'Towards an understanding of inequity', *Journal of Abnormal and Social Psychology*, Vol. 67, pp. 422–36.

Armstrong, M. and Brown, D. (2006) *Strategic Reward: Making it Happen.* London: Kogan Page.

Armstrong, M. and Murlis, H. (1998) *Reward Management: A handbook of remuneration strategy and practice.* London: Kogan Page.

Armstrong, M., Thompson, P., Brown, D. and Cotton, C. (2005): *Reward Management: Report on a one-day conference held on 13th July 2005, organised jointly by e-reward and the Chartered Institute of Personnel and Development.* London: CIPD.

CIPD (2007) *Reward Management: Annual Survey Report 2007.* London: CIPD.

Doeringer, P.B. and Piore, M.J. (1970) *Internal Labour Markets and Manpower Analysis.* Washington, DC: Office of Manpower Research, US Department of Labor.

Grabham, A. (2003) 'Composition of Pay', *Labour Market Trends*, August.

IRS (2006) 'Making the most of reward'. *IRS Employment Review*, 19 May, pp. 27–9. London: IRS.

Jacques, E. (1962) 'Objective measures for pay differentials', *Harvard Business Review*, January–February, pp. 133–7.

Kersley, B., Forth, J., Bryson, A., Bewley, H., Dix, G. and Oxenbridge, S. (2005) *Inside the Workplace: First Findings from the 2004 Workplace Employment Relations Survey.* London: DTI.

Kersley, B., Alpin, C., Forth, J., Bryson, A., Bewley, H., Dix, G. and Oxenbridge, S. (2006) *Inside the Workplace: Findings from the 2004 Workplace Employment Relations Survey.* Abingdon: Routledge.

Kessler, I. (2001) 'Reward System Choices', in J. Storey (ed.), *Human Resource Management: A Critical Text*, 2nd edn. London: Thomson Learning.

Kessler, I. (2005) 'Remuneration Systems' in S. Bach (ed.), *Managing Human Resources: Personnel Management in Transition*, 4th edn. Oxford: Blackwell.

Lazear, E.P. (1995) *Personnel Economics.* Boston: Massachusetts Institute of Technology.

Office for National Statistics (2006) *2006 Annual Survey of Hours and Earnings.* London: ONS.

Poole, M. and Jenkins, G. (1998) 'Human Resource Management and the Theory of Rewards: Evidence from a national survey', *British Journal of Industrial Relations*, Vol. 36, No. 2, pp. 227–47.

Purcell, J. and Hutchinson, S. (2006) *Rewarding Work: The Vital Role of Line Managers.* London: CIPD.

Smith, I. (1993) 'Reward management: A retrospective assessment', *Employee Relations*, Vol. 15.

Suff, R. (2006) 'Investing in Excellence at the Crown Prosecution Service', *IRS Employment Review*, No. 841, 17 February, pp. 24–7.

Thompson, M. (1998) 'Trust and Reward', in S.J. Perkins and S.J. Sandringham (eds), *Trust, Motivation and Commitment.* Farringdon: Remuneration Research Centre.

Thorpe, R. (2000) 'Reward Strategy', in R. Thorpe and G. Homan (eds), *Strategic Reward Systems.* London: Financial Times/Prentice Hall.

Torrington, D.P. and Tan Chwee Huat (1994) *Human Resource Management for South East Asia.* Singapore: Simon & Schuster.

White, G. (2000) 'Determining pay', in G. White and J. Druker (eds), *Reward Management: A Critical Text.* London: Routledge.

An extensive range of additional materials, including multiple choice questions, answers to questions and links to useful websites can be found on the Human Resource Management Companion Website at **www.pearsoned.co.uk/torrington**.

CHAPTER 27

SALARIES

1 Introduce and assess the operation of traditional grading structures and pay spines

2 Explain the concept of 'broadbanding'

3 Appraise different approaches to job evaluation

4 Examine the legal framework for reward management

The most important component of the reward package, at least for most employees, is their monthly or weekly salary. Because this also represents the lion's share of the pay bill for most organisations, it is important both that it is seen to be fair and that it is administered accurately and professionally. Failing to do so is likely to lead an organisation to lose some of the trust of its employees, making them less likely to maximise their efforts and more likely to seek alternative employment. So effective methods which appear to be fair in the way they operate need to be found in order to establish how much each job-holder should receive in the form of base pay. In addition, care must be taken to ensure that the organisation complies with the various regulations which apply in this area of activity.

On what basis though should we determine how much each job-holder should be paid? Should the decision be based on market worth (i.e. what other employers pay people doing similar jobs) or on the significance of a particular type of job to the success of the organisation? Interestingly, as far as employees are concerned, the latter is the preferred approach (*see* Dickinson 2006). Surveys of employee views suggest that market rates produce pay structures which are considered to be unfair because they do not take full account of other factors such as the responsibility that is shouldered by job-holders, the skills and knowledge they are required to bring to the job, the type of conditions they are required to work in or their individual performance. Determining appropriate differentials is therefore anything but a straightforward matter. There is a general recognition that some jobs are worth more than others because their overall contribution is greater or because they carry more responsibility, but measuring these attributes in any kind of objective way is very difficult to achieve in practice.

SALARY STRUCTURES

Most organisations of any size have in place some form of grading structure which is used as the basis for determining the basic rate of pay for each job. Moves towards person-based and performance-related reward in recent years have tended to be used to determine the level of bonus or progression within a grading structure. They have thus been used *in addition* to and not instead of established job-based systems.

The traditional approach involves developing a salary structure of groups, ladders and steps, whereby different groups or 'families' of jobs in an organisation are identified, each having a separate pay scale. Increasingly the term 'job family' is being replaced with 'career framework' (IDS 2006, p. 2), but the principle is the same. It is illustrated in Figure 27.1.

Job families

The first element of the structure is the broad groupings of salaries, each group being administered according to the same set of rules. The questions in making decisions about this are to do with the logical grouping of job-holders, according to their common interests, performance criteria, qualifications and, perhaps, bargaining arrangements and trade union membership. Massey (2000, p. 144) suggests the following as a typical seven-way division of jobs into distinct families:

1 Executives

2 Management

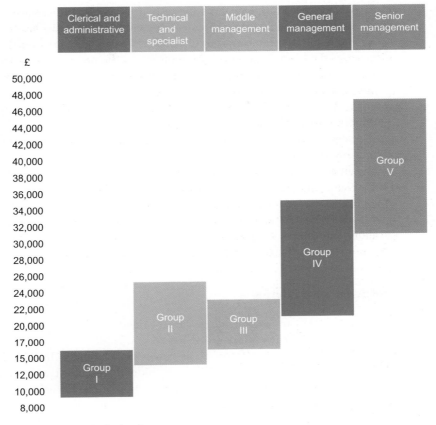

Figure 27.1 Typical salary groups

3 Professional

4 Technical

5 Administrative

6 Skilled manual

7 Manual

The broad salary ranges are then set against each group, to encompass either the maximum and minimum of the various people who will then be in the group or – in the rare circumstance of starting from scratch – the ideal maximum and minimum levels.

As the grouping has been done on the basis of job similarity, the attaching of maximum and minimum salaries can show up peculiarities, with one or two jobs far below a logical minimum and others above a logical maximum. This requires the limits for the group to be put at the 'proper' level, with the exceptions either being identified as exceptions and the incumbents being paid a protected rate or being moved into a more appropriate group.

Salary groups will not stack neatly one on top of another in a salary hierarchy. There will be considerable overlap, recognising that there is an element of salary growth as a result of experience as well as status and responsibility. No overlap at all (a rare arrangement) emphasises the hierarchy, encouraging employees to put their feet on the salary ladder and climb, but the clarity of internal relativities may increase the dissatisfaction of those on the lower rungs and put pressure on the pay system to accommodate the occasional anomaly, especially if climbing is not well supported. Overlapping grades blur the edges of relativities and can reduce dissatisfaction at the bottom, but introduce dissatisfaction higher up.

Another reason why pay scales for different job families usually overlap is to accommodate scales of different length. A family with a flat hierarchy will tend to have a small number of scales with many steps, while the steep hierarchy will tend to have more scales, but each with fewer steps. One of the main drawbacks of overlapping scales is the problem of migration, where an employee regards the job as technical at one time and makes a case for it to be reclassified as administrative at another time, because there is no further scope for progress in the first classification. Another aspect of migration is the more substantive case of employees seeking transfer to other jobs as a result of changes in the relative pay scales, which reduce rigidity in the internal labour market.

Ladders and steps

Because employees are assumed to be career oriented, salary arrangements are based on that assumption, so each salary group has several ladders within it and each ladder has a number of steps (often referred to as 'scales' and 'points'). In the traditional model increments are awarded annually, reflecting individual seniority. Hence the new starter normally enters employment with the organisation at the lowest rung of the ladder in the grade for the job. At the end of each completed year of service individuals are then awarded an increment until after six or seven years they reach the top of the ladder – the ceiling for the relevant grade. At this point pay progression stops, except for any annual cost of living rise. The only way in which an individual can gain a higher income within the organisation is to secure promotion to a more highly graded job. This involves moving up on to a new ladder, at which point annual incremental pay awards commence again. Such approaches are still common in the public sector, although, as in many private sector organisations, incremental progress is increasingly linked to satisfactory performance, skills acquisition or the achievement of agreed objectives.

The number of ladders will vary from organisation to organisation depending on particular circumstances, but for many large organisations offering a potential long-term career path it would be usual for there to be five or six separate ladders or grades for each job family. IDS (2006, p. 30) give the following example of the approach used at Zarlink Semiconductors. Here there are six ladders for each job family, descriptors being used to indicate broadly which jobs are graded at which level:

1 entry

2 developing

3 working

4 senior (team leader)

5 specialist (manager)

6 principal (director)

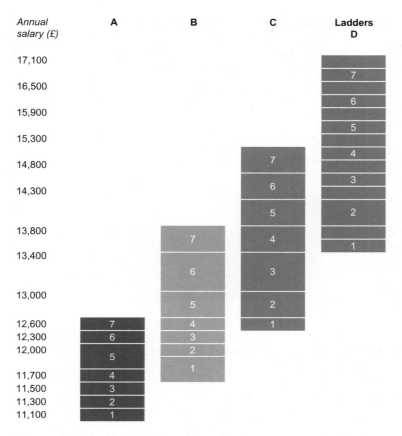

Figure 27.2 Ladders and steps in a salary group

As with groups there is considerable overlap, the top rung of one ladder being rather higher than the bottom rung of the next. Taking a typical general employee group as an example, we could envisage four ladders, as shown in Figure 27.2. The size of the differential between steps varies from £200 to £600 according to the level of the salary, and the overlapping could be used in a number of ways according to the differing requirements. Steps 6 and 7 on each ladder would probably be only for those who had reached their particular ceiling and were unlikely to be promoted further, while steps 4 and 5 could be for those who are on their way up and have made sufficient progress up one ladder to contemplate seeking a position with a salary taken from the next higher ladder.

The figures attached to the ladders in this example are round, in the belief that salaries are most meaningful to recipients when they are in round figures. However, ladders are sometimes developed with steps having a more precise arithmetical relationship to their relative position, so that each step represents the same percentage increase. Equally, some ladders have the same cash amount attached to each step. Some commentators place importance on the relationship of the maximum to the minimum of a ladder, described as the span, and the relationship between the bottom rung of adjacent ladders, referred to as the differential. A span of 50 per cent above the minimum or 20 per cent on either side of the midpoint is common.

The self-financing increment principle

It is generally believed that fixed incremental payment schemes are self-regulating, so that introducing incremental payment schemes does not mean that within a few years everyone is at the maximum. The assumption is that just as some move up, others retire or resign and are replaced by new recruits at the bottom of the ladder. However, this will clearly not be the case when staff turnover is low, nor will it be the case in very tight labour markets where it is necessary to appoint external candidates to points on the scales which reflect their market worth rather than simply starting them at the base of the grade as would typically occur in the case of an internal promotion.

ACTIVITY 27.1

If incremental scales cease to be self-financing through lack of labour market movement, what advantage is there to the employer in keeping them?

Why not one big (happy) family?

An important question is whether there should be subgroupings within the organisation at all, or whether all employees should be paid in accordance with one overall salary structure. Internal relativities disappear; there is only a differential structure. This arrangement has many attractions, as it emphasises the integration of all employees and may encourage them to identify with the organisation as a whole, it is administratively simple and can stimulate competition for personal advancement. It also allows more flexibility in the pay that is arranged for any individual and removes the problem that tends to occur with a family approach whereby some necessary but peripheral jobs do not readily fit into any of the major families of jobs in the organisation.

Interest in the development of single pay structures has increased in recent years for a number of reasons. It has accompanied a more general preference among employers for taking an organisation-wide approach to a whole range of HR initiatives. New technologies often demand a more flexible workforce, leading to a blurring of the organisational distinction between groups of workers. Harmonisation of the terms and conditions of employment follows, so that all employees work the same number of hours, are given the same training opportunities and enjoy the same entitlement to occupational pensions, sick pay and annual leave. Such practices have also been conspicuously imported into British subsidiaries of Japanese and American companies, which typically have longer experience of single-status employment practices. Moreover, substantial increases in the occurrence and frequency of corporate mergers and acquisitions means that payment systems can become overwhelmingly complex when previously separate organisations are brought together for the first time. The result is a tendency to simplify as a means of achieving a workable harmonised salary system.

Interest has also arisen following recent judgments in which courts have awarded equal pay to employees who have sought to compare their jobs with those of other individuals in wholly different job families. As a result, employers who continue to operate different mechanisms for determining the pay of different groups of employees have had difficulty in defending their practices when faced with equal value claims.

The argument against such a system is that it applies a common set of assumptions that may be inappropriate for certain groups. In general management, for instance, it will probably be an assumption that all members of the group will be interested in promotion and job change; this will be encouraged by the salary arrangements, which will encourage job-holders to look for opportunities to move around. In contrast, the research chemist will be expected to stick at one type of job for a longer period, and movement into other fields of the company's affairs, such as personnel or marketing, will often be discouraged. For this reason it will be more appropriate for the research chemist to be in a salary group with a relatively small number of ladders, each having a large number of steps; while a general management colleague will be more logically set in a context of more ladders, each with fewer steps.

There are other reasons too for sticking with or moving towards a structure composed of a number of different distinct job families. Key is the flexibility it gives employers to respond efficiently to developments in specific labour markets. As a result, when one group of staff become harder to recruit and retain because demand for their skills increases, pay rates can be adjusted upwards without the need to incur the costs associated with a general pay rise for all employees.

Moreover, in practice it is very difficult to develop a single pay structure which is acceptable to all parties in an organisation. The more diverse the skills, values or union affiliation of the employees, the more difficult is such a single job family. The factors used to compare job with job always tend to favour one grouping at the expense of another; one job at the expense of another. The wider the diversity of jobs that are brought within the purview of a single scheme, the wider will be the potential dissatisfaction, with the result that the payment arrangement is one that at best is tolerated because it is the least offensive rather than being accepted as satisfactory.

ACTIVITY 27.2

In what type of situations do you think a single, integrated pay structure would be appropriate? Where would such a pay structure be inappropriate? What are the most likely management problems in each case?

WINDOW ON PRACTICE

Since 2003 the National Health Service, like many public sector organisations, has been moving towards a single streamlined pay structure for all its staff except doctors and dentists. It started by securing agreement with its many trade unions to pilot a scheme in 12 NHS Trusts. The new pay scales that resulted formed part of a wider package of measures being introduced by the government under the heading 'agenda for change'.

The new pay structure radically simplified established NHS pay practices. Instead of each professional group negotiating its own grading structure, the agenda for change approach created a standard pay scale which covers everyone. Six hundred and fifty different pay grades were replaced with just 16 pay bands (two spines each with eight grades) along with harmonised terms and conditions which apply across the whole NHS.

All existing jobs were allocated to one of the eight new bands using a job evaluation scheme which takes account of five factors:

- the level of responsibility held by the job-holder;
- the extent of knowledge, training and experience needed to do the job;
- the extent to which the job-holder has freedom to act independently;
- the level and type of skills deployed by the job-holder;
- the nature of the working environment and amount of effort required to carry out the job.

The number of incremental steps varies from band to band. Band 1 (mainly for lower-skilled ancillary and clerical roles) contains four steps, while Band 7 (specialist nurses and section managers) contains nine. Progression is mainly based on seniority, so after each completed year of service, the employee is awarded one increment and climbs a step. But two steps in each band (the second from the bottom and one higher up the scale) can only be attained if the job-holder also satisfies a competency-based assessment.

Sources: IDS (2003b) 'Pay modernisation in the NHS', *IDS Report* No. 884, July. London: IDS; and Department of Health website (**www.doh.gov.uk/agendaforchange**).

BROADBANDING

Attention has increasingly been given in recent years to the introduction of 'broadbanding' as a way of retaining the positive features of traditional pay scales while reducing some of the less desirable effects (*see* Armstrong and Brown 2001; CIPD 2007). One of these less desirable effects is the built-in incentive to focus on being promoted rather than on performing well in the current job. This can lead to individuals playing damaging political games in a bid to weaken the position of colleagues or even undermine their own supervisors. Inflexibility can also occur when individuals refuse to undertake duties or types of work associated with higher grades. Moreover, in making internal equity the main determinant of pay rates within an organisation, rigid salary structures prevent managers from offering higher salaries to new employees. This tends to hinder effective competition in some labour markets.

Broadbanding essentially involves retaining some form of grading system while greatly reducing the numbers of grades or salary bands. The process typically results in the replacement of a structure consisting of ten or a dozen distinct grades with one consisting of only three or four. Pay variation within grades is then based on individual performance, skill or external market value rather than on the nature and size of the job. The great advantage of such approaches is their ability to reduce hierarchical thinking. Differences in pay levels still exist between colleagues but they are no longer seen as being due solely to the fact that one employee is graded more highly than another. This can reduce feelings of inequity provided the new criteria are reasonably open and objective. As a result, teamwork is encouraged as is a focus on improving individual performance in order to secure higher pay.

In theory, therefore, broadbanded structures increase the extent to which managers have discretion over the setting of internal differentials, introduce more flexibility and permit organisations to reward performance or skills acquisition as well as job size. Their attraction is that they achieve this while retaining a skeleton grading system which gives order to the structure and helps justify differentials. Time will tell how acceptable such approaches are to the courts when it comes to judging equal value claims (*see* the section below, 'The legal framework for pay and reward', under 'Equal Value').

WINDOW ON PRACTICE

The Britannia is the UK's second largest mutual building society. It employs approximately 4,000 staff – 1,500 in its branches and 2,500 in its head office. Until 2002 the society operated a traditional hierarchical grading system consisting of 16 separate grades. Once employees were paid at the top of the scale for their particular grade, the only way they could earn more was to apply for promotion. Excellence and experience in their current job could not be further rewarded. This approach was seen by managers to be too rigid and inflexible to enable the society to meet its staffing objectives satisfactorily. In particular it was believed to be providing a disincentive to enhanced individual performance and effective employee development.

The decision was thus taken to move to a far simpler, broadbanded system. Instead of 16 grades there are now just six bands into which all employees have been assimilated. Instead of 670 quite tightly defined job descriptions, there are now 38 more flexibly written role profiles. For each band a midpoint is identified which is set broadly at the market rate for the majority of jobs that are covered by the relevant role profiles. Where individual employees sit within the broad bands depends on their performance. The best performers are paid above the midpoint, the poorer performers below it. Annual pay rises thus reflect market rates (aiding effective recruitment and retention), but also reward individual effort.

Source: Dennis 2005.

JOB EVALUATION

One of the main tasks associated with the administration of weekly or monthly salary payments is setting the differential gaps. It is necessary always to juggle the three factors of performance, market rate and equity. It is rarely possible or wise to pay people only according to their performance or contribution, and linking payment only to developments in the labour market can make working relationships very difficult. There is always the vexed question of how much more than Y and how much less than Z should X receive? The relative contribution of each individual of the three is difficult to measure, so some acceptable assessment of each job is made. The difficult problem of assessing performance is overlaid with the even more difficult problem of making comparisons.

The best-established way of tackling this problem is to use a form of job evaluation, a technique which appears to be used by more and more UK employers each year. Steady growth was reported during the 1990s despite the approach being criticised by advocates of greater flexibility in pay determination (IRS 1998). Large-scale surveys (*see* Thompson and Milsome 2001; IDS 2003a; CIPD 2004 and 2007) confirm the continuation of this trend in more recent years, also providing evidence of further likely take-up in the future. Much of the recent growth has been in the public sector, local authorities and the NHS being examples of major employers establishing new schemes in recent years, but the surveys suggest that job evaluation is very widely used in the private sector as well. Moreover, few organisations abandon it, once introduced. The maxim that 'job evaluation is the one management tool that refuses to go out of fashion' thus continues to hold true.

Job evaluation is the most common method used to compare the relative values of different jobs in order to provide the basis for a rational pay structure. Among the many definitions is this one from ACAS:

> Job evaluation is concerned with assessing the relative demands of different jobs within an organization. Its usual purpose is to provide a basis for relating differences in rates of pay to different in-job requirements. It is therefore a tool which can be used to help in the determination of a pay structure. (ACAS 1984)

It is a well-established technique, having been developed in all its most common forms by the 1920s. In recent years it has received a series of boosts. First, various types of incomes policy between 1965 and 1974 either encouraged the introduction of job evaluation or specifically permitted expenditure above the prevailing norm by companies wishing to introduce it. In the 1980s the use of job evaluation became the hinge of most equal pay cases. More recently organisations have found it useful as part of moves towards single-status contractual arrangements and resolving pay issues following organisational mergers.

Despite its popularity it is often misunderstood, so the following points have to be made:

- Job evaluation is concerned with the job and not the performance of the individual job-holder. Individual merit is not assessed.

- The technique is systematic rather than scientific. It depends on the judgement of people with experience, requiring them to decide in a planned and systematic way, but it does not produce results that are infallible.

- Job evaluation does not eliminate collective bargaining where trade unions are recognised. It determines the differential gaps between incomes; it does not determine pay levels or annual pay rises.

- Only a structure of pay rates is produced. Other elements of earnings, such as premia and incentives, are not determined by the method.

The chief reason for the introduction of job evaluation is to achieve fairness in pay policy and to increase employees' sense of fairness. It is also commonly used as a tool in organisation restructuring and in harmonising the terms and conditions enjoyed by different groups of employees, for example following a merger or acquisition, or the signing of a single-status agreement with a trade union. Another important reason for the increased use of job evaluation is the need to comply with the Equal Pay Act 1970, as modified in 1984, which places as central in assessing equal pay claims the question of whether or not a job evaluation scheme is in use.

There are many methods of job evaluation in use and they are summarised by Armstrong and Murlis (1998, pp. 81–102), Smith and Nethersall (2000) and IDS (2003a). Where a non-analytical or 'whole job' scheme is used a panel of assessors examines each job as a whole, in terms of its difficulty or value to the business, to determine which should be ranked more highly than others. No attempt is made to break each job down into its constituent parts. By contrast, an analytical scheme requires each element or factor of the job to be assessed. Since 1988 it has been the practice of courts only to accept the results of analytical schemes in equal pay cases.

The most widely used analytical schemes are based on points-rating systems, under which each job is examined in terms of factors such as skill, effort and responsibility. Each factor is given a weighting indicating its value relative to the others and for each factor there are varying degrees. A score is then given depending on how demanding the job is in terms of each factor, with the overall points value determining the relative worth of each job – and hence its grade in the organisation's pay structure.

Traditionally the analysis was carried out by a panel of managers and workforce representatives examining each job description in turn and comparing it, factor by factor, against grading definitions. In recent years there has been increased interest in computer-assisted job evaluation systems which award scores to each job on the basis of information gathered from job analysis questionnaires.

A well-known set of factors, weightings and degrees was devised for the National Electrical Manufacturers Association of the United States, but the International Labour Organisation has produced a list of the factors used most frequently (*see* table below). It would be unusual for more than a dozen of these to be used in any one scheme, most taking account of six to ten different factors.

The points values eventually derived for each job can be plotted on a graph or simply listed from the highest to the lowest to indicate the ranking. Then – and only then – are points ratings matched with cash amounts, as decisions are made on which points

Accountability	Effort	Problem solving
Accuracy	Initiative	Resources control
Analysis and judgement	Judgement	Responsibility for cash/
Complexity	Know-how	materials, etc.
Contact and diplomacy	Knowledge and skills	Social skills
Creativity	Mental effort	Supervision given/received
Decision making	Mental fatigue	Task completion
Dexterity	Physical demands	Training and experience
Education	Physical skills	Work conditions
Effect of errors	Planning and coordination	Work pressure

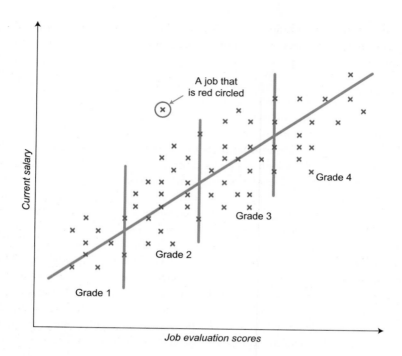

A job that
is red circled

Current salary

Grade 4

Grade 3

Grade 2

Grade 1

Job evaluation scores

Figure 27.3
Job evaluation
analysis

ranges equate with various pay grades. This process is illustrated in Figure 27.3, each cross representing a job. The most common approach involves using a graph on which one axis represents the *current* salary for each job evaluated and the other the number of *job evaluation points* awarded. A line of best fit is then drawn and each job assigned to a grade. Salary-modelling software is widely available to help with this process.

It is virtually inevitable that some jobs will be found to be paid incorrectly after job evaluation has been completed. If the evaluation says that the pay rate should be higher then the rate duly rises, either immediately or step by step, to the new level. The only problem is finding the money, and introducing job evaluation always costs money. More difficult is the situation where evaluation shows the employee to be overpaid. It is not feasible to reduce the pay of the job-holder without breaching the contract of employment. There have been two approaches. The first, which was never widespread and appears almost to have disappeared, is buying out. The overpaid employee is offered a large lump sum in consideration of the fact of henceforth being paid at the new, lower rate. The second and more general device used is that of the personal rate or **red-circling**. An example could be where the rate for the job would be circled in red on the salary administrator's records to show that the employee should continue at the present level while remaining in that post, but a successor would be paid at the lower job-evaluated rate.

A widely used proprietary scheme is the Hay Guide Chart-Profile Method (E-reward 2003), which is particularly appropriate for the evaluation of management jobs. The method is based on an assessment of four factors; know-how, problem solving, accountability and working conditions. Jobs are assessed by using each of three guide charts, one for each factor. A profile is then developed for the job showing the relationship between the factors, a ranking is eventually produced and the rates of pay of the jobs considered in order to produce a new pay structure. At this stage comes one of the greatest advantages of this system. The proprietors have available a vast amount of comparative pay data on different undertakings using their system, so their clients not only can compare rates of pay within their organisation (differentials and internal relativities) but also can examine their external relativities. This and other proprietary systems developed by firms of consultants are described by Armstrong and Murlis (1998, pp. 602–15) and by IDS (2000).

WINDOW ON PRACTICE

In 2002 three local careers services serving the West Midlands merged to form the Coventry, Solihull and Warwickshire Partnership (CSWP). It is a not-for-profit organisation which is independent, but each of its three constituent parts was once part of a local authority. Following the merger it became apparent that it was very unsatisfactory to continue employing staff on three completely different sets of terms and conditions. Not only were holiday entitlements and mileage allowances different, but the merger also brought about a situation in which people doing essentially the same job were paid different amounts because the grading systems used by each of the three legacy organisations differed considerably.

It was therefore decided to draw up a new set of terms and conditions that would apply to everyone (i.e. a single-status arrangement) and a new payment system consisting of 18 grades and 66 spinal column points (i.e. steps) on to which all existing staff would be assimilated. The system was devised by the Hay Group using their job evaluation system, the hope of managers being that subcontracting the work to an independent consultancy would make the results more acceptable to employees.

However, officials of UNISON (the recognised trade union at CSWP) were unhappy about some of the details and refused to recommend acceptance of the new package of terms and conditions when their members were balloted about it in 2003. As a result it was soundly rejected in the vote, despite the fact that the majority of staff would benefit financially from their regrading and that those who did not would have their pay red-circled indefinitely. A general pay rise of 3.5 per cent was also associated with acceptance of the deal. A subsequent analysis of the reasons established that a lack of communication by managers with employees about the implications of moves to a single-status arrangement was responsible, along with a dislike among staff for the pressure they had been put under to accept the whole deal as a condition for receiving the 3.5 per cent rise.

Over the following two years negotiations with UNISON continued resulting in some concessions being made on the details of the new pay structure. Moreover, senior managers took care to consult more effectively with staff, staging roadshows at which they explained the implications for staff and gave everyone an opportunity to express their views. A further ballot was held and this time the new deal was accepted.

Source: IRS 2006.

EMPLOYEE PARTICIPATION IN JOB EVALUATION

The degree of participation by non-managerial employees in job evaluation varies from one business to another. In some cases the entire operation is conducted from start to finish without any employee participation at all. Some degree of participation is more common and is sensible if acceptance of a new scheme is to be gained. Apart from negotiating on pay levels and bargaining units, the main opportunities for employee contribution are discussed below.

Job families

Employees collectively need to consent to the family structure and they can probably add to the deliberations of managers about what that structure should be, as they will be well aware of the sensitive points of comparison.

Job descriptions

Traditionally job descriptions have been crucial to the evaluation and it is common for job-holders to prepare their own, using a pro-forma outline, or for supervisors to prepare them for jobs for which they are responsible. Superficially, this is an attractive method, as there is direct involvement of the employee, who cannot claim to have been misrepresented. Also, it delegates the task of writing job descriptions, enabling it to be completed more quickly. The drawback is similar to that of character references in selection. Some employees write good descriptions and some write bad ones: some overstate while others understate. Inconsistency in job descriptions makes consistency in evaluation difficult.

An alternative is for job descriptions to be compiled by job analysts after questioning employees and their supervisors, who subsequently initial the job description which the analyst produces, attesting to its accuracy.

Panel evaluation

The awarding of points is usually done by a panel of people who represent between them the interests and expertise of management and employees. This is not only being 'democratic', it is acknowledging the need for the experience and perspective of job-holders as well as managers in arriving at shrewd judgements of relative worth. Naturally, panel memberships alter so that employees are not asked to evaluate their own jobs. Although there is an understandable general tendency for employee representatives to push ratings up, and for management representatives to try to push them down, this usually smooths out because both parties are deriving differential rankings and not pay levels. The only potential conflict of interest will be if employee representatives and managers have divergent objectives on the shape of the eventual pay structure, with big or small differential gaps.

Job analysis questionnaires

Proprietary, computer-assisted job evaluation methods involve trained analysts putting a series of detailed questions to job-holders from a multiple-choice questionnaire. The results are then fed into a computer which generates a score for each job. There is therefore no need for a panel to reach decisions based on written job descriptions. While there is clearly direct employee involvement in providing answers to the job analysis questionnaire, the absence of a panel including workforce representatives can reduce the level of employee influence on the outcome of the exercise. This is particularly the case with those propriet-ary schemes which are customised to meet the needs of the purchasing organisation.

THE LEGAL FRAMEWORK FOR PAY AND REWARD

Equal value

One of the major reasons for the growth in job evaluation in recent years has been the development of equal pay law. When assessing the validity of equal pay claims, tribunals employ the principles of job evaluation as a starting point, appointing a job analyst to undertake a comparison of the content of different jobs if necessary. Importantly, from the employer perspective, this means that the use by an organisation of an analytical job evaluation scheme can be a very effective defence when an equal pay claim is brought. The employer can simply claim that the jobs in question have both been evaluated and been found to be of different value for specific reasons. Provided the scheme itself is free of sex bias, this should serve to deter aggrieved employees from bringing cases in the first place.

The Equal Pay Act 1970 established that a woman could bring a case to an employ-ment tribunal claiming entitlement to equal pay with a man working at the same estab-lishment if the claimant and her chosen comparator were engaged in 'like work' or work rated as equivalent under an employer's job evaluation study. A man can equally bring a case comparing his pay to that of a female colleague but this has rarely occurred in practice outside the field of pension entitlements. An amendment to the Act, which came into effect in 1984, broadened the definition of 'equal value' so that it became possible for a case to be brought if the claimant believes that her work is equal to that of her com-parator in terms of the demands made upon them. This amendment followed a European Court ruling which judged the existing Equal Pay Act to fall short of the stand-ard established by the EEC Equal Pay Directive. Since then other European Court rulings have further extended the scope of equal value law. You will find further information and discussion exercises focusing on debates about equal pay issues on this book's com-panion website, **www.pearsoned.co.uk/torrington**.

Like work

When presented with a claim for equal pay an employment tribunal will first seek to establish whether the claimant is engaged in 'like work' with the more highly paid man she has named as her comparator. The work does not have to be identical to justify equal pay under this heading, but must be either the same or of a broadly similar nature. In practice this means that the difference in pay can only be justified if there is 'a differ-ence of practical importance' in the work done or if there is 'a genuine material factor' which justifies the higher rate of pay enjoyed by the male comparator.

An example of a difference of practical importance might be the level of responsibil-ity of the man's job when compared to that of the claimant. An employer might, for example, be justified in paying a man more than his female colleague working on a comparable production line if the articles being manufactured by the man were of substantially greater value. Similarly a discriminatory payment could be justified if a man worked under less supervision than a woman engaged in otherwise like work. A common example would be a man working without supervision on night shifts.

Where there is no practical difference of this kind a discriminatory payment can only be justified where there is a 'genuine material factor other than sex' which can explain the difference in pay levels.

Work rated as equivalent

Cases brought under this section of the Act relate to jobs which are different in nature but have been rated as equivalent under the employer's job evaluation study. The existence of such a study can also provide the basis of an employer's defence in equal value claims. A definition of a job evaluation scheme is included in the Act:

> A woman is to be regarded as employed on work rated as equivalent with that of any man if her job and his have been given an equal value, in terms of the demand made on a worker under various headings (for instance, effort, skill, decision), on a study undertaken with a view to evaluating in these terms the jobs done by all or any of the employees in an undertaking. (Equal Pay Act 1970, s. 1(5))

Case law has further narrowed the definition of acceptable job evaluation schemes. In the case of *Bromley* v. *H & J. Quick* (1988) the Court of Appeal ruled that the identification of benchmark jobs and paired comparisons was 'insufficiently analytical' as this did not involve evaluation under headings as required by the Act. The widely used method of job evaluation whereby only a sample of benchmark jobs are analysed cannot, therefore, be relied upon as a basis for an employer's defence. The jobs of the applicants and their chosen comparators must each have been evaluated analytically. In addition, a tribunal will look at the means by which scores derived from a job evaluation scheme are used to determine the rate of pay and will take account of a job evaluation study which has been completed but not implemented.

To be acceptable to a tribunal the job evaluation scheme in use must also be free of sex bias. Employers should ensure, therefore, that the factor weightings do not indirectly discriminate by overemphasising job requirements associated with typical male jobs, such as physical effort, at the expense of those associated with jobs predominantly undertaken by women, such as manual dexterity or attention to detail.

WINDOW ON PRACTICE

In recent years the number of cases brought to tribunals under the work rated as equivalent heading has grown hugely. At the time of writing (early 2007) there are several thousand individual and group-based claims awaiting a hearing, the vast majority being brought by public sector workers. This situation has come about because of the moves to single-status payment structures of the kind referred to above. What has happened is that employers have carried out extensive job evaluation exercises and have decided as a result that significant groups of predominantly female staff should be assimilated to new salary scales at a higher level or grade than that which determines their current level of pay. In other words, the job evaluation exercises have rated these women's jobs as equivalent to those of male colleagues who have hitherto enjoyed higher pay. Under equal pay law women in this position not only have the right to be upgraded in respect of future work, but also have the right to receive back-pay for up to six years to compensate them for the fact that they have effectively been underpaid for the work they have done in the past. Employers faced with this situation have typically sought to reach financial settlements with the individuals affected or with their union representatives. However, this has proved difficult to achieve in many cases because no-win-no-fee lawyers have advised the women concerned to take their cases through the tribunal system and not to settle for anything less than full back-pay plus interest.

Many of the employers affected are local authorities with very limited scope for increasing their wage bills. The result is downward pressure on wage settlements for other groups of workers, threats to services and upward pressure on council tax bills for the general public. In November 2006 the Local Government Employers' Association warned that the total likely cost associated with claims already in the tribunal system was likely to be over £3 billion (Fuller 2006).

Work of equal value

A woman who is not engaged in like work, work of a broadly similar nature or work rated as equivalent is still entitled to bring an equal pay claim if she believes her work to be of equal value. In these cases the claimant names as her chosen comparator a man employed by the same undertaking who may be engaged in work of a wholly different nature. If the tribunal decides that there are grounds to believe that the work is of equal value, it will then appoint an independent expert, nominated by ACAS, to carry out a job evaluation study. The report of the expert will then be used by the tribunal as a basis of the decision on whether or not to make an award of equal pay to the claimant. A woman may bring an equal value claim in this way even if she has male colleagues engaged in like work and paid at the same rate as she.

A number of significant equal value cases have been brought to tribunals over the years. In *Hayward* v. *Cammell Laird* (1984) a cook was awarded pay equal to that of men employed as joiners and laggers, but only after an appeal to the House of Lords three years after making the initial complaint. In 1990 the shopworkers' union USDAW dropped an equal value case against Sainsbury's when the employer agreed to carry out a job evaluation exercise. The union had claimed that predominantly female check-out operators were engaged in work of equal value to that of predominantly male ware-housemen. This led to an 11 per cent rise in Sainsbury's retail wage bill and to a series of similar USDAW settlements with other major retailers during 1990 and 1991. The impact of these cases has been very substantial, leading to the restructuring of pay arrangements across industry and the public services.

Genuine material factor defences

If it is established, to the satisfaction of an employment tribunal, that the claimant is engaged in like work, work rated as equivalent or work of equal value, the employer must show that the difference in the respective rates of pay is not due to sex discrimination but to a 'genuine material factor not of sex'. There are many defences which potentially fall into this category, some of which are described in Chapter 23. Among the most significant, as far as job evaluation is concerned, is the practice of red-circling whereby an individual's rate of pay is protected for a period following redeployment or a new job evaluation exercise. In most cases, provided it can be clearly shown that the red circle was awarded for reasons other than the individual's sex, this will be an acceptable material factor defence.

WINDOW ON PRACTICE

The Ontario Pay Equity Act

A major purpose of equal pay law is the reduction of inequality between payment for jobs which are principally performed by men and those which are mostly carried out by women. Although improvements have occurred since the 1970s when the legislation was first brought in, women's gross average hourly earnings remain around 80 per cent of men's (Shaw and Clark 2000). Equal pay law is thus failing to achieve one of its principal aims, or is doing so too slowly. This has led many to argue that the current law is inadequate and that more radical approaches are needed.

A model often cited by supporters of change is the approach used in the Canadian province of Ontario, where an inspectorate has a policing role. This means that there is less need for individual women or their representatives to prepare court actions. The following are the key features of the Ontario pay equity regime:

* Employers of more than 100 people are required to have written policies which identify 'female' job classes – defined as being over 60 per cent female.

* They then have to carry out job evaluation to establish whether or not there is a discrepancy between male and female classes.

* Where there is, they have to draw up a 'pay equity plan' setting out what they intend to do to narrow the gap – that is, make pay equity adjustments – over a number of years if necessary.

* There are derogations similar in nature to the UK's genuine material factors which employers can deploy to defend unequal pay.

Aileen McColgan (1993, p. 251) makes the following observation about the system:

> The potential of Ontario's legislation lies in its effective reversal of the burden of proof. Rather than encouraging employers to ignore issues of equal pay save in the unlikely event of an individual's complaint, the Pay Equity Act obliges them, in co-operation with any bargaining agent, to scrutinise their own pay practices for evidence of discrimination and eliminate it.

The National Minimum Wage

Since 1999 most workers in the UK have been entitled in law to be paid a minimum hourly rate for the work that they do. The rate of the National Minimum Wage (NMW) is not linked to any formula, but is set by the Secretary of State for Trade and Industry after consultation with a body of experts and representatives from industry known as the Low Pay Commission. The aim is always to set the highest rate possible that will not appreciably have an adverse impact on employment levels. In practice the level of the NMW is increased on 1 October each year, and in recent years the increases have been well in excess of the prevailing rate of inflation. In early 2007 it stood at £5.35 an hour.

Not everyone, however, is entitled to the full amount. There are some groups who are excluded altogether such as people engaged in family work (au pairs, nannies, etc.), people working in sheltered work schemes run for homeless persons, apprentices, barristers' pupils and students undertaking periods of work experience as part of a course of higher education. Other groups are only entitled to a lower 'development rate' which is set at around 80 per cent of the full rate (£4.45 an hour in 2007). This applies to people who are aged 18–22 and those over that age who are in the first six months of a new job during which at least 26 days are being spent training to achieve a National Vocational Qualification (NVQ) or Scottish Vocational Qualification (SVQ). Finally, there is a third, lower 'youth rate' for 16–17 year olds which is around 60 per cent of the full adult rate (£3.30 an hour in 2007).

In practice it can be very difficult for employers to establish that they are in fact paying staff at or above the National Minimum Wage. One reason is the complexity of the regulations on what payments and payments in kind can and cannot be included as part of someone's salary for NMW purposes. For example, the regulations state that over-time and on-call payments must not be included and thus, in effect, must be paid in addition to the NMW. On the other hand, employers are entitled to include in their calculations a sum to compensate for live-in accommodation, meaning that live-in staff may be paid slightly less than the NMW because they enjoy this type of benefit. Staff meals, however, cannot be included, nor can tips which are paid in cash. However, where tips are paid by customers on credit cards and distributed to staff through the payroll they can be included and thus form part of the hourly rate and not a supplement. There are also quite complicated rules about times when people are and are not deemed to be working for the purposes of the payment of the NMW, while further complexity arises in situations where people are paid entirely on a piecework basis and do not there-fore receive an hourly rate (e.g. where people are paid for the amount of work they do, not the amount of time spent doing it).

The government has appointed a team of inspectors to investigate incidents of wilful refusal to pay the NMW. They have the right to inspect records of hours worked and wages paid so as to establish whether or not the NMW has been and is being been paid. Where an employer knowingly refuses to comply with the NMW regulations, it can be charged with a criminal offence and fined. Until January 2007 the maximum fine was £5,000. Since then it has been calculated according to the following formula:

> Twice the rate of the minimum wage at the time of the charge multiplied by the number of employees who have been paid below the level of the NMW multiplied by the number of working days they have not been paid the NMW.

In addition, of course, workers who are found not to have been paid the NMW are entitled to receive their full entitlement in the future and to receive back-pay too by way of compensation.

ACTIVITY 27.3

At the time that the National Minimum Wage was introduced some groups representing employers argued that it would have a negative impact on both the level of unemployment and the level of inflation. Why do you think there is a danger of these effects when minimum wages are introduced? Why do you think they have not occurred in practice in the UK as a result of the National Minimum Wage?

Deductions from wages

A third way in which the administration of salaries is regulated concerns situations in which employers make deductions from wage packets for one reason or another. All employees in the UK are entitled in law to receive an itemised pay statement which sets out the gross rate of pay for the month or week and any deductions that have been made. The Employment Rights Act 1996 sets out what deductions can lawfully be made, the implication being that other types of deduction are unlawful and can lead to action in the employment tribunal. The list of permissible deductions includes those authorised by legislation such as tax and national insurance contributions and those authorised in the contract of employment such as trade union subscriptions or pension fund contributions. Sometimes courts issue 'attachment orders' requiring an employer to pay a fine or a debt on behalf of an employee and to make an equivalent deduction from the pay package, and from time to time mistakes are made in salary administration resulting in overpayments to employees that need to be recovered. In both these situations deductions are lawful. Importantly, however, it is unlawful for an employer to levy any kind of fine on an employee as a punishment when a disciplinary offence has been committed or where an individual's performance in the job is unsatisfactory. In such circumstances along with any others in which underpayments of agreed wages are made, aggrieved employees have the right to take their case to an employment tribunal and to argue that they should be reimbursed.

SUMMARY PROPOSITIONS

27.1 Traditional salary structures assign each job to a grade in which there are a number of incremental steps.

27.2 Recent years have seen moves towards single pay spines covering all jobs in an organisation. Separate scales for different 'job families' remain common.

27.3 Another recent development is a move towards broadbanded structures which reduce the number of grades in each salary scale to allow managers greater flexibility in setting pay levels for individual employees.

27.4 Job evaluation involves using a standard system to measure the size or importance of jobs in an organisation. Systems can be analytical or non-analytical. Modern computerised systems are highly analytical in nature.

27.5 Key decisions in designing job evaluation schemes concern which factors to include and what weighting to give to each.

27.6 A major reason for the growth in the use of job evaluation in recent years has been the development of equal value law which uses the principles of job evaluation as the basis for deciding cases.

27.7 Other matters that affect the administration of salaries include the rules of the National Minimum Wage system and rules that restrict the deductions that employers can lawfully make from employees' wage packets.

GENERAL DISCUSSION TOPICS

1 'Job evaluation does not produce equitable payment: it merely produces a ramshackle method of justifying the status quo.' Do you agree with this statement?

2 What would be the main arguments for and against introducing legislation that is similar to the Ontario Pay Equity Act in the UK?

3 What do you think would be the major organisational problems associated with a move from a narrow to a broadbanded payment structure?

FURTHER READING

Armstrong, M. and Baron, A. (1995) *The Job Evaluation Handbook*. London: IPD.
Hastings, S. (2000) 'Grading systems and estimating value', in G. White and J. Druker (eds), *Reward Management: A Critical Text*. London: Routledge.
IDS (2003a) 'Job evaluation is alive and well despite market-driven pay', *IDS Report*, No. 875, February. London: IDS.
Lawler, E. (1990) *Strategic Pay*. San Francisco: Jossey Bass.

IDS (2003a) and Armstrong and Baron (1995) provide the best practical guides to job evaluation processes, including case studies from different sectors. The most widely quoted critique of job evaluation is found in Lawler (1990), in which the author sets out the case for the adoption of new approaches in many organisational scenarios. Hastings (2000) provides a good summary of various other critical perspectives.

Armstrong, M. and Brown, D. (2001) *New Dimensions in Pay Management*. London: CIPD.
IPD (1997) *The IPD Guide on Broadbanding*. London: IPD.

A great deal has been written about broadbanding in recent years and the likelihood that it will be adopted to a greater extent in the future. The best general introduction to the topic is IPD (1997), a more detailed account being provided by Armstrong and Brown (2001).

Leslie, S., Hastings, S. and Morris, J. (2003) *Equal Pay: A practical guide to the law*. London: The Law Society.

Rubery, J. (ed.) (1998) *Equal Pay in Europe? Closing the Gender Wage Gap*. London: Macmillan.

Shaw, S. and Clark, M. (2000) 'Women, pay and equal opportunities', in R. Thorpe and G. Homan (eds), *Strategic Reward Systems*. London: Financial Times/Prentice Hall.

Equal pay issues are debated and discussed in many books and articles. Good starting points are Shaw and Clark (2000) and Leslie *et al.* (2003). The book of articles edited by Jill Rubery (1998) contains detailed analysis of pay equity issues in different industries in Germany, Italy and the UK.

REFERENCES

ACAS (1984) *Job Evaluation*. London: Advisory, Conciliation and Arbitration Services.

Armstrong, M. and Brown, D. (2001) *New Dimensions in Pay Management*. London: CIPD.

Armstrong, M. and Murlis, H. (1998) *Reward Management*. London: Kogan Page.

Chartered Institute of Personnel and Development (2004) *Reward Management 2004: A survey of policy and practice*. London: CIPD.

Chartered Institute of Personnel and Development (2007) *Reward Management: Annual Survey Report 2007*. London: CIPD.

Dennis, S. (2005) 'Rejecting pay hierarchy: broadbanding at Britannia', *IRS Employment Review* No. 828, 29 July.

Dickinson, J. (2006) 'Employees' preferences for the bases of pay differentials', *Employee Relations*, Vol. 28, No. 2 pp. 164–83.

E-reward (2003) 'What is happening to job evaluation today: a large-scale survey', **www. e-reward.co.uk**.

Fuller, G. (2006) 'UK councils facing up to £3bn in equal pay claims', *Personnel Today*, 13 November.

Hastings, S. (2000) 'Grading systems and estimating value', in G. White and J. Druker (eds), *Reward Management: A Critical Text*. London: Routledge.

IDS (2000) *Job Evaluation*, IDS Studies Plus, Autumn. London: IDS.

IDS (2003a) 'Job evaluation is alive and well despite market-driven pay', *IDS Report*, No. 875, February. London: IDS.

IDS (2003b) 'Pay modernisation in the NHS', *IDS Report*, No. 884, July. London: IDS.

IDS (2006) 'Job Families', *IDS Study* No. 814, January. London: IDS.

IPD (1997) *The IPD Guide on Broadbanding*. London: IPD.

IRS (1998) 'There is value in job evaluation', *IRS Employment Trends*, No. 665, October.

IRS (2006) 'Three into one does go: harmonisation at CSWP', *IRS Employment Review* No. 842, pp. 31–5.

McColgan, A. (1993) 'Equal Pay: A New Approach', in A. McColgan (ed.), *The Future of Labour Law*. London: Cassell.

Massey, C. (2000) 'Strategic reward systems – pay systems and structures', in R. Thorpe and G. Homan (eds), *Strategic Reward Systems*. London: Financial Times/Prentice Hall.

Shaw, S. and Clark, M. (2000) 'Women, pay and equal opportunities', in R. Thorpe and G. Homan (eds), *Strategic Reward Systems*. London: Financial Times/Prentice Hall.

Smith, P. and Nethersall, G. (2000) 'Job Evaluation', in R. Thorpe and G. Homan (eds), *Strategic Reward Systems*. London: Financial Times/Prentice Hall.

Thompson, P. and Milsome, S. (2001) *Reward Determination in the UK*. London: CIPD.

LEGAL CASES

Bromley v. *H. & J. Quick* [1988] ICR 623.

Hayward v. *Cammell Laird Shipbuilders Ltd* [1984] TLR 52.

An extensive range of additional materials, including multiple choice questions, answers to questions and links to useful websites can be found on the Human Resource Management Companion Website at **www.pearsoned.co.uk/torrington**.

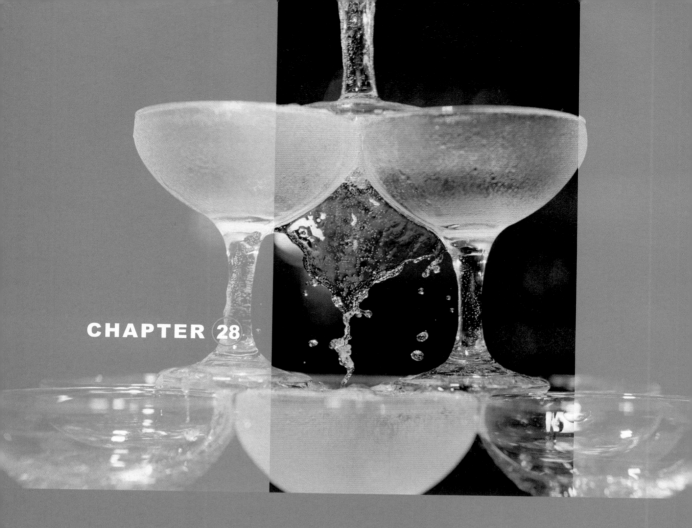

CHAPTER 28

INCENTIVES

THE OBJECTIVES OF THIS CHAPTER ARE TO:

1 Set out the major choices faced by employers contemplating setting up or reviewing incentive payment schemes

2 Explore the question of how many people are paid different types of incentive in the UK

3 Outline the main forms of payment by results (PBR) schemes and discuss their advantages and disadvantages

4 Debate the merits of individual performance-related pay (PRP)

5 Introduce skills-based pay and discuss its major advantages and disadvantages

6 Outline the major forms of profit-sharing schemes that operate, including those sponsored by the government

Incentive payments remain one of the ideas that fascinate managers as they search for the magic formula. Somewhere there is a method of linking payment to performance so effectively that their movements will coincide, enabling the manager to leave the workers on automatic pilot, as it were, while attending to more important matters such as strategic planning or going to lunch. This conviction has sustained a continuing search for this elusive formula, which has been hunted with all the fervour of those trying to find the Holy Grail or the crock of gold at the end of the rainbow.

In recent years incentives of all kinds have been the source of much debate among HR professionals, consultants, trade unionists and academic writers. While particular attention has been given to the pros and cons of individual performance-related reward systems, much has also been written in support of and against the use of team-based incentives and those which reward the acquisition of defined skills. Profit sharing and employee share ownership have been the subject of significant government initiatives and have thus also become topics about which a great deal is written.

BASIC CHOICES

While incentive payment systems are common in the UK, there are millions of employees who do not receive this kind of reward and many employers who use them only in a limited way (often in the remuneration of senior managers). It is thus perfectly possible, and some would argue desirable, to recruit, retain and motivate a workforce by paying a simple, fixed rate of pay for each job in the organisation. There is other equipment in the HR manager's toolkit which can be used to reward effort and maintain good levels of job satisfaction. The most fundamental question is therefore whether or not to use an incentive payment system at all. In the opinion of Sisson and Storey (2000, pp. 123–4) many organisations in the UK have introduced schemes in recent years for 'ideological reasons' as a means of impressing stock market analysts, reinforcing management control or undermining established collective bargaining machinery. These, they suggest, are poor reasons which have generally met with little long-term success. Incentive schemes should only be used where they are appropriate to the needs of the business and where they can clearly contribute to the achievement of organisational objectives.

There is a long tradition in the academic literature of hostility to incentive schemes in general and those which focus on the individual in particular. In 1966, Frederick Herzberg argued that pay was a 'hygiene factor' rather than a 'motivator'. He claimed that its capacity to motivate positively was limited, while it can very easily demotivate when managed poorly. It follows that there is little to be gained and a great deal to lose from the introduction of incentive schemes. Others (for example, Thompson 2000) have focused on the way that incentives are perceived by employees as tools of management control which reduce their autonomy and discretion. This, it is argued, causes resentment and leads to dissatisfaction and industrial conflict. A third source of criticism is the considerable additional costs which invariably mount up when organisations introduce incentive schemes. Cox (2006, p. 1493) labels these 'costly side-effects' and shows that they are both considerable and largely unanticipated at the time a new scheme is introduced.

A different school of thought argues in favour of incentives on the grounds that they reward effort and behaviours which the organisation wishes to encourage. As a result they not only are a fair basis for rewarding people, but also can enhance organisational effectiveness and productivity. Advocates of **expectancy theory** hold this position with their belief that individual employees will alter their behaviour (e.g. by working harder or prioritising their actions differently) if they believe that in so doing they will be rewarded with something they value. Hence, where additional pay is a valued reward, employees will seek it and will work to secure it. A positive outcome for both employer and employee is achievable provided the incentive is paid in return for a form of employee behaviour which genuinely contributes to the achievement of organisational objectives.

In addition, many reward specialists point to a significant **sorting effect** which leads employees who are willing and able to perform to a higher standard to be attracted to jobs in which their superior relative contribution will be properly rewarded. At the same time, it is argued, existing employees who perform relatively poorly are more likely to seek alternative employment than colleagues who perform well and are rewarded for doing so. Hence, over time, the quality of employees rises as a result of the presence of incentive schemes. Conversely, of course, it can be plausibly argued that employers who fail to recognise superior individual contribution in their payment systems are more likely to lose higher-performing people because they perceive themselves to be being inadequately rewarded for their skills and efforts.

The research evidence is patchy on the question of how far incentives actually lead to performance improvements at the organisational level. Some studies suggest a correlation between superior performance and some types of incentive scheme (e.g. Huselid 1995; Lazear 2000; Piekkola 2005; and Gielen *et al.* 2006), while others (e.g. Thompson 1992 and Pearce *et al.* 1985) have found no significant evidence of any link. In any case, as Corby *et al.* (2005, pp. 5–6) point out, there are very few published studies which focus on performance or productivity levels before and after the introduction of a new scheme. What we have are correlation studies which link superior organisational performance to the presence of incentive schemes, but no proof of any causal relationship. Much seems to depend on the circumstances. Incentives are not universally applicable, but can play a role in enhancing individual effort or performance where the conditions and scheme design are right. Problems occur when the wrong system is imposed, on the wrong people, in the wrong circumstances or for the wrong reasons.

Where an incentive scheme is used, the next choice relates to the way the scheme is to operate. There are two basic approaches that can be used: bonus payments and incremental progression. In the case of the former, the employee is rewarded with a single payment (possibly made in stages) at the end of a payment period. In the case of profit sharing it will often be an annual payment, while sales commission is usually paid monthly. Whatever the timing, the key principle is that the pay is variable. Good performance in one period is rewarded, but the same individual could earn rather less in the next if his or her performance deteriorates. Some writers refer to such systems as putting 'pay at risk', because earnings vary from period to period depending on how much incentive is earned. The alternative approach involves making incremental progression dependent on the individual's contribution. The reward takes the form of a general pay rise over and above any cost of living increment being paid in a particular year. The incentive payment thus becomes consolidated into overall earnings and is not variable or 'at risk' after it has been earned.

What in your view are the main advantages and disadvantages of these alternative approaches from a management perspective? Would you be more motivated by the prospect of a pay rise or a one-off bonus payment?

Another basic choice concerns the extent of the incentive. In practice this is a decision of rather greater importance than the type of incentive scheme to be used, although it is given rather less coverage in the literature. There is a world of difference, in terms of cost and employee perception, between a scheme which rewards people with three per cent or four per cent of salary and one which pays a sum equivalent to 25 per cent. Studies undertaken in the USA, reported by Bartol and Durham (2000, p. 14), suggest that the minimum level of bonus or pay rise 'necessary to elicit positive perceptual and attitudinal responses' is between five per cent and seven per cent of salary. Piekkola (2005), in her studies of links between incentives and firm performance in Finland, found that a positive impact on productivity only began to kick in once the incentive exceeded 3.6 per cent of salary. Lesser payments are thus unlikely to provide meaningful incentives and will have only a peripheral impact. According to Hendry *et al.* (2000, p. 54) this has been a major problem for schemes introduced in the public sector where incentives have tended to be worth a maximum of only two per cent or three per cent of salary. Armstrong and Murlis (1998) offer the following advice:

As a rule of thumb, those whose performance is outstanding may deserve and expect rewards of 10% and more in their earlier period in a job. People whose level of performance and rate of development is well above the average may merit increases of between 7 and 9%, while those who are progressing well at the expected rate towards the fully competent level may warrant an increase of between 4% and 6%. Increases of between 0% and 3% may be justified for those who are not making such good progress but who are still developing steadily. Performance-related increases of less than 2–3% are hardly worth giving. Much also depends on current market movement and this affects expectations. (Armstrong and Murlis 1998, pp. 286–9)

The final choice concerns the level at which the incentive will be paid. Some schemes reward individuals for individual performance, others reward a group of employees or team for their collective performance. Finally there are schemes which share incentive payments out among all employees in the organisation or within individual business units. Team-based incentives have tended to get a better press in recent years than individual incentives, a major problem with the latter being their tendency to undermine teamworking in situations where it is an important contributor to competitive advantage (*see* Pfeffer 1998, pp. 218–20), but the different forms of incentive are by no means mutually exclusive. It is possible, for example, to reward a salesperson with three types of incentive, one from each level. The basic pay would thus be enhanced with commission calculated individually, with a performance-based payment made to all in his/her sales team to reflect excellent customer feedback, and finally with a profit-related bonus paid to all employees in the organisation. Indeed, the more recent research suggests that employers are increasingly mixing different types of incentive scheme so as to enable them to help meet a range of distinct organisational objectives. It is not at all uncommon, as a result, for more senior employees to have an opportunity to earn additional income from three or four different types of bonus, some individual, some group based, some leading to a pay rise, others resulting in a one-off bonus payment. The schemes themselves also appear to be becoming increasingly sophisticated and administratively complex (IDS 2005, p. 7; CIPD 2007, p. 15).

WINDOW ON PRACTICE

Peter and Patrick are sales consultants for a financial services company and both had business targets for a six-month period. Peter met his target comfortably and received the predetermined bonus of £6,000 for reaching on-target earnings. Patrick failed to reach his target because his sales manager boss left the company and poached two of Patrick's prime customers just before they signed agreements with Patrick, whose bonus was therefore £2,000 instead of £6,250.

Joanne was a sales consultant for the same company as Peter and Patrick. Before the sales manager left, he made over to her several promising clients with whom he had done considerable preparatory work and who were not willing to be 'poached' by his new employer. All of these signed agreements and one of them decided to increase the value of the deal tenfold without any reference to Joanne until after that decision was made, and without knowing that she was now the appropriate contact. Her bonus for the period was £23,400.

Henry is a production manager in a light engineering company with performance pay related to a formula combining output with value added. Bonus payments were made monthly in anticipation of what they should be. One of Henry's initiatives was to increase the gearing of the payment by results scheme in the factory. Through peculiarities of company accounting his bonus payments were 'justified' according to the formula, but later it was calculated that the production costs had risen by an amount that cancelled out the value-added benefits. Also 30 per cent of the year's output had to be recalled due to a design fault.

Patrick had his bonus made up to £6,250. Joanne had her bonus reduced to £8,000, but took legal advice and had the amount cut restored, whereupon Peter and Patrick both threatened to resign until mollified by *ex gratia* payments of £2,000 each. Peter resigned three months later. Henry was dismissed.

THE EXTENT TO WHICH INCENTIVES ARE PAID

There is conflicting evidence about how widespread incentive payments are in the UK and about whether or not they are becoming more or less common. Until 2005, each year the government's New Earnings Survey selected a sample of over 100,000 employees from across the country and asked their employers to fill in a form outlining their earnings in the previous tax year. One of the questions asked was about incentive payments 'such as piecework, commission, profit sharing, productivity and other incentives/ bonuses'. The survey results persistently showed that only around 15–20 per cent of employees were receiving such payments, most of which was accounted for by traditional piecework or payment-by-results systems operated in manufacturing organisations. The incidence of individual incentives paid to non-manual workers was low. Only around 10 per cent were recorded as receiving such payments in 2003 (Office for National Statistics 2003). The New Earnings Survey has now been superseded by the Annual Survey of Hours and Earnings (ASHE) which no longer includes a general question about incentive payments. Instead it simply records the amount of earnings that are comprised of 'bonuses and commissions' in each payment period (i.e. each week or month). As a result, data about annual bonuses and pay rises that are linked to performance criteria are not captured (Office for National Statistics 2006).

In any event, other surveys have long painted a rather different picture. The authors analysing the 2004 Workplace Employment Relations Survey (Kersley *et al.* 2006, pp. 190–1) concluded that around 40 of the workplaces in their sample operated either a payment by results or a merit pay incentive scheme, while 21 per cent operated some form of share-ownership scheme. Around 30 per cent paid profit-related bonuses to at least some employees. Even allowing for a strong degree of overlap between schemes as a result of employers operating different payment systems simultaneously, these figures suggest that incentive payments form at least some part of some peoples' reward packages in a majority of UK workplaces. The 2004 Employment Relations Survey also found evidence of substantial growth in the incidence of individual performance-related payment systems since the previous survey conducted in 1998.

The CIPD's annual survey of reward practice covers a much smaller sample of employers, but it too suggests both high usage of incentives in the UK and considerably increased usage of incentives over recent years. In 2007 70 per cent of CIPD's respondents reported using 'cash-based/incentive plans'. Sixty-four per cent used individual-based schemes, 27 per cent used team-based schemes, while 53 per cent used schemes that 'are driven by business results'. While such approaches are used by a sizeable minority of employers in the public and voluntary sectors, it is in the private sector that activity is focused.

It is not easy to reconcile the diverse results produced by these surveys. One possibility is that the different results may reflect the different samples used. The ONS New Earnings Survey covered workplaces of all sizes, including the very smallest, while the others tend to focus on somewhat larger employers. It could therefore be the case that incentive schemes are largely used in bigger firms with more sophisticated management practices. Another possibility is that a high proportion of the schemes in operation reward employees with performance-based incremental payments (that is, a pay rise) rather than a one-off annual or monthly bonus. These would not have been picked up by the New Earnings Survey, which asks specifically about the amount of incentive payment received in the previous tax year. A further possibility is that many of the schemes in operation only apply to senior managers and not to the generality of staff. Either way, there is clear evidence of growth in the extent to which employers make use of incentive payment systems.

ACTIVITY 28.2

What other factors might account for the different results picked up by these surveys? How could a survey be designed which would give definitive information about the extent of incentive payments in the UK?

PAYMENT BY RESULTS SCHEMES

Historically, the most widely used incentive schemes have been those which reward employees according to the number of items or units of work they produce or the time they take to produce them. This approach is associated with F.W. Taylor and the phase in the development of personnel management described in Chapter 1 under the heading 'Humane bureaucracy'. Little attention has been paid to the operation of piecework schemes in recent years and there is some evidence to show that they are in decline, both in terms of the proportion of total pay which is determined according to PBR principles and in terms of the number of employees paid in this way. However, PBR is still widely used in some shape or form by employers of manual workers, and it is apparent that new schemes are commonly introduced in manufacturing organisations (Cox 2006).

Individual time saving

It is rare for a scheme to be based on the purest form of piecework, a payment of X pence per piece produced, as this provides no security against external influences which depress output such as machine failure or delays in the delivery of raw materials. The most common type of scheme in use, therefore, is one where the incentive is paid for time saved in performing a specified operation. A standard time is derived for a work sequence and the employee receives an additional payment for the time saved in completing a number of such operations. If it is not possible to work due to shortage of materials or some other reason, the time involved is not counted when the sums are done at the end of the day.

Standard times are derived by the twin techniques of method study and work measurement, which are the skills of the work study engineer. By study of the operation, the work study engineer decides what is the most efficient way to carry it out and then times an operator actually doing the job over a period, so as to measure the 'standard time'. Work-measured schemes of this kind have, however, been subject to a great deal of criticism and are only effective where people are employed on short-cycle manual operations with the volume of output varying between individuals depending on their skill or application.

The main difficulty, from the employee's point of view, is the fluctuation in earnings that occurs as a consequence of a varying level of demand for the product. If the fluctuations are considerable then the employees will be encouraged to try to stabilise them, either by pressing for the guaranteed element to be increased, or by storing output in the good times to prevent the worst effects of the bad, or by social control of high-performing individuals to share out the benefits of the scheme as equally as possible.

Measured daywork

To some people the idea of measured daywork provides the answer to the shortcomings of individual incentive schemes. Instead of employees receiving a variable payment in accordance with the output achieved, they are paid a fixed sum as long as they maintain a predetermined and agreed level of working. Employees thus have far less discretion over the amount of effort they expend. Theoretically, this deals with the key problem of other schemes by providing for both stable earnings and stable output instead of 'as much as you can, if you can'.

The advantage of measured daywork over time-saving schemes, from the management point of view, is the greater level of management control that is exercised. The principal disadvantage is the tendency for the agreed level of working to become a readily achievable norm which can only be increased after negotiation with workforce representatives.

Group and plant-wide incentives

Sometimes the principles of individual time saving are applied to group rather than individual output to improve group performance and to promote the development of teamworking. Where jobs are interdependent, group incentives can be appropriate, but it may also put great pressure on the group members, aggravating any interpersonal animosity that exists and increasing the likelihood of stoppages for industrial action. Group schemes can also severely reduce the level of management control by allowing the production group to determine output according to the financial needs of individual group members.

A variant on the group incentive is the plant-wide bonus scheme, under which all employees in a plant or other organisation share in a pool bonus that is linked to the level of output, the value added by the employees collectively or some similar formula. The attraction of these methods lies in the fact that the benefit to the management of the organisation is 'real' because the measurement is made at the end of the system, compared with the measurements most usually made at different points within the system, whereby wages and labour costs can go up while output and profitability both come down. Theoretically, employees are also more likely to identify with the organisation as a whole, they will cooperate more readily with the management and each other, and there is even an element of workers' control. The difficulties lie in the fact that there is no tangible link between individual effort and individual reward, so that those who are working effectively can have their efforts nullified by others working less effectively or by misfortunes elsewhere.

Commission

The payment of commission on sales is a widespread practice about which surprisingly little is known as these schemes have not come under the same close scrutiny as incentive schemes for manual employees. They suffer from most of the same drawbacks as manual incentives, except that they are linked to business won rather than to output achieved.

ACTIVITY 28.3

A problem with sales commission is its tendency to reward the quantity of goods sold without having regard to the quality of service provided by sales staff. In which circumstances might this have negative consequences? How could a commission-based incentive scheme be adapted to incorporate measures of quality as well as quantity?

DISADVANTAGES OF PBR SCHEMES

The whole concept of payment by results was set up to cope with a stable and predictable situation, within the boundaries of the workplace. External demands from customers were irritations for others – such as sales representatives – to worry about. The factory was the arena, the juxtaposed parties were the management on the one hand and the people doing the work on the other, and the deal was output in exchange for cash. The dramatic changes of the past twenty years, which have swept away stability, dismantled the organisational boundary and enthroned the customer as arbiter of almost everything have also made PBR almost obsolete.

According to the New Earnings Survey the proportion of manual workers receiving PBR payments steadily declined between 1983 and 2003, and there is every reason to believe that this decline has continued in the years since. This trend can be explained, in part, by changing technologies and changes in working practices. A payment system that puts the greatest emphasis on the number of items produced or on the time taken to produce them is inappropriate in industries where product quality is of greater significance than product quantity. Similarly a manufacturing company operating a just-in-time system will rely too heavily on overall plant performance to benefit from a payment scheme that primarily rewards individual effort.

In addition to the problem of fluctuating earnings, described above, there are a number of further inherent disadvantages which explain the decline of PBR-based remuneration arrangements.

Operational inefficiencies

For incentives to work to the mutual satisfaction of both parties, there has to be a smooth operational flow, with materials, job cards, equipment and storage space all readily available exactly when they are needed, and an insatiable demand for the output. Seldom can these conditions be guaranteed and when they do exist they seldom last without snags. Raw materials run out, job cards are not available, tools are faulty, the stores are full, customer demand is fluctuating or there is trouble with the computer. As soon as this sort of thing happens the incentive-paid worker has an incentive either to fiddle the scheme or to negotiate its alteration for protection against operational vagaries.

Quality of work

The stimulus to increase volume of output can adversely affect the quality of output, as there is an incentive to do things as quickly as possible. If the payment scheme is organised so that only output meeting quality standards is paid for, there may still be the tendency to produce expensive scrap. Operatives filling jars with marmalade may break the jars if they work too hurriedly. This means that the jar is lost and the marmalade as well, for fear of glass splinters.

Renewed emphasis on quality and customer satisfaction means that employers increasingly need to reward individuals with the most highly developed skills or those who are most readily adaptable to the operation of new methods and technologies. PBR, with its emphasis on the quantity of items produced or sold, may be judged inappropriate for organisations competing in markets in which the quality of production is of greater significance than previously.

The quality of working life

There is also a danger that PBR schemes may demotivate the workforce and so impair the quality of working life for individual employees. In our industrial consciousness PBR is associated with the worst aspects of rationalised work: routine, tight control, hyper-specialisation and mechanistic practices. The worker is characterised as an adjunct to the machine, or as an alternative to a machine. Although this may not necessarily be the case, it is usually so, and generally expected. Payment by results in this way reinforces the mechanical element in the control of working relationships by failing to reward employee initiative, skills acquisition or flexibility. There is also evidence to suggest that achieving high levels of productivity by requiring individuals to undertake the same repetitive tasks again and again during the working day increases stress levels and can make some employees susceptible to repetitive strain injuries.

The selective nature of the incentive

Seldom do incentive arrangements cover all employees. Typically, groups of employees are working on a payment basis which permits their earnings to be geared to their output, while their performance depends on the before or after processes of employees not so rewarded, such as craftsmen making tools and fixtures, labourers bringing materials in and out, fork-lift truck drivers, storekeepers and so forth.

The conventional way round the problem is to pay the 'others' a bonus linked to the incentive earned by those receiving it. The reasoning for this is that those who expect to earn more (such as the craftspeople) have a favourable differential guaranteed as well as an interest in high levels of output, while that same interest in sustaining output is generated in the other employees (such as the labourers and the storekeepers) without whom the incentive earners cannot maintain their output levels. The drawbacks are obvious. The labour costs are increased by making additional payments to employees on a non-discriminating basis, so that the storekeeper who is a hindrance to output will still derive benefit from the efforts of others, and the employees whose efforts are directly rewarded by incentives feel that the fruits of their labour are being shared by those whose labours are not so directly controlled.

Obscurity of payment arrangements

Because of these difficulties, incentive schemes are constantly modified or refined in an attempt to circumvent fiddling or to get a fresh stimulus to output, or in response to employee demands for some other type of change. This leads to a situation in which the employees find it hard to understand what behaviour by them leads to particular results in payment terms. This same obscurity is often found in the latest fashion in PRP. In a recent unpublished study comparing performance management in two blue-chip companies, less than half the people in management posts claimed to understand how the payments were calculated. Many of those actually misunderstood their schemes!

PERFORMANCE-RELATED PAY

Arguments about the advantages and disadvantages of individual PRP have been some of the most hotly contested in recent decades. The topic has formed the basis of numerous research studies and remains one which attracts much controversy, as was shown in recent debates about the introduction of PRP for teachers working in state schools. The main reason is the apparent contrast between the theoretical attractiveness of such systems – at least from a management perspective – and their supposed tendency to disappoint when operated in practice. While there are many different types of scheme available, all involve the award of a pay rise or bonus payment to individual employees following a formal assessment of their performance over a defined period (normally the previous year). Two distinct varieties of scheme can be identified.

1 **Merit-based systems** simply involve the immediate supervisor undertaking an appraisal of each subordinate's work performance during the previous year. This will typically be done following a formal appraisal interview and often requires the completion of standard documentation drawn up by an HR department. A proportion of future remuneration is then linked to a score derived from the supervisor's assessment. Some systems require supervisors to award a percentage mark against different criteria, while others oblige them to assess individual performance as 'excellent', 'good', 'satisfactory' or 'inadequate'. Merit-based systems are generally regarded as unsatisfactory because they allow considerable scope for assessors to make subjective judgements or to allow personal prejudice to colour their assessments. There is also a tendency to give undue weight to recent events at the expense of achievements taking place early in the appraisal period.

2 **Goal-based systems** are more objective, but are not appropriate for all kinds of job. They are, however, particularly well suited for the assessment of managerial work. Here the supervisor and subordinate meet at the start of the appraisal period and agree between them a list of objectives which the appraisee will seek to meet during the coming months. Examples would be the completion of particular projects, the establishment of new initiatives, undertaking a course of training or making substantial progress towards the solving of a problem. Many employers nowadays seek to link individual objectives directly to defined organisational goals for the year as a means of reinforcing their significance and ensuring that all are pulling in the same direction. At the end of the year the employee is assessed on the basis of which objectives have or have not been met. A score is then derived and a bonus payment or pay rise awarded. Where performance in a job can meaningfully be assessed in this

way, such systems are recommended because they are reasonably objective and straight-forward to score. Where the nature of the job involves the consistent achievement of a defined level of performance, and cannot usefully be assessed in terms of the achievement of specific objectives, the goal-based approach has less to offer. It may still be possible to assess part of the job in this way, but there will also have to be a merit-based element if the appraisal is to reflect all of a person's activity during the appraisal period.

ACTIVITY 28.4

Make a list of five jobs that you consider would be best rewarded by a merit-based system and five more that are best rewarded via the goal-based approach.

The attractions of PRP

It is not difficult to see why PRP has attracted the interest of managers, consultants and government ministers. Its theoretical attractions are considerable and include the following:

- attracting and retaining good performers;
- improving individual and corporate performance;
- clarifying job roles and duties;
- improving communication;
- improving motivation;
- reinforcing management control;
- identifying developmental objectives;
- reinforcing the individual employment relationship at the expense of the collective;
- rewarding individuals without needing to promote them.

In short PRP aims to provide a flexible and cost-effective means of distributing rewards fairly between the good and poorer performers while also contributing towards improved organisation performance. Moreover, it is based on principles to which most people, employees as well as managers, seem to adhere (Brown and Armstrong 2000, pp. 11–13). Most of us are very happy to see individuals rewarded for superior perform-ance and/or effort and would like payment decisions to be based on such criteria. The problems arise when attempts are made to put the principles into practice. A system which is fair and objective in theory can easily fail to achieve these objectives when implemented.

Critiques of PRP

Performance-related pay attracted a great amount of criticism from academic researchers in the 1980s and 1990s during a period when its virtues were frequently asserted by HR managers and consultants. The attacks came from several quarters.

Occupational psychologists tended to question the ability of PRP to motivate positively (e.g. Kohn 1993), while sociologists saw it as a means of reinforcing management control at the expense of worker autonomy (e.g. Hendry *et al.* 2000). A further source of criticism has come from those who suspect that PRP is used as a means of perpetuating gender inequality in payment matters (e.g. Rubery 1995). However, the most colourful and damning criticisms have come from management thinkers such as W. Edwards Deming who advocate Total Quality Management approaches (*see* Chapter 11) and for whom PRP represents exactly the wrong kind of initiative to introduce. The whole basis of their philosophy is the substitution of 'leadership' for 'supervision', removing organisational hierarchies and managing people with as little direction and control as possible. They see PRP as having the opposite effect. It reinforces the hierarchy, enhances the power of supervisors and strengthens management control.

For many critics, including those cited above, PRP has fundamental flaws which cannot be overcome. Kohn, for example, argues that incentives can only succeed in securing temporary compliance. Their use cannot change underlying attitudes, while the attempt to do so ultimately damages the long-term health of an organisation by undermining relationships and encouraging employees to focus on short-term aims:

> Managers who insist that the job won't get done right without rewards have failed to offer a convincing argument for behavioural manipulation. Promising a reward to someone who appears unmotivated is a bit like offering salt water to someone who is thirsty. Bribes in the workplace simply can't work. (Kohn 1993, p. 60)

A second stream of criticism is more moderate, arguing that PRP can have a role to play in organisations, but that its positive effects are limited. Moreover, while not fundamentally flawed, PRP is very difficult to implement effectively in practice. As a result, systems fail as often as they succeed. The arguments are summarised well by Gomez-Mejia and Balkin (1992, pp. 249–55), Cannell and Wood (1992, pp. 66–101), Pfeffer (1998, pp. 203–4) and Purcell (2000). The major points made by these authors are as follows:

- Employees paid by PRP, especially where the incentive is substantial, tend to develop a narrow focus to their work. They concentrate on those aspects which they believe will initiate payments, while neglecting other parts of their jobs.

- PRP, because of its individual nature, tends to undermine teamworking. People focus on their own objectives at the expense of cooperation with colleagues.

- PRP, because it involves managers rating employees, can lead to a situation in which a majority of staff are demotivated when they receive their rating. This occurs where people perceive their own performance to be rather better than it is considered to be by their supervisors – a common situation. The result is a negative effect on the motivation of the staff who are unexceptional, but loyal and valued. These are often the very people on whom organisations depend most.

- Employees are rarely in a position wholly to determine the outcomes of their own performance. Factors outside their control play an important role, leading to a situation in which the achievement or non-achievement of objectives is partially a matter of chance.

- Even the most experienced managers find it difficult to undertake fair and objective appraisals of their employees' performance. Subjective judgements are often taken into account leading to perceptions of bias. Some managers deliberately manipulate ratings for political reasons, allowing their judgement to be coloured by the effect they perceive the outcome will have on particular employees. Low ratings are thus avoided, as are very high ratings, where it is perceived this will lead to disharmony or deterioration of personal relationships.
- In organisations subject to swift and profound change, objectives set for the coming year may become obsolete after a few months. Employees then find themselves with an incentive to meet goals which are no longer priorities for the organisation.
- PRP systems tend to discourage creative thinking, the challenging of established ways of doing things and a questioning attitude among employees.
- Budgetary constraints often lead managers to reduce ratings, creating a situation in which excellent individual performance is not properly rewarded.
- It is difficult to ensure that each line manager takes a uniform approach to the rating of his or her subordinates. Some tend to be more generously disposed in general than others, leading to inconsistency and perceptions of unfairness.
- When the results of performance appraisal meetings have an impact on pay levels, employees tend to downplay their weaknesses. As a result development needs are not discussed or addressed.
- PRP systems invariably increase the paybill. This occurs because managers fear demotivating their staff by awarding low or zero rises in the first years of a system's operation. Poorer performers are thus rewarded as well as better performers.

Using PRP effectively

Despite the problems described above it is possible to implement PRP successfully, as is shown by the experience of case study companies quoted by Brown and Armstrong (2000), IRS (2005a and 2005b) and IDS (2005). It will only work, however, if it is used in appropriate circumstances and if it is implemented properly. Part of the problem with PRP has been a tendency in the HR press to portray it as universally applicable and as a panacea capable of improving performance dramatically. In fact it is neither, but is one of a range of tools that have a useful if limited role to play in some situations. Gomez-Mejia and Balkin (1992) specify the following favourable conditions:

- Where individual performance can be objectively and meaningfully measured.
- Where individuals are in a position to control the outcomes of their work.
- Where close teamworking or cooperation with others is not central to successful job performance.
- Where there is an individualistic organisational culture.

In addition, Brown and Armstrong (2000) rightly point to the importance of careful implementation and lengthy preparation prior to the installation of a scheme. More-over, they argue that PRP should not be looked at or judged in isolation from other forms of reward, both extrinsic and intrinsic. Success or failure can hinge on what else is being done to maximise motivation, to develop people and to improve their job security.

Ultimately PRP has one great advantage which no amount of criticism can remove: it helps ensure that organisational priorities become individual priorities. Managers can signal the importance of a particular objective by including it in a subordinate's goals for the coming year. If the possibility of additional payment is then tied to its achievement, the chances that the objective concerned will be met increase significantly. Organisational performance is improved as a result. Where the achievement of such specific objectives forms a relatively minor part of someone's job, PRP can form a relatively minor part of their pay packet. Other rewards can then be used to recognise other kinds of achievement.

WINDOW ON PRACTICE

Many job descriptions for supervisory positions include reference to responsibility for ensuring that the appropriate health and safety at work regulations are adhered to. Few supervisors, however, left to themselves would see this aspect of their work as a priority. In one organisation known to the authors it was decided to try to raise the profile of health and safety issues by including objectives in this field into managers' annual performance targets. It therefore became clear that the level of PRP in the following year would, in part, be determined by the extent to which the health and safety objectives had been met. The result was the swift establishment of departmental health and safety committees and schemes whereby staff could bring safety hazards to the attention of supervisors.

SKILLS-BASED PAY

A further kind of incentive payment scheme is one which seeks to reward employees for the skills or competencies which they acquire. It is well established in the United States and, according to IRS (2003), has attracted a good deal more interest among British employers. It is particularly prevalent as a means of rewarding technical staff, but there is no reason why the principle should not be extended to any group of employees for whom the acquisition of additional skills might benefit the organisation.

There are several potential benefits for an employer introducing a skills-based pay scheme. Its most obvious effect is to encourage multiskilling and flexibility enabling the organisation to respond more effectively and speedily to the needs of customers. A multi-skilled workforce may also be slimmer and less expensive. In addition it is argued that, in rewarding skills acquisition, a company will attract and retain staff more effectively than its competitors in the labour market. The operation of a skills-based reward system is proof that the sponsoring employer is genuinely committed to employee development.

Most skills-based payment systems reward employees with additional increments to their base pay once they have completed defined skill modules. A number of such schemes are described in detail in a study published by Incomes Data Services (1992). Typical is the scheme operated by Venture Pressings Ltd where staff are employed on four basic grades, each divided into 10 increments. Employees progress up the scale by acquiring specific skills and demonstrating proficiency in them to the satisfaction of internal assessors. New starters are also assessed and begin their employment on the incremental point most appropriate to the level of skills they can demonstrate. In many industries it is now possible to link payment for skills acquisition directly to the attainment of National Vocational Qualifications (NVQs) for which both the setting of standards and the assessment of individual competence are carried out externally.

A skills-based pay system will only be cost effective if it results in productivity increases which are sufficient to cover the considerable costs associated with its introduction and maintenance. A business can invest a great deal of resources both in training its workforce to attain new skills, and in rewarding them once those skills have been acquired, only to find that the cost of the scheme outweighs the benefit gained in terms of increased flexibility and efficiency. Furthermore, in assisting employees to become more highly qualified and in many cases to gain NVQs, an employer may actually find it harder to retain its staff in relatively competitive labour markets.

The other major potential disadvantage is associated with skills obsolescence. Where a business operates in a fast-moving environment and needs to adapt its technology regularly, a skills-based payment system can leave the organisation paying enhanced salaries for skills which are no longer significant or are not required at all. Employers seeking to introduce skills-based systems of payment therefore need to consider the implications very carefully and must ensure that they only reward the acquisition of those skills which will clearly contribute to increased productivity over the long term.

ACTIVITY 28.5

A number of commentators praise skills-based pay as a system which avoids some of the pitfalls associated with PRP schemes. Look back at the list of practical problems with PRP schemes above and consider which do and which do not apply to skills-based incentive systems.

PROFIT SHARING

There are a number of different ways in which companies are able to link remuneration to profit levels. In recent years the government has sought to encourage such schemes and has actively promoted their establishment with advantageous tax arrangements. Underlying government support is the belief that linking pay to profits increases the employee's commitment to his or her company by deepening the level of mutual interest. As a result, it is argued that such schemes act as an incentive encouraging employees to work harder and with greater flexibility in pursuit of higher levels of take-home pay. Other potential advantages for employers described by Pendleton (2000, pp. 346–51) are better cost flexibility, changed attitudes on the part of employees and the discouragement of union membership.

Cash-based schemes

The traditional and most common profit-sharing arrangement is simply to pay employees a cash bonus, calculated as a proportion of annual profits, on which the employee incurs both a PAYE and a national insurance liability. Some organisations pay discretionary profit bonuses on this basis, while others allocate a fixed proportion of profits to employees as a matter of policy. **Gainsharing** is a variation on cash-based profit sharing which is widely used in the USA and which can be used in non-profit-making organisations as well as those operating in the commercial sector. Here the bonus relates to costs saved rather than profit generated in a defined period. So if a workforce successfully achieves the same level of output at lower overall cost, the gain is shared between employer and employees.

Between 1987 and 2000 the government operated an approved profit-related pay scheme which became increasingly popular. By 1996 there were over 14,000 schemes in operation, covering 3.7 million employees. The attraction was the ability profit-related pay schemes gave employers to give pay rises to all employees, while recouping the cost through tax concessions. The scheme was phased out and has now been replaced by the Share Incentive Plan (*see* below).

Share-based schemes

There are several methods of profit sharing which involve employees being awarded shares rather than cash. Here too there are government-sponsored schemes in operation which involve favourable tax treatment. There are several distinct schemes available for employers to use some of which are more tax efficient than others. Traditionally senior managers have been paid, in part, through share-based reward systems, but companies are increasingly seeing an advantage in extending these arrangements to a greater proportion of their staff. The purpose is to increase commitment by giving employees a significant financial stake in the future of the business they work for, at the same time helping to align employees' interests with those of shareholders. The result should be improved staff retention and higher levels of individual performance, but it is difficult to prove that such outcomes result in practice from the introduction of these schemes. For most ordinary employees the level of reward is too low and the extent to which their actions impact on a firm's performance too indirect, for there to be a clear-cut incentive effect. Cohen (2006) provides a concise and clear guide to the whole range of systems. The two most common are the following:

1 **Savings-Related Share Option** schemes permit companies to grant share options to directors and employees in a tax-effective manner. This means that they are given the opportunity to buy shares in their own companies at a future date, but at the current price. The hope is that the value will have increased in the meantime, allowing the purchaser to cash in a tidy profit. This particular government-sponsored scheme requires participants to put between £5 and £250 of their monthly pay aside and then to use the proceeds of the accumulated fund, after three, five or seven years, to buy shares at a discount of 20 per cent of the price they were when the plan started.

2 **Inland Revenue Approved Share Incentive Plans** (previously called All-Employee Share Schemes) allow employees to obtain shares in their own companies while avoiding tax and national insurance contributions. Employers can give such shares to employees to a maximum value of £3,000 per year. Some can be given in recognition

of individual or team performance, making it possible to award some employees more shares than others. Where employees subsequently hold these shares for three years or more, there is no tax liability when they are sold. In addition, under the scheme, employees can buy up to a further £1,500 worth of shares out of pre-tax income and subsequently avoid a proportion of the tax owed when they are sold. Companies are also allowed to give 'free' matching shares for each share purchased by an employee under the scheme. Employers as well as employees gain tax advantages from operating these schemes. Deductions in corporation tax can be made equivalent to the amount of salary used by employees to purchase shares, as well as monies used in establishing and operating the scheme.

Disadvantages of profit-related schemes

The obvious disadvantage of the schemes described above from the employee's point of view is the risk that pay levels may decline if the company fails to meet its expected profit levels. If no profit is made it cannot be shared. Share values can go down as well as up. Companies are not permitted to make guarantees about meeting payments and will have their schemes revoked by the Inland Revenue if they do so. In any event it is likely that profit-based incentives will vary in magnitude from year to year.

For these reasons it is questionable to assert that profit-sharing schemes do in fact act as incentives. Unlike PRP awards they do not relate specifically to the actions of the individual employee. Annual profit levels are clearly influenced by a whole range of factors which are both internal and external to the company. An employee may well develop a community of interest with the company management, shareholders and other employees but it is unlikely seriously to affect the nature of his or her work. Furthermore, both poor and good performers are rewarded equally in profit-related schemes. The incentive effect will therefore be very slight in most cases and will be restricted to a general increase in employee commitment.

SUMMARY PROPOSITIONS

28.1 Incentive schemes should be used where they are appropriate to the needs of the business and where they can clearly contribute to the achievement of organisational objectives.

28.2 Incentive payment schemes either involve the payment of a bonus or form the basis of incremental progression systems. In either case, the reward should represent at least seven per cent of salary if there is to be a meaningful incentive effect.

28.3 The extent to which different types of incentive arrangement are used in the UK is unclear. There is evidence of growth in recent years, but the majority of employees are not covered by such schemes.

28.4 Methods of payment by results include individual time saving, group incentives, measured daywork, plant-wide schemes, productivity schemes and commission.

28.5 Performance-related pay systems are either merit based or goal based. They have been the subject of notable debate in recent years, many researchers finding a mismatch between their theoretical attractions and practical outcomes.

28.6 Skills-based pay involves linking incentives to the achievement of defined competencies or qualifications. It rewards what people bring to the job rather than the results of their efforts.

28.7 Profit sharing has been promoted by governments for many years. The Share Incentive Plan is the latest attempt to encourage employees to hold shares in their own companies.

GENERAL DISCUSSION TOPICS

1 What are the relative advantages of: (a) a system of straight salary that is the same each month, and (b) a system of salary with an individual performance-related addition so that the total payment each month varies?

2 In what circumstances might it be appropriate to base individual payment on team performance?

3 What do you think about Peter, Patrick, Joanne and Henry in the Window on practice box early in this chapter?

FURTHER READING

Brown, D. and Armstrong, M. (2000) *Paying or Contribution: real performance-related pay strategies.* London: Kogan Page.

Kohn, A. (1993) 'Why Incentive Plans Cannot Work', *Harvard Business Review*, September–October, pp. 54–63.

The debate about the merits of individual performance-related pay is so polarised that it is rare to find a balanced account that sets out the views of those who are for and those who are against. It is best to read the partisan accounts. Kohn's (1993) article contains an eloquent and damning critique of such schemes, while Brown and Armstrong (2000) paint a more positive picture.

Incomes Data Services (IDS).

Industrial Relations Services (IRS).

Information about trends in the design of incentive payment schemes is regularly provided in the IDS and IRS publications. They also commonly feature case studies which show exactly how the various schemes operate in practice as well as regular surveys of current practice that can be used for benchmarking processes.

Thorpe, R. and Homan, G. (eds) *Strategic Reward Systems.* London: Financial Times/Prentice Hall. Several chapters in this book concern incentive payment systems of one kind or another. The book includes extensive material on PRP, skills-based pay, gainsharing, profit-sharing and team-based incentives.

REFERENCES

Armstrong, M. and Murlis, H. (1998) *Reward Management*, 4th edn. London: Kogan Page.
Bartol, K.M. and Durham, C.C. (2000) 'Incentives: Theory and Practice', in C. Cooper and E. Locke (eds), *Industrial and Organizational Psychology*. Oxford: Blackwell.

Brown, D. and Armstrong, M. (2000) *Paying for Contribution: real performance-related pay strategies*. London: Kogan Page.

Cannell, M. and Wood, S. (1992) *Incentive Pay: Impact and Evolution*. London: IPM.

CIPD (2007) *Reward Management: Annual Survey Report 2007*. London: CIPD.

Cohen, S. (2006) *Employee Share Plans: Supporting business performance*. London: CIPD.

Corby, S., White, G. and Stanworth, C. (2005) 'No news is good news? Evaluating new pay systems', *Human Resource Management Journal*, Vol. 15, No. 1, pp. 4–24.

Cox, A. (2006) 'The outcomes of variable pay systems: tales of multiple costs and unforeseen consequences', *International Journal of Human Resource Management*, Vol. 16, No. 8, pp. 1475–97.

Gielen, A.C., Kerkhofs, M.J.M. and Van Ours, J.C. (2006) *Performance-related pay and labor productivity*, IZA Discussion Paper 2211. Berlin: Institute for the Study of Labor (IZA).

Gomez-Mejia, L. and Balkin, D. (1992) *Compensation, Organizational Strategy and Firm Performance*. Cincinnati, Ohio: South Western Publishing.

Hendry, C., Woodward, S., Bradley, P. and Perkins, S. (2000) 'Performance and rewards: cleaning out the stables', *Human Resource Management Journal*, Vol. 10, No. 3, pp. 46–62.

Herzberg, F. (1966) *Work and the Nature of Man*. Cleveland, Ohio: World Publishing.

Huselid, M. (1995) 'The impact of HRM practices on turnover, productivity and corporate performance', *Academy of Management Journal*, June.

IDS (1992) *Skills-based pay*, IDS Study No. 500. London: IDS.

IDS (2005) *Bonus Schemes*. IDS Study No. 794. London: IDS.

IDS (2003) *Bonus Schemes*, IDS Study No. 742. London: IDS.

IRS (2005a) 'Pay 4 Performance at Yorkshire Water', *IRS Employment Review*, No. 833, pp. 31–5.

IRS (2005b) 'Performing flexible reward at Severn Trent Water', *IRS Employment Review*, No. 834, pp. 30–3.

Kersley, B., Alpin, C., Forth, J., Bryson, A., Bewley, H., Dix, G. and Oxenbridge, S. (2006) *Inside the Workplace: Findings from the 2004 Workplace Employment Relations Survey*. Abingdon: Routledge.

Kohn, A. (1993) 'Why Incentive Plans Cannot Work', *Harvard Business Review*, September–October, pp. 54–63.

Lazear, E.P. (2000) 'Performance Pay and Productivity', *American Economic Review*, Vol. 90, No. 5, pp. 1346–61.

Office for National Statistics (2003) *New Earnings Survey*. London: The Stationery Office.

Office for National Statistics (2006) *2006 Annual Survey of Hours and Earnings*. London ONS.

Pearce, J.L., Stevenson, W.B. and Perry, J.L. (1985) 'Managerial compensation based on organizational performance: A time series analysis of the effects of merit pay', *Academy of Management Journal*, Vol. 28, pp. 261–78.

Pendleton, A. (2000) 'Profit-sharing and employee share ownership', in R. Thorpe and G. Homan (eds), *Strategic Reward Systems*. London: FT/Prentice Hall.

Pfeffer, J. (1998) *The Human Equation: Building profits by putting people first*. Boston: Harvard Business School Press.

Piekkola, H. (2005) 'Performance-related pay and firm performance in Finland', *International Journal of Manpower*, Vol. 7, No. 8, pp. 619–35.

Purcell, J. (2000) 'Pay per view', *People Management*, 3 February, pp. 41–3.

Rubery, J. (1995) 'Performance-related pay and the prospects for gender pay equity', *Journal of Management Studies*, Vol. 32, No. 5, pp. 637–54.

Sisson, K. and Storey, J. (2000) *The Realities of Human Resource Management*. Buckingham: Open University Press.

Thompson, M. (1992) *Pay and Performance: The Employer Experience*. Institute of Manpower Studies Report 218. London: IMS.

Thompson, M. (2000) 'Salary progression systems', in G. White and J. Druker (eds), *Reward Management: A Critical Text*. London: Routledge.

An extensive range of additional materials, including multiple choice questions, answers to questions and links to useful websites can be found on the Human Resource Management Companion Website at **www.pearsoned.co.uk/torrington**.

PENSIONS AND BENEFITS

THE OBJECTIVES OF THIS CHAPTER ARE TO:

1 Introduce the different types of pension scheme provided by the state, by employers and by financial services organisations

2 Explain the causes and significance of current trends in the provision of occupational pensions

3 Outline the roles played by HR professionals in the field of occupational pensions

4 Distinguish between statutory sick pay (SSP) and occupational sick pay (OSP)

5 Assess recent developments in the provision of company cars by UK employers

6 Explore the potential of flexible benefits systems in the UK context

Employee benefits commonly used to be known as 'fringe benefits', suggesting a periph-eral role in the typical pay packet. The substantial growth in the value of most benefits packages over the past ten or twenty years means that the title 'fringe' is no longer appropriate. An increasing proportion of individual remuneration is made up of addi-tional perks, allowances and entitlements which are mostly paid in kind rather than cash. The total value of benefits 'paid' by employers to employees commonly represents between 20 per cent and 50 per cent of an organisation's salary budget, depending on what is included. Pensions alone can easily account for 20 per cent, to which must be added the costs of providing some or all of the following: company cars, sick pay, meals, live-in accommodation, parking facilities, private health insurance, crèche facilities, mobile phones, Christmas parties, staff discounts, relocation expenses and any holiday or maternity allowances paid in excess of the required statutory minima. Smith (2000a, p. 153) shows that these extra elements of pay are distributed unevenly between members of staff. Those earning at the top of the scale (especially directors and senior managers) tend to gain rather more than average employees, 30 per cent or 40 per cent of their take-home pay being accounted for by benefits of various kinds.

Despite these developments, there remains a big question-mark over how far employees value the benefits provided to them by their employers or appreciate the extent of the costs involved in their provision. A survey of 13,000 employees carried out by Towers Perrin (IRS 2000, pp. 5–9, Thompson and Milsome 2001, pp. 55–62) found that a major-ity were dissatisfied with the level of benefits provided and that only 21 per cent were interested in improving the package by reducing their take-home pay. They concluded that 'traditional benefits are not a significant factor in the recruitment, retention and motivation of most employees' because there was 'a misalignment between their needs and the extent to which their employers are meeting those needs'. This does not mean, of course, that employers can easily stop offering benefits. While the full cost may not be appreciated by employees, they are generally in favour of the benefits and would resent their removal. Poor publicity would also inevitably follow the withdrawal of rewards such as pensions which are generally seen as being the hallmark of a good employer. The alternative courses of action involve communicating the true value of benefits to employees more effectively and providing them with a degree of choice as to which benefits they wish to receive. The latter approach, involving the provision of 'flexible' or 'cafeteria' benefits, has become very common in the USA and has received a great deal of attention in the UK too. You will find further information and discussion exercises about the objectives of benefits strategies on this book's companion website, **www.pearsoned.co.uk/torrington**.

PENSIONS

The role of employers in providing pensions has moved up the public policy agenda for several reasons in recent years, but underlying all of them are the long-term demo-graphic trends which have called into question the ability of the established UK pension system to provide an adequate income to older people after they retire. First and fore-most people are living increasingly longer and thus require a bigger pension to provide them with an income across their years of retirement. In 1950 men aged 65 in the UK could expect to live for a further 12 years on average, and women for a further 15. The figures are now 19 years for men and 22 for women, and with rapid developments in medical science there is every reason to expect life expectancy rates to accelerate further in the coming fifty years. It is likely, according to many projections that over half of the people born in the 1980s will live into their nineties and beyond. Secondly, fewer children are being born, birth rates in the UK having been at below replacement rates since the late 1960s (Pemberton *et al.* 2006, p. 4). These trends are soon going to lead to a steady increase in the **dependency ratio**, by which is meant the proportion of retired people vis-à-vis working people in the economy. At present in the UK 27 per cent of the adult population is aged over 65. By 2050 according to the Government Actuary, the proportion will be 48 per cent (Turner 2004, p. 4). Demographic trends are thus leading us steadily towards a situation in which the funding of adequate pensions using established approaches is going to become harder and harder to achieve. The trend for more young people to stay at school until the age of 18 and for many more to go on to university makes the problem more acute because it further reduces the proportion of the population which is economically active.

The UK is by no means unique in facing this long-term problem. Indeed, in many other industrialised countries the situation is worse because fertlity rates are lower still and there is a tradition of greater reliance on the state to provide pension income than has hitherto been the case in the UK. Everywhere it is increasingly being realised that action needs to be taken now in order to avoid a future scenario in which either the elderly live in unacceptable poverty or taxation has to be increased to economically unsustainable levels in order to fund a decent level of state pension.

In the UK the situation has been made worse over the past 10 years by some most unwelcome trends in the occupational pensions sector. Until the 1990s the UK could boast that it had one of the most extensive and well-funded systems of occupational pension provision in the world. Well over half of the workforce were members of reasonably generous, well-funded occupational pension schemes provided for them by their employers, while millions of retired employees drew a substantial income from the schemes which supplemented their state pensions. This system was likened by commentators who drew international comparisons to the goose that laid the golden egg. It meant that the UK had a great deal less to worry about from population ageing than other countries because so much more of our pension income was sourced privately through both individual savings and these huge long-established occupational pension funds. Unfortunately, the goose has now stopped laying the golden eggs and the long-established system is in terminal decline. Employers are less likely to offer membership of occupational schemes than they were, and where they still do, it is on a less satisfactory financial basis when seen from the perspective of most employees.

A combination of factors is responsible, but the core problem is the hugely increased costs that are now associated with the provision of good pensions for staff. This is due to taxation changes, to increased life expectancy and to the need to keep topping up pension funds whenever the stock market suffers falls of the kinds it has in recent years.

The government has responded to this situation in a way that most commentators have welcomed, although some argue that the plans they have put in place do not go far enough. In 2002 Adair Turner (now Lord Turner), a former Director General of the Confederation of British Industry (CBI) was appointed by the Department for Work and Pensions to lead an extensive review of future pension provision in the UK. The Turner Commission has since produced three substantial reports setting out their findings and recommendations. The government accepted the vast majority of these and brought forward a Pensions Bill in 2006. At the time of writing this complex and highly significant piece of legislation has yet to become law, but there is every reason to believe that it will become the Pensions Act 2007. It aims to encourage later retirement and significantly greater levels of saving into pension funds. It also makes important changes to the established state pension system which are aimed particularly at improving the position of women. At the same time other steps have been taken by the government to ease the pressures on the pension system caused by demographic trends. The equalisation of state pension ages between men and women is such a step, as in many respects is the recent substantial growth in immigration. Other measures include new incentives for people who are not working (e.g. single parents and early retirees) to re-enter the workforce.

ACTIVITY 29.1

The UK has always been unusual in having such a substantial occupational pensions sector. There is a similar system in the Netherlands and in the Republic of Ireland, but in most EU countries most employers see no reason why they should be involved in the provision of pensions. Why do you think these differences persist? What arguments would you advance to persuade a company based in an EU country of the need to offer occupational pensions to employees in a new UK subsidiary?

State schemes

The state runs two schemes: a basic scheme and the State Second Pension (S2P) scheme. The latter replaced SERPS (the State Earnings Related Pension Scheme) in 2002, but people who contributed to SERPS have all their accrued entitlements under that scheme protected. Every employee is obliged to contribute a standard amount to the basic scheme, which currently provides an old age pension at the age of 65 for men and 60 for women. By 2020 the pensionable age for both men and women will be 65 and in the 10 years prior to this date there will be a gradual phasing in of the new pensionable age for women. The Pensions Act 2007 pushes back the state pension age for men and women once equalisation has been achieved. It will increase to 66 from 2024, to 67 from 2034 and to 68 from 2044. The Act also states that from 2012 annual uprating of the basic state pension will be determined in line with growth in the average earnings of UK workers 'subject to affordability and the fiscal position'. At present the level of the pension goes up each year in line with prices.

Anyone earning above a 'low earnings threshold' determined by the government (£12,500 a year in 2007) makes payments towards S2P through their national insurance contributions. At present both contributions and the final pension are earnings related, but this position is planned to change over the coming decades. At the same time that the level of the basic state pension becomes earnings related, a flat rate for S2P will be phased in. It is anticipated that this process will be completed for people retiring after 2030.

The state pension schemes are organised on a pay-as-you-go basis. This means that there is no state pension fund as such, and the money that is paid to today's pensioners comes from today's taxes and national insurance contributions. The money that will be paid to today's contributors, when they become pensioners, will come not from the investment of their and their employers' contributions, but from the contributions of the workforce and their employers in the future. This is why there is growing concern about the ability of future governments to be able to fund state pensions for many more retired people beyond a basic subsistence level.

Occupational schemes

The UK has had, for many years, one of the most extensive and effective systems of occupational pension provision in the world. There are 96,200 separate schemes in operation with combined assets worth approximately £800 billion. Just under 10 million people are members of occupational pension schemes, while around eight million pensioners draw an income from their funds (Government Actuary 2006, p. 19). Although there has been some reduction recently in the proportion of the workforce covered by occupational pensions, they remain by far the most significant employee benefit in terms of their cost to employers.

In general, occupational schemes provide an additional retirement pension on top of the state pension, providing better and wider-ranging benefits than the state schemes and a great deal more flexibility. They are most often found in large organisations and the public sector, but some smaller organisations also run such schemes. Men and women have equal access to occupational schemes and, since 1990, have had to be treated equally in respect of all scheme rules. Yet, in spite of this, men and women continue to fare differently in terms of pensions benefits due to the typical pattern of women's employment being different from male patterns and women's longer average life expectancy. A higher proportion of managerial and professional workers have occupational pensions than other groups, unskilled workers being the least likely to be in schemes. It is no longer lawful for an employer to exclude part-time or temporary workers.

With the exception of one or two in the public sector, occupational schemes do not pay their pensioners in the pay-as-you-go manner operated by the state, but create a pension fund, which is managed separately from the business. The advantage of this is that should the organisation become bankrupt, the pension fund cannot be seized to pay debtors because it is not part of the company. The money in the pension fund is invested and held in trust for the employees of the company at the time of their retirement. However, where a company becomes insolvent at a time when its pension fund is in deficit, employees can lose all or part of their pensions. This has happened in one or two high-profile cases recently, leading the government to establish a central fund which will compensate people to an extent in such circumstances in the future.

Larger organisations traditionally administer their own pension funds through an investment or fund manager. The manager will plan how to invest the money in the fund to get the best return and to ensure that the money that is needed to pay pensions and other benefits will be available when required. An actuary can provide mortality tables and other statistical information in order to assist planning and must be hired regularly to carry out a formal actuarial assessment of the scheme's assets and liabilities. Smaller organisations tend to appoint an insurance company or a bank to administer their pension funds, and so use their expertise. Pension funds can be invested in a variety of different ways, and are often worth more than the market value of their sponsoring companies. As a result they have come to dominate investment on the stock market.

During the 1990s as the worth of stocks and shares increased, the typical pension fund found itself in surplus. It thus had more assets than it needed to pay its liabilities. As a result benefit levels were increased and many employers were able to enjoy lengthy 'contribution holidays', meaning that they did not have to put any money into their funds. In recent years this position has changed radically as stock markets have fallen, life expectancy has risen, the amount of taxation levied on the funds has been increased and costly new regulations have been imposed. By the end of 2002 all but nine of the FTSE 100 companies (i.e. the largest in the country) had pension funds in deficit, the combined shortfall amounting to £77 billion. This was equivalent to 93 per cent of their annual operating profits. The figures for smaller companies were even worse, their fund deficits representing over 130 per cent of operating profits (IRS 2003). Since then the position has improved slightly, but deficits are still the norm. In 2005 the total deficits of the FTSE 100 companies amounted to £64.6 billion and the FTSE 350 to £78.5 billion. According to the National Association of Pension Funds it will not be for a further 10 years before most employers are able to claim that their funds are once again fully funded (NAPF 2007). Occupational funds take three main forms.

1 **Defined benefit schemes** dominated for the past thirty or forty years, but the number of people with access to them has declined hugely in the last four or five years. Virtually all the public sector schemes still take this form, but two-thirds of the private sector schemes have now been closed to new members (NAPF 2007). They remain operational only for the purposes of paying pensions to retired members and for the benefit of employees who joined before their closure. Here contributions are made into a single organisation-wide fund which is invested on behalf of members by a fund manager. Retired employees then draw a pension from the fund calculated according to a defined formula. Most defined benefit schemes take the final salary form, in which the value of the pension is determined by the level of salary being received by each individual at the time of retirement. In the private sector it is common for this to be calculated on a 'sixtieths' basis, whereby the retiree is paid an annual pension equivalent to 1/60th (1.67 per cent) of his or her final salary multiplied by the number of years' pensionable service he or she has completed. In the public sector it is usual for the figure to be based on 'eightieths', with a tax-free lump sum being paid in addition at the time of retirement. In either case the size of pension is heavily related to the length of scheme membership, the maximum pension payable equalling two-thirds of final salary. Examples of final salary calculations are given in Figure 29.1.

Figure 29.1
Final salary schemes – examples of various contribution periods with a 1/60th and a 1/80th scheme

Sixtieths scheme

Final salary	= £24,000
Contributions for 5 years	= 1/60 × 24,000 × 5
Pension	= £2,000 per year
Final salary	= £24,000
Contributions for 25 years	= 1/60 × 24,000 × 25
Pension	= £10,000 per year
Final salary	= £24,000
Contributions for 40 years	= 1/60 × 24,000 × 40
Pension	= £16,000 per year

Eightieths scheme

Final salary	= £24,000
Contributions for 25 years	= 1/80 × 24,000 × 25
Pension	= £7,500 per year
Lump sum	= 3/80 × 24,000 × 25 = £22,500

Another form of defined benefit scheme bases the pension calculation on the average salary earned over a period of 5, 10 or 20 years prior to retirement rather than on pay in the final year. Unless most of someone's pensionable service has been spent earning close to the final salary level, such schemes are less generous than the final salary variety in terms of the amount of pension paid. High levels of inflation also reduce the value of pensions calculated on an average salary basis. The government has signalled that it wishes over time to convert some of the public sector schemes from the final salary to an average salary formula, while also removing the right enjoyed by many public sector workers to retire on a full pension at the age of 60. Such proposals have been met with strong resistance from the workers concerned and have led to instances of industrial action. However, in the future it is likely that further attempts will be made to move in this direction because the cost to the taxpayer of funding existing schemes is substantial and hard to justify when workers in the private sector are seeing the value of their occupational pensions fall and their retirement ages increase.

Most defined benefit schemes are contributory. This means that monies are paid into the fund on a regular basis by both the employer and the employee. In the case of employees the contribution is fixed as a percentage of salary (typically five per cent), a sum which is subject to tax relief. Employers, by contrast, are obliged only to pay in sufficient funds to ensure that the scheme remains solvent. When the pension fund is in surplus, as many were in the 1980s and 1990s, employers can take 'contribution holidays'. By contrast, when the fund is in deficit, the employer has to contribute whatever is necessary to ensure that assets are sufficient to meet possible liabilities.

This means that the amount of employer contribution can vary considerably, year on year, in an unpredictable fashion. In 2006 contribution rates for employers were averaging 15–16 per cent of salary (NAPF 2007). Employers, like employees, gain from tax relief on contributions paid.

In some industries, as well as parts of the public sector, it has been traditional for occupational pensions to be non-contributory. In such schemes the employee makes no contribution at all, but nonetheless draws a pension calculated according to the final salary. Civil servants benefit from this kind of arrangement, as do many employees in the banking and finance sectors. Defined benefit schemes typically offer extra benefits such as ill-health pensions for those forced to retire early and death-in-service benefits for widows and widowers.

2 **Defined contribution schemes** (also known as money purchase schemes) are organised in a totally different way from defined benefit arrangements, and there are no promises about what the final level of pension will be. Employees and employers both contribute a fixed percentage of current salary to these schemes, usually five per cent or six per cent on a monthly basis. The pension benefits received are then entirely dependent on the money that has been contributed and the way in which it has been invested. Where investments perform well, a good level of pension can be gained. Where investments are disappointing, the result is a low level of pension. Further uncertainty derives from the way in which money purchase schemes result in the payment of a single lump sum to the employee when he/she retires. This is then used to buy an annuity from an insurance company from which a weekly or monthly income is paid for life. Annuity rates vary considerably from year to year, and there is also considerable variation between the deals offered by different providers. In essence this means that the risk associated with pension investments is carried by the

employee in a defined contribution arrangement, rather than by the employer as in a final salary scheme. For this reason defined contribution schemes are generally less satisfactory than defined benefit schemes when seen from an employee's perspective. Investments have to perform unusually well while inflation remains low for a money purchase scheme to give an equivalent level of benefit. However, despite these drawbacks, money purchase schemes are more flexible and more easily transferable than defined benefit arrangements. For people changing jobs frequently or working on a self-employed basis for periods of time, particularly during the early years of a career, they can thus be a more attractive option.

In recent years there has been a strong trend away from defined benefit schemes and towards defined contribution provision. At the time of writing 66 per cent of all UK schemes are of the money purchase variety, compared with only five per cent in 1990 (NAPF 1992 and 2007). The majority of newly established schemes take the defined contribution form, while many organisations now offer only a money purchase scheme to new employees. The trend has coincided with a period in which long contribution holidays have come to an end and in which the amount of regulation to which defined benefit schemes are subject has increased substantially. Employers have thus taken the opportunity to reduce their own liabilities and to move to a form of provision which is more predictable financially from their point of view, but which is likely to pay a far lower level of pension to their employees when they retire.

3 Hybrid schemes too are becoming more common, although as yet they represent a small minority of UK pension funds. These, in various different ways, combine elements of the defined benefit and defined contribution forms of provision. The most common form is the 'money purchase underpin' which is basically a final salary arrangement, but one which calculates pensions and transfer values on a money purchase basis where these are higher. Such schemes seek to combine the best aspects of both main types of scheme. They offer a generous, secure and predictable pension, but also incorporate the flexibility associated with defined contribution schemes.

ACTIVITY 29.2

Which of these three types of occupational pension scheme would you find most attractive at the current stage in your career? Under what circumstances might you change your preference?

Group personal pensions

Since the 1980s there has been substantial growth in the market for personal pensions. Self-employed people have always needed to be concerned with making their own provisions for retirement, as they have been excluded from joining S2P, and before that SERPS. More general attention has been focused on this area due to increasing job mobility and the perceived greater portability of personal pensions. A personal pension is arranged, usually through an insurance company, and the individual pays regular amounts into his or her own 'pension fund' in the same way that he or she would with a company fund. The employer may also make a contribution to the fund, but at present very few employers have chosen to do so.

An alternative arrangement is a Group Personal Pension plan (GPP) set up by an employer instead of an occupational pension scheme. From a legal and taxation perspective a GPP is no different from any individual personal pension arrangement, but charges are lower because the employer is able to arrange a bulk discount. The scheme is administered by an insurance company, the employer making contributions as well as the employee. Pensions are calculated on the same basis as an occupational money purchase scheme, but tend to be less extensive because employees are responsible for paying some of the administrative charges. From an employee perspective a GPP is inferior to an occupational pension scheme, but is better than a situation in which no employer provision is made at all. Such arrangements are mainly entered into by small firms, but one or two big companies have also set them up in place of conventional occupational pensions. A key difference is that a GPP is contract based rather than trust based. This means that unlike an occupational pension a GPP has no board of trustees appointed to oversee the running of the scheme; instead a contract is signed with an external provider.

Stakeholder pensions

A new form of government-sponsored pension arrangement, the stakeholder pension, was established in 2001. These are aimed primarily at the five million or so middle income earners (that is, those earning in the £15,000 to £25,000 a year range) who do not have access to an occupational scheme. The aim is to reduce the number of people in future decades who are reliant on state pensions for their retirement income.

A stakeholder pension scheme can be operated by an employer, a financial services company or a trade union. They operate along money purchase lines and are regulated by established authorities. Charges are kept low because providers are obliged to follow minimum standards set by the government. Employers are not obliged to make contributions to a stakeholder pension, but must provide access to one through their payroll. If employees join a scheme, for example one provided by their trade union, the employer is therefore obliged to make deductions via the payroll out of pre-tax income. Views vary on whether or not the stakeholder scheme can be hailed as a success. Supporters point to the fact that over 1.4 million plans have now been set up, while critics stress that 80 per cent of these are 'designation only' which means that no money has actually been invested in them. Moreover, because many of the schemes which are being used are set up by employers to replace existing money purchase plans, it would seem that relatively few of the five million target group are actually benefiting in practice.

WINDOW ON PRACTICE

The Pensions Act 2007 includes very significant measures aimed at forcing both employees and employers to contribute to pension funds. Central is the concept of 'Personal Accounts' which will, once established, effectively make occupational pension provision of a kind available to all employees. As such it substantially extends the principles underlying stakeholder pensions.

From 2012 employers who do not provide a superior occupational pension or GPP will be required to pay a contribution of 3 per cent of all employees' earnings between £5,000 and £33,000 a year into a personal account. Employees will pay a contribution of 4 per cent, a further 1 per cent being paid in as a result of tax relief. Employees will be permitted to opt out, but they will be automatically enrolled by their employer into either an occupational scheme or the new personal accounts scheme. The latter will be commercially provided but will operate within strict government regulations.

OCCUPATIONAL PENSIONS AND HRM

While occupational pension schemes are governed by a board of trustees which includes member representatives, in most organisations the pensions manager and pensions department are part of the HR function. It is thus important that HR professionals are familiar with the types of scheme offered and the main operating rules so that they can give accurate and timely advice to staff and to potential recruits. They also need to be familiar with the regulatory environment for occupational pensions, which has changed considerably in recent years. Aside from new legislation outlawing discrimination on grounds of sex or against part-time and temporary staff, several other important regulatory changes have been made and new regulatory bodies established. The Pensions Act 1995 sets out in detail what information must be disclosed to scheme members on request and what must be sent to them automatically each year. The Act also requires all occupational funds to meet a defined minimum funding level so that they are always able to meet their liabilities in the event of the employing company being wound up. Moreover, strict restrictions are now placed on 'self-investment', making sure that fund assets cannot be invested in property or other business ventures controlled by the sponsoring organisation. However, the most important single piece of legislation was the Social Security Act 1985 which put in place a series of measures to protect 'early leavers', ensuring that people who switch employers during their careers do not suffer substantial loss in the value of their pensions.

Early leavers now have one of three options in making their pension arrangements when they begin work for a new employer. One option is to claim back the contributions that the individual has made into the former employer's pension scheme. Deductions are made in accordance with tax laws, and of course the employer's contribution is lost, but a substantial sum can be reinvested in the new employer's scheme or in a personal pension. Another alternative involves opting for a preserved pension. With a final salary scheme, if there were no inflation, and if the individual progressed very little up the career ladder, a preserved pension from an old employer plus a pension from the recent employer would equate well with the pension he or she would have received had he or she been with the new employer for the whole period. However, if these conditions are not met, which in recent times they have not been, individuals who have had more than one employer lose out in the pension stakes. Past employers are required to revalue preserved pensions in line with inflation (to a maximum of five per cent), but the value of such a pension remains linked to the level of salary at the date of leaving.

The third option is usually preferable, but is only open to people who have completed two years' membership of a scheme. This involves the transfer of the pension from the old employer's fund into that of the new employer. The process is straightforward in the case of a money purchase scheme, because the worth of each person's pension is readily calculated. It is simply the value of the employee's contributions, plus those of the employer, together with funds accrued as a result of their investment. The process is more complicated in the case of a final salary scheme, the transfer value being calculated according to standard actuarial conventions which take account of the employee's age, length of pensionable service, the level of salary at the time of leaving and the current interest rate. All things being equal, 'early leavers' still fare worse than 'stayers' in terms of final pensions, but the difference is a great deal less than used to be the case.

Aside from giving advice and taking overall responsibility for pensions issues, HR managers are concerned with determining their organisations' pension policy. Is an occupational pension to be offered? If so, what form should it take? What level of contribution is the employer going to make? It is quite possible to make a judgement in favour of generous occupational provision simply on paternalistic grounds. Many organisations have thus decided that they will offer pensions because it is in the interests of their staff that they should. Occupational schemes represent a convenient and tax-advantageous method of providing an income in old age; it therefore makes sense to include a pension in the total pay and benefits package. The problems with such a commitment, particularly in the case of defined benefit schemes, are the cost and the fact that the long-term financial consequences are unpredictable. This, combined with the fact that many employees do not seem to appreciate the value of an occupational pension, is one of the reasons that many employers have been questioning their commitment to final salary schemes and to pension provision in general.

Research suggests that interest in and understanding of occupational pensions varies considerably from person to person (Goode 1993; Taylor 2000). Older people, professional workers and those working in the financial services sector usually have a clearer perception of their value than other groups of staff. For these groups pensions are important, and their labour market behaviour will be affected as a result. A firm which does not offer a good pension will thus find it harder to recruit and retain them than one which does. By contrast, a firm which largely employs younger people, and/or workers in lower-skilled occupations, may find that it makes more sense to offer additional pay in place of an occupational scheme. You will find further information and discussion exercises about the HR perspective on occupational pensions on this book's companion website, **www.pearsoned.co.uk/torrington**.

ACTIVITY 29.3

It has been argued that by making occupational pensions readily transferable, by increasing the complexity of the regulatory regime and by increasing taxation levied on pension funds, successive governments have provided a major disincentive to employers considering the establishment of a scheme. To what extent do you agree with this point of view?

SICK PAY

As with pension schemes, the provision of sick pay is seen as the mark of a good employer. Sick pay is an important issue due to the need for control and administration of absence. Research suggests that sickness absence represents around four per cent of working time (CBI 2000), although there are large differences between sector and job type. The HR manager and the HR department have a variety of roles to play in relation to sick pay, particularly since the introduction of statutory sick pay (SSP) in 1983 when state sick pay in addition to occupational sick pay became managed by the employer.

Statutory sick pay

Statutory sick pay is a state benefit that has been in existence for several decades. It provides a basic income (£70.05 per week in 2007) to employees who are incapable of going to their normal place of work as a result of illness. SSP, however, is not claimed from a benefit office; it is administered by employers and paid through the payroll according to regulations set out in statute.

Since 1994 employers have been required to take full financial responsibility for SSP for the first four weeks of absence, after which they can claim back a portion of the costs from the state through reduced employer national insurance contributions. However, the method of calculation used now ensures that smaller employers are able to claim back a very considerably higher proportion of the costs than larger employers who usually have to fund it all themselves. Most employees are entitled to state sickness benefit; however, there are some exceptions: employees who fall sick outside the EU, employees who are sick during an industrial dispute, employees over pensionable age and part-timers whose earnings are below the lower earnings limit (£82 per week in 2007). These groups, as well as self-employed people, are obliged to claim state incapacity benefit instead from the Benefits Agency. SSP is built around the concepts of qualifying days, waiting days, certification, linked periods, transfer to the Department for Work and Pensions (DWP) and record periods.

Qualifying days are those days on which the employee would normally have worked, except for the fact that he or she was sick. For many Monday-to-Friday employees this is very straightforward. However, it is more complex to administer for those on some form of rotating week or shift system. Sick pay is only payable for qualifying days.

Waiting days have to pass before the employee is entitled to receive sick pay – at present the number of days is three. These three days must be qualifying days, and on the fourth qualifying day the employee is entitled to sickness benefit, should he or she still be away from work due to sickness.

Certification from a doctor is required after seven days of sickness absence. Prior to this the employee provides self-certification. This involves notifying the employer of absence due to sickness by the first day on which benefit is due – that is, immediately following the three waiting days.

Linked periods of illness mean that the three waiting days do not apply. If the employee has had a period of incapacity from work (PIW) within the previous eight weeks, then the two periods are linked and treated as just one period for SSP purposes, and so the three waiting days do not have to pass again.

The employer does not have to administer SSP for every employee indefinitely. Where the employee has been absent due to sickness for a continuous or linked period of 28 weeks the responsibility for payment passes from the employer to the state. A continuous period of 28 weeks' sickness is clearly identifiable. It is not so clear when linked periods are involved. An employee who was sick for five days, back at work for four weeks, sick for one day, at work for seven weeks and then sick for two days would have a linked period of incapacity of eight days. Alternatively, an employee who was sick for four days, back at work for ten weeks and then sick for five days would have a period of incapacity this time of five days. The DWP requires employers to keep SSP records for three years so that these can be inspected.

Occupational sick pay

There is no obligation on employers to pay employees for days of absence due to sickness beyond what is required under the state's SSP scheme. However, most employers choose to do so via a benefit known as occupational sick pay (OSP). The most common approach is to continue paying the full salary for a set period of time, but other schemes involve reducing the pay rate for days taken off as a result of illness. In either case a sum in excess of the statutory minimum is paid, the portion accounted for by SSP being reclaimed from the state where possible. Paying the full salary is straightforward for those staff who receive a basic salary with no additions. It is more difficult to define for those whose pay is supplemented by shift allowances or productivity bonuses.

Occupational sick pay arrangements tend to be most generous in unionised environments and in the public sector, although professional and managerial employees are usually well covered in most organisations. The common public sector approach involves paying full pay for the first six months of an illness, once three years' service have been completed, before moving the employee on to half-pay for a further six months. Thereafter OSP ceases. At the other end of the scale are employers who pay no OSP at all. They take the view that occupational sick pay will be abused and so pay only what is due under the state scheme. Another approach involves paying a predetermined flat rate in addition to money provided via SSP.

Occupational sick pay schemes also vary according to the period of service required. Some employers provide sick pay for sickness absence from the first day of employment. Others require a qualifying period to be served. For some this is a nominal period of four weeks, but the period may be three or six months, or a year or more. There is a major difference here between OSP and SSP. With SSP pay is available immediately after employment has begun.

We covered the methods used by employers to reduce absence in Chapter 15.

COMPANY CARS

A form of employee benefit which is a great deal more common in the UK than in other countries is the company car, but they are a good deal less common than they used to be. In 2000 84 per cent of companies offered a car to at least some of their staff. By 2006 the proportion had fallen to 64 per cent (IRS 2006a). Managers from overseas often take some persuading that cars are necessary to attract and retain high-calibre managers, but the received wisdom is that they are. Their importance to employees is demonstrated by the comparative lack of take-up of cash alternatives where these are offered (Smith 2000a, p. 161). After pensions, they are the second most significant employee benefit in cost terms, and are provided for some employees by over 90 per cent of large and medium-sized companies.

There are a number of sound reasons underlying the provision of company cars. First, for some there is a need as part of their jobs to travel very widely and regularly. Not everyone can be assumed to own a reliable car, so it is sometimes necessary to provide one simply to enable an employee to carry out his/her day-to-day job duties. In the case of sales representatives and senior managers the impression created when travelling on company business can be important. It is therefore often considered necessary to provide them with upmarket and up-to-date models to ensure that clients and potential clients are suitably impressed. A case can also be made on cost efficiency grounds for people who clock up a great number of business miles each year. The cost of paying them a reasonable mileage allowance to drive their own cars is often greater than the cost of providing them with a company vehicle; it costs £12,000 a year to reimburse someone who has travelled 30,000 miles at 40p per mile.

However, most possessors of company cars do not fit either of the above categories. Their car entitlements simply come as an expected part of the pay package for middle and senior managers. As such, they signify the achievement of a certain level of status. Indeed, in many companies the cars offered become steadily more imposing as people climb up the corporate hierarchy. Being upgraded to a more impressive car thus signifies in a very manifest way the company's approval. Downgrading, of course, has the opposite effect.

One of the reasons that company cars are so significant in the UK is historical, because before April 1994 they were a highly tax-efficient benefit. It was a good deal cheaper to drive a company car than to purchase one's own out of taxed income, so it made sense for people to be 'paid' in part with a car. This is now far from being the case.

The current tax regime introduced in April 2002 encourages employers to lease or purchase cars which are environmentally friendly. Until then company cars were simply taxed according to the number of miles driven on company business, the annual tax paid by the driver being equivalent to a percentage of the car's list price. The more business miles clocked up, the less tax was paid. In addition there were substantial discounts for people who drove older cars. Now the tax paid depends on carbon emissions or engine size and there are no reductions for people who drive a great number of miles or use an older vehicle. So there is a substantial incentive for people who drive a great deal as part of their jobs to use smaller cars or larger ones with low carbon emissions. Most employers offer cash alternatives equal to the tax payable on the car, but many of those eligible choose not to take these up despite the fact that there are no longer any obvious tax advantages associated with driving a company car. This is partly because company cars tend to be more expensive than models individuals could justify buying from their own income, but mainly because of the substantial savings that still accrue in terms of insurance, maintenance and repair costs. The tax changes have, however, led to a preference for 'trading down'. This means that where a choice is given, employees are increasingly opting for a smaller car and more cash in their pay packets.

According to IDS (2006a, pp. 6–7) employers are increasingly distinguishing between the way they treat 'status drivers', for whom a car comes as part of a senior employee's standard remuneration package, and 'need drivers'. The latter group comprise people who are required to drive as part of their job. They may not therefore be highly paid, and might well if offered a cash alternative prefer to purchase an inexpensive or second-hand car which is fine for their personal purposes, but which is inappropriate in terms of the image it presents of their organisation when on company business. For this reason a majority of companies are now either abandoning cash alternatives for 'need drivers' or stipulating that the money must be used to purchase an 'appropriate' car which is 'fit for purpose'.

A major policy choice faced by employers in the provision of cars is whether to buy or lease their fleet. There are advantages and disadvantages associated with both approaches, much depending on the nature of the deal that is struck with a leasing company. Where the company is reputable and where the agreement provides for insurance, maintenance and repair of vehicles, the financial case for leasing is strong.

ACTIVITY 29.4

Assume that you have been offered a new job which comes with either the use of a new company car or a cash allowance. The salary is £35,000 per year. The car is worth £15,000, giving you an annual tax bill of £5,250. This is also the amount being offered by way of an annual cash allowance. Which option would you choose and why?

LONDON ALLOWANCES

Most larger employers pay a standard, organisation-wide allowance or salary weighting to employees working in central London. In some cases such allowances are also paid to employees working in the region around London. The purpose is to attract and retain staff who are obliged to live and commute in the capital where the cost of property, transport and parking is so much higher than it is elsewhere in the country. The typical level of allowance is between £5,000 and £7,000 a year, the highest sums being paid by the finance houses of the City and the lowest by the retailers. Recent years have seen considerable increases in the London weighting supplements paid to public sector workers. In 2006 police officers were being paid £6,333 a year and teachers at the top of the pay scale £6,558 over and above national rates (IDS 2006b, p. 2). In the private sector the level of allowances has tended to rise more slowly than wage inflation generally and has often been frozen for a number of years. This has occurred either because employers are increasingly moving towards the development of wholly separate London-based salary scales, or because moves towards broadbanding (*see* Chapter 27) allow higher wages to be paid to London-based staff without the need for a separate supplementary payment. Over time, therefore, the flat-rate allowance has thus become a less significant part of the total pay packet. Instead employers are tending to target resources on the groups who are hardest to recruit. In tight labour markets this means that there is now a greater differential between pay rates in and out of London than was the case ten years ago.

A more general trend, mainly in the private sector, is a move away from national pay scales and regional weightings altogether. Instead systems which allow organisations to pay different levels of salary to people doing the same or similar work in different regions of the country are being introduced (see IRS 2006b). Increasingly, salaries are determined with reference to what other local employers are paying, rather than to what other employees of the same organisation but based elsewhere in the UK are paid. While this may well seem deeply unfair to those who receive lower pay as a result, it can be seen as being a fair approach because it means that pay reflects the variable cost of living in different parts of the country. Data from the government's Annual Survey of Hours and Earnings on what major groups of employees are being paid is now freely available from the Office of National Statistics website. This breaks wages down by occupation for each local authority area, allowing employers to establish very easily whether they are paying below, at or above 'the going rate' in specific locations.

FLEXIBLE BENEFITS

Flexible benefits or 'cafeteria plans' have proliferated in the United States over recent years where they are specifically recognised in the tax regime. By contrast, take-up of the idea in the UK has tended to be slow (Smith 2000b, p. 379). However, several high-profile organisations have now moved towards greater flexibility and there is unquestionably a great deal more interest in the approach developing among UK employers more generally. This is being driven by tight labour market conditions and is often linked to the type of initiatives in the work-life balance arena we discuss in Chapter 31.

The case for flexible benefits from an HRM perspective is strong, but the systems themselves can prove to be very costly to operate. The approach involves giving individual employees a choice as to how exactly their pay packet is made up. The overall value of the package is set by the employer, but it is for employees to choose for themselves what balance they wish to strike between cash and the different kinds of benefit. Those who have children, for example, can opt for benefits that are of value to them such as childcare vouchers, access to a company crèche or additional holidays. A young person in his or her first job might well prefer to forgo most benefits in return for higher take-home pay, while an older person may wish to purchase additional years of pensionable service in exchange for cash or perhaps a car.

There are a number of good reasons for considering such an approach. First, it helps ensure that employees are only provided with benefits which they are aware of and appreciate. Resources that would otherwise be wasted by providing unwanted benefits are thus saved. The employer gets maximum value per pound spent, while at the same time allowing employees to tailor their own 'perfect' benefits mix. The result should be improved staff retention and a better motivated workforce.

WINDOW ON PRACTICE

In 1998 a large-scale merger took place between two of the world's largest professional services firms – Price Waterhouse and Coopers & Lybrand. The merged firm, called PricewaterhouseCoopers, employs 150,000 people in 150 different countries. While the two organisations were culturally similar, they had rather different traditions in the provision of benefits. Rather than continue with different people employed on different sets of terms and conditions, partners decided to harmonise everyone as soon as was possible. This process was made a great deal easier and less contentious by the decision to develop a new flexible benefits scheme called 'Choices'. It allows employees to trade cash for additional holiday, a choice of car, childcare vouchers, retail vouchers, insurance of various kinds and a pension. No one was required to alter their existing benefits package as a result of the merger unless they wished to.

Source: O. Franks and D. Thompson (2000) 'Rights and rites of passage', *People Management*, 17 February.

Flexible benefits plans take many different forms, the main distinction being between those that are 'fully flexible' and those that allow a degree of flexibility within prescribed limits. The former allow employees a free hand to make up their own package and to change it at regular intervals. Under such a regime an employee could theoretically swap all benefits for cash, or could double his or her holiday entitlement in exchange for a pay cut. A degree of restriction is more common, a specified core of benefits being compulsory, with flexibility beyond that. Under such a scheme all employees might be required to take four weeks' holiday and invest in a minimal pension, but be allowed freedom to determine whether or not they wished to benefit from private health insurance, gym membership, discounts on company products, etc. Typical plans also permit some choice of the make and model of car.

A third approach is administratively simpler but is more restrictive in terms of employee choice. This involves 'prepackaging' a number of separate benefits menus designed to suit different groups of employees (rather like a pre-set banquet menu in a Chinese restaurant). Employees must then opt for one package from a choice of five or six, each having the same overall cash value. One is typically tailored to meet the needs of older staff, another is for those with young families, a third for new graduates and so on.

A number of disadvantages with flexible benefits systems can be identified which may well explain their relatively slow development in the UK. These are summarised by Smith (2000b) as follows:

> Objections include difficult administration; problems connected with handling individual employee choices; the requirement for complex costing and records; difficulty in getting employees to make effective choices; employees making mistakes (for example leaving themselves with inadequate pension cover); employees' circumstances changing over time leaving his or her package inappropriate and giving the employer the costly headache of re-designing the package; and finally the possible hiring of expensive specialist or consultant skills and financial counselling to support the move to flexibility.

Uncertainty about the future tax position may also be a deterrent, especially where changes have the potential to throw a whole system out of kilter (as happened in 1997 when the Chancellor of the Exchequer substantially extended taxation on pension fund investments). Good advice about how to overcome these obstacles, together with examples of UK-based schemes in operation, is provided in IDS (2005). A case study outlining the approach taken by Lloyds TSB, which operates one of the largest UK schemes, is provided in IRS (2003).

SUMMARY PROPOSITIONS

29.1 Between 20 per cent and 50 per cent of the typical employer's pay bill is spent on the provision of supplementary benefits. Evidence suggests that most employees do not appreciate the true financial value of such benefits.

29.2 Occupational pensions are a tax-efficient means of providing funds for retirement in excess of what is provided by state and personal pension schemes.

29.3 Occupational pensions take one of three forms: defined benefit, defined contribution and hybrid. Employers can choose as an alternative to set up a group personal pension or to provide a stakeholder pension under the government's scheme. In recent years employers have been closing their defined benefit schemes and offering defined contribution schemes and group personal pensions instead.

29.4 Employers are required to facilitate the payment of statutory sick pay to employees who are away from work as a result of an illness. Most pay occupational sick pay in addition either as a result of moral obligation or in order to attract, retain and motivate their workforces.

29.5 Company cars are commonly provided by UK employers for senior staff. The tax regime introduced in 2002 aimed to discourage demand for larger cars which are not environmentally friendly.

29.6 In theory flexible benefits plans have a great deal to offer employees. It is likely that their use will grow more widespread in the next few years.

GENERAL DISCUSSION TOPICS

1 Why do you think so few people seem to have an appreciation of the value of their occupational pensions and other benefits? What could be done to raise awareness of the costs involved in their provision?

2 Draw up three flexible benefits packages: one aimed at new graduates, one at employees in their thirties, and one for those aged over 50.

FURTHER READING

Chartered Institute of Personnel and Development.
CIPD provides up-to-date information about organisational policy on pensions and benefits, as well as about priorities for benefits managers, in this annual survey (published in February each year).

CIPD (2002) *Pensions and HR's role: a guide*. London: CIPD.
This useful guide reviews all the current pressures facing organisations seeking to offer decent occupational pensions for their employees and puts forward suggestions about possible ways forward from an HR perspective.

Employee Relations.
A special edition of *Employee Relations* published in 2000 also focused on occupational pensions from an HR point of view.

Incomes Data Services (IDS).
Industrial Relations Services (IRS).
Extensive coverage to these issues is given in the IDS and IRS publications listed in the References below.

Smith, I. (2002a) 'Benefits', in G. White and J. Druker (eds), *Reward Management: A Critical Text*. London: Routledge.

Smith, I. (2002b) 'Flexible plans for pay and benefits', in R. Thorpe and G. Homan (eds), *Strategic Reward Systems*. London: Financial Times/Prentice Hall.

These two chapters provide the best introductions to flexible benefits in the UK context.

REFERENCES

CBI (2000) *Focus on Absence*. London: CBI.

Franks, O. and Thompson, D. (2000) 'Rights and rites of passage', *People Management*, 17 February.

Goode, R. (1993) *Pension Law Reform: The Report of the Pension Law Review Committee*, Volume 2: Research. London: HMSO.

Government Actuary (2006) *Occupational Pension Schemes: Thirteenth Survey*. London: Government Actuary's Department.

IDS (2005) *Flexible Benefits*, IDS Study No. 811, December. London: IDS.

IDS (2006a) *Company cars and business travel*, IDS Study No. 817. London: IDS.

IDS (2006b) *London Allowances*, IDS Study No. 827. London: IDS.

IRS (2000) 'Managing benefit provision', *IRS Pay and Benefits Bulletin*, No. 487, January. London: IRS.

IRS (2003) 'Banking on flexible benefits at Lloyds TSB', *IRS Employment Review*, No. 768, January. London: IRS.

IRS (2006a) 'Benefits and allowances 3', *IRS Employment Review*, No. 853, 18 August. London: IRS.

IRS (2006b) 'Spotlight on the regions', *IRS Employment Review*, No. 856, 6 October. London: IRS.

NAPF (1992) *Seventeenth Annual Survey of Occupational Pension Funds*. London: National Association of Pension Funds.

NAPF (2007) *Annual Survey of Occupational Pension Funds 2006*. London: National Association of Pension Funds.

Pemberton, H., Thane P. and Whiteside, N. (2006) *Britain's Pension Crisis: History and Policy*. Oxford: British Academy.

Smith, I. (2000a) 'Benefits', in G. White and J. Druker (eds), *Reward Management: A Critical Text*. London: Routledge.

Smith, I. (2000b) 'Flexible plans for pay and benefits', in R. Thorpe and G. Homan (eds), *Strategic Reward Systems*. London: Financial Times/Prentice Hall.

Taylor, S. (2000) 'Occupational pensions and employee retention: debate and evidence', *Employee Relations*, Vol. 22, No. 3, pp. 246–59.

Thompson, P. and Milsome, S. (2001) *Reward Determination in the UK*. London: CIPD.

Turner, A. (2004) *Pensions: Challenges and Choices. The First Report of the Pensions Commission*. London: HMSO.

An extensive range of additional materials, including multiple choice questions, answers to questions and links to useful websites can be found on the Human Resource Management Companion Website at **www.pearsoned.co.uk/torrington.**

INTERACTIVE SKILL 6: NEGOTIATION

Negotiation has developed into a major mode of decision making in all aspects of social, political and business life, even though there is always a feeling that it is no more than a substitute for direct, decisive action. In employment we have the institutions of collective bargaining as a means of regulating some parts of the employment relationship between employer and organised employees. The essence of the process is to find not just common ground between two parties but a new relationship with greater constructive potential than the one that preceded it. To some this is the cornerstone of industrial democracy and the effective running of a business, but to others it is seen as impairing efficiency, inhibiting change and producing the lowest, rather than the highest, common factor of cooperation between management and employees. There is growing concern among union leaders as well as in parts of management that there is a lack of both experience and expertise in bargaining.

This Focus on skills deals directly with that field of expertise. Because negotiation has been out of fashion, most of the academic work on negotiation is of relatively long standing, although there is a recent thorough review in Hiltrop and Udall (1995) and a particular angle described in Grint (1997). There have also been a number of more practical books recently, including Kennedy (1998).

> for over a decade it has been possible to shape an HR career without coming into contact with unions. Industrial relations expertise has been lost as those who forged their skills in the 1970s have moved on, many into retirement . . . Some employers are looking outside their organizations to bring in industrial relations expertise. But this cannot be a permanent solution. (Roberts 2002, p. 37)

The objectives of this Focus on skills are to:

1 Examine the place of conflict in the employment relationship, its sources, benefits and drawbacks

2 Explain bargaining strategies and tactics

3 Explain the negotiating sequence

4 Consider some aspects of bargaining with individuals

Since the summer of 2000 British trade unions have had restored to them a statutory right to recognition by an employer that had been removed twenty years before. Recognition means the right to require an employer to negotiate on matters such as hours, pay and holidays: not to consult, but to negotiate. A useful summary is in Younson (2000).

Is negotiation rightly viewed as an activity that is only second best to unilateral decision making? If the outcome is no more than compromise, the choice seems to be between negotiation and capitulation. Some would argue that capitulation by one side would be a better outcome for both than a compromise that ignores the difficulties and dissatisfies both. There is, however, an alternative to splitting the difference in negotiation and that is where the differences in view and objective of the parties are accommodated to such an extent that the outcome for both is better than could have been achieved by the unilateral executive action of either.

Negotiation takes place because the parties have some goals that are common to both and some goals that conflict. Employer and employees usually share the common goal of keeping the business in operation, but some of their other goals may conflict. Consequently the two parties negotiate settlements because the attempt by one to force a solution on the other either would fail because of the other's strength or would not be as satisfactory a settlement without the approval of the other party.

Traditionally, negotiation on employment matters has been assumed to deal with the collective aspects of the relationship between the management or the employers and the unions or the workers. Here, however, we include material on the negotiation of the bargain between the management and an individual person or consultancy selling services.

The nature of conflict in the employment relationship

The approach to collective negotiations depends on the view that conflict of interests is inevitable between employer and employee because there is an authority relationship in which the aims of the two parties will at least sometimes conflict. A further assumption is that such conflict does not necessarily damage that relationship.

This has led some commentators to discuss negotiation in terms of equally matched protagonists. The power of the two parties may not actually be equal, but they are both willing to behave as if it were. Negotiation thus has the appearance of power equalisation in the search for a solution to a problem. When both sides set out to reach an agreement that is satisfactory to themselves and acceptable to the other, then their power is equalised by that desire. Where the concern for acceptance by the other is lacking, there comes the use of power play of the forcing type described later:

> negotiators seek to increase common interest and expand cooperation in order to broaden the area of agreement to cover the item under dispute. On the other hand, each seeks to maximize his own interest and prevail in conflict, in order to make the agreement more valuable to himself. No matter what angle analysis takes, it cannot eliminate the basic tension between cooperation and conflict that provides the dynamic of negotiation. (Zartman 1976, p. 41)

The relative power of the parties is likely to fluctuate from one situation to the next; this is recognised by the ritual and face-saving elements of negotiation, where a power imbalance is not fully exploited, both to make agreement possible and in the knowledge that the power imbalance may be reversed on the next issue to be resolved.

The classic work of Ann Douglas (1962) produced a formulation of the negotiating encounter that has been little modified by those coming after her. However, this needs further thought when applied to negotiations between representatives of management and representatives of employees about terms and conditions of employment because of the clear inequality of power and access to resources between them.

Sources of conflict in the collective employment relationship

Most texts on organisational behaviour include sections on reducing conflict, and management talk is full of the need for teamworking, corporate culture and collaboration, so why do we find one area of working life where conflict is readily accepted, even emphasised?

Although the processes of civilisation tend to constrain it there is a natural human impulse to behave aggressively to some degree at some time. One outlet for aggression is in negotiations within the employing organisation, which is a splendid arena for the expression of aggressiveness and bravura without actually incurring the physical risks that would be involved in violent combat. Dr Johnson summed up the attractions of vigorous disagreement when he said, 'I dogmatise and am contradicted, and in this conflict of opinions I find delight'. Probably the main source of industrial relations conflict is divergence of interests between those who are classified as managers and those who are seen as non-managers. One group is seeking principally such things as efficiency, productivity and the obedience of others to their own authority. The members of the other group are interested in these things, but are more interested in features such as high pay, freedom of action, independence from supervision, scope for the individual and leisure. To some extent these invariably conflict.

Potential benefits of such conflict

Although it is widely believed that conflict of the type described here is counterproductive, there are some advantages.

Introducing new rules

Employment is governed by a number of rules, formal rules that define unfair dismissal and the rate of pay for various jobs, as well as informal rules such as dress codes and modes of address. Management/union conflict is usually a disagreement over the rules and the bargain that is struck produces a new rule: a new rate of pay, or a new employment practice. It may be the only way of achieving that particular change, and it is a very authoritative source of rule making because of the joint participation in its creation.

Modifying the goals

The goals that management set can be modified as a result of conflict with others. Ways in which management's goals will be unpopular or difficult to implement may be seen for the first time and modifications made early instead of too late. A greater range and diversity of views is brought to bear on a particular matter so that the capacity for innovation is enhanced, but modification of goals can be difficult for managers to accept.

Clash of values

More fundamental is the possible clash of values, usually about managerial prerogative. Managers like to believe and proclaim that management is their inalienable right, so that those who question the way their work is done are ignorant or impertinent. Non-managers may regard management as a job that should be done properly by people who are responsive to questioning and criticism.

Competitiveness

One of the most likely sources of conflict is the urge to compete for a share of limited resources. Much of the drive behind differential pay claims comes from competing with other groups at a similar level, but there may also be competition for finance, materials, security, survival, power, recognition or status.

Organisational tradition

If the tradition of an organisation is to be conflict prone, then it may retain that mode obdurately, while other organisations in which conflict has not been a prominent feature may continue without it. It is axiomatic that certain industries in the United Kingdom are much more likely to display the manifestations of extreme conflict in industrial relations than others. Indicators such as the number of working days lost through strikes show a pattern of distribution which varies little between different industries year by year. The nature of the conflict can range between the extremes of pettiness, secrecy, fear and insecurity on the one hand, to vigorous, open and productive debate on the other, with many organisations exhibiting neither.

Understanding of respective positions

Combatants will come to a better understanding of their position on the issue being debated because of their need to set it forth, develop supporting arguments and then defend those arguments against criticism. This enables them to see more clearly what they want, why they want it and how justifiable it is. In challenging the position of the other party, they will come to a clearer understanding of where they stand, and why.

Potential drawbacks of such conflict

The above advantages may not be sufficient to balance the potential drawbacks.

Waste of time and energy

Conflict and the ensuing negotiations take a great deal of time and energy. Conflict can be stressful when over-personalised, and individuals become obsessed with the conflict itself rather than what it is about. Negotiation takes much longer than simple management decree.

Emotional stress for participants

People vary in the type of organisational stress to which they are prone. To be involved in negotiation is stressful for some people, while others find it stimulating.

Accommodating conflict often causes some inefficiency through the paraphernalia that can accompany it: striking, working to rule, working without enthusiasm, withdrawing cooperation or the simple delay caused by protracted negotiation.

Risks

Negotiation may be the only way to cope with a conflictual situation, but there is the risk of stirring up a hornets' nest. When conflict is brought to the surface it may be resolved or accommodated, or it may get worse if the situation is handled badly.

The quality and amount of communication is impaired. Those involved are concerned more to confirm their own viewpoint than to convey understanding, and there are perceptual distortions such as stereotyping and cognitive dissonance. The attitudes behind the communications may also become inappropriate as there are greater feelings of hostility and attempts to score off others.

Bargaining strategies

Managers and managements adopt various strategies to cope with conflict. We need to recognise these and appreciate some of the likely effects.

Avoidance

To some extent conflict can be 'handled' by ignoring it. For a time this will prevent it surfacing so that it remains latent rather than manifest: the danger being that it is harder to deal with when it eventually does erupt. Opposing views cannot be heard unless there is apparatus for their expression. The management of an organisation can fail to provide such apparatus by, for instance, not having personnel specialists, not recognising trade unions and not recognising employee representatives. If the management organise the establishment as if conflict of opinion did not exist, any such difference will be less apparent and its expression stifled. This strategy is becoming harder to sustain because of the developing legal support for employee representation, but it has obvious short-term advantages.

Smoothing

A familiar strategy is to try to resolve conflict by honeyed words in exhortation or discussion where the emphasis is on the value of teamwork, the assurance that 'we all agree really' and an overt, honest attempt to get past the divergence of opinion, which is regarded as a temporary and unfortunate aberration. This is often an accurate diagnosis and represents an approach that would have broad employee support in a particular employment context, but there is always the risk that smoothing ignores the real problem, like giving a massage to someone who has suffered a heart attack.

Forcing

The opposite to smoothing is to attack expressions of dissent and deal with conflict by stamping it out. This is not easy and has innumerable, unfortunate precedents in both the political and industrial arenas.

Compromise

Where divergence of views is acknowledged and confronted, one possibility is to split the difference. If employees claim a pay increase of £10 and the management say they can afford nothing, a settlement of £5 saves the face of both parties but satisfies neither. However common this strategy may be, and sometimes there is no alternative, it has one major drawback: both parties fail to win.

Confrontation

The fifth strategy is to confront the issue on which the parties differ. This involves accepting that there is a conflict of opinions or interests, exploring the scale and nature of the conflict and then working towards an accommodation of the differences which will provide a greater degree of satisfaction of the objectives of both parties than can be achieved by simple compromise. This sounds ambitious, but we suggest that this is the most productive strategy in many cases and offers the opportunity of both parties winning. It is important that both parties recognise that they are confronting *the issues* on which they are divided rather than the individuals with whom they are negotiating. This is the strategy we consider here.

ACTIVITY 6.1

Consider an industrial dispute or disagreement which you have recently witnessed or read about.

1 Was the management strategy one of avoidance, smoothing, forcing, compromise or confrontation?

2 Was this an inappropriate strategy?

3 If the answer to the last question was 'yes' why was an inappropriate strategy used?

Bargaining tactics

In preparing for negotiation there are a number of matters that the parties must review before they begin.

Resolution or accommodation

Conflict can be *resolved* so that the original feelings of antagonism or opposition over the issues that have brought the conflict to a head vanish. This type of outcome has a romantic appeal and will frequently be sought in industrial relations issues because so many people feel acutely uncomfortable when involved in relationships of overt antagonism.

Alternatively, the conflict may be *accommodated*, so that the differences of view persist, but a modus vivendi, some form of living with the situation, is discovered. In view of the inevitability of the conflict that is endemic in the employment relationship, accommodation may be a more common prospect than resolution, but an interesting question for a negotiator to ponder when approaching the bargaining table is: which is it – resolution or accommodation?

Tension level

Most negotiators feel they have no chance to determine the timing of encounters. This is partly due to reluctance; managers in particular tend to resort to negotiation only when necessary, and the necessity is usually a crisis. A more proactive approach is to initiate encounters, at least trying to push them towards favourable timings.

A feature of timing is the tension level. Too much, and the negotiators get the jitters, unable to see things straight and indulging in excessive interpersonal vituperation: too little tension, and there is no real will to reach a settlement. Ideal timing is to get a point when both sides have a balanced desire to reach a settlement.

Power balance

Effective negotiation is rarely limited to the sheer exploitation of power advantage. The best settlement is one in which both sides can recognise their own and mutual advantages (Fowler 1990, pp. 11–16). The background to any negotiation includes the relative power of the disputants. Power parity is the most conducive to success:

> Perceptions of power inequality undermine trust, inhibit dialogue, and decrease the likelihood of a constructive outcome from an attempted confrontation. Inequality tends to undermine trust on both ends of the imbalanced relationship, directly affecting both the person with the perceived power inferiority and the one with perceived superiority.
> (Walton 1969, p. 98)

The greater the power differential, the more negative the attitudes.

Synchronising

The approaches and reactions of the two parties need a degree of synchronising to ensure that an approach is made at a time when the other party is ready to deal with it. Management interpretation of managerial prerogative often causes managers to move quickly in search of a solution, virtually pre-empting negotiation. When what they see as a positive overture is not reciprocated, they are likely to feel frustrated, discouraged and cross; making themselves in turn unready for overtures from the other side.

Openness

Conflict is handled more effectively if the participants are open with each other about the facts of the situation and their feelings about it. The Americans place great emphasis on this, as openness is more culturally acceptable in the United States than in the United Kingdom, but we note their concern that negotiators should own up to feelings of resentment and anger, rather than mask their feelings behind role assumptions of self-importance.

WINDOW ON PRACTICE

John Dunlop is known as one of the great theorists of industrial relations and the processes in collective bargaining (see Dunlop 1984). David Farnham summarises the ten points of his framework for analysing the negotiating process:

1. It takes agreement within each negotiating group to reach a settlement between them.
2. Initial proposals are typically large, compared with eventual settlements.
3. Both sides need to make concessions in order to move towards an agreement.
4. A deadline is an essential feature of most negotiating.
5. The end stages of negotiating are particularly delicate, with private discussions often being used to close the gap between the parties.

→

6 Negotiating is influenced by whether it involves the final, intermediate or first stages of the conflict-resolution process.

7 Negotiating and overt conflict may take place simultaneously, with the conflict serving as a tool for getting agreement.

8 Getting agreement does not flourish in public.

9 Negotiated settlements need procedures to administer or interpret the final agreement.

10 Personalities and their interactions can affect negotiating outcomes.

Source: D. Farnham (1993) *Employee Relations*. London: IPM, p. 337.

The negotiation sequence

In the various stages of the negotiating encounter aspects of ritual are especially important. They can make for formality and awkwardness rather than relaxed informality, but these ritual steps are not time-wasting prevarication: they are an inescapable feature of the process, which is summarised in Figure 6.1.

Agenda

The meeting needs an agenda or some form of agreement about what is to be discussed. The nature of the agenda can have an effect on both the conduct and outcome of the negotiations. It affects the conduct of the encounter by revealing and defining the matters that each side wants to deal with. It is unlikely that other matters will be added to the agenda, particularly if negotiations take place regularly between the parties, so that the negotiators can begin to see, before the meeting, what areas the discussions will cover.

The sequence of items on the agenda will influence the outcome as the possibilities of accommodation between the two positions emerge in the discussion. If, for instance, all the items of the employees' claim come first and all the management's points come later, the possibilities do not turn into probabilities until the discussions are well advanced. An agenda that juxtaposes management and employee 'points' in a logical fashion can enable the shape of a settlement to develop in the minds of the negotiators earlier, even though there would be no commitment until all the pieces of the jigsaw were available. Many negotiations take place without an agenda at all, sometimes because there is a crisis, sometimes because neither party is sufficiently well organised to prepare one. Morley and Stephenson (1977, pp. 74–8) review a number of studies to draw the conclusion that agreement between negotiators is facilitated when there is the opportunity for them to experience 'orientation', considering on what to stand firm and on what to contemplate yielding, or where there is an understanding of the issues involved. An agenda is a prerequisite of orientation.

Information

Both parties need facts to support their argument in negotiation. Some information will be provided to employee representatives for the purposes of collective bargaining and

Figure 6.1
The negotiating
process

both sets of negotiators have to collect what they need, analyse it so that they under-stand it, and confirm that the interpretation is shared by each member of their team.

Strategy

The main feature of preparation is for each set of negotiators to decide their strategy. Probably the most helpful work on negotiation strategy has been done by Fowler (1990), with his careful analysis of bargaining conventions and possibilities. Here we limit our considerations to four aspects of strategy.

Objectives

What do the negotiators seek to achieve? They need clear and helpful objectives. The most useful objectives are those that envisage improvements which could flow from a changing of the employment rules, changes in efficiency, working practices, manning levels, shiftwork patterns, administrative procedures, flexibility, cost control, and so forth. Unless both parties to the negotiations want something out of the meeting there is little scope for anything but attrition.

Roles

Who will do what in the negotiations? A popular fallacy is that negotiation is best con-ducted by 'everyone chipping in when they have something to say' and 'playing it by ear'. This is the style for a brainstorming, problem-solving group discussion; negotia-tion is quite different. Problem solving implies common interests; negotiation implies conflicting interests between groups who are opposed in debate. Negotiators need a specific role, in which they remain. The roles are:

1 **Chair.** In the majority of cases the management provide this function, and one of the management team will chair the discussion and control the meeting.

2 **Advocate.** Each party requires one person who will be the principal advocate to articulate the case and to examine the opposing case. This provides focus to the discussion and control of the argument. Although it is common for the roles of chair and advocate to be combined in one person for status reasons, this can put a great strain on the individual, who is combining two roles that are not compatible.

3 **Specialists.** The third role is that of specialist. There is one person who fully understands the details of the management proposal or arrangement that is being questioned, another to provide expert comment on any legal points, and so forth. The important emphasis is on what the specialist does *not* do. One would not expect this particular negotiator to become involved in the general debate, as this is confusing and moves control from the advocate. The specialist's role is to provide advice when required, rather like the civil servants who regularly pass notes to ministers appearing before House of Commons Committees. Negotiating does not benefit from free-for-all, unstructured discussion.

4 **Observers.** There is no need for all those attending to speak in order to justify their presence. There is an important role for those who do no more than observe the discussions. They get less emotionally involved in the interplay and point scoring, and are able to evaluate the situation as it develops. When there are adjournments the observers often initiate the discussions within their team as strategy is redefined and further tactics considered.

Predicting counterclaims

No strategy survives intact the first encounter with the opposition, but its chances are improved if the negotiators have tried to predict what they will hear from the opposition. In this way they will be prepared not only to advance their own arguments, but also to respond to arguments put to them.

Unity

Because negotiations are the confrontation of different sets of interests, each team works out a united position before negotiations begin and expresses that unity in negotiation. If the position is to be modified, then they will agree the modification. This is another aspect of the vital difference between this activity and problem solving. It is the differences between the parties that have to be handled; differences within the parties are simply a nuisance.

The negotiation

Setting

The number of people representing each side will influence the conduct of negotiations. The larger the number, the greater the degree of formality that is needed to manage the meeting; this is an argument in favour of negotiations between very small teams. On the other hand, meetings between two or three people in 'smoke-filled rooms' give rise to allegations of manipulation and are difficult for members of trade unions to countenance in view of their dependence on democratic support. Another problem is that different phases of negotiation call for different arrangements. Relatively large numbers can be an advantage at the beginning, but are often a hindrance in the later stages:

> it is not uncommon for the trade union side to field a sizeable team – a union official, perhaps, supported by a shop stewards' committee. It is unwise for a single manager to attempt to negotiate alone with such a team. Negotiation demands a high level of concentration and quick thinking and it is difficult for one person to maintain full attention to everything that is said, and to detect every nuance in the discussion. This does not mean that the management team must equal the trade union team in size. Indeed, to go beyond a fairly small number runs the risk of poor coordination between team members and the possibility that differing views will emerge within the team as negotiations proceed. (Fowler 1990, p. 35)

When asked to suggest an appropriate number, most experienced negotiators opt for three or four on each side.

Negotiating

The opening stage of the negotiations is one of *exploration*. Negotiators begin by making it clear that they are representing the interests of people who are much more important than the negotiators themselves: 'the membership', 'the board' and 'the shareholders' are just a sample of the powerful decision makers behind the negotiators. They also emphasise the strength and righteousness of their case as well as the impossibility of any movement from the position they are declaring. Both sides know but do not acknowledge that there will be movement from the positions that they are busy declaring to be immovable. The displays of strength are necessary for the negotiators to convince themselves that they are right and to impress the opposition, who have previously only been able to see the rightness of their own position.

The substantive element of this phase is to clarify what the differences are and how important or intransigent each feature of the opposing case is. By the time it draws to a close the negotiators should be quite clear on the matters that divide them, where and how. This, of course, is an important part of the process: differentiation precedes integration.

An important part of the ritual at this point is for the participants to keep down the level of interpersonal animosity. This is a part of the emphasis on their representative role that has already been mentioned. Different behaviours are needed later that depend on an open, trusting relationship between the negotiators, so this must not be impaired by personal acrimony at the opening.

After the differences have been explored, there is an almost instinctive move to a second, integrative stage of the encounter. Here negotiators are looking for possibilities of movement and mutual accommodation:

Douglas distinguishes between the public role-playing activities of the first stage and the 'psychological' (individual) activities of the second stage as being concerned, respectively, with inter-party and interpersonal exchange. Behaviourally the inter-party exchange is characterized by official statements of position, ostensibly committing the party or parties to some future action congruent with that position. The interpersonal exchange, on the other hand, is characterized by unofficial behaviours which do not so commit the parties in question. (Morley and Stephenson 1970, p. 19)

This second stage is *bidding and bargaining*. The statements made by negotiators are much more tentative than earlier, as they sound out possibilities, float ideas, ask questions, make suggestions and generally change style towards a problem-solving mode. This has to be done without any commitment of the party that is being represented, so the thrusts are couched in very non-committal terms, specifically exonerating the party being represented from any explicit authorisation of what is being said. Gradually, the opportunities for mutual accommodation can be perceived in the background of the discussion. We can now incorporate the idea of target points and resistance points advanced by Walton and McKersie (1965).

The target point of a negotiating team is the declared objective, what they would really like to achieve. It will be spelled out in the exploration phase. The resistance point is where they would rather break off negotiations than settle. This point is never declared and is usually not known either. Although negotiators frequently begin negotiations with a feeling of 'not a penny more than . . .', the point at which they would actually resist is seldom the same as that at which they think they would resist. Normally the resistance points for both parties slide constantly back and forth during negotiations.

Decision making

Through the stage of bidding and bargaining all the variations of integration will have been considered and explored, even though negotiators will have veered away from making firm commitments. The third phase of their encounter is when they reach an agreement, and it is interesting to pause here with the comment that agreement is inevitable in all but a small minority of situations, because the bargainers need each other and they have no one else with whom to negotiate. The employees want to continue working for the organisation. Even if they take strike action, they will eventually return to work. The management need the employees to work for them. Employees collectively cannot choose a different management with whom to negotiate and managers can seldom choose a replacement workforce with whom to bargain. They have to reach agreement, no matter how long it takes.

After an adjournment the management will make an offer. The decision about what to offer is the most difficult and important task in the whole process, because the offer can affect the resistance point of the other party. The way in which the other's resistance point will be affected cannot be predetermined. A very low offer could move the other's resistance point further away or bring it nearer; we cannot be sure until the negotiations actually take place.

The offer may be revised, but eventually an offer will be accepted and the face-to-face negotiations are over, but the full process is not yet complete.

Negotiations on the contract for collective consent are thus significantly different from those of other types of bargaining in which people engage. The negotiations to purchase a second-hand car or a house may seem at first sight to be similar, but in both of those situations either party can opt out at any stage and cease to deal any further. The possibility of losing the other is always present, just as is the possibility of negotiating with a different 'opponent'. For this reason the political analogies are more helpful. A peace treaty has to be agreed between the nations that have been at war, and no one else.

Recapitulation

Once a bargain has been struck the tension of negotiation is released and the natural inclination of the negotiators is to break up and spread the news of the agreement that has been reached. It is suggested that they should resist this temptation and first recapitulate all the points on which they have agreed and, if necessary, make arrangements on any minor matters still outstanding that everyone had forgotten.

In the wake of a settlement there are usually a number of such minor matters. If they are dealt with there and then they should be dealt with speedily because of the overriding relief at reaching agreement that is felt. If discussion of them is deferred because they are difficult, then agreement may be hard to reach later as the issues stand on their own, instead of in the context of a larger settlement.

Written statement

If it is possible to produce a brief written statement before the meeting is ended, both parties to the negotiations will be greatly helped. The emphasis here is on producing a brief written statement *before* the meeting ends, not as soon as possible afterwards. This will help all the negotiators to take away the same interpretation of what they have done and make them less dependent on recollection. In most circumstances it can also be used to advise non-participants: retyped as a memorandum to supervisors, put up on noticeboards, read out at union meetings, and so on. This will reduce the distortion that can stem from rumour. Until the agreement is in writing it rests on an understanding, and understanding can easily change.

Commitment of the parties

So far agreement has been reached between negotiators only, and it is of no value unless the parties represented by those negotiators accept it and make it work. This requires acceptance at two levels: first in words and then in deeds.

Employee representatives have to report back to their membership and persuade them to accept the agreement. To some extent management representatives may have to do the same thing, but they customarily carry more personal authority to make decisions than do employee representatives.

Although this is a difficult and uncertain process, it is no more important than the final level of acceptance, which is where people make the agreement work. Benefits to the employees are likely to be of the type that are simple to administer, such as an increase in the rates of pay, but benefits to the business, such as changes in working practices and the variation of demarcation boundaries, are much more difficult. They may quickly be glossed over and forgotten unless the changes are painstakingly secured after the terms have been agreed.

WINDOW ON PRACTICE

Ordinary citizens rarely know exactly what takes place behind the scenes in politics, so the following is an unsubstantiated anecdote. In March 2007 there was widespread astonishment when a power-sharing agreement was reached in Northern Ireland between Dr Ian Paisley and Mr Gerry Adams, representing diametrically opposed political views about the political future of Ulster. This was after a very long period of violent confrontation and hundreds of murders. After the agreement a story emerged about how this remarkable changes had been brought about. The British government minister sent to govern the province because earlier attempts at devolved government had failed was Peter Hain. According to the story he used his considerable unilateral powers to propose certain changes, such as introducing new charges for the domestic supply of water and removing grammar schools. Some of the changes alarmed Dr Paisley and his supporters, while others alarmed Mr Adams and his supporters. Both sets of supporters lobbied their leaders, who asked Mr Hain to withdraw the proposals. Apparently Mr Hain said, in suitable diplomatic language, that he would not be able to withdraw the measures unless an agreement was reached by 26 March 2007. The surprise settlement on 26 March enabled self-government to be restored. The truth of this story is not known, but it is a neat example of how even the most outspoken representatives depend absolutely on the interests of those they represent.

ACTIVITY 6.2

1 Why is the process (as well as the result) of negotiating important to both management representatives and employee representatives?

2 Is the process of negotiation important to the members of management and the employees who are represented, but not participating in the negotiations; or are they only interested in the result?

Negotiating with individuals

The majority of people at work are employed at the rate for the job, even though there may be some marginal variations in individual circumstances. There are, however, a small number of people who genuinely negotiate an individual arrangement. Sometimes they are employees, more often they are freelance providers of specialist services.

Although there are not the same elaborate rituals that surround the collective bargain, there is still a fundamental conflict of interest in that the two parties are not 'on the same side', but there is also the key difference in that the parties can walk away from each other. They are not (yet) bound to each other by a contract of employment; the employer can readily decide to contract with a different supplier and the supplier of services will not be wholly dependent on a single employer. Also the employer is keen that the supplier should produce a *performance*, not simply honouring the agreement with poor grace, but performing at a high level.

Some individuals get great satisfaction from the idea of negotiating their own deal. It gives them a clear sense of their own value and a feeling of autonomy, being in control of their own destiny. It was earlier suggested that collective negotiations are at least partly a way of people dealing with their aggressive tendencies. In individual situations it is slightly different in that the gaming element is stronger and everyone becomes his or her own entrepreneur.

The negotiating process is broadly the same in that the first stage is to muster all the information that is needed. Exactly what is the task to be done? What is the standard to which it has to be completed? What are the timescales? What latitude is there? When the parties sit down to negotiate, there is again the general searching stage of defining the negotiating range, clarifying what is wanted and hearing what the supplier wants and needs. The employer has the useful advantage that the prospective supplier has to tender, knowing that there are, or may be, others tendering for the same work, so the supplier has to pitch the tender at a level attractive enough to interest the employer not only in the price but also in the quality of service being offered.

Those employing services have to know what they can and cannot do. William Oncken (1984) has coined the term 'freedom scale' to describe the degree of discretion you want to enjoy. His scale is:

- Level 5 = Act on your own, routine reporting only.
- Level 4 = Act, but advise at once.
- Level 3 = Recommend, then take resulting action.
- Level 2 = Ask what to do.
- Level 1 = Wait until told.

Although Level 5 sounds very status-full and macho, employers may prefer in some negotiations to have less freedom, so that they cannot be expected to commit themselves without time for thought. Remember the representation element that was so central to collective negotiation.

WINDOW ON PRACTICE

Roger Fisher and William Ury (1986) suggest four basic rules to govern any negotiation:

1 Separate the people from the problem. Don't focus on the clash of personalities or bruised egos, but on the problem that needs resolution.

$\rightarrow$

2 Focus on interests, not positions. If you get locked into a particular position, you may not achieve the real objective of your negotiation. Always be looking for alternative possibilities.

3 Make the pie bigger. Generate other possibilities beyond what your 'opponent' is asking for by thinking of options that are of low cost to you and of high benefit to them.

4 Insist on using objective criteria. Prevent the negotiation becoming a contest of wills by looking for objective standards or criteria that can be used by both parties to test the reasonableness of any position that is adopted.

SUMMARY PROPOSITIONS

6.1 The practice of negotiation is based on a need to resolve or accommodate matters on which there is a conflict of interest about the appropriate rate for the job between those who employ and those who are employed.

6.2 In collective issues negotiation can clear the air, introduce new rules, modify an unworkable management position or produce better understanding of respective positions.

6.3 Among the problems of negotiation are the waste of time, the stress and the risks.

6.4 The most common bargaining strategies are avoidance, smoothing, forcing, compromise or confrontation.

6.5 Aspects of preparation are setting the agenda, collecting information, deciding a strategy, agreeing objectives and roles.

6.6 The stages in collective negotiation are exploration, bidding and bargaining, decision making, recapitulation, agreeing a written statement and ensuring the commitment of the parties.

6.7 In individual negotiations a negotiator will want to get agreement to an appropriate position of the 'freedom scale'.

GENERAL DISCUSSION TOPICS

1 In 1735 Benjamin Franklin said that 'necessity never made a good bargain'. Do you agree with this when applied to collective negotiations?

2 Is negotiation necessary in payment matters or is it just a form of game playing that appeals to people who like doing deals?

FURTHER READING

Fisher, R. and Ury, W. (1986) *Getting to Yes: Negotiating agreement without giving in.* New York: Penguin.
This is very sound on the basics and probably the most thorough recent treatment.

Hiltrop, J.M. and Udall, B. (1995) *The Essence of Negotiation.* Hemel Hempstead: Prentice Hall International.
A relatively recent thorough treatment of the process, it has an especially useful review of the literature.

Kennedy, G. (1998) *The New Negotiating Edge*. London: Nicholas Brealey.
Written by a professor in a business school, who combines academia with running an international consultancy, this book combines some of the merits of both spheres of work. It proposes an approach to negotiating that is a modification of what is set out here. It is described as trading behaviour with four stages: prepare, debate, propose and bargain.

Scott, W.P. (1981) *The Skills of Negotiating*. New York: Wiley.
This book has probably the best explanation of the interactive skills involved in negotiating.

WEB LINKS

Most websites deal with negotiating sales but two that could be useful are:

www.core-solutions.com (a consultancy, Core Solutions); and

www.unison.org.uk/bargining (the trade union, UNISON).

REFERENCES

Douglas, A. (1962) *Industrial Peacemaking*. New York: Columbia University Press.
Dunlop, J.T. (1984) *Dispute Resolution*. London: Auburn.
Farnham, D. (1993) *Employee Relations*. London: IPM.
Fisher, R. and Ury, W. (1986) *Getting to Yes: Negotiating agreement without giving in*. New York: Penguin.
Fowler, A. (1990) *Negotiation Skills and Strategies*. London: IPM.
Grint, K. (1997) *Fuzzy Management*. London: Sage.
Hiltrop, J.M. and Udall, B. (1995) *The Essence of Negotiation*. Hemel Hempstead: Prentice Hall International.
Kennedy, G. (1998) *The New Negotiating Edge*. London: Nicholas Brealey.
Morley, I. and Stephenson, G.M. (1970) 'Strength of case, communication systems and the outcomes of simulated negotiations', *Industrial Relations Journal*, Summer.
Oncken, W. (1984) *Managing Management Time: who's got the monkey?* Englewood Cliffs, NJ: Prentice-Hall.
Roberts, Z. (2002) 'A Square Deal', *People Management*, Vol. 8, No. 18, September, pp. 37–40.
Walton, R.E. (1969) *Interpersonal Peacemaking: Confrontations and third party consultation*. Reading, Mass.: Addison-Wesley.
Walton, R.E. and McKersie, R.B. (1965) *Towards a Behavioural Theory of Labour Negotiations*. London: McGraw-Hill.
Younson, F. (2000) 'How to handle a union recognition claim', *People Management*, Vol. 6, No. 15.
Zartman, I.W. (1976) *The 50% Solution*. New York: Anchor Press/Doubleday.

REVIEW OF PART 6

When Friedrich Engels came to Manchester from Germany in the 1840s he acted as agent for his family firm at what is now known as Jackson's Mill, for many years housing the Chemical Engineering Department of the University of Manchester. Looking out of his small first floor office he saw the squalid hovels of his workers in nearby Ancoats, with overcrowding, lack of sanitation and a level of poverty such that the average life expectancy was less than 30. This was a life-transforming experience for the young man who had left behind the elegant buildings and broad thoroughfares of Dresden. He wrote *The Condition of the Working Classes in England in 1844* and four years later collaborated with Karl Marx to write *The Communist Manifesto*. Here was the economic analysis that was to provide the intellectual underpinnings of the labour movement and of trade unionism for a hundred years. Fundamentally antagonistic, the interests of capitalists and workers were bound to cause class conflict and struggle as those who controlled the means of production wrestled to extract a surplus from the producers.

The management of employee relations is not now quite so stark, but the processes rest on the same fundamental premise of conflict between two different sets of interests, and much of that is about money. How will it be distributed? Who will decide on fair shares? How will the inevitable disagreements be dealt with? How will the employee voice be heard? Pay is the mechanism of exchange at the centre of the employment contract. It not only rewards contribution and determines standard of living, it also reflects social status and financial security. Every aspect of human resource management has an important impact on the lives of all those involved, whether they be managing or managed, although the distinction between those who manage and those who are managed is hardly clear. Pay has a more significant impact on people's lives than some of the matters we have considered in this book.

CASE STUDY PROBLEM

Cavendish Hall Hotel

Daphne Jones has recently been appointed as personnel manger of the Cavendish Hall Hotel, a 200-bedroom, four-star country house hotel located in rolling hills a few miles south of a major northern industrial conurbation. The hotel provides a wide range of conference and banqueting facilities and is a popular wedding location. Despite poor reviews from guests concerning the cost of drinks and the quality of the food on offer, the hotel is financially successful, having recently recorded increased annual profits.

Soon after her appointment Daphne decides that it is necessary and desirable to introduce a new payment system which links reward to individual effort and competence. She is concerned that the present system of paying everyone in a job role the same rate irrespective of their individual performance is unfair and tends to demotivate the best performers. She therefore decides to take a different approach when determining this year's annual pay rises.

1 Each member of staff will receive a 1 per cent salary increase irrespective of performance to take account of the increased cost of living.

2 Each line manager will be required to score his or her staff on the basis of their individual performance over the past year. There are four options:
   - excellent
   - good
   - satisfactory
   - unsatisfactory

3 Staff scored as 'excellent' will receive a 4 per cent pay rise (3 per cent plus the 1 per cent cost of living increase), those marked as 'good' will receive 3 per cent and those as 'satisfactory' 2 per cent. People who are marked as 'unsatisfactory' will simply receive the 1 per cent cost of living increase.

The hotel has not hitherto operated any kind of formal performance management system. There are no annual appraisals or development reviews. Managers vary greatly in the extent to which they communicate with their staff at all, let alone to discuss their individual performance. For many the only indicator they have that they are doing a good job is the amount they receive from guests in the form of tips. As a result, when the new scheme is announced in a series of staff meetings, there is enormous excitement. There is massive anticipation among staff in the days and weeks running up to the announcement of the pay awards.

At the last minute, however, there are hitches and as a result the announcement is delayed for a week. This occurs because Daphne finds herself to disagree profoundly with the scores awarded by two of her managers:

George Clapham, the head porter, has awarded all his staff excellent ratings. When Daphne questions him about this he replies that he thinks all his lads are wonderful, that they have all worked very hard over the last year and that they all deserve the full 4 per cent. Surely, Daphne argues, he cannot give Graham Dudd an excellent rating? Not only has he been absent most of the past year, but he is regularly found away from his post chatting up chambermaids in the staff room.

George argues that Graham means well and is very much liked by his colleagues. Daphne insists he is downgraded to 'satisfactory'.

Henry Oldham-Down, the head chef, has awarded two of his senior staff excellent ratings, but has rated all the commis-chefs and kitchen porters as 'unsatisfactory'. When questioned about this, Henry says that they are all 'crap' and a waste of space as far as he is concerned and that giving them the 1 per cent cost of living rise is much more than they deserve. Daphne lists some names of kitchen staff who she thinks do a good job. After each name is mentioned Henry just says 'crap'.

Daphne insists that one or two of the staff are upgraded to 'satisfactory'.

The following week letters are sent to all staff telling them how they have been rated by their managers and what the implications are for their pay. At the end of the letter is a sentence that asks staff who are unhappy with their pay rises to see Daphne Jones.

The following day a long line of disappointed staff forms outside Daphne's office. There is a perceivable drop in morale and this leads to reduced effort. In the coming weeks absence rates increase and guest complaints rise. There are particular problems in the kitchen, leading several guests to write very strongly worded letters of complaint.

Daphne is not surprised that poor performers are disappointed, but she finds it hard to understand why so many strong performers who have been rated 'good' are so negative about the whole exercise. What is more, she finds herself under fire from the Finance Director of the company which owns the hotel. He says that the pay bill is now too high and that it will have to be cut back next year.

The General Manager of Cavendish Hall thinks that the problems with the scheme have mainly been caused by different managers rating people according to different criteria. Next year, he says, we will use a forced ranking system. This will mean that each line manager will be asked to rank his or her staff in order of performance. The top 25 per cent will then receive the excellent rating and highest pay rise. Those in the second quartile will be scored as 'good' and those in the third and fourth quartiles as 'satisfactory' and 'unsatisfactory' respectively. This system also means that a budget can be set and that it will be adhered to in practice.

Required

1 What was wrong with the design of the payment system?

2 What was wrong with the way it was introduced?

3 What do you think of the new 'forced ranking system' that is planned for next year?

4 What alternative type of system would you argue should be introduced and why?

As we come to the close of the book, we have a different sort of Part. We are not considering activities in a specific functional grouping, but issues that tend to influence all functional areas. The ethical dimension of management in general and HR management in particular has aroused great interest recently, although the bulk of the small literature is yet to produce many really useful insights. In many western countries, particularly the UK, the matter of the balance between hours spent working and hours spent at home has recently received a great deal of attention.

The nature of the HR function is undergoing some changes and those engaged in the area need to be aware of these and how changes may move forward. The effectiveness of the HR function is frequently questioned so all HR people need to consider how valuable their contribution is and how it can be effectively measured, especially by the proper deployment of information technology and by measuring changes in human capital. The future of work is a fundamental consideration in human resource management, as the approaches and methods used clearly must fit the evolving practice in employment rather than being locked either into a set of practices that are no longer appropriate or in a fantasy world envisaged by HR practitioners, but not rooted in reality. We conclude our series of interactive skills by considering the activity of chairing meetings. HR people spend a great deal of time in these, but do they know how best to manage them?

ETHICS AND CORPORATE SOCIAL RESPONSIBILITY

THE OBJECTIVES OF THIS CHAPTER ARE TO:

1 Introduce the topic of ethics and corporate social responsibility

2 Consider the particular aspects of ethics that affect HRM

3 Review the variations of ethical practice across national boundaries

4 Suggest particular ethical questions facing HRM people in the future

WINDOW ON PRACTICE

In January 2004 the Treasury Select Committee of the British Parliament criticised chief executives of large insurance companies for taking big pay rises at a time when the profitability of their companies and the value of endowment policies were falling, both after a period during which endowment policies had been mis-sold. Between 1999 and 2002 the value of payouts from endowment policies had declined by an average of 25 per cent, the companies' share prices had declined by 50 per cent and the chief executives' remuneration had risen by amounts between 45 per cent and 70 per cent to sums ranging up to £1.3 million. The chairman of the committee said, 'The industry is going downhill like a slalom skier . . . Why do you think you're worth so much?'

Source: Based on A. Senior (2004) 'MPs attack insurers over chiefs' pay', *The Times*, 28 January, p. 26.

This could be a starting point for the fourth general discussion topic at the end of this chapter.

THE ETHICAL DIMENSION

Human resource management has always had an ethical dimension. In Chapter 1 we defined the first phase of its evolution as a preoccupation with social justice, and when the second phase of preoccupation with developing bureaucracy began it was the development of *humane* bureaucracy. The odd thing is that practitioners have for so long been trying to bury this aspect, while academic commentators have grumbled that personnel practitioners fail to deliver on it. Forty years ago it was possible to write a chapter in a book on personnel management with the title 'The Social Role of Personnel' (Torrington 1968, pp. 147–60) and generate a series of reviews that all vehemently disagreed with the implicit proposition that there actually *was* a social role for the personnel manager in the business. In 1977 Peter Anthony reminded his readers of an earlier statement by Michael Fogarty at an IPM conference, 'the business of business is business' before adding his own comment, 'it is the business of the industrial relations specialist to make sure that the business can get done'.

Since then there has been some increase of interest in ethics, but now it is not a vain attempt of the nice personnel people to act as the conscience of the company. Instead, it is a much more general management interest. Kenneth Blanchard is an American academic and consultant of considerable reputation, including being the author of the best-selling *The One-Minute Manager*. He teamed up with Norman Vincent Peale, who had written in 1952 *The Power of Positive Thinking*, which had sold no fewer than 20 million copies. Together they produced a slim, popular book about ethics in management which they described as follows:

ethical behaviour is related to self-esteem. We both believe that people who feel good about themselves have what it takes to withstand outside pressure and to do what is right rather than do what is merely expedient, popular or lucrative. We believe that a strong code of morality in any business is the first step toward its success. We believe that ethical managers are winning managers. (Blanchard and Peale 1988, p. 7)

It is interesting that the idea is 'sold' as a means to an end rather than as an end in itself, and it sounds almost as 'expedient, popular or lucrative' as the alternative that they are disparaging. We will return to the general management interest in business ethics later in the chapter, but we can get Blanchard and Peale in clearer perspective if we consider some definitions.

Any dictionary will indicate that ethics can be both singular and plural. In the singular it relates to:

the moral value of human conduct and the principles that ought to govern that conduct.

The plural form describes:

a social, religious or civil code of behaviour considered to be correct, especially that of a particular group or profession.

In the business context we can therefore understand ethics as a part of the culture of the individual business corporation that sets norms of behaviour by which people in the business will abide because the norms have some moral authority as well being convenient. It is also a set of guidelines followed by people in a particular group or profession because it makes practical sense in enabling them to do their jobs. Barristers will not represent two different clients if there is likely to be a conflict of interest between the clients. Doctors will generally refrain from sexual relationships with their patients. In both cases there are sound practical reasons, quite apart from any moral dimension. The medical profession is, however, an interesting point of comparison because the importance of ethics is so obvious, public discussion of medical ethics is regular, academic examination of medical ethics is widespread and there is a history that goes back at least 2,400 years to the Greek 'Father of medicine' Hippocrates. Among the contemporary attempts to formulate a universal code of ethics, the most widely reported is described by Gillon (2003) as having four principles, their longevity being demonstrated by three of them being given a definition in Latin as well as in English:

Beneficence – a practitioner should act in the best interest of the patient. (*Salus aegroti suprema lex.*)

Non-maleficence – 'first, do no harm' (*primum non nocere*).

Autonomy – the patient has the right to refuse or choose their treatment. (*Voluntas aegroti suprema lex.*)

Justice – concerns the distribution of scarce health resources, and the decision of who gets what treatment.

Gillon explains how this affects the individual practitioner:

> The best moral strategy for justice that I have found for myself as a health care worker is first to distinguish whether it is I or an organisation, profession, or society itself that has to make a decision. For example, 'how should I respond to a particular patient who wants an abortion?' is distinct from, 'what is this hospital's organisational view on abortion?' and 'what is the medical profession's collective view on abortion?' and 'what is society's view as expressed in law and practice?'
>
> Firstly, for decisions that I must take myself I must try to exclude decisions that have no moral basis or justification. Neither pursuit of my own self interest – for example, accepting bribes from patients, hospitals, or drug manufacturers – nor action that discriminates against patients on the basis of personal preference or prejudice can provide a just or morally acceptable basis for allocating scarce health care resources or for any other category of justice. Moreover, it is not my role as a doctor to punish patients; withholding antibiotics from smokers who do not give up smoking or refusing to refer heavy drinkers with liver damage induced by alcohol for specialist assessment on the grounds that they are at fault is not a just or morally acceptable basis for rationing my medical resources. (Gillon 2003, p. 267)

Although these comments are directed at medical practitioners or health care workers, it is an interesting intellectual exercise to substitute the word 'employee' for 'patient' to see how helpful and practical they might be for HR people.

Early management concern with ethics

The early management concern with ethics was discussed in Chapter 1, where comments were made about some of the Victorian philanthropists, such as Lord Leverhulme. An American contemporary was Andrew Carnegie, who was born in Scotland but made a considerable fortune after emigrating to the United States and devoted the last years of his life to giving most of it away. In 1900 he wrote a book called *The Gospel of Wealth*, which set out a statement of corporate social responsibility that was quite as paternalist as that of his British counterparts. He believed that corporate social responsibility had two principles, charity and stewardship. The more fortunate in society had an obligation to aid the less fortunate (charity) and those with wealth should see themselves as owning that wealth in trust for the rest of society by using it for purposes which were socially legitimate (stewardship).

Carnegie was very influential, largely because he dispensed charity on such a massive scale, but the paternalism gradually drew more and more criticism and the involvement in social responsibility waned. It was more or less destroyed altogether by Milton Friedman, who argued that those in business were not qualified to decide on the relative urgency of social needs. He contended that managers who devoted corporate resources to pursue personal interpretations of social need might be misguided in their selection and would unfairly 'tax' their shareholders, employees and customers:

There is one and only one social responsibility of business: to use its resources and energy in activities designed to increase its profits as long as it stays within the rules of the game, engaging in open and free competition, without deception and fraud. (Friedman 1963, p. 163)

Renewed interest in business ethics

The 1980s saw the return of interest in business ethics, although to many people it remains an incongruous concept:

Many persons educated in the humanities (with their aristocratic traditions) and the social sciences (with their quantifying, collectivist traditions) are uncritically anti-capitalist. They think of business as vulgar, philistine, and morally suspect . . . Three accusations come up.

(a) In pursuit of profits, won't businesses act immorally whenever necessary?

(b) Aren't executive salaries out of line? Isn't dramatic inequality wrong?

(c) Isn't it wrong to subject workers and middle managers in their mature years to so much insecurity? Isn't it wrong to let people go abruptly and without a parachute? (Novak 1996, pp. 7–8)

That was an American perspective, but it would be echoed by many people in Europe. There is also the more general feeling that any commercially driven activity has dominant motivations that are inevitably opposed to social considerations. Another version of the same view, echoing Friedman, is that those in management positions should *not* make moral judgements as they have no authority to do so. Instead they should respond to public opinion as expressed by customers' purchasing decisions, demonstrations by pressure groups or trade unions or by government legislation.

WINDOW ON PRACTICE

One relatively recent form of control on management decision making is whistle-blowing, which describes the practice of an employee metaphorically blowing a whistle to attract attention from the outside to some ethical malpractice within the business. Originally this was done by lone individuals taking great risks with their employment, but the method has now altered through the establishment of a charity, Public Concern at Work, which gives free legal advice to potential whistle-blowers. Its director claims that most issues are now settled within the business:

90 per cent of clients who follow our advice report a successful outcome. This has much to do with our policy that, if raised responsibly within the organisation, concerns about malpractice will be addressed properly by those in charge. (Dehn 1997)

An alternative point of view sees business practice as a product of its past:

> Wealth or value creation is in essence a moral act. The individual entrepreneurs who first organised production systematically were steeped in largely Nonconformist religious convictions that blocked most customary routes to advancement in British society of the eighteenth and early nineteenth centuries [who] . . . shared a belief that their works on this earth would justify them, that the Kingdom of Heaven was to be built by them, here and now. (Hampden-Turner and Trompenaars 1993, p. 3)

These authors then argue that the moral values that drive wealth creation are rooted in the national and organisational cultures of the wealth-creating corporations, although that is frequently forgotten because of the prominence given to the 'value-empty' discipline of economics, of which Milton Friedman was the supreme example:

> The qualities of work performed by these corporations depend as much on the durable values of their work cultures as they once depended on the values of their founders. In our survey of 15,000 executives we found that culture of origin is the most important determinant of values. In any culture, a deep structure of beliefs is the invisible hand that regulates economic activity. (Friedman 1963, p. 4)

The need for ethical guidelines

The logic supporting the need for ethical guidelines is that actions in business are the result of decisions by human beings, and human beings tend to seek justification for their actions beyond the rule of value for money. Frequently this takes the form of grotesque rationalisation. The various Mafia families apparently have a very robust code of conduct, based on strong family cohesion and a convenient interpretation of the Roman Catholic faith. This 'justification' enables them to peddle drugs, launder money, run large-scale prostitution and extortion, to say nothing of killing people, without a sense of guilt. Osama bin Laden apparently is motivated by a personal interpretation of Islam that legitimises terrorism.

Fortunately most people do not resort to such extreme behaviour, but will still seek to justify to themselves actions they take that can have unpleasant consequences for other people. The person who is totally rational in decision making is a rare creature in business life. In Chapter 25 there was an account of Milgram's work, which showed people acting in a most extreme way when they were put in an 'agentic state', whereby the responsibility lay somewhere else, absolving individuals of any guilt or responsibility associated with their actions. Recent concern about responsibility for fatal accidents has created great interest in the concept of corporate manslaughter. Who is responsible for a train crash, the train driver or those in overall charge of the business who did not arrange for suitable training, supervision or other facilities?

Moral justification

Sometimes the moral justification comes from a value system that is independent of the business itself and where individual opinions can be sharply divided. Some doctors and nurses are happy to work in abortion clinics, while others refuse, as some people are passionately committed to the woman's right to choose and others are equally passionately pro-life. Some people are enraged about the destruction of green land to build motorways, while others are enthusiastic. Other actions and decisions are more generally supported by the external value system. Few would disagree that people at work should be honest and that claims about a product or service should be accurate. Most would also agree with the general proposition of equal opportunity for all, although there may be sharp disagreement about what exactly that means in practice.

Ethical principles

Some standards of ethics derive from voluntary agreement by members of a particular industry, such as editors of national newspapers, or statutory 'watchdogs' such as those monitoring the activities of privatised public utilities. The problem of pensions and similar financial services being mis-sold has produced the Personal Investment Authority, which has quite swingeing powers intended to prevent a repetition of that sort of problem. Then there are the ethical standards that are generated within a particular business. The Royal Dutch/Shell Group of Companies relies largely for its international effectiveness on the values shared by all its companies and employees. No new joint venture will be developed unless the partner company accepts them.

> The business principles are a set of beliefs which say what the Shell group stands for and covers in general terms its responsibilities to its principal stakeholders, its shareholders, employees, customers and society. They are concerned with economic principles, business integrity, political activities, the environment, the community and availability of information. (Haddock and South 1994, p. 226)

These principles were first set out in 1976 and were not imposed from the top, but were a codification of already accepted behaviour. The principles are revised from time to time and one of the challenging tasks for the central HR function was to introduce a code of practice relating to drugs and alcohol, which took considerable discussion and consultation before agreement could be reached.

Individuals encounter moral dilemmas frequently in their working lives and are likely to find them very difficult. In carrying out research a few years ago about performance appraisal practice in a large building society, it was possible to see the rise in sickness absence at the time of the annual appraisal discussion, and this was most marked among appraisers: those who had to pass on bad news. We saw in Chapter 25 that few managers wish to take over responsibility for grievance and discipline from HR people, and making the decision to dismiss someone for almost any reason other than gross misconduct is a most unpopular management task because it seems that the interests of the business are being considered at the expense of the interests of individual employees. At times like this managers are very anxious to find some justifying framework for their actions.

ACTIVITY 30.1

Eric was deaf, mute and suffered from cerebral palsy. He had been unemployable all his adult life, but in his late twenties he started to follow round the local authority refuse collectors emptying dustbins. As the lorry reached the end of a street, Eric would go ahead of it and drag dustbins out from behind the houses to the front. His handicap made it a very slow and painful process, but it was something he could do and he worked until he dropped with exhaustion. This completely unofficial arrangement was accepted by the refuse collectors as they were able to complete their rounds more quickly and they were on an incentive payment arrangement and Eric's participation enabled them to complete their rounds in slightly less time. At the end of the week they had a collection and gave Eric a few pounds. This transformed his life, as he had a purpose and had some mates.

1 Do you feel that Eric was being exploited by the refuse collectors? Local authority officials heard about what Eric was doing and said it had to stop.

2 Why do you think they made this decision? Do you agree with it? A personnel manager in the neighbourhood heard about Eric and arranged for him to be taught to operate a sewing machine. He was then employed in the personnel manager's factory to maintain and repair all the overalls: a straightforward job carried out skilfully and conscientiously.

3 Do you feel that Eric was being exploited by the personnel manager?

4 As Eric was able to draw invalidity benefit, do you feel that the job should have been offered first to someone who was able-bodied? In the following three years investigations twice demonstrated that the overalls could be repaired more cheaply by subcontracting the work to another company, but that decision was not taken. Eric carried on as an employee.

5 Why do you think they did not make that decision? Do you agree with it?

Codes of ethics

By the early 1990s one-third of leading British companies had a written code of ethics, which was nearly double the number in 1987. The key issue with ethical codes is the extent to which they are supported by the people to whom they apply. They are not rules that can be enforced by penalties for non-compliance. It is necessary that they are understood, appreciated and willingly honoured by the great majority of those who are affected. There will then be considerable social pressure on the few who do not wish to comply. Imposing ethics is very tricky. While examining equal opportunities some years ago, researchers found an interesting situation in an American computer company with a rapidly growing British subsidiary. The company had a high-profile commitment to 'positive action to seek out and employ members of disadvantaged groups'. This was reinforced in the annual appraisal system for managers, who had to indicate what they had done in the last 12 months to implement a 'programme of employment and develop-ment for minorities'. The company annual report made a claim that this initiative was advancing at all international locations. In Britain, however, it was found in prac-tice that:

> Without exception, all managers to whom we spoke ignored that part of their appraisal . . . They put a line through the offending clause and wrote 'not applicable in the UK' . . . despite the corporate objective of 'citizenship', applicable in the UK, requiring recruitment officers to seek out the disadvantaged in the community . . . Suggestions by the researchers that such an active recruitment policy was an obligation on the part of management . . . invoked the reaction, 'we're not a welfare organisation'. (Torrington, Hitner and Knights 1982, p. 23)

ETHICS AND HUMAN RESOURCE MANAGEMENT

Criticisms of the HRM approach to ethics

Some academics have criticised HR managers for management failures in the employment field and derided them as powerless because of their inability to carry out 'simple' tasks such as introducing genuine equality of opportunity and humanising the workplace. Forty years ago Flanders criticised them, and their managerial colleagues, for getting the balance wrong between who did what in management:

> Confusion over the role of personnel management can produce a compromise that gets the worst of all worlds. In major areas of industrial relations policy – such as employment, negotiations, communications and training – line management may shed all the details of administration, while retaining ultimate authority and an illusion of responsibility. (Flanders 1964, p. 254)

WINDOW ON PRACTICE

One of the most telling caricatures of the HR manager comes from a Tyneside shop floor:

> Joe, an old labourer, is trudging through the shipyard carrying a heavy load on his shoulders. It is a filthy, wet day and the sole of his shoe is flapping open. The personnel manager, passing at the time, stops him, saying 'Hey Joe, you can't go round with your shoe in that state on a wet day like this' and reaching into his back pocket takes out a bundle of bank notes. Joe beams in anticipation. 'Here' says the personnel manager, slipping the elastic band off the bundle of notes, 'put this round your shoe, it will help keep the wet out'.
> (Murray 1972, p. 279)

The most vigorous denunciation of personnel people for not putting the world to rights has been from Tim Hart (1993) with his onslaught on HRM, which had three points of criticism:

1 HRM is amoral and anti-social because it has moved away from the principles of the famous social philanthropists who realised that the standard economic paradigm of labour utility needed to be tempered with social and religious values. HRM ignores the pluralistic nature of work organisations and personnel managers have abandoned their welfare origins.

2 Personnel managers, aided and abetted by the Institute of Personnel Management, have lost their claim to independent professional standing, as HRM is a managerial rather than professional approach, producing a purely reactive response to situations.

3 HRM is ecologically destructive because it consolidates an exploitative relationship between people at work which is then reproduced in our approach to relationships in the wider society and with our environment.

Other management specialists do not receive these criticisms, either because their activities are more limited in their social implications or because their academic commentators are more interested in the technical than the social aspects of what they are doing.

HR interest in ethics

The 'welfare' concept

HR people have long held a strong interest in ethics, although it was usually caricatured as welfare. Some of the academic critics argue that personnel managers should remain aloof from the management hurly-burly so that 'professional values will be paramount and prevail over other interests' (Hart 1993, p. 30). The problem with that simplistic argument is that HR people do not have a separate professional existence from the management of which they are a part. HRM is a management activity or it is nothing. The company doctor and the company legal adviser are bound by codes of professional ethics different from those of managers, but they are employed for their specialist, technical expertise and they are members of long-established, powerful professional groupings with their own normal places of work. When they leave their surgeries or their courtrooms to align themselves with managers in companies, they are in a specialised role. They can maintain a non-managerial, professional detachment, giving advice that is highly regarded, even when it is highly unpopular. Furthermore they advise; they do not decide. For instance, any dismissal on the grounds of ill health is a management decision and not a medical decision, no matter how explicit and uncompromising the medical advice may be.

HR specialists do not have separate places and conventions of work which they leave in order to advise managements. They are employed in no other capacity than to participate closely in the *management* process of the business. They do not even have the limited degree of independence that company accountants have, as their activities are not subject to external audit, and it is ludicrous to expect of them a fully fledged independent, professional stance, although there is a move in that direction since the professional body became chartered. The chartered personnel practitioner can only retain that particular cachet after regular reassessment of professional competence.

The change in general management orientation during the 1980s and 1990s towards the idea of leaner and fitter, flexible organisations, downsizing, delayering, outplacement and all the other ideas that eventually lead to fewer people in jobs and fewer still with any sort of employment security have usually been implemented by personnel people. HR and personnel managers cannot behave like Banquo's ghost and be silently disapproving of their colleagues' actions. What they can do is to argue vigorously in favour of what they see as the best combination of efficiency and justice, but they can only argue vigorously if they are present when decisions are made. If they are not generally 'on side', they do not participate in the decision making and they probably do not keep their jobs. Either they are a part of management, valued by their colleagues, despite their funny ideas, or they are powerless. There are no ivory towers for them to occupy, and no more employment security for them than for any other member of the business.

The 'deviant innovator'

In the different era of the 1970s Legge (1978) propounded her formulation of the conformist and deviant innovator as alternative strategies for the personnel manager to pursue. The conventions of employment security then, especially those of managers, were such that personnel specialists could perhaps pursue a deviant path with impunity. Now it is more difficult:

> The 'deviant innovator' bolt hole based on a plea to consider the merits of social values and to ponder the value of an independent 'professional stance' appeared to be offering a less secure refuge. (Storey 1992, p. 275)

They can still take such an approach, if they are valued by their managerial colleagues for the wholeness of their contribution, and if they accept the fact that they will often lose the argument: they cannot do it by masquerading as an unrepresentative shop steward. They have no monopoly of either wisdom or righteousness, and other members of the management team are just as likely as they are to be concerned about social values.

Job enrichment and humanising the workplace

HR managers have not abandoned their interest in welfare; they have moved away from an approach to welfare that was trivial, anachronistic and paternalist. In the HR vocabulary the term 'welfare' is code for middle-class do-gooders placing flowers in the works canteen. Personnel managers increasingly shun the traditional approach to welfare not for its softness, but because it is ineffectual. It steers clear of the work that people are doing and concentrates on the surroundings in which the work is carried out. It does not satisfy the HR obsession with getting progress in the employment of people, and it certainly does not do enough to satisfy the people who are employed. In many undertakings HR specialists are taking their management colleagues along with them in an enthusiastic and convinced attempt to give jobs more meaning and to humanise the workplace. Their reasoning is that the business can only maintain its competitive edge if the people who work there are committed to its success, and that commitment is volitional: you need hearts and minds as well as hands and muscle. Investment in training and the dismantling of elaborate, alienating organisation structures do more for employee well-being than paternalistic welfare programmes ever did.

ETHICS ACROSS NATIONAL BOUNDARIES

The international dimension of the social responsibility question has still to be developed. Logging operations in South America are ravaging the rainforests, which are essential to life continuing on the planet. Error, or neglect, in the management of manufacturing processes can produce a tragedy like that of Chernobyl in Ukraine or the various discharges of crude oil that have occurred all over the world. We have already referred to the concern about values in Shell, yet this business suffered serious difficulties about its plans for the disposal of the Brent Spar oil rig. Since the first formal warning by the American Surgeon General about the risks of smoking, tobacco consumption has been falling in western countries, so the tobacco companies have increased their marketing in less developed countries, which is widely regarded as a most dubious practice.

Ethical standards vary. The Recruit affair was a major Japanese scandal involving allegations of corruption among the country's most senior politicians. In the aftermath there was much American criticism of Japanese business practices and a flurry of righteous indignation in western newspapers about the need to use 'slush funds' in various countries to obtain business. Becker and Fritzsche (1987) carried out a study of different ethical perceptions between American, French and German executives. Thirty-nine per cent of the Americans said that paying money for business favours was unethical. Only 12 per cent of the French and none of the Germans agreed. In the United States Japanese companies have been accused of avoiding the employment of ethnic minority groups by the careful location of their factories (Cole and Deskins 1988, pp. 17–19). On the other hand, Japanese standards on employee health and safety are as high as those anywhere in the world (Wokutch 1990). In South East Asia the contrast in prosperity between countries such as Malaysia and Singapore on the one hand and Indonesia and the Philippines on the other means that there are ethical questions about the employment of illegal immigrants that are superficially similar to those applying to Cubans and Mexicans in the United States, but which do not occur in other parts of the world. There are very low wages and long working hours in China; and in Europe, Britain initially refused to accept the social chapter of the Maastricht Treaty harmonising employment conditions across the European Union.

The most remarkable recent case in the area of ethics has been the long-running saga of the American company Enron, an energy company employing 21,000 people and with revenues of $111 billion in 2000. *Fortune* magazine named Enron 'America's Most Innovative Company' for six consecutive years.

At the end of 2001 it was revealed that Enron's reported financial condition was sustained mostly by institutionalised, systematic, and creatively planned accounting fraud. After a long and complex trial the directors of the company paid large sums in compensation. The scandal also caused the dissolution of the Arthur Andersen accounting firm.

The disparate nature of ethical standards between countries will be one of the key HR issues to be addressed in the future. There will gradually be a growing together of national practice on working hours, but it will take much longer for rates of pay to harmonise. One can visualise common standards on health and safety developing much more quickly than equality of opportunity between the sexes and across ethnic divisions.

It seems that games are played between governments and multinational companies:

> Corporations in the international arena . . . have no real desire to seek international rules and regulations . . . that would erode the differential competitive advantage which accrues as a consequence of astute locational decisions. Indeed the strategies are centred on endless negotiations, or the ability to play off the offer from one nation against that of another . . . Examples of this strategy can be found in the recent negotiations over CFC restrictions, ozone depletion and the preservation of the Amazon rain forest. (McGowan and Mahon 1992, p. 172)

Fisher and Lovell (2006, p. 433) report the extent to which HRM in India is regarded by some as being ethically hypocritical:

> HRM ignores context, in particular the tradition of strong unions in India and the illegality of retrenchment, which means that voluntary retirement is the most common method of downsizing in India.

SOME CURRENT AND DEVELOPING ETHICAL DILEMMAS

We conclude this chapter by suggesting some of the less obvious ethical dilemmas for those in management positions. Issues such as the environment and equalising opportunity are extensively discussed, but there are others that receive less attention.

Life in the business

What sort of quality does working life have and what sort of quality will it have in the future? Twenty years ago a team of experts were employed at government expense in a Quality of Working Life Unit. Their task was to suggest ways in which that quality could be improved, mainly through job redesign initiatives. Since then the general belief is that quality of working life has declined, partly through overwork and partly through fear of losing employment. At the beginning of the twenty-first century workplace stress is one of the most common causes of absence and the place of work is an arena where newspapers would have us believe that harassment, poor supervision and bullying are rife, to say nothing of problems with passive smoking.

> Few people go off to work these days with a song in their hearts . . . many people dread each day because they have to work in places where they feel abused and powerless. What is happening to us? Why are talented, productive people being thwarted and sabotaged? Why do we treat each other so badly? Why are tyrannical bosses tolerated? Does the bottom line really justify the hurt and frustration we experience? (Wright and Smye 1996, p. 3)

As we saw at the beginning of this book, we now lack the comfortable feelings of security that the employing organisation used to provide. Whether people really are more or less secure in their jobs is debatable, but there is no doubt that they *feel* less secure. Furthermore, delayering and downsizing to become leaner and fitter has mainly affected people in middle-range posts, who used to be the most secure and who valued their security most highly.

As the gradual shift in organisation from entity to process continues we shall have to find ways that make work less stressful and more satisfying, despite the absence of certain of its traditionally most attractive features: security and community.

Information technology and the workplace

We have plenty of predictions of what the computer, the Internet and the microprocessor can do and what will in due course logically happen: manufacturing will progressively be taken over by robots, there will be rapid transfer and manipulation of data, the paperless office, people working from home instead of coming into a centre, and so forth: the golden age of the post-industrial society and the worldwide web. The ethical dilemma is to wonder what will be done to make up for what the computer will take from us: the conviviality and communal feeling of organisational life.

Managers have long had the opportunity to spend more of their time, and make more of their decisions, by rational planning and operational research methods than in fact they do. The strange thing is that there continues to be a preference among managers in general and HR managers in particular to spend their time talking with people and to make their decisions as a result of discussion and shrewd judgement. Will managers now begin to eschew face-to-face discussion in favour of face-to-terminal decision making, or will they continue to confer and keep busy while others feed to them an ever-increasing flow of processed information requiring interpretation, evaluation and further discussion? Research findings suggest that managers work in the way that they do at least partly because they like it that way:

> The manager actually seems to prefer brevity and interruption in his work. Superficiality is an occupational hazard of the manager's job. Very current information (gossip, hearsay, speculation) is favoured; routine reports are not. The manager clearly favours the . . . verbal media, spending most of his time in verbal contact. (Mintzberg 1973, pp. 51–2)

The date and male gender of that quotation may be significant. Most of the studies of managerial work have been of men and of men and women working in a male-dominated culture. It may be that the increasing proportion of managerial jobs done by women will alter the stereotype. The women authors of *Corporate Abuse* are quite clear about the need to care for souls:

> Studies of work flow suggest there is five times more opportunity to experience joy in the workplace on a daily basis than in the home environment if it is a workplace that is in tune with the needs of the soul . . . Once we have a community of fully nurtured souls, the possibility of creativity is limitless. Everyone in the workforce will be tapped into his or her own power source as well as being part of a larger community of effort and partnership. (Wright and Smye 1996, pp. 248–9)

This rings strangely in management ears, but maybe this is the way to rediscover the sense of community that employing organisations used to provide.

How great will the influence of the computer on HRM work actually become? How will we make up for what the computer takes away? If there is a general tendency for people to work at home, taking their terminal with them, how popular will that turn out to be? It is over a century since the household ceased to be the central productive unit and the men, and later the women, began to spend a large part of their waking hours at a different social centre: the factory, shop or office – the organisational entity. To be housebound has become a blight. We can see how it used to be:

> In 1810 the common productive unit in New England was still the rural household. Processing and preserving of food, candlemaking, soap-making, spinning, weaving, shoemaking, quilting, rug-making, the keeping of small animals and gardens, all took place on domestic premises.
>
> Although money income might be obtained by the household through the sale of produce, and additional money be earned through occasional wages to its members, the United States household was overwhelmingly self-sufficient . . . Women were as active in the creation of domestic self-sufficiency as were men. (Illich 1981, pp. 111–12)

Since that time we have dismantled, or allowed to wither, all the social mechanisms that supported that self-sufficiency, and developed instead the social institution of the workplace as the arena for many of our human needs, such as affiliation, interaction, teamworking and competition. It really seems most unlikely that the move away from working in the household will be reversed. In every country of the world roads and railways are jammed with people at the beginning and end of the day going to work or returning, despite the tendency for the organisational entity to decline.

The world wide web may not turn everyone into a home-worker, but it is still having a significant impact. There is the slightly isolating nature of the work that computerisation produces. The individual employee is not one of many in a crowded workshop, but one of a few scattered around a mass of busy machines. The clerical employee spends more time gazing at a computer terminal and less talking to colleagues. What employee behaviour will this engender and what attitudes will be associated with that behaviour?

WINDOW ON PRACTICE

Susan is not a high-flier, but an extremely competent and conscientious PA/secretary who is happy to work part-time so as to maintain an active family role. She explains what she has progressively 'lost':

> When I started I worked for one boss. He was a bit of a pain at times, but I got very involved, partly because he was so disorganised. He relied on me and I could follow all the ups and downs of his office politics. There was good camaraderie with other secretaries, who really ran the place. Not at all PC, but interesting and worthwhile. Nowadays there is more concentration on just doing the basic job of setting out letters and endless hours staring at that bloody screen. I feel more and more isolated.

As more people become able to use the computer there is a net loss of jobs. This has been seen in its most dramatic form in the publishing of newspapers, where typesetting has been eliminated through journalists typing their copy directly at a computer terminal.

The central ethical dilemma seems to be that we are allowing information technology gradually to take away the social institution of the organisation on which we have become so dependent. How will this scenario unfold?

ACTIVITY 30.2

What difference has the computer made to your working life so far? What further effect do you expect it to have in the next five years? How readily would you be (or are you) a home-worker?

Employment

If employing organisations are not to provide the security of a job for life, how will people find employment, both as a way of earning their livelihood and as a means of finding their place in society? There has been much brave talk of people managing their own careers and concentrating on ensuring their continuing employability. Charles Handy enunciated his concept of portfolio living, whereby people put together a portfolio of different activities so that they could control their own lives without becoming dependent on a single employer. This is fine for the able, well educated and independently minded, but human society has not evolved to the point where that description fits everyone; it probably fits only a minority.

There have always been large proportions of any society who were dependent. The golden age of Ancient Greece was based on slavery, as was the earlier Pharoanic period in Egypt. The lord of the manor had his tenants, mass production required masses of people and the world has always required large numbers for their armies. Not only were there dependent people, but society depended on them. We are now moving into this strange new world where there seems to be no place for that large proportion of the population.

It is unrealistic to expect every middle-aged redundant unskilled operative or every school-leaver without GCSEs to develop their own flexible employability. They need someone or something to provide them with the opportunity to work. Current economic wisdom is that jobs can only come through the activity of the market. This is one of the common political debating points: where are the jobs going to come from? Surely, however, it is one of the salient questions for human resource management. If personnel managers have social responsibility, how will *they* improve job prospects in the economy?

Self-improvement

For a long time we have lived with inflation that was, in many ways, the engine of growth. Not only did we spend in order to avoid higher prices next month, but we always felt we were making progress when our take-home pay kept going up. Rationally we know that we were not necessarily doing better at all, but it vaguely *felt* as if we were. Recently the level of inflation has been so firmly controlled that we no longer have that spurious feeling of making progress, as cost-of-living adjustments either do not exist or seem so small.

Without the mirage of progress provided by inflation, people need to have a more genuine sense of being able to do better. We have already considered the advantages and drawbacks of relating pay to performance, which is the main way in which it has been possible recently to see an improvement in one's material circumstances, but this really pays off only for a minority.

Delayering has taken out another yardstick of progress, as the scope for promotion is much reduced. This may reduce costs and may replace the phoney improvement of promotion by the possibility of real improvement through finding new opportunities, but we should remember that the business that is 'lean and mean' feels very mean indeed to the people who are inside it.

A nice HR challenge is to develop novel aspects of corporate culture that will recognise achievement and give a sense of progress for all those who seek it, without generating envy:

> Conspicuous privilege, ostentation, and other forms of behaviour, even when not necessarily wrong, typically provoke envy. Unusually large salaries or bonuses, even if justified by competition in a free and open market, may offer demagogues fertile ground on which to scatter the seeds of envy. It is wise to take precautions against these eventualities. (Novak 1996, p. 144)

Personal (note: not personnel) management

One ethical challenge in HRM is to ensure that the processes of management are seen to be carried out by people who can be seen, talked to, argued with and persuaded.

While it is clearly important for managers to avoid an over-preoccupation with procedural trivia, which reinforces the status quo and inhibits change, management is not all about strategy, and HRM has only a modest strategic element. It is the operational or technical aspects that require the skill and confer the status. Is there anything harder for a manager to do well than carry out a successful appraisal interview? Are there many more important jobs to be done than *explaining* strategy, or making the absolutely right appointment of someone to a key role? This is operational management for HR specialists, yet so often we find that they have retreated to the strategy bunker to think great thoughts and discuss the shape of the world with like-minded people consuming endless cups of coffee, while the appraisal and the selection and the communication is left to 'the line'.

There used to be a management approach known as MBWA, or management by walking about. This exhorted managers to get out of their offices and walk about to see what was going on and to be available. We have already referred in this chapter to the apparent preference among managers to spend their time in face-to-face discussion rather than in solitary activities. The trouble is that more and more of their contacts are with other managers rather than with people in the front line.

We suggest that it is important to maintain the work of HR as largely 'a contact sport', dealing face to face with people in all sorts of jobs in all parts of the business, so that, although the business employs the HR manager, there is an agent of that employing business with whom that manager can reason and debate.

Future HR managers will need a shrewd strategic sense and a set of operational managerial skills. They will also need an ethical sense, able to set management action in its context, understanding the implications for the enterprise, for each person and for the community at large. Many aspects of management work can be developed into a science: successful HRM is an art.

WINDOW ON PRACTICE

There has recently developed an interest in corporate social responsibility or CSR. Reviewing this development Stefan Stern (2004) made the following comment:

> CSR is bound to fail in companies where it is adopted simply for reasons of public relations . . . It may be successful in changing attitudes to your company in the short term, but if your activities are morally dubious they will eventually be exposed. CSR, if it is to mean anything, cannot be a bolted-on attitude or a departmental annexe . . . It is not about 'putting something back' – it is about how you make your money in the first place. (. . . In any case, if you really feel the need to 'put something back', doesn't that suggest you have taken too much already?) (Stern 2004, p. 35)

SUMMARY PROPOSITIONS

30.1 In the business context, ethics are part of the corporate culture that sets norms of behaviour by which people in the business will abide because they have some moral authority as well as being convenient.

30.2 Ethical standards vary between different national cultures, making international standards difficult.

30.3 Ethical codes are only valid if they are appreciated and willingly implemented by the great majority of those to whom they apply.

30.4 Personnel management has always had a strong ethical dimension, although personnel managers and the practice of HRM are regularly criticised for failure in social responsibility.

30.5 The CIPD has a code for its members, setting standards of conduct in accuracy, confidentiality, counselling, developing others, equal opportunities, fair dealing and self-development.

30.6 Among current and developing ethical dilemmas are the quality of life in the business, information technology in the workplace, employment, self-improvement and personal management.

GENERAL DISCUSSION TOPICS

1 The chapter opens by explaining that personnel managers for years played down their ethical/welfare role. Why do you think this was?

2 To what extent do you regard Tim Hart's criticisms as valid?

3 What examples can members of the group produce that would put you in the position of feeling that the demands of your job were in conflict with what you regarded as being right? How would you deal with this and how do the Milgram experiments on obedience explain, or fail to explain, your actions?

4 Most people agree that differences in rates of pay according to value or effort are justified, but that some differences are 'obscene'. What criteria would you suggest for setting pay differentials within a business that both are seen as fair and are effective in being able to attract and retain appropriate people from the labour market?

FURTHER READING

Fisher, C. and Lovell, A. (2006) *Business Ethics and Values*, 2nd edn. Harlow: Prentice Hall.
McEwan, T. (2001) *Managing Values and Beliefs in Organisations*. Harlow: Prentice Hall.
Both of these books provide useful reviews of ethical issues for managers in general. Both are up to date and have sections of particular interest to HRM people.

People Management (2003), 10 July.
This issue of the journal is dedicated to examining corporate social responsibility.

Redman, T. and Wilkinson, A. (2001) *Contemporary Human Resource Management*. Harlow: Prentice Hall.
There is an excellent chapter on employment ethics by Peter Ackers in this volume.

REFERENCES

Anthony, P.D. (1977) *The Conduct of Industrial Relations*. London: Institute of Personnel Management.

Becker, H. and Fritzsche, D.J. (1987) 'A comparison of the ethical behavior of American, French and German managers', *Columbia Journal of World Business*, Winter, pp. 87–95.

Blanchard, K. and Peale, N.V. (1988) *The Power of Ethical Management*. London: Heinemann.

Cole, R.E. and Deskins, D.R. (1988) 'Racial factors in site location and employment patterns of Japanese auto firms in America', *California Management Review*, Fall, p. 11.

Dehn, G. (1997) 'Blow the whistle, save a life', *The Times*, 8 April.

Fisher, C. and Lovell, A. (2006) *Business Ethics and Values*, 2nd edn. Harlow: Prentice Hall.

Flanders, A. (1964) *The Fawley Productivity Agreements*. London: Faber & Faber.

Friedman, M. (1963) *Capitalism and Freedom*. Chicago: University of Chicago Press.

Gillon, R. (2003) 'Four Scenarios', *Journal of Medical Ethics*, Vol. 29, pp. 267–8.

Haddock, C. and South, B. (1994) 'How Shell's organisation and HR practices help it to be both global and local', in D.P. Torrington (ed.), *International Human Resource Management*. Hemel Hempstead: Prentice Hall International.

Hampden-Turner, C. and Trompenaars, F. (1993) *The Seven Cultures of Capitalism*. New York: Doubleday.

Hart, T.J. (1993) 'Human resource management; time to exorcize the militant tendency', *Employee Relations*, Vol. 15, No. 3, pp. 29–36.

Illich, I. (1981) *Shadow Work*. London: Marion Boyars.

Institute of Personnel and Development (1996) *Code of Professional Conduct*. London: IPD.

Legge, K. (1978) *Power, Innovation and Problem-solving in Personnel Management*. Maidenhead: McGraw-Hill.

McGowan, R.A. and Mahon, J.F. (1992) 'Multiple games, multiple levels: gamesmanship and strategic corporate responses to environmental issues', *Business and the Contemporary World*, Vol. 14, No. 4, pp. 162–77.

Mintzberg, H. (1973) *The Nature of Managerial Work*. London: Harper & Row.

Murray, J. (1972) 'The role of the shop steward in industry', in D.P. Torrington (ed.), *Handbook of Industrial Relations*. Epping: Gower.

Novak, M. (1996) *Business as a Calling: work and the examined life*. New York: Free Press.

Senior, A. (2004) 'MPs Attack Insurers over Chiefs' Pay', *The Times*, 28 January, p. 26.

Stern, S. (2004) 'The Perils of CSR', *Royal Society of Arts Journal*, January.

Storey, J. (1992) *Developments in the Management of Human Resources*. Oxford: Blackwell.

Torrington, D.P. (1968) *Successful Personnel Management*. London: Staples Press.

Torrington, D.P., Hitner, T.J. and Knights, D. (1982) *Management and the Multi-Racial Workforce*. Aldershot: Gower.

Wokutch, R.E. (1990) 'Corporate social responsibility, Japanese style', *Academy of Management Executive*, May, pp. 56–72.

Wright, L. and Smye, M. (1996) *Corporate Abuse*. New York: Macmillan.

An extensive range of additional materials, including multiple choice questions, answers to questions and links to useful websites can be found on the Human Resource Management Companion Website at **www.pearsoned.co.uk/torrington**.

CHAPTER ③1

WORK-LIFE BALANCE

THE OBJECTIVES OF THIS CHAPTER ARE TO:

1   Analyse the drivers for work-life balance

2   Outline the legislative context

3   Explore a range of work-life balance practices

4   Assess the benefits of work-life balance

5   Assess the barriers to, and problems with, work-life balance

At this early stage in the twenty-first century there is increasing evidence that, for some, the value of work is changing. While the 1980s were characterised by the idea that 'lunch is for wimps', there has been a shift, perhaps encouraged by increasing work intensification and pressure, towards valuing a slower and gentler pace, which allows more room for personal interests, environment and family. In 2001 41 per cent of managers in an Institute of Management survey felt that the quality of working life had got worse over the previous three years (Institute of Management 2001). In the 1990s the notion of 'downshifting' appeared, which has been described as swapping a life of total commitment to work and possible high rewards, for less demanding, or part-time work or self-employment, or a combination of the three. This notion has been considerably expanded to form a wide range of legitimate work options under the banner of work-life balance or work-life integration which is being supported by government initiatives and is a key issue, rather than a key practice, in organisations not only in the UK but across Europe, America and such eastern countries as Japan. The latest Workplace Employment Relations (WER) survey (Kersley *et al.* 2006) found increasing use of flexible working options compared with the previous 1998 survey.

DRIVERS FOR WORK-LIFE BALANCE

Much of the pressure for work-life balance policies originates from the changing demographic make-up of our potential workforce, changing social roles, the changing responsibilities of organisations and legislative pressure. Increasing numbers of women in the workforce wishing to combine family and work responsibilities is an obvious driver for what were initially called 'family-friendly' polices (Kodz *et al.* 2002) and which quickly became work-life balance policies. This legacy does cause some problems for the implementation of work-life balance as we discuss later. The ageing population and workforce is another demographic change which has raised the importance of work-life balance for employers. Older employees may wish, or financially need, to remain in work, but work fewer hours or different shift patterns. The government recognises this and in its *Opportunity Age* strategy (DWP 2005) there is the identified goal of increasing flexibility for older workers so they can combine work with family and other commitments and any health problems.

WINDOW ON PRACTICE

Asda embraces work-life balance

Staff retention is important to Asda and they have developed a raft of policies and cultural initiatives to support this. Retaining and recruiting older workers is an important part of this. They began in their store in Broadstairs where they wanted to mirror the profile of local residents, 50 per cent of whom were over 50. Asda have used some creative approaches, for example recruitment channels through bingo halls and tea dances, often attracting people who were not even looking for a job. They were also very aware that older workers did not want to work fixed full-time hours and have developed a variety of flexible options to meet this need. In order to support personal commitment Asda encourage managers to 'just say yes' when employees need to take time off or swap shifts, and then worry about the shift rota later. Some policies specifically designed for older workers are 'Benidorm leave' which is the opportunity to take up to two months off over the winter, so that a longer stay in a warmer place is possible, and 'grandparent's leave' where new grandparents can take up to a week's unpaid leave to help with childcare support. Asda have found that employing older workers has provided a more stable and motivated and flexible workforce

Source: Summarised from R. Suff, (2005) 'Extending working life', *IRS Employment Review*, No. 838, pp. 45–8.

A recent study by the Royal College of Nursing (RCN) identified the large number of nurses, working very difficult shift patterns, over the age of 50 who were going to retire. Many of these nurses would have been prepared to stay on in work if they had access to shift patterns which allowed them a better work-life balance, or if they could work part time at the same job level. Such is the level of concern that the government has sponsored a drive to improve work-life balance in the NHS (Mahoney 2002). In addition, the fact that people are living longer means that many employees or potential employees have caring responsibilities, not only for children, but also for elderly parents.

In a tight labour market with a shortage of needed skills employers are forced into developing policies which can attract and retain groups of workers who might previously have left the organisation. Lloyds TSB, for example, felt that to attract and retain the workers that they needed, they needed to demonstrate that they were a progressive employer in terms of work-life balance policies. IRS (2002) found that the most popular reasons for employers to introduce work-life balance policies were recruitment and retention, and CIPD (2005) found that retention was the key driver. The importance of this issue is underlined by the fact that the government is encouraging work-life balance, and began a campaign for this in 2000.

A further influence is the need for employers to respond to what is now termed 'a 24/7 society'. Noon and Blyton (1997) argue that individual working hours are being decoupled from operating hours, and that more flexibility is needed to cover round-the-clock peaks and troughs. They argue that this now applies to a much wider range of business areas than hotels, hospitals and continuous processes operations. Financial services and retail operations are now subject to similar pressures. There is much evidence of work intensification over the past two decades and this faster pace has been associated with much greater levels of stress in organisations. Holbeche and McCartney (2002) found that employees were experiencing anxiety, work overload, loss of control, pressure, long hours and insufficient personal time. Such experiences are likely to encourage a reassessment of values in workers, and there is also evidence that younger people entering the labour market are much less willing to sacrifice their personal lives for total commitment to work. Values and expectations appear to be changing.

Associated with such changes organisations have been facing, and sometimes losing, lawsuits in respect of stress resulting from work. From a legal perspective employers have a duty of care, so in terms of self-protection work-life balance measures have an attraction. On a more positive note there is some evidence that employers are more concerned about promoting a healthy working environment and are more aware of their social responsibilities as an employer.

In conjunction with David Blunkett, the then Secretary of State for Education and Employment, the Employers for Work-life Balance Alliance was set up in 2000. It comprised 22 employers who exhibited good practice in work-life balance and served to offer advice to other organisations. The alliance has now disbanded but in its place Investors in People has developed a work-life balance model which offers guidance for employers.

ACTIVITY 31.1

'Work-life balance is just another fad. In a few years time it will be superseded by another issue.' To what extent do you agree with this statement and why?

THE LEGISLATIVE CONTEXT: FAMILY-FRIENDLY LAW

In recent years a significant contribution to the development of workplaces which offer a better work-life balance has been made by the government and by EU institutions. This has involved the introduction of new regulations which require employers to take account of the needs of people with family responsibilities as well as substantial improvements to existing statutory rights. Campaigners pressing for greater family-friendly working practices would like to see a much further extension of this kind of legal right, and this may well happen over time. For now though the government has chosen to take an incremental rather than a radical approach to policy development in this area, taking care to balance the interests of employees and employers. The major ways in which the law plays a part in promoting family-friendly working practices are set out in the following paragraphs. The Working Time Regulations 1998, which are also often reviewed in this context, were discussed in Chapter 22.

Ante-natal care

A well-established statute gives pregnant employees the right to take reasonable time off work to attend medical appointments connected with a pregnancy without losing any pay. The right is expressed as follows:

> not to be unreasonably refused time off for the purposes of attending ante-natal care appointments.

This means that permission must be sought and gained before the leave is taken. There is no general right simply to leave the employers' premises and then later state that this was for the purposes of attending ante-natal care appointments. If an employer unreasonably refuses a request, a claim can be taken to an employment tribunal. In many cases the employer's action will constitute sex discrimination and will lead to compensation being awarded. More common are situations in which the time off is agreed to, but not on a paid basis, or in which employers insist that any 'lost' time is made up at a later date. In such cases the tribunals make an award equal to any salary that has been lost. A common situation in which an employer can reasonably refuse a request is where the woman concerned works on a part-time basis and could arrange her appointment at a time when she is not working.

Maternity leave

The right for a mother to take time off before, during and after her baby is born has applied for many years, but the UK's regulatory regime was altered significantly in 2000 and rights were extended further in 2003 and 2007. The aims were both to increase the amount of time a woman could take off work for maternity reasons, and to simplify administrative requirements.

The scheme specifies three different types of maternity leave:

- ordinary maternity leave (OML);
- compulsory maternity leave (CML);
- additional maternity leave (AML).

OML applies to all workers but there is no qualifying period of service. It can last for up to 26 weeks (i.e. six months) and can start at any time within 11 weeks of the date that the baby is expected to be born. Unlike the old scheme, no information needs to be supplied to the employer in writing, nor are any statements of intentions about taking further leave or returning to work required. The woman must, however, inform her employer of the week in which she expects to have her baby and give three weeks' notice of her intention to take the leave. OML normally begins on the intended date (i.e. on the date the employee informed the employer that it would start), but it starts automatically at an earlier time if the baby arrives early or if the woman is absent for a pregnancy-related reason in the four weeks prior to the expected date of birth.

During OML the contract of employment continues in all respects except for pay. The woman is entitled to retain any contractual benefits such as company cars, portable computers and mobile phones, and her holidays continue to accrue. Any health insurance provided by the employer is retained and all the general duties owed by employers to employees and vice versa continue (*see* Chapter 6). Moreover, there is a general right for the woman to return to the same job on the same terms and conditions following OML. All pay rises and other improvements to terms and conditions must be honoured so that after her return to work the contractual situation is as if the maternity leave had not occurred. The only exception is where the job becomes redundant during OML, in which case the right is to return to a suitable alternative job with similar terms and conditions. It is important to remember that the right is to return to the same *job* and not necessarily to the same *work*. It may be that changes have been made in her absence that mean the detailed work the woman does on her return may be somewhat different.

CML is straightforward. It is simply the two weeks after the birth, during which there is now a compulsory period of maternity leave. The onus is on the employer to make sure that no work is done during this period. Except in the case of very premature births, CML and OML overlap, so CML only applies where a woman decides she does not wish to exercise her right to OML.

AML can only be taken by employees. It runs for a further 26 weeks following on from the end of OML, giving women in this position the right to take a full year of leave following a birth. However, the contractual position during OML and AML is wholly different. Unless the contract of employment states otherwise, terms and conditions of employment do not remain in place during AML. The only exceptions are notice provisions (on either side), redundancy compensation, the right to disciplinary and grievance procedures and the basic duty of trust and confidence. In other respects the contract of employment is suspended during this time. Annual leave continues to accrue but only to the four weeks required by the Working Time Regulations. The right to return after AML is to the same job *if reasonably practicable*. Otherwise it is to a suitable job on no less favourable terms and conditions.

Whether a woman just takes OML or exercises her right to take AML, she is entitled to return to work before the full period of leave elapses, but to exercise this right she must give eight weeks' notice to her employer. There is no longer any requirement to inform the employer in writing of a return to work after 26 weeks (or 52 weeks in the case of AML). The assumption must be that the woman will return at this time.

Maternity pay

Public sector employers as well as many larger companies continue to pay their employees during maternity leave, but this is not a legal requirement. Regulations specify only that Statutory Maternity Pay (SMP) is paid through the payroll to all those who are entitled to receive it. SMP is payable for 39 weeks for employees who have completed 26 weeks' service with their employers at the fifteenth week prior to the week that the baby is due, and who earn more than the lower earnings limit for national insurance purposes (£84 a week in 2007). Women who do not qualify for SMP have to claim state maternity allowance from the Benefits Agency from the start of their leave.

SMP is paid at the 'higher rate' for the first six weeks (90 per cent of salary) and thereafter at the 'lower rate' (£108.85 per week in 2007). Employers can claim a portion of their SMP payments back from the government through reduced future national insurance contributions.

Parental, paternity and adoption leave

European law gives both parents of a child the right to take up to 13 weeks' unpaid leave during the first five years of the child's life or during the five years following the adoption of a child. If the child is disabled, 18 weeks may be taken during the first 18 years of the child's life. In the UK this right currently only extends to *employees* who have completed a year's continuous service with their employer. It is only available to parents who have caring responsibilities for the child and the leave must be for the purpose of caring for that child. Interestingly, in this area of law, multiple births give multiple rights. So parents of triplets are entitled to take 39 weeks' leave.

As with the Working Time Regulations (*see* Chapter 22), employers may if they wish enter into a formal **workplace agreement** with their employees setting out how the principles of the law are to be applied locally. In the absence of such an agreement, a statutory default scheme applies which sets out how parental leave schemes should operate in practice. Included are clauses which restrict parents to a maximum of four weeks' parental leave per calender year and which give a 'right to return' equivalent to that for additional maternity leave (AML).

In addition to the right to take unpaid parental leave, since April 2003 UK law has given fathers of new babies the right to take two weeks' paid paternity leave within the first 56 days of the birth. However, this only applies to employees who have been employed for six months, 14 weeks before the expected date of the birth. As with parental leave, only fathers who expect to have responsibility for the child's upbringing are eligible. Paternity leave is paid at the same rate as the lower rate of statutory maternity pay (SMP), while return-to-work arrangements and contractual entitlements are the same as those for ordinary maternity leave (OML). Here though, multiple births do not give multiple rights.

When parents adopt a child, only one is entitled to take full adoption leave on the same basis as the maternity leave scheme outlined above, with pay during the first six months. The other is then entitled to take unpaid parental leave and two weeks' paid adoption leave. The payment arrangements rules about entitlement, notification procedures and contractual entitlements are as for maternity and paternity leave respectively.

Time off for dependants

Further European law gives workers a right to take reasonable amounts of time off during working hours for urgent family reasons, employers being informed of the intention to take the leave 'as soon as is reasonably practicable'. The UK legislation which gives effect to the relevant directive dates from 2000. It specifies the following situations in which such leave can be taken:

- to provide assistance when a dependant falls ill, gives birth or is injured;
- to make arrangements for the provision of care for a dependant who is ill or injured;
- on the death of a dependant;
- due to unexpected disruption or termination of the arrangements for the care of a dependant;
- to deal with an incident involving a child during the time when an educational establishment has care of that child.

'Dependants' are defined as spouses, children, parents or people who live in the same household as the worker, but they only become 'dependants' once they rely on the worker for assistance when ill, either directly or through arrangements made with a third party. Tenants, lodgers and employees are specifically excluded. The term 'reasonable' is not defined in the Act, but guidance issued by the Department of Trade and Industry (DTI) suggests that it should not normally be more than two days (i.e. enough time to deal with an immediate crisis and arrange longer-term care). This law does not therefore give a parent the right to take weeks of time off to care for a child during the whole duration of an illness. As with ante-natal care, the right is not to have a reasonable request turned down, and over time the courts will have to determine what is and what is not reasonable. What, for example, should happen if the employer knows that a mother's husband is unemployed and available to care for a sick child?

The right to request flexible working

A significant family-friendly measure is the right to request flexible working. It goes some way to meeting the demands of campaigners that parents with child-rearing or caring responsibilities should be able to work part time as a right, but it falls short of this position by some margin. The right is for parents of young children and people with caring responsibilities for infirm adults to request any form of flexible working, but it is likely to be used principally by women returning from maternity leave who would like to cut or alter their hours.

The regulations set out a procedure which requires the parent or carer to write formally to their employer asking for a one-off change in terms and conditions, together with an explanation as to how the request could be accommodated in practice. The employer can turn the request down, but only if one of the following eight reasons applies:

- burden of additional costs;
- detrimental effect on ability to meet customer demand;
- inability to reorganise work among existing staff;
- inability to recruit additional staff;
- detrimental impact on quality;
- detrimental impact on performance;
- insufficiency of work during the periods the employee proposes to work;
- planned structural changes.

When a request is turned down, the employee has a right to make a formal appeal, but if this is unsuccessful must wait for a further year before being allowed to make another request to work flexibly. The grounds on which complaints can be made to an employment tribunal are narrow because the right is only to *make a request* to work flexibly. According to the regulations tribunals are not invited to give consideration as to whether the refusal was itself justified on business grounds or not. However, this situation has effectively changed as a result of the ruling in the case of *Hardys & Hansons PLC* v. *Lax* (2005) – at least as far as requests made by women are concerned. Here the regulations were used in tandem with sex discrimination law to bring about a situation in which employers' reasons are subject to scrutiny by tribunals. Mrs Lax won her case. Her request to return to work following maternity leave on a job-share basis had been turned down, despite such an arrangement being possible. The employers' objections had been 'greatly exaggerated'.

Debates about family-friendly legislation

Views are divided about how, and indeed whether, further extensions of the family-friendly rights outlined above would be justified. Some mooted changes are uncontroversial, such as allowing a couple to choose whether it is the mother or the father who exercises the right to take additional maternity leave (AML), but others are strongly resisted by employers' associations. These include paying women at the higher rate of SMP throughout ordinary maternity leave (OML), giving employees returning from maternity leave a legal right to work part time and requiring larger employers to provide access to crèche facilities. Many employers argue that such measures would unacceptably add to their costs and make them less competitive internationally. There is also evidence of growing discontent about such measures from employees who do not have families, and a fear that too much regulation of this kind actually serves to hinder rather than help women's employment prospects by acting as a 'disincentive to hiring women of prime child-bearing age' (Lea 2001, p. 57).

However, strong public policy arguments can also be put in favour of family-friendly legislation and these hold sway in current government circles. In short, it is believed that such measures are needed to provide gateways which allow parents (particularly mothers) to combine working with their family responsibilities and hence to put much needed skills and experience at the disposal of the economy. They also serve to encourage single mothers and those with unemployed partners to come off welfare benefits and to take up paid employment instead. Helping fathers to take a greater share of domestic responsibilities contributes to this aim as much as removing the barriers which discourage mothers from returning to work following a pregnancy. In a tight labour market, where skills shortages are common, a compelling case can thus be made for family-friendly regulation on purely economic grounds (*see* Collins 2002, pp. 454–5).

ACTIVITY 31.2

Where do you stand in this debate about family-friendly legislation? Does it serve to underpin economic prosperity or reduce international competitiveness? What further measures would you welcome and which would you oppose?

WORK-LIFE BALANCE PRACTICES

Work-life balance options focus on three different types of work flexibility. First, there is flexibility in terms of the number of hours worked; second, the exact timing of those hours; and, third, the location at which the work is carried out. Clearly some options may reflect all three types of flexibility. While the legislation only addresses the need of parents and other carers, there is a strong lobby for flexible work options to be potentially available for all employees. There are many possible work-life balance options, and clearly not all of these options are appropriate for all jobs or employees, and employers will need to be convinced of the business benefits of any work-life balance option. In addition work-life balance will mean different things to different people, depending on their age, life circumstances, values, interests, personality and so on. At present flexible options are predominantly taken by women (IRS 2002). Part-time working remains the most available and most popular (*see*, for example, CIPD 2005; Kersley *et al*. 2006), and is now so common that it is often not recognised as a flexible approach. In our own research in a variety of functions in the health service (Hall and Atkinson 2006) we found that part-time work was rarely identified as flexible work to achieve work-life balance, even though it was very much in evidence, and informal approaches to work flexibility such as unplanned time off and individual agreements about start and finish times were the most commonly mentioned and used. Table 31.1 lists the main options.

Some items on this list are self-evident, but others require an explanation. While flexitime has been used for some time the systems tended to be formal, with limits, and there is currently an emphasis on less formal approaches and a more ad hoc approach to flexible hours, with, for example, days off for urgent domestic issues and time made

Table 31.1 Options for achieving work-life balance

Part time	Term-time working	Unpaid leave
Flexitime	Job share	Unpaid sabbaticals
Compressed week	Self-rostering	Work from home
Annual hours	Shift swapping	Informal flexibility

up later. Compressed hours allow an employee to work perhaps a nine-day fortnight by working a little extra each day to allow for one whole day off. Self-rostering has been used particularly in the health service and allows nursing teams to design shift patterns and staffing around the demands of work (for example getting the right mix of skills on each shift and taking account of patient care needs) and their own needs. IDS (2000) has produced a useful volume containing case studies of six organisations explaining how each has implemented work-life balance.

WINDOW ON PRACTICE

Work-life balance at Lloyds TSB

Lloyds TSB has won praise for its work-life balance policies, and Rana (2002a) highlights the key role of the line manager as being open to new ideas and coming up with a work-life solution to meet both individual and business needs. Lloyds TSB introduced Work Options in March 1999 and in 2002 just under 3,600 employees were working flexibly as a result of this. An important foundation of policy at Lloyds TSB is that applications to work flexibly are now 'reason neutral', as it was felt that taking a reason into account forced managers into making value judgements. Now all that matters is making a viable business case.

Originally work-life balance policies were not embraced as fully as the bank would have liked; in particular men did not feel that it was legitimate to work flexibly and felt that doing so would damage their careers. This position is gradually improving and 16 per cent of those using work options are men and 18 per cent are managers.

However, there is still some way to go. A union representative explained that flexible options did not sit easily with the old culture of long hours and unclaimed overtime pay, and that employees were still inhibited in requesting flexibility. The representative was also concerned that staff shortages may limit the viability of many work options.

Source: Summarised from E. Rana (2002a) 'How does it really work in practice?', in *The Guide to Work-life Balance*. London: CIPD.

Glynn *et al.* (2002) suggest that in fixed-hours cultures, such as a supermarket, work-life balance policies which detail specific options for flexibility will help. In a long-hours culture, like consultancy work, they argue that it is harder to achieve work-life balance, and a more viable option is to allow individuals more informal discretion to work their hours at the times and in the location that best suit business and personal needs.

There is some evidence that the public sector makes much better provision for work-life balance (*see*, for example, Murphy 2006) and Walton and Gaskell (2001) give some excellent examples of senior public sector employees working in a variety of flexible ways. Case 31.1 on this book's companion website, **www.pearsoned.co.uk/torrington**, focuses on the public sector.

WINDOW ON PRACTICE

Gap years for grown-ups

Saga Magazine (2003) reports on the increasing trend for those in their fifties and sixties to take off into the unknown for a gap year. While some of these may be retired, many are still in employment and are taking a year out, returning to work refreshed and with a new perspective on life with rediscovered drive and enthusiasm. Examples given in the article are individuals who feel they have had little freedom in the past due to work and family commitments, and want to do something while they are still fit and active.

There can be powerful advantages in the work environment from employers making such long periods of leave available, not only in retaining people who might otherwise give up their job, but as one of their interviewees explained, 'I don't bother with the trivia now. And I came back to my job far more resilient, resourceful and tolerant.'

BENEFITS OF WORK-LIFE BALANCE

Work-life balance practices have been shown in some instances to reduce absence (especially unplanned absence), raise morale and increase levels of job satisfaction. Murphy (2006) reports that organisations in an IRS survey found flexible working had a positive impact on retention, recruitment and absenteeism, and these perceptions were shared by respondents to the CIPD survey (2005) who also report very positive impacts on motivation.

WINDOW ON PRACTICE

Benefits experienced

Scott (2007) reports on the Britannia Building Society, which found that absence and employee turnover have both reduced as a result of their flexible working policy. Absence dropped from 3.06 per cent in 2004 to 2.35 per cent in 2006 and turnover from 18.94 per cent in 2004 to 12.6 per cent in 2006. Whilst they had adopted flexible working before 2004 it was ad hoc and inconsistent so improvements were made by getting board commitment, engaging people across the business in focus groups and including the input of representatives into a new HR policy on flexible working. Britannia also claim that there is a direct link with customer satisfaction.

Phillips (2007) reports on Ellis Fairbank, Recruitment Consultants, who state that flexible working for all staff has increased productivity and helped to attract top talent. They also found lower absence, reduced employee turnover and raised morale. The Consultancy used flexible working in their advertising campaign to attract staff.

Such advertising is a surprisingly underused practice. The CIPD (2005) in their survey found that only 36 per cent of respondent employers to their survey used flexible working in their recruitment advertising compared with 74 per cent who communicate this information in staff handbooks.

Sources: Summarised from A. Scott (2007) 'Flexible Working cuts absence', *People Management*, Vol. 13, No. 6, p. 15, 22 March; and L. Phillips (2007) 'Add muscle with flexible work', *People Management*, Vol. 13, No. 5, p. 10, 8 March.

Increased levels of performance have also been found as employees are less tired and so work more effectively when they are working. Kodz *et al.* (2002) in their research found that productivity and quality of work had both improved, as had staff retention and the ability to recruit staff. Perry-Smith and Blum (2000) found that bundles of work-life balance policies were related to higher organisational performance in a US survey of 527 firms. In the early 1970s the UK experienced some intensive industrial action which caused the government to introduce a three-day week throughout the economy, accompanied by regular power cuts to conserve energy. For that short period industrial production dipped by less than the 40 per cent that working hours were reduced. Control and choice are important characteristics of working life and Kodz *et al.* found that

there is increasing acceptance that choice, control and flexibility are important in work, that personal fulfilment is important *outside* work, and, further, that satisfaction *outside work may enhance employees' contribution to work.* (Kodz *et al.* 2002, p. 1, italics in original)

In our own research we found that informal flexibility was highly valued and associated with employee discretionary effort in terms of supporting colleagues, and patients where appropriate, and being available and flexible to cover emergencies. As employees appreciated the flexibility they were given they expressed the desire to give something back and recognised the need for 'give and take'.

Sabbaticals in particular can give individuals space and time to develop in other ways. Davidson (2002) reports on Elan, an IT company, that funds sabbaticals for employees to develop in new ways if there is a possibility this can transfer back into the workplace. They have supported such interests as horse whispering, surfing, performance music and neuro-linguistic programming and argue that 'sabbaticals give people the security of knowing they have a job to return to, and they bring fresh ideas back into the workplace' (p. 37).

In a baseline study covering employers and employees, conducted by the Institute for Employment Research at the University of Warwick and IFF Research Ltd (Hogarth *et al.* 2001), 91 per cent of employers and 96 per cent of employees felt that people work better when they can balance their work with other aspects of their lives. Employers can also find that such policies can meet business needs for flexibility and can be a way of addressing diversity issues.

Some employers have argued that staff on shorter working hours are still producing the same amount of work that they did on full-time hours; however, this was found to be, at least in part, due to the fact they were working longer than part-time paid hours, as the Window on practice in the following section demonstrates.

Case 31.2 on this book's companion website, **www.pearsoned.co.uk/torrington** presents two different perspectives on the value and importance of work-life balance.

BARRIERS TO, AND PROBLEMS WITH, WORK-LIFE BALANCE

The take-up gap

There is considerable evidence that the demand for flexible work options is much greater than the take-up so far, and this has been referred to as the take-up gap. Hogarth *et al.* (2001) report that 47 per cent of employees not currently using flexitime would like to do so, and 35 per cent would like a compressed week. The desire to work different or more flexible hours is a significant determinant of employees moving jobs either within or between employers (Boheim and Taylor 2004) to achieve the flexibility they desire; the researchers also point to rigidities in the British labour market which does not offer enough jobs with flexible hours. Some work-life balance strategies cost the organisation money and financial limits are set for such practices to be viable. The AA experienced difficulties in setting up teleworking at home. Productivity was greater than that of site-based staff, but in order to offset the cost of technology and infrastructure such workers had to be more than 1.5 times as productive as site staff. To gain such productivity tight management and measurement of home-based teleworkers is necessary (Bibby 2002).

Policies and some line managers may limit access to work-life balance to certain groups, which is clearly evidenced in the latest WER survey (Kersley *et al.* 2006). There is also evidence that some employers fail to have a strategic approach to work-life balance, but use such practices in a fire-fighting manner, to deal with situations when they reach breaking point (*see*, for example, a case study of a Further Education college in Glynn *et al.* 2002). Whilst organisations can sometimes easily provide reduced hours work for, say, administrative and sales staff, it is much more difficult to do this with professional staff. Anecdotal evidence suggests that many professionals moving from full- to part-time work find that they are really expected to do a full-time job in part-time hours and with part-time pay. In respect of nurses Edwards and Robinson (2004) found that the lack of a strategic approach to reducing hours resulted in a dissatisfactory situation for both part-timers and full-timers alike as shown in the Window on practice below.

WINDOW ON PRACTICE

Part-time working for qualified nurses

Edwards and Robinson (2004) researched part-time working for nurses in three NHS trusts and found that flexible working had evolved reactively as a response to requests from full-time nurses wishing to work part time. Senior and middle managers reported that nursing culture did not support part-time working and that some line managers were unenthusiastic. Whilst line managers perceived that part-time working aided retention and to some extent recruitment they identified disadvantages as communication and information flow; management and supervision including continuity of service and nurse availability; and work orientation (for example not wanting responsibility or promotion or to take on new tasks and roles). Nursing staff themselves reported that there was a tendency for management to give part-time staff different and often less central roles. On a range of activities including: acting as a team leader; attending management, practice development and research meetings; shadowing senior staff; and developing clinical guidelines, the researchers found that part-time staff were always less involved than full-time staff. Part-timers were also less satisfied with their training and career progression than full-time staff. The researchers identified a circle of skills erosion and being limited to a narrow range of tasks for part-timers, which diminishes flexibility for part-timers and does not provide the best return for the employers. Edwards and Robinson identified that problems resulted from the way that part-time working was implemented in that part-timers occupied jobs normally designed for full-timers which were not necessarily suited to or planned for part-timers. Whilst the employers had acquiesced in responding to requests for part-time work they had made minimal additional effort to adjust the systems of work organisation to support part-time working.

Source: Summarised from C. Edwards and O. Robinson (2004) 'Evaluating the Business Case for Part-time Working amongst Qualified Nurses', *British Journal of Industrial Relations*, Vol. 42, No. 1, pp. 167–83.

There is evidence in the literature that work-life balance requests for childcare reasons would be dealt with more favourably than requests on any other basis. The association that work-life balance practices have with women bringing up children creates two problems. The first is that work-life balance is 'ghettoised' (*see*, for example, Rana 2002b), as something done for women with children who are not interested in real careers. The second is that this causes alienation from the rest of the workforce who are not allowed these special privileges. In particular, working part time has been a popular option in combining work and other commitments, and yet there is considerable evidence that this limits career development (*see*, for example, MacDermid *et al*. 2001).

WINDOW ON PRACTICE

Who is entitled to work-life balance? A cautionary tale

In a government office there is a work-life balance policy with a range of options available. The options, however, are seen as being available only for women with children and this is causing much resentment among other staff. One manager, however, arranged, informally, in a specific year to have Friday afternoons off so that she could take her disabled husband up to the Lake District, avoiding the stressful Friday evening rush hour. To do this she worked extra time every other day of the week to make up her full-time hours. There were no problems resulting from this arrangement. She requested that the arrangement should continue the following year, but was told that she now had to make a formal application. She did this and was turned down on the basis that it was not compatible with work demands, and that she was needed in the office on a Friday afternoon. Stunned by this the manager wrote back explaining that she had two children, and it was on this basis that she needed the Friday afternoon off. Her application was granted.

ACTIVITY 31.3

Discuss the following statement. To what extent do you agree or disagree with it, and why?
    'Employees should be equally entitled to work-life balance options, as long as business needs are met. It doesn't matter whether the reason is childcare, the desire to engage in sports activities, do extra gardening, or just loll around on the sofa watching television.'

The take-up of work-life balance options is often equated with lack of commitment to one's career or to the organisation. In the baseline study Hogarth *et al.* (2001) found that two-thirds of male employees felt that their career prospects would be damaged if they worked part time, and CIPD (Rana 2002b) found strikingly similar results in their survey of work-life balance.

In addition there are many employees who are committed to full-time hours because financial commitments mean that they require full-time pay. This severely limits the type of flexibility that they feel is appropriate for themselves. Heavy workloads may prevent requests for flexible working, and where departments are inadequately staffed flexible options are severely curtailed. High levels of work, combined with pressure from the organisational culture, may also have unexpected consequences for those employees opting to reduce their hours to part time from full time, as is shown in the Window on practice.

WINDOW ON PRACTICE

Unpaid work

Glynn *et al.* (2002) in their research for the Institute for Employment Studies found examples of individuals reducing their hours to part time, but actually continuing to work more like their original hours as the workload had not reduced. As one interviewee who had done this explained:

> I end up working almost full time, just not visibly in the office. I do it at home once the kids are in bed.

Managers appeared to be aware of these situations, and one manager explained:

> she produces almost exactly the same amount, of the same quality, as when she was working full time . . . she feels she has to prove she's still committed . . . she's not actually working less, she's working the same but in a different location . . . at a different time . . . she's not being paid for it and her access to other benefits [is] reduced . . . I worry that it is not sustainable for her.

Source: Summarised from C. Glynn, I. Steinberg and C. McCartney (2002) *Work-life balance: The role of the manager*. Horsham: Roffey Park Institute.

Furthermore, in many organisations individuals have to be proactive and come up with flexible solutions which meet business needs and this is difficult when there are few precedents and a lack of understanding of what is available or possible. In our own research (Hall and Atkinson 2006) we found that although the Health Trust was keen to support work-life balance and had an appropriate policy few employees were aware of what was available or knew how to locate the policy. In their Work Foundation survey Visser and Williams (2006) report that focus group participants felt that work-life balance options were not well communicated to them. In addition the majority of organisations in an IRS survey had no procedure for employees to use to request flexible working (IRS 2002).

The CIPD survey (Rana 2002b) reports that 74 per cent of respondents believed that working hours is not an indication of commitment, 84 per cent felt that individuals working part time were not less committed and 77 per cent believed that organisations should allow employees to attend to personal commitments in working time, and then make the time up. However, while these figures demonstrate that there have been some shifts in attitudes, culture remains a major barrier to take-up. Long-hours cultures with early and late meetings are hard to shift. It is argued that more middle and senior manager role models are needed of flexible working and that there need to be work-life balance champions.

Managers' role in implementing work-life balance

Whether or not there is a work-life balance policy in existence, it is often line managers who will be the 'main arbiters of whether work-life balance policies become a reality

. . . both by their attitudes and management practices' (Glynn *et al.* 2002, p. 5). The Work Foundation found that managers were the main barrier to introducing and implementing work-life balance policies (CIPD 2003). Managers have to manage performance targets of the team and often feel that flexible working damages this, and flexible working for some may mean higher workloads for others. There is a pressure on line managers to be fair and their decisions about who can work flexibly and in what way are under scrutiny and may result in a backlash. On top of this managers may receive a bonus for meeting team performance targets, which may be jeopardised by flexible working. We have said before that there is a general lack of a strategic approach to work-life balance and one of the consequences of this is that when employees reduce their hours the remainder of the work tends to be reallocated to the remaining full-time workers. Murphy (2006) in an IRS survey found that employers appeared not prepared to pick up the costs associated with work-life balance. MacDermid *et al.* (2001) found that managers had three concerns relating to employees working reduced hours. The first concerned helping employees develop professionally while not working full time; the second was what to do if more employees wanted to work reduced hours as it could be a nightmare to manage a host of different alternative work arrangements; and third, it was felt that some jobs were just not do-able on anything less than a full-time basis.

WINDOW ON PRACTICE

Managing part-time working in the police service

Dick (2004) reports on the impact of part-time working for police officers in a large metropolitan constabulary in the north of England. There was no HR strategy which addressed the aims for implementation and management of part-time working. Officers put forward a proposal for part-time working which set out how their hours should be scheduled. There was a view in the HR department that line managers were resistant to part-time working but Dick found a number of contradictions and difficulties for managers in dealing with this issue.

Operational policing is a demand-led activity 365 days a year with unpredictable events. There is a tradition of staying behind at the end of a shift to complete work, to work extra shifts at short notice and be on call over 24 hours. This was a clear issue as part-timers in this case had often opted for reduced hours so that they could be available at specific times to deal with childcare responsibilities. Managers of part-time officers felt they could not force them to work extra hours when needed due to fear of a backlash and an industrial tribunal. Only one part-timer thought the culture of always being available was a legitimate response to the demands of the job, others felt that a more creative approach was possible, and felt that solutions were possible through culture change.

Managers often objected to part-time working because of the lack of consistency of supervision that this would entail. In order to meet the demand for part-time working managers often put part-timers in a non-central role, but this brought with it the perspective that part-timers were being marginalised. Dick identified that previously

→

managers were not able to recoup the hours lost when an officer started to work part time, but a new policy to enable this had just been introduced. Also part-timers were able to negotiate the shifts they desired with the consequence that full-timers got more than their fair share of unpopular shifts, and Dick identified a possible change to paying part-timers for the specific shifts they actually work which was not happening at the time.

This is a good example of the way that work is constructed according to a set of rules based on what works for a full-time officer, but which causes serious problems when applied to part-timers.

Source: Summarised from P. Dick (2004) 'Between a rock and a hard place: The dilemmas of managing part-time working in the police service', *Personnel Review*, Vol. 33, No. 3, pp. 302–31.

Managing workers who are not visible (working at home, for example) is a particular concern for line managers. Felstead *et al.* (2003) report the fear that working at home is a 'slacker's charter', but they also found that home-workers themselves had fears about not being able easily to demonstrate their honesty, reliability and productivity. Some managed this by working more hours than they should in order to demonstrate greater output. To counteract this fear, managers in Felstead's study introduced new surveillance devices, set output targets and brought management into the home via home visits. Managers also felt that home-working represented a potential threat to the integration of teams and the acceptance of corporate culture, and that it impeded the transmission of tacit knowledge. There is also a concern that only some employees have the characteristics to be successful home-workers, and Felstead *et al.* (2003) develop this idea in some detail.

It is becoming apparent that a range of key management skills is needed in managing flexibility. For example Janman (2002) suggests that key skills are communication, empowerment, performance management and coaching. Glynn *et al.* (2002) are more specific in their recommendations. They suggest that line managers need to be able to 'push back' work demands from other parts of the organisation which they feel are unrealistic; plan and schedule; delegate in a fair and equitable way and understand the capacity and skills of those who report directly to them. They suggest that it is important for managers to be able to crack down hard on individual breaches of trust without cracking down across the board.

The Work Foundation (CIPD 2003) suggests that implementing work-life balance requires managers to shift the way that they measure staff, requiring more effort in judging performance and output rather than time spent doing the job. Managers clearly have to learn how to manage at a distance. But all this needs to be supported by the organisational culture:

To thrive, work-life balance needs a supportive organizational culture that has sympathetic values and practices at its core. Arguably, training practitioners have one of the most important and strategic roles in creating and supporting that culture through imaginative and appropriate training programmes. (McCartney 2003, p. 39)

Unfortunately Kodtz *et al.* (2002) found that line managers felt abandoned and did not get the support that they needed.

McCartney goes on to give the example of Ford Europe which provides seminars related to work-life balance topics such as stress management, how individuals should manage their own working arrangements, maternity and returning to work and new fathers' workshops. Also reported is BT, which offers e-learning packages on skills to enable balance, optimising the performance of flexible teams and judging which roles are suitable for home-working.

Limits on access to work-life balance

So far we have treated work-life balance as an option potentially available for a majority of employees, but this is not the case in reality. Felstead *et al.* (2003) reveal that the option to work at home is usually the privilege of the highly educated and/or people at the top of the organisational hierarchy. People in these jobs, they suggest, have considerably more influence over the work processes they are engaged in. They also report that although more women work at home than men, there are more men who have the choice to work at home. Nolan and Wood (2003) also note that work-life balance is not for the lower paid. They report that five per cent of such employees hold more than one job, and usually work in low-paid, low-status jobs in catering and personal services. A similar scene is painted by Polly Toynbee (2003). She also reports that many of these low-paid workers work for agencies and thus are distanced from the ultimate 'employer'. In these circumstances work-life balance policies are unlikely to be available in any case. Even working only for one employer Toynbee reports a hospital porter saying, 'You can't survive, not with a family, unless you do the long, long hours, unless you both work all the hours there are' (p. 59). Felstead *et al.* (2002) highlight an assumption in the work-life balance literature, which portrays working at home as always a 'good thing'. They argue that what is important is the *option* to work at home, as some people work at home doing low-paid unsatisfying jobs with no choice of work location, such conditions not necessarily being conducive to work-life balance.

White *et al.* (2003) argue that organisations are using flexibility to attempt to offset the damage being caused by high-performance work practices, but they argue that flexibility is only enjoyed by a small proportion of the workforce at the moment, and in any case only has a small effect on the problem. They argue for more fundamental changes in working practices with safeguards to protect work-life balance, such as giving teams themselves the responsibility for addressing work-life balance issues when setting output targets for themselves.

> Successful implementation of flexible working is a culture-change programme, one that has relatively distinct goals in terms of values and beliefs, processes and behaviours. Viewing flexible working as culture change places the topic firmly on the strategic agenda. (Janman 2002, p. 17)

Few organisations monitor and evaluate the take-up of work-life balance options or measure their costs and benefits (IRS 2002). However, McCartney (2003) found that in BT the company used an annual survey, webchats, career life-planning discussions, and employee networks to do this.

SUMMARY PROPOSITIONS

31.1 Demographic factors, the changing composition of the workforce, recruitment and retention problems, work intensification and the 24-hour society are all drivers for work-life balance initiatives.

31.2 There is increasing legislation encouraging employers to support work-life balance, but the emphasis is on family-friendly measures, and not on work-life balance for all.

31.3 Work-life balance policies generally provide options around how many hours are worked, exactly when these hours are worked and where they are worked.

31.4 When employees are given some control over their work-life balance they are likely to be more satisfied with work, have greater commitment to work, be more productive and stay longer in the organisation.

31.5 Barriers to work-life balance include understaffing, line manager fears, worries about career damage, lack of a strategic approach to reduced hours working and organisational culture.

GENERAL DISCUSSION TOPICS

1 It is important to measure the costs and benefits of work-life balance. In what ways could this be done?

2 Discuss a range of measures that could be taken in an organisation to help line managers manage work-life balance successfully.

FURTHER READING

CIPD (2005) *Flexible Working: The Implementation Challenge*. London: CIPD.
Examples of good practice in both public and private sector organisations, incorporated with some of the results from the CIPD's 2005 flexible working survey.

Duggan, M. (2003) *Family-Friendly Policies: A handbook for employer and employee*. Welwyn Garden City: Emis Publishing.
This book on family-friendly employment legislation is comprehensive.

IDS (2006) *Flexitime Schemes*, IDS Studies, No. 822. London: IDS.
This IDS HR Study focuses on formal flexitime systems and includes brief cases from 30 well-known organisations. Characteristics of systems described include recording methods, normal hours, bandwidth of flexible hours, lunch breaks, accounting periods and how debit and credit hours are managed.

Kossek, E. and Lambert, S. (eds) (2005) *Work and Life Integration: Organisational, Cultural and Individual Perspectives*. London: Lawrence Erlbaum Associates.
A useful book as a broad, rather than just an individual approach to work-like integration is taken. The book is equally appropriate for practitioners and academic study, as there is a dual focus on theory and practical aspects.

Holder, R. and Bradshaw, B. (2002) *Balancing Work and Life*. London: Dorling Kindersley Ltd.

This is a useful, practical handbook which focuses on the steps readers can take in order to balance their work life with other aspects of their life. The book guides the reader through exercises which help them to recognise what success means for them as a person, understand themselves better, make changes in their work life and sustain these. The emphasis is on issues that are within the individual's control whether or not the organisation has any work-life balance policy or flexible options available.

McColgan, A. (2000) 'Family Friendly Frolics: The Maternity and Parental Leave etc Regulations 1999', *Industrial Law Journal*, Vol. 29, No. 2.

This provides a sharply critical and thought-provoking appraisal of the measures taken by the government. The author shows how the UK has a great deal further to go in terms of legal provision if parents here are to enjoy the kind of rights that are common in many other EU countries.

Rabinowitz, S. (2007) 'Book Reviews: Work, family, and life interfaces: a selective book review', *Career Development International*, Vol. 12, No. 2, pp. 108–28.

Review an interesting selection of eight books published in 2005/6 focusing on the work-life interface giving a flavour of developments in thinking and including multicultural and multidisciplinary perspectives.

REFERENCES

Bibby, A. (2002) 'Home start', *People Management*, Vol. 8, No. 1, 10 January, pp. 36–7.

Boheim, R. and Taylor, M. (2004) 'Actual and preferred working hours', *British Journal of Industrial Relations*, Vol. 42, No. 1, pp. 149–66.

CIPD (2003) 'Managers obstruct flexibility', *People Management*, Vol. 9, No. 18, p. 9.

CIPD (2005) *Flexible Working: Impact and Implementation: An employer survey*. London: CIPD.

Collins, H. (2002) 'Is There a Third Way in Labour Law?', in J. Conaghan, R.M. Fischl and K. Klare (eds), *Labour Law in an Era of Globalization: Transformative Practices and Possibilities*. Oxford: Oxford University Press.

Davidson, E. (2002) 'What lies beneath', *People Management*, Vol. 8, No. 25, pp. 36–7.

Dick, P. (2004) 'Between a rock and a hard place: The dilemmas of managing part-time working in the police service', *Personnel Review*, Vol. 33, No. 3, pp. 302–31.

DWP (2005) *Opportunity Age: meeting the challenges of ageing in the 21st century*, March, at **www.dwp.gov.uk/opportunity_age**.

Edwards, C. and Robinson, O. (2004) 'Evaluating the Business Case for Part-time Working amongst Qualified Nurses', *British Journal of Industrial Relations*, Vol. 42, No. 1, pp. 167–83.

Felstead, A., Jewson, N. and Walters, S. (2003) 'Managerial control of employees working at home', *British Journal of Industrial Relations*, Vol. 41, No. 2, June, pp. 241–64.

Felstead, A., Jewson, N., Phizacklea, A. and Walters, S. (2002) 'The option of working at home: another privilege for the favoured few', *New Technology, Work and Employment*, Vol. 17, No. 3, pp. 204–23.

Glynn, C., Steinberg, I. and McCartney, C. (2002) *Work-life balance: The role of the manager*. Horsham: Roffey Park Institute.

Hall, L. and Atkinson, C. (2006) 'Improving Working Lives: Flexible Working and the role of employee control', *Employee Relations*, Vol. 28, No. 4.

Hogarth, T., Hasluck, C., Pierre, G. with Winterbotham, M. and Vivian, D. (2001) *Work-life Balance 2000: Results from the baseline study*. Research Report 249. London: DfEE.

Holbeche, L. and McCartney, C. (2002) *The Roffey Park Management Agenda*. Horsham: Roffey Park Institute.

IDS (2000) *Work-life balance*, IDS Study, No. 698, November. London: IDS.

IDS (2006) *Flexitime Schemes*, IDS Studies, No. 822. London: IDS.

Institute of Management (2001) *The Quality of Working Life Report*. London: Institute of Management.

IRS (2002) 'Hanging in the balance', *IRS Employment Review*, No. 766, 30 December, pp. 6–11.

Janman, K. (2002) 'How to . . . improve work-life balance in your organisation', *The Guide to Work-life Balance*. London: CIPD.

Kersley, B., Alpin, C., Forth, J., Bryson, A., Bewley, H., Dix, G. and Oxenbridge, S. (2006) *Inside the Workplace: Findings from the 2004 Workplace Employment Relations Survey*. London: Routledge.

Kodz, J., Harper, H. and Dench, S. (2002) *Work-life Balance: Beyond the Rhetoric*, Institute for Employment Studies Report No. 384. Brighton: Institute for Employment Studies.

Lea, R. (2001) 'The Work-Life Balance and all that: The re-regulation of the labour market', IoD policy paper. London: Institute of Directors.

McCartney, C. (2003) 'Addressing the balance', *People Management*, Vol. 9, No. 17, 28 August, p. 39.

MacDermid, S., Lee, M., Buck, M. and Williams, M. (2001) 'Alternative work arrangements among professionals and managers', *Journal of Management Development*, Vol. 20, No. 4, pp. 305–17.

Mahoney, C. (2002) 'Only intensive care can save NHS staff', *in The Guide to Work-life Balance*. London: CIPD.

Murphy, N. (2006) 'Work: Our flexible friend', *IRS Employment Review*, No. 850, 7 July, pp. 8–15.

Nolan, P. and Wood, S. (2003) 'Mapping the future of work', *British Journal of Industrial Relations*, Vol. 41, No. 2, pp. 165–74.

Noon, M. and Blyton, P. (1997) *The Realities of Work*. London: Macmillan Business.

Perry-Smith, J. and Blum, T. (2000) 'Work-family human resource bundles and perceived organizational performance', *Academy of Management Journal*, Vol. 43, pp. 1107–17.

Phillips, L. (2007) 'Add muscle with flexible work', *People Management*, Vol. 13, No. 5, 8 March, p. 10.

Rana, E. (2002a) 'How does it really work in practice?', *in The Guide to Work-life Balance*. London: CIPD.

Rana, E. (2002b) 'Balancing Act Earns UK respect', *in The Guide to Work-life Balance*. London: CIPD.

Saga Magazine (2003) 'See the world and change your life', April, pp. 47–50.

Scott, A. (2007) 'Flexible Working cuts absence', *People Management*, Vol. 13, No. 6, 22 March, p. 15.

Suff, R. (2005) 'Extending working life', *IRS Employment Review*, No. 838, pp. 45–8.

Toynbee, P. (2003) *Hard Work: Life in low-pay Britain*. London: Bloomsbury.

Visser, F. and Williams, L. (2006) *Work-life Balance: Rhetoric vs Reality*. London: The Work Foundation and Unison.

Walton, P. and Gaskell, L. (2001) 'Pliable Alternatives', *People Management*, Vol. 7, No. 6, 22 March, pp. 26–31.

White, M., Hill, S., McGovern, P., Mills, C. and Smeaton, D. (2003) ' "High performance" management practices, working hours and work-life balance', *British Journal of Industrial Relations*, Vol. 41, No. 2, June, pp. 175–95.

LEGAL CASES

Hardys & Hansons Plc v. *Lax* [2005] EWCA Civ 846, 7 July 2005.

An extensive range of additional materials, including multiple choice questions, answers to questions and links to useful websites can be found on the Human Resource Management Companion Website at **www.pearsoned.co.uk/torrington**.

CHAPTER 32

THE CHANGING HR FUNCTION

THE OBJECTIVES OF THIS CHAPTER ARE TO:

1 Identify and explain current models relating to the roles and structure of the HR function

2 Explore the extent to which the HR function operates strategically

3 Examine the extent of outsourcing and shared services and the benefits and drawbacks of these approaches

4 Explore the role of line managers in HRM

5 Debate and critique the current developments in HR roles and structures

The personnel/HR function has developed considerably since its earliest welfare role, through a range of different incarnations. There is a long history of the specialist function analysing its role in the organisation and promoting the way in which such roles need to develop in order for the function to gain greater power and credibility. Much emphasis has been placed therefore on a strategic role. If HR is strategic to business success (Boxall and Purcell 2003) then HR needs to be a strategic player and the role of business strategist will be a key role for HR specialists in the future (Cleland *et al.* 2000).

Analysing HR roles has been a useful way to reflect what is going on in the function and how it is changing, but sometimes roles and role structures are used in the normative sense of what the function should be doing and where it should be aiming.

The function is again in a period of key change and this is reflected by the attention given to this topic in journals. For example a whole issue was devoted to this topic in *Human Resource Management Journal* (2001), in *Human Resource Management* (2005), and in *Personnel Review* (2006).

ANALYSIS OF HR ROLES AND STRUCTURES

One earlier well-known example of the analysis of HR roles is by Tyson and Fell (1985) who identified three roles using a construction management metaphor: architect; clerk of works and contract negotiator, but perhaps the most frequently quoted is Storey's (1992) four roles (handmaiden, regulator, changemaker and adviser) which he identified at the threshold of the move from personnel management to HRM.

In 1997 Ulrich proposed an HR role set which has had a significant influence on the way in which HR has subsequently been structured in the UK, and elsewhere. On the basis of work with leading-edge organisations in the USA he proposed four HR roles, using the metaphors of employee champion; administrative expert; change agent; and strategic partner. He further identified the summary role of business partner, explaining that HR fulfils this role if the four roles above are all effectively achieved. Ulrich's four 1997 roles are as follows:

- **Strategic partner** – aligning HR and business strategy, identifying HR priorities through organisational diagnosis.

- **Administrative expert** – the traditional role of designing the firm's infrastructure to enable the design and delivery of HR processes, producing administrative efficiency.

- **Employee champion** – concerned with the day-to-day needs of employees, linking employee contribution to business success, and increasing commitment and competence. Involves personal contact with employees and provides a means for employees to voice their opinions, and helps maintain the psychological contract.

- **Change agent** – involved in transformation and cultural change such as identifying and framing problems and working to solve them.

One of the fundamental features of Ulrich's approach is his view that HR effectiveness can only be achieved if all business needs relating to HR are met, and therefore all roles are fulfilled. Thus, Ulrich argues that HR must deliver on both an administrative level and a strategic level. This has been echoed elsewhere, with comments that operational HR excellence is an essential precursor for the involvement of HR professionals at a strategic level (e.g. Caldwell 2003; CIPD 2006a). This is a clear change of thinking from the earlier views which exhorted HR to move from administration to strategy, as in the characterisation of HRM as being in opposition to traditional personnel management (*see*, for example, Storey 1992) It has been argued that Ulrich's model has been the biggest reconception of the HR function since the personnel versus HRM debate and a cursory glance at the advertisements in *People Management* will show the influence that it has had on job titles and the apparent structure of the HR function. However whilst making the case for strength from the combining of roles, Ulrich does acknowledge the paradox created by trying to fulfil all roles, such as representing employee needs at the same time as implementing a management agenda.

On the basis of further research Ulrich and Brockbank (2005a, 2005b) provided a view of the way in which HR roles had evolved since 1997, and this new analysis focuses on what an HR professional has to do to create value. In the new synthesis of roles, most of the roles have new titles. These are: Employee advocate; Human capital developer; Strategic partner; Functional expert; and the compound role of Leader. However, the roles reported in 2005 can be linked back to the earlier model, as shown in Table 32.1.

Roles in Ulrich and Brockbank (2005b)	Explanation of 2005 role	Equivalent role in Ulrich (1997)
Employee advocate	Caring for, listening to, understanding and responding to employee needs, covering issues such as grievances, the impact of strategy on employees, equality, diversity, health and safety, discipline. All these are played out in a context of the realities of the firm and the performance standards required of individuals.	Employee champion
Human capital developer	Based on the premise that people are a critical asset of the organisation and thus need to be developed proactively with a focus on maximising their potential and contribution in the future. Such human capital developers would be located in Centres of HR Expertise, and often act as coaches working on behaviour and attitudes.	Employee champion
Strategic partner	Multiple dimensions including business expert, change agent, knowledge manager and consultant	Combination of Strategic partner and Change agent
Functional expert	Application of the HR body of knowledge through HR practices. There are two categories of HR practices, those for which HR has direct responsibility (such as recruitment) and those for which responsibility is indirect (such as communications). Some practices are delivered through administrative efficiency and others through policies and interventions.	An expansion of Administrative expert
Leader	Leading the HR function, establishing the function's agenda within the firm and acting as a role model demonstrating the importance of HR in the way they lead their own function. Also contributing to the leadership of the organisation. This role requires that the functions of the four roles above are met.	Similar to the Business partner role in that it requires the functioning of all other roles, but goes beyond this.

Table 32.1 Comparison of HR roles in the Ulrich and Brockbank (2005b) model and the Ulrich (1997) model

We can make some interesting observations about how roles have evolved, in Ulrich's view, over the period. For example the Employee advocate role is now a single clear role rather than being combined with people development as in the old Employee champion role. This reflects the recent imperative to explore and understand the employee voice and employee well-being and a recognition that these are important for the individual and the organisation and were underrepresented in earlier thinking and practice in HRM.

The Human capital developer role reflects increasing attention to the management and development of human capital and the role of HR in this. It is resonant of role titles, both academic and professional, with 'human capital' in the title and in other analyses of HR roles such as the 'human capital steward' in Lengnick-Hall and Lengnick-Hall's analysis, 2003. We discuss the concept of human capital in more detail in Chapter 2 and in Chapter 33.

Whilst one of the key and differentiating features of the 1997 roles was the prominence of the Administrative expert role, in that it was of equal value to other roles, it is interesting to see that administration has now been subsumed in a role reflecting functional expertise. This may reflect a further distancing from administrative aspects as these are outsourced.

Note that while these new roles have been published much of the debate in professional journals and in academia still relates to both the original 1997 roles and the new roles. This is due partly to publishing time-lags, but also to the huge impact that the original model has had, and reflects the gradual process by which organisations absorb and implement new ideas.

ACTIVITY 32.1

Using a sample (say, between 3 and 6) of the most recent issues of *People Management* analyse the job advertisements in order to answer the following questions:

1 How do the job titles quoted compare with the roles identified by Ulrich (1997) and Ulrich and Brockbank (2005b)?

2 Select those advertisements containing job titles much as 'Strategic partner' or 'Business partner' or 'HR partner' (or equivalents). What are the key objectives and job content for each of these roles? What types of variation are there between the job titles and within each job title?

3 To what extent do salaries for 'Strategic partner' and other HR roles differ, and to what extent do they vary within 'Strategic partner' type roles?

4 Using a similar sample of magazine issues from 2003 for comparison, how have job titles and objectives/content changed overall?

What has emerged from Ulrich's work, much of which is suggested in the 1997 text, is a restructuring of the HR function into what is often referred to as the three-legged structure. This structure comprises:

- **strategic/business roles** working with senior managers and business leaders on business issues, strategic organisational change and design;
- **shared service centres, outsourcing contractors, and HR intranet support,** all focusing on administrative and routine issues; and
- **centres of HR expertise** providing specialist support to the service centres, providing expert advice and being involved in the design of HR policy and activities.

There is evidence that in many large organisations (*see*, for example, Robinson 2006) this structure has replaced the integrated model where one HR team carried out this full range of roles. The CIPD is beginning a research project to find out how widely adopted this structure is and what evidence there is of effectiveness.

HR STRATEGIC ROLE

There is much evidence that the strategic or business partner role is the one which has been most attractive to organisations. For example an examination of advertisements for HR posts in *People Management* at the time of writing shows that around 25–30 per cent of job titles advertised are Business Partner or Strategic Partner, compared with early 2003 when these titles were rarely, if at all, used. HR needs to be credible to offer a strategic contribution and it has been suggested that such credibility needs to come from being involved in a wider range of business agendas, and there is some evidence of this happening (*see* the Window on practice that follows).

WINDOW ON PRACTICE

Broader business involvement for HR professionals

Robinson (2006) reports on the first stage of a CIPD-sponsored research project which aims to explore the changing face of the HR function. One part of this first stage was to convene a panel of academics and senior HR professionals from the Royal Bank of Scotland, Dell, PwC, Centrica, Standard Chartered Bank, Barclays and Diesel. HR professionals agreed that HR needs to be involved in a wider range of business agendas, such as branding, ethics, risk management and corporate social responsibility (CSR) as well as change, and that these would be central to the HR of the future, as would involvement in creating 'employer of choice' status and selling the customer brand.

Source: Summarised from V. Robinson (2006) 'Three legs good?',
People Management, Vol. 12, No. 21, 26 October, pp. 62–4.

It is worth noting however that the term business partner is often used as a synonym for strategic partner, and used interchangeably (Francis and Keegan 2006; Robinson 2006), although this is not what Ulrich was suggesting. In addition there is further evidence that different organisations are interpreting the role in a variety of ways. For example Pickard (2004), suggesting that business partners are emerging as the dominant model, explains how in Vauxhall 'partners are working with the business, developing close relationships with line managers and helping to solve issues'. In other organisations partners are roles of a more strategic nature, providing consultancy to senior managers and becoming involved in the wide range of business issues, as above, and in the Prudential example quoted by Pickard in the same article.

In a local government context Griffiths (2005) reports an Employers' Organisation survey which found that 68 per cent of senior HR managers had a strategic partner role as their primary role; however the survey report suggests reasons for this high figure, one of which is that there are varied interpretations of that role. Furthermore Truss *et al.* (2002) identify ambivalence over the precise meaning of the word 'strategic'.

WINDOW ON PRACTICE

HR specialists' perceptions of their roles

The 2003 CIPD survey (CIPD 2003) asked HR specialists about their perceptions of their primary role:

- 33 per cent saw their primary role as strategic partner (and 56 per cent saw this as their primary role in the future),

- 28 per cent saw their primary role as change agents (and 30 per cent saw this as their primary role in the future),

- 24 per cent saw their primary role as administrative experts (and 4 per cent saw this as their primary role in the future),

- 12 per cent saw their primary role as employee champion (and 6 per cent saw this as their primary role in the future).

CIPD (2003) *HR Survey: Where we are, where we're heading.* London: CIPD.

Articles and books abound on how to become a strategic partner (*see*, for example, Goodge *et al.* 2004; and Reilly and Williams 2006), with other roles seemingly down-played. One interpretation of this is that the HR function is finally gaining prized strategic involvement giving it credibility and power in organisations.

The focus on HR's strategic involvement was a fundamental part of the move towards HRM from personnel management. However recent prescriptive literature appears to display similar levels of exhortation, and research suggests that while some progress may have been made towards strategic involvement there remains a wide gap between rhetoric and reality.

In addition to the lack of clarity about the nature of the strategic role, another problem with assessing the extent of strategic involvement is that many surveys on the HR roles are completed by HR specialists alone, and it has often been demonstrated that others in the organisation will not necessarily share the view of the HR specialist on this, and other topics. A recent example of this is a survey which included an assessment of the HR strategic role in India, where Bhatnagar and Sharma (2005) found that line managers and HR managers differed significantly in their assessment of HR's strategic partner role, with HR managers having a much more positive view of their involvement in this capacity.

Caldwell's (2004) interviewees were mostly optimistic about the growing links between HR policy and business strategy, but this rarely was sufficient for them to be defined as a 'business partner', even though 16 of the 24 respondents were represented in the board-room. The general view was that HR people are at the implementation end of strategy. We must therefore question the extent to which changes in role titles actually reflect changes in roles carried out.

WINDOW ON PRACTICE

HR partners: A worldwide picture

Griffiths reports on a worldwide survey of 1,057 HR professionals carried out by Mercer HR Consulting. The survey covered Australia, Canada, the USA, 11 countries in Asia, 16 in Europe and 15 in Latin America, and found that becoming a business partner is a priority across the world, with the greatest emphasis on this in Europe. The driver for this change appeared to be the need for HR to add greater value to the organisation. There was a general recognition that more business talent was needed in HR, in particular business understanding and cross-functional skills. The survey found that HR specialists spent half as much time on strategic partnership working as they desired, and twice as much time on administration as they desired. When commenting on the survey, Diez (a Partner at Mercer Consulting) warned that the HR function had to prove itself with high performance in terms of HR services before it could persuade chief executives that it should be a business partner. However Europe and Asia were found to be behind the rest of the world in their plans to restructure processes and make use of e-HR. Only 42–43 per cent of organisations in these countries had such plans, compared with 93 per cent of organisations in Latin America and 89 per cent in Australia.

Source: J. Griffiths (2004a) 'Partnership drives worldwide change',
People Management, Vol. 10, No. 17, 2 September, p. 12.

The extent to which the HR function becomes involved in both organisational and human resource strategy development is dependent on a range of factors, the most often quoted being whether the most senior HR person is a member of the board of directors. The ultimate in strategic involvement is the presence of an HR board director and this has previously been used as a proxy for strategic involvement. Sparkes (2001) identifies a key role for the HR director as promoting the connection between organisational strategy, culture and people strategy. He maintains that being an HR director means that 'we can almost guarantee that a human element is built into everything strategic from the start' (p. 45).

There is some historical evidence to suggest that HR board membership has increased and surveys suggest that around three-fifths of larger organisations have an HR director (*see*, for example, Hall and Torrington 1998), although some surveys indicate lower percentages. However we found, as did Truss *et al.* (2002), that strategic HR roles can come and go depending on the context. Recent examples of HR directorships doing just this include Arcadia (Topshop, Burtons and other high street names), where the HR director for over 10 years resigned and will not be replaced by another HR director, with no reasons being given (*People Management* 2006d); and Thorntons who scrapped the HR director post believing it to be a luxury the company could not afford (Griffiths 2004b). Griffiths (2005) quotes Warner (the corporate director of people and property at Hertfordshire County Council) who says that HR has dropped off the top table in recent times, but who also suggests that HR should not have an automatic right to be on the board, and that the function has to earn its place.

Saratoga, the human capital metrics business of PwC, in its *Key Trends in Human Capital Survey 2006* found little evidence of an increasing strategic influence for HR: in fact the number of HR board directors of FTSE 100 companies had fallen to six, and Phelps, the partner in HR services at PwC, said one of the reasons behind the trend was the lack of skilled, strategically minded HR professionals (*People Management* 2006b).

There is evidence that HR managers have to prove themselves before being given a seat on the board (*see*, for example, Hall and Torrington 1998) so building key competencies is essential. Barney and Wright (1998) suggest that one of the real reasons why HR professionals are not involved in strategic planning is that they are not displaying the required competencies. This continues to be an issue.

It is suggested that HR managers need to use business and financial language; describe the rationale for HR activities in terms of added value; use strategic thinking, act as a business manager first and an HR manager second; appoint line managers into the HR function; concentrate on priorities as defined by the business; understand the business they work in, display business acumen, use relationship building and networking skills, and offer well-developed change-management skills that can be used immediately

Sheehan (2005) argues that the business expertise and credibility of the senior HR specialist can either support or prevent strategic HR integration. Vicky Wright (President of the CIPD) considers that HR will never get to the strategy table unless it delivers at a basic operational level, and identifies the most common problem as HR's lack of business understanding. She also points to the need to link business priorities with the HR strategy agenda (using creativity and innovation), and to develop personal competencies to ensure that they can interact successfully with bosses and peers at board level. At a 2006 CIPD seminar three themes emerged when HR directors talked about their relationship with their chief executives:

building their confidence and interpersonal skills; preparedness to take accountability; use of analysis and information to support their argument. (Wright 2006)

In our own research we found (Hall and Torrington 1998), as did Kelly and Gennard (1996), that board membership was generally identified as desirable, for as Sparkes (2001) suggests, it improves HR's understanding of the business context in which HR strategies need to be developed and implemented. However, board membership does not guarantee the involvement of specialists in strategy, and it is not necessarily seen as essential to strategic involvement. This is perhaps why currently very little attention is given to assessing the percentage of organisations with an HR director.

Other factors influencing the role of the HR function in strategic concerns include the overall philosophy of the organisation towards the value of its people, its culture, the mindset of the chief executive, and the working relationship between the chief executive and the most senior HR person.

These influences are not particularly easy to manipulate, but what the HR function *can* do is look for opportunities in these areas, and *use* them. Building a good working relationship with the chief executive is critical. For example Stiles (2001) confirms the power of the chief executive in selecting who should be appointed to the board.

Guest and King (2001) argue that, as senior managers and board members appear to have limited knowledge of research linking people management and performance, there is an opportunity for enthusiastic HR managers/directors to feed new ideas to chief executives. Increasingly, HR managers need to become closer to their accounting colleagues. In addition, the function needs to prepare itself by thinking strategically, identifying a functional mission and strategy and involving line management in the development and implementation of human resource strategy.

 The extent to which the HR function makes a strategic contribution to the organisation is the focus of Case 32.1, 'People issues are central to the success of any organisation', on this book's companion website, **www.pearsoned.co.uk/torrington**.

OUTSOURCING HR

HR administration, for example pensions, payroll and recruitment, has typically been outsourced. But more specialist aspects have been subject to outsourcing too, such as training and legal work. IDS (2003) argues that the delivery channels for outsourcing HR administration involve e-HR and HR service centres. We will deal with these separately, while recognising that there may be some overlap in approach.

The drivers for outsourcing HR are frequently quoted as reducing costs and improving service delivery. Outsourcing appears to encourage the measurement of the value of HR, and IDS (2003) suggests that this comes about through the need for service-level agreements and key performance indicators with a greater focus on customer satisfaction. Cooke *et al.* (2005) in the USA identify a wide range of benefits from outsourcing such as allowing a firm to concentrate on its core business; gaining from the specialist supplier's economies of scale and learning from them; shifting the burden of risk and enabling greater numerical flexibility; and the ability to keep costs down due to competitive tendering processes. Outsourcing has also been introduced as a vehicle for effecting changes that would be hard to implement internally. For example in large organisations outsourcing has been used to bring different parts of the organisation together to reduce costs, apply common standards and share best practice (*see*, for example, Pickard 2002), and to provide access to innovative IT solutions. A further advantage that is claimed is that the internal HR function can now concentrate on driving the direction of HR rather than carry out more mundane tasks.

WINDOW ON PRACTICE

HR outsourcing at the BBC

Pickard (2006) provides details of the HR outsourcing deal between the BBC and Capita. The deal is worth £100m and involves the transfer of around 260 staff from the BBC to Capita, and is expected to save the BBC £50m. The contract is part of a wider transformation of HR at the BBC involving more than 200 redundancies, and focused on making the function more strategic and on providing better value for money. The deal is Capita's first end-to-end HR outsourcing project, but it has already held contracts for single functions such as payroll. The services to be outsourced are:

- recruitment
- pay and benefits, but not pensions
- assessment and outplacement and some training and development
- HR administration
- relocation
- occupational health
- disability access services

HR remaining in the BBC has been centralised and includes pensions and training and development; a Business Partner model has been introduced in the divisions.

Bectu (the broadcasting union) has opposed the outsourcing deal. Most of the staff affected are administrative staff and the relocation to Capita involves some staff moving to Belfast from London, although others will move to different locations in London (depending on their involvement in specific tasks). Capita has said that those whose new jobs are in Belfast, but who are unwilling to move, will be offered alternative jobs in Capita, but not necessarily related to BBC work.

Source: J. Pickard (2006) 'Conflicting Schedule', *People Management*, Vol. 12, No. 5, 9 March, pp. 14–15.

Unilever grants £1bn contract

The outsourcing contract awarded by Unilver to Accenture is the world's most extensive one to date. It affects 40 per cent of its global HR function of 3,300 staff.

Globally, 1,200 jobs will be lost, 250 of these in the UK. (The losses will be dealt with through redeployment, transfers, natural wastage and voluntary redundancy.)

The seven-year deal will affect 2,000,000 staff in 100 countries and covers HR administration and learning services. The aim is to create a simpler, more agile global function.

Source: Summarised from *People Management* (2006e) 'Unilever grants £1bn contract', Vol. 12, No. 12, 15 June, p. 10.

BT renews Accenture deal for a decade

BT renewed its HR outsourcing contract with Accenture after much speculation that it would move to another contractor. The contract is for 10 years and is worth £306m covering 87,000 staff. Towards the end of the original contract BT and Accenture acknowledged that they had problems with clarification of responsibilities and with communications, but have now developed a new model for managing the relationship, and key issues have been written into the new contract.

Source: *People Management* (2005b) 'BT renews Accenture deal for a decade', Vol. 11, No. 3, 10 February, p. 8.

However, time is needed to select and develop a relationship and trust with a service provider. Rippin and Dawson (2001) also identify the importance of fit with the service provider and warn that organisations choosing to outsource in order to save costs should not expect immediate returns. Outsourcing the whole of HR (sometimes called end-to-end outsourcing) is also a very different proposition from outsourcing differentiated activities, which has been happening in an ad hoc manner for a much longer time. Blackburn and Darwen Borough Council, for example, has outsourced all its HR to Capita, including strategic HR (IDS 2003), which is the one part that most organisations retain in-house. Main (2006) suggests the lack of success of some outsourcing experiences is due to the fact that outsourcing is seen as a way to get rid of a problem (such as cost and inadequate computer systems) and the view that once activities are outsourced management responsibility for them ends. He suggests all this has hampered the development of end-to-end outsourcing, and that, as an alternative, companies have gone for shared service centres and have outsourced separate HR functions such as training, administration and payroll to separate providers.

ACTIVITY 32.2

We noted that outsourcing the whole of the HR function is a different proposition from outsourcing some specific aspects. In the context of your own organisation, or one that you are familiar with:

1 If you were to outsource some specific aspects of HR, what would they be and why would you choose them?

Or

What aspects of HR are already outsourced, how effective has this proved to be and why?

2 If you were to outsource the whole HR function what reactions would you anticipate from employees and line managers, why do you think they would react like this and what could be done to support them through this change?

Or

If your organisation has already outsourced the entire HR function how effective has this proved to be and why?

Some organisations have clearly experienced advantages from outsourcing, although many of these are based in the USA and there is a question as to the extent to which such an approach should be applied in the same way in the UK. Hammond (2002), using survey evidence, reports that firms in the UK are resisting outsourcing. He argues that BP experienced only limited success when it outsourced to Exault, and that outsourcing is a different proposition for such big companies as opposed to smaller organisations. This same survey found that managers have a number of fears about outsourcing HR, such as loss of control, loss of the personal touch and doubts about the quality and commitment of external staff. However, the research reported was commissioned by Northgate Information Solutions and this fact needs to be taken into account when interpreting the results, as this company has a product to sell. John Hofmeister, director of HR at the Royal Dutch/Shell group, attacks outsourcing as leading to the corrosion of HR departments, and he argues that only high levels of internal HR staffing can lead to and maintain high levels of HR practices (*People Management* 2002). In a slightly different vein Gratton (2003) argues that outsourcing combined with other trends such as devolution fragments the HR function, and she identifies a growing alienation between different providers (outsourcing agencies, line managers and remaining specialists in the HR function). She argues that HR would provide greater added value as a unified whole than when broken down into different fragments. Gratton proposed four mechanisms through which the function can be integrated to provide greater added value. The four mechanisms are: operational integration (e.g. using standardised technology to present a consistent front to the employee); intellectual integration (through a shared knowledge base); social integration (meaning that the function has a clear sense of where it is going and there is collective buy in to performance); and emotional integration (using bonds of friendship and reciprocity and a sense of shared identify and meaning). One of the major challenges is for the HR function to pull together the separate outsourced and segmented elements (CIPD 2006a).

Such outsourcing has been dogged with many problems, to the extent that some organisations have brought HR back in-house (*see*, for example, CIPD 2006a), and Brockett (2006b) quotes Marcia Roberts (Chief Executive of the Recruitment and Employment Confederation) as saying that as a potential outsourcing agency for recruitment 'you often find yourself replying to tenders and dealing not with HR but with the purchasing department – which is more likely to be concentrating solely on cost'. In terms of possible adverse consequences Cooke *et al.* (2005) identify the potential loss of skill, knowledge and capacity, a reduction in the quality of services, the loss of employee morale, short-term disruption and discontinuity, and damage to long-term competitiveness. It has been suggested by a senior HR practitioner that outsourcing is 'not a threat for the function or the business, but a threat to the individual' (CIPD 2006a, p. 5).

In spite of these concerns, it is predicted that outsourcing will continue to increase, in particular outsourcing overseas – sometimes referred to as 'offshoring', although in some cases this form of outsourcing may be to wholly owned subsidiaries or may be the movement of an internal service centre (Crabb 2003). India is a favoured destination but Eastern Europe is also popular. However, cultural and legal differences will inevitably restrict the range of activities that can be successfully outsourced in this way. The popularity of the outsourcing idea is underlined by the fact that the CIPD now runs a course entitled 'Outsourcing HR' to help specialists understand the procurement process. According to a recent survey (CIPD 2006c) there is only a minor interest in offshoring HR compared with other functions, with just seven per cent claiming to have done this or to be planning to do this.

WINDOW ON PRACTICE

HR's role in offshoring

Whilst we have noted the lack of interest in offshoring HR tasks, support within an organisation for general outsourcing can bring major HR challenges. A survey conducted by CIPD in 2006 (CIPD 2006c) identified HR support for offshoring as consulting with unions, workforce planning, employee redeployment, contributing to the internal communications strategy and training. The survey found that in less than 60 per cent of organisations was the HR function involved in the strategic decision to offshore, and even in planning specific requirements of projects, the HR function was only included in 70 per cent of organisations. Problems generally experienced in offshoring, as reported in this survey, included negative impact on staff morale (55 per cent); managerial control becoming more difficult (48 per cent); the possibility of UK job losses (44 per cent); language problems (33 per cent) and risk of disruption to supply (24 per cent). These issues clearly have implications for the work of the HR function as well as having a relevance to the offshoring of the HR function or part of it.

CIPD (2006c) *Offshoring and the role of HR*. London: CIPD.

Key issues for implementing the offshoring of HR include a careful choice of partner so that there is sufficient fit, clear performance specifications, IT system compatibility, reassurance regarding the impact on HR staff, line managers and employees, promotion of new arrangements, good contract management and monitoring of performance.

WINDOW ON PRACTICE

How to manage an HR outsourcing contract

Main (2006) identifies eight key points:

1 Sign the contract but do not abdicate the responsibility

2 Develop core competence in contract management

3 Ensure board-level support

4 Select a partner that works to understand you

5 Establish a collaborative relationship

6 Consider setting up the contract as a joint venture

7 Understand what you currently get out of HR

8 Retain ownership of the HR policy and strategy

Source: Summarised from C. Main (2006) 'How to manage an outsourcing contract', *People Management*, Vol. 12, No. 13, 29 June, pp. 44–5.

Case 32.2 on this book's companion website, **www.pearsoned.co.uk/torrington**, focuses on HR outsourcing.

HR SHARED SERVICES

Some organisations argue that a better alternative to outsourcing is to use an HR service centre or shared service centre (*see*, for example, Pickard 2002). Shared service centres are sometimes referred to as partnership service centres or insourcing, depending on the circumstances. For example the Window on practice shows how Rotherham Borough Council has entered into a strategic partnership with BT.

WINDOW ON PRACTICE

Rotherham Brought Together (RBT)

IDS (2003) reports how Rotherham Borough Council and BT created RBT. RBT is responsible for HR administration and payroll, the management of IT functions, procurement, customer contact and revenues and budgets.

Five hundred council staff have been seconded to RBT on their existing terms and conditions, and new appointees will be on the same conditions. For its part BT has invested heavily in RBT, and will initially take the profit from the operation. However, after a certain level of profit has been achieved the profit will be shared with Rotherham BC.

RBT includes an integrated HR/payroll system, self-service HR through an intranet, and an HR service centre to deal with transactional and operational HR issues. The first port of call is intended to be the intranet and then the service centre, but for some issues such as discipline and grievance a specialist adviser will be made available.

Alongside the creation of RBT line managers have been given more responsibility for HR, and HR staff have been centralised, although some senior HR staff remain in Rotherham BC with a remit which includes strategy, policy, OD, and culture change, among other issues.

There is a plan for RBT to take on work from other clients in the future.

Source: Summarised from IDS (2003) *Outsourcing HR administration*, IDS Study Plus, Spring. London: IDS.

London bodies plan shared services

The Greater London Authority (GLA) and the Metropolitan Police (Met) are both planning shared service centres.

The Met plan to open their first centre in 2008 and it is designed to deal with front-line queries and to provide self-updating access and HR services for both managers and employees. Such centres would be backed up by Centres of Excellence.

In the GLA the service centres are intended to group transactional functions such as payroll, pensions, absence management and occupational health, an approach already used by Transport for London. A framework is being developed for greater integration across the GLA group.

Source: J. Brockett (2006a) 'London bodies plan shared services', *People Management*, Vol. 12, No. 11, 1 June, p. 10.

MoD shares HR operations

The Ministry of Defence (MoD) has set up a dedicated in-house agency called the People, Pay and Pensions Agency (PPPA) to act as a shared services operation dealing with transactional HR issues. There will be two shared service centres, in Manchester and Bath, and they will cover payroll, absence management, discipline services, health and welfare. This covers 80,000 non-military staff and It is expected to save £283m over the next 10 years.

The move is intended to support attempts to devolve more HR responsibility to line managers, and to enable the professional HR function to concentrate more on strategic issues. The strategic HR team is made up of Business Partners and a core strategic team focusing on such areas as talent management. In parallel with these changes the overall HR function is being reduced from 3,000 HR managers at the end of 2004 to 1,700 by 2008.

Source: R. Manocha (2006) 'MoD shares HR operations', *People Management*, Vol. 12, No. 5, 9 March, p. 10.

Shared services save RBS £11m

In 2004 the Royal Bank of Scotland (RBS) launched a shared services HR system to support 130,000 employees in eight divisions. The system is designed to allow managers and employees access to HR services on-line, and the bank claims to have saved £11m in each year of its operation. The on-line system was designed to replace paper and telephone transactions, but was introduced with a 'soft launch' where other methods of contact were allowed alongside the on-line self-service method. The next step is to introduce compulsory self-service by agreeing dates when other transaction channels are cut off.

Source: *People Management* (2006c) 'Shared services save RBS £11m', Vol. 12, No. 5, 9 March, p. 13.

IDS (2003) suggests that developing an HR service centre is often the linchpin in a company's drive to achieve a more efficient form of HR delivery, and suggests that this is primarily achieved by streamlining and centralising routine HR processes and transactions. In addition such a service centre is usually the primary point of reference for line managers with HR queries. The benefits IDS identifies are savings from lower transaction costs, the removal of unneeded duplication, a more consistent HR approach across the whole of a company and an HR service which is more customer focused and more responsive to business needs.

Service centres may be HR centres or may be a shared centre with other functions, such as IT or finance. Other terms used are 'HR call centre' or 'client centre'. In terms of operation many centres have staff based in the 'back office' dealing with administration and transactions, and different staffing for the 'front office' where enquiries from line managers are handled. Alternatively staff may be organised in teams by specialist function or client group (IDS 2003). Staff at the service centre would have electronic access to personal employee details and HR policies and so on.

One of the advantages of such centres is the metrics that can be derived to assess their performance. Examples are call waiting time, call count, call length, time taken to resolve queries, accuracy and satisfaction measures from users. There is usually a system of escalation where queries can be fed up to the next level if the original call centre operator cannot resolve them, so for example there would be access to a functional specialist for non-routine or complex queries.

One form of shared services is to have an online or e-HR self-service system, as in the RBS example in the Window on practice above. Such systems may offer cost saving advantages, but can pose special problems of their own inducing feelings of remoteness, dehumanisation and lack of customer friendliness. *People Management* (2006a) reports on a study by Roffey Park Institute which investigated line manager perceptions of e-HR. The two negative aspects reported most frequently were that line managers felt they had insufficient training on the system, and that employees were penalised when they did not keep their records up to date. Managers also felt that they spent too much time on HR administration and that on-line help available was of poor quality. We explore different aspects of e-HR in more detail in Chapter 33.

WINDOW ON PRACTICE

HR service centres: task limits

Recruitment administration is a task that a service centre would be likely to take on, and IDS (2001) provides an example of how this would work in practice. IDS suggests that:

- Service centre staff would:
    - Place advertisements
    - Issue application forms
    - Receive application forms
    - Deal with candidate management
    - Provide information for shortlisting and interviewing
    - Arrange interviews and assessment dates
    - Prepare and send offer and rejection letters
    - Draw up and send out contracts
    - Request references
    - Send out starter packs
    - Enter new starters on records system
    - Monitor equal opportunities

- Line managers, perhaps supported by a local HR adviser, would:
  - Determine the need for the vacancy
  - Confirm/draw up job and person specifications
  - Define selection and assessment processes
  - Shortlist
  - Carry out interviews
  - Make the final selection decision
  - Co-determine the salary package

Source: Summarised from IDS (2001) *HR Service Centres*, IDS Study, No. 707, April.

The problems with the service centre structure are that local knowledge and business solutions may be lost in the changeover, many low-level administrative roles are created with little potential for career development and there may be an obsession with measurement at the expense of service delivery.

THE ROLE OF LINE MANAGERS IN HR

The literature has for some time been replete with articles about the decentralisation and devolution of HR management as methods of integrating HR activities with day-to-day line management. We use the word devolution here to mean the reallocation of HR tasks to managers outside the HR function, keeping this separate from the relocation of HR specialists to lower levels of the business, in order to work closely with line managers in specific departments or sections in the organisation (which we consider to be decentralisation). Here we concentrate on the line taking ownership of HR activities, enabling HR specialists to act as a consultant, coach, facilitator and strategic partner, which has been identified as a key plank of HRM, being different from a traditional personnel management approach (*see*, for example, Storey 1992). Such devolution of operational day-to-day HR tasks has been described by Hope-Hailey *et al.* (2005) as devolving the employee champion role.

The advantages of this approach to restructuring HR activities have been identified as allowing HR specialists to focus on strategic rather than operational concerns, and a strengthening of the relationship between the employee and his or her manager, resulting in a more positive management approach to employee performance. The importance of the role of the line manager in delivering HR is well documented, especially by Hutchinson and Purcell (2004), as in their research they found that first-line manager behaviour is:

the most important factor explaining the variation in both job satisfaction and job discretion, or the choice that people have over how they do their jobs. It is also one of the most important factors in developing organizational commitment. (p. ix)

Hutchinson and Purcell suggest that line managers bring HR policies to life, and in the extract quoted above show how line managers have a direct impact on employee performance.

However, the difficulties of devolving HR activities to first-line managers have also been consistently highlighted. In our research, we found that implementation was difficult, sometimes being described as a game of tennis where although there was a deliberate policy to devolve HR activities, and managers were encouraged to take them on, these often bounced straight back to HR specialists (Hall and Torrington 1998). The idea that line managers need to take on more day-to-day HR activities has been countered by line managers' lack of skills and interest in this. For example Hope-Hailey *et al.* (2005) on the basis of their research found that line managers neither were motivated nor had the ability to take on people management responsibilities. Interestingly McConville (2006) in the context of the NHS, the Armed Forces and the Fire Services, found that middle managers wanted to be proactive in HR, were committed to it, and exceeded their job requirements to carry out HR activities, but their already substantial workload created the greatest barrier. Caldwell (2004) found that managers resisted taking full ownership of HR and conversely HR professionals wanted to retain control over HR policy. His interviewees were generally reluctant to take devolution 'too far', as ultimately too much devolution may result in the HR role itself being devalued. Our evidence supports this, that HR specialists were keen to hand over the responsibility for day-to-day HR activities, but were less keen to hand over authority for them and the associated budgets. A number of aspects of line manager involvement in HR activities have been identified as problematic, including the lack of consistency of HR decisions and lack of integration resulting in more difficulties in implementing HR strategy.

Maxwell and Watson (2007), on the basis of their investigation into line manager and HR manager perspectives of line management involvement in HR in Hilton Hotels, propose three types of line manager buy-in which are key to their active involvement in HR activities. These are:

- a conceptual understanding of the reasons for their involvement;
- the ability to implement these activities effectively through a clear HR role and having sufficient capability; and
- belief that their involvement in HR is valuable.

Interestingly the authors also found a general lack of shared understanding between line managers and HR specialists about the role of line managers in HR, and some indications that the more similar the perceptions of HR and line managers, the better the hotel performance, whereas the more divergent their perceptions, the weaker the hotel performance.

CRITIQUE OF THE DEVELOPMENT OF HR ROLES AND STRUCTURES

The evidence suggests that while it is difficult successfully to change HR roles, as they are socially constructed and depend on the expectations of other members of the role set (*see*, for example, Truss *et al.* 2002), there have been changes in the overall level of line manager involvement in HR, in the use of outsourcing and shared service centres and in the emphasis on strategic roles.

Reality of HR: strategy or administration?

Brewster and Less (2006) conducted research in 60 international non-governmental organisations (NGOs), many small, but including some large ones such as the Roman Catholic Church. They found HRM issues were neglected and not regarded as strategic, and that the emphasis was on campaigning programmes, rather than on enhancing the employee experience and performance. Where HR specialists did exist they were rarely represented at senior levels. Yet internally there was dissatisfaction with HR, particularly among fieldworkers. HR managers felt their role was purely administrative and reactive, and that they lacked involvement in strategic planning and had no presence on trustee boards. Line managers lacked the skills to promote employee commitment via concern for employee capability and work-life balance.

Source: C. Brewster and S. Less (2006) 'The success of NGOs hinges on their people – but HR is neglected in the sector', *People Management*, Vol. 12, No. 6, 23 March, p. 44.

One interpretation of these developments is that the HR function is finally gaining prized strategic involvement giving it credibility and power in organisations. However not only do we need to separate the rhetoric from real changes, but these developments in the function are not without their problems. As Hope-Hailey *et al.* (2005) suggest on the basis of their investigation into the banking industry, the HR function may be able to become more strategic, but the employee experience may deteriorate. The concentration on strategic roles appears to have gone hand in hand with the abandonment of the role of employee champion. There is considerable evidence to suggest that the employee champion role is still equated with tea and sympathy, and that concern for employee well-being is seen as a signal that the HR function is being dragged back to its old welfare role (*see*, for example, Francis and Keegan 2006; Beckett 2005; and Pickard 2005), with consequent loss of status and credibility. In an interview one senior CIPD adviser stated that 'nobody wants to be an employee champion. They all think it's ideologically unsound' (Francis and Keegan 2006).

In case studies of the HR function in large local authorities Harris (2006) found increasing use of self-service and outsourcing which appeared to undermine the role of employee champion. She suggests that as the HR function becomes distanced from the workforce and line managers, the consequent loss of knowledge on operational issues means that the function is less able to act as an employee advocate. She found that employees were less likely to see HR as a form of support and advice and suggests they are more likely to approach the union or use legal redress, making the employment relationship more adversarial. She proposes that this loss of touch hinders rather than enables a strategic role.

Along the same lines Francis and Keegan (2005) in their research, which involved interviews with key CIPD staff, HR practitioners, HR course leaders, students and union representatives, found the employee champion role was disintegrating in almost all of the organisations they looked at. They found growth of the business partner role and the parallel restructuring of the HR function which appeared to downgrade the employee-facing role, a reduction in the number of HR specialists (as can be seen also in our Window on practice examples) and the devolution of face-to-face HR to line managers. They identified a loss of employee trust and confidence and a cost to employee well-being. Respondents believed employees were losing out because line managers did not have time to prioritise HR issues, or their training, and often HR advisers were geographically distant. As HR specialists vanish, they suggest, employees are more likely to turn to unions for support and advice.

The unions are already aware of this trend and Harry Donaldson (Regional Secretary of GMB Scotland) commented that unions were worried about HR shifting its focus away from the workforce and away from 'traditional HR' which was associated with welfare and trust. Given that line managers do not always have the necessary skills, he suggested that the chasm thus created between HR and the workforce would be filled by the unions (*People Management* 2005a).

Not only do these developments have potential consequences for employees, they also have consequences for HR practitioners. Francis and Keegan (2006) found that HR practitioners do not consider employee champion roles as career-enhancing moves, and in 2005 Francis and Keegan reported that HR professionals were further concerned that the 'people' element of the job was diminishing. They suggested the people element is a key reason why many enter the profession, and that changes are resulting in disenchanted HR professionals. In addition they found evidence of an increasing split between strategic and non-strategic HR roles. Not only does this split hinder strategic parts of the role and therefore the fulfilment of the HR role overall, but HR professionals perceive that people are parachuted into the top HR jobs from outside the profession (Francis and Keegan 2006), a development which clearly limits career progression for HR professionals.

In terms of the HR function as a whole devolution (to line managers) and decentralisation (from the centre to specific business units) create problems for consistency and integration. Caldwell (2003) also suggests that the decentralisation of HRM to the business unit level has resulted in HRM being under more pressures associated with costs, value and delivery and suggests that this has been the driver for the fragmentation or balkanisation of HR into specialist subtasks with some parts outsourced externally or to the line. Caldwell suggests that the main risk here is de-professionalisation of the function, and that decentralisation may cause the HR contribution to constantly shift, thereby diminishing the clarity of its role or function. He suggests that the function remains dogged by ambiguity and conflict.

There is however a view that Ulrich's work has been misinterpreted and that by roles he meant tasks to be achieved rather than discrete jobs. In spite of this the current focus on Ulrich's roles and structures appears to be based on the assumption that what is good for the organisation is good for the employee. Francis and Keegan (2006) put this well when they say that current models, like earlier ones, are premised upon the assumption of mutuality of interests between all stakeholders – employees, managers, consultants and HR professionals. And Hope-Hailey *et al.* (2005) suggest Ulrich's conception of roles is at best unitarist or at worst naive. The emerging consensus appears to be that there is too much emphasis on models and not enough on skills, people and delivery in context, and that there is a need for the HR function to be agile and flexible in response to the needs of the organisation and consequently for the less rigid application of models (*see*, for example, CIPD 2006a).

SUMMARY PROPOSITIONS

32.1 For many years categorisations of the HR role have been proposed. These include Tyson and Fell (1985); and Storey (1992). The most recent proposal is from Ulrich and Brockbank (2005a) who identify these roles: employee advocate; human capital developer; strategic partner; functional expert; and leader, with a compound role.

32.2 Alongside these role definitions a three-legged HR department structure appears to be evolving: a strategic/business partner group; an administrative/transactional group, usually comprising shared services, e-HR and/or outsourcing; and a centre of functional expertise group.

32.3 The strategic partner role has been most attractive to organisations. The extent to which HR specialists are involved in HR strategy is influenced by the environment of the business, its culture, the perspective of the chief executive, HR board membership and the qualities, characteristics and working relationships of the most senior HR specialist.

32.4 Whilst there have been some early problems with outsourcing, this continues to be pursued by many organisations, and often involves cost savings and staff reductions.

32.5 Devolution of HR activities to line managers enables HR professionals to focus on strategic issues. But line managers often do not have the required motivation, skills or time to carry out HR activities effectively.

32.6 There are concerns that the focus on the business partner role has been at the expense of the employee champion/advocate role, with the consequence that employee well-being is compromised.

32.7 The current trends in HR roles and structure are fragmenting the HR function, resulting in a lack of integration and consistency, and difficulties in effective strategic HR.

GENERAL DISCUSSION TOPICS

1 Does it really matter whether the most senior HR person is on the board of directors, or are personal work relationships, political alliances and personal track records more important?

2 'Outsourcing may be an effective solution in the medium term, but it brings short-term disruption and long-term damage to organisational capability and success.' To what extent do you agree or disagree with this statement?

3 Debate the following comment: 'There has always been a debate about the extent to which day-to-day HR activities should be shared between the professional function and the line. In essence nothing has really changed.'

FURTHER READING

Reilly, P. and Williams, T. (2006) *Strategic HR: Building the Capability to Deliver*. London: Gower.

It is refreshing to find a find a book on the HR role which is set in a UK rather than a US context. The purpose of the book is not to sell an approach but to enable practitioners to work through the reasons for adopting a particular approach and how this might be pursued. The authors draw on experiences of the HR role in the UK and how it is evolving, and provide a sound critique of the challenges and barriers to be overcome. They emphasise the development of capability rather than purely focusing on structures and processes.

Simms, J. (2005) 'Right to Buy', *People Management*, Vol. 11, No. 17, 1 September, pp. 32–7.

This is an illuminating article on the relationship between the HR and procurement functions in the purchase of external HR services such as outsourcing. The article reports the results of a Reed/CIPD/Chartered Institute of Purchasing and Supply (CIPS) survey, and finds that the two disciplines worked collaboratively in HR outsourcing in nearly two-thirds of FTSE 100 companies. However HR professionals had concerns that procurement put cost before quality, used over-legalistic contract specifications and paid little regard to business relationships. On the other hand procurement specialists found HR to be lacking in financial awareness, unable to specify requirements and outcomes and hazy about what constitutes success or failure. Examples and guidance are provided to show how the two specialisms can work together.

Khatri, N. and Budhwar, P. (2001) 'A study of strategic HR issues in an Asian context', *Personnel Review*, Vol. 31, No. 2, pp. 166–87.

This article investigates strategic HR issues which are often neglected. Rather than focusing on strategic content issues, the research reported here concentrates on the structure of the HR function and its strategic relationships; HR competencies; the nature of HR strategy (for example formal or informal); and HR outsourcing. Although the study is located in a very specific context – the electronics and components sector and the machinery and equipment sector in Singapore – the literature review and results are both very useful and informative and straightforward reading.

WEB LINK

www.saratogapwc.co.uk (the website of Saratoga, the human capital metrics business of PricewaterhouseCoopers)

REFERENCES

Barney, J. and Wright, P. (1998) 'On becoming a strategic partner: the role of human resources in gaining competitive advantage', *Human Resource Management*, Vol. 37, No. 1, pp. 31–46.

Beckett, H. (2005) 'Perfect Partners', *People Management*, Vol. 11, 1 April, pp. 16–23.

Bhatnagar, J. and Sharma, A. (2005) 'The Indian perspective of strategic HR roles and organizational learning capability', *The International Journal of Human Resource Management*, Vol. 16, No. 9, pp. 1711–39.

Boxall, P. and Purcell, J. (2003) *Strategy and Human Resource Management*. Basingstoke: Palgrave Macmillan.

Brewster, C. and Less, S. (2006) 'The success of NGOs hinges on their people – but HR is neglected in the sector', *People Management*, Vol. 12, No. 6, 23 March, p. 44.

Brockett, J. (2006a) 'London Bodies Plan shared services', *People Management*, Vol. 12, No. 11, 1 June, p. 10.

Brockett, J. (2006b) 'Outsourcing "endangers HR"', *People Management*, Vol. 12, No. 21, 26 October, p. 10.

Caldwell, R. (2003) 'The Changing Roles of Personnel Managers: Old Ambiguities, New Uncertainties', *Journal of Management Studies*, Vol. 40, No. 4, pp. 983–1004.

Caldwell, R. (2004) 'Rhetoric, facts and self-fulfilling prophesies: exploring practitioners' perceptions of progress in implementing HRM', *Journal of Management Studies*, Vol. 35, No. 3, pp. 196–215.

CIPD (2003) *HR Survey: Where we are, where we're heading.* London: CIPD.

CIPD (2006a) *The HR Function: A report on an event to discuss the changing shape of the HR function.* London: CIPD.

CIPD (2006b) *The Changing HR function: The key questions.* London: CIPD.

CIPD (2006c) *Offshoring and the role of HR.* London: CIPD.

Cleland, J., Pajo, K. and Toulson, P. (2000) 'Move it or lose it: an examination of the evolving role of the human resources professional in New Zealand', *International Journal of Human Resource Management*, Vol. 11, No. 1, pp. 143–60.

Cooke, F., Shen, J. and McBride, A (2005) 'Outsourcing HR as a competitive strategy? A Literature review and an assessment of implications', *Human Resource Management*, Vol. 44, No. 4, Winter, pp. 413–32.

Crabb, S. (2003) ' HR faces offshore boom', *People Management*, Vol. 9, No. 4, 20 February, p. 7.

Francis, H. and Keegan, A. (2005) 'Slippery slope', *People Management*, Vol. 11, No. 13, 30 June, pp. 26–31.

Francis, H. and Keegan, A. (2006) 'The changing face of HRM: in search of balance', *Human Resource Management Journal*, Vol. 16, No. 3, pp. 231–49.

Gennard, J. and Kelly, J. (1997) 'The Unimportance of labels: The diffusion of the Personnel/HRM Function', *Industrial Relations Journal*, Vol. 28, No. 1, pp. 27–42.

Goodge, P., Strange, J. and Dalziel S. (2004) 'How to build a career as an HR Partner', *People Management*, Vol. 10, No. 13, 30 June, pp. 42–42.

Gratton, L. (2003) 'The Humpty Dumpty effect', *People Management*, Vol. 9 No. 9, 1 May, p. 18.

Griffiths, J. (2004a) 'Partnership drives worldwide change', *People Management*, Vol. 10, No. 17, 2 September, p. 12.

Griffiths, J. (2004b) 'Thorntons scraps HR Director post', *People Management*, Vol. 10, No. 14, 15 July, p. 9.

Griffiths, J. (2005) 'Local Heroes?', *People Management*, Vol. 11, No. 5, 10 March, pp. 12–13.

Guest, D. and King, Z. (2001) 'Personnel's Paradox', *People Management*, Vol. 17, No. 19, 27 September, pp. 24–9.

Hall, L. and Torrington, D. (1998) *The Human Resource Function: The Dynamics of change and development.* London: Financial Times Pitman Publishing.

Hammond, D. (2002) 'Firms resist outsourcing', *People Management*, Vol. 8, No. 12, 13 June, p. 8.

Harris, L. (2006) 'Have council changes eroded HR's role as employee champion?', *People Management*, Vol. 12, No. 21, 26 October, p. 72.

Hope-Hailey, V., Farndale, E. and Truss, C. (2005) 'The HR department's role in organizational performance', *Human Resource Management Journal*, Vol. 15, No. 3, pp. 49–66.

Hutchinson, S. and Purcell, J. (2004) *Bringing Policies to Life: The vital role of front-line managers in people management.* Executive Briefing. London: CIPD.

IDS (2001) *HR Service Centres*, IDS Study, No. 707, April.

IDS (2003) *Outsourcing HR administration*, IDS Study Plus. London: IDS.

IRS (2001) 'HR in 2001: the HR audit', *IRS Employment Trends*, No. 728, May, pp. 4–10.

Kelly, J. and Gennard, J. (1996) 'The role of personnel directors in the Board of Directors', *Personnel Review*, Vol. 25, No. 1, pp. 7–24.

Lengnick-Hall, M. and Lengnick-Hall, C. (2003) *Human Resource Management in the Knowledge Economy*. San Francisco: Berrett-Koehler Inc.

McConville, T. (2006) 'Devolved RM responsibilities, middle-managers and role dissonance', *Personnel Review*, Vol. 35, No. 6, pp. 637–53.

Main C. (2006) 'How to manage an outsourcing contract', *People Management*, Vol. 12, No. 13, 29 June, pp. 44–5.

Manocha, R. (2006) 'MoD Shares HR operations', *People Management*, Vol. 12, No. 5, 9 March, p. 10.

Maxwell, G. and Watson, S. (2007) 'Perspectives on line managers in human resource management: Hilton International's UK Hotels', *International Journal of Human Resource Management*, Vol. 17, No. 6, pp. 1152–70.

People Management (2002) 'HR departments are corroded by the extent of outsourcing', Vol. 8, No. 20, 10 October, p. 10.

People Management (2005a) 'Address people needs, not just business needs, advises GMB', Vol. 11, No. 6, 24 March, p. 10.

People Management (2005b) 'BT renews Accenture deal for a decade', Vol. 11, No. 3, 10 February, p. 8.

People Management (2006a) 'E-HR can alienate managers', Vol. 12, No. 4, 23 February, p. 16.

People Management (2006b) 'HR "is still not strategic enough"', Vol. 12, No. 6, 23 March, p. 13.

People Management (2006c) 'Shared services save RBS £11m', Vol. 12, No. 5, 9 March, p. 13.

People Management (2006d) 'Arcadia strips HR of its place on the board', Vol. 12, No. 9, 4 May, p. 10.

People Management (2006e) 'Unilever grants £1bn contract', Vol. 12, No. 12, 15 June, p. 10.

Pickard, J. (2002) 'A source of inspiration', *People Management*, Vol. 8, No. 14, 11 July, pp. 36–42.

Pickard, J. (2004) 'One step beyond', *People Management*, Vol. 10, No. 13, 30 June, pp. 26–31.

Pickard, J. (2005) 'Part, Not Partner', *People Management*, Vol. 11, No. 21, 27 October, pp. 48–50.

Pickard, J. (2006) 'Conflicting Schedule', *People Management*, Vol. 12, No. 5, 9 March, pp. 14–15.

Reilly, P. and Williams, T. (2006) *Strategic HR: building the capability to deliver*. London: Gower.

Rippin, S. and Dawson, G. (2001) 'How to outsource the HR function', *People Management*, Vol. 7, No. 19, 27 September, pp. 42–3.

Robinson, V. (2006) 'Three legs good?', *People Management*, Vol. 12, No. 21, 26 October, pp. 62–4.

Sheehan, C. (2005), 'A model for HRM strategic integration', *Personnel Review*, Vol. 32, No. 2, pp. 192–209.

Sparkes, J. (2001) 'Job's a good un', *People Management*, Vol. 7, No. 20, 11 October, pp. 44–7.

Stiles, P. (2001) 'The impact of the board on strategy: an empirical examination', *Journal of Management Studies*, Vol. 38, No. 5, pp. 627–50.

Storey, J. (1992) *Developments in the Management of Human Resources*. Oxford: Blackwell.

Townley, B. (2004) 'Managerial Technologies, Ethics and Managing', *Journal of Management Studies*, Vol. 41, No. 3, pp. 425–45.

Truss, C., Gratton, L., Hope-Hailey, V., Stiles, P. and Zaleska, J. (2002) 'Paying the Piper: choice and constraint in changing HR functional roles', *Human Resource Management Journal*, Vol. 12, No. 2, pp. 39–63.

Tyson, S. (1995) *Human Resource Strategy*. London: Pitman.

Tyson, S. and Fell, A. (1985) *Evaluating the Personnel Function*. London: Hutchinson.

Ulrich, D. (1997) *Human Resource Champions: The Next Agenda for Adding Value and Delivering Results*. Boston: Harvard Business School Press.

Ulrich, D. and Brockbank, W. (2005a) 'Role Call', *People Management*, Vol. 11, No. 13, 16 June, pp. 24–8.

Ulrich, D. and Brockbank, W. (2005b) *The HR Value Proposition*. Boston: Harvard Business School Press.

Wright, V. (2006) 'Shaping up for strategy', *People Management*, Vol. 12, No. 21, 26 October, p. 7.

An extensive range of additional materials, including multiple choice questions, answers to questions and links to useful websites can be found on the Human Resource Management Companion Website at **www.pearsoned.co.uk/torrington**.

CHAPTER ③③

INFORMATION TECHNOLOGY AND HUMAN CAPITAL MEASUREMENT

THE OBJECTIVES OF THIS CHAPTER ARE TO:

1 Explore the contribution of information technology to the effective and efficient provision of HR

2 Identify a variety of approaches to measuring HR and human capital

3 Explain a range of simple measures which are frequently used

4 Explore the use of scorecards and other strategic frameworks in measuring human capital

5 Identify types of human capital reporting and the role of these

Technology is being used increasingly and in a variety of ways to support HR activities and, arguably, to give HR professionals more time for more strategic matters. Some of this extra time is being redirected to a range of human capital evaluation activities that are also supported by a more advanced use of technology. We have already explored some of the research which shows how different HR activities affect the bottom line, and how critical intangible assets are to a firm's value. This focus is growing in importance. Traditional accountancy measures are inadequate to reflect the value of people to the organisation. Measures are needed to demonstrate how people are an asset adding value to the business rather than just a cost. Measurement of HR has become increasingly important but many HR specialists resist the concept and methods of measurement and IRS (2003) reports that less than half of respondents to its survey calculate measures of HR value.

THE CONTRIBUTION OF TECHNOLOGY TO EFFECTIVE AND EFFICIENT HR PROVISION

There is a wide range of ways in which technology can contribute to the HR function and we have discussed many of these so far in this text, for example the use of technology to enhance recruitment and selection activities and to widen the range of learning experiences, and a broad summary of the potential uses of technology to support HR activities is given in Table 33.1.

In this section therefore we will focus on technology as a means of providing and manipulating HR information via HRIS (human resource information systems) and technology as a means of delivering HR as in e-HR which we touched upon in Chapter 32. In the latter part of this chapter we will see how such systems also have the potential to provide a major input into Human Capital Measurement (HCM)

Table 33.1 Potential uses of technology to support HR activities: a 2006 CIPD view

People development and performance management	Online appraisal systems such as 360° feedback Training needs analysis Career management and succession planning
Resource management	Online recruitment and selection Induction packages HR planning and forecasting Time and attendance
Employee relations and communications	Intranet Shared service centres Organisational development (OD) approaches Team development
HR information and accounting	Intranet Employee and manager self-service HR metrics/human capital
Retention and reward	Payroll Total reward statements Employee self-service in creation of flexible rewards packages Reward modelling Pensions administration

Source: CIPD (2006a) *HR and Technology: Beyond Delivery, A Change Agenda*. London: CIPD.

HRIS

HRISs, in one form or another, have been around for about three decades, and debate continues about how they are and should ideally be used. Early systems were basic administrative tools containing employee data, with operational, analysis, modelling, and interactive facilities gradually being exploited over time. However Ball (2000) found that HRISs were still being used primarily for administrative rather than analytical ends and exploitation remains painfully slow and patchy. One of the key attractions of technology for the HR function is that it can reduce time on administrative chores to free this up for more strategic activities. However the introduction and enhancement of HRIS is usually accompanied by staff cuts, and Gardener and her colleagues (2003) found that although the technology did free up time in one sense it also created a need to spend time on IT support and training.

In terms of the contribution that technology makes to the HR function, Zuboff (1988) makes a very useful distinction between automating current activities, so that they are done more efficiently and require fewer staff, and informating. This latter is explained as supplying new forms of information which requires new ways of thinking, for example by carrying out activities in a different way, carrying out new activities, integrating data across the whole organisation, making access to the data available to different users, rather than replicating current activities and ways of doing things. The tendency to automate rather than informate severely restricts the potential of any HRIS.

If we link this view of the potential of technology with the HR capability model of Reddington *et al.* (2005), the variable contribution of HRISs to HRM becomes clearer. Reddington *et al.* suggest that three primary drivers promote HR capability:

- 'operational' (i.e. improving cost effectiveness by reducing the costs of its services and headcount);
- 'rational' (i.e. improving its services to employees and line managers who are increasingly demanding); and
- 'transformational' (i.e. addressing the key strategic drivers of the organisation).

Automating in Zuboff's terms clearly addresses the operational driver, and we have seen evidence of this in reducing HR headcounts, and automating may also make some contribution to the rational driver. Informating, however, is essential to progress the transformational driver and also to satisfactorily progress the rational driver, and this is essential for HRISs to make a significant contribution to HCM. So if technology is to make a real contribution to the HR function we need to go beyond automating. The evidence for this is patchy but there are some good examples of new approaches, if we think more broadly of the examples of the use of technology we have quoted in previous chapters. But these are often highlights in an overall picture of basic provision.

In the 2005 CIPD survey on People Management and Technology (CIPD 2005) just over three-quarters of the respondents reported use of an HRIS, and just over half of these had a single integrated HR system, but few (16 per cent) were integrated with other IT systems in the wider organisation, which is important for informating. The three key functions of an HRIS were reported as absence management (85 per cent), training (75 per cent) and reward (75 per cent), and these are also the three most likely to be run as an integrated system within HR. Analysis showed that the greater proportion of functions that are integrated as part of the HRIS, the more likely that the system would be used to aid human capital reporting, comply with supply-chain partner requirements, improve profitability, reduce headcount and deliver against economic criteria. Interestingly, respondents said that if they were to introduce their system again almost three-quarters would seek greater integration and more clarity with providers; slightly fewer respondents said they would arrange more training.

The five most popular reasons for introducing an HRIS are: improving quality (91 per cent), speed (81 per cent) and flexibility (59 per cent) of information, reducing the administrative burden on the HR department (83 per cent) and improving services to employees (56 per cent). Again there is more evidence of automating than of informating. In terms of who the intended users of the HRIS are, 99 per cent identified members of the HR department; 46 per cent identified line managers elsewhere in the business, while 32 per cent included employees. This suggests that some progress is being made in this respect towards informating. Tansley and colleagues (2001) provide an excellent insight into an organisation trying to develop an HRIS intended to encourage transformational change in the organisation and going beyond automating. This system is shown in the next Window on practice.

WINDOW ON PRACTICE

Developing an integrated HRIS: a cautionary tale

Tansley and her colleagues report on an engineering company that was developing an HRIS as part of a business-wide Enterprise Resource Planning System (ERS). This approach meant not only that all HR information would be integrated but that it would also be integrated with other IT systems in the business. This new system was considered to be one of the most important changes in the organisation and an opportunity to break with the past and move to an HRM style of people management. It was to be designed to allow access beyond the HR function i.e. to other line managers and employees and beyond the organisation, e.g. to any outsourced functions, such as payroll. Whilst the HR project team (designing the HR part of the ERS) were aware that success depended on changing attitudes and the culture of the business, line managers were unfortunately excluded from the planning process. The first stage of work for the project planning team was to map HR processes, but difficulties arose as owners of some of the processes felt their previous work was ignored. There was also an attempt to find a standard 'one best way' to carry out different processes, and this caused problems with different parts of the business, who wanted to tailor things to meet their own needs. A further problem was that each HR process was mapped separately, thereby missing the potential of seeing and doing things differently, and preventing adoption of a more strategic approach. Whilst the HR project manager saw the process as an opportunity to think anew and do things differently others did not want to think so radically and preferred to keep things the same (especially those who were the process owners). Many had difficulties with the idea of devolving HR to line managers and there was a view that senior HR managers were gradually distancing themselves from the project as it was seen to be political suicide to give HR away. Training on the system was confusing as improved versions were constantly being produced. In retrospect, many said they had not understood the full potential of the system.

The researchers concluded that the company had used IT to reproduce, extend and improve on current HR processes by automating HR data, and that it was thus able to add some value at an operational level and reduce headcount. However the opportunity of informating and reconfiguring the nature of HR work and roles was missed.

Source: C. Tansley, S. Newell and H. Williams (2001) 'Effecting HRM-style practices through an integrated human resource information system. An e-greenfield site?', *Personnel Review*, Vol. 30, No. 3, pp. 351–70.

e-HR

One of the difficulties with e-HR is that it can be defined in a wide range of ways. It can include HR and corporate intranets containing static information, interactive HR and corporate intranets, email-based initiatives and the Internet. The emphasis here is on intranets. The CIPD (2005) found that 71 per cent of respondents claimed their organisation had an intranet with an HR facility, with larger organisations being more likely, not surprisingly, to have them. Of respondents 98 per cent say that the main purpose is to provide access to HR information and 88 per cent say it is to provide a facility for downloading forms. An intranet can also allow employees the facility to interact with the system to input information or make choices where applicable, which the CIPD terms an HRSS (HR self-service) system. Twenty-two per cent of respondents had such a system. CIPD survey's findings on the purpose of introducing such system are shown in Table 33.2.

The CIPD found that access to such self-service systems was limited as only 64 per cent of organisations reported that all employees have access to this, and only 32 per cent said that all employees have been trained to use the system. As with other initiatives, much of the drive for such systems has come from the need to liberate the personnel function from its administrative tasks to allow it to focus on more strategic matters (Trapp 2001) and indeed the CIPD found that this was precisely the view of its respondents. Some identified problematic aspects such as the need to spend more time on the computer, leaving less time for face-to-face activities. Another disadvantage cited was software costs and training time to use such systems. Such systems are often introduced

Table 33.2 The uses of an HR self-service system from the People Management and Technology Survey 2005

Personal details updated	79%
Applications for jobs online	76%
Requests for training	67%
Access to e-learning	53%
Submission of time-management information	53%
Posting and answering queries	31%
Administration of flexible benefits	25%
Administration of queries	21%

Source: CIPD (2005) *People Management and Technology: Progress and Potential*. London: CIPD.

along with HR service centres, the intention being that the system should be the first port of call, before the service centre. In this way the pressure on service centres should be reduced in the long run. Different surveys have produced very different results concerning the extent of use (*see*, for example, Trapp 2001; compare this with IRS 2002b), and we will not dwell on the figures. However, it is generally agreed that more sophisticated applications are still not very common and are most likely to be found in IT or related companies. IRS (2003) found that improvement in communications (73 per cent) was most frequently cited as the specific reason for introducing e-HR, followed by reduction of routine administration (60 per cent), whereas only 37 per cent said they were looking specifically for cost savings. Tyler (2001) also suggests empowering employees as another reason for introduction. In terms of the static information they hold, intranets are likely to contain HR policies, rules and regulations, details of training courses, standard forms, staff handbooks, induction information and information on benefits.

ACTIVITY 33.1

We referred to the 'loss of the personal touch' in the introduction to this discussion of these alternative means of providing HR services.

How important is 'the personal touch' to the employees of today, and why do you think this is so?

More sophisticated systems include such features as the ability to update one's personal details (password access), reviewing and changing the flexible benefits that one has chosen, checking one's remaining leave entitlement and requesting leave, submitting expense claim forms, asking questions (such as pension projection figures), performance management and salary review tools. IRS (2002b) identifies three user groups of such systems: HR service centres or the HR function, line managers and employees. In terms of employees such systems are often referred to as self-service or self-management systems.

Some of these applications will clearly require changes in the organisational culture. In addition there are concerns about the loss of the personal touch and security of information (Trapp 2001). There are also issues about the access to computers and the computer literacy of some staff. Some companies have introduced kiosks where computers can be used by a range of staff, but there are issues about the extent to which staff will prefer to use their coffee breaks booking holidays on the computer.

Web case 33.1 on this book's companion website, **www.pearsoned.co.uk/torrington**, focuses on the use of technology in HR.

MEASURING HR AND HUMAN CAPITAL

The research referred to in previous chapters (especially Chapter 11 on Strategic aspects of performance) has a very clear focus on identifying and measuring a range of best practices in terms of workforce organisation and management (such as self-managing teams, high training spend, reduced status differentials) and relating these to impact on productivity and profitability. This is a very specific approach to 'proving' that HR practices affect bottom-line performance. In this chapter we later focus on this type of measurement in the context of specific organisations, but we begin by taking a wider perspective and will review a broader and simpler range of measures which are used to demonstrate how the HR function and HR capital contribute to the organisation.

HR measures are sometimes talked about in the context of measuring the contribution of the HR function. An example of such measures might be the staffing costs of the HR function, recruitment speed, training delivery, management satisfaction with HR advice and services, and so on. The Window on practice provides one of many approaches to such measurement.

WINDOW ON PRACTICE

HR survey: What do managers need from the function?

Cathy Cooper (2001) reports on how Fidelity International redesigned its annual manager survey so that it became a meaningful tool in helping the company to improve people management. The original survey which had been used for five years tended to be a 'popularity contest for HR'. The first stage in redesign was to investigate what the survey should focus on. To this end an external consultant was employed to hold focus group sessions with HR staff to establish the strengths and weaknesses of the department. The survey manager then held one-to-one interviews with managers to establish their concerns. The interview data were then used to frame topics for the survey. The approach taken in the survey was to ask how well all managers, including HR, managed their people rather than how well or badly HR was doing. The survey was designed to take 10 minutes to complete and respondents were asked to identify the extent to which they agreed or disagreed with a number of statements. Respondents were invited to make any additional comments they wished. Some questions were retained, however, to get specific information on HR's performance. The survey was delivered by the company intranet to make responding easy. Of the 500 managers they invited to participate they received completed questionnaires from over half.

The results of the survey were used to develop 12 broad goals for the HR function with which individual objectives will be aligned. Senior managers have been involved in deciding how the goals could best be met, and then HR directors and their teams in different locations will develop a project action plan.

Source: Summarised from C. Cooper (2001) 'Win by a canvass', *People Management*,
Vol. 7, No. 2, 25 January, pp. 42–4.

Such factors are clearly the responsibility of the people in the HR function and are under their control. They are designed to show how the HR function adds value to the organisation and can provide a way of capturing how that value is improved over time. Most HR measures, however, are within the control partly of members of the HR function, and partly of others in the organisation, particularly where HR is devolved to line managers. For example absence and employee turnover are typical measures in many organisations. But to what extent are absence levels, for example, the result of the absence policy (and HR may or may not have designed this alone)? Other factors that may have an effect are: the way the policy is implemented by line managers, the influence of other policies (such as work-life balance), the influence of the way that work is structured and commitment to peers (as for example in self-managing teams)? The list could go on. It could be argued that the HR function has an ultimate responsibility for all of this. In reality, however, this is not a tenable view. There is also a very great emphasis on partnership in HR, requiring many activities to be business driven and owned rather than HR driven and owned. Thus many HR measures represent aspects of human capital in the organisation on which the HR function has some influence. IRS (2002a) in its survey found that respondents commented on the inherent difficulty of identifying the contribution of the HR function in many measures.

ACTIVITY 33.2

Employee turnover is frequently measured in organisations. Identify which aspects of the organisation have an influence on this and who in the organisation would be seen as having a responsibility for these aspects.

We move on now from the specific contribution of the HR function to discuss human capital measurement (HCM), which has attracted considerable attention, with some organisations setting up dedicated roles and units to undertake HCM, either within or attached to the HR function. We identified broadly above the ultimate purpose of measurement in that it identifies the contribution of people to the performance of the organisation and enables the organisation to improve this contribution. This contribution is as we have noted previously very difficult to disentangle from other factors in the situation and is also difficult to measure quantitatively. As we showed in the earlier part of this chapter many HRISs still focus on administration at the expense of analysis and evaluation, thereby possibly limiting what the organisation can achieve in this area. We have discussed previously the nature of human capital and the resource-based view (in Chapter 2) and human capital and knowledge management (in Chapter 12) and it may be useful to read or re-read these sections before moving on.

There is considerable evidence that there exists no single measure or set of measures that represent the value of human capital in the organisation (*see*, for example, Kingsmill 2003). This is largely because every context is different and, as Elias and Scarborough (2004) discovered, different organisations are driven by different things in their human capital measurement. They found that approaches differed in two significant ways. One major area of difference concerned whether the whole or part of the workforce was covered in human capital reporting; the other concerned whether a strategic, holistic and aggregate (such as balanced scorecard) approach was taken or whether individual aspects were reported. Interestingly they found that most organisations in their sample reported on individual aspects. CIPD (2006b) identifies three different levels of sophistication of human capital data: basic; intermediate and higher, which we explain below.

At a **basic level** it is suggested that actions include the collection of basic data (*see* the examples discussed above) and the use of existing data to communicate to managers essential departmental information on such matters as absence, accidents, turnover and so on. In addition trends and patterns in the data are identified and causes investigated. The outcome of this exercise is to provide measures of efficiency and effectiveness so that identified problems can be tackled, for example to reduce absence or accidents or to improve the diversity profile. These basic measures represent the 'individual' measures that Elias and Scarborough (2004) found to be most common.

At an **intermediate level** CIPD (2006b) suggests that actions involve designing data collection for specific human capital needs, such as designing an employee attitude survey to measure satisfaction, and then using this data to inform the development of people policies and procedures. In addition correlations are investigated, say, between levels of satisfaction and potential antecedents such as levels of training, flexible working, line manager coaching, and so on. The final action is to communicate to line managers which processes influence desired outcomes such as satisfaction, and therefore highlight the value of these processes. The outcome at this level is to provide measures of processes in order to aid the design of the most appropriate HR model for the context, and to communicate to managers why the processes are important and what they can achieve, as well as how to implement them.

At the **higher level** CIPD suggests that actions include the identification of key performance indicators in relation to business strategy and the collection of qualitative and quantitative data specifically to measure these, and to feed these data into a model such as the balanced scorecard. Managers are then provided with a range of indicators on a range of measures which they can use to monitor the progress of their department. The resulting data can be used to inform decisions and communicate human capital measures to a range of audiences. The outcome at this level is to identify the drivers of the business, to provide better informed internal decision making and to report externally on progress in relation to strategy.

We focus on simple basic measures initially and then move to the higher-level ones.

Frequently used basic measures

IRS (2002a) divides measures into hard and soft measures, with training days, for example, being a hard (objective) measure and employee satisfaction, for example, being a soft measure. In its survey IRS found that employers most frequently calculated absence rates (96 per cent), employee turnover (98 per cent) and expenditure on training (88 per cent). However, these figures are based on a small sample, so actual percentages should be treated with caution. Other popular measures were employee relations indicators (such as number of grievances and tribunal cases), training days, cost to fill vacancies, time to fill vacancies, HR costs as a proportion of profit or total costs and time spent communicating with staff. Only nine per cent of the organisatons surveyed measured productivity.

In terms of soft measures, IRS (IRS 2002a) found that 85 per cent of the sample measured employee satisfaction, 72 per cent measured line manager satisfaction, 68 per cent measured senior manager satisfaction and 60 per cent measured customer satisfaction. Employee satisfaction was considered to be the most effective soft measure.

Such measures are frequently collected in an ad hoc manner, are not integrated or tied in with business strategy and may not result in action being taken. The CIPD Factsheet (2006b) on human capital provides a very useful framework in which to understand the different areas of human capital that may be evaluated. CIPD suggests that the data collected fall under five broad headings: performance data; demographic data; recruitment and retention data; training and development data; and opinion data. In the following section we give some examples of the more popular and simple measures using the categorisation proposed by the CIPD (2006b).

Performance data – specific example: absence analysis and costing

CIPD suggests that performance data may include performance management data, productivity and profitability data, customer satisfaction and loyalty data. Absence and attendance clearly comes into this category. For aggregate analysis the **absence rate** is the number of days of absence, that is, when attendance would have been expected, of all employees. The **absence percentage rate** is this figure divided by the total number of actual working days for all employees over the year, multiplied by 100. This simple percentage figure is the one most often used and enables the organisation's absence level to be compared with national figures, or those of other organisations in the same sector.

The **absence frequency rate** is the number of spells of absence over the period, usually a year. Comparing this and the absence percentage rate gives critical information about the type of absence problem that the organisation is experiencing.

Absence data, as well as enabling external comparisons, can be analysed by department, work-group, occupation, grade and so on. In this way the analysis will throw up problem areas, and additional analysis can be undertaken to try to identify the causes of differing levels of absence in different parts of the organisation. The data may be supplemented by information from questionnaires or interviews with employees or line managers.

The purpose of producing this information is to understand the causes and extent of absence in order to manage it effectively. So, for example, such analysis may result in a new absence policy, employee communications about the impact of absence, appropriate training for line managers, changes to specific groups of jobs and the introduction of a new type of attendance system such as flexitime. The information provides a base for future monitoring. Absence data can be analysed further to provide benchmarks of 'high', 'medium' and 'low' absence levels in the organisation, and can be used to set improvement targets. This analysis can also be used to trigger specific management actions when an employee reaches different benchmark levels. For example, a trigger may be the number of days or number of spells per year or, as in the Bradford factor (*see* Figure 15.2 on p. 345 for the formula), a combination of both.

The costing of absence needs to have a wider focus than just the pay of the absent individual. Other costs include:

- line manager costs in finding a temporary replacement or rescheduling work;
- the actual costs of the temporary employee;
- costs of showing a temporary employee what to do;
- costs associated with a slower work rate or more errors from a temporary employee;
- costs of contracts not completed on time.

These costs can be calculated and provide the potential for productivity improvement.

Performance data – specific example: relating the workforce to organisational performance

Various analytical methods relate the contribution of the workforce to organisational performance. This analysis can be used to control headcount, and to measure organisational effectiveness and compare it with that of similar organisations. The information can also be used to communicate to employees what their contribution is to the business. Turnover per employee and profit per employee can be calculated in order to monitor performance and to demonstrate to each employee the importance of cost consciousness. If an employee of an organisation employing 3,000 employees realises that profit per employee is only £900 this means far more to that individual than expressing profit as £2.7 million. Cost consciousness suddenly becomes important as the fragile and marginal nature of profits is demonstrated. A further calculation expresses the cost of employees in relation to the total costs of production. To work this out, turnover less profit (that is, the cost of production) is compared with employee costs (salary plus on-costs). The percentage of production costs accounted for by employees will vary markedly according to the nature of the business. For example, in some pharmaceutical businesses people costs will account for 70 per cent of all production costs (due to a heavy emphasis on research and development) whereas in a less people-intensive business, as found in other parts of the manufacturing sector, people costs may only account for around 15 per cent. Changes in the percentage of people costs over time would need to be investigated. People costs are a good way of communicating to employees just how important they are to the success of the business.

Demographic data – specific example: equal opportunities analysis

CIPD defines these as data on the composition of the workforce, and these may include equal opportunities analysis which aims to provide an organisational profile of, most frequently, ethnic origin, gender, age and disability. The resulting percentages from this can be compared with national and local community figures to give an initial idea of how representative the organisation is. Further analyses break these figures down to compare them by department, job category and grade. It is in this type of analysis that startling differences are likely to be found, for example as shown in Figure 33.1.

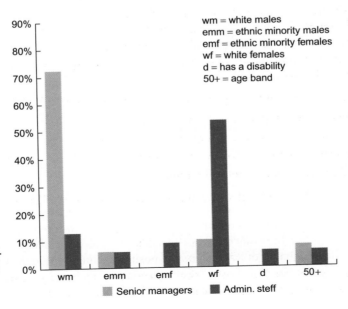

Figure 33.1
Breakdown of senior manager staff group and administrative staff group

wm = white males
emm = ethnic minority males
emf = ethnic minority females
wf = white females
d = has a disability
50+ = age band

The information gleaned can be used to:

- question the extent and spread of disadvantaged groups in the organisation;
- identify specific barriers to a more representative spread;
- formulate appropriate policy and action plans;
- set targets to be achieved and to monitor year on year compared with these base figures.

Other analyses can be carried out to show promotion, internal moves and secondment figures for disadvantaged groups compared with advantaged groups, for example white males. Further mention is made of these and the recruitment system in the following section.

ACTIVITY 33.3

1 What basic metrics does your HR function calculate?

2 What is the purpose of each one?

3 How are the results translated into action?

4 To what extent are these measures related to business strategy?

5 To what extent are these measures integrated?

Recruitment and retention data – specific example: turnover analysis and costing

We cover this aspect in Chapter 9 on Staff retention.

Training and development data

Typical training and development data include annual training days per employee, training spend per employee, existence of personal development plans for what percentage of the workforce and for which job roles, and the elapsed time between an employee joining an organisation and being involved in an induction programme. Other measures may cover the number of accredited or trained coaches and mentors, or the competencies/skills of staff as judged by a variety of measures.

Opinion data

Whilst opinion survey data are not new, considerably more attention has been given to such data of late. For example in the National Heath Service there is an annual employee opinion survey which focuses on employee views of hours worked, appraisal, training, teamwork, injuries, harassment, work-life balance, job satisfaction, work pressure, intention to leave, quality of leadership, and positive feelings within the organisation, as well as other issues. Hospital Trusts are able to compare their ratings against the national picture and can also break down their data by job type.

Basic measures can be benchmarked externally against other similar organisations which would allow a meaningful comparison, such as competitors. They can also be benchmarked internally by comparing departments, different locations and so on. IRS (2002a) found that around one-third of the organisations it surveys regularly carried out external benchmarking and the same percentage regularly carried out internal benchmarking.

Whilst the measures described above can clearly add value, much of this work is done in an ad hoc manner and lacks strategic integration. We turn now to the higher, strategic end of the spectrum of HCM.

Strategic frameworks and scorecards for HCM

Higher-level approaches are more representative of human capital management, which the Accounting for People Task force defined as 'an approach to people management that treats it as a high level strategic issue rather than an operational matter "to be left to the HR people" and seeks systematically to analyse, measure and evaluate how people policies and practices contribute to value creation' (Kingsmill 2003, p. 5). The emphasis is not just on measurement, but on using this measurement approach as a management tool for effecting change and improvement. Such an approach addresses the problem often found in measurement, namely that the wrong things are measured (*see*, for example, Chartered Management Institute 2006, quoted in IRS 2006; Gratton 2004).

Through the use of a strategic framework or model the organisation can identify what drives the performance of employees in relation to the organisation's strategy. These drivers can then be expressed as a range of measures with indicators, and targets can be set at about the levels that need to be achieved. These targets are often cascaded down to employee level, and form the base for the 'hard' metrics approach to performance management as opposed to the 'soft' good management approach to performance management which we discussed in Chapter 13.

There are a variety of models that can be used and Matthewman and Matignon (2005) identify six such frameworks: the human resource benchmarking model; the balanced scorecard; the human capital monitor; the human capital index; the engagement model; and the organisational performance model. We look at the Human Resource Scorecard and Mayo's Human Capital Monitor in more detail below, and the Window on practice is about the Royal Bank of Scotland Group who use the engagement model.

WINDOW ON PRACTICE

Royal Bank of Scotland Group's HCM

The Royal Bank of Scotland, as part of its vision for the future, has included 'being the most admired bank', and it is accepted that the contribution made by employees is vital to achieving this, in order to add value for customers and shareholders. The board therefore requires monthly reports of people-based information (such as training and absence). Another closely related goal is to become 'the most admired employer' and to do this the bank has identified the need to 'build a compelling employee proposition that attracts, engages and retains the best talent'. The overall employee proposition consists of total reward; work itself; recognition; performance and development; leadership; relationships; product brands and reputation; and work-life balance plus physical environment. These are shown in Figure 33.2 within the full Integrated Human Capital Model. The organisation as a whole needed to develop a good understanding of how each of these impacts on whether employees join, stay or leave the bank. Once this evidence is gathered it can inform the HR strategies that are required to achieve the goal. In the broader human capital model the bank believes that the make-up of the employee proposition determines employee engagement and that levels of engagement influence employee performance. The model is intended to be used as a diagnostic tool for businesses within the group. For example it can be used to explain why staff doing similar types of work within different businesses have differing levels of performance. The model is owned by a small HR research and measurement team who act as consultants to the nine businesses in the group. The model can also be used to show how HR strategies and improvements impact both on engagement and on a range of business metrics, as shown in the model. The bank has decided that employee engagement is a more relevant measure than, say, commitment or satisfaction, and incorporates both of these. Engagement is characterised by an employee who scores highly on a range of questions focusing on 'How much do I want to and actually do improve our business results?' In terms of HR data collected, a range of inputs is shown on the left of the model, the top input, 'global people data', being the HRIS (called the 'HR management system' – HRMS) that is used in the bank.

The model is about improving future performance, rather than just reporting on past performance, and statistical correlations between employees (often segmented by, say, age, jobs, tenure) and engagement gives a better line of sight between HR interventions and profitability.

Source: IDS (2004) 'The Royal Bank of Scotland',
Human Capital Measurement, IDS HR Study No. 783, pp. 33–6.

Considerable attention has been given to the use of scorecards, such as the balanced scorecard (Kaplan and Norton 1992) and, later, the HR scorecard (Becker *et al.* 2001), in linking people, strategy and performance. These are perhaps the best-known score-cards, but many different scorecards have been developed over the last decade or so. Such scorecards utilise a range of measures of HR which are viewed as critical to the success of the business strategy, and which move the process of measurement on from an ad hoc to a strategic and integrated approach. Kaplan and Norton widened the perspective on the measurement of business performance by measuring more than financial performance. Their premise is that other factors which lead to financial performance need to be measured to give a more rounded view of how well the organisation is performing. This means that measures of business performance are based on measures of

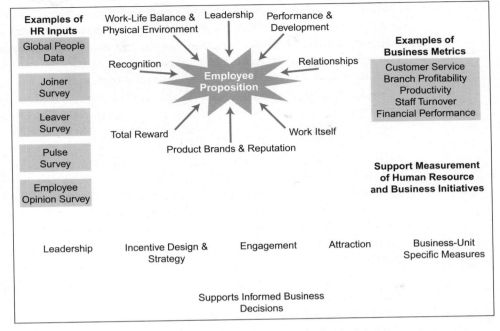

Figure 33.2
The Royal Bank of Scotland Group's Integrated Human Capital Measurement model

(Source: IDS (2004) 'The Royal Bank of Scotland', *Human Capital Measurement*, IDS HR Study No. 783, p. 34)

strategy implementation in a range of areas. Kaplan and Norton identify three other areas for measurement in addition to financial measures: customer measures, internal business process measures and learning and growth measures. In each of these areas critical elements need to be identified and then measures devised to identify current levels and to measure progress. Some organisations implementing this scorecard have developed the learning and growth area to include a wider range of HR measures.

Becker *et al.* (2001) argue that it is important to have a 'measurement system [that] convincingly showcases HR's impact on business performance' (p. 4), otherwise, they argue, the HR function cannot show how it adds value and risks being outsourced. The system they suggest focuses on 'HR architecture', and by this they mean the 'sum of the HR function, the broader HR system, and the resulting employee behaviours' (p. 1). This is therefore a broad view of HR measurement, as we discussed at the beginning of this chapter. Becker and his colleagues have designed a seven-step process to clarify and measure HR's strategic influence:

Step 1. Clearly define business strategy in a way that involves discussing how the strategy can be implemented and communicated.

Step 2. Develop a business case for HR as a strategic asset explaining how and why HR can facilitate business strategy – Becker and his colleagues suggest how current research relating HR to firm performance can be useful here.

Step 3. Create a strategy map – which should involve managers across the organisation, and needs to address the critical strategic goals, identify the performance drivers for each goal, identify how progress towards goals can be measured, identify barriers to goal achievement, identify required employee behaviour for goal achievement, question whether the HR function is developing employee competencies and behaviours needed to meet the goals, and if this is not happening, what needs to change.

Step 4. Identify HR deliverables from the strategy map – which may include performance drivers and enablers; for example low turnover, high levels of specific competencies and so on may be needed to reduce product development time.

Step 5. Align HR architecture with the deliverables in step 4. Policies can be developed to result in these deliverables – for example policies encouraging low turnover may be supported by family-friendly and work-life balance policies, diversity policies, career development opportunities and so on.

Step 6. Design a strategic HR measurement system. This requires that valid measures of HR deliverables are developed. For example in specifying low turnover it would be important to identify which particular staff groups this applies to, whether voluntary turnover only is to be calculated, whether internal job moves are included and so on.

Step 7. Implement management by measurement – Becker and his colleagues suggest that once the measurement system has been developed this can then become a powerful management tool.

In designing measures Becker and his colleagues suggest that HR efficiency as well as deliverables need to be measured. Efficiency measures tend to be cost measures, for example cost per new hire, or HR cost per employee. They suggest that these are both lagging indicators. Leading indicators can also be measured. These are defined as measures of 'high-performance work system' and HR system alignment. The high-performance work system appears to be defined in terms of best-practice-type measures, for example hours of training received each year by each employee, or percentage of the workforce regularly undergoing annual appraisal. HR system alignment indicates the extent to which the high-performance work system is tailored to business strategy via supporting each HR deliverable. Useful lists of HR deliverables and efficiency measures can be found in Ulrich (1997).

An alternative framework for monitoring, measuring and managing human capital is the 'human capital monitor' and this has been developed in the UK by Andrew Mayo (2001). The human capital monitor is designed to connect the intrinsic value of the human capital in the organisation with the working environment. It includes processes and systems which impact on employees' behaviour together with the value that is created by people. As with the previous models discussed this is not specifically designed for the HR function to monitor itself. The model adds together the value of people as assets (box 1) and the motivation and commitment (box 2) to produce the people contribution to added value (box 3). The model is shown in Figure 33.3.

The first box in the model, people as assets, provides a method of balancing people costs with a measure of the value that they contribute. Mayo argues that calculating the value of people is important for four reasons. First, resourcing decisions should be about more than just cost; second, it is important to understand relative values of individuals and teams; third, it helps make informed investment decisions showing the relative benefits of investing in people as opposed to other assets; and finally, it enables the company to monitor whether its talent is increasing or decreasing. To demonstrate the types of measures that Mayo suggests, we use the example of capability, where the following measures are provided: personal behaviour; business and professional know-how; network of contacts; qualifications and experience; attitudes and values. In terms of maximising human capital we will look at potential. Here Mayo suggests that success in acquisition could

THE HUMAN CAPITAL MONITOR

People as assets	**People motivation and commitment**	**People contribution to added value**
Human asset worth = Employment costs × Individual asset multiplier (IAM)/1000	Measures – How successful are we?	The value added to each stakeholder
IAM = a function of • capability • potential • contribution • values alignment	**The work environment that drives success**	• Financial • Non-financial
Maximising human capital • Acquisition – How successful • Retention are we? • Growth – What drives success?	• Leadership • Practical support • The work group • Learning and development • Rewards and recognition	• Current • Future

Between the first and second boxes is a "+" sign, and between the second and third boxes is an "=" sign.

Figure 33.3
Mayo's human capital monitor

(Source: Adapted from A. Mayo (2001) *The human value of the enterprise: Valuing people as assets – monitoring, measuring and managing.* London: Nicholas Brealey, p. 65.)

be measured by total human asset worth, average IAM (individual asset multiplier) of new recruits and the increase in strategically important core capabilities. The drivers for acquisition of potential include employer brand and acceptance rates, among others.

We turn now to the second box concerning motivation and commitment. Here Mayo suggests such measures as absence levels, satisfaction surveys, attrition rates and reasons for leaving, among others. He suggests five influencing factors as listed in the model, and for the work group, for example, he proposes two measures: team assessments of working practices and a team stability index.

In the final box, people contribution to added value, Mayo suggests that the focus should be on wealth creation, which is a much broader concept than profit, as some of the wealth created can be reinvested in the business. To this end he compares a conventional income statement with a value-added financial statement, which goes beyond seeing people as just costs. In assessing current value Mayo suggests that work needs to be analysed into work which creates value and non-value added work (such as re-doing work, duplication, computer downtime, cross-charging and so on), and that the percentage of each type of work needs to be a focus. He argues that building future value is dependent on innovation and that measures of this need to be derived.

Case 33.2 on this book's companion website, **www.pearsoned.co.uk/torrington**, focuses on human capital.

HUMAN CAPITAL REPORTING

Elias and Scarborough (2004) liken internal and external human capital reporting to management accounting and financial accounting, in that the first is internal and aimed at managing the organisation in an increasingly better way whereas the second is for external consumption. Currently there is minimal external reporting of human capital but a greater extent of internal reporting, which we suggest is a necessary precursor.

The British government's White Paper, *Modernising Company Law* (2002), suggested that the largest 1,000 companies should publish an annual operating and financial review (OFR), and experts believed this would need to include a review of the ways that employees are managed (*People Management* 2002a). However this planned requirement has now been scrapped and a simpler version will now be required which meets the minimum demands of the EU Accounts and Modernisation Directive (EAMD) (Scott 2005). The report now required is entitled the 'Business Review', forms part of the Director's Report, and actually came into force in April 2005. The Business Review requires 'a balanced and comprehensive analysis of the business', and that human capital management issues should be included 'where material'. The scrapping of the OFR raised fears that human capital reporting would have less priority in the business; however the Business Review does apply in some form to all organisations except small firms. Angela Baron suggests that the better the information an organisation has on its human capital the more likely it is that business benefits will accrue (Manocha 2006), and it has been suggested that many companies that have prepared for the OFR will go ahead and produce the more extensive report. The Department for Business, Enterprise and Regulatory Reform (DBERR) has not discounted the possibility of the OFR being resurrected.

Matthewman and Matignon (2005) state that human capital reporting needs to be tailored to the goals, needs and character of each organisation. However the variety of internal and voluntary external reporting appears to be one of the factors that seem to hold back some form of mandatory external reporting. Whilst the Kingsmill Report (2003) declared that there could be no single approach to HCM others have not given up on this. For example Ruth Spellman of the IiP has set up a Human Capital Management Standards Group with the aim of establishing a universal set of metrics which can be used by organisations of any size and in any sector (IRS 2006). A less ambitious project is in the public sector where the Public Sector People Management Association is currently developing a template to allow all local authorities to evaluate the impact of human capital (Stuff 2007).

Other barriers to external reporting have been identified by Elias and Scarborough (2004) as a lack of interest among important external audiences, and Huselid (2003, quoted in Stiles and Kulvisaechana 2003) suggests a major problem is the lack of sophisticated HRISs and a fear that human capital information is too sensitive to reveal to competitors. In addition he suggests that there are concerns from unions and employees that such information might be divulged. The type of information which is most likely to be reported externally, according to Huselid, includes the percentage of employees in stock plans; average pay; revenue per employee; training expenditure and compensation.

WINDOW ON PRACTICE

External Reporting at Yell

Yell provides external information on human capital in both its Annual Report and its Corporate Responsibility Report, produced for the first time in 2005. Yell defines corporate responsibility reporting as 'providing our shareholders and other stakeholders with confidence that Yell is a well-managed and responsible company'.

Barr, the HR Director, says that the measures reported result from an ongoing dialogue with stakeholders. Currently the report covers employee retention (broken down by sales, non-sales), training and development (including average training hours per person), equality and diversity (including gender by job role and employee opinion survey data), health and safety (including accident rates).

Source: S. Welfare (2005) 'The tip of the iceberg: human capital reporting', *IRS Employment Review*, No. 837, 16 December, pp. 8–13.

SUMMARY PROPOSITIONS

33.1 Technology has an important role in freeing up HR professionals to work on more strategic issues. However most HRISs automate existing processes rather than informating. HRISs contribute to human capital management, and more sophisticated systems which facilitate informating have the potential to make a much greater contribution.

33.2 Ad hoc measures of human capital are likely to include absence and turnover analysis and equal opportunities monitoring, but these measures are frequently not strategically integrated and do not necessarily lead to action.

33.3 Strategic frameworks enable a more sophisticated approach to human capital measurement and management. For example the balanced scorecard (Kaplan and Norton 1992), the HR scorecard (Becker *et al.* 2002) and the human capital monitor (Mayo 2001) have all been used as a framework. Such frameworks integrate measures and relate them to organisational strategy.

33.4 Human capital reporting can be both internal and external, but most organisations focus on the former rather than the latter.

GENERAL DISCUSSION TOPICS

1 'Quantitative measures mean nothing. The way that questions are asked, the subjective understanding of what the question means, biased response patterns, and the way that data are analysed and presented, all mean that statistics can be made to say whatever the author of them wishes.' To what extent do you agree or disagree with this statement, and why?

2 'HCM is too complex and resource intensive for any but the largest of organisations.' What factors support this statement, and how could you argue against it?

FURTHER READING

IDS (2001a) *HR Intranets*, IDS Study, No. 713.
This is a very useful guide to a wide range of HR intranet usage. The study explores the challenges of intranets, design, promotion required, content and application, and includes seven case studies: Shell, Argos, Cisco Systems, Prudential, Ford, ICL and Cable and Wireless.

Likierman, A. (2005) 'How to measure the performance of HR', *People Management*, Vol. 11, No. 16, pp. 64–5.
Sound and punchy advice on measuring HR.

Neary, D. (2002) 'Creating a company-wide on-line performance management system: A case study at TRW Inc', *Human Resource Management*, Vol. 41, No. 4, Winter, pp. 491–8.
An interesting example of an IT-based system across 100,000 employees based in 36 countries. Explains the design and implementation of the system.

Stuff, P. (2006) 'Benchmarking the benchmarkers', *Employment Trends, IRS Employment Review*, No. 853, pp. 22–4.
Reviews a variety of levels of benchmarking, from basic hard data, to benchmarking processes, to strategic benchmarking. In addition it looks at different benchmarking approaches, including internal; competitive; functional; and generic. A useful summary article with company examples.

Toulson, P. and Dewe, P. (2004) 'HR accounting as a measurement tool', *Human Resource Management Journal*, Vol. 14, No. 2, pp. 75–90.
New Zealand based study which aims to find out why HR counting is important, to whom, and its links with organisational and HR strategies.

WEB LINK

www.accountingforpeople.gov.uk (the website of the Task Force on Human Capital)

REFERENCES

Ball, K. (2000) 'The use of human resource information systems: a survey', *Personnel Review*, Vol. 30, No. 6, pp. 677–93.

Becker, B., Huselid, M. and Ulrich, D. (2001) *The HR Scorecard: Linking People, Strategy and Performance*. Boston: Harvard Business School Press.

CIPD (2005) *People Management and Technology: Progress and Potential*. London: CIPD.

CIPD (2006a) *HR and Technology: Beyond Delivery, A Change Agenda*. London: CIPD.

CIPD (2006b) *Human Capital Factsheet*. London: CIPD.

Cooper, C. (2001) 'Win by a canvass', *People Management*, Vol. 7, No. 2, 25 January, pp. 42–4.

Crabb, S. (2003) 'HR faces offshore boom', *People Management*, Vol. 9, No. 4, 20 February, p. 7.

Elias, J. and Scarborough, H. (2004) 'Evaluating Human Capital: an exploratory study of management practice', *Human Resource Management Journal*, Vol. 14, No. 4, pp. 21–40.

Gardener, S., Lepak, D. and Bartol, K. (2003) 'Virtual HR: The impact of information technology on the human resource professional', *Journal of Vocational Behaviour*, Vol. 63, pp. 159–79.

Gratton, L. (2003) 'The Humpty Dumpty Effect', *People Management*, Vol. 9, No. 9, 1 May, p. 18.

Gratton, L. (2004) 'Means to an end', *People Management*, Vol. 10, 2 September, p. 20.

Hall, L. and Torrington, D.P. (1998) *The Human Resource Function: The dynamics of change and development*. London: Financial Times Pitman Publishing.

Hammond, D. (2002) 'Firms resist outsourcing', *People Management*, Vol. 8, No. 12, 13 June, p. 8.

Higginbottom, K. (2002) 'Prudential outsources HR in US', *People Management*, Vol. 8, No. 2, 24 January, p. 10.

IDS (2001a) *HR Intranets*, IDS Study, No. 713, August.

IDS (2001b) *HR Service Centres*, IDS Study, No. 707, April.

IDS (2003) *Outsourcing HR administration*, IDS Study Plus, Spring.

IDS (2004) 'The Royal Bank of Scotland', *Human Capital Measurement*, IDS HR Study, No. 783, pp. 33–6.

IRS (2002a) 'Measure for measure', *IRS Employment Review*, No. 754, June, pp. 8–13.

IRS (2002b) 'e-HR: evolution or revolution?', *IRS Employment Review*, No. 764, 25 November, pp. 8–14.

IRS (2003) 'HR goes strategic', *IRS Employment Review*, No. 733, 4 April, pp. 9–14.

IRS (2006) 'Human Capital Reporting: rising from the ashes', *IRS Employment Review*, 18 August, p. 8.

Kaplan, R. and Norton, D. (1992) 'The balanced scorecard – measures that drive performance', *Harvard Business Review*, January–February, pp. 71–9.

Kingsmill, D. (2003) *Accounting for People Report*. London: Task Force on Human Capital.

Manocha, R. (2006), 'Review puts reporting back on agenda', *People Management*, Vol. 12, No. 1, 12 January, p. 9.

Matthewman, J. and Matignon, F. (2005) *Human Capital Reporting: An internal perspective, A Guide*, London: CIPD.

Mayo, A. (2001) *The human value of the enterprise: Valuing people as assets – monitoring, measuring and managing*. London: Nicholas Brealey.

People Management (2002a) 'Human Capital Review', Vol. 8, No. 15, 25 July, p. 9.

People Management (2002b) 'HR departments are corroded by the extent of outsourcing', Vol. 8, No. 20, 10 October, p. 10.

Pickard, J. (2002) 'A source of inspiration?', *People Management*, Vol. 8, No. 14, 11 July, pp. 36–42.

Reddington, M., Withers, M. and Williamson, M. (2005) *Transforming HR: Creating Value Through People*. Oxford: Elsevier Butterworth-Heinemann.

Rippin, S. and Dawson, G. (2001) 'How to outsource the HR function', *People Management*, Vol. 7, No. 19, 27 September, pp. 42–3.

Scott, A. (2005) 'Scrapping OFRs "an astonishing U-turn"', *People Management*, Vol. 11, No. 24, 8 December, p. 10.

Stiles, P. and Kulvisaechana, S. (2003) *Human Capital and Performance: A literature Review*. Cambridge: Judge Institute of Management, University of Cambridge.

Stuff, R. (2007) 'A strong public performance', *IRS Employment Review*, No. 865, 16 February, pp. 6–9.

Tansley, C., Newell, S. and Williams, H. (2001) 'Effecting HRM-style practices through an integrated human resource information system. An e-greenfield site?', *Personnel Review*, Vol. 30, No. 3, pp. 351–70.

Trapp, R. (2001) 'Of mice and men', *People Management*, Vol. 7, No. 13, 28 June, pp. 24–32.

Tyler, E. (2001) 'The click step', *People Management*, Vol. 7, No. 8, 19 April, pp. 50–2.

Ulrich, D. (1997) 'Measuring human resources: an overview of practice and a prescription for results', *Human Resource Management*, Vol. 36, Fall, pp. 303–20.

Welfare, S. (2005) 'The tip of the iceberg: human capital reporting', *IRS Employment Review*, No. 837, 16 December, pp. 8–13.

Zuboff, S. (1988) *In the age of the SMART Machine*. New York: Basic Books.

An extensive range of additional materials, including multiple choice questions, answers to questions and links to useful websites can be found on the Human Resource Management Companion Website at **www.pearsoned.co.uk/torrington**.

CHAPTER 34

THE FUTURE OF WORK

THE OBJECTIVES OF THIS CHAPTER ARE TO:

1   Outline the likely demand for skills in the UK over the next twenty years

2   Introduce the debate about whether the workforce will need to upskill or downskill in the future

3   Set out the major demographic trends in the UK and their consequences for the supply of skills

4   Discuss the major consequences for HR practices arising from a changing workforce profile

5   Debate the merits of the argument that traditional employment practices will change radically in the future in response to environmental trends

6   Put the case for focusing on labour market and regulatory developments as well as developments in product markets when considering the future of work

In a business world that is increasingly seen as being subject to instability and change, managers are right to be interested in likely future developments so that they can prepare effectively and, hopefully, keep one step ahead of their competitors. Business history is littered with examples of big, powerful corporations that have failed to survive because they did not adapt fast enough in the face of unstoppable developments in technology, changes in customer demand or the innovations of competitors. In a global economy governments are also right to be interested in the same developments so that they can put in place measures which will give their organisations the best chance of competing effectively internationally. The trouble is, as Mark Twain famously wrote, 'prediction is difficult, especially when predictions relate to the future'. People have very different ideas about the ways in which our business environment will evolve in future decades, and they can't all be right.

Differences of opinion about the likely future of working life are particularly diverse. On the one hand there is a highly influential school of thought associated (in the UK) with the work of writers such as Charles Handy and Susan Greenfield which predicts a radically different future for work in western industrialised countries. Not only will the nature of the work people do be different from that done by most workers today, the radical view foresees a future in which the very idea of the 'job' will become increasingly outdated. Forms of self-employment and subcontracting will be the norm, as 'knowledge workers' pursue 'portfolio careers', moving from assignment to assignment and retraining regularly in order to make a living. Others agree that the future of work will develop in important ways, but reject the idea that we are heading quickly and inexorably towards radically different working lives. They expect to witness evolution rather than revolution as current trends continue steadily to adjust expectations about work and the demand for and supply of workers. This is the main message that has come out of many recent studies carried out under the auspices of the ESRC's Future of Work research programme (*see* Nolan 2004 and Taylor 2002). A third view stresses the significance of the changes we have witnessed in the past twenty or thirty years and predicts a future for work which, by contrast, is rather more stable than we have become used to. Instead of further transformation, the tendency will be for earlier changes, such as the move from a mixed to a market economy, the feminisation of the workforce, the rise of the service sector, globalisation of business activity, and the rise of employment law, to bed in as western countries enjoy a period of relative economic stability by the standards of recent history. According to this view, the future of work has to a considerable degree 'already happened'. We now need to adjust more fully to the consequences of developments which are clearly permanent and not temporary.

THE FUTURE DEMAND FOR WORKERS

If current trends are maintained we can expect to see continued increases, year on year, in the number of jobs being created by British organisations. In 2006 there were 37.1 million people of working age in the UK, of whom 30.8 million were in work. Around 1.5 million were unemployed and actively seeking work, while a further 7.9 million people of working age were defined as being 'economically inactive' (ONS 2006a). The total number of jobs has grown steadily in recent years to reach its current peak of 26.7 million. The figure decreased during the recessions of the early 1980s and early 1990s, but the long-term trend has been upwards for over sixty years.

Importantly, this increase in the amount of employment in the UK has occurred at a time when many major industries have seen the introduction of labour-saving technologies and when millions of jobs have effectively been 'exported' to developing countries where labour costs are much cheaper. Major industrial restructuring has occurred, yet the demand for labour over the long term has increased steadily. Provided the economy continues to grow, we can thus expect to see further increased demand for people on the part of employers over the coming decade.

But what sort of skills will employers be looking for? Here too long-term trends paint a clear picture which there is every reason to believe will continue for the foreseeable future. The official method used to classify occupations in the UK was changed in 1999, so it is not possible to make a precise comparison of today's figures with those produced by government statisticians before then. Nonetheless an obvious long-term pattern can be seen in the two sets of statistics presented in Tables 34.1 and 34.2. These show a pronounced switch occurring over a long period of time, and continuing strongly in more recent years, away from skilled, semi-skilled and unskilled manual work towards jobs which require higher-level and more specialised skills. The major growth areas have long been in the professional, technical and managerial occupations.

The change in the occupational profile of the UK workforce has largely been driven by the revolutionary shift that has occurred in the nature of our industries during the past thirty years. In 1978, which was the first year that data was collected on employment by sector, seven million people worked in manufacturing and a further one and a half million in the energy, water, farming and fishing industries. These have all hugely declined since then. Manufacturing now employs only three million (12 per cent of all jobs). Agriculture

Table 34.1
Changes in occupations, 1951–1999

Occupation	% in 1951	% in 1999
Higher professionals	1.9	6.4
Lower professionals	4.7	14.9
Employers and proprietors	5.0	3.4
Managers and administrators	5.5	15.7
Clerks	10.7	14.9
Foremen, supervisors and inspectors	2.6	3.1
Skilled manual	24.9	12.7
Semi-skilled manual	31.5	23.0
Unskilled manual	13.1	5.9

Source: *Labour Force Survey* statistics accessed at **www.statistics.gov.uk**.

Table 34.2
Changes in occupations, 2001–2006

Occupation	% in 2001	% in 2006
Managers and senior officials	12.9	14.7
Professional occupations	11.7	12.7
Associate professional and technical occupations	13.2	14.2
Administrative and secretarial	14.9	13.5
Skilled trades	9.5	8.4
Personal services	7.5	8.3
Sales and customer services	8.6	8.6
Process, plant and machine operatives	8.7	7.4
Elementary occupations	13.2	12.1

Source: *Labour Force Survey* statistics accessed at **www.statistics.gov.uk**.

United Kingdom
Millions

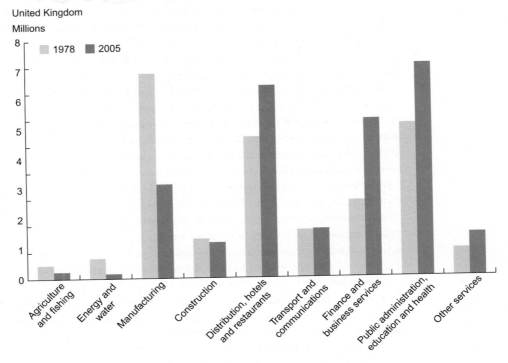

Figure 34.1
Employee jobs:
by industry,
1978 (Quarter
2) and 2005
(Quarter 2)

(Source: ONS (2006a: 7))

and fishing account for just 200,000 jobs; energy and water for fewer still (*see* Figure 34.1). The big growth areas have been in retailing, distribution, hotels and restaurants, finance, business services, public administration, education and health. Employment in the financial services sector has grown especially quickly, more than doubling since 1978.

In the most recent years the biggest growth areas in terms of jobs have been in the public sector. Public sector employment fell during the 1990s. Having peaked at 5.9 million in 1991, it reached a 'low point' of 5.1 million in 1998 before climbing back to 5.9 million again. Over 300,000 new jobs have been created in the NHS since 1998 and over 200,000 in education. The expansion of local and central government has led to the creation of 128,000 jobs, a further 45,000 being created in the police service (ONS 2006a, p. 26). Another major employment trend since the 1970s has been a substantial growth in the proportion of people working in small businesses. The small firms sector now employs 55 per cent of the UK workforce.

ACTIVITY 34.1

Why do you think countries such as the UK have seen so great a transformation in their industrial structure since the 1970s? Why are there so many fewer manufacturing jobs and so many more jobs in the service sector? Why are organisations so much more likely to employ small numbers of people than was the case fifty years ago?

One of the most vigorously contested debates among labour market economists concerns the nature of the skills that employers will be looking for in the future, a debate that has very important implications for government education policy, which, as a result, is itself controversial (*see* Grugulis *et al.* 2004). In recent years a highly influential group has argued that in the future economies such as the UK's will see a speeding up of the trends identified above. Influenced by figures such as Manuel Castells of Berkeley University in California, it has become common for policymakers to believe that a 'new economy' is rapidly developing which will increasingly be dominated by companies which are 'knowledge-intensive' in nature. According to this 'upskilling thesis', lower-skilled jobs will be rarer and rarer in industrialised countries. Because they can be done far more cheaply in developing economies, they will increasingly be exported overseas.

It follows that the governments such as the UK's should prepare the workforce as best it can for the challenges of a 'high-skill, high-wage economy' in which those who do not have a relevant higher education are going to struggle to make a living. Hence we see the rapid expansion of universities, heavy investment in schools and the provision of all manner of schemes designed to equip unemployed people with new skills.

Critics of Castells tend to look to the writings of a very different American academic guru figure – Harry Braverman. His theories derive from a Marxian perspective as well as from observations of the activities of corporations in the 1960s and 1970s. This contrasting 'deskilling thesis' argues that businesses competing in capitalist economies will always look for ways of cutting their labour costs, and that they do this in part by continually reducing the level of skills required by the people they employ. It follows that, far from leading to a demand for higher-level skills and knowledge, the advent of an economy based on information and communication technologies will *over time* reduce such demand.

Both schools draw on widely documented trends to back up their positions. The upskillers draw attention to the fact that the major growth areas in labour demand are in the higher-skilled occupational categories. Demand for graduates is increasing, demand for lower-skilled people is less strong, and is decreasing in some industries. They also draw attention to the emergence of skills shortages in many industries as employers find it steadily harder to recruit people with the abilities and experience they need.

By contrast, the downskillers draw attention to the growth of call-centre-type operations which use technology to reduce the amount of knowledge and expertise required by customer services staff, and to the increasing use of bureaucratic systems which reduce the number of situations in which people have a discretion to make decisions. They also point to the strong growth in industries such as retailing and hotels which are characterised by employment of people who need only be low skilled and who are relatively low paid. They thus forecast a situation in which the workforce is heavily overqualified and in which graduates are increasingly employed in jobs for which no degree is necessary. They also argue that many of the 'skills' that employers say are in short supply are not in fact 'skills' at all, but are merely 'attributes' or 'characteristics'. The target here is an evolving business language that refers to 'communication skills', 'interpersonal skills', 'teamworking skills', 'problem-solving skills' and 'customer-handling skills'. These, it is argued, have nothing whatever to do with a knowledge-based economy and cannot be gained through formal education.

As with all debates that concern the likely future direction of society, it is difficult to reach firm conclusions about this debate. However, in truth what appears to be happening is that we are seeing the emergence of an 'hourglass' occupational structure in the UK in which half of the jobs are of the 'high-skill/high-pay' variety, and the other half are 'low skill/low pay' (Grugulis *et al.* 2004: 6). The metaphor of the hourglass was originally advanced by Nolan (2001). But it has been popularised and expanded in the highly influential article by Goos and Manning (2003) entitled 'McJobs and Macjobs: the growing polarisation of jobs in the UK'. What seems to be happening is the following:

- Increasing numbers of people are being employed in relatively highly paid, secure, professional and managerial occupations in the finance, private services and public sectors.

- Lower-skilled jobs in manufacturing along with many lower-paid clerical and administrative roles are being 'exported' to countries in Eastern Europe and South East Asia where cheaper labour is readily available.

- But, at the same time, the growing number of higher-paid people are using their disposable income to purchase services which cannot be provided from overseas. Hence there is a simultaneous and rapid growth in demand for hairdressers, beauticians, restaurant workers, and people to work in the media, tourist and entertainment-oriented industries.

- There also remains a great demand for, and shortage of, some groups of skilled workers – plumbers, builders, decorators, etc., whose jobs also, by their nature, cannot be so easily exported.

For the foreseeable future, therefore, we are likely to see growth in demand *both* for people who have gained a higher education or who have specialised higher-level skills *and* for people who have strong interpersonal skills (or attributes) to work in the expanding personal services sector. From a public policy point of view, this means that government is broadly correct to put more investment into higher education, but that it is equally important to make available high-quality, specialised forms of vocational education so that the future needs of all industrial sectors are properly provided for. This latter area is one in which the UK has been conspicuously weaker than other European countries for many years.

WINDOW ON PRACTICE

In 2006 the Confederation of British Industry (CBI) published a survey of employers which revealed a lack of basic educational skills among new recruits. According to respondents the big problem in the UK is a lack of basic numerical skills among school leavers, but good reading and writing skills are also in short supply. The problem extends to graduate recruits too. The survey suggests that 23 per cent of employers are unhappy with levels of literacy among their graduates and that 13 per cent are concerned about numeracy levels. The response, according to the CBI, is for one in three employers to provide remedial tuition in reading, writing and arithmetic.

Source: M. Green (2006) 'Employers alarmed at skills shortage', *Financial Times*, 21 August.

THE FUTURE SUPPLY OF WORKERS

The UK population currently stands at 59.8 million. This accounts for 13 per cent of the European Union population, eight per cent of the total European population and just under one per cent of the world's total population. Unlike that of most European countries, the UK population is currently growing (Jeffries 2005). This is for two reasons:

1 Birth rates currently exceed death rates. Each year approximately 700,000 babies are born in the UK, while 615,000 people die – a net gain of 85,000 people.

2 Each year it is estimated that around 150,000 more people migrate into the country than emigrate out of it. Total immigration is now in excess of half a million a year.

The population is therefore growing at a rate of nearly a quarter of a million people each year (ONS 2006b). Official estimates state that the total UK population will reach 65 million by 2050, but this figure will be reached a good deal sooner if current levels of immigration continue. This upward trend in the UK population represents a reversal of the position in the in the 1970s and early 1980s – a period of substantial net emigration and relatively low birth rates.

The birth rate increased substantially after the Second World War and continued at relatively high levels until the late 1960s. Over a million babies were born at the peak in 1964. This created the large 'baby boom' generation who are now in their forties and fifties. From 1964 onwards the UK saw a sharp decline in its birth rate, which reached a low point in 1977 when only 657,000 babies were born (i.e. fewer than the number of deaths). This was due in part to the relatively low number of births in the country in the war years (1939–45), in part to the wide availability of the contraceptive pill and abortion, and partly to changes in social attitudes leading to later marriages. The downward trend was reversed somewhat in the 1980s as the baby boomers had children, but fertility rates remain at relatively low levels historically. As a result of these patterns, we have an ageing population. There are many more people in the UK in their forties and fifties than there are in their twenties and thirties (*see* Figure 34.2).

ACTIVITY 34.2

Why do you think that people, on average, choose to have fewer children than they did a generation ago? Can anything be done to reverse the trend? How far should governments see it as their role to encourage more births?

This will mean that there are many more retired people in the future than there are at present, but at the same time the number of adults of working age is projected to increase rather than decrease. Official estimates state that there will be 40.5 million people who are over school leaving age and below retirement age in 2020 as a result of continued net immigration and the equalisation of male and female state pension ages at 65 from 2010. The average age of this group will increase substantially because there will be a higher proportion of older people in the workforce and because younger people are projected

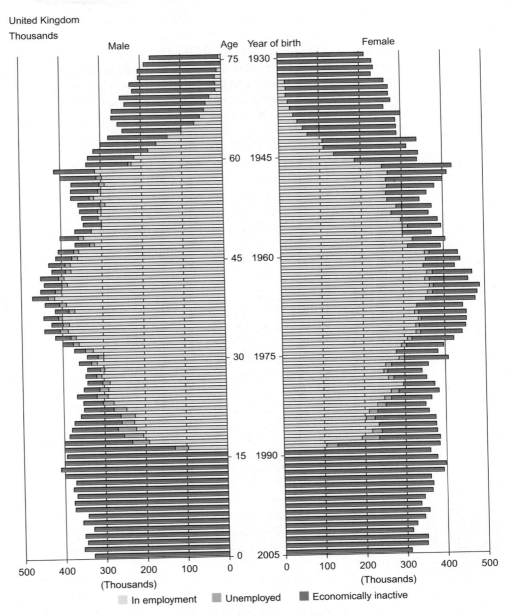

Figure 34.2
Population
structure: by
age, sex and
economic
activity,
autumn 2005[1]

United Kingdom
Thousands

Male   Age   Year of birth   Female

(Thousands)   (Thousands)

☐ In employment   ☐ Unemployed   ■ Economically inactive

(Source: ONS (2006a) Labour Force Survey.   [1] Not seasonally adjusted)

to choose to stay on in full-time education for longer, on average, than they currently do
(Smith *et al.* 2005). We can thus conclude with a degree of confidence both that the
supply of labour will increase in the coming two decades and that the profile of the
workforce will age significantly.

However, there are important regional differences that it is important to note. The
structure, density and growth of the population are by no means likely to be uniform
across the whole country. The highest concentrations of older people, for example,

are in the resort towns along the south and eastern coasts. Christchurch in Dorset is officially the 'oldest' place in the UK where 33.2 per cent are entitled to draw a state pension. By contrast, pensioners are few and far between in inner London. Tower Hamlets boasts the lowest proportion (only 9.8 per cent), but the numbers are also low in some commuter towns close to London and in cities with large student populations.

The highest concentrations of children are found in Northern Ireland where fertility rates are much higher than elsewhere in the country, while young adults are concentrated in university towns and cities, reflecting the fact that there are now 1.4 million full-time students in the UK. As far as England is concerned, between the 1930s and 2001 the major trend was a movement of people from the north of the country to the south, the southern regions gaining 30,000 people a year on average during this period. Since 2001 there has been an apparent reversal of this long-term trend, the north gaining 35,000 people per year at the expense of the south (Champion 2005). However, as a result of migration and falling fertility rates the populations of Scotland and Wales are both falling. In both countries there are considerably more deaths than births each year and relatively high levels of net emigration.

We can also predict with some certainty that there will be greater diversity among the workforce in terms of ethnicity and national origin as a result of net immigration.

All around the world international migration is increasing. As far as the UK is concerned this means that the long-term trend is towards greater levels of both emigration and immigration (Horsfield 2005). Until the early 1990s the UK had been broadly in balance as far as international migration was concerned for around twenty years. Indeed, for much of the 1970s and during the early 1980s more people left the UK each year than entered it. Since 1993 this trend has changed. Every year there are now substantially more immigrants than emigrants, a gap which widens year on year. People leaving the UK tend to be older on average than the new arrivals. Many leave in order to retire in sunnier climes, while others seek new opportunities in Australasia, the USA, Canada and EU countries. A fair proportion of annual emigration each year involves people who were born overseas returning to their countries of origin, for example following a period studying in a UK university. Historically the main source of immigrants into the UK has been from new Commonwealth countries such as India, Pakistan, Bangladesh and from the Caribbean. However, more recently we have seen a substantial growth in people arriving from other developing countries (such as Somalia) and especially from the countries which joined the European Union in May 2004 (i.e. Poland, Slovakia, Hungary, Cyprus and the Baltic states).

As a result of net immigration the proportion of the UK population which was born overseas increases each year, the vast majority of these people being of working age (Randall and Salt 2005). At the time of the 2001 census just under five million UK residents had been born overseas. This represents 8.3 per cent of the population. This is a great deal higher than was the case at the time of previous censuses. In 1991 the figure was 6.7 per cent, and in 1951 only 4.2 per cent. Here too, however, there is considerable regional variation. Forty-eight per cent of immigrants arriving in the UK settle in London and the south east of England, the largest numbers settling in inner London. The London borough of Brent boasts the highest proportion of foreign-born residents (46.6 per cent). By contrast, the lowest levels (under 3 per cent) are found in the English-Scottish border regions.

If current trends continue the supply of labour across the UK as a whole should be sufficient to meet the growing demand for labour. Chronic skills shortages will be avoided provided government and employers continue to invest in the education and development of people. Importantly, in these respects the UK is a great deal better placed than many of its competitor countries where the population is falling and is ageing at a far faster rate than is the case in Britain. Fertility rates in many southern and eastern European countries have now fallen well below 1.5, meaning that each couple produces on average fewer than 1.5 children. A fertility rate of 2.1 is required to maintain a stable population, yet it is 1.32 in Germany, 1.28 in Italy, 1.27 in Spain and only 1.26 in Poland (United Nations 2005). In the UK immigration allows the maintenance of steady population growth, despite historically low fertility rates (1.66 in 2006). This is in contrast to the position of many countries where immigration rules are more restrictive or where low wages and relatively high unemployment make them less attractive to economic migrants.

The statistics suggest, however, that employers in many regions will continue to face some skills shortages. Provided unemployment remains relatively low, this will tend to push wage rates up beyond the rate of price inflation. The result, as has been the case for the past fifteen years, will be greater pressure on organisations to improve labour productivity by reorganising, merging to achieve economies of scale and outsourcing activities where they can be supplied more efficiently by external providers. It will also be necessary for employers willingly to employ more older people than they have tended to be accustomed to doing. Indeed, in order to meet their demand for labour it is likely that organisations are going to have to target older groups and take steps to make employment attractive to them. There are three distinct groups who have not traditionally found themselves to be in great demand by recruiters:

- people over the age of fifty who are still working,
- people who have taken early retirement/redundancy,
- people who are over the state retirement age.

In the case of the first group, traditional full-time jobs will be sought. The others are more likely to be looking for part-time work or some other form of flexible working. Research strongly suggests that most people have a preference for phased retirement as opposed to full-time work until a retirement day and then leisure (HSBC 2006). Employers who can provide flexibility of this kind will be in a far stronger position to compete for the services of older workers than competitors who do not. Another consequence of an ageing population will be the presence among younger employees of more people with responsibility for caring for elderly relatives. Attracting and retaining them will also require flexible working options.

Aside from flexibility, the other major element that needs to be in place in order to attract and retain older people is a culture which fully respects and values their contribution. A great deal of research has been carried out in recent years looking at attitudes to older workers among managers and younger employees. The conclusion is that people commonly stereotype older workers, just as they tend to stereotype young workers. Older workers tend to be seen as being reliable, stable, mature and experienced, but also as difficult to train, resistant to change, over-cautious, poor with technology, slow and prone to ill health. Organisations which are serious about employing more older people will need to tackle such stereotyping and to ensure that opportunities for development are provided for people of all ages.

However, at the same time, employers need to recognise that people do change as they age and do contribute different qualities than younger colleagues. They thus need to be managed somewhat differently from an HR perspective. It will be necessary, for example, to tailor reward packages to suit the needs of older workers as well as younger ones. Clearly this will include pension arrangements, but may also incorporate other benefits which older employees value more than younger employees such as health insurance.

Organisations often seek a workforce which reflects its core target market. This is particularly true of creative and media industries which need younger employees to ensure that they are in touch with the needs, aspirations and concerns of people in the key 18–30 group. This is a major source of age discrimination in the labour market which is likely, over time, to change. Instead of seeking employees who match their consumers by age, employers will want people of any age who reflect the values and attitudes of more broadly-aged target markets.

The changes to HR practice required as a result of increased numbers of workers from overseas are less profound but equally important. The key here is to make sure that the organisation both gains and retains a reputation for fairness in its labour markets. Once an organisation is perceived to be prone to acting in a discriminatory fashion towards members of ethnic minorities or migrant workers, the reputation is hard to shake off, making it harder to recruit and retain a skilled workforce. In this area perceptions of managers about the fairness of their policies and practices is irrelevant. The perception of the target labour market is all that matters, so we can expect to see organisations in the future 'bending over backwards' to ensure not just that they are committed to equal opportunities and diversity, but that they are seen to be too.

ACTIVITY 34.3

According to the demographers at the United Nations several European countries are going to see substantial falls in their populations over the next forty years due to low fertility rates. It is estimated that the German population will fall from 83 million to 79 million by 2050, and the Italian population from 58 million to 51 million. In Russia the projected fall is from 143 million to 112 million By contrast the British and French populations are projected to increase modestly during this period, while in Turkey the population will increase hugely from 77 million today to 101 million in 2050.

What do you think are the main long-term implications for organisations in these different European countries? What will the effect be on the labour market? What will be the effect on the capacity of public sector organisations to deliver vital public services?

FUTURE CONTRACTUAL ARRANGEMENTS

While there is general agreement among commentators about the nature of the work we will be carrying out in the coming decades and the profile of the workforce that will be employed to carry it out, there is considerable disagreement about the types of contract (both legal and psychological) that will be prevalent. For some years now a diverse group of futurologists have gained considerable influence by predicting substantial changes in this area. The most prominent figure in the UK is Charles Handy, who has published a series of books in which he argues that radical change is in store (*see* Handy 1984, 1989, 1994 and 2001). A broadly similar analysis has been developed by Davidson and Rees Mogg (1997), Rifkin (1995) and Bridges (1995), and more recently by Susan Greenfield (2003a and 2003b). While each of these writers, and others who have advocated the evolution of a similar future for the world of work, justify their conclusion somewhat differently, all predict a switch in the dominant form of work from employment to various forms of self-employment. Moreover, where employment continues, people will be far more likely to work from home (connected to others electronically) and to work for small, highly specialised companies and will neither have nor expect long-term job security.

For Handy the future is one in which portfolio careers will dominate. People will move from employer to employer regularly, often working for two concerns at the same time. There will be periods of self-employment and periods of employment, the conventional working life being likened to that of an actor auditioning for work and moving from production to production on stage, screen and television. There will be periods in between assignments when we will be under-employed, and other periods when we have more than enough work on our plates. Davidson and Rees-Mogg (1997, p. 237) prefer the example of film production companies which assemble a group of talented specialists to work on a project, but when it is over 'the lighting technicians, cameramen, sound engineers and wardrobe specialists will go their separate ways'. Others, including Greenfield (1993, p. 92) go further in arguing that 'the concept of the "job" as we know it may disappear altogether' and that 'firms will perhaps bid for employee time almost on a day-to-day basis'. Insecurity of employment, according to this view, will soon become the norm.

The analysis on which these writers base their predictions is thoughtful and logical and can be persuasive. At root they all argue that greater volatility in the world of employment is inevitable as organisations experience increasing volatility in their product markets. Because employers will no longer operate in markets which are at all stable and predictable, it follows that they will be unable to guarantee any kind of stable employment. For most analysts, increased volatility is seen as being a product of increased competition. Sparrow (2002) uses the term 'hyper-competition' to describe a business environment in which lean, highly productive organisations make use of the latest information and communications technologies to sell their goods and services to anyone, anywhere in a fast-evolving, knowledge-based global economy. In such a world, it is argued, no organisation can be viable if it burdens itself with large numbers of dependent employees expecting to enjoy lengthy, stable careers. Instead organisations will continually be expanding and retracting, forming and dissolving, and hiring different people, with different skill-sets on an 'as needs' basis. Greenfield's conclusion is the same, but for her the change will arise not as a result of increased competition, as she predicts greater cooperation and less competition, but simply because increased technical specialisation will mean that the most efficient and effective enterprises will be those which are small and highly flexible. Rifkin argues that traditional jobs will disappear because technological advances will create a world in which machines do many of the jobs currently performed by people. His future is a world of under-employment in which there are not enough jobs to go round, forcing a large proportion of the workforce either into self-employment or into a working life of short-term employment as and when opportunities arise.

A number of arguments have been advanced in opposition to this radical vision of an employment-free future world of work. Nolan (2004) has led the assault in the UK, drawing on empirical data indicating that in most respects, despite evidence of increased volatility in product markets, traditional, long-term, full-time employment is showing no sign whatever of withering away. Indeed, in some respects the trend is towards greater security, albeit in smaller enterprises. He is contemptuous in his criticisms of those who continue to peddle what he sees as misleading myths:

> Scarcely a week passes without a well-paid visionary heralding the demise of paid work and employment or the growing salience in the new economy of the 'free-worker'. Attention to detail is invariably slight. The great variance in the patterns of work and the consequences of past upheavals in employment are routinely ignored. (Nolan 2004, p. 7)

He goes on to make reference to the real trends that are observable in both the UK and the USA, to many of which we have referred in this and in earlier chapters:

- employment levels (i.e. the number of traditional jobs) are rising and not falling;
- the vast majority of workers continue to be employed in permanent jobs;
- job tenure rates have remained broadly stable for decades;
- around a third of the workforce has been employed (already) for ten years or more by their current employer;
- self-employment has not grown appreciably over the past decade;
- the number of temporary workers has fallen substantially over the past ten years.

While this evidence is very convincing, it is too early to condemn Handy, Rifkin and Greenfield as having been hopelessly wrong in their predictions. It is possible that over the coming few decades they will be proved right. But it is fair to point out that, at least in the case of Handy, the same claims were being made twenty-five years ago about what the world of work would be like today, and in many respects the opposite has turned out to be the case.

One possible reason that the predictions of these futurologists may prove to be inaccurate is their over-reliance on an analysis of what is likely to happen to product markets, ignoring in the process other determinants of employment arrangements such as labour market pressures and the regulatory environment. The evidence suggests that they are right about increasing competition and the need for organisations to become more specialised, flexible and productive, but that they are wrong to ignore other factors in the evolving business environment which serve to push organisations in an opposite direction to that which they would prefer given a free hand. For example, it is very often claimed that in the future, because employers will be unable to guarantee long-term employment, they will instead provide their workers with a capacity for greater 'employability'. People will be recruited and motivated, not with the promise of job security, but with skills development and work experience which will help them to build successful portfolio careers. This is a logical prediction if it is assumed that employers do not have to compete with one another for relatively scarce skills. However, as we have seen throughout this book, in recent years the trend has been towards tighter labour markets in which people increasingly have a choice about where they work and are willing as well as able to switch employers when they become dissatisfied. It is at least arguable that most would-be workers prefer secure employment to employability and portfolio career-building. If so the organisations that will be most successful in attracting and retaining people will be those which maximise job security by offering employment on a permanent basis.

Moreover, in a world in which the quality of staff increasingly provides the key to achieving competitive advantage, it is probable that employers will prefer to nurture high levels of commitment and discretionary effort from their people, rather than hiring and firing them on an as needs basis. In other words, employers may well conclude that a committed, productive workforce is not compatible with highly flexible organisation structures, and that the former is a better route to establishing competitive advantage than the latter.

The potential influence of regulation also needs to be taken into account. In the UK there is general agreement among employers and the political establishment that the best way of securing high levels of employment over the long term is to minimise labour market regulation so as to free businesses of costs which make them less competitive internationally. However, much employment regulation now originates at the European level and would not, for the most part, be on UK statute books were it not for Britain's membership of the European Union. The political establishments of the other larger EU countries have tended to take a different view, believing increased social protection to be necessary as a means of promoting greater security of employment. A perception of insecurity, in their view, tends to reduce people's willingness to spend and to put their savings in riskier types of investment vehicle. The result is less economic growth and a greater propensity to stagnation and recession (European Commission 2000). The outcome, as we have seen in recent years, has been a plethora of new employment legislation aiming to increase security by making it increasingly hard for employers to hire and fire either cheaply or easily. This creates a situation in which any journey on the part of employers towards much more flexible organisational forms is made harder both to embark on and to complete.

Finally it is necessary to point out that some economists are increasingly questioning the commonly held view that the business environment of the future will necessarily be characterised by greater volatility, at least as far as the western industrialised countries are concerned. Indeed already they observe far greater levels of economic stability pertaining in countries such as the UK and the USA that have moved farthest down the road away from manufacturing and towards the establishment of knowledge-based service industries. Kaletsky (2006), for example, argues strongly that manufacturing activities are the major source of volatility and that exporting these overseas, leaving home-based employees to focus on product design and marketing, actually serves to guarantee greater security of employment in a global economy. He gives the title 'platform companies' to organisations like Nokia, Dell and L'Oreal which sell their products internationally, but subcontract the entire manufacturing process to other companies:

> Because the manufacture of physical goods is the most volatile and capital-intensive part of the business process, outsourcing [overseas] does not just transfer jobs and factories – platform companies also outsource to China and other developing countries much of the economic volatility that goes with capital investment, inventory cycles and the unionised factory environment. (p. 21)

Could it be therefore that long-term, stable employment, far from being consigned to the dustbin of history, will actually become more common in the future as organisations increasingly outsource the more volatile elements of their operations and concentrate instead on higher-skilled, value-adding activities? Only time will tell, but an analysis of the major current labour market trends is consistent with this possibility.

WINDOW ON PRACTICE

In recent years the UK government has made major investments in new technology as a means of improving standards of service delivery in the public services and reducing costs. In 2004 the Gershon Report entitled 'Transformational Government' was published. This identified £21 billion of possible annual savings across government that could be gained by greater efficiency generated by IT. To date the government claims to have saved £9.8 billion.

In order to deliver the government's ambitious agenda in this field, there is a need to recruit IT professionals with the experience and knowledge to develop highly complex systems. This task is proving difficult because there are relatively few people with the required skills and many potential competitors for their services. Critics say that the government will continue to be restricted in its ambitions until it accepts, as it has been reluctant to do, that it needs to pay people at or above the market rate for their services, while also creating clear career paths so that IT people, once recruited, can develop careers by moving across the different government departments. Historically IT people have tended to be hired on a subcontracted basis to work on one-off projects. This no longer works effectively as a means of sourcing scarce skills because private sector competitors are able to offer the prospect of longer-term career growth.

Source: R. Newing (2005) 'Technology: Rethink on careers as IT skills shortages loom', *Financial Times*, 15 June.

SUMMARY PROPOSITIONS

34.1 The likely future direction of employment practices in the UK has attracted a great deal of attention in recent years and has led to several hotly contested debates.

34.2 The occupations which are growing fastest are higher-level professional, technical and managerial jobs in the public and private sectors, and lower-paid jobs in the private services sector.

34.3 The working population in the UK is likely to grow at a slower rate in the future than it has in the recent past. It is also going to age and become more ethnically diverse.

34.4 Labour markets are likely to tighten further, leading to more skills shortages and a demand for skilled workers from overseas.

34.5 A radical vision for the future of work has been advocated by several influential management thinkers in recent years. They predict many fewer jobs, less job stability and more self-employment.

34.6 The radical vision is increasingly being challenged by researchers who maintain that the organisation of work is unlikely to alter radically in the foreseeable future.

GENERAL DISCUSSION TOPICS

1 What are the major trends in your own organisation's future demand for skills? To what extent do you foresee these being harder to source in the future and why?

2 What purpose does a study of current demographic trends serve from the point of view of the HR function in organisations?

3 Why do you think management writers continue to predict a revolution in the way work is organised in industrialised countries, despite the presence of evidence suggesting a continuation of the approaches that are currently prevalent?

FURTHER READING

Robert Taylor, formerly labour affairs editor of the *Financial Times*, has published five excellent papers over the past few years focusing on different aspects of the future of work. These draw on the large range of academic research that has been contributed to the Economic and Social Research Council's Future of Work programme. You can download these papers without charge at **www.leeds.ac.uk/esrcfutureofwork**.

The government's Office of National Statistics (ONS) also has an excellent website which can be used to gain access to a large range of authoritative articles and statistics concerning demographic trends and the demand and supply of skills in the UK. You will find summaries of the most recent trends in their annual publications *Social Trends* and *Labour Market Review*.

REFERENCES

Bridges, W. (1995) *Jobshift: how to prosper in a workplace without jobs*. London: Nicholas Brealey.

Champion, T. (2005) 'Population movement within the UK', in Office of National Statistics, *Focus on People and Migration*. London: HMSO.

Davidson, J.D. and Rees-Mogg, W. (1997) *The Sovereign Individual: The coming economic revolution. How to survive and prosper in it*. Basingstoke: Macmillan.

European Commission (2000) *The Future of Work*. London. Kogan Page.

Goos, M. and Manning, A. (2003) 'McJobs and Macjobs: the growing polarisation of jobs in the UK', in R. Dickens, P. Gregg and J. Wadsworth (eds), *The Labour Market Under New Labour*. Basingstoke: Palgrave.

Green, M. (2006) 'Employers alarmed at skills shortage', *Financial Times*, 21 August.

Greenfield, S. (2003a) *Tomorrow's People*. London: Penguin/Allen Lane.

Greenfield, S. (2003b) 'Flexible Futures', *People Management*, 23 October, pp. 52–3.

Grugulis, I., Warhurst, C. and Keep, E. (2004) 'What's happening to "Skill"?', in C. Warhurst, I. Grugulis and E. Keep (eds), *The Skills That Matter*. Basingstoke: Palgrave.

Handy, C. (1984) *The Future of Work*. Oxford: Blackwell.

Handy, C. (1989) *The Age of Unreason*. London: Business Books.

Handy, C. (1994) *The Empty Raincoat: Making Sense of the Future*. London: Hutchinson.

Handy, C. (2001) *The Elephant and the Flea: Looking Backwards to the Future*. London: Hutchinson.

Horsfield, G. (2005) 'International migration', in Office of National Statistics, *Focus on People and Migration*. London: HMSO.

HSBC (2006) *The Future of Retirement: What the World Wants*. London: HSBC.

Jeffries, J. (2005) 'The UK population: past, present and future', in Office of National Statistics, *Focus on People and Migration*. London: HMSO.

Kaletsky, A. (2006) 'Why the sun is rising over Britain, not Japan', *The Times*, 10 November, p. 21.

Newing, R. (2005) 'Technology: Rethink on careers as IT skills shortages loom', *Financial Times*, 15 June.

Nolan, P. (2001) 'Shaping things to come', *People Management*, 27 December.

Nolan, P. (2004) *Back to the Future of Work*. At **www.leeds.ac.uk/esrcfutureofwork/downloads/ events/colloquium_2004/nolan_paper_0904.pdf**.

ONS (2006a) *Labour Market Review 2006*. London: HMSO.

ONS (2006b) *Social Trends 2006*. London: HMSO.

Randall, M. and Salt, J. (2005) 'The foreign-born population', in Office of National Statistics, *Focus on People and Migration*. London: HMSO.

Rifkin, J. (1995) *The End of Work: The decline of the global labour force and the dawn of the post-market era*. New York: Puttnam.

Smith, C., Tomassini, C., Smallwood, S. and Hawkins, M. (2005) 'The changing age structure of the UK population', in Office of National Statistics, *Focus on People and Migration*. London: HMSO.

Sparrow, P. (2002) 'The Future of work', in D. Holman, T. Wall, C. Clegg, P. Sparrow and A. Howard (eds), *The New Workplace: a guide to the human impact of modern working practices*. Chichester: Wiley.

Taylor, R. (2002) *Britain's World of Work – Myths and Realities*. At **www.leeds.ac.uk/ esrcfutureofwork**.

United Nations (2005) *World Population Prospects: The 2004 Revision*. New York: United Nations.

An extensive range of additional materials, including multiple choice questions, answers to questions and links to useful websites can be found on the Human Resource Management Companion Website at **www.pearsoned.co.uk/torrington**.

INTERACTIVE SKILL 7: CHAIRING MEETINGS

Part 7 has been a mixture of topics having in common the single feature that they potentially affect all of the functional areas dealt with in the earlier parts of the book. For that reason our examination of an interactive skill now considers an activity that deals with coordination in a rather different way: making meetings work. Meetings do not constitute the whole of management but they are an inescapable part of the management process and they are frequently less successful than they should be. Leading, or chairing, meetings is a challenging skill but a rewarding aspect of human resource management. Chairing is a position that is associated with authority. Company boards, benches of magistrates, Cabinet committees, employment tribunals, political parties, debating societies are among the many activities that are led by the person in the chair. Professors in universities are appointed to chairs, not because they are too weary or lazy to stand up, but because the occupation of a chair represents authority.

WINDOW IN PRACTICE

In courts of law there is a standard opening to proceedings whereby everyone present stands for the entry of the judge or the magistrates. If there is more than one person on the bench, the chair for the central person usually has a higher back than the others to emphasise the authority of the office that person holds.

The objectives of this Focus on skills are to:

1 Review some of the different types of meeting HR people have to chair

2 Explain the stages of running a meeting: preparation, conduct of the meeting itself, follow-up and implementation of proposals

Types of meeting

HR specialists have many meetings to chair, including selection panels, meetings with union officials, health and safety committees, job evaluation groups and many more. It is not sufficient just to know why a meeting is being held for it to be a success: the processes by which a meeting works have to be understood as well. In one of our research projects 433 meetings were observed, and many showed the chair to have such limited understanding of the basic mechanics of meetings that there was inadequate discussion, understanding and action about important matters. Poor meetings not only fail to achieve objectives, they also do harm, as members become frustrated about lack of progress or about not being able to get their point of view across. It is not just the fault of the person in charge: all participants have to learn meeting mechanics. The analogy of the orchestra is apt. The conductor is responsible for the final quality of the coordinated act, but every instrumentalist has to make a distinctive, but not individualistic, contribution that blends with all the others.

We have to pay careful attention to the details of running the meeting. Good intentions and the importance of the matter to be considered are not enough on their own. The person in charge takes the blame for things not being right. Those who feel overlooked or outmanoeuvred are merciless with those who have overlooked them, however unintentional this was by the person in the chair. The person in charge may feel very uncomfortable and may lose respect in the eyes of colleagues, but something is still usually achieved: catharsis for group members and some information exchange.

The basic necessities are a clear format, purpose and preparation, with the leader being in control. Those attending the meeting can then concentrate on content rather than fretting about the way the meeting is being conducted. People will only attend and make a success of meetings they see as useful.

WINDOW ON PRACTICE

An ICI plant manager has on the wall of his office a framed citation confirming that he is a full member of 'The Institution of Meetings Engineers'. This is obviously a spoof, non-existent body dreamt up by a few engineers who felt that most meetings were a waste of time. The inscription included phrases such as, 'Members shall attend all meetings called, regardless of their value . . . Any member falling asleep shall have membership suspended until he wakes up . . . A member finding a meeting useful should send a full report to the General Secretary of the Institution before seeking medical attention.'

Many readers will empathise with those comments, having attended meetings which seem pointless, or boring, or too long, or all three. People who can chair meetings effectively are a rare breed, highly regarded by their colleagues.

Preparation

Making effective arrangements for a meeting help it to be an effective meeting. Here is a series of check questions.

Who should attend the meeting?

A large group will ensure that a wide range of interests is represented, so that there should be few problems of people complaining that they were excluded. Large numbers are usually appropriate when pressing matters of major importance are to be discussed and a lot of people have to be informed quickly. The problems are that the more people who attend, the more likely it is that the business will grind to a halt. Also the more people who attend, the less likely it is that there will be any useful discussion.

A small group makes discussion easier and more productive as there are fewer people competing to have their say and it is easier for the person in the chair to blend together a range of contributions in finding a consensus.

Ideally you want people either who have expertise in the matter being discussed or who have a stake in it. This ensures focus for the discussion and should help outcomes, as there is an old axiom that people will support that which they have helped to create. Observers or free-loaders can be a nuisance as they do not have the discipline of having to deliver on whatever is agreed and may therefore become more concerned to make an impression as someone with bright ideas rather than thinking of practical solutions.

You may want a variety of personalities and styles to ensure a lively discussion.

What is the brief or terms of reference of the meeting?

Does this meeting have the power to take a decision, to make a recommendation, or simply to exchange information? All of these are equally valid objectives, but it helps to be clear on this basic question of what sort of meeting it is.

Sometimes there is a limit to how wide the discussion can usefully range. Some aspects will be outside the competence of the meeting and such discussion could distract those present from dealing with the matter they should be discussing. An example is where a decision has already been made elsewhere that cannot be changed. If it has been decided elsewhere that a plant should close, there will then be a number of other meetings to decide how that decision should be implemented. It is rarely appropriate for a management meeting to try and get that decision changed. If members spend time deploring the decision that has been made, it might be worth while if they then are able to move on, having expressed their feelings.

As well as explicit terms of reference that define the range of discussion, there may well be some conclusions that would be unacceptable. The chair needs to have sufficient nous to be aware of what these are and to whom they would not be acceptable, so that they can either be ruled out in discussion or questioned if suggested.

What should the agenda be?

There are two questions about the agenda, one more obvious than the other: what do we need to consider, and in what order?

The content of the agenda is usually drafted and proposed by the chair or, in more formal meetings, the chair in consultation with the secretary. The topics for consideration need to be clearly described, so that members of the group can come to the meeting with a clear understanding of them and with a focus on the key issues. There is a risk in putting too many items on the agenda so that some are rushed, or put off to another occasion.

The sequence of items can be affected by the consideration of which chicken needs to come before which egg. Getting the right things early on the agenda can make it easier to resolve later matters provided they are in the right order; otherwise decisions are half made and then deferred 'until we have dealt with item X'.

With meetings where there are minutes to review, matters arising and any other business can take up a lot of time unless there is careful planning.

ACTIVITY 7.1

Reflect on a meeting you attended recently that you felt was not well organised and run. Were the terms of reference for the meeting clear to all attending? Was the sequence of items on the agenda conducive to a successful meeting? Would the meeting have been more effective if the sequence had been different?

What about the physical location and arrangements?

How often have you attended a meeting where one or more of the following occur:

- Two people do not come because they were not told about it (or so they say).
- Three people arrive late because they could not find the room.
- Two of the late arrivals immediately leave to try and borrow chairs from another room because there are not enough.

- Coffee arrives ten minutes after the meeting has started and is served (or distributed) by catering assistants who swap comments with each other in loud voices such as, 'One more down here, Flo'.

- Several people mutter that they had specifically asked for tea, whereupon Flo produces a docket and reads out what it says so as to clear Flo and her colleague of any responsibility for the fact that tea has not been provided.

- After half an hour a succession of people arrive for a completely different meeting, because the room has been double-booked (or so they say. Probably they forgot to book it. You're sure that *you did* book it, aren't you?).

- The room is noisy, too hot or too cold, the wrong shape or in the wrong place, and the toilets are miles away.

Incidents like these can wreck a meeting, or at least send the chair into convulsions, yet most of them can be avoided with good organisation, so that you merely have to contend with the people who have brought the wrong papers or do not know what is going on as they have not opened their e-mail since last month.

What is the meeting for?

The person leading the meeting needs a clear view of what type of meeting it is going to be. This will affect the way it is run and the way in which those attending are asked to participate.

The meeting may be *to convey information*. Then the sole focus is on the chair, who is passing on information, or analysis or news to a gathering of those who need to know. The only role for others attending the meeting is to listen, perhaps ask questions and probably mutter explanations and reiterations to each other to check their understanding. The reason for doing this in a meeting rather than distributing a memorandum is to give the opportunity for further clarification through questions; there is also the symbolic impact of information being passed on personally rather than impersonally. It is therefore usually done for matters of weight and significance.

If a meeting is *to share information* the chair is the coordinator rather than the fount of all wisdom. A health or social work case conference is a typical example and the chair needs skill to elicit constructive participation, and to encourage a free flow of information at the same time as preventing such a free flow that the meeting becomes chaotic and loses any sense of direction.

A meeting *to make a decision* will have a different style again. The expertise needed to make the right decision is distributed among the members of the group, so that much of the time is spent sharing information, but there has to be joint ownership of, or support for, the decision that is eventually made. A board meeting is the obvious example and the actual dynamics of the encounter itself will vary according to the relative status and authority of those present. The chair may be so dominant that the meeting is to win the support of members to a decision that is already made. In other situations it is necessary for a consensus to be identified as the discussion develops so that it can be articulated for everyone to accept or modify until it wins general acceptance and commitment. Some decisions are reached by voting. Although these are not common in management meetings, it is still essential that the chair moves to a vote only when a consensus is apparent. A majority of one is scarcely a majority at all and talking should continue until the weight of opinion is more substantial.

Conduct of the meeting itself

How can contributions be stimulated and controlled?

For each item on the agenda, the chair needs to consider:

- Who has something to say?
- How can I get them to say it?
- How can I keep the long-winded brief?
- When should I nudge the meeting towards a decision/the next item?

Few people are accustomed to expressing a point of view in a meeting, and most are likely to find it inhibiting. They speak best when asked to do so, and when speaking on something about which they are knowledgeable. Leaders of meetings get contributions by asking people to speak, picking up non-verbal cues of a desire to speak or reaction to what someone else has said. Statements of fact rather than expressions of opinion are the easiest way for people to make their first contribution. Experienced members of groups can help the less experienced by 'shaping' the clumsy or over-emotional comments of their colleagues and agreeing with them (for example: 'I would like to agree with what Hilary was saying and make the further point . . .' NOT, 'I think Hilary was trying to say . . .').

Inexperienced leaders of meetings sometimes show their worry about losing control by constantly emphasising the limited time available, but this makes it harder for people to make coherent contributions. People speak more effectively and come to the point more quickly when not under time pressure.

Curbing the excesses of the verbose is a true test of chairing skill. Making a succinct and focused contribution is a competence not found often among people attending meetings, so the chair has to be skilled not only in eliciting contributions, but also in closing people down when they are running out of control. Here are some suggestions:

- Use eye contact with the speaker to indicate encouragement or discouragement. When you begin to lose interest, or become mildly irritated, the speaker will receive that silent message and will usually respond to it.
- For those who will not respond, use more direct signals, such as looking away or looking anxiously at your watch.
- Use focus questions. If the speaker is rambling on and on, you must focus what is being said by interrupting with a question to focus the speaker and to elicit an answer that is likely to be brief. Examples are:
  - 'How long will it take for X's performance to improve?'
  - 'What will it cost?'
  - 'Have you got it cleared?'

Bringing people in

An aspect of control is finding ways to bring people into the discussion at the time when their contribution is most appropriate. Ways to do it are like this:

- Pick out someone who you think should have a relevant or constructive comment to make and invite him or her: 'What is your view, Henry?' or 'I wonder if Sheila could help us with the exact figures . . .' or, 'Well I know that Harry has direct experience of this sort of problem . . .'.

- Pick out someone whose body language indicates a potential willingness to speak. This might be a raised hand, or an obviously angry reaction to a comment from someone else, a worried expression, a vigorous nod of agreement or a sudden change in someone's demeanour showing that he or she has just had a brainwave. The tricky thing is to decide who to bring into the discussion when, bearing in mind that people raising their hands or looking angry will have to have their say eventually.

Keeping it going

A meeting is best chaired when the chair takes part constantly in the discussion, not necessarily expressing an opinion, nor declining to do so, but watching the pattern develop and helping everyone to see the pattern and concentrate on it.

- Summarise sparingly, but summarise well. It is pointless to summarise every individual contribution, as the contributors will not see that their own, crystal-clear, succinct comments need any summarising from anyone else. Summarising is needed when there are a number of contributions that have to be pulled together and a pattern found.
- An exception to the last sentence is where a person has not expressed him- or herself at all well, and is prepared to acknowledge it: 'I have not put that very clearly, but do you see what I am driving at?' Because you have been listening closely, you are able to move things forward by saying something like, 'Well what I got from that was . . . Have I got it right?' The person will then confirm that you got it right or will modify it. Either way the person will be grateful to you. Do not say, 'I think what you were trying to say was . . .'. That shows you to be patronising and the other person to be inadequate.
- Be ready to summarise where the discussion has reached, but do not summarise in search of a conclusion until you are confident that there is at least a partial consensus among all those present. Picking the right time is risky but unavoidable. If you go for a conclusion too quickly, you may not carry the meeting with you and you seriously undermine your necessary authority. Leaving it too late makes everyone fed up because things are dragging on. People grumble about meetings, but they rarely grumble about the (very few) meetings that are well run.
- Where things are really difficult, try getting a series of partial solutions. This is trying to split up an issue into parts and identifying a part where there appears to be general agreement and confirming that with the rest of the group, even if it is conditional on some other problem being resolved later. This helps the group by giving everyone a sense of some agreement and progress. Once there are two or three small matters on which there is agreement, it is surprising how much more progress can be made.

And what about your own input?

The person chairing the meeting is not simply enabling everyone else to have their say, like the Speaker of the House of Commons. There is usually a strong personal contribution to be made, often a leading contribution. People will want to hear what you have to say, maybe looking to you for a lead, but you still need to carry them with you.

There are basically two alternative approaches: playing the waiting game or leading from the front. Playing the waiting game is setting up the discussion of different points by a brief, summary introduction of the issue and eventually shaping the discussion with your own views and reaction. Leading from the front is setting out your position and then inviting suggestions. Neither is better than the other; they are simply different approaches that suit different situations and people.

Winding it up

Finally the chair sums things up by reiterating the points upon which agreement has been reached and the nature of that agreement. There may well be further points of clarification and even argument, but the chair has to nail down what people will accept and commit to. Equally important is to sum up the remaining points of disagreement, again with as much succinct clarity as possible. This is when you might just get your lucky break, because your summary might make someone realise that he or she really has been a bit petty and it is time for a magnanimous gesture. Also someone may have been doggedly hanging on to a position in the hope of movement elsewhere and is now prepared to shift because he or she is simply not going to win their argument. No one likes to be the reason for a group failing to agree.

ACTIVITY 7.2

On the basis of the suggestions in the last few pages formulate some forms of words that would be effective for your own personal style in various aspects of chairing a meeting, such as:

- Stimulating and controlling contributions
- Curbing the verbose
- Bringing people in
- Keeping it going
- Making your own input

Members of the group need to disperse feeling that their time has been well spent and that they had their day, knowing what has been agreed and what is outstanding, and knowing what happens next.

Follow-up

When the meeting has finished, the leader of the meeting still has work to do.

Minutes or report of the meeting

Formal meetings have minutes. Less formal meetings have notes. Informal meetings may not have any agreed record at all, but people will still have made jottings in their diary, on a clipboard or in the margin of the agenda. You have no control over what notes people at the meeting make for their own use, but the way you run the meeting will, of course, affect what they write.

The more formal minutes or notes will be written by the secretary, if there is one, or by the chair. The purpose is to produce a stimulus to appropriate action, not to write historical analysis. Sometimes it is important to describe the discussion and issues, so that those not in attendance can understand not simply what was agreed but at least some of the reasoning. In other cases it is sufficient simply to list the action points and who is responsible for following them through.

Activity 7.3 has the framework of an administrative drill for a committee secretary to follow. To make this illustration concrete we are assuming a meeting once a month on Day 28.

ACTIVITY 7.3

Day **Phase One: MINUTES AND PRELIMINARIES**

1, 2   Write draft of minutes for yesterday's meeting, including notes of action items.

5   Clear minutes with chair and confirm date and time of next meeting.

6, 7   Type, copy and distribute minutes.

10   Book room for next meeting.

Phase Two: AGENDA

18   Ask committee members for items to be included on next agenda.

21   Discuss order of agenda and inclusion/deferment of items with chair.

Suggested sequence:

(a)   Announcements (apologies, introduction of new members, chair's points).

(b)   Minutes of previous meeting and matters arising, where matter involves brief report. Matters arising for further discussion to be separate agenda items.

(c)   Items requiring decision but involving little controversy.

(d)   Most difficult item.
        (possible break)

(e)   Next most difficult item.

(f)   Items requiring discussion but not decision.

(g)   Easy items.

(h)   Any other business.

(i)   Provisional date of next meeting.

Phase Three: RUN-UP

22   Circulate agenda and other papers to members, with note of date, time and venue.

26   Check seating, catering, visual aids.
        Collate all papers, past minutes, apologies.

28   Attend meeting and take notes for minutes.

Implementation of proposals

The meeting will have ended with general understanding that various actions would follow. Some of these will follow at once, as people scurry away to make their phone calls or look up information. Other actions will be forgotten unless there is a reminder. This is where the circulation of the minutes can be useful. Other actions will probably need the chair to push them along and pull together actions by different people as the situation changes in the days after the meeting.

SUMMARY PROPOSITIONS

7.1 Chairing meetings is an aspect of management that is crucial to making and implementing management decisions.

7.2 Key aspects of preparing for a meeting are: who should attend, what is the brief, what is the agenda, what about physical location and arrangements, what is the meeting for: to convey information, to share information or to make a decision?

7.3 Key features of conducting the meeting itself are: how contributions can be stimulated and controlled, bringing people in, keeping it going, making your own input and winding it up.

7.4 An administrative drill for a meeting secretary deals with minutes and preliminaries, agenda and run-up.

GENERAL DISCUSSION TOPICS

1 What advantages and drawbacks do you see in an arrangement where everyone takes it in turn to chair a meeting of a particular group?

2 Why do so many people complain about the amount of time they spend in meetings?

3 To what extent could videoconferencing or a web-based chat room be an alternative to a conventional meeting?

FURTHER READING

Harvey, J. (2002) *Chairing Meetings*. London: BMJ Publishing Group Ltd.
Suggestions for medical doctors by a medical doctor.

WEB LINKS

Many organisations offer guidance on chairing meetings. Putting 'chairing meetings' into your search engine will provide pages of possibilities. Among the possibilities are:

www.propellertraining.com

www.Convoko.com

www.marywardcentre.ac.uk

REVIEW OF PART 7

This final part of the book has covered some diverse topics, having in common the fact that they can not be pigeon-holed in a specific area of HR practice like those of Parts 2–6. They are also issues that have come to the fore more recently than the main areas of HR work, where practice is long established, no matter how often it has to be modified and brought up to date. Another common feature is that they cannot be parcelled up and 'passed to Personnel'. They are aspects of management that have an HR dimension and indicate the fact that HRM is increasingly a part of all management that cannot simply be dumped somewhere, although the need for specialised, expert input will grow and some administrative aspects should sensibly be collected together.

As with everything else we have looked at, there are important social and political aspects to the first two chapters on ethics and work-life balance, and the last on the future of work, while the measurement of human capital almost implies questioning the value of everything that has gone before in this book, and reviewing the changing nature of the HR function is a useful exercise for all those looking forward in their careers. Chairing meetings is a skill that all managers need.

In the opening chapter we offered a philosophy for human resource management that included:

> Only by satisfying the needs of the individual contributor will the business obtain the commitment to organisational objectives that is needed for organisational success, and only by contributing to organisational success will individuals be able to satisfy their personal employment needs. It is when employer and employee – or business and supplier of skills – accept this mutuality and reciprocal dependence that human resource management is exciting, centre stage and productive of business success.

That is a tough ask of any HR person, yet nothing less will do.

Offshoring to India

Since 2000 dozens of large corporations based in the UK, USA and Canada have transferred parts of their operations to cities such as Bangalore and Mumbai in India. In the main the activities that are 'offshored' are those carried out in call centres, such as customer enquiries, telemarketing and back-office administration. It is estimated that 150,000 such jobs will have been switched from the UK to India by 2010. Most of the larger finance companies either have made such a move or are actively considering doing so. The same is true of many e-businesses, mail-order retailers and other service sector companies. Rail and airline enquiries may well soon be answered down the phone from India, while some larger legal firms rely on secretarial services based in India to type up dictated letters. Offshoring has clearly become a major business trend.

The potential advantages are very evident. The salary that has to be paid to a call-centre worker in India is around 20 per cent of the figure required to secure the services of someone in the UK. This means that call centres in India operate at around 40 per cent of their cost in the UK once international telephone charges have been taken into account. Setting up a 850-seat centre in India costs about £20 million, but can easily yield annual savings of £15 million once it is established. Savings of that kind are just too significant to pass up in highly competitive industries that must cut costs wherever possible if they are to survive and grow.

Moreover, by Indian standards, these are well-paid jobs which attract highly educated people, including graduates, who perform more effectively and more quickly than the typical UK call-centre worker. Employers report that as well as having lower salary expectations, Indian employees are more adaptable to change and more responsive to management demands than their UK counterparts. Their level of spoken English is generally very high too. It is thus argued that costs are saved and quality is increased when an organisation offshores its operations to India.

Offshoring has been criticised vigorously by trade unions representing the British workers whose jobs are put at risk by the offshoring trend. They argue that it is no more than a 'corporate fashion' which cannot be justified over the longer term. They point to the very high levels of staff turnover that are found in many Indian call-centre operations and to persistent power maintenance problems. Over the long term, the critics argue, shortages of appropriately qualified staff will emerge as the Indian economy develops its own high-tech industrial sector. Cost savings will thus reduce substantially within 10 years. Critics also point to well-publicised instances of poor-quality services being provided by some Indian operations.

It appears that in order to be successful, a great deal of effort must be put into training Indian staff to adopt western personas, particularly in the telesales operations.

They have to make 200 calls to the UK or the USA on each shift that they work, and these yield more sales if the operator poses as someone called Jack or Cathy and is able to chat about the weather in the UK or the latest television programmes.

Required

1 Companies transferring their call-centre operations to India can either outsource to one of the established India-based providers (which typically operate 10,000-seat centres), or set up their own bespoke operation via a subsidiary company. What are the major advantages and disadvantages of each of these options from the perspective of the corporation?

2 Critics of offshoring often claim that the practice is unethical, when seen from the perspective of both UK and Indian employees. To what extent do you agree with this view and why? What steps might be taken by a company that aims to be a champion of corporate social responsibility to ensure that it acted ethically when offshoring?

3 A great deal of customer demand for call-centre services is concentrated in the evenings and at weekends, and this is also the prime time for selling goods and services to UK and US-based consumers via cold calling. What implications does this have for the achievement of a work-life balance for Indian call-centre workers?

4 Some companies have already outsourced parts of their HR function to India – mainly basic back-office tasks such as payroll administration, the maintenance of databases and intranet systems, generation of standard letters and sets of documentation and benefits administration. How much further do you think this process could be taken? To what extent would it be feasible to offshore some of the advisory functions carried out by HR specialists as well as the basic administrative tasks?

Sources

Crabb, S. (2003) 'East India companies', *People Management*, 20 February, pp. 28–32. Articles downloaded from the BBC News website (**www.bbc.co.uk**).

Glossary

The terms in this glossary have been taken selectively from the text. Rather than repeating definitions that are already in the text, we have selected those terms which are neologisms that may not appear in a dictionary, or are invented words, like outsourcing, which do not yet appear in a dictionary. We also include terms, like bureaucracy, which require more interpretation than we have provided in the text.

Benchmarking. Originally a benchmark was a mark on a work bench that could be used to measure off a standard size. This idea of comparative measurement is used in HRM to describe the process of checking some aspect of work in one's own business against an external standard, like the average number of days lost through absence across the working population as a whole, or in a particular industry, by age, occupation, gender and so forth. It is slightly different from 'yardstick', which is literally a measuring stick a yard long. This is sometimes used as a rough and ready measure for some aspect of management effectiveness, but it lacks the dimension of external comparison.

Best fit/Fit. In many fields of human endeavour there is an aim to find and implement the one best way, or the right way of doing things. An alternative is to work out the best way of doing things in this or that situation. There is no single approach or method that is always right.

Bottom line. A term derived from accountancy, where it is the final total in a profit and loss statement or other financial document. In management generally it is used as the ultimate criterion or most important factor: financial viability.

Brand. A term taken from marketing to describe a company or product name that is very distinctive and powerful. Examples are Coca-Cola, Microsoft, Rolls-Royce or Virgin. It was illustrated by the Retail Director of a fashion chain who said, 'If I buy a ready meal from X and I don't like it, I take it back. If I buy it from Marks and Spencer, either I haven't followed the instructions or there is something wrong with my cooker.' To HR people the company brand can be very important in matters of commitment and recruitment.

Bureaucracy has become almost a term of abuse, describing rigidity, lack of responsiveness by staff, lack of willingness to take responsibility and too much emphasis on the rules. It is, however, a time-honoured method of making any large organisation work. In contemporary business usage it describes a type of centralised social order that makes things happen by having guidelines of policy, procedure and precedent to empower role-holders to do their jobs, conferring appropriate authority for action as well as limiting the scope for individual whim or prejudice. It is therefore both more acceptable and more practical as a method of organisation for any large undertaking than relying on the autocratic alternative of everything being decided by a small number of people at the centre, while everyone else waits and grumbles. Human resource managers are occasionally derided by some of their colleagues in other functions for their apparent preoccupation with the 'rules' of procedure and employment law. These colleagues are, of course, wrong, but bureaucracy has a serious inherent flaw in that it always grows, requiring frequent pruning and review.

Career. The whole issue of careers is explored in Chapter 19, but the idea of a career involving moving from job to job is relatively recent. For most people a career was an occupation, like nursing or teaching or carpentry or bricklaying. It was only in bureaucracies that people looked for a promotional ladder. In most of the long-standing professions a career was a lifetime of doing the same job, although perhaps introducing a change of emphasis. A clergyman was a clergyman, even though a few might become deans or bishops. A writer was a writer, although there might be moves from writing poetry to writing novels. An architect is an architect, a dentist is a dentist, a driver is a driver. In some areas the idea of moving 'up' has been created artificially by inventing new pay grades and titles. Until the 1970s British nursing had three levels: nurse, sister and matron. In order to provide a career structure, new jobs were introduced: nursing officer, senior nursing officer and principal nursing officer. The flattening of hierarchies is changing the emphasis. There is now a greater number of sideways, cross-functional moves rather than vertical moves, thus the increasing trend for careers to involve changes in occupation.

Casual work is where someone is employed on a temporary and probably irregular basis without any obligation on either party to further employment when a spell is complete.

Change/Initiatives are often regarded as invariably desirable, particularly by consultants trying to sell you something. Although constantly advocated in HRM, they have to be balanced against other issues such as stability and security.

Furthermore few changes in HR practice can be made quickly and easily. The ideas are usually easy or obvious. Getting them accepted and making them work requires a great deal of hard work, which means that changes have to be worth the trouble and not just some transitory idea that will have been overtaken by something else in six months' time. 'Initiative fatigue' is a term used to describe the experience of some people who have scarcely got used to one new initiative before another is imposed that contradicts the first.

Clocking on (or in) is a term still in common usage, although the practice is not now widespread. In the heyday of large-scale production businesses, manual employees registered their arrival for work by operating an automatic time-recording machine, usually by punching a hole in a personal card. Sometimes they clocked out as well as on. This gave a reliable record of hours worked and enabled pay calculations to be made. Although initially seen as a way to be fair, it eventually became a symbol of close, overbearing control – 'The tyranny of clocking on'. It has become less common although variants are used by, for example, security staff who clock their arrival at various parts of the premises at regular times during the night, or by managers of motorway service stations to demonstrate that they have recently checked the cleanliness of the toilets. A refinement and extension of clocking is the tachograph in road-haulage vehicles.

Coach/Mentor/Protégé. A coach is someone who gives specialised training and guidance as well as

general support and encouragement. This may be to an individual, like a tennis player, or to a team, as in cricket. A mentor gives the same sort of service to an individual in what is often a very close personal relationship, requiring from the protégé a high degree of trust in the integrity and goodwill of the mentor. A protégé is someone who is guided by a mentor, acknowledging a need for that person's greater standing and expertise. Tiger Woods is the world's most successful golfer, but still needs a coach: he is not the coach's protégé. One of the most ghastly bits of management jargon is the word 'mentee', presumably invented by someone who could not cope with three syllables, as an alternative to protégé.

Commitment is widely used in contemporary HR to describe the quality of being dedicated to the cause, and various methods are used (see Chapter 9, for example) to develop this quality among the members of the workforce in their dedication to the cause of company success. Some may be committed to a career or to the employment security that is associated with the success of the business, while others are committed to the success of their career perhaps at the expense of the business, and others have no commitment at all. In these circumstances the value of the brand may be important.

Competitive advantage. Any business has to be competitive, no matter how much many of its members may not like the idea. A school has to be seen by parents to be at least as good as other schools, otherwise parents will remove their children and the pupils will not have self-respect. Commercial organisations seek competitive advantage for more immediate reasons of survival, but schools, hospitals, charities and churches will all decline and may close if they do not meet the current needs and expectations of their 'clients', although they will quite rightly cavil at the terms 'customers' or 'clients'.

Contingency is a word much used in sociology and organisation theory. Apart from its normal usage of describing a possible future event that cannot be predicted with certainty, in management it is used to differentiate from the absolute. Solutions to problems are seldom invariably right: it depends on the particular circumstances of the event.

Contract/consideration. In this book the use of material about contract is mainly about legal agreements, although there is also the reference to psychological contracts. The fundamental principle of a legal contract is that there must be consideration. A contract is a spoken or written agreement that is intended to be enforceable at law, but the offer of agreement by one party only becomes legally enforceable when there is consideration from the other party, that is an undertaking of some sort, to do something or to stop doing something or to abandon a claim. An offer of employment, for instance, is not legally binding on the employer making the offer until and unless the prospective employee accepts the offer and agrees to provide the work (consideration) that the employer is offering. This same sense of reciprocity is equally fundamental

to the psychological contract: there must be an agreed exchange. Contracting out (from a pension scheme, for instance) involves withdrawing from an agreement and thereby relinquishing the benefits that would otherwise have been received.

Culture/Organisational culture. In management circles interest in culture is an attempt to grasp the realities of collective life in a department or organisation that cannot be easily seen and described with such identifiers as job titles, departments and organisation charts. It is an aspect of the hard/soft distinction. Recently it has been especially important in explaining the differences in management practice in various countries, but organisational culture refers to the beliefs, conventions and general patterns of behaviour that characterise a particular organisation.

Delayering is a method of downsizing that reduces the number of people in a hierarchy by removing a tier in the organisational structure.

Demographics describes statistical data relating to the age and gender structure of the population. This is an important element in understanding the labour market.

Diversity is subtly different from equality and refers principally to the value to management of making the most of employees from two distinct groups, women and those from ethnic minorities, rather than assuming that core employees are white and male. Although these two groups have been the main focus of debate and action, there has

recently been greater attention being paid to other groups, such as those who are potentially discriminated against on the grounds of age or disability.

Downsizing describes an approach to increasing organisational efficiency by reducing the number of people employed in the business and therefore reducing the costs associated with their employment. The main methods are delayering and outplacement/outsourcing.

Employee relations/Industrial relations are not simply different terms for the same activities; they denote a significant change of emphasis. Concern with industrial relations developed when the emphasis was on collective relationships within an industry, such as engineering, agriculture or teaching. Each business within the ambit of that industry observed the terms and conditions agreed between employers' representatives and unions, which bound every employer. Employee relations have little regard for industry criteria and focus on collective arrangements within an individual business.

Employee voice is a term that has only come into use during the twenty-first century, largely as a result of the globalisation issue that was discussed in Chapter 4. At a time when trade union membership is not as widespread in European countries as it was, and is unknown in many other countries, employee voice refers to a wide variety of processes and structures which enable people to contribute to decision making in the place where they work and perhaps to influence decision making in other places that affect the place where they work.

Environment. We typically think nowadays of the physical environment in which we live and the environmental issues that are of concern: pollution, greenhouse gases, GM crops, vulnerable species and so forth. In HRM it is more likely to refer to the social, political and legal environment of the business.

Flexibility is something managers try hard to achieve and trade unions and the legal system try to limit. The flexible workforce makes managerial life easier by giving more scope to managers to manipulate the labour supply, as do flexible hours arrangements. Flexibility agreements with unions reduce rigidity in work practices. All these practices reduce the problems of bureaucracy but the advantages for employees may be more mixed. Flexible hours are probably the most attractive, but there are always disadvantages for employees with flexibility initiatives that at least slightly erode their personal security.

Globalisation/internationalisation are both terms coined recently to describe two slightly different aspects of modern business. Many companies work internationally, importing materials and resources and exporting products and services. If their business expands they may appoint agents in overseas countries to represent their interests, or they may establish overseas subsidiaries. The company remains, with a distinctive national head office and branding. Globalisation represents a distinctive further step as the company operates major businesses in different countries and regions. Its national identity is submerged beneath its global

identity and branding. As these businesses grow larger and therefore more powerful, some commentators and pressure groups grow very concerned that their commercial interests can destabilise and harm the economies of individual countries, especially smaller countries in the developing world.

Grievance/discipline. Everyone who is employed has a contract in two parts. The first part is the wage/work bargain. One party to the contract pays money and provides benefits to the other party, who provides work in exchange. The second part of the contract is the psychological contract, referred to throughout this book, where what is exchanged between the two parties is a less tangible – but no less important – form of satisfaction. Both parts of the contract are maintained through the mutual satisfaction of the parties. When something happens to reduce the level of satisfaction of either party HRM uses the terms 'grievance' or 'discipline' to describe the processes whereby satisfaction may be restored.

Hard/Soft. Hard data are precise and can be accurately measured by numbers and statistical calculation. Soft data are less precise but may be more important in planning. They include judgement, assessment and informed guesswork.

Hierarchy is the system of organisation which ranks all the people according to their status or authority. This is used for all manner of purposes, ranging from the trivial, like who has the biggest office and who is allowed to travel first class, to the identification of who is empowered to do what, as

the hierarchical system includes titles or labels to make sense of the jobs that people do. In Britain the growth of hierarchy received a boost when an early management theorist, E.F.L. Brech, advanced his theory of the span of control, saying that no manager should supervise directly the work of four or five subordinates, *whose work interlocks*. Many people accepted the theory but conveniently forgot the last three words.

Human capital. Economists, rather reluctantly, conceded that any economic analysis of an organisation or an economy needed to include the concept of a value or cost assigned to skills, knowledge or experience of the population. It has proved a more acceptable and useful concept than the sterile accountancy technique of human asset accounting. Its main value to HR practitioners is the idea that human capital requires investment.

The Human Relations School. A school of thought that developed in the 1930s as a reaction against the perceived mechanical thinking of Scientific management. It aimed to develop high productivity by concentrating on the well-being of the individual worker and the surrounding social relationships in the workplace, with an emphasis on adapting the task to the worker rather than adapting the worker to the task.

Marketplace/Labour market. The importance of both these concepts (taken from Economics) in HRM is to emphasise that people management can never be entirely inward in focus. The business has to operate in a context in which there is a market for its products or service, and the business has to survive in that market no matter how inconvenient it may be for the people inside the business. Equally there is an external market for labour and skills, which cannot be ignored. Even employees totally loyal to the business will be aware of prevailing conditions elsewhere, not only how much people are paid but also conditions of work, hours and fringe benefits.

Matrix is a term that has recently come into popular currency because of film and television programmes using it in a very specialised way. In management it has long been used to describe a particular form of organisation in which levels of specialisation, accountability and responsibility are set out in vertical columns crossed by horizontal lines, with points of intersection identifying individual people who have a line of communication in one direction (line management) as well as a distinct accountability to someone else. An office manager, for instance, might be responsible for most things to the immediate superior, but accountable to the HR manager for health and safety issues. 'The line' is often mentioned in this book and refers to the vertical line of accountability.

Meta-analysis is an analysis with combines a number of existing analyses already carried out by others into one summary analysis. Meta is a scientific term indicating a change in condition, such as in metamorphosis. In social sciences it denotes something beyond, of a higher-order kind.

Mission/Aims/Objectives/Targets. These are all terms used quite loosely in management jargon and are in a rough hierarchy from the broad to the specific. Mission comes from religion and is used in a business to describe what the organisation is for, what its purpose is. It is fashionably set in a mission statement and is typically vague and general, but can be useful in developing commitment. Aims and objectives describe the more specific purposes of individual functions, departments, teams or individuals within the mission framework. Targets are very specific and usually short term as stages on the way for teams and individuals to achieve longer-term objectives.

Occupational health. Many businesses describe their medical departments as 'Occupational Health', regardless of the skills possessed by the people who work in them, but it is worth bearing in mind that occupational medicine is a defined specialism, not general practice in an occupational setting. Both doctors and nurses can acquire qualifications in occupational medicine, but they are most likely to be needed in a business with specific hazards, like radiation or toxic materials.

Outplacement/Outsourcing. There is a small difference between these two terms. Outplacement describes taking a complete activity and shifting it to a supplier, while outsourcing describes looking outside the business for human resources.

Peers is an equivocal term in Britain because it has two meanings. One is to describe members of the aristocracy: earls, baronets, dukes, marquesses and viscounts. In this book, and in more general usage, it describes people of the same age, status, ability or qualification as oneself. A peer group is therefore a group of one's equals, not one's superiors.

Performance. Everyone wants effective performance. The individual wants the satisfaction of achievement and results, managers want individuals to be effectively coordinated and productive, customers want a good product and good service at the right price, governments want efficient businesses in a growing economy. Achieving performance is complicated. It is not simply paying people lots of money, although not paying people enough money may well inhibit performance. It is not simply being nice to people and releasing them from supervision, as without supervision they may do the wrong things. Achieving effective performance also varies according to the work done. A symphony orchestra requires members of great expertise at different instruments, yet all must work to an identical score under the strict leadership of the conductor, with very little scope for individual flair. The jazz quartet is more loosely coordinated, with many individual riffs. Those working for a courier firm or in the operating theatre of a hospital can only perform well by following a tight schedule arranged by someone else. Those working in an advertising agency have a much looser rein in order to encourage their creativity.

Portfolio is a collection of items that represent a person's work. Very familiar for people whose work can best be demonstrated by examples, like painters or cartoonists, it is also now much used by all classes of worker to demonstrate their skills and accomplishments, thereby justifying a qualification to practise.

Reactive/Proactive. This distinction is important in HRM because there is a natural emphasis in people matters to await developments and deal with them (reactive). Many HR people report that they spend much of their time putting right problems created by the impetuosity or thoughtlessness of their colleagues in other functions. There is also a need, however, to create opportunities for growth and change and to think ahead of issues so that problems can be averted. A well-rounded HR/personnel function is able to maintain a balance between both types of approach, vigorously and calmly sorting out problems or disasters but also taking matters forward in a creative way when the problems are all under control.

Recruitment/Selection. Recruitment is the process whereby a business seeks applicants either generally or for particular vacancies. Potential applicants are interested but there is no mutual obligation. Selection is the process whereby not only does the employer choose between two or more interested applicants, but applicants also select, deciding how much further they wish to pursue their original enquiry. The end of the process is a legally binding agreement.

Resourcing. This term has only recently come into common usage and means simply providing the needed resources. For HR people this is providing the human resources that are needed, although some pedantic academics (like at least one of your authors) dislike

the term 'employee resourcing' as it is the employing organisation that is being provided with resources; not the employees. Also employees are not the only source of human resources for the business. Consultants or subcontractors are alternative sources.

Ritual is a series of actions or a type of behaviour that is invariably followed, in accordance with a convention. Developed originally to help people feel secure in the mysteries of religious practices, rituals are widespread in contemporary society (the ritual of going to the pub on Friday after work, the ritual of the pre-match huddle, the ritual of Prime Minister's Question Time). All provide the benefit of enabling people to feel comfortable and accepted in a social situation, and are therefore important in many employment situations where there is a felt need to conform to existing conventions. The selection interview is the most obvious. Other examples are the 'leaving do', collections before a marriage, negotiations, and the office party.

Scenario. A method of envisaging the future is to bring together various bits of evidence, both hard and soft, and fit them together in a way that describes a reliable version of the future in X years' time.

Scientific management. The first modern theory of management, formulated by F.W. Taylor and using the principles of industrial engineering to raise productivity by adapting the worker to the machine or the process. It relied heavily on adjusting the worker's earnings to the level of individual output. The basic ideas remain in place and are

at the root of many payment systems, but most management academics and commentators throughout the last three-quarters of the twentieth century disparaged and deplored the 'mechanistic and inhuman' practices spawned by scientific management.

Sex/Gender. The word sex is pretty clear in its meaning as describing either a range of interesting activities, or to describe the biological distinction between male and female. Until recently gender was a grammatical term to distinguish between classes of noun or pronoun in some languages, loosely based on natural distinctions of sex: masculine, feminine or neuter. It is now also used to refer to social and cultural differences between the sexes.

Statutory rights. Rights of the individual citizen or citizens that derive explictly from a statute or Act of Parliament.

Stress presents managers with two problems. An employee may be absent from work suffering from stress, but this is a condition that is easy to fake and not easy to diagnose. How does a manager detect malingering and take appropriate action? More significantly, a manager may exacerbate or cause stress in someone. How can this be avoided and what remedies are available to employees? A further complication is that stress is not necessarily undesirable. Any football fan will suffer periods of intense stress when the wrong team is winning a match, but this only makes sweeter the euphoria when the right team wins. Stress can be stimulating as well as harmful and some jobs are best done and most enjoyed where there is frequent stress followed by achievement (journalists' deadlines and surgical crises being two examples).

Tells. 'I love you' is a statement by one person to another that is normally accompanied by certain actions and behaviours that demonstrate to the recipient how sincere the feeling is. Sometimes, however, we say things that we do not believe, or of which we are unsure. Then the listener may try to guess what we really mean, not just what the words say. We give clues to our uncertainty or our truthfulness by what we do,

especially what we cannot help doing. These are tells. Blushing shows we are embarrassed, many people put their hands to their mouths when they feel guilty. HR managers need to learn what tells to look for in situations like selection, where not all candidates are strictly accurate in what they say, or in appraisal, where people may be very guarded in what they say.

Tribunal here refers almost only to the three-person panel that makes up the employment tribunal that decides matters of employment law, although it can be any sort of body used to settle disputes. It is not always made up of three people, but

it is normal to have an odd number to avoid deadlock.

Unitarist/Pluralist. For HRM these terms come from industrial relations analysis. A unitarist thinker believes that all authority and all responsibility is centred in one place or person, so that senior management can, and must, decide on all key issues, while other people involved simply have to accept the consequences. The pluralist says that is both unacceptable and impractical. Employees have a legitimate interest in the business that cannot be disregarded; the local community is another important stakeholder.

Index

Note: text within windows on practice and activities has not been indexed